THE ENCYCLOPEDIA OF
LANGUAGE
AND
LINGUISTICS

THE ENCYCLOPEDIA OF
LANGUAGE
AND
LINGUISTICS

Volume 7

Editor-in-Chief
R. E. ASHER
University of Edinburgh, UK

Coordinating Editor
J. M. Y. SIMPSON
University of Glasgow, UK

PERGAMON PRESS
OXFORD • NEW YORK • SEOUL • TOKYO

UK   Pergamon Press Ltd, Headington Hill Hall, Oxford OX3 0BW, England

USA   Pergamon Press, Inc, 660 White Plains Road, Tarrytown, New York 10591-5153,
            USA

KOREA   Pergamon Press Korea, KPO Box 315, Seoul 110-603, Korea

JAPAN   Pergamon Press Japan, Tsunashima Building Annex, 3-20-12 Yushima, Bunkyo-
            ku, Tokyo 113, Japan

First edition 1994

Library of Congress Cataloging in Publication Data
The encyclopedia of language and linguistics / R. E. Asher, editor-in-chief ;
    J. M. Y. Simpson, coordinating editor.
        p.   cm.
    Includes index.
    1. Language and languages—Encyclopedias.   2. Linguistics—
Encyclopedias.   I. Asher, R. E.   II. Simpson, J. M. Y.
P29.E48   1994
403—dc20   93–37778

British Library Cataloguing in Publication Data
A catalogue record for this book is available from the British Library.

ISBN 0–08–035943–4

∞™   The paper used in this publication meets the minimum requirements of the American National Standard for Information
Sciences—Permanence of Paper for Printed Library Materials, ANSI Z39.48–1984.

Printed and bound in Great Britain by BPCC Wheatons Ltd, Exeter

Contents

Executive Editorial Board

R

Radical Interpretation

The scenario of 'radical interpretation' is that of an individual—perhaps a field linguist—who finds herself amongst a people with which her own culture has had no previous contact, and who must try to come to understand them and their language. Philosophers in what may be called the 'interpretationist' school in recent analytic philosophy have thought that, by considering how she might proceed with her task, light may be thrown on the nature of mental and semantic concepts. The tactic has a broadly verificationist inspiration: their idea is that one can find out what meaning and the mind are, by seeing how one detects them in others.

1. W. V. O. Quine

Use of the scenario for this purpose first came to prominence with the publication in 1960 of Quine's *Word and Object* (see *Quine, Willard van Orman*). The discussion in ch. 2 of 'radical translation' is a landmark in the philosophy of language, and all debate about the nature of meaning since is necessarily informed by, even if it rejects, Quine's approach. Quine subscribed to behaviorism about meaning, holding that, insofar as it is fixed at all, 'meaning is a property of behavior.' Accordingly, he set out to consider how much of ordinary semantic notions can be constructed from a basis of purely physical facts about the 'natives' disposition to verbal behavior. His true concern was thus not so much epistemic as metaphysical: not to see how we might in practice seek to determine the meanings of native sentences, but rather to explore how, as David Lewis has put it, 'the facts (about behavior) determine the facts (about meaning).' Quine used the scenario as a heuristic device to explore this latter question; although his verificationist leanings mean that for him the metaphysical question of if and how the facts are fixed becomes one with the question of how they might, at least in principle, be verified. Quine considered how a translator might arrive at a correct 'translation manual' from the natives' language into her own. He concluded, notoriously, that the data of natives' dispositions to verbal behavior does not suffice to narrow the choice down to just one: all the constraints available on the translator's task leave many manuals equally acceptable. The most disturbing element in this thesis of the 'indeterminacy of translation' was Quine's claim of the 'inscrutability of reference': there is no basis to discriminate between alternative 'analytical hypotheses' about sentences which assign different references to terms and predicates, where these yield logically equivalent translations for whole sentences. So, in Quine's example, it is indeterminate whether native talk is about rabbits, rabbit parts, or rabbit time-slices. This thesis about reference has been convincingly argued against by Evans, but it is now generally recognized that some considerable indeterminacy in translation exists (see *Indeterminacy of Translation*).

2. D. Davidson

Quine was concerned solely with how the meaning of native sentences might be discovered by a translator. But it is now generally recognized that this task can be accomplished only simultaneously with another: the 'interpretation' of the speakers of the language to be translated—that is, the ascription to them of beliefs, desires, and other mental states. The impossibility demonstrated by Quine of constructing sentence meanings from facts about speakers' dispositions to verbal behavior is part of the more general falsity of behaviorism. Behaviorism is false because there is no simple, one-by-one relation of the mental states of persons to their observable behavior: what a person does in response to a given stimulus depends not just on what she believes, but also on what she wants, and there is no principled limit on the further mental states which may crucially affect her response. Similarly, what the sentences of a subject's language mean has no implications for her behavior except as mediated by her mental states. Thus Davidson (see *Davidson, Donald*), continuing the investigation of mental and semantic concepts by means of the radical interpretation scenario, noticed how meaning and belief 'conspire' together to determine which sentences a subject holds true (and hence which she will assent to). In Davidson's work the primary focus switches to the mental: his concern is with how a 'radical interpreter' might ascribe mental states to the natives. He holds that the essential nature of the mind can be illuminated by this method. He uses it to argue, for example, that beliefs are by nature mainly true. One must, he claims, use a principle of 'charity' in interpreting others—that is, ascribe to them mainly true beliefs; and he makes a characteristic interpretationist move from this claim about the inevitable method of interpretation, to a conclusion about the nature of belief itself. The product of a successful interpretation exercise will be both an ascription of beliefs, etc., to the natives, and a theory of meaning for their language. Davidson argues that, while explicit reduction of sentence meaning to non-semantic notions is impossible, by giving an account of how such an interpretation of a community can be achieved, one gives all that is needed by way of philosophical explanation of the nature of meaning. He holds that a theory of truth can serve as a theory of meaning, and has suggested that telling the radical interpretation story can also serve as all that is needed by way of philosophical explanation of what truth is. It has, however, been questioned whether the same story can illuminate both truth and meaning (see *Meaning: Philosophical Theories; Truth*).

3. State of the Art

That meanings cannot be constructed from speakers' dispositions, as Quine showed, is now generally recognized. But while Quine drew the moral that ordinary semantic notions are not scientifically respectable, most nowadays would conclude instead that his standard for respectability was too severe. But the appeal to radical interpretation in the philosophical elucidation of the mental and semantic remains much in evidence. Doubts about Davidson's work focus on two main issues. It is uncontroversial that an interpretation must 'make sense' of the individual(s) to be interpreted, and that this requires seeing a certain pattern in the interrelations amongst their mental states, and in how these states relate to the meanings of sentences of their language. But whether this requires the dominant role for 'charity' urged by Davidson, or exactly what this comes to, has been contested. More radically, the methodology behind the radical interpretation approach to meaning and the mind may be questioned. It assumes that an account of what mental states and meanings are is to be extracted from an account of how one goes about ascribing them to others; but the true relation of priority may be the reverse: it is not until there is a philosophical account of the nature of the mind, that it will be possible to determine how, if at all, one can come to know the mental states of others.

Bibliography

Blackburn S 1984 *Spreading the Word.* Clarendon Press, Oxford

Davidson D 1984 *Inquiries into Truth and Interpretation.* Clarendon Press, Oxford

Evans G 1975 Identity and predication. *Journal of Philosophy* 72: 343–63

Goldman A 1989 Interpretation psychologized. *Mind and Language* 4: 161–85

LePore E (ed.) 1986 *Truth and Interpretation: Perspectives on the Philosophy of Donald Davidson.* Blackwell, Oxford

Lewis D 1974 Radical interpretation. *Synthese* 27: 331–44

McGinn C 1977 Charity, interpretation and belief. *Journal of Philosophy* 74: 521–35

Quine W V O 1960 *Word and Object.* MIT Press, Cambridge, MA

E. M. Fricker

Radulphus Brito (c.1275–1320)

Brito was one of the most important of the Modistae. Nothing is known of his birthplace and date, or of the place of his death. He became Master of Arts in the Faculty of Philosophy in Paris and then Master of Theology—incepted 1311–12. He was Provisor of the Sorbonne from 1315 to 1320. His career was devoted to scholarship and belongs to the last decade of the thirteenth and the first decade of the fourteenth century. He was author of the Priscian Minor commentary and commentaries on Aristotle (see *Linguistic Theory in the Later Middle Ages*).

Bibliography

Brito R 1980 *Quaestiones super Priscianum Minorem,* 2 vols. Fromann-Holzboog, Stuttgart

Bursill-Hall G L 1988 The Modistae revisited. In: Rosier I (ed.) *L'Héritage des grammairiens latins de l'Antiquité aux Lumières.* Société pour l'information grammaticale, Paris

Covington M A 1984 *Syntactic Theory in the High Middle Ages: Modistic Models of Sentence Structure.* Cambridge University Press, Cambridge

Enders H W 1975 *Sprachlogische Traktate des Mittelalters und der Semantikbegriff,* Mitteilungen des Grabmann-Institut. Schöningh, Paderborn

Kelly L G 1990 Composition and the verb in 'Grammatica Speculativa'. In: Bursill-Hall G L, Ebbeson S, Koerner E F K (eds.)

De ortu Grammaticae: Studies in Medieval Grammar and Linguistic Theory in memory of Jan Pinborg. Benjamins, Amsterdam

Pinborg J 1975a Die Logik der Modistae. *Studia Mediewistyczne* 16: 39–97

Pinborg J 1975b A note on some theoretical concepts of logic and grammar. *Revue Internationale de Philosophie* 113: 286–96

Pinborg J 1976 Some problems of semantic representations in medieval logic. In: Parret H (ed.) *History of Linguistic Thought and Contemporary Linguistics.* de Gruyter, Berlin

Pinborg J 1980 Radulphus Brito on universals. *Cahiers de l'Institut du Moyen Age Grec et Latin* 35: 56–142

G. L. Bursill-Hall

Rājarājavarma, A. R. (1863–1918)

Easily the most authoritative of grammarians in Malayalam in his times and after, A. R. Rājarājavarma hailed from a princely family of erstwhile Travancore. He was a pioneer of the renaissance of Malayalam at the beginning of the twentieth century. A gifted poet in both Malayalam and Sanskrit and a skilled translator of Sanskrit poetry and prose into Malayalam, he excelled as a farsighted contributor to the overall planning and development of the Malayalam language. A great teacher who produced distinguished students, he was referred to as the Pāṇini of Kerala after his magnum opus *Kēralapāṇinīyam,* which presents a descriptive-cum-historico-comparative treatment of the Malayalam language on the lines of the Pāṇinian tradition (see *Pāṇini*) and that of western grammarians such as Robert Caldwell (see *Caldwell, Robert*).

The first edition of *Kēralapāṇinīyam* (1968) was in sūtra-vṛtti-bhāṣya (aphorism, gloss, and commentary) style (see *Sūtra*); it contained 357 formulaic rules and their explanation in detail. The work was thoroughly recast in its second edition (1917) in the kārikā-bhāṣya (verse and commentary) style, comprising 194 rules. Statements in the *Kēralapāṇinīyam* pertain to sociocultural and historical matters; separation of Malayalam and Tamil; phonology, sandhi, parts of speech, inflectional and derivational morphology, differences between case suffixes and postpositions; nominal and verbal compounds; syntactic relations; and etymology. Rājarājavarma evinces a remarkable insight into fundamental principles of coining technical terms acceptable to the speech community.

His other writings include graded grammars of Malayalam, restatements of Sanskrit grammar, textbooks on literary composition, poetics, and metrics; annotation of a Kathakaḷi play; translations in simple Malayalam of famous Sanskrit poems and plays; and original compositions in Malayalam of varying length from single quatrains to an historic epic.

Born in the Lakshmipuram palace in Changanachery, Rājarājavarma spent his formative years in the Anantapuram palace in Haripad, studying Sanskrit grammar and literature, poetics, astrology, and logic under his illustrious uncle, Kēralavarma, reputed as the Kālidāsa of Kerala. He was the first from the princely class to attend a public school and have formal education in English. So was he to take a BA degree and to join the government service. A graduate in chemistry, he won the prestigious Ross gold medal for his MA in Sanskrit (1891) from the University of Madras.

He held, successively, the positions of Inspector of the Sanskrit School; Principal, Sanskrit College; Professor of Sanskrit and Dravidian languages and the first Indian Principal of the Maharaja's College, Trivandrum. He also served on various boards and committees, including the one that considered the establishment of the first University in Kerala. His influence in shaping the sensibilities of the Keralite in matters of literary appreciation, education, and culture was considerable.

See also: Malayalam.

Bibliography

Ezhuthachan K N 1975 *The History of the Grammatical Theories in Malayalam*. Dravidian Linguistics Association, Trivandrum
Sankaranarayanan C[handrika] 1985 *A. R. Rājarājavarma—malayālattinṭe rājaśilpi*. State Institute of Languages, Trivandrum

V. R. Prabodhachandran Nayar

Ralph of Beauvais (fl. c. 1175)

Few details of Ralph of Beauvais's life are known. He was born in England, went to France (Hunt 1980: 50) by 1140, was a pupil of Abelard—a claim which may be difficult to prove—and taught at Beauvais. He enjoyed a high reputation; cf. Gerald of Wales (Hunt 1980: 49). He was at the height of his fame in the late 1160s and early 1170s; in the second half of the twelfth century Ralph and his followers created a 'school,' principally concerned with syntax, and using examples taken from classical authors to substantiate their grammatical rules. The very important *Glose Promisimus* (including the Promisimus nos succincta brevitate festinare ad literam . . . , Oxford, Bodleian. Cod. Laud Lat. 67, f1.20–88v) has close links with Ralph's school; other members of this 'school' included Petrus Hispanus (non-Papa; see *Petrus Hispanus*), Robert Blund (of Lincoln), and Robertus de Paris—their treatises have survived (cf. Kneepkens).

Bibliography

Fredborg K M 1980 Universal grammar according to some 12th century grammarians. *HL* **7(1–2)**: 69–84
Fredborg K M 1988 Speculative grammar. In: Dronke P (ed.) *A History of Twelfth-Century Western Philosophy*. Cambridge University Press, Cambridge
Hunt R W 1980 Studies on Priscian in the twelfth century, vol. II. In: Bursill-Hall G L (ed.) *Collected Papers on the History of Grammar in the Middle Ages*. Benjamins, Amsterdam
Kneepkens C H 1978 Master Guido and his view of government: On twelfth-century linguistic thought. *Vivarium* **16(2)**: 108–41
Kneepkens C H 1981 Robert Blund and the theory of evocation. In: Braakhuis H A G, Kneepkens C H, Rijk L M de (eds.) *English Logic and Semantics from the end of the Twelfth Century to the time of Ockham and Burleigh*, Acts of the 14th European Symposium on Medieval Logic and Semantics, April 23–27, 1979. Ingenium, Nijmegen
Kneepkens C H 1987 'Suppositio' and 'supponere' in 12th century grammar. In: Jolivet J, Libera A de (eds.) *Gilbert de Poitiers et ses contemporains aux origines de la Logica Modernorum*. Bibliopolis, Rome
Ralph of Beauvais 1982 *Glose super Donatum*. Ingenium, Nijmegen
Ralph of Beauvais 1993 *Liber Tytan*. Artistarium, Nijmegen

G. L. Bursill-Hall

Ramaswami Aiyar, L. Vishwanatha (1895–1948)

L. V. Ramaswami Aiyar was born in 1895 at Trichur, Kerala State, India, the only son of L. V. Ramaswami Aiyar, an inspector of government schools. He took his BA degree in geology in 1914 and BL degree in 1916 from the University of Madras through the Presidency College and Law College. After a brief stint as a lawyer, he worked for some time as a teacher in various schools and took his MA degree in English by private study. In 1925 he became a lecturer in English at the Maharaja's College in Ernakulam (Kerala State) which had been his alma mater for predegree study.

A rare polyglot, Ramaswami Aiyar was well-versed in 18 languages, foreign and Indian (e.g., German and Malayalam), classical and modern (e.g., Sanskrit and Bengali), and even in tribal languages like Brahui and Kurukh. He published three books and wrote 199 essays on Dravidian linguistics published in more than 18 journals both in India and abroad. The topics dealt with by Ramaswami Aiyar are broadly; (a) Malayalam linguistics; (b) Tamil linguistics; and (c) comparative Dravidian. He had a unique grasp of the grammatical structures of Tamil and Malayalam which served him well in the study of comparative Dravidian.

His book *A Brief Account of Malayalam Phonetics* is the first of a series of phonetic studies of modern Indian languages published in India or elsewhere. His magnum opus *The Evolution of Malayalam Morphology* (1936) was the first historical grammar of a Dravidian language and, incidentally, also a historical grammar of Old and Middle Tamil in its broad outlines. His classic essay 'Morphology of the Old Tamil Verb' (*Anthropos* 1938) is also the first descriptive study of the verbs of a Dravidian language with a historico–comparative perspective. His essays on comparative Dravidian, which number approximately 96, were published in many different journals, for example, *Anthropos*, *Indian Historical Quarterly*, and *Educational Review*, and they constitute a contribution to the comparative study of Dravidian languages which has not been equalled by any individual since Dr Caldwell (see *Caldwell, Robert*).

During his lifetime, Ramaswami Aiyar was acknowledged as an authority on Dravidian philology throughout the world by scholars such as Emeneau (USA; see *Emeneau, Murray Barnson*), Burrow (UK; see *Burrow, Thomas*), Jules Bloch (France; see *Bloch, Jules*), Schrader (Germany), and S. K. Chatterji (India; see *Chatterji, Suniti Kumar*). He died of diabetes on January 31, 1948, the day after the death of Mahatma Gandhi. Romain Rolland's French biography of Gandhi, translated into English by Ramaswami Aiyar, was a bestseller.

Bibliography

Antony C L 1978 Biographical notes on L. V. Ramaswami Iyar. *International Journal of Dravidian Linguistics* **VII**: 2–3

Chatterji S K 1950 Necrology: Professor L. V. Ramaswami Aiyar, M.A.B.L. *Indian Linguistics* **11**: 26–29

Kamatchinathan A 1992 Collected works of L. V. Ramaswami Aiyar: A bibliography (Unpublished manuscript)

Subramoniam V I, Gopinathan N B 1978 Ramaswami Iyer and Seshagiri Prabhu. *Pioneers in Linguistics* **1**: 1–62

A. Kamatchinathan

Ramus, Petrus (1515–72)

Pierre de la Ramée, a French humanist, mathematician, and philosopher, better known as Petrus Ramus, is credited with having introduced formalism to Linguistics and has sometimes been hailed as a precursor of modern structuralism.

He was born at Cuts (Vermandois) in 1515. He evinced his hostility to the Aristotelian and scholastic tradition in his MA thesis (1536), which brought about the disapproval of the Sorbonne. He nevertheless became a professor in the Royal College (Collège de France) in 1551, after being the Principal of the Collège de Presles (1545). Embracing the Reformation (1561), he had to give up his professorship, which he resumed after the Amboise peace treaty, from 1563 to 1567. After touring Switzerland and Germany (1568–70), he went back to Paris, where he was assassinated in the massacre of St Bartholemew (August 26, 1572).

Ramus's linguistic thought, which constantly evolved, has been described as 'prestructuralist,' because it is essentially founded on the study of variation and distribution of word forms, and not on semantic criteria. After dividing the contrasting areas of grammar, dialectic, and rhetoric, Ramus, claiming Plato's authority, exclusively used dichotomy in analyzing linguistic material, which led him to reduce the traditional distinctions between several terms to binary oppositions. While he set down his theory in his *Scholae grammaticae*, Ramus also wrote grammars of Latin, Greek, and French (the last-mentioned with reformed spelling). Breaking away from Latin tradition, he rejected the then used expression 'parts of speech' (*partes orationis*) and classified words (*voces*) into two categories (declinable/undeclinable), which, once redistributed, produced four categories, associated in pairs: nouns–verbs, adverbs–conjunctions. Establishing such wide word classes and so few syntactic rules enabled him to avoid recategorizing words from one class into another, but compelled him to acknowledge that their associations were constantly disrupted. Ramus gathered those disruptions under the name of 'anomalies,' giving up the usual system of figures of construction. In 1572 Ramus introduced the Latin system of cases into his French grammar, previously built on a study of how the forms were arranged, which shows the failure of a purely formal grammar (Chevalier 1968).

Influenced by Rudolph Agricola and collaborating with Omer Talon, Ramus carried out a redistribution of the fields between dialectic and rhetoric; as regards the latter, he intended both to evince a creative opposition to the received texts of antiquity and to promote the French language (Meerhoff 1986).

The extreme formalism of Ramus may set him apart in the history of linguistics. Ramism has nevertheless left deep marks, and has particularly influenced Sanctius (see *Sanctius, Franciscus*), Port-Royal (see *Port-Royal Tradition of Grammar*), and north European grammarians.

Bibliography

Chevalier J-C 1968 *Histoire de la syntaxe*. Droz, Geneva

Demaizière C 1983 *La grammaire française au XVIe siècle: Les grammairiens picards*, 2 vols. Atelier Reproduction des thèses/-Didier, Lille/Paris

Meerhoff K 1986 *Rhétorique et poétique au XVIe siècle en France: Du Bellay, Ramus et les autres*. Brill, Leiden

Ong W J 1958 *Ramus, Method and the Decay of Dialogue*. Harvard University Press, Cambridge, MA

Padley G A 1976 & 1985 *Grammatical Theory in Western Europe 1500–1700* The Latin Tradition & Trends in Vernacular Grammar, I. Cambridge University Press, Cambridge

Ramus P 1559 *Grammatica* [*Latina*]. A. Wechelus, Paris

Ramus P 1562 *Gramere* [*fransoeze*]. A. Wechelus, Paris

Ramus P 1569 *Scholae in liberales artes*. E. Episcopius, Basle

B. L. Colombat

Rask, Rasmus Kristian (1787–1832)

Rask was born on November 22, 1787, and died on November 14, 1832. In his short life he attained a lasting reputation, especially as the father of historical–comparative linguistics. Possibly his own aim was otherwise; he published on a wide front. But his significant contributions were within a narrow compass.

After school in Odense he went to the University of Copenhagen, but left without a degree. Self-teaching fueled his interest in literature (especially saga and epic) and in language. Two extended foreign visits, to Iceland in 1813–15 and across India in 1816–23 (with long stays in Stockholm and St Petersburg en route), added ideas and data to his reading. His titular chair at Copenhagen University from 1818 was owed to his work on the genetic linkage of the Nordic languages and his Indian journey was permitted as a historical research enterprise. He was professor of literary history from 1825, but his final appointment (1831) was in oriental languages.

A brief 'Aapologia pro studiis suis' was found in his papers, composed towards the end of his life. Here he professes to seek the systemic and organic nature of language. Its 'inner form' is to be discovered by empirical methods, and his whole tendency is typological. It is not surprising that his output included work on Old English and Frisian, on Lappish–Finnish and Danish (with a good deal on orthography), on Avestan, and even grammars of Spanish and Italian. Much was foundation work; but his 'pell-mell approach' (to quote Hjelmslev; see *Hjelmslev, Louis Trolle*) betrays excessive enthusiasm. Possibly the tussle between this and the precise philological demands of his employers (and their realistic assessment of his real strengths) led to his later psychological difficulties and early death.

Without doubt, his fame rests on two publications only: the *Vejledning* (1811) and the *Undersögelse* (1818). Both concentrated on Icelandic, the first as a concomitant to Rask's interest in early literature and the second because it was a prize essay which had to conform to the organizers' aim of establishing proto-Nordic.

The 1811 study was based on thirteenth-century Icelandic and completed by 1809, when Rask was 22 years old. As well as helping to locate the North Germanic tongues in history it contained the first uncovering of the process which Grimm later called 'Umlaut,' the effect of certain sounds (which may then be lost) on the vocalism of the preceding syllable. The *Undersögelse* was perhaps inspired by the appearance in 1809 of the second volume of J. C. Adelung's *Mithridates*. When the Danish Academy announced the competition in 1811 Rask entered, won the prize in 1814, and then gained funding for the publication which came in 1818. The work abounded in principles essential to the genetic–historical enquiry which then dominated the nineteenth century. These included: that, for all the centrality of grammar, historians have in practice to work with phonology; and that cognate languages display systematic sound-correspondences which can be stated as pretty tight rules. Other matters were sometimes well seen (e.g., that Baltic and Slavic are distinct groups), and sometimes not (he havered over Celtic and did not adduce Indian evidence). But in many ways Rask was more clear-minded than Grimm, whom he so notably influenced, as on the essential separateness of the two great German(ic) sound shifts.

So much is there, and is right, as to method and as to detail in this pioneering enterprise on comparative–historical linguistics that Rask can rest content with his achievement. He has the lasting admiration and gratitude of the profession.

See also: Grimm, Jacob Ludwig Carl.

Bibliography

Rask R K 1811 *Vejledning til det Islandske eller gamle Nordiske sprog.* Schubote, Copenhagen
Rask R K 1818 *Undersögelse om det gamle Nordiske eller Islandske sprogs oprindelse.* Gyldendal, Copenhagen
Rask R K 1932–35 *Udvalgte Afhandlinger*, 3 vols. Levin and Munksgaard, Copenhagen
Antonsen E H 1962 Rasmus Rask and Jacob Grimm: Their relationship in the investigation of Germanic vocalism. *Scandinavian Studies* **34**: 183–94
Koerner E F K 1989 *Practicing Linguistic Historiography.* Benjamins, Amsterdam
Pedersen H 1924 *Sprogvidenskaben i det nittende Aarhundrede.* Gyldendal, Copenhagen
Sebeok T A (ed.) 1966 *Portraits of Linguists*, 2 vols. Indiana University Press, Bloomington, IN

N. E. Collinge

Rastafarianism

Rastafarianism is a messianic cult originating in Jamaica but now practiced elsewhere in the West Indies, the UK, the USA, Canada, Australia, and New Zealand, and also in Europe and the former colonies of France, Holland, and Spain. Its roots can be traced back to the teachings of Marcus Mosiah Garvey, who is said to have declared, on leaving Jamaica for the USA in 1916: 'Look to Africa for the crowning of a Black King: he shall be the Redeemer.' When, in 1930, the then Ras ('prince') Tafari was crowned Emperor of Ethiopia and given the titles Haile Selassie I, King of Kings and Lion of the Tribe of Judah, Garvey's followers in Jamaica recognized that his words had been prophetic and the Ras Tafari movement was born.

Rastafarian beliefs are centered on the divinity of Haile Selassie, who is seen to be the returned Christ. The divinity is addressed as *Jah*, as in the Bible (Psalm 68: 4) and much of Rastafarian doctrine involves the reinterpretation of the Bible to apply specifically to Black people, who are said to be the true Israelites, exiled as slaves in 'Babylon' (a term used by Rastafarians to refer to Jamaica, the Western world generally, or even the police). In the early days of the movement, repatriation to Africa was seen as the only means of redemption, but more recently greater emphasis has been placed on liberation in situ; a general consciousness of African roots, a sense of history, and a positive self-image to counter the negative one imposed by Babylon since the days of slavery.

There is no special ceremony involved in becoming a Rastafarian: one simply has to recognize the presence of Ras Tafari within—to experience a revelation of self-knowledge. However, many of the symbolic practices of Rastafarians identify them as separate from mainstream (White or colonial) society. As well as restricting themselves to a practically vegetarian diet, composed only of naturally produced food (*I-tal*), they identify themselves with the Nazarites of the Bible in abstaining from strong drink and, in the case of men, by allowing their hair and beards to grow (see Numbers 6: 5). The resulting 'locks' or 'dreadlocks' are the most distinctive external trait of the Rastafarian. Since these 'locks' are curly, they also give positive value to a typically Afro–Caribbean physical trait which had been viewed negatively in colonial society.

Like these physical symbols of Rastafarian identity, the language used by Rastafarians is one that was formerly heavily stigmatized. The use of Jamaican Creole by Rastafarians has contributed to a greater acceptance of this variety, both in Jamaica and in the UK, where it is beginning to be used by young Afro–Caribbeans whose parents came from other islands.

Apart from conferring status on Jamaican Creole, Rastafarianism has contributed several distinctive words, some of which have been adopted by non-Rastafarians. Many of the words coined by Rastafarians have multiple meanings and some involve a play on homophones. The most important of these, because of its centrality to the cult and its subsequent use in many compounds is *I*, which involves a play on the homophones *I* and *eye*, incorporating concepts of identity and vision. In Rastafarian language, the pronoun *I* or *I-and-I* is used for both *I* and *we*, emphasizing the oneness of all Rastafarians if not all humanity. Cashmore (1979: 170) quotes a Rastaman as saying: 'I and I are one people . . . Ras Tafari is in all of I.' *I* is also substituted for the first syllable of several English words and names: *I-drin* for *brethren*; *I-vid* for *David*; and *I-tal* for *vital*. This last example, the word for food acceptable to Rastafarians, is 'fast becoming part of Jamaican speech' (Barrett 1977: 141), and words for common Jamaican foods are being remodeled on the Rastafarian pattern: thus *Callalu* is now called *Illalu*. Other English words are refashioned in order to substitute 'positive' morphemes for 'negative' ones. Thus *appreciate* and *create* become *apprecilove* and *crelove*, whilst *understand* becomes *overstand*.

On the other hand, Rastafarians tend to give positive meanings to words which are negative in standard English: *dread* is thus a term of great approbation amongst Rastafarians, for whom *Natty Dread*, immortalized in song by Bob Marley, has become a folk-hero. (The same semantic shift is found in the use of *bad* and *wicked* in US and British Black English respectively, and can possibly be attributed to the underlying influence of African languages which have this trait.)

In the UK and the USA as well as Jamaica, Rastafarian words are entering the general vocabulary as a result of the popularization of Rastafarian beliefs and practices, largely through the medium of Reggae music.

See also: Black English in Education: UK.

Bibliography

Barrett L E 1977 *The Rastafarians*. Sangsters Book Store, Kingston, Jamaica/Heinemann Educational, London

Bones J 1986 Language and Rastafari. In: Sutcliffe D, Wong A (eds.) *The Language of the Black Experience*. Blackwell, Oxford

Cashmore E 1979 *Rastaman: The Rastafarian Movement in England*. Allen & Unwin, London

Edwards V 1986 *Language in a Black Community*. Multilingual Matters, Clevedon

Garrison L 1979 *Black Youth, Rastafarianism and the Identity Crisis in Britain*. ACER Project, London

J. C. Beal

Rationalism

The term 'rationalism' is standardly used in histories of philosophy to contrast with 'empiricism.' Rationalists (from the Latin *ratio* 'reason') are said to maintain that knowledge can be arrived at by reason alone, independently of the senses, while empiricists (Greek *empeiria* 'experience') take it that there can be no knowledge which is not ultimately derived from sensory inputs. The classification is perhaps most familiar in textbooks of seventeenth- and eighteenth-century philosophy, where the 'British empiricists,' Locke, Berkeley, and Hume, are routinely contrasted with the 'continental rationalists,' Descartes, Spinoza, and Leibniz (see *Locke, John*; *Descartes, René*; *Leibniz, G. W.*). But this blunt and schematic contrast is in many respects misleading; the 'rationalist' Descartes, for example, insists on the vital importance of sensory observation in testing scientific theories, while the 'empiricist' Locke, though asserting that 'all our knowledge is founded in experience,' nonetheless stresses the crucial role played, in the development of knowledge, by the mind's own active faculties for combining, comparing, and abstracting from sensory data.

1. Innate Ideas

Despite its problems, the rationalist/empiricist distinction does provide a useful focus for a number of central issues in the philosophy of language. The most important of these is the issue of 'innateness' (see *Innate Ideas*). Rationalists like Descartes, following a tradition that goes back as far as Plato, maintained that the human mind at birth is already imprinted with certain innate 'ideas'—a term which covered both concepts (such as the concept of God or of triangularity) and also propositions or principles (such as the principle of noncontradiction in logic). This implies, in effect, that there is a kind of innate language—a language of thought—which all human beings are born knowing. The term 'knowing' is a slippery one in this context, since it is clear that young children, for example, do not possess any *explicit* awareness of principles like the law of noncontradiction; and this led Locke and others to dismiss the whole notion of innate ideas. To this innatists replied that the knowledge in question might be present *implicitly*; in a suggestive analogy used by Leibniz in his *New Essays on Human Understanding* (ca. 1704), the human mind at birth is likened to a block of marble—not a uniform block indifferently suited to receive any shape the sculptor may choose to impose on it, but one already veined in a certain pattern. In this metaphor, the blows of the sculptor's hammer are likened to sensory inputs: without them there could be no sculpture, just as without sensory inputs there could be no knowledge. But though the hammer blows are necessary, the internal veining is also necessary to explain the final shape. And similarly, a crude empiricism that appeals to sensory input alone is insufficient to explain knowledge of certain fundamental and universal principles of logic and mathematics; an innate prestructuring of the human mind must also be invoked.

2. A Universal Language of Thought

There is some similarity between the issues addressed in these early debates and the linguistic controversy over Noam Chomsky's notion of a 'universal grammar' (see *Radical Interpretation*). Just as Chomsky argues that the mind must be endowed from birth with certain deep structural principles which enable the young child to learn any language on the basis of very meager and defective linguistic data, so the earlier 'rationalists' argued for the theory of innate ideas by citing human ability to perceive and acknowledge fundamental conceptual and logical truths, whose validity is recognized as extending far beyond those cases which have actually been perceived by the senses. In both cases, what makes the argument persuasive, or at the very least challenging, is its insistence on the need to explain the gap between the limited actual empirical input in early life and the richness and scope of the eventual abilities (whether logical or linguistic) which all human beings normally develop.

The idea of a universal language of human thought is a pervasive one in rationalist philosophy, and is not confined to discussions of the innateness question. In the seventeenth century, the notion is often connected with a belief in a divine creator who has illuminated our minds with (at least some of) the fundamental principles which govern the universe as a whole. In a famous pronouncement, Galileo declared in *Il Saggiatore* (1623) that 'The great book of the universe cannot be understood unless one can read the language in which it is written—the language of mathematics.' Some years later, Descartes announced his revolutionary program for the mathematicization of physics in closely similar terms. The qualitative language of earlier scholastic philosophy was resolutely to be avoided; all scientific explanations were to be couched in quantitative terms. 'I recognize no matter in corporeal objects,' wrote Descartes, 'apart from what the geometers call quantity . . . i.e., that to which every kind of division, shape and motion is applicable' (*Principles of Philosophy* 1644). Part of what this new program involved was a rejection of the ordinary language of the senses, with its supposedly 'commonsense' vocabulary of terms like 'warm,' 'wet,' 'hard,' 'heavy,' 'bitter,' 'smooth.' Such terms may be applied on the basis of sensory experiences which are vivid enough, yet the rationalists argued that they lacked the transparency and precision of mathematical terms. 'Sensible properties are in fact occult properties,' wrote Leibniz later in the seventeenth century, 'and there must be others more manifest which could render them more understandable.'

3. *Characteristica Universalis*

A recurring dream of rationalism was that of a *characteristica universalis*—a clear, precise, and universal symbolic alphabet in terms of which the whole of human knowledge might be represented. It is probably fair to say that the philosophical consensus nowadays is that any such aspiration is radically misconceived. Briefly, there seem to be two major obstacles in its way. The first is the problem of 'commensurability': it is hard to see how the languages of different branches of science (and perhaps even of different theories within the same branch) can be readily intertranslatable, or reducible to a common currency of 'neutral' or universal symbols. And the second is the problem of 'justification': it is hard to see how traditional rationalism could defend its claim to have discovered the master vocabulary or canonical language which describes the universe 'as it really is.' Many of the issues involved here are complex and still unresolved. What is clear is the enduring importance of the rationalist tradition in philosophy, if only because so much contemporary philosophy of language and theory of meaning defines itself by its opposition to that tradition.

Bibliography

Cottingham J 1984 *Rationalism*. Paladin Books, London
Chomsky N 1966 *Cartesian Linguistics: A Chapter in The History of Rationalist Thought*. Harper and Row, New York

J. Cottingham

effective; that all curriculum subjects could be taught in German (as opposed to Latin); and that he could show how unity of language, government, and religion could be secured throughout the Empire.

From 1612–18 Ratke worked in Frankfurt, Weimar, and Augsburg. It was during this period that the young Comenius heard of his work. Unfortunately, Ratke's colleagues Jung and Helwig abandoned him in Augsburg leaving him to travel on to Köthen alone. In Köthen, Ratke and his new staff produced more than thirty textbooks—the *Köthen Series*—within two years. However, Ratke ended his term in Köthen in prison. From 1620 until his death in 1635 Ratke wrote a series of further works which remained unpublished until 1970–71.

The intellectual appeal of Ratke's grammars lies in the fact that they were conceived within a coherent theory of the curriculum. His aphorism *Omnia primum in Germanico* was the first step in securing the vernacular as medium of instruction in Germany. Another—*Ex Germanico in alias linguas*—introduced the vernacular as a curriculum subject. Using the instrument of 'harmony,' the grammars of other languages were to be taught on a basis uniform with the vernacular. Ratke published parallel universal and particular grammars in and for German, Latin, Greek, Italian, and French.

Important vernacular German grammars in the Ratkean tradition were produced by Gueintz, Schottel, Harsdörfer, and von Zesen.

Bibliography

Ising E 1959 *Wolfgang Ratkes Schriften zur deutschen Grammatik (1612–1630)*. Akademie Verlag, Berlin
Padley G A 1985 *Grammatical Theory in Western Europe 1500–1700: Trends in Vernacular Grammar I*. Cambridge University Press, Cambridge
Ratke W 1619 *Grammatica Universalis: Pro didactica Ratichii*. Köthen
Ratke W 1970–71 *Allunterweisung: Schriften zur Bildungs-, Wissenschafts- und Gesellschaftsreform*, 2 vols. Volk und Wissen, Berlin
Rhenius J (ed.) n.d. *Methodus Institutionis nova quadruplex*. Leipzig
Walmsley J B 1987 Towards a historiography of Ratke's writings in the English-speaking world. *History of Education* **16**: 11–27
Wells C J 1985 *German: A Linguistic History to 1945*. Oxford University Press, Oxford

J. B. Walmsley

Ratke, Wolfgang (1571–1635)

Wolfgang Ratke (Ratichius) was until recent times variously dismissed as a charlatan or hailed as a great and original thinker.

Ratke was born on October 18, 1571 in Holstein, attended the Johanneum in Hamburg, and Rostock University. Motivated—as earlier English grammarians had been (cf. Sonnenschein; see *Sonnenschein, Edward Adolf*)—by the disharmony in grammatical terminology, Ratke presented in 1612 a *Memorandum* (the Frankfurt *Memorial*) to the Electors of the German Empire in which he claimed that language teaching could be made more

Raumer, Rudolf von (1815–76)

Rudolf von Raumer was born near Hanover on April 14, 1815, the son of Professor Karl von Raumer. In 1832 he entered the University of Erlangen to read Classical and Oriental Philology. In 1834 he went to Göttingen, where the brothers Grimm, who were friends of his family, introduced him to the Old Germanic languages (see *Grimm, Jacob Ludwig Carl*). In 1840 he returned to Erlangen, where he remained until 1864. He died on August 30, 1876.

Von Raumer's first publication, a short paper on aspiration and the Germanic sound shift, appeared in 1837. In this he describes the two sound shifts of Germanic. He regards the aspirates of Greek and Sanskrit as being pronounced, not as fricatives (as in modern languages) but as stops with a following *h*-element, and the Sanskrit palatals as stops with a following *y*-element, and not affricates. In this youthful work the foundations of von Raumer's later works were laid.

Von Raumer's early philological works consisted of short papers; he published no full-length book until his *Geschichte der germanische Philologie* of 1870. This is a history of Germanic philology from the Reformation to von Raumer's own day, almost half the book being devoted to the life and works of the brothers Grimm; it breaks no new ground philologically.

The collected philological works of 1863 is only a single volume, but is of great significance to Indo–European phonetics and phonology. It contains papers defining his views on aspirates and palatals, the classification of vowels and consonants, on voice (which was not fully understood until much later), on *h*, and on German spelling, and also on the relationship between the Semitic and Indo–European languages, which he believed to have had a common origin.

Von Raumer's wide range of interests included religion, language, and philosophy. In the 1840s he wrote articles on the development of German culture. He also worked for a radical revision of German spelling, which in his time was based on historical principles and allowed of certain variations. He was a leading figure in the spelling reform which was finally adopted in 1880.

In phonetics, von Raumer was a pioneer in the use of physiology for the purpose of showing phonetic relations. He distinguished between spoken and written language and regarded the spoken word as the basis for phonetic research. He made a clear distinction between letter and sound; prior to his time 'letter' had been used indiscriminately to designate a written letter or spoken sound. He also distinguished between and described aspirates and spirants.

Bibliography

Arens H 1969 *Sprachwissenschaft: der Gang ihrer Entwicklung von der Antike bis zur Gegenwart*, 2nd edn. Alber, Munich
Hender C 1877 Rudolf Heinrich Georg von Raumer. In: 1970 *Allgemeine deutsche Biographie*, 2nd edn., vol. 27. Duncker and Humblot, Berlin
Raumer R von 1863 *Gesammelte sprachwissenschaftliche Schriften*. Heyder and Zimmer, Frankfurt
Raumer R von 1870 *Geschichte der germanischen Philologie, vorzugsweise in Deutschland*. Oldenbourg, Munich
Raumer R von 1967 Linguistic–historical change and the natural–historical definition of sounds. In: Lehmann W P (ed.) *A Reader in Nineteenth Century Historical Indo–European Linguistics*. Indiana University Press, Bloomington, IN

E. C. Dove

Readability

In its general sense, 'readability' is an attribute of a text, referring to whether or not it is interestingly and attractively written, and easy to understand. In its more technical usage, the study of readability relates to the systematic examination of a wide range of factors that in combination have been found to be associated with the interest and difficulty levels of texts.

The study of readability has been a cause of debate, mainly because its analysis of the surface features of texts, and the relating of these to likely comprehensibility, has been taken by some commentators as representing an atheoretical approach to the study of what makes a text readable. Furthermore, the indiscriminate application of readability formulas, which predict probable comprehension using counts of surface text features, has been criticized by some as being dangerous and unreliable. The current consensus view of readability formulas is that they can, under certain circumstances, offer useful indications of the comparative levels of difficulty of texts. Readability formula scores are, however, only estimates, and while they can make some useful general comparisons, they are not to be trusted in the more sensitive task of matching individual readers to texts (see *Reading Inventories, Informal*).

1. The History of the Study of Readability

The serious study of readability began in the USA in the 1920s, and had two main areas of focus: basal reading schemes (that is, series of books for beginning readers), and content area reading (that is, school textbooks on subjects such as mathematics, history, or science; see *Reading Teaching: Materials*). The vocabulary of school texts was given close attention following the publication in 1921 of Thorndike's *A Teacher's Word Book of 10,000 Words*. Trends towards extending education to a wider population led teachers to consider more carefully whether the books then in schools were too difficult for a new generation of students who were the first in their families to attend secondary school. Thorndike's study of word frequencies was seminal since it provided a principled basis for estimating vocabulary difficulty, based on mean word frequency. This in turn led to the first readability formulas.

A second catalyst for readability studies came from journalism and mass communications research. Studies in these areas began in the 1930s and were given further impetus by World War II, in which adult literacy needs were addressed by many psychologists and reading specialists, and during the 1940s some of the most widely used readability formulas were devised.

2. Readability Formulas

Klare (1963) and Harrison (1980) have given detailed accounts of the development of readability formulas. Nearly all formulas, including those devised in the 1920s, had a similar genesis and share certain characteristics. Most formulas were derived by selecting a number of texts or passages and analyzing the relationship between a group of linguistic variables and some criterion, such as comprehension test scores or teachers' ratings of difficulty. The formula is then constructed by combining arithmetically the statistics identified as the most highly predictive, such as word length or sentence length. The most widely used formula is that of Flesch (1948). Flesch developed a number of formulas, but the best-known is his 'reading ease formula':

Reading Ease Score
$$= 206.835 - (0.846 \times \text{sylls}/100\text{w}) - (1.015 \times \text{wds}/\text{sen})$$

In the formula, *sylls/100w* stands for the mean number of syllables per 100 words, and *wds/sen* for the mean number of words per sentence. The reading ease score itself is a notional comprehension score out of 100, in which 100 indicates a very easy and 0 a very difficult passage.

This formula is typical of many in that it includes one vocabulary variable—the count of syllables per word—and one syntactic variable—the mean number of words per sentence.

3. Criticisms of Readability Formulas

The Flesch formula has been shown to be one of the most valid and reliable, but it also demonstrates most of the weaknesses for which readability formulas have been attacked. First, the vocabulary variable does not take account of word frequency: in English there are many short rare words and many long frequently used ones, and the formula would be insensitive to this. Second, no account is taken of repetition; if a long or difficult word is glossed and then repeated, the passage containing it presumably is less difficult to comprehend than a similar passage containing many different long words, but the formula does not allow for this. Third, sentence length is a very crude index of syntactic complexity; periodic sentence constructions with simple clause structure would be rated as difficult, while compressed, embedded, or elliptical constructions would be assessed as relatively easy. Fourth, many critics have pointed out that such formulas are insensitive to disruptions in coherence; if the sentences (or indeed all the words within them) were randomly reordered, the formula score would remain unchanged, while the comprehensibility of the passage would certainly be altered.

Such criticisms sound damning, but the fact that readability formulas have been used in hundreds of studies suggests that they have some merits. To understand these merits, one must accept that readability studies are based on correlations, not causal relationships. From a statistical standpoint, if certain variables correlate highly with actual difficulty, then it is reasonable to include them in a predictive formula. Many dozens of studies have confirmed that vocabulary is by far the best single predictor of text difficulty, and for this reason it is included in nearly all formulas. Flesch's variable of syllables per word may seem arbitrary, but it has certain advantages; it has been found to correlate more highly with actual vocabulary difficulty than a count of mean word length, as expressed in letters per word, and it is much easier to apply reliably than counts of word frequency. Word frequency counts have many problems, such as how to treat irregular plurals, proper names, abbreviations, and compound words, and every problem potentially adds to unreliability in application.

Equally, while a count of the mean number of words per sentence is crude, it does in fact account for most of the variance attributable to grammatical structure. Many attempts have been made to include more complex grammatical variables in readability studies, but when this is done, other problems can occur. First, readability formulas are derived from multiple regression analyses, and it is axiomatic that each new variable added gives less additional predictive accuracy than the last, but adds a full measure of error. For this reason, formulas tend to have no more than three or four variables. Some studies have begun with over 100 syntactic variables, including indices of embeddedness, frequency of passives, and other verb forms associated with difficulties in comprehension, but complex formulas derived from them have not proved to be any better at predicting difficulties associated with grammatical structure than a simple measure of sentence length. For all its weaknesses, therefore, the Flesch formula remains a perfectly adequate one, and the more complex analyses available today have not really improved upon it.

If a formula is misused, however, even its author would declare the results invalid. Such circumstances could occur, for example, if a formula derived from an analysis of school textbook prose were applied to poetry. There is also some doubt over the appropriateness of using a formula to analyze very brief segments of text, such as labels, instructions, or individual sentences, though this issue is partly one of sampling adequacy.

4. Sampling Adequacy and Readability

Even if one concedes that under certain circumstances it can be valid to apply a readability formula, there remains the problem of sampling. Some studies have shown that readability estimates based on 100-word samples of text can be misleading. A number of formula developers suggested that three such samples should be taken as a minimum, and their results averaged. This has not prevented the sale of computer programs to estimate readability which will not permit the user to sample more than a single 100-word passage. However, such a weak sampling procedure may be useless: Fitzgerald (1981) used a computer to estimate the readability of five high-school textbooks, then went on to calculate the critical number of passages needed to be 80 percent certain that there would be no more than one year's difference between the sample mean and the overall mean. She found that in one case it was 72 samples, which amounted to nearly half the book.

The problem here relates not to the number of samples, but to the relatively modest information on mean sentence length obtainable from a 100-word sample. In beginning reading texts there may be 10 or more sentences in a 100-word passage, but in textbooks sentences in the range 30–50 words long are common (see *Textbooks*). This means that a 100-word passage offers an adequate basis for estimating mean word length, but an inadequate one for estimating sentence length. One solution is therefore to analyze 250-word samples, rather than ones of 100 words. Such a procedure does not degrade the validity of a formula, and it may well increase its reliability.

5. Nonformula Approaches to Estimating Readability

A nonformula approach to estimating readability which has been widely used is the 'Fry graph' (1977), which is reproduced in Fig. 1. One feature of this graph is that it extends up to USA grade level 17, and thus claims to analyze material beyond school and up to college level. One other feature is that the location of the point indicating the mean grade level of the passage gives further information concerning the relative difficulty of the passage: if it is above the median line, one might expect the passage to be, in relative terms, more difficult in vocabulary than grammar; if it is below the line, one would expect the reverse to be the case.

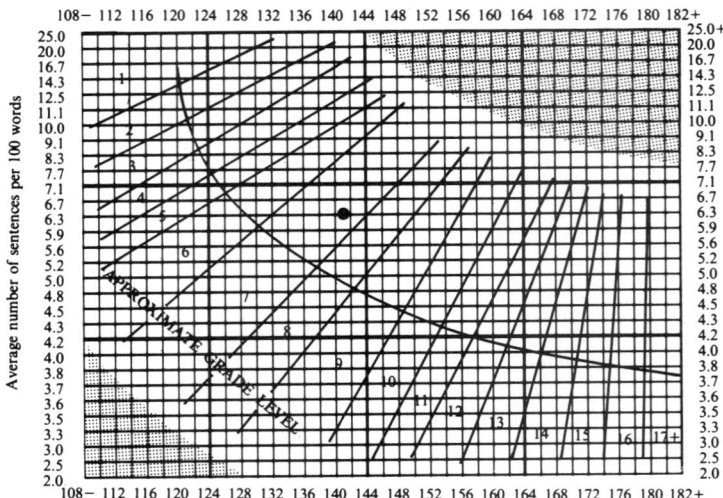

Average number of syllables per 100 words

Directions: Randomly select 3 one hundred word passages from a book or an article. Plot average number of syllables and average number of sentences per 100 words on graph to determine the grade level of the material. Choose more passages per book if great variability is observed and conclude that the book has uneven readability. Few books will fall in gray area but when they do grade level scores are invalid.

Count proper nouns, numerals, and initializations as words. Count a syllable for each symbol. For example, '1945' is 1 word and 4 syllables and 'IRA' is 1 word and 3 syllables.

Example:

	Syllables	Sentences
1st Hundred Words	124	6.6
2nd Hundred Words	141	5.5
3rd Hundred Words	158	6.8
Average	141	6.3

Readability 7th grade (see dot plotted on graph)

Figure 1. Fry graph for estimating readability—extended (Fry 1977).

6. Cloze Procedure and Readability

During the 1960s, cloze procedure was seen by some as a potentially exciting new practical and theoretical basis for readability analysis and validation. Major studies in the 1960s and 1970s used cloze scores to measure relative text difficulty in what was then thought to be a more valid and reliable way than had hitherto been considered possible. This was because cloze treated every passage in the same way, and researchers were not faced with problems of attempting to equalize comprehension question difficulty. Words were deleted on a regular basis, generally every fifth, seventh, or tenth word, and readers had to replace them. The mean cloze score provided an index of the comprehensibility of the passage, and this could be compared with scores derived from other passages using the same group of readers. It was hoped that this would offer more valid readability data.

In the event, this promise was not fulfilled. It is now accepted that what cloze measures is redundancy, rather than comprehension, and these differ in important ways. For example, in a complex science passage, a reader might readily supply a missing word in a cloze test, because it collocates with another in a different part of the passage, but this may have little to do with whether it is understood or not. Conversely, in a literary text, a reader might supply an incorrect but grammatically acceptable synonym, which would be scored as wrong in a cloze test.

Other studies have called into question the sensitivity of cloze to intersentential constraints. Scrambling the sentence order of a text has only a small effect on cloze scores, but has been found to seriously disrupt recall and comprehension. For these reasons cloze is currently used less widely in readability research.

7. The Future of Readability Research

Readability research has been regularly discredited, but it refuses to pass away. This is perhaps because the issue of making reading material more comprehensible to a wide audience is the goal of most authors and publishers. Psychologists and linguists have castigated readability research, but it is still being used to help produce more readable newspapers, consumer material, and legal documents. Uncritical use of readability formulas can produce nonsensical prose, but provided users avoid the fallacy of assuming that correlation is causation, readability measures may still have a limited role to play.

Current initiatives are attempting to take account of the enormous influence that cognitive psychology has had upon our understanding of the reading process since the early 1970s. Studies of text structure, and of the reader's knowledge of text structure, are having a major impact upon how comprehension is viewed, and such studies are now being recognized as important in readability analysis (see *Reading, Theories of*). Similarly, a reader's prior knowledge of the specific topic dealt with has a significant effect on his or her ability to cope with a text. These interactions are unique for each individual, as are those related to motivation and interest level. The effect of all these factors is difficult to quantify, but it is recognized that a complete analysis of readability must take account of them.

Bibliography

Fitzgerald G G 1981 How many samples give a good readability estimate?: The Fry Graph. *Journal of Reading* **24**: 404–10
Flesch R F 1948 A new readability yardstick. *Journal of Applied Psychology* **32**: 221–33
Fry E 1977 Fry's readability graph: Clarifications, validity and extension to level 17. *Journal of Reading* **21**: 242–52
Harrison C 1980 *Readability in the Classroom*. Cambridge University Press, Cambridge
Klare G R 1963 *The Measurement of Readability*. Iowa State University Press, Ames, IA
Thorndike E L 1921 *A Teacher's Word Book of 10,000 Words*. Columbia University, New York

C. Harrison

Reading: Acquisition

When people think about children acquiring reading skills, they usually think of learning to read words—'cracking the code.' However, the real purpose of reading is finding out the meaning of the text, and this aspect of reading acquisition will be reviewed later in the article. There is a very large body of research into how children learn to read, and the best method of teaching them, and this article is necessarily very selective. Almost all of the research has been on reading words, and the balance of this article reflects this bias.

The first section outlines a variety of reading-related skills that children acquire in the early years of school, and considers which, if any, of these skills are prerequisites for learning to read. The second section surveys some current methods of teaching children to read, and the third gives an account of some important aspects of the development of reading skill. In the final section, comprehension is considered: both its normal development, and the causes of comprehension difficulties.

1. Reading-related Skills

Children who are learning to read already possess a wide variety of relevant skills and will acquire many others. Many of these skills are either prerequisites for reading or are related to it in other, less direct ways.

However, many children who cannot yet read have vague or even wholly misguided conceptions about it. Even those who do not will find much of the terminology used in reading lessons new. They may not be familiar with the idea of talking about language. They may lack the necessary knowledge about words, syllables, and phonemes that are prerequisites for an analytic approach to reading. To master the art of reading they will have to learn to pay attention to features of language that they have previously ignored. Although children beginning school have a good command of spoken language, which they can produce and comprehend effectively, they lack the ability to analyze and reflect on the form of language, independent of its meaning. The ability to think and talk about language is sometimes described as a 'metalinguistic' skill, one level up from the basic linguistic skills required for using language to talk about the world.

Before discussing the development of specific reading-related skills, it is necessary to make one methodological point. Many of the findings about how the development of these skills relates to progress in reading are only correlational—they show that the age at which a child acquires a certain skill reflects the age at which that child develops a particular reading ability. However, it is a truism that correlations are not necessarily indicators of causal relations. Furthermore, even when there is a causal relation, a correlation cannot show which direction it runs in. The skills considered could, therefore, be related to reading in various ways. Ehri (1979) identifies four types of relation. First, skills may be 'prerequisites': skills upon which reading builds, and which must be acquired before reading can be learned. Second, they may have the role of 'facilitators': skills which may speed progress in beginning reading, but which are not essential. Third, they may be consequences of learning to read: skills that develop through practice at reading rather than vice versa. Finally, there may be no direct link between a skill and reading ability at all—they may be incidentally correlated, perhaps because each is related to some other factor, such as intelligence. Because a variety of explanations are possible for a correlation between a particular skill and reading ability, it is not always clear that training in that skill will improve reading. Training can only be useful if a skill is either a prerequisite for or a facilitator of reading development.

One method by which causal relations can be tested uses a mixture of longitudinal and training studies. Longitudinal studies establish which of two abilities develop first in the individual child. Since abilities that develop later cannot cause the development of abilities that develop earlier, longitudinal studies rule out whole sets of causal hypotheses. But abilities that develop earlier do not necessarily cause the development of abilities that develop later, even if the two are strongly correlated. The development of both may be caused by a third factor—a general facility with language, for example. However, if training the ability that develops early has a specific effect on the ability that develops later, and if more general training does not have the same effect, then a causal relation is indicated.

However, combined longitudinal and training studies are difficult and time-consuming to carry out, and their importance has only recently been recognized. There is, therefore, some uncertainty about which skills are necessary for reading to begin. It follows that the concept of 'reading readiness' must be questioned. Readiness tests are intended to assess whether a child is ready to begin formal reading instruction. They assess the perceptual, cognitive, and linguistic skills assumed to be used in reading (for example, visual and auditory matching, letter-sound relations), so that appropriate prereading instruction can be given, if necessary. But reading-readiness skills will only be helpful if the skills taught are prerequisites for beginning reading. As will become clear from the evidence below, learning to read may foster some 'readiness skills,' rather than vice versa.

1.1 Understanding of Printed Language Concepts

Between the ages of 3 and 5 years children's ideas about reading change dramatically, as do their ideas about the components of written language. For instance, 3 year olds are more likely than older children to misassess their reading ability, thinking that they can read when they cannot. By 5 years, most children know if they are unable to read, and know about the importance of words. Preschool children may not know about the directional constraints in reading, and also typically have some difficulty in understanding reading and writing terminology—they often cannot distinguish between letters, words, and sentences or between letters and numerals. Thus, it cannot be assumed that children start school with any clear concept of reading. They probably know that they will learn to read, but may not know what this means. Children's early knowledge of the language and terminology of reading has been shown to correlate with their later reading skill. However, an explicit understanding of reading-related concepts may not be a prerequisite for reading. Reading instruction may encourage children to develop a more analytic approach and to learn more about the terminology, rather than vice versa, though without some basic concepts, such as an understanding of the left-to-right rule in English, reading will not progress very far.

1.2 Letter Recognition

Children's knowledge of letter names when they start school is a good predictor of reading progress during the first year, but is not related to later success in reading. However, teaching children letter names does not improve their reading, and children can learn to read without being able to name any letters. It is likely that, rather than letter knowledge having a causal role in reading acquisition, some common variable, such as an interest in written materials, underlies both letter naming and reading.

Children often have difficulty discriminating between letters that are mirror images of one another. This difficulty has nothing to do with visual discrimination, but is probably related to the need to pay attention to orientation, which will not have been important to the child previously. Although many objects have a canonical orientation, they do not assume a different identity when their orientation changes.

1.3 Word Consciousness

'Word consciousness' or 'lexical awareness' is the ability to recognize that both writing and speech are made up of distinct entities called words. Although the concept of a word is one that literate adults take for granted, it is not necessarily an obvious one to young children. Some 5 year olds still find it difficult to recognize words as distinct units. (An excellent review of research on word consciousness is given by Linnea Ehri (1979), who also addresses some of the broader issues about the relation between word consciousness and reading.)

Performance on some tasks that measure word awareness skills is correlated with early reading ability. For example, in beginning readers, reading skill correlates with ability to judge whether a sound is made up of one word or two words or whether it is a word at all. Reading ability is also related to the ability to pick out the word or words that differ between two sentences. More surprisingly, first-grade children have difficulty detecting word boundaries in printed materials, despite the fact that there are clear visual cues to where one word ends and the next begins. The ability to pick out printed words develops with increased reading proficiency.

It has not been clearly established whether teaching word consciousness skills enhances reading. Some children are aware of words before they begin to read, so word consciousness is not simply a consequence of learning to read. However, there is no evidence that it is essential for reading to begin.

1.4 Phonemic and Linguistic Awareness

Children may begin to read by learning to recognize whole words as visual patterns, more or less as 'logographs.' But learning an adequate reading vocabulary in this way would place an enormous, and unnecessary, burden on memory. Children learning an alphabetic writing system can capitalize on the fact that the written symbols are (to a greater or lesser extent) associated with phonemes (see *Writing Systems: Principles and Typology*). Once children have grasped this principle, which is regarded by many as the key to learning to read, they will be able to gain independence in reading, and be able to recognize for themselves words that they have never before seen written.

In particular, children must learn the rules that relate written letters or groups of letters to sounds. However, in English, these rules are complex as there is often no one-to-one correspondence between letters and sounds. Such rules are called 'grapheme-phoneme correspondence' rules (GPC rules) because they state the relation between small units of written language (graphemes) and small units of spoken language (phonemes). To apply grapheme-phoneme correspondence rules, children have to be able to break written words into parts, and put the parts back together once the corresponding sounds have been determined (these skills are called 'segmentation' and 'blending'). The use of these rules demands at least an implicit mastery of the phonemic system of the language. The phonemes or sound segments produced by application of the rules must then be blended to produce a pronunciation for the word as a whole.

However, before they can apply an analytic strategy to word decoding, children must become aware of the phonemic segments into which words can be divided. Without such awareness, decoding using grapheme-phoneme correspondence rules and blending are impossible. But experiments with young children (4- to 5-year olds) have shown that they find segmentation of words into phonemes almost impossible. Children are much better at dividing words into syllables and putting syllables together to form words. Such data clearly show that the younger children have difficulty making explicit the phonemic distinctions needed for many approaches to reading, although they are perfectly able to perceive differences at the phonemic level (e.g., they know that two words that differ in one phoneme are not the same). Prereading success on the phoneme segmentation task predicts reading success in the second grade. Young children's difficulty in this area is probably related to the fact that phonemes, unlike syllables, do not have acoustic boundaries separating them in speech.

Furthermore, phonemes overlap in speech, largely because of a phenomenon known as 'coarticulation.' The way the parts of the mouth move means that, for example, the articulation of /b/ will depend on the following vowel. The first part of *bat* is pronounced differently from that of *but*. The very first bit of the word contains information about the vowel as well as about the /b/ (see *Speech Development: Acoustic/Phonetic Studies*). Thus, when a word is broken into its constituent sounds, and these are said individually—for example, *cat* into /k/, /a/, and /t/—only approximations to the underlying phonemes can be derived. Therefore, no matter how fast the consecutive phonemes are spoken, they will not blend together to form *cat* unless they are distorted.

More general phonemic awareness skills have also been shown to be related to early reading. Even very obvious features of words, such as their spoken or written length, may be difficult for children to perceive. For example, prereading children perform at chance level when shown two cards and asked to say which shows the word *mow* and which *motorcycle*. They do not understand even this highly-salient feature of writing—that the word that looks longer has the longer pronunciation.

Young (kindergarten) children experience even greater difficulty in tasks that require them to be aware of more subtle phonemic differences between words, such as deciding whether two words begin with the same sound, or whether two words rhyme. The lack of phonemic awareness in young children is also indicated by their performance on sound deletion tasks. For instance, when asked to say what remained when a particular sound was removed from a word (e.g., /h/ removed from *hill*), children with a mental age below 7 are unable to perform the task at all, and for more advanced children middle sounds (e.g., /s/ in *nest*) are harder than initial or final ones. Performance on this phoneme deletion task has been shown to correlate with reading skill in the first and second grades.

In an important and influential study, Bradley and Bryant (1978) addressed the question of whether there is a causal link between phonemic analysis skills and reading. They compared backward readers (10-year olds) not only with normal readers of the same age, but with normal children (6-year olds) who had the same reading age as the backward readers. They asked children to detect the odd-one-out in sequences of four spoken words (either on the basis of alliteration, or of rhyme), and to produce words that rhymed with other words that they read out. The older normal readers showed the best performance, but the important finding was that the backward readers were poorer on such tasks than the younger normal readers, even though they had, presumably, had much more experience of written language. Bradley and Bryant argue that phonemic analysis skills do not simply develop through exposure to print, but that they are causally related to reading—phonemic awareness helps children learn to read. In a later longitudinal study, they provided further evidence for this idea. They showed that performance on the odd-one-out task at 4- or 5-years was a good predictor of reading achievement, but not of mathematical ability, three years later. They also found that training in categorizing picture names by their sounds improved reading and spelling skills

in nonreaders who were lagging behind in phonemic awareness, but only when it was supplemented by teaching with plastic letters that demonstrated to the children how words that have sounds in common often have common spelling patterns. The improvement in reading was long-lasting—when the children were retested at 13, those given phonological training were still ahead of the control groups (who were either given no training, or training in an unrelated skill) in reading and spelling, but the children trained in the connection between sounds and letters were still ahead of all other groups. In this study, as in the previous one, there were no differences between the groups in arithmetic—the training effect was restricted to reading and spelling. These studies by Bradley and Bryant have shown that training to rectify a deficiency in the skill of sound categorization can improve reading generally. But it is also possible that learning to read improves phonemic awareness.

Ellis and Large (1988) have suggested that the causal relation between reading and phonemic skills (they used syllable- and phoneme-segmentation, and rhyming and blending tasks) changes over the first few years of schooling. In a longitudinal study, they showed that the phonemic skills of those children who were nonreaders at age 5 predicted their reading ability at 6. However, once reading ability begins to develop, it causes the development of reading-related skills. For those children who had begun to read, reading skill at 5, and again at 6, predicted phonemic skills one year later. Ellis has suggested that the ability to read 'makes sense of' sound skills and fosters their development. Work with adults also suggests that learning to read using an alphabetic system allows phonemic awareness to develop. Chinese adults (who were fluent only in a logographic script) did poorly on phonemic segmentation tasks by comparison with those who could read an alphabetic script (see *Chinese Writing System*). Similar results have also been found when Portuguese illiterates and ex-illiterates are compared on segmental analysis tasks. The poor performance of illiterate adults on such tasks suggests that learning to read has a causal role in the development of phonemic awareness. However, whatever the precise relation between such skills and reading, young children should find an analytic approach to reading difficult.

1.5 Orthographic Awareness
The orthography, or writing system, of a language such as English comprises more than just an alphabet (see *English from the Introduction of Printing*). There are also rules about which sequences of letters are admissible. For example, the orthographic rules of English would be violated by a word beginning *zn-*. Furthermore, some letters appear more often in certain positions in words, and some of the permissible sequences of letters are more common than others. Just as words within sentences are to some degree predictable—for example, one expects articles to be followed by nouns—so are letters within words. To the extent that a letter is highly predictable it is said to be 'redundant.'

In one type of experiment to investigate orthographic awareness, children are asked to make explicit judgments, for instance, saying which of two nonwords they think are more 'word like.' Their ability to perform this task increases with age and with reading fluency. However, studies that have investigated how orthographic structure affects speed of word identification or naming have found no improvement with age beyond the initial stages of learning to read. But, in a task that more closely approximates reading—lexical decision (deciding whether a string of letters is or is not a word)—younger children are more influenced by the orthographic features of letter strings than older children. The nonwords are either similar or dissimilar, orthographically, to real words. In this sort of task, younger children take longer to reject the wordlike nonwords.

2. Approaches to Teaching Reading

The two main methods currently in use to teach children to read are the 'whole word' (or look-and-say) approach, and the 'phonics' (or code-based) approach, though a method gaining in popularity is the 'real books' or 'apprenticeship' approach.

The contribution of the skills discussed in Sect. 1 to children's reading development may depend on how they are taught to read. Letter orientation, order, and attention to salient features of words will be important for approaches that emphasize sight recognition of words, with little attention to letter-to-sound rules. Differentiation of letters, the association between sounds and letters and blending of sounds will be more important for phonics approaches.

2.1 Whole Word (Look-and-Say)

As has already been seen, it is difficult for young children to segment and analyze words into their component features. In this approach the overall shape and gross visual features of the word are stressed, and not its component letters, so analytic skills are not necessary. The assumption behind this method is that children should be taught to read the way skilled readers do, by recognizing words 'directly' without having to analyze them into their component letters. Children are taught to recognize a small set of words from cards. These first words are those that occur very frequently in print, and ones which will be in their first reading books. Once children have built up a basic sight vocabulary they progress to the first reading book in the scheme, in which almost all the words are taken from the flashcards. The method also circumvents the problem that, in English, there are numerous exceptions to any simple set of grapheme-phoneme correspondence rules.

An approach that is related to the whole-word approach which has been widely used is the language experience approach. This approach combines learning to read with learning to write, and relates reading to the child's own experiences and spoken language. The correspondence between spoken and written language is stressed. From the start, children are encouraged to make up written sentences about things that are of interest to them. For instance, they might write their own captions for pictures, and then put together a series of such captioned pictures to make a 'story' booklet, which then becomes a text for learning to read. In one such scheme, children have their own word file or dictionary. The file contains basic words from reading books, each on a small card, together with the child's individual words, which are written on blank cards by the teacher. The philosophy of this approach is that learning to read should be related to functions of language with which children are already familiar, in particular its communicative function. The first words taught are based on children's own experiences. By using these words to compose written sentences about events that are meaningful to them, children learn both about reading and about its connection with writing. One advantage of the language experience approach is that the real function of written words—that they convey meanings—is emphasized from the outset. A second advantage is that this approach can be tailored to individual children's language capabilities and vocabulary, as well as relating reading to topics that are of interest to them.

The whole-word method has numerous disadvantages and limitations. The argument that children should be taught to identify words the way that skilled readers do is contentious. Skilled readers may access word meanings directly (without phonological recoding), but beginning readers may, nevertheless, benefit from training in decoding. Indeed, there are occasions when skilled readers need to recode phonologically, for example to identify words that are in their spoken vocabulary, but which they have not met before in written form. Equipped with only the ability to recognize words as visual patterns, beginning readers will have no tools for deciphering new and untaught words. They need to learn the alphabetic principle.

2.2 Phonics

Phonics approaches to the teaching of reading stress the importance of GPC rules. Children taught this way learn the sounds that the letters of the alphabet usually make, so that they can pronounce unfamiliar printed words. They may have to attain a certain level of proficiency in producing the appropriate letter-to-sound correspondences before they are exposed to words. This approach provides children with a more general reading skill. In principle, they should be able to 'sound out' any new word they come across. In practice, however, things are not so straightforward. Grapheme-phoneme correspondences in most of the languages that use an alphabetic writing system are irregular to a greater or lesser extent, and a letter may be associated with several different sounds. Furthermore, as discussed in the previous section, a letter's sound often depends on the surrounding letters. A more serious problem for phonics methods arises from the difficulty that young readers have in dividing words into their parts. Most 5-year olds find it impossible to perform the word segmentation and blending that are fundamental to the phonics approach.

2.3 The 'Psycholinguistic' Method

Finally, an approach to reading instruction based on Goodman's 'psycholinguistic guessing game' account of reading requires consideration (see, for example, 1967). This account assumes that readers begin with numerous expectations about the meaning and purpose of the text, and use the print only to confirm or disconfirm these predictions. Smith, another proponent of this approach, argues that, since adults can access word meanings directly without first deriving a phonological representation, there is no reason to teach children to read by this 'unnatural' method. He further argues that the reading speed of skilled readers proves that they cannot be attending to every letter. Fluent readers make use of all kinds of information—syntactic, semantic, and pragmatic—in recognizing words, and Smith's view is that beginners should be taught to read in the same way. He argues that decoding is not only an unnatural and difficult method of learning to read, but that it can be positively harmful. He proposes that in 'making sense' of the text, children will learn whatever rules they need to. In other words, children should 'learn to read by reading'—by deriving hypotheses from the context and from prior knowledge of what the text is about (for a summary of these ideas see Smith 1973).

However, Smith is not explicit about how children should be taught. He simply suggests that children should be immersed in interesting, meaningful materials. Nevertheless, his ideas have been very influential in educational circles, and a method that is becoming increasingly popular—the real books or apprenticeship approach—has been motivated by the ideas of Smith and Goodman. In this approach, the similarities between learning to read and learning to speak are stressed, and the emphasis is on books with motivating content and an interesting story line. There is little attempt at formal teaching in the initial stages, which are similar to the sorts of initiation into reading that the child might experience at home. First, children simply listen to an adult reading to them, while following the story in a book, then they attempt to read along with the adult until they feel able to 'read' some or all of the text themselves.

However, apart from Smith's failure to explain exactly how children should be taught, there are a number of flaws in his arguments. For example, there is no good evidence that skilled readers rely heavily on context to help them identify clearly printed words in normal reading. Such guesswork may sometimes be useful in identifying a visually unfamiliar word or even for working out the meaning of a wholly new word. But, in general, contextual information is usually available too late to aid word identification in skilled readers. Smith's theory predicts that skilled readers make greater use of context in word identification but, as will be seen below, the evidence suggests the reverse.

Finally, there is no reason to believe that the best way to teach reading is to train young children in the skills used by adults. Reading cannot simply be a guessing game. There must be some decoding of the printed text so that the guesses can be confirmed or disconfirmed. Furthermore, decoding usually needs to be taught. It cannot be expected to materialize as a by-product of intelligent guesswork, though some children are undoubtedly able to work out the rules for themselves, with little formal instruction. Interesting accounts of the characteristics of children who learn to read before they go to school can be found in Clark (1976).

2.4 Assessment of Teaching Methods

It is difficult to make an objective assessment of methods of teaching reading, because there are so many factors that cannot be controlled. Indeed, it has been suggested that children's progress in learning to read is much more closely related to the quality of their teacher than to the program used. Some children seem to learn by any method, and some fail by any method. However, presumably some methods produce better results on average than others.

Chall (1979) surveyed research on the relation between teaching method and reading achievement. Her conclusion

was that an early emphasis on phonics led to better reading by the time the children had reached the fourth grade than did a whole-word approach, at least as far as reading new words and reading aloud were concerned. However, teaching method had little effect on comprehension, or on interest and involvement in reading. A more recent review of this research (Johnson and Baumann 1984) also confirms that early intensive instruction in phonics produces readers who are more proficient at pronouncing words than are those taught by a whole-word approach. There is little evidence on the efficacy of the apprenticeship approach because it is too new to have been properly assessed.

3. The Development of Reading

3.1 Stage Models of Reading

There are various models that attempt to give an account of the stages that children go through as they learn to read (for an example of such a model see *Disorders of Reading and Writing*). In general, such models propose that the child progresses from learning words as unanalyzed wholes to a more analytic approach in which grapheme-phoneme and orthographic rules are used. For instance, two such models are similar in proposing three stages:

(a) a logographic stage in which familiar words are recognized as visual patterns, using salient visual features, and new words cannot be identified at all;

(b) an alphabetic phase, in which the child learns and uses GPC rules and can tackle novel words and decode nonwords;

(c) an orthographic phase where the child learns the conventions of the English orthography, and identifies words by making use of orthographic units, without the need for phonological conversion.

A detailed comparison and critique of these two models, and a related one, can be found in Stuart and Coltheart (1988), who argue that the way in which children approach initial reading is not invariant, but depends on what skills they have available to them: for instance, children who already have some phonological skills may not enter the logographic phase at all.

3.2 Meaning Access: Direct or Mediated

The conversion of a written word into its spoken form may be a useful way of recognizing that word, even in skilled readers. The ability to carry out this so-called phonological recoding may be an important part of the development of reading. Phonological recoding in word recognition requires the use of spelling-to-sound rules, such as the GPC rules discussed earlier.

Since the sight vocabularies of beginning readers are relatively underdeveloped in comparison with their aural vocabularies, phonological coding is important for these readers in retrieving the meanings of words that they have heard but never before encountered in print. However, even beginning readers can recognize some words directly, from their visual appearance. Although the research in this area has produced somewhat inconsistent results, most evidence suggests that phonological recoding skills are relatively late in developing. Children progress from accessing the lexicon without the use of phonology to the use of both phonology and direct (visual) access. However, some studies have shown the reverse pattern: that young children rely more on phonological information in word recognition than older children. These discrepant results may have arisen because of the sorts of stimuli used in the experiments: high frequency, concrete words might invite direct access, whereas less frequent, abstract words may require phonological mediation. Of course, the relative use of different strategies in word recognition may depend not only on age, reading ability, and type of word, but also on the method used to teach reading.

Words could also be converted to a phonological form after they are recognized, by simply looking up the pronunciation in the mental dictionary. So, even if children can access the meanings of words directly, phonological recoding may play some part in their reading strategies, and those of skilled readers, because it provides a more durable medium than visual coding for storing early parts of a sentence so that they can be combined with what comes later. There is good evidence that children use postlexical phonology to aid comprehension. Indeed, older children and adults find it hard to suppress phonological coding even when it is disadvantageous (e.g., in remembering lists of phonologically-confusable picture names). Even Japanese subjects reading Kanji, a logographic script, store the symbols in a phonological rather than a visual or semantic form (see also *Japanese Writing System*). In these cases, a phonological code cannot be produced from the pictures or logographs by using GPC rules. The word must be accessed from the visual pattern and its phonological form retrieved and used as a memory code.

3.3 Use of Context in Reading

A number of experimental studies have investigated changes in children's use of context as their reading skill develops. However, a distinction must be made between the use of context to correct or prevent errors, and the use of context to speed word recognition. In general, older readers are better at using context to make predictions (e.g., guessing what the next word might be) or to check them, but they do not use context as much as younger readers to identify words in the normal course of reading. The use of context in reading has played an important role in some theories of reading acquisition. Certain theorists (notably, Frank Smith) have based their ideas for teaching reading on the premise that good readers are better at using contextual information to help them decipher words. However, there is no evidence to support this hypothesis at the level of word recognition and, in any case, most content words are not very predictable, so that use of context will not compensate for inadequate word decoding. In fact, all the experimental evidence on the effects of context on word recognition points to the opposite conclusion—the use of context decreases as reading skill increases (for a review, see Stanovich 1982). There is no doubt that contextual and perceptual information work together in word recognition—they interact. However, the primary use of context in poorer readers is to compensate for the fact that they cannot recognize words from their perceptual properties alone.

4. Reading Comprehension

4.1 The Development of Comprehension Skills

One might assume that, once children have learnt to decode the words in text reasonably efficiently, comprehension will follow automatically. Since children learning to read have, for some years, been understanding spoken language, one would expect the skills they have learnt to transfer to understanding language in written form. However, this does not always seem to be the case. Reading comprehension is highly correlated with listening comprehension but, in fact, children's listening comprehension may not be as highly developed as one would expect from their level of language development—many children who have reading comprehension problems also have listening comprehension problems. However, there are also a number of reasons why beginning readers might have problems that are specific to reading. Both of these possibilities will be discussed here in relation to the development of comprehension skills.

Writing is not simply 'speech written down.' The language of books is a particular language register that children may not be familiar with unless they have had many books read to them before and as they learn to read. In addition, written language does not have all the supporting cues (stress, intonation, gestural, and facial expression) that accompany everyday oral interactions. If children are to read with understanding, they need to be initiated into this 'language of books.'

A second problem is that young children may be so engrossed in the word-decoding aspect of reading that they do not have the cognitive capacity to simultaneously carry out comprehension processes. In addition, the rapid loss of information from short-term memory makes it difficult for very slow readers to 'hold' information from early in a sentence so that they can integrate it with what comes later. If word recognition is slow and labored, much of the prior context may have been forgotten by the time the current word has been recognized. Decoding skills will obviously improve with practice so, as children get older, they can devote more attention to comprehension. Indeed, it has been shown that in the later primary school years, comprehension skills replace decoding skills as the most important predictors of overall reading ability. A related problem is that beginning readers may think that 'getting the words right' is the point of reading, and may not connect this activity with having stories read to them. It may not be until children's word recognition skills become relatively fast and automatic, that they are able to give their full attention to comprehending the content of the text.

In the remainder of this section, consideration is given to comprehension skills where there is likely to be some overlap between written and spoken language understanding. However, it should be borne in mind that some of the processes may be more difficult to carry out in the case of written text, for the reasons given above.

Understanding a text results in a mental representation of the state of affairs the text describes—a mental model of the text. Even after the individual words have been identified and grouped into phrases, clauses, and sentences, a number of other skills will also be necessary to construct such models. The meanings of individual sentences and paragraphs must be integrated, and the main ideas of the text identified. In many cases, inferential skills will be needed to go beyond what is explicitly stated, since authors necessarily leave some of the links between parts of the text implicit. The development of children's ability to make inferences from text is considered later, and also a number of more specific skills that are necessary for comprehension. For story understanding, these include: identifying the main characters and their motives, following the plot, and deriving the main theme. In the case of expository texts, the skills include identifying the topic, differentiating between important and trivial information, following the argument, and extracting the gist meaning of the passage.

The development of children's ability to monitor their own comprehension—to be aware of whether they have adequately understood a text—is also reviewed. As reading progresses beyond the beginning stages, such 'metacognitive' skills become increasingly important. Although beginning readers also need to make use of metalevel knowledge (the technical vocabulary of reading), comprehension processes are much more dependent than word recognition and decoding on metacognitive abilities. Children need to be aware that they have not adequately understood a piece of text, and to know what to do to remedy their lack of understanding.

4.1.1 Understanding the Structure of the Text

Many recent theories of comprehension have drawn attention to the fact that information in a text is hierarchically structured. This structure arises because each text is focused round one or more main ideas, with subsidiary ideas and trivial details subordinated to the main ones. Proper understanding of a text depends on an understanding of the main point, and on sensitivity to the relative importance of the other ideas (see *Discourse Processing*).

During the primary school years there is a marked increase in children's ability to pick out the main idea of a text, and to judge the relative importance of different aspects of a text. Even at 12, most children are only able to distinguish explicitly between the very important and very unimportant information (and not between intermediate levels). In contrast, children's recall of text is very sensitive to level of importance (as determined by adults): even 5-year olds are more likely to recall the main events in a text than the trivial details. This discrepancy between awareness of levels of importance and the effect of importance on recall may be related to children's developing metacognitive skills (see below)—children may pay more attention to the more important ideas in a text, even though they cannot explicitly identify which those ideas are.

Another important element in comprehension is understanding how the ideas in a text are related, and one way to assess children's understanding of the logical structure of texts is to ask them to tell stories themselves. Research has shown that children gradually develop the ability to tell coherent narratives and that, like adults, they expect certain types of information to be present in stories. When expected information is missing, it is often added in retelling, so that the story corresponds to what was expected. Similarly, when a story relates events out of order, the normal order is often restored in retelling and, as children get older, they are more likely to reproduce an ill-structured story in a well-structured form (for a review, see Baker and Stein 1981). The ability to understand how ideas are interconnected in a story probably develops even before children learn to read.

4.1.2 Making Inferences from Text

Inference has many roles in comprehension (for a review, see Oakhill and Garnham 1988: ch. 2). In particular, inferences are crucial to the process of connecting up the ideas in a text, since many things are left implicit. The emerging mental model of the text will indicate where such gaps arise and, therefore, which of the multitude of possible inferences need to be made. There have been numerous studies of the development of children's inferencing skills. In general, these studies support the idea that young children can make the same inferences as older ones, although they do not do so spontaneously, and only do so when prompted or explicitly questioned.

A related important question is whether inferences are drawn as a text is understood, or only later. It is quite feasible that neither younger nor older children make optional (i.e., elaborative) inferences during comprehension, but that older children are superior at answering inferential questions because they are able to recall a greater proportion of the explicit information in the text, from which they can make inferences retrospectively. The available data are compatible with this explanation of developmental trends.

4.1.3 Comprehension Monitoring

Comprehension monitoring is necessary as a means of assessing whether one's understanding is adequate, so that appropriate action can be taken to overcome any comprehension difficulties. This is one of the metalinguistic skills that children acquire as their linguistic skills develop. All readers monitor their comprehension to some extent but, in general, younger children are less likely to realize that they do not understand, or to know what to do about it if they do realize (for a review, see Garner 1987). They are, for example, unable to detect that crucial information is missing from a text, or to spot even gross inconsistencies. However, there is no good evidence that metalinguistic awareness is causally related to comprehension skill. It may be that the process of learning to read increases the child's language awareness, rather than the other way round.

Children's ideas about reading, which can be elicited in interviews, also provide some indication of their metacognitive awareness. A typical finding is that younger children generally have fewer resources to help them deal with comprehension failures.

4.2 Theories of Poor Comprehension

The problems of poor comprehenders—children who have adequate word recognition skills, but who do not understand what they read as well as might be expected, will now be considered (for a review of this area, see Oakhill and Garnham 1988: ch. 5). Three main types of theory have been advanced to account for children's comprehension difficulties. The first is that children have problems at the level of single words. One obvious possibility is that poor comprehenders have inadequate vocabularies—they may be able to decode many words whose meanings they do not know. In general, vocabulary size is a good indicator of reading comprehension skill perhaps, in part, because both depend on general linguistic experience. However, procedures that are effective in increasing vocabulary do not necessarily improve comprehension. Furthermore, it is possible to identify groups of children who are matched on vocabulary who nevertheless differ markedly in comprehension skill. Another potential problem at the level of words is that poor comprehenders' word recognition, though accurate, is not automatic. Some authors (notably, Perfetti, see for example, 1985) have shown that good comprehenders recognize words more rapidly than poor comprehenders and they argue that this lack of automaticity creates a 'bottleneck' in working memory. On this view, poor comprehenders have less capacity available for comprehension processes—not because they have smaller working memories, but because they make less efficient use of them. However, although there are several sources of evidence that poor comprehension and slow decoding go together, there is probably no direct causal link between the two. It may be precisely because decoding is such a basic part of reading that children who read more decode faster. Furthermore, speed and automaticity often go hand in hand with a large vocabulary and accurate decoding. When these two factors are taken into account, fast decoding is not such a reliable indicator of good comprehension.

Some work has suggested that good comprehenders, like older children, make greater use of context in reading. In general, good comprehenders are better at using context as a check on their decoding, but they do not make so much use of context as poor comprehenders to speed word recognition.

A second view is that comprehension problems arise at a higher level of text processing. One hypothesis is that poor comprehenders fail to make use of the syntactic constraints in text. Work to explore this idea has shown that poor comprehenders tend to read word-by-word, and do not spontaneously group text into meaningful phrases. Other studies that have investigated sensitivity to syntactic structure more directly have shown that, rather than using the syntactic and semantic cues in a text to integrate the meanings of the individual words, poor comprehenders seem to treat each word separately. These processing characteristics might, at least in part, be related to differences in working memory between good and poor comprehenders.

The third view is that poor comprehenders' problems arise beyond the sentence level—at the level of text integration and inference. Many studies indicate that good and poor comprehenders differ in the extent to which they integrate the information in a text, and in their use of inferences. Such studies show that the making of inferences not only helps the skilled comprehenders to understand the text, but also to remember it. If poor comprehenders make fewer inferences than good ones, one must always ask whether it is because they have poorer inferential skills, or whether they cannot remember the information on which the inferences are based. This question is particularly important because many measures of text comprehension impose demands on memory. However, the evidence suggests that the poor comprehenders's inferior inference skills cannot be explained in terms of poor memory for the text, but that poor comprehenders are less good at working memory tasks than their skilled counterparts. Since working memory is important in making inferences and in the construction of a meaning representation of the text, it is not surprising that poor comprehenders are deficient in these text-comprehension skills.

Other text-level skills differentiate between good and poor comprehenders. In Sect. 4.1.3 it was seen that young children are often poor at monitoring their comprehension, and fail to realize that they have not understood a text. Good comprehenders, like older children, seem to have a better awareness of what comprehension is and when it has been successful. There is evidence that poor comprehenders' problems arise, at least in part, because they fail to monitor their comprehension, or make less use of monitoring strategies (see Garner 1987, for a review). Again, working memory may play a part in such processing—readers with deficient working memories will have little scope for the sorts of processes required to monitor comprehension.

Of course, each of the possible explanations of poor comprehension may be right—each may characterize the difficulties of a distinct group of poor comprehenders, or may partly explain an individual child's problem. In general, though, it seems that children with a specific comprehension deficit have particular difficulties in making inferences from and integrating the ideas in text. Poorer readers also have metacognitive deficits. They often have inadequate conceptions of reading, and may not realize that the primary purpose is to make sense of the text, focusing on reading as a decoding, rather than a meaning-getting, process. Fortunately, a variety of procedures designed to help such children have proved quite successful (for a review, see Oakhill and Garnham 1988: ch. 6).

In general, children who are poor at understanding text are also poor at understanding spoken language. Many studies have found differences between good and poor text comprehenders even in listening tasks. Such findings again support the idea that decoding speed and automaticity can only be part of the poor comprehenders' problem. The skills on which good and poor comprehenders differ also suggest that they will experience difficulty with listening too. Problems with syntax, memory, and metacognitive monitoring would certainly be expected to be general comprehension problems, and not restricted to reading. This does not, of course, mean that reading is no more than decoding plus oral comprehension skills. There are many important differences between oral and written language, but children who have trouble understanding written language often have trouble with spoken language too. So, although slow decoding might contribute to reading comprehension problems, particularly in the initial stages of learning to read, it is unlikely to be their only cause.

See also: Language Acquisition in the Child; Reading Processes in Adults; Reading, Theories of; Children's Early Reading Development; Reading Difficulties; Disorders of Reading and Writing.

Bibliography

Baker L, Stein N L 1981 The development of prose comprehension skills. In: Santa C, Hayes B (eds.) *Children's Prose Comprehension: Research and Practice*. International Reading Association, Newark, DE

Bradley L, Bryant P E 1978 Difficulties in auditory organisation as a possible cause of reading backwardness. *Nature* **271**: 746–47

Chall J S 1979 The great debate: Ten years later, with a modest proposal for reading stages. In: Resnick L B, Weaver P A (eds.) *Theory and Practice in Early Reading*, vol. 1. Lawrence Erlbaum, Hillsdale, NJ

Clark M M 1976 *Young Fluent Readers*. Heinemann Educational, London

Ehri L C 1979 Linguistic insight: Threshold of reading acquisition. In: Waller T G, MacKinnon G E (eds.) *Reading Research: Advances in Theory and Practice*, vol. 1. Academic Press, New York

Ellis N, Large B 1988 The early stages of reading: A longitudinal study. *Applied Cognitive Psychology* 2: 47–76

Garner R 1987 *Metacognition and Reading Comprehension*. Ablex, Norwood, NJ

Goodman K S 1967 Reading: A psycholinguistic guessing game. *Journal of the Reading Specialist* 6: 126–35

Johnson D D, Baumann J F 1984 Word identification. In: Pearson P D (ed.) *Handbook of Reading Research*. Longman, London.

Oakhill J, Garnham A 1988 *Becoming a Skilled Reader*. Blackwell, Oxford

Perfetti C A 1985 *Reading Ability*. Oxford University Press, Oxford

Smith F 1973 *Psycholinguistics and Reading*. Holt, Rinehart and Winston, New York

Stanovich K E 1982 Individual differences in the cognitive processes of reading. Vol. II: Text-level processes. *Journal of Learning Disabilities* 15: 549–54

Stuart M, Coltheart M 1988 Does reading develop in a series of stages? *Cognition* 30: 139–81

J. Oakhill

Reading Difficulties

For most children, learning to read involves the integration of a system for processing written language with one which already exists for processing spoken language. When learning to read in an alphabetic script such as English (see *Writing Systems: Principles and Typology*), the child has to learn that printed words convey meanings, that the printed letters (graphemes) in written words map onto the individual speech segments (phonemes) of spoken words (see *Phoneme*) and that there are irregularities in these mappings (see *English Spelling: Rationale*). In addition, when reading continuous text, the child has to integrate the meanings of words in phrases and sentences, using knowledge of syntax and text integration (see *Discourse Processing*). The attentional resources which these various processes require are considerable and place limitations on the extent to which the novice can be expected to read well. This is especially true if the child has basic language deficiencies.

Children experience difficulties learning to read for two main reasons. They may be generally slow in all curriculum areas, perhaps because of a global language difficulty. These children are usually described as 'backward' or simply, poor readers. On the other hand, they may have a specific reading difficulty (or 'dyslexia'). Arguably, these children have more specific language problems than generally backward readers (Hulme and Snowling 1988). From a linguistic perspective, they have specific difficulties with one or more of the component subskills which contribute to fluent reading.

1. Phonological Difficulties

It is widely held that phonological awareness is one of the best predictors of reading achievement, even when the substantial effects of IQ are partialled out (Goswami and Bryant 1990; see *Literacy and Phonological Awareness*). Moreover, phonological deficits, including difficulties with phoneme segmentation and nonword repetition, are characteristic of dyslexic children, who also have difficulty using phonological short-term memory codes (see *Disorders of Language, Phonological*). It is therefore not surprising that the primary problem which they have with reading is in the use of phonological strategies (see *Language Acquisition: Phonological Studies*). This can be seen most directly in their approach to reading nonsense words (words which are new to them). There have been many studies showing that dyslexics have nonword reading deficits which are out of proportion to the problems that they have in reading words. Moreover, case-study evidence concerning such individuals (described as developmental phonological dyslexics) has shown that the striking discrepancy between word and nonword reading skill is not transient; it may persist throughout development, imposing a constraint upon reading unfamiliar materials, such as technical or foreign words.

2. Morphological Problems

The development of alphabetic competence (the appreciation that there are mappings between sounds and letters), must be accompanied by increasing proficiency with orthographic processing (Frith 1985). Words in English orthography vary in the directness of mapping sound onto spelling. Some words (e.g., *cat*) have a simple pattern where each phoneme is represented by a single letter; in other cases more complex (e.g., *head*) or obscure relationships (e.g., *yacht*) exist. Many are nevertheless rule-governed, and dictated by morphological factors (e.g., sign-signature; see *Morphology*). These 'opaque' orthographic conventions, violating the simple application of letter-sound rules, are gradually learned (see *Morphophonemics*). However, some dyslexic children are unable to make this advance; their reading remains alphabetic, proceeding on the basis of sound. Thus, they have more difficulty in reading irregular words than regular or nonsense words. These children have been described as developmental surface dyslexics. Their reading development is 'arrested' at a later stage than that of phonological dyslexics (see *Disorders of Language: Morphological Implications*).

3. Syntactic Deficits

A number of recent studies have suggested that dyslexic readers have difficulties with syntactic processing, for example, problems with judgments of grammatical well-formedness, and a delay in the acquisition of certain syntactic structures (Shankweiler and Crain 1986; see *Language Acquisition: Grammar; Parsing: Psycholinguistics*). A problem with these studies, is that certain syntactic structures—e.g., some types of relative clause—may only be encountered with any frequency in written language (see *Relative Clauses; Written and Spoken Language: Relationship*). It follows that poor readers will have had less exposure to these than good readers and, hence, will have difficulty in dealing with them. Thus, it remains equivocal whether syntactic processing problems actually affect the *reading* process.

4. Semantic Deficits

The reading difficulties which characterize dyslexic children are specific difficulties with decoding processes. However, there are also children who can decode well but who have comprehension difficulties. Indeed, a syndrome of 'hyperlexia' in which decoding skills are precocious has been posited. These children are proficient in the use of phonics (see *Reading Teaching: Methods*). Detailed examination of their reading comprehension shows that it is generally in line with (poor) vocabulary development (see *Language Acquisition: Vocabulary*). Thus, the existence of 'hyperlexia' indicates that the development of single-word reading skills can advance without the support of comprehension. This pattern of performance can also be observed in children learning to read in a second language (see *Second Language Processing: Reading*).

5. Knowledge of the World

Reading for meaning involves the integration of information gleaned from a text with the reader's existing knowledge of the world. Oakhill and Garnham (1988) review studies showing that young readers and poor comprehenders have difficulties in making inferences from, and integrating the ideas in, texts. It has also been shown that readers of low verbal ability have more difficulty in choosing story-appropriate completions for sentences during reading, regardless of grammatical category, than children of higher verbal ability but similar decoding skill. Moreover, when subsequently asked to answer questions about texts they read, they can answer those requiring memory for facts as well as controls can, but they have difficulty with those on which they have to bring general knowledge of the world to bear.

6. Conclusions

It is clear that there are numerous *specific* difficulties which children can encounter when learning to read. Collectively, these difficulties extend beyond single-word processing and may affect reading comprehension. The capacity of individual children to overcome such difficulties will depend upon the interaction of their cognitive strengths and weaknesses with the teaching they receive (Snowling 1987).

See also: Reading: Acquisition; Reading: Testing; Miscue Analysis; Children's Early Reading Development; Literacy and Metalinguistic Awareness; Reading, Theories of; Sentence Types and Clause Subordination; Disorders of Reading and Writing; Reading and Writing Disorders: Intervention.

Bibliography

Frith U 1985 Beneath the surface of developmental dyslexia. In: Patterson K E, Marshall J C, Coltheart M (eds.) *Surface Dyslexia*. Routledge and Kegan Paul, London

Goswami U, Bryant P 1990 *Phonological skills and learning to read*. Erlbaum, Hove

Hulme C, Snowling M 1988 The classification of children's reading difficulties. *Developmental Medicine and Child Neurology* **37**: 167–69

Oakhill J, Garnham A 1988 *Becoming a skilled reader*. Blackwell, Oxford

Shankweiler D, Crain S 1986 Language mechanisms and reading disorder: A modular approach. *Cognition* **24**: 139–68

Snowling M 1987 *Dyslexia: A Cognitive Developmental Perspective*. Blackwell, Oxford

M. J. Snowling

Reading Inventories, Informal

The informal reading inventory (IRI) consists of graded passages of text which the learner is asked to read aloud. Questions are then asked about their understanding of what they have read. On the basis of this performance, the teacher can decide the level of difficulty of text with which the pupil can cope. Although a form of assessment, the technique is seen as more natural and closer to the classroom situation than a formal reading test (see *Reading: Testing*). As Powell (1971: 642) has explained, 'the strength of the IRI is not as a test instrument, but as a strategy for studying the behavior of the learner in a reading situation and as a basis for instant diagnosis in the teaching environment.'

The use of the IRI can be traced back to the 1920s, although Betts (1957) is usually credited with popularizing and carefully describing the technique in the 1940s and 1950s; he identified several levels of student functioning in reading: 'independent,' 'instructional,' and 'frustration,' according to the number of errors made and the questions answered correctly.

Pikulski (1990), comparing four IRIs, reported considerable variety in respect to the grade levels covered; the length of passages used; the source of passages (whether they were specially written; whether they were based on readability formulas; whether they were selected from basal readers or taken from literature books); the use of pictures; the range, type, and number of questions used for each passage; the criteria adopted for the instructional level; the time needed to give the IRI; and the type of text used (expository or narrative, or both). Questions to assess understanding could be factual, inferential, or terminological; conclusion or evaluation questions were used rarely.

Sometimes the literature refers to 'curriculum IRIs.' This is where the teacher constructs his/her own IRI by using passages from the reading scheme or basal series being used in the classroom.

The development of 'miscue analysis' has had considerable influence on how 'errors' are perceived (see *Miscue Analysis*). More recent IRIs have taken such research into consideration, and published versions provide detailed information as to what should be recorded as an error. So the effective use of the IRI depends on users who have a good understanding of the nature of the reading process and are familiar with the flexible diagnostic use of IRIs to provide insights into how the learner is coping with the process and developing appropriate strategies.

Generally, the IRI is now seen as a way to evaluate reading less formally; as an attempt to match readers with the texts that are likely to be experienced in the classroom; and as a technique to enable teachers and reading specialists to answer specific teaching questions and to understand the nature of a child's reading. For all these purposes, it is necessary that the results are seen as tentative.

Bibliography

Betts E A 1957 *Foundations of Reading Instruction*. American Book Co., New York
Johnson M J 1987 *Informal Reading Inventories*. International Reading Association, Newark, DE
Pikulski J J 1990 Informal reading inventories. *The Reading Teacher* **43**: 514–16
Powell W R 1971 Validity of the IRI reading levels. *Elementary English* **48**: 637–42

E. Goodacre

Reading Processes in Adults

Reading may be defined in the most general terms as the extraction of meaning from print, though already at this point the objection may be raised that readers do not so much extract meaning from print, but rather engage in an active construction of meaning based on the signs provided by the print. The impossibility of providing a more precise definition is apparent when considering that reading encompasses processes as different from one another as understanding a 'STOP' sign, studying a complex textbook, and reading a long novel for pleasure. All that can be said with a fair degree of certainty is that the skills readers use for the extraction of meaning from print are extremely complex, automated to a fairly high degree, and highly flexible, comprising a number of different styles (see *Word Recognition and Lexical Access*; *Parsing: Psycholinguistics*; *Discourse Processing*).

The complexity of reading is partly caused by the fact that reading, apart from using the linguistic and cognitive mechanisms involved in any receptive skill (e.g., lexical access, syntactic parsing, inferencing), also involves visual and perceptual mechanisms whose primary function is not the reception of linguistic signals. It employs two distinct routes to meaning: a 'phonological' route involving mapping written symbols onto their sound equivalents prior to accessing meaning, as well as a 'direct' route, so called because it incorporates no intermediate stage involving sounds but rather consists of direct access from the orthographic representation of the word to its stored form in the reader's memory. In addition, in contrast to the listener, the reader can control the reception of the linguistic input by means of eye movements, and is thus far more active than the listener is. The complexity of reading is further manifest in the ability of readers to handle both print and handwriting, though understanding of how the latter is processed is extremely partial.

The degree of automaticity in reading is not completely clear. The eye does not move over the page in an automatic way—its movement is guided by the content of what is being read. Yet at lower processing levels, such as recognition of features, letters, and possibly words, the mechanism is nevertheless largely automated, so that cognitive attention is being freed to deal with higher-level operations.

The flexibility of the reading process has led researchers to identify a number of reading styles, which have great importance in educational contexts. The choice of reading style seems to be a result of two factors. First, 'reading purpose' has been found to influence the way readers structure their progress through long stretches of text. Related to that are the findings that the attention readers pay to different types of words in sentences (e.g., function words vs. content words) varies according to the task they have been set. Thus clarifying reading purpose seems to be an important metacognitive skill. Second, 'text type' seems to generate different types of reading behavior. Thus research into reading style and reading purpose confirms reading as an extremely flexible activity, with the reader being able to control a large repertoire of behaviors.

1. The Physical Basis of Reading

The most important point about the physical process of reading is that eye movements during reading are not smooth; the eye moves in short leaps, known as 'saccades,' typically lasting approximately 20–35 msec and spanning 7–9 characters. Saccades are ballistic movements; that is, they are fully planned before execution, and nothing can be done to change them once execution has been initiated. Between saccades the eye rests on a specific spot on the page; these periods, each lasting approximately 250 msec, are known as 'fixations.' Perceptual processing of printed information occurs only during fixations: no information can be processed visually during saccades. Approximately 10–15 percent of saccades are regressions to previously fixated words. The latency of oculomotor movements, which is approximately 125–175 msec, means that the decision about where to move next must be taken within the first 50 msec or so of each fixation. Although not all information regarding the word being fixated is processed by that time, the decisions are sensitive and quick enough for readers to exhibit preferred fixation locations (between the beginning and middle of a fixated word) as well as to be able to skip short words, in which case the fixation on the previous word tends to be longer.

During fixations, the most sensitive region of the eye, the fovea, rests on the word being fixated. The structure of the eye means that the visual angle that can be seen with sufficient visual acuity subtends only 2 degrees. However, at the same time information perceived in the parafoveal region of the eye (subtending an additional 5 degrees to either side of the fovea) is also being processed. The importance of parafoveal information has been demonstrated in eye movement studies showing that when fewer than 14 characters to the right and four characters to the left of the point of fixation are visible to the reader, reading is impaired. The information gleaned from the text via the parafovea usually refers to spaces and hence to the number of words in the vicinity of fixation as well as to their shape; it is instrumental in determining the length of the next saccade and the locus of the next fixation. Information is thus acquired from a large area, from letters and from spaces, all of which contribute to the control of eye movements so that it might be useful to think of three different perceptual spans: the letter identification span, which is the area from which letter information is extracted; the word identification span, which is the area from which word identification proceeds; and a total information span, from which useful information is extracted. One aspect of eye movements which is still not well understood is the way information from different fixations is integrated across saccades to form a fairly continuous and relatively error free progression across the page.

Finally, it is important to mention the 'return sweep,' which is the movement from the end of the line to the beginning of the next line. These are fairly complex movements since they are initiated before the end of the line is reached and involve a long movement to an area which has not been previewed parafoveally.

2. Investigating Reading

Because reading is a mental process, it cannot be directly investigated. Researchers are confined to examinations of its external manifestations or of external evidence demonstrating that comprehension has taken place. This lays a great proportion of reading research open to criticism concerning its ecological validity; that is, the extent to which a given methodology compares with a real-life reading situation. Such criticism may, for example, query the extent to which our understanding of reading is helped by 'lexical decision' tasks (timing subjects' decisions on words, nonwords, or letter arrays as constituting words). Another type of criticism may ask how far one naturalistic activity, such as oral reading, reflects another, such as silent reading. Also, laboratory demands mean that readers are put in a studying mode rather than a simple reading mode during experiments (Anderson and Pearson 1984). The answer to these criticisms is that, in spite of sometimes seeming far removed from what happens in reading itself, many methodologies highlight different features of processing that may be vitally important to any reader.

For the sake of convenience, it is possible to place methodologies on a number of axes. The first important distinction is 'process' versus 'product' orientation. Since the product of reading is usually some kind of comprehension or integration into existing memory structures, some researchers claim that by probing changes in these structures (by asking comprehension questions or requiring subjects to recall passages they have read) reading can be examined. However, such procedures clearly place the object of the investigation at one further remove from the process. Process-oriented research, on the other hand, attempts to discover what actually happens while reading is going on, by examining the different outward manifestations, such as eye movements, gaze duration, recording of oral reading, and introspection. In this case, it is the intrusive nature of most process-oriented research which has often been subject to criticism.

A further methodological consideration is the 'unit of investigation,' beginning with letters and words; continuing with phrases, clauses, and sentences; and ending with whole texts, with ecological validity presumably increasing with length of text. Finally, it is useful to think of methodologies in terms of the 'level' at which they tap into the reading process. Some methodologies investigate fairly low-level behavior, such as word recognition (though this is not to say that such low-level behavior is not influenced by higher level processes); others investigate fairly high-level cognitive behavior, such as note-taking and summarizing.

Methodologies are often bound to a certain level of investigation. Not all methodologies can provide insights at all cognitive processing levels. For example, fairly complex instrumentation is needed for investigations aiming to provide a detailed and accurate time course for reading activities. Some methodologies may also encourage a certain type of reading, thus limiting the generalizability of their findings to the process as a whole.

All of these reservations should be borne in mind when considering the research methods surveyed below; furthermore, it is important to remember that this is only a small number of the variety of ways researchers look at reading.

2.1 Eye-movement Research

The text appears on a cathode ray tube (CRT) and an invisible infrared ray, directed at the eye, reflects eye movements during reading. The sensitivity of this method has enabled researchers to come up with a wealth of information regarding fixation patterns and constraints. The main objection raised by critics is that the subject's head must be mechanically restrained throughout the experiment, possibly leading to a distortion of the behavior under examination.

2.2 Subject-paced Methods

The text appears on a computer screen at a rate determined by the subject, who presses a button to advance the display; the units according to which the display moves are predetermined by the experimenter: clauses, groups of words, single words, etc. Some experimenters include a 'look-back' facility. The main advantages of this method are its relative accessibility and ease of use in a variety of settings, including educational research, and that it may be used to probe the process at various levels. Its main disadvantage is that in its most sensitive form, where the text is read word by word, its ecological validity is lowest, since subjects are deprived of the ability to use parafoveal information.

2.3 Rapid Serial Visual Presentation (RSVP)

The experimenter controls the presentation of the text totally. The main advantage is the ability to vary presentation speed and to check for comprehension at greatly increased speeds.

2.4 Miscue Analysis

This method, used extensively by Goodman (1970) and his coworkers, analyzes the mistakes readers make while reading aloud. Its impact on educational methods and on theories of second-language reading has possibly been greater than that of any other methodology (see *Miscue Analysis*).

2.5 Tachistoscopic Methods

The tachistoscope allows the researcher to control the mode and length of presentation of isolated words and to probe the subjects' reaction to them. Two tasks commonly investigated in this way are naming (i.e., reading a word aloud—note the need for a special name for this task) and lexical decision.

2.6 Letter-detection Methods

Subjects are asked to read a text and to circle any occurrence of a letter, group of letters, or word. It has had some impact on the consideration of attention and automaticity in reading and has led to some fruitful discussion of the units of reading.

2.7 Introspection and Think Aloud

Here subjects are asked to introspect about their reading while it is going on. This approach, which regards reading from a problem-solving point of view, is mainly suitable for the investigation of higher-level cognitive processes of which the reader is conscious.

3. Models of Reading

It is convenient to group models of reading into two types. Sequential models (Sect. 3.1) attempt to chart the time course of reading; that is, what actually happens from the moment the reader first sets eyes on the line of print. Componential approaches (Sect. 3.2), on the other hand, attempt to analyze reading into its component processes and to examine what type of knowledge the reader utilizes, with the temporal interaction of these components relegated to a secondary place.

3.1 Sequential Models

3.1.1 Bottom-up Models

Possibly the best example of such models is still Gough's (1972) linear, unidirectional model which, in spite of being a fairly early attempt, nevertheless captures many of the essentials of bottom-up models. Aptly presented under the title 'One Second of Reading,' it begins with the visual input of a single fixation, during which purely visual information about letter features is taken in, creating an 'iconic image' on the retina. The letters are then scanned in from the iconic image, identified in a serial manner, and stored in a 'character register.' They are then decoded and mapped onto a 'lexical entry' using some kind of letter–sound correspondence. The meanings assigned to the words as a result of lexical search are then stored in 'primary memory.' This memory store compiles the words (once again, in a serial fashion) until enough words have accumulated for the entire store to be comprehended. They are then cleared through the application of syntactic and semantic rules. Gough calls the mechanism performing these syntactic and semantic operations 'Merlin,' and the place where the sentences are stored is TPWSGWTAU (the place where sentences go when they are understood), two names which serve as an indication of the state of our knowledge about this part of the process.

3.1.2 Top-down Models

Clearly, even the most extreme bottom-up model such as Gough's takes into account the reader's contribution to the process, in the form of knowledge of pattern recognition rules, decoding rules, syntactic, and semantic rules. What top-down models stress, however, is the active contribution of the reader to the lower-level processes; beginning with intake of visual information and going on to decoding. The serial processing of letters and words described in Sect. 3.1.1, where each stage must be completed before the next one is allowed to take place, is rejected. The stress is on reading efficiency, minimizing the reader's dependence on visual elements and maximizing dependence on meaning cues: the memorable phrase used by Goodman (1970) to describe reading is 'a psycholinguistic guessing game.'

Goodman's model may serve as a suitable contrast to Gough's: it sees the reader as engaged in a tripartite ongoing process of 'prediction,' 'confirmation,' and 'correction,' preceded by recognition-initiation and followed by termination of reading. According to the model, the reader hypothesizes about what will be read, samples the text to test the hypothesis, and then, upon confirmation of the hypothesis, forms new hypotheses and begins anew. This process is carried out in a series of cycles: 'optical,' 'perceptual,' 'syntactic,' and 'meaning.' The model thus claims that only a small portion of the text is actually perceived: only when a hypothesis is disconfirmed does the reader decode all letters and words. It is important to emphasize that the guessing that Goodman (1970) describes is not the overall, generalized type of guessing which enables readers to skip whole sentences or passages: what is meant is guessing at a far lower level of letter and word recognition.

3.1.3 Interactive Models

Intuitively attractive though top-down models are, they have been criticized for being too vague to generate useful research hypotheses, as well as contradicting subsequent research findings. One reasonable expectation, if such models were correct, would be to find that good readers rely on context more than poor readers. Yet a large number of studies have shown that the opposite is true: it is poor readers who rely on context more. Good readers decode faster and therefore do not need the context as much as poor readers do. Furthermore, the constant hypothesis testing which top-down models would have the reader engage in seems extremely time-consuming. On the other hand, a large body of experimental evidence has shown that surrounding context facilitates word recognition and that readers do not decode each letter. Recent models of reading, therefore, present the reading process as a constant interaction between top-down and bottom-up processes. They introduce compensatory mechanisms or other ways through which higher-level cognitive processing might influence lower level decoding strategies. They also often take account of the attentional limitations of the human mind, and make use of the notion of automatic versus controlled processing, hypothesizing that certain elements of reading are automatized, so that attentional capacity can be devoted to higher-level operations.

3.2 Componential Approaches

As far as the components of reading are concerned, it is clear that readers need to engage in a large variety of cognitive operations in order to extract meaning from text. Componential approaches have usually tried to deal with those aspects of reading that are engaged in constructing meaning from discourse. However, it has proved impossible to form a definitive list of universally applicable components apart from, possibly, knowledge of the meanings of words (Oakhill and Garnham 1988). The notion of flexibility helps explain why this is so: because of the great variation in texts, genres, and reader purposes, both in real life and in experimental conditions, there is little hope of finding any but an extremely general common denominator. Anything more complex than that is dependent upon the intricate interplay of all factors, with any single factor becoming critical only when brought to prominence by some feature of the text or of the reader: at all other times the necessary component skills of reading are integrated to a degree that makes it impossible to distinguish between them.

In spite of this complexity, there have been a large number of attempts to compile lists of reading skills and components. The classification of reading into five styles offered by Pugh (1978) seems both useful and adequate. 'Scanning' is basically a matching activity, in which the reader attempts to locate a group of symbols. 'Search reading' is searching for words from a semantic field. 'Skimming' involves using the author's structure to construct an overview of the text. 'Receptive reading' is an author-directed activity in which the reader attempts to uncover what the writer intended to convey. 'Responsive reading' uses the writer's words as a prompt for the reader's own activity.

The sections below discuss some of the important component skills readers make use of for the comprehension of discourse. This list can only serve to hint at the complexity of the issues and is extremely partial. Note that it includes many components that are not specific to reading: reading is a specialized activity which calls upon cognitive skills which are used for other purposes as well.

3.2.1 Resolving Anaphoric Relations

To form a coherent representation of discourse in the mind, the reader constantly needs to resolve anaphoric references (by means of pronouns, repeated or new noun phrases, and ellipsis) to previously mentioned nouns (see *Anaphora*; *Discourse Processing*). Although assigning anaphoric reference is often a matter of making inferences, the difference is that in contrast to inferences, which may often be optional, resolving anaphora is a prerequisite for comprehending discourse. Doing so entails a complex combination of grammatical rules, discourse conventions (rather than rules), and knowledge of the world. This complexity means that the making of anaphoric linkages, which begins with the encoding fixation, must continue to be carried out over a succession of fixations.

3.2.2 Activating Schemata

Schemata, the abstract memory structures in which knowledge is organized, have been shown to play a crucial role in comprehension (see *Discourse Processing*). As investigating recall protocols has shown, readers who do not possess, or who are unable to activate, an appropriate schema, often interpret a text according to their own schemata, reach false conclusions about it, and store a misrepresentation of the text. Schema theory and schema-oriented research thus emphasize the active contribution the reader makes to understanding the text, and are on a reader-driven end of the scale. However, the top-down process in this case operates on a far more general scale than the one that Goodman (1970) hypothesizes.

Both content schemata (knowledge of the world) and formal schemata (knowledge of the conventions of text genres) play a role in attention allocation, although the type of attention that is paid is not clear. However, it has been demonstrated that readers spend more time on segments of texts that are relevant to their purpose, and seem to be more engrossed in the segments that are connected to

the schema that has been activated than in other segments (Wilson and Anderson 1986). Thus, though the mechanism for schema activation is not clear, activating the right schema for the right text is crucial for comprehension.

3.2.3 Inferencing

Two points must be made. First, making inferences is an essential part of comprehension. Writers cannot possibly make all the information in a text explicit; they must rely on the reader to make the necessary inferences in each case. Second, the number of inferences that can usually be drawn even from one or two sentences is extremely large; readers cannot possibly make all of them. Thus a mechanism must exist for the reader to make only those inferences that are necessary and sufficient for comprehension of the text. There is also the question of when the inferences are made; since there is such a large number of possible inferences, it is possible that readers draw them only when forced to do so, that is, when integration of the new context into a coherent representation of the discourse necessitates an inference (see *Inference*).

3.2.4 Comprehension Monitoring

Baker and Brown (1984: 355) identify 'three main types of metacognitive skills: awareness, monitoring and deployment of compensatory strategies.' Thus an important characteristic of skilled adult readers is their ability to assess the degree to which comprehension has taken place and, when in doubt, to decide on an appropriate course of action: ignoring parts of the text; automatically correcting the internal representation (i.e., assuming that the text is corrupted or erroneous and going on reading); reinspecting the text, either through a regressive fixation (in case of localized comprehension difficulties) or going back to a previous section. A common metaphor in the literature is the ability to drive more slowly and shift gears when reaching an uphill slope in a car. Adult readers may well take comprehension monitoring for granted, and it may be partly automatized; yet this is not, on the whole, an automatic skill. It entails an understanding of what reading is done for, an acceptance that the printed word is not sacred, and the ability to compare the world as appearing from the text with the reader's own perception of the world. Thus younger readers, as well as poor readers, have been shown not to notice what for an adult reader would be fairly blatant inconsistencies in texts. This tallies well with the existence of a fairly large number of training studies indicating the developmental, learned nature of this skill, as well as its educational importance. Comprehension monitoring literature often looks at reading for remembering and reading for meaning as two different activities.

All levels of reading are monitored, beginning with spelling and typographical errors and ending with the ability to pick up inconsistencies across a large portion of text.

4. Reading in Different Languages

The overview of reading presented above is overwhelmingly based on research conducted on reading in English. Any generalization from these findings to other languages should be made with extreme caution, given the great differences between languages and the problems of comparing research crosslinguistically, resulting from the difficulty of experimentally equating languages. Yet the body of evidence suggests that differences may exist in the reading processes between languages, with differences in writing systems, orthography, morphology, and syntax all contributing to the development of correspondingly different reading processes (see *Writing Systems: Principles and Typology*).

At the physical level of eye movement, fixation durations in Chinese, Japanese, and Hebrew tend to be longer than in English, whereas saccade length is shorter than in English. This reflects a greater density of information, both visual and linguistic, in these three languages, yet it is difficult to separate the contribution of orthographic and morphological components of this phenomenon. Another finding is that the asymmetry of the perceptual span is reversed for readers of languages written from right to left: information is extracted from 14 characters to the left of fixation and 4 characters to the right (see Sect. 1 above). The size of the perceptual span is likewise dependent on the density of text in the appropriate language (Rayner and Pollatsek 1989).

At the lowest cognitive level involved, that of letter and word recognition, readers may be using different strategies depending on the 'orthographical depth' or 'shallowness' of the script (that is, the degree to which script-sound correspondences are regular and unambiguous). Readers of orthographically shallow languages, where such correspondences are extremely regular, may have no incentive for developing a *direct* route to meaning. Indeed, it has been suggested that readers of Serbo–Croat, for example, may be constrained by the orthography to use only a phonologically mediated route, and in Spanish it has been demonstrated that word recognition is slower than in English, with words being processed in a clearly linear fashion. On the other hand, in an orthographically deep language such as Hebrew, using as it does a phonemically impoverished orthographic code, there is evidence suggesting that readers may be relying on orthographic rather than phonemic codes for lexical access. This might be even more characteristic of readers of logographic languages such as Chinese, although it must be stressed that, contrary to popular belief, Chinese orthography does in many cases provide phonological clues to the pronunciation of the word, and Chinese readers may be using more of a mixture of strategies than is commonly believed. Other languages may exhibit even more striking phenomena: proficient readers of Arabic have been shown in experimental conditions to process letters as visual stimuli rather than linguistic stimuli.

At higher levels of processing, eye movement research has shown that readers of German, unlike readers of English, tend to fixate on short function words. This is attributable to the fact that in German, many function words are inflected for case and gender, thus containing important morphological information. Subject-paced reading studies have shown that readers of Spanish do not use certain parsing procedures which can be shown to be used by English readers (Mitchell, et al. 1990).

The little evidence there is of the differences in reading strategies in various languages has two important implications: first, it serves to emphasize the flexibility of the reading process; second, it highlights the problematic question of the transfer of reading skills from a first language to a second (see *Second Language Processing: Reading*).

See also: Reading: Acquisition; Writing Systems: Principles and Typology; Psycholinguistics—Overview; Second Language Processing: Reading; Reading Teaching: Materials; Reading: Testing; Line Breaks and Reading; Readability; Miscue Analysis.

Bibliography

Anderson R C, Pearson P D 1984 A schema-theoretic view of basic processes in reading comprehension. In: Pearson P D (ed.) *Handbook of Reading Research.* Longman, New York

Baker L, Brown A L 1984 Metacognitive skills and reading. In: Pearson P D (ed.) *Handbook of Reading Research.* Longman, New York

Goodman K 1970 Reading: A psycholinguistic guessing game. In: Singer H, Ruddell, R B (eds.) *Theoretical Models and Processes of Reading*, 2nd edn. International Reading Association, Newark, DE

Gough P B 1972 One second of reading. In: Kavanagh J F, Mattingly I G (eds.) *Language by Ear and by Eye: The Relationships between Speech and Reading.* MIT Press, Cambridge, MA

Mitchell D C, Cuetos F, Zagar D 1990 Reading in different languages: Is there a universal mechanism for parsing sentences? In: Balota D A, Flores d'Arcais G B, Rayner K (eds.) *Comprehension Processes in Reading.* Lawrence Erlbaum, Hillsdale, NJ

Oakhill J, Garnham A 1988 *Becoming a Skilled Reader.* Basil Blackwell, Oxford

Rayner K, Pollatsek A 1989 *The Psychology of Reading.* Prentice Hall, London

Pearson P D (ed.) 1984 *Handbook of Reading Research.* Longman, New York.

Pugh, A K 1978 *Silent Reading: An Introduction to its Study and Teaching.* Heinemann Educational, London

Wilson P, Anderson R C 1986 What they don't know will hurt them: The role of prior knowledge in comprehension. In: Orasanu J (ed.) *Reading Comprehension: From Research to Practice.* Lawrence Erlbaum, Hillsdale, NJ

A. Paran

Reading Recovery

Reading recovery is a program created as a 'prevention strategy designed to reduce dramatically the number of children with reading and writing difficulties in an education system' (Clay 1987: 36). It was developed initially in New Zealand during the late 1970s by Marie Clay.

Children who are identified early on in their school careers as being within the bottom 20 percent of readers in their class receive individual daily lessons from a specially trained teacher. Once the children are able to work comfortably at the average class level they leave the program. It is claimed that this standard is achieved by about 80 percent of children on the program within a 12–20-week period. Because the reading ability of a child selected for the program is relative to its class scores there may be significant differences between schools in the reading levels of their reading recovery groups.

Unlike many other educational innovations which tend to spread on a fairly random basis, the introduction, dissemination, and development of reading recovery has been, and will continue to be, regulated very tightly. Access to the program by teachers is rigorously controlled. Class teachers must participate in a year of part-time training by 'teacher leaders' who have themselves undertaken a year-long full-time course of training. The number of training institutions is small and within countries whole networks are set up to maintain the purity of the procedures. Since the program's inception, reading recovery has been introduced to Australia (1984), USA (1984), Canada (1988), and the UK (1990).

Each reading recovery session is structured within a 'lesson frame.' During a 30-minute session a child: (a) reads familiar materials; (b) reads yesterday's new book; (c) engages in some writing; (d) is introduced to, and reads, a new book chosen from a collection organized into 20 levels. During these four phases the teacher keeps records and interacts with the child, introducing strategies as appropriate. Once the session is finished the child returns to the classroom and experiences regular class teaching. The pedagogic orientation is toward helping the child develop a range of strategies within meaningful contexts rather than forcing her/him to learn sets of discrete skills (DeFord, et al. 1991).

The adherents of reading recovery claim great success for the program. Only a limited number of studies have examined these claims, most of which have been carried out by people involved in developing and teaching reading recovery. There are even fewer long-term studies of the consequences of reading recovery. The studies tend to support the claims but there are still questions to be examined. One problem is that there is really nothing to compare the program with; the degree of control over the implementation and teaching of the program seems unique. Thus, for some educationalists, it remains to be seen whether it is the particular literacy strategies, the degree of one-to-one teaching, or the systematically controlled application of the program which are critical for success.

Reading recovery is inevitably a very expensive program to implement and maintain, and the rigid control of the program means there can be no cost cutting. The absence of substantial long-term studies means that the cost-effectiveness of the program remains uncertain.

See also: Reading Teaching: Methods; Children's Early Reading Development; Reading Difficulties.

Bibliography

Clay M 1987 Implementing reading recovery: Systematic adaptations to an educational innovation. *New Zealand Journal of Educational Studies* 22: 35–58

DeFord D, Lyons C, Pinnell G 1991 *Bridges to Literacy: Learning From Reading Recovery*. Heinemann, Portsmouth, NH

N. Hall

Reading Teaching: Materials

In past centuries, people learnt to read from the Bible and *Pilgrim's Progress*. In the late twentieth century scores of books are written for the specific purpose of teaching children to read. In Britain they are called 'reading schemes,' in North America 'basal reading programs.' Typically, a reading scheme is 'any set of books which has

a common theme and authorship, follows a progression of difficulty such that the earliest books or materials can be read to some extent by beginning readers, ascends in level of difficulty, style and content, and is marketed with associated materials such as teachers' manuals, prereading activities, workbooks, and kits' (Winch 1982: 76). Writers have to create texts that enable learners to induce the complex relationships between the marks on the page and their own oral language. There are a number of ways in which this can be done.

1. Phonic Schemes

Phonic schemes aim to simplify the learner's task by using a high proportion of words that have regular spellings. In the early stages, this usually means words with short vowel sounds represented by single vowel letters and with consonant sounds represented by the letter or letters most frequently associated with them, e.g., 'cap,' 'bed,' 'milk,' 'strong,' 'funny.' Later, words with long vowels or diphthongs represented by common vowel digraphs or by a vowel letter plus ⟨-e⟩ may be included, e.g., 'wait,' 'tree,' 'mine,' 'boat,' 'food.' It is never possible for all the words to be regularly spelt since so many of the unavoidable grammatical words in English use infrequent spelling patterns, e.g., 'the,' 'was,' 'of,' 'one.' If pupils have understood the alphabetic principle and have learnt the most frequent grapheme–phoneme correspondences, then it should be possible for them to read a considerable number of regular words without having had to memorize them visually. Phonic reading schemes are therefore generally characterized by a relatively high number of different words ('types') in each text. This gives the writer some scope for writing a reasonably interesting story and for avoiding unnatural levels of word repetition. However, the linguistic disadvantage of a high proportion of phonically regular words is that it tends to produce an arhythmic text— because so many of the words are monosyllables—which may also have an unhelpful amount of unintended rhyme. There is research evidence that the worst examples, e.g., *The cat can bat the pan*, are 'inordinately difficult to process' (Adams 1990: 322). Later phonic schemes have avoided these excesses; a British example is *New Way* (1987).

2. 'Sight' Schemes

A quite different approach to simplifying the beginning reader's task is to select words that are visually distinctive in the hope that the child will remember the appearance of the whole word without having related its component letters to their phonemic equivalents, e.g., 'aeroplane,' 'adventure,' 'elephant,' 'tortoise.' This approach, which is sometimes called 'look and say,' requires writers to control strictly the number of word types both within and between books in a scheme in order to lighten the burden on the reader's memory. Such vocabulary control necessarily means that the words that do appear have to be repeated frequently. Although repetition is needed if children are to develop a vocabulary of words recognized on sight, it can have two detrimental effects. The first is the occurrence of grammatical structures not usually found other than in reading schemes (leading to a style sometimes known as 'read-erese'), for example:

See the children play.   (1)

Fly fast, big aeroplane!   (2)

The second is the violation of the normal information structure of a written discourse, where there is an expectation that—apart from passages in which the author explicitly summarizes what has gone before—each new sentence will introduce some new information. In reading books where the same words are recycled repeatedly, the information gets recycled too, for example:

> My house has a roof. It is a red roof. The roof of my house is red.   (3)

With text like that, the motivation for continuing to read has to come from something external, such as the desire to learn to read or to please the teacher, because the meaning alone is not enough to carry the reader forward. A sight scheme with less obtrusive vocabulary repetition is *Reading 387* (1978), widely used in both Britain and North America.

A particular type of sight reading scheme selects a high proportion of the vocabulary on the basis of a word frequency list. The best known example in Britain is the *Ladybird Keywords* (1964) scheme. This was devised in the light of research that showed, among other things, that just 12 words—'a,' 'and,' 'he,' 'I,' 'in,' 'is,' 'it,' 'of,' 'that,' 'the,' 'to,' 'was'—constitute roughly a quarter of all adults' and children's reading material. The authors believed that, if children learnt to read from books that repeated these and other high frequency words very often, they would rapidly be able to read a wide range of texts. Unfortunately, this ignores the fact that short words that are not picturable are very hard for young children to remember; also, a heavy concentration of them produces remarkably arid language, for example:

> He will let us go in with him.   (4)

Later sight schemes, e.g., *Story Chest* (1982) put more emphasis on meaning and less on strict vocabulary control.

3. Modified Orthography

A more radical approach to the particular problem of the complexity of the English writing system is to modify it. Various approaches have been tried, including diacritics, color coding, and a revised alphabet (see Southgate and Roberts 1970). The only one that has had any significant take-up within the British education system is i.t.a. (the initial teaching alphabet), which was designed by Sir James Pitman. During the 1960s and early 1970s it was adopted by 10 percent of English schools that had infant classes but later it was virtually abandoned and is of only historical interest. Even so, it is worth a brief account because it illustrates some of the problems that, despite generous funding and official recognition and support, beset attempts to revise English orthography (see *Spelling Reform Proposals: English*).

The i.t.a. contains 44 characters, including 24 from traditional orthography (TO) ($\langle x \rangle$ and $\langle q \rangle$ are omitted). The 20 additional characters are similar in design to traditional graphemes; indeed, 14 of them are digraphs consisting of two familiar letters joined by a ligature. The aim of the system is to provide, as far as possible, a one-to-one relationship between sounds and symbols while retaining

sufficient similarity to TO to make transfer easy. So postvocalic $\langle r \rangle$ is retained in words like *farm* $\langle \text{farm} \rangle$, even though most English speakers of English do not pronounce the $\langle r \rangle$ in that position. Although it is possible to find words in which every character is new, for example, *chose* $\langle \text{chœs} \rangle$, the majority of words undergo only slight changes, for example, *little* $\langle \text{littl} \rangle$, *morning* $\langle \text{morniŋ} \rangle$.

The problems that led to the demise of i.t.a. in the classroom were largely practical: parents' opposition; the paucity of reading materials available in i t a; the difficulty for teachers of managing the transition phase, when some of their pupils were on i.t.a., some on TO and some between the two; and so on. There was one shortcoming, though, that arose from a failure to exploit fully the advantages of a regularized alphabet: i.t.a. was not associated with any one particular reading scheme, and several TO schemes were transliterated into i.t.a. This meant that when sight schemes with severely restricted vocabulary were transliterated, all the problems of unnatural grammar and static discourse were carried over to the new medium, despite the fact that, with the benefit of consistent grapheme–phoneme relationships, pupils should not have been so dependent on visual memory and should have been able to decode a wider vocabulary.

4. 'Language Experience' Materials

An alternative to using published reading materials as a basis for early reading lessons is to use books that children write themselves—in other words, to foster a closer relationship between the teaching of reading and writing than is usual (see *Writing: Process Approach to Teaching*). This is most likely to happen when a school adopts a 'language experience' (or 'whole language') approach. Obviously very young children have not got sufficient manual skill to produce handwriting that will be sufficiently legible for other children to read. However, the widespread use in primary schools of computers with concept keyboards and simple word-processing programs means that even 5-year olds can create little stories that become part of the classroom reading stock.

Another method used in some British schools to help beginners to write is called 'breakthrough to literacy.' This is a set of materials and techniques that was a product of the Schools' Council Programme in Linguistics and English Teaching (see *Schools Council (UK): English Teaching Program*). Children have a small plastic stand and a sentence maker, which is a folder containing small pieces of card, some with a high-frequency word printed on them, and some blank for the child's own words. When they want to write a sentence, the children select the words they need from the sentence maker and arrange them in sequence in the stand. Their finished work can be transcribed by the teacher and the resulting books made available to all the children.

The biggest advantage of reading materials that derive from language experience approaches is that the language comes from the children themselves, so there is no risk of the unnaturalness of 'readerese.'

5. 'Real' Books

During the 1980s, a small but influential group of educationists in Britain led a movement against published reading schemes. They advocated that children should be taught to read using so-called 'real' books (a misleading label, since it implies that any book written with the express purpose of teaching children to read is somehow not 'real'). The emphasis is on the quality of the writing and illustrations in the books offered to children, rather than on the vocabulary control and graded progression from one level to another that characterize reading schemes. Vast numbers of fine books for young children are published every year. The idea is that a selection should be available in the classroom; that the child should choose any book and 'read' it with the support of the teacher or another adult. This 'apprenticeship' approach (Waterland 1985) puts the enjoyment of reading before the acquisition of skills and allows the child to learn from the behavior of a skilled practitioner, but it obviously makes substantial demands on teachers' time.

A comparison of the language of reading schemes and 'real' books (Perera 1993) shows that the latter generally have longer sentences, a greater variety of sentence length, more polysyllabic words, and less word repetition. Together, these features lead to more natural-sounding language than is found on the whole in reading schemes. However, the high rate of introduction of new words can cause reading difficulty. A particular problem is that there may be no overlap of vocabulary from one book to the next that the child chooses.

6. Trends in the 1990s

Since the 1970s there have been changes both in the kinds of books used in the teaching of reading and in the way they are used by teachers (Department of Education and Science 1990). In the 1970s, it was fairly common for a school to have just one reading scheme and for children to work their way through all its books and any associated activities. During the 1980s, there was a tendency to use reading schemes more flexibly: many schools stocked a number of different schemes, with the result that teachers were to some extent able to tailor a reading program to individual needs. Trends in the 1990s point to some blurring of the earlier rigid distinction between reading schemes and other books, with teachers making both kinds of books readily available to young learners.

As far as the reading materials themselves are concerned, conscious attempts are made to avoid racist, sexist, or social class bias; there is awareness of the need for language and story structure that will accord with the child's expectations; there is a measure of integration of sight and phonic approaches within one scheme (e.g., *Oxford Reading Tree* 1986); and there is an increased use of a wider range of genres, including nonfiction and poetry, as well as the traditional story texts.

See also: Reading Teaching: Methods; Children's Early Reading Development; Reading: Theories of.

Bibliography

(a) Reading Schemes
Breakthrough to Literacy 1970 Longman for the Schools' Council, London
Ladybird Keywords Reading Scheme 1964 Wills and Hepworth, Loughborough
New Way 1987 Macmillan Education, London
Oxford Reading Tree 1986 Oxford University Press, Oxford
Reading 360 1978 Ginn, Aylesbury
Story Chest 1982 Arnold-Wheaton, London

(b) References
Adams M J 1990 *Beginning to Read*. MIT Press, Cambridge, MA
Beard R 1987 *Developing Reading 3–13*. Hodder and Stoughton, London
Department of Education and Science 1990 *The Teaching and Learning of Language and Literacy*. HMSO, London
Perera K 1993 'The good book': Linguistic aspects. In: Beard R (ed.) *Teaching Literacy: Balancing Perspectives*. Hodder and Stoughton, London
Southgate V, Roberts G R 1970 *Reading—Which Approach?* University of London Press, London
Waterland L 1985 *Read with Me: An Apprenticeship Approach to Reading*. Thimble Press, Stroud
Winch G 1982 The use of reading schemes: A comparative study. In: Burnes D, Campbell A, Jones R (eds.) *Reading, Writing and Multiculturalism*. Australian Reading Association, Adelaide

K. Perera

Reading Teaching: Methods

Distinctions between different methods of teaching reading are not always easy because of their inevitably overlapping nature. The long-standing debate between 'phonic' methods, which emphasize the learning of letter–sound relationships, and 'whole word' methods, which emphasize the learning of the recognition of words to build up a 'sight vocabulary,' has recently been superseded by other debates related to the use of specifically written schemes for the teaching of reading and other, 'real books,' particularly picture books, which have won praise for their literary merit. Debates have also been widened to embrace the different ways of bridging the gap between competence in spoken language and the emergence of literacy.

1. Historical Perspectives on the Teaching of Reading

For several centuries the 'alphabetic' method of teaching reading was widespread. This method involves saying the names of the letters, from which words can be recognized and pronounced (e.g., 'eff-oe-ex' *fox*). There is obviously a good deal of overlap between this method and the 'phonic' method which began to be used increasingly from the middle of the nineteenth century onwards. Phonics draws attention to particular aspects of the written 'code': the relationships between the phonemes of the language and the graphemes (letters) of the alphabet which can represent them (e.g.,/iː/: *seat, seen, thief*). There is, therefore, no easy division between the two methods, because all the consonant letter names contain a phoneme (e.g., *bee, dee, eff*), and the vowel letter names consist of 'long' phonemes ('ay,' 'ee,' 'ie,' 'oe,' and 'ue') with which they are commonly associated.

By the early twentieth century, many new books specifically written for the teaching of reading reflected a phonic emphasis. Subsequent years, though, saw an increasing concern over the artificial language embodied in such books, which appeared overcontrived and lacking in interest and meaning (e.g., *Is it in? Or is it on? It is an ox. An ox is at it*). The outcome of this disillusionment was a shift in the middle of the twentieth century to methods which gave greater emphasis to meaning, particularly through the teaching of whole words and sentences. This shift also reflected the growing influence of the Gestalt school of psychology and its assumption that humans prefer to perceive things as 'wholes.' However, this was followed by a countermovement from those who feared that whole word methods created too great a dependency on the teacher because learners literally had to 'take the teacher's word' for what the print represented and were not necessarily able to develop analytic and synthetic strategies for decoding the text on their own.

2. Post-1945 Perspectives

Such was the unsatisfactory and uncompromising nature of this continuing debate between 'code-emphases' and 'meaning-emphases' that a major study was set up to study the results from research in the field over the past 50 years as objectively as possible (Chall 1967, 1983). This study reported that, on balance, code-emphasis approaches give better results, at least for the first 3 years of schooling, and recommended a code-emphasis for beginning reading instruction. These conclusions are even more confidently made in the second edition of the report (Chall 1983).

The 1970s and 1980s saw the development of finer distinctions between methods of teaching reading, particularly those which seemed more 'natural' in the experiences which they offered children. Most prominent among these were 'linguistically informed phonics,' 'the use of grammatically appropriate texts,' and broader, 'story-based methods.' There was growing interest too, in the support which the teacher can give the learner–reader in interacting with text in ways which emulate skilled reading behavior, by using 'shared' and 'paired' methods of teaching.

2.1 Linguistically Informed Phonics

'Linguistically informed phonics' represents an attempt to counter arguments that the phoneme–grapheme correspondences of English orthography are highly irregular and that trying to teach them directly can be misleading. Research has shown that there are several hundred of these correspondences, even in the words which children are likely to be using in the early years of schooling. Linguistically informed phonics (Morris 1990) is based on studies which suggest that English orthography is, in fact, highly patterned, with only a few words diverging completely, especially when relationships in word meanings are taken into consideration (e.g., phot*o*graph and phot*o*graphy; h*ear* and h*ear*d). Underlying this method is the identification of the 44 phonemes of the English accent known as RP (received pronunciation) and the grouping of the graphemes which are most commonly associated with them into vowel sounds (e.g., /ei/: *a*pe, r*ai*n, pl*ay*) and consonant sounds (e.g., /ʃ/: *sh*op).

2.2 Grammatically Appropriate Texts

There has not been a grammatical method as such in recent years, but there has been increasing attention to the syntax of the texts which are used in the teaching of reading. This attention has been evident in both specifically written 'reading schemes' and in the use of the 'language experience approach,' which can result in children interacting with texts which reflect the use of nonstandard dialects (see *Reading Teaching: Materials*).

In the writing of reading schemes, there has been increasing concern to ensure that the syntax adopts the more common patterns of children's speech and largely avoids the kinds of syntactical structures with which children may be less familiar, such as passive verb forms, unnecessarily long subjects in sentences, and separated sequences, especially subjects from verbs.

The 'language experience' approach provides for a more child-centered range of grammatical possibilities. The emphasis here is on encouraging learners to compose and create texts which they write themselves or have written for them by teachers or parents, who may use word-cards and other apparatus to facilitate the transcription process. In this method, talking, listening, reading, and writing can be utilized together and major concessions can be made to nonstandard variations in children's own dialects. Language experience approaches are, by their very nature, very adaptable and can be used to support a range of different methods.

2.3 Story-based Methods

'Story-based methods' take whole texts as a starting point and share an emphasis on narrative discourse and its 'story grammar,' related to setting, main characters, plot, and denouement. As children have the story read to them, perhaps several times, its entertaining content can provide a meaningful and perhaps multilayered context for building up word recognition and word analysis skills as well as an increasing use of contextual cues to anticipate and predict sequences in orthography, grammar, and meaning.

In recent years, story methods have been associated with an increasing concern to monitor the quality of the texts used in the teaching of reading. This has been prompted by the growing recognition of the high quality of young children's picture books and the ways in which these books can be grouped to facilitate learning. It is assumed that the resulting grouping of books, perhaps discreetly labeled or color-coded, will be more likely to provide support for children in building up independence in reading competence. Other arguments suggest that, given the great skill of many contemporary writers and book illustrators in creating compulsive storylines and themes, they should also be respected as 'teachers of reading' (Meek 1982).

2.4 Paired and Shared Reading

While story methods can be supported by whole word and phonic aspects, the teaching approaches most associated with them tend to be various forms of 'paired' or 'shared reading.' Paired reading involves simultaneous oral reading of an appropriate text by child and adult. As soon as the child feels able to read independently, he or she taps on the table or chair and continues alone until a significant error is made or a word cannot be read; then the paired reading cycle is restarted (Morgan 1986). 'Shared reading,' sometimes referred to as an 'apprenticeship approach,' involves a less structured approach, in which the child reads with the adult any book which has appeal. Initially the child may only listen and follow the sequence of pictures or text, but eventually will begin to make up or retell the story while beginning to follow the lines of print. Competence with known texts can lead on to more accomplished behavior with unknown texts as confidence with decoding and the use of contextual cues grows. As yet, there is relatively little systematic research on the dynamics of shared and paired reading, such as the influence of the choice of texts, the cumulative relationship between different texts and also the role of the adult in responding to apparent differences in children's learning styles and in supporting their reading development by using other materials and teaching methods.

While shared reading can be used with any text, it has come to be associated with the use of texts which are not part of a specifically written scheme, so-called 'real books.' This in turn has led to a polarization (at least in the UK) of the kind that was associated with phonic and whole word methods. In some ways this more recent polarization is equally misleading and even more unsatisfactory. The distinction between the two types of book is based on the assumption that books written as part of reading schemes lack authenticity because, by their very nature, they are too contrived and fail to reflect the organic kind of writer–reader relationship apparent in many of the fine picture books.

At the same time, it can also be argued that some schemes contain creatively written and ingenious books, while picture books can reflect all manner of questionable contrivance in their design and content. It also has to be borne in mind that, whatever kinds of books are used, other teaching approaches may have to be provided to consolidate children's learning of the structure of the orthography itself. Schemes often include such provision; a 'real book' approach may require it even more, because it involves an ever-changing context in terms of vocabulary, style, and register, and replaces structure with serendipity in book choice and with idiosyncrasy in decisions about the kinds of direct teaching which are needed.

3. Current Perspectives

There is, then, no clear conclusion to be drawn on the superiority of one method over another and there is much to be said for recommending an informed, adaptable eclecticism. In the early 1990s, the debate is still distinguished by a number of tensions, for instance between those who have an overriding concern for the literary quality of the texts used in the teaching of reading (e.g., Waterland 1988) and those who are concerned with the significance of phonological processing in early reading development (e.g., Goswami and Bryant 1990; see also *Literacy and Phonological Awareness*). There is also an increasing interest in the ways in which children can be helped to build 'bridges' between their competence in oracy and their emerging abilities in literacy, by shared reading, language experience approaches, the use of functional print in the environment, and the use of texts which draw upon the patterns of children's speech (Donaldson 1989). Furthermore, there is a growing recognition of the enormously important role which parents can play in fostering children's reading, by exploiting uses of literacy in a domestic setting and by directly helping children to respond to the texts recommended by schools (see *Home Language and School Language*).

The challenge of promoting universal literacy can therefore be pursued on several complementary fronts. Nevertheless, success in this pursuit will only be possible if the pedagogical implications of research can be drawn together from a variety of perspectives, as has been done so successfully by Marilyn Jager Adams (1990). This balanced eclecticism seems to be the most flexible way of ensuring that teaching approaches are commensurate with the individuality which children inevitably bring to the process of learning to read.

See also: Reading, Theories of; Children's Early Reading Development.

Bibliography

Adams M J 1990 *Beginning to Read.* MIT Press, Cambridge, MA
Beard R 1990 *Developing Reading 3–13*, 2nd edn. Hodder and Stoughton Educational, Sevenoaks
Chall J S 1967 *Learning to Read: The Great Debate*. McGraw-Hill, New York
Donaldson M 1989 *Sense and Sensibility: Some Thoughts on the Teaching of Literacy*. University of Reading, Reading
Goswami U, Bryant P 1990 *Phonological Skills and Learning to Read*. Lawrence Erlbaum, Hove
Meek M 1982 *Learning to Read*. Bodley Head, London
Morgan R 1986 *Helping Children Read*. Methuen, London
Morris J M 1990 *The Morris–Montessori Word List*. Montessori Centre, London
Waterland E 1988 *Read With Me: An Apprenticeship Approach to Reading*, 2nd edn. Thimble Press, Stroud

R. Beard

Reading, Theories of

The primary focus of reading theory has been on the processes involved in skilled reading. In keeping with the information processing metaphor that has been dominant in cognitive psychology, theorists have proposed multicomponent accounts of one or more reading subskills—letter and word recognition, sentence understanding, text comprehension—which are used at different levels of written language. The recent appearance, however, of models in the connectionist (neural net) parallel distributed processing (PDP) framework has provided a provocative challenge to traditional theoretical orthodoxy in this field.

1. Issues That Divide Theories

Historically theorists have differed on the principles which govern how the components of reading skill operate together. 'Top-down' theorists hold that a reader's higher-order cognitive functions (intentions, hypotheses, prior knowledge) control the mechanisms involved in lower-order letter and word recognition, sentence parsing, and the like. In contrast, 'bottom-up' theorists contend that lower-order mechanisms operate in modular fashion uninfluenced by higher-order cognitive functions and processing strategies. According to this view, higher-order processes can operate only on the outputs from lower level components. 'Interactive' theorists allow for considerable crosstalk between components at different levels so that interpretation of text is the result of 'top-down' and 'bottom-up' shared control.

In recent years, the issues that divide theories have shifted somewhat. The one serious contender as a 'top-down' theory, the reading as hypothesis testing ('psycholinguistic guessing game') notion, has received little empirical support. Contrary to the theory, the mark of a skilled reader is not in superior use of context and hypothesis generation, but lies rather in accurate and efficient context-free word recognition (Rayner and Pollatsek 1989; see *Reading Difficulties*).

While current theorists still differ on the principle of modularity, perhaps more importantly they also differ on the assumptions they make about the nature of memory. Some prefer an 'entries in a computer file' metaphor of memory, while others favor the notion of parallel distribution representations. According to the computer file metaphor, the memory of an item is a stored copy which may be retrieved as in a computer database. In the PDP account, the memory of an item involves the construction of a pattern of activity distributed over many neuron-like units, with each unit involved in representing many different items. In models of reading, pools of units are postulated with separate pools corresponding to orthographic, phonological, semantic, etc., representational primitives. Stored in memory are the strengths of the connections built up through experience between units in the network which allow patterns of activity to be recreated. So PDP networks would appear ideal for handling 'interactive' processing, but traditional distinctions have become blurred by the appearance of 'bottom-up' PDP models which simulate 'top-down' effects.

2. Approaches to Theories of Skill at Different Levels of Written Language

2.1 Letters

How early visual processing leads to the perception of letters is not addressed by current models of the reading process. Many multicomponent theories include an abstract letter identification process prior to word recognition. It is not clear, however, how different forms of a letter (e.g., upper and lower case, italic, handwritten) converge on its 'abstract identity.'

2.2 Letters and Words

The most explicit multicomponent account of word reading is Dual Route Theory (DRT) which holds that there exist independent lexical and nonlexical routes for processing words. The lexical route directly maps a word's visual characteristics (via abstract letter identities) onto a lexical representation stored in memory which in turn 'addresses' the word's meaning and its phonology (for word naming). The nonlexical route 'assembles' a word's phonology by parsing the letter string into orthographic units, assigning phonemic values to the parsed subword units, and blending the assigned phonemes into a whole phonological representation: the output from this process may then be used to access lexical or semantic information as well as for word naming. The lexical route is considered necessary for reading irregular words and the rapid reading of regular words, the nonlexical route, for reading unfamiliar words and nonwords.

Oral reading data from patients with acquired and developmental dyslexia support the dissociation in DRT

between addressed and assembled phonology (see *Reading Difficulties*). However, DRT, is not a fixed set of postulates. Indeed, several versions of DRT have been proposed in response to various empirical challenges (e.g., the effect of lexical analogies on nonword reading). As a consequence, several of the basic assumptions of DRT have been modified with the result that the theory has lost much of its former modular flavor. Patterson and Morton (1985), for example, argue that the addressed and assembled routes are separable but not necessarily independent, while Balota (see Balota, et al. 1990) has proposed that lexical access does not precede the retrieval of meaning but that these processes instead operate in cascade so that they occur in a continuous manner. With such revisions DRT risks becoming virtually indistinguishable from interactive accounts.

Interactive models were originally motivated to account for the effects of context (words) on letter perception (letters in words are identified more accurately than letters in nonwords or consonant strings). These effects were successfully simulated by McClelland and Rumelhart (1981) using a model which allowed for interactive activation operating in cascade among feature, letter, and word recognition units so that activity in units at higher (word, letter) levels could contribute to the activity in units at lower (letter, feature) levels. The model can account for a variety of context effects including the oft-reported illusory perception of letters (in words) that are not in fact there. There is considerable debate, however, on whether there is empirical justification to extend the model so as to include the influence of syntactic and semantic constraints on word recognition.

The McClelland and Rumelhart model shares with DRT the 'entries in a computer file' metaphor. In this respect more recent connectionist PDP models are quite revolutionary for such models have no 'entries' in memory that are 'accessed' or 'activated.' Seidenberg and McClelland (1989) implemented a connectionist PDP neural net model consisting of a network with orthographic (input), phonological (output), and hidden units. The weights on the connections between the sets of units in the network reflect what the system has learned about the structure of English orthography. Each time a word is perceived, patterns of activation are created in the network which depend jointly on what the network *knows* and the current effect on the network of the word in question. Word recognition, therefore, does not involve accessing an entry in memory, but is instead a constructive process. The model is considerably less interactive than the McClelland and Rumelhart model and its implementation of phonology is somewhat primitive. Nevertheless, with this somewhat minimal architecture the model simulates many aspects of normal reading. It performs very poorly, however, with nonwords, and the extent to which the model in its present form can account for impaired reading is unclear.

2.3 Words, Sentences, and Text

The processes involved in comprehension are hypothesized to include extracting word meaning, apprehending syntactic structure, assigning thematic roles to phrases, making links within and between sentences, and ultimately building a mental representation of the content of the text.

Word meaning has been traditionally conceptualized in terms of lists of semantic features or in terms of more global structures (prototypes). Semantic feature and prototype notions, however, have difficulty accounting for polysemy (see *Polysemy*). A model by Hintzman (1986) provides a more promising approach to this problem. Hintzman proposes an instance-based system with no fixed representations in memory. Rather, each episodic experience with a 'word in context' produces a trace in memory. The meaning of a word, then, is embodied in the accumulation of its individual episodic experiences, with each new experience contributing to the word's continually evolving meaning. At the time of word meaning retrieval, the precise trace that is activated depends on the context in which the word occurs.

A central issue for theories of sentence understanding has to do with the nature of the parsing mechanism which carries out structural analyses which specify the relations among words. Theorists are divided on whether semantic and discourse processes affect the workings of the parser. As a result there have appeared both modular as well as highly interactive PDP accounts (see Balota, et al. 1990) of sentence parsing.

According to Kintsch and van Dijk (1978) several processes are involved in constructing a mental representation of an entire text. A text's constituent propositions are extracted and linked together to form a coherent text base which in turn is used to develop a macrostructure which captures the text's essential information or gist. At the same time, a 'situation model' is formed which integrates textual information with the reader's prior knowledge. Thus, the ultimate representation created by the reader involves not only the local and global meaning of the text but inferences based upon these meanings and the reader's knowledge of the world. Kintsch and van Dijk's theory is underspecified in several crucial respects (e.g., how propositions are formed, how inferences are made, etc.). Nevertheless, the theory has undoubtedly been the most influential account of text comprehension over the past decade and has stimulated a significant body of research into the nature of inference generation and the extent to which knowledge of the world (as embodied in situation models, 'schemas,' 'scripts,' 'frames,' 'scenarios,' etc.) influences inferences made during on-going reading (see Graesser and Bower 1990).

3. Reading Acquisition

Theories of skilled reading do not speak directly to practical issues of reading instruction. What are needed are theories of reading skill acquisition. Unfortunately, acquisition has received relatively little attention by reading theorists. There are signs, however, that this situation may be changing. A general outline of a theory of word reading development has been proposed by Frith (1985). Frith argues that there are phases in the development of word reading skill which are marked by the appearance of different learning strategies for processing different aspects of printed words: first using salient graphic features, then using grapheme–phoneme correspondences (GPCs), and finally employing larger orthographic subword units in recognizing words. Frith argues further that word reading and spelling normally develop *out of step* so that the alphabetic GPC strategy appears first in spelling and only later in reading, while the orthographic strategy surfaces first in reading and only later in spelling (see *Children's Early Reading Development*;

English Spelling: Children's; *Writing Instruction*). Although no mechanism is proposed for how changes occur, failure to advance from one phase to another is thought to result in different patterns of impairment in reading (see *Reading Difficulties*). More recently, Adams (1990) has proposed a somewhat broader outline for a highly interactive theory of reading acquisition from the connectionist PDP perspective. The PDP framework would appear particularly suited to the development of models of acquisition since PDP networks 'learn.' Of critical importance for such models will be the assumptions made about the nature of representational primitives at different levels in the system and how they are learned. Considerable work, moreover, needs to be done by network theorists developing and evaluating different learning algorithms (see Caudill and Butler 1990).

4. Conclusion

The state of theory in reading in the early 1990s is very much in flux. This state is much welcomed and speaks to the high level of energy that exists in the discipline. However, research is still very far from producing an overall comprehensive theory that provides a realistic account of the processes involved in skilled reading. Such a theory will have to address not only the nature of reading skill but also how skill in reading is acquired.

Bibliography

Adams M J 1990 *Beginning to Read*. MIT Press, Cambridge, MA
Balota D A, Flores d'Arcais G B, Rayner K 1990 (eds.) *Comprehension Processes in Reading*. Erlbaum, Hillsdale, NJ
Caudill M, Butler C 1990 *Naturally Intelligent Systems*. MIT Press, Cambridge, MA
Frith U 1985 Beneath the surface of developmental dyslexia. In: Patterson K E, Marshall J C, Coltheart M (eds.) *Surface Dyslexia*. Erlbaum, London
Graesser A C, Bower G H 1990 (eds.) *Inferences and Text Comprehension*. Academic Press, New York
Hintzman D L 1986 'Schema abstraction' in a multiple-trace memory model. *Psychological Review* **93**: 411–28
Kintsch W, Dijk T A van 1978 Toward a model of text comprehension and production. *Psychological Review* **85**: 363–94
McClelland J L, Rumelhart, D E 1981 An interactive activation model of context effects in letter perception, Part 1: An account of basic findings. *Psychological Review* **88**: 375–407
Patterson K E, Morton J 1985 From orthography to phonology: an attempt at an old interpretation. In: Patterson K E, Marshall J C, Coltheart M (eds.) *Surface Dyslexia*. Erlbaum, Hillsdale, NJ
Rayner K, Pollatsek A 1989 *The Psychology of Reading*. Prentice Hall, Englewood Cliffs, NJ
Seidenberg M S, McClelland J L 1989 A distributed, developmental model of word recognition and naming. *Psychological Review* **96**: 523–68

G. E. MacKinnon

Reading: Testing

Reading is the ability to comprehend the thoughts and feelings of others through the medium of written text. It is an amplifier of human abilities. Illiteracy impoverishes the individual and society; reading enriches. Reading tests can encourage literacy in many ways.

J. P. Guilford, a twentieth-century psychologist, underlined the importance of test theory and its applications: 'No other contribution of psychology has had the social impact equal to that created by the psychological test. No other technique and no other body of theory in psychology has been so fully rationalized from the mathematical point of view' (cited in Pumfrey 1977: 1). This observation is equally valid in relation to the varied uses of different types of reading tests in describing, analyzing, predicting, and increasing control of reading development.

1. Reading Tests

Reading tests are efficient means of systematically eliciting valid information concerning both inter- and intraindividual differences in readers' attainments in, and attitudes towards, various aspects of reading. The information obtained by such means can be used to improve both individual and institutional decision making concerning teaching methods and resources, thereby enhancing readers' attainments and progress in reading.

Reading tests can be used in assessing graphophonic, syntactic, and semantic aspects of reading attainments. In addition, affective aspects of reading can be tested using a variety of attitude scales.

In the early 1990s, reading tests that sought to provide 'formative' (process-related) rather than 'summative' (outcome-related) assessments of pupils' reading were in demand (see Sect. 5 below).

2. Uses of Reading Tests

The following are the 13 major uses of reading tests:
   (a) To monitor and make explicit the reading attainments and attitudes to reading of individuals and groups at a given point in time.
   (b) To encourage the development of high standards in reading at individual, local, regional, and national levels.
   (c) To improve communication between interested parties by minimizing ambiguities when describing the reading standards of individuals and groups.
   (d) To compare the reading attainments and attitudes towards reading of pupils within a class.
   (e) To identify starting points for instruction.
   (f) To measure the progress made by individuals and groups.
   (g) To evaluate the efficacy of various approaches to the teaching of reading.
   (h) To identify the pattern of an individual's strengths and weaknesses in various aspects of reading.
   (i) To assist in matching reading materials and methods to the reader.
   (j) To help in the early identification of reading difficulties.
   (k) To increase teachers' understanding of the processes involved in the development of reading.
   (l) To enhance professional accountability.
   (m) To facilitate reading research.

3. Classification of Reading Tests

There is a vast range of reading tests available. They can be grouped into three broad categories: informal, normative, and criterion-referenced tests. Each provides differing types of information. All three are complementary. Each type has its own strengths and weaknesses. These must be considered in relation to the uses to which the information they provide is to be put (Pumfrey 1985).

3.1 Informal Reading Tests

The teacher of reading is continuously observing the reading-related behaviors of pupils. The theoretical basis of reading development adopted and the specific instructional objectives and methods of teaching employed determine the aspects of pupils' reading to which attention will be directed. Everyday work with the learner, irrespective of age or attainments, provides opportunities for systematic and extended sampling of reading attainments, progress, and attitudes towards reading in a variety of genres. Systematic observation in a particular instructional context provides opportunities for a variety of informal reading tests directly related to ongoing instruction to be developed.

One of the more valuable techniques that has been developed for use with individuals is known as the 'informal reading inventory' (IRI). It is informal in the sense that a wide variety of textual materials can be used. There is no normative comparison with other pupils' performances. The purpose of an IRI is to identify whether a text from which the pupil is working is suited to the child's current reading attainments. This applies irrespective of the content of the text or the level of complexity of the material. The IRI technique is valuable to any teacher of any subject at any level where textual material is in use (see *Reading Inventories, Informal*). IRIs have also been developed for use with groups of pupils (Johnson, et al. 1987).

Linked to the use of individual IRIS is 'oral miscue analysis.' The reader's deviations from the correct decoding of the printed material are not construed as 'mistakes,' but as 'miscues.' Goodman, the psycholinguist, considers that their study provides 'a window on the reading process.' A variety of tests have been developed in this field (e.g., Goodman, et al. 1987; see *Miscue Analysis*).

3.2 Normative Reading Tests

Normative reading tests concentrate on providing valid information concerning individual differences in various aspects of pupils' reading attainments. The two key characteristics of such tests are that they have deliberately been designed to discriminate between pupils and that the test norms are established on a defined group. This enables the relative attainments of individuals and groups to be validly assessed. Questions such as 'How well does this pupil/ class/school/LEA score in relation to the population on which the test was standardized?' can be answered.

A refinement of the approach leads to standardized diagnostic attainment tests. These provide a number of scores for the individual pupil on different aspects of the reading process. Results can be presented in the form of a profile. From such profiles, a pupil's relative strengths and weaknesses can be identified and ideas for teaching developed.

The interpretation of standardized reading test profiles is a complex subject. Technical aspects of test theory and of the nature of reading must be appreciated if the information is to be interpreted correctly. For example, an understanding of the reliabilities of the subtest scores and of their intercorrelations must be simultaneously considered in identifying areas of relative strength and weakness and planning instructional programs.

3.3 Criterion-referenced Reading Tests

Criterion-referenced tests are frequently based on detailed task analyses of the content of reading instruction. Their constructors often concentrate on a particular domain, e.g., regular consonant–vowel–consonant (CVC) words. Such tests are often called 'domain-referenced reading tests' to highlight their content specificity.

These tests are based on the premise that all pupils need to master certain specified common aspects of reading if they are to develop skills at progressively higher levels. Attention is concentrated on a comparison of the child's abilities in relation to the mastery of processes and materials that it is deemed necessary and reasonable that a pupil achieves. For example, it might be considered that every pupil learning to read English needs to be able to read the 12 words in English that comprise approximately 25 percent of typical written material encountered by pupils. The immediate recognition of these 12 words could be considered a criterion of early reading performance. The aim is that *all* pupils master this specified material. If this instructional objective is achieved, the fact that such a 12-word test no longer serves to discriminate between the pupils, in terms of their relative reading attainments in this particular task, is educationally irrelevant. Such tests enable a starting score to be identified and progress to be measured in relation to the individual and the group.

It has been argued that educationists have concentrated their attention on normative rather than on criterion-referenced tests of reading. One consequence is that too many pupils are doomed inevitably to being labeled as *relative* failures. In fact, the two approaches to testing are complementary.

The relationship between criterion-referenced and normative tests can be seen in performance examinations in music. In the UK examinations in music are based on grades extending from one to eight. The tests can be taken by individuals of any age. The competencies expected at each grade level are clearly specified. What candidates need to know and do is made explicit. However, not all those taking the examination pass. Some obtain higher scores than others. If every candidate passed Grade 1 for a given instrument with a mark of 100 percent, there would probably be a demand that the absolute standard be raised.

Turning to reading, irrespective of whether a normative test or a criterion-referenced one is used, some pupils will learn more rapidly than others. Every criterion-referenced reading test has a normative aspect, and vice versa.

4. Selecting a Reading Test

Selecting a reading test requires the potential user to be clear concerning the purpose(s) for which information is required (see Sect. 2 above). Questions also must be asked concerning:

(a) Goals of instruction: ('Is my interest in attainments in, or attitudes towards, reading?');
(b) Sources of information: ('Will the information I require be best obtained from informal, normative, or criterion-referenced tests?');
(c) Level of interpretation: ('Am I interested only in describing the pupil's attainments or do I wish to obtain more detailed information that will be of diagnostic utility?'); and
(d) Stage of reading development: (e.g., 'Is my interest with prereading skills or with higher-order reading skills requiring inferential comprehension?').

5. Reading Tests: Developments

Most reading tests provide means of quantifying the products of a reading curriculum via the pupil's reading test performances. Reading tests of various types may provide either quantitative or qualitative information at different levels of measurement. Normative reading tests can provide raw scores, reading ages, percentiles, and a variety of scales based on z scores (mean $= 0$; standard deviation $= 1$). The latter convey the same information on different numerical scales. For example, they include ones with means of 100 and standard deviations of 15 and others having means of 50 and standard deviations of 10. Criterion-referenced reading test results are frequently reported as the number or percentage of items correct in relation to mastery of a prescribed domain.

Criterion-referenced reading tests are seen by teachers as of greater motivational importance to pupils and greater educational utility to themselves than normative tests.

Interest is increasingly turning towards the importance of the processes involved in reading (Glaser, et al. 1988). It is claimed that qualitative insights into processes underpinning an individual's interactions with text can be obtained using IRIS or other diagnostic reading tests. Additionally, attitude scales provide assessments of pupils' perceptions of affective aspects of reading such as its enjoyment and utility.

The importance of testing pupils' reading in the educational context in which they are learning is also receiving increasing attention. Formative, summative, and contextual thrusts are apparent in the Standard Assessment Tasks being used in relation to the National Curriculum in England and Wales (see *National Curriculum: English (England and Wales)*).

6. Using Reading Tests

Reading tests vary in their complexity. Training in the administration and interpretation of reading tests is essential if the information that such tests can provide is to be of maximum use.

7. Sources of Information

Extensive sections describing reading tests can be found in the following compendia: Mitchell 1985; Hammill, et al. 1989. The Educational Testing Service at Princeton, NJ, in the USA, can produce extensive lists of tests of all types. More specialist sources are: Buros 1975; Vincent, et al. 1983; Pumfrey 1985, 1991; Vincent, et al. 1986; and Gorman, et al. 1988.

Bibliography

Buros O K 1975 *Reading Tests and Reviews II*. Gryphon Press, Lincoln, NB
Glaser S M, Searfoss L W, Gentile L M (eds.) 1988 *Re-examining Reading Diagnosis: New Trends and Procedures*. International Reading Association, Newark, DE

Goodman Y, Watson D J, Burke C L 1987 *Reading Miscue Inventory: Alternative Procedures*. Heinemann Educational, London

Gorman T P, White J, Brooks G, Maclure M, Kispal A 1988 *Language Performance in Schools*. HMSO, London

Hammill D D, Brown L, Bryant B R 1989 *A Consumer's Guide to Tests in Print*. Pro-Ed, Austin, TX

Johnson M S, Kress R A, Pikulski J J 1987 *Informal Reading Inventories*, 2nd edn. International Reading Association, Newark, DE

Mitchell J V (ed.) 1985 *The Ninth Mental Measurement Yearbook*. Buros Institute of Mental Measurement, Lincoln, NB

Pumfrey P D 1977 *Measuring Reading Abilities: Concepts, Sources and Applications*. Hodder and Stoughton, London

Pumfrey P D 1985 *Reading: Tests and Assessment Techniques*, 2nd edn. Hodder and Stoughton, London

Pumfrey P D 1991 *Improving Children's Reading in the Junior School: Challenges and Responses*. Hodder and Stoughton, London

Vincent D, Green L, Francis J, Powney J 1983 *A Review of Reading Tests*. NFER-Nelson, Windsor

Vincent D, Pugh A K, Brooks G (eds.) 1986 *Assessing Reading*. Macmillan Education, London

P. D. Pumfrey

Reading and Writing Disorders: Intervention

This article is concerned with intervention procedures which are applicable to those whose disorders of written language are associated with visual-linguistic rather than visual-perceptive impairment (see *Disorders of Reading and Writing*).

1. Developmental Disorders of Reading and Writing

Intervention starts at the prereading stage with children who are at risk because they have difficulty in acquiring spoken language. Parents are shown how to give these children a richer language base through reading to them, teaching them rhymes and rhyming games and awakening their interest in how words sound as well as in what they mean. In addition, the children may be encouraged to take an interest in writing by making squiggles on a sheet of paper. This is a step towards appreciating that such squiggles have meaning for other people. Where there are persisting problems of verbal language, the teaching of reading and writing will be incorporated in the intervention program.

Most language-delayed and language-disordered children have difficulty in remembering words and this affects their spoken and written language since the learning of words in context, with plenty of opportunity to practice them, will be a continuing feature. It is important to emphasize context because words are not only understood better in context, they are recalled more easily.

Children with disorders of the dyspraxic and the phonological–syntactic type require considerable work on word segmentation. They lack the ability to break words into their component parts and rebuild them. Work on this skill makes use of both auditory and visual avenues. The word is said in its entirety by the instructor and then written in segmented fashion. The child copies the segments saying them aloud. Finally, the whole word is presented and said

and the child attempts to copy it. The number of stages in the process and the number of times it is repeated depend on the amount of difficulty experienced by the child.

The same groups of children also need auditory training particularly focused on rhyming words. As their ability to appreciate sound components of words improves, they are taught how to break down and reassemble sound clusters or blends and they are then some way to being prepared for alphabet use.

Children who are hyperlexic need help on the same lines as autistic children (see *Disorders of Language, Developmental: Intervention*) focusing on meaningful communication and comprehension. It is important that the child's precocious reading skills are not emphasized to the detriment of spoken language although some therapists use the strengths of word recognition or sentence recognition as a step forward to the development of verbal comprehension.

Learning disabled children show reading and writing deficits either as the most conspicuous feature of the disability or as part of their general lack of linguistic competence. In the latter case, written work will concentrate on extracting and conveying a number of different meanings using the same kind of strategies as for spoken language. In other instances the teacher must take the child back to the point of written language acquisition where deviation occurs. This may be in visual-perceptual skills or impaired segmentation or lack of phoneme–grapheme correspondence. The strategies developed at that point have apparently proved unsuccessful and must be exchanged for more useful ones as indicated above.

2. Acquired Disorders of Reading and Writing

Reading disorders are associated with almost every form of aphasia as are writing disorders. They are related to the kind of aphasia and are usually treated concurrently with spoken language (see *Language Loss: Intervention*). The patient's ability to recall the alphabet, to copy words and sentences, and to read aloud or silently, are part of the assessment. In addition to linguistic disturbances, the patient may have suffered paralysis of the right hand and arm. If this is not too severe he may prefer to use it for writing. In either case, printing may be immediately easier than cursive writing but the latter should be used as soon as possible.

Early rehabilitation is devoted towards reestablishing the individual components of the written code, letters, numbers, words, and sentences. This involves matching, copying, writing a simple sequence such as the alphabet or the days of the week or spontaneous writing of familiar material and dictation. If the condition is one of global aphasia, the therapist may prefer to concentrate first on comprehension of spoken language and then teach word identification at a simple level.

Comprehension of reading may be affected through disorder at the semantic or the syntactic level and must be tackled differently. Strategies employed will be associated with those for verbal language following language loss in adulthood (see *Language Loss: Intervention*).

Continuous practice is necessary and patients are required to read and write at some level every day. A first step towards narrative may be diary keeping, first in note form then with full sentences. Written material may be read aloud or silently. Unfortunately, the selection of reading material is difficult since simple stories tend to be infantile and thus insulting, but it may be possible to make use of material compiled for use in teaching English as a foreign language.

As with spoken language, the amount of importance the individual attaches to the reading skill varies with occupation and interest. The same kind of sensitivity and understanding is therefore required from the therapist as for intervention in spoken language.

See also: Disorders of Reading and Writing; Pathology: Intervention; Disorders of Language, Developmental: Intervention; Language Loss: Intervention.

Bibliography

Snowling M (ed.) 1985 *Children's Written Language Difficulties.* NFER-Nelson, Windsor
Wallach G, Butler K (eds.) 1984 *Language Learning Disabilities in School Age Children.* Williams and Wilkins, Baltimore, MD

B. Byers Brown

Realism

Dictionaries of philosophy tend to define the philosophical doctrine of realism along the following lines: realism is the view that the entities one takes to exist, do so independently of our minds and mental powers. Realism thus explicated is then contrasted with idealism, which holds that the items of everyday experience or scientific investigation are in some sense mental constructs (see *Truth*; *Epistemology*; *Universals*).

1. Historical Context

Historically two specific forms of realism are often distinguished: (a) medieval realism regarding the existence of properties; (b) the dispute between direct realists on the one hand and phenomenalists and representationalists on the other. In the first dispute, realists argued that predicates such as 'is wise' stand for mind-independent correlates—here the property of wisdom, just as names such as 'Socrates' stand for independently existing objects. Their opponents argued that 'is wise' can apply meaningfully and truly to mind-independent objects without it being the case that it too stood for some mind-independent entity. Insofar as predicates designate anything at all, they designate mind-dependent entities such as concepts (see *Properties and Predication: Formal Theories*; *Concepts*).

Direct realists in perception argued for a distinction between first the act of perceiving, second its content—e.g., that a tree is in front of me—and finally the object of perception. The latter, where it exists, is a mind-independent entity, the direct realist maintains, whereas the act of perceiving and its content are clearly mind-dependent. Opponents of direct realism reject the distinction between act, content, and object in perception and hence maintain that the immediate objects of perception are mind-dependent entities—ideas, sense data, and so forth. Both disputes, then, exemplify the general pattern—realism affirms mind-independence for some sort of entity, idealism or antirealism denies it.

2. 'Realism' in Current Philosophy

In current analytical philosophy 'realism versus antirealism' seems to be used to cover two somewhat different sets of problems. The first concerns scientific realism which is usually contrasted with forms of instrumentalism. The instrumentalist distinguishes between observational and theoretical sectors of language and maintains that only sentences of the former sector are objectively true or false. Theoretical sentences are instrumentalistically useful to the extent that their observational consequences turn out to be true but truth for the theoretical sector consists in nothing more than such predictive utility. For the scientific realist, by contrast, even if one can draw a significant distinction between observational and theoretical sectors, which some doubt, there is no difference in respect of truth: sentences from either sector are rendered true or false by a mind-independent world. Scientific realism is also often taken to include the antiskeptical view that science inevitably progresses, if correctly pursued, closer and closer to the truth, and that the theoretical terms of current science are not empty but refer to mind-independent entities with natures of roughly the same type as we ascribe to them.

The extreme instrumentalist denial that the concept of truth applies to scientific theory (found in some logical positivists) did not survive Tarski's demonstration of the definability of truth for certain formal languages (see *Tarski, Alfred*). But instrumentalistic views are common amongst philosophers influenced by the positivists or by pragmatism. W. V. O. Quine, for instance, draws a fairly sharp observation/theory distinction and denies there is any mind and theory-independent distinction of fact not reflected in a difference in observational data (see *Quine, Willard van Orman*). His views incline towards a relativism regarding truth for those theories compatible with, but transcending, the empirical facts. Similarly relativistic views on scientific truth can be found in many other influential philosophers (in the early writings of T. S. Kuhn, for instance) and are incompatible with the realist view of a mind-independent realm of facts against which theories can be measured absolutely for truth or falsity.

As well as scientific realism, 'realism' is also currently used as a name for certain fallibilistic doctrines. The fallibilist about a certain class of beliefs holds that such beliefs, even if arrived at in optimal conditions for belief formation, can be wholly false. The linguistic turn of modern philosophy has led to fallibilism being interpreted as a semantic doctrine: that truth for sentences transcends the evidence for them. A tension thus emerges between the skepticism of fallibilism and the antiskepticism of the scientific realists (who often claim the semantic doctrine of fallibilism has little to do with traditional realism). Nonetheless the idea of mind-independence needs explicating—antirealists agree the world is independent of, for example, the will—and fallibilism offers one fairly clear way of doing so. On the other hand, traditional realism did not involve radical skepticism towards sentences such as 'there are physical objects,' the very reverse in fact. Even if the fallibilist evinces no actual doubt regarding this sentence but holds merely that our opinions and the truth on this matter might have come apart, realists with a naturalistic approach to cognition might demur. Conversely one might take a fallibilist view towards, say, mathematics while denying that it deals with mind-independent entities. A compromise is to characterize realism towards a class of entities as the view that some beliefs (typically linguistically expressed) *about* them are fallible. Antirealist fallibilism in mathematics then consists in denying that mathematics is about anything. Explicating just what 'aboutness' comes to, is the major difficulty with this proposal.

Fallibilism is taken to be the key realist notion by philosophers skeptical of its truth such as Hilary Putnam and Michael Dummett (see *Putnam, Hilary*; *Dummett, M. A. E.*). They agree of course that one is often wrong; that, for example, the objects one applies terms to in actual linguistic practice are often not those one ought to apply them to if one is to respect the objective content of the expression. But they insist objective content is rooted in our linguistic practices too. Empiricist views of sentence meaning—the meanings transmitted and learnt in language-learning cannot transcend the empirical circumstances of the learning—then lead them to suggest the notion of truth is identified or replaced with epistemic notions such as verifiability or justified assertibility and to deny that beliefs arrived at in optimal circumstances can be false. Thus metaphysical doctrines such as realism are held to depend on theories from the philosophy of language.

Critics of such views counter that they rest on poor epistemology. Skeptics about the notion of nondeductive justification will find the notion of justified assertibility dubious. And Chomskyans will charge the antifallibilists with a crude empiricist theory of the acquisition and transmission of linguistic meaning, holding by contrast that the empirical circumstances of language learning may act only as a catalyst activating a largely innate cognitive state of understanding which can transcend its experiential inputs. Even if the general negative arguments against realism fail, however, the task of establishing it as correct for particular cases, for example, for microphysical objects, quantum mechanical states, abstract objects, and so forth, is still a substantial and unrealized one.

See also: Reference, Philosophical Issues concerning.

Bibliography

Devitt M 1984 *Realism and Truth*. Blackwell, Oxford
Dummett M 1978 *Truth and Other Enigmas*. Duckworth, London
Kuhn T S 1970 *The Structure of Scientific Revolutions*. University of Chicago Press, Chicago, IL
Putnam H 1978 *Meaning and the Moral Sciences*. Routledge and Kegan Paul, London
Quine W V O 1981 *Theories and Things*. Harvard University Press, Cambridge, MA

A. Weir

Reasoning

The study of reasoning has entered into a new phase since the 1970s. For two thousand years the 'science of reasoning' was, essentially, the Aristotelian tradition (see *Aristotle and Logic*); then in the nineteenth and twentieth centuries it took a distinctly mathematical turn: but since the 1970s it has returned to studying 'real reasoning'—reasoning which people actually use in order to convince one another—and

this is leading to new ideas about the nature, structure, and evaluation of reasoning, particularly from the perspectives of informal logic, linguistics, and cognitive psychology.

1. Historical Background

Though the Stoics invented propositional logic (see *Aristotle and the Stoics on Language*), Aristotle was undoubtedly the key figure in the 'science of reasoning' until the nineteenth century. Aristotle distinguished three different kinds or aspects of reasoning. These were: (a) 'analytic'—the science of demonstrative reasoning, the kind of reasoning which is characteristic of mathematics; (b) 'dialectic'—the science of argumentative dialogue; and (c) 'rhetoric'—the science of persuasion. Aristotle's analytic is the beginning of what is called 'logic' and is to be found mainly in his *Prior Analytics* and *Posterior Analytics*. His theory of argumentative debate is to be found in his *Topics* and *De Sophisticis Elenchis*, and his theory of good and convincing oratory is to be found in his *Rhetoric*. The theory of the syllogism (see *Syllogism*) is probably Aristotle's most famous contribution to the theory of reasoning and is still widely studied. A syllogism is an argument with two premises and a conclusion, where all three sentences are of one of the following forms, (A) 'All As are Bs,' (E) 'No As are Bs,' (I) 'Some As are Bs,' (O) 'Some As are not Bs,' and the premises have one term in common, as in:

All crocodiles are amphibious creatures	(A)
No amphibious creatures are lovable	(E)

Therefore

No crocodiles are lovable.	(E)

where 'amphibious creature' is the term common to both premises. Prior (1962) contains an excellent account of Aristotle's theory of the syllogism.

In the medieval world Aristotle's theory of the syllogism was studied; 'disputations' were conducted according to strict rules deriving from the theory of dialectic; and rhetoric also remained of central importance. However, with the rise of science, dialectic and rhetoric declined in importance and the study of reasoning became increasingly the study of analytic. Furthermore, the methods by which reasoning was studied became increasingly mathematical. Some of the most important figures in this development were Leibniz (see *Leibniz, G. W.*), Bolzano, Boole (see *Boole, George*), and De Morgan, but by far the most important was Gottlob Frege (1848–1925; see *Frege, Gottlob*), and modern logic is universally recognized to date from the publication of his *Begriffsschrift*; (1879; see *Logic: Historical Survey*).

2. The Influence of Frege

Frege was a mathematician who was mainly interested in studying mathematical reasoning by mathematical methods. He generalized certain mathematical ideas, notably those of 'variable' and 'function,' to produce the notational ideas which are now universally used to articulate the logical form of sentences and the logical structure of reasoning. The essentials of this notation are variables, predicates, and quantifiers. Variables, like x, y, z, function in logical notation very much as variables function in mathematical expressions, i.e., they mark a 'gap' in an expression which can be filled by a name or which can be quantified over to yield a true or false sentence. 'Predicate letters,' like F, G, and H, stand for something different from ordinary grammatical predicates and something more like mathematical functions. For example, in *All crocodiles are amphibious creatures* the grammatical subject is 'all crocodiles' and the grammatical predicate is 'are amphibious creatures.' In logic, 'all' is a 'quantifier,' a word of quantity, and the *logical* predicates are ' . . . is a crocodile' and ' . . . is an amphibious creature.' Logical predicates are commonly thought of as 'what is left' when names are removed from simple sentences; for example, *John is a crocodile*, *John is scalier than Mary*, and *John is between Mary and Peter* yield the logical predicates 'x is a crocodile,' 'x is scalier than y,' and 'x is between y and z,' written Fx, Gxy, and Hxyz respectively, where the variables mark gaps as explained above. The *quantifiers* are the words 'all' and 'some' (and their synonyms), and are commonly written $\forall x$ and Ex respectively. To return to the simple example, *All crocodiles are amphibious* is construed as saying, 'For all x, if x is a crocodile then x is an amphibious creature' which is written in logical notation as $\forall x (Fx \supset Gx)$.

Frege's system provided a considerably more powerful and flexible instrument for representing patterns of reasoning involving quantifiers than did Aristotle's syllogistic, and the Fregean tradition, with important contributions from Bertrand Russell (see *Russell, Bertrand*) and others, dominated thinking about reasoning until the 1970s. It produced many remarkable results, especially about mathematical reasoning: some of the most notable of these were Church's theorem that elementary predicate logic is undecidable, Tarski's theorem that 'truth' cannot be defined within elementary arithmetic (see *Tarski, Alfred*), and Gödel's theorems that one cannot prove the consistency of elementary number theory without assuming it and that one cannot completely axiomatize elementary number theory. This remarkable tradition is the theoretical basis of the whole of the modern computing and information technology industry and much research is continuing along these lines (see *First Order Logic*).

3. Recent Developments

However, since the 1970s there has been an upsurge of interest in the study of reasoning which derives from several quite different perspectives, including those of informal logic, argumentation theory, and cognitive psychology.

3.1 Informal Logic

The informal logic tradition has emerged mainly in North America, among logicians and philosophers who used to teach modern formal logic partly in the hope of improving students' reasoning skills. Partly because this hope was not realized, and partly because of the difficulty of *applying* modern logic to much 'real reasoning'—reasoning of the kind people actually use in order to try to convince others—modern informal logic focuses on the study of such real reasoning. It pays particular attention to the language and structure of reasoning, and to fallacies. Though there were earlier works in this tradition, the publication of Michael Scriven's book, *Reasoning* (1976), is widely regarded as the moment when the subject came of age. Good examples of works in this tradition are Govier (1985); Johnson and Blair (1977); and Freeman (1988).

3.2 Argumentation

The 'argumentation' tradition has arisen mainly in Holland, and derives its inspiration particularly from the speech–act theory of J. L. Austin (see *Austin, J. L.*) as developed by J. R. Searle. However, it also owes a great deal to modern logic, to the theory of dialectic, and to Perelman's work on rhetoric. Argumentation theory also focuses on 'real argumentation'; it describes its program as belonging to 'normative pragmatics,' and it assesses argumentation by reconstructing it in terms of an ideal dialectical model (for this approach to the study of argument see especially Van Eemeren, et al. 1984, 1987).

3.3 Cognitive Psychology

In recent years cognitive psychologists have given increasing attention to the study of reasoning. Interesting developments here, with far–reaching implications for the whole field, are particularly associated with the work of Philip Johnson-Laird, especially with his contention that people reason, not by any kind of reference to 'logical rules' (as Piaget (see *Piaget, Jean*) and many others have thought), but by means of 'mental models' (for a good exposition of these ideas see Johnson-Laird 1983, 1991).

4. Summary

In summary, the study of reasoning began with the ancient Greeks, remained in the Aristotelian tradition for nearly two thousand years, then took a mathematical turn, and has in the latter part of the twentieth century returned to a broad approach to the subject, and is focusing, in the 1990s, on real reasoning—reasoning of the kind people actually use with a view to convincing others, and which is only rarely about crocodiles!

See also: Logic: Historical Survey; Propositional Calculus; Predicate Calculus; Inference; First Order Logic.

Bibliography

Blair J A, Johnson R H 1980 *Informal Logic; The First International Symposium*. Edgepress, Pt Reyes, CA
Eemeren F H van, Grootendorst R, Kruiger T 1987 *Handbook of Argumentation Theory*. Foris, Dordrecht
Eemeren F H van, Grootendorst R 1984 *Speech Acts in Argumentative Discussion*. Foris, Dordrecht
Freeman J B 1988 *Thinking Logically*. Prentice Hall, Englewood Cliffs, NJ
Frege G 1879 *Begriffsscrift*. Louis Nebert, Halle
Govier T 1985 *A Practical Study of Argument*. Wadsworth, Belmont, CA
Johnson R H, Blair J A 1977 *Logical Self-Defense*. McGraw-Hill, New York
Johnson-Laird P N 1983 *Mental Models*. Cambridge University Press, Cambridge
Johnson-Laird P N 1991 *Deduction*. Lawrence Erlbaum, Hove
Kneale W, Kneale M 1962 *The Development of Logic*. Oxford University Press, Oxford
Perelman C, Olbrechts-Tyteca 1969 *The New Rhetoric: A Treatise on Argumentation*. University of Notre Dame Press, Notre Dame, IN
Prior A N 1962 *Formal Logic*. Oxford University Press, Oxford
Scriven M 1976 *Reasoning*. McGraw-Hill, New York

A. Fisher

Reconstruction and Unwritten Languages

And perhaps the Druids were in the right, who, as Julius Caesar tells us, did not make use of letters, to record their philosophy and theology, though they knew the Greek letters, because they thought the use of them impaired the memory.

(Lord Monboddo 1774)

1. The Comparative Method and Unwritten Languages

This title recalls the old question, can the comparative method (henceforth CM) be applied successfully to unwritten languages? 'Unwritten' in this context was usually associated with so-called 'primitive' or 'exotic' languages, and thus the question has the corollaries, (a) is change in unwritten/primitive/exotic languages fundamentally different from change in written languages?, and (b) is sound change regular in unwritten/exotic languages (regular sound change being a cornerstone of the CM)? The CM has been applied successfully to cases of unwritten/exotic languages so often and so consistently that one would expect the doubt to have been abandoned long ago. However, the unfortunate fact is that the question continues to recur. For example Baldi (1990: 11) asks:

The comparative method relies on sound correspondences; what, then, can it do in language families where sound correspondences are irregular and inconsistent? Boretzky (1984), for example, has argued that change in the Arandic languages of central Australia seems to proceed more by abrupt lexical replacement through borrowing than by gradual phonological change.

Therefore, it is important to reaffirm (a) that the question of written versus unwritten language is irrelevant for the CM, and has been irrelevant throughout the history of linguistics; (b) that sound change is not fundamentally different in written and unwritten languages; and (c) that the myth of linguistic primitivism affecting the applicability of the CM should remain refuted once and for all. Writing is not the issue, but rather the data relevant for comparative reconstruction. Hopefully, this re-examination of these issues will contribute to greater understanding of comparative reconstruction in general.

2. A Misperceived History

Though surprising to some, the CM has been applied successfully to unwritten (exotic) languages from its very inception to the time of writing, and the question about evidence from unwritten languages was present even in the CM's earliest application. The Hungarian Jesuit mathematician Joannis Sajnovics (1770) attempted to test claims that Hungarian, Lapp, and Finnish were related. On an astronomy research trip to the Norwegian Arctic, he elicited Lapp words and transcribed them in an orthography he devised himself. These 'field' data were the basis for his application of the CM which demonstrated that Hungarian, Lapp, and Finnish were related; nevertheless, he reasoned that to convince skeptics he must use previously published data. Thus in his published report (Sajnovics 1770) he employed none of his own data which had approached Lapp as an unwritten language, but selected examples from the only source available to him, Leem's textbook (1748) and lexical samples (1768–81) of Lapp, though these were recorded in an inadequate Danish orthography with Danish glosses, both of which were major obstacles to Sajnovics (Stipa

1990: 209–11). Thus the issue of data from unwritten languages has existed from the very beginning of the CM.

In spite of the popular association of historical linguistics with written Indo–European languages, comparative linguistics has an equally long association with 'exotic' unwritten languages. It is revealing to recall that a year before the publication of Sir William Jones's (1788) famous discourse, often heralded as the discovery of Indo–European and the foundation of comparative linguistics, Jonathan Edwards (in 1787 in an address to the Connecticut Society of Arts and Sciences) declared that 'the language of the several [Algonquian] tribes in New England ... are radically the same [i.e., from the same mother tongue]'; Edwards cited data comparing Delaware, Natick, Mohegan, and Ojibwa, actual data being something Jones's discourse lacked. Edwards concluded:

It is not to be supposed, that the like coincidence is extended to all the words of those languages. Very many words are totally different. Still the analogy is such as is sufficient to show, that they are mere dialects of the same original language.

(Quoted in Andresen 1990: 45)

Edwards's observations did not go unnoticed, since their publication went through several editions. Thus, comparative linguistics involving unwritten/exotic languages has an age and pedigree equal to the better-known developments involving Indo–European tongues. Edwards is not a unique case. Based on comparative word lists, Barton (1797: xlv) 'show[ed], that the language of the Cheerake [Cherokee] is not radically [same mother language] different from that of the Six-Nations.' Heckewelder (1876: 118) considered evidence in North America for different 'principal languages, branching out ... into various dialects, but all derived from one or the other of the ... mother languages.' Concerning Iroquoian languages, Heckewelder found:

This language in various dialects is spoken by the Mengwe or Six Nations, the Wyandots or Hurons, the Naudowessies, the Assinipoetuk, ... All these languages, however they may be called in a general sense, are dialects of the same mother tongue, and have considerable affinity with each other ... It is sufficient to compare the vocabularies that we have ... to see the great similitude that subsists between them.

(Heckewelder 1876: 119–20)

It may be worth mentioning that there were a number of earlier cases, for example, Ximénez's (ca. 1702) discovery that all the Mayan languages of Guatemala belong to a single family (see Ximénez 1952); Gilij's (1782) demonstration that Maipure, Güipunave, and Cávere (an Arawakan language) are related, in which he recognized sound correspondences (see Gilij 1965); etc. (see also other cases cited in Stipa 1990).

Furthermore, it must be noted, perhaps to the surprise of many, that sound change played a prominent role in early comparative studies of American Indian languages (recall that Leskien's (1876) declaration that 'sound laws suffer no exceptions' dates from 1876, though sound correspondences had played an important role in the work of several earlier comparative linguists). Gatschet (1876: 13) dealt with the 'sound shifts in related (American Indian) languages among which the far-reaching laws of consonantal sounds of the Indo–European languages also hold' (with examples presented from 'Pueblo' languages). Similarly,

Otto Stoll (1885) presented a number of sound correspondences and associated sound changes among Mayan languages, concluding:

> These changes follow regular phonetic laws and bear a strong affinity to the principle of 'Lautverschiebung' (Grimm's law), long ago known as an agent of most extensive application in the morphology of the Indo–Germanic languages.
>
> (Stoll 1885: 257)

Given the history of comparative linguistic work on unwritten languages and even the early employment of the notion of regular sound change in such studies, one might wonder why there has been so much bother about the recurring question of whether the CM was applicable to unwritten languages.

3. Comparative Reconstruction and Writing

The CM requires that something be compared. Somewhat paradoxically, for an unwritten language to be compared, data from it must be recorded. For unwritten or 'preliterate' languages, this means the written transcription of spoken (descriptive) data. The question about reconstruction and unwritten languages, then, is really not about writing per se, but rather about the kind of written evidence used in comparisons, that is, about whether or not there is an older tradition of written texts—languages lacking such a tradition have often been considered 'exotic' or 'primitive,' and it is essentially about these that the question of the applicability of the CM has been raised. Two facts bear emphasis here: (a) the value of written documents for the successful application of the CM has been overrated; and (b) the supposition that linguistic change in unwritten, so-called primitive (or exotic) languages may behave differently from change in languages with a tradition of writing must be abandoned.

3.1 Reconstruction in Families with both 'Written' and 'Unwritten' Languages

A brief look at language families to which the CM has been applied successfully reveals that it is quite common for these families to exhibit a mix of some languages with a written tradition and others which are largely unwritten. For example, Uralic, with an old and strong tradition of comparative linguistics, includes Hungarian (with attestations from the eighth century onward), several other 'written' languages (e.g., Finnish, Estonian, etc.), and languages with no real tradition of writing (Vogul, Ostyak, some Samoyed languages; Stipa 1990: 356–57). Semitic includes languages with some of the earliest known written documents, together with Ethiopian relatives which have scarcely been recorded by linguists. Sapir's (1913, 1915–19) reconstruction of Uto–Aztecan, which demonstrated conclusively for the first time the validity of this family, was one of the earliest rigorous demonstrations of the applicability of the CM to unwritten languages; it also relied on the assumption of the regularity of sound change. Nevertheless, it involved mixed written and unwritten languages, that is, abundant written colonial material for Nahuatl, but Sapir's field notes for Southern Paiute. Families with a mixture of 'written' and 'unwritten' languages are very common, and comparative reconstruction in them goes on essentially without comment or question, though the written sources naturally require philological interpretation (see below).

Even when writing is available, it sometimes provides little or no real advantage for reconstruction. For example, a few Austronesian languages (a very large family) have early written materials; there are Old Cham inscriptions (from 829 AD), Old Malay inscriptions (682–686 AD), and Old Javanese texts (from the ninth to fifteenth centuries; Blust 1990: 133–36). However, as Blust (1990: 136) points out, Old Javanese 'had already changed more than many modern Austronesian languages, and the study of Old Javanese texts . . . contributes little to higher-level reconstruction that cannot be gained from the study of modern Javanese.' He concludes:

> In short, the comparative enterprise in Indo–European linguistics was significantly simplified through the use of attested ancestral stages of the modern languages (particularly Indo–Iranian and Romance) while nothing of the kind can be said for Austronesian.
>
> (Blust 1990: 136)

That is, as these cases show, the existence of unwritten languages (languages with no long written tradition) has not been an obstacle to comparative reconstruction, and the presence of old writing is not always an advantage.

3.2 The Overrated and Misperceived Role of Writing

As pointed out by Haas (1969: 20):

> Since the existence of written languages . . . was of greater strategic importance in the development of our knowledge of Indo–European, some scholars came to believe that the historical and comparative study of languages was impossible without written records of earlier stages of the same or related languages.

This belief persisted in spite of the fact that the comparative study of unwritten/exotic languages has had a long and successful history, as mentioned above. Bloomfield (1925) resolved to disprove once and for all the assertion that the reconstruction of a protolanguage could not be successfully accomplished in the absence of written records of earlier stages of the language (see Haas 1969: 22). Bloomfield's famous Algonquian proof shows, though this was not his primary intention, how writing can not only be overrated, but can sometimes actually be an obstacle to reconstruction. Bloomfield employed mixed 'written' and 'unwritten' source materials on the Algonquian languages he compared, older written sources for some, his own field data for others. He relied in part on earlier records from missionaries and traders and on his own field records for Menomini and Cree; his Fox and Ojibwa material were written down by William Jones, a native speaker of Fox. It will immediately be seen how this provides an important lesson about the value of written sources.

Bloomfield's (1925, 1928) famous proof of the applicability of the CM in unwritten languages was based on the following correspondence sets and reconstructions for Central Algonquian, which he extracted from these sources:

Fox	Ojibwa	Plains Cree	Menomini	PCA	
hk	šk	sk	čk	*čk	(1)
šk	šk	sk	sk	*šk	(2)
hk	hk	sk	hk	*xk	(3)
hk	hk	hk	hk	*hk	(4)
šk	šk	hk	hk	*çk	(5)

Bloomfield postulated the reconstruction of *çk for set (5) as distinct from the others on the bases of scant evidence, but under the assumption that sound change is regular and the difference in this correspondence set (though exhibiting only sounds that occur in different combinations in the other sets) could not plausibly be explained in any other way. Later, his decision to reconstruct something different for this set was confirmed when Swampy Cree was discovered to contain the correspondence *htk* for set (5), distinct in Swampy Cree from the reflexes of the other four reconstructions. Based on this Bloomfield (1928: 100) concluded:

> As an assumption, however, the postulate [of sound-change without exception] yields, as a matter of mere routine, predictions which otherwise would be impossible. In other words, the statement that *phonemes change* (sound-changes have no exceptions) is a tested hypothesis: in so far as one may speak of such a thing, it is a proved truth.

Moreover, Jones's renditions of Ojibwa are important to the point to be made here. Since Fox does not contrast *sk* and *šk*, Jones (as a native speaker of Fox) failed to recognize and record the contrast in Ojibwa. Had the written material available to Bloomfield not failed to represent this contrast, Swampy Cree would not have been the only extant witness to the distinctness of set (5). (The missionary and trader records are even less accurate representations of the languages; see Hockett 1970: 500–16). As Bloomfield (1946: 88) reported it:

> The fuss and trouble behind my note in Language [Bloomfield 1928] would have been avoided if I had listened to O[jibwa], which plainly distinguishes sk (< PA çk) from šk (< PA šk); instead, I depended on printed records which failed to show the distinction.

The truth of the matter in the case of Central Algonquian is that the older written materials were rather an obstacle to reliable reconstruction by the CM, and it was the accurately recorded field data, the usual currency of 'unwritten' languages, which led to the correct solution. Hereby hangs an important tale: written representations require interpretation. They are all in some sense one step removed from the spoken language. Comparative reconstruction which depends on older written documents can be no better than the linguist's ability to extract relevant information from these representations to interpret the phonology of the languages involved. In the case of some extinct languages and other highly changed languages, the older writing available may be a very imprecise reflection of the spoken language; getting accurate indications of the phonology underlying such languages is at times like trying to reconstruct the nature of the snail from its fossil shell. Hockett (1970: 502) drew the lesson to be derived from Bloomfield's Central Algonquian experience blatantly:

> Written records are a means to an end, and there is no justification for holding them in high esteem, or even in reverence (as is sometimes the case) EXCEPT as indirect evidence for what one is trying to discover.

Faber (1990: 619) goes even more to the grain of the matter:

> While extension of the comparative method to instances in which some of the languages to be compared are known primarily or exclusively through written remains is desirable, it brings with it additional complications. These complications involve for the most part reconstruction of the phonetic and phonemic system underlying a particular orthography, in addition to explicit recognition of the fact that the original reduction of the language to writing, whether systematic or haphazard, involved a loss of information. As a result, reconstructions which are based in part on epigraphic corpora are necessarily more distant

approximations to the ancestor language than are reconstructions based exclusively on directly observed data.

Hittite illustrates this point. While Hittite has radically revised linguists' understanding of Indo–European phonology, it was written in a highly imprecise cuneiform syllabary on clay tablets from 1650 to 1200 BC, and several aspects of its phonetic interpretation are still in dispute. For example, did it have four or five vowels? Did it have an [o]? Did Hittite have contrastive vowel length, or, what does the doubling of vowels in the texts mean? What do the frequent double stops in the orthography represent? What is the phonetic nature of the contrast between double stops (corresponding generally to voiceless stops of the traditional Indo–European reconstruction) and single stops (corresponding to voiced and voiced aspirates of traditional Indo–European)? Hittite writing also had as yet unclear extra ('pleonastic') vowels, thought by many not to be involved in the pronunciation of the word (see Baldi 1983: 159–60).

In part, the prejudice in favor of old written traditions reflects a hold over from an earlier stage of comparative linguistics where language change was thought to take place in discrete stages of progress and decay. The languages of so-called 'savage' people were thought to be 'primitive' relics which had not yet evolved (progressed, through processes of compounding and agglutination) to the state of greater perfection which it was believed that the older written Indo–European languages, in particular Sanskrit, had attained; modern languages were typically viewed as just decayed reflections (due to analogy and sound changes, which were assumed to be operative only in this later phase) of their more perfect ancestors. Thus, the old written languages, thought to be more perfect, were allotted a special status. By the time of the neogrammarian movement (see Osthoff and Brugmann 1878), comparative linguistics adopted a uniformitarian position, where language change was no longer held to take place in discrete stages of either progress or decay, but where languages were seen to undergo the same kinds of changes at all times throughout their histories. With this reorientation, written language was accorded less of a special status and attention turned more toward spoken language, in particular to dialects (see Osthoff 1883), and attention to dialectology promoted the development of phonetics, techniques for recording forms of spoken language (see Sievers 1876). Thus, speaking of the principle that sound laws are without exception, Delbrück affirmed in his influential neogrammarian introduction to linguistics:

> This natural constitution of language is not manifested in the cultivated tongues, but in the dialects of the people. The guiding principles for linguistic research should accordingly be deduced not from obsolete written languages of antiquity, but chiefly from the living popular dialects of the present day.
>
> (1974: 61)

> It is of far greater importance to collect further facts from living languages, in order to draw conclusions from them with regard to the ancient languages.
>
> (1974: 126)

Thus, the uniformitarian reorientation led linguists to view spoken language, not written, as the more valuable for linguistic research (see Christy 1983: 35–36, 55, 58). By 1900, Henry Sweet (1900: 79) was able to report:

It is now an axiom of scientific philology that the real life of language is in many respects more clearly seen and better studied in dialects and colloquial forms of speech than in highly developed literary languages.

Hoenigswald (1990: 379) provides a worthwhile summary of the real value of writing for reconstruction:

That written records add to the fullness of our basic knowledge and give us a 'free ride' into the past is of course true, but it does not change the uncertainty which hangs over our inferences. That written records allow us direct observation of changes along something that can come rather close to a direct line of descent is also true, but it still does not solve the problem of how to describe, classify, and 'explain' the changes. The most interesting use of written records lies in their availability for the task of confirming or disallowing inferences, as in the case of Latin and Proto–Romance. It should, however, be understood that neither the comparative method nor internal reconstruction depend[s] on written records.

4. Misconceptions about 'Primitive' Languages and Their Implications for the CM

In some cases, past misconceptions about so-called 'primitive' languages have caused doubts about whether the CM is applicable to exotic and unwritten languages. Unfortunately, some of these misgivings linger on even today.

4.1 The Myth of Imprecise Sounds

Some had doubted that the CM could be applied to exotic languages based on the commonplace nineteenth-century belief that such languages were imprecise, with vague or fluctuating articulations defying description and transcription. Thus, for example, two famous American Indian scholars reported:

In many languages, as is well known, there are elementary sounds of an indeterminate nature, which seem to float between two, and sometimes even three or four, diverse articulations.
(Horacio Hale 1884: 233)

In spite of the significance attached to the phonetic elements, they are, in many American languages, singularly vague and fluctuating.
(Daniel Brinton 1888: 8)

It is now known, of course, that the imprecision is not a fault in these languages, but lies rather in the inability of those recording the languages to represent them accurately. Heckewelder (1876: 374) recognized this long ago:

To this you will add the numerous errors committed by those who attempt to write down the words of the Indian languages, and who either in their own have not alphabetical signs adequate to the true expression of the sounds, or want an *Indian ear* to distinguish them. I could write a volume on the subject of their ridiculous mistakes.

Boas's (1889) article 'On alternating sounds' explained away this misconception about the nature of so-called 'primitive' languages, though its throes had some continued reverberations, for example, in Rivers's (1922: 20) Presidential address to the Royal Anthropological Institute (Henson 1974: 37). Thus, Boas removed one obstacle to the application of the CM to unwritten languages.

4.2 The Myth of Rapid Change

Another misconception of the past, which still produces some faint echoes today, is that unwritten exotic languages 'change with a rapidity that soon renders reconstruction so tenuous as to be meaningless' (Haas 1969: 27). For example, in Sayce's (1874) famous *The Principles of Comparative Philology* the reader is taught:

If . . . we really want to see the principle of Phonetic Decay in its full activity and importance we must turn our eyes to unwritten dialects rather than to that particular dialect which has accidentally been stereotyped into the standard language of literature. Here the various processes which change and develop language go on unchecked.
(Sayce 1874: 20–21)

. . . as a general rule, tribes in a low state of civilisation . . . are continually changing the character of their idioms, so that in the course of a single generation two neighbouring villages become mutually unintelligible.
(Sayce 1874: 46–47)

The dialects of barbarian tribes are perpetually altering. There is nothing to preserve them—neither traditions, nor ritual, nor literature.
(Sayce 1874: 80)

Similarly, Edward Tylor (1881: 142), in the first textbook of anthropology, instructed that:

Indeed, anyone who will attend to how English words run together in talking may satisfy himself that his own language would undergo rapid changes like those of barbaric tongues, were it not for the schoolmaster and the printer, who insist on keeping our words fixed and separate.
(Henson 1974: 10)

Payne (1899: 92) concluded that 'from 20 to 40 years is probably a liberal allotment for the average life of a very low savage language.' (see Christy 1983: 48, 54.)

Abundant descriptive and historical linguistic work with exotic and unwritten languages has overwhelmingly demonstrated the inaccuracy of the rapid-change assumption. Nevertheless, the idea has been slow to die. For example, Pulgram (1961: 32) still espoused it:

In some linguistic families, notably Amerindian and African, prehistory is but a few decades distant. Any thrust into the past will involve the linguist in reconstruction . . . By the time the Amerindian or African linguist has reached, speaking in terms of the genealogical tree . . . , the third or fourth generation, which perhaps carries him backward no farther than a century, he faces a proto-language of his own making that has an exceedingly small degree of verisimilitude.
(Haas 1969: 27)

Sometimes associated with the myth of rapid change in unwritten languages is the notion held by some (Powell 1891; Boas 1920; Schuchardt 1928, etc.) that unwritten languages may borrow so extensively and become so mixed that it may be impossible in some cases to determine a single genetic ancestor, to classify them, or to recover their past through comparative reconstruction (cf. Greenberg 1953: 266). Through the in-depth study of abundant cases, it is now known both that extensive borrowing is possible in all areas of the grammar and lexicon, and that written and unwritten languages do not behave differently in this regard. For languages transmitted naturally (from one generation to the next) such intensive contact and borrowing pose no insurmountable problem for classification and the application of the CM (Thomason and Kaufman 1988).

4.3 The Regularity of Sound Change in So-called 'Primitive' Languages

There is now, in the early 1990s, no longer any doubt about the regularity of sound change in unwritten (exotic) languages, though in the past this regularity was frequently questioned, based on misconceptions concerning so-called 'primitive' languages. With an allusion to these misconceptions, Sapir (1931: 74) summarized the now almost universal attitude:

Is there any reason to believe that the process of regular phonetic change is any less applicable to the languages of primitive peoples than to the languages of the more civilized nations? This question must be answered in the negative ... If these laws are more difficult to discover in primitive languages, this is not due to any special characteristic which these languages possess but merely to the inadequate technique of some who have tried to study them.

As is now well-known, Bloomfield (1925, 1928) demonstrated the validity of the assumption of the regularity of sound change for unwritten 'primitive/exotic' languages, responding to doubts about the applicability of the CM to 'exotic' languages, for example, the misgivings of Meillet and Cohen (1924: 9) in their famous book, *Les langues du Monde*:

> One may well ask whether the languages of America (which are still for the most part poorly known and insufficiently studied from a comparative point of view) will ever lend themselves to exact, exhaustive comparative treatment; the samples offered so far hold scant promise ... it is not even clear that the principle of genealogical classification applies.

(See also Meillet 1925: vi–vii.) Rivet (1925) recognized that the lack of regular phonetic correspondences in some 'exotic' languages might lie in the fault of the transcription, but he nevertheless considered it possible that these languages might not conform to 'rules as strict as those found in the Indo–European language' (Rivet 1925: 26; see also Andresen 1990: 189).

It was against these sentiments that Bloomfield (1925: 130) directed his famous article:

> I hope, also, to help dispose of the notion that the usual processes of linguistic change are suspended on the American continent. (Meillet and Cohen, *Les langues du monde*, Paris, 1924, p. 9). If there exists anywhere a language in which these processes do not occur (sound-change independent of meaning, analogic change, etc), then they will not explain the history of Indo–European or any other language. A principle such as the regularity of phonetic change is not part of the specific tradition handed on to each new speaker of a given language, but is either a universal trait of human speech or nothing at all, an error.

Sapir (1929: 160–61), who had already engaged in the comparative reconstruction of a number of American Indian language families, seconded Bloomfield:

> The methods developed by the Indo–Europeanists have been applied with marked success to other groups of languages. It is abundantly clear that they apply just as rigorously to the unwritten primitive languages of Africa and America as to the better known forms of speech of the more sophisticated peoples ... The more we devote ourselves to the comparative study of the languages of a primitive linguistic stock, the more clearly we realize that phonetic law and analogical leveling are the only satisfactory key to the unravelling of the development of dialects and languages from a common base. Professor Leonard Bloomfield's experiences with Central Algonkian and my own with Athabaskan leave nothing to be desired in this respect and are a complete answer to those who find it difficult to accept the large-scale regularity of the operation of all those unconscious linguistic forces which in their totality give us regular phonetic change and morphological readjustment on the basis of such change. It is not merely theoretically possible to predict the correctness of specific forms among unlettered peoples on the basis of such phonetic laws as have been worked out for them—such predictions are already on record in considerable number. There can be no doubt that the methods first developed in the field of Indo–European linguistics are destined to play a consistently important rôle in the study of all other groups of languages.

(See also Sapir (1931): 78.) Since Sapir and Bloomfield's early work, the assumption that sound change is regular has proved itself useful and valid in case after case of work on exotic and unwritten languages.

4.4 The Applicability of the CM to Exotic Languages

Some doubts about the applicability of the CM to exotic languages seem to stem from an often imprecisely articulated belief that change in exotic languages may somehow be fundamentally different from that typical of written languages. Frequently, Australian languages have been implicated in these doubts (see, for example, Sommerfeld 1938: 187–88). More recently, Boretzky (1982, 1984) has made similar claims, which have been cited approvingly by Mühlhäusler (1989; see also Baldi 1990: 11). Boretzky contrasts Aranta (in Australia) and Kâte (in New Guinea) with Slavic and Romance—'exotic' with 'European.' Boretzky objects that in exotic languages semantic slots are likely to be filled either by difficult-to-relate morphs, or, conversely, that the phonological differences are so small (in Arandic) that there is no scope for reconstruction; he thinks that change in the Arandic languages proceeds more by abrupt lexical replacement through borrowing than by gradual phonological change (Hoenigswald 1990: 377). This, however, does not invalidate the CM for these languages. Dixon (1990: 398) shows that 'it is quite clear that Australian languages change in a regular fashion, in the same way as Indo–European and other families.' In fact, it was through a demonstration of regular changes that Hale (1964, 1976) was able to show that the languages of northeastern Queensland with many short monosyllabic words, formerly thought to be quite aberrant, in fact developed regularly from a normal Pama–Nyungan type language. Vocabulary may present difficulties in Australia, but lexical borrowings are a fact of linguistic life that the CM has to contend with everywhere, not just in Australia or New Guinea (see Dixon 1980: 254; Johnson 1990: 430). Moreover, as Hoenigswald (1990) points out, Boretzky is wrong when he assumes that the CM was developed only in work on Indo–European languages and applies well only to these languages. Comparative work in a number of families (Uralic, Dravidian, Athabaskan, Mayan, Algonquian, Uto–Aztecan, Austronesian, and Sino–Tibetan, among others) has contributed to the development of the CM and to greater understanding of linguistic change in general.

5. Conclusions

The CM applies to both written and unwritten languages. Change in unwritten or exotic languages is not fundamentally different in its nature from that which goes on in languages with a tradition of writing. Sound change is equally regular in written and unwritten languages. Abundant comparative research involving unwritten and exotic languages from all over the world has demonstrated time and again the legitimacy of reconstruction by the CM for unwritten as well as written languages.

Bibliography

Andresen J T 1990 *Linguistics in America 1769–1924*. Routledge, London

Baldi P 1983 *An Introduction to the Indo–European Languages*. Southern Illinois University Press, Carbondale, IL

Baldi P (ed.) 1990 *Linguistic Change and Reconstruction Methodology*. Mouton de Gruyter, Berlin

Barton B S 1797 *New Views on the Origin of the Tribes and Nations of America*. B. S. Barton, Philadelphia, PA

Bloomfield L 1925 On the sound system of Central Algonquian. *Lg* 1: 130–56

Bloomfield L 1928 A note on sound-change. *Lg* 4: 99–100

Bloomfield L 1946 Algonquian. In: Hoijer H (ed.) *Linguistic Structures of Native America*. The Viking Fund, New York

Blust R 1990 Summary report: Linguistic change and reconstruction methodology in the Austronesian language family. In: Baldi P (ed.) 1990

Boas F 1889 On alternating sounds. *AmA* 2: 47–53

Boas F 1920 The classification of American languages. *AmA* 22: 367–76

Boretzky N 1982 Das indogermanische Sprachwandelmodell und Wandel in exotischen Sprachen. *Zeitschrift für vergleichende Sprachforschung* 95: 49–80

Boretzky N 1984 The Indo–Europeanist model of sound change and genetic affinity and its application to exotic languages. *Diachronica* 1: 1–51

Brinton D G 1888 The language of palaeolithic man. *American Philosophical Society* **1888**: 3–16

Christy C 1983 *Uniformitarianism in Linguistics*. John Benjamins, Amsterdam

Delbrück B 1974 *Introduction to the Study of Language: A Critical Survey of the History and Methods of Comparative Philology of the Indo–European Languages*. John Benjamins, Amsterdam

Dixon R M W 1980 *The Languages of Australia*. Cambridge University Press, Cambridge

Dixon R M W 1990 Summary report: Linguistic change and reconstruction in the Australian language family. In: Baldi P (ed.) 1990

Faber A 1990 Interpretation of orthographic forms. In: Baldi P (ed.) 1990

Gatschet A 1876 *Zwölf Sprachen aus dem südwesten Nordamerikas (Pueblos-und Apache-Mundarten; Tonto, Tonkawa, Digger, Utah)*. Hermann Böhlau, Weimar

Gilij F S 1965 Ensayo de historia americana. (trans. Tovar A) In: *Fuentes para la Historia Colonial de Venezuela*, Vol. 3. Biblioteca de la Academia Nacional de la Historia, Caracas

Greenberg J 1953 Historical linguistics and unwritten languages. In: Kroeber A (ed.) *Anthropology Today*. University of Chicago Press, Chicago, IL

Haas M 1969 *The Prehistory of Languages*. Mouton, The Hague

Hale H 1884 On some doubtful or intermediate articulations: An experiment in phonetics. *Journal of the Royal Anthropological Institute* 14: 233–43

Hale K 1964 Classification of the Northern Paman languages, Cape York Peninsula, Australia: A research report. *Oceanic Linguistics* 3: 248–65

Hale K 1976 Phonological developments in particular Northern Paman languages, and, phonological developments in a Northern Paman language: Uradhi. In: Sutton P (ed.) *Languages of Cape York*. Australian Institute of Aboriginal Studies, Canberra

Heckewelder J 1876 *History, Manners, and Customs of the Indian Nations Who Once Inhabited Pennsylvania and the Neighboring States*. The Historical Society of Pennsylvania, Philadelphia, PA

Henson H 1974 *British Social Anthropologists and Language: A History of Separate Development*. Clarendon Press, Oxford

Hockett C 1948 Implications of Bloomfield's Algonquian studies. *Lg* 24: 117–31

Hockett C (ed.) 1970 *A Leonard Bloomfield anthology*. Indiana University Press, Bloomington, IN

Hoenigswald H 1990 Is the 'comparative' method general or family-specific? In: Baldi P (ed.) 1990

Johnson S 1990 Social parameters of linguistic change in an unstratified aboriginal society. In: Baldi P (ed.) 1990

Leem K 1748 *En Lappisk grammatica efter den dialect, som bruges af Field-Lapperne udi Porsanger-Fiorden, samt et register over de udi samme grammatica anførte obervationers indhold*. Nidrosiæ, Copenhagen

Leem K 1768–81 *Lexicon Lapponicum bipartitum: Lapponico–Danica-Latinum & Danico-Latino-Lapponicum*. Nidrosiæ, Copenhagen

Leskien A 1876 *Die Declination im Slavisch–Litauischen und Germanischen*. S. Hirzel, Leipzig

Meillet A 1925 *La méthode comparative en linguistique historique*. H. Aschehoug, Oslo

Meillet A, Cohen M 1924 *Les langues du monde*. E. Champion, Paris

Mühlhäusler P 1989 On the causes of accelerated linguistic change in the Pacific area. In: Breivik L, Jahr E (eds.) *Language Change: Contributions to the Study of its Causes*. Mouton de Gruyter, Berlin

Osthoff H 1883 *Schriftsprache und Mundart*. Richter, Hamburg

Osthoff H, Brugmann K 1878 *Morphologische Untersuchungen auf dem Gebiete der indogermanischen Sprachen*. S. Hirzel, Leipzig

Payne E J 1899 *History of the New World Called America*, vol. 2. Oxford University Press, Oxford

Powell J W 1891 *Indian Linguistic Families of America North of Mexico*, Seventh annual report, Bureau of American Ethnology. Government Printing Office, Washington DC

Pulgram E 1961 The nature and use of proto-languages. *Lingua* 10: 18–37

Rivers W H R 1922 The unity of anthropology. *Journal of the Royal Anthropological Institute* 52: 12–25

Rivet P 1925 Les Australiens en Amérique. *BSL* **26**: 23–63

Sajnovics J 1770 *Demonstratio idioma ungarorum et lapponum idem esse*. Typis Collegii Societatis Jesu, Tyrnaviae

Sapir E 1913, 1915–19 Southern Paiute and Nahuatl: a study in Uto–Aztecan. *Journal de la Société des Américanistes de Paris*, Part 1, **10**: 379–425; Part 2, **11**: 433–88

Sapir E 1929 The status of linguistics as a science. *Lg* **5**: 207–14

Sapir E 1931 The concept of phonetic law as tested in primitive languages by Leonard Bloomfield. In: Rice S (ed.) *Methods in Social Science: A Case Book*. University of Chicago Press, Chicago, IL

Sayce A H 1874 *The Principles of Comparative Philology*. Trübner, London

Schuchardt-Brevier H 1928 *Hugo Schuchardt-Brevier: Ein Vademecum der allgemeinen Sprachwissenschaft*. Niemeyer, Halle

Sievers E 1876 *Grundzüge der Lautphysiologie zur Einführung in das Studium der Lautlehre der indogermanischen Sprachen*. Breikopf and Härtel, Leipzig

Sommerfeld A 1938 *La langue et la société*. H. Aschoug, Oslo

Stipa G 1990 *Finnisch–ugrische Sprachforschung: Von der Renaisance bis zum Neupositivismus*, Mémoires de la Société Finno–Ougrienne, 206. Suomalias–Ugrilainen Seura, Helsinki

Stoll O 1885 Supplementary remarks to the grammar of the Cakchiquel language. *Proceedings of the American Philosophical Society* 22: 255–68

Sweet H 1900 *The History of Language*. Dent, London

Thomason S, Kaufman T 1988 *Language Contact, Creolization, and Genetic Linguistics*. University of California Press, Berkeley, CA

Tylor E 1881 *Anthropology; An Introduction to the Study of Man and Civilisation*. Macmillan, London

Ximénez F 1952 *Arte de las tres lenguas Cakchiquel, Quiche y Tzutuhil*. Microfilm collection of manuscripts on Middle American cultural anthropology, 36. University of Chicago Library, Chicago, IL

L. Campbell

Redundancy

'Redundancy' is an informal, pretheoretical notion often appealed to in linguistic theorizing. It is applied both to actual language usage (manifested in behavior or texts) and to the grammars and theories that linguists develop to account for language structure. The concept of redundancy occurs in two related senses: (a) predictability, and (b) unnecessary repetition.

Information theory considers samples of language (texts) as unidimensional strings of symbols (see *Information Theory*). To the extent that one can, given a string of words, or letters, or whatever, surely predict the next word or letter, the text in question displays redundancy. More generally, one can consider the predictability of a symbol as determined by its preceding and following context. A text in which the individual unit symbols are highly predictable is very redundant. Information theory has developed mathematical techniques for describing the redundancy of texts; the inverse notion, defined with precision in information theory, but not widely current in linguistics, is 'entropy' (see *Entropy*).

This information–theoretical concept of redundancy, while mathematically sophisticated, is linguistically crude. It makes no distinction, for instance, between the syntax and the semantics of a text. An item may be predictable because of its semantic content, as in the example *The . . . is the world's largest land-dwelling mammal.* Here, the word *elephant* is predictable by virtue of its meaning. One makes this prediction on the basis of one's knowledge of the world, in this case of zoology. But take another word from the same example: *The elephant is . . . world's largest land-dwelling mammal.* Here, there is only one word, *the* (or perhaps marginally *this*), which can fill the gap, and the word *the* is therefore predictable, but now on the basis of its being required in the grammatical structure of a sentence of this type. Here the prediction requires knowledge of English grammar, rather than of any extralinguistic domain.

Linguistic theorists typically regard the redundancy of languages in their syntax as falling within the scope of linguistic theory, but most would eschew any responsibility to account for the redundancy (in the sense of predictability) in the semantics of language usage. In other words, linguistic theory attempts to account for *how* people say what they say, as molded by the rules of the grammars of languages, but not for *what* people say. People sometimes, of course, say the most predictable things, such as 'Good morning'; and at other times they say the most unpredictable things. This is of no relevance to the core of linguistic theory, which concerns itself not with language behavior, whether redundant (predictable) or not, but with language system.

Examples of redundancy (=predictability) in languages, ascribable to their grammatical systems, including their phonology and morphology, are such facts as the following: (a) in English, a stop consonant immediately following a word-initial /s/ is predictably voiceless and unaspirated; (b) in German, a noun phrase acting as the direct object of the verb *folgen* is predictably in the dative case; and (c) in French, an attributive adjective modifying a singular feminine noun is also, predictably, singular and feminine. Clearly, this kind of redundancy in language is exactly what

grammar focuses on. In fact all rules of grammar which state a contingent but predictable correlation between two or more structural elements, such as case, number, gender, word-order, etc., address some redundancy in language itself. In this sense, the redundancy in language, the extent to which its forms follow clear constraining rules, the 'structuredness' of language, is the central object of a theoretical linguist's attention.

Turning to the sense in which redundancy identifies unnecessary information in some stretch of language usage, this is more evident in the semantics of texts. For instance, if one says, 'That female woman is my sister,' it would be agreed that there is one word too many. There is simply no need to modify *woman* with *female*, as all the information in *female* is already encoded in *woman*. Here, actually, core linguistic theory, in the shape of lexical semantics, can illuminate the redundancy, which arises through the avoidable repetition of a semantic feature. However, the usual way in which lexical semantics defines its goals in this area is not in terms of redundancy, but of a distinct, though closely related notion, tautology. A tautology is a necessary truth, such as *Every woman is female.* In the normal usage of linguists, a tautology is distinguished from an instance of semantic redundancy. The tautology *Every woman is female* could not be shortened without loss, unlike the redundant *That female woman is my sister.* (One might say that it is 'pragmatically redundant' to utter a tautology, as any hearer would be expected to know its content already, and so perhaps the whole utterance could remain unsaid, 'without loss,' but this is evidently a different matter from the semantic redundancy of *female woman.*)

The element of necessity distinguishes the case of syntactic, morphological, and phonological redundancy (discussed earlier), on the one hand, from the case of semantic redundancy, on the other. A speaker of French has no choice but to express the feminine gender three times in a phrase such as *une femme fameuse*; the grammar of the language makes this necessary. But the French speaker can in some sense choose whether or not to say *une femme femelle*, and in fact generally chooses not to, in order to avoid the redundancy.

A Martian looking at human languages might judge that their syntactic, morphological, and phonological redundancy was also 'unnecessary' in some strict sense. Perhaps, in some strict but unrealistic sense, some of the structuredness of languages *is* unnecessary; the British schoolchild learning French has probably often ruefully felt the French insistence on gender and number agreement to be 'unnecessary.' The commands specified by computer operating systems to get machines to do one's bidding do not typically exhibit anything like such a high degree of grammatical structuredness as natural language samples do. But here lies the clue to the function of much, if not all, of the redundancy in language. Computer command languages are not beset by the massive ambiguity inherent in natural language, and are used in relatively noise-free channels, compared to human language. As any student of computational linguistics knows, natural language texts are rife with local ambiguities, that is, places in a string where several interpretations are possible. But typically many such local ambiguities are resolvable by elements occurring elsewhere in the string. The correlation of elements of structure at some distance apart by grammatical rules compensates for much of the local ambiguity, and makes correct interpretation of larger-sized units (e.g., whole sentences) relatively trouble-free.

The linguist accepts redundancy as one of the facts of language to be accounted for by grammars and linguistic theories. The linguist writes grammars, often in a quasi-mathematical format devised expressly for the purpose of describing natural languages. Such a quasi-mathematical notation is itself a kind of language, in fact a metalanguage, to which the notion of redundancy can be applied. A motif running through much of the grammatical theorizing of the past thirty years has been the elimination of redundancy from the metalanguage used for the formulation of (generative) grammars. An instance is the development of X-bar theory, of which a simplified account is given below.

Once, generative grammarians proposed phrase structure rules such as (1):

NounPhrase   → Determiner + Noun

VerbPhrase   → Auxiliary + Verb (+NounPhrase)

AdjectivePhrase   → (Intensifier+) Adjective

PrepositionalPhrase → Preposition + NounPhrase.   (1)

One immediately observes a certain pattern, or predictability, here. There is a consistent correlation between the category of the mother phrase and the category of one of its daughters, the head. To eliminate this restatement of the same type of information, arguably a kind of redundancy, from grammars, a new convention was introduced into the metalanguage of grammar writing. This convention replaced the names of the categories Noun, Verb, Adjective, and Preposition by a variable 'X,' so that (with a little extra work to be done on the ordering of elements) the four rules above could be reduced to one, namely (2):

XPhrase → Complement of X + X   (2)

Certain rules formulated by linguists, usually involving the content of entries in the lexicon, have been specifically labeled as '(lexical) redundancy rules.' These can be morphological, or phonological, as the rules which specify, for English, that all vowels are voiced. The central idea is to replace the superfluity of information found in the linguistic item itself, be it a lexical entry, a phrase, or an entire sentence, with a single statement in the grammatical metalanguage. Some intuition of what it is, or should be, unnecessary to say more than once is clearly also at work here.

J. R. Hurford

Redundancy Rules in Phonology

Phonological systems in all languages exhibit 'redundancy.' Not all logically possible combinations of features occur as segments, nor do all logically possible sequences of segments occur in morphemes. The values of certain features are redundant and can be predicted in terms of the values of other features. Rules which describe such predictable

or redundant features are known as 'redundancy rules' or 'morpheme structure rules.'

1. Redundancy Rules

In generative phonology, it has been assumed since Halle (1959) that there are two distinct types of rules, phonological rules proper and (lexical) redundancy rules or morpheme structure rules. Phonological rules relate underlying or phonological representations to phonetic representations and account for alternations. For example, the voicing alternation in many English suffixes, plural [s] ~ [z] (*cats* [s], *dogs* [z]), 3 SG PRES agreement [s] ~ [z] (*kicks* [s], *hugs* [z]), PT [t] ~ [d] (*wished* [t], *loved* [d]) is usually accounted for by a phonological rule which changes the underlying [+voice] specification of these consonantal suffixes to [−voice] when they immediately follow consonants that are [−voice]. Redundancy rules, on the other hand, state generalizations about dictionary entries or underlying representation of morphemes.

Lexical representations or dictionary entries are generally assumed to be redundancy free—that is only unpredictable information is specified. Redundant feature specifications are left blank and filled in by redundancy rules (see *Representations in Phonology*). Redundancy rules that state redundancies within a single segment are known as 'segment structure rules.' For example, in a language with five underlying vowels *i*, *u*, *e*, *o*, and *a*, all vowels need not be specified in underlying representations for the features [back], [round], [high], and [low]. Since *a* is the only low vowel, it is possible to represent it simply as [+low] and write a redundancy rule:

$$[+\text{low}] \rightarrow \begin{bmatrix} -\text{round} \\ -\text{high} \\ +\text{back} \end{bmatrix} \qquad (1)$$

to fill in the specifications of [+round], [−high], and [+back]. If a vowel is [+high] or [−back] it is predictably [−low]. These relationships can also be stated in redundancy rules:

$$\begin{Bmatrix} [-\text{back}] \\ [+\text{high}] \end{Bmatrix} \rightarrow [-\text{low}] \qquad (2)$$

Similarly the relationship between backness and roundness for the nonlow vowels can be expressed by a redundancy rule utilizing a Greek letter variable, eliminating the need to specify nonlow vowels for both the features [round] and [back]:

$$\begin{bmatrix} -\text{low} \\ \alpha\text{back} \end{bmatrix} \rightarrow [\alpha\text{round}] \qquad (3)$$

The alpha (α) in this rule is a variable with two possible values '+' or '−' (see *Abbreviatory Conventions*). The rule states that nonlow vowels have the same value for the feature [round] as for the feature [back]: plus for back vowels and minus for front vowels.

Redundancy rules that state restrictions or constraints on sequences of segments within morphemes or lexical items are called 'sequence structure rules.' For example, if a language allows only homorganic nasal obstruent clusters within morphemes, (e.g., *ŋk*, *nt*, *mp*, but not *ŋt*, *mk*, etc.) the place features for nasals preceding obstruents can be left unspecified in lexical entries and filled in by a sequence structure rule that copies the place specification for the nasal from the following obstruent.

2. Rules versus Conditions

In early works in generative phonology, morpheme structure rules were ordered with phonological rules and not always clearly distinguished from them. In a language with the five underlying vowels discussed above, a phonological rule epenthesizing the vowel *e* would have been ordered before the segment structure rules stating that nonlow vowels have the same value for [round] as for [back] and the rule stating that [−back] vowels are [−low]. In this way the values of [round] and [low] could be supplied to the epenthetic vowel by the segment structure rules discussed above. For example, the Spanish rule of epenthesis, which inserts *e* before word initial clusters beginning with *s* (/slobakya/ > [esloβakya] 'slovakia' cf. [tʃekosloβakya] 'Czechoslovakia'), could insert a vowel specified simply as [−back −high]. The specifications of [−low] and [−round] for the epenthetic *e*, as well as underlying *e* (e.g., *tela* 'fabric'), would be supplied by the same redundancy rules if they were ordered after the epenthesis rule. Similarly, if nasal assimilation occurred across morpheme boundaries as well as within morphemes, a single rule of nasal assimilation would have been formulated to fill in redundant place features for nasals in nasal obstruent clusters within morphemes as well as to change features in clusters arising through morpheme combinations. For example, the same rule could be used to fill in the place of articulation features of nasals in nasal obstruent clusters in English morphemes (*si*[ŋ]*k*, *hi*[n]*t*, *wi*[m]*p*) and to change features of the nasal in the negative prefix *in-* when it precedes an obstruent (*i*[ŋ]-*conceivable*, *i*[n]-*tolerable*, *i*[m]-*possible*, cf. *i*[n]-*articulate*).

In an influential article, Stanley (1967) argued that the practice of ordering morpheme structure rules with phonological rules is problematic and that morpheme structure rules should be clearly distinguished from phonological rules. Indeed he suggested that 'morpheme structure rules' (MSRs) be replaced by 'morpheme structure conditions' (MSCs) which state generalizations about fully specified (underlying) lexical representations. His argument proceeded in two stages. First he argued that morpheme structure rules should apply in a block before phonological rules to guarantee that the input to the phonological rules be fully specified, that is, that the input to the phonological rules contain no blanks. Stanley argued that this was necessary because if phonological rules operate on partially specified representations, certain misuses of blanks are possible. Specifically, it can be shown that a blank can function as a third value, distinct from both plus and minus, if phonological rules apply to partially specified representations. Stanley then argued that rather than filling in blanks in lexical entries, morpheme structure conditions should state true generalizations about fully specified lexical representations, for otherwise it is arbitrary which feature is left blank in certain cases (see below).

Stanley's argument that phonological rules cannot apply to partially specified representations proceeds as follows: given a rule R, [+A] → [+B] and a representation with no specification for [+A], [A, −B], whether R applies or not, the unspecified value can function as a third value, distinct

from both '+' and '−.' The assumption that R does not apply to this representation has been called the 'submatrix convention' of rule application whereas the assumption that R applies to such a representation is known as the 'distinctness convention' of rule application. For example, assuming the submatrix convention of rule application, a rule voicing intervocalic obstruents ([−son] → [+voi]/V___V) would not apply to a segment unspecified for [son] between vowels, whereas with the distinctness convention this rule would apply to such a segment.

Consider first the submatrix convention of rule application, the segments (4):

$$
\begin{bmatrix} +a \\ b \\ c \end{bmatrix}
\begin{bmatrix} +a \\ +b \\ c \end{bmatrix}
\begin{bmatrix} +a \\ -b \\ c \end{bmatrix}
\tag{4}
$$

and the rules (5):

$$
\begin{aligned}
&\text{(i)} \quad [+a] \to [-c] \\
&\text{(ii)} \quad [+b] \to [+c] \\
&\text{(iii)} \quad [-b] \to [+c] \\
&\text{(iv)} \quad [-c] \to [+b]
\end{aligned}
\tag{5}
$$

If these rules are applied in the order given, the following derivations result:

$$
\begin{array}{ccc}
\begin{bmatrix} +a \\ b \\ c \end{bmatrix} & \begin{bmatrix} +a \\ +b \\ c \end{bmatrix} & \begin{bmatrix} +a \\ -b \\ c \end{bmatrix} \\
\text{(i)} & \text{(i)} & \text{(i)} \\
\downarrow & \downarrow & \downarrow \\
\begin{bmatrix} +a \\ b \\ -c \end{bmatrix} & \begin{bmatrix} +a \\ +b \\ -c \end{bmatrix} & \begin{bmatrix} +a \\ -b \\ -c \end{bmatrix} \\
\text{(iv)} & \text{(ii)} & \text{(iii)} \\
\downarrow & \downarrow & \downarrow \\
\begin{bmatrix} +a \\ +b \\ -c \end{bmatrix} & \begin{bmatrix} +a \\ +b \\ +c \end{bmatrix} & \begin{bmatrix} +a \\ -b \\ +c \end{bmatrix}
\end{array}
\tag{6}
$$

Since the first segment emerges distinct from both the second and the third, and since it was distinct from neither to start with, the blank has functioned as a third value, distinct from both plus and minus. This is problematic if one is committed to the position that features are binary. It is also problematic if one assumes that plus and minus specifications, but not blanks, contribute to complexity, because the cost-free blank is functioning on a par with plus and minus, but does not contribute to complexity. With the distinctness convention of rule application, the same three segments can also be rendered distinct by applying the following rules in the order given:

$$
\begin{aligned}
&\text{(iii)} \quad [-b] \to \begin{bmatrix} -a \\ -c \end{bmatrix} \\
&\text{(iv)} \quad [+b] \to [+c] \\
&\text{(v)} \quad [-a] \to [+b]
\end{aligned}
$$

$$
\begin{bmatrix} +a \\ b \\ c \end{bmatrix}
\begin{bmatrix} +a \\ +b \\ c \end{bmatrix}
\begin{bmatrix} +a \\ -b \\ c \end{bmatrix}
$$

$$
\begin{array}{cc}
\text{(iii)} & \text{(iii)} \\
\downarrow & \downarrow \\
\begin{bmatrix} -a \\ b \\ -c \end{bmatrix} &
\begin{bmatrix} -a \\ -b \\ -c \end{bmatrix}
\end{array}
\tag{7}
$$

$$
\begin{array}{ccc}
\text{(iv)} & \text{(iv)} & \\
\downarrow & \downarrow & \downarrow \\
\begin{bmatrix} -a \\ b \\ +c \end{bmatrix} &
\begin{bmatrix} +a \\ +b \\ +c \end{bmatrix} &
\end{array}
$$

$$
\begin{array}{cc}
\text{(v)} & \text{(v)} \\
\downarrow & \downarrow \\
\begin{bmatrix} -a \\ +b \\ +c \end{bmatrix} &
\begin{bmatrix} -a \\ +b \\ -c \end{bmatrix}
\end{array}
$$

The misuse of blanks can be avoided if the well-formedness condition is adopted. The well-formedness condition requires that no derivations occur in which a rule $[+A] \rightarrow [+B]$ is available to apply to a representation unspecified for [A], that is, [A]. As Stanley notes, however, the well-formedness condition is problematic because it is not possible to determine, except by running through a (potentially) infinite number of derivations, whether a grammar is well-formed. He concludes that the input to the phonological rules should be fully specified (see *Representations in Phonology*).

In Stanley's theory, sequence structure conditions replace sequence structure rules and segment structure conditions replace segment structure rules. Three types of morpheme structure conditions are distinguished: if–then conditions, positive conditions, and negative conditions. All morpheme structure rules can be translated into if–then conditions. An if–then condition states that if a lexical representation meets some condition x, it must also meet some condition y. For example, a morpheme structure rule:

$$
[+\text{low}] \rightarrow \begin{bmatrix} +\text{back} \\ -\text{high} \\ -\text{round} \end{bmatrix}
\tag{8}
$$

can be stated as an if–then condition on fully specified matrices: If a vowel is low, then it is also back, nonhigh, and unrounded.

Positive conditions state certain generalizations that cannot be otherwise stated. For example, if a language has morphemes only of the shape CVCV, this cannot be stated with an if–then condition. Such a generalization can be stated with a positive condition P(C):CVCV. Negative conditions state combinations of features that cannot occur, eliminating the arbitrariness that occurs in cases of interdependent features. For example, in a language with vowel harmony (see *Vowel Harmony*) there are co-occurrence restrictions such that certain combinations of vowels do not occur in morphemes. In native morphemes in Igbo, for example, all vowels are [+advanced tongue root] ([+ATR]) or [−advanced tongue root] ([−ATR]). In such a case it would be arbitrary to choose the first (or last) vowel in a morpheme as the one specified for [ATR] and to predict the specifications of the other vowels by a morpheme structure rule. A negative condition, on the other hand, expresses the fact that sequences of vowels that disagree in specification for [ATR] are prohibited:

$$
\sim \begin{bmatrix} +\text{syll} \\ \alpha\text{ATR} \end{bmatrix} C_0 \begin{bmatrix} -\text{syll} \\ -\alpha\text{ATR} \end{bmatrix}
\tag{9}
$$

(where '$\sim$' means that what follows is not permitted; C_0 indicates any number of consonants).

Chomsky and Halle (1968) adopt most of Stanley's proposals (e.g., that MSCs replace MSRs, that phonological representations are fully specified; see *Generative Phonology*). However, unlike Stanley, they suggest that redundant features are not specified in lexical representations of morphemes. They suggest that in a language in which the longest morpheme contains x segments, the set of logically possible fully specified representations with x or fewer segments which satisfy all the morpheme structure conditions of the language is constructed. This is the set of possible morphemes for the language. Every lexical representation is specified so that it is distinct from all but one of the fully specified representations which satisfy the morpheme structure conditions. Each partially specified lexical representation selects one fully specified representation from the set of fully specified representations. In this way the partially specified lexical representations become fully specified and the input to the phonological rules is fully specified. It should be noted that this proposal, unlike that of Stanley, does not remove the arbitrariness of which feature is unspecified in the case of interdependent features.

According to this view, morpheme structure conditions are filters. A 'filter,' unlike a rule, does not change or fill in features. It can either reject representations that are ill-formed and accept representations which satisfy its conditions as do Chomsky and Halle's MSCs, or it can block the application of rules that would create ill-formed representations.

Chomsky and Halle (1968) outline an alternative view in their discussion of markedness whereby (see *Markedness*; *Generative Phonology*) lexical representations are specified with u's (for unmarked values) and m's (for marked values) as well as '+' and '−.' Problems associated with blanks do not occur because lexical entries no longer contain blanks. Moreover, many redundancy rules need not be stated in grammars of individual languages since universal marking conventions will change u's and m's into '+' and '−.'

3. Phonetic Constraints

Most generative phonologists have not considered it necessary to state constraints on the distribution of segments and features in phonetic representations, although it is well-known that such constraints exist. Shibatani (1973) argues, however, that surface phonetic constraints, which state constraints on feature and segment combinations at the phonetic level, should be explicitly stated. He suggests that there are also three types of surface phonetic constraints: positive; if–then; and negative constraints.

In discussions of morpheme structure rules or conditions, it is often claimed that a speaker's ability to distinguish possible (but accidentally nonoccurring) from impossible forms is evidence for morpheme structure rules or conditions. Chomsky and Halle (1968), for example, suggest that speakers can distinguish accidental gaps in their lexicons (i.e., forms that could be English but are not) such as *brillig*, *karulize, thode,* from forms such as *gnip, rtut,* and *psik,* which could not be English. They claim that this ability indicates the existence of morpheme structure conditions. Shibatani correctly observes, however, that it is often constraints on surface phonetic forms, not on the underlying shape morphemes, that are utilized in sorting out these possible from impossible forms. Indeed, he suggests that morphemes with initial *gn* clusters must be assumed to account for alternating forms like *gnosis/agnostic* and *gnathism/ agnathous,* and hence the impossibility of *gnip* cannot be due to a MSC. Rather, he claims, it is due to the surface phonetic constraint in English against word (or syllable) initial stop–nasal clusters. Similarly, he observes that native speakers of German reject nonsense words such as [bund] and [tag] as possible words. This is because German disallows syllable final voiced obstruents, not because there is a German MSC which disallows word (or syllable) final voiced obstruents. Indeed, it is well-known that morphemes in German must contain final voiced obstruents to account for alternations such as [bunt] 'federation'/[bundəs] (genitive).

4. Duplication and Domain

There are several problems with morpheme structure rules or conditions as conceived in Chomsky and Halle (1968) and Stanley (1967). First, as has been noted by many (including Stanley, Chomsky, and Halle), MSRs or MSCs often duplicate phonological rules. That is, whenever the same restrictions hold within morphemes as across morpheme boundaries, the same statement will occur twice, once as an MSC and once as a phonological rule. For example, in a language with vowel harmony, there will be an MSC stating that certain sequences of vowels are prohibited and a phonological rule eliminating these same sequences when they arise through morpheme combinations. This duplication is problematic because an analysis with two separate but identical statements misses a generalization. If the same restriction holds within morphemes and across morpheme boundaries, a single rule, not two, is indicated.

Ringen (1988) suggests that this duplication problem is solved by abandoning Stanley's proposal that the input to the phonological rules be fully specified. She suggested that phonological rules be allowed to fill in features as well as to change features, and that feature changing applications should be permitted only to derived forms. Derived forms are understood to be forms arising through the combination of morphemes or application of a phonological rule. For example, the obstruent cluster in English *dogs* /dɔg + z/ is derived because it arises through the combination of morphemes. The final obstruent in German *Tag* [tak] is derived because it results from the application of a phonological rule, in this case a rule that devoices syllable final obstruents (cf. [tagə] plural). This suggestion has been incorporated into lexical phonology (see *Lexical Phonology and Morphology*) and underspecification theory (see *Underspecification*).

A second problem with morpheme structure rules and conditions as conceived by Chomsky and Halle (1968) and Stanley (1967) is that most, if not all, are actually constraints or rules whose domains are not morphemes per se. Segment structure rules state redundancies in segments, not

morphemes. Those morpheme structure rules or constraints that duplicate phonological rules are constraints that are true of 'domains' that are larger than morphemes. Other putative morpheme structure rules or constraints are actually constraints on syllables (see *Syllable*) or words (see *Word, Phonological*). In fact it has been suggested that there are actually no constraints on morphemes at all.

5. Underspecification

If it is assumed that the input to the phonological rules is fully specified, an MSC stating that all vowels are [−nasal] will be posited for a language like English regardless of whether lexical representations are fully specified (as assumed by Stanley) or partially specified (assumed by Chomsky and Halle). If, however, the assumption that the input to the phonological rules consists of fully specified representations is abandoned, it is not necessary to formulate an MSC stating that English vowels are underlyingly [−nasal]. This is because they are not [−nasal], they are unspecified for nasality. This is the position of many generative phonologists who now reject the assumption that the input to the phonological rules is fully specified. Redundancy rules are assumed to be rules that apply late in derivations (e.g., English V → [−nasal]), rather than early in derivations as assumed in classical generative phonology. A rule specifying vowels as [−nasal] would not apply to all vowels, only to those that had not been specified [+nasal] by a vowel nasalization rule.

Some phonologists have proposed constraints on rule application to ensure that features are always binary. Others now accept the position that features are not binary, arguing that some are 'privative,' some 'binary,' and others 'ternary.' Privative features have only one value: they are either present or absent. It has recently been suggested that [voice] is an example of a privative feature. Voiced segments are specified with the feature [voice], voiceless segments do not have this feature. The claim that voice is (universally) privative embodies the claim that no phonological rule will ever need to refer to the absence of voice, since such reference is impossible. Binary features have two values '+' and '−.' Ternary features have three values. If one adopts the position that features may be specified as '+,' '−,' or unspecified, for example, [+nasal], [−nasal], [nasal], and if rules can refer to '+,' '−,' or the absence of specification, then the feature [nasal] is ternary because it has three values, +, −, and 0 (unspecified).

Much research remains to be done to determine which features should be unspecified, how redundancy rules interact with phonological rules, whether all features are binary, and whether some features remain unspecified on the surface in some languages (see *Underspecification*).

Bibliography

Chomsky N, Halle M 1968 *The Sound Pattern of English.* Harper and Row, New York

Halle M 1959 *The Sound Pattern of Russian.* Mouton, The Hague

Ringen C 1988 *Vowel Harmony: Theoreticai Implications.* Garland, New York

Shibatani M 1973 The role of surface phonetic constraints in generative phonology. *Lg* **49**: 87–106

Stanley R 1967 Redundancy rules in phonology. *Lg* **43**: 393–436

C. O. Ringen

Reduplication

'Reduplication' refers to the affixation of a morpheme whose phonological form depends in all or in part on the phonological form of the stem to which it attaches. For example, in Agta, various plurals are formed by prefixing to a stem a copy of the first consonant–vowel–consonant sequence of the stem:

(a) takki 'leg'	tak-takki 'legs'	
(b) mag-saddu 'leak' (v)	mag-sad-saddu 'leak in many places'	
(c) bari 'body'	bar-bari kid-in 'my whole body'	(1)

The phonemic content of the Agta plural prefix illustrated in (1) changes completely with the host stem. This phonological dependence characterizes reduplicating affixes, which may prefix, suffix, or infix to stems.

1. The Form of Reduplication

Reduplication may be 'full' or 'partial.' In full reduplication, the entire phonological form of a stem is repeated in the reduplicating affix. For example, Warlpiri uses full morpheme reduplication to form the plural of some nouns:

(a) kurdu 'child'	kurdu-kurdu 'children'	
(b) kamina 'girl'	kamina-kamina 'girls'	(2)
(c) mardukuja 'woman'	mardukuja-mardukuja 'women'	

In partial reduplication, only some of the phonological material from the stem appears in the affix, as in the Agta examples in (1).

Although a reduplicating affix is phonologically dependent on a stem, the affix might include some change or deformation of the stem's phonological material. For example, Akan employs a reduplicating verbal prefix that copies the first consonant and vowel of the verb stem but makes the copied vowel [+high]. Yoruba nominalizes verbs with a prefix that copies the first consonant of a stem but places an /i/ after this copied consonant, regardless of the first stem vowel.

2. The Function of Reduplication

Reduplication is most often found to express certain semantic features. On nouns, reduplication often indicates plurality; on verbs, it often signals repetitive or intensive aspect. However, cross-linguistically, reduplicating affixes serve any function that any affix with its own phonological form may serve, including all derivational and inflectional functions. As far as morphological function is concerned, then, reduplication is indistinguishable from other forms of affixation.

3. Formalizing Reduplication

In partial reduplication, the reduplicating affix is some specifiable prosodic constituent, such as a syllable or foot, of some characterizable phonological shape. This observation suggests that reduplication is not some transformation based on a factorization of the stem into segments and a reorganization and repetition of some of the segments. A transformational account might predict that reduplication will copy any specifiable subpart of the stem in any order without regard to the prosodic constituency of the output. Rather, the reduplicating affix, like affixes that have their own phonological material, may be assigned a particular prosodic structure. In reduplication, phonological material from the stem is 'borrowed' and mapped onto the prosodic structure of the affix.

Exactly how to perform this borrowing and mapping is a matter of theoretical debate. For example, Steriade (1988) claims that all partial reduplication is full reduplication with truncation of the copy. The truncation parallels what occurs in nicknames (hypocoristics). She observes that truncation and simplification reduce morphemes to certain canonical prosodic shapes in a language. Partial reduplication, then, would specify the unmarked prosodic shape that serves as the target for the reduction of a full copy of the stem.

On the other hand, McCarthy and Prince (in press), extending the analysis introduced by Marantz (1982), suggest that the reduplication affix has as its lexically specified phonological form the prosodic structure characterizing the output of Steriade's truncation processes. On this account, reduplication involves a parsing of the stem's phonological material according to the metrical structure of the stem and the subsequent association of phonological material from the stem to the prosodically characterized reduplicating affix. The association of phonological material to an independent prosodic 'skeleton' occurs outside reduplication in the nonconcatenative root and pattern morphology familiar from Semitic languages (McCarthy 1981). In nonconcatenative morphology, the phonemic content (the 'melody') and the prosodic skeleton are independent morphemes; in reduplication, the skeleton is the reduplicating affix while the 'melody' is borrowed from the stem.

4. Interactions between the Morphology and Phonology of Reduplication

Problems in explaining the form and location of reduplication affixes appear to arise in the cases of infixing reduplication and the so-called 'bracketing paradoxes.' In infixing reduplication, the reduplicating affix appears inside the stem to which it attaches and its phonological form is determined by the subportion of the stem to which it attaches, not by the phonological form of the entire stem. Infixing reduplication places reduplicating affixes in the same prosodic positions within a word as the infixing of affixes that have their own, fixed phonological form. Thus the positioning of infixing reduplication poses no new problems for morphological theory. However, that the form of the reduplicating affix is determined by the subportion of the stem to which the affix attaches and not by the entire stem to which it is morphologically related strongly suggests that the copying in reduplication is phonological, not morphological. That is, the copying in reduplication is dependent on the prosodic phonology of words, not directly on their internal morphological structure.

Bracketing paradoxes arise when the copying in reduplication seems to depend on a bracketing of a word distinct from its morphological structure. For example, in Kihehe (=Hehe) (Odden and Odden 1985), a full morpheme reduplicating prefix forming the moderative of a verb stem will copy the inflectional infinitival morpheme when this morpheme syllabifies with the stem, as shown in (3b):

(a) kú-tova-tóva 'to beat a bit'
    inf-beat-beat   (3)
(b) kw-iita-kw-iita 'to pour a bit'
    inf-pour-inf-pour

In (3a) the infinitive prefix *ku-* does not syllabify with the stem and is not copied by the moderative verb forming reduplicating affix. In (3b), on the other hand, the infinitive prefix, *kw-* before a vowel, does syllabify with the stem and thus is copied by moderative reduplication.

The example in (3b) illustrates that, phonologically, sometimes the infinitival prefix is bracketed with the verb stem before the reduplicating affix is attached, allowing the affix to copy both the stem and prefix. The example in (3a), in contrast, illustrates that, phonologically, sometimes the reduplicating affix attaches to the stem before the infinitival prefix is affixed and thus copies only the stem. However, the morphological structures of the verbs involved always have the infinitive morpheme—inflectional morphology—bracketed outside the derivational moderative affix. Such 'bracketing paradoxes' or mismatches between phonological and morphological bracketings argue for a separation of the morphological and phonological structure of words. Since reduplication is sensitive to the syllabification and thus the phonological structure of words, the copying in reduplication should occur in the phonology, not the morphology.

Also indicating that the copying of reduplication is essentially phonological is the interaction of reduplication with the operation of phonological rules. Kiparsky (1987) among others has argued that the copying in reduplication in certain cases must follow the application of specific phonological rules to the stem. On standard assumptions about the organization of grammar, copying in reduplication should occur before any phonological rules if reduplication were strictly morphological. Alternatively, given the assumptions of lexical phonology and morphology, the interleaving of morphological and phonological processes should allow the application of certain phonological rules before the copying in reduplication. However, the evidence from bracketing paradoxes clearly shows that lexical phonology and morphology wrongly equates the morphological and phonological structures and thus the morphological and phonological derivations of words. Given that the morphological and phonological structures are independent, evidence that the copying in reduplication follows the operation of certain phonological rules provides further support for the conclusion that the copying in reduplication is part of the phonology, not the morphology.

5. Conclusion

In function as well as form, reduplication proves to be regular affixation, not one of a class of 'processes' potentially distinct in morphology from the arrangement of morphological 'items' known as morphemes. The various mechanisms needed to derive the correct phonological form for the reduplicating affix have been shown to be independently motivated in affixation. The lone possible exceptional 'process' associated with reduplication is the copying of phonological material from a stem. However, research on bracketing paradoxes and on the interaction of reduplication and phonological rules shows that whatever this copying is, it is phonological, not morphological—ordered among phonological processes and dependent on the phonological, not the morphological bracketing of a word. Thus it belongs, together with the 'spreading' of features and the attachment and delinking of association lines, among the types of autosegmental phonological mechanisms.

See also: Morphology, Nonconcatenative.

Bibliography

Kiparsky P 1987 *The Phonology of Reduplication*. Stanford University, Stanford, CA

McCarthy J 1981 A prosodic theory of nonconcatenative morphology. *LIn* 12: 373–418

McCarthy J, Prince A in press *Prosodic Morphology*. MIT Press, Cambridge, MA

Marantz A 1982 Re Reduplication. *LIn* 13(3): 435–82

Odden D, Odden M 1985 Ordered reduplication in Kihehe. *LIn* 16: 497–503

Steriade D 1988 Reduplication and syllable transfer in Sanskrit and elsewhere. *Phonology* 5: 73–155

A. Marantz

Reference and Anaphor Resolution in Natural Language Processing

It is usually easy for a human to decide what a pronoun (or other definite reference) in a text is referring to. However, attempting to give the same ability to a computer program that processes natural language reveals the extraordinary complexity that is involved in this seemingly effortless task. Resolving an anaphor requires knowledge from all levels of language—the lexicon, syntax, semantics, and discourse pragmatics—as well as knowledge of the world itself.

1. Anaphors and Back-references

By an 'anaphor' we mean any abbreviated back-reference to an entity mentioned, explicitly or implicitly, earlier in a text or conversation. Pronouns are the paradigm case (example (1)). However, other proforms may also be anaphoric; example (2) shows the proadjective *such* and example (3) the proverb *to do so*:

Nadia offered a peanut to one of the marmosets. *It* ignored *her*.   (1)

Nadia is looking for an experienced LISP programmer to work   (2)
on her project, but *such* programmers are hard to find.

Nadia sings sea shanties when she's happy. Chrysanne *does so*   (3)
when she's sad.

(Note that this definition of anaphors as back-references is similar, but not identical, to the use of the term in government-binding theory; see *Binding*; *Anaphora*.) Anaphors are usually also taken to include pronominal forward references, as in (4); although strictly speaking such usages are 'cataphors,' not anaphors, many of the problems in their resolution are the same:

> For *her* ill-advised remarks about the Duchess, Nadia (4)
> paid a heavy price.

Not all pronouns are anaphoric; exceptions include the *it* of cleft sentences (*It doesn't matter where she is*) and the so-called 'weather' and 'time' *it* (*It's raining*).

Definite noun phrases can also act as anaphors,

> Nadia offered a peanut to one of the marmosets. *The marmoset* (5)
> ignored her

In (5), the definite noun phrase *the marmoset*, like *it* in (1), can be understood only through the earlier text, *one of the marmosets*.

To resolve an anaphor is to determine the entity it refers to, its 'referent.' This usually involves finding some word or phrase in the preceding text that acts as the 'antecedent' of the anaphor; the anaphor and the antecedent (which may itself be an anaphor) are said to be 'coreferential.' For example, in text (1), the antecedent of the pronoun *her* is the word *Nadia* and the referent of *her* is the person Nadia; the antecedent of *it* is *one of the marmosets* and the referent is the particular marmoset.

2. Simple Methods and their Limitations

At first glance, the antecedent of an anaphor might seem simply to be the most recent preceding noun phrase that matches it in gender and number (and perhaps, in some languages, other morphological features as well). Indeed, this is often the case, but not invariably so:

> Nadia put the wine on the arm of the chair. *It* slid off. (6)

In (6), *it* refers to the wine, not the more recently mentioned chair or its arm. In general, a text will often provide a number of potential antecedents for an anaphor; the task of resolution is to choose the best candidate. Two important factors in resolution are semantic coherence and focus.

'Semantic coherence' is the preference for the most sensible or plausible reading of a sentence; in (6), it makes more sense for the wine to be sliding off the arm, than, say, the arm to be sliding off the chair (or the chair off the arm). To determine whether a particular reading is plausible, it often suffices to determine whether or not selectional restrictions have been violated (see *Selectional Restrictions*; *Disambiguation: Role of Knowledge*).

A 'focused' item is one that is highlighted or given prominence by the text (see *Topic and Comment*). For example, in (6), the wine is more central to the discussion than the place that it was put. The more highly focused an entity in the discourse is, the more likely it is that it will subsequently be referred to anaphorically, and hence the more likely it is that the antecedent of an anaphor is a highly focused entity. Focus is, at least partly, a matter of syntax; the direct object of a verb is more highly focused than the subject, for example.

Syntax may also play a role in precluding coreference:

> Nadia thinks that Sue hates *her*. (7)

> *She* sings whenever Nadia is in the bath. (8)

In (7), *Sue* is the most recent noun phrase that matches *her*, but cannot be the antecedent, because in English a pronoun that is the object of a verb must be reflexive if coreferential with the subject (*Sue hates herself*). Similarly, *she* in (8) cannot be a cataphor whose antecedent is *Nadia*, as English prohibits a pronoun c-commanding a nonpronominal antecedent (see *C-Command*).

Several algorithms have been constructed that attempt to resolve anaphors on the basis of the role of syntax in focus and coreference. One such method (Hobbs 1978) is to traverse parse trees in an optimal order, so that noun phrases are encountered in decreasing order of their likelihood of being the correct antecedent (subject to matching and plausibility). Another is to use the structure of the sentence to determine the most highly focused entities to choose among (Sidner 1983).

Although such methods perform at an accuracy of up to 90 percent, they suffer from a number of weaknesses. First, most will always give some answer, even though it might be wrong; that is, they cannot say 'can't decide between these two' or (unless there is no candidate antecedent at all) 'don't know.' Second, the methods are generally limited to antecedents that match the anaphor; but an anaphoric definite noun phrase need only refer to something related to the antecedent:

> Nadia accidentally dropped her radio, damaging *the case*. (9)

In (9), the mention of the radio permits subsequent anaphoric definite references to its components and other concepts associated with it. Third, determining the relative plausibility of alternative antecedents can, in the most general case, require complex inference (see *Disambiguation: Role of Knowledge*; *Knowledge Representation for Natural Language Processing*), as shown by the differing more plausible resolutions for *she* in these two texts:

> Nadia phoned Chrysanne because *she* wanted to ask (10)
> for help with the marmosets.

> Nadia phoned Chrysanne because *she* was the person (11)
> most likely to be able to help with the marmosets.

Fourth, the methods are limited to anaphors whose antecedents are present in the recently preceding text. But, as shown in Sect. 3 below, an antecedent can be a long distance back in the text. In fact, there need be no explicit textual antecedent at all. For example, an anaphor may refer to a collection of things mentioned:

> Nadia was playing chess in the garden with Chrysanne (12)
> when *they* heard a loud bang.

> Nadia examined each peach carefully. Most of *them* were (13)
> rotten.

In (12), *they* means the set that contains Nadia and Chrysanne (but not chess or the garden). In (13), *them* refers to the set of all peaches that Nadia examined.

3. The Role of Discourse Structure

The problems of simple anaphor resolution methods are solved, at least in part, by methods that take into consideration the structure of the discourse itself (see *Discourse*), and explicitly construct or maintain a list of the entities that it makes 'referable' at any time.

For example, Grosz (1978) collected examples of so-called 'task-oriented dialogs'—specifically, the discourse that ensued as a novice assembled an air-compressor under the guidance of an expert. Grosz found that the structure of the discourse, including its use of anaphora, mirrored that of the task itself, each subtask having in effect its own subdialog. Anaphors often found their antecedents in much earlier dialog on the same subtask, even if another subtask intervened. For example, the novice might begin the task of assembling the pump platform, and mention it by name. A number of required subtasks would then be performed, with no mention of the platform; but when they were complete and the main task resumed, the platform would often be referred to anaphorically. From these observations, Grosz developed a model of anaphor resolution that used knowledge of the structure of the topic of the discourse. In the model, following the discourse structure and resolving anaphors are mutually dependent processes: the completion of the subdialog associated with a subtask enables anaphoric references to entities on 'the next level up,' and the occurrence of such references is often the linguistic cue that the subdialog is complete. This can be formalized in terms of there being a hierarchy of focus spaces making available possible antecedents for anaphora. The weakness of this model is its restriction to highly structured domains of discourse in which the structure can be known in advance, though there have been attempts to generalize the model.

Working with logical forms derived from sentences, Webber (1979) developed a method for determining exactly what entities are made available by a sentence for subsequent reference, i.e., what entities are evoked by the sentence for possible subsequent anaphoric reference. Her rules enable any anaphor resolution method to consider exactly the right set of candidates, including sets not explicitly mentioned. For example, in (13) above, the phrase *each peach* would lead to the component $\forall x(\mathrm{peach}(x)\ldots)$ in the logical form; from this, Webber's rules would add the set of peaches mentioned to the list of evoked entities. Webber did not, however, cover all types of anaphors or evoked entities in her rules, and because it requires the sentence to be converted to logical form first, which implies having a full understanding of it, her method is primarily applicable to anaphors whose antecedents occur in a preceding sentence rather than the same one.

4. Shallow, Hybrid Systems

It can be seen that the resolution of anaphors requires not just knowledge of linguistic structure but also, where inference, associations, or plausibility ranking is required, considerable knowledge of the world. Because this can be extremely difficult and time-consuming in computer systems—indeed, general solutions are at present unknown—attempts have been made to consolidate the 'shallow' methods, including perhaps simple forms of inference, to extend them as far as possible. Carter (1987) gives a good example of such a system.

Bibliography

Carter D 1987 *Interpreting Anaphors in Natural Language Texts.* Ellis Horwood, Chichester
Grosz B J 1978 The representation and use of focus in dialogue understanding. In: Walker D E (ed.) *Understanding Spoken Language.* North-Holland, New York
Hirst G 1981 *Anaphora in Natural Language Understanding: A Survey.* Springer, Berlin
Hobbs J R 1978 Resolving pronoun references. *Lingua* **44**: 311–38
Sidner C L 1983 Focusing in the comprehension of definite anaphora. In: Brady M, Berwick R C (eds.) *Computational Models of Discourse.* MIT Press, Cambridge, MA
Webber B L 1979 *A Formal Approach to Discourse Anaphora.* Garland, New York

G. Hirst

Reference Group

Individuals are influenced by an exceedingly small fraction of the numerous others to whom they are exposed throughout their lives. The reference group literature is concerned with the determinants and consequences of these selective audiences. The 'reference group' label, however, is a misnomer because individuals are impacted on by various types of 'reference others.' Indeed, the reference group literature is difficult to review because it encompasses three types of 'reference influence' that have been studied, particularly in sociology, psychology, and symbolic interactionism. This article begins by examining major concepts, ideas, and implications, then it considers the relevance of language for the understanding of reference others.

1. Individual, Reference Relationship, and Reference Other

The reference group literature entails considerable debate concerning the necessity and validity of various concepts. Viewing the reference group literature as a loose conceptual scheme rather than a rigorous theory, a useful typology encompasses three components (Schmitt 1972). First, the 'reference other' is the other that is influencing the individual. The reference other is described in terms of its 'empirical status,' e.g., individual, group, imaginary other; and 'membership status,' i.e., does the individual belong to the group that is influencing him? Second, 'reference relationship' is the type of influence the reference other has over the individual. As explained below, there are three types of influence: comparative, normative, and identification–object. The type of influence is described in terms of its 'scope,' e.g., extent of internalization of norms, and its 'role character,' i.e., how many roles does the influence encompass? Third, the individual is the object of the influence being extended by the reference other. The individual is described in terms of 'perception of the reference relationship,' e.g., objective or subjective; and 'awareness of the reference other,' i.e., does the individual symbolically take the reference other into account?

1.1 Comparative Reference Relationship

Pioneering reference group studies focused on the influence of comparative reference others on self-evaluations, but it is evident in the late twentieth century that individuals often compare themselves to reference others in various contexts (Hyman and Singer 1968). Such comparisons generate 'self-feelings.' 'Relative gratification' or 'relative deprivation' is experienced when the individual feels relatively 'better off' or 'worse off' than the comparative reference other regarding the characteristic being evaluated. Researchers have given more attention to relative deprivation, apparently because feelings of deprivation lead to dissatisfaction and disruptive actions, including protest and revolution.

Feelings of gratification and deprivation are relative feelings. A student may feel deprived when comparing his or her C paper to a student with an A paper, but yet feel quite gratified when comparing that same C paper with a student who received the grade of F. Pragmatically, individuals making comparisons and their reference others, including organizers of social movements, employers, teachers, and therapists, can attempt to modify relative feelings by changing the comparative reference others that are being used as points of comparison.

Group members often compare themselves to other members in competitive groups that entail visible differences in economic, prestige, or power structures (Gecas 1982: 7). In mass societies with elaborate communication systems, individuals, also, frequently compare themselves to persons in groups of which they are not members. Individuals make comparisons because of a need for more information, concerns about self-esteem, and cultural socialization. There is empirical support for Festinger's 'Social Comparison Theory' which holds that individuals compare themselves with persons similar to themselves. Associate professors, for example, will compare their salary increases to those of other associate professors (Singer 1981). Much of the supporting evidence, however, is based on laboratory studies. Disconfirming evidence also exists, as in the case of the blind who use the sighted for certain comparisons.

Comparative reference relationships account for otherwise inexplicable findings involving 'absolute' deprivation, situations in which people appear deprived in some objective sense. Stouffer's study of American soldiers in World War II found that better-educated inductees were less likely to feel deprived by being drafted than lesser-educated inductees (Hyman and Singer 1968). The lesser-educated men compared themselves with friends and acquaintances, many of whom had been deferred because they were working in draft-exempt jobs. The better-educated men compared themselves with their friends and acquaintances, many of whom were also drafted.

Variations on the reference group concept expand its scope in several ways. One can think in terms of extended social networks rather than narrowly defined groups (see *Sociometry*). One can consider cases wherein a social system is being compared with another system, rather than an individual person with another person. Misconceptions entailed in social comparisons have important consequences and social systems may sometimes force individuals to adopt harmful referents for comparison (see *Labeling Theory of Social Deviance*).

1.2 Normative Reference Relationship

Earlier reference group studies brought attention to the normative influence of reference groups, discussing conformity, anchoring groups, and groups that set and enforce norms. The views that reference others can influence norms and values and that changes in reference others often bring about shifts in attitudes have been confirmed.

Investigators of normative reference others have been the most prolific in detecting the conceptual complexities of reference relationships (Hyman and Singer 1968). The 'negative reference group' concept made it apparent that individuals sometimes reject the norms and values of their reference others. Some Americans, for example, have lived their lives fighting Communism. The concept of 'saliency' underscored that the influence of reference others may be momentary and situational. Merton and Kitt's writings that introduced ideas about reference groups into sociology underscored that individuals have more than one reference group and that these 'multiple reference groups' may be 'sustaining' or 'conflicting.' Individuals often resolve reference group conflict in the direction of their most important or most salient reference other. Sometimes, however, individuals live with conflict by internally compartmentalizing the conflict or by using coping mechanisms. True marginal persons cannot resolve conflict involving the values of different reference others and must cope with it.

Shibutani contended that a reference group is that group whose perspective is used by the person as the frame of reference in the organization of his or her perceptual field. This view was particularly crucial in the development of the normative reference group literature because it clarified that the reference other could be either imaginary or empirical and either a membership or nonmembership other; provided a way of studying individuals in mass societies as they assumed the perspectives of various 'social worlds,' such as sport or art; and more clearly anchored reference group leads in symbolic interactionism. Following Shibutani's view of reference others as 'perspectives,' symbolic interactionists underscored the need to clarify the conceptual status of the reference other and to intensively study individuals in relation to their audiences and communication channels.

1.3 Identification–Object Reference Relationship

Certain of the early reference group theorists stressed that reference groups were the groups in which an individual aspires: (a) to maintain or (b) to attain membership. Recognizing that the underlying dimension of this aspirational version of reference groups concerned the emotional bond between the individual and the reference other, Schmitt (1972: 49) later concluded that an identification–object reference relationship exists between the individual and a reference other if the individual's degree of positive or negative sentiment toward the reference other is sufficient to direct his or her overt or covert behavior toward the reference other as an object. While individuals will often be normatively influenced by their identification–object reference other, this is not necessarily the case. A man who has successfully improved his class standing may dearly love his working-class parents but have left their values behind. Even in the usual instance where an individual has a normative and an identification–object relationship with the same reference other, the concept of identification–object relationship underscores that the reference other is an object of the individual's feelings rather than a source of attitudes and values.

Although individuals may have identification–object relationships with their membership or nonmembership reference others, the identification–object relationship is particularly helpful in accounting for how groups of which individuals are not members come to have a normative influence over them. Individuals may begin to socialize themselves to what they perceive to be the norms of non-membership groups before they are ever exposed to their influence, a process called 'anticipatory socialization.' Non-membership groups are, of course, prevalent in mass societies with high rates of social mobility. Studies of social class have often explicitly or implicitly considered identification–object reference relationships. Turner, for example, has explicated the role of reference others in the lives of future-oriented persons. Unfortunately, only minimal attention has been given to the identification–object relationship even though it is one of the central processes through which all three types of reference relationships are originated and maintained. Consequently, feeling is stressed in the following discussion of language and reference others.

2. Language: Overview and Six Directives

Reference others do not have a *de facto* existence, being dependent on the relationship of individuals to them. Consequently, reference others must be cast within a social psychological perspective, such as symbolic interactionism, that does not minimize the intentionality of the individual as do many versions of structuralism and semiotics. The following discussion of language is consistent with symbolic interactionism, a school that recognized the crucial role of language for human behavior. Language is living linguistic categories that make common understandings possible. These linguistic categories are: (a) verbally or nonverbally shared, (b) experienced, and (c) given meaning by being incorporated and interpreted within the individual's ongoing interactions. Following Burke's (1950: 43) contention that language is a symbolic means of eliciting cooperation in beings that necessarily respond to symbols, six directives that highlight the interplay between language, feeling, and perspectives are offered.

2.1 Language as 'Doorway' to Feelings and Perspectives

Language provides the individual with an entrance mode, a doorway, to others' feelings and perspectives. Lieberson cautiously concluded in his study of language and ethnic relations in Canada, that at least one group will learn to communicate with the other in almost any contact setting involving groups with different native languages. Based on his classic study, *Wayward Puritans*, Erikson (1966) implies that the constitution of deviance occurs through a language that makes shared perceptions possible.

Emotions, as well as perspectives, are facilitated through language. Elkin found that the expressions used by American soldiers in World War II gave the soldiers a unique universe of discourse that enhanced their solidarity. Denzin concluded that three languages had to be learned before alcoholics could benefit from Alcoholics Anonymous: (a) the meta-language of emotionality, (b) the language of direct feeling and emotion, and (c) the language of Alcoholics Anonymous. The languages that were spoken had to be experienced and felt emotionally before Alcoholics Anonymous could become a reference group for an alcoholic.

2.2 The Dampening of Feelings and Perspectives Through Language

Lifton's *The Nazi Doctors* is monumental evidence of the power of rhetoric to influence perspectives and feelings. The step between periodic violence and a system of total genocide was facilitated by the medicalization of killing (see *Medicalization*)—the imagery of killing in the name of healing. Just as doctors would remove a gangrenous appendix from a diseased body, they would remove the Jew—a gangrenous appendix—from the body of mankind. Central to the medicalization of killing was the dampening or deamplification of language—with its attendant numbing, denial, and derealization. Euphemisms, code terms, and the medical metaphor were common definitions of genocide that provided Nazi doctors with an opportunity to locate meaning within, and to experience an emotional anesthesia regarding, their human atrocities. A manual of the time issued by the University of Berlin called on German physicians to become a 'cultivator of the genes,' a 'physician to the *Volk*,' and a 'biological soldier.' Although the Nazi doctors did not literally believe the euphemisms, the daily use of such language enabled them to live symbolically in a world of derealization, disavowal, and nonfeeling.

2.3 Feelings and Perspectives Through Expansion of Language

Snow and his associates demonstrated how social movement organizations (SMOs) enhance participation through frame alignment processes. These researchers cast their conclusions around the concept of frame, i.e., a shared definition, but language expansion was clearly a fundamental agent through which SMOs influenced perspectives and feelings. The SMOs efforts concentrated on recruiting members. Language was fundamental to their persuasive tactics.

Frame amplification involved making a value or belief surrounding an issue more salient. Peace activists, for example, sought to redefine their public image as a movement by revitalizing dormant values such as the right to redress grievances and express dissent. Frame extension entailed attracting members on the basis of values and beliefs that are incidental to SMOs, but important to potential recruits. Slogans such as 'Let's Save 6th Street—Austin's Neighborhood,' were crucial linguistic devices that appealed to the values and beliefs of potential members.

2.4 Preserving Feelings and Perspectives Through Language

Feelings and perspectives must be preserved for reference relationships to be maintained. As the shared realities in membership groups, for example, become increasingly differentiated from the realities of outsiders, members rely on each other more and more for the validation of their perspectives (Turner 1970: 82). Language preserves and validates feelings and perspectives through: (a) emotional reminders, and (b) vocabularies of motive.

Emotional reminders are verbal and nonverbal symbols that call out emotional memories and feelings. During President Reagan's controversial visit to the Bitburg cemetery in Germany, 'Holocaust Stories' and photographs, diaries, monuments, and war mementos called out memories of the Holocaust (Schmitt 1989). Language, of course, has the capacity to retain meaning in various external forms.

Mills's seminal statement concerning 'vocabularies of motive' pointed out that language provides ready-made explanations of behavior for situated activities. Motive is linguistic conduct.

What is reason for one man is rationalization for another. The variable is the accepted vocabulary of motives, the ultimates of discourse, of each man's dominant group about whose opinion he cares.

(Mills 1940: 910)

Vocabularies of motive temper the impact of past and future problematic behaviors on reference relationships (Mills 1940; Lindesmith, et al. 1988: 144-51).

2.5 Feelings and Perspectives Through Laminated Language

Linguistic labels were 'laminated,' i.e., layered one on another, in order to influence the feelings and perspectives of participants within the social world of professional football regarding the 'nonstrike teams' that the owners created during the 1987 National Football League strike in the USA. Owners labeled the teams 'replacements' in an attempt to minimize differences between nonstrike and strike teams. Striking players called them 'scabs' to delegitimate them. Fans who enjoyed the new teams named them, for example, 'Spare Bears' and 'Care Bears.' Sport writers generated more complicated and mocking laminations, e.g., 'The Seachicks,' 'Phoney-Niners'; and 'Rhinestone Cowboys' (Schmitt 1991).

The fact that the laminated football labels were circulated through various mass media forms is noteworthy. The media have important influences on language and meaning. They create new words with new meanings; extend the meaning of existing words; substitute new meanings by displacing older ones; and, primarily, stabilize existing conventions of meaning for the words in our language (DeFleur and Ball-Rokeach 1989: 267).

2.6 Feelings and Perspectives About Language

Individuals sometimes develop feelings about language that may impede or facilitate reference relationships. Labov (1972) found that youth who were not members of street groups read significantly better than members because success in school was irrelevant to prestige within the street groups. But some members were quite articulate regarding objects that were important to the group, including language in ritual insults and verbal routines with girls.

Many contemporary women argue that language is male-dominated and that using language alienates women from their own reality (see *Sexism*). Lantz (1958: 467) found in his study of Coal Town that natives resented the 'damn hunkie talk' and the peculiar language gestures of the immigrants. This made communication and interaction extremely difficult.

See also: Symbolic Interactionism.

Bibliography

Burke K 1950 *A Rhetoric of Motives*. Prentice-Hall, Englewood Cliffs, NJ

DeFleur M L, Ball-Rokeach S J 1989 *Theories of Mass Communication*. Longman, New York

Denzin N K 1987 *The Recovering Alcoholic*. Sage, Newbury Park, CA

Elkin F 1946 The soldier's language. *The American Journal of Sociology* 51: 414–22

Erikson K T 1966 *Wayward Puritans*. John Wiley, New York

Gecas V 1982 The self-concept. In: Turner R H, Short Jr J F (eds.) *Annual Review of Sociology*. Annual Reviews Inc., Palo Alto, CA

Hyman H H, Singer E (eds.) 1968 *Readings in Reference Group Theory and Research*. Free Press, New York

Labov W 1972 *Language in the Inner City*. University of Pennsylvania Press, Philadelphia, PA

Lantz H R 1958 *People of Coal Town*. Columbia University Press, New York

Lieberson S 1970 *Language and Ethnic Relations in Canada*. John Wiley, New York

Lifton R J 1986 *The Nazi Doctors*. Basic Books, New York

Lindesmith A R, Strauss A L, Denzin N K 1988 *Social Psychology*. Prentice-Hall, Englewood Cliffs, NJ

Mills C W 1940 Situated actions and vocabularies of motive. *American Sociological Review* 5: 904–13

Schmitt R L 1972 *The Reference Other Orientation*. Southern Illinois University Press, Carbondale, IL

Schmitt R L 1989 Sharing the Holocaust: Bitburg as emotional reminder. In: Denzin N K (ed.) *Studies in Symbolic Interactionism*. JAI Press, Greenwich, CT

Schmitt R L 1991 Strikes, frames, and touchdowns: The institutional struggle for meaning in the 1987 National Football League Season. *Symbolic Interaction* 14: 237–59

Shibutani T 1955 Reference groups as perspectives. *American Journal of Sociology* 60: 562–69

Singer E 1981 Reference groups and social evaluations. In: Rosenberg M, Turner R H (eds.) *Social Psychology: Sociological Perspectives*. Basic Books, New York

Snow D A, Rochford Jr E B, Worden S K, Benford R D 1986 Frame alignment processes, micromobilization, and movement participation. *American Sociological Review* 51: 464–81

Turner R H 1970 *Family Interaction*. John Wiley, New York

R. L. Schmitt

Reference, Philosophical Issues concerning

The problem of reference—in the broadest terms, that of how words relate to the world—is fundamental in semantics and the philosophy of language (see *Philosophy of Language*). Analytic philosophy, particularly in the pioneering work of Gottlob Frege, Bertrand Russell, and Ludwig Wittgenstein, places reference and truth at the center of philosophical analyses of language, treating as semantic or meaning paradigms, on the one hand, the relation between a name and an object and, on the other, the relation between a sentence and a state of the world (see *Frege, Gottlob*; *Russell, Bertrand*; *Wittgenstein, Ludwig*; *Truth*). In theoretical linguistics problems about reference, naming, and truth have figured both in the development of semantic theory and in pragmatic theories of speech acts (see *Formal Semantics*; *Pragmatics*). This article, which presents central philosophical issues concerning reference through the perspective of a certain broad-based program in the philosophy of language, should be read in conjunction with the articles on names and descriptions (see *Names and Descriptions*) and indexicals (see *Indexicals*), which complement the treatment here by focusing on specific modes of reference.

1. Philosophical Theories of Language

We talk and think about the world, or so it seems. Whole utterances tell us how a speaker believes, or wants, the world to be. They represent some state or aspect of the world; in the favored jargon, whole sentences specify 'states of affairs.' Thus, if Max says *Times are tough* he speaks the truth only if the economic life of his society is in recession. But it is not just whole sentences that are about the world; parts of sentences also have representational functions. Those chunks from which utterances are built refer to individuals and kinds in the world. Reference is a relation between an expression and an object or kind. Paradigms of 'singular reference' are proper names, demonstratives, and definite descriptions; 'singular' because a name—'Chomsky,' for example—refers in a particular use, if it refers at all, to just one object. 'General terms,' 'table,' 'electron,' and the like, refer not to particular objects but to kinds or (as some prefer to think of it) to the properties that all tables or electrons share.

Little in the philosophy of language is uncontroversial, and the theory of reference is no exception. In a provocatively sceptical work, Stephen Schiffer (1987) has reminded us that the problems with which philosophers have struggled may be artifacts of their conception of language. He thinks that all that is bedrock is:

> we humans have noise and mark making proclivities, and, like earthworms and flounders, we survive for some finite period of time in the environments into which we are born.

> (Schiffer 1987: 1)

The rest is philosophers' theory which, in Schiffer's view, is mostly pretty bad theory. Schiffer is right at least to the extent that we cannot take talk of meaning, or truth, or reference for granted. The ideas that 'Kripke' is the name of Kripke, that 'tiger' refers to tigers, that the sentence *the moon is made of green cheese* is false, despite their common-sense appearance, involve theoretical ideas about language. So they must be judged by the usual standards (inchoate though they be) that apply to all theories. Because humans have been immersed in language so long, philosophical reflection on language must take its point of departure from human responses to this long experience, to what is called 'folk theory.' Philosophers' theories of language are mostly rival attempts to systematize, debug, and extend this folk theory. We should not too prematurely follow Schiffer and resign ourselves to the failure of all these attempts.

As a species we have invested a huge chunk of our cognitive resources in language. Learning a language is probably the most intensive and the most critical achievement of any child, and no child comes empty minded to the job; the human larynx certainly, and the human brain most probably, are adapted to that task. So it seems reasonable to conclude that our noise and marking activities are adaptive, and are so in virtue of some feature(s) of the marks and noises so produced. It is of course a further step to the idea that the function of language is to represent our physical and social world. But we need a theory of those features that make our investment in language pay, and our only starting point is the theory we have, a theory in which reference and truth play a central role in capturing the relations between language and the world.

2. The Theory of Reference: An Outline of an Ambitious Program

What is reference, and what is its place in an overall account of the nature of language? These questions are best answered by articulating and evaluating an ambitious semantic program, namely one which aims to explain meaning via reference and sentence structure, and then to give

an account of reference that appeals to nothing semantic. The ultimate aim of this theory of reference is to explain the relationship between linguistic representation and the world represented. That requires that it rely on no semantic notions, else it presupposes the very relationship to be explained. This program (hereafter the ambitious program) has four enabling assumptions; those who think it *too* ambitious take it that at least one of these is false.

2.1 The Need for a Theory of Meaning

The first assumption is that what is needed, and can legitimately be looked for, is a theory of meaning. General truths about the nature and organization of language are to be discovered. Thus what is needed, in some broad sense, is a theory. Looking for a theory of *meaning* makes the working assumption that the folk-theoretic notion of meaning—that notion which informs our unreflective modes of speaking about meaning—is not hopelessly compromised. Thus defenders of the ambitious program suppose that our intuitive notions of meaning will need to be clarified and revised rather than abandoned in favor of something completely different. Neither part of this assumption is uncontroversial. Schiffer, for example, challenges the need for theory, and Quine (see *Quine, Willard van Orman*), among others, is sceptical of the prospects of finding a definition of meaning which is not either vacuous or circular (see *Meaning: Philosophical Theories*; *Analyticity*).

2.2 Meaning and Truth-conditions

The second assumption is that one fundamental element of sentence meaning is a sentence's truth-conditions. A minimum condition of successful translation, for example, is that the translating sentence have the same truth-conditions as the sentence translated. Moreover, if the point of language is to enable us to represent our physical and social world, and if truth is our fundamental mode of evaluating representation, then two sentences sharing truth-conditions share a very significant property. They will be true and false in just the same circumstances. An explanation of a sentence's truth-conditions does not tell us all we need to know about a sentence's meaning. There is some interesting difference between *Edward is not very clever* and *Edward is a dork* but both sentences share something very important. The idea that sentence meaning is captured through a theory of truth-conditions is not quite as coarse grained as might seem. Even if *Cordates are vertebrates* and *Renates are vertebrates* have the same truth-conditions in virtue of the fact that all and only renates are cordates, it by no means follows that the explanation of the two sentences having that truth-condition is the same. So a theory of meaning focused on truth-conditions need not count the two sentences as semantically equivalent.

Of course, this assumption rests on fallible and controversial ideas. It is by no means universally agreed that a basic function of language is the representation of the speaker's world, nor that representation is best understood by appeal to truth. It is quite widely argued that an epistemic notion, verification, is the central element of sentence meaning. The logical positivists (see *Logical Positivism*) thought that the meaning of a sentence is determined by its method of verification, that is by the conditions under which it would be rational to accept the sentence into one's belief system, and sophisticated versions of this view are still extant.

2.3 Decompositional and Atomic Theories of Meaning

The ambitious program develops a 'decompositional' theory of meaning, a theory that explains a sentence's meaning by appeal to the semantics of the words it contains and its structure. The argument for a decompositional theory is simple and strong. Natural languages are productive, that is, they are unbounded. There is no longest sentence of English. We can add to any sentence without turning the meaningful into the meaningless. Of course, as sentences get longer, they become harder to keep track of both in production and comprehension. So they become less communicatively salient. But there is a slow fade out of intelligibility, not a line between sense and nonsense. Moreover, languages are systematic. We do not learn to speak a language sentence by sentence. To acquire a new word is to acquire the capacity to speak and understand a range of new sentences; the same is true of mastering a new syntactic construction. In learning a language we learn words one by one together with techniques for combining them into more complex constructions. These facts suggest that a theory of meaning should consist of three parts. One is a theory of word meaning; on this view word meaning is the most fundamental semantic property. A second is a theory of sentence structure; syntax tells us how words are organized into phrases, and phrases into sentences. The third part is a theory of 'projection rules.' These tell us how the meanings of the words of a constituent and its structure explain that constituent's meaning.

A theory of meaning conforming to this pattern is an 'atomic' theory; a theory which takes the reference of a term to be its key semantic property is 'referential atomism.' Most agree that languages are productive and systematic (though some of those developing 'connectionist' models of human cognitive architecture deny this), but many deny that a theory of meaning should be atomic. Defenders of molecular theories of meaning, for example, take the sentence to be fundamental. Theorists as different as Davidson (see *Davidson, Donald*), Dummett (see *Dummett, M. A. E.*), and Grice have resisted the inference from productivity to atomism. They do not deny that words have meaning. Instead they take the meaning of a word to be derived from the meaning of sentences in which it appears (though it has proven difficult to give an explicit account of this derivation). Word meaning does not explain sentence meaning but is derived from it. This approach is supported by the fact that the most interesting semantic properties are properties of sentences. The units of linguistic communication and representation seem to be sentences. Even one word utterances like *Idiot!* are best construed as sentences, not bare words; they seem to have truth values.

It may well be true, as Davidson, Quine, and Dummett in their differing ways have argued, that sentence meaning is more evidentially basic than word meaning. Davidson, following Quine, has urged that confronted with the speakers of an untranslated language, we have some reasonable hopes of determining which sentences they assent to, which sentences they 'hold true,' and that this is the empirical basis of a theory of meaning. One could quarrel with the conception of Quine and others concerning the evidential

resources for the semantic theory. But more importantly, the atomists' case is that word meaning is explanatorily fundamental, not that it is evidentially fundamental. There is no doubt that the physical behavior of macroscopic objects has been, and is, evidentially fundamental in the development of physical theory, but talk of middle-size objects traveling slowly is not the most fundamental level of explanation in physical theory. Similarly, the evidential primacy of facts about sentences establishes nothing about explanation. A semantic theory which reduces all other semantic notions to word meaning may get its crucial confirmation from facts about sentences (see *Meaning: Philosophical Theories*).

2.4 Naturalized Semantics

The final enabling assumption of the ambitious program is that we should look not just for a semantic theory but for a naturalized semantic theory. The 'naturalist' demand derives from an epistemic idea and a metaphysical idea. The epistemic idea is that philosophical theories enjoy no special status. They differ from the theories of the natural sciences in important ways; for example, they are less precisely formulated and much harder to bring into contact with data. But they share with the sciences their fallible and provisional character. So semantic theory is empirical and provisional. The idea is that semantic theory is a protoscience that will one day jettison its prefix. The further commitment is that semantic theory be physicalist. It is notoriously difficult to formulate precisely the requirements of a physicalist ontology, and its bearing on the 'special sciences' (the social sciences, psychology, linguistics, and biology). But the intuitive idea is that the properties, mechanisms, and processes posited in the special sciences must be explicable by more fundamental ones, and, while it is hard to come up with a general formula, particular cases are often clear enough. If cognitive psychologists posit, for example, a capacity to access a special pictorial memory, they owe an explanation of the mechanism of access, an explanation appealing to simpler psychological or neural mechanisms. So the ambitious program is committed to giving an account of the relation between words and the world, not just taking that relation as primitive. It is most plausible to suppose that the semantic can be explained by the psychological. So naturalist programs have reductive intentions towards semantics.

There is a lot of scepticism about the prospects for naturalizing semantics. Both Kripke (see *Kripke: Philosophy of Language*) and Putnam (see *Putnam, Hilary*) argue that the reductive intent is unnecessary and incapable of fulfillment. It is just a mistake to think of the human sciences in general, and semantics in particular, as protosciences. For one thing, that is to miss the normative element of a theory of meaning. No regularity of behavior, or psychological disposition underlying that regularity, can give sense to the notion of a term being misapplied. Suppose that some benighted tourist points at a wallaroo and says *Lo! A kangaroo*. They have said something false. But that is so only if their tokens of 'kangaroo' apply to all and only kangaroos, not to kangaroos *and* wallaroos. But they have just demonstrated that their 'kangaroo'-using disposition is the disposition to apply the term to both varieties of macropod. Since such dispositions and their ilk are, in his view, about the only facts the naturalist has to trade in, Kripke is decidedly sceptical about the prospects for an account of reference in naturalistic terms with sufficient resources to give a robust account of misrepresentation.

So defenders of the ambitious program propose to develop a theory of meaning with reference as its core semantic notion, deriving a theory of sentence meaning from that core. But they do not take referential relations to be primitive; on the contrary, these are to be explained by appeal to more fundamental facts.

3. Description Theories and Causal Theories

Traditional theories of reference, concerning either singular or general terms, were not naturalist theories. Consider, for example, the theories that have been offered for general terms, such as *photon* and *tiger*. These are both examples of natural kind terms, one theoretical, the other observational.

3.1 Theoretical and Observational Terms

Theoretical terms have been the focus of intense debate in philosophy of science. In the heyday of logical empiricism, the idea was to explain the semantics of 'photon' and kindred terms by reducing their semantics to the semantics of the observation language; perhaps by direct definition, perhaps more subtly. Not just evidence but also meaning depended on observation; hence the 'logical' in 'logical empiricist.' But attempts to explain the meaning of theoretical terms by appeal to observational ones simply have not succeeded. So it has been supposed that the semantics of theoretical terms is derived from the role they play in the theories that contain them. The term 'species,' for example, derives its semantic properties from its role in the theories of evolution, ecology, and population genetics, the theories that essentially appeal to that notion. So 'species' means something like 'evolving interbreeding ecologically coherent populations,' for that is how these theories characterize species. The idea was originally proposed as a theory of the meaning of theoretical terms, but unless a term's meaning is to be completely decoupled from its reference, we can take it to be a theory of reference as well: the term refers to all and only those biological entities that (perhaps only approximately) fit that characterization.

This conception of the semantics of theoretical terms faces serious problems, for it follows that the semantics of a term change not just when the theory undergoes revolutionary restructuring, but whenever the theory is significantly modified. Though a number of philosophers have embraced some version of the idea that theory-change entails meaning-change, it has implausible consequences. It becomes difficult to explain how even those who accept differing versions of the same basic theory routinely succeed in communicating with each other, and still more difficult to explain the successful communication between those whose views are very far apart. But Darwin and Owen, for example, despite their very different views on the nature of species, understood each other perfectly well; understanding was a precondition of their deep disagreement. Moreover, this view of the semantics of theoretical terms makes it difficult to give an account of the cumulative aspects of scientific change.

So these theories of the semantics of theoretical terms may not work on their own lights, but even were they to

work, they are inadequate by the atomist's lights. For term meaning is explained by appeal to other semantic facts. Logical empiricists attempted to reduce the meaning of 'photon' and its ilk to the semantics of observation terms. The defenders of 'theoretical role' semantics explained term meaning by appeal to the meaning of the sentences that jointly make up a theory. We have here no explanation of representation by a more fundamental class of fact.

3.2 Componential Analysis

'Theoretical role' semantics at best explains some semantic facts by appeal to others; the same might well be said of many theories of the meaning of words like 'tiger' or 'sloop.' These terms have received less explicit attention in the philosophical literature, but there has been a substantial theory of word meaning developed in linguistics and related disciplines, a theory known as 'componential analysis' (see *Componential Analysis*). The idea is simple, and is also common in philosophy: these terms acquire their meaning from definitions. 'Tiger' means 'large, carnivorous, striped Asian feline'; 'Sloop' means 'a one-masted cutter with a fixed bowsprit.' Once more, this idea is naturally seen both as a theory of meaning and as a theory of reference; the term refers to those entities which fit the definition. As a general view of the semantics of natural kind or artifact terms, this story has problems. Putnam has pointed out that *tigers are carnivores* is very different from the genuinely definitional *triangles are three-sided*, for it is both contingent and empirically corrigible. Fodor (1981) has pointed out that it is in fact extremely difficult to construct extensionally correct definitions in which the defining terms are more conceptually basic than the defined term.

There is a deeper problem for componential analysis. Definitions do not yield an explanation of the relationship between language and the world. Rather, in Devitt's felicitous phrase, they 'pass the semantic buck'; they explain the meaning, and hence the reference, of the term defined, only insofar as some further adequate explanation can be given of the semantics of the defining terms. 'Passing the buck' is not pointless if it is passed to terms that are in some way special; terms whose semantic properties can be explained, not just presupposed. Logical empiricists thought that observation terms were special, but the official 'antipsychologism' of that movement, the ban on appeal to psychological process, prevented them from giving any explanation of the semantics of observation terms. Many contemporary semantic theories are far from being antipsychologistic. But the clear failure to reduce theoretical language to observation language, and the difficulty of reducing quite ordinary terms to a reasonably small set of more basic ones, threatens our ability to profitably 'pass the buck.'

3.3 Singular Terms

Kripke has constructed a similar argument about names. He has argued that names cannot be abbreviated descriptions because a name has the same bearer, or none, in every possible world. In his terminology, names are referentially 'rigid.' But the reference of a description, or even a cluster of them, can vary from possible world to possible world. Hence there can be no semantic equivalence between names and descriptions (see *Names and Descriptions*). In some respects then, Kripke supports John Stuart Mill's view of names, namely, that while names, like other terms, might have connotations, those connotations do not determine the reference of the name; 'Kripke' does not refer to Kripke in virtue of any connotation of 'Kripke.' Proponents of 'direct reference' theories of names have taken his arguments to support the stronger thesis that there is nothing to the semantics of names but their denotation; more about this in Sect. 4.

Kripke's provocative metaphysical views have aroused much debate, but Devitt has pointed out that his arguments 'from ignorance and error' are clearer and more convincing, for they do not rest on corrigible metaphysical intuitions. Kripke points out that 'descriptivist' theories of names imply that we can use a name to designate its bearer only if we can identify that bearer, if not in a police lineup then at least in knowing some unique characteristic of the bearer. He goes on to illustrate the implausibility of this view. Human language (unlike many animal systems of communication) is not stimulus bound. We can speak of the elsewhere and elsewhen. Given our cognitive limitations, and the stimulus freedom of language, referring to Einstein had better not closely depend on knowing about Einstein. Putnam has made much the same kind of point about general terms. But the most critical point against the description theory of names is not that it forges too close a link between referring and knowing, for no doubt suitably cunning amendments to the theory might be able to finesse that problem. Rather, it is a buck-passing theory.

3.4 Causal Chains

So what kind of theory might avoid buck-passing? Since the early 1970s or so, causal hypotheses about reference have been explored (see Field 1972; Devitt 1981; Devitt and Sterelny 1987). The central idea is that the referential relation is constituted by a causal chain between a term token, and its reference. Let us follow Putnam in imagining how this might go for natural kind terms. Joseph Banks disembarks at Botany Bay, and is confronted by the first kangaroo anyone in his speech community has seen. There is causal commerce between him and the roo, as a result of which Banks says 'We will call these animals "kangaroos".' There is a causal chain between the term token and its bearer in virtue of which the term refers to kangaroos. Others hear him talk of kangaroos, or read his letters about them, and acquire a causal connection to kangaroos indirectly, via Banks's linguistic behavior. They 'borrow' their reference from his.

Naturally, this sketch is oversimplified. The introduction of a natural kind term involves not just an ostensive but also a structural component. A term is introduced into the language by perceptual contact with samples of the kind. But the extension of the term goes beyond these samples, concerning all those objects having the same nature as the samples. In a first approximation, the nature of kinds is determined by internal structure. So the term 'kangaroo' applies to all animals having the same internal structure as that of the samples; the term 'plutonium' to that stuff having the same internal structure of the samples produced through the Manhattan Project. Having the same nature, then, is a matter of scientific discovery; internal structure is discovered only through empirical investigation. The link

between referring and knowing is cut, for the introduction of the term does not depend on the term's coiner knowing the nature of this structure, and hence the nature of the 'same kind as' relation. It follows that the users of a natural kind term need not, and often do not, know necessary and sufficient conditions for membership of the kind. Indeed they may not just be ignorant, they may be quite mistaken without prejudice to their capacity to use the name to refer to a kind. We have here not just an account of how kangaroos got their (English) name; it is an account of what reference is. On this view, the referential relation is just an appropriate type of causal chain between represented and representation.

4. Causal Theories and Semantic Data

Causal theories of reference are partly motivated by the problems of semantic buck-passing. But they also help to meet problems for theoretical role views of reference. Reference often seems to be stable over major scientific change; Cuvier and Huxley both used 'species' to refer to species despite their work at opposite sides of a great scientific divide. However, because nothing fits the characterization that Cuvier gave of species—for example, he thought they were immutable—that poses a problem for theoretical role views and other related views of reference. We want to say that Cuvier was wrong in what he wrote about species, not that he wrote about, literally, nothing. Putnam's theory, in cutting the link between the capacity to refer and the capacity to characterize a kind correctly, explains how reference can be stable over theory change. Kripke took the rigidity of names, and the fact that our capacity to use a name is insensitive to our epistemic grip on its bearer, to count against description theories and in favor of causal ones. But Field and Devitt have emphasized the fact that causal theories might be ultimate theories of reference. For causal relations between the speaking mind and bespoken world are physical facts.

4.1 Fregean Problems and Description Theories

The ambitious program confronts two distinct classes of problem. It faces the naturalization problem; the fundamental semantic notion must be explicable nonsemantically, otherwise there is an unexplained relation at the root of the theory (see Sect. 5). Further, though, and simultaneously, the theory must do justice to the semantic phenomena. In the literature on names that has dominated discussions of reference, the semantic agenda has been developed around problems associated with Frege (see *Names and Descriptions*). A theory of names, the idea has been, must do justice to the following facts:

(a) The sentence *Mount Egmont = Mount Taranaki* differs in some very important way from *Mount Egmont = Mount Egmont* even though Mount Egmont is Mount Taranaki.

(b) The sentence *Alfred believes that Mount Egmont is the highest mountain in New Zealand's north island* differs in some important way from *Alfred believes that Mount Taranaki is the highest mountain in New Zealand's north island*, again, despite the identity.

(c) The sentence *Vulcan is the closest planet to the sun* is meaningful even though *Vulcan'* is an empty name.

Though they have received less attention, similar phenomena arise for general terms. Consider, for example, empty terms. Piltdown man was a fraud, hence the species *Dawsoni* never existed; still *Eoanthropus Dawsoni was the precursor to homo sapiens* is meaningful, though false.

Description theories of names and general terms have many problems. It was on semantic grounds that Putnam rejected abbreviation accounts of general terms and Kripke descriptivist theories of names. But whatever their other troubles, description theories do justice to these problems. If names are abbreviated descriptions, it is no surprise that distinct but coreferential names are not semantically equivalent. If names are abbreviated descriptions, then a name is meaningful but empty if its associated description fails uniquely to designate some object. Russell's theory of descriptions (see *Russell, Bertrand*) thus solves the problem of the meaningfulness of empty names, granted an account of general terms.

The problem of belief contexts is tougher, but a common idea is that in such contexts it is not merely the reference of the name that is relevant to the truth-conditions of the belief sentences in which it appears; the mechanism of reference is also relevant. Frege christened mechanisms of reference 'sense' (see *Sense*). Though 'Mount Egmont' and 'Mount Taranaki' refer to the same mountain, their mechanisms of reference, the descriptions associated with them, are not the same; hence the two belief sentences have distinct meanings.

Some at least of this machinery can be applied to general terms. These too have a mechanism of reference of some kind. Though Weismann believed that the germ plasm was responsible for inherited similarities between organisms, he did not believe that DNA was responsible for those similarities, unaware as he was of the identity of germ plasm and DNA. Perhaps we can appeal to distinct mechanisms of reference to explain the differences between these belief sentences, and the apparently related difference between *Germ plasm is germ plasm* and *Germ plasm is DNA*. Of course, within buck-passing semantics, this idea is of restricted utility; for it cannot be deployed for those general terms to whom the referential buck is ultimately passed. A logical empiricist might argue that meaningful observational predicates are never empty, and that coextensive observational terms are semantically interchangeable, but this position is very difficult to defend for those who admit a wider range of undefinable general terms.

4.2 Causal Theories and the Fregean Problems

Causal theories of reference may well be able to meet the Fregean problems in the same way that description theories do, by holding that a term's mechanism of reference is semantically relevant. The mechanism of reference, on the causal account, is not a description but a causal network linking term token to reference (see Devitt and Sterelny 1987). Distinct causal networks link tokens of 'Mount Taranaki' and 'Mount Egmont' to Mount Taranaki, one network ultimately deriving from the linguistic behavior of Maori-speaking New Zealanders and the other, English-speaking New Zealanders. Because the two tokens refer in virtue of their linkage to distinct networks, *Egmont is Taranaki* differs in meaning from *Egmont is Egmont*.

For the same reason, belief sentences differing only in the substitution of one name for the other differ in meaning. A name can be meaningful but empty through being associated with a causal network similar to that of standard names, but which is not grounded in any object. The substitution of causal networks for descriptions in this revised approach to Frege's problem has the advantage of being extendable to the parallel problems with general terms, and without the restriction implicit in buck-passing theories.

The idea of deploying causal theories to reconstruct the notion of sense is very controversial; most see the causal theory as a theory of 'direct reference,' a theory that dispenses with Frege's notion of sense and his agenda of problems for the semantics of singular terms (see Wettstein 1986; Almog, et al. 1989). Proponents of 'direct reference' do not of course deny that there is some interesting difference between *Alphonse believes that Samuel Clement wrote Huckleberry Finn* and *Alphonse believes that Mark Twain wrote Huckleberry Finn*; they just deny that there is a semantic difference between them, for there is just one proposition—the set of worlds in which Twain wrote the book—for Alphonse to be related to. Explaining the difference between the sentences is a job for pragmatics or psychology or both, but not for semantics, the proper role of which is an explanation of the information load of linguistic representation (see Almog, et al. 1989). This division of labor may be appropriate, though troubles plague it. Direct reference theorists have mostly concentrated on singular reference, yet Fregean problems seem to arise for general terms as well. Even within singular reference, most attention is paid to identity and opacity. It is hard to see what account of the meaningfulness of sentences essentially containing an empty name can be given by those who abjure any surrogate for the notion of sense.

4.3 Other Problems for Causal Theories

However the Byzantine disputes between different factions of causal theorists might resolve themselves, causal theories can probably handle Frege's problems. But they face some of their own. The causal theory, like the description theory, is not fully general. There are a raft of examples that do not fit it. Some natural kind terms have been introduced not by encounter with samples but by prediction; 'neutrino' and 'black hole' are famous examples. The same can be true of names; 'Nemesis' has been introduced as the name for a hypothesized companion of the sun that disturbs the Oort cloud every 26 million years. Rather more prosaically, architects sometimes name their buildings, and parents their children, before these have progressed beyond planning. At the time of their introduction, these terms do not depend for their semantic properties on a causal chain between term and thing. There is within language some passing of the semantic buck, and the causal theorist must accommodate that.

Moreover the causal theories seems to deem impossible something that clearly is possible: reference change. Simple versions of the theory imply that the reference of a term is fixed by the acts that introduce that term into the language; all future use depends on those introducing uses. Yet reference clearly can change; 'Aotearoa' is now widely used in New Zealand as an alternative name for New Zealand, but it originally named only the north island. The same is true of general terms. We use 'consumption' as a Victorian synonym of TB, but they used it for a much wider range of respiratory complaints. 'Gay' is another general term that has shifted reference vigorously in recent times. Clearly, causal theorists need a more complex account in which an expression's reference will depend not just on the introducing use but also on the ongoing uses; on not just their initial 'grounding' on their bearers but on reencounters, 'regroundings' on them. Empty names and general terms are also trouble. The introduction of a term always has some cause, yet some are empty. 'Phlogiston' does not designate oxygen even though oxygen was the usual salient cause of the experimental results culminating in the introduction of 'phlogiston.' 'Santa Claus' is empty despite a connection with a real historical figure and its 'regrounding' on assorted impostors.

No consensus has emerged; there is even debate about just what the phenomena are, let alone which theory best handles them. The most devoted defender of causal semantics could not claim that they offer a complete and satisfactory account of the phenomena in their domain. Still, sophisticated causal theories do a fairly good job with the most pressing items on their semantic agenda. The story is much less cheerful when the reduction of the semantic to the nonsemantic is considered.

5. Naturalizing Reference

The ambitious program is in trouble if reference turns out to be inexplicable. Quine, as noted earlier, has long been sceptical that any account of meaning can be had. In arguing against the analytic/synthetic distinction he claimed that sameness of meaning, hence meaning, can be explained only by other semantic notions (see *Analyticity*). There is no escape from the circle of semantic concepts. So these notions have no place in real science, however attractive they may be. Quine is right in demanding that semantic properties be explained or abandoned; defenders of causal theories hope however to show he is too pessimistic about the prospects of explaining meaning.

The reductive task is formidable. Late-twentieth-century attempts rely on the notion that representation is a causal relation. As we have seen, the root idea is that the 'tiger'–tiger connection depends in some way on the causal connections between 'tigers' and tigers. But the causal relations in question are crucially ambiguous. Consider the relations between Max's uses of 'tiger' and that set of tigers Max has encountered. His 'tiger's, surely, apply to these tigers and to all the others. But how could that be so? He has no causal connection with the rest. Somehow the term's range of application must be generalized beyond the grounding set, and by just the right amount. It must apply to all tigers, but not more: not to all large carnivores, all felines, all tigerish looking things, or to everything that is either a tiger or will be born next year. It must include all tigers; not all except those born in the New York Zoo. Even the notion of the grounding set itself is problematic. For consider the causal chain. It goes via the sensory impressions of tigers, tiger surfaces, tigers, the causal history of there being tigers near Max. So why aren't Max's uses of 'tiger' about tigerish retinal projections or tiger surfaces rather than tigers? Ambiguity problems seem to arise in one way or another for all attempts to explain representation.

5.1 The Appeal to Psychology

The natural way to resolve these indeterminacies is to appeal to the psychology of the language speaker, to what the speaker intended or believed. Max refers to tigers, not their characteristic retinal projections, because he intends to speak of a kind of animal. Responses along these lines threaten naturalistic semantics with circularity. For the response seems to be presupposing just the same capacities in thought that are to be explained in talk; causal theories of reference totter on the edge of being buck-passing theories after all. Psychological processes can appropriately be appealed to in giving a theory of meaning for natural language. But it is not much of an advance to presuppose the very properties of mental representation that are to be explained in linguistic representation. Moreover, in appealing to a speaker's knowledge, a more cognitive theory threatens to return causal theories to the descriptive theories from which they were in flight.

Names pose the same problem. On the Kripkean view, names are introduced into the language in formal or informal naming ceremonies. Max acquires a jet black kitten with fierce yellow eyes and proposes to his friends that they call her 'Satan.' Thus Satan is named, a name for the cat, not a cat surface or a temporal slice of a cat. Those present, in virtue of their interaction with the cat and the name, acquire the semantic ability to designate that cat by that name. This story is plausible, but it clearly presupposes that sophisticated perceptual, intentional, and linguistic capacities are already in place (see *Intentionality*).

Naturalist semantics thus faces a dilemma. Representation seems to be a species of causal relation. Yet causal relations do not seem sufficiently determinate. They leave too many candidates as the content of any given term. Winnowing these candidates requires one to move back inside the mind. In turn, this threatens the project with circularity.

5.2 'Semantic Bootstrapping'

There is a natural strategy for escaping this dilemma, which might be called 'semantic bootstrapping.' Perhaps there is a hierarchy of terms: from pure causal terms through descriptive–causal terms to descriptive terms. A pure causal term is one for which no descriptive knowledge of the referent is required. It can be acquired atomically, hence no threat of circularity arises. This base could play a role in the explanation of the reference of some nonbasic ones, names, perhaps, or natural kind terms. The descriptive knowledge required for their acquisition might require only base level concepts. This larger class could then play a role in our story for others, and so on. Successful bootstrapping would simultaneously explain both the nature of the referential relation, and explain how terms with those referential properties could be acquired.

Tough problems confront this proposal. Can the less basic be explained by the more basic in some way that does not presuppose that nonbasic terms are defined? There is very good reason to deny that many concepts are definable. So descriptive elements must be built into a causal theory of reference in ways compatible with its original demonstration that our capacity to refer to the world's furniture does not in general depend on identifying knowledge of that to which we refer.

Still more serious is the problem of actually finding basic terms. Sensory terms at first sight seem candidates, but even for them the ambiguity problem arises. Does 'red' (when first acquired by some child) name a color or a shade of that color, or even an intensity level of light? Concepts for which no problem of ambiguity arise look decidedly thin on the ground. So our basis for bootstrapping our way to the rest of our conceptual equipment may not be available.

6. Linguistic Representation and Mental Representation

This problem suggests that the Kripkean story may not be the right story of primitive content, but rather plays a role in the explanation of more cognitively sophisticated linguistic and mental representation, representations whose content presupposes a conceptual backdrop. Causal semantics then is faced with the problem that the cognitive capacities it relies on in explaining reference seem to presuppose the representational capacities that we most want explained. Trading in the problems of linguistic representation on the problem of mental representation might be progress. For one thing, there is that latter problem anyway. For another, it might be that the psychological problem is more tractable than the linguistic one, even though the trade-in constrains the solution. If we psychologize semantics, we can hardly explain mental representation by appeal to linguistic representation, as some have hoped.

How then might we hope to explain the mental capacities on which causal semantics depend? There seem to be only three options in the literature: reliable correlation, or indication; biological function; and functional role. All have problems.

6.1 Indication

The essential intuition behind indication theories is that representation is reliable correlation; a concept is a tiger concept just when its tokening covaries with the presence of tigers in the vicinity. Concept tokens are counterfactually dependent on their object; Max would not produce 'tiger' tokens unless confronted with tiger instances. Indication seems best suited to explain perception; it is obviously hard to extend indicator theories to mental representation in general, and from concepts for ostensively definable kinds to other concepts. Yet it seems that the causal semantics of names and natural kind terms require an account of the 'aboutness' of intentions and beliefs, not just perceptions. But the most severe problem for indication is misrepresentation. Leopards, practical jokes, noises in the undergrowth can all cause Max nervously to token 'tiger,' yet that concept is not the concept of tigers and anything else that goes grunt in the night. No-one tokens the tiger-concept only when tigers are present. Moreover, indication does not seem to deliver an account of the representational properties of even basic concepts, for indication is a relation not between a representation and an object or kind of object, but a relation between a representation and a state of affairs, the state of affairs of there being a tiger here now. For a defense of indication theories, see Dretske (1981, 1988) and Stampe (1986).

6.2 Teleology

One popular response to the problems of historical causal theories and of indication is to appeal to the biological function of a representation-forming mechanism. A mechanism has its biological function in virtue of its evolutionary history, so this appeal is uncontroversially naturalistic. Further, it seems to have the potential to solve the problem of misrepresentation. Robins feed their chicks when they gape and screech. But robins are vulnerable to cuckoos. In feeding a young cuckoo, the robin represents it, indeed misrepresents it, as her chick. For the biological function of the representation is to direct the robins in feeding their chicks, not to direct them in feeding their chicks or cuckoos, nor to feed retinal images or chick surfaces. That mechanism evolved because it led to robin ancestors feeding robin chicks, and despite the fact that it sometimes led them to feed cuckoos.

The proposal to add teleological elements to the causal story seems very attractive. For an appeal to the biological function of a representation is thoroughly naturalistic, yet does give more discriminatory machinery. We can specify the circumstances in which a mental state represents rather than misrepresents: it represents when the token is caused by circumstances of the same kind as those selectively responsible for the existence of the type. Beavers have the cognitive capacity to have tokens that represent the immediate presence of a wolf, because wolf-here-now circumstances were critical to the evolution of that capacity. So a beaver represents when she tokens that thought when confronted with a wolf, misrepresents when she tokens it in other circumstances. The appeal to teleology allows to specify the circumstances in which representation is veridical in a nonintentional, nonarbitrary way.

Teleological theory looks to be a very plausible account of the semantics of innate structures, and it may well be that there will be an important teleological element in our total theory of mental representation. But the attempt to extend the teleological story to the human propositional attitudes, and hence to the cognitive capacities that causal theories of names and general terms presuppose, faces great difficulties. Human beliefs do not have evolutionary histories. Very few human beliefs have been available to the ancestral population long enough to be the subjects of an evolutionary history. Moreover, the representational structures that are the standard examples of teleological semantics are fixed, isolated, innate. Beavers' representations of danger, ducklings' mother-thoughts, and frogs' musings on flies seem likely to be unstructured; they don't have component representations. Human intentions and beliefs, representations that are implicit in causal theories of reference, are complex. For creatures whose representational systems are languages of thought, the fundamental relationship is not between some way the world is and a sentence in the language of thought. It is rather between elements of the world—individuals and kinds—and concepts. A teleological semantics needs to be recast as a theory of reference.

It is at best an open question whether teleological theories explain enough of our capacities for mental representation to get causal theories of reference off the ground. Millikan (1984) and Papineau (1987) have both defended ambitious teleological programs, but have yet to win many converts.

6.3 Functional Role

Can the representational capacities implicit in causal theories of reference be explained by looking upstream from the formation of the concept rather than, or as well as, downstream to its causes? There is some plausibility in the idea that a concept is a cow concept rather than a cow-appearance concept or a cow-or-thin-buffalo concept because of the way it is used in the cognitive system (see *Concepts*). 'Two factor' theories of content have been quite popular in the literature on the mind (see Field 1978; Lycan 1988). They take content to be fixed by some combination of causal relations between mind and world, and functional relations within the mind. Unfortunately there are important problems in recruiting two factor theories to the problem of explaining the nature of primitive referential relations.

First, in their normal formulation two factor theories presuppose a solution to referential semantics, taking their problem to be accounting for an extra dimension of content, a functional notion that explains the differences between referentially identical representation. Field (1978) and Lycan (1988) take referential semantics and functional role to be independent vectors; if so, functional role is no use in eliminating indeterminacies of reference.

Second, functional role theories concentrate on inference, but an appeal to inference seems unlikely to explain the reference of concepts. For concepts do not have inferential roles. Only sentences, or sentence-like representations, do. Moreover, an inferential role theory of content may leave us with a holistic theory of content. For the inferential productivity of a representation depends on the other intentional states of the system. The belief that wallaroos are edible prompts the belief that the moon is full if you happen also to believe that wallaroos are edible when the moon is full. Holistic theories of representation are problematic in making representation idiosyncratic; people never act the same way because they mean the same thing, because they never do mean the same thing.

7. Conclusion

The ambitious program is ambitious, but it is a worthy ambition. It deserves pursuit, for success would enable us to integrate our folk and scientific conceptions of ourselves qua language users. A failure (in the absence of an alternative route for the reduction of the semantic to the more fundamental) would force us either into the wholesale rejection of our folk theory of ourselves as thinkers and talkers or into dividing our self conception into two incommensurable chunks, a scientific and a folk image. The relation between these chunks would be obscure, and their joint truth would be still more so. The ambitious program is not yet triumphant, but neither has it failed.

Bibliography

Almog J, Perry J, Wettstein H (eds.) 1989 *Themes From Kaplan*. Oxford University Press, Oxford
Davidson D 1984 *Inquiries into Truth and Interpretation*. Clarendon Press, Oxford
Devitt M 1981 *Designation*. Columbia University Press, New York
Devitt M, Sterelny K 1987 *Language & Reality*. Blackwell/MIT Press, Oxford
Dretske F 1981 *Knowledge and the Flow of Information*. Basil Blackwell, Oxford
Dretske F 1988 *Explaining Behavior: Reasons in a World of Causes*. Bradford/MIT Press, Cambridge, MA
Dummett M 1975 What is a theory of meaning, vol. 1. In: Guttenplan S (ed.) *Mind and Language*. Clarendon Press, Oxford
Dummett M 1976 What is a theory of meaning, vol. 2. In: Evans G, McDowell J (eds.) *Truth and Meaning*. Clarendon Press, Oxford
Field H 1972 Tarski's theory of truth. *Journal of Philosophy* **69**: 347–75
Field H 1978 Mental representations. *Erkenntnis* **13**: 9–61
Fodor J 1981 *Representations*. Bradford/MIT Press, Cambridge, MA
Kripke S 1980 *Naming and Necessity*. Harvard University Press, Cambridge, MA
Kripke S 1982 *Wittgenstein on Rules and Private Language*. Harvard University Press, Cambridge, MA
Lycan W 1988 *Judgement and Justification*. Cambridge University Press, Cambridge
Millikan R G 1984 *Language, Thought and Other Biological Categories*. Bradford/MIT Press, Cambridge, MA
Papineau D 1987 *Reality and Representation*. Basil Blackwell, Oxford
Putnam H 1975 *Mind, Language and Reality: Philosophical Papers*, vol. 2. Cambridge University Press, Cambridge
Putnam H 1981 *Reason, Truth and History*. Cambridge University Press, Cambridge
Quine W V O 1960 *Word and Object*. MIT Press, Cambridge, MA
Schiffer S 1987 *Remnants of Meaning*. Bradford/MIT Press, Cambridge, MA
Stampe D 1986 Verification and a causal account of meaning. *Synthese* **69**: 107–37
Wettstein H 1986 Has semantics rested on a mistake? *Journal of Philosophy* **83**: 185–209

K. Sterelny

Reference: Psychological Approaches

'Reference' is the term used to describe the relationship between utterances and their objects of communication in the world. In the same way that symbols on a road map refer to the different towns and routes they represent, so utterances refer to the different individuals, events, times, and places about which they are being used to communicate.

Thus the reference relationship anchors utterances to their objects of communication. Different components of the utterance can be used to pick out different sorts of referent in the world. For instance in (1), the two noun-phrases *Harry* and *the man in the stove pipe hat* refer to two different individuals, the adverb *yesterday* refers to a particular time when the event took place, and the main clause refers to the event itself:

Yesterday, Harry bumped into the man in the stove pipe hat.   (1)

Reference has attracted particular attention in psychology, because its interpretation depends heavily on the context of the utterance, whether that be in the nonlinguistic situation or the surrounding text. For instance, in the example above the time referred to by *yesterday* can only be determined in relation to the time the utterance was produced, part of the general speech situation. References of this sort, which point outside the text, are termed 'exophoric.' However, in written language it is more common to have 'endophoric' or text-internal reference. For instance, if (1) had been embedded in a larger story, the referent for

Harry or *the man* ... would usually be fixed in relation to a previous description introducing those individuals into the narrative.

Both exophoric and endophoric reference are of interest to psychologists mainly because they pose problems about how a listener or reader establishes the intended relationship between the expression and its referent. This raises psychological issues both about the mental representation of the referent and the cognitive processes involved in mapping referential expressions onto their intended referents.

1. Varieties of Reference

1.1 Exophoric Reference and Deixis

Although the bulk of psychological work has been concerned with text-internal reference, exophoric reference also raises a number of fascinating psychological questions concerning how the referent is established during language comprehension.

One such problem arises from 'deixis,' which is a term used to describe the way some referential expressions incorporate a pointing-like gesture as part of their meaning (see Bühler 1934—relevant extracts also in Jarvella and Klein 1982—for the first modern treatment). This pointing function is most apparent with the demonstratives *this* and *that*, personal pronouns such as *I* or *you*, and some spatial or temporal adverbials such as *here* and *now*. These expressions and many others point to their referents in relation to the speaker's perspective on the scene. For instance, to establish the referent for *this* the listener has to determine what the speaker might have in mind at that time, helped often by a physical pointing gesture.

The bulk of the psychological work on deictic reference has been directed at how speakers learn to use these expressions appropriately (Clark 1977), and this has shown that a full understanding of their use is only acquired relatively late in language acquisition. The developmental results almost certainly reflect the conceptual problem children have in taking into account the listener's perspective in language use. There is also some work on the use of deictics by more mature speakers particularly in relation to descriptions of space (see Jarvella and Klein 1982, and Miller and Johnson-Laird 1976 for a fuller discussion).

Although exophoric reference has not attracted the attention paid to text-internal reference, it does illustrate in a very clear way the psychological issues involved in referential communication. For any reference to succeed, the communicators have to take account of various aspects of the context of utterance to establish a common focus of attention on the referent. In the case of deixis this usually means establishing a common perspective on the scene. In the case of text-internal endophoric reference it means establishing a common focus of attention on the relevant antecedent information in the text.

1.2 Endophoric Reference and Anaphora

Much of the psychological work on reference has been concerned with how a reader establishes text-internal reference relationships, and in most cases interest has centered on referential noun phrases. Such endophoric relations usually occur through what is called 'anaphora,' or reference in relation to a description encountered earlier in the text. This can be illustrated in the brief passage (2):

> John noticed that a window had been left open. *He* walked over to *the window* and closed *it* firmly. (2)

The second sentence in (2) contains three examples of anaphoric reference, two with the pronouns *he* and *it* and one in the form of the definite noun phrase *the window*. These are all relatively straightforward cases, where the interpretation of the anaphoric noun phrases is as coreferential with the antecedents in the text. Thus *he* is coreferential with *John*, and *the window* and *it* with the antecedent *a window*. However, there are more interesting cases of anaphoric reference where the referential relationship between antecedent and anaphor may be less direct, for instance, in (3).

> John was most impressed with the new orchestra. *The violins* were playing beautifully. (3)

Here the noun phrase *the violins* is anaphorically related to the antecedent *orchestra* in the sense that the reader will take it to refer to the violins in that particular orchestra, but the relation is not one of strict coreference.

The two main issues in the psychological work have been establishing when and how anaphors are interpreted during the course of comprehension and determining what kind of mental representation of the context the reader needs to do this.

2. The Psychological Framework for Interpreting Reference

Whether a reference is made endophorically or exophorically its success ultimately depends on the speaker or writer ensuring that his audience is attending to the same thing that he has in mind in making it. In effect, successful reference requires coordination on a 'common focus of attention,' and it is how this coordination may be achieved which is one of the key issues in psychological accounts of referential communication. The problem is considered first in relation to spoken dialogue and then, more specifically, in relation to resolving anaphoric references in written discourse.

2.1 Reference in Spoken Dialogue

In dialogue, the conversants need to establish coordinated interpretation of reference. The speaker should formulate his descriptions to take into account the listener's current knowledge about and perspective on the referential domain while at the same time the listener has to take into account the speaker's perspective.

This requirement for coordinated language processing goes beyond the simple point that reference is sensitive to context. It has led some researchers to argue that successful reference depends upon establishing a special kind of context which is in common to the communicators. This common context is sometimes called 'mutual knowledge' and it comes from a recognition by speaker and listener of the knowledge which they share that is relevant to the interpretation (see Clark and Marshall 1981). For instance, if in trying to fix a meeting you said to a friend *I'll meet you at the concert* the referential description *the concert* would only be felicitous if you both had mutual knowledge about the significance of the one particular concert which you, as speaker, had in mind. This might come from a previous agreement to go to that concert, or just from the fact that you both know that you will both be playing at it. Whatever the basis of the knowledge it should be mutual, that is recognized by each as shared knowledge.

Although there is a general consensus about the importance of mutual knowledge for successful reference in principle, there is some controversy about whether communicators regularly infer such knowledge as a prerequisite to normal conversation (see Smith 1982) for a general debate). Some researchers have championed the contrary position that real communication depends just as much on having a prior state of mutual ignorance. But whichever position is taken on the issue of mutual knowledge inference, it is clear that establishing reference in dialogue requires some interaction between the speaker and listener.

There has been a lot of work exploring this interactional side to reference. The original investigations were directed specifically at the development of referential communication skills and employed a simple communication task where a child had to describe a sequence of rather abstract pictures (tangrams) to another child in such a way that they could exactly replicate the sequence (see Krauss and Glucksberg 1969). The main findings from these studies were that children younger than about 5 or 6 years tend to produce idiosyncratic descriptions—a picture resembling a hat might be described as *mummy's hat* and a subsequent different picture as *another mummy's hat*. As a consequence the references often failed because the child had not taken proper account of the listener's relevant knowledge. More recent studies indicate that adults may initially produce somewhat idiosyncratic descriptions in this kind of task, but then they will use the subsequent interaction to repair any misunderstanding. An example of such an exchange (4–7) (from Clark and Wilkes-Gibbs 1986) is:

Uh, person putting a shoe on. (4)

Putting a shoe on? (5)

Uh huh. Facing left. Looks like he's sitting down. (6)

Okay. (7)

Perhaps the strongest evidence that reference in dialogue depends upon a special common context of the sort Clark and his colleagues have proposed comes from the observation that people who have overheard, but not partaken in the dialogue have a great deal of trouble identifying the referent (see Schober and Clark 1989).

The main thrust of work on reference in dialogue, therefore, has been to establish the role of the interaction in achieving a coordinated interpretation of referential descriptions (see Garrod and Anderson 1987 and Clark 1985 for fuller discussion).

2.2 Reference in Reading and the Interpretation of Anaphors

The psychological work on understanding reference in reading addresses a somewhat different set of issues about interpretation relative to a context. This is mainly because it centers around anaphors and these impose special processing requirements.

There are many different forms of anaphoric reference associated with different linguistic devices but the most important difference in relation to comprehension is that between pronominal anaphora as opposed to full noun-phrase anaphora. On the surface, these two forms seem to be equivalent, thus in (8–9) the pronoun is interchangeable with the definite description:

A man walked into the room. (8)

He/The man sat down in the corner. (9)

But this is not always the case, as for instance in (10) below:

Julia usually goes to Valentino's for lunch, because
she fancies the waiter there, for dinner she prefers
to eat at La Grande Bouffe where the food is better
but *he*/the waiter* is not nearly so handsome. (10)

The difference relates to the fact that referential pronouns, at least in written material, require an explicitly mentioned antecedent and then have to take their reference from this. The interpretation of fuller definite noun phrases on the other hand is not so rigorously conditioned by previously mentioned discourse referents. Thus in (10), the second mention of *the waiter* is taken to refer to a different individual but one who is playing the same role in the situation as the antecedent.

Whether the reference is with a pronoun or a fuller description the first processing issue raised is that of the immediacy of interpretation of the anaphor. The question is whether the reader accesses the prior context immediately and forges the link between anaphor and antecedent before trying to interpret the rest of the sentence or leaves all such context-dependent interpretation until after an initial context-free analysis of the sentence has been made. This question was of interest to psycholinguists because in the 1970s it was widely believed that the comprehension process occurred in stages. It began with the identification of letters and words, then syntactic structure, then sentence meaning, and so on, with each stage building on the output of the previous one. So according to this account it was only at the final stage that the full contextual significance of the sentence was arrived at (see Fodor, et al. 1974 for a general discussion of this position).

A number of experimental techniques have been devised to try and establish exactly this point of anaphoric resolution. Most of the techniques involve having a reader carry out some secondary task which gives evidence that the anaphor has been resolved and at the same time marks the point in the processing of the sentence when this has happened. For example, Garrod and Sanford (1985) presented readers with passages of text like the following:

Elizabeth was a very inexperienced swimmer and wouldn't have gone into the pool if the lifeguard hadn't been standing nearby. But as soon as she was out of her depth she started to panic and wave her hands about in a frenzy.

These texts acted as context for one of four critical sentences whose subject was an anaphor for one of the characters in the story. The critical sentences also contained a misspelling of the main verb as in (11–14):

Within seconds Elizabeth *senk* [beneath the surface] (11)

Within seconds Elizabeth *jimped* [into the pool] (12)

Within seconds the lifeguard *senk* [beneath the surface] (13)

Within seconds the lifeguard *jimped* [into the pool] (14)

The sentences were so constructed that in half the cases (e.g., in (12) and (13) above) the sentence was contextually anomalous at the point of the misspelled verb. In other words, so long as the reader had established exactly who *Elizabeth* and *the lifeguard* were they would know that she could sink but not jump and he jump but not sink at that point in the story. Hence, being aware of the anomaly in the verb depended upon having already interpreted the immediately preceding anaphor.

The misspellings were included to establish whether or not the reader was sensitive to these anomalies at the point of encountering the verb, since time to detect such misspellings is known to reflect the degree to which the word fits into its context. By measuring exactly when readers could detect the misspellings during the course of reading the sentence, it was possible to demonstrate that the anaphors had been interpreted before encountering the verb.

This and other such studies where eye fixations have been recorded during reading (see Rayner and Pollatsek 1990) indicate that anaphors in general receive a contextually sensitive interpretation almost immediately they are encountered. The only exception to this general rule is with certain contexts of interpretation for pronouns. Thus when the proper name and definite description anaphors in (11–14) are replaced with pronouns, only the pronoun referring to the antecedent introduced by proper name (i.e., *Elizabeth*) is resolved immediately. This almost certainly reflects the fact that *Elizabeth* is treated as the main character or 'thematic subject' in the prior text, while *the lifeguard* only plays a secondary role. As will be shown below, interpretation of pronouns, unlike fuller definite descriptions, is very sensitive to the degree to which the intended antecedent is in the focus of the reader's attention at the time the pronoun is encountered.

Apart from casting doubt on the adequacy of the stages account of sentence processing, evidence for the immediacy of anaphoric resolution raises a number of questions about how the context can be made so readily available during processing. This is particularly puzzling given that readers forget the exact wording of what they have just read almost instantly (at least beyond the last sentence encountered). The most promising hypothesis is that the reader carries in mind a skeletal representation of the currently relevant discourse referents, against which any anaphor can be matched. Such a representation is referred to as a 'discourse model' and corresponds in certain ways to the representations proposed in some contemporary accounts of the formal semantics of reference and anaphora (see, for example, *Discourse Representation Theory*; Kamp 1981).

Two processing questions arise from the assumption that antecedent referents are mentally represented in such a model. First, the question of what referent information becomes incorporated into the model, and second, the question of how it is retained there as the reader proceeds through the text. Psychologists have tended to look at these questions in relation to the 'common focus of attention' framework introduced above. So they assume that referent information can enter and leave the reader's focus of attention as the discourse proceeds and it is the status of this information which is so important to resolving pronominal reference (see Chafe 1972 on 'foregrounding' as a related approach in linguistics; see also *Foregrounding*).

It is easy to create examples where there seems to be a mismatch between the reader's current focus of attention on antecedent referents and the writer's intended interpretation. For instance (15) throws most people on a first reading.

> If an incendiary device should land nearby, don't lose your
> head. Put it in a bucket and cover it with sand. (15)

In (15), the most strongly focused antecedent seems to be *your head* rather than *an incendiary device* and so this is initially treated as antecedent for the pronoun *it*. Here the degree of focus reflects both the recency of mention of the antecedent and, possibly, the fact that it is in a main as opposed to subordinate clause. However, recency of mention is by no means the main factor in determining antecedent accessibility, since in the example (16) readers take the pronoun to refer to the first-mentioned matching antecedent *the feedpipe* rather than the most recently mentioned one *the chain* even when they are quite ignorant as to what these things are.

> The feedpipe lubricates the chain, and *it* should be adjusted to
> leave a gap half an inch between itself and the sprocket. (16)

In this case, antecedent focusing seems to be associated with the effect of sentence topic which overrides recency of mention.

There are a number of such factors which have been identified as affecting the ease with which a reader can interpret pronouns which all seem to correlate with the degree to which the antecedent referent is 'in mind' at the time of encountering the pronoun. The correlation can be established by interrupting readers at various points in a text and having them write continuation sentences. The referents included in these sentences tend to relate to just those antecedents that may readily be pronominalized. In contrast to pronouns, the interpretation of other forms of anaphoric device such as definite descriptions and proper names is affected less by the degree of antecedent focus.

However, there is evidence that the interpretation of full noun-phrase anaphors may be determined by a somewhat different kind of antecedent focusing which comes from the reader's representation of the situation portrayed in the text. It is common to find cases where a definite description is used in the absence of an explicitly mentioned antecedent, yet still receives a contextually conditioned referential interpretation. For instance in (18) below, the phrase *the car* is taken to refer to the vehicle that *Keith* in (17) used to drive to London.

> Yesterday, Keith drove to London. (17)

> *The car* kept breaking down. (18)

In cases like this where there is 'situational' reference, the evidence is that readers can often make an immediate contextual interpretation even in the absence of a matching discourse antecedent. However, this will only happen when the context clearly indicates a situation which 'affords' antecedents to match the reference, as in examples (3) and (10) above for instance (see Garrod and Sanford 1990 for a detailed discussion).

Taken together, the work on pronominal and other forms of anaphora has broad implications for psychological theories of language processing. These include the idea that the contextual interpretation of sentences proceeds incrementally as each word and phrase is encountered and that the whole process depends upon having ready access to a rich mental representation of what has gone before. This representation contains not only skeletal information about the referents which are currently in focus, but also information about the currently relevant reference situation or scenario. (A general account of the significance of reference to psychological models of reading can be found in Sanford and Garrod 1981.)

See also: Psychological Semantics; Coherence: Psychological Approaches.

Bibliography

Bühler K 1934 *Sprachtheorie: Die Darstellungfunktion der Sprache*. Fischer, Stuttgart

Chafe W 1972 Discourse structure and human knowledge. In: Carroll J B, Freedle R O (eds.) *Language Comprehension and the Acquisition of Knowledge*. Winston, Washington, DC

Clark E 1977 From gesture to word: On the natural history of deixis in language acquisition. In: Bruner J S, Garton A (eds.) *Human Growth and Development: Wolfson College Lectures*. Oxford University Press, Oxford

Clark H H, Marshall C R 1981 Definite reference and mutual knowledge. In: Joshi A K, Sag I A, Webber B L (eds.) *Elements of Discourse Understanding*. Cambridge University Press, Cambridge

Clark H H, Wilkes-Gibbs D 1986 Referring as a collaborative process. *Cognition* 22(1): 1–39

Clark H H 1985 Language use and language users. In: Lindzey G, Aronson E (eds.) *The Handbook of Social Psychology*, 3rd edn. Harper and Row, New York

Fodor J A, Bever T G, Garrett M F 1974 *The Psychology of Language: An Introduction to Psycholinguistics and Generative Grammar*. McGraw-Hill, New York

Garrod S, Anderson A 1987 Saying what you mean in dialogue: A study in conceptual and semantic coordination. *Cognition* 27: 181–218

Garrod S, Sanford A 1985 On the real-time character of interpretation during reading. *Language and Cognitive Processes* 1: 43–59

Garrod S, Sanford A 1990 Referential processes in reading. In: Balota D A, Flores d'Arcais G B, Rayner K (eds.) *Comprehension Processes in Reading*. LEA, Hillsdale, NJ

Jarvella R J, Klein W 1982 (eds.) *Speech Place and Action: Studies in Deixis and Related Topics*. John Wiley and Sons, Chichester

Kamp H 1981 A theory of truth and semantic representation. In: Groenendijk J, Janssen T, Stokhof M (eds.) *Formal Methods in the Study of Language*. Mathematical Centre Tracts, Amsterdam

Krauss R M, Glucksberg S 1969 The development of communication competence as a function of age. *Child Development* 40: 255–56

Miller G A, Johnson-Laird P N 1976 *Language and Perception*. Cambridge University Press, Cambridge

Rayner K, Pollatsek A 1990 *The Psychology of Reading*. Prentice Hall, Englewood Cliffs, NJ

Sanford A, Garrod S 1981 *Understanding Written Language: Explorations in Comprehension Beyond the Sentence*. John Wiley and Sons, Chichester

Schober M F, Clark H H 1989 Understanding by addressees and overhearers. *Cognitive Psychology* 21: 211–32

Smith N V 1982 (ed.) *Mutual Knowledge*. Academic Press, London

S. Garrod
A. Sanford

Reflexives and Reciprocals

Reflexive constructions (as in *The man killed himself*) and reciprocal constructions (as in *The boy and the girl like each other*) have been the subject of great interest from the point of view of linguistic typology and comparison, and from the point of view of various generative theories of syntax. The typologically oriented studies have been concerned not only with establishing the types and subtypes of the reflexive and the reciprocal constructions but also with their histories. On the other hand, the generative approaches to reflexives and reciprocals have concentrated on certain subtypes of the constructions, whose properties pose challenges to the given theories.

1. Reflexives

Before discussing reflexive constructions, it is best to define a prototypical reflexive situation: in a prototypical reflexive situation (RefS), a participant acts on himself or herself, rather than on any other: *The man killed himself*. A language may, but need not, have a special reflexive marker (RefM), or construction (RefC) to encode reflexive situations. And a RefS need not be encoded by means of a RefC, even in a language that does have one. This is typically the case with verbs that encode activities that one more commonly performs on oneself rather than on anybody or anything else; witness *The man shaved* (meaning 'The man shaved himself').

Conversely, a construction used to encode reflexive situations may be used with other, nonreflexive, functions, as in *The king himself opened the festival*, where *himself* has an emphatic rather than a reflexive function (see Sect. 4 for more examples).

As far as reflexive markers are concerned, three main types can be distinguished: (a) nominal reflexives, where the marker exhibits properties characteristic of nouns or pronouns in the language; (b) verbal reflexives, where the marker is part of the morphology associated with verbs (an affix, a clitic, or a particle); and (c) possessive reflexives, where the marker exhibits properties characteristic of certain possessive forms, such as possessive adjectives.

A nominal reflexive strategy is found in, for example, English: the reflexive elements exhibit properties characteristic of the pronouns, such as gender and number variation (*himself*, *herself*, *themselves*), and they function as noun phrases.

A verbal reflexive strategy is found in, for example, Nkore–Kiga (a dialect of Rwanda), where the RefM is a prefix on the verb:

Nganwa n   -aa-ye -shereka.   (1)
Nganwa PRES PROG-he-REFM-hide
'Nganwa is hiding (himself).'

A possessive reflexive strategy is found in, for example, Russian, where the RefM agrees in all the relevant features with the noun it modifies:

On ljubit svoju   rodinu.   (2)
he he.loves REFM.FEM.SG.ACC country.FEM.SG.ACC
'He loves his (own) country.'

The distinction between nominal reflexives and verbal reflexives, although clear in theory, is not always so in practice. Since verbal reflexives typically develop from nominal reflexives (see Sect. 4), there are cases where the RefM is neither purely of the nominal nor purely of the verbal type; French *se* is a case in point.

Two basic kinds of nominal and possessive reflexive systems can be distinguished on the basis of the availability of reflexive markers for the grammatical persons: one in which there is a RefM available for each grammatical person, and one in which there are RefMs only for the third person. That is, if a language has any reflexive marking at all, it will have it for the third person, and possibly for the other persons as well. Normally, it is only in the third person that ambiguity between a reflexive and a nonreflexive interpretation may arise in the absence of an explicit reflexive strategy.

In a reflexive situation, one participant plays two (or even more) roles, for example agent and patient, or agent and possessor. Alternatively, one can say that in a reflexive situation the participants playing certain roles (agent and patient) are nondistinct. In clauses with nominal and possessive RefCs, the relevant participant is encoded (at least) twice; each mention encodes one of the two (or more) roles. That is, nominal and possessive RefCs highlight the fact that a single participant is involved in a situation in multiple roles. In clauses with a verbal RefC, the relevant participant is encoded only once; what is highlighted there is the nondistinctness of the participants playing certain roles in a situation.

Even though nominal and possessive RefMs do refer to participants, they do not have independent reference; their referents are determined elsewhere, usually, though not necessarily, in the same clause. It is the existence of an anaphoric relation between a RefM and its antecedent that circumscribes the range of the phenomena to be considered here. Thus besides prototypical reflexives, included here are also, for example, benefactive, goal, logophoric, and emphatic reflexives.

The range of reflexive functions acquired by nominal reflexives is considerably greater than those acquired by verbal and possessive reflexives; their phonological independence and their (pro)nominal properties permit them to occur in a much larger set of syntactic environments. It is because of this relatively great flexibility and the resulting variety of anaphoric relations with their antecedents that nominal reflexives have received considerably more attention in the linguistic literature than the other two types. This survey also will concentrate on nominal reflexives.

Before investigating the range of RefCs found in languages, it is useful to determine the properties of the prototypical RefC. In a prototypical RefC of the nominal type, the RefM and its antecedent occur in the same clause; the RefM functions as a direct object, and the antecedent functions as a subject; the RefM encodes a patient, and its antecedent encodes an agent; and there is only one noun phrase that functions as antecedent. However, none of these properties of the prototypical RefC is necessary. There are languages where only subjects can be antecedents of reflexives, e.g., Chinese, but other languages allow nonsubject arguments to be antecedents, e.g., English: *The next day, when the giant's grandmother had turned Jack back into himself, he set off for home.*

There may be further restrictions on what kind of noun phrase may function as antecedent; in Chinese, the antecedent must not only be subject, but it must also be animate (at least metaphorically).

Languages commonly allow non patient reflexives and non agent antecedents: *He likes himself too much* and *He bought himself a brand new car.*

There are differences among languages as to the kinds of argument positions—besides direct objects—in which RefMs may appear. English permits indirect-object reflexives and certain kinds of oblique reflexives: *I sent the parcel to myself,* and *She is in love with herself.* English does not always allow locative reflexives, but there are languages that do so quite freely; compare the following sentence (3) from Dutch and its English gloss (where *him* is coreferential with *John*):

Jan   zag een slang naast zich.   (3)
John saw a   snake near REFM
'John saw a snake near him.'

English and some other languages also allow nominal reflexives in nonargument positions, in modifying positions within noun phrases: *Have you seen the picture of yourself in today's paper?*.

Some languages allow reflexives in subject position; in such cases the antecedent is outside the clause in which the RefM occurs. Reflexives of this kind are usually referred to as 'logophoric'; they occur in clauses embedded under certain verbs, called 'logophoric' by Kuno (1987). Kuno defines logophoric verbs as those that encode various speech acts and mental events or states and that take as their arguments noun phrases that encode the speaker, the experiencer, or the addressee. In the following example (4) of a logophoric reflexive from Chinese, the RefM may have as its antecedent either the subject of its own clause (*Lisi*) or the subject of the higher clause (*Zhangsan*):

Zhangsan juede Lisi dui ziji   mei xinxin.   (4)
Zhangsan think Lisi to REFM no confidence
'Zhangsan thought that Lisi had no confidence in himself/him.'

In terms of the syntactic configuration of a RefM and its antecedent, the commonest situation is for the two to occur in the same clause; they are 'clause mates.' However, a number of languages allow 'long-distance' anaphora, where the RefM and its antecedent are in separate clauses, but still within the same sentence. Long-distance anaphora is characteristic of logophoric reflexives (see the Chinese example (4) above). In fact, in Chinese and some other languages such long-distance anaphora is in principle unbounded; provided certain conditions are met, there is no limit on how many clause boundaries may intervene between a RefM and its antecedent. In English, long-distance anaphora is found with emphatic reflexives, for example, *Mr Smith said he could not comment on rumors that the bank wanted to replace some management staff, including himself.* It is also found with 'picture-noun' reflexives: *The [picture of herself/song about herself] that Mary [painted/composed] in a couple of hours won the first prize.*

Some languages, English among them, permit the antecedent to be not just outside the clause where the RefM occurs, but even outside the sentence (Zribi-Hertz 1989). And in Japanese—for some speakers—the RefM need not have any overt, syntactic antecedent at all; in such cases the RefM refers to the speaker(s):

Zibun-wo Naomi-ga aishi-teru.   (5)
REFM-DO Naomi-SU love -PROG.PRES
'Naomi loves me.'

The antecedent of a reflexive is typically a single noun phrase, but there are languages, such as English, that allow split antecedents: *Mary whispered secret things to Paul about themselves.*

Reflexive constructions are normally used not only when it is the whole of a participant that is affected by his or her own action (as in *The man killed himself*), but also when only part of him or her is. In some cases, the partitive nature of the reflexive is overt; in addition to the RefM, the sentence also contains specification of the part affected, as in Czech:

Učesala   si   vlasy.   (6)
she.combed REFM.DAT hair.PL.ACC
'She combed her hair.'

The body part affected by the action is treated as a patient; the RefM encodes a beneficiary.

However, the partitive nature of a reflexive may be covert: it is the participant as a whole that is treated as affected by the action, either because the exact identity of the part affected is not relevant or not known, or, because of the nature of the event, the identity of the part affected is self-evident, as in the next two Czech examples, respectively:

Umyla   se.   (7)
she.washed REFM.ACC
'She washed (not necessarily the whole of her body).'

The next example (8) is broadly synonymous with the overt partitive reflexive (6) above:

Učesala   se.   (8)
she.combed REFM.ACC
'She combed her hair.'

2. Reciprocals

As will be seen in what follows, there are some similarities between reflexive and reciprocal constructions; much of what has been said above about reflexives applies, *mutatis mutandis*, to reciprocals as well. As with reflexives, it is necessary to make a distinction between reciprocal situations (RecS) on the one hand and reciprocal markers (RecM) and reciprocal constructions (RecC) on the other. In a prototypical reciprocal situation, there are two participants that play identical pairs of roles vis-à-vis each other, e.g., agent and patient, as in *The two boys punched each other*. A reciprocal situation need not be encoded by means of a RecC even in a language that does have one. This is typically the case when the relations in the type of situation being encoded are normally or necessarily reciprocal, as in *They met at five o'clock*; but cf. Dyirbal (Australian):

Balagara   ḏaymbal-ḏaymbal-bari -ɲu bu bi -ŋga.
two (people).NOM find   -find   -RECM -PAST half way-LOC
'The two people met each other halfway.'   (9)

Conversely, a construction used to encode reciprocal situations may have other, nonreciprocal functions (see Sect. 4 for examples).

Two basic types of reciprocal markers can be distinguished: (a) nominal reciprocals, where the marker exhibits properties characteristic of nouns or pronouns; and (b) verbal reciprocals, where the marker is part of the morphology associated with verbs (an affix, a clitic, or a particle). The English RecMs *each other* and *one another* are of the nominal type (they function as noun phrases); the Dyirbal RecM (9) is of the verbal type.

Even though they represent participants, nominal RecMs (like nominal RefMs) do not have independent reference; their referents are determined elsewhere, typically (though not necessarily) in the same clause. Again, one can use the existence of an anaphoric relation between a RecM and its antecedent to define the range of phenomena to be discussed here.

RecCs are not restricted to encoding situations with only two participants involved in mirror image relations to each other. They may be used to encode situations with more than two participants playing a pair of roles, regardless of whether each of the participants stands in a reciprocal relation to all the others or only to some of them. Thus in *The members of the winning soccer team congratulated each other* it is not necessarily the case that each player exchanged congratulations with every other member of the team. (A discussion of such uses of the English RecM *each other* may be found in Langendoen 1978.)

In many languages, the RecCs are also used to encode 'chaining' (or 'linear configurational') situations, where (most of) the participants play identical pairs of roles, but not vis-à-vis each other, as in the Japanese example and its English gloss:

Shitai-ga kasanari -a   -tte iru.   (10)
corpse-SU pile on top-RECM-PROG PRES
'The corpses are piled on top of one another.'

As is the case with reflexives, it is nominal reciprocals that exhibit a greater range of uses relative to verbal reciprocals. In a prototypical nominal RecC, the RecM is a direct object, the antecedent is a subject, and the two are in the same clause. In many languages, the RecM may occur in positions other than direct object; witness English *They often buy presents for each other*, and *They were sitting next to one another*. They may also occur in modifying positions within noun phrases: *They wrote malicious articles about each other*, and *They praised each other's efforts*.

The antecedent of a reciprocal is typically a subject, but some languages, English among them, allow nonsubject antecedents: *He kept goading them against each other*.

Prototypically, a RecM and its antecedent are in the same clause, but there are languages, such as English, that do allow long-distance anaphora: *The counselor warned the couple that preoccupation with each other's shortcomings would only make the situation worse.*

3. Reflexives and Reciprocals in Modern Syntactic Theories

Reciprocal and, even more so, reflexive constructions have received a considerable amount of attention in various generative theories of syntax. It is the nominal subtypes of the constructions that the theories have concentrated on; this is because of the anaphoric relations between the reflexive and the reciprocal markers and their antecedents. When both types of construction are discussed, it is usually assumed that they are subject to the same rules. In generalized phrase structure grammar (see *Generalized Phrase Structure Grammar*), it has been suggested that the anaphoric relations can be handled by means of general feature-instantiation principles. In relational grammar (see *Relational Grammar*), multiattachment is used as the mechanism to account for (at least some) reflexives. It is in the framework of the government and binding theory that reflexives and reciprocals have received most attention by far, and the subsequent discussion will focus on the treatments of the constructions within this theory.

In government and binding, reflexives and reciprocals are explicitly assumed to be elements of the same kind, called 'anaphors' (as opposed to 'pronominals' and 'R-expressions' (referential expressions); see *Anaphora*). The distribution of anaphoric elements is said to be governed by the following binding condition: an anaphor is bound in its governing category (Chomsky 1981: 188; see also *Binding*). In broad terms this means that an anaphor and its antecedent must be clause mates, but detailed research on the anaphoric elements in a number of languages has revealed a considerable number of difficulties with the anaphor binding condition. The problems most often discussed have to do with anaphora across noun–phrase boundaries (with picture-noun reflexives), anaphora across clause boundaries, nonoccurrence of anaphoric elements in certain environments where pronominals are unexpectedly required instead, and alternation between anaphoric elements and pronominals in what appears to be one and the same structural position. There are other problems that are less frequently discussed, but that are nevertheless important as well: anaphora across sentence boundaries (is this kind of anaphora to be handled in a syntactic theory that assumes the sentence to be the highest level of syntactic analysis?), reflexives without syntactic antecedents, and split antecedents. Another problem is that the category of anaphoric elements in a language need not be homogeneous; i.e., the various anaphoric elements need not be subject to exactly the same rules. For example, 3rd person reflexives on the one hand, and 1st and 2nd person reflexives on the other, need not exhibit exactly the same properties (they do not in English); there may be differences between the reflexives and the reciprocals (as there are in English; see Lebeaux 1983), and there may even be differences between two subtypes of a construction (see Rosen 1981 for a discussion, within the framework of relational grammar, of the differences between the two types of reflexive in Italian). (A summary of many of the problems with the mainstream government and binding approaches to reflexives can be found in Zribi-Hertz 1989.)

The various attempts to overcome the problems with anaphoric elements fall basically into two categories: (a) those which are purely structural; and (b) those which supplement syntactic conditions with other, nonstructural conditions. A purely structural approach may, for example, posit two different underlying structures for sentences in which an anaphor appears to alternate with a pronominal. A great deal of work has also gone into defining and refining the concept of 'governing category' crucial to the binding conventions. For example, a governing category may be required to contain an 'accessible' subject or to contain an 'independent' tense. The notion of 'command' (the antecedent commanding the anaphor), crucial to binding, has also received a considerable amount of attention, and different kinds of the command relation have been proposed. It has also been suggested that unbounded anaphora be handled in logical form rather than in the syntactic component of the theory (see *Generalized Phrase Structure Grammar*).

On the other hand, there are approaches to anaphora that claim that attempts at purely syntactic accounts are bound to be unsuccessful, and that there are semantic, pragmatic, and/or discourse factors that must be taken into consideration as well. For example, Kuno (1987) argues that English reflexives are used if and only if the referent is a direct recipient or target of the event encoded in the sentence. This generalization is said to account for sentences like the following: *John left his family behind him* and *John fell in love with himself.* Kuno also uses the notion of 'empathy' to account for certain uses of English reflexives: subject to a number of qualifications, a sentence where a reflexive pronoun and its antecedent are clause mates must be interpretable as involving the speaker's empathy with the referent of the reflexive. Picture-noun reflexives also are sensitive to empathy: they are best when the speaker empathizes with the referent of the reflexive. The antecedent of a picture- noun reflexive must be (construable as) an actual speaker/perceiver; i.e., picture-noun reflexives are logophoric phenomena. In fact, long-distance reflexive anaphora in all the languages for which the phenomenon has been reported (whether of the picture-noun type or not) involves logophoricity. According to Kuno, the use of English reflexives is governed, besides syntactic constraints, by a number of nonsyntactic constraints, such as speech act empathy hierarchy, topic empathy hierarchy, and awareness condition. It is not only English reflexives that are sensitive to empathy, but reflexives in other languages (e.g., Japanese, Korean, and Turkish) as well. As far as English reciprocals are concerned, Kuno suggests that they are typically used to encode situations where there is active interaction of the participants and where the participants are aware of each other's involvement in the situation.

A somewhat different analysis of English reflexives, although in some ways related to Kuno's, is the discourse-oriented approach of Zribi-Hertz (1989). According to Zribi-Hertz, a serious problem with the mainstream government and binding treatment of reflexives is that its assumptions about English reflexives are based on sentences in isolation. When one considers discourse (see *Discourse*), it becomes clear that nearly all of those assumptions are inadequate. English reflexives cannot introduce new participants into discourse; that is, they must be bound, but not necessarily in their governing category (and with 1st and 2nd person reflexives the antecedent need not be explicit). Zribi-Hertz introduces the semantic/pragmatic concepts of '(minimal) subject of consciousness,' and 'domain of point of view.' The subject of consciousness is the participant whose thoughts or feelings are conveyed in a given portion of discourse; this concept is related to Kuno's notion of logophoricity. The domain of point of view is a portion of discourse characterized by one and only one narrative viewpoint. According to Zribi-Hertz, most of the syntactic constraints on reflexives that hold for simple clauses may be violated in discourse as long as the reflexive and its antecedent (the minimal subject of consciousness) occur within one and the same domain of point of view.

4. Historical Developments of Reflexives and Reciprocals

In sharp contrast to the studies of anaphora in the various generative syntactic theories stand typological studies of the constructions, the most detailed ones being Faltz (1985), Geniušienė (1987), and Kemmer (1992). These studies aim at developing typologies of the constructions (see Sects. 2 and 3 above), but they are also interested in the origin of the constructions and in their subsequent developments, in the range of functions that are acquired by constructions which at some time had (only) a reflexive or a reciprocal function.

Verbal reflexives typically develop from nominal reflexives: over time, an erstwhile nominal element loses its original properties and gravitates more and more to the verb. Nominal reflexives have, according to Faltz (1985), two main sources. One is emphatic pronouns; in the early stages of the development such pronouns are used to emphasize that an event is directed at the performer himself or herself rather than at any other participant, which is the more common kind of case. Over time, the emphatic function may be lost, and the elements acquire a purely reflexive function. (In some languages, English among them, the reflexives still have an emphatic function.) The other main source of nominal reflexives is nouns such as 'body' and 'soul'; over time, such nouns are grammaticalized into reflexive markers.

Reciprocal markers often develop from reflexives. In many languages, the reciprocal and the reflexive functions are marked in the same way; Imbabura Quechua is one such language:

Wambra-kuna riku-ri   -rka.   (11)
child   -PL see -RECM/REFM-PAST.they
'The children saw each other/themselves.'

It is not uncommon for a language to have more than one nonpossessive reflexive and/or reciprocal construction. In such cases, the two or more constructions are not (fully) synonymous: as discussed by Haiman (1983) and Kemmer (1992), there is a direct correlation between, on the one hand, the degree of structural separateness of a RefM or a RecM (e.g., an independent element vs. an affix) and its phonological size (in terms of the number of syllables), and, on the other hand, the degree of conceptual independence of the participants involved in the situation being encoded and/or the degree of conceptual independence of the relations that hold among the participants: greater structural separateness and greater phonological size are associated with greater conceptual independence, and lesser structural separateness and smaller phonological size are associated with lesser conceptual independence.

Both reciprocals and, especially, reflexives, tend to acquire a number of other functions, more or less directly related to the source functions. The range of functions that reflexive and reciprocal markers may develop are discussed in detail in Geniušienė (1987) and in Kemmer (1992). The following brief survey of the functions that reflexives and reciprocals may develop is not exhaustive; it contains only those kinds of developments that are relatively common.

As mentioned above, reflexives often develop into reciprocals. They also develop into middle-voice markers, as in Lithuanian:

Mes   su -si   -jaudinome dėl   atsitikim-o.   (12)
we.NOM PFV-'REFM'-excited   because of incident-GEN
'We got excited because of the incident.'

(The distinction between reflexives and the middle voice is not a sharp one; rather, the two categories merge into one another. Furthermore, different linguists may define the two categories in different ways.)

Reflexive markers sometimes develop a 'deagentive' function: they are used to encode spontaneous events, events not attributed to any external agency, as in French:

La   porte s'   -est fermée   (toute seule). (13)
ART door 'REFM'-AUX close.PASS PARTCP all   alone
'The door closed (by itself).'

Closely related to the spontaneous-event marking function is a range of functions that can be loosely characterized as 'passivizing.' In both the spontaneous-event and the passivizing functions, the subject of the sentence encodes the entity undergoing the event; the difference is that in the former no external agent is implied, whereas in the latter there is an agent, implied or expressed. The following are examples of an agentless passive from Northern Paiute (Uto–Aztecan) and an agented passive from Romanian:

Nopi na   -a'taa -'kɨ -'ti yaʔa.   (14)
house 'REFM'-sit.PL -CAUS -PRES here
'Houses are put up here.'

Casa   s   -a   construit   de un englez. (15)
house.DET 'REFM'-PERF build.PASS PARTCP by an Englishman
'The house was built by an Englishman.'

Originally reflexive markers can also develop a 'depatientive' function: the event is directed at a patient, but the patient is not encoded. Such sentences typically express general or habitual situations: the event is directed at any entity of a certain kind, as in see the next example from Georgian:

ʒaɣl -i i   -kbin -eb -a   (16)
dog -NOM 'REFM'-bite -THEM -it
'The dog bites.'

Reciprocal constructions are used in a number of languages to signal joint involvement of two or more participants in an event, as in the example from Ainu:

Tun   newa u   -rešpa wa okai ruwe ne.   (17)
two people LOC 'RECM'-live PROF dwell PART PART
'They were living there together.'

And like reflexives, reciprocals may also acquire a depatientive function, as in To'aba'ita (Austronesian):

Roo wane kero kwai -labata'i.   (18)
two man they.DU 'RECM'-harm
'The two men harm (others).'

In many languages, clauses that contain a reflexive or a reciprocal construction exhibit reduced transitivity, even if they contain verbs that are otherwise transitive (see *Transitivity*). When the reflexive or the reciprocal markers have some additional, nonreflexive, nonreciprocal uses, it is sometimes suggested that they have a core function of detransitivization. On the other hand, one can argue that such reduced transitivity is a reflection of the semantics of the reflexive and the reciprocal constructions. Prototypical reflexive and prototypical reciprocal situations are neither like prototypical intransitive nor like prototypical transitive situations: although they contain an agent and a patient, the two are not (fully) distinct from each other; in a sense, they can be regarded as members of one set. This intermediate status of reflexive and reciprocal situations may be reflected in their encoding: clauses with reflexive and/or reciprocal constructions may be intermediate between (fully) intransitive and (fully) transitive clauses.

Bibliography

Chomsky N 1981 *Lectures on Government and Binding.* Foris, Dordrecht

Faltz L M 1985 *Reflexivization: A Study in Universal Syntax.* Garland, New York

Geniušienė E 1987 *The Typology of Reflexives.* Mouton de Gruyter, Berlin

Haiman J 1983 Iconic and economic motivation. *Lg* **59**: 781–819

Kemmer S E 1992 *The Middle Voice: A Typological and Diachronic Study.* Benjamins, Amsterdam

Kuno S 1987 *Functional Syntax: Anaphora, Discourse and Empathy.* University of Chicago Press, Chicago, IL

Langendoen D T 1978 The logic of reciprocity. *LIn* **9**: 177–97

Lebeaux D 1983 A distributional difference between reciprocals and reflexives. *LIn* **14**: 723–30

Rosen C G 1981 The relational structure of reflexive clauses: Evidence from Italian (Doctoral dissertation, Harvard University)

Zribi-Hertz A 1989 Anaphor binding and narrative point of view: English reflexive pronouns in sentence and discourse. *Lg* **65**: 695–727

F. Lichtenberk

Register in Literature

'Register' describes variation in language according to use. It captures the intuition that there are functionally distinct varieties of language in such contexts of situation as sport, science, or advertising. Such variation contrasts with variation by user, or dialectal variation. Literary texts are often characterized by an allusiveness to nonliterary registers. This makes relevant the social meanings of the language alluded to, deploying its context into the text. Such 'reregistration' (Carter and Nash 1983: 129) is arguably central both to intertextuality (see *Intertextuality*) and the literariness of literary texts. The question remains open whether literature itself defines a register.

1. Register as Meaning Potential

Although register is sometimes used loosely in sociolinguistics, stylistics, and applied linguistics to label a 'way of speaking,' the term itself is particularly associated with the systemic–functional school of linguistics and with the functionalist stylistics associated with that school (for references see Birch 1989: 25–29, 139–45; Birch and O'Toole 1988: vi–ix; 1–11). Thus, the notion finds its place within the linguistics of M. A. K. Halliday and his associates and has undergone considerable development as a technical term. In its early use a situation type was claimed to determine uniquely frequencies of linguistic forms, producing, appropriately to the situation, a characteristic textual pattern of superficial lexical and grammatical items (see Halliday, et al. 1964: 87–98). It is worth noting at the outset that register has always been a probabilistic entity and therefore is, like 'dialect,' vague in the absence of quantifiable situational parameters. It nevertheless remains an intuitively valuable analytic tool (see *Dialect and Dialectology*).

In *Language as Social Semiotic* (Halliday 1978) the concept of register has a role in a much more comprehensive sociological linguistics. The strength of this theory is that it connects text to the social system and the context of culture. A text is an interactive semantic process (see *Text*). It is interpreted as an instantiation of meanings, semantic choices from the totality of potential contrasts of meaning encoded in grammar but which originate in social life. An analyst can interpret these social meanings and their historical–ideological context of culture in any text. Literary and nonliterary texts are the same in this respect.

We begin with the social system, since it is here meanings are made. The multidimensional sources of human significance are interactively created and exchanged in semiotic systems (see *Structuralism and Semiotics, Literary*). This 'making of meaning' occurs in social institutions and their recurring social contexts or situation types. Such situations are themselves semiotic constructs—we can recognize them and what they 'mean' within our culture. Each type has three dimensions relevant to potential meanings (1):

field = social activity performed
tenor = social roles enacted
mode = the role of language in the situation. (1)

'Mode' includes both channel (written, spoken, etc.) and genre (literary, 'narrative,' 'lyric,' etc., and nonliterary, 'interview,' 'casual conversation,' 'argument,' etc.) (see also *Genre*). The genres, or rhetorical norms, available in a culture precode language to perform the social activities and roles of each situation type and thus enable language to play the constitutive part which the social system demands of it as regards 'field' and 'tenor'.

The language system functions in these contexts of situation and, Halliday argues, it has been shaped to do so. 'What can be meant' falls into three functional domains which serve the three aspects of situations. Language functions (2):

ideationally = to represent experience
interpersonally = to enact social relationships
textually = to create text relevant to situations. (2)

Each function interprets the 'meaning potential'—'what can be meant'—in a given situation type. Out of the whole range of potential semantic contrasts, speakers statistically enact only *some* in a situation. This situationally constrained set of options is a register; 'the necessary mediating concept that enables us to establish the continuity between a text and its sociosemiotic environment' (Halliday 1978: 145). By analyzing these meaningful choices, as realized in the grammar and lexis instanced in a text, we can interpret its register and thus how the text is functioning to both enact and create a social situation (see *Functional Relations*).

2. The Interpretation of Text

The above theory provides a framework for the statement of ideational, interpersonal, and textual meanings. It is the task of linguistic analysis to analyze such patterns of encoded choice. But a reader's interpretation also involves contextualization of textual patterning at a higher level. This process is relative to the reader's social positioning, critical practices, and ideological interest within the context of culture. Some 'higher level semiotics' of the culture (see

Sect. 1 above) become relevant. A literary text, produced and consumed in situations within the social institution of 'literature,' also makes relevant a 'literary universe of discourse' and 'literary norms and assumptions' including the body of other literary and literary critical texts. It is the job of the linguist to describe this process of interpretation—how a text might be understood. And although subjective relativity and hence indeterminacy of readings is normal, it is also assumed that there is some community of the plausible which is replicable across readers based on common linguistic and cultural resources (Halliday 1971; Birch 1989; see *Interpretation*).

There is no mechanical procedure for interpreting, merely various heuristic practices. However, some textual patterns are prominent. If this prominence figures in interpretation in terms of higher level semiotics, then it is seen as 'motivated prominence' or 'foregrounding' (Halliday 1971; see also *Foregrounding*; *Style: Definitions*).

The analyst approaches foregrounded patterns first of all in terms of the choices they exhibit according to the functions of language. How is a world represented (see *Representation*; *Mind-style*)? How does the speaker reveal him or her self and manipulate the addressee? How does the 'texture of the patterning relate it relevantly to itself, its cohesion, and to its contexts of situation and culture, its coherence in terms of higher level semiotics (see *Cohesion and Coherence in Literature*)? The analyst intertwines description with higher level interpretation, each guiding the other.

Most analyses concentrate on the 'representativeness' of a text world in terms of the semantics of processes and participants (see *Representation*). Halliday (1971) studies Golding's *The Inheritors* in this way and contrasts the represented world of a Neanderthal community with that of early man. In an influential article, Burton (in Carter 1982: 194–214) subjects a passage from Plath's *The Bell Jar* to a similar analysis and pointedly interprets the foregrounded representation in terms of the higher level semiotic of feminism. Two articles which survey this approach are Kennedy (in Carter 1982: 83–99) who analyzes Conrad's *The Secret Agent* and Joyce's *Two Gallants*, and Simpson (1988) where the opening of Le Carré's *The Little Drummer Girl* is treated. Much of this analytic work has a usefully pedagogic orientation (see Carter 1982, especially the Introduction: also Brumfit and Carter 1986; Carter and Simpson 1988). In the work of Fowler (1981; 1986) we find emphasis on all three functional domains but increasingly on the interpersonal dimension of literary texts, an orientation he explicitly connects to the dialogism of Bakhtin (see *Dialogism*, see also as regards the interpersonal, Weber in Carter and Simpson 1989: 95–111; Toolan in Birch and O'Toole 1988).

3. Sovereignty and Reregistration

The functional patterning of a text is also interpreted in terms of the field, tenor, and mode of its context of situation. The situations enacted provide another route upwards to higher level meanings.

In literary texts such contextualization is on two levels (Halliday 1978: 146). On the first level, the text is related to the social situation of its *own* production and consumption. One can talk of the 'field' of verbal art, the 'tenor' of the authorial presence (the 'implied' author and reader) and the

genre, the conventions of which preshape and enable these. This is the context of literary theory and the sociology of literature. Halliday (1978: 145–50) provides such a context for a Thurber fable. The second level is produced by a general feature of the first level. In literary texts, the immediate social environment does not determine the form, except via its genre. Compare this with a practical situation like buying a bus ticket where the language actually achieves the buying and this determines what is meant. By contrast, the literary text 'creates its own immediate context of situation'; the text is 'self-sufficient' (Halliday 1978: 140–46). By deploying a pattern from *anywhere* in the language, the author recreates that situation and its higher level meanings and thus a virtual reality, the text world, through language. For example, deployment in written mode of the register of casual speech 'creates' a virtual situation in which inferable 'personae' spontaneously speak.

Carter and Nash (1983) label this feature of literary texts 'sovereignty.' They write, 'this denotes the self-supporting capacity of the text, its power to generate and develop a pattern of meaning, without reference to externals and without requiring of its readers any prior knowledge other than the common stock of experience' (Carter and Nash 1983: 130). This generic displacement from the exigencies of immediate demands permits a literary text to utilize any register and paradoxically, through its very self-sufficiency, to integrate the social meanings made outside the literary universe of discourse into the literary text. This process is termed 'reregistration' (Carter and Nash 1983: 129). The imported meanings both add an extra layer of contextual meaning to the text (a form of equivalence not noted by Jakobson 1960) and the allusive register items take on new meanings or interpretative potential in the new text. Reregistration is an important contributor to the characteristic polysemy or semantic density of literary texts (Carter and Nash 1983: 120, 140). This register identification across texts is one important dimension of intertextuality (see *Intertextuality*).

Carter (in Steele and Threadgold 1987: 442) illustrates reregistration by demonstrating the language of the travel brochure or geography book in a work of fiction and cites the use of journalistic and historical forms in Rushdie's *Midnight's Children* and *Shame*. Auden's employment of 'officialese' in *The Unknown Citizen* is cited by Carter and Simpson (1988: 22; see also Fowler 1981: 29–32 for an analysis of the registers of bureaucracy). O'Toole (in Birch and O'Toole 1988: 12–30) demonstrates the interaction of two registers in Reed's *Naming of Parts*. Carter and Nash (1983: 129) point out how even a single technical expression like 'double indemnity' from the register of insurance when deployed as the title of a crime novel takes on a new relevance and generates an extra layer of meaning in that literary context. Simpson (1988: 12ff) investigates reader responses to the Le Carré passage mentioned above (Sect. 2). He finds that 'the basic novelistic format has been overlaid by elements of a tourist–travelogue register' and his informants recognize this as well as the text genre as 'thriller–spy novel' (see Simpson 1988 for further references to examples of reregistration).

4. Issues and Outlooks

Is literature itself a register? This is the issue of literariness (see *Literary Language*). We ask whether the functioning of language in literary situations itself generates characteristic patterns of choice. Some sources talk as if this was the case (see Halliday 1983: xi). Others adamantly deny it (Halliday in the foreword to Birch and O'Toole 1988: vii; Simpson 1988).

Reregistration suggests that literary situations do not constrain authorial options because linguistic patterns from any situation can be deployed. If register is a probabilistic 'linguistic' pattern of semantic options, then all patterns are unpredictably equiprobable in a literary text. However, it has recently been claimed that such deployments, producing 'register mix,' are a characteristic of many texts. O'Toole writes ' . . . texts are not simply 'instances' of register but institutionally determined, multi-registerial discourses . . . ' (Birch and O'Toole: 111–25). Hudson (1980: 49) sees register as the output of a speaker's internalized norms. In this respect, a speaker's utterance would convey, like a dialect or accent, that particular mix of social meanings he or she opted for out of a multiplicity of norms, perhaps in a situation of normative conflict or lack of focus. The statistical realization of this register mix would precisely convey that mix of meaning.

In spite of sovereignty and reregistration, it is clear that literary texts do function in first-level social situations, those in which they are produced and consumed, and these must somehow relate to their linguistic patterns. The normative nonlanguage factor that relates situation to text patterns is not register but genre. It is there that we find the normative dimension of literariness (see *Genre*).

It is also through genre, as a contingent historical part of situations, that the language itself is related upwards to the social institutions (education, publishing, literary criticism, etc.) and social practices (methods of reading, generic conventions, etc.) that construct literariness with respect to its function in societies (see Fowler 1981; Kress, in Birch and O'Toole 1988: 126–41). Pointing downwards to language choice, the genre specifies those sociohistorical clusters of text pattern that are recognizably 'literary,' for example, Simpson's 'basic novelistic format' above. Such a text will mix and interweave reregistered items and generic texture in a rich brew which exhibits literariness, no feature of which is found only in literature. This 'pattern of patterns' functions to enable the inferential methods of reading which have evolved in literary institutions, which in turn function ideologically in some historical context of culture. It is a matter of terminology, but the first level generic features of literary texts might be seen as registerial, although paradoxically the whole 'mix' cannot, because of reregistration.

The main recent research in social semiotics integrates it with other contemporary trends. Some relates register to broader discursive practices and links functionalist stylistics to poststructuralist thought, Foucault in particular (see Halliday in Birch and O'Toole 1988: 31–44; Halliday 1987); Threadgold in Steele and Threadgold 1987: 549–97; Threadgold in Birch and O'Toole 1988: 169–204; see also *Foucault, Michel*). Another trend is towards the critical analysis of language, ideology, and power (see Kress in Birch and O'Toole 1988: 126–41; see also *Criticism, Linguistic; Discourse Analysis and Literature; Ideology*). Social semiotic approaches to literature can also be closely related to discourse and pragmatic approaches in that all equally approach literary texts as a use of language in context (see *Literary Pragmatics; Discourse Analysis and Literature*).

See also: Genre.

Bibliography

Birch D 1989 *Language, Literature and Critical Practice*. Routledge, London
Birch D, O'Toole M (eds.) 1988 *Functions of Style*. Pinter, London
Brumfit C, Carter R (eds.) 1986 *Literature and Language Teaching*. Oxford University Press, Oxford
Carter R (ed.) 1982 *Language and Literature: An Introductory Reader in Stylistics*. Allen and Unwin, London
Carter R, Nash W 1983 Language and literariness. *Prose Studies* **6(2)**: 123–41
Carter R, Simpson P (eds.) 1988 *Language, Discourse and Literature*. Unwin Hyman, London
Fowler R 1981 *Literature as Social Discourse*. Batsford Academic, London
Fowler R 1986 *Linguistic Criticism*. Oxford University Press, Oxford
Halliday M, McIntosh A, Strevens P 1964 *The Linguistic Sciences and Language Teaching*. Longmans, London
Halliday M 1971 Linguistic function and literary style: An inquiry into the language of William Golding's *The Inheritors*. In: Chatman S (ed.) *Literary Style: A Symposium*. Oxford University Press, New York
Halliday M 1978 *Language as Social Semiotic*. Arnold, London
Halliday M 1983 Foreword. In: Cummings M, Simmons R *The Language of Literature: A Stylistic Introduction to the Study of Literature*. Pergamon Press, Oxford
Halliday M 1987 Language and the order of nature. In: Fabb N, Attridge D, Durant A, MacCabe C (eds.) *The Linguistics of Writing*. Manchester University Press, Manchester
Hudson R 1980 *Sociolinguistics*. Cambridge University Press, Cambridge
Jakobson R 1960 Concluding statement: Linguistics and poetics. In: Sebeok T (ed.) *Style in Language*. MIT Press, Cambridge, MA
Simpson P 1988 Access through application. *Parlance: The Journal of the Poetics and Linguistics Association* **1(2)**: 5–28
Steele R, Threadgold T (eds.) 1987 *Language Topics: Essays in Honour of Michael Halliday*, vol. ii. Benjamins, Amsterdam.

W. Downes

Regressive Metonomy

'Regressive metonomy' is a disorder of spoken discourse involving elaborate definition, due to a specific psychiatric condition such as psychosis or dementia. It is classified as one of the symptoms of Ganser's Syndrome. In Whitlock's example (1967) the patient explained that the picture of a house which he drew was 'an amalgamation of building materials' and another patient when asked where to identify where he was replied 'the Department of Education in Illness.'

See also: Ganser's Syndrome.

Bibliography

Whitlock F A 1967 The Ganser Syndrome. *British Journal of Psychiatry* 113 (Jan–June): 19–29

Regular Negation

The term 'regular negation' is used to describe a class of words and phrases whose semantic behavior resembles that of anti-additive expressions. Typical examples are noun phrases of the forms *no* N, *nothing*, *none*, *neither* N, and *no one*, adverbs like *nowhere* and *never*, and the determiner *no*. Among the sentential connectives, the word *without* can be shown to belong to the class of regular negations, as can the expressions *not* and *it is not the case that*. The negative force of a regular negation is stronger than that of other negative expressions in that it satisfies the entire first law of De Morgan.

See also: Antiadditive Expressions; Negative Expressions.

F. Zwarts

Reichenbach, Hans (1891–1953)

The philosopher Hans Reichenbach was born in Hamburg, Germany. He attended the Technische Hochschule in Stuttgart, and the Universities of Berlin, Munich, and Göttingen. In 1915 he received his degree at the University of Erlangen with a thesis on probability.

His academic career commenced at the Technische Hochschule in Stuttgart in 1920. In 1926 Reichenbach was appointed at the University of Berlin. After the Nazis had seized power he escaped to Turkey. He taught at the University of Istanbul from 1933 until 1938, when he was appointed at the University of California. Reichenbach lectured at Columbia University (1947) and at the Sorbonne in Paris in 1952.

Reichenbach was closely associated with the development of logical positivism in the 1920s and 1930s. With Rudolf Carnap (see *Carnap, Rudolf*) he was editor of *Erkenntnis* (later called *Journal of Unified Science*), the official journal of this movement, which was initiated by the Vienna Circle.

Reichenbach's writings on probability and induction are considered classics. He made important contributions to the study of time, space, and geometry. He investigated the consequences of relativity theory and he was deeply involved in the conceptual difficulties of physical theory, especially in those surrounding quantum mechanics.

1. The Analysis of Conversational Language

Firmly rooted in the logistic tradition and inspired by the necessity of teaching in several languages, Reichenbach sought to adapt the methods of logic to the study of natural language. To this end he focused on the analysis of grammatical categories. He dismissed the categories of traditional grammar—nouns, adjectives, and verbs—in favor of the logical classifications function, argument, and logical term. In particular, he rejected the distinction between verbs and adjectives, the latter, he contended, being on a par with the tense of a verb.

According to Reichenbach, tenses of verbs belong to a class of descriptions in which the individual referred to is the act of speaking. On this so-called 'token reflexive' analysis, a present tense statement like *I see John* says that an event, the seeing of John, occurs now, where 'now' means the same as 'the time at which the token "I see John" is uttered.' Reichenbach called the temporal point of the token the 'point of speech' (S). In addition to this, Reichenbach introduced two other temporal points the 'point of event' (E) and the 'point of reference' (R), the latter providing a relatively fixed point about which the events related may be ordered, while the former is the temporal point at which the event being talked about took place.

According to this three-point structure the analysis of simple past is provided in the following table:

$$\text{———X———X———}$$
$$\text{E, R} \qquad \text{S}$$

The present perfect is analyzed as:

$$\text{———X———X———}$$
$$\text{E} \qquad \text{S, R}$$

and the past perfect is analyzed as:

$$\text{———X———X———X———}$$
$$\text{E} \qquad \text{R} \qquad \text{S}$$

The analysis of other tenses is in the same spirit.

Although severely criticized by some, Reichenbach's theory of tenses still is of great importance to current work on the subject.

Bibliography

Reichenbach H 1947 *Elements of Symbolic Logic*. Macmillan, New York

F. Veltman

Reinecke, John E. (1904–82)

Reinecke was born in Kansas, and died in Honolulu, Hawaii. He received his BA in education from Kansas State Teachers' College, 1925, moved to Hawaii in 1926, and taught at various high schools on the Big Island 1926–35. In 1932, he married Aiko Tokimasa, with whom he collaborated in studies of Hawaiian Creole English and in the labor movement. He moved to Connecticut in 1935. He received his PhD from Yale University in race relations in 1937, and traveled in the southeastern USA. He was appointed assistant professor of sociology at the University of Hawaii 1937–38, but not reappointed because of his liberal political views and active involvement on behalf of the labor movement. Reinecke taught at various high schools on Oahu 1939–48. He was dismissed with revocation of his teaching certificate, because of his political views and vigorous defense of the labor movement in his writings and actions. In 1951 he was reduced to selling the local newspaper, and arrested by the FBI in August 1951 and charged with violating the Smith Act. In June 1953, he and six others ('the Hawaii Seven') were found guilty of all charges and sentenced to five years in prison and fined $5000. While the case was on appeal, he was employed as a researcher and labor negotiator by Unity House in Honolulu (1958–68). His conviction was overturned by the Ninth Circuit Court of Appeals in San Francisco in 1958. In the mid-1960s, encouraged by Stanley Tsuzaki of the University of Hawaii, he returned to the study of the sociolinguistics of pidgin/creole languages. His teaching certificate was restored in 1976 by the Hawaii State Board of Education and he was exonerated from all charges. In 1978, by special act of the Hawaii legislature, an out of court settlement of $250,000 was paid to Reinecke and his wife for the violation of their constitutional rights.

During his 'first' sociolinguistic period, both his MA thesis of 1935 and his dissertation of 1937 represent remarkable pieces of work. Reinecke was one of the pioneers in founding the sociology of language as a border discipline between sociology and linguistics, and was the first researcher to apply these new insights to the sociology/linguistics of pidgin/creole languages. The 1937 dissertation is still eminently worthy of publication, with annotations. Until comprehensive surveys of pidgin and creole languages and linguistics half a century later to some extent superseded it, it was regarded as the most comprehensive and ambitious work ever attempted in the pidgin/creole field.

Reinecke's 'second' sociolinguistic period, from about 1965 to his death in 1982, resulted in the belated publication of his thesis, the compilation (with four collaborators) of the impressive annotated bibliography of pidgin/creole languages, and the founding and six-year editorship of the general newsletter of the field, the *Carrier Pidgin*.

He was a charismatic figure, on the Islands and elsewhere, a force to be reckoned with in the labor movement, the cultural history of Hawaii, the sociology of language, and pidgin/creole linguistics. 'John Reinecke embodied a rare combination of qualities: humanism, scholarship, and activism. The very act of studying pidgin and creole languages constitutes a form of social protest against the injustice done to their speakers. Hence, his work on behalf of the labor movement was not the only form of activism that he supported. Creole language study was the other horse pulling the cart. [For him,] labor and linguistics were thus complementary' (Gilbert 1987b: ix).

See also: Pidgins and Creoles; Pidgins and Creoles: Morphology; Pidgins, Creoles, and Change.

Bibliography

Gilbert G G (ed.) 1987 *Pidgin and Creole Languages: Essays in Memory of John E. Reinecke*. University of Hawaii Press, Honolulu, HI

Hancock I 1982 Focus on creolists (1): John E. Reinecke. *The Carrier Pidgin* **10(1)**: 1–2

Reinecke J E 1937 Marginal languages: A sociological survey of the Creole languages and trade jargons. (Doctoral dissertation, Yale University)

Reinecke J E 1969 *Language and Dialect in Hawaii: A Sociolinguistic History to 1935*. University of Hawaii Press, Honolulu, HI

Reinecke J E, Tsuzaki S M, DeCamp D, Hancock I F, Wood R E (eds) 1975 *A Bibliography of Pidgin and Creole Languages*. University of Hawaii Press, Honolulu, HI

Sato C J, Reinecke A T 1987 John E. Reinecke: His life and work. In: Gilbert G G (ed.) 1987

G. G. Gilbert

Reinisch, Simon Leo (1832–1919)

Simon Leo Reinisch has been called the 'father of Egyptology and Africanistics in Vienna' and is still considered as the pioneer and creator of Cushitic linguistics (see *Cushitic*; *Ancient Egyptian and Coptic*).

He was born on October 26, 1832 in Osterwitz, Styria, the fifth child of Josef Reinisch and his second wife, Elisabeth Spieler. At an early age he showed himself to be an especially gifted child and, after completing his schooling at the Gymnasium in Graz, in 1854 he was enrolled at the University of Vienna. There he began his involvement with Oriental languages, and in particular Ancient Egyptian, to which he was to devote the rest of his life. In 1864, three years after graduating, Reinisch was invited by Archduke Ferdinand Maximilian, the younger brother of the Emperor, to catalog his collection of Egyptian artifacts housed at Miramar. Shortly after that, when Maximilian became Emperor of Mexico, he sent Reinisch to Egypt to add to his collection, and then in 1866 called him to Mexico to be his private secretary. During the year that Reinisch spent there in Maximilian's service, he worked on the indigenous languages of Mexico, with a particular interest in pre- and early post-Columbian manuscripts, which he cataloged. He also prepared a number of grammars of Mexican languages, none of which, unfortunately, ever reached publication.

In 1868 he was appointed lecturer in Egyptian archaeology, and in 1873 Professor in Egyptian language and archaeology, at the University of Vienna. During this time he used his profound knowledge of a wide range of languages—Classical European, Ancient Oriental, and now Native American—to embark upon the question of the common origin of human languages. To his lectures on Egyptian and Coptic in Vienna he began to add unofficial classes on African languages, notably those of the Sudan and the Horn of Africa. The first of his African journeys took place in 1875–76, to the Bogos in Eritrea, to which he returned in 1879–80. The linguistic data that he collected during these journeys provided the material for over 20 books and articles, including several grammars, such as those of Bilin, Chamir, Quara, Kunama, Saho, and Beja, some of which are still the most extensive descriptions of these languages to date.

Reinisch had begun his studies at a time when modern linguistic science was in its infancy and much of the methodology that he used is necessarily now out of date. This is true not only in phonological analysis, but also in the fields of language comparison and historical linguistics. Nonetheless, the actual language data that Reinisch recorded are still invaluable.

Reinisch's service to the field of Oriental languages was recognized by his country when, first, in 1884, he was elected a full member of the Academy of Sciences and then, in 1899, he was awarded the title of Hofrat. He retired in

1903 to his estate in his native Styria, where he died on December 24, 1919.

Bibliography

Mukarovsky H G (ed.) 1987 *Leo Reinisch—Werk und Erbe.* Österreichische Akadamie der Wissenschaften, Vienna
Zaborski A 1976 Cushitic overview. In: Bender M L (ed.) *The Non-Semitic Languages of Ethiopia.* African Studies Center, Michigan State University, East Lansing, MI

D. L. Appleyard

Relational Grammar

Relational grammar (RG) is a theory of grammar developed primarily by David Perlmutter and Paul Postal. In this theory grammatical relations are taken to be primitive. The theory is multistratal. In a passive clause like *Tom was seen by Fred*, *Tom* is a direct object in the initial stratum which advances to subject in the final stratum displacing the initial stratum subject *Fred*.

1. Basic Notions

RG recognizes the following grammatical relations: subject, direct object, indirect object, and a number of oblique relations such as locative, instrumental, and benefactive. Subject, direct object, and indirect object are called terms and with the obliques they form the following hierarchy:

$$\text{subject} \quad \text{direct object} \quad \text{indirect object} \quad \text{obliques} \qquad (1)$$
$$1 \qquad\qquad 2 \qquad\qquad 3$$

The terms are often referred to by their position on the hierarchy, a subject being 1, a direct object 2, and an indirect object 3. 1 and 2 are called nuclear relations, and 2 and 3 are collectively object relations.

Clause structure is represented by networks of arcs. An arc is a curved arrow joining a tail node and a head node. Each arc bears a label for a relation and one or more coordinates indicating the stratum or strata at which the relation is held. The structure of the active clause (2a) is shown in (2b). (The lowercase c stands for coordinate and the subscript numeral indicates the level or stratum. P stands for predicate.)

Fred saw Tom   (2a)

(2b)

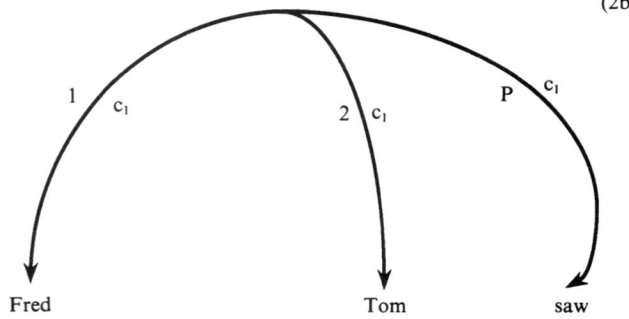

Fred   Tom   saw

The structure of the corresponding passive (3a) is displayed in (3b):

Tom was seen by Fred   (3a)

(3b)

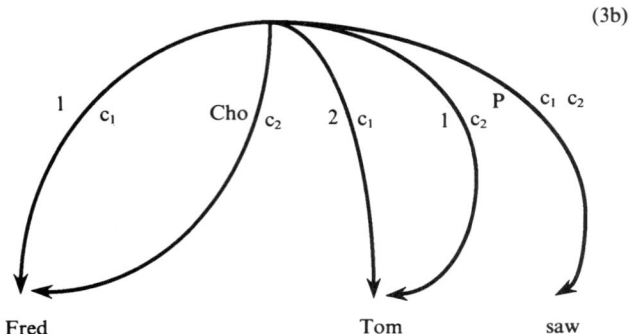

Fred   Tom   saw

Example (2b) indicates that the active clause is interpreted as having a single stratum in which *Fred* holds the subject relation, *Tom* the direct object relation and *saw* the predicate relation. The passive equivalent (3a) has two strata. As can be seen from (3b), the initial stratum is the same as the sole stratum of the active clause, but the second and final stratum involves revaluations. The initial 2 *Tom* advances to 1 and forces the initial 1 *Fred* to demote to *chômeur* (Cho). The word *chômeur*, which is French for unemployed person, denotes the relation held by nominals that are displaced from term status (1, 2, or 3). *Fred* in (3a) lacks properties of the corresponding term. It is an optional, peripheral prepositional phrase unable to control verb agreement.

Relational networks are difficult to read when more than two strata are involved and it is common practice to use instead a stratal diagram with one arc for each relation and 'horizontal arcs' to mark off the strata. Here is the stratal diagram equivalent of the relational network in (3b):

(4)

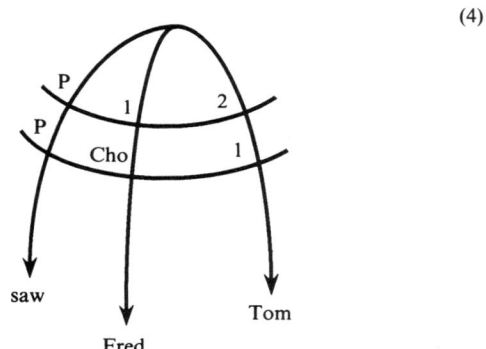

saw   Fred   Tom

In early RG the assignment of initial grammatical relations was made in accordance with a principle known as the universal alignment hypothesis whereby agents, experiencers, and cognizers were taken to be initial 1s, patients and themes to be initial 2s, and recipients initial 3s. This hypothesis in its strong form has been abandoned, but it remains generally true that agents are taken to be initial 1s and patients or themes initial 2s. The alignment principle can be seen at work in the treament of the two constructions used with *give* in English.

The construction with *to* is held to reflect initial grammatical relations directly while the double object construction is interpreted as involving the advancement of an initial indirect object to direct object. The relational networks for (5a) and (5b) are given in (6a) and (6b) respectively:

Fred gave a book to Tom (5a)

Fred gave Tom a book (5b)

(6a)

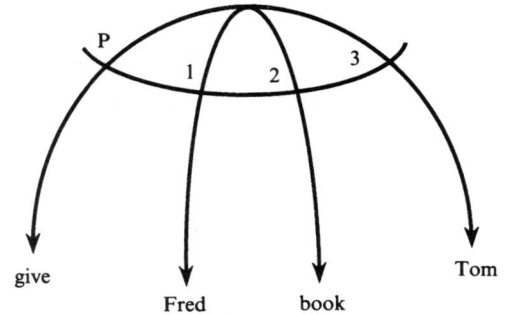

(6b)

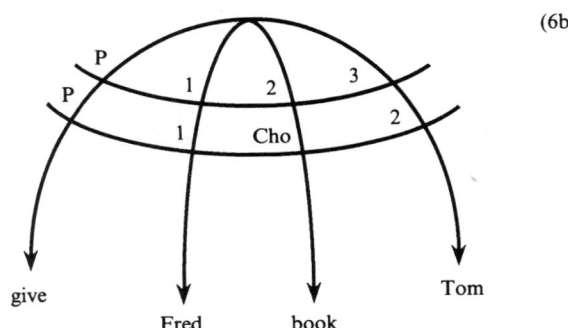

Some syntactic evidence for the interpretation given in (6b) lies in the fact that the putative 2 can be advanced to 1 via passive. Correspondence with (5b) produces *Tom was given a book by Fred*. The relations borne by the nominals in the three strata of this passive are displayed in (7) which is a stratal chart. Each column shows the career of a nominal through the strata. The stratal chart is a convenient substitute for relational networks and stratal diagrams:

Tom was given a book by Fred (7)
```
3      2      1
2      Cho    1
1      Cho    Cho
```

In some varieties of English one can have a passive of the form *A book was given Tom by Fred*. This can be interpreted as the result of 2–1 advancement (passive) with 3–2 advancement in a subsequent stratum:

A book was given Tom by Fred (8)
```
2      3      1
1      3      Cho
1      2      Cho
```

However, the analysis presented in (8) is controversial within RG. Bickford (1987) seeks to constrain RG theory by not allowing 3–2 advancement to follow 2–1 advancement since he finds no language where such a configuration is needed. He points out that there is little evidence to show that nominals like *Tom* in (8) are direct objects and suggests that they may be indirect objects that are not flagged (marked) as such.

The relational network is unordered. Surface structure order is handled by linearization rules which are normally based on final grammatical relations. The basic word order of English, for instance, can be specified as: 1–P–2–3–nonterm.

RG recognizes a class of overlay relations which can be held in addition to the central relations (1, 2, 3, obliques, and *chômeur*). These include topic, overweight, focus (illustrated in (23a, b)), relative, and question (see *Topic, Focus, and Word Order*). In the relative clause of *I saw the book which you wrote*, the pronoun *which* would bear the 2 relation and the overlay relation of relative. The linearization rules would place relative first in the clause.

2. Relational Laws

RG does not allow unconstrained revaluation. In order to characterize language as narrowly as possible, RG proposes well-formedness conditions on revaluations including the following:

(a) Stratal Uniqueness Law. There can be only one dependent bearing a particular term relation in a particular stratum.

(b) Final 1 Law. Every final stratum must have a subject. This does not mean there must be a surface subject. In *Go away!* there is a second person final 1 that is deleted in surface structure.

(c) Oblique Law. A dependent bearing an oblique relation bears that relation in the initial stratum. In other words, no revaluations to oblique.

(d) Motivated *Chômage* Law. *Chômeurs* are not created spontaneously, but as the result of advancement, ascension (see Sect. 6.2), or dummy birth (Sect. 5.5).

(e) *Chômeur* Advancement Ban. A *chômeur* cannot advance.

Here is a summary of licit revaluations:

Advancements	Demotions	(9)
2–1	1–2	
3–1	1–3	
Oblique-1	1-*Chômeur*	
3–2	2–3	
Oblique-2	2-*Chômeur*	
Oblique-3	3-*Chômeur*	

3. Motivation

RG began as a reaction to transformational grammar in which subject and direct object were defined in terms of structural configuration, the subject being the relation held by the noun phrase immediately dominated by the sentence node and the direct object being the relation held by the noun phrase immediately dominated by the verb phrase node (10). In such a system subject and object are derived entities, whereas in RG they are undefined primitives. An important argument put forward by Perlmutter and Postal (1983) in support of RG as opposed to transformational grammar concerned the universal characterization of the passive. They claimed that RG could characterize the passive universally in terms of the advancement of 2 to 1 from a transitive stratum, whereas an attempt to capture the universal character of the passive in structural terms would have to cope with language particular differences. In Tzotzil, for instance, active and passive have the same word order whereas in English the agent/experiencer and patient/theme change positions. In Russian the *chômeur* appears in the instrumental case whereas in English it appears in a prepositional phrase.

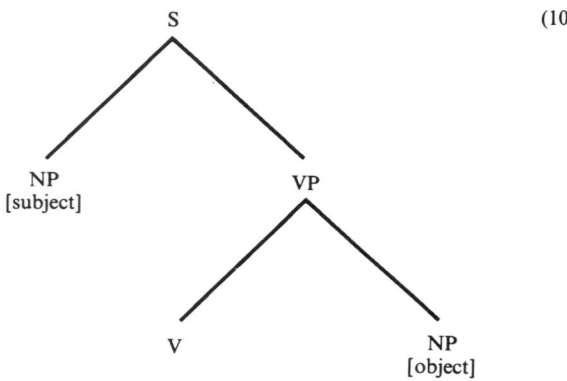

(10)

4. Arc Pair Grammar

Arc pair grammar (APG) is an offshoot of relational grammar developed by Paul Postal and David Johnson in the late 1970s (Johnson and Postal 1980). Example (11) is the APG relational network for the passive sentence *Tom was seen by Fred* previously given as (3a):

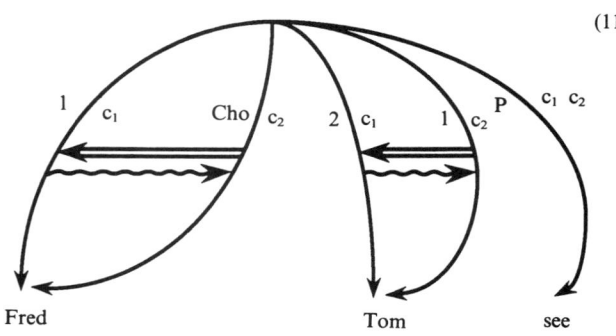

(11)

Two notions peculiar to APG that are shown in (11) are the sponsor relation and the erase relation. The initial 1 is said to sponsor the Cho arc. This is indicated by the wiggly arrow. The Cho arc on the other hand erases the initial 1 arc, i.e., replaces it at a later stratum. The erase relation is indicated by a double arrow. Example (11) illustrates that the initial 2 sponsors the final 1 and the final 1 erases the initial 2. The initial 1 is referred to as the predecessor of the Cho arc; conversely the Cho arc is the successor of the initial 1 arc.

5. Some Clause-internal Revaluations

5.1 Unaccusatives

RG distinguishes intransitive subjects that are initial 1s from intransitive subjects that are initial 2s. In English one can form a pseudo-passive with verbs like *sleep, dream, ski,* and *jump* but not with verbs like *exist, melt,* and *vanish*:

The bed was jumped on by the children (12)

*The bed was existed in by the children (13)

RG attributes the difference to a difference in initial stratum relations. Predicates like *jump* are analyzed as having an initial 1 and predicates like *exist* as having an initial 2. The former group are called unergative predicates (a stratum with a 1 but no 2 is unergative); the latter group unaccusative (a stratum with a 2 but no 1 is unaccusative). With

unaccusative predicates the initial 2 advances to 1 in accordance with the Final 1 Law (Perlmutter and Postal 1984: 85):

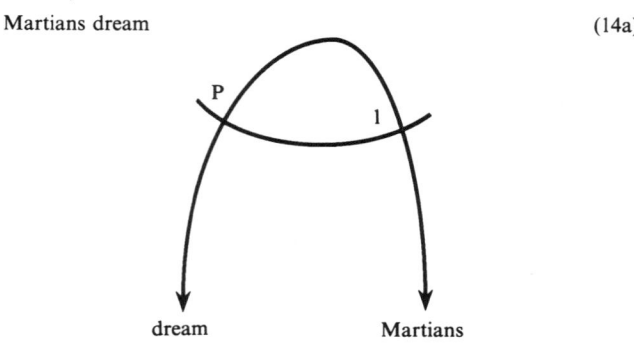

(14a)

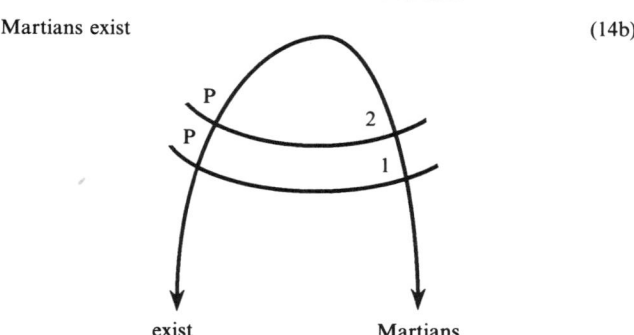

(14b)

The failure of unaccusative predicates to allow pseudo-passives is attributed to the 1 Advancement Exclusiveness Law (1AEX) which limits advancements to subject to one per clause. The relational network for the pseudo-passive, it is argued, would have 2–1 advancement plus the advancement of an oblique to 1. Here is a stratal chart showing the analysis of *The bed was existed in by the children*.

2	Loc	P	(15)
1	Loc	P	
Cho	1	P	

children	bed	exist

Rosen 1984, developing earlier work of Perlmutter, demonstrates that in Italian intransitive predicates fall into two classes with respect to at least three separate criteria. Verbs like *arrivare* 'to arrive,' *venire* 'to come,' and *partire* 'to leave' conjugate with *essere* 'to be' in the compound tenses; allow the proclitic *ne* 'of it,' 'of them' as in *Ne sono venuti tre* (of-them are come three) 'Three of them came,' and appear in absolute constructions like *Partiti gli amici, Giovanni si è addormentato* 'The friends having departed, Giovanni fell asleep.' On the other hand verbs like *dormire* 'to sleep,' *telefonare* 'to telephone,' and *tacere* 'to be silent' conjugate with *avere* 'to have,' do not allow the proclitic *ne*, and do not appear in absolute constructions. The first group are interpreted as unaccusative, the second group as unergative. The behavior of the putative unaccusative initial 2s parallels the behavior of initial 2s in transitive strata. The proclitic *ne*, for instance, can be used to refer to an initial and final 2 as in *Ne ho visti tre* (of-them I-have seen three) 'I saw three of them.'

5.2 Antipassive and 2–3 Retreat

In a great number of languages there are two-place intransitive constructions which are a regular alternative to the transitive construction or peculiar to certain predicates. There are two analyses available in RG which involve interpreting such constructions as having an initial transitive stratum. If there is evidence that the nonsubject complement is an indirect object, then the intransitive construction can be interpreted as reflecting 2–3 retreat. If the nonsubject complement is neither a 2 nor a 3, then it can be considered a *chômeur*. The following pair of sentences (16) is from Yup'ik Eskimo. Example (16a) is a transitive sentence, and (16b) the intransitive counterpart. In this dialect the detransitivized construction is used to express a nonspecific patient, as here, or it is used in the negative (Blake 1990: 41):

Qimugte-m neraa	neqa	(16a)
dog-ERG eat:3s:3s	fish	
'The dog ate the fish.'		

Qimugta ner'uq neq-mek		(16b)
dog eat:3s fish-ABL		
'The dog ate fish.'		

In the transitive sentence (16a) the subject is marked by the ergative case and the direct object is in the unmarked absolutive case. In the intransitive counterpart the subject is in the absolutive and the erstwhile direct object in the instrumental and hence a candidate for interpretation as a *chômeur*. However, the Motivated Chômage Law (Sect. 2) specifies that a dependent cannot go into *chômage* spontaneously. Postal's solution to this problem is to analyze sentences like (16b) as follows (Postal 1977):

1	P	2	(17)
2	P	Cho	
1	P	Cho	
qimug-	ner-	neq-	

In the second stratum the initial 1 demotes to 2 and pushes the initial 2 into *chômage*. In the final stratum the 2 advances to 1 in accordance with the Final 1 Law.

The construction in (16b) as analyzed in RG is called antipassive, but a note on terminology is in order here. The term antipassive in the general literature is usually used to cover detransitivized constructions in ergative languages, but in RG a distinction is made between 2–3 retreat (see (23b)) and antipassive and the term is not restricted to ergative languages.

5.3 Inversion

In some languages one finds nominals marked like indirect objects which exhibit subject properties. This happens with a verb like Italian *piacere a* 'to please to' as in (18):

A Giorgio piace Roma	(18)
to George pleases Rome	
'George likes Rome.'	

For such a predicate RG supplies an 'inversion analysis.' The experiencer is taken to be an initial 1 that demotes to 3 and the theme is taken to be an initial 2 that advances to 1 in accordance with the Final 1 Law:

1	2	P	(19)
3	2	P	
3	1	P	
Giorgio	Roma	piacere	

Some evidence for the analysis is provided by the fact that

the inversion nominal (*Giorgio* in (18)) behaves like a subject in that it can control the missing subject of various nonfinite constructions. In (20) *Giorgio*, the subject, controls the missing subject of the infinitive *far(e)*. In (21) it is the putative inversion nominal that controls the missing subject of *lasciar(e)* (adapted from Perlmutter 1982):

Giorgio mi ha rimproverato tante volte da farmi paura.
George me has reproved so:many times to make:me fear
'George rebuked me so many times that he scared me.' (20)

A Giorgio è talmente piaciuta una compagna d'ufficio da lasciarci.
To George is so pleased a companion-of-office to leave:us
[lit.] 'To George was so pleasing an office co-worker that he left us.'
'George was so taken with a girl at the office that he left us.' (21)

This is significant when one considers that an 'ordinary indirect object' (initial and final 3) does not have these control properties. RG is able to distinguish between indirect objects that are initial 3s and those that are initial 1s.

5.4 Dummies

Nonreferring nominals like *it* in *It rained* and *there* in *There's a fly in the soup* are treated as dummies and do not appear in the initial stratum but have a *birth* in a later stratum. Here is an analysis of *There's a fly in the soup* (22). Note that *be* is taken to be an unaccusative predicate so *fly* is an initial 2. The dummy is introduced in the second stratum as a 2. It pushes the initial 2 into *chômage* in accordance with the Stratal Uniqueness Law and then advances to 1 in accordance with the Final 1 Law:

(22)

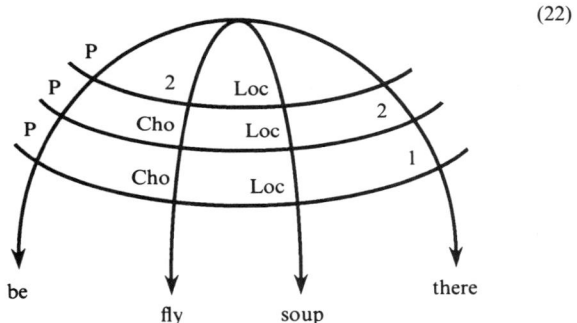

6. Some Multinode Analyses

6.1 Cross-clausal Multiattachment

In a sentence like *Rosa will go to buy the meat*, *Rosa* appears in the main clause, but is also understood to be the subject of the dependent verb. In early transformational grammar *Rosa* would have appeared as the subject of the nonfinite clause in deep structure and been deleted under identity with the controlling nominal in the governing clause by a transformation known as 'equi noun phrase deletion.' In RG *Rosa* would be multiattached. Here is an example from K'ekchi (23). The example illustrates two points: cross-clausal multiattachment (*Rosa* is a 1 in both clauses) and a clause-internal multiattachment arising from the fact that *Rosa* heads an overlay arc (focus) as well as a central relation arc (1). The fact that *Rosa* is focused is apparent from its position before the verb in what is a verb–object–subject language (Berinstein 1985: 137–38):

Lix Rosa ta:-øxic chi lok'oc re li tib	(23a)
Rosa FUT-3ABS-go PREP buy:INF DAT the meat	
'It's Rosa who will go to buy the meat.'	

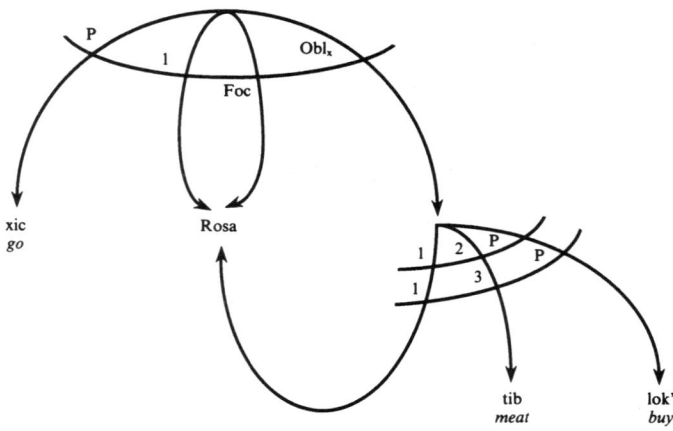

6.2 Ascension

The verb *seem* can take a subject that is sensitive to the selectional restrictions of a dependent verb rather than to *seem* itself. For such predicates an 'ascension' or raising analysis is used. In *Fred seems to work* (24), for instance, *Fred* is taken to be an initial stratum subject of *work* that ascends to become a dependent of *seem*. *Seem* itself is taken to be an unaccusative predicate with a clause as initial 2:

Fred seems to work   (24a)

(24b)

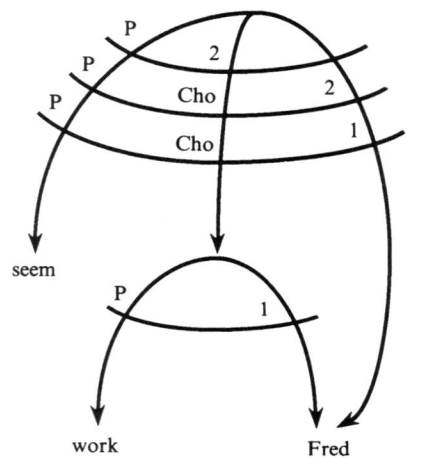

When *Fred* ascends it takes on the relation of the dependent out of which it ascends in accordance with the Relational Succession Law (ascendees assume the grammatical relation of their host).

Ascension analyses are also posited for sentences like *I expect the glass to fall* where *glass* ascends to become the final 2 of the governing clause, and also for sentences with predicates such as *be tough*, *be easy*, etc., as in *John is easy to please*. This would be analyzed as involving the ascension of *John* from initial 2 of *please* to second stratum 2 and final stratum 1 of *be easy*.

Besides cross-clausal ascension RG also posits ascension out of possessor phrases. Consider the following pair of sentences (25) from Stoney (Frantz 1981:30):

Ma-thiha n-uzazach   (25a)
my-foot 2s-wash
'You washed my foot.'

Thiha ma-n-uzazach   (25b)
foot 1s-2s-wash
'You washed my foot.'

In (25a) the possessor is expressed as a proclitic or prefix to the possessed, whereas in the synonymous or nearly synonymous (25b) the erstwhile possessor is expressed as a direct object realized via a prefix on the verb. RG seeks to relate pairs like this in the following way. Sentence (25a) would be taken to reflect initial stratum relations directly with the first person POSS(essor) a dependent of the H(ead) *thiha* 'foot.' Example (25b) on the other hand would be interpreted as reflecting the ascension of the possessor out of the possessor phrase into the clause proper. This analysis is displayed in (26). Note that the ascendee takes on the relation borne by its host (namely direct object) in accordance with the Relational Succession Law and pushes the initial direct object into *chômage* in accordance with the Stratal Uniqueness Law.

(26)

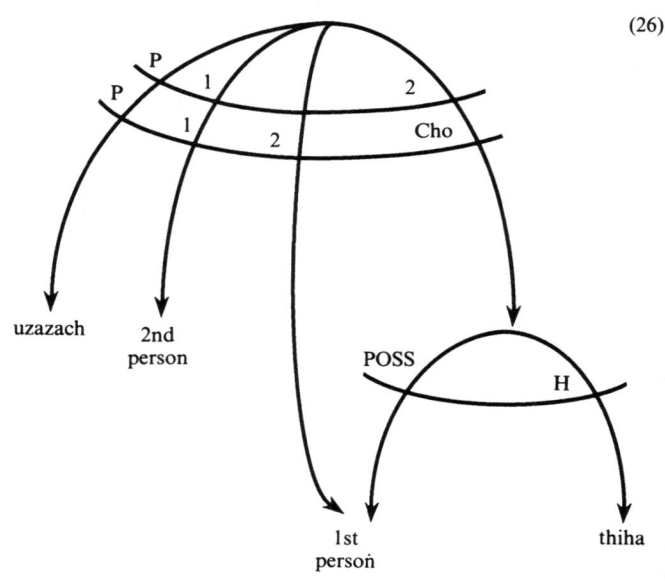

7. Clause Union

If the synonymous sentences (27a and b) are compared one can see that while (27a) contains two clauses, (27b) has amalgamated the two, as evidenced by the position of the clitic pronouns which are proclitic to the finite modal *deve* though they represent arguments of the infinitive *spiegare*:

Ugo deve spiegar-te-lo.   (27a)
Ugo must explain-thee-it

Ugo te lo deve spiegare   (27b)
Ugo thee it must explain
'Ugo must explain it to you.'

RG provides an analysis in terms of 'clause union' which is applicable here. (27a) is given a biclausal analysis and (27b) is given a biclausal analysis in the initial stratum, but one in which there is a union in a later stratum. The analysis of (27b) is given in (28):

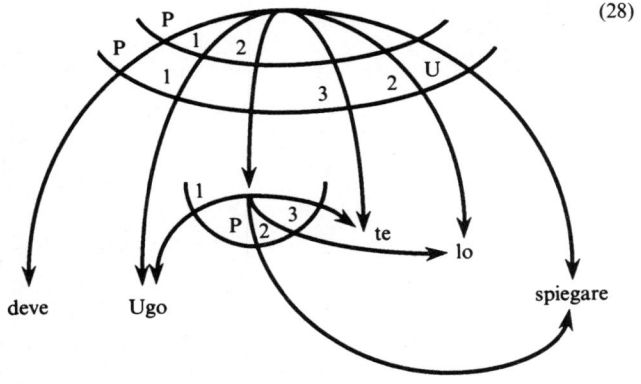

(28)

Ugo is an initial 1 in both the upstairs (matrix) and downstairs (embedded) clauses (multiattachment). In the second stratum, the union stratum, *te* and *lo* ascend into the higher clause. *Spiegare* ascends to become a union predicate which can be considered a predicate *chômeur* and indeed, in the analysis of Davies and Rosen presented below, this notion is used. Essentially such an analysis provides for the dependents of a downstairs verb to ascend and become dependents of an upstairs verb leaving the downstairs verb stripped. It has the advantage that it is applicable in cases where the upstairs and downstairs verbs are not even adjacent.

Most of the examples of clause union in the literature concern 'causative clause union.' In Italian, for instance, the verb *fare* 'to make' is used to form the causative of verbs as illustrated in the following (Davies and Rosen 1988: 71) where the position of *mi*, a final 3 expressing the recipient of *regalare*, is indicative of union:

Il babbo mi ha fatto regalare una torta da Nino   (29)
the daddy me has made give   a   cake by Nino
'Father made Nino give a cake to me.'

RG also extends biclausal analyses to morphological causatives. The following example (30) is from Georgian (Davies and Rosen 1988: 71):

Mamam   Ninos   miacemina   torti čemtvis   (30)
father:ERG Nino:DAT he:caused:give:her:it cake me:for
'Father made Nino give the cake to me.'

The biclausal analysis is shown in (31). Note that *mama* is an initial 1 in the upstairs clause. This means that the initial 1 of the downstairs clause must be revalued. As can be seen

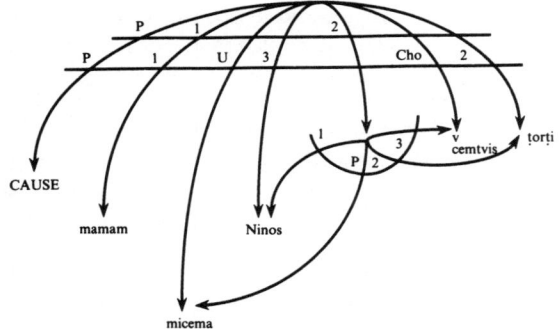

it revalues to 3 which in turn means that the downstairs 3 must revalue. It becomes a *chômeur* as in (31).

Davies and Rosen 1988 have also proposed a new analysis in which unions are interpreted as multipredicate uniclausal constructions. Example (32) displays the new analysis of (27b) above; the older analysis is in (28):

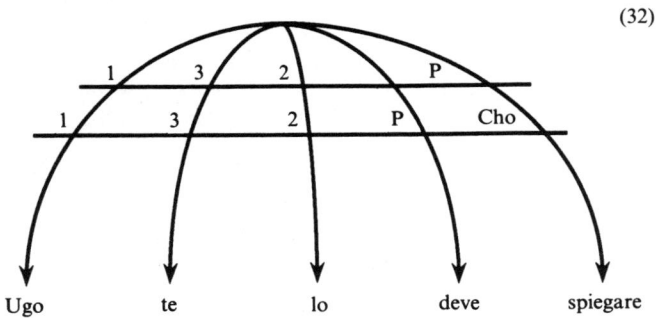

(32)

In this analysis there is only one clause node and the inner clause consisting of the lexical verb and its dependents occupies the first stratum. The modal predicate is introduced in the second stratum and puts the inner predicate in *chômage*.

Here is the uniclausal analysis (33) of the Georgian sentence given above as (30) with a biclausal analysis as (31):

		P	1	2	3	(33)
P	1	Cho	3	2	Cho	
CAUSE	mama	micema	Nino	torti	čem	

The inner clause consists of *micema* and its dependents. The causative predicate is introduced in the second stratum which puts the lexical predicate in *chômage*.

There are a number of arguments in favor of the new analysis. Under the old analysis violations of the Motivated *Chômage* Law occur. Consider *čem* 'me' in (31). It heads a *chômeur* arc in the second stratum, but it does not head a term arc in an earlier stratum with the same tail, i.e., in the same clause. According to the Motivated *Chômage* Law it should. This deficiency is made good under the new analysis as can be seen from (33) since *čem* does head a term arc in an earlier stratum of the same clause.

A second argument concerns the asymmetry between union and ascension. In ascension the ascendee takes over the relation of the host pushing the host or the remnant thereof into *chômage* under the Relational Succession Law (see Sect. 6.2). However, in unions it is the raised nominals that are put in *chômage* when they encounter occupied relations. Under the new analysis there are no raised nominals or ascendees in clause union.

8. Overview

RG is one of a number of theories that began as a reaction to transformational grammar, but whereas some saw transformational grammar with its deep, intermediate, and surface structures and a proliferation of transformations as too unconstrained and moved in the direction of surface structure only models, Perlmutter and Postal retained multilevel analyses and indeed allowed rules to make reference to any level (global rules). The distinctive feature of RG is that it deals in grammatical relations as primitives. Its limitation up to the present has been that it generates relational networks consisting of predicates, central relations, and overlay relations but not surface structures. With a few exceptions, some within the framework of arc pair grammar, it has not spelt out the realization in terms of linear sequences of morphemes. It has not dealt with the internal structure of noun phrases, for instance.

Given the large number of competing theories the future of RG must be in some doubt, but it is certain that RG has made a contribution of permanent value that is translatable into other frameworks. This would include the explication of the hierarchical nature of grammatical relations, the unaccusative hypothesis, and the notion of *chômage*.

Bibliography

The principal sources are two volumes of papers:
> Perlmutter D (ed.) 1983 *Studies in Relational Grammar 1*;
> Perlmutter D, Rosen C (eds.) 1984 *Studies in Relational Grammar 2*.

A general overview is provided in Blake B J 1990 *Relational Grammar*.

Berinstein A 1985 *Evidence for Multiattachment in K'ekchi (Mayan)*. Garland, New York

Bickford J A 1987 Universal constraints on relationally complex clauses (Doctoral dissertation, University of California)

Blake B J 1990 *Relational Grammar*. Routledge, London

Davies W, Rosen C 1988 Unions as multi-predicate clauses. *Lg* **64**: 52–88

Frantz D 1981 Grammatical relations in universal grammar. Indiana University Linguistics Club, Bloomington, IN

Johnson D, Postal P 1980 *Arc Pair Grammar*. Princeton University Press, Princeton, NJ

Perlmutter D 1982 Syntactic representation, syntactic levels, and the notion of subject. In: Jacobson P, Pullum G (eds.) *The Nature of Syntactic Representation*. Reidel, Dordrecht

Perlmutter D (ed.) 1983 *Studies in Relational Grammar*, vol. 1. University of Chicago Press, Chicago, IL

Perlmutter D, Postal P 1983 Toward a universal definition of the passive. In: Perlmutter D (ed.) 1983

Perlmutter D, Postal P 1984 The 1-Advancement exclusiveness law. In: Perlmutter D, Rosen C (eds.) 1984

Perlmutter D, Rosen C (eds.) 1984 *Studies in Relational Grammar*, vol. 2. University of Chicago Press, Chicago, IL

Postal P 1977 Antipassive in French. *Lingvisticae Investigationes* **1**: 333–74

Rosen C 1984 The interface between semantic roles and initial grammatical relations. In: Perlmutter D, Rosen C (eds.) 1984

B. Blake

Relative Clauses

The typical case of a relative clause is a clause which modifies a noun. For example in the phrase *the man who is old*, the clause *who is old* modifies the noun *man*, specifying which man we are talking about. We can see that a relative clause resembles an attributive adjective, by comparing the phrase *the old man*, where the adjective *old* modifies the noun *man* by specifying which man we are talking about. Part of the interest of relative clauses is that they can be built in many different ways; even in English there is a variety of different ways of building relative clauses. In linguistic research, relative clauses have often functioned as core data in claims about fundamental syntactic issues.

1. Relative Clauses in English

A relative clause acts as a modifier by restricting the semantic domain covered by a syntactic constituent (typically a noun). For example, in *the man who I know very well*, the relative clause *who I know very well* restricts the semantic domain of *man*, restricting it from any man down to specifically the man who I know very well. A construction of this type can also be called a 'restrictive relative clause' to distinguish it from another construction which in English is almost identical in form but different in function, a 'non-restrictive relative clause' (also called appositive relative clause). This fact shows that like other modifiers, relative clauses can be 'imitated' in syntactic position and form by constituents which do not modify in the sense of restricting reference but simply add further information. An example of a nonrestrictive relative clause is found in *John, who I know very well*; here, the relative clause *who I know very well* does not restrict the semantic domain of *John*, but simply adds extra information. This article will follow common practice in using 'relative clause' informally to mean 'restrictive relative clause.'

Keenan and Comrie (1977) and Comrie (1981) define 'relative clause' (= restrictive relative clause) in terms of its function, and their definitions, slightly changed here, will be used in this article. A restrictive relative clause specifies a set of objects in two steps: (a) a larger set is specified, the domain of relativization, and (b) the domain is restricted to some subset of which a certain proposition (the 'restricting sentence') is true. In English the domain of relativization is expressed in surface structure by the head nominal (*man*), and the restricting sentence is expressed by the restricting clause (*who I know very well*). In some languages, such as Turkish, the restricting sentence is expressed by a noun phrase, which by this definition is therefore called the relative clause even though it is not syntactically clausal. This definition thus defines 'relative clause' in terms of its semantic function rather than its syntactic structure.

In a relative clause like *The man whose books I read* it is useful to distinguish and name the parts. Here the head is *man*, but it could include another modifier, so that *old man* could function as a head for a relative clause. The restricting clause is *whose books I read* (Keenan and Comrie find the restricting sentence or proposition by reconstructing this clause as *I read his books*). The fronted *wh*-phrase *whose books* can be called the relative phrase; there is no consistent term for this item, which in English can include *that* or a *wh*-pronoun like *who*. There is a gap after *read* where the object, which we would expect for a transitive verb like *read*, is missing. Keenan and Comrie suggest the term NPrel as the name for 'the NP in the restricting sentence that is coreferential with the head NP as the NP relativized on'; here the NPrel is the possessive pronoun *his*.

English relative clauses typically take a nominal head, which is the head of the noun phrase containing the relative clause. Nonrestrictive relative clauses can in addition take as heads many types of phrase including even verb phrases as in *John luckily escaped, which I unluckily didn't*, but restrictive relatives appear to take only nominal heads. More than one relative clause may be attached to a single head, as in (Jespersen's example) *Can you mention anyone that we know who is as talented as he is?* It is possible to extrapose a relative clause, as in *The man arrived yesterday that I wanted to introduce you to.*

Relative clauses found in English can be classified according to the presence or absence of various key components—

the relative phrase, the head, and tense. A relative clause without a relative phrase is called a bare relative clause or a contact clause, an example being *the man I like*. The object is the most common function to be relativized in this type of clause; dialects of English differ in whether they allow a subject gap in a bare relative, but these tend to be generally acceptable in existential sentences such as *there is a man wants to see you*. A relative clause which apparently lacks a head is called a free relative clause, also sometimes called a headless relative (though some argue that the head is present syntactically but phonologically empty, and hence that this is a misleading name). Examples include *I liked who I met* and *I like whoever I meet*; here there appears to be no head preceding the relative phrase *who/whoever* (analysis 1 below), though it has alternatively been argued (analysis 2 below) that *who/whoever* is not the relative phrase but is itself the head (followed by a bare relative):

I liked [NP   [s   who   I met]]   (1)
I liked [NP who [s   I met]]   (2)
        head   relative phrase

Finally we can classify relative clauses acording to their tense. There are various types of nonfinite relative clause in English, including the *-ing* participial type with a subject gap *the man reading the book*, the passive type *a vase broken by dropping it on the floor*, the *to*-infinitive type *a person to fix the washing machine*, and the *for-to* type *a problem for you to puzzle over*.

The presence or absence of key features is one type of distinction between relative clauses in English; another is the choice of relative phrase. English allows a wide range of relative phrases. These include most of the *wh*-words (with dialectal variation, for example in whether *what* can be used), as in *the place where I was born* or *the question why I was asked here*. A *wh*-word compounded with *ever* forms a relative phrase which can be used in free relatives, as in *whoever arrives first has to make the pasta*, or *eat whatever you like*, or *do it however you want* (*wh*-ever words are used also in '*wh*-ever adj' structures as in *whenever possible*). A *wh*-word inside a phrase can make that phrase able to function as a relative phrase, as in *the man whose mother I met* or *the place in which I was born*. Ross (1967) called this phenomenon 'pied piping,' using an analysis in which the *wh*-word is moved to the front of the sentence from the base-generated position inside the sentence, and when it moves it can take the surrounding constituents with it; the term 'pied piping' draws an analogy with the fairytale Pied Piper of Hamlyn taking the rats with him when he leaves the town. Ross demonstrated that pied piping could result in a sentence in which the *wh*-word is embedded very deeply in the relative phrase, and cited the example *reports the height of the lettering on the covers of which the government prescribes should be abolished*. Pied piping is subject to certain island restrictions, described by Ross, and Bresnan and Grimshaw add that pied piping does not occur in free relatives. Sometimes a preposition is both pied-piped and repeated in its place in the sentence. In older English a 'pied-piped' combination of 'preposition + *wh*-phrase' can be substituted by a compound with the structure 'where-preposition' (*in which* becomes *wherein*, etc.).

In addition to *wh*-words, certain conjunctions can act as relative phrases, most prominently *that*, as in *the man that I saw*. In southern standard English *that* is the oldest surviving relative phrase (from Old English) and was the most commonly used in Middle English; examples of *that* in early modern English include its use in nonrestrictives and with inanimate heads, but in these two contexts, *that* has been replaced by *wh*-words (partly under the influence of Latin-inspired traditional grammar). In addition to *that*, words like *as* and *but* can also act as relative phrases, as in the following examples from Jespersen (again dialects differ in acceptability of these): *such women as knew Tom*; *none but are shipwrecked*. In addition to these overt relative phrases, some syntacticians argue that there is also a relative phrase which is not phonologically realized. This null relative phrase would for example be found in the gap position at the front of a contact clause (in analysis 2 above); in this analysis, a relative clause would always have a relative phrase, overt or null. Some syntacticians argue that *that* is not itself a relative phrase but is simply a subordinating conjunction or complementizer and is accompanied by a null relative phrase, as in the following analysis:

I liked [NP the man [s that   [e]   I met]]
                  relative phrase

As a final comment on English relative clauses, it is worth noting that this is an area which has interested prescriptive grammarians, including issues such as whether *whom* should be used, whether a preposition can be 'dangled' (stranded) at the end of a sentence, and which relative pronoun should be used in restrictive and nonrestrictive relative clauses.

2. Relative Clauses in Other Languages

Few languages have been found which lack relative clauses, though Comrie (1981) cites the Australian language Warlpiri as a possible exception. As Keenan and Comrie point out, given their semantic definition which we are using here, relative 'clauses' are not always actually clauses. For example, the following Turkish relative clause is expressed syntactically by a noun phrase which is headed by a nominalized verb (nominalized with the suffix *diğ*) and has a genitive subject (*Hasan-ın*). The noun phrase which expresses the relative clause itself carries possessive morphology, and in effect 'possesses' its head *patates-i*:

[NP Hasan-ın Sinan-a ver -diğ-i] patates-i   yedim
    Hasan -of Sinan-to give his   potato-ACCUSATIVE I-ate
'I ate the potato that Hasan gave to Sinan'

Typological distinctions involving relative clauses include the position of the head relative to the clause, the grammatical functions within the clause which the NPrel can occupy, the extent to which the clause is nominalized, and whether the clause forms a constituent with its head. Lehmann (1984) provides an extensive crosslinguistic survey of relative clauses, while Peranteau, et al. (1972) is a seminal collection of papers on the analysis of relative clauses in many languages.

In English the head is outside the relative clause, and the clause follows the head; this type of clause can be called a postnominal relative clause. In some languages (e.g., Turkish) the clause precedes the head, and so can be called a prenominal relative clause. Tagalog is a language in which the clause is found in both prenominal and postnominal positions. There is however another possible relation between the head and the relative clause, which is that the head might be contained inside the relative clause which modifies it; clauses like this are called 'internally headed'; an example from Bambara is:

```
tye  ye    ne ye  no    min   ye san
man  PAST  I  PAST horse which see buy
'The man bought the horse that I saw'
```

This is classified as an internally headed clause because the apparent syntactic structure is:

```
tye  ye    [ne ye  no    min   ye ] san
man  PAST  I  PAST horse which see   buy
                   head
           subject object      verb
```

Comparing this with a simple sentence, we can see that *no* ('horse') fills the object position inside the sentence (where in English there would be a gap). Bambara is typical of languages which allow internally headed relative clauses in that it has an Object–Verb word order.

```
ne ye   no    ye
I  PAST horse see
'I saw a horse'
```

Crucially, in the relative clause structure *no* is also interpreted as the head modified by the relative clause (there is no external head, as there is in English, where *horse* would be the external head). We look at the syntactic analysis of internally headed relative clauses in Sect. 3.

Typically the internally-headed relative clause is treated as a nominal constituent (e.g., a noun phrase), as indicated morphologically by a relative marker, nominalizing suffix or case suffix. The internally headed relative clause is interpreted in a way similar to an externally headed clause (i.e., the S or nominalized S is interpreted similarly to a [NP head [S relative clause]] construction. The internal head may be marked as such, as in Bambara, where the relative marker *min* follows the internal head, or may not be marked, in which case ambiguity may arise if there is more than one NP inside the clause which could be interpreted as the head; an example of this ambiguity is the following Imbabura Quechua sentence which can mean either 'the town you are coming to is small' or 'the town you are coming from is small'; there is no indication in the clause to show whether the NPrel should be interpreted as 'from-place' or as 'to-place':

```
Kan shamu-shka         llajta-ka    uchilla-mi
you come-NOMINALIZER   town-TOPIC   small-VALIDATOR
```

Sometimes the head of the relative clause is represented by a full noun phrase both outside and inside the relative clause, thus appearing as a mixture of internally- and externally-headed relative. Clauses of this type are called correlatives (the term 'corelative' is also used); the following example is from Hindi:

```
[Ādmī ne       jis    cākū  se   murgī  ko
 man  ERGATIVE which knife with chicken ACCUSATIVE
 mārā thā], us   cākū  ko          Rām ne       dekhā
 killed    that knife ACCUSATIVE   Ram ERGATIVE saw
'Ram saw the knife with which the man killed the chicken'
```

Here, the NPrel is realized as a full NP *jis caku* inside the clause (as with an internally headed relative clause); but it is also realized as a full NP *us caku* outside and following the clause (as with an externally headed, prenominal relative clause). Lehmann (1986) distinguishes a type of clause

which he calls 'adjoined'; an adjoined relative clause is not a constituent with its head (incidentally, indicating again the difference between head of a relative and head in the X-bar sense). Lehmann characterizes the Hindi correlative as an 'adjoined' type of relative clause.

In English, a pronoun may be found in the place where we expect a gap, as in *the books which I don't remember who read them*; here, *them* fills an expected gap after *read*. The acceptability of these sentences varies according to dialect and register; they can be used as ways of getting around island constraints as in the quoted example, where a gap would be illegitimate because it violates the complex noun phrase constraint. Jespersen calls these 'exhausted relative clauses' and Sells (1984) names the pronoun an 'intrusive pronoun'; both terms indicate that the pronoun in English sentences of this kind is seen as somehow syntactically alien, a filler inserted as an aid to comprehension. Sells argues that this is distinct from the resumptive pronoun—another widely found type of gap-filling pronoun (as in the following Hebrew example), where the pronoun has a clear syntactic function, acting as an operator-bound variable:

```
ha'iš  še    pagasti  oto
the man that I-met    him
'the man that I met'
```

An NPrel can be chosen from some syntactic positions more easily than others; the subject position is generally the most accessible position for relativization from (i.e., the NPrel corresponds to the subject of the relative clause). Resumptive pronouns tend to be used for NPrel which are in less accessible positions, as Arabic demonstrates: a resumptive pronoun can be used in all grammatical positions except subject.

In some languages there is a morphological matching between the external head and the NPrel. Comrie (1981) gives as an example Persian, where the external head of the relative clause may be a subject in its own sentence, but if it is related to an NPrel in the relative clause which is an object, the upper subject may carry object marking (accusative case). Thus agreement between the upper subject and the lower object takes priority over grammatical function marking in the upper clause:

```
Zan-i-rā               [ke didid]      injā-st
woman ACCUSATIVE       that you-saw    here-is
'the woman that you saw is here'
```

In Ancient Greek, the matching works in the opposite direction: a genitive external head may lead the relative phrase in the relative clause also to take genitive case, even though it relates to a direct object NPrel.

3. Syntactic Theory and Relative Clauses

Relative clause constructions have been of interest in their own right and for the insights which they offer into the organization of the grammar. One example of more general insights involves syntactic islands. When syntactic islands were first identified in the mid 1960s, relative clause constructions offered some of the earliest examples; Chomsky's A-over-A constraint and Ross's complex noun phrase constraint both drew on the fact that a noun phrase can be extracted out of a verbal complement inside another noun phrase, but not out of a relative clause inside another noun phrase.

A second area in which relative clauses have offered more general insights is in their instantiation of a hierarchy of grammatical functions. Crosslinguistically, the NPrel in a restrictive relative clause can come from grammatical functional positions ranging from subject to 'object of comparison,' but which NPrels are acceptable varies from language to language. Keenan and Comrie (1977) showed that in a language the existence of one possible NPrel could usually be related to the existence of other possible NPrels. They showed this in two stages. First they argued that it was possible to identify a universal set of possible relative-clause formation strategies; a language could use one or more of these strategies. Then they showed that each strategy used by a language could be used to extract NPrels from one or more positions, and that where several NPrels were possible for a particular strategy, those NPrels formed a continuous subset of the following ordered set, which they called the 'accessibility hierarchy':

subject—direct object—indirect object—oblique argument NP—
genitive or possessor NP—object of comparison

To show how this works, consider English. Keenan and Comrie's relativization strategies are differentiated according to the position of the head (three options—before, after, or inside the clause), and according to whether the grammatical function of the NPrel is unambiguously indicated on the relative phrase (or some other element in the clause). Thus one relativization strategy in English is to construct a postnominal relative clause using a relative phrase like *who* (which does not by itself mark the grammatical function of the NPrel). Using this relativization strategy it is possible to relativize from subject position and from direct object position:

The man who saw you   (NPrel is in subject position)
The man who I saw   (NPrel is in object position)

A different relativization strategy ('English strategy 2') must be used for extraction from other positions; this involves the use of a preposition or a morphological change of the *wh*-word to indicate the grammatical function of the NPrel, as in:

The man who I gave it to   (NPrel is in indirect object position)
The man whose book I saw   (NPrel is in possessor position)

Keenan and Comrie's point is that a particular strategy picks out a continuous segment of possibilities along the hierarchy, which means that if it is possible to use 'English strategy 2' to relativize from indirect object and from possessor, it must also be possible to use it to relativize from oblique argument NP since this is between the other two on the hierarchy, and this is shown by the following example:

The box that I put the money in   (NPrel is oblique argument NP)

Similarly, since 'English strategy 2' cannot be used to relativize direct objects, we can predict accurately that it can also not be used to relativize subjects (i.e., neither objects nor subjects are relativized using a preposition, or a morphologically marked relative phrase). Keenan and Comrie argue that there is always a strategy which can be used to relativize subjects (which are the most accessible on the hierarchy). In addition to suggesting a hierarchical organization, Keenan and Comrie's findings are of more general interest in that they provide evidence for the existence of specific grammatical functions. For example, by showing that a relativization strategy in a language may distinguish between indirect object and oblique argument they demonstrate that these are potentially distinct grammatical functions in a language. Their account also provides strong evidence for the notion of subject, as well as for the special status of the subject (at the top of the hierarchy, and always relativizable). Keenan and Comrie address the issue of subject languages where the notion of subject is in some doubt, including Tagalog, ergative languages (like Basque), and 'topic' oriented languages (like Lisu), and suggest that the notion of subject is nevertheless useful here too. For example, they address the issue of Dyirbal relative clauses, where only absolutive NPs can be relativized, and ergative NPs cannot. They argue, in keeping with the accessibility hierarchy, that the absolutive NPs are the subjects in both transitive and intransitive sentences (going against the traditional analysis whereby absolute NPs in transitive sentences are interpreted as equivalent to object rather than subject). Revisions have been suggested to Keenan and Comrie's claims. Lehmann (1986) suggests that subhierarchies should be distinguished depending on whether the NPrel depends on a verb (e.g., a subject NPrel) or a noun (e.g., a possessor NPrel). Lehmann also points to certain tendencies: adjoined relative clauses (which are typically the least nominal) tend to allow relativization of the largest range of syntactic functions, and prenominal relative clauses tend to allow relativization of the smallest range. Maxwell (1979) suggests that while the hierarchy is basically correct, a better account is given by a different characterization of the strategies of relativization, which he bases on work by Givon.

Another area in which relative clauses appear to offer some more general insight is into the nature of appositive modifiers, of which nonrestrictive relative clauses are one example. English nonrestrictive relative clauses differ from restrictive relatives most obviously in that they are spoken with an intonational break (like parentheticals). In many languages, this is the only difference between the two (in some languages there is not even an intonational break). However, English nonrestrictive relative clauses in addition appear to show minor syntactic differences from restrictive relative clauses, and there have been many attempts to relate these syntactic differences to the difference in semantic function between the two types of clause. The syntactic differences include: (a) nonrestrictive relatives use a narrower range of relative phrases, being unable to use *that* or phrases where the *wh*-element is embedded and noninitial, so that while *whose mother*, is acceptable as a relative phrase in a nonrestrictive relative, *the mother of whom* is not; (b) nonrestrictive relatives escape weak crossover (leftness condition) effects which restrictive relatives are subject to, giving a distinction between *the man, who his mother loves, arrived yesterday* and **the man who his mother loves arrived yesterday*; (c) the nonrestrictive relative seems to be in some sense syntactically disconnected from its head; for example a negative polarity item (like *any*) in the nonrestrictive clause cannot be licensed by the determiner (like *only*) of the head: **only the tourists, who have any imagination, go to visit Sicily.* Various explanations have been given of the difference between the two types of clause. One type of account is to place the nonrestrictive relative clause higher in the phrase than the restrictive relative clause (e.g., at a higher bar-level in an X-bar system). An alternative, which is differently realized by different writers, is to say that the nonrestrictive relative is not syntactically a constituent of the noun phrase at some level of syntactic structure; parallel to parentheticals, some authors suggest that a nonrestrictive relative clause is in fact never syntactically part of the sentence which contains it, but that the relation is a discourse one. The issue of the difference between restrictive and nonrestrictive relative clauses, though it has been extensively discussed, is made problematic by several factors, which include the fact that English is one of the few languages ever cited in evidence, and even in English some have claimed that in actual usage the differences are lost; moreover, as Jespersen points out, it is sometimes difficult to decide whether a particular relative clause should be classified as restrictive or nonrestrictive.

Syntacticians have paid particular attention to the head of the relative clause, in two cases where it is not immediately clear that there is an external head. In free relatives, the issue is whether there is a head or not; in internally headed relatives the issue is whether there is an external head. For free relatives, Bresnan and Grimshaw (1978) argue that the *wh*-phrase is the external head and is not the relative phrase at the front of the relative clause; the relative clause is then interpreted as a contact clause; thus the structure is *I'll buy [NP what [S you're selling]]*. Among their evidence is the fact that the distribution of the free relative matches the category of the *wh*-phrase, that any subject–verb number agreement must involve the *wh*-phrase, and that there is no pied-piping; they argue on the basis of this that there is no movement to create the gap in a free relative (and show that for example in Tok Pisin, where there is no *wh*-movement, a pronoun fills in the gap in the clause). Opposite arguments have also been mounted that the *wh*-phrase is in fact the relative phrase, and that there is *wh*-movement in a free relative. The problem of the head in free relatives has troubled linguistics for a long time; Jespersen discusses alternative proposals by Onions and Sweet (and provides his own proposal, which is similar to that of Bresnan and Grimshaw). Turning now to internally headed relatives, typically these have been analyzed in the generative framework by giving them syntactic structures similar to externally headed relatives; for example, Speas (1990) suggests, discussing internally headed relatives in Navajo, that the internal head is moved at the level of logical form to become the external head.

In summary, relative clauses have provided insights into broader issues in linguistic theory and universal grammar, as well as presenting a range of interesting problems which are specific to the construction. Few of the questions raised by relative clauses have been answered definitively, and it seems likely that relative clauses will continue to offer a rich source of interest for future linguistic research.

Bibliography

Bresnan J, Grimshaw J 1978 The syntax of free relatives in English. *Linguistic Inquiry* 9: 331–91

Comrie B 1981 *Language Universals and Linguistic Typology*. Basil Blackwell, Oxford

Jespersen O 1928 *A Modern English Grammar on Historical Principles*, Part III. George Allen and Unwin, London

Keenan E L, Comrie B 1977 Noun phrase accessibility and universal grammar. *Linguistic Inquiry* 8: 63–99

Lehmann C 1984 *Der Relativsatz: Typologie seiner Strukturen, Theorie seiner Funktionen, Kompendium seiner Grammatik.* Narr, Tübingen

Lehmann C 1986 On the typology of relative clauses. *Linguistics* 24: 663–80

Maxwell D N 1979 Strategies of relativization and NP accessibility. *Language* 55: 352–71

Peranteau P M, Levi J N, Phares G C (ed.) 1972 *The Chicago Which Hunt: Papers from the Relative Clause Festival.* Chicago Linguistic Society, Chicago, IL

Ross J R 1967 Constraints on variables in syntax (Doctoral dissertation, Massachusetts Institute of Technology)

Sells P 1984 Syntax and semantics of resumptive pronouns (Doctoral dissertation, University of Massachusetts)

Speas M 1990 *Phrase Structure in Natural Language.* Kluwer Academic, Dordrecht

N. Fabb

Relevance

Grice's 'maxim of relation' (viz: 'be relevant') (see *Conversational Maxims*) has been elevated to the status of an overriding principle governing communication and cognition by Sperber and Wilson (1986; see *Pragmatic Principles*). The principle of relevance is at the center of their claim of a new approach to the study of human communication. 'Relevance theory' (RT) purports to be a unified theory of cognition to serve as a foundation for studies in cognitive science (see *Cognitive Science*). Relevance theory offers insights into, among other things, inferencing, implicature, irony, and metaphor (see *Irony*; *Metaphor*). Its refinements in the study of implicature are presented briefly in Sect. 5 below. The aims of RT are ambitious, but it does have some defects which limit its usefulness. The theory relies heavily on the explication of the workings of a formal deductive system for its substance, rests on restricted, asocial conceptions of communication, language-users, and their cognitive environments, and ignores developments in both discourse analysis and artificial intelligence (see *Discourse*; *Artificial Intelligence*; *Communication*).

1. The Principle of Relevance

Sperber and Wilson formulate the 'principle of relevance' as follows:

> Every act of ostensive communication communicates the presumption of its own optimal relevance.
>
> (1986: 158)

(See Sect. 2 below for an explanation of the term 'ostensive.') The term 'relevance' is used in a technical sense to refer to the bringing about of contextual effect. An utterance is only relevant if it has some contextual effect (see *Context*). In Sperber and Wilson's words:

> The notion of a contextual effect is essential to a characterization of relevance. We want to argue that having contextual effects is a necessary condition for relevance, and that other things being equal, the greater the contextual effects, the greater the relevance.
>
> (1986: 119)

There are varying degrees of relevance. Sperber and Wilson claim that there is an inverse correlation of effort and relevance. In other words, the more processing it takes to work out what a speaker intends by an utterance, the less relevant that utterance is. As various critics have pointed out, this begs the questions: 'relevant to what?' (e.g., Clark 1987) and 'relevant to whom?' (Wilks 1987).

2. Ostensive-inferential Communication

Ostensive and inferential communication (see *Inference*) are two sides of the same process; a process which, Sperber and Wilson argue, is achieved because of the principle of relevance. A communicator is involved in ostension; a communicator's audience is involved in inferencing. A communicator's ostensive action comes with a 'guarantee of relevance' (1986: 50), such that what makes the intention behind the ostensive act manifest to an audience is the principle of relevance.

3. Informative and Communicative Intentions

A distinction in RT, upon which Sperber and Wilson place considerable importance, is between, 'informative' and 'communicative' intentions, which underlie all communication. In the informative intention, a speaker (S) intends a hearer (H) to recognize S's intention to inform H of something: S intends to make manifest to an audience a set of assumptions (on 'manifestness' and 'assumptions,' see Sect. 4 below).

In the communicative intention, S intends H to recognize the informative intention; it is therefore a second-order informative intention.

4. Cognitive Environments, Assumptions, and Manifestness

Sperber and Wilson initially define assumptions as 'thoughts treated by the individual as representations of the actual world' (1986: 2). They give precedence to the cognitive function of language in RT. But a strength of it is its ability to include nonpropositional (see *Proposition*; *Propositional Attitudes*) and expressive (see *Expressive Power*) elements, to account for vague, ambivalent meanings or 'impressions,' which may not be verbally communicated. The authors account for explicitness of an informative intention in terms of the degree to which an assumption is made manifest. Before going into detail about degrees of manifestness, however, a fuller description of assumptions is needed.

Assumptions are composed of a structured set of concepts. A concept is located in the memory store (see *Memory: Organization*) and contains an address (its point of access in memory) and one or all of the following entries: encyclopedic, logical, and lexical (Sperber and Wilson 1986: 83; see *Lexicon*). The human information-processor (see Sect. 5.3 below) manipulates the conceptual content of assumptions. The processing device has access to assumptions from four sources: (1) direct perception; (2) decoding of the encoded utterances of others; (3) its own memory store, and (4) deduction from assumptions accessible from sources 1 to 3. Together these assumptions from four sources make up an individual's cognitive environment.

In Sperber and Wilson's model, H can infer S's assumptions on the basis of knowledge of S's cognitive environment. They define a cognitive environment as follows:

> A cognitive environment is merely a set of assumptions which the individual is capable of mentally representing.
>
> (1986: 46)

Differences in the cognitive environments of two people are simply differences in individual possession of facts, experience, and ability; people's stocks of assumptions vary according to their physical environments and cognitive abilities. On the basis of a complex of assumptions, H can infer the relevance of S's ostension. Sperber and Wilson argue that this capacity to infer relevance is the fundamental human information-processing activity. (They compare this human capacity to various nonhuman information-processing abilities, one of which is the instinctive ability of a frog to track insects.)

The authors account for variations in the strength of assumptions in terms of the degree to which they are made 'manifest' to an individual. An assumption actually 'entertained' by an individual is knowledge of which s/he has a mental representation (see *Representation*). Other assumptions are only potential; these are possible assumptions, which an individual may (but need not) have mental representations of, which are hence potentially part of his/her manifest knowledge. An individual's cognitive environment is all his/her manifest knowledge: 'An individual's total cognitive environment is the set of all the facts that he can perceive or infer: all the facts that are manifest to him' (1986: 39). The most strongly manifest (i.e., 'most readily assumable') assumptions are those derived directly from perceptual sources, and those with long processing histories. The weakest are assumptions that can only be derived with effort: potentially computable implications from entries in memory store, or deductions that can be made from other assumptions.

5. The Identification of Implicatures

In RT, the principle of relevance governs the recovery of implicatures; a speaker's expectations about how to be maximally relevant are the means by which implicatures can be worked out. The authors' exploration of implicature offers two useful innovations: a distinction between implicated premises and implicated conclusions, and an alternative to an untenably clearcut divide between determinate and indeterminate implicatures. Only the second of these innovations results from the elevation of the maxim of relevance to the status of an overriding principle.

6. An Asocial Model

In *Relevance*, human beings are viewed as information processors with an inbuilt capacity to infer relevance. This single capacity is assumed to be the key to human communication and cognition. Around this assumption, the authors build a model which they claim offers a unified theory of cognition, to serve as the foundation for an approach to the study of human communication. A drawback of the model, however, is its lack of any social element.

6.1 Individuals and Cognitive Environments

Relevance theory hinges on S's intention to inform and H's corresponding recognition of this intention. This recognition requires H to infer a connection between some action performed by S and S's intention in carrying it out; in other words, H constructs a teleological explanation for S's action (see *Teleological Explanations*). Teleology alone, however, is not enough for a theory of social action (see *Action Theory and the Production of Speech*; *Sociology in Language*). *Relevance* presents an intentionalist view of action (see *Intentionality*). In it, people are depicted as individuals who confront unique problems in communication. In the real world, however, people are social beings who are working within preexisting conventions (see *Convention*). This latter view of the language-user and the nature of communication is practiced in studies of discourse analysis, especially in certain later developments (e.g., Fairclough 1989; see *Discourse*; *Power and Language*).

In Sperber and Wilson's model, differences between people are depicted solely as differences between individuals' cognitive environments. These differences are assumed to stem from variations in physical environment and cognitive ability between people. Considerations of culture and society are notably absent in the characterization of individuals' cognitive environments. In *Relevance*, the authors work with a 'commonsensical' view of all individuals sharing essentially the same epistemological organization of the real world. This is not to say that Sperber and Wilson are claiming that the assumptions making up people's cognitive environments are necessarily facts; they insist that they are presenting a cognitive approach rather than an epistemological one. In this insistence, they are stressing that they are not concerned with the truth or falsity of assumptions. But even a cognitive approach must rest on some conception of epistemology; if this conception is not explicitly focused on, it will nevertheless be present but in an unreflective form.

The consequences of such disregard are serious. For if language analysts are to construct a teleological explanation for someone's action, they need to make assumptions about that person's knowledge structures. The analysts assume the actor's assumptions. Similarly, the hearer in Sperber and Wilson's model needs to make assumptions about the speaker's knowledge structures. The authors claim that H can infer (and therefore assume) S's assumptions on the basis of knowledge of S's cognitive environment. But they do not attend to how H might know (or make guesses at) S's cognitive environment. (For further discussion, see Mey and Talbot 1988.)

6.2 Assumptions and Manifestness

A cognitive environment is the total of an individual's manifest knowledge, a whole set of assumptions derivable from the four sources mentioned in Sect. 4 above. Within the framework given, there is no way of discussing any divergence of assumptions according to class, gender, or ethnicity. In the absence of any cultural perspective, the knowledge manifest to different individuals is largely the same (typical examples include knowledge of the weather, the pleasantness of sea air, and the price of cars). The effect is highly ethnocentric; one is left with the impression that everyone lives in the same kind of white, middle-class, educated world. While this may be true, to some extent, of the linguists and cognitive scientists comprising the authors' audience, it is a seriously inadequate provision of social context for a study of either communication or cognition (see *Pragmatics*). This ethnocentric bias is displayed particularly clearly by the authors' examples of derivable

assumptions that are weakly manifest (e.g., 'Chomsky never had breakfast with Julius Caesar') (1986: 40). Their ad hoc choice of unrelated facts known both to themselves and their readers for the potentially endless production of negative assumptions betrays an unsystematic approach.

As an alternative to the concept of mutual knowledge which they consider to be problematic (and which indeed has its own problems—see *Shared Knowledge*), Sperber and Wilson put forward the concept of 'mutual manifestness' of assumptions. They dislike mutual knowledge because, as they see it, such a concept relies on positing consciously held knowledge which S and H both, by definition, know for certain that they share. As they say, this degree of certainty is an impossibility, rendering the concept useless:

> Mutual knowledge must be certain, or else it does not exist; and since it can never be certain it can never exist.
>
> (1986: 19–20)

In order to provide a viable alternative to this excessively rigid and unsatisfactory concept of mutual knowledge, Sperber and Wilson suggest instead the 'mutual manifestness' of knowledge. Similarities in individuals' cognitive environments make mutually manifest assumptions possible. However, mutually manifest knowledge is itself a problem; it has little more to offer than the concept of mutual knowledge that it is intended to replace. As knowledge-which-is-there-to-be-mutually-assumed it is in principle no different from mutual knowledge (see Gibbs 1987a, 1987b for discussion). In the absence of any social element, with which to locate and specify kinds of knowledge that might be mutually accessible to different individuals, this is inevitable.

6.3 The Mind as Information Processor

In RT, thought processes are assumed to be exclusively matters of information processing by a 'device.' The human mind is conceived to be a 'deductive mechanism' which has the capacity to manipulate the conceptual content of assumptions from a range of sources (see Sect. 4 above) and no more than this. Sperber and Wilson operate with the same kind of reductionist conception of human mental processes as is found in transformational generative grammar, namely the 'black box' (see *Generative Grammar*; *Chomsky's Philosophy of Language*). This view of the mind severely limits the scope of human mental activity and precludes any sociocultural perspective on the individual's construction of knowledge. Sperber and Wilson's favorite metaphor for the human mind is the computer. They limit their object of enquiry accordingly to how the human mind functions as a computer, i.e., to human information processing.

7. Conclusion

Sperber and Wilson's basic premise is that 'Human cognition is relevance oriented' (1987: 700). Their aim in creating RT was to provide a unified theory of cognition for studies in cognitive science. Such a unified approach was eagerly awaited and anticipated as a major breakthrough. When *Relevance* appeared in print in 1986 it was favorably received in many places and has made some contribution to developments in pragmatics (in particular, in the identification of implicatures; see Sect. 5 above). It generated a good deal of debate in the late 1980s. From the perspective of the early 1990s, however, RT does not appear to have had much lasting influence or effect; nor has it proved to supply the unified theory that was anticipated.

See also: Communication; Representation; Discourse; Cognitive Science; Sociology in Language; Sociolinguistics; Pragmatics.

Bibliography

Clark H H 1987 Relevance to what? *Behavioral and Brain Sciences* **10(4)**: 714–15
Fairclough N 1989 *Language and Power*. Longman, London
Gibbs R W 1987a Mutual knowledge and the psychology of conversational inference. *Journal of Pragmatics* **11(5)**: 561–88
Gibbs R W 1987b The relevance of Relevance for psychological theory. *Behavioral and Brain Sciences* **10(4)**: 718–19
Mey J L, Talbot M M 1988 Computation and the soul (Review article of Sperber and Wilson's *Relevance*). *Semiotica* **72(3/4)**: 291–339
Sperber D, Wilson D 1986 *Relevance: Communication and Cognition*. Basil Blackwell, Oxford
Sperber D, Wilson D 1987 Precis of *Relevance: Communication and Cognition*. *Behavioral and Brain Sciences* **10(4)**: 695–754
Wilks Y 1987 Relevance must be to someone. *Behavioral and Brain Sciences* **10(4)**: 735–36

M. M. Talbot

Relevant Logic

An orthodox account of logical consequence requires that one proposition is a consequence of others if the latter cannot be true and at the same time the former false. This view would seem, however, to ignore any connection of relevance between the propositions involved (see *Entailment*). An alternative account, designed to explicate this notion of logical relevance of one proposition to another, was developed by Anderson and Belnap out of earlier work by Ackermann. It is called 'relevant,' or 'relevance,' logic.

1. Relevance

Anderson and Belnap focused on two aspects of relevance:

1.1 Meaning-connection

If one proposition entails another, there must, they said, be some connection of meaning between them. How can this be explicated in the context of modern formal logic? Anderson and Belnap concentrated initially on propositional logic, and within that on so-called first-degree entailments, entailments of the form A→B, where A and B contain no occurrences of the entailment connective '→,' but only truth-functional connectives '&' (and), '∨' (or), and '∼' (not). Belnap proposed a test of meaning-connection relevance in this context, that of variable-sharing. A necessary condition for A to entail B is that A and B (combinations of propositional variables) should share a variable (see *Truth Functions*; *Propositional Calculus*).

1.2 Derivational Utility

Variable-sharing can be criticized as over-technical and parochial, and difficult to generalize beyond propositional logic. An alternative criterion which Anderson and Belnap developed is based on the idea of the use of an assumption in a chain of derivations. Only what has actually been used in some essential way is relevant. However, what is essential is difficult to pin down. It cannot mean 'necessary,' given that they accept the validity of $(p{\rightarrow}q){\rightarrow}((q{\rightarrow}p){\rightarrow}(p{\rightarrow}q))$; and it must be restricted to occurrences or tokens, since they reject $p{\rightarrow}(p{\rightarrow}p)$.

2. Entailment and Relevant Implication

Anderson and Belnap's first interest was in the logic of entailment, E, which respects considerations of both relevance and necessity. Before long, however, a theory of a non-modal conditional connective was developed, called the calculus of relevant implication, R. In the early 1970s, it was discovered (by Maximova) that extending relevant implication by an S4-type modal connective, yielding the system $R^{\square}$, did not give a theory identical to that of entailment, and since then interest in the calculus E of entailment has waned in favor of R and $R^{\square}$ (see *Modal Logic*).

3. Semantics

3.1 Relational Semantics

At the end of the 1960s, relevant logic was well-worked out as a formal syntactic theory, but it had no real semantics. Following Kripke's lead in providing a set-theoretic semantical analysis of modal logic, several authors independently hit upon the way to provide a similar semantics for relevant logic (see *Kripke: Philosophy of Language*). The preferred version has settled on a relational semantics, in which the conditional '→' receives its truth-condition relative to a ternary relation of accessibility between worlds or indices: 'A→B' is true at x if B is true at z whenever A is true at y and $Rxyz$—where $Rxyz$ can be read as 'x and y are compossible at z' (see *Modal Logic*; *Formal Semantics*).

3.2 Other Semantic Analyses

The ternary relation $Rxyz$ obeys the same principles as a basic relation of spherical geometry: 'z lies within the minor arc of the great circle through x and y.' The worlds semantics also has an algebraic counterpart—the Lindenbaum algebra is a distributive lattice with a semigroup operation, called a De Morgan monoid, whose prime filters correspond to the worlds. By focusing on the semigroup operation ∘ and all the filters one can also develop an elegant operational semantics, whose truth clause for '→' reads: 'A→B' is true at x if and only if whenever A is true at y, B is true at $x∘y$.

4. Decidability

It was thought for some time that R (and E) were decidable, that is, that there was an effective method for testing for validity in them. No proof could be found, however, and eventually in the early 1980s Urquhart established their undecidability.

Perhaps the most famous thesis valid in classical logic but invalid in R and E is the inference from A ∨ B and ∼A to B, Disjunctive Syllogism. The corresponding rule form, that if A ∨ B and ∼A are in some theory T then so is B, is known as the Gamma conjecture for T. (γ was Ackermann's name for this rule in his forerunner of E.) E and R are Gamma-theories. Much work in the 1970s and 1980s focused on $R^{\#}$, effectively Peano arithmetic based on R.

To much surprise, this was found in 1987 not to be a Gamma-theory.

5. Quantified Relevant Logic

With the exception of the study of $R^{\#}$, much of the work on relevant logic has concentrated on the propositional fragment (indeed, in its first phase, the first-degree part—theses A→B where A and B contain no arrows—dominated discussion), perhaps in the belief that the extension to first order and quantifiers was relatively straightforward. In point of fact, there are two tricky problems here. The first concerns the correct analysis of *All As are B*. If it is represented as $(\forall x)(Ax \to Bx)$, with the '→' of relevant logic, while *Some As are B* remains as $(\exists x)(Ax \ \& \ Bx)$, then *Not all As are B* and *Some As are not B* are no longer equivalent. This is counter-intuitive. Second, straightforward extensions of the proof theory and semantics in fact result in incompleteness, as shown in Fine 1984. This was rectified in Fine 1988 by revising the semantics. Quantified relevant logic is still a fairly unstable theory.

See also: Predicate Calculus; Quantifiers; Formal Semantics; Deviant Logics.

Bibliography

Anderson A R, Belnap N D 1975, 1992 *Entailment*, 2 vols. Princeton University Press, Princeton, NJ
Dunn J M 1986 Relevance logic and entailment. In: Gabbay D M, Guenthner F (eds.) *Handbook of Philosophical Logic*, vol. III. Reidel, Dordrecht
Fine K 1988 Semantics for quantified relevance logic. *Journal of Philosophical Logic* 17: 27–59
Fine K 1989 Incompleteness for quantified relevance logics. In: Norman J, Sylvan R (eds.) *Directions in Relevant Logic*. Kluwer, Dordrecht
Read S 1988 *Relevant Logic*. Blackwell, Oxford
Routley R, Plumwood V, Meyer M K, Brady R T 1982 *Relevant Logics and Their Rivals*. Ridgeview, Atascadero, CA

S. Read

Reliability/Validity

In social research, reliability and validity are two criteria for judging the quality of measurements. 'Validity' refers to whether the measurement technique captures the intended meaning of the variable. 'Reliability' refers to the dependability of the technique.

1. Measurement and Concepts

Measurement is a central issue in social research. Both description and explanation depend on the researcher's ability to devise and execute procedures for observing and classifying those observations in terms of variables. More specifically, this task involves the classifying of those being observed in terms of the 'attributes' comprising the 'variables' under study.

In a simple example, the gender of respondents might be measured in a survey: that is, each respondent would be identified with one of the attributes—male or female—comprising the variable, gender. The procedure for accomplishing this would be straightforward, perhaps by asking respondents to check one of two boxes: [ ] Male, [ ] Female. Because this item taps what is generally meant by the term 'gender,' it is probably a valid measure, and as such would be expected to be reliable as well.

To distinguish between validity and reliability further, consider this illustration. Imagine stepping on a bathroom scale that registered a weight of 130 pounds. Now imagine stepping repeatedly on the same scale, with the following results: 115, 140, 120, 190, etc. That scale would be judged an unreliable measuring device. By contrast, if it faithfully reported 130 every time the same person stepped on it, it would be judged reliable. Notice, however, that the scale's reliability does not guarantee its validity. If the person really weighed 110 or 210 pounds, the scale would be judged reliable but invalid.

The issues of reliability and validity apply to all social research measures. Unfortunately, most variables of interest are not as tidy as weight and gender, and thus the nature of social research variables must be examined. Most of the variables of interest to linguistics are themselves linguistic, for example, the various ways a word may be pronounced by different speakers, but many other variables may be associated with variations in language and thus be important for sociolinguistic studies.

All variables begin as 'concepts': ideas that represent experiences and thinking. Some common social science concepts would include social class, bureaucracy, alienation, kinship. Variables are concepts comprised of sets of mutually exhaustive attributes or characteristics. Thus, reviewing the list of concepts just presented, social class is a variable: comprised of attributes such as lower class, middle class, and upper class.

Bureaucracy is *not* a variable, however. It could, however, be seen as one of the attributes comprising Max Weber's variable, 'forms of social organization' (the other attributes being 'charismatic' and 'traditional'; see also *Weber, Max*).

Alienation is a variable, comprised of attributes such as low, medium, and high. Finally, kinship is not a variable per se, though 'type of kinship system' could be a variable used to describe societies; the attributes might include: patrilineal, matrilineal, egalitarian, for example.

From this perspective, measurement is a matter of identifying units of analysis with the attributes comprising the variables under study. In a linguistic survey of Canada, it might be required to measure the variable, 'language used at home,' with the attributes of that variable being 'English,' 'French,' and other languages.

The examples given above should illustrate that variables are constructed by the researcher rather than existing in nature. Consider the example of 'social class.' Though it might be comprised of the attributes, lower class, middle class, and upper class, this structure might be inappropriate to some research purposes. W. Lloyd Warner, in his examination of 'Jonesville,' distinguished lower-lower, upper-lower, lower-middle, upper-middle, lower-upper, and upper-upper classes. A Marxist analysis, on the other hand, might require attributes such as proletariat, bourgeoisie, etc.

The process of specifying the nature of variables prior to measurement is called 'conceptualization.' Choices are made among options and ambiguities are clarified.

'Operationalization,' the next step in this process, specifies the concrete procedures (operations) that will result in measurements of the variable in question. The statement of precisely how a variable will be measured and what observations will correspond to specific attributes on that variable is called the 'operational definition' of the variable.

Thus, in a survey of college students, the variable, grade point average, might be measured by asking respondents to answer the question: 'Approximately what was your grade point average as of the end of last term?' Or, alternatively, the researchers might be able to extract grade point averages from the registrar's files and add that information to the data collected by the questionnaire. The operational definition, in the latter instance, would be 'the grade point average recorded in the Registrar's student files.'

It is the operational definition of a variable—specifying what observations will be made and how those observations will be converted into attributes of the variable in question—that can be evaluated in terms of its validity and reliability. There are several aspects of each.

2. Validity

The validity of a measurement refers to the extent to which it measures what the researcher intends, or whether it actually measures something else. Asking students to report their own grade point averages, for example, might be criticized as possibly measuring what the respondents would like the researcher to think about them more than their actual scholastic achievement.

There is a basic, philosophical issue to be acknowledged before proceeding with this evaluation, however. Virtually all the variables studied by social scientists reflect concepts which were products of the mind. Their meanings are ultimately only what people agree they are. 'Social class,' for example, does not exist in nature, but only as a concept created for the purpose of organizing a set of observations regarding differential wealth, power, prestige, etc. Therefore the question of whether a particular operational definition of a variable really measures that variable rests on agreement as to the meaning of the variable in the first place, and people often differ in their use of such terms. This caveat notwithstanding, there are useful grounds upon which to judge the validity of measurements.

2.1 Face Validity

Despite some disagreements as to the meanings of concepts, there has to be some level of agreement or else people could not communicate through the use of the terms that refer to those concepts. 'Face validity' refers to the extent of agreement between a measurement and the common consensus as to what the concept in question means. Thus, despite disagreements regarding the meaning of social class, few would deny the relevance of measuring annual income in that context.

It is worth noting that annual income is an imperfect measure of social class, even of wealth. Someone with a trillion dollars in their home safe yet earning no annual income is undeniably wealthy. Or conversely, imagine someone with a substantial income but even more substantial debts: such a person might be bankrupt on balance. Still, annual income has face validity as a measure of social class, whereas a measure of, say, height would not: being able to see over other people's heads is not what is commonly meant by 'upper class.'

2.2 Criterion-related Validity

Another standard of validity involves its predictive power. Often, variables are measured in order to estimate some future behavior. Thus, a test of 'marital compatibility' might be devised in the hope of predicting whether prospective marriages would be successful or not. A study examining the extent to which the test actually correlated with the subsequent success or failure of marriages would provide a standard by which to evaluate the adequacy of the test.

Other examples where 'criterion-related validity' might easily apply could include college entrance exams as predictors of college performance, drivers' tests as predictors of driver safety, measures of political attitudes as predictors of voting behavior, etc.

2.3 Content Validity

Given that social science variables typically reference a diversity of meanings, the measurement of a variable can also be judged on the extent to which it successfully captures the different aspects of that variable.

Thus, for example, Charles Glock (1965) delineated five major dimensions of 'religiosity': belief, ritual, cognitive (knowledge), experiential, and consequential (the impact of religion in a person's life). It would be reasonable to ask, therefore, which dimensions were tapped by a particular measurement of religiosity. If a measure of religiosity that used only church attendance and praying before meals was constructed, that measurement technique could be reasonably criticized as omitting several meanings commonly associated with the term. Of course, it might be appropriate to limit the measurement, in terms of the aims of the particular study; in such a situation, it might be wiser to relabel the measurement as 'religious ritual.'

By the same token, it might be asked whether a particular measure of 'prejudice' focuses on prejudice against one or a few groups or somehow captures the idea of prejudice in general. Measures of liberalism and conservatism may tap only domestic or foreign-policy dimensions or both; similarly, liberalism and conservatism can refer strictly to politics or to morality, lifestyle, and other social issues. As a criterion of quality, content validity asks that the label assigned to a measurement cover whatever breadth of meaning is commonly associated with that term.

2.4 Construct Validity

'Construct validity' refers to how well the measurement of a particular variable articulates the place of that variable within a network of causal relationships with other variables. Whereas criterion-related validity tests the extent to which a measurement relates to other measures of the variable in question, construct validity is a matter of the measurement relating to measurements of other variables as expected on logical, theoretical grounds.

Thus, for example, a measure of alienation might be developed, based on answers to a number of questionnaire items. On theoretical grounds, there may be a number of expectations about alienated people: they might be less likely to vote, less likely to marry, and more likely to contemplate suicide than would be the case for less alienated people.

It would be reasonable to expect therefore that the measure of alienation would be negatively correlated with voting and marrying and positively correlated with reports of contemplated suicide. The failure of any one of these correlations should give cause for questioning the validity of the theoretical expectations; the failure of all should also call into question the construct validity of the measure itself.

3. Reliability

Whereas validity is a matter of measuring what it is said is being measured, reliability merely asks whether the measuring has been carried out dependably. The basic metaphor for reliability is repeated measurements of the same thing—with the same result produced each time, for example, earlier in this article using the same bathroom scale repeatedly, getting the same weight each time was discussed.

Unfortunately, many social science measurements do not lend themselves to such straightforward reliability-testing. In a survey, for example, the same question cannot be asked repeatedly. And even if it could be, the respondent would remember his or her earlier answer and simply give it again.

Despite these difficulties, there are techniques that provide tests of reliability in social research.

3.1 Test–Retest Method

Having said that the same question cannot be asked repeatedly of the same respondent, it is nonetheless sometimes possible to repeat questions to a more limited extent. In a lengthy questionnaire, for example, it might be possible to ask the same question in different locations without drawing the respondent's attention to what is being done.

In studies that involve data-collection at more than one point in time, the same question can be asked at different times, allowing an evaluation of the consistency of responses. This practice sometimes produces surprising results, however.

When Sacks and Krushat (1980) asked many of the same health and demographic questions in two surveys, three months apart, they found that only 15 percent of the respondents gave exactly the same answers. Whereas all subjects were presumably three months older, one seemed to have become five years younger. One respondent's mother aged 20 years in three months. One woman reported a missing ovary in the first survey but had evidently found it by the time of the second survey.

3.2 Split–Half Method

The test–retest method can be approximated through a somewhat different technique, if the researcher has several indicators of the variable in question. If the several indicators offer *valid* measures of the variable, then they should be correlated highly with each other. Whether they do so in fact can be taken as a test of reliability.

To give a simple example, suppose it is required to measure how 'fat' respondents are: how wide they are in relation to their height. As measures of their width, they could be asked to report the size of their waists, chests, thighs, forearms, necks, and hips. It seems obvious that any

of these measures, in relation to height, offers a valid measure of how fat respondents are. In practice, however, the reports might not correlate as well as would be expected, due to the fact that people may be aware of their waistline measurements but not know the other measurements. Many of their reports, then would be estimates of less than perfect reliability.

In testing the reliability of social science indicators, the several indicators might be randomly assigned to two subsets: each providing a valid measure of the variable. All the indicators would be included in a single questionnaire. Each set of indicators would then be used to classify respondents in terms of the variable, and the two classifications would be correlated.

3.3 Standardized Measures

Since science is a cumulative enterprise, with current research growing out of and beyond the past, it is sometimes possible to choose measures that have been developed, tested, and generally accepted as reliable measures of particular variables. The US Census Bureau, for example, has established numerous definitions and measurement techniques addressing a number of demographic concepts. In addition to profiting from previous reliability testing, it is possible to compare findings with those of other studies using the same measures.

Many measures are standardized informally, by the weight of repetition among researchers addressing a particular concept. The Srole Anomia Scale is an example of this.

3.4 Coder Reliability

The question of reliability is not limited to asking questions and getting answers from respondents. Sometimes the measurement process includes the coding of textual materials, such as answers given to open-ended questions (e.g., 'What do you consider the biggest problems facing the nation today?'). To support quantitative data analysis, such answers must be converted to standardized code categories (e.g., 'crime,' 'pollution,' 'recession,' etc.). This process has two stages: (a) establishing the set of appropriate codes and (b) actually assigning textual responses (e.g., 'It's not safe to walk the streets anymore') to the appropriate code category (e.g., 'crime').

The coding of textual materials involves subjective judgments on the part of the coder(s). When more than one person does the coding, there is a danger that they will have somewhat different interpretations of the code categories and will not make comparable assignments. The easiest method for checking against this possibility is to select some subset of the materials (40 or 50 questions, for example) and have all the coders process the selected materials. You can then determine the 'intercoder reliability.'

Even if all the coding was done by one person, it would be good practice to recode some of the materials, after a suitable passage of time, to see if the interpretation is consistent.

4. Tension Between Reliability and Validity

The best measurements are those ranking high in both validity and reliability. It is worth noting in conclusion, however, that a certain tension exists between the two qualities. Increasing one often reduces the other.

Imagine a study with the aim of classifying people in terms of their religiousness. A fairly reliable measure would be represented by asking the question, 'How many times, if any, did you attend worship services during the past week?' The number of times reported would then constitute a scale of religiousness. Names might even be given to levels on the scale: 'extremely religious' for attending worship services seven or more times during the week, 'very religious' for 2 to 6 times, 'religious' for attending once, etc.

The above measure is probably a *reliable* one in that people should be able to recall accurately how many times they attended worship services during the past week. Its *validity* is subject to question, however, since attendance at worship services is only a small part of what would normally be meant by the term 'religiousness.' Moreover, one can think of reasons why a 'truly religious' person might not have attended worship services (e.g., hospitalized that week) or why nonreligious people might have attended (e.g., brought unwillingly by an insistent spouse or parents).

A more valid approach might involve unstructured, hourlong conversations with respondents, probing their beliefs about supernatural matters, their support of religious institutions, a wide range of religious practices, feelings, and behaviors regarding moral/ethical matters, etc. By the end of each interview, the researcher might be confident about gauging how religious that person really was. In any event, the interviewer would feel more confident of the judgment than if the only information available was the answers people gave to the simple question about worship services.

While the latter approach can offer more validity, it comes at a price in terms of reliability. Different interviewers, for example, might judge the same respondent differently. A respondent's inability to express complex ideas and feelings might lead to an inaccurate assessment. Many other factors conspire to make this more valid measurement technique potentially a less reliable one.

The solution to this dilemma is to use a variety of measurement techniques—varying in validity and reliability—whenever possible. These several indicators of a variable can be compared and perhaps combined in the analysis.

See also: Scaling; Social Class; Sociology Language.

Bibliography

Babbie E 1989 *The Practice of Social Research*. Wadsworth, Belmont, CA
Burgess R 1986 *Key Variables in Social Investigation*. Routledge and Kegan Paul, London
Carmines E G, Zeller R A 1979 *Reliability and Validity Assessment*. Sage, Beverly Hills, CA
Miller D 1983 *Handbook of Research Design and Social Measurement*. Longman, New York
Sacks J, Krushat W M 1980 Reliability of the health hazard appraisal. *American Journal of Public Health* July: 730–32
Veltman C 1986 The interpretation of the language questions of the Canadian census. *Review of Canadian Sociology and Anthropology* 23(3)

E. Babbie

Religion

Religion has always played a role, often a very significant and even crucial one, in the history of language and linguistics, and for that reason this encyclopedia contains more than 80 articles in the religion subject area. There are articles on all the major world religions: Baha'ism, Buddhism, Christianity, Confucianism, Hinduism, Islam, Jainism, Judaism, Shintō, Sikhism, Taoism, and Zoroastrianism, as well as on Cargo Cults, Mormonism, New Religious Movements, Quakerism, Rastafarianism, and American Indian, Australian Aboriginal, Ancient Near Eastern, Celtic, Melanesian, and Ecstatic religions.

They focus on four main areas, some of them covered in separate articles: (a) sacred texts such as the Bible, the Buddhist canon, the Qur'ān, and the Vedas; (b) special religious languages and language varieties such as Avestan, Christian Syriac, Church Latin, Church Slavonic, Ge'ez, Biblical Hebrew, Jewish Aramaic, Pahlavi, and Pali, as well as those used in blessing, cursing, euphemism, evangelism, meditation, glossolalia, preaching, and the like; (c) views about language such as those enshrined in the biblical story of the Tower of Babel and the racist myth of an Aryan superlanguage, and belief in the magical power of words and names; and (d) the influence of religion on the history of linguistics due to such factors as the need for accurate transmission of sacred texts and oral traditions from generation to generation, and the impetus of missionary activities, especially Buddhist and Christian, to translate them into the vernacular.

1. Sacred Texts

Sacred texts have a central role to play in most religious traditions and the language in which they are written and read is often crucial. Sacred scripts or 'hieroglyphics' were sometimes invented with a special religious function, and exquisite calligraphy evolved as in Islamic art and the great monastic manuscript traditions of medieval Europe.

In Islamic doctrine, the Qur'ān represents the actual words of the deity delivered directly, in Arabic, to Muhammad in the early seventh century AD, and must only be read in Arabic. Thus for the majority of ordinary Muslims throughout the world, who have no knowledge of Arabic, translation into the vernacular is officially discouraged and the Qur'ān is recited in the original language with amazing devotion and accuracy, but minimal understanding. Similar conservatism applies to the reading of Sanskrit texts in modern Hindu temples, Avestan texts in Zoroastrian worship, and the Bible in Hebrew, even in the more liberal or progressive Jewish synagogues (see *Hinduism*; *Zoroastrianism*; *Judaism*). In some cases it is the language of a widely used translation that assumes this role as in some varieties of Christianity where Greek, Latin, Slavonic, Syriac, Ge'ez, and other versions, not to mention the King James Authorized Version, have been treated with the same awe as if they were the original text (see *Bible Translations, Ancient Versions*; *Christian Syriac*; *Church Latin*; *Church Slavonic*; *Ge'ez*). The same applies to some versions of the Buddhist canon which are in most contexts preferred to the original Pali (see *Buddhism, Japanese*; *Buddhist Canons: Translations*).

2. Special Languages

In addition to the languages of their sacred texts, many religious communities employ special languages or language varieties for other purposes. Glossolalia or 'speaking in tongues' is a conspicuous example where utterances in a language unknown to virtually everybody present has an important prophetic function (see *Glossolalia*). Untranslateable or 'nonsense' languages are a feature of religious rites among the Australian aborigines of northern Arnhem land (see *Australian Aboriginal Religions*), while some American Indian medicine men use an incomprehensible language when talking to each other or to supernatural powers (see *American Indian Religions, North*; *American Indian Religions, South*). Probably as much for social and political reasons as for spiritual ones, Rastafarians have evolved a distinctive mode of speech among themselves, unintelligible to the outsider (see *Rastafarianism*). The same applies to the cargo cults and several other new religious movements. Monastic sign language is another example of a special language evolved within a purely religious context (see *Alternate Sign Languages*).

There are many examples of the belief that everyday language is not sacred enough for religious purposes. They include the use of Sumerian in ancient Near Eastern rituals long after it had ceased to be a living language (see *Ancient Near Eastern Religions*), of Sanskrit in Hindu worship (see *Mantra*), and of Ge'ez in Ethiopian Christianity, Syriac in Eastern Christianity (in Kerala in South India, for example, to this day), Hebrew in Judaism, and, until the twentieth century, Latin in the Roman Catholic Church all over the world.

The notion that no human language at all, ancient or modern, natural or artificial, is adequate, appears both in the well-known Quaker predilection for silent worship (see *Quakerism*) and in the 'language-transcendent' meditation techniques of some varieties of Buddhism and Christianity (see *Meditation*).

Within the context of a religious community meeting regularly for worship, special varieties of language are often used for public prayer, hymn-singing, and preaching, partly to heighten people's awareness of the sacredness of the moment, and partly to highlight the continuity of what they are doing with the worship of other communities elsewhere (see *Hymns*; *Prayer*; *Preaching*). Thus, for example, Jews all over the world using precisely the same Hebrew words as their ancestors have used for generations, as they celebrate Passover or Yom Kippur ('the Day of Atonement'), experience a sense of solidarity as 'God's people' which would not be possible if any other language was used.

The same applied until the twentieth century to the use of Church Latin in the Catholic Mass, and to the distinctive English of the 1661 Book of Common Prayer in the Church of England. The introduction of the vernacular into worship places the emphasis more on communication and the fuller participation of the people, although the precise wording of the modern Catholic 'Missal' and of the Anglican 'Alternative Service Books' is still controlled by the ecclesiastical authorities. Conservative opposition to using the vernacular in worship is common as in the case of the Anglican 'Prayerbook Society,' dedicated to preserving the use of the 1661 Book of Common Prayer (see *Christianity in Europe*).

The dynamics of prayer in which human individuals believe they are engaged in dialogue with a deity or saint, also determines the variety of language adopted (see *Prayer*). In the language of hymns, too, metrical constraints, the popularity of traditional melodies, and other factors lead to the survival of bizarre archaisms which would rarely be heard outside that special context. Frequently, tension between a desire to uphold an ancient religious tradition, by preserving Latin or Hebrew or Sanskrit, for example, and a move towards making public worship more generally intelligible, has produced interesting compromises (see *Hymns*). The need to train preachers in the use of a language variety designed to elicit the appropriate response, has produced elaborate homiletical strategies down the ages, particularly in Christian tradition (see *Evangelism*; *Preaching*).

3. Beliefs about Language

Belief in the power of language to influence reality is expressed in many ways all over the world. In European tradition this implies a Platonic view of language in which there is a direct connection between the world of names and the world of things (see *Magic*). The Chinese doctrine of the 'rectification of names' (*Cheng-ming*) was similarly based on the belief that there is (or ought to be) a formal correspondence, between names and functions, titles and duties, especially in politics (see *Confucianism*). In Hindu philosophy the sacred sound *om* was understood to be the consummation of the Vedas and as such to denote their ultimate referent Brahman, source of all intelligibility and being (see *Mantra*).

Personal names are believed to have special powers, and great care is taken by many communities to protect their children by naming them according to a set of carefully controlled rules. Some African tribes give their children unattractive names to make them uninviting to evil spirits. In some American Indian and Australian Aboriginal communities, the name of a recently deceased person is taboo, and even words that resemble it are meticulously avoided. Jews at one time changed the names of their children to deceive the angel of death, and the name of their God was believed to be surrounded by such a powerful aura of sacredness that it was never to be pronounced except by the High Priest in a very special ritual context. Some Christians apply a similar taboo to the name 'Jesus' in the late twentieth century (see *Names: Religious Beliefs*; *Taboo, Religious*).

Written language has a special role to play in this respect as beliefs about the Hebrew alphabet and the Tetragrammaton in Jewish tradition illustrate (see *Alphabet: Religious Beliefs*). Egyptian hieroglyphics, Nordic runes, and Chinese characters also have a long and fascinating history of magical uses and beliefs.

Several religious traditions believe in the creative power of the divine word or command: in Ancient Egyptian tradition the god Ptah created heaven and earth by his word. The same creative power is attributed to the word of the god Prajapati in Hinduism, and to the creator god of Jews, Christians, and Muslims. In Hindu iconography, the god Siva Nataraja ('Lord of the Dance') is represented as producing the sound which creates, sustains, and destroys the world. Highly complex mythological and doctrinal elaborations of this concept appear in Hinduism, Christianity, and elsewhere (see *Hindu Views on Language*; *Word of God*).

Primary myths about the origin of language, on the other hand, are surprisingly rare. The biblical stories of Ham, Shem, and Japheth, the three sons of Noah, and of the Tower of Babel (see *Babel*), an elaborate West African example from the Dogon of Mali, and a passing reference in Greek mythology seem to be exceptions. Maybe the focus on language as a key to understanding human nature and society is a modern one.

In striking contrast to this situation are the many modern 'secondary myths,' clearly motivated by political and social factors, including sixteenth-century claims that Adam and Eve spoke a Teutonic language and that the Mayan script was of Semitic origin, and more recently, quite blatant attempts to prove the superiority of the Aryan race—or the Semites or the Africans—by the use of linguistic evidence (see *Myths About Language*).

4. Influence of Religion on Linguistics

The belief that, to be effective, ritual utterances, frequently in a language or language variety other than that of the priests performing them, have to be recited with absolute accuracy, has had profound effects on the history of language and linguistics. In the first place, it means that religious authorities insist on a very large part of their educational programs being devoted to language teaching. Thus the training of Catholic priests, Jewish rabbis, Muslim imams, and Hindu brahmins had to include the study of the ancient language in which their scriptures and their liturgy were written—Latin, Hebrew, Arabic, Sanskrit, respectively—whatever their mother tongue was, and whatever the language of the people they would be working among. At the same time, religious schools are set up in which children are taught at least the rudiments of the appropriate language to enable them to recite texts correctly from an early age. Muslim Qur'ān schools are a good example (see *Islam in Africa*). In many cases religious institutions exert, or are bound by, legal authority to preserve and protect the sacred language. This applies as much to the vernacular wording of the modern Catholic Mass and the English of the Church of England liturgy, as to the sacred languages of Judaism, Islam, and Hinduism. The effect on the survival or spread of such languages and language varieties, as also on perceptions of their superiority above indigenous or colloquial languages and dialects, can readily be appreciated (see *Linguistic Imperialism*).

Second, elaborate scribal and grammatical techniques were worked out to ensure that the sacred text was accurately transmitted. Thus ancient languages which might have been totally forgotten have been preserved in the context of religious institutions of many types. A very large proportion of the linguistic material that has survived from the ancient world is of a religious nature, preserved in temple libraries and the like (see *Ancient Near Eastern Religions*). Scribes engaged in copying a sacred text, the Jewish masoretes, for example, worked under the strictest rules governing every aspect of their craft. They also devised elaborate systems of 'pointing' to preserve correctly every minute phonological detail, including cantillation marks, after Hebrew had ceased to be their first language. This

and other developments, especially contact with Arabic grammarians, led eventually to the emergence of Hebrew linguistics (see *Grammarians, Hebrew*).

In early Hindu tradition, by contrast, the primary form of language was speech, not writing. The Vedas are regarded as *śruti* 'hearing,' to be transmitted word-perfect from generation to generation. Here too the linguistic precision required led not only to some astonishing feats of memory, but also to the appearance of some remarkable pioneers in the history of linguistics, of whom Pāṇini is certainly the most celebrated.

Finally, the communication, interpretation, and translation of sacred texts have influenced language and linguistics in a number of significant ways. The history of Bible translation is by far the best documented example of this (see *Bible Translations: Ancient Versions*). In many languages, such as Gothic and Old Church Slavonic, as well as countless modern spoken languages in Africa and Asia, the Bible was the first text to be written down. In many cases new writing systems had to be devised, while others like the Korean Han'gŭl system, came to be more widely used as a result of the efforts of Bible translators, so that they were no longer the possession of an intellectual elite (see *Christianity in East Asia*). It is probably true to say that, because of European colonial and postcolonial educational policies, there is still very little published in most of the African languages except for church purposes (see *Christianity in Africa*).

Important contributions to all branches of linguistics have been made as a result of the activities of Christian scholars and missionaries, from the early pioneering work of men like the Jesuit Matteo Ricci (1552–1610) in China and the eighteenth-century English Baptist William Carey in India, not to mention St Jerome (see *Bible Translations, Ancient Versions*) and Martin Luther (see *Luther, Martin*), to the more recent and more technical research associated with the Protestant Bible Societies, the Vatican (where incidentally there is still a thriving Latin Department), and the Summer Institute of Linguistics. As a result of their work, many languages and dialects were recorded for the first time, and the first grammars and dictionaries produced. Theological controversies, like the 'term question' in nineteenth-century China, focused for the first time on important semantic issues (see *Chinese: Translation of Theological Terms*), and some recent advances in comparative semitic linguistics are due to the activities of a new generation of biblical scholars (see *Bible*).

The effect of Buddhist missionary activities, especially in Central and Eastern Asia, has been considerable too, but less well-documented. It appears that Buddhist teachings were from the beginning translated into regional languages and dialects. The early history of translation into Chinese, for example, can be traced for 1,000 years, from the earliest attempts by polyglot monks in the second century BC, to the establishment of official translation bureaus. It was for the purpose of translating the Buddhist canon into Tibetan that the Tibetan script was created in the seventh century AD, and this in turn was used as a model for the Mongolian writing system, created under the patronage of Kublai Khan in the thirteenth century (see *Buddhist Canons: Translations*).

Bibliography

Gill S D 1981 *Sacred Words: A Study of Navajo Religion and Prayer*. Greenwood Press, Westport, CT

Gomez L O 1987 Buddhist views of language. In: Eliade M (ed.) *Encyclopedia of Religion*, vol. 8, pp. 446–51. Macmillan, New York

Samarin W (ed.) 1976 *Language in Religious Practice*. Newbury House, Rowley, MA

Tambiah S J 1968 The magical power of words. *Man* NS 3: 175–208

Wheelock W T 1987 Language. In: Eliade M (ed.) *Encyclopedia of Religion*, vol. 8, pp. 438–46. Macmillan, New York

J. F. A. Sawyer

Religious Language

Already in their myths of origin one can detect in Jewish and Christian traditions a concern with words and language. In the book of Genesis, God is represented as 'speaking' words of creation and the human being, made in the image of God, is given the task of naming the animals. In the same book, the arrogance of the human architects of the tower of Babel is punished by confusing the human languages and scattering the people across the earth. In Christian mythopoetic language, God incarnate in Jesus the Christ is also the Incarnate 'Word' of God. The words of Jesus and those of the early Christian communities are preserved in the Bible, which itself has become, in some Christian contexts, the 'Word' of God almost on a par with the Incarnate Word.

This article will address two clusters of interest in Christian religious language; the first concerns the elementary but profoundly religious question of how it is that God can be spoken of at all given God's transcendence. That is, can God be 'named' by us? The second concerns the critical interpretation of texts received as sacred within the Christian tradition.

1. How can God be 'Named?'

The unnameability of the deity within Judaism and Christianity follows from God's holiness. God is represented in the Book of Exodus as too holy to be named or imaged by human beings, revealing Himself to Moses as 'I AM who I AM.' While it would be anachronistic to attribute to the authors of this early text the concern with metaphysical ultimacy that was to preoccupy later thinkers, scripture evidences changes in the conception of God from a polytheism in which the God of Israel is the greatest of the gods towards a heightened and radical monotheism. God, as creator of all that is, is in a strict sense incomparable with any 'thing.'

A pure and late Christian expression of this insight can be found in Anselm's Proslogion, a text which continues to impress modern writers, if not for its success in demonstrating the existence of God, then for the subtlety of the means by which Anselm (ca. 1033–1109) tries to name God, His designation of the God he addresses as 'that than which nothing greater can be conceived' avoids the pitfalls of saying either that God is the greatest of all things or of suggesting one could adequately conceive (comprehend) the

deity. God for Anselm could not be so conceived because God is God and not a creature to which human language could adequately apply. Similar reflections are found in the work of Anselm's Jewish near contemporary, Moses Maimonides (1135–1204), who writes of the Tetragrammaton (the divine name) that 'the majesty of the name and the dread of uttering it, are connected with the fact that it denotes God Himself, without including in its meaning any names of the things created by Him' (*A Guide for the Perplexed*).

Thomas Aquinas (1224–74) made use of a variety of sources in his deliberations on the knowledge of God and the speaking of God: Aristotle, of course, but also Augustine and neo-Platonist thinkers like Denys the Areopagite. Aquinas argued that God could be known and named principally as creator. This is the basis of his so-called 'proofs' for the existence of God, but also for his discussion of the language adequate to God. In the *Summa Theologiae* (Ia. 13) Aquinas discusses the inadequacy of human words for speaking of God, but suggests that there may be a very few terms which might be predicated of God literally by means of what he calls 'analogy'. Analogy for Aquinas is not the crude proportionality suggested by some later writers but rests on his conviction that some terms like 'good' and 'wise' signify perfections which inhere perfectly in God and flow from God to creatures. By analogy, human beings could say, for instance, that God is wise, without being able fully to grasp what wisdom in the Godhead might be. While Aquinas employs a theory of meaning which one would be unlikely to advance in the early 1990s, he nonetheless stands in an ancient tradition of reflection on religious language which, in its linking of the theological and the mystical and its sensitivity to the limitations of human language of the Divine, continues to be of importance.

A quite different sensibility is apparent following the Enlightenment in the British philosophers who, in the course of their writings, readdressed questions of the meaningfulness of religious language. David Hume (1711–76) in *The Dialogues Concerning Natural Religion* proceeds like a Ciceronian skeptic, demonstrating the poverty of the then popular arguments for God's existence from evidence of design in the world. No arguments from natural circumstances could, to Hume's mind, give any idea of the divine nature. Such 'analogies' (here meaning something like 'comparisons' and thus used in a different sense than that of Aquinas) could as easily prove the world to be the product of an immature or senile deity as of a good and powerful one. Natural knowledge of God, it is argued, is useless and humans must rest on the revealed. But since Hume elsewhere makes it clear that the gravest doubts must be cast on any claims to revelation, one is left with the position that, when speaking of God, a truly agnostic silence is best. Hume's *Dialogues* set an agenda for English-language philosophy of religion which is still being addressed. One of the most strident twentieth-century offspring of this debate is A. J. Ayer's *Language, Truth and Logic*, one of whose stated objectives was to show that religious language was 'literally' meaningless.

In this century religious language has become a more explicit topic for theologians and philosophers of religion. As Ayer's logical positivism disintegrated under the weight of its own contradictions, theists found the emphasis on diversity of linguistic tasks and modes favored by ordinary language philosophy to be useful. Ian Ramsey's *Religious Language* (1957) pioneered an interest in models in religious language, and subsequently metaphor, too, has emerged as an important topic, with parallels drawn between the use of models and metaphors in religious language and in the language of scientific theory construction. Wittgenstein has had an important and lasting influence. His notion of the diversity of linguistic tasks and functions ('language-games') has been much used, and even abused; its most extreme variant being forms of a 'Wittgensteinian fideism' wherein religious language is meaningful to religious adherents but not to others. Paul Ricoeur has shown a sustained interest in religious language running from his early book on *The Symbolism of Evil*, through works on metaphor, narrative, and biblical interpretation. Ricoeur's work is useful in bringing together continental and analytical philosophical concerns, for instance, with reference and narrative. More recent philosophy of religious language in the analytic tradition has been interested in questions of reference and realism, conceptual and linguistic relativism, and the status of 'God' as a proper name.

2. Religious Language and the Interpretation of Texts

The books which make up the Hebrew scriptures, written and compiled over many centuries, are already works of theological interpretation with later writings glossing and building upon the earlier, a tradition continued in Rabbinic exegesis. The early Christians, after some debate, retained the holy books of the Jews but set about providing Christian rereadings of them, a task which guaranteed from the outset that Christian theology must concern itself with the interpretation of religious language. Already in the letters of St Paul, new Christian interpretations are being given of books like Genesis. Early interpretation assumed the texts to be oracular and this, in conjunction with the conviction that the books of the 'Old Testament' must be read as pointing to Christ, led to the view that all scripture must have some edifying meaning. Typological and allegorical methods of interpretation were employed to discern this and it was widely held that all scriptures had two senses, literal and spiritual. By the fourth century AD, Augustine was already cautioning against overly allegorical readings of scripture (see Augustine, *De Genesi ad litteram*). By medieval times exegetes looked for four senses of scripture: literal or historical, allegorical, moral, and anagogical or prophetic. Many of the early theologians were also students of rhetoric and, while their interpretations may at times seem odd to the modern reader, their works displayed considerable sensitivity to the specific natures of the texts before them.

Modern biblical interpretation might be said to begin with the Renaissance and Reformation. Reformers like John Calvin (1509–64) were skilled in the new tools of literary analysis and eager to get behind the accretion of church teachings to the texts themselves in the original languages. Yet while consensus could be reached on the desirability of straightforward readings of the Biblical texts, it proved more difficult and indeed impossible to achieve uniformity in the interpretation of the Biblical texts.

The Romantic philosopher–theologian Friedrich Schleiermacher (1768–1834) is credited with elevating the study of interpretation to a science, which he called 'hermeneutics.' Schleiermacher's own concern was psychological and concerned with the gap between the reader and the mind of the author, but later nineteenth-century writers like Wilhelm Dilthey emphasized historical and cultural dimensions of the interpretive task, subjects of note to the then rapidly developing discipline of Biblical studies.

In the twentieth century, the works of Martin Heidegger and Hans-Georg Gadamer, while not themselves addressed directly to religious matters, have been influential for theological hermeneutics, especially in studies dealing with parable, narrative, text, and rhetorical criticism.

3. Questions

While questions of truth and reference will always be of importance, work on religious language in the late twentieth century shows a movement away from straightforward interest in the justification of religious claims towards the literary particularities of religious texts. Biblical rhetoric is enjoying renewed attention and narrative has emerged as an important if elusive analytic category. Questions familiar to secular literary criticism arise inevitably when considering the biblical texts: what constitutes a text? who is the reader? how do texts inform texts? It is not surprising that literary critics like Northrop Frye, Frank Kermode, and Robert Alter continue to find the biblical literature of interest.

Questions about the validity of received interpretations of canonical literature have led naturally to study of the link between power, ideology, and language. As Paul Ricoeur has said, 'to narrate is already to explain.' Arguing that interpretations of religious language themselves are never neutral, liberation and feminist theologies propose new interpretive strategies that challenge reigning views on texts and meanings. New ways of naming and knowing God are being sought by theologians.

It also appears that nontheologians, especially those influenced by French philosophy, are taking a renewed interest in religious language. Following Heidegger's essay on 'The Onto-Theological Constitution of Metaphysics' some of this interest was initially hostile to the theological and metaphysical presence in language. However, writings show that religious language may be once more recommending itself to nonreligious critics, with special interest being shown in the task, native to traditional negative theology, of 'saying the unsayable.' Noteworthy, too, is the work on female symbolics and the language of love which has drawn French postmodernist critics like Julia Kristeva and Luce Irigiray to reconsider Christian religious language.

Bibliography

Ackroyd P R, Evans C F (eds.) 1970 *The Cambridge History of the Bible: From the Beginnings to Jerome.* Cambridge University Press, Cambridge

Burrell D B 1986 *Knowing the Unknowable God: Ibn-Sina, Maimonides, Aquinas.* Notre Dame University Press, Notre Dame, IN

Kerr F 1986 *Theology After Wittgenstein.* Basil Blackwell, Oxford

Palmer R E 1969 *Hermeneutics.* Northwestern University Press, Evanston, IL

Ramsey I T 1957 *Religious Language.* SCM Press, London

Ricoeur P 1984 *Time and Narrative.* University of Chicago Press, Chicago, IL

Soskice J 1985 *Metaphor and Religious Language.* Oxford University Press, Oxford

J. Martin Soskice

Renaissance Linguistics: French Tradition

Linguistic description of French was unknown in France before the sixteenth century. The first works relating to the grammar of French were written in England, starting from the mid- to late-thirteenth century and settling into a set group of texts (dialogues, orthography, morphology, lexicon) by the end of the fourteenth century. The most complete grammar of French and one of the best dictionaries of French available before 1600 was John Palsgrave's *Lesclarcissement de la langue françoyse* (1530; see Kibbee 1991).

In France the study of French got a later start, beginning only in the 1530s after Geoffroy Tory's appeal to bring French under the control of rules (in the *Champ fleury,* 1529). This motivation emphasized morphology more than syntax, and evolved into a tradition of grammatical description continued by Louis Meigret (1550), Robert Estienne (1557), and Ramus (Pierre de la Ramée; 1562 and 1572). A parallel tradition of grammars for the learning of French as a second language developed in France and the Low Countries, with Jean Pillot (1550), Jean Garnier (1558), Gabriel Meurier (many works, starting from 1553), and Antoine Cauchie (1570). The study of the French lexicon developed in a flourishing dictionary tradition, although it remained during the sixteenth century a tradition of bilingual dictionaries, primarily French–Latin (Robert Estienne, continued and amplified by his understudies), with some French–Greek works (Budé and Henri Estienne). Collections of real and imagined etymologies (Perion 1555, Trippault 1580, H. Estienne 1565 (Book III), and Guichard 1610) added an historical component to the lexical field. These reference works provided the raw material for a lexical debate focusing on the acceptable expansion of vocabulary, primarily through introduction of dialectal and archaic words and the creation of neologisms. It involved translators, lexicographers, lawyers, and men of letters, featuring Du Bellay and Ronsard from the literary perspective as well as Henri Estienne, Abel Mathieu, and many others from a more linguistic background.

A lively orthographic debate raged at the midpoint of the century, pitting proponents of univocity (one letter should equal one sound) against conservators of etymological spelling. Meigret and Ramus led the charge of the reformers (religious as well as orthographic) and the movement largely died with them. (Meigret died ca. 1558; Ramus in the St Bartholomew's Day massacre of 1572.)

The subjective essays on French often draw on all these traditions. The evaluation of the vernacular attempted to define the 'naive puissance' of French, those features of French which distinguished it from its rivals, both ancient and modern. Henri Estienne, in his diatribes against Italian (especially 1578 and 1579), is the best-known polemicist for the French language, a tradition which continues to this day (but usually outside linguistic circles).

1. Morphology and Syntax

The grammarians of the sixteenth century started from the grammatical categories developed in the Greco–Latin tradition (especially Priscian and Donatus). This tradition is strong in the description and classification of morphology, less so in the description of syntax. Already in the 1520s, Robert Estienne published guides to the conjugation of French verbs and declension of nouns, manuals designed to help translators accurately render Latin into French. Thus his grammar (1557) lists three different ways of forming the pluperfect 'conjunctive,' using the forms which, in the twentieth century, would be called the past conditional, the pluperfect subjunctive, and the pluperfect indicative. The three are distinguished only by the conjunction used at the beginning of the clause, but since each can be used to translate the Latin pluperfect subjunctive, they are grouped in one category. Because these efforts did not describe French on its own terms, the first descriptions of French frequently include such categories as 'optative' mood in the verb conjugations and full six-case nominal and pronominal declensions. Applying such categories to French required grammarians to turn to semantic rather than morphological definitions of grammatical features, a move which paved the way for more abstract mentalist grammars in the seventeenth century.

Syntax in these grammars was generally limited to questions of agreement. Peculiarities in popular usage (e.g., *j'aimons*) were universally condemned while the agreement of the past participle was a point of contention between the latinizing grammarians (Dubois) and those who felt more constrained by usage. Syntactic arguments were often invoked to resolve problems of morphological classification, particularly by Meigret and Ramus, but syntax in its own right held less interest for the grammarians of the sixteenth century than did morphology.

1.1 Jacques Dubois (Sylvius; 1478–1555)

The first grammar of French published in France was the *Isagoge in linguam gallicam* (1531), written by Jacques Dubois, a Picard physician whose medical writings were far more successful. It is divided into two parts, the *Etymologica* and the *Grammatica Latino–gallica.* The first part is an inventory of Latin–French letter correspondences, in which Dubois took no notice of the effect of context. Thus he notes that Latin ⟨a⟩ can end up in French as ⟨a⟩, ⟨e⟩, ⟨i⟩, ⟨o⟩, ⟨ou⟩, ⟨ea⟩, ⟨ai⟩, or ⟨au⟩ without specifying in which contexts each of these changes took place.

In the grammar, Dubois sought to put French under the control of rules by reestablishing some parts of Latin usage that French had abandoned. His grammar follows the linguistic categories of Donatus, and explains how Latin forms are rendered in French. As he considered the differences between French and Latin 'corruptions,' he sometimes recommended the substitution of Picard forms and practices for those of Paris, finding that his native dialect was closer to Latin. Meigret attacked the *Isagoge* for its failure to observe and follow usage, while Robert Estienne condemned the dialectal features. It was never reprinted.

1.2 Louis Meigret (?1500–?58)

Louis Meigret, born into a well-known Lyons family, was an active translator, proponent of orthographic reform, and the author of the *Tretté de la grammere françoeze* (1550), a much stronger effort in the description of French than the work of Dubois. He opens with a description of the sounds of French, a study which profited from his attempts at orthographic reform. Because of the radical reforms he proposed, he was forced to consider sounds rather than letters, a major advance which was largely ignored once the orthographic question was settled in favor of more traditional spelling. The rest of the grammar is devoted to the eight parts of speech, with the article (definite article only) inserted before the section on nouns. Meigret leans towards semantic definitions of grammatical categories, but he does invoke morphology to deny the existence of neuter gender and nominal declension in French.

1.3 Robert Estienne (1503–59) and Henri Estienne (1531–98)

Robert Estienne's *Traicté de la grammaire françoise* (1557) is a catalog of French morphology, derived in part from his earlier guides to conjugation and declension, in part from the works of Dubois and especially Meigret. Estienne admits in his preface that the complaints about the orthography of Meigret's *Tretté* inspired his own efforts. Estienne's grammar is remarkable only for the clarity of its layout, testimony more to his skills as a printer than to his skills as a grammarian. Robert Estienne deserves much greater recognition for his lexicographic work (see Sect. 3).

Robert's son, Henri, wrote the *Hypomneses de gallica lingua* (1582) as a supplement to his father's grammatical work, adding a long description of sounds, and devoting the last 60 pages to assorted problems in syntax and semantics, including changes in meaning between preposed and postposed adjectives and various aspects of article usage. Although hardly complete, these often rich commentaries venture into new areas in the description of French.

1.4 Ramus (Pierre de la Ramée; 1515–72)

Ramus was an ardent opponent of scholastic philosophy, which earned him the enmity of conservative Catholic theologians at the Sorbonne. He wrote widely on philosophical, rhetorical, and grammatical questions, treating Latin and Greek grammar in the 1550s before writing the *Gramere* (1562), which he revised and transformed into traditional orthography in the *Grammaire* (1572). His basis in philosophy led Ramus to question methodological practices in grammatical description, and he makes significant innovations in his insistence on using formal distinctions and complementary distribution to define grammatical categories. This organizational consistency, however, leads to many grammatical inconsistencies.

The *Gramere* is divided into two parts, like Dubois's, etymology and syntax. Etymology includes the description of sounds and derivational and inflectional morphology. The strict application of his formalistic approach forces him to consider synthetic comparatives (e.g., *meilleur*) in the first part, and analytic comparative (*plus beau*) in the second. The confusion in the definition of moods leads him to reject the category altogether. The basic information included in these works is taken mainly from Meigret. In

the second edition, inspired by Henri Estienne's *Traicté de la conformité du langage françois avec le grec* (1565), Ramus pleaded for French grammar to be considered on its own terms, not in the light of Latin, but it was precisely his own reliance on Latin models that led him astray in many of his arguments.

2. Orthography and Pronunciation

Pronunciation *per se* was rarely dealt with directly in French treatises of the sixteenth century. Instead, grammarians concentrated on the relationship between letters and the sounds they represent. The reformers insisted on a principle of strict univocity (one letter = one sound), while conservatives found a variety of reasons to maintain traditional spelling. Still, in debating the merits of different spelling systems, the grammarians had to confront real issues in the description of the French sound system, such as the lack of orthographic symbols to represent the French sounds which did not exist in Latin (e.g., [ʃ], [ʒ], [z], [v], nasal vowels, schwa, etc.).

Towards the end of the century, the most significant efforts in the description of the French sound system came in works destined for foreign learners of French. Jacques Bellot (fl. 1580–90), a native of Caen who taught French in England, developed a crude descriptive method for describing point and manner of articulation in phonetics. Claude de Sainliens (Hollyband; ? –1597), whose *French Schoolemaister* (1573) and *Frenche Littelton* (1576) remained basic texts for teaching French to English speakers well into the seventeenth century, offered a strong defense of traditional orthography in his *De pronuntiatione linguae gallicae* (1580), although he used diacritics to mark silent letters. Théodore de Bèze (1519–1605) wrote his excellent study *De francicae linguae recta pronuntiatione tractatus* (1584) for German-speaking students in Switzerland.

The orthographic debate was launched by Tory's *Champ fleury*, in which the printer from Bourges noted the variety of pronunciations represented by the letters ⟨e⟩ and ⟨c⟩. Tory inspired an unknown author from Abbeville (Picardy) to compose the *Tres utile et compendieux traité de l'art et science d'orthographie gallicane* (1529), a work which proposed a more conservative (i.e., more Latinate) spelling in order to better distinguish homonyms. Dubois follows this line of reasoning when he proposes that *lisons* (from *lire*), be written *ligons* because in Latin there is a ⟨g⟩ (*legamus*). To accommodate French pronunciation and Latin etymons, Dubois experimented with some new symbols such as ⟨g̊⟩ for the /s/ in *lisons*. In the same year as Dubois's treatise (1531), Tory introduced the use of the cédille. In 1533 appeared the *Briefve doctrine pour deuement escripre selon la proprieté du langaige francoys*, possibly written by Clément Marot. This work tries to regularize the use of various diacritics in French, including the apostrophe, grave and acute accents, cedilla, circumflex accent, and the diaeresis. Many of these innovations were incorporated into the last section of Etienne Dolet's *La Maniere de bien traduire d'une langue en aultre. D'advantage. De la punctuation de la langue Francoyse. Plus, Des accents d'ycelle* (1540).

2.1 *Louis Meigret, Guillaume des Autels (1529–81), and Jacques Peletier du Mans (1517–82)*

Louis Meigret also reacted quickly to Tory's appeal, composing a manifesto for orthographic reform (*Traité touchant le commun usage de l'escriture françoise auquel est debattu des faultes et abus en la vraye et ancienne puissance des letres*) and a sample text in his new orthography (his translation of Pliny the Elder). However, his reforms were considered too radical, and these works, written ca. 1531, were not printed until 1542 and 1543 respectively, and then only after they had been put into more standard orthography. A second edition of the treatise appeared in 1545. After some minor reforms incorporated into Meigret's translation of Cicero (1547), the real breakthrough occurred in 1548, with the publication of Meigret's translation of Lucian's *Philopseudes*, printed entirely in Meigret's reformed orthography by Christian Wechel. This translation inspired responses from Jacques Peletier du Mans (*Dialogue de l'orthografe e prononciacion françoeze* and *Apolojie à Louis Meigret Lyonnais*, 1550) and Guillaume des Autels (*De l'antique escriture de la langue française et de sa poesie, contre l'orthographe des Maigretistes* (1548; published at the behest of Philippe Le Brun under the pseudonym Glaumalis de Vezelet). Peletier du Mans had already published (1545) in the introduction to his translation of Horace a letter outlining his sympathetic but cautious views on orthographic reform. To these critics Meigret responded with his usual venom, in the *Défenses de Louis Meigret touchant son orthographie française contre les censures et calomnies de Glaumalis de Vezelet et de ses adhérents* and *La response de Louis Meigret à l'Apolojie de Jacques Peletier* (both 1550). Des Autels fought back with his *Replique de Guillaume des Autels aux furieuses defenses de Louis Meigret* (1551), which Meigret parried with the *Reponse de Louis Meigret à la dezesperée repliqe de Glaomalis de Vezelet, transformé en Gyllaome des Aotels* (1551).

Meigret identified three problems with French spelling: *superfluité* (letters which are not pronounced), *diminution* (sounds pronounced which are not reflected by letters), and *usurpation* (one letter is pronounced like another). By far the most common offense against reason in French orthography is the first, a weakness Peletier du Mans was willing to attack. However, he opposed most changes designed to remedy the second and third types of orthographic heresy (according to Meigret), which required more radical changes of habit.

The conservatives, represented by des Autels, argued that traditional spelling clarified the diachronic relationships between etymons and contemporary words as well as the synchronic relationships between words of the same family. The maintenance of these etymological letters also helped foreigners learning French, presumably because they would already be conversant with Latin. Second, no spelling system could represent all the varieties of pronunciation: each person would spell differently. Third, as pronunciation changed from period to period spelling would be in a constant state of flux. These arguments, aided by the inertia of a literate public unwilling to master a new system, won the day, and spelling reform ever since has limited itself to minor points (e.g., the acceptance in 1835 of the spelling *-ais* for the imperfect endings). Meigret himself was forced

to abandon his reformed orthography by printers who preferred profit to reason; the last translations he composed were printed in traditional orthography.

2.2 *Ramus, Honorat Rambaud (fl. 1580), and Laurent Joubert (1529–83)*

In the last part of the sixteenth century, some appeals for reformed orthography continued to be heard—Ramus in the first edition of his *Gramere*, Rambaud in the *Declaration des abus que l'on commet en écrivant, et le moyen de les éviter et représenter naïvement les paroles* (1578), and Joubert in the *Dialogue sur la Cacographie fransaise* (a supplement to his *Traité du ris*, 1579). Rambaud went so far as to create a whole new alphabet of 52 characters which, while simplifying sound-letter correspondences, complicated all other aspects of reading. Joubert's dialogue blames the confusion in French spelling on Germanic influence, which, according to him, encouraged clusters of consonants (e.g., *prebstre*) lacking in the other Romance languages. By the end of the century orthographic theory and practice had settled down into a somewhat reformed position: the exaggerated etymological letters had been dropped, but many unpronounced letters, in particular ⟨s⟩ in word-final and preconsonantal position, remained.

3. Lexicography

All the dictionaries relating to French in the sixteenth century were bilingual dictionaries, but the amount of information about the French words increased steadily, approaching French definitions of French words. That stage was finally reached with Nicot's dictionary (1606). As Latin word-lists such as Alexander Neckham's *De ustensilibus* and John of Garland's *Synonyma* (twelfth century) grew into large manuscript dictionaries such as Giovanni Balbi's *Catholicon* (fourteenth century), the French glosses to these works became more and more informative about the vulgar language. The humanists, however, were repulsed by the medieval Latin additions to these dictionaries. Robert Estienne's work as a lexicographer grew out of his printing business, where he produced scholarly editions of newly discovered or newly collated Latin manuscripts. As the number of such editions grew, and as the translation of those editions into French became a more popular and more profitable enterprise for the printing world, the quantity and quality of French lexicography improved.

Robert Estienne's Latin and Latin–French dictionaries served as the lexicographic model for dictionaries produced all over Europe, establishing the selection of words included, the examples provided, the order followed. The words had to be found in classical authors, the examples, where possible, in editions Estienne himself produced. Estienne replaced the topical organization preferred in most earlier dictionaries with an alphabetic organization that simplified the use of dictionaries as a reference tool.

The first Estienne-produced dictionary, the *Thesaurus linguae latinae* (1531), already included French equivalents, which were expanded in the 1536 edition. In 1538 he published his first fully bilingual dictionary, the *Dictionarium latino–gallicum* (Latin–French), which he reversed in 1539 to produce the *Dictionnaire françois–latin*. Estienne expanded this work, numbering about 9,000 entries, to 13,000 entries in the 1549 edition. A major step towards the creation of a French–French dictionary was the inclusion of French words drawn from sixteenth-century French authors in the 1549 edition. The work was reissued in 1564 by Thierry and in 1573 by Jean Nicot (1530?–1600), and the French added to or replaced by German, Dutch, and English in a number of lexicographic works published abroad. Thus Estienne's dictionaries had a great influence on lexicography and on the teaching of the French language across Europe. Furthermore, within France, they served to stabilize French vocabulary and standardize forms as they remained the principal lexical reference works until the dictionary of the *Académie française* (1694).

4. History of the French Language in the Sixteenth Century

In the sixteenth century, the history of the French language served as primary evidence in the history of French institutions. The history of those institutions was itself crucial to the debate on the role of the monarchy, in turn related to the Wars of Religion. French clearly had close affinity to Latin, and thus to Italian and Spanish. However, humanist admiration for Greek, Reform interest in Hebrew, and concurrent bursts of celtomania and xenophobia led to theories of the origin of the French language which resolutely pursued the implausible.

The thesis that French had Greek origins was supported by a number of Classical and biblical sources (Léon Trippault provides a summary in an appendix to his *Celt–hellenisme, ou etymologic des mots francois tirez du graec. Plus. Preuves en general de la descente de nostre langue*, 1580). Many historians of French claimed that the Gauls spoke Greek or some closely related language. In this way native gallican interests could be allied with the most prestigious of the ancient languages (and opposed to Italian/Latin). This linkage took on political significance in works such as François Hotman's *Franco–gallia* (1573), in which evidence from diachronic linguistics was adduced to provide an historical basis for elected, constitutional monarchy and customary law, as opposed to divine-right absolute monarchy and Roman law.

At the same time, other scholars sought to establish links between Hebrew and French. Guillaume Postel (*Linguarum duodecim characteribus differentium alphabetum, introductio, ac legendi modus longè facilimus*, 1538) provided a basis for this work, which received occasional mention in the works of Joachim Perion (*Dialogorum de linguae Gallicæ origine, eiusque cum Græca cognatione, libri quatuor*, 1555) and Trippault, and culminated in Estienne Guichard's *L'harmonie étymologique des langues hébraïque, chaldaïque, syriaque, en laquelle par plusieurs Antiquitez et Etymologies de toute sorte se demonstre evidemment que toutes les langues sont descendues de l'Hébraïque* (1610).

Such historical evidence was necessarily impressionistic, generally based on word-lists of fewer than 500 entries (Joachim Perion, Léon Trippault). The dangers of basing such conclusions on small lists of words led the more linguistically sophisticated Henri Estienne to argue not for a Greek origin of French, but rather closer affinity between constructions of modern French with ancient Greek (*Traicté de la conformité du langage françois avec le grec*, 1565). Even in these small word-lists many of the etymologies were erroneous, for greater emphasis was placed on

semantic similarity than on regular sound (letter) changes. One or two similar letters and a plausible story relating the meaning of French and Greek words were enough to establish the etymological link.

As the sixteenth century wore on, the flaws in this method became apparent. Abel Mathieu (*Devis de la langue françoyse*, 1559; *Second devis et principal propos de la langue françoyse*, 1560) established that many of the legitimate etymologies relating French to Greek words were words only recently introduced into French, in the wave of neologisms that accompanied the translation of Classical works into French. This theme was picked up by Etienne Pasquier (*Recherches sur la France*, 1560) and Claude Fauchet (*Recueil de l'origine de la langue et poesie françoise*, 1581), who first traced the history of medieval French literature. The absence of the supposedly Greek words in those texts helped destroy the myth of the Greek origins of the French language. Equally important, a new attitude towards etymology, insisting on methodical links between letters rather than on subjective impressions based on a limited portion of the complete lexical corpus, and a recognition of the difference between Vulgar Latin and Classical Latin, improved the accuracy of historical speculation. Jacques Bourgoing, counselor to the king, demonstrated the usefulness of the comparative method to correct the errors of the Grecophile etymologists in his *De origine usu et ratione vulgarium vocum linguæ Gallicæ, Italicæ, & Hispanicæ, libri primi sive A, centuria una* (1583), thus setting the foundation for seventeenth-century historical work, such as Ménage's *Les origines de la langue française* (1650).

5. Subjective Appreciation of Language

The establishment of standard languages and the competition for preferred status among the modern languages in the sixteenth century inspired a number of observations, both within grammatical works and in special volumes dedicated to the subject, concerning the relative merits of European languages. Works such as Du Bellay's *Deffence et illustration de la langue françoyse* (1549) and Ronsard's *Abrégé de l'art poétique* (1565) served this purpose on the literary side, while Henri Estienne provided the most pointed remarks from a more linguistic frame of mind (*Deux dialogues du nouveau langage françois italianizé*, 1578; *Project du livre intitulé de la precellence du langage françois*, 1579). The authors of such comments directed their attacks not only at competing vernaculars (especially Italian), but also at 'nonstandard' forms of their own language. Early in the century dialectal forms were viewed approvingly as enriching the word-stock of French, but as religious intolerance grew in the period of the Wars of Religion so too did linguistic intolerance. Meigret attacks what he labels the 'effeminate' usage of the court as well as the Picardisms of Dubois, only to be attacked himself for dialectal features of his native Lyonnais. Picard, Gascon, and Norman pronunciation are noted and rejected in orthographic and pronunciation texts, and a number of other dialects are noted (disapprovingly) in dictionaries. Thus the stage was set for the linguistic absolutism of Malherbe, Vaugelas, and Bouhors in the seventeenth century.

Bibliography

Brunot F 1906 *Histoire de la langue françoise des origines à 1900, Tome II: seizième siècle*. A. Colin, Paris

Catach N 1968 *L'orthographe française à l'époque de la Renaissance: Auteurs, Imprimeurs, Ateliers d'imprimerie*. Droz, Geneva

Chevalier J-C 1968 *Histoire de la syntaxe: naissance de la notion de complément dans la grammaire française (1530–1750)*. Droz, Geneva

Kibbee D A 1991 *For To Speke Frenche Trewely. The French Language in England, 1000–1600: Its Status, Description and Instruction*. Benjamins, Amsterdam

Livet C-L 1859 *La grammaire française et les grammairiens du xviᵉ siècle*. Didier, Paris

Stengel E 1976 (1st edn. 1890) *Chronologisches Verzeichnis französischer Grammatiken vom Ende des 14. bis zum Ausgange des 18. Jahrhunderts nebst Angabe der bisher ermittelten Fundorte derselbe*. Benjamins, Amsterdam

Swiggers P, Hoecke W van 1989 *La langue française au xviᵉ siècle: usage, enseignement et approches descriptives*. Peeters, Louvain

Thurot C 1966 (1st edn. 1881) *De la prononciation française depuis le commencement du xviᵉ siècle, d'après les témoignages des grammairiens*. Slatkine Reprints, Geneva

D. A. Kibbee

Renaissance Linguistics: General Survey

The Renaissance was an intellectual movement extending over several centuries which sought to assimilate the whole of Europe's ancient heritage. The veneration for the achievements of antiquity resulted in an extensive and irreversible enlargement of perspectives in all spheres of intellectual life. This emulation of ancient models is perhaps better known now than the intellectual fermentation associated with it. While Renaissance architects like Brunelleschi who designed buildings in the style of Ancient Rome and Renaissance poets from Petrarch to Milton who composed in the meters and style of the Latin writers are well known, there is a tendency to overlook Renaissance thinkers like Marsilio Ficino (1433–99), who added to the existing canon ancient philosophers, like Plato (see *Plato*), whose works had been largely unknown hitherto. Renaissance linguistics, if the term may be coined, represents an analogous expansion of horizons, both in the number of languages studied and the theoretical frameworks utilized.

The literary facet of the Renaissance is usually called 'humanism' and its practitioners 'humanists.' The intensive study of Roman authors began in several smaller northern Italian cities in the thirteenth century, gathered increasing momentum in the fourteenth century, spread in the fifteenth century to neighboring Spain, France, and Germany, and by the sixteenth century had embraced the whole of western Europe. The resulting emphasis on Latin literature strained traditional pedagogy by making it a desirable goal to know enough Latin to enable one to compose in the language as well as the Ancients had done. In this way, standards of linguistic competence were raised to hitherto unknown levels.

As for the attitude of the early humanists to the immediate past, one can say that they ignored rather than rejected the Aristotelianized grammar of the High Middle Ages and the modistic treatises of that period (see *Aristotle*). They did not, in fact, discard all features of medieval grammar. For instance, they continued to use many syntactic concepts which had come into vogue in the previous three hundred years, such as 'agent,' 'patient,' and 'antecedent.' Thus, contrary to a common misconception, the humanistic grammatical writing of the fifteenth century was no mere nostalgic return to ancient models coupled with a blanket rejection of medieval grammar. The grammatical tradition had been rich and variegated in medieval Italy, and much of this long-standing grammatical practice survived more or less intact into the fifteenth century and beyond.

In any case, a conscious antithesis between medieval scholasticism and Renaissance humanism was slow to develop, and this was especially true of basic approaches to grammatical analysis. The early Renaissance humanists, notably Petrarch (1304–74) and Coluccio Salutati (1331–1406), despite their disdain for many aspects of scholasticism, were content to use the grammatical literature available in their day, much of which had been produced only recently. What was novel was their determination to restrict grammar to its original propaedeutic function as the most basic of the liberal arts, the gateway to knowledge, and the indispensable tool for the study of the revered classical authors. The link between logic and grammar, together with the connection with philosophical speculation, was accordingly dissolved; grammar resumed its original lowly status as the humble foundation stone in the edifice of belles-lettres.

But grammar had developed considerably in the previous three centuries of scholasticism; the humanists could not have put back the clock even if they had wished to do so. In any case, their ambitions were extremely exacting, for what they attempted to do was to acquire not merely superficial grammatical correctness but also something of the genuine style of the Roman writers of the classical period, a quality which they referred to as *elegantia*. Accordingly, stylistic precepts and rhetorical considerations begin to play as important a role as grammatical rules. An early example is the treatise *De compositione* (1420) by Gasparino Barzizza (1360–1430), which deals with such topics as word order and choice of vocabulary.

The most successful of the stylistic manuals written by the humanists was the massive *Elegantiae linguae Latinae* of Lorenzo Valla (1407–57), completed in the mid-1440s. This famous work, countless printed editions of which were destined to appear, is lexicographical and phraseological in character: it is chiefly a collection of words, locutions, and syntactic constructions, backed up by examples from the classical authors. Valla presents no systematic grammatical apparatus and no system of syntactic analysis, confining his attention to those aspects of style which can be discussed in connection with isolated words.

In this way, in matters of grammatical doctrine the fifteenth-century humanists were not especially innovative. The seminal work was the *Regulae grammaticales* by the humanist educator Guarino Veronese (1370–1460), which was in circulation by 1418. It deviates from the average fourteenth-century grammar only in dispensing with dialectical subtleties and in being concisely formulated. Guarino aimed to provide just enough material to enable his students to read and write Latin correctly. The *Regulae grammaticales* comprises a tightly organized syntax in the style of Guarino's fourteenth-century predecessors and a series of short chapters on a variety of topics (irregular noun inflection, comparatives, relative pronouns, syntactic figures, etc.).

In the second half of the fifteenth century, humanists began to move away from the sketchy grammars of Guarino and others. Thus, in 1468 Niccolò Perotti (1429–80) composed a manual entitled *Rudimenta grammatices*, which was printed in 1473 by Rome's first printing press. Although this work was not especially original (the central syntactic section, for example, is an expansion of the corresponding portion of Guarino's *Regulae grammaticales*), it starts out with a morphology and concludes with a treatise on epistolary style. From this novel combination of parts Perotti in effect produced the first comprehensive grammar and stylistics of Latin, and its success is attested by the scores of editions which appeared both in Italy and elsewhere in the late fifteenth and early sixteenth centuries.

More ambitious still was the *Introductiones Latinae* by the Spanish humanist Antonio de Nebrija (1444–1522), the first printed edition of which appeared in Salamanca in 1481. Nebrija's grammar, which remained in use longer than any other Latin grammar written in the fifteenth century, covers elementary morphology, syntax, orthography, metrics, and also contains an orthographical dictionary. From 1495 on, editions also include a copious commentary by the author, in which Nebrija painstakingly explains the material covered in the grammar. This is a far cry from the sparse *Regulae grammaticales* of Guarino Veronese.

Serious lexicographical work also began in the fifteenth century. Niccolò Perotti, for example, wrote a voluminous commentary on Martial's epigrams, entitled *Cornucopiae* (it appeared posthumously in 1489), which was in effect a vast treasure-house of Latin vocabulary. Nebrija also contributed to Latin lexicography by publishing a Latin–Spanish dictionary and a Spanish–Latin dictionary. In the sixteenth century, important new Latin lexica were compiled by Ambrogio Calepino (Reggio 1502) and Robert Estienne (Paris 1531). The latter's *Latinae linguae thesaurus* continued in use well beyond the Renaissance.

Overt hostility to medieval grammar became more pronounced from the mid-fifteenth century on. While Guarino Veronese did not explicitly refer to his medieval predecessors, Lorenzo Valla forcefully attacked both the medieval lexicographers and the modistic grammarians, and wrote a treatise correcting mistakes in the *Doctrinale*, a popular metrical grammar written about 1200 by Alexandre de Villedieu. Valla's main charge against the lexicographers and the Modistae was that they were purveyors of corrupt Latinity and hence impostors. A more concentrated attack on the *Doctrinale* was made by Giovanni Sulpizio in the 1470s. Sulpizio argued that that work was too obscure and confusing to be an effective pedagogical tool. Alexander Hegius (died 1498), on the other hand, aimed his fire at the modistic grammarians in his *Invectiva contra modos significandi*, composed in 1486 and published in his *Dialogi* (Deventer 1503). Again, Jan Despauter in the Low Countries wrote a whole series of textbooks in the early years of the sixteenth century which were aimed at supplanting the *Doctrinale*, although his criticisms of Alexandre de Villedieu were more moderate in tone than those of his immediate humanist predecessors.

By the middle of the fifteenth century a new element had entered the grammatical tradition, namely firsthand acquaintance with the whole corpus of Roman grammatical literature. Medieval grammarians had been familiar with only Donatus (see *Donatus*) and Priscian. From the early years of the fifteenth century on, as humanists discovered more and more manuscripts of Roman authors, the number of available ancient grammatical works increased. At the Council of Constance, for instance, Poggio Bracciolini discovered two complete manuscripts of Quintilian's *Ars oratoria*, a work which introduced the humanists to the state of grammatical knowledge and speculation in the first century AD. By the 1460s, most of the Roman grammatical literature known today had been unearthed. Not surprisingly, this newly discovered grammatical literature influenced the style of grammatical writing. In revealing that the Romans themselves had disagreed on important issues of grammatical doctrine these works also stimulated a re-evaluation of traditional grammar. Thus, Giulio Pomponio Leto (1428–98), who made a careful study of Varro's *De lingua Latina* and published the first printed edition of that work in 1471, adopted Varro's theory of tenses, analyzing *amavero* 'I shall have loved' as a future perfect indicative, rather than a future subjunctive, as had been customary hitherto (see also *Varro, Marcus Terentius*; *Varro and Early Latin Language Science*).

Fundamental criticism of the grammatical tradition appears first in Lorenzo Valla's *Elegantiae linguae Latinae* in the mid-fifteenth century and becomes more marked in the sixteenth century. The most influential work in this vein was the *De causis linguae Latinae* by Julius Caesar Scaliger (1484–1558), first published in Lyons in 1540 (see *Scaliger, Julius Caesar*). Scaliger censures the wrongheadedness of the terminology and definitions used hitherto by grammarians. Earlier in the sixteenth century, the English humanist Thomas Linacre (d. 1524) wrote a more modest theoretical treatise (*De emendata structura Latini sermonis*, London 1524) which was also influential, especially on the Continent. Linacre's syntactic theory included a heavy reliance on the notion of ellipsis, which had been a popular device in the Middle Ages, and it was wholeheartedly embraced by the Spanish humanist Francisco Sánchez de las Brozas (1523–1600) in a textbook entitled *Minerva* (Salamanca 1587), which was to enjoy a considerable vogue outside Spain after it was republished in Holland in the mid-seventeenth century.

Petrus Ramus (1515–72; see *Ramus, Petrus*) attempted an impressive-sounding pedagogical reform in France from the 1540s, and wrote a set of grammatical textbooks, including grammars of Latin and Greek, and a theoretical work entitled *Scholae grammaticae* (Paris 1559), which also influenced Francisco Sánchez. Another comprehensive manual of Latin grammar which contained commentaries of a theoretical character was written by the Portuguese Jesuit Manuel Alvares (*De institutione grammatica*, Lisbon 1572, and many subsequent editions).

The revival of classical learning attempted by the humanists ipso facto encouraged the use of Latin for all purposes. However, scholars in the West were also led for the first time to take up the serious study of Greek. The study of the language was inaugurated when Manuel Chrysoloras (died 1415) began to teach in Florence in February 1397. The textbook which he wrote for his Italian pupils, the *Erotēmata*, was the first Greek grammar widely used in Italy. Chrysoloras's pupil Guarino Veronese made an abridgment of it for the use of his students and translated it into Latin. In his grammar, Chrysoloras simplified the uneconomical presentation of Greek morphology customary in the grammars used in the Byzantine East.

The fifteenth century then saw the progressive development of Greek studies in Italy. By the end of the century several grammars had been written and published in printed editions: the *Eisagogé* of Theodorus Gaza (died ca. 1475), for instance, included sections on syntax and metrics. The grammar of Constantine Lascaris appeared regularly in a bilingual Greek–Latin version; it also contained a syntax. However, in spite of competition, Chrysoloras's *Erotēmata* remained the most popular Greek grammar in Renaissance Italy. A pioneering contribution to Greek lexicography was the *Thesaurus Graecae linguae* (Geneva 1572) by Henri Estienne (1528–98), widely used as a reference work until the nineteenth century.

Together with these contemporary works some of the older Greek grammatical literature also became available, such as the grammar of Manuel Moschopulus (thirteenth century) and the *Syntax* of Apollonius Dyscolus (see *Apollonius Dyscolus*), a copy of which was brought to Italy by Giovanni Aurispa from a trip to the Byzantine East in 1423. This was probably the first grammatical work of Greek antiquity to reach the West; it was subsequently published by the famous Venetian printer Aldo Manuzio together with the grammar of Theodorus Gaza in 1495. The now famous *Technē grammatikē* attributed to Dionysius Thrax was unknown in the West during the Renaissance (see *Dionysius Thrax, The Technai, and Sextus Empiricus*).

Knowledge of Greek in the West never equalled that of Latin. The majority of scholars did not know the language well enough to read it with ease and made their acquaintance with Greek literature and philosophy from translations. Many of the foremost Greek scholars of the Renaissance, both Greeks and Westerners, spent their energies translating Greek literature into Latin. Important new translations of Aristotle's works, for example, were done in the fifteenth century (see *Aristotle*).

All over western Europe, the slow rise of the vernaculars, which had already begun in the Middle Ages, continued in the fifteenth and sixteenth centuries. In Italy, the vernacular had been used for literary purposes in the fourteenth century by the great triad Dante, Boccaccio, and Petrarch. In the fifteenth century, there followed the sonnets of Lorenzo de' Medici, Luigi Pulci's *Morgante*, and Angelo Poliziano's *Stanze per la giostra*. The first Italian to use the vernacular for scholarly purposes was Leon Battista Alberti (1404–72). In the 1440s, he composed the two treatises *Della tranquillità dell'animo* ('On the tranquillity of the soul'), and *Della famiglia* ('On the family'), and defended the use of the vernacular in the prefaces to those works. Moreover, about 1450 Alberti wrote a grammatical sketch of Italian, which he left unpublished. This work did not become widely known to scholars until it was discovered in the late nineteenth century.

It may seem strange to us that in defending the use of the vernacular Alberti did not argue that Italian was a living language and therefore more natural to use than a dead language such as Latin, but instead that the vernacular is a more universal medium of communication than Latin in

not being confined to the learned. He insisted, furthermore, that the vernacular is capable of being as expressive as Latin, a fact which he said was demonstrated by the achievement of the great Italian writers of the fourteenth century. Hence, it was to a large extent the prior *literary* use of the vernacular that made it worthy to be used for scholarly purposes on an equal footing with Latin.

An interesting problem arose in the case of the rise of Italian which was caused by the fact that there was no dominant political power which could impose the use of one particular Italian dialect on the whole peninsula. Italian scholars tried to solve the problem of the choice of a standard dialect by the use of abstract arguments. Three different solutions were suggested: first, the variety of Italian which had been used by Dante, Boccaccio, and Petrarch, which was a Tuscan dialect; second, the contemporary spoken dialect of Florence and Tuscany, which already differed appreciably from the language of the great fourteenth-century writers; and third, a pan-Italian 'courtly' variety of the language, a common denominator of the speech of the upper classes all over Italy.

Pietro Bembo, a Venetian, defended the use of the archaic Tuscan language of the Italian classics in a dialogue composed in the early years of the sixteenth century and published in 1525. The contemporary dialect of Tuscany was championed, not surprisingly, by a number of scholars from that area, notably Machiavelli and the members of the Florentine Academy. The idea of a 'courtly' dialect was vigorously promoted by Giangiorgio Trissino and also by Baldassare Castiglione, the author of *Il cortigiano*. Bembo's solution eventually triumphed after it had been adopted by Leonardo Salviati in his influential *Avvertimenti* (1584–86) and also by the Accademia della Crusca in its Italian dictionary, published in the early years of the seventeenth century.

The first grammar of Spanish to appear in print was the work of the Salamanca humanist Antonio de Nebrija and was published in 1492. In Spain, after the political unification of the Iberian peninsula under Ferdinand and Isabella, the choice of a literary dialect caused none of the problems which were to occur in Italy. The first Portuguese grammar was written by Fernão de Oliveira and appeared in Lisbon in 1536.

In the case of French, a grammatical tradition had developed in England in the late Middle Ages, exemplified by the *Donait français* (1409), which was commissioned by John Barton. Some of the French grammars which appeared in the early sixteenth century were also written by Englishmen, e.g., Alexander Barcley (1521) and John Palsgrave (1530). Palsgrave's grammar is especially comprehensive. The first French grammar to appear in France was written by Jacques Dubois (see *Dubois, Jacques (Sylvius)*); it was in Latin and was entitled *In linguam Gallicam isagoge* (Paris 1531).

The descriptive framework used in these vernacular grammars was, not surprisingly, the traditional Latin one. This is particularly obvious in the case of Nebrija's Castilian grammar, which bears a strong textual affinity to the same author's Latin grammar. It is also significant that a great deal of attention is devoted in these early vernacular grammars to orthographic questions. The ideal was to achieve a consistent spelling system with a separate symbol for each sound. Nebrija proposed such a system in a treatise published in 1517 (*Orthographia del castellano*), in which the basic theoretical notions were the same as those that he had expounded earlier in a treatise on the pronunciation of Latin and Greek (*De vi ac potestate litterarum*, Salamanca 1503). In France, the cause of orthographical reform was espoused by Louis Meigret (*Le tretté de la grammere françoeze* 1550; see *Meigret, Louis*) and somewhat later by Petrus Ramus (*Gramere* 1562). It cannot be said that any of these reforms had much practical success.

In the sixteenth century, the linguistic horizon of western Europe was broadened in other ways. First, the voyages of discovery and the ensuing commercial and colonial enterprises of the Portuguese and the Spanish (and later the Dutch, French, and English) brought Europeans into contact for the first time with the languages of the Levant, Africa, India, the Far East, and the New World. Second, the study of Hebrew (and later Aramaic and Arabic) introduced scholars to a radically different grammatical framework: the first full-scale grammar of Hebrew to appear in the West appeared in Pforzheim in 1506, written in Latin by Johann Reuchlin (1455–1522). These twin factors had the effect of putting an end to the linguistic isolation of western Europe.

The results of these widening perspectives were complex. Since no generally agreed-on methodology existed for conducting linguistic research, the work done on the newly discovered exotic languages sometimes bore an amateurish stamp. The aim was, at least, clear: missionary-linguists needed to produce practical grammars which could be used in the task of converting the natives to Christianity. At the same time, they were led to face the problem of accounting for the extraordinary linguistic diversity with which they were confronted, and penetrating the process whereby so many different languages had arisen. Their curiosity was mainly stimulated by vocabulary, and the conceptual tool used to approach the problem was the etymological theory that the West had inherited, ultimately, from the Stoics (see *Aristotle and the Stoics on Language*). There was also a further factor: the Biblical account of the building of the Tower of Babel seemed to imply that Hebrew was the original language of mankind and that all other languages were distortions of this primitive Hebrew. The story of the Flood gave rise to the notion that the languages of Noah's progeny were related to each other in the same way as his descendants. By the first half of the sixteenth century scholars had been made aware for the first time of the close affinity between Hebrew and Arabic. In this way, the genealogical notion of language relationship began to be taken more seriously. Scholars, therefore, imagined that they could make lexical comparisons between Hebrew and the languages spoken in the world in their own day and use them to arrive at the origins of words and discover the genealogy of the languages themselves.

The notion that there were several parent languages each of which in the course of time gave rise to a group of related languages was clearly expressed in a brief essay on the genetic affiliations of the languages of Europe (*Diatriba de Europaeorum linguis*) by Joseph Scaliger (1540–1609; see *Scaliger, Joseph Justus*), written in 1599 and published in 1610. However, there were at this time no criteria for determining which words in a language had been inherited from its parent language and which had been borrowed from other sources. The most daring etymological theorist of the period, Johannes Goropius Becanus (*Origines Antwerpianae* Antwerp 1569) indulged in the fantasy of deriving all languages from his native Dutch, but in so doing he launched the idea that the languages of Europe are later divergent continuations of the language of the ancient Scythians, an Iranian tribe living on the steppes of southern Russia in antiquity. His etymologies were greeted with incredulity by contemporaries, but his example set a trend.

Other important works on language relationships which appeared in the sixteenth century were Guillaume Postel's *De originibus* (Paris 1538; see *Postel, G.*), Theodore Bibliander's *De ratione communi omnium linguarum* (Zurich 1548), and Conrad Gesner's *Mithridates* (Zurich 1555). Postel explicitly claims that Hebrew was the first language of mankind, that Arabic, Aramaic, and Ethiopic were corrupt forms of Hebrew, and that even Greek had adopted many expressions and turns of phrase from it. He also endorses the Biblical account of the sons and descendants of Noah as a basis for drawing inferences about the early relationships of languages and peoples. It is noteworthy that he defends the extreme naturalist position presented in Plato's *Cratylus* (see *Plato*), exemplifying in this way the increasing influence of that dialogue on the philosophy of language in the sixteenth century after its translation in the late fifteenth century by Marsilio Ficino. Postel also represents the crude beginnings of language typology: he contrasts the 'grammatical' languages (Latin and Greek) with what he calls the 'natural' languages (Hebrew and the other Semitic languages; see *Hebrew*; *Semitic Languages*). Inflections, he claims, were borrowed into Latin and Greek from the latter languages. As fanciful as these ideas undoubtedly are, they testify to the powerful impact of the study of Hebrew on the general linguistic ideas of the time.

The main thesis of Bibliander's *De ratione communi* is that there is no language which cannot be described grammatically. Bibliander is remarkable in that he was not only familiar with Hebrew but also with one of the Slavic languages, namely Polish, and emphasizes the fact that such languages are as grammatically organized as Latin and Greek. Like Postel, he is scornful of suggestions that some languages have no grammatical rules at all. Significantly, it was to a large degree the *grammatical* similarity of Hebrew to Arabic and Ethiopic which was used to demonstrate that they are related (*affines*) to one another. Conrad Gesner's *Mithridates* (1555), a less ambitious book than Bibliander's, was an attempt to survey all known languages in the world and included specimens of many of them in the form of the Lord's Prayer.

Grammars of non-European languages began to be written soon after missionaries arrived in large numbers in the New World in the third decade of the sixteenth century. The earliest grammar of a Native American language to appear in print was Maturino Gilberti's *Arte de la lengua de Michuacan* (Mexico City 1558). The most notable of them were the *Arte de la lengua mexicana y castellana* by Alonso de Molina (Mexico City 1571) and the Quechua grammar by Domingo de Santo Tomás (Valladolid 1560). These were all the work of members of the mendicant orders or the Society of Jesus. Not surprisingly, the framework used in them was the familiar Latin one (indeed, Nebrija's

Introductiones Latinae was the model most often referred to in these grammars). However, the Latin framework had the advantage of being familiar to all churchmen. Moreover, a conscientious investigator who spent most of a lifetime in the field could achieve comprehensive coverage. But since most grammars of exotic languages were published outside Europe for local consumption, it was difficult for a coherent tradition of grammatical expertise to develop. There is evidence, however, that grammarians did not start out from scratch, but were given special training and familiarity with the work of people who had studied the same or similar languages previously.

Bibliography

Ferguson W K 1948 *The Renaissance in Historical Thought: Five Centuries of Interpretation.* Houghton Mifflin, Cambridge, MA

Padley G A 1976 *Grammatical Theory in Western Europe 1500–1700: The Latin Tradition.* Cambridge University Press, Cambridge

Padley G A 1985 *Grammatical Theory in Western Europe 1500–1700: Trends in Vernacular Grammar,* 2 vols. Cambridge University Press, Cambridge

Percival W K 1975 The grammatical tradition and the rise of the vernaculars. In: Sebeok T A (ed.) *Current Trends in Linguistics. Vol. 13: Historiography of Linguistics.* Mouton, The Hague

Rowe J H 1974 Sixteenth and seventeenth-century grammars. In: Hymes D (ed.) *Studies in the History of Linguistics: Traditions and Paradigms.* Indiana University Press, Bloomington, IN

W. K. Percival

Renaissance Linguistics: Italian Tradition

Interest in language during the Renaissance in Italy was probably stronger than at any time in the ancient or medieval past, to judge by the quantity of writings devoted to it. This interest was stimulated by the cultural and political conditions of the age, but was also strongly governed and in some ways limited by them. In spite of these constraints, considerable advances were made in areas such as the understanding of the ancestry of Italian, phonetic analysis, and the establishment of the grammar and lexicography of the vernacular.

1. Cultural and Political Background

Educated Italians had two written languages at their disposal. The vernacular had already been well established as a literary language alongside Latin by three great authors of the late thirteenth and fourteenth centuries, Dante Alighieri (1265–1321), Francesco Petrarca (Petrarch) (1304–74), and Giovanni Boccaccio (1313–75), all from Florentine families. But the rise of humanism, to which the study of classical Latin and to a lesser extent Greek was central, meant that Latin retained great prestige and was esteemed by some as worthier than the vernacular. The latter continued to be cultivated by writers in the fifteenth century, particularly during its last quarter. However, the Italian written vernacular did not develop in the same way as in nation states such as England or France. Italy was disunited, a patchwork of states which were often mutual rivals and some of which came under French or Spanish domination after 1494. There was no political capital, therefore, to provide

spoken and written linguistic unity. Nevertheless, there was a natural tendency towards some degree of uniformity throughout the peninsula (Italians still belonged to a cultural community); and this was encouraged by a practical motive—the growth of the printing industry, centered in Venice, and the consequent search for a wider readership—as well as by the triumph of the doctrine (expounded most notably by the Venetian nobleman Pietro Bembo (1470–1547), and dominant by the 1530s) that, if the vernacular was to be a worthy alternative to Latin, it had to be treated with the same seriousness: one should therefore imitate the language of the best authors alone, and this meant the Florentine of Petrarch and to a lesser extent Dante for poetry, that of Boccaccio for prose. This difficult process was accompanied by debates (known as the *questione della lingua* 'the language question') over the rival claims of Latin and the vernacular; over the extent to which written use of the vernacular could be influenced by non-Tuscan varieties, or by contemporary Tuscan, or by the spelling and syntax of Latin itself; and hence over the name to be given to the literary language (e.g., Italian, Tuscan, Florentine, or just the *volgare*). These debates were made all the more acrimonious by the strong challenge which was made to the cultural leadership of Florence, particularly after the death of Lorenzo de' Medici in 1492.

Given this background, interest in language was naturally strong; but it was also partisan. It was often conditioned by the writer's place of origin and by his views on the status of the literary vernacular and on its name and nature. It also tended to focus on the literary rather than the spoken language (as indeed had been the case with grammars of classical languages from the Alexandrian school up to the Middle Ages).

2. Diachronic and Comparative Linguistics

2.1 The Relationship of Latin and Greek

It was widely believed in the fifteenth century that Latin derived from Greek: the classical myth of the transference of 'letters' from ancient Greece to Rome was taken to refer not just to the alphabet but also to language itself (Aeolic, or Attic, or generically Greek). An isolated opponent of this idea was the Sienese theologian Bartolomeo Benvoglienti (d. 1486). More influenced by the myth of the Tower of Babel than by humanistic ideas, he held that the language of the ancient Romans had not been brought from Greece but was a sister language indigenous to Italy. There was still uncertainty in the sixteenth century. Bembo wrote in his *Prose della volgar lingua* (1525) that Latin came from Greek; but Lodovico Castelvetro (ca. 1505–71), of Modena, used the Babel myth in order to criticize this view in his *Giunte* to the *Prose* (written 1549–63).

2.2 The Vernacular: Ancestry and Change

Debates in the early part of the period on the language or languages used in ancient Rome formed the basis of the study of the development of the vernacular. In the first half of the fifteenth century some were still influenced by the medieval view (seen for instance in Dante's *De vulgari eloquentia*) that there was a necessary distinction between a literary language governed by 'art' and an unregulated vernacular which was a product of 'nature.' In a discussion which took place in Florence in 1435, Leonardo Bruni (ca.

1370–1444), a Tuscan, supported the idea that the Roman 'unlettered' had spoken a *sermo vulgaris*, distinct from *sermo litteratus* in the same way as the contemporary vernacular was distinct from Latin. (Bruni did not identify the *sermo vulgaris* with the vernacular, however, nor did he despise the latter, which he believed had a right to its own separate existence.) Flavio Biondo of Forlì (1392–1463) argued, though, that Latin had been the language used by all levels of society, albeit with differences according to the cultural levels of speakers. Writing about 15 years later, Poggio Bracciolini (1380–1459) suggested that the variety of spoken Latin had been due to the movement into Rome of neighboring peoples who spoke different languages.

Biondo attributed the evolution of Latin into the vernacular to the influence of the Germanic invasions. He was no supporter of the vernacular and for him this change was a process of corruption. But the Florentine Leon Battista Alberti (1404–72), while still talking of the corruption of the vernacular, used Biondo's argument to support the younger language: if the ancient Romans had chosen to write in a language which was that of all society, not just of an elite, then his contemporaries should likewise use the vernacular in order to reach a wider audience (proem added to *Della famiglia*, Book III, in 1437).

The Latin–vernacular relationship was often analyzed in the sixteenth century with terms from the natural world. In Pierio Valeriano's *Dialogo della volgar lingua* (after 1524), Gian Giorgio Trissino (1478–1550) describes the Italian vernacular as the daughter of Latin, while Spanish is merely Latin which has grown old. From the 1530s onwards the idea of 'corruption' was developed, particularly by Claudio Tolomei (ca. 1492–1556), Girolamo Muzio (1496–1576), and Benedetto Varchi (1503–65), in a way that would favor the vernacular, with recourse to the Aristotelian distinction between corruption leading merely to *alteratio* (a change of accidents not substance) and that leading to the *generatio* of a new substance, in this case the vernacular. The contrast between 'dead' languages (such as Latin) and 'living' ones was made in 1540 by Alessandro Citolini (ca. 1500–ca. 1583), who may have derived it from Tolomei, the central figure in the 'Sienese school.' Tolomei made the important distinction (described in his *Cesano*, printed 1555 but composed probably in the 1530s) between an uninterrupted tradition from Latin to the vernacular and the later borrowing of learned words, leading to doublets such as *pieve* and *plebe*.

Castelvetro developed these ideas into a concept similar to that of 'vulgar Latin.' Continuing his attack on Bembo's *Prose*, he argued that there had been a continuity between a low form of spoken Latin and the vernacular. The modern *lingua vulgare*, he wrote, was not used in the same form in republican Rome, but, if one ignores changes in gender, inflection, etc., such a language (for which evidence is found in comedies and in writers like Apuleius) was used among the uneducated. Castelvetro also studied the social and psychological reasons which led to the gradual spread of this language during the late Empire and the barbarian invasions. He attributed regional differences in the vernacular to a variety of reasons: in the north of Italy, to the colder climate (which meant that Latin was pronounced more imperfectly there than in Tuscany) and to exchanges of words with peoples beyond the Alps; in the south, to a preference for speaking Greek.

Castelvetro was an outstanding student of etymology and of historical grammar, analyzing for instance the formation of the future tense and of the conditional mood in Italian and recognizing the importance of analogy in the evolution of verb forms.

Relationships between the vernacular and ancient languages other than Latin were also explored, often for the purpose of ennobling the ancestry of the modern language. The idea of a continuity between the lexicon of Etruscan and of Tuscan was expressed by Niccolò della Luna (1410–after 1450) and was developed, with varying degrees of caution, by Tuscans in the sixteenth century. Tolomei (in the *Cesano*) estimated that over two-thirds of Tuscan words came from Latin, but that lesser contributions came from Etruscan and the Germanic languages; however, he recognized that Etruscan words had become part of Latin first. A Florentine, Pier Francesco Giambullari (1495–1555), used the forgeries of Giovanni Nanni of Viterbo (1432?–1502) (published under his Latinized name of Annius in 1498) in order to expound in the 1540s (and hence in the climate of cultural nationalism of Cosimo de' Medici's state) the theory that, after the Flood, Noah had brought Aramaic to Etruria. Aramaic was thus the source of Etruscan, which was older than Greek, and which in turn became the core of Tuscan (*Il Gello*, 1546).

Evidence for a Greek lexical and even morphological substratum was also investigated. Benvoglienti gave a list of words which could be derived from Greek and compared the definite articles in Greek and the vernacular. Raffaele Maffei, in a work printed in 1506, also produced evidence that Greek had left its legacy in the lexicon of the vernacular. According to Valeriano, Trissino believed that, while Latin was the mother of the vernacular, the Greek of the 'Grecianized Romans' who migrated from Constantinople after the Lombards had been driven out of Italy was its foster mother and the source of its definite articles.

Two later contributions to this debate came from Ascanio Persio (1554–1610) in his *Discorso intorno alla conformità della lingua italiana con le più nobili antiche lingue e principalmente con la greca* (1592) and Angelo Monosini in his *Floris italicae linguae libri* (1604). Persio, from Matera in the Basilicata, was able to distinguish between Greek words which had come through Christian Latin and those which came from the living Greek still used in the south. His title suggests knowledge of Henri Estienne's (ca. 1531–98) *Traicté de la conformité du langage françois avec le grec* (1565; see *Renaissance Linguistics: French Tradition*); however, while the Frenchman was arguing for a direct link with ancient Greek, Persio (like Monosini) acknowledged that Latin was the main source of 'our Italian language.'

Filippo Sassetti (1540–88), a scholar turned merchant, noted during his travels in India some similarities between words in Sanskrit and Italian; but his observations were not taken further.

The Florentine Vincenzio Borghini (1515–80) made brief but perceptive contributions to the study of linguistic history, many of which he unfortunately left unpolished and unpublished: for example, essays on why languages change, on how and why loan words enter languages, and on the causes of semantic change (which he gave as changes in the thing designated, a tendency to move from general to narrower meanings, and changes in customs).

3. Spelling Systems and Phonetic Analysis

Two of the principal factors which led to proposals to modify spelling were the movement to establish the autonomy and dignity of the vernacular and its literature alongside Latin, and the desire to support one variety of the vernacular against others. Discussions of orthography could lead in turn to the analysis of the sounds of Tuscan and of other contrasting pronunciations. Experimentation with new spelling systems began, in one exceptional case, in the manuscript age, but it was particularly associated in Italy with the introduction of printing and with varieties of italic type, a new style first used for a complete book in 1501.

Such new spelling systems shared the aim of helping readers to understand the written language more easily, avoiding confusion between words which would otherwise be written in the same way. They could also give some help with pronunciation, at least by indicating some stresses and in a few cases by marking open and closed *e* and *o* or voiced and voiceless *z* (whose distribution varies regionally). A variety of strategies were used separately or in combination: (a) assigning existing variant letter forms to different sounds (e.g., *i* for the vowel but *j* for the semiconsonant [j], *u* for the vowel but *v* for the consonant, *z* for [ts] but *ç* for [dz]); (b) using diacritics such as grave, acute, or occasionally circumflex accents on vowels; (c) borrowing characters from the Greek alphabet; (d) replacing etymological spellings (e.g., preferring *i* to *y* and *f* to *ph*, so that there was one symbol for one sound, or using *-tt-*, which reflected pronunciation, rather than *-ct-* or *-pt-*).

The first two of these resources were used by Alberti in his manuscript grammar of 1437–41 (see Sect. 4), and again, in print this time, in the 1540s by Tolomei and Giambullari. The first three were used by Trissino in his printed alphabets of 1524 and 1529; his use of epsilon and omega (to be linked with his personal enthusiasm for Greek culture; see Sect. 2.2) aroused particular hostility for many years thereafter. However, only two reforms were to have lasting effect. One was the introduction of accents to distinguish between certain monosyllables (e.g., *è* 'is' versus *e* 'and') and to mark oxytone words (e.g., *andò*) and the use of the apostrophe to indicate the loss of a vowel where two words came into contact. This began, in print, with a Petrarch printed by Aldo Manuzio (ca. 1450–1515) and edited by Bembo in 1501, and was then extended by other printers and editors. The other reform was the gradual elimination (by authors, printers, and their editors) of most Latinizing spellings in the course of the sixteenth century. This was favored by the return towards prehumanistic, fourteenth-century literary models, and guidance in this direction was first given in Fortunio's *Regole* (see Sect. 4).

Since the linguistic interests of Italians were predominantly in the written language, it is not surprising that by far the best description of the articulation of Tuscan should have come in a work by a foreigner, the *De italica pronunciatione et orthographia* (1569) of the Welsh doctor Siôn Dafydd Rhys (1534–ca. 1609). Other major contributions included the published and unpublished works of Tolomei (such as *Il Polito*, 1525, an excellent analysis of the relationship between spelling and speech, with a good understanding of the primacy of speech and of the social dimensions of the problem), and the descriptions of articulation in the *Elementi del parlar toscano* of Giorgio Bartoli (d. 1583).

4. Grammar

In the study of Latin grammar, some innovations appear in the *Regulae* of Guarino Veronese (1374–1460), written before 1418, which dispensed with such concepts of the medieval *modistae* as the *suppositum* (subject) and *appositum* (predicate), and *transitio* and *intransitio* (respectively, the relation between verb and object and between verb and subject). Lorenzo Valla's (ca. 1407–57) *Elegantiae* (finished in 1449) re-examined in detail the morphological, syntactic, and lexical distinctions offered by Latin. A number of humanist grammars written in the second half of the century based themselves on grammars of the fourth and fifth centuries (Donatus and Priscian) rather than on medieval sources.

Grammarians of the vernacular naturally took Latin grammar as their blueprint. One of the purposes of the first grammar, written by Alberti as early as 1437–41, was precisely to show that Tuscan could be analyzed with the same criteria as Latin. However, the use of a Latin-based framework made it difficult to deal with innovations of the vernacular such as definite and indefinite articles, the conditional mood, the loss of the neuter gender, and of distinctive case endings. There was much debate over the status of the 'signs of case' (e.g., *a, di, da* and compounds like *al, del, dal*).

Another potential problem was that of the type of vernacular to be analyzed. Alberti wrote before the rise of imitation of the fourteenth-century literary tradition and he therefore chose contemporary spoken Florentine usage. But his precocious grammar found no imitators. Grammars written by non-Tuscans in the sixteenth century codified the usage of the great Tuscan authors of the fourteenth century and were intended to help readers to model their own writings on them. Thus the *Regole grammaticali della volgar lingua* (1516) of Giovan Francesco Fortunio (ca. 1470–1517), of Pordenone, provided a guide, based on Dante, Petrarch, and Boccaccio, to morphology and spelling, the areas in which non-Tuscans needed most guidance. The third book of Bembo's *Prose*, the work which provided the most influential statement of the argument for imitation in the vernacular, included a grammar based chiefly on Petrarch and Boccaccio; the dialog form used by Bembo helped him to avoid the schematic and the technical. Later grammars, however (including recastings of Bembo's), were easier for readers to consult. That of Marco Antonio Ateneo Carlino (Naples, 1533) used as models two modern authors (Bembo himself and Jacopo Sannazaro, 1456?–1530) as well as Petrarch. The first grammar to treat syntax separately, if briefly, was that of Rinaldo Corso (1525–ca. 1580; Venice, 1549). A much fuller treatment of syntax is found in Giambullari's *Regole della lingua fiorentina* (1552) and owes much to a work by an Englishman, Thomas Linacre's (ca. 1460–1524) *De emendata structura latini sermonis* (1524). Giambullari's grammar is part of a reaction on the part of Florence to the way in which non-Tuscans had appropriated what Florentines considered to be their language; the usage which he describes is based on the living usage of his cultured contemporaries, but he also takes earlier writers into account.

Bembo was the only outstanding linguistic scholar of the sixteenth century to publish a complete grammar. However, of the others, Tolomei and Vincenzio Borghini both planned to write grammars and left various sketches on grammatical topics; Castelvetro's works (mostly published posthumously) dealt with aspects of grammar, including its historical dimension (see Sect. 2.2); and Lionardo Salviati (1539–89), a Florentine, wrote at length on nouns and articles in his *Avvertimenti* on Boccaccio's *Decameron* (1584–86).

5. Lexicography

Although there were some fifteenth-century antecedents (e.g., Venetian–German and vernacular–Latin glossaries), lexicography flourished, like grammar, only from the second quarter of the sixteenth century. From then on, the purpose of dictionaries and glossaries was, as with grammars, to describe fourteenth-century literary Tuscan; another similarity was that, for a long time, their compilers came from outside Tuscany.

After some relatively unsuccessful attempts in the 1520s and 1530s—Niccolò Liburnio's (ca. 1474–1557) *Tre fontane* (Venice, 1526); Lucilio Minerbi's (ca. 1490–after 1522) *Vocabolario*, printed with the *Decameron*, also in Venice, in 1535; Fabricio Luna's (d. 1559) *Vocabulario di cinque mila vocabuli toschi*, Naples, 1536—a notable improvement in lexicography was marked by works produced in the 1540s by two authors from the Ferrara area; Alberto Acarisio's (1497?–1544?) *Vocabolario, grammatica et orthographia de la lingua volgare* (1543), which is much better organized than its predecessors, explains words with definitions (in the vernacular) or synonyms (vernacular or Latin), and offers information on the register of some words; Francesco Alunno's (1484?–1556) *Le ricchezze della lingua volgare* (1543), based on Boccaccio, which was partly a dictionary, partly a concordance (the meaning of many entries is left unexplained), and (like Acarisio's dictionary) included a grammar; and Alunno's encyclopaedia-cum-dictionary *La fabrica del mondo* (1546–48). Both Acarisio and Alunno showed an interest in contemporary non-Tuscan usage, and Alunno gave separate lists of foreign, dialectal, or technical words which conform with those found in his approved authors. In the *Ricchezze* Alunno noted where Italian words have cognate forms in other languages (e.g., *città* has similar forms in Latin, Spanish, French, and English), and he stressed that Boccaccio did not limit his vocabulary to Tuscan. But a strict adherence to Tuscan and to archaizing principles underlay the first Florentine dictionary, the *Vocabolario* (1612) of the Accademia della Crusca. The compilers made some methodological progress over predecessors such as Alunno by giving more emphasis to definitions rather than synonyms.

6. Translation

The first modern Italian treatise on translation was Bruni's *De recta interpretatione* (ca. 1420). It arose out of his experiences in translating from Greek into Latin, but he saw its conclusions as equally valid for translations into the vernacular. The qualities which he considered essential, but which had been lacking from medieval translations, included an excellent knowledge of both languages being used, a sense of style, and the ability to imitate the characteristic style of the source text.

In the sixteenth century, discussions on translation were given new impetus by the Latin–vernacular rivalry, by new ideas about dead and living languages and comparative linguistics, and (in some cases) by Protestant sympathies and by anticlericalism. Among the general questions raised were those of whether knowledge should be vulgarized, whether translation affects the expression of concepts, and whether new words were needed in the vernacular.

Some took a liberal attitude to these problems. In Sperone Speroni's (1500–88) *Dialogo delle lingue* (Venice, 1542), the philosopher Pietro Pomponazzi says that all languages are of equal worth and that Greek philosophical works could and should be translated into the vernacular. Giovan Battista Gelli (1498–1563), in his *I capricci del bottaio*, Ragionamento v (1546), repeated Bruni's advice and urged Tuscans to translate sacred scriptures, works of learning, and even everyday legal documents, creating neologisms where necessary; this would enrich their language as well as having spiritual, educational, and practical benefits.

Others were more cautious. Castelvetro wrote (in a letter of 1543) that some concepts were so bound up with words that they were untranslatable; there was a risk of providing inappropriate 'clothes' for concepts in other languages. As for the question of neologisms, he tried to use the natural words of his own language in his translation of Aristotle's *Poetics*. Tolomei (in a letter also of 1543) approved of the principle of making works available in other languages but said that a poet inevitably lacked originality when translating another poet. Borghini, like Castelvetro, warned of the difficulties of translating concepts (because of the differences between languages, customs, etc.) and of the problems of inventing new words.

7. Nonliterary Varieties of the Vernacular

It was seen above (Sect. 2.2 and Sect. 3) that the Italian Renaissance showed a certain degree of interest in the social use of language and in spoken language. A recognition that, when one considered language in general as a means of human communication, the spoken word had primacy over the written word, spread in the sixteenth century with the reaction, particularly strong in Tuscany, against the humanistic attitude typified by Bembo's assertion (in the *Prose*) that no language could truly exist without a writer. In practice, however, varieties of the vernacular other than the literary tended to be mentioned, if at all, only in the course of the study of the written language. Dialect or regional synonyms might, for instance, be used in Latin–vernacular dictionaries or in glossaries designed to help non-Tuscans to read works from the literary canon. In discussions on the literary vernacular, considerable use was made of the potential parallel between the linguistic situation in Italy (where Italians saw that they shared a literary language in the making but argued about whether it was Tuscan or 'common') and the five 'dialects' of ancient Greece, Attic, Ionic, Doric, Aeolic, and the 'koiné' or common dialect. It was in this context that the term *dialetto* was introduced in the mid-sixteenth century and then used in contrast with *lingua*.

The few descriptions of dialect phonology came from outside the mainstream of vernacular culture. The humanist Paolo Pompilio (ca. 1455–91) mentioned some regional pronunciations in 1488; but the first detailed (and affectionate) description of a dialect appeared only in 1606, the *Prissian da Milan della parnonzia milanesa* by G. A. Biffi.

An outstanding example of a scholar who examined non-literary varieties of Tuscan was Borghini. He studied the language of artisans and of rustic or female speakers, as well as of nonliterary texts. But the main aim of such research was to provide authority for rare forms in the texts of fourteenth-century authors.

See also: Italian.

Bibliography

Malmberg B 1973 *La traduzione: Saggi e studi.* Lint, Trieste
Migliorini B 1984 *Storia della lingua italiana*, 2nd edn. Faber and Faber, London
Padley G A 1988 *Grammatical Theory in Western Europe 1500–1700: Trends in Vernacular Grammar*, II. Cambridge University Press, Cambridge
Ramat P, Niederehe H-J, Koerner K (eds.) 1986 *The History of Linguistics in Italy.* Benjamins, Amsterdam
Tancke G 1984 *Die italienischen Wörterbücher von den Anfängen bis zum Erscheinen des 'Vocabolario degli Accademici della Crusca' (1612).* Niemeyer, Tübingen
Tavoni M 1990 La linguistica rinascimentale: L'Europa occidentale. In: Lepschy G C (ed.) *Storia della linguistica*, vol. 2. Il Mulino, Bologna
Trabalza C 1908 *Storia della grammatica italiana.* Hoepli, Milan

B. Richardson

Renaissance Linguistics: Spanish Tradition

The origin of Spanish Renaissance linguistics can be traced to Italy in the 1440s, to the work of Lorenzo Valla (1407–57). His ideas, goals, and methods decisively influenced early Spanish humanism. One of Valla's goals was the recovery of Classical Latin, rescuing it from what he perceived as the clumsiness and corruption of Medieval and Church Latin. Recovery of the language of Cicero and Virgil would make possible the rediscovery of Classical learning. Valla also wanted to discredit the canon of medieval grammarians, and the scholastic philosophers who had provided the intellectual basis for medieval thought. Valla's tool to achieve both goals was philological exegesis (the use of grammar, rhetoric, and history to establish the validity of part or all of a text), which was not of his invention, but which he developed and perfected (see *Philology and History*).

Humanist questioning of Medieval Latin texts presented a problem for the Church, since much of Church doctrine had resulted from readings of those texts. The Church was also troubled by humanism's rejection of scholastic philosophy, because it served as the base for medieval theology. The resulting conflict between the Church and humanism greatly affected grammatical studies during the Renaissance, to some degree everywhere in Europe, but particularly in Spain.

During the early Renaissance an interest in 'vernacular humanism' paralleled the interest in 'Classical humanism.' The concern with correct usage of Latin was transferred to the vernacular languages, and it led to the writing of both grammars and treatises on the merits and values of these languages. For Spanish, one of these treatises deserves special consideration, the *Diálogo de la Lengua* (1535; written in Naples, first published in Madrid in 1737) by Juan de Valdés (ca. 1495–1541). It is an attempt to do for the Spanish language what Pietro Bembo (1470–1547) had done for Tuscan (Italian) in his *Prose della Volgar Lingua* (1525). The development of national states and the need for a unifying official language added to interest in the study of the vernaculars.

Early humanists were not interested in explanatory theories of grammar; their objective was to describe the language of the great figures of Classical antiquity, not to explain the nature of language and how it worked. Moreover, the theoretical approach to language with which they were familiar, 'speculative grammar,' had been developed within Aristotelian scholasticism, which they rejected. However, towards the end of the first half of the sixteenth century, when the goals of the humanist movement had been achieved, interest in theory again developed. As far as linguistics is concerned, the Renaissance can be divided into two major periods. The first one is dominated by descriptivism, the second one by an interest in explanatory theories of language and grammar. In Spanish Renaissance linguistics one finds the same two periods, the second one beginning toward the 1580s. Each one of these periods in Spain will be dominated by one major figure, Nebrija and Sanctius, respectively. Those topics of Spanish linguistics that overlap the above temporal division will be treated separately.

1. The Early Renaissance in Spain

Lorenzo Valla's ideas and methods spread to Spain quickly, earlier than to other parts of Europe. This is partially explained by the Spanish (Aragonese) presence in Italy. In 1440 Valla, while acting as secretary of Alfonso V of Aragón, wrote his *Declamatio de Falso Credita et Ementita Donatione Constantini*, where he first used the philological method to expose as fraudulent the document used by the Church to claim the Italian territories of the former Roman Empire. Obviously this favored Alfonso's claim to territories in Italy.

A more important factor was Antonio de Nebrija's humanistic training in Italy. In 1463, at age 19, Nebrija left the University of Salamanca to continue studying at the Spanish College in Bologna. He spent 7 years in Italy studying the ideas and methods of humanist philology. When he returned to Spain in 1470 Nebrija had become a devoted follower of Valla.

1.1 Antonio de Nebrija (1444–1522)

Antonio (also Elio Antonio) de Nebrija (or Lebrija, for his place of birth in southern Spain) dominated the early Renaissance in Spain through the volume, quality, and diversity of his work. He is the first to cover all the fields and languages of interest to early humanism. He wrote grammars of Latin (including a 1486 version in Castilian, for Queen Isabella) as well as one of Castilian. He also wrote bilingual dictionaries of Latin and Castilian, and studies on the orthography and pronunciation of Classical Latin, Greek, and Hebrew. Nebrija also wrote dictionaries of Latin legal and medical terminology, a book on history and archaeology of Spain, and other diverse works, including poetry composed in classical Latin.

Nebrija's first major work, his *Introductiones Latinae* (Salamanca 1481) appeared while he was teaching at the University of Salamanca. It was an immediate success; by the time of its author's death the book had gone through at least 50 editions or printings, in Spain and abroad. After Nebrija's death the *Introductiones* was published several times during the sixteenth century in France and Italy. An English translation of the 1486 Castilian version appeared in England in 1631. In Spain the *Introductiones* was the most popular text for teaching Latin until the eighteenth century. Its success was determined mostly by its didactic nature. Nebrija was an admirer of the Latin (Byzantine) grammarian Priscian, but he realized, and said so, that Priscian wrote for students whose first language was Latin, while he was writing for students with no knowledge of Latin when they arrived in school; the book was the first one consciously written for students of Latin as a second language.

His dictionaries, Latin–Spanish (1492), Spanish–Latin (ca. 1495), were models of lexicography; they represented a complete break with the medieval tradition in this kind of work. His Spanish grammar, *Gramática de la Lengua Castellana* (Salamanca 1492), was the first complete one for a modern language. It includes books (sections) on syntax and on Spanish for foreigners, in addition to the traditional sections on orthography, pronunciation, prosody, and morphology. Rather than simply adapting and translating from Latin, Nebrija in the *Gramática* develops a new grammatical terminology for Spanish.

In 1502 Nebrija joined the group set up in Alcalá by Cardinal Jiménez Cisneros to publish a polyglot Bible, but he abandoned Alcalá when Cisneros forbade changes in the Medieval Latin version. On returning to the University of Salamanca he tried to publish a list of biblical errors deriving from a poor knowledge of Latin, Greek, and Hebrew, but the Grand Inquisitor prohibited the publication and ordered Nebrija to surrender the list, which he did. Nebrija's problems with the Church and the Inquisition had no grave consequences, but only because of his friendship with the leaders of the Spanish Church, and with the Spanish monarchs Ferdinand and Isabella. Later grammarians would not find dealing with the Inquisition as easy.

Nebrija spent his last years as a professor at the University of Alcalá, which had been founded by Cardinal Cisneros. In recognition of the importance of Nebrija's scholarship and continuing productivity Cisneros said in the decree of appointment that the Spanish grammarian would draw a salary whether he taught or not.

1.2 Other Descriptive Grammars

Several grammars on Spanish were published before 1580, but only one in Spain proper, Baltasar Sotomayor's *Grammática* (1565), which compares Spanish and French to facilitate the learning of the latter. Four were published in the Spanish territories of the Low Countries, in Amberes (Antwerp), or Lovaina (Louvain), all to facilitate the learning of Spanish. Two are anonymous (1555, 1559), but the authors of the others were Gabriel Meurier and Cristóbal Villalón (both 1558). Meurier's includes French as well as Spanish, while Villalón's is the best of this whole group. Two grammars appeared in Italy during this period, those of Giovanni Mario Alessandri (1560) and Giovanni Miranda (1565). None is comparable in intent or content to Nebrija's.

Latin grammars were published by Bernabé de Busto (Salamanca 1533) and Bachiller Thámara (Antwerp 1550), both in Spanish, but only four works on the Classical languages written during this period, all by the same author, deserve any consideration, and only because the author, Francisco Sánchez de las Brozas (usually referred to in Spanish as 'el Brocense,' and in other languages as 'Sanctius') is the major figure of the second part of the Renaissance in Spain. Two of his introductory textbooks on Latin were published in Lyon in 1562; another one, written in Spanish, was published in Spain in 1576. Sanctius published an introductory Greek grammar in Antwerp in 1581. His major work, the *Minerva*, will be discussed below, in the second period of the Renaissance.

Certainly worthy of mention is the work on Amerindian languages done by Spanish missionaries in the New World. They had composed by 1571 five grammars of Mexican languages (one of Tarasco and four of Nahua) and one of the Quechua of Peru. All had attached vocabularies in the local language and Spanish. This was achieved while there were many modern European languages, English and German among them, for which full grammars had not yet been written.

2. The Late Renaissance in Spain

Descriptive grammars of Spanish continued to appear during the second part of the Spanish linguistic Renaissance; many of them, by authors of other nationalities, were published abroad, in England, France, Germany, and Italy. Of those published in Spain the only one worthy of mention is Bartolomé Jiménez Patón's *Instituciones de la Gramática Española* (Baeza 1614).

The first dictionary of Spanish, by Sebastián de Covarrubias (1539–1613), the *Tesoro de la Lengua Castellana o Española*, was first published in Madrid in 1611. Covarrubias includes archaisms, neologisms, loanwords (many of Amerindian origin, e.g., *canoa* 'canoe,' *hamaca* 'hammock'), and vulgarisms, labeling them as such. Definitions are usually precise and concise but complete, except when dealing with terms related to history, geography, the arts, religion, mythology, or to the exotic. The entries for the latter resemble those of the medieval encyclopedic treatises, as do many of his often incorrect etymologies. The book, however, is of great value for its documentation of the lexicon of the period, and for the interpretation of the writings of Covarrubias's contemporaries.

2.1 Sanctius (1523–1600)

Francisco Sánchez de las Brozas (Sanctius or 'el Brocense') was born in western Spain, but spent his early life in the service of the Portuguese court. After returning to Spain at age 20 he dedicated himself almost entirely to the academic life. He studied at the Universities of Valladolid and Salamanca, and in 1554 became a *praeceptor* 'lecturer' at the Trilingual (Latin, Greek, Hebrew) College of the latter university. In 1573 he obtained the Chair of Rhetoric, and later those of Greek and Latin, all at Salamanca. In addition to those books mentioned above he wrote treatises on rhetoric, philosophy, and theology, as well as translations, and editions of literary works.

In 1584 Sanctius was ordered to appear before the Inquisitorial Tribunal in Valladolid, was reprimanded for his textual interpretation, and warned that future errors would be severely punished. In 1593, the year of his retirement from the university, he was again investigated by the Inquisition. Sanctius died before the end of his trial, and was denied burial honors. The Inquisition's preoccupation with Renaissance philology and grammar is evident from the pejorative use of the word *gramático* 'grammarian' during the trial, when addressing Sanctius. This explains why Sanctius (and later Correas, see below) never wrote a treatise on grammatical theory, on linguistics as such. His ideas on the subject have to be culled from a book that is in appearance nothing more than a study of Latin grammar, his *Minerva: seu de Causis Linguae Latinae* (Salamanca 1587).

Sanctius' approach to grammar and language can be placed in the same mentalist, rationalist, tradition of medieval speculative grammar which developed the ideas first posited in Aristotle's *Peri hermeneias*. The full title of his *Minerva* (see above) shows that he acknowledged a debt to Julius Caesar Scaliger's (1484–1558) *De Causis Linguae Latinae* (1540); his influence on the Port-Royal grammarians was expressly recognized by one of the authors (Claude Lancelot) of the *Grammaire Générale et Raisonnée* (1660).

There are, however, major differences between Sanctius and those that precede or follow him. Sanctius is the only one to postulate an underlying structure that is syntactic rather than semantic in nature, as well as the only one to postulate a grammatical or syntactic system, rather than a purely logical one. He will constantly justify what he says by referring to *grammaticae ratio* 'grammatical system or logic.' His underlying structure not only includes elements that must be understood as deleted from the surface; it also includes grammatical forms that, as Sanctius shows, are essential at that level but cannot appear in the surface. In the *Minerva* the perfect grammarian is defined as one who in Cicero's or Virgil's books will identify which words are nouns, which are verbs, as well as other matters that concern only grammar, even if he does not understand the meanings of the words. Not until much later can one find a statement that so clearly upholds the autonomy of grammar. Sanctius did not develop a system of rules to relate his two levels of syntactic structures, but the *Minerva* is nearer to modern generative grammar than any other work written before the twentieth century.

2.2 Other Theoretical Grammarians

Two other Spanish grammarians of the seventeenth century show a major interest in grammatical theory, Correas and Caramuel. The former applied and developed the ideas of Sanctius, the latter represented a return to late medieval grammatical thought.

Gonzalo Correas (1571?–1631) was born in the same area of western Spain as Sanctius. Correas taught Greek and Hebrew at the University of Salamanca. He published grammars of Greek, Latin, and Spanish (and a now lost one on Hebrew), edited and translated Classical works, compiled a collection of Spanish proverbs and popular sayings, and composed some minor poetry in Greek, Latin, and Spanish. In his time he was very well-known for several treatises proposing the radical reform of Spanish orthography.

Correas was the most important follower in Spain of the author of the *Minerva*. Like Sanctius, Correas never wrote a linguistic treatise as such. His ideas on grammatical theory and universal grammar appear in the *Arte Grande de la Lengua Castellana*, an excellent and lengthy grammar of Spanish finished in 1626 but not published until this century, and in the *Trilingüe de Tres Lenguas* (Salamanca 1627), which includes grammars of Spanish, Latin, and Greek, all written in Spanish. Correas held that grammar (i.e., syntax) was for the most part common to all languages, and made use of this idea in writing the *Trilingüe*. In his treatment of syntax he closely follows Sanctius.

Juan Caramuel y Lobkowitz (1606–82) was a bishop who subscribed to the ideas of Scholasticism. His only book on grammar, the *Grammatica Audax* (Frankfurt 1654), dealt with Latin. He was a follower of the medieval *Modistae* and their speculative grammar, particularly of Thomas of Erfurt, whose *De Modis Significandi sive Grammatica Speculativa* (ca. 1305) was at the time attributed to J. Duns Scotus (Caramuel claimed to be a follower of Duns Scotus). Caramuel's *Grammatica* anticipates the semantic and logical position of the authors of the Port-Royal grammar.

3. The Preoccupation with Orthography

The first treatment of the writing system of Spanish appears in Enrique de Villena's *Arte de Trovar*, completed in 1433. It is an interesting work, but it should be studied in the context of the Middle Ages rather than here. The first to treat this subject in the Renaissance was Antonio de Nebrija in his 1492 *Gramática de la Lengua Castellana* and later in his *Reglas de Orthographía en la Lengua Castellana* (Alcalá de Henares 1517). Nebrija is perfectly aware of the difference between letter and sound of language; in the *Reglas* he very clearly states that a letter is nothing but a mark or figure through which a sound of language is represented. In the same book he says that humans can make an infinite number of sounds, but that each language has a limited number of specifically linguistic sounds, showing his awareness of what modern linguistics calls 'phonemes.'

Writing after the invention of printing, Nebrija shared with many of his contemporaries the preoccupation with the standardization of orthography, to the point of suggesting that the standardized form be enforced by royal decree. Spelling, Nebrija says, should show a one-to-one relationship between letters and sounds; both in the *Gramática* and in the *Reglas* he insists on requiring that one write as one speaks, and vice versa. Nebrija proposed the reform of Spanish orthography to make it adjust to the above ideal of biuniqueness. This concern with the correspondence between speech sounds and letters will be shared up to the late twentieth century by most Spanish grammarians.

The most interesting proposals for spelling reform during the later Renaissance are those of Mateo Alemán, a major literary figure whose *Ortografía Castellana* (Mexico 1609) reflected the changes which had taken place in Spanish pronunciation since Nebrija's time, and those of Gonzalo Correas, whose *Nueva i Zierta Ortografía Kastellana* (Salamanca 1624) and *Ortografía Kastellana Nueva i Perfeta* (Salamanca 1630), reflect in their titles some of the changes he proposed.

4. Historical Linguistics

As stated previously, during the early Renaissance vernacular humanism ran parallel to Classical humanism, very often in the same author. Proponents of the merits of the vernacular languages were familiar with the mostly mythological histories of Latin and Hebrew, and felt the need to give a similar historical background to their own languages. Nebrija in the introduction to his Spanish *Gramática* gave a nutshell history of the Spanish language; he correctly saw Castilian as developing from the 'corruption' of Classical Latin. Since he perceived the latter as the most perfect of languages, claiming it as the ancestor could not but enhance Castilian, even if corruption was the link between the two. The idea, essentially correct, was embraced by grammarians and authors of treatises on language during most of the sixteenth century. However, perception of Spanish as an imperial language, spoken by the rulers of the Low Countries, most of Italy, and immense territories in the New World, Asia, and the Pacific Ocean, made scholars desire an even more illustrious beginning for the language. Spain was not in this alone; most of Europe was making fantastic claims for the particular vernacular of each country.

In this context, in 1588, 'relics' were found in Granada, among which were manuscripts supposedly dating from the first century AD, some written in Latin, others in Castilian. Some of the documents in Castilian were attributed to St Cecil, disciple of St James the Apostle, patron of Spain. Until the end of the seventeenth century, when the Vatican declared that the 'relics' were false, they served to validate claims that Castilian developed independently, rather than being a 'corruption' of Latin, and was at least as old as the latter. The first history of the Spanish language, Bernardo José de Aldrete's (1560–1641) *Del Origen y Principio de la Lengua Castellana o Romance que Oi se Usa en España* (Rome 1606), was written to combat this so-called 'theory of early Castilian.' José de Aldrete, although he himself was a member of the clergy, published his book in Rome to avoid conflict with the Spanish Church and Inquisition. For the same reason, rather than questioning the authenticity of the 'relics,' he said that the documents were written in Spanish not because the language was spoken in the first century AD, but because St Cecil had worked the miracle of writing in a language which would not exist until a thousand years later. By giving a miracle as an alternative explanation, José de Aldrete obviously hoped to safeguard his work from attacks by the Church. José de Aldrete's book is more modern than any written on historical linguistics up to the end of the eighteenth century.

5. Dialects and Sociolects

A number of the grammarians working with the vernaculars during the Renaissance noted the geographic and social variety occurring in those languages. As early as 1535 Juan de Valdés in his *Diálogo de la Lengua* said that there were many varieties of Castilian because it was spoken in many regions, each region having vocabulary items and pronunciation that were peculiar to it. He points out two reasons for this variety: diversity of realms, and contact with speakers from neighboring regions. In his *Del Origen y Principio* Bernardo José de Aldrete devotes one whole chapter to dialects, calling them by that same name. José de Aldrete states that there are as many dialects of one same language as there is geographic diversity. He points to differences between rural and urban speech. He goes on to say that there is diversity even within a city, if it is large enough, as well as between speakers from lowlands and mountains in rural areas.

Sebastián de Covarrubias' *Tesoro* is the first Spanish dictionary which gives a definition of dialect. It is, Covarrubias says, that which is peculiar to each language, through which we distinguish the speech of Old and New Castile, of Andalusia, and of other regions, where, even though the same Castilian language is spoken, there are different manners of pronunciation and of forming vocabulary; and all other nations have these same differences that distinguish people from one province from those of another. Covarrubias often points out the regional and social usage of the words he defines.

Gonzalo Correas in his *Arte grande* called for a standard or norm, that of pure Castilian. This notwithstanding, he criticized some aspects of the language in Castile. Throughout the book he discusses regional differences, those that are morphological or syntactic as well as those that occur in pronunciation and vocabulary. He even recognized social variety, indicating that this occurs because of age, social class, sex, profession or occupation, and rural or urban condition. More importantly, Correas stated that each social variety, each sociolect, was as valid within its context as any other, specifically indicating that the linguistic style of the court and nobility was only one part of each language, other styles being just as good and as elegant for their speakers and circumstances.

Dialectology and sociolinguistics did not come into their own until much later. However, modern linguists will not find fault in the above ideas of the Spanish Renaissance concerning geographic and social variety.

Bibliography

Breva-Claramonte M 1983 *Sanctius' Theory of Language: A Contribution to the History of Renaissance Linguistics.* Benjamins, Amsterdam

Lépinette B 1989 Contribution à l'étude du *Tesoro* de Sebastián de Covarrubias (1611). *Historiographia Linguistica* 16: 257–310

Padley G A 1976 *Grammatical Theory in Western Europe 1500–1700: The Latin Tradition.* Cambridge University Press, Cambridge

Padley G A 1985 *Grammatical Theory in Western Europe 1500–1700: Trends in Vernacular Grammar I.* Cambridge University Press, Cambridge

Quilis A, Niederehe H-J (eds.) 1986 *The History of Linguistics in Spain.* Benjamins, Amsterdam

Robins R H 1979 *A Short History of Linguistics*, 2nd edn. Longman, London

Tusón J 1982 *Aproximación a la Historia de la Lingüística.* Teide, Barcelona

J. C. Zamora

Renou, Louis (1896–1966)

A prolific and versatile scholar, Louis Renou was one of the foremost indologists of the twentieth century. Born on October 28, 1896, he took his *agrégation* in 1920, his academic career having been interrupted by service in World War I. His first important publications appeared in 1925. These included two doctoral theses, the main one on the perfect tense in the Vedic hymns (Renou 1925) and the subsidiary one comprising a critical edition and French translation of the section on India in Ptolemy's *Geography*.

Renou's interest in India had been aroused by the Sanskrit scholar Sylvain Lévi and his first important appointment was to the chair of Sanskrit and Comparative Grammar at the University of Lyon (1925–28). In 1929 he became professor at the Ecole des Hautes Etudes and in 1937 in the Faculté des Lettres at the Sorbonne. He was Membre de l'Institut and Chevalier de la Légion d'Honneur.

His doctoral research proved to be an indication of the direction Renou was to take subsequently. In the broad pattern of his work there are two main strands: the study of the Vedas and the study of grammar. His study of the language of the Vedas led to the publication of a grammar of Vedic (Renou 1952). As with his work of a similar sort on classical Sanskrit, this was intended to be purely descriptive and deliberately avoided a discussion of the prehistory of the language or indeed of any questions of historical linguistics. He published several translations of Vedic hymns and conceived as a major task a complete translation of the *Ṛgveda*. Sadly he died before this was completed.

Published work by Renou on classical Sanskrit language is essentially of two sorts. First, there are teaching grammars (e.g., Renou 1930) and monographs on aspects of the grammar of Sanskrit. Second, he produced studies on the work of the Sanskrit grammarians. An important publication emerging from this research was a new translation of Pāṇini's *Aṣṭādhyāyī* (1947–54; see *Pāṇini*). His translation was based on the seventh-century exegetical work, *Kāśikāvṛtti*, and in collaboration with a Japanese scholar, Yutaka Ojihara, he published a translation of this (1960–67), completed after his death. Published over a longer period than either of these was his translation of the twelfth-century grammatical treatise *Durghaṭavṛtti* of Śaraṇadeva (1940–56). One offshoot of these studies was a book on Sanskrit grammatical terminology (Renou 1942). A major combined outcome of his work on Vedic and classical Sanskrit was the series of *Etudes védiques et pāṇinéennes*, which was started in 1955 and the sixteenth volume of which appeared in the year after his death.

The wide range of Renou's other publications includes lexicographical and bibliographical works. There are also important works to which his main contribution was that of editor. Among these are editions of the text of the *Upaniṣads* with a French translation, and general studies of Indian civilization. His interests also extended to Indian religion and this led to his being invited to deliver the Jordan Lectures in Comparative Religion in the University of London in 1951 (Renou 1953).

Bibliography

Filliozat J 1967 Louis Renou et son œuvre scientifique. *Journal asiatique* **255**: 1–30

Renou L 1925 *La valeur du parfait dans les hymnes védiques*. Champion, Paris
Renou L 1930 *Grammaire sanscrite*, 2 vols. Adrien-Maisonneuve, Paris
Renou L 1942 *Terminologie grammaticale du sanskrit*, 4 parts. Champion, Paris
Renou L 1947–54 *La grammaire de Pāṇini, traduite du sanskrit avec des extraits des commentaires indigènes*, 3 parts. Klincksieck, Paris
Renou L 1952 *Grammaire de la langue védique*. IAC, Lyon and Paris
Renou L 1953 *Religions of Ancient India*. University of London, London

R. E. Asher

Reported Speech

Language is an autoreflexive sign system which affords the possibility of referring to itself. Speech can be used to report an infinite variety of things, including speech and thought. It can be used to make a distinction between one's own words and those of another, as well as between using a word in its proper sense and mentioning it as a vital function of language. However, the structural means of speech reporting vary widely across languages. The study of reported speech, therefore, calls for a survey and comparison of the linguistic means that have been developed for this purpose. Since, in principle, every aspect of an utterance can be reported, such an endeavor involves all structural levels of the linguistic system as well as the contextual and situational imbedding of linguistic utterances.

1. Types of Reported Speech

Three types of reported speech are commonly distinguished, direct speech (*oratio recta*), indirect speech (*oratio obliqua*), and quasidirect discourse or *style indirect libre* (Bally 1912). The latter are more complex communicative strategies than the first one. Speech reporting that makes use of direct speech invokes the original speech situation and conveys, or claims to convey, the original speaker's exact words. This implies that such a report encompasses two deictic centers: that of the original speech situation and that of the actual speech situation. A speech report that makes use of indirect speech has only one deictic center: that of the actual situation. The point of view of the reported utterance and the report is the same. Speech reporting through quasidirect discourse is characterized by the presence of two deictic centers which, however, are not indicated explicitly by reference to another speaker or speech event. That another's speech is being reported must be inferred from certain grammatical features whose occurrence can only be interpreted coherently if a hidden speaker is assumed. Consider these examples:

Direct speech. He looked at her furiously and said: (1) 'Why can't you stop it? Really! Why do you go on with this comedy?'

Indirect speech. He looked at her furiously and asked (2) her why she could not stop it, and why she continued with the comedy.

. He looked at her furiously. (3)
Why couldn't she stop it? Really! Why did she go on
with this comedy?

The main difference between these three kinds of reported speech lies in the point of view of report and reported speech event. In (1) two points of view are distinguished, as evidenced by the third- and second-person pronouns which refer to the same individual who is the addressee of the reported speech event, hence *you*, and a person talked about in the report, hence *she*. The point of view of the reported speech event is shifted to that of the report in (2), and the addressee of the reported speech event is referred to with a third-person pronoun throughout. This is also the case in (3). However, here this feature which points to indirect speech is combined with other features such as uninverted word order and an exclamation (*Really!*) indicating the speaker's point of view rather than the reporter's.

Although point of view is a useful criterion for making the above threefold distinction, it cannot capture the finer differences between the various kinds of reported speech. Closer inspection of the grammatical means employed for this purpose blurs the distinction. Moreover, direct and indirect speech are not equally clearly distinguished in all languages.

2. Grammatical Means of Speech Reporting

The grammatical problem of speech reporting is that the reported speech must be integrated into the report. This can be done by text-deictic pronouns, by complementation, or by treating the reported phrase as a sentential object. Languages differ in strategies which are encoded in the grammar. Among the more common devices used for integrating reported speech and for distinguishing types of reported speech are tense, mood, embedding, and pronominalization.

2.1 Tense

Many languages have rules by means of which the tense forms in indirect speech are adjusted to those of the report. In English an utterance using present tense (*I am late.*) will be backshifted to preterit if reported with past time reference (*He said he was late.*). A past tense form in a complement clause of indirect speech is thus to be interpreted as present in the original utterance. Other languages with rigid sequence of tense rules are Latin and French. However, not all languages that have a morphological tense system have a sequence of tense rules. For example, in Russian and other Slavonic languages tenses in indirect speech are not adjusted to the report. The shifting of tenses in reported speech is hence not a logical consequence of a tense system, but a conventional way of using it.

2.2 Mood

Some languages employ the subjunctive mood to mark reported utterances in indirect speech, e.g., German. Tense and mood often interact. In German, mood is more important than tense. In general, past tense forms distinguish the subjunctive mood more clearly than present tense forms and are therefore often favored where the requirement of harmonizing the tenses of report and reported phrase would demand a present tense form. In long reports the subjunctive mood is often the only indication that sentences are to be understood as indirect speech.

Mood is relevant for speech reporting not only as a formal category but as a means of indicating the illocutionary force of an utterance. Reported phrases in indirect speech have no force of their own. When integrated into a report, sentences are therefore stripped of grammatical indications of interrogative, imperative, hortative or other moods. Instead of being reenacted the mood of the original utterance must then be rendered by means of report verbs ('to inquire'), conjunctions ('whether'), adverbials ('longingly') or other descriptive words. In direct speech illocutionary force indicating mood is expressed, while in indirect speech it is described.

2.3 Embedding

The strategies of embedding an utterance into a report can be considered along a dimension of integration created between the two parts. At one extreme the reported and reporting parts are only loosely linked, for instance, by a text-deictic pronoun referring to a preceding sentence (*This is what Bill said*). At the other extreme there are highly integrated constructions such as the Latin 'accusative with infinitive' where the subject of the reported sentence is turned into the direct object of the reporting matrix sentence. Between these extremes are various patterns of complementation and subordination. Complementizers like *that* are sometimes thought to be typical of indirect speech, but in some languages, for example, Yoruba, they also occur in direct speech reports. The distribution of some complementizers is also commonly restricted to speech reporting. Some languages have special quotative markers. While it is more common that indirect speech is marked in such a way, some languages, such as Kartvelian, use enclitic quotative markers for direct speech. Embedding is also achieved by treating the reported part as a sentential object, as in Japanese where the direct object marker -*o* can be attached to a reported utterance.

Speech reporting constructions are highly integrated when the reporting part or the reported part or both are not syntactically self-sufficient. In this sense indirect speech is more highly integrated than direct speech. But, while in indirect speech the reported part is typically more dependent than in direct speech, the reporting part is often not syntactically complete in both direct and indirect speech reporting. Many report verbs like 'say' are transitive. Where they are used as introducers of direct speech, the reported part must be considered as an object-like component of the matrix sentence.

2.4 Pronominalization

Languages that distinguish direct and indirect speech have different pronominalization strategies for the two constructions (Li 1986). Referential constraints on pronouns are often the only criterion for differentiating direct and indirect speech, and vice versa; other criteria for diagnosing a report as direct or indirect may be needed in order to disambiguate pronominal reference:

Jim said I was wrong. (4)

If (4) is to be read as direct speech, the first-person

pronoun refers to the subject of the matrix sentence, *Jim*, whereas an indirect reading would make it refer to the speaker of (4). Establishing pronominal reference in opaque contexts is one of the most intricate areas of semantics (Partee 1973).

Disambiguation of pronouns in reported speech often depends on contextual information. Some languages have developed fourth-person or 'logophoric' pronouns (Hagège 1974) which are used to refer to individuals whose point of view is being reported in indirect discourse as opposed to individuals outside the reported speech. Reflexive pronouns like 'herself' are sometimes used in a similar function as in (Kuno 1975):

John said to Mary that dancers like herself were a   (5)
pleasure to watch.

3. Attitudes to the Report

In addition to reporting a speech event, a reporter can express his own attitude towards the report, for example, by identifying with its content or calling it into doubt. One way of doing this is by using descriptive report verbs such as 'purport,' 'maintain,' 'lie,' rather than neutral ones like 'say.'

Grammatical and lexical devices for indicating the speaker's commitment to the report or the reliability of its source are also common. Many languages use adverbs to differentiate degrees of authenticity. The hearsay quality of a report can also be indicated by unspecific pronouns (*They say . . .*), by modal verbs, such as German *sollen*, or auxiliaries, such as Japanese *sōda*.

4. Sociocultural Conventions of Speech Reporting

Direct speech is sometimes described as more authentic than indirect speech, because the latter allows the reporter to introduce additional information from his own point of view. However, the faithfulness of a report must not be confused with the stylistic means of its presentation. The use of all forms of reported speech is governed by sociocultural conventions (Vološinov 1973). A clear distinction must therefore be made between the stylistic means of reported speech and the communicative function of quoting. Verbatim quotation and constructed dialogue make use of the same stylistic means, direct speech, but they imply very different claims to factual truth. There is evidence that societies differ with respect to the authenticity expected of direct speech in reports of actual speech events. It has been suggested that verbatim quotation depends on writing as the technique of linguistic repetition (Goody 1977).

5. Future Research

Many aspects of reported speech warrant further research. One of the most general tasks is to find culture-specific and possibly universal criteria for the accuracy of reported speech. This involves the question of which features of utterances are to be taken into account when reporting them. Very important in this regard is the rendering of intonation, both in direct and indirect speech (Fonagy 1986). Whether literacy has shaped the Western notion of the identity of utterance tokens is a related question. Further, the hypothesis that the grammatical encoding of a clear distinction between direct and indirect speech was

influenced by written language usage needs to be investigated. And more should be known about the differences between written and spoken speech reports.

Speech reporting involving other languages, dialects or translations has received little attention, although it is a promising research ground regarding linguistic questions about the identity of reported utterances and their integration into a report, as well as sociolinguistic and sociopsychological issues concerning the perception of and attitudes towards individual and group-defining features of speech.

Bibliography

Bally C 1912 Le style indirect libre en français moderne. *Germanisch–Romanische Monatsschrift* **4**: 549–56, 597–606

Banfield A 1982 *Unspeakable Sentences: Narration and Representation in the Language of Fiction*. Routledge and Kegan Paul, Boston, MA

Fonagy I 1986 Reported speech in French and Hungarian. In: Coulmas F (ed.) *Direct and Indirect Speech*. Mouton de Gruyter, Berlin

Goody J 1977 *The Domestication of the Savage Mind*. Cambridge University Press, Cambridge

Hagège C 1974 Les pronoms logophoriques. *Bulletin de la Société de Linguistique de Paris* **69**: 287–310

Kuno S 1975 Three perspectives in the functional approach to syntax. In: *Papers from the Parasession on Functionalism*. Chicago Linguistic Society, Chicago, IL

Li C 1986 Direct speech and indirect speech: A functional study. In: Coulmas F (ed.) *Direct and Indirect Speech*. Mouton de Gruyter, Berlin

Partee B H 1973 The syntax and semantics of quotation. In: Kiparsky P, Anderson S (eds.) *A Festschrift for Morris Halle*. Holt, Rinehart and Winston, New York

Vološinov V N 1973 *Marxism and the Philosophy of Language*. Seminar Press, New York

Wierzbicka A 1974 The semantics of direct and indirect discourse. *Papers in Linguistics* **7**: 267–307

F. Coulmas

Representation

Certain intellectual and cultural trends, and technological developments, originating in the nineteenth century, have formed a set of commonsense beliefs about the relationship between the communicative media and 'reality': the philosophy of utilitarianism; the rise of sociology; realism and naturalism in nineteenth-century fiction; the rise of newspapers (and all the 'information-gathering' services that support them) and their claim of objectivity; the development of still and moving photography, sound recording, and now ever more advanced audiovisual technologies. It is in the nature of these trends to insist that an objectively existing reality can be represented faithfully in language or images (or statistics, etc.).

This naive realism, product of a dominant empiricist and authoritarian climate, has been in this century repeatedly challenged by artistic avant-gardes: cubism, trans-sense poetry, the *nouveau roman*, etc. It has also been subjected to academic critique in different domains, including art history and the sociology of knowledge. Until recently, realism of representation has not been much questioned in linguistics, partly because of an uncritical acceptance of the communication or channel model in which language is a conduit for conveying ideas unaltered from one brain to another; partly because of the problematic nature of one area of theory, the Sapir–Whorf hypothesis (see *Sapir–Whorf Hypothesis*).

An alternative conception of representation in language is basic to critical sociolinguistics (see *Critical Sociolinguistics*; see also *Criticism, Linguistic*). Representation is regarded as a process of construction, not as a modeling. Informally, the proposal is that, whatever 'natural' structure the world might have, our experience of it is shaped to a large degree by the social (cultural, political, etc.) and ideological relationships within which we are positioned. Language has a reciprocal, dialectical, relationship with this constructed reality. On the one hand, conceding the plausibility of 'natural kinds' such as color, shape, directionality, etc., it may be proposed that much of the semantics of a language answers to the life of its speakers: this is easy enough to demonstrate as far as lexical inventory and structure are concerned, anyway. Reciprocally, as the structure of language encodes the categories of thought by which a society manages its reality, it crystallizes them, aiding the simplification of the perceived world and facilitating the transmission of received values.

1. Interdisciplinary Sources

Berger and Luckmann's central thesis is indicated in the title of their book, *The Social Construction of Reality* (1976). Reality as we perceive it and conceive of it is relative to specific cultures, specific kinds of social organizations. It is a product of social interactions among individuals, and of institutional structures and relationships. The structure of the socially constructed world we experience is affirmed when we communicate with one another, and Berger and Luckmann point out that 'conversation' has a particularly significant role in reality-maintenance. Because conversation is casual and uncritical, the ordinary terms which represent our commonsense beliefs can be mentioned without emphasis or enquiry—contrast the language of the classroom or of the law.

A parallel set of ideas, which have been most influential in linguists' formulation of the theory of representation, is found in the work of Michel Foucault (see *Foucault, Michel*). Central to Foucault's contribution is the idea of 'discourse' (see *Discourse*) a system of prohibitions and conventions, culturally originating, about what can be spoken about and how (cf. register as 'range of semantic potential' in Halliday 1978; see also *Register in Literature*; for a detailed exposition, see *Discourse, Ideology, and Literature*).

In E. H. Gombrich's treatise *Art and Illusion* (1960), representation in the visual arts is not a rendering of a subject but the construction of a way of seeing: an illusion in his striking term. Analyzing many familiar examples, he demonstrates how the deployment of the technical properties of the medium manages the illusion. That most apparently 'natural' of properties of visual representation, perspective, was a historical development. Techniques based on converging lines with attendant differences in size in representations of objects known in world-knowledge to be equivalent in size, guided viewers to sense an illusion of depth and three-dimensionality in their experience of a flat painting.

Gombrich's approach is based on an exemplary union of historical circumstances, variety and change of technical procedures, and the contribution of the viewer's internalized knowledge. The latter dimension of his theory accords well with 'schematic' approaches to language comprehension in psycholinguistics: people understand language in terms of schematized knowledge that they project on to texts (see de Beaugrande and Dressler 1981: ch. 5; Garnham 1985: ch. 7; Johnson-Laird 1983).

The Sapir–Whorf hypothesis contains two claims (see also *Sapir–Whorf Hypothesis*; *Sapir, Edward*; *Whorf, Benjamin Lee*). 'Linguistic relativity' argues (contrasting native American and European languages) that the structures of languages differ in fundamental ways, particularly as the semantics and syntax represent spatial and temporal aspects of experience, and material processes. 'Linguistic determinism' suggests that speakers are constrained to perceive and think along the lines afforded by the structure of their language. As far as relativity is concerned, 'difference of structure' needs defining very carefully. 'Determinism' in the form implied by Whorf is untestable. However, there is some psycholinguistic research to the effect that the simplicity with which a concept is coded has an influence on the accessibility and the memorability of that concept (Carroll 1964; Clark and Clark 1977); coding varies from language to language, even for the so-called 'natural categories.'

The cross-linguistic comparisons which Whorf makes are not central to the linguistic theory of representation, and rather serve to muddy the water; more important is that an individual language provides alternative ways of coding a concept or an event. Alternative wordings or phrasings segment or package experience in ideologically distinct ways.

2. Representation in Functional–systemic Linguistics

Halliday's *Introduction to Functional Grammar* has a section 'Clause as Representation' which begins in a Whorfian manner. He asks the reader to imagine a natural scene, birds flying overhead: 'perceptually the phenomenon is all of a piece; but when we talk about it we analyze it as a semantic configuration'; and there are different ways of analysis—'birds are flying in the sky' or 'it's winging' (1985: 101–02). The implication is that alternative linguistic expressions encode differently structured experiences. Halliday locates representational alternativity within what he calls the 'ideational' function of language: 'it is through this function that the speaker or writer embodies in language his experience of the phenomena of the real world' (1971: 332). This representational function is served by systems of linguistic options of which the most important are lexis and transitivity (see *Transitivity*). Lexis (vocabulary) is taxonomically organized: systems of words categorize the objects, qualities, and events recognized by the culture into sets of hierarchical relations (see *Sense*; *Structural Semantics*), providing an organized mapping of experience; the structure is value-laden—'girl' is opposed to both 'boy' and 'man'; alternatives are richly available which signify different orientations—'money,' 'capital,' 'investment,' 'loot,' 'bread,' etc. In Halliday's terms, transitivity refers to the semantic structure of the clause: who does what to whom, who experiences what, and so on (1985: ch. 5); choices made in the transitivity system are fundamental to the way in which a text offers a perspective on an event.

Halliday's most memorable demonstration (1971) of the construction of a mode of experiencing through linguistic structure concerns a fictional text—William Golding's *The Inheritors*. This is a classic study of the way in which a fictional world is constructed, consistent and foregrounded transitivity choices defamiliarizing (see *Formalism, Russian*) experience for the reader by staging an illusion of the causally restricted cognitive world of 'Neanderthal Man.' This study makes it clear how fundamentally important the linguistic theory of representation is for our understanding of the way in which language is structured to create fictional worlds and 'mind-styles' (see *Mind-style*), but here we are talking about the deliberate textual strategies of a professional novelist.

The crucial point about representation is that the linguistic construction of reality is not limited to deliberate fictional technique: the principle pervades language. Recall Berger and Luckmann on conversation, the casual way in which we share and maintain our society's categorization of experience by uncritically mentioning the terms in which it is divided up and sorted. The same ideological working is found in familiar modes of public discourse: the news media (Fowler 1991), rules and regulations, official documents, interviews, etc., have all been shown to encode commitments to specific systems of values, ways of representing the world (Fowler, et al. 1979). These values, which are conveyed in recognizably distinct genres (see *Genre*) or registers (see *Register in Literature*) of language (advertisement for women, right-wing newspaper editorial, letter from bank, etc.), are institutionally grounded: they are representations of the world in terms appropriate to the social and economic needs of the organizations that utter them. Representation, which is always from some specific point of view, can be seen not just as an innocent process but a social practice, conscious or not.

Bibliography

Beaugrande R A de, Dressler W 1981 *Introduction to Text Linguistics*. Longman, London

Berger P L, Luckmann T 1979 *The Social Construction of Reality*. Penguin, Harmondsworth

Carroll J B 1964 *Language and Thought*. Prentice-Hall, Englewood Cliffs, NJ

Clark H H, Clark E V 1977 *Psychology and Language: An Introduction to Psycholinguistics*. Harcourt Brace Jovanovich, New York

Fowler R 1991 *Language in the News: Discourse and Ideology in the Press*. Routledge, London

Fowler R, Hodge R, Kress G, Trew A 1979 *Language and Control*. Routledge and Kegan Paul, London

Garnham A 1985 *Psycholinguistics: Central Topics*. Methuen, London

Gombrich E H 1960 *Art and Illusion*. Phaidon, London

Halliday M A K 1971 Linguistic function and literary style. In: Chatman S (ed.) *Literary Style: A Symposium*. Oxford University Press, London

Halliday M A K 1978 *Language as Social Semiotic*. Arnold, London

Halliday M A K 1985 *An Introduction to Functional Grammar*. Arnold, London

Johnson-Laird P 1983 *Mental Models*. Cambridge University Press, Cambridge

R. Fowler

Representation, Mental

The notion of representation is a familiar, if philosophically problematic, one. It becomes more problematic, and less familiar, when modified with the epithet 'mental.' Nevertheless, the notion of mental representation is crucial both in cognitive psychology and cognitive science. It is also crucial in linguistics itself, at least for those who accept Chomsky's views that grammars describe part of the contents of the minds of language users, and that linguistics is correctly construed as part of cognitive psychology.

1. Representation and Mental Representation

It is a fundamental assumption of cognitive psychology and cognitive science that explanations of behavior make reference not only to inputs and outputs but to information encoded in the mind. In order to provide an information processing account of a particular ability it is necessary, therefore, to describe how inputs, outputs, and stored information are internally encoded. It is natural to think of these encodings as depending on a mental representation scheme or language. Following Jerry Fodor (1975) this language is usually referred to as the language of thought, though different mental faculties may use different representational schemes. Although this view of mental processing is widely accepted, it raises a very difficult question: what is a mental representation?

One can make a start on answering this question by considering everyday types of representation that are easier to understand. A simple two-dimensional town map represents space spatially. In general, however, there need be no such direct correspondence between what is represented and how it is represented. British Ordnance Survey maps represent the third spatial dimension using contour lines, and they represent things in the landscape by symbols that may (church with a tower) or may not (coach station) resemble what they represent. In such a representational scheme, the correspondence between what is represented and the elements of the scheme must play a role in both the production and the use of particular representations—only in aberrant cases will it not do so. In particular, resemblance is not sufficient for representation, as a consideration of portraits, particularly those of identical twins, shows. Causation is crucial in determining what something represents. Indeed, some philosophers (e.g., Fodor 1990) have suggested purely causal theories of how a mental state comes to represent something in the world.

There is little difficulty understanding how maps work. But maps require people to create and interpret them. We, as mapmakers, create the representational schemes that allow us to make particular maps and, thus, to achieve our navigatory goals. And we, as map users, have the goals that make maps useful. Mental representations differ from maps in both respects. First, the meanings of the elements of a system of mental representation are not arbitrarily stipulated. They arise from natural effects that the environment has on people or animals. However, not every effect that the world has on an animal gives rise to a mental representation. For an effect to be a representation, it must have the function of providing information about what it represents. Second, although natural effects can have representational functions imposed upon them, mental representations typically have functions that derive from the natural goals of people or animals. Furthermore, an account of mental representations cannot be based on the idea of a person inside the head setting them up and using them—homunculus theories cannot explain cognition.

If the job of cognitive scientists is to discover the representational schemes used by the mind, that job is very different from a mapmaker's. Mapmakers decide what to represent, taking into account how their maps will be used, and they stipulate a representational scheme to encode the relevant information. Depending on the mapmaker's skill, the map may or may not be easy to use. Cognitive scientists have to assess the purpose of a piece of mental apparatus, to postulate a representational scheme that, together with processes to operate on it, satisfies that purpose. Then they must try to find evidence that that scheme is used. This process is a complex one, not only because cognitive scientists cannot look and see what the elements of the representational scheme are, but also because they have to make inferences about processes as well as representations. The representational scheme needed to perform a task depends on what processes act upon the representations allowed by the scheme.

The philosopher Fred Dretske (1988) contrasts mental representations with maps by classifying them as a type, indeed the most important type, of natural representation system. He claims that natural representation systems are the source of intentionality in the world. Intentionality is the 'aboutness' which philosophers take to be a defining characteristic of mental phenomena. A map is 'about' the terrain it represents, but only derivatively. Its aboutness derives from the fact that people interpret it as being about a certain part of the world. The aboutness of mental representations is not derivative, and it is for this reason that mental representations are so important and so difficult to understand. It is also for this reason that the study of maps can only take us so far in understanding the concept of mental representation.

Dretske analyzes the notion of representation in terms of indication. One thing indicates another if its occurrence provides information about what it indicates. Because of the rich correlational structure of the world, there are many instances of indication. A bear's paw prints in the snow indicate that a bear has passed this way. The ringing of a door bell indicates that someone is at the door (and also, for example, that current is flowing in the door bell's electric circuit). Certain patterns of activity in a person's visual cortex indicate that they have seen a chair (to anyone or anything that can register them). For Dretske, there is no misindication. If signs are misinterpreted, they are being used as representations.

An indicator becomes a representation if it is given the function of indicating the state of something else. Now misrepresentation is possible. If a car's fuel gauge jams, it does not really indicate that the tank is full. But since it has been given the function of indicating how much fuel is in the tank, it misrepresents how full it is. Misrepresentation

can be a nuisance, or worse. However, the possibility of misrepresentation goes hand in hand with a very useful property of representational schemes: their elements can be recombined at will. Maps of imaginary countries can be drawn. I can mentally represent not only what the world is like, but how I want it to be, how I think you falsely believe it to be, and so on. Thus, although natural systems of representation derive from natural indicators of things in the real world, particular representations can be decoupled from the world. They need not be caused by what they represent.

2. Neural Substrates and Connectionism

Cognitive scientists assume that the mind is a mechanism, in the very general Turing machine sense, and that its physical substrate is the brain. Thus, every mental state is associated with a corresponding brain state. If that mental state is a complex representational one, each element of the representation is associated with some aspect of that brain state. For most of our cognitive abilities, no more can be said at present. It is not even known whether equivalent mental states are always associated with the same brain state. And even when a good deal is known about the underlying neural substrate—as in the case of low-level visual processing, for example—it has been argued (e.g., by David Marr 1982) that questions about representational schemes and the processes that act on them can often be addressed independently of questions about neural substrates, via an information processing analysis of the relevant ability.

It is, of course, possible to take a purely functionalist approach to cognition in general and to mental representations in particular. Functionalism holds that the correct, or best, theory of a particular mental ability is the one that best explains the psychological data. The mental representations people use are the ones postulated in that theory. On one interpretation this view is vacuous, because the decision about which explanation is best may be influenced by nonpsychological factors, such as compatibility with what is known about brain structure. On another interpretation functionalism is a substantive, though almost certainly false, doctrine. On this interpretation, considerations about brain structure are irrelevant to choosing the best psychological theory.

Since about 1980 the substantive version of functionalism has been challenged by people working in the parallel distributed processing (PDP) or connectionist framework. Connectionists attempt to reproduce human behavior using networks of simple processing elements whose properties resemble those of brain cells or clusters of them. The behavior of a connectionist machine may suggest that it is following a set of rules (couched in a language of thought). However, nothing in the machine corresponds to the rules in the way that a piece of code in a traditional computer model of the mind does.

The correct interpretation of connectionist models has been a matter of intense debate. It is known that connectionist machines can simulate traditional serial computers (von Neumann machines), just as von Neumann machines can simulate connectionist machines. However, connectionist machines as they are used in cognitive modeling do not perform such simulations. How should such machines be described? On one view they do not contain representations of the rules they appear to be following. Rules are traditionally represented symbolically, and connectionism has been described as a subsymbolic approach to cognition. A contrasting view is that connectionist machines represent rules indirectly, and usually in a distributed fashion. Trying to decide which account is correct is complicated by the fact that many connectionist machines do not exactly follow the rules that their designers wanted them to, so it is not surprising that they do not represent those rules. In one famous example, a network was trained to produce the past tenses of English verbs from their stem forms (Rumelhart and McClelland 1986). However, a detailed analysis of the performance of the machine (Pinker and Prince 1988) showed its knowledge to be lacking in many respects. In particular, it had not encoded the fact there are no phonological conditions on whether the regular (-*ed*) rule can be applied. Some connectionist systems do follow (usually much simpler) sets of rules exactly, and properties of their (matrix algebra) descriptions may correspond to information that one would intuitively want to say is represented in the system. However, this representation is not so obvious as a traditional symbolic one. So connectionist machines raise in an acute form the question of when information is represented explicitly and when implicitly.

The contrast between implicit and explicit representation can be illustrated with a simple example from semantic memory. Sparrows are represented as a subclass of birds. Birds are represented as being able to fly, unless there is specific information to the contrary. There is no specific information that sparrows cannot fly. From the explicitly encoded information it can, therefore, be inferred that sparrows can fly—that information is implicitly represented. Whether information is encoded explicitly or implicitly determines how easily a particular task can be performed. Implicit information should take longer to compute than explicit information takes to retrieve. It may appear from this example that the contrast between explicit and implicit representation is a clear one. However, it is not, as the questions raised by representation in connectionist networks show. Indeed, although the contrast between implicit and explicit representation has become increasingly important recently, it remains unclear whether there is one distinction or several.

Although connectionist machines raise important questions about how mechanisms encode rules and follow them, their existence in no way bears upon the very difficult philosophical questions about rule following raised by Wittgenstein (1953), which have sometimes been taken to challenge Chomsky's (e.g., 1972) idea of linguistic rules in the mind. The description of a connection machine (or, for that matter, a von Neumann machine) as following a rule is part of a description of its behavior by us. Wittgenstein's questions about how people follow rules turn into questions about what we, as cognitive scientists expect of a machine that we describe as following a certain set of rules. It does not matter whether those rules are encoded explicitly, or only implicitly.

Bibliography

Chomsky N 1972 *Language and Mind*. Harcourt Brace Jovanovich, New York
Dretske F 1988 *Explaining Behavior: Reasons in a World of Causes*. MIT Press, Cambridge, MA
Fodor J A 1975 *The Language of Thought*. Crowell, New York
Fodor J A 1990 *A Theory of Content and Other Essays*. MIT Press/Bradford Books, Cambridge, MA
Marr D 1982 *Vision: A Computational Investigation into the Human Representation and Processing of Visual Information*. Freeman, San Francisco, CA
Pinker S, Prince A 1988 On language and connectionism: Analysis of a parallel distributed processing model of language acquisition. *Cognition* **28**: 73–193
Rumelhart D E, McClelland J L 1986 On learning the past tenses of English verbs. In: McClelland J L, Rumelhart D E, et al. *Parallel Distributed Processing: Explorations in the Microstructure of Cognition. Vol. 2: Psychological and Biological Models*. MIT Press, Cambridge, MA
Wittgenstein L 1953 *Philosophical Investigations* (trans. Anscombe GEM). Blackwell, Oxford

A. Garnham

Representations in Phonology

Structuralist phonologists (see *Phonology, Post-Bloomfieldian*) distinguished three significant levels of phonological representation:

(a) the *phonetic* level: a record of utterances showing all phonetic detail;

(b) the *phonemic* level: a record showing only those phonetic properties which are distinctive (see *Distinctiveness*) that is, omitting from (a) all phonetic detail which was predictable;

(c) the *morphophonemic* level: a representation of utterances taking into account alternations between phonemes (see *Morphophonemics*).

Only when (b) had been established could any work in morphology be carried out; and, as a result of this, (c) could in turn be established.

In orthodox generative linguistics, the grammar of a language is viewed as a device which consists of three essential components: a syntactic component, a semantic component, and a phonological component. The relationship among these components is such that the rules of the syntactic component generate an infinite set of syntactic structures which are given a semantic representation by the semantic component and a pronunciation by the phonological component (see Fig. 1). The phonological component of a grammar basically consists of a set of rules which applies to the output of the syntactic component and, in doing so, describes how each sentence is to be pronounced. In the phonological component (see *Generative Phonology*), it was claimed that only *two* important levels need to be distinguished:

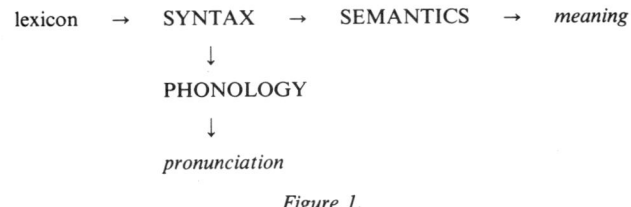

Figure 1.

(d) the *phonological* level: rather like (c) above;
(e) the *phonetic* level: near to (a), but not exactly equivalent to it (see *Phonemics, Taxonomic*).

Before these two levels can be expounded (Sects. 3 and 4 below), some preliminary discussion is necessary.

Insert figure

	λ	n
CONSONANTAL	−	+
SYLLABIC	0	0
NASAL	0	+
LONG	−	0
VOICE	0	0
CONTINUANT	0	0
STRESS	0	0
HIGH	+	0
BACK	−	0
etc.		

Figure 2.

1. Readjustment Rules

It is often said that phonological rules apply to the output of the syntactic component. While this statement is essentially true, it must nevertheless be observed that in order for this very output to become the actual input of the phonological component, a number of (slight) modifications must be carried out. These modifications are brought about by 'readjustment rules,' whose main task it is to turn a *syntactic* surface structure (i.e., the output of the syntactic component) into a *phonological* surface structure (i.e., the input to the phonological component). This task is important because, in the syntactic surface structure, one may encounter formatives (morphemes, items) such as PAST, PLURAL, etc., which have not yet been given an adequate phonological shape and to which phonological rules could not possibly apply. Furthermore, this readjustment component is responsible for #-insertions and occasional junctural changes without which the domains (stems, words, phrases) for the proper application of the phonological rules could not be established.

The output of the syntactic component—the syntactic surface structure—is a string of lexical and grammatical formatives. This string is represented with labeled brackets specifying not only the substrings which make up the constituents of the surface structure but also the categories (S, NP, N, V, etc.) to which they belong. The lexical formatives have a lexical representation in the lexicon. This representation, in addition to having phonological properties, has syntactic and semantic properties, which will not be treated in this article. The grammatical formatives, on the other hand, appear in the syntactic surface structure as (phonologically empty) abstract objects.

2. Lexical Representation

The phonological properties of a lexical item appear in the lexicon in the shape of a two-dimensional matrix. In such a matrix, the columns represent segments and the rows represent distinctive features (a segment, therefore, is a matrix with only one column).

In the lexicon, each lexical item (morpheme, formative) is represented by only those distinctive features which are necessary to distinguish it from every other lexical item in the language. That is, only the *nonredundant* features appear in the lexical matrix. Sometimes it is said that at this point distinctive features serve a classificatory purpose because here their function is basically to classify each item in such a way that it is distinct from all other items. Because of this, lexical matrices are also called 'classificatory' matrices.

In the lexical matrix, the phonological segments will be characterized as ' + ,' ' − ,' or '0' with respect to a given feature. That is, the segment in question can be positively specified, negatively specified, or unspecified. The phonological properties in the lexical matrix for the item *inn* would be represented roughly as shown in Fig. 2.

A phonological segment is left unspecified for a particular feature if the value of that feature can be predicted by general rules. Such rules are called redundancy rules (see *Redundancy Rules in Phonology*), and two types may be distinguished. First, segment structure rules fill in features that automatically follow from the remaining features of a given segment (in English, for example, [VOICE] need not be specified in the case of nasals). Second, sequence structure rules fill in features that automatically follow from the surrounding segments (in English, for example, only /s/ can occur word-initially before a stop, and it is therefore sufficient to write [+ CONSONANTAL] in this position, for the remaining features will be added at a later stage by means of sequence structure rules).

Since the function of redundancy rules is to fill in blanks (0's) in matrices, it is important to know where these rules are to be situated in the overall grammar. Although a number of linguists have been rather unclear about this aspect (even in Chomsky and Halle (1968) there is some confusion), it should be pointed out that the general assumption is for redundancy rules to be part of the readjustment component. Since this component links up syntax and phonology, it follows that, at the input stage of the phonological component, phonological representations will be fully specified. One might say that redundancy rules turn incompletely specified (lexical) representations into fully specified (phonological) representations.

3. Phonological Representation

As stated earlier, the readjustment rules prepare syntactic surface structures for entrance into the phonological component of the grammar. The input or starting point of this component is called the 'phonological level,' or the 'phonological surface structure,' or the 'systematic phonemic level.' On that level, 'phonological representations' are found, although, again, in the literature a variety of names exists, all of which refer to the same object. In addition to 'phonological representation,' one may encounter terms such as 'underlying representation,' 'morphophonemic representation,' or 'systematic phonemic representation.'

The phonological segments occurring in phonological representations are said to constitute the systematic phonemes of the language. There is no reason to suppose that this inventory will correspond in any strict way to the segments that appear on the phonetic level. Indeed, one may find segments in the underlying phonological representation which never occur in phonetic surface forms (for example, /œ/—a low front rounded vowel—and /x/—a voiceless velar fricative—were claimed to be systematic phonemes of English but do not appear as such phonetically).

The only fundamental constraint governing the relation between the systematic phonemes and their phonetic realization (or representation) is the 'naturalness condition.' This condition implies that phonological segments do not constitute an arbitrary code but are closely related to the representations that are needed to state phonetic properties. This closeness is reflected by the fact that both phonological and phonetic representations are formulated in terms of the same distinctive features. To put it somewhat differently, systematic phonemes automatically pass into their phonetic equivalents except when phonological rules prevent such universal mapping from taking place. In short, all phonetic characterizations not assigned by any phonological rule are considered to be the same as the phonological (underlying) categorizations. One only posits 'unnatural' underlying representations such as the above-mentioned /æ/ and /x/ when these have simplifying effects on the overall grammar.

The crucial task of the phonologist, therefore, will be to set up phonological (underlying) representations and to discover the rules that map them onto phonetic surface forms. This is generally carried out in close accord with a principle known as the 'unique underlier condition.' This principle states that every nonsuppletive (i.e., regular or predictable) alternation is to be accounted for by assigning to each morpheme a single, phonologically specified underlying representation, with the allomorphy derived by general rules. The idea implicit in this principle is that when a number of forms are felt to be related, this relatedness should be expressed by positing a common source. The very nature of this 'common source' has always been of major concern to generative phonologists and has engendered the fundamental debate on what is known in the literature as the 'abstractness controversy' (see *Generative Phonology: Abstractness Controversy*). The central issue of this debate concerned the extent to which ('deep') underlying representations could diverge from ('surface') phonetic ones—a rather important issue, especially in view of the fact that standard transformational–generative theory allowed phonologists virtually unlimited freedom in going about their task.

The systematic phonemic representation thus shows some affinities with the morphophonemic level of taxonomic linguistics. The phonological representation is said to be morphophonemic in nature precisely because for each morpheme a single underlying form is set up from which all other forms are derived. For example, given the forms *electric* [ɪléktrɪk] and *electricity* [ɪlektrísətɪ] one observes that the stem-final consonant is realized as [k] or [s]. The latter realization is the result of a process known as 'velar softening'; /k/ becomes [s] before suffixes such as *-ity*, *-ism*, *-ify*, and *-ize* (e.g., *elastic—elasticity*; *critic—criticize—criticism*). A straightforward description of these facts can be obtained by stating that the [k] of *electric* and the [s] of *electricity* are manifestations of the same segment. That is, both [k] and [s] can be traced to some unique underlying segment, say, /k/. This procedure can be depicted (in a slightly simplified fashion) as in Fig. 3.

Once the last phonological rule of the grammar has been applied, all # and + boundaries are automatically erased

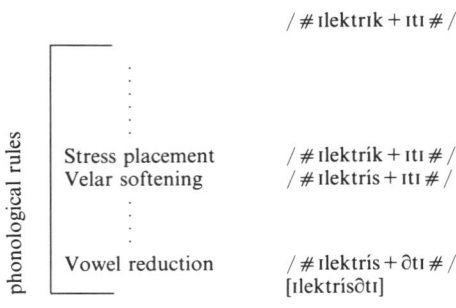

Figure 3.

by virtue of a general convention. It is by applying this convention that one moves from the output of the rule of velar softening to the phonetic representation [ɪlektrísətɪ]. The ordered set of successive representations figuring between the phonological representation / # ɪlektrik + ɪtɪ # / and the phonetic representation [ɪlektrísətɪ] is known as the 'derivation' of [ɪlektrísətɪ]. The phonological representation constitutes the input of the derivation, and the phonetic representation is its output. The item [ɪlektrísətɪ], being the result of the application of some phonological rules, may be referred to as a derived form.

Since phonological rules apply one at a time, a string (word, phrase, sentence) may have many phonological representations between the systematic phonemic and the phonetic representation. However, in generative phonology, none of these is considered to have any theoretical importance. Of particular interest is the fact that no significance is attached to the classical phonemic representation (renamed by generative phonologists as 'taxonomic phonemic representation' or 'autonomous phonemic representation'). Generative phonologists have argued, often convincingly, that the recognition of such a level is not at all necessary (see *Phonemics, Taxonomic*). To all intents and purposes, any representation figuring between the phonological and phonetic levels could be referred to as an 'intermediate representation.' This position was taken up strongly by early generative phonologists, but has not found favour with all followers: lexical phonologists, for example (see *Lexical Phonology and Morphology*), see the phonological representations at the boundary between the lexical and postlexical components as closely equivalent to taxonomic phonemic representations (Mohanan 1986).

4. Phonetic Representation

As pointed out, many generative phonologists recognize only two important levels of representation. One distinguishes between the level of underlying (phonological) representation and the level of pronunciation. Whereas the former is generally referred to as the systematic phonemic level, the latter is also known as the 'systematic phonetic level.'

At the systematic phonemic level, sentences consist of (phonologically converted) morphemes/formatives and junctures. At the systematic phonetic level, the strings consist of sequences of feature columns which correspond, roughly, to the phones of a traditional description. These feature matrices will differ from those at the systematic phonemic level in that they can be viewed as physical scales on which a value for a given phonetic segment can be specified not only in terms of *plus* and *minus* values but also in terms of integers (numerical values). This number is an indication of the *extent* to which the phonetic segment is characterized by the corresponding phonetic property (for example, [*n*STRESS], [*n*NASAL], where *n* may indicate the degree of stress or the degree of nasalization). The phonetic properties in the phonetic matrix for the item *inn* would be represented roughly as shown in Fig. 4.

	λ	n
CONS	−	+
SYL	+	−
NAS	2	+
LONG	−	−
VOI	+	+
CONT	+	−
STRESS	1	−
HIGH	+	−
BACK	−	−
etc.		

Figure 4.

In this matrix, [1STRESS] implies that the initial phonetic segment has main stress, and [2NASAL] implies that it is partially nasalized.

The phonetic features, which make up phonetic matrices, involve three sets of phenomena: (a) they refer to independent elements in the perceptual reality of the speaker–hearer; (b) they are mental instructions indicating how the articulatory system is to perform; and (c) they represent aspects of vocal-tract behavior which are under the voluntary control of the speaker.

It is important to bear in mind that systematic phonetic representations—and therefore also the features in terms of which they are specified—refer to a perceptual reality and that they *do not* describe a physical or acoustic reality. At best, the relationship between phonetic representations and actual speech signals is only indirect.

Such a systematic phonetic representation basically corresponds to an 'idealized' narrow phonetic transcription, which differs from the 'physical phonetic representation' (the exact physical and physiological description of a concrete utterance by means of instruments). Hence, this phonetic transcription does not constitute a direct record of the actual utterance—it is a representation of what the speaker–hearer considers to be the phonetic properties of a sentence, based on a hypothesis of its syntactic surface structure and on his/her knowledge of the phonological rules. In short, it corresponds to the speaker–hearer's interpretation, which may be quite different from what is actually found physically.

5. Distinctive Features and Complex Segments

The phonological characterization of a lexical item in the lexicon, as well as the description of the phonological and phonetic levels (together with the rules connecting these levels), are formulated by means of distinctive features. The set of distinctive features provides a universal referential framework which allows for the various sounds of a language to be categorized in relation to each other and also for speech sounds to be compared across languages.

As indicated earlier, the distinctive features occurring in lexical matrices have a classificatory function and may be referred to as 'classificatory features' (although in actual practice the term 'phonological features' is also generally used here); those occurring in phonetic representations have a phonetic function and are called 'phonetic features'; and, finally, the distinctive features occurring in underlying representations have a phonological function and are called 'phonological features.' The last are clearly *phonological* because at the systematic phonemic level (as opposed to the systematic phonetic level) the interpretation of the features is never direct, as underlying segments are not articulated.

The matrices at the phonological level are set up on a strictly binary basis. The proposed binary features were designed to capture the phonological oppositions found in languages, but not necessarily the different phonetic realizations of those oppositions (hence the name 'distinctive' features). To say, for example, that an underlying segment is [−NASAL] does not mean that it is articulated without nasality: recall that the vowel in the lexical item *inn* is underlyingly [−NASAL], but it is nasal phonetically.

Although the notion that phonological features (as opposed to phonetic features) are binary has been questioned on a number of occasions, binarity is generally justified on the grounds that (a) there are many oppositions which are undoubtedly binary in nature ([±VOICE], [±NASAL], etc.), and therefore one should uphold this principle for all the other distinctive features as well; and (b) it would be rather awkward to compare languages and evaluate descriptions if some features were binary and others *n*-ary.

In generative phonology, the distinctive feature is the minimal unit of description. In point of fact, it is considered to be the only unit that has any linguistic status (alphabetical symbols such as *p*, *b*, *t*, *d*, etc. being merely ad hoc abbreviations of feature bundles such as [+CONS, −SYL, −CONT, −SON, −STRID, etc.]). Although segments were at first assumed to have no linguistic status at all, it is difficult to reconcile this idea with what happens in actual practice, for at this same time a feature [SEGMENT] was introduced in order to distinguish junctures ([−SEGMENT]) from true units ([+SEGMENT). Implicit in this practice would seem to be the assumption that segmentation must be given linguistic status after all.

Further evidence testifying to the importance of segmentation concerns the discussion in the literature of what is known as the 'complex segment.' On the systematic phonemic level, each segment is represented as a bundle of specified (−/+) features. As far as these representations are concerned, attention must be drawn to a rather important controversial issue, namely, the characterization of phenomena such as diphthongs, prenasalized consonants, postnasalized consonants, affricates, contour tones, etc., all of which exhibit inherent sequential properties. Clearly, the first part of an affricate is [−CONTINUANT] and its second part is [+CONTINUANT]. Similarly, the first part of a prenalized stop is [+NASAL] and its second part is [−NASAL]. Instead of using atomic features such as [DELAYED RELEASE] or [PRENASAL], which obfuscate the internal changing state of the segment, some phonologists have introduced the distinction between simple versus complex

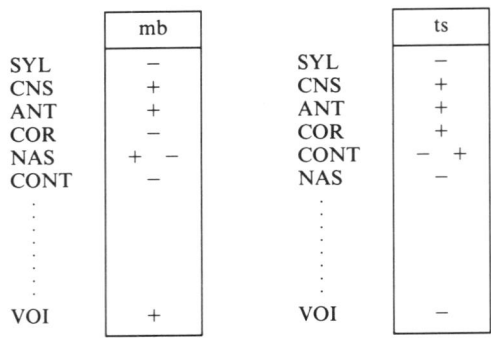

Figure 5.

segments. A 'complex segment' is a segment which has, for at least one feature, a complex specification consisting of a sequence of two or more simple specifications. The phonetic correlates of these specifications are taken to appear in temporal succession. By way of illustration, consider the phonological matrices for the prenasalized stop /mb/ and the affricate /ts/, as shown in Fig. 5.

The linear arrangement of the features [NASAL] and [CONTINUANT] within one segment characterizes the beginning and end points of the segment. It should be emphasized, though, that such a solution violates the definition of the notion 'segment' as conceptualized within orthodox generative phonology, for segments are assumed to have no subparts. Yet, sequences of features within one segment constitute subsegments and hence create an altogether different relationship to the entire segment, namely, one of subdivision.

The controversy about the phonological representation of complex segments has played a major role in bringing about a fundamental change in phonological research from the late 1970s onward, whereby 'strict segmentalism' has been abandoned in favour of an essentially nonlinear model of phonological representation (see *Nonlinear Phonology*).

Bibliography

Botha R 1971 *Methodological Aspects of Transformational–Generative Phonology*. Mouton, The Hague

Chomsky N, Halle M 1968 *The Sound Pattern of English*. Harper, New York

Dell F 1980 *Generative Phonology and French Phonology*. Cambridge University Press, Cambridge

Fischer-Jørgensen E 1975 *Trends in Phonological Theory*. Akademisk Forlag, Copenhagen

Goldsmith J A 1990 *Autosegmental and Metrical Phonology*. Basil Blackwell, Oxford

Mohanan K P 1986 *The Theory of Lexical Phonology*. Reidel, Dordrecht

Postal P 1968 *Aspects of Phonological Theory*. Harper, New York

D. L. Goyvaerts

Resultatives

The term 'predicate' is used in at least two ways in modern linguistics. First, in a sentence like:

John gave another piece of pie to the man at the desk. (1)

gave could be called the predicate, since it is the word which denotes the event or the state being spoken about, while *John, another piece of pie,* and *the man at the desk* are arguments of this predicate, since they are role-players or participants in the event (that is, they are assigned a property by way of being participants in an event or state). Another use of the term is to talk of a predicate that consists of an entire verb phrase (or VP), which takes, then, only one argument: the subject of the clause. In that case *gave another piece of pie to the man at the desk* is the predicate in (1) and *John* is its only argument.

With either use of the term, the predicate looked at above is called a primary predicate. Perhaps the defining characteristic of a primary predicate is the presence of a verb; a primary predicate is or contains a verb or is accompanied by a copular (or linking) verb. In (1) *gave*, the event word, is a verb. However:

That new kitten is a naughty scamp. (2)

is not about an event, but about a state, and the words *a naughty scamp* denote the property assigned to *that new kitten*. It is debatable whether the copular *is* in (2) is part of the property or is merely a grammatical formative that carries the tense of the clause. In either case, the predicate here (*is a naughty scamp* or *a naughty scamp*) is a primary predicate because of the presence of *is*.

Not all predicates are primary, however. Phrases that do not contain a verb nor are accompanied by a copular verb can be predicated of other phrases in the sentence:

Jack left her house [furious]. (3)

John ate the meat [raw]. (4)

[Penniless], Mary was hopeless. (5)

We considered Paul [an asset]. (6)

In all of these sentences it could be argued that there are two predicates, the primary one and a secondary one, in brackets. For example, in (3) it could be argued that John is assigned two properties: one of having left (her house) and one of having been furious. Of course, there is a semantic relationship between the two properties—in (3) John performed the act of leaving (her house) while he was in a state of fury. Likewise, various semantic relationships could be found between the primary and secondary predicates in (4)–(6), where it is important to notice that the secondary predicate can be predicated of a subject (as in (3) and (5)) or of a direct object (DO) (as in (4) and (6)). Some have argued, then, that instead of having two predicates, sentences like (3)–(6), have complex predicates. In (3), for example, John would be assigned the complex property of leaving (her house) while being furious.

If the analysis in which sentences like (3)–(6) have two predicates is accepted, the next question becomes whether these sentences have single clauses, or whether each predicate demands its own clause. For example, is (3) to be analyzed as in:

Jack [[left] [her house] [furious]]. (7)

where the VP has three major constituents: the verb (V), a noun phrase (NP), and an adjective phrase (AP), or as in:

Jack [[left] [her house] [PRO furious]]. (8)

where the VP has three major constituents: the V, an NP, and a so-called small clause? In (8) the small clause consists of an AP and its subject argument, which is a phonetically null item (an inaudible grammatical item) represented by the term PRO, which in turn is semantically controlled by (that is, interpreted as equivalent to) *Jack*.

This debate stems from a variety of theoretical and empirical concerns. Perhaps the most major concern involves the relationship between syntax and semantics. If the syntax is isomorphic to the semantics, then each predicate should be contained in a separate clause. While mapping from syntax into semantics (or vice versa) would be ideally simplified if these two components of the grammar were isomorphic, it is not logically necessary that they be isomorphic and there is a growing body of linguistic literature that argues that they are far from isomorphic. The empirical concerns, on the other hand, are language specific. In a given language there might be data that are more perspicaciously accounted for with one analysis than with the other.

In spite of all these debatable issues, there is much of interest that can be said for sure about issues of predication. Here, one particular kind of secondary predicate, known as the resultative, will be looked at:

> I cut her hair [short]. (9)

In (9) I cut her hair and, as a result, it became short. Some sentences are ambiguous as to whether or not a secondary predicate is resultative:

> John made the tea weak. (10)

(10) could describe the situation in which John added water to the tea and the tea became weak (the resultative reading), or another in which John made the tea and it came out weak (the nonresultative reading).

Generally, a transitive sentence with an AP resultative which has the form in (11) can be paraphrased as in (12):

> X Verbs Y [Z]. (11)

> X causes Y to become Z by Verbing Y. (12)

Here Z stands for the AP resultative.

The semantic interaction between resultatives and Vs shown in (11)–(12) has been accounted for in various ways, not all of which are necessarily discrete from one another, where some propose that the resultative forms a complex predicate with the V (as in Green 1973); some treat the resultative and the V as a single, discontinuous lexical item (like *take . . . to task*, as in Bolinger 1971); and some argue that the resultative is an argument of V (as in Carrier and Randall 1988). Many have argued that resultatives are syntactic sisters to V and to the NP they are predicated of (such as McNulty 1988). Some have argued that the semantic difference between secondary predicates like that in (3) (a depictive) and resultatives is paralleled by a syntactic difference (such as McNulty 1988; but see also Demonte 1989; Rapoport 1992). Likewise there has been much discussion over whether or not resultatives form small clauses (as in van Voorst 1983; Hoekstra 1988).

Another point of contention is whether or not resultatives are limited to particular syntactic categories. Of course, secondary predicates are not verbal (by definition). But beyond that, the question is open. One thorny issue is whether or not resultatives can be prepositional phrases (PPs). Simpson (1983, 1986) explicitly states that resultatives can be of the category AP, NP, or PP (that is, all the major categories other than VP):

> I painted the car [AP yellow]. (13)

> I painted the car [NP a pale shade of yellow]. (14)

> I cooked the meat [PP to a cinder]. (15)

Many agree with Simpson in admitting PPs as resultatives. For example, in Hoekstra (1988), where Dutch is compared to English, every example of a resultative predicating of an internal argument of the primary predicate is a PP. Pustejovsky (1989) argues that any phrase which can denote a state can be a resultative, including PP. Van Voorst (1983) argues for Dutch that directional PPs are predicates inside small clauses, occupying the same syntactic position resultative APs occupy. All the data and arguments presented by van Voorst are consistent with the analysis of the directional PPs as resultatives.

An explicit claim that PPs cannot be resultatives is found in Rapoport (1992: fn. 11), who says the PP in examples like (5) modifies the V rather than being predicated of an NP. It would seem, moreover, that some works embody the implicit claim that PPs cannot be resultatives. For example, some say that particular languages lack resultatives, including Green (1973) for French, Merlo (1986, 1988) for Italian, and Rapoport (1986) for Hebrew. But if PPs are admitted as resultatives, these languages surely have resultatives. This point is re-examined below.

Below are listed some of the arguments for including PP among resultative types. Via these arguments the major syntactic diagnostics for recognizing resultatives will become evident.

First, PPs such as the following will be dealt with:

> She scrubbed the dirt {[out of her skirt]/ [from her skirt]/ [off the step]/ [away]}. (16)

> I slapped him {[into a stupor]/ [out of his hysteria]}. (17)

(For evidence that *away* is a PP, see Jackendoff 1973.) In these examples the PPs are directional or spatial with a verb that is not inherently a motion verb (as in (16)), or they are state PPs (as in (17)). The discussion below will be limited to these sorts of PPs. In particular, examples with locational PPs where the V is a motion verb (such as *go, run, dance, fly*) will not be discussed, since the matter of whether or not such PPs with such Vs can truly be predicates is much more complex.

First, consider their sense. The paraphrase test in (10)–(12) cannot be used as it now stands, since the Z of (11) would not be an AP in (16)–(17), but a PP, and most PPs are not grammatical as predicates in the position immediately following a form of the verb *become* (a fact that has nothing to do with whether or not they can be resultatives or any other kind of predicate). Instead, in each instance it is necessary to ask whether the PP describes a state or location that is predicated of the DO and that is the result of the primary predicate's action on the DO. On that basis locational PPs like those in (16) are at least borderline resultatives semantically and are worthy of further testing, and state PPs like those in (17) seem to be clear resultatives.

Second, many have claimed that there are restrictions on which element can be the subject of a resultative. Some have argued that the subject of a resultative must be the affected argument of the V (in the sense of Tenny 1987) or a patient of the V (as in Simpson 1986). Simpson (1983) claims that resultatives in English are predicated of deep objects only. If Simpson's claim were correct, a diagnostic for resultatives could be formulated immediately: resultatives should not be predicated of objects of P. And, in fact, they cannot. (18)–(19) form minimal pairs:

I slapped her [silly]. (18)

*I slapped at her [silly]. (19)

PPs behave precisely as other resultatives here:

*She scrubbed at the dirt {[out of her skirt]/ [from her skirt]/ [off the step]/ [away]}. (cf. (16)) (20)

*I slapped at him {[into a stupor]/ [out of his hysteria]}. (cf. (17)) (21)

A caveat is in order here: Not all PPs that concern the endpoint of the V's action are predicates, however; some are degree modifiers of the action.

I beat him [to a pulp]. (22)

I beat him [to the point of exhaustion]. (23)

The PP in (22) must be a resultative, whereas that in (23) can be a modifier of the V (and, perhaps ambiguously a resultative, as well). In (22) the PP can be predicated only of the DO. But in (23) it is unclear whether the subject or the DO or even the people watching become exhausted; the PP tells us that the beating went on too long—it is a degree modifier of the V. Accordingly, if all nominals that are potential arguments of the PPs are removed, the predicative PP in (22) becomes ungrammatical, but the modifier PP in (23) is still acceptable:

*The fight went on [to a pulp]. (24)

The fight went on [to the point of exhaustion]. (25)

Third, another diagnostic based on Simpson's claim also involves assuming the validity of the work in Burzio (1986), who argues that superficially intransitive verbs fall into two classes, those that have deep subjects and those that have deep objects which move into subject position (called ergatives or unaccusatives). If Burzio is correct, Simpson's generalization above can be accepted, and this diagnostic formed: resultatives should be able to be predicated of a subject with an unaccusative V only. Of course, with intransitive sentences that contain a resultative AP the pattern of paraphrase given above in (11)–(12) will not hold. Instead, a semantic correlation of the following type is looked for:

X Verbs [Z]. (26)

X Verbs to the point of becoming Z. (27)

(Again, if Z is a PP and not an AP, this paraphrase test will not hold.) This seems true: in (28)–(31) the contrast between the unaccusatives *bleach* and *fry* and the intransitives *cry* and *drink* can be seen. Here the resultatives are APs (where an asterisk indicates that no good resultative reading is available):

The shirt bleached [white] in the sun. (28)
(cf. The sun bleached the shirt [white].)

The bacon fried [crisp]. (29)
(cf. Let's fry the bacon [crisp].)

*The boy cried [sick]. (30)

*The boy drank [sick]. (31)

The same contrast occurs with resultatives that are PPs:

The shirt bleached [to the purest white]. (cf. (28)) (32)

The bacon fried [to a crisp]. (cf. (29)) (33)

*The boy cried [into a stupor]. (cf. (30)) (34)

*The boy drank [out of his mind]. (cf. (31)) (35)

The correlation between deep transitivity and the possibility of a resultative is so strong that fake objects can be found, often reflexive objects (Simpson 1983), with otherwise intransitive Vs, where the fake object and the resultative must both appear:

The boy cried his eyes [blind]. (36)
The boy cried himself [sick]. (cf. (30))

The boy drank the pool [dry]. (37)
The boy drank himself [sick]. (cf. (31))

These objects are fake in that they are neither subcategorized for by the primary predicate nor are they assigned a theta role by (that is, nor are they arguments of) the primary predicate. Once more, the correlation holds also for PP resultatives:

The boy cried his eyes [out]. (38)
The boy cried himself [into a stupor]. (cf. (34))

The boy drank the pool [down to the bottom]. (39)
The boy drank himself [out of his mind]. (cf. (35))

By three diagnostics, then, the relevant PPs in (16) and following examples (both state and locational with non-motion verbs) are resultatives: they have the sense of resultatives; they are predicated of DOs but not objects of prepositions (OPs); they are predicated of surface subjects only of unaccusative Vs. These three diagnostics are the most common ways of identifying resultatives. If these diagnostics and the above arguments are valid, then not only can PPs be resultatives, but a variety of languages that have been claimed not to have resultatives, such as the Romance languages, certainly do. In (40), for example, there is a PP resultative in Italian:

Ho intrecciato i fiori [a forma di ghirlanda]. (40)
'I wove the flowers [into a garland].'

In fact, the Romance languages have AP resultatives, as well as PP ones, where a particular semantic restriction holds, as is seen by looking at Italian. Many of the examples below have grammatical counterparts in French, Spanish, Portuguese, Catalan, and probably throughout the Romance languages.

It seems that in a sentence with a resultative AP, the primary predicate must be interpreted as focusing on the endpoint of the activity denoted by that predicate. Resultative APs, then, can occur in sentences in which the primary predicate is one with an instantaneous effect on the DO, such as:

Quel macellaio taglia le carni [sottili]. (41)
'That butcher cuts meats [thin].'
Mia figlia ha cucito la gonna [troppo stretta].
'My daughter sewed the skirt [too tight].'

If the effect of the primary predicate on the DO is not instantaneous, but achieved only gradually, via duration or repetition, an AP resultative is allowed only if it is somehow emphasized so that the addressee's attention is drawn to the endpoint of the event of the primary predicate. Thus, for example, in each pair of sentences in (42) the first is not acceptable, but the second is fine or at least much better than the first for many speakers:

*Ho stirato la camicia [piatta]. (42a)
'I ironed the shirt [flat].'
Ho stirato la camicia [piatta piatta].
'I ironed the shirt [very flat].'

?*Hanno riscaldato l'acqua [bollente]. (42b)
'They heated the water [boiling].'
Hanno riscaldato l'acqua [tanto calda che non ci si poteva entrare].
'They heated the water [so hot that no one could get in].'

?*Ha strappato la lettera [fine]. (42c)
'He ripped up the letter [fine].' (in small pieces)
Ha strappato la lettera [fine fine].
'He ripped up the letter [very fine].'

?Abbiamo pettinato i capelli [lisci]. (42d)
'We combed the hair [smooth].'
Abbiamo pettinato i capelli [lisci come seta].
'We combed the hair [smooth like silk].'

?Li abbiamo scoloriti [bianchi]. (42e)
'We bleached them [white].'
Li abbiamo scoloriti [quasi, ma non perfettamente, bianchi].
'We bleached them [almost, but not perfectly, white].'

However, while being interpretable as focusing on the endpoint of its activity is necessary for the V, it is not sufficient:

*Ho macchiato la camicia [rossa]. (43)
'I stained the shirt [red].'

The outcome, then, is a strategy for interpreting sentences that have resultative APs. But Vs will have to be marked in the lexicon as to whether or not they allow resultatives. That is, resultative arguments (as opposed to resultatives with fake object sentences, which are not arguments—as in (36)–(39) above, which have no grammatical counterpart in Italian or any of the Romance languages) will appear in the predicate–argument structure and in the subcategorization frame of a verb. For those Vs which allow resultatives, the ease with which the V can be read as focusing on the endpoint of its activity in a given sentence in a given pragmatic context (as shown below) determines the ease with which a sentence with a resultative will be interpreted.

It is now time to consider how pragmatic context enters. A given activity can have an instantaneous effect on one object but not on a different object, simply because of the physical nature of the objects and not for any grammatical reason. For example, if we hammer on metal, we do not expect an instantaneous effect, but if we hammer on tin foil, we do. A resultative AP turns out to be better in the sentence describing the second event than in that describing the first. Alternatively, a given object might be instantaneously affected by one activity but not by another. So a sentence about a machine that can flatten metal in an instant is more acceptable than a sentence in which a person is hammering on metal. The grammaticality judgments marked below are common to the speech of many, although the contrasts are not always strong.

*Gianni ha martellato il metallo [piatto]. (44)
'Gianni hammered the metal [flat].'
?Gianni ha martellato la carta stagnola [piatta].
'Gianni hammered the tin foil [flat].'
?Quella pressa idraulica ha {pestato/ pressato} il metallo
piatto (subito subito).
'That hydraulic press {smashed/ pressed} the metal
flat (in an instant).'

Likewise, in a situational context in which the addressee's point of attention is naturally the endpoint of an activity, a V whose effect is felt only after some duration of the activity can nevertheless cooccur with a resultative:

Quell'anitra, l'hai cucinata [saporita]. (45)
'That duck, you cooked it [tasty].'

(Context: a debate over whether the shirt in question (46)
got ironed flat or into pleats.)
—Ho stirato la camicia [piatta piatta].
'I ironed the shirt [very flat].'
—No, hai stirato la camicia [pieghettata].
'No, you ironed the shirt [pleated].'

(The response in (46) is the example of interest here. Many people find it acceptable.)

Similarly, imperatives can set up an endpoint-focused context. That is, when we order someone to beat eggs, we often do not care how they get to the desired result so long as they do. Quite generally, resultatives with imperatives about cooking are considered more acceptable than their statement counterparts:

Sbatti le uova [cremose]. 'Beat the eggs [creamy].' (47)
(cf. ?*Maria sbatte le uova [cremose].
'Maria is beating the eggs [creamy].')
Macinatele [fini]. 'Grind them [fine].'
(cf. ?Le avete macinate [fini].
'You have ground them [fine].')

Also, if the V is of low information with respect to the type and manner of activity, where the major information of the V is the endpoint of the activity, resultative APs are acceptable, even if the activity has to be iterative or durative before the desired effect on the object is achieved. *Caricare* 'load' is such a V. Material can be loaded onto or into a location by doing many different types of actions (in contrast to ironing, for example, which involves a highly specified action). Resultatives are easily allowed with this V, where intensification of the AP makes it that much more colloquial:

Gli operai hanno caricato il camion [pieno]. (48a)
'The workers loaded the truck [full].'

Gli operai hanno caricato il camion [pieno al massimo]. (48b)
'The workers loaded the truck [full to the brim].'

In sum, it appears that AP resultatives in Italian are more readily accepted: (a) with instantaneous-effect Vs (41); (b) if modified or intensified (42); (c) with instantaneous effect situations (44); (d) in situations that focus the addressee's attention on the endpoint of an activity (45)–(46); (e) with certain imperatives (47); and (f) with Vs that naturally focus on the endpoint of the activity they denote (48). Given that resultatives concern the endpoint of the primary predicate's action by definition, the interpretation strategy that exists in Italian is natural. Other languages may have somewhat different restrictions on the types of sentences that can occur with resultatives, but, presumably, all such restrictions should follow either from the nature of resultatives themselves or from independent grammatical factors in the language.

Finally, it is worth noting that Levin and Rapoport (1988) have argued that the ability of a language to take a resultative follows from the existence or not of a process of lexical subordination in the language (a concept similar to lexical conflation in Talmy 1975, 1985). Lexical subordination is also claimed to be responsible for at least two other grammatical phenomena. One is the use of a manner-of-movement verb to show change of location. In English, for example, the verb *float* can be used to show simple manner of movement (as in (49)), or manner plus change of location (as in (50)):

The bottle floated in the cave.	(49)
The bottle floated into the cave.	(50)

The second is the use of a manner-of-speaking verb with a DO that expresses the thing spoken (Zwicky 1971, Mufwene 1978), as in:

She mumbled her adoration.	(51)

Significantly, Italian exhibits both phenomena:

Il fiume serpeggia al mare.	(52)
'The river snakes (its way) to the sea.'	
Carolina ha sussurato la sua ammirazione per il poeta.	(53)
'Carolina whispered her admiration for the poet.'	

Thus, it may well be that the process of lexical subordination is the cornerstone for the resultative construction.

While this article gives a brief overview of some of the major theoretical debates involving the analysis of resultatives and of some of the more characteristic limitations on the data in Romance languages, the analysis of resultatives is only beginning to receive wide attention. The debates are bound to change, perhaps drastically, over the next few years, as additional languages are examined.

Bibliography

Bolinger D 1971 *The Phrasal Verb in English.* Harvard University Press, Cambridge, MA

Burzio L 1986 *Italian Syntax: A Government-Binding Approach.* Reidel, Dordrecht

Carrier J, Randall J 1988 From conceptual structure to syntax: Projecting from resultatives (Unpublished manuscript, Harvard University and Northeastern University, Cambridge and Boston, MA)

Demonte V 1989 Remarks on secondary predicates: C-command, extraction, and reanalysis. *Linguistic Review* 6: 1–39

Green G 1973 A syntactic syncretism in English and French. In: Kachru B, et al. (eds.) *Issues in Linguistics.* University of Illinois Press, Urbana, IL

Hoekstra T 1988 Small clause results. *Lingua* 74: 101–39

Jackendoff R 1973 The base rules for prepositional phrases. In: Kiparsky P, Anderson S (eds.) *A Festscrift for Morris Halle.* Holt, Rinehart and Winston, New York

Levin B, Rapoport T 1988 Lexical subordination. *Chicago Linguistic Society* 24: 275–89

McNulty E 1988 The syntax of adjunct predicates (Doctoral dissertation, University of Connecticut)

Merlo P 1986 Secondary predication in Italian and English (Doctoral dissertation, University of Venice

Merlo P 1988 Secondary predicates in Italian and English. In: Powers J, de Jong K (eds.) *Proceedings of the Fifth Eastern States Conference on Linguistics.* Ohio State University, Columbus, OH

Mufwene S 1978 English manner-of-speaking verbs revisited. In: Farkas D, et al. (eds.) *Papers from the Parasession on the Lexicon.* Chicago Linguistic Society, Chicago, IL

Pustejovsky J 1989 The generative lexicon (Unpublished manuscript, Brandeis University)

Rapoport T 1986 Nonverbal predication in Hebrew. *Proceedings of West Coast Conference on Foreign Languages* V. Stanford University, Stanford, CA

Rapoport T 1992 Secondary predication and the lexical representation of verbs. *Machine Translation* 4: 4

Simpson J 1983 Resultatives. In: Levin L, Rappaport M, Zaenen A (eds.) *Papers in Lexical–Functional Grammar.* Indiana University Linguistics Club, Bloomington, IN

Simpson J 1986 Resultative attributes (Unpublished manuscript, Massachusetts Institute of Technology)

Talmy L 1975 Semantics and syntax of motion. In: Kimball J (ed.) *Syntax and Semantics. Vol. 4.* Academic Press, New York

Talmy L 1985 Lexicalization patterns: Semantic structure in lexical forms. In: Shopen T (ed.) *Language Typology and Syntactic Description. Vol. 3: Grammatical Categories and the Lexicon.* Cambridge University Press, Cambridge, MA

Tenny C 1987 Grammaticalizing aspect and affectedness (Doctoral dissertation, Massachusetts Institute of Technology)

Voorst van J 1983 Anaphor binding and directional PPs in Dutch. *CLS* 19: 386–95

Zwicky A 1971 In a manner of speaking. *LIn* 2: 223–32

D. J. Napoli

Reuchlin, Johann (1455–1522)

The three areas of language, literature, and mysticism provide a suitable framework for a brief review of the German savant Johann Reuchlin's lasting contribution to Semitic studies.

First, there is his expertise as a Hebraist. Under the influence of Pico (1463–94), the 'father' of Christian Kabbalah, Reuchlin developed a consuming interest in Jewish mysticism. In order to gain access to the Kabbalah he resolved to perfect his knowledge of Hebrew by employing Jewish teachers. Thanks to his instructors, Reuchlin's passion for all things Hebraic remained undiminished for the rest of his life. He never tired of stressing the importance of Hebrew for a proper understanding of the Bible. 'I assure you,' he wrote in 1508, 'that not one of the Latins can expound the Old Testament unless he first becomes proficient in the language in which it was written. For the mediator between God and man was language, as we read in the Pentateuch; but not any language, only Hebrew through which God wished his secrets to be made known unto man.' To encourage and help students, he published a grammar-cum-dictionary, the *De rudimentis hebraicis* (1506). This was followed in 1512 by the Hebrew text of the seven penitential psalms, with translation and commentary (*in septem psalmos poenitentiales*), likewise intended for beginners. Finally, six years later, he published the *De accentibus et orthographia linguae hebraicae*, a treatise on accents, pronunciation, and synagogue music. Reuchlin's importance for linguistic study is that he established philology as a recognized discipline, independent of theology, an approach which led him to criticize and correct the Vulgate at several points.

Reuchlin's high regard for postbiblical Jewish literature emerged in 'the battle of the books,' a bitter controversy which raged for almost a decade. In 1510, the Emperor Maximilian, at the instigation of the Dominicans, ordered the destruction of all Hebrew books inimical to Christianity. Reuchlin was asked to assist by deciding which ones should be condemned. He reacted by coming to the defense of Jewish literature. This concern for the preservation of the Jewish literary heritage sprang not from any philo-Semitic feelings, for he was no friend of the Jews, but from educational and humanitarian motives. He was convinced that the loss of the Hebrew language would harm Christian biblical scholarship. As an ex-lawyer, he also knew that the Jews had rights. Whatever their disabilities, they had received guarantees from popes and emperors that their books would not be destroyed. Though he claimed that he was defending Christian rather than Jewish interests in the action he took, Reuchlin had the satisfaction before he died of knowing that he had won 'the battle of the books,' a victory for Jews and Christian humanists alike.

Pico studied Kabbalah for two reasons: to confirm Christian truth and to confute the Jews from their own literature. When he was prevented by death from pursuing further studies, his mantle fell upon Reuchlin who expressed the hope that he would 'soon accomplish precisely what Pico promised.' His first contribution was the *De verbo mirifico* (1494), where he demonstrates the practical value of Jewish mystical techniques for attaining union with Christ. The 'wonder-working word' of the title is YHSVH, the letters of the Hebrew form of the name 'Jesus.' This was followed by the *De arte cabalistica* (1517), the author's *magnum opus*, which represents the climax of his Kabbalistic studies. Written in dialogue form, it is essentially an apologia for the Christian study of Kabbalah.

Reuchlin's contribution in the three areas of language, literature, and mysticism marks a turning point in the Church's attitude towards Hebrew and Jewish literature.

Bibliography

Geiger L 1871 *Johann Reuchlin: sein Leben und seine Werke*. Duncker and Humbolt, Leipzig

Goodman M, Goodman S 1983 *Johann Reuchlin: On the Art of the Kabbalaha*. (Eng. transl.). Abaris Books, New York

Overfield J M 1984 *Humanism and Scholasticism in Late Mediaeval Germany*. Princeton University Press, Princeton, NJ

G. Lloyd Jones

Réunion: Language Situation

The most widely used language among the 596,693 inhabitants (1990) of the French Overseas Department of Réunion, who are of mixed European, African, and Chinese origin, is Réunion Creole French, which is progressively gaining in status. The official language is French and this is also the language of education. Adult literacy stands at about 80 percent.

Rhaeto–Romance

The Rhaeto–Romance (R–R) languages are a tenuous entity consisting of the Romansch dialects of Grisons, Switzerland; the Ladin dialects of the Dolomitic Alps in south Tyrol, Italy; and the Friulian dialects around Cividale and Udine. Although there are perhaps 40,000 speakers of Romansch, 10,000 of Ladin, and nearly 500,000 speakers of Friulian, almost all speakers of these dialects also speak either German or an Italian dialect, often as their first language.

The 'unity' of Rhaeto–Romance is based on a small number of phonological and morphological features (nominal plurals in -*s*; second person singular verbal desinences in -*s*; palatalization of velars before -*a*; retention of /kl-/ consonant clusters) which are not only shared with French (and various Italian dialects north of the La Spezia–Rimini isogloss) but which are not even common to all R–R dialects: in both Ladin and Friulian, for example, many masculine nouns form their plural with -*i*, as do the majority of Italian dialects. Although R–R unity has been asserted by major scholars such as G. I. Ascoli, T. Gartner, and G. Rohlfs, it has also been challenged by others, among them C. Battisti and G. Pellegrini. Mutual intelligibility has never been a relevant issue, nor has there ever been any period when the languages were standardized or associated with a single political entity.

In fact, even to speak of three major dialects is to oversimplify the social and political situation greatly. Romansch alone had five major dialects (the Rhenish dialects of the Surselva and Sutselva; the Albula pass dialect of Surmeiran; and the Engadine dialects of Puter and Vallader) for which orthographic traditions date back to Bifrun's (Puter) Bible translation of 1561. Attempts have twice been made to create a standardized '*Romonsch fusionau*' (1864) or '*Rumantsch Grischun*' (1985) whose orthography would not favor the morphology or phonetic structure of any of the Swiss dialects.

Ladin is represented by the radically different dialects of Fassa, Gardena, Ampezzo, Livinallongo, and the Gadera Valley. In addition to the central Koiné of Friulian, there are dialects with distinct features from Erto in the west, to the Carnic Alps along the Austrian border, to Gradisca near the border with Slovenia.

In their morphosyntactic typology, the various R–R dialects exhibit the differing influences of the prestige or reference languages which are spoken around them. Romansch, and the Ladin dialects of Gardena and the Gadera Valley, under heavy German influence, exhibit the familiar verb-second word order of German, in addition to innumerable borrowings and calques from German. Friulian and all the Ladin dialects share with the majority of the northern Italian dialects the cliticization and doubling of subject pronouns which produces structures like '(He) he—comes.'

Although heavily influenced by German, the Surselvan dialect of Romansch is unique in R–R (and perhaps in all of Romance) in having preserved the inherited (-*us*/-*um*) distinction of Latin, and having transformed it into a distinction between attributive (<- *um*) and predicative (<- *us*) forms of the masculine singular adjective: thus, for example, (*il ei*) *bun-s* '(he is) good' contrasts with (*in*) *bien* (*um*) '(a) good (man).'

J. Haiman

Rhetoric: Anthropological Perspectives

The word rhetoric, in the popular sense, has associated with it the stigma of empty, flowery talk, or impressive speech saturated with falsehood. Remembering also that a rhetorical question is really not intended to elicit an answer, one often regards rhetoric as suspiciously false and dishonest. This connotation of rhetoric, however, is not in accord with its meaning as a discipline of study since the times of Aristotle. Rhetoric refers to the art of oratory, or persuasive speaking—the art of effective argumentation with the view to influencing opinion.

Persuasive communication is used in many spheres of life, for example, counseling, cajoling, and even deceiving. It is a vital mode of discourse in business, politics, and negotiation. Rhetoric was of central concern in early Greek society, where speech was a dominant force, and has been found to be of great significance in nonliterate communities as a whole. That oratory is of tremendous importance in oral societies is not surprising since in the relative absence of writing, and modes of electromagnetic communication, speaking constitutes the single most important mode of interaction.

Even so, certain cultures within the nonliterate world have been particularly known for their eloquence. The Athenians, in Ancient Greece, were well known for being great talkers. Similarly, certain cultures in Africa, such as the Ashanti, Anang–Ibibio, and the Bantu have long been associated with skilful oratory by several anthropologists and explorers. The Anang of Nigeria, for instance, are said to have derived their name from their ability to speak wittily and meaningfully on any occasion.

1. Power of the Word

The power of the spoken word is well-recognized in nonliterate societies. Being the embodiment of acoustic energy, the spoken word has an immediate impact, the capacity to make or break. According to a Yoruba proverb, 'Speech is like an egg, when dropped it shatters.' And according to an Arab saying, 'Words can bring you an elephant, and also bring you to the foot of the elephant.' In certain societies, the spoken word in such religious contexts as divination may have the power to alter reality; and according to Judeo–Christian tradition, the world was created by the spoken word. In everyday life, those endowed with the power of effective speech are held in high social esteem due to the facility with which they contain situations of stress through persuasion.

An important corollary of the power of speech, as against the written word, is the basic risk involved in all face-to-face communication. The spacial and temporal link between the speaker and hearer puts discourse participants at considerable risk since unlike in writing where evaluation is delayed, there is here an instant evaluation of each other's communicative competence. The stakes in oral communication are high, and they become higher in public speaking where speakers have to contend with a wider audience. This is partly the reason why good orators are highly prized in nonliterate societies.

2. Acquisition

In several parts of the nonliterate world, the skilful control of words is highly valued, and most cultures do not organize formal training in the art since it comes naturally with constant exposure to traditional speech. According to an Akan adage, speech is free, 'The spider did not sell speech.' Yet grammatical knowledge is not the be-all of language learning. The sociocultural rules governing the use of language are considered equally important. Rituals observed on the birth of a child in several African societies attest to this. During the naming ceremony, the child is initiated into the moral values of speaking. The official, using water and gin in alternation, baptizes the child's tongue, to initiate him into the essence of truth and social sensitivity in the exercise of the spoken word. Generally speaking, children who acquire verbal wit at an early age are considered as sages; they are closely watched and earmarked for relevant sociopolitical positions in future. Where formal training in oratory exists, such children naturally have a greater advantage.

2.1 Training

Formal training in oratory is common in Burundi among the Tutsis, and may also be found in the West Indies. Among the people of St Vincent in the West Indies, where 'talking sweet' is highly valued in various forums such as tea meetings, parents do not only encourage their children to learn the techniques of oratory. They enter into agreement with men of proven rhetorical abilities to formally train their children in manner of delivery, fluency, and self-comportment in public speaking (Abrahams 1977: 123). In Burundi, where the ideals of oratorical ability are stressed among the upper classes, aristocratic boys are given formal education in speech-making from the age of ten. The content of the training includes impromptu speeches, formulas for petitioning a superior for gift, composition of praise poems, self-defensive rhetoric, funeral orations, voice modulations, and gestural comportment on stage (Finnegan 1970: 449). As a result of this, Tutsi aristocrats, as against the peasants, are well-known for their elegance in speech. Among the Maori of New Zealand, even though oratory may be learned by a natural process in the countryside, city-born children can learn oratorical skills in the universities, training colleges, Maori Studies courses at high school, and culture clubs. Furthermore, some ethnic groups run courses inviting young migrants home to learn the art of public speaking (Salmond 1975: 51).

3. Sociopolitical Roles

In several societies there is no formal training in oratory. Children attend forums for debate and acquire speaking skills, customary lore, and genealogies by listening to elders. Among the Akan of Ghana, a child may carry his father's stool and follow him to the chief's palace during meetings; he may sit and listen, learn proverbs and their use, and thereby sharpen his rhetorical skills. Skills in public speaking also come with, or are expected of, certain social and political positions. It is a fact that several traditional offices require considerable forensic skills in the exercise of duties. In most cultures in Africa and Polynesia, certain positions like chiefship, headship of lineages, and jury membership require considerable skills in rhetoric to exercise effective control over the issues at stake, particularly in dispute settlement.

Chiefs, prior to their installation, go into several weeks of seclusion where their attention is drawn to certain formal norms of communication (Finnegan 1970: 453). Even so, most chiefs and elders acquire skills in oratory on the job. Ineloquent chiefs are generally disliked. In Ghana, there are occasional instances of chiefs who have been destooled on account of oratorical incompetence.

Apart from traditional office bearers, the generality of the population may equip themselves with various speaking styles and formulas, to lend vitality to conversation, argue effectively in public debates, or present a case in court.

3.1 Speech Specialists

To help contain the hazards of public speaking, as well as enhance political positions, the exercise of rhetoric may be delegated by dignitaries to surrogates and other speaking agents. Professional orators exist in several cultures of Africa, South America, and Polynesia, who perform public orations on behalf of patrons. This has been reported of the Maori, Samoan, Fijian, Tikopian, Tongan, and the Balinese communities (Bloch 1975). In a large part of such Polynesian cultures, high-ranking officials avoid risking their integrity in face-to-face behavior by hiring orators to speak on their behalf. Among the Samoans, it is done so that 'the source of authority and wisdom represented by the chief is protected by having the lower ranking orator to expose himself to potential retaliation and loss of face' (Duranti 1988: 22). Among the Tongan nobles, oratory is the task of ceremonial attendants. In Tikopia, chiefs do not address public assemblies, they give instructions to *maru* to speak for them (Firth 1975: 35). And among the Balinese, a Malayo–Polynesian people, orators or speech specialists are appointed by patrons for various speaking engagements (Hobart 1975: 77). Patrons may be traditional office-bearers, government officials, or agents of political parties.

The use of surrogate orators is also very common in Africa, particularly along the west coast. It is common among the Akan, Kru, Ga, Ewe, and several ethnic groups in northern Ghana, Burkina Faso, Benin, and Côte d'Ivoire. Among the Akan, frequent references have been made by missionaries and anthropologists to the 'linguist,' or intermediary known locally as *okyeame*, through whom the chief receives messages from his audience, and also speaks to them. On receiving the chief's message, which may have been heard in low tone by the audience, the orator has the discretion to edit the royal word—elaborate it with metaphor, proverb, and other rhetorical devices; paraphrase it, or merely repeat it if well-spoken (Yankah 1989: 82). Without the orator's supplement, the patron's speech act is considered incomplete as a formal utterance. This mode of manipulating the rhetoric of patrons in formal assemblies is also known among the Wishram Chinook of Washington, and the Cuna Indians of South America (Hymes 1972: 61; Sherzer 1975: 26).

3.2 Gender

Rhetoric in several traditional communities is male dominated. In certain cultures, women are generally forbidden to express themselves in public. Among the Maori, old women may only provide preludes to oratory through wailing, and singing of ancient songs, but they dare not speak in public assemblies. 'Only the cock was made to crow,' say the men, 'if the hen tries, wring her neck' (Salmond 1975: 51). Among the Balinese, no female orators are known, even though women may be elected to represent their households in the assembly (Hobart 1975: 77). In Malagasy, an orator must be male, since women are supposed to be endowed with less tact and subtlety than men (Keenan 1973: 228). Among the Akan of Ghana, key positions that require the exercise of rhetoric, such as chief, orator, and lineage head, have been typically male dominated. Furthermore, the chief's palace, which is the most common ground for rhetoric and formal argument, is not always open to women. They are prohibited from entering the premises when they are in their menses. The proverb, 'The hen knows the dawn of day, yet it looks to the cock's crow,' is often quoted by the Akan to demonstrate the woman's secondary status in public speaking. Even so, current trends point to a gradual recognition of women in speaking roles. Not only are women chiefs occasionally found. There are a few instances of male chiefs having appointed women as their orators (*akyeame*), on the basis of their prior competence or potential. It is not surprising that despite the proverb quoted above, the following is also gaining currency, 'The hen also knows the dawn of day.'

Women's verbal wit is also evident in all-female forums, like the courts of queen mothers, where women office holders (including orators and jury members) assert their oratorical skills without censure.

4. Moments of Rhetoric

Occasions that attract rhetoric differ from culture to culture, yet they are often formal and centered on public domains. They range from litigation in court in most parts of Africa, where persuasive speeches are given by litigants to influence juries, to the macaronic diction given by 'men of words' in the West Indies at feasts and tea meetings. Among the people of St Vincent, home ceremonies and send-offs provide fitting occasions for speech making. Yet festival ceremonies like Christmas, weddings, concert and tea meetings attract specialist orators who competitively test out their skills in eloquence. At tea meetings, for instance, speakers present the gospel and emancipation stories in ornate speech (Abrahams 1977: 121). Among several ethnic groups in Africa, sermons, funerals, marriage ceremonies, and even public donations provide fitting opportunities for speakers to assert their forensic skills. Among the Akan, a public donation or drink gift is not merely presented. It is accompanied by a brief speech often replete with proverbs, archaisms, idioms, and other rhetorical devices. A flowery acceptance speech is also expected from the recipient or his orator.

Among the Ilongot of the Philippines, bride price meetings are great occasions for *purung* oratory (Rosaldo 1973). In Malagasy, marriage requests attract the most elaborate use of *kabary*, ceremonial speech, which is highly allusive. Here, two speechmakers are required: one representing the girl's family, and the other representing the family of the boy. The two orators then start a contest in which they try to outdo each other in rhetorical skills (Keenan 1973).

Among several communities in the Western Pacific, such as Samoa and Tonga, oratory centers around *fono*, formal assemblies of elders where political matters are discussed.

Generally, though, rhetoric pervades most verbal interactions in traditional societies. A beggar in Burundi may petition a patron for a new pair of shoes in poetic style, referring metaphorically to his ragged shoe held together by a safety pin, 'One does not hide one's misfortunes; if one tries to hide them they will nevertheless soon be revealed. Now I know a poor old man, broken in health and ill; there is a spear stuck in his body and he cannot be saved' (Finnegan 1970: 450).

5. Norms

Rhetoric in traditional societies often follows rigid formats of presentation and modes of comportment when executed in a public forum. In certain cases, speaking rights may be restricted. Among the Maori, speakers must qualify by age, seniority of birth, and competence. Furthermore, rules of precedence in keeping with social and political hierarchies are closely observed. Thus the order in which individuals speak in a group sometimes depends on seniority. Among the Ashanti (Akan), judicial hearings provide another example of rigid sequencing. Members of the jury made up of various subchiefs express their opinion, beginning with the highest in rank (apart from the king), followed successively by the next lowest rank. The last to express his opinion and pronounce judgment is the King of Ashanti, known as *Kasapreko*, 'the Ultimate Speaker.' Also, where a chief has more than one orator present at a formal meeting, they sit in order of rank, the highest ranked sitting closest to the patron.

5.1 Poise

Other norms observed include that of self-comportment while speaking. In Tikopia, the stance of a speaker in a formal assembly is usually restrained. He may walk up and down and gesticulate, or stand still with hands folded (Firth 1975: 37). Among the Ilongot of northern Philippines, the orator does not stand; he sits with his hands at his sides. Gestures are generally limited to the shoulders (Rosaldo 1973: 210). Among the Akan, speakers in a public forum are expected to conform to certain norms of deference, including standing, lowering the wrap-around cloth to expose one's shoulder, and removing the feet from footwear, all as a sign of respect for the elders present. Also, under no circumstances must a speaker gesticulate exclusively with the left hand.

5.2 Orator's Staff

When Akan chiefs' orators are speaking, there is an additional requirement: they are expected to hold in their left hand their staff of authority, without which they are incompetent to speak on behalf of the chief. Such staffs often embody proverb designs that are chosen to suit specific occasions. Thus an orator-diplomat prosecuting a case on the chief's behalf may hold the proverb design, 'A good case is briefly argued,' and one pleading a cause may hold the staff design, 'One making a request is no nuisance.' The proverbial designs are thus rhetorical in themselves, and often reinforce the speaker's argument or rhetorical stance (Yankah 1989: 99–100).

5.3 Intermediation

More importantly, Akan speakers in a formal forum do not directly speak to their addressees. Rhetorical communication, particularly in the royal domain, is triadic: it has to be routed through a speech intermediary (orator), who relays the message to the intended addressee and transmits the reply accordingly, often couching it in ornate, elegant style. This mode of formal communication is common almost throughout West Africa. In the Philippines and Polynesia, a reflex of triadic communication is evident in the avoidance of direct eye contact between the orator and his opponent. Among the Ilongot, the orator's eyes are cast sideways, past his opponent, since eye contact is a metaphor for mutual concord (Rosaldo 1973: 210).

6. Style

Even though the style of rhetoric differs from culture to culture, it is characterized in most traditional societies by the saturated use of artful witty language, formulaic expression, metaphor, proverb, honorific terms of address, and politeness expression. In such societies, a conscious effort is made by speakers to preserve the ideal sphere of interactants, through the avoidance of language that could pose a direct threat to face (Brenneis and Myers 1984). A great degree of redundancy is thus to be expected, even though there is room for creativity and dramatic surprise particularly in moments of tension. An extreme example of fixed, predictable rhetoric may be found among the Balinese of Indonesia, where traditional assembly speeches are so prescribed that there are no open conflicts, and open argument is punished. The use of insulting language at the assembly attracts a purification ceremony (Hobart 1975: 73).

Linguistic and literary devices used in oratory may be exemplified from the language of Akan oratory. Formal rhetoric in Akan is characterized by proverbs, metaphor, and politeness expressions. The latter refers to terms of politeness, or courteous addressives expressing deference or solidarity. Expressions of deference in formal speech include traditional titles, or appellations in reference to dignitaries of higher social status. The most common title is *Nana* used in reference to the elder or chief.

Terms of respect, such as *oburu* and *aberaw*, may also be suffixed to greetings, or expressions of formal thanks, or request. Their use denotes the speaker's respect for the referent's social or political identity. Another stylistic mark of politeness in Akan rhetoric is the apologetic formula and disclaimer often used to signal an imminent or apparent profanity, verbal taboo, or proverb. Apologizing for an imminent proverb signals rhetorical humility on the part of the speaker; it implies that the speaker does not seek to teach a lesson to the august assembly through the wise saying. Alternatively, an apology may mean, 'My sharp words are not directed at the entire assembly; they have a narrower target of reference.'

It is, however, the intense use of metaphor and proverb that marks Akan rhetoric. Such devices animate rhetoric through their poetic luster. Proverbs and metaphors may be used to embellish discourse, or in reference to themes of sociocultural delicacy that may otherwise offend dignified audiences in a public forum.

Below is an example of formal rhetoric by an elder representing his wing, during court proceedings in Kumasi, the seat of the Ashanti state in Ghana. This was during a heated discussion of a disputed succession to a throne. The speech was directed at a subchief who had expressed opposition to the new chief's installation by making rude remarks that appeared to impugn the king's integrity. Note the use of apologies, proverbial expressions, and appellations.

We of this division beg to say
That Nana A., my apologies, has betrayed his thoughts
He has jumped a conflagration
Spilling dust into his own eyes
A, my apologies, has allowed his eyes
To outstrip his eyebrows

It is said, if you dance too skilfully
You betray your slave ancestry
We want A. to understand
That we are fed up with his excesses
His arrogance and uproar
And to you, Chief of Y,
My apologies, *Oburu*
You who are supporting his cause
Does the Bosomtwe god not taboo the monkey's head?
You who, my apologies, are violating the Almighty King
Remember you swore an oath
In the hands of Daasebre—Object-of-unlimited-thanks
You are in violation of the law
Arrest them, let's impose a heavy fine!

In this passage, the speaker uses proverbs, apologies, and polite terms of address not only to distinguish himself as an experienced orator, but also to soften the impact of his verbal attack on a fellow elder.

The use of oblique language and terms of politeness pervades most rhetoric in traditional society. In moments of tension, the challenge becomes that of creatively registering dissent, protest, or displeasure within the scope of the politeness frame.

Bibliography

Abrahams R 1977 The training of the man of words in talking sweet. In: Bauman, R (ed.) *Verbal Art as Performance*. Newbury House, Reading, MA

Bauman R, Sherzer J (eds.) 1989 *Explorations in the Ethnography of Speaking*, 2nd edn. Cambridge University Press, Cambridge

Bloch M (ed.) 1975 *Political Language and Oratory in Traditional Society*. Academic Press, London

Brenneis D L, Myers F 1984 *Dangerous Words: Language and Politics in the Pacific*. New York University Press, New York

Duranti A 1988 Intentions, language and social action in a Samoan context. *Journal of Pragmatics* 12: 13–33

Finnegan R 1970 *Oral Literature in Africa*. Clarendon Press, Oxford

Firth R 1975 Speech-making and authority in Tikopia. In: Bloch M *Political Language and Oratory in Traditional Society*. Academic Press, New York

Gumperz J J, Hymes D (eds.) 1986 *Directions in Sociolinguistics*. Basil Blackwell, Oxford

Hobart M 1975 Orators and patrons: Two types of political leader in Balinese village society. In: Bloch M (ed.) *Political Language and Oratory in Traditional Society*. Academic Press, New York

Hymes D 1972 Models of the interaction of language and social life. In: Gumperz J J, Hymes D (eds.) *Directions in Sociolinguistics*. Holt, Rinehart and Winston, New York

Keenan E 1973 A sliding sense of obligatoriness: The polystructure of Malagasy oratory. *Language in Society* 2: 225–43

Rosaldo M 1973 I have nothing to hide: The language of Ilongot oratory. *Language in Society*. 2: 193–223

Salmond A 1975 Mana makes the man: A look at Maori oratory and politics. In: Bloch M (ed.) *Political Language and Oratory in Traditional Society*. Academic Press, New York

Sherzer J 1975 Namakke, sumakke, koirmakke: Three types of speech event. In: Bauman R, Sherzer J (eds.) *Explorations in the Ethnography of Speaking*. Cambridge University Press, Cambridge

Yankah K 1989 *The Proverb in the Context of Akan Rhetoric: A Theory of Proverb Praxis*. Peter Lang, New York

K. Yankah

Rhetoric, Classical

Rhetoric, the art of speaking, that is, of speaking in such a manner as to impress the hearers and influence them for or against an opinion or a certain course of action, exists implicitly or explicitly in any society. It is essential to cultural, political, and social activities as such, in so far as these demand a display of uninterrupted speech, or monologue. As a formalized type of knowledge, it has been studied and practiced by the ancient Greeks since the fifth century BC; it was developed by the Sophists of Athens, who learnt it from Sicily (Corax and his pupil Tisias, both of Syracuse), discussed by Plato and Aristotle—the creator of a systematic and scientific *Rhetoric*—continued by the Alexandrian hellenists, and later by the Romans (Cicero, Quintilian), for whom the oratorical skill had an ethical bearing as attached to the art of living. The evolution of classical rhetorics was seriously inhibited when Christian culture became powerful. St Augustine declared that the Holy Spirit does not need language to communicate itself to humans; the revealed Truth is known beforehand, established by theology, and not inferred from rhetorically structured reasoning. Nevertheless, this knowledge survived through the Renaissance humanists; it was an important component of their philology (grammar, dialectics, and rhetorics), and it remains essential to the modern concept of elegant, written, artistic 'prose.' Classical rhetoric is taken up literally by structuralist *rhétorique générale* and also, though more vaguely, by deconstructionism (see *Grammatology*). It is the historical source of modern discourse analysis and pragmatics (see *Discourse Analysis and Drama*; *Pragmatics*).

1. Greek Rhetoric

According to Cicero, who refers to a lost work of Aristotle, the Sicilian citizens banished by the tyrants, returned from exile after the latter's expulsion (467 BC), and instituted a number of civil processes for the recovery of their confiscated property. They needed a rule-governed art of speaking in public to deal with these questions, a *forensic* rhetoric. Corax—'the artificer of persuasion'—was the first known author of a handbook of rhetoric. He divided speech into three parts as a minimum (exordium, arguments, and epilogue), and described the typical content of each of the parts. His students or clients learned their speeches by heart and eventually delivered them in court.

Gorgias of Leontini (483–375 BC) is said to have learnt from Tisias, who accompanied him when he visited Athens as an ambassador—to obtain help against Syracuse. His approach to rhetoric is stylistic; ornamentation, poetical words, unusual figures, symmetries and antitheses, almost metrical sentences and periods—elaborated, artificial details creating a new, persuasive prose. His rhetoric is mainly used in 'epideictic' or display oratory (show-speeches, funeral orations, praise, etc.); this branch is regarded as inferior to forensic and to the noblest 'deliberative,' oratory. Among his followers are Agathon, Polus, Licymnius, Evenus, Alcidamas, Polycrates, Callippus, and Thrasymachus. When Western, or Sicilian, rhetoric met the Eastern, properly Greek thought, it became Sophist philosophy, the first professional, paid philosophical teaching. Protagoras, who was the first to call himself a Sophist, was also a grammarian; Prodicus, Hippias, Theodorus, and Theodectes belong to this much discussed group of 'persuaders.' Other Attic orators are Isocrates and the famous politician Demosthenes.

Plato deals with the subject of rhetoric in two of his dialogues, the *Gorgias* and the *Phaedrus*. In the first of these, persuasion is opposed to the acquisition of knowledge. The rhetorician is not an expert; he merely produces beliefs, false or true. He manipulates the ignorant multitude in law courts and public assemblies. Socrates claims that rhetoric is not a true art and that it does not lead to justice, even though it seems to do so. In the second dialogue, rhetoric is opposed to dialectics—as later in Stoic philosophy, where these were the two branches of logic—and severely criticized; but there is now for Plato a true art of rhetoric: if an already settled question is to be communicated, the orator must know the minds of his hearers, and he must know to adapt his arguments to these minds, and do it in the right moment. This is a psychological and pedagogical view of rhetoric.

Aristotle's *Rhetoric* (written about 330 BC) is a positive study of oratory, aiming at the deliberative genre. In its three books, he discusses, respectively, logical proofs and their dialectics; psychological proofs, referring to human emotions and characters; and questions of style and arrangement. In modern terms: the content, the communication itself, and the expression of the discourse. In the first book, Aristotle defends rhetoric as a way to truth and justice; this applies especially to deliberation, because here the subject is contingent and uncertain—no one deliberates about what is certain. Proofs are nonartificial (five types: laws, witnesses, contracts, torture, oaths) or artificial; the latter are ethical, emotional, or logical. Logical proofs are deductive or inductive. The three kinds of rhetoric are defined as follows: the deliberative kind exhorts or dissuades, its time is the future (what has to be done, what will be expedient or harmful?), and it makes the hearer a judge of the future; the forensic kind accuses or defends, its time is the past (what has been done, is it just or unjust?), and it makes the hearer a judge of the past; the epideictic kind praises or blames, its time is the present (what is being done, is it noble or disgraceful?), and it makes the hearer at least a critic of the orator's skill. Deliberative oratory deals with politics and legislation. Its questions concern what is good, and what is expedient; it must take into consideration the relation between form of government and such values as freedom, wealth, and education. Forensic oratory deals with wrongdoing, its causes and motives, and it must consider human actions in general, and their voluntary and involuntary motives (four voluntary ones:

habit, reason, anger, desire; three involuntary ones: chance, nature, compulsion). There are two kinds of justice and hence of injustice: legality, which refers to written laws, and equity, referring to unwritten laws. Epideictic oratory refers to virtue and vice. The orator shows here his own moral character, and what he thinks of that of the audience. As induction (use of examples) prevails in deliberative, and deduction (enthymeme) in forensic, comparison (amplification) is suitable to epideictic oratory. Having thus determined the first component, the content, in the first book, Aristotle now considers communication itself, in the second book. Here, communication itself is considered, trustworthiness is explained to be based on the impression that the speaker creates of himself, especially in deliberative oratory, and on the frame of mind of the judge, especially in forensic oratory. A knowledge, and therefore an analysis, of emotions is needed: anger and slight; mildness; love and friendship; hatred; fear; shame and shamelessness; benevolence; pity; horror; envy; emulation; contempt. Moral habits and personal character are related to emotions. Finally, a study of the form of the proofs is presented: examples are historical statements, invented scenes, or fables. Enthymemes are either simple maxims or unfolded syllogisms. These are demonstrative or refutative. Apparent enthymemes (fallacies) are classified. The logic of objections is discussed. Amplifications are enthymemes intending to show that a matter's importance is great or small. In the third book, Aristotle deals with expression. The language should sound slightly removed from commonplace, but its artificiality must be concealed; it must be clear and natural, but nevertheless discreetly uncommon. Metaphors are recommended, for they are both ordinary and produce a 'foreign' air, if they are suitable. Composition must avoid obscurity. There are devices for obtaining dignity of style (an art of discreet naming), and for obtaining propriety of style (emotional relevance). The language must have rhythm (but not meter); Ciceronian 'numerus' maintains this idea. Periods are important units; they should be balanced as to rhythm and meaning. Styles are different: written style is more refined than oral agonistic (polemic)—the epideictic is close to writing, the deliberative close to agonistic, and the forensic comes in between. The arrangement of the parts of a speech includes an exordium (a sort of prelude), a narrative statement, the central proof, and a peroration or epilogue. These parts differ in deliberative, forensic, and epideictic oratory.

The last of the Attic orators 'worthy to be called by that name' (Quintilian) is Demetrius (ca. 350–283 BC); political oratory gradually declined, and was succeeded by the rhetoric of the schools, characterized by a highly artificial and exaggerated style, the so-called Asianism.

2. Roman Rhetoric

The politician, writer, and rhetorician Marcus Tullius Cicero (*De Oratore, Brutus, Orator*) wants to unite wise thinking and beautiful speaking—unlike Socrates, who had separated these aims, according to Cicero—and thus to practice at the same time the arts of '*docere*' (proving), '*delectare*' (pleasing) and '*movere*' (affecting emotionally). Quintilian is the author of another principal work, the twelve books of *De institutione oratoria*. Technically, Aristotelian rhetoric is maintained and formalized, and it can be said that it achieves in Roman rhetoric a definitive form in which it has survived for two thousand years, remaining the main source of all modern research on linguistic performance.

The three branches become 'genres': *genus deliberativum*, *genus iudiciale*, and *genus demonstrativum* (the epideictic). One of Cicero's classifications shows the following tree-structure:

```
1   doctrina docendi → orator; oratio; quaestio
2.1 orator → res; verba
2.2 oratio → docere; movere
2.3 quaestio → consultatio; causa
3.1 res → collocatio; inventio
3.2 verba → actio; elocutio
3.3 docere → narratio; confirmatio
3.4 movere → principium; peroratio
3.5 consultatio → actio; cognitio
3.6 causa → exornatio; veritas
```

Besides the 'referential' concerns (2.3), the central 'morphological' issues concern *inventio* and *elocutio* (in 2.1), whereas the 'syntactic' domain (2.2), also called *dispositio*, treats the parts of speech, its sections or components. The parts of (3.4) of course embed or surround those of (3.3).

In fact, *elocutio* becomes the most important technical chapter of the entire doctrine (Lausberg 1963). Under this heading is found, in particular, the list of *tropi* and that of *figurae*—the 'tropes' being typical ways of conceptualizing the content (by periphrasis, synecdoche, antonomasia, emphasis, litotes, hyperbole, metonymy, metaphor, irony), and the 'figures' being typical ways of 'phrasing' the expression (e.g., by using repetition, comparison, parallelism, ellipsis, antithesis, parenthesis, examples, syllogisms, rhetorical questions, exclamations, etc.). The tropes have been taken up by recent cognitive research (Lakoff and Johnson 1980), and the existing theoretical literature on metaphor is now immense.

3. Concluding Remarks

The study of linguistic performance in dialogue and monologue is an essential dimension of general linguistics. The forms of address, the 'turn taking' in dialogue, and—in dialogues consisting of exchanges of monologues—the 'strategies' of integrating performative, tense sequences (Weinrich 1964) and constative, relaxed sequences in monologue, the choices of lexical, grammatical and, as we now say, *stylistic* devices in any performance, are important for our understanding of how a language evolves historically (Sweetser 1990) by selection from a range of possibilities. This study is also of crucial interest to our knowledge of the human psyche, manifested chiefly by language, bodily and verbal; cognition and emotion are perhaps not structured, but at least regulated decisively by language, and certainly best known from the rhetorical peculiarities through which they are signified, as shown also by Freudian psychoanalysis. On the other hand, political systems, rules, and laws must be based on a regulation of discourse, and have to determine what can, cannot, and must be said where and when. Rhetoric is in this respect the necessary bridge between political science and linguistics.

The study of oratory is thus relevant to linguistics proper, to psychology and to political thought. It is above all an indispensable component of any philosophy; if the discipline of logic is the formal study of propositional synonymies and parasynonymies, the general cause of these phenomena must be—as Aristotle saw and insisted—the fact that propositions are made up of language and related to thoughts in such a way that the 'same thought' can underlie different 'logoi' or sentential expressions. The basis of logic is rhetoric, understood as the study of this fundamental relation between thought and language. Dialectics, the art of dialogue (Perelman 1989), is itself based on our relative knowledge of the elementary mystery of *someone saying something to somebody* in general—an obvious but still enigmatic condition of human existence as an ontologically established syntagm relating language, mind, and world.

See also: Stylistics; Discourse; Manipulation; Kinesics.

Bibliography

Aristotle 1982 (transl. Freese J H) *'Art' of Rhetoric*. Harvard University Press, Cambridge, MA
Cauquelin A 1990 *Aristote: Le Langage*. Presses Universitaires de France, Paris
Fontanier P 1977 *Les figures du discours*. Flammarion, Paris
Groupe μ (Dubois J, Edeline F, Klinkenberg J M, Minguet P, Pire F, Trinon H) 1970 *Rhétorique générale*. Larousse, Paris
Lakoff G, Johnson M 1980 *Metaphors We Live By*. University of Chicago Press, Chicago, IL
Lausberg H 1963 *Elemente der literarischen Rhetorik*. Max Hueber, Munich
Marsais C Du 1967 *Traité des tropes*. Slatkine, Geneva
Morier H 1989 *Dictionnaire de poétique et de rhétorique*, 4th edn. Presses Universitaires de France, Paris
Patillon M 1990 *Elements de rhétorique classique*. Nathan, Paris
Perelman C 1989 *Rhétoriques*. Editions de l'Université de Bruxelles, Bruxelles
Sweetser E 1990 *From Etymology to Pragmatics: Metaphorical and Cultural Aspects of Semantic Structure*. Cambridge University Press, Cambridge
Weinrich H 1964 *Tempus*. Verlag W. Kohlhammer, Stuttgart

P. Aa. Brandt

Rhyme

The origins of formalized rhyme in the West are mysterious, but almost certainly to be found in Latin hymnology; it is likely that these Christian hymns owe rhyme, in their turn, to Mithraism and the Zoroastrian *Avesta* (Draper 1957, 1965). But rhyme has embedded itself in the various Western systems of versification at differing levels of metrical assimilation. Regular English verse, for instance, thanks to the principle of recurrence which governs syllable-stress meter (see *Meter*), does not regard rhyme's line-demarcative function as crucial, whereas in syllabic, phrase-accented French verse, rhyme is called upon to define, and bestow full metricality on, the line. In fact, rhyme in English verse is an unsystematized, if not simply ornamental (Hill 1969; Lewis 1987), verse resource. English verse makes no structurally significant distinction between masculine and feminine rhymes, as French does and as German can, even though it is familiar with the terms (masculine = rhyme on stressed syllable alone, feminine = rhyme on stressed syllable + following unstressed syllable(s)). Nor does English verse automatically differentiate, as French verse does, degrees of richness in rhyme (number of homophonic phonemes in the rhyme cluster). As a result, rhyme in English has a prolific but unstable terminology, whose terms relate not to the phonetic finesses of full rhyme, but to the various kinds of approximation to, or departure from, full rhyme (Rickert 1978).

1. The Phonetics of Rhyme

Full end-rhyme in English consists of the pairing of two line-terminal stressed syllables, which share identical vocalic and postvocalic sounds, but usually have dissimilar prevocalic consonants (homophones which are homographs belong to the special effects of pun-rhyming, while repetitions relate to special formal features: refrains, the sestina). Even if English rhyme is not metrically line-demarcative, it derives much of its significance from its line-terminal position. It constitutes an important acoustic landmark in the text, transforming the tonic value of stress into a phonic value, and thus helping to activate and organize its acoustic environment. Rhyme, also, in creating stanzas, creates a sequence of structural intervals, which may be equal (*abab*) or unequal (*abba*); varying intervals allow the rhyme-pairs to operate at different levels of consciousness, or with differing intensities of impact, and differing intonational and modal configurations. In the heroic couplet, on the other hand, rhyme-pairs may bespeak a tireless, consistent, intellectual acuity. If rhyme organizes lines in stanzas, acoustically affiliating or dissociating consecutive lines, then it might be proposed that, if a certain scheme, say *abab*, is to be affirmed, *a* needs in some sense to rhyme 'against' *b*. But the rhymes of the first stanza of Gray's 'Elegy,' for example—/deɪ/; /liː/; /weɪ/; /miː/— share many features: open syllables, front unrounded vowels, length (glide and long). It is, in fact, in Gray's particular interests here to minimize differentia: the darkening, emptying landscape, the wearied, elegiac tone, the gradual, uninterrupted withdrawal into self. Rhyme analysis has yet to develop a classification of phonetic proximity/distance which will provide some sense of how conniving or adversative adjacent rhyme-pairs can be.

2. Rhyme and Phonosemantics

Few would disagree with Jakobson's general axiom about the indivisibility of the acoustic and the semantic in rhyme: 'Rhyme necessarily involves the semantic relationship between the rhyming units' (1960: 1367). But what the semantic relationship should or might be remains a subject of debate. Wimsatt's broad view that rhymes 'impose upon the logical pattern of expressed argument a kind of fixative counterpattern of alogical implication' (1954: 153) has much in common with the formalists' privileging of relationships of disparity and incongruity in rhyme. Perloff (1970) has tried to restore the balance in the direction of the neutral or congruent, and at the same time to provide a more thorough classification of the kinds of semantic association available in rhyme, viz. semantic congruity: symbol-rhyme, causal rhyme, synonym-rhyme, metonymy-rhyme, symbolic association-rhyme and semantic disparity: antithesis-rhyme, irony-rhyme, pun-rhyme. Nemoianu (1971) believes that there are very few genuinely neutral rhymes (which he calls 'secondary')—he identifies three

directions in rhyme's semantic activity: diffuse (atmospheric, play of sound-symbolism), horizontal, and vertical. He also produces a rhyme classification by content criteria: classical (confirmatory), ironic (see Perloff), substantial (semantic prominence), secondary (neutral). Corresponding to this classification is a classification by function: parallelism (classical), cementation of new aesthetic product (ironic), break in grammatical norms (substantial), demarcation between lines (secondary). These taxonomic suggestions have not excited much response.

3. Rhyme and Morphosemantics

Part of Wimsatt's argument about the 'alogical' semantics of rhyme rests on the proposition that, while it makes sense for words with the same morphological structures to be coupled, rhymes unjustifiably couple heterogeneous roots. In terms of modern morphemic thinking, it would be truer to say that, since rhyme and assonance are so frequently the ways in which morphemic similarity manifests itself, one can assume that rhyme is in fact evidence of morphemic similarity. Rhyme, therefore, may either create new morphosemantic relationships through its process of acoustic attraction, or it may reinforce already existing morphemic convergences and, at the same time, their semantic univocality. Thus, if *ow* in *glow* and *flow* means 'steady' (with *gl* a phenomenon of light and *fl* a phenomenon of movement), then *blow* will be a steady expiration or a methodically delivered injury, while *low* will suggest a relatively unchanging state. Equally, *limb* is more poetically attractive than *leg* because it has the grace factor supplied by *im* in *slim* and *trim*, and perhaps a coquettish coloring derived from *prim* and *whim* (see Bolinger 1950). Naturally these phono-morphemic systems are not great respecters of grammatical categories (see *Sound Symbolism*).

4. Rhyme and Word Class

Pioneering work on the combinations of word-class characteristically involved in rhymes has been done by Herbert (1940). Herbert's conclusions bring no surprises and his statistical methods for assessing the quality of poets are crude. But the understanding of the grammar and syntax of rhyme, and of the relative frequency of parts of speech in the rhyme position, which his study initiates, will in turn facilitate an understanding of what it might mean, as a conscious poetic gesture, to rhyme a noun with, say, an adverb, and indicate what kinds of grammatical transference—adverbialization of nouns, substantivalization of prepositions—rhyme can engineer.

Much rhyme theory works from an assumption of equivalence or equation between the two rhyme words (i.e., a synchronic view). But Perloff's causal rhyme reminds us that possibilities of linear and temporal sequence also act along rhyme's vertical axis. There are two principal senses in which this is so. First, rhyme-pairs can create alternative, if truncated, syntagms, if their parts of speech are syntactically consecutive (adj + noun, verb + adv, noun + verb, etc.). Second, rhyme order affects the status of the words of the rhyme pair: the first word is the proposal, the given, the innocent, the rhyme of expectation, while the second is the answer, the thought-up, the guileful, the rhyme of fulfillment or surprise; the first rhyme word 'sets up' the second, is the 'straight man,' while the second is full of artifice and display.

5. Amplified Rhyme

To concentrate exclusively on rhyme words or rhyme schemes is to risk overlooking the 'length' of rhymes, the phenomenon of 'amplified' or 'reinforced' rhyme. It is not just line-terminal words that rhyme, but whole lines. In the couplet:

Love, Hope, and Joy, fair pleasure's smiling train,
Hate, Fear, and Grief, the family of pain
(Pope, *An Essay on Man*, Epistle 2, LL. 117–18)

one might suppose that the phonetic and graphemic antitheses between the two sets of line-initial nouns are ironically highlighted by the rhyme *smiling train/family of pain*, with its distinction between the close corporateness of *family* and the looser discipleship of *train*. But the parallelism of the nouns is reinforced in the amplification of the /eɪn/ rhyme by /f/, /m/, /l/, /ɪ/, /p/, prefiguring the burden of the following couplet:

These mix'd with art, and to due bounds confin'd,
Make and maintain the balance of the mind.
(lines 119–20)

If rhyme seems to have the ability to suffuse whole lines and give an overriding orientation to syntax, it is because rhyme, with its own special dictionary, seems to be a repository of hard-earned human wisdom, of proverbial truths— ambition/perdition; name/fame/blame/shame—or a transcendental language precipitated out of common language, atemporal, with an authority beyond any particular verse instance. But lines 117–18 from Pope above may reveal to us that rhyme's ability to be transfixative and unrevisable is established against an equal and opposite capacity to be highly contingent and unstable. The very fact that the rhyme so provocatively parades acoustic fit as the key to its paradigms, encourages us to find *Cain*, or *strain*, or even *gain*, as substitutes for *pain*; and since the acoustic imperative ultimately overrides considerations of semantic and/or syntactic appropriacy, one might, without any loss of poetic right, equally substitute *Spain*, or *rain*, or *Jane*, or *sane* or *vain* (with the noun in the following line).

6. Rhyme and Half-rhyme

But in the end, however strong acoustic imperatives are for full rhyme, our awareness of these imperatives is activated by rhyme's line-terminal position. And it is position alone which can give full-rhyme status to rhymes with weak phonetic claims (half-rhymes, pararhymes). How far automatic acoustic linkages play a part in the operation of half-rhymes is impossible to determine. If *bland*, for example, rhymes with *clash*, and if *clash* rhymes with *rush*, would the reading mind, unaided, sense any connection between *bland* and *rush*? That is, does the principle of transitivity—x = y, y = z ∴ x = z—apply to half-rhymes, as it does to full rhymes? If it does, then half-rhyme radically increases the constituents of rhyme families. If it does not, then half-rhymes are nonce creations which make no suppositions about other possible partners. Closely related to this question is another: does half-rhyme represent something evolutionary in language—an acquired subtlety of ear—or is it

a regressive step, the embryonic or unachieved rhyme rather than full rhyme superseded?

If much work has still to be done on the phonetic relativities of rhyme, so too there is work to be done on the history of rhyme and its generical connections. By the former is meant the changing pairings of loaded lexical items like *earth*, *reason*, *heart*, *wife*, the changing contexts of particular combinations (*reason/treason*; *mind/blind*; *grave/brave*; etc.), and what these tell us about evolving culture and ideology. By the latter is meant the way that particular rhymes may operate to define or stabilize the genres in which they occur; the rhymes of the first stanza of Wordsworth's 'Strange fits of passion have I known,' for instance, tell us what kind of hybrid the lyrical ballad is, for, if *tell/befell* is the business of balladry, the publicization of event, then *known/alone* is the Romantic counterthrust, the disturbing knowledge of self acquired in solitude.

Bibliography

Bolinger D L 1950 Rime, assonance and morpheme analysis. *Word* **6**: 117–36
Draper J W 1957 The origin of rhyme. *RLC* **31**: 74–85
Draper J W 1965 The origin of rhyme: A supplement. *RLC* **39**: 452–53
Herbert T W 1940 The grammar of rimes. *SewR* **48**: 362–77
Hill A A 1969 A phonological description of poetic ornaments *LangS* **2**: 99–123
Jakobson R 1960 Closing statement: Linguistics and poetics. In: Sebeok T A (ed.) *Style in Language.* MIT Press, Cambridge, MA
Lewis R 1987 Riming in French. *FMLS* **23**: 1–10
Nemoianu V 1971 Levels of study in the semantics of rhyme. *Style* **5**: 246–64
Perloff M 1970 *Rhyme and Meaning in the Poetry of Yeats.* Mouton, The Hague
Rickert W E 1978 Rhyme terms. *Style* **12(1)**: 35–46
Wimsatt W K Jr 1954 One relation of rhyme to reason. In: Wimsatt W K Jr *The Verbal Icon: Studies in the meaning of poetry.* University of Kentucky Press, Lexington, KY

C. Scott

Rhythm

To describe rhythm as a principle of repetition or recurrence is to desemanticize and to displace it; rhythm is a perceptual experience not to be dissociated from the particularity of its context (in poetry, the verse-instance); it is part of the dynamic of perception and cognition, rather than an anterior or posterior pattern. Thus in Chatman's account (1965: 18–29), 'primary' rhythm ('simple periodic return of a given stimulus') is not meaningfully rhythmic; only 'secondary' rhythm—the grouping, differential highlighting, 'interpretation,' of primary rhythm—is. The perception of rhythm is a psychological need, the means whereby phenomena are made sense of, and sensory stimuli are absorbed as subjective percepts. Rhythm compels the text to recover its status as enunciation (process), to resist being something that already exists, the enunciated (product). Free verse in particular has explored rhythm as an improvised relationship between language and the reading subject.

1. Rhythm and Meter

Is rhythm (a) a superordinate of meter, with meter constituting merely one manifestation of it (rhythms of weak and strong, or long and short, or high and low)? Or is rhythm (b) the actualization of meter in the variables of language, standing in tension with meter's abstract regularity? Or is rhythm (c) something anticipated and encompassed by the superordinate meter? If rhythm is regarded as a psycho-physiological universal (cf., biorhythms), with its sources in pulse, respiration, muscular coordination, then it will be set against meter as the animate against the mechanical, the contingent against the abstract, the experiential against the intellectual. Position (a) is represented by I. A. Richards; his affective approach to literary value inevitably entails an organic view of rhythm, and explicitly defines meter as 'its specialized form' (1963: 134). According to (b), rhythm emerges from meter at the point at which the demands of 'natural' speech outweigh or replace metrical demands, and at which the fixity of meter is submerged in the complex diversity of utterance. This position can be associated with the new criticism and structuralism (e.g., Wimsatt and Beardsley 1959; Fowler 1966). We should remember, however, that, for the formalists, it is not so much rhythm's irregularity that deviates from meter, as the reverse: meter itself is deviation, part of the organized violence practiced on language by poetic form. But the distinction between rhythm and meter is invalidated by position (c), the position of many generative metrists (see *Meter*). By proposing models which make 'irregularity,' 'variation,' and 'deviation' actively constitutive of meter, generative metrists build linguistic variables into a predictive set of metrical options. By the same token, rhythm is neutralized as a value, and is merely a feature of metrical complexity or of nonmetricality. In other words, in generative terms, rhythm and meter combine as performance and competence, surface structure and deep structure, with a clear privileging of meter, which determines what is possible within the rules of rhythmic transformation. Rhythm is thus assimilated to meter as a dimension of its complexity, rather than standing in tension against it, as a fundamentally different principle.

2. The Location of Rhythm

Plato described 'rhythm' as 'the name for order in movement' (*Laws* 2.665a) and the kinetic element is crucial. If we think of rhythm as interval, we risk thinking of it spatially; if we think of it as movement, we involve it with duration, in the Bergsonian sense, as something indivisible, qualitative, and indissolubly linked with ongoing inner experience. Symmetry and proportion as spatial percepts can only become rhythm through the motions of the eye. Rhythm is thus not accessible in the text, but only in the linear reading of the text. It is to do with response, and with what activates and informs response, the transformation of figures into configuration; as Bridges (1922: 55) puts it: '[Rhythm] is more than mere movement; it is rather a coordination of movements that appeals to the feelings or emotions.'

Inasmuch as rhythm is a multilevel experience (see Cureton 1985), it is the channel through which a text engages the reader at different points along the continuum from the subconscious to the conscious. But there is no way of knowing what selector mechanisms operate in reading, which rhythmic aspects are highlighted or suppressed, how many and what combinations of level are achieved; but at the very least, it is dangerous to assume, in poetry, that meter is always the dominant, if not exclusive, source of rhythmic experience.

Many would argue not only that to place rhythm in the space between text and reader is to mystify it and remove it from investigation, but also that rhythm must be replaced in the text, and specifically in the patterns of structural differentia which derive from Saussurean linguistics (see *Saussurean Tradition in Twentieth-century Linguistics*). But, outside meter, this project has been little pursued. And as long as rhythm is where prosodic analysis makes room for paralinguistic features (tempo, pausing, loudness, tone, intonation, etc.), and as long as rhythm is treated as a multilevel phenomenon, it will elude quantification and measurement.

3. Rhythm and Meaning

Not surprisingly, meter only becomes meaningful for the generative metrists when it is nonmetrical. Halle and Keyser (1971: 171) explain the unmetricality of Keats's line:

How many bards gild the lapses of time

by proposing that 'the poet is purposely moving outside of the meter in order to caricature metrically the sense of the line. The line is literally what it speaks of figuratively, "a lapse of time".' Of course, if one values visceral, noncultural contacts with language, of the kind that Barthes celebrates in *jouissance* (as opposed to 'pleasure'), then questions about the hermeneutics of rhythm will be beside the point. But one might venture that rhythm has at least a phatic function, in establishing a channel of communication, or that it means in the sense of giving shape to meaning, of facilitating its emergence, or that it guarantees intelligibility—nonsense poetry can be uttered with all the paralinguistic evidence of apparent meaningfulness because of the rhythm which subtends it. Rhythm can certainly have meaning if it acts as a code (Morse). It can also aspire to a semantic function in those prosodies in which meter, because minimally coded, is actually supplemented by, or implicated in, the variables of rhythm: French verse can use the variable configurations of an alexandrine hemistich $(2+4, 4+2, 3+3,$ etc.) to project, or at least identify, impulses (expansion, contraction) or attitudes or personae (voices).

4. Rhythm and Euphony

The notion of rhythmicity, as something which organizes the perception of pattern in a text and facilitates its absorption, is frequently yoked with that of euphony. This is particularly so where rhythm is regarded not as primarily expressive or imitative, but as aesthetic, as a servant of harmony. The debate about euphony (see Bishop 1975, 1985) derives from proposals made by Grammont (1923). Grammont argues that vowel modulation (varying point of articulation) and the careful disposition of modulating groups produce the captivating music of verse. Bishop is anxious to establish the part played in euphony by items expressly omitted by Grammont: consonants, short and imparisyllabic lines, patterns that cross metrical boundaries (caesura, line). He goes on to propose three 'laws' of euphony: identity (repetition), proximity (sounds produced in the same vicinity), and progression (e.g., avoidance of clusters, of dissonant sequences, of maximal articulatory leaps) a more comprehensive classification of euphonic categories is to be found in Gauthier (1974). Ironically, the correlation of lingual ease and aural pleasure which underpins theories of euphony returns the aesthetic to the imitative and physiological, to propositions about the mouth as site of sexual/erotic activity or as the 'translator' of cardiac, pulmonary, and gastric noises.

Bibliography

Attridge D 1982 *The Rhythms of English Poetry.* Longman, London

Bishop L O 1975 Phonological correlates of euphony. *FR* **49(1)**: 11–22

Bishop L O 1985 Euphony: A new method of analysis. *LangS* **18(4)**: 342–62

Bridges R 1929 Humdrum and harum-scarum: A paper on free verse. *London Mercury* **7**: 54–63

Chatman S B 1965 *A Theory of Meter.* Mouton, The Hague

Cureton R D 1985 Rhythm: A multilevel analysis. *Style* **19(12)**: 242–257

Fowler R 1966 'Prose rhythm' and metre. In: Fowler R (ed.) *Essays on Style and Language: Linguistic and Critical Approaches to Literary Style.* Routledge and Kegan Paul, London

Gauthier M 1974 *Système euphonique et rythmique du vers français.* Klincksieck, Paris

Grammont M 1923 *Le Vers français: Ses moyens d'expression, son harmonie.* E Champion, Paris

Halle M, Keyser S J 1971 *English Stress: Its Form, Its Growth, and Its Role in Verse.* Harper and Row, New York

Meschonnic H 1982 *Critique du rythme: Anthropologie historique du langage.* Verdier, Lagrasse

Richards I A 1963 *Principles of Literary Criticism.* Routledge and Kegan Paul, London

Wimsatt W K Jr, Beardsley M C 1959 The concept of meter: An exercise in abstraction. *Proceedings of the Modern Language Association of America* **74**: 585–98

C. Scott

Richards, I. A. (1893–1979)

In a career lasting sixty years, I. A. Richards made major contributions to semantics, literary theory and criticism, theories of metaphor and translation, elementary reading and second-language training, and world literacy.

Born in Sandbach, Cheshire on February 23, 1893, the son of a Welsh chemical engineer, Richards attended Clifton and Magdalene College, Cambridge, where he received first-class honors in 1915. Four years later he began teaching in the new English program at Cambridge. Collaboration with C. K. Ogden led to *The Meaning of Meaning* (1923), called the best-known work on semantics ever published. They were known for their novel adaptation of American pragmatism and behaviorism in conjunction with native British philosophical psychology and their context theory of meaning. By contextualism they meant that a word or utterance gains its full meaning only through its surrounding context, interpreted in psychological and

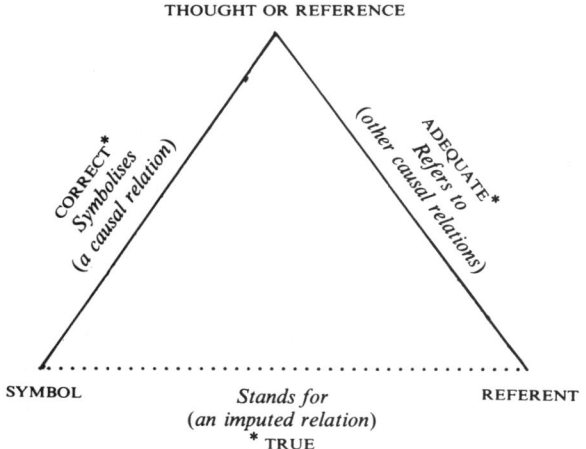

Figure 1. Triangle of interpretation.

physical terms, which they depicted in a triangle of interpretation (Fig. 1). The authors defined two broad uses of language: referential (asserting or describing facts) and emotive (the expression of feeling). Besides these uses, they outlined five functions of language, each more or less present in a given utterance, though Richards eventually enumerated seven functions: indicating, characterizing, realizing, valuing, influencing, controlling, and purposing. Their theories anticipated themes in logical positivism and the Vienna Circle.

In *Principles of Literary Criticism* (1924) and *Practical Criticism* (1929) Richards examined literary language (*Science and Poetry* (1926) was a popularization). *Principles of Literary Criticism* offers a psychological theory of value, a theory of communication, and an analysis of poetry that places strong emphasis on complexity, irony, and synthesis ('poetry of inclusion'), thereby revealing the influence of literary modernism. *Practical Criticism* sifts through hundreds of student reports on poems and categorizes types of misreading (for example, stock responses, irrelevant associations, doctrinal adhesions, and sentimentality). Many supposedly well-prepared students had made faulty readings and foisted them upon the authors. The book proposes the method of 'close reading' to determine 'sense,' 'feeling,' 'tone,' and 'intention,' and lays particular emphasis on the proper kind of belief brought to reading, as well as the sincerity of response. Both books contain a critique of the media industry, then in its infancy. Together they exerted a broad impact on the study of literature. Richards has been referred to as the father of new criticism, which stressed close textual analysis and dominated academic literary studies from the 1940s to the 1960s.

Coleridge on Imagination (1934) virtually founded Coleridge studies in the twentieth century, while *The Philosophy of Rhetoric* (1936) contains a revolutionary theory of metaphor. Hitherto metaphor was analyzed in terms of idea and image, the idea assuming the principal role with regard to meaning. Instead, Richards granted parity to the two halves of the metaphorical copula, calling them 'tenor' (principal subject) and 'vehicle' (what the principal subject is compared to). These interact to form the metaphor, which is the whole double unit, a new creation, not the vehicle alone. Neither tenor nor vehicle go through the metaphorical process unchanged: metaphor is a 'transaction between contexts.'

During the 1930s Richards became absorbed in Basic English, an 850-word version of normal English devised by Ogden in the 1920s as an auxiliary international language. Sojourns in China convinced Richards of the possibility of using Basic English as a way into standard English. In 1939 he transferred to Harvard University where he developed the *Language Through Pictures* series (with Christine M. Gibson) and pioneered the use of audio-visual media in the teaching of beginning reading and second-language training. For students to possess major texts on which to develop their understanding of language and culture, he translated into simplified English Plato's *Republic* (1942) and Homer's *Iliad* (1951). *Beyond* (1974), on the relation of man to god in Homer, Job, Plato, Dante, and Shelley, is his humanistic testament. In his later career he also turned to writing poetry and published four collections.

In 1974 Richards returned to Cambridge, England. In spring 1979 he embarked on a lecture tour of China with the general subject of English as a second language. He fell seriously ill and was taken back to Cambridge where he died on 7 September.

Bibliography

Brower R, Vendler H, Hollander J (eds.) 1973 *I. A. Richards: Essays in His Honor*. Oxford University Press, New York

Hotopf W H N 1965 *Language, Thought and Comprehension: A Case Study of the Writings of I. A. Richards*. Routledge and Kegan Paul, London

Richards I A, Ogden C K 1923 *The Meaning of Meaning*. Kegan Paul, Trench, Trubner, London

Richards I A 1924 *Principles of Literary Criticism*. Kegan Paul, Trench, Trubner, London

Richards I A 1929 *Practical Criticism: A Study of Literary Judgment*. Kegan Paul, Trench, Trubner, London

Richards I A 1974 *Beyond*. Harcourt Brace Jovanovitch, New York

Russo J P 1989 *I. A. Richards: His Life and Work*. Johns Hopkins University Press and Routledge, Baltimore and London

Shusterman R 1988 *Critique et Poésie selon I. A. Richards: De la Confiance positiviste au Relativisme naissant*. Presses Universitaires de Bordeaux, Bordeaux

J. P. Russo

Riddle

The riddle, a verbal art miniature built on a playful inversion of interrogation, challenges the wit of adults and children in virtually every known human society. Its formal economy masks a bold engagement with the conceptual foundations of culture, just as its accessible discourse style conceals a highly self-conscious deployment of linguistic resources. In short, the riddle is deceptively ingenuous; beneath its compact verbal surface lurks a serious exercise in cultural reflexivity. Even the routinized pattern of verbal exchange provides real opportunities for social intrigue as people come together to jointly create and sustain riddling sessions.

1. The True Riddle

Aristotle states in *The Poetics* that 'the essence of a riddle is, while speaking of actual facts, to make impossible combinations.' The true riddle (the focus of attention in this essay) features what folklorists call a 'block element,' that is, a germ of authentic puzzlement, an apparent semantic impasse that after all submits to sense-making procedures. Speech economies often include various riddle-like productions that fall into the broader category of 'interrogative ludic routines' but lack the pivotal block element. Also to be distinguished from the true riddle is the puzzle, which generally centers on a logical rather than an epistemological problem, and is often the object of far more intellectual effort than the riddle.

Each true riddle parades its moment of ambiguity in the compass of a verbal game allotting to one player the authority to initiate and resolve a common focus of puzzlement, and to the other the right and duty to announce (if known) or to improvise (if not known) a solution. The one who poses and finally resolves the riddle occupies the seer's role, holding the key to what sometimes appears as a magical dispelling of incongruity. The player who responds has the right (in most riddling traditions) to discover this key independently, and thereby emerge as a heroic solver of riddles.

Broadly, the true riddle may be defined as a verbal game founded on a playful adaptation of the interrogative system, which progresses from a state of conceptual dissonance to a state of conceptual harmony by foregrounding and then removing nuances of linguistic and conceptual incongruity. Riddles invert the standard questioning protocol by lodging the answer to the question with the questioner, and designating the person who is asked the question as the person who implicitly lacks the answer. In the jargon of speech-act theory, the speech act of riddling systematically reverses the polarity of the felicity conditions that hold sway in canonical questioning (Austin 1962; McDowell 1979: 30).

Riddles manipulate available sources of incongruity to create a semantic uneasiness, compelling one to entertain apparently contrary-to-fact presuppositions. If a riddle asks *What's black and white and red all over?* or *What has eyes but cannot see?* or *What is blue and white and has two cherries on top?* or *What's taller sitting than standing?*, in every case the respondent is backed into an untenable semantic corner, forced to accept what appear to be impossible stipulations (that something is simultaneously three different colors, that something with eyes might nonetheless be blind, that a blue and white object might have cherries on top, that something might be taller when it sits than when it stands).

In this way riddles create momentary epistemological dilemmas that cry out for resolution, and resolution comes, in a satisfying release of tension, when the solution is provided. Conceptual harmony is achieved when the semantic duplicity is unmasked, and the counterfactual presupposition can be set aside. A newspaper is black and white and *read* all over; a potato has *eyes* though such eyes are not lenses for viewing; the bubble lights on top of a police car can be thought of as *cherries*; a dog is indeed taller sitting than standing. Points of systematic communicative dysfunction are trotted out for display and then dispelled in the riddle's progress, a trajectory that Roger Abrahams (1972) has referred to as 'epistemological foreplay.'

2. Riddling

Riddles are customarily aired in riddling sessions, so the speech event known as riddling is a vital component in any comprehensive account of the riddle. Riddling entails two participant roles: the riddler, who poses and resolves the riddle, and the riddlee, who attempts and then requests a solution. Riddling fosters active participation: bystanders and onlookers are easily incorporated as members of the riddlee contingent, and individuals can readily migrate from one participant role to the other. Riddling partakes of the conversational ethos by virtue of its reciprocal, participatory design, but channels this ethos into a rather predictable, game-like sequence of player moves.

Each participant role encompasses a specific purpose and a set of conventional moves. The riddler becomes the authority figure in the interlude between posing and solving the riddle. Other players respond to this person's initiatives, and must at last submit to his or her decisive announcement of the solution. The riddler acquires by the riddling contract a license to run the show, but in turn assumes responsibility for a plausible arousal and removal of conceptual dissonance. In some traditions and on some occasions, riddlers may exhort the riddlees and provide clues to keep them engaged. Often, the riddler may disavow a potentially correct solution in favor of another preferred solution. Riddlees too find ways to enhance their options. They may ask for clarification, solicit clues, offer possible solutions, and at last surrender and clamor for the solution. Their turn at conversational dependency buys them the thrill of a successful riddle act, with its movement from confusion to enlightenment. At the same time, each riddlee can anticipate a turn at riddler, and a moment as authority figure.

In some riddling traditions, the participant moves are highly formulaic, and riddling takes on a distinctly ritualistic aura. The West African tone riddle is a rhythmic conjoining of verse isolates into poetic couplets (Giray-Saul 1983; Yankah 1983). Among the Tambunan Dusun of North Borneo riddling formulas with characteristic pitch contours punctuate every moment in the riddling encounter (Williams 1963). These discourse markers endow the riddling with a clearly defined aural structure; they dramatize its inherent principles of speech organization. Other riddling traditions may be less formally constituted but nonetheless channel discourse into patterned utterance sequences diagnostic of the riddling game.

Riddling sessions can be viewed in their entirety as extended discourse units, sometimes acquiring the feel of a symposium, with an emergent topic of common focus, sometimes unleashing—especially among child riddlers—rounds of legalistic negotiation as individual players seek to adapt this simple rule structure to their advantage. Riddling frequently interacts with other forms of verbal art, notably with various forms of traditional narrative, providing for a refreshing interplay of contrastive performance genres: riddles activate a rapid exchange of verbal moves, whereas narratives engage audiences in a protracted spate of single-author talk. In every speech community, riddles must be factored into the flow of talk in accordance with local principles of speech etiquette.

3. Ludic Transformation

The riddle is a finite exercise in transmuting the world of ordinary experience into an alien world of infinite possibility. It accomplishes a process of ludic transformation, a playful reconstitution of reality, a flirtation with alternative classificatory systems. Ludic transformation may attack the verbal code, as an exercise in native linguistics, or it may attack the conceptual code of unspoken assumption, the set of enthymemes held in common within a given social group. Its favored methods, repeated throughout the world's riddling corpuses, include homophony, metaphor, and anomaly.

Homophony, understood loosely as the ability of a phonetic sequence to trigger discrepant semantic interpretations, provides abundant ammunition to the world's riddlers. The coincidence of different lexemes on a single phonetic string, as in the classic newspaper riddle cited above, or the historical process of polysemic extension of meaning, create a pool of semantic wrinkles readily exploited in the riddle format. Ambiguities derivative from grammatical processes may facilitate the riddler's craft, as in this example:

What has four wheels and flies?
A garbage truck.

This ludic transformation begins with the polysemy inherent in the word *flies*, but is aided and abetted by uncertainty introduced in deletions associated with the grammatical process of compounding separate sentences (*What has four wheels?* and *What has flies?*).

Riddles working at the level of linguistic ambiguity force a reassessment of language resources and indeed, of the very nature of natural languages. They reveal human speech as a perverse instrument of human purpose, as able equally to deceive or confuse as to render with clarity. There is preliminary evidence associating an increase in language-based ludic transformation with riddling traditions of modern, urban populations (McDowell 1979).

Metaphoric ludic transformation makes use of unorthodox methods for referring to a familiar object, in the process suggesting an affinity between objects that are not normally conceived of as kindred. *A thousand lights in a dish* is resolved into *the stars in the night sky*, evincing the trope known in Classical rhetoric as the *diagram*, in which pairs of related terms retain a constant relationship to one another (a:b::c:d). Thus, 'lights in a dish' serves as an innovative descriptive phrase for 'stars in the night sky,' and the riddle proposes an overarching theme running through various domains of experience, a theme which might be labeled 'atomistic objects in a concave holder.' Elli Kőngás-Maranda (1971) argues that riddles identify unifying principles in the cosmology, what she calls the 'superset,' and in a similar vein James Fernandez (1980) attributes to riddles a puzzlement that is ultimately edifying in its discovery of transcendent propositions composing an integrated world view.

Finally, ludic transformation may simply place before our eyes empirical observations that contradict the way we normally think about things. A dog (like other four-legged creatures) is in fact taller sitting than standing (*What is taller sitting than standing?*); one long ball of twine would in fact reach the moon (*How many balls of string would it take to reach the moon?*); smoke does appear to rise exclusively (*What goes up and never comes down?*). Riddles founded on anomaly direct one's attention to the experiential richness of the surrounding world, which always defeats attempts to impose tidy conceptual order.

4. The Riddle's Mission

Riddles entertain and challenge, but their mission transcends these immediate pleasures. Even though the different kinds of ludic transformation move in different directions, taken collectively they precipitate a general deconstruction of received cultural systems. Riddles centered on linguistic duplicity unmask the expressive neutrality of language, which can as easily deceive as inform; riddles centered on metaphoric associations propose fleeting, alternative visions of conceptual order; and those centered on anomaly reveal the poverty of ordinary classificatory systems. On balance, the riddle forces a sophisticated, slightly ironic stance toward cultural resources. Riddles function as a cultural instrument for measuring the limits of culture, by revealing the arbitrary and tentative character of standard expressive and conceptual equipment (Hamnett 1967). Freed from a slavish fidelity to these cultural resources, the veteran of riddling can now bend them to his or her own purposes. Stripped of their necessity, these resources acquire in their own right a new vitality, a new malleability. In the final analysis, the riddle's mission is to advance a critical perspective on habitual modes of thought and expression, and in the process to energize the jaded conventions routinely used to contain people's experience of the world.

Bibliography

Abrahams R 1972 The literary study of the riddle. *Texas Studies in Literature and Language* xiv: 177–97

Aristotle (transl. Bouchier E S) *The Poetics*. Blackwell Oxford

Austin J L 1962 *How To Do Things With Words*. Clarendon Press, Oxford

Blacking J 1961 The social value of Venda riddles. *African Studies* **20**: 1–32

Fernandez J 1980 Edification by puzzlement. In: Karp I, Bird C S (eds.) *Explorations in African Systems of Thought*. Indiana University Press, Bloomington, IN

Giray-Saul E 1983 A West African riddling tradition: The *solem kueese* of the Mossi of Upper Volta. In: Anyidoho K, Avorgbedor D, Domowitz S, Giray-Saul E (eds.) *Cross Rhythms: Occasional Papers in African Folklore*. Trickster Press, Folklore Institute, Bloomington, IN

Hamnett I 1967 Ambiguity, classification and change: The function of riddles. *Man n.s.* 2/3 379–92

Kõngäs Maranda E 1971 The logic of riddles. In: Kõngäs Maranda E, Maranda P (eds.) *Structural Analysis of Oral Tradition*. University of Pennsylvania Press, Philadelphia, PA

McDowell J H 1979 *Children's Riddling*. Indiana University Press, Bloomington, IN

Pepicello W J, Green T 1984 *The Language of Riddles: New Perspectives*. Ohio State University Press, Columbus, OH

Williams T 1963 The form and function of Tambunan Dusun riddles. *Journal of American Folklore* **76**: 95–110

Yankah K 1983 The poetics of the Akan riddle. In: Anyidoho K, Avorgbedor D, Domowitz S, Giray-Saul E (eds.) *Cross Rhythms: Papers in African Folklore*. Trickster Press, Folklore Institute, Bloomington, IN

J. McDowell

Riff

SEE Berber Languages

Ritual

There is no generally agreed definition or concept of 'ritual.' In this article, data from Vedic ritual will be used to characterize a concept of ritual in terms that display similarities and dissimilarities between ritual and language and between the science of ritual and linguistics.

Both ritual and language are rule-governed activities that may be characterized in terms of the rules that govern their use and that are made explicit in their description and analysis. In ritual, these rules have rarely been studied, but in language, they fall within several domains that provide the methodology adopted here in order to find out where ritual belongs.

If a distinction is made between phonology, syntax, semantics, and pragmatics, it should be observed first that there is no clearly demarcated domain in ritual that corresponds to phonology, not because there could not be such a domain but because it is not clearly demarcated since ritual activities (which include, for example, starting a fire, killing an animal, crossing a bridge, producing sound, meditating silently, sprinkling, bathing, lifting one or both hands) range over almost the entire realm of human activities and have not, so far, been the subject of a generally accepted scientific treatment.

Adopting a logical terminology, the three remaining linguistic domains are defined roughly as follows: syntax is concerned with the relations between linguistic expressions, semantics with the relations between those expressions and meanings, and pragmatics with the relations between expressions, meanings, and users or contexts of use. If in these definitions 'linguistic expressions' are replaced by 'ritual activities' then it will be possible to explore to what extent there are corresponding ritual domains, which may be referred to provisionally as 'ritual syntax,' 'ritual semantics,' and 'ritual pragmatics.'

1. Ritual Syntax

Vedic rituals constitute a hierarchy of many levels in which, for example, D (*darśapūrṇamāsa*, 'full and new moon ceremonies') occupies a lower rank than P (*paśubandha*, 'animal sacrifice'). Thus, D may be embedded in P, but P cannot be embedded in D. The embedding mechanisms involve rules that are recursive, a feature discovered by the ancient Indian grammarians who also noted that the recursiveness of ritual is similar to the recursiveness of grammar.

Rituals consist of sequences of smaller units, namely 'rites.' If rituals are referred to by capital letters and rites by small letters, rituals may be defined by phrase structure rules where sequential order is expressed by concatenation, e.g.:

$$D \rightarrow d_1 \cdots d_m$$

If D is embedded in P, the rites of D will occur, generally in the same sequence, between the rites of P, e.g., as follows:

$$p_1 \cdots p_j d_1 \cdots d_m p_{j+1} \cdots p_n,$$

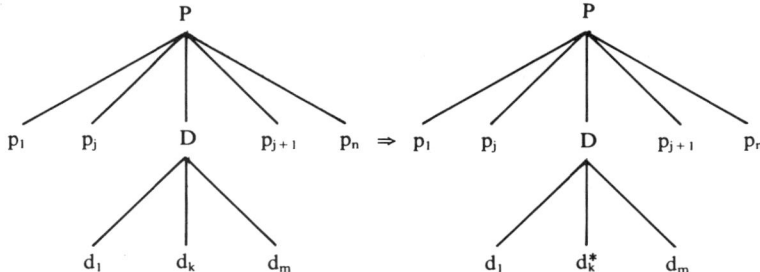

Figure 1.

where $1 \leqslant j < n$. In general, in such an embedding, at least one of the rites that are embedded will be modified. For example, D involves a recitation of 15 *samidheni* ('kindling') verses, but when D is embedded in P, 17 such verses are recited. Assuming that the rite with 15 verses is d_k ($1 \leqslant k \leqslant m$) and the rite with 17 verses is d_k^*, a rule can be postulated that operates within the described context, that is, a transformational rule between the trees shown in Fig. 1. In whatever way these regularities are described— here they are described by transformations, Chomsky has since used 'binding theory,' and others have used other mechanisms—it is clear that these structures in ritual syntax and in the syntax of natural languages are the same.

The same cannot be said for self-embedding structures that are generated by rules of the type:

A → BAB

which lead by repeated application to structures such as:

$\cdots$ BBBBBABBBBB $\cdots$

that are common in ritual but rare to nonexistent in language. For example, each layer of the brick altar of the Agnicayana ritual is laid down after an Upasad rite is performed, and another Upasad rite is performed immediately afterwards; the initial Upasad is preceded by the Pravargya rite, and the final Upasad is followed by another performance of the Pravargya. Similarly, at the beginning and end of each consecration of such a layer, the Adhvaryu recites the same mantras. Again, the well-known Aśvamedha horse sacrifice is preceded and followed by the Odana rite of preparing a rice stew. These structures exhibit self-embedding because when such sequences consist of more than one step they occur in the opposite order at the beginning and at the end.

From these examples of transformational rules (with their implied phrase structure rules) and self-embedding rules it may be concluded that ritual syntax is in some respects similar and in others dissimilar to the syntax of language.

2. Ritual Semantics

Neither rituals nor rites refer to meanings in the manner in which linguistic expressions refer to meanings or in any other systematic manner. Philosophers or theologians (rather than ritualists) frequently provide rituals with interpretations which may be regarded as 'meanings' although many of them are obvious rationalizations. In India and in Asia generally, these interpretations change constantly whereas the rituals remain the same. Thus fire rites which

originally were part of the Vedic ritual have been incorporated in Hindu and Buddhist rituals and provided with interpretations that have nothing to do with whatever interpretations, if any, were assigned to them originally. Moreover, there is no function that assigns meanings to rituals on the basis of the alleged meanings of their constituent rites.

In general, Indologists (e.g., Louis Renou) have observed that there are no close connections between mythology and ritual in Vedic religion, Hinduism or Tantrism, and anthropologists (e.g., A van Gennep) have noted that such rites as sprinkling may indicate fecundity, repulsion, or something else. Since semantic rules, which are an essential part of language, do not occur in ritual, ritual has no semantics and should not be referred to, even in metaphorical terms, as a language or be conceived of in linguistic terms.

3. Ritual Pragmatics

Austin (1962: 14–15) formulated conditions for the felicity of performatives which may be regarded as falling within pragmatics. The use of rites, and especially of mantras, is governed by similar conditions: they can only be used by the appropriate person and at the appropriate time and place; they have to be executed correctly; and mantras have to be recited with the correct degree of loudness, at the correct pitch, and at the correct pace. Most of these conditions are more extensive and more stringent than anything that applies to the normal use of a natural language such as English or Sanskrit.

4. Mantras

Rites are often accompanied by mantras, that is, ritual chants or recitations. According to the Indian science of ritual, there is a one-to-one correspondence between rites and mantras (e.g., *ekamantrāṇi karmāṇi* 'each act is accompanied by one mantra': *Āpastamba Śrauta Sūtra* 24.1.38). The properties of ritual syntax are therefore also properties of the syntax of mantras which are similarly, like the rites to which they are attached, devoid of meaning. This was recognized by the ancient Indian ritualist Kautsa: *anarthakā mantrāḥ* 'mantras are without meaning.'

Mantras possess other syntactic properties that are not found in language. For example, they abound in three-, four-, or fivefold repetitions that may be recursively combined, as, for example, in:

$A^3(BC^5)^3A^3$

where X^3 means: X X X. Such structures are closer, in form and function, to musical structures or configurations found in bird songs than to anything found in the syntax of natural languages.

When linguistic utterances containing mantras are translated from one language into another, the mantras are not translated but quoted: they do not change although they may be adapted (like geographical names) to the phonology of the receiving language. Like rituals and individual rites, mantras remain invariant over long stretches of time and space, even when crossing linguistic, social, geographical, cultural, or religious boundaries—traveling, for example, from India to East and Southeast Asia as far as Japan or Bali. Rites and mantras are accordingly attributed to an *Urzeit*:

yajñena yajñam ayajanta devās
tāni dharmāṇi prathamāny āsan

'with ritual the gods performed ritual;
these were the first ordinances' *(Ṛgveda 1.164.50)*

and mantras assigned to a primordial realm beyond language:

yato vāco nivartante
aprāpya manasā saha

'from which words return,
beyond the reach of mind' *(Taittirīya Upaniṣad 8.4.1)*

Mantras are always archaic. The most celebrated Indian mantra, *om*, typifies what Jakobson called 'the most natural order of sound production,' an opening of the mouth followed by its closure.

Since ritualization and mantra-like sound production are common among animal species, these and other facts combine to suggest that, in the course of evolution, language developed from ritual through the intermediary of mantras. Language originated when meanings were attached to mantras, which must have happened by chance, perhaps playfully. It was selected because of its almost miraculous power to communicate and deal with the world. That the syntax of natural languages came from ritual before there was any semantics explains, amongst other things, why syntax is, from the semantic point of view, so illogical, inefficient, and roundabout. This independence from semantics accounts likewise for the need to go beyond 'natural' language and construct the rational but artificial languages of mathematics, logic, computers, and whatever else the future may have in store.

Ritual and mantras are found among many animals but religion, like language, is confined to humans. That ritual and mantras came to be connected with religion is due to the latter's intrinsic nature. For religion is not merely archaic, it is also characterized by an urge to find meaning which is an extrapolation from the systematic reference to meanings that characterizes language. After language had begun to attach meanings to mantras and then to words, sentences and other linguistic utterances that linguists and philosophers are still in the process of dissecting, religion went on to make sense of trees, animals, and mountains, then ritual, the universe, and man himself. More truly human than the attribution of life to everything that is referred to as 'animism,' this impulse to make sense must also have come into being by chance. It was selected because it was so reassuring, probably at a point in time not very long after the origin of language, on all counts the most bewildering event in the development of the human animal.

See also: Mantra; Hinduism; Australian Aboriginal Religions; American Indian Religions, North; Origin and Evolution of Language; Origins of Language.

Bibliography

Austin J L 1962 *How to do Things with Words*. Oxford University Press, Oxford
Gennep A van 1911 De la méthode à suivre dans l'étude des rites et des mythes. *Revue de l'Université de Bruxelles*, pp. 502–23
Renou L 1953 *Religions of Ancient India*. Athlone Press, London
Staal F 1985 Mantras and bird songs. *Journal of the American Oriental Society* **105**: 549–58
Staal F 1989 *Rules without Meaning: Ritual, Mantras and the Human Sciences*. Peter Lang, New York

F. Staal

Ritwan

SEE Algonquian

Robins, Robert Henry (1921–   )

R. H. Robins was born on July 1, 1921 in Broadstairs, Kent, and was educated at Tonbridge School and New College, Oxford. After an interruption of several years due to World War II he graduated in 1948 with first class honours in Literae Humaniores. In the same year he was appointed to a lectureship in Linguistics at the School of Oriental and African Studies, University of London, joining the Department of Phonetics and Linguistics which was headed by J. R. Firth (see *Firth and the London School*). In 1966 he was appointed Professor of General Linguistics, and in 1986 was elected a Fellow of the British Academy. On his retirement, the University conferred on him the title of Emeritus Professor. His wife Sheila took an active interest in his work throughout her life and accompanied him abroad on many occasions, be it to conferences or visiting appointments (at the Universities of Hawaii, Washington (Seattle), Minnesota, Salzburg and South Florida). Of the many offices he held and is now holding, special mention should be made of his presidency of the Henry Sweet Society for the History of Linguistics of which he is a founder member, of his secretaryship and presidency of the Philological Society (1961–88, 1988–92), and his active involvement with the International Committee of Linguists, first as the British representative and subsequently as its president.

Robins is probably most widely known as the author of a textbook on general linguistics (1964), now in its fourth edition (1989), which has been translated into several European languages as well as into Malay and Japanese. The scope of that work reflects his broad conception of the subject. It covers principles and concepts of European linguistics, especially the work of Trubetzkoy and Saussure (see *Trubetzkoy, Nikolai Sergeyevic*; *Saussure, Ferdinand (-Mongin) de*), and of American structuralism and generative grammar (see *American Structuralism*; *Generative Grammar*). For, although trained in Firthian methods and known as the chief interpreter of Firth's not always easily accessible ideas ('What did Professor Firth mean when he said . . . ?'), Robins conducted teaching and research in

Firthian theory (contextual semantics and prosodic phonology) but not to the exclusion of competing models. Nor has he ever bowed to fashion. At a time when it was widely held in American structuralist circles that languages can differ in unpredictable and unlimited ways, he published a paper on noun and verb as universal grammatical classes, and when morpheme-based models of grammatical analysis were all the rage, whether in an item-and-arrangement or an item-and-process version, he wrote a paper 'In defence of WP,' pointing out that the word-and-paradigm model of traditional European grammar has certain distinct advantages where highly fusional languages are concerned. These and other papers are conveniently accessible in Robins (1970) while a bibliography up to 1985 is to be found at the end of the Festschrift which marked his 65th birthday (Bynon and Palmer 1986).

The development of linguistic theory in the wider cultural setting of its time is a topic which has occupied Robins throughout his career. His first book-size publication was a work on ancient and medieval grammatical theory in Europe (1951) while his textbook (1967) spans the entire period from classical antiquity to the present and 'takes in' important non-European developments, especially the Sanskrit and Arab grammarians. Robins (1973) is a more detailed review of nineteenth- and twentieth-century theory, above all with regard to historical and typological comparison. Robin's latest publication, at the time of writing, is a work on the Byzantine grammarians.

Bibliography

Robins R H 1951 *Ancient and Mediaeval Grammatical Theory in Europe*. Bell, London
Robins R H 1958 *The Yurok Language: Grammar, Texts, Lexicon*. University of California Press, Berkeley, CA
Robins R H 1970 *Diversions of Bloomsbury: Selected Writings on Linguistics*. North-Holland, Amsterdam
Robins R H 1973 *Ideen- und Problemgeschichte der Sprachwissenschaft*. Athenaeum, Frankfurt am Main
Robins R H 1989 *General Linguistics: An Introductory Survey*, 4th edn. Longman, London
Robins R H 1990 *A Short History of Linguistics*, 3rd edn. Longman, London
Robins R H in press *The Byzantine Grammarians*. Mouton de Gruyter, Berlin
Bynon T, Palmer F R (eds.) 1986 *Studies in the History of Western Linguistics: In Honour of R. H. Robins*. Cambridge University Press, Cambridge

T. Bynon

Rock Music

Since the 1950s, rock music has become an essential part of twentieth-century (sub)culture. As a symbol of protest for many thousands of youngsters against the values of their elders, as an expression of the young people's existence, but also as a largely commercialized commodity of the music industry, this music has succeeded in creating its own language within the multimedia world. The language of rock music—that is, the language used in song texts and when speaking about and within the music 'scene'—is closely linked to the diverse forms of rock music.

1. The Communicative Situation

Rock music as a language of sounds is embedded in behavioral language (e.g., dancing movements, facial expressions), in the language of social staging (e.g., clothes, accessories, hair cut, show elements), in pictorial language (e.g., posters, record covers, films, videos), and in verbal language. The latter is mainly used by the makers of rock (text writers and interpreters), but also by professional intermediaries acting as the 'multipliers' of rock language (journalists, program designers, moderators) and by the consumers of rock music—predominantly young people. Depending on the text type (e.g., interview, show, letters from the readers), makers, intermediaries, and consumers of rock music can either assume the role of the text originator or that of the text recipient, in accordance with the respective position of the partners involved—in a primarily one-way communication situation. The speaker's utterances reach the audience either directly (in concerts and festivals) or indirectly by means of sound carriers such as records, cassette tapes, CD's, sound films, or music videos. The mass media press, radio, television, as well as music publishing houses and discos, ensure an unrestricted dissemination of rock music language. The topics treated in rock music are closely connected with the emotional and social needs of the makers and consumers of rock music: song texts mainly verbalize protest and feelings; in the other media, the music and its interpretation, styles, playing techniques, and instruments, along with fans, stars, and rock music management predominate.

2. Specific Forms of Utterances

Except in song texts, the trademark of rock music language is a vocabulary characterized by terminological and group-specific elements. Terminology is used when treating essential topics such as instruments (e.g., *lead guitar*), styles (e.g., *heavy metal, thrash*), musicians (e.g., *keyboardist, hip-hop group*), and show business (e.g., *gig*). The language of rock music—like rock music itself—is a product of acculturation: its terminology derives from serious music (e.g., *staccato*), from jazz (e.g., *jam session*), from communication engineering and electronics (e.g., *phase-shifter*), as well as from the literary–philosophical beat and hip movements (e.g., *groove*) or from the drug-using subculture (e.g., *dope-men*). The group-specific aspect appears in the use of hyperboles and trendy words taken from the youth language (e.g., *her voice had sounded eerily perfect; a cool title*), from colloquial style and slang (e.g., *my fave band; to kick her ass; muthafuckin' cookies*), from metaphors and comparisons (e.g., *rock god; he whirled like a dervish; we were rough as a badger's ass for so many years*), but also from group-specific word formations that aim at economy in expression (e.g., *Hendrix-inflected guitar work; teenage angst monster; lip-sync number; antitechno band*).

Frequently, almost identical themes have to be verbalized so that variation in expression is of great importance. Such variations can usually be found in the large number of synonyms (e.g., *funk groups = funk acts = funksters*).

As rock music shows a large range of styles and trends which exist only for a short time, there is a strong need to invent new terms. The language of rock music is a good example of a rapidly changing language: a whole language history to be observed within one single generation.

Naturally, this phenomenon is primarily limited to the English-speaking countries, where the most important method of enlarging the vocabulary is by forming new group-specific expressions or coining new terminology (e.g., rhythmic American poetry, also known as *rap: rap music; rapper; rap entertainer; rap-mania; rap language; rap clothes; rap movie; rap comedy show; rap commercials*). Outside English-speaking countries, increasing the vocabulary generally means taking over English–American words and/or blending them with elements of the vernacular.

3. Conditions and Aims of Communication

There are many different conceptions of music, styles, cultural influences, and economic conditions that determine rock music. So rock music is an aesthetic, a socio-psychological, as well as an economic phenomenon. The same applies to the language of rock music. Its aesthetic function is fulfilled by the lyrics, but also by wordplay and figurative expressions, all of which make the language elastic, expressive, and dynamic. The socio-psychological function lies mainly in the use of terminology and youth language. The 'correct' use of terminology increases the speaker's prestige and is useful for his orientation and self-characterization. The language of young people is highly entertaining, if used with detached irony. But it also helps to define, intensify, and stabilize groups. It tends to strengthen the feeling of belonging to a peer group and is a means of protest against the culture and the way of life of grown-ups. Together with the music, it plays an important part in the socialization of young people. Thus, the language of rock music, by its use of overappraising and exaggerating terms, serves to promote star cult, allowing young people to satisfy their needs for identification. Expressions taken from colloquial language or slang also exhibit a kind of intimacy between stars, professional intermediaries, and fans; at the same time, they help to distinguish the 'rock family' from the world and norms of adults.

As is the case with rock music itself, the language of rock music is a highly important economic factor. Thus, the use of trendy words proves that their user is up-to-date; many idioms serve purely as signals: their only communicative aim is to highlight the users' unique features and to attract the attention that is necessary for the texts and their originators to survive in the rough competition of big rock business.

Bibliography

Frith S 1988 *Music for Pleasure: Essays in the Sociology of Pop.* Polity, Cambridge

Hibbert T 1983 *Rockspeak! The Dictionary of Rock Terms.* Omnibus, London

Hudson K 1983 *The Language of the Teenage Revolution.* Macmillan, London

Ortner L 1982 *Wortschatz der Pop-/Rockmusik: Das Vokabular der Beiträge über Pop/Rockmusik in deutschen Musikzeitschriften*, Sprache der Gegenwart 53. De Gruyter, Berlin

L. Ortner

Rohlfs, Gerhard (1892–1986)

Gerhard Rohlfs was born on July 14, 1892 in Berlin where he graduated in 1920. He held chairs at the Universities of Tübingen (1926–38) and Munich (1938–57). In 1922, his prize-winning essay, *Das romanische habeo-Futurum und Konditionalis*, attracted considerable attention. He plunged into controversy (from which he was never to be far removed) with his opposition to the 'idealist' school of linguistics as represented by Karl Vossler (see *Vossler, Karl*) and Eugen Lerch. His involvement in the *Sprach- und Sachatlas Italiens und der Südschweiz* (1928–40; see also *Jaberg, Karl; Jud, Jakob*) led to major publications both on the languages and linguistic history of the area (southern Italy, including Sicily) for which he had had special responsibility in connection with the atlas and on the Italian language in general. He interested himself in the origins of the Greek-speaking communities in the south of Italy, arguing on linguistic grounds (and against the prevailing view that they dated from the Byzantine period) that they constitute remnants of Magna Graecia (i.e., of the Greek cities founded in the area from the eighth to the fifth centuries BC). His historical grammar of the Italian language and its dialects is authoritative. In the wider field of Romance linguistics, he published a two-volume manual (1950–52; mainly on Gallo–Romance and Italo–Romance, and with a strong bibliographical orientation), complemented by a similar volume (1957) on Hispanic linguistics, and a study (1954) of the lexical differentiation of the Romance languages. He also worked on onomastics (with especial reference to Italy), the history of the French language, Gascon, Romansch, and Romanian, and produced a Vulgar Latin reader. He took a lifelong interest in the relations (which, in his view, had in certain cases been exaggerated by some scholars) between Latin or the Romance languages on the one hand and non-Romance languages (including Oscan, Basque, Germanic, Serbo-Croat) on the other; in particular, he argued repeatedly against the view that a feature of contemporary Tuscan pronunciation, the *gorgia toscana*, is to be attributed to the persistence of an Etruscan speech-habit. He died on September 12, 1986 in Tübingen.

Bibliography

Christmann H H 1987 Gerhard Rohlfs (1892–1986). *Zeitschrift für romanische Philologie* **103**: 698–712

Rohlfs G 1949–54 *Historische Grammatik der italienischen Sprache und ihrer Mundarten*, 3 vols. Francke, Bern

Rohlfs G 1950–52 *Romanische Philologie. Vol. I: Allgemeine Romanistik, Französische und provenzalische Philologie.* Winter, Heidelberg

Rohlfs G 1954 *Die lexikalische Differenzierung der romanischen Sprachen.* Bayerische Akademie der Wissenschaften, Munich

Rohlfs G 1957 *Manual de filología hispánica: Guía bibliográfica crítica y metódica.* Instituto Caro y Cuervo, Bogotá

G. Price

Role and Reference Grammar

Role and reference grammar (RRG) is the name given to a framework of grammatical description developed by W. Foley and R. Van Valin, with contributions from colleagues, from the mid-1970s onwards. RRG differs markedly from all other models of grammar in that its theoretical constructs have been primarily developed inductively from detailed investigations of non-European 'exotic' languages.

Consequently, insightful description has been favored in this approach over rigorous formalization, and perhaps RRG is best interpreted as a framework for grammatical description rather than an explicit model of grammar, at least in terms of the way the latter is widely conceived. RRG does share traits with other models in that it is lexically based (as are lexical functional grammar and head-driven phrase structure grammar; see *Head-driven Phrase Structure Grammar*) and monostratal (as are the previous two mentioned and generalized phrase structure grammar; see *Generalized Phrase Structure Grammar*), but contrasts with these in being functionally oriented. RRG assumes that the use of language in human communication and social interaction is fundamental to understanding much of its structure (this assumption it shares with systemic functional grammar; see *Systemic Theory*).

1. Basic Assumptions of RRG

RRG can be characterized as starting from a functional approach to grammatical description, that is, grammatical units and constructions are analyzed, first, in terms of their functional role in a linguistic system, and only second, in terms of their 'formal' (structural) properties. 'Function' in this context refers to communicative function, the use of language in human verbal interaction to transmit information. The forms of language are studied in the light of the functions they serve. Indeed, a central research strategy of RRG is to investigate the relationship between form and function in language, how the same form can have several functions and how different functions may be encoded in the same form. This research strategy contrasts strongly with formal models of grammar, which describe only language structure and this in formal, structural terms and have scant regard for linguistic functions. Formal approaches to grammar view language predominantly as a cognitive or psychological system, an internal mental representation of linguistic forms and rules. Formal theories understand a model of grammar to be a formal specification of the constraints on those aspects of human intelligence manifested in language (Chomsky's 'language competence') and the construction of such as part of the development of a general theory of mind in cognitive science. RRG, on the other hand, regards the social basis of a linguistic system, in its use as the device for verbal interaction between participants, as fundamental. Its concern is to research how humans in social formations use language to create and sustain meanings. A grammar in RRG must provide an explicit account of the ways in which language is linked to knowledge of and interaction with the world: the linguistic resources for the representation of events and actions upon the world to realize pragmatic goals.

The linguistic resources for the representation of events is classically semantics and those for goal-oriented actions on the world is pragmatics. Thus, the study of grammar in RRG is especially the study of how semantic and pragmatic factors constrain the syntactic patterns of a language. Hence syntax is not autonomous, in the sense claimed by formal models. For RRG the syntactic structure is viewed as the outcome of the interplay between the speaker's interaction to communicate propositionally formulable information (semantics), and the constraints imposed by the social and linguistic context in which it occurs (pragmatics). Syntax is not entirely reducible to semantics and pragmatics; all languages have some arbitrary formal patterns, largely the result of diachronic drift, such as the prenominal adjective position of English. However, the syntactic options in a language, for example, active and passive, are the result of the interaction of these factors, and this is what is highlighted in grammatical work in RRG. Language is a system for making meanings: when speakers choose one syntactic option over another, they are creating meaning and this is what RRG wants to uncover.

RRG has two basic goals: (a) the development of an explanatory framework for universal grammar (UG), and (b) the development of a framework of grammatical analysis that relates directly to the study of language in the sociocultural world. RRG is concerned largely with substantive universals, generalizations about the possible formal and functional elements of language. It seeks to answer why certain languages have particular constructions, while others do not. Formal models typically are more interested in formal universals, generalizations about the abstract formal properties of grammar, usually constraints on the application of rules. As a descriptive strategy, the models of UG in formal approaches are employed to impose very strong conditions on the terms in which the grammar of any individual language may be couched. RRG attempts to be a more flexible framework, falling somewhere between the two extremes of describing each language in its own terms, which makes crosslinguistic comparison difficult, and describing each language in universal terms which commonly results in obscuring the actual language in favor of a picture demanded by the theory.

2. Basic Theoretical Constructs

RRG is a completely nonderivational framework. Instead of deriving related sentences from an abstract underlying form, it pairs meaning representations to various structural realizations, by uncovering the various contextual conditions which determine these realizations. It is, thus, one of a class of 'unification grammars' (Schieber 1986) developed during the late 1980s and early 1990s. RRG, indeed, derives its name from an early impulse toward its formulation by two important papers in the mid-1970s by Paul Schachter (Schachter 1976, 1977) in which he demonstrates how the choice among various clause structures in Tagalog is determined by an interaction of semantic (role) factors and contextual/pragmatic (reference) factors. This insight was taken as basic and served as a foundation for much of the later RRG theorizing on clause structure.

2.1 Clausal Grammar

RRG analyzes clause structure in all languages as being comprised of two layers: a core layer which includes the verb and its associated 'core' (i.e., 'subcategorized') arguments, and a peripheral layer, which includes oblique nominals, temporal, and locational setting constituents or other adverbial-like modifiers. In addition, it visualizes clause-level grammar as being comprised of two separate, major systems; one specifying the semantic relationships between the constituents, especially between the verb and its core arguments, and the other concerned with the discourse, pragmatic status of these constituents. RRG differs significantly in its analysis of both of these systems from what is offered in other theories.

Basic to the network of semantic relationships in the clause is a system of verb classification developed in RRG from earlier work by Dowty (1979), who in turn modified Vendler (1967). RRG contrasts with earlier and present day theories in that it does not take 'semantic roles' of NPs, that is, the 'core roles' of Fillmore (1968) or the θ-roles of government and binding theory, as primitive concepts. Rather, the semantic primitives are a set of atomic predicates, through which the semantic properties of different verb classes are represented; the semantic roles are interpreted automatically from these representations. Vendler (1967) and Dowty (1979) distinguish four large classes of verbs: activities (*run, eat*), accomplishments (*smash, eat a lolly*), achievements (*spot, die*), and states (*know, be good*). Dowty (1979) further adds a distinction between predicates controlled by a willful deliberate agent (*look at*), and those not (*see*). Each of the verb classes is assigned a logical structure. The logical structure of a verb consists of a basic atomic 'stative' or 'activity' predicate, plus one of a set of operator atomic predicates like BECOME (a change in state, location, etc.), DO (performed willfully by an agent), or CAUSE (one event is a prior condition for another). Stative predicates are primitive and allow no further decomposition; 'be good' has the logical structure *good'(x)* and 'know,' *know'(x, y)*. Achievement predicates consist of an atomic stative predicate plus BECOME: 'die' is *BECOME (dead'(x))*, while 'realize' is *BECOME (known'(x, y))*. Uncontrolled activity predicates are also primitive and not decomposable: 'fall' is *fall'(x)* and 'smell' is *smell'(x, y)*; but controlled activity predicates consist of an activity predicate plus DO: 'smile' is *DO (x,[smile'(x)])*, while 'eat' is *DO(x,[eat'(x,y)])*. Accomplishment predicates are the most complex; note that *Egbert smashed the vase* expresses that Egbert does some action which brings it about that the vase gets smashed. Accomplishment predicates express a causative relation (the atomic predicate CAUSE) between a usually unspecified activity (represented in the logical structure by *do'*) and a resulting change in state *BECOME (predicate'(x))*. So, the logical structure for 'smash' would be *[DO (x, do'(x))] CAUSE [BECOME (smashed'(y))]*, read as x deliberately does an action (DO) such that x causes y to become smashed.

RRG adopts this basic schema from Dowty (1979), but extends it with further atomic predicates and uses the logical structures to define semantic roles. For example, it adds the primitives *be-at'(x, y)* for locational verbs like *stand on* and *have'(x, x)* for possession. The semantic role of agent is defined as x in the configuration DO (x), that is, deliberate performer of an action, and PATIENT as y in *state'(y)*, an entity in a state. The full inventory of logical structure primitives and definitions of semantic roles is as follows:

1	State predicates			(1)
	A Locational	be-at'(x, y)	x = theme	
			y = location	
	B Nonlocational			
	1 state	predicate'(x)	x = patient	
	2 perception	see'(x, y)	x = location	
			y = theme	
	3 cognition	know'(x, y)	x = location	
			y = theme	
	4 possession	have'(x, y)	x = location	
			y = theme	

2	Activity predicates			(2)
	A Controllable			
	1 uncontrolled	predicate'(x)	x = effector	
	2 controlled	DO (x, [predicate'(x)])	x = agent	
	B Motional	go'(x)	x = theme	

Additional roles introduced above: 'theme,' the entity whose location is at issue; 'effector,' the nonvolitional performer of the action; and 'location,' the place/entity at which the event occurs. It must be repeated that all these semantic roles are not primitives in RRG, they are simply read off the logical structure representations.

What are primitive in RRG are two fundamental 'macro roles'—'actor' and 'undergoer.' This is a basic dichotomy across all verb classes between an argument which expresses the participant which performs, effects, instigates, or controls the situation denoted by the predicate (the actor), and the argument which expresses the participant which does not perform, instigate, or control any event, but rather is affected by it (the undergoer). The opposition between these two is a fundamental organizing principle for the structure of the clause. The notion of actor is not equivalent to agent, nor is undergoer equivalent to patient (although actor and undergoer do bear more than a small resemblance to the notions of 'logical subject' and 'logical object' in other approaches). The choice of actor and undergoer reflects the perspective on the event (Fillmore 1977). Note the effect of the different actor choices in *Fred rented the flat to Egbert*, and *Egbert rented the flat from Fred*; these denote the same commercial transaction, but the perspective is different; whichever participant is chosen as actor is ascribed the primary responsibility for the event. Similar alternations occur with undergoer choice: *Egbert drained the water from the pool*, and *Egbert drained the pool of water*. Again the same event is denoted by both sentences, but the choice of undergoer reflects the speaker's perspective as to which entity is primarily affected (there is also a secondary consideration of which nominal is focused; see *Information Structure*).

Actor and undergoer each instantiate a number of semantic roles, as defined by the logical structures. With a logical structure that indicates a multiple of semantic roles, the interpretation of one as actor and another as undergoer is managed by a 'hierarchy of accessibility':

Actor:	agent		(3)
	effector		
	location		
	theme		
Undergoer:	patient		

The preferred choice for actor is agent, then effector, and then location, while for undergoer, it is patient, then theme, and then location. Thus, if present, the agent must be actor and the patient, undergoer: if these are lacking, the choices will then proceed down and up the hierarchy respectively. To illustrate the workings of this system consider the following logical structure:

[DO(Egbert, [do'(Egbert)])] CAUSE [do'(poker)] CAUSE [BECOME (broken' vase)] (4)

Egbert is an agent, *poker*, an effector, and *vase*, a patient. Both *Egbert* and *poker* are possible actors, but because agent outranks effector on the hierarchy, *Egbert* must be actor; *poker*, being outranked, is realized as a prepositional phrase with *with* (see discussion in Foley and Van Valin 1984: 53–63, 81–95). *Vase*, a patient, is necessarily the undergoer, so the sentence corresponding to this logical structure must be *Egbert broke the vase with the poker*.

Note that the above discussion of clause structure was phrased in semantic terms, employing logical structure representations of the meaning of verbs and the semantically based macro roles of actor and undergoer, rather than syntactic notions like the grammatical relations subject and object; these are rejected as language universals and hence necessary theoretical primitives by RRG on the grounds that there are no necessary and sufficient conditions for their definitions and that many languages provide no evidence for their existence. Indeed, some languages provide quite strong arguments against the postulation of these as universal, necessary, theoretical constructs. In RRG, actor and undergoer fill the role of logical (deep) subject and object in other theories, while (surface) subject largely corresponds to the notion of 'pivot.' Pivot is the basic theoretical construct of the system of clause-level grammar dealing with the discourse and pragmatic status of constituents. The pivot of a clause is the nominal within it which is most crucially involved; it is the nominal around which the construction is built. In English, the pivot of a clause is its subject; the actor in an active clause and the undergoer in a passive clause. Many complex constructions in English involving clause combinations revolve around the notion of subjects. For example:

Ellipsis of subject in complements (5)
(a) Fred wants to see Marsha
(b) *Fred wants Marsha to see
(c) Fred wants to be seen by Marsha

Subject of complement as object of matrix verb (6)
(a) John expects that Paul will catch the wombat
(b) John expects Paul to catch the wombat
(c) *John expects the wombat Paul to catch
(d) John expects the wombat to be caught by Paul

Ellipsis of subject in coordinated clauses (7)
(a) Oscar went to the store and spoke to Bill
(b) *Oscar went to the store and Bill spoke to
(c) Oscar went to the store and was spoken to by Bill

All three constructions (5–7) employ the notion of subjects. When the subject is actor, the usual active clause is found. English is a language in which the unmarked choice of pivot is actor. When the undergoer is to be pivot, a passive construction must be used; this backgrounds the actor to an oblique prepositional phrase. Note that the ungrammatical examples above are so, because the undergoer has been chosen as pivot, but the clause has not been rearranged as passive; when this is done, as in the final examples, the sentences are grammatical.

One of the great advantages of using the notion of pivot as opposed to subject is that it is not necessarily tied to the semantic notions with which subject is contaminated. English is a language in which the unmarked choice for pivot is the actor, with the marked choice, the undergoer, being licensed by the passive construction. There are other languages, some so-called 'ergative' languages, in which the unmarked choice for pivot is undergoer, and the marked, actor. ABsolutive is the case of the pivot in Dyirbal of Australia (Dixon 1979)

				(8)
Undergoer = Pivot			Actor	
balan	dyugumbil	bangul	yaṛangu buṛa-n	
FEM ABS	woman ABS	MASC ERG	man ERG see-PT	

'the man saw the woman'

If the actor is to be pivot, a construction called the 'antipassive' must be used which allows the actor to be in the ABSOLUTIVE case (hence, pivot), while the undergoer appears in the oblique DATIVE case. This is functionally parallel to the passive of English:

				(9)
Actor = Pivot				
bayi	yaṛa	bagun	dyugumbilgu buṛal-ŋa-ɲu	
MASC ABS	man ABS	FEM DAT	woman DAT see-ANTIPASSIVE-PT	

'the man saw the woman'

The pivot of Dyirbal functions completely analogously to that of English; nearly all complex constructions involving the combinations of clauses revolve around it. But such heavy dependence on the notion of pivot is not necessary. Some languages, for example, Mayan languages, may have more than one pivot type, using, say, actor as the pivot for some constructions, and the undergoer for others. And some languages, Archi or Acehnese, may lack pivots altogether, so that their complex syntax revolves around strictly semantic notions like the macro roles of actor and undergoer. RRG simply makes this concept available as a theoretical construct for the grammar of any language; it does not require that all languages make use of it. In this way RRG has an advantage over approaches which take grammatical relations like subject and object as primitives, requiring them to be present in the grammars of all languages. The crosslinguistic evidence suggests that they are not.

2.2 Interclausal Grammar

While the analysis of the systems of clause level grammar in RRG is unique, it is in the area of interclausal grammar that RRG is most innovative. The RRG approach here is radically different from anything attempted elsewhere. RRG does not begin from unquestioned pretheoretical constructs like clause and sentence, but sees these as crosslinguistically highly problematic. Hence, it chooses to atomize these into simpler, more primitive concepts, in terms of which clause and sentences can be defined.

Clauses are composed in RRG of a core and a periphery. The core in turn is made up of the nucleus (i.e., the verb) and its associated core (i.e., subcategorized) arguments, particularly the actor and undergoer. The periphery contains the arguments expressing the spatiotemporal setting of the event, as well as secondary participants in the event, e.g., beneficiaries (these all are commonly termed oblique nominals). Clause structure can then be represented in these terms thus:

$$P^{[(ADV)(NP)(NP)]}P \quad C^{[NP...(NP)]}N\frac{[Predicate]}{NUCLEUS}N C \qquad (10)$$

PERIPHERY	CORE

Note the nucleus is included within the core.

The theory of juncture in RRG is concerned with how these three subclausal units can be combined to form larger complex constructions. There are three types of juncture. A nuclear juncture is one with a complex nucleus, i.e., containing more than one predicate. This complex nucleus takes a single set of core arguments. Nuclear junctures are commonly found in serial verb constructions, such as this from Barai of Papua New Guinea:

$$C^{[fu\ fase}\ N^{[fi\ isoe]}N]C \qquad (11)$$
he letter sit write
'He sat writing a letter.'

Note the complex nucleus takes the two core arguments *fu* 'he' and *fase* 'letter' as a whole, although *fase* 'letter' is semantically subcategorized only by *isoe* 'write.' A core juncture is any one involving the nominal constituents of the core unit, either when a unit fills the slot of a nominal constituent in a core, as in complement constructions:

$$C^{[NP[Egbert]}NP\ N^{[believes]}N\ NP^{[that\ Hortense\ stole\ the\ aardvark]}NP]C \qquad (12)$$

Or when a core argument is shared between two units:

$$\overset{U}{\overparen{\qquad}}\qquad\overset{A}{\overparen{\qquad}}$$
$$C^{[Egbert}\ N^{[believes]}N\ Hor]C\quad C^{[tense}\ N^{[to\ have\ stolen]}N\ the\ aardvark]C \qquad (13)$$

Hortense is both the undergoer of *believe* (note the passive *Hortense is believed by Egbert to have stolen the aardvark*) and the actor of *have stolen*. A peripheral juncture is one not involving constituents of the core. This could be a case in which one unit functions as a peripheral nominal of another, so-called subordinate adverbial clauses:

While Egbert wasn't watching, Hortense stole the aardvark (14)

or in which two units with completely independent cores and peripheries are strung together:

Hortense stole the aardvark but Egbert was watching *Flipper* on cable TV (15)

In addition to the theory of 'juncture,' RRG also proposes a theory of 'nexus' needed to describe interclausal grammar. Nexus refers to the type of syntactic relationship between the units in the juncture. The nature of the syntactic relationship is a function of the behavior of the units in the juncture with respect to a set of 'operators.' Each of the three unit types, nuclear, core, and peripheral, has a set of corresponding operators. For the nucleus, the most common operator crosslinguistically is 'aspect.' Aspect then can have all the members of a complex nucleus within its scope. Note that the aspect marker in the following Barai construction modifies both verbs in the serial verb construction:

fu fase fi isoe va (16)
he letter sit write CONT
'He is sitting, writing a letter'

('Deontic') 'modality' is an operator on the core unit. It expresses a relationship between a core argument, the actor, and his/her intended accomplishment of an action. Note that the deontic modal *can* modifies both units in the following core juncture:

Egbert can sit playing his bassoon for hours (17)

(Egbert can both sit and play his bassoon for hours—scope over the whole core juncture.) Finally, the most common peripheral operators are 'tense' and 'illocutionary force.' Note the scope of the tag *didn't he?* in this conjoined construction:

John went to work, but forgot his briefcase, didn't he? (18)

This is a peripheral juncture; the linkage involves no core constituents between the two units. Yet the question indicated by the tag applies to both members of the conjunct.

The theory of operators plays a crucial role in the theory of nexus. Units in a juncture can be combined in any one of three different types of nexi. Subordinate nexus is where one unit is embedded as a (nominal) constituent of another unit. This nexus is not possible in nuclear junctures, for they lack nominal constituents, but core subordinate and peripheral subordinate constructions are common:

Core:	Hortense's stealing of the aardvark disturbed Egbert	(19)
Peripheral:	Because Hortense stole the aardvark, Egbert went to look for another one	(20)

Subordinate nexus is [+embedded], but there are two types of [−embedded] nexi: 'coordinate' and 'cosubordinate.' These are found in all three types of juncture. The difference between them involves the scope of operators. Units in a cosubordinate nexus in a particular juncture are necessarily under the scope of the operator(s) of that juncture type; they are thus [+dependent]. Units in a coordinate nexus are not; they are [−dependent]. Consider these examples of cosubordinate and coordinate nexus in nuclear and peripheral juncture in Barai and English respectively:

Nuclear cosubordinate: (21)
fu kai fu-one kume fie va
he friend he-POS call listen CONT
'He was calling and listening for his friend'

Nuclear coordinate: (22)
fy vazai ufu furi numu akoe
he grass cut PRF pile throw away
'He finished cutting, and then piled and threw away the grass'

In the cosubordinate example (21), the aspectual marker *va* CONT, a nuclear operator, has scope over both verbs, while in the coordinate example, the aspectual *furi* PRF only modifies the verb immediately before it:

Peripheral cosubordinate:	John went to work, but forgot his briefcase, didn't he?	(23)
Peripheral coordinate:	John went to work, but did he forget his briefcase?	(24)

Illocutionary force is a peripheral operator, so the questioning in the above examples illustrates this. In the cosubordinate example (23), the illocutionary force is realized in the question tag, which has scope over both conjuncts, while in the coordinate example (24), the question only applies to the second conjunct. The first is a statement.

Juncture and nexus combine to produce eight possible clause linkage types:

nuclear–cosubordinate (25)

nuclear–coordinate (26)

core–cosubordinate (27)

core–subordinate (28)

core–coordinate (29)

peripheral–cosubordinate (30)

peripheral–subordinate (31)

peripheral–coordinate (32)

These range from the most stripped down and fused linkage types at the top to the most elaboratedly coded and weakly linked ones at the bottom. In addition these are unmarked relationships for juncture and nexus; these are nuclear–cosubordinate, core–subordinate, and peripheral–coordinate. If a language has only one linkage type for a particular juncture, it will be these. There may be more, but at least these will be present. The range of linkage types across languages seems to vary widely, from three or four to the full eight. The relationship between particular linkage types and specific interclausal semantic relations is a further, important area of study within RRG (see Foley and Van Valin 1984: 264–304).

Bibliography

Dixon R M W 1979 Ergativity. *Lg* **55**: 59–138

Dowty D R 1979 *Word Meaning and Montague Grammar*. Reidel, Dordrecht

Fillmore C J 1968 The case for case. In: Bach E, Harms R T (eds.) *Universals in Linguistic Theory*. Holt, Reinhart and Winston, New York

Fillmore C J 1977 The case for case reopened. In: Cole P, Sadock J (eds.) *Syntax and Semantics. Vol. 8: Grammatical Relations*. Academic Press, New York

Foley W A, Van Valin R D 1984 *Functional Syntax and Universal Grammar*. Cambridge University Press, Cambridge

Schachter P 1976 The subject in Philippine languages: Topic, actor, actor–topic, or none of the above. In: Li C N (ed.) *Subject and Topic*. Academic Press, New York

Schachter P 1977 Reference-related and role-related properties of subjects. In: Cole P, Sadock J (eds.) *Syntax and Semantics. Vol. 8: Grammatical Relations*. Academic Press, New York

Schieber S M 1986 *An Introduction to Unification-Based Approaches to Grammar*. Center for the Study of Language and Information, Stanford University, Stanford, CA

Vendler Z 1967 *Linguistics in Philosophy*. Cornell University Press, Ithaca, NY

W. A. Foley

Role Theory

Role theory is often traced back to William Shakespeare's famous lines in *As You Like It*:

All the world's a stage,
And all the men and women merely players;
They have their exits and their entrances;
And one man in his time plays many parts . . .

Use of the term rests on two complementary commonsense observations. On the one hand, different people, when they find themselves in similar positions, behave and even think and feel similarly. On the other hand, the same individual, when placed in different positions, behaves, and often thinks and feels, differently. Furthermore, each role includes a cluster of expected behaviors—a *gestalt*—so that it is viewed as odd, inconsistent, or wrong when the physician sweeps up his own office, the parson frequents gambling parlors on his day off, or a child takes charge of family finances.

1. Definitions

A social role can be formally defined as: a comprehensive pattern for behavior and attitude; constituting a strategy for coping with a set of recurrent situations; socially identified, more or less clearly, as an entity; subject to being played recognizably by different individuals; supplying a major basis for identifying and placing people in society; and constituting a framework from which meanings are assigned to people's individual actions.

There are many useful ways to classify roles, but an initial distinction can be made among four types. First are 'basic' roles such as gender and age roles. These are roles that individuals carry with them and are expected to play in almost every situation. They are partial determinants of eligibility to perform many specific roles and of how those more specific roles are to be played. 'Position' or status roles are more specific and are attached to formally designated positions in groups, organizations, and larger formalized social units. They include family roles, occupational roles, political office roles, and roles associated with participation in particular activities such as golfer, surfer, and stamp collector. 'Functional group' roles are behavior patterns that emerge informally in the course of sustained interaction in any group. For example, someone may play the role of leader without any formal group decision; others may play devil's advocate, mediator, or counselor. 'Value' roles are the roles that develop about strongly positively or negatively valued activity, such as the role of hero, saint, group exemplar, murderer, or thief.

Basic roles are embedded in culture so that thinking and acting in terms of them seem automatic, though aspects of them are often written into law for reinforcement. Position roles in social institutions such as the family are culturally defined, often with legal enforcement, while position roles in organizations are defined through some decision process accepted as legitimate for that organization. By contrast, both functional group roles and value roles are quite informal and based on images conveyed in the culture. In the course of sustained group interaction, individuals may wittingly or unwittingly pattern their behavior so as to play a particular role with some consistency. Furthermore, people tend to categorize each other informally, and to interpret each other's behavior and behave toward each other according to the functional group roles. Once people are labeled in value terms, they are expected to continue to behave consistently with the label, so that heroes must live up to their prior achievements and criminals are constantly suspected of more evil doing.

Among the first social scientists to use the concept was the German sociologist, George Simmel. Brought to America, the concept was prominently embodied in four streams of scholarship. Robert E. Park and George Herbert Mead used it in laying the foundations for symbolic interactionism, a school of thought stressing human flexibility and creativeness, and using social interaction as the starting point for understanding larger social systems. Jacob Moreno used the concepts of role and role playing in his psychodrama and sociodrama as a way of making people aware of their own systems of interpersonal relationships, as an opening stage in psychotherapy. Kurt Lewin used the concept role to extend the insights of *Gestalt* psychology to a social psychology that stressed the structure and interrelationship of the social settings that link actors to one another. The most influential formulation of role was that of the anthropologist, Ralph Linton, who saw it as the key to refining the concept of culture so as to acknowledge that not everyone subjected to a common culture shared the same set of understandings.

2. Structural versus Interactional Role Theory

Linton's conception of roles as the sets of norms attached to particular statuses, culturally transmitted to the incumbents and interactants of given roles, accorded well with the behaviorist orientation of the early twentieth century. However, the overly mechanistic and consensual view of roles was challenged from two quarters. Robert Merton (1957) replaced impersonal cultural norms with 'expectations' conveyed by incumbents in the appropriate 'role set.' Like school superintendents who must accommodate their role enactment to the demands of teachers, students, parents, and school board members, role incumbents must deal with the divergent expectations produced by the diverse interests and points of view of a set of closely related other-roles. Because there are several alternate strategies for reconciling these diversities, there is room for considerable variability and innovation in role behavior.

Scholars in the symbolic interactionist tradition, incorporating the idea of role as a *gestalt*, posed a more fundamental challenge to structural versions of role theory. Interactionists argued that in most situations roles are vague and ill-defined, but individuals act as if they were clear-cut. The implicit assumption that roles are real and that people are enacting roles provides the framework within which individuals attempt to interpret each other's behavior and to shape roles for themselves. Interaction is a highly tentative process, crucially hinging on 'role taking'—imaginatively placing oneself in the position of other interactants so as to infer the roles they are playing and how they are playing them—and 'role making'—improvising a role for oneself that enables one to deal with others.

3. Role Differentiation

Whichever approach is taken, fundamental questions that arise are why and how various behaviors and attitudes become differentiated and grouped into roles, how actors are allocated to particular roles, and how roles are actually enacted. The principle that the division of labor becomes more complex, with tasks assigned to more and increasingly specialized roles, as the size of an organization or society increases and as the nature of the tasks becomes more complex, has been abundantly documented. Much less progress has been made, however, in understanding the principles that govern the way that tasks and attitudes are grouped and separated to form roles. Robert F. Bales demonstrated that artificial groups, meeting for several successive sessions, and assigned formal tasks to accomplish, often tended to develop two complementary leader roles (see *Interaction Process Analysis*). By concentrating on getting the job done, the task or instrumental leader created tensions in the group and had little time for dealing with members' interpersonal problems. If these tensions were not to disrupt group functioning, there had to be a social–emotional or expressive leader, who worked with members to relieve tensions and resolve interpersonal frictions. At one time this observation was proposed as the explanation for the nearly universal pattern of role differentiation in families, between husband as instrumental leader and wife as expressive leader. However, further research suggested that differentiation between instrumental and expressive leadership roles only evolved when group members lacked sufficient incentive for achieving group goals. On this and other grounds, use of Bales's observation to justify traditional family role patterns is discredited.

It has been proposed that the pattern of role differentiation is shaped by considerations of functionality, tenability, and representationality. Functionality refers to a division of labor that minimizes incompatibility of goals and means and conflicts of interest within roles, and accommodates to the differentiations of ability and disposition in the pools from which role incumbents are recruited. Representational differentiation separates and combines elements so as to accentuate value differences and similarities, and is often an overlay on functional differentiation. A role is tenable when there is a tolerable balance between the rewards and costs of playing the role to the incumbents. What role construction is tenable depends upon the power that incumbents bring to the role and what configuration of behavior and attitude harmonizes with incumbents' self conceptions.

4. Role Allocation and Learning

The obverse of role differentiation is role allocation, the 'assignment' of individuals to particular roles. According to a substitutability principle, discordant or ineffectual role relationships often can be resolved alternatively by redifferentiating the roles or by reallocating individuals or categories of individuals among existing roles. When role theory is approached structurally, an important distinction is made between allocation by ascription or achievement. Ascription means that individuals are required to perform certain roles and not others by accident of birth or life stage, according to cultural or legal mandate. Achieved roles are acquired through the individual's own efforts or conduct, and include most roles except gender and age in modern societies.

The interactional approach sees role allocation as the everchanging product of negotiation in interpersonal and intergroup relationships. An important feature of this negotiation is a process of 'altercasting,' of attempting to manipulate situations so as to cast relevant others into those roles that enable individuals to seize the desired roles for themselves. Altercasting on an institutional scale is illustrated by the way in which blind people are coerced into playing a stereotypic blind role in order to receive services from social agencies and to have harmonious dealings with strangers and acquaintances (Scott 1969).

Whether ascribed or achieved, roles must be learned in order to be enacted. Thornton and Nardi (1975) have proposed that learning involves four stages. First is the anticipatory stage, in which one hears or reads about the role or observes a role model, but without directly experiencing the role. Understanding at this stage is superficial, often idealized and unrealistic. It is followed by a stage of formal learning in which the role is learned through attention to rules and regulations, official declarations, and cultural norms. Transition to this stage begins with entry into trade or professional school, apprenticeship, or directly into the role. It typically characterizes the early experience in the role when the individual is guided by formal rules and values. As one gains experience in a role one begins to learn that the role is not generally enacted strictly according to the formal rules, and one learns the role as it is more informally understood by experienced incumbents. In a final stage, the incumbent becomes sufficiently secure in performing the role to begin to develop unique variations on the standard formal and customary informal role. The role is thus modified so as to fit uniquely the personality of the incumbent. Starting from a structural framework, this outline of stages concludes by stressing individual variability, consistent with an interactional approach.

The interactional approach calls attention to the fact that roles are normally learned in pairs or sets. Since role-playing depends upon role-taking significant other-roles, individuals must learn a good deal about these other-roles in order to master their own roles. While the learning of other-roles is usually limited to the anticipatory and formal stages and tends to be biased by the focal role's role-standpoint, individuals are sometimes able, in an emergency or other unusual situation, to assume and play the other-role when it has been abandoned. This process of 'role appropriation' has been observed when a child unexpectedly fills in for a temporarily incapacitated parent.

5. Role Enactment

Most social roles can only be enacted in interaction with relevant other-roles, and the nature of that interaction supplies the role's meaning. An important contribution of structural role theory has been to think of roles as consisting of rights and duties. The tenability of a role depends in large part on the balance between rights and duties, as it relates to the incumbents' relative power in the situation. A role is thought to be legitimate or fair if duties are balanced with rights. However, as interactionists point out, balance is largely in the eye of the beholder.

Seen interactionally, the balancing of rights and duties also means reciprocity, since one role's rights become another role's duties. At the very minimum, implementation of rights in one role requires that other-roles involve a duty not to prevent the focal role incumbent from exercising those rights. But the reciprocity is often much more active, as when the child's right to food and lodging implies an obligation for parents to provide those benefits, and as the employee's right to be paid for working implies the employer's duty to pay the worker. There is also another kind of reciprocity, in that what the focal role provides for the other should be in reasonable balance with what the other-role provides for the focal role. Thus 'exchange theory' and role theory come together at this point. It is a major proposition of role theory that discontent, interrole friction, poor role performance, and disruptions of the role system result from incumbents' conviction that relationships are unfair because of an absence of reciprocity or balance in any of these respects. Again, interactionists caution that judgments, that contributions are not equivalent and feelings of unfairness are often the consequence rather than the cause of disenchantment in role relationships.

Roles can be enacted with varying degrees of 'role adequacy,' and people tend to be evaluated within an organization and as persons on the basis of the adequacy with which they perform their roles. Besides personal skills and ability and disposition or motivation, role adequacy depends upon opportunity and resources. Role adequacy is also affected by 'intrarole conflict,' the presence of relatively incompatible expectations inherent in the role. Such incompatibility may be a consequence of the role set (as already discussed) or of an incompatible combination of tasks, as in the role of teacher who must be both educator and disciplinarian in a neighborhood of unruly children.

A further obstacle to adequate role performance can be 'interrole conflict.' Role conflict refers to the experience of incompatible obligations from two or more of a person's roles. An example would be a minister of a church whose religious responsibility is to accept a very modest salary gratefully, but who, as a father, feels obligated to secure the best education for his children that money can buy. Role conflict can be a fairly moderate or quite intense experience, depending upon how deeply and equally committed the individual is to the roles involved and how irrevocable the consequences of a particular decision may be. For example, conflict between a business trip and a meeting of one's monthly bridge group is usually resolved with a minimum of stress by opting for the business trip because commitment to the occupational role is much stronger than commitment to the bridge group, and because consequences of missing the bridge group occasionally are not serious or irrevocable. By contrast, commitment to family roles such as parent, husband or wife, son or daughter, and brother or sister, is usually high. Nevertheless, in daily life, conflicts involving family roles are often resolved without great stress by temporarily setting aside family commitments because the effects are minor and temporary, and there are abundant opportunities to compensate. But when the life, safety, or health of a family member is at stake so that the consequences of failing to carry out one's responsibilities could be severe and irrevocable, the experience of role conflict will be intense unless the conflicting role is easily set aside.

Two quite different kinds of interrole conflict are 'role value conflict' and 'role overload.' Value conflict is the more serious because it means that the more adequately the individual performs one role, the more he or she is dishonored in terms of the other role. But with the growing multiplicity of roles people play in modern societies, much more research has been devoted to role overload—the simple problem of not having enough time to perform all of one's responsibilities or of being unable to be in two places at the same time.

The term 'role strain' is sometimes used to describe the state of personal stress in the role-conflicted individual (Goode 1960), or the person who is unable to perform an allocated role adequately, according to his or her own standards, for any of the reasons reviewed. The ways in which people try to resolve role strain will be quite different, depending upon whether the cause of role strain is role conflict, inability to perform a task, or some other condition.

There are several ways to deal with role conflict. One way is 'role abandonment,' that is, opting for the responsibilities of one role and neglecting the responsibilities of the other. But abandonment can be permanent or temporary. The executive whose business trips conflict with bridge club meetings may resign from the bridge club, or the volunteer fireman whose emergency duties too often conflict with family or occupational responsibilities may resign from the volunteer fire brigade. More often role abandonment is attempted as a one-time solution. But such one-time abandonment usually carries penalties or at least requires assurances of more serious commitment to the abandoned role in the future. For example, the father who is absent on his daughter's birthday because of a business trip will be expected to bring home a special gift and treat his daughter to some special entertainment as a 'peace offering' on his return.

When commitment to both roles is high, people often try to resolve role conflict either by contriving to perform both roles in some way, or by performing only part of their responsibilities to each role. For example, one may attempt to attend two conflicting meetings, leaving one early and getting to the other late. Or one might try to perform the responsibility that could be completed in less time first, before taking up the more time-consuming responsibility. Needless to say, this approach is often counterproductive, with the result that both roles are performed poorly, if at all. Still another resolution might be called double role abandonment. Early research showed that workers who were pressured by their employers to hold one opinion (employee role) and by their union officials to hold a different opinion (union member role) often lost interest in the issue entirely. Whatever resolution is chosen, the stress of severe role conflict can affect concentration, motivation, and attitude toward the roles in question.

While the association of role overload with stress in modern societies had long been accepted as proved, Samuel Sieber (1974) challenged the necessary connection between multiple roles and role stress. According to a principle of 'role accumulation,' benefits (rights) often accumulate faster than duties when one assumes additional roles. One can often combine the duties of two or more roles into a single act, or use the benefits gained from one role as resources to help meet obligations of another role. This reasoning also led to questioning the common assumption that women who attempted to combine homemaker and professional roles suffered exceptional role strain. Several studies have now shown that levels of satisfaction are often higher among women who combine these two roles than among women who are involved in either homemaking or career exclusively. Specific outcomes are clearly affected by whether the single or dual role is a matter of personal choice or not and other variables not yet fully explored. Likewise, there is still much to be learned about the conditions that determine whether multiple roles will intensify role strain or lead to a rewarding role accumulation.

6. Organizational Roles

Most position roles are units in the division of labor by which some organization or institution functions. Consequently the content and arrangement of roles reflect the goals of the organization or institution. To insure that this is the case, organizations vest certain roles with the authority of 'legitimate role definers,' whose incumbents can change the organizational role structure and evaluate role performance in the organization. In order to minimize disruptive 'role ambiguities,' intrarole conflicts, and other role-related threats to organizational functioning, highly formal descriptions of roles and their interrelationships are typically evolved. However, even in such rigidly formalized organizations as the military and police, incumbents of each organizational role develop their own shared informal role

definitions. These informal roles incorporate practices which the role incumbents agree upon (informally) as the appropriate way to enact the role. They provide a role that is either more functional, more tenable, or more acceptable representationally than the formal role. They fill in remaining ambiguities in the formal role; for example, police must not use excessive force in making arrests, and police officers look to their peers to help define what is and is not acceptable force. They indicate which aspects of the role should contribute most to the incumbents' sense of self-fulfillment. They take account of compromises that must be made on pragmatic grounds, but which are unlikely to be admitted publicly in formal role descriptions.

Whether the informal role fosters the goals of the organization or undermines them depends upon the functionaries' degree of enthusiasm for organizational goals and their relationships toward organizational authorities. For example, the common practice of factory employees evolving their own standard of what constitutes a good day's work and informally sanctioning both under- and overachievers may be either a hostile slowdown of production or a means for keeping production at an optimum level consistent with maintaining worker well-being.

While role ambiguities and intrarole conflicts are generally considered to be damaging to organizational functioning, there is evidence to suggest that this is not always the case. For one thing, overly specific role statements may impair needed flexibility to deal with the unforseen. For another, some ambiguity and intrarole conflict can serve as a challenge, making role performance more interesting to the incumbent and encouraging innovations that may improve organizational functioning.

7. Roles in Society

The role that one plays and the adequacy with which it is played largely determine one's standing in an organization. For most roles there is little carryover of standing from one organization to another. But the implications of one's basic roles and value roles usually transcend any particular organizational setting. In addition, some highly valued position roles, such as one's profession, supply an important basis for standing in the society and not merely in the workplace.

Every society provides for certain situational or temporary roles that serve to exempt incumbents from normal responsibilities in most of their roles. Best known among these is the sick role. Talcott Parsons identified the sick role as a set of balanced rights and duties. When suitably certified as sufficiently ill—normally by a physician in modern societies but in other ways in other societies—role incumbents are temporarily relieved from many responsibilities in their occupational, family, community, and even friend roles and are entitled to be treated compassionately, provided that they are seriously cooperating with their physician and others in an effort to recover from the illness. The concept of how ill one must be and the criteria by which one is certified as ill, along with the kind of ministrations expected from family and friends and the range of responsibilities from which one is relieved vary greatly among different cultures and subcultures. Bereavement is another universally accepted exempting role. Other roles such as the drunken role and the stress role have their culturally specific configurations and are recognized as exempting roles under some circumstances in some cultures.

8. Role and Person

Because each individual plays different roles in different situations and at different life stages, and because people generally know each other by the roles they have an opportunity to see them play, the question for individuals and for those who know them is: who is the real person beneath the various role facades? Often people must play roles with which they would not want to be personally identified, and even more often, they are concerned that the person revealed through a single role will be mistaken for their whole person. Under these circumstances, people often engage in 'role distancing' by feigning detachment from the roles they are playing or making light of their role performance.

For those behavioral scientists who believe there is a 'person' behind the various roles, it has been proposed that each individual's role repertoire is organized into a hierarchy of salience. The individual's self-conception is built around the most salient roles. The hierarchy is partly determined by cultural selection of 'master roles,' such as one's occupation in the United States and one's family roles in more traditional societies. But it also varies uniquely from individual to individual, based on one's personal socialization experience. The most salient roles are those to which the individual is most committed, and which the individual should perform most conscientiously. For the salient roles there is a process of role–person merger, indicated by a tendency to continue playing the role even in situations where it is not called for, to resist giving up the role even in exchange for a more advantageous role, and internalization of attitudes and beliefs appropriate to the role.

Role–person merger is caused in part by how others view one and is governed by an 'appearance' principle, that in the absence of contradictory cues people tend to accept each other as they appear to be; an 'effect' principle, that the greater the effect of one's particular role on others, the more they conceive one as the person revealed in that role; and a 'consistency' principle, that one is identified as a person on the basis of observed behavioral consistencies between situations. In spite of a 'consensus' principle, that we tend to see ourselves as others see us, individuals are also active in shaping their self-conceptions by emphasizing roles they play best and with greatest autonomy, and by identifying most strongly with roles in which they have invested the most effort, creativeness, and personal sacrifice.

Situational compartmentalization is the most important tactic by which people handle the variety of roles they play during a given span of time. However, the life course is characterized by a great many 'role transitions,' when people give up one role to take on another. These transitions, from only child to sibling, from single to married, to parenthood, to empty nest, from dependent child to self-supporting adult, through occupational promotions and demotions, to retirement, and many others, can take place smoothly or with much stress. Transitions to roles with less favorable privileges-to-obligations ratios, such as divorce, widowhood, unemployment, and often retirement are inherently stressful. In most other transitions the stress is attendant on mastering and being accepted in the new role, so the stress level reflects the degree of difference between the old and new role and, inversely, the social support from the role set in the new role. In some instances, the stress is less in acquiring a new role than in divesting oneself of the old role. Helen Ebaugh (1988) has examined the difficult experience of former nuns, formerly married persons, former convicts, and former alcoholics, who continue to be known as exnuns, exconvicts, divorcees, widows, and ex-alcoholics while attempting to assume new roles for themselves.

9. Role Change

Historic changes in gender roles, age roles, family roles, occupational roles, and others have been extensively documented and analyzed. Roles may divide like an amoeba, or coalesce; new roles may be created or old ones die out. Research, however, has mostly dealt with changes in the content of continuing roles. The impetus for change usually comes from broader cultural change in values connected with the focal role; social structural changes that modify demand for the services provided by the role, the availability of resources, or social support for performance of the role; or the size and personal qualifications of the pool of potential recruits to the role. These changes can work indirectly through modifying the role's supporting network or by inducing change in other-roles that are part of the role set, or directly by creating role–person misfit. If these conditions are not relieved by reallocation or by negotiating idiosyncratic roles for the misfits, they contribute to either dysfunctionality, untenability, or inappropriate representationality in the role.

Whether the impetus for change will lead to negotiated change in the role depends upon the costs of alternatives, structural autonomy of the role, unity and mobilization of role incumbents, mobilized client demand for services that the revised role would render, cultural credibility of the changed role pattern, and institutional support for change. If the role change would encroach on the rights and duties of other roles, active resistance and conflict can be expected, depending upon the costs of the change to the encroached and their unity and mobilization in resisting change, and on the scarcity and monopolizability of skills held by the focal role incumbents and the role's support structure. If enough of these conditions are sufficiently unfavorable for change, the outcome can be resignation. But if the balance is favorable, changes in the focal role and accommodating changes in the role set should follow.

10. Conclusion

Linguistically, social roles are among the most important nouns, naming the categories of persons who participate in language. From the perspective of the sociologist, all kinship terms such as *mother*, *father*, or *cousin* name roles. But the lexicon of roles is vast, including for example professional roles (*doctor*, *judge*), positions in sports (*quarterback*, *coach*) and nonfamily personal relationships (*leader*, *lover*). Indeed, to the sociologist any term that identifies a position in a social system can be understood as the name of a role.

One can speak of a grammar of roles, because every role exists in relation to other roles and each particular relationship entails expectations concerning how role incumbents will communicate. A leader is expected to speak authoritatively, while a follower is expected to cheer the leader's words. A judge pronounces judgments. A quarterback calls plays but listens to the advice of the coach. A doctor gives diagnoses and prescriptions. Lovers share intimate words that must not be uttered in public. As researchers pay increasing attention to the linguistic variations that exist within a speech community, they will be well advised to examine the effect of role playing upon language.

As we have seen, most roles can be assigned to one of four categories: basic roles, position or status roles, functional group roles, and value roles. Structuralist analysis emphasizes the consensual character of norms that define roles, while symbolic interactionists describe a more tentative process in which roles are taken and made. Sociologists of both schools have examined how behaviors and attitudes coalesce to form differentiated roles, and they also study how roles are allocated to individuals, learned by them, and enacted reciprocally with other roles. Of special interest to sociolinguistics, organizations vest certain roles with the authority to define and transform other roles. Throughout life, individuals play a variety of roles, more or less adequately, managing role transitions, changes, and communications with others concerning the genuine person who wears all the masks. Language is the medium through which roles are created, and each role in turn shapes the language of the person who plays it.

See also: Exchange Theory; Social Psychology; Sociology of Language; Symbolic Interactionism.

Bibliography

Allen V L, van de Vliert E 1984 *Role Transitions*. Plenum, New York
Biddle B J 1979 *Role Theory: Expectations, Identities, and Behaviors*. Academic Press, New York
Ebaugh H R F 1988 *Becoming an EX: The Process of Role Exit*. University of Chicago Press, Chicago, IL
Goode W J 1960 A Theory of role strain. *American Sociological Review* 25: 483–96
Heiss J 1981 Social Roles. In: Rosenberg M, Turner R H *Social Psychology: Sociological Perspectives*. Basic, New York
Kahn R L, Wolfe D M, Quinn R P, Snoek J D 1964 *Organizational Stress: Studies in Role Conflict and Ambiguity*. Wiley, New York
Merton R M 1957 The role set. *British Journal of Sociology* 8: 106–20
Scott R A 1969 *The Making of Blind Men*. Russell Sage Foundation, New York
Sieber S 1974 Toward a theory of role accumulation. *American Sociological Review* 39: 567–78
Thornton R, Nardi P M 1975 The dynamics of role acquisition. *American Journal of Sociology* 80(4): 870–85
Turner R H 1990 Role change. *Annual Review of Sociology* 16: 87–110
Zurcher L A 1983 *Social Roles: Conformity, Conflict, and Creativity*. Sage, Beverly Hills, CA

R. H. Turner

Roles

Although 'role' is a central theoretical concept in research on linguistic interaction, notions about roles are notori-ously diffuse, and there is little general consensus as to how they should be defined operationally. Role theory is not a single, well-defined approach, but a mixture of perspectives derived from social anthropology, sociology, and social psychology that focus on different, sometimes only indirectly related, aspects of human interaction.

1. The Concept of Roles

The term 'role' comes from the Latin *rotula* 'rolled up script' or 'lines recited by an actor in a theater.' Interest in roles stems from a decision to view linguistic interaction metaphorically as a dramatic performance following a script that assigns speakers various parts or functions in interaction, and determines how these are performed, interpreted, and coordinated in different situations. A role is not a concrete human quality, but a hypothetical functional or behavioral attribute of an idealized 'Homo sociologicus,' i.e., a model member of society with a position in some group or interpersonal relationship, who performs analytically distinguishable activities in connection with this position. 'Role' is a theoretical category between 'self' and 'other,' an attempt to conceptualize the interface between the individual and the group. It combines psychological notions of personality and individual motivation, and social anthropological notions of group identity and behavior.

2. Roles and the Group

From the standpoint of the group, roles are positions to be filled or functions to be performed in the social system in some designated situation. Sociologists traditionally describe them as collective expectations about, or behavioral enactments of, rights and duties associated with an individual's status in the group (based on age, sex, ethnic background, class, education, occupation, etc.). Roles are not absolute natural laws, but they are socially binding, and not to conform to them is to run the risk of being regarded as a deviant member of the group. Role expectations, in this view, are shared reciprocally by members of the group, reinforced in the group by rewards and sanctions (role pressure), and reflected in conventional speech (and other) activities of individual members of the group. Linguistic analyses of, for example, male/female, doctor/patient, teacher/pupil, etc., interaction often characterize group role expectations as primary constraints on conventional choices and interpretations of speech styles and strategies in different contexts.

3. Roles and the Individual

From the standpoint of the individual, roles are simply convenient interactional strategies that can be learned, interchanged, ignored, or modified as needed in response to changing situational requirements. No role is final, and all roles are essentially subjective, flexible, and personal. Symbolic interactionists describe speakers as bundles of roles, claiming that it is only through social interaction that speakers develop the concept of the 'me' as seen by the others. A speaker's roles are continuously redefined by the process and results of interaction. Consequently, in the symbolic interactionist view, speakers have 'multiple roles'- and 'multiple selves'—as many, potentially, as there are interactions. Here, role theory and personality theory more or less intersect, and linguistic studies focus on phenomena such as self-presentation, face-saving, code-switching, speech accommodation, uncertainty in initial interaction, and so on.

4. Roles and Partners

From the standpoint of partners in interaction, roles are continuously claimed, projected, interpreted, confirmed, rejected, and renegotiated during conversation. Above all, they must be continuously 'coordinated' so that the interaction can flow smoothly. Ethnomethodologists focus on procedures partners use to recognize, select, invoke, and organize appropriate role activities in the context of a particular face-to-face interaction. How partners introduce innovation and change in the interaction, for example, agreeing to alter some speaking role, or establishing a new role, depends on a common body of shared global assumptions, and on some type of shared situational assumptive framework that the partners negotiate with each other. Linguistic studies of negotiations of this sort focus on partners' practical coordination of activities such as opening and closing conversations, introducing, shifting, or ending topics, taking turns, maintaining interaction, repairing misunderstandings, and so on.

5. Roles and Interpersonal Relationships

From an interpersonal standpoint, roles suggest underlying attitudes and intentions toward partners that must also be continuously modified and renegotiated during interaction. Social psychologists point out the tendency of individuals, due to different personality characteristics, goals, and personal preferences, to establish particular types of relationships with each other in given situations (dominant/ submissive, affiliative/nonaffiliative, involved/uninvolved). The negotiation of levels of power, affiliation, and intimacy in conversation is performed by means of subtle verbal, nonverbal vocal, and kinesic signals of assertiveness/ unassertiveness and positive/negative affect of various intensities. Multimodal studies of face-to-face speech focus on phenomena such as verbal immediacy, specificity of reference, directness and indirectness, intonation, facial expression, gaze, and other emotive activities that signal information about, and are used to strategically regulate, interpersonal relationships in conversation (see *Kinesics*).

6. Role as Metaphor

The widely different notions of, and approaches to, roles in modern linguistics reflect a lack of general agreement among scholars about what roles are, concretely, and how they may best be defined and investigated. Roles are not observable realities, but *metaphors*, and can thus only be analyzed systematically as hypothetical constructs within some clearly defined overriding conceptual framework.

See also: Metaphor; Situation Semantics; Interactionism; Code-switching and Mixing; Conversation Analysis; Conversational Maxims; Ethnomethodology.

Bibliography

Biddle B J, Thomas E J 1979 *Role Theory: Concepts and Research.* Krieger, Huntingdon, NY
Dahrendorf R 1973 *Homo Sociologicus.* Routledge and Kegan Paul, London
Goffman E 1971 *Relations in Public.* Allen Lane, London
Hesterman R C 1981 *Role Theory.* Exposition Press, Pompano Beach, FL
Ickes W, Knowles E S 1982 *Personality, Roles, and Social Behavior.* Springer-Verlag, New York
Linton R 1936 *The Study of Man.* Appleton-Century, New York

R. W. Janney
H. Arndt

Roman *Ars Grammatica,* including Priscian

The Roman *ars grammatica* comprises Roman grammatical works written between the third and the sixth century AD. They are all intended as textbooks in the schools or as handbooks for teachers. The majority consist of descriptions of Latin morphology focusing on the word classes ('parts of speech'), but many of the works also include treatments of phonology, metrics, and stylistics, which in some instances are taken by the authors as being as important as purely grammatical matters. The standard textbooks of the Roman *ars grammatica* tradition (especially Donatus' two grammars of the fourth century AD) were to form the basis for grammar teaching and grammar writing in Europe for more than a thousand years.

1. Background

The term *ars grammatica* means 'the art of grammar' and is a translation of Greek *téchnē grammatikē* with the same meaning. It is also likely that the Roman *ars grammatica* originated from the Greek genre of the *téchnē grammatikḗ*, but owing to the lack of Greek grammatical texts and the dating problems within Greek linguistics, notably the uncertainty of the dating of Dionysius Thrax's *téchnē grammatikḗ*, the exact nature of the connection between the two grammatical traditions remains unclear.

Just as in the Greek world, the Roman grammatical textbooks are basically designed for providing a metalanguage and method for analyzing those literary texts (mainly metrical texts like the works of Homer and Virgil) which were used as the principal textbooks in the schools. Gradually, however, the aim of the grammarians becomes basically linguistic, and literary considerations fade into the background, perhaps due to the increasing divergence between the spoken and written languages and the need for teaching a standardized literary language in the schools. But it may have also been due to the establishment of a well-organized school system and a professionalism among the teachers, who preferred a fixed curriculum.

The works labeled *ars grammatica* cover a wide variety of subjects and approaches to language and, in comparison with the few reminiscences of Greek grammar from antiquity, are impressive both in quality and quantity. The extant grammatical texts, however, represent but a part of the Roman grammatical literature. In some of the works that remain available we find references to grammarians otherwise unknown to us or to grammars now lost. Furthermore, the name of the author of many of the extant works is unknown or uncertain (cf. Kaster 1988 for a well-documented and thorough description of the lives and works of Greek and Roman grammarians). In many instances a grammar is attributed to a famous person known to have written an *ars grammatica* (e.g., Remmius Palaemon) or another famous person (e.g., St Augustine). It is common for the grammarians to copy each other extensively, often without acknowledging their sources.

All grammars and other linguistic texts by Roman grammarians except Varro and Quintilian have been published by Keil 1855–80. Accordingly, Keil's editions have had a major impact on the study of Roman linguistics. Unfortunately, many of his texts are badly in need of a new textual edition; it must be said that the study of Roman linguistics is seriously hampered by the lack of philologically reliable editions of those texts available (for further literature on the Roman grammatical tradition, cf. Barwick 1922 and Hovdhaugen 1982).

2. The Roman Grammarians

The first extant *ars grammatica* is the work in three books by Marius Plotius Sacerdos (third century AD). The work is badly organized and apparently starts with prepositions and verbs (the manuscript is fragmentary in the beginning). After the parts of speech have been discussed, there is an extensive treatment of the ablative case and a possible seventh case in Latin. The second book is devoted to syllable quantity and phonotactic matters as well as to a classification of stems and words according to their final sounds and syllables. The third book is entirely devoted to metrics.

The African grammarian Flavius Sosipater Charisius (fourth century AD) wrote an extensive *Ars grammatica* in five books, which treats morphology (including an extensive classification of words into inflectional classes), stylistics, and metrics and which also includes a short phonology (i.e., a description of the letters and their pronunciation), a list of synonyms, a list of words with different genders in Greek and Latin, and so forth. A characteristic feature of Charisius' work, and one which is unique in the *ars grammatica* tradition, is that on most controversial points he quotes extensively the views of other authors (many of them unknown from other sources). To some extent his grammar is a compilation or reader of Roman grammatical literature.

Diomedes (fourth or fifth century AD) wrote an *Ars grammatica* in three volumes, which in many respects follows the arrangement of Sacerdos, except that the second book contains just a short sketch of phonology and then treats stylistics and poetical matters, including cases of correct and incorrect Latin. Furthermore, in contrast to Sacerdos but in line with Charisius, he includes numerous references to and examples from Greek.

The most influential Roman grammarian of the fourth century was Aelius Donatus, who wrote two grammars: *Ars minor* and *Ars major*. The *Ars minor* only treats the word classes and is written as a dialogue between the teacher who asks and the pupil who answers. The *Ars Major* also includes a short phonology and aspects of correct and incorrect Latin. Table 1 gives a survey of the contents of Donatus' very influential *Ars major* (of these topics only sections 7–15 are included in the *Ars minor*).

The *Ars grammatica* attributed to Marius Victorinus (fourth century AD) illustrates another type of *ars grammatica*. Victorinus discusses in his preface what grammar should be and stresses the literary nature of his grammar

Table 1.

1. On voice	12. On participles
2. On letters/sounds	13. On conjunctions
3. On syllables	14. On prepositions
4. On metrical feet	15. On interjections
5. On accents	16. On barbarism (*barbarismus*)
6. On punctuation	17. On syntactic faults (*soloecismus*)
7. On parts of speech	18. On other errors
8. On nouns	19. On irregularities (*metaplasmus*)
9. On pronouns	20. On rhetorical figures (*schema*)
10. On verbs	21. On tropes
11. On adverbs	

and its importance for literary studies, but limits his treatment to phonology, orthography, and metrical aspects of the syllable. A similar approach is found in the *Ars* attributed to Atilius Fortunatianus (fourth century AD?), which is mainly a book on metrics but which contains in the beginning some short chapters on vowels, consonants, and syllables. Victorinus also wrote a short elementary *ars* in the form of questions and answers (a format that apparently starts with Donatus's *Ars minor* and which becomes very popular in late antiquity and the Middle Ages) but which, unlike Donatus's *Ars minor*, contains a lot of Greek examples, something that may be due to Victorinus being a Christian.

Consentius (date uncertain) and Phocas (fifth century AD) both limited their *Artes* to the noun and verb. Consentius also wrote a separate treatise about grammatical and stylistic errors.

The teaching of grammar beyond the elementary stage usually consisted in the teacher's reading a paragraph from a grammar and then commenting on it. Some teachers published their commentaries, thereby creating an important new grammatical genre and demonstrating the versatility and originality of Roman linguistics. Most influential were the commentaries on Donatus's *Ars major* by Marius Servius Honoratus (fourth century AD) and by Pompeius (fifth century AD). Pompeius is especially important since he most clearly represents the semantically oriented approach to grammatical analysis which can already be found implicit in Servius (on whom Pompeius to a large extent based his work) and Phocas and which would prove to be central in Priscian and medieval linguistics.

In contrast to the monolingual Greek grammar, Latin linguistics was bilingual, covering both Latin and Greek. Many authors of an *ars grammatica* neglected Greek, however, and had no Greek examples in their texts (e.g., Donatus, Sacerdos) while others (e.g., Charisius, Diomedes, and Priscian) extensively compared their analysis with Greek and quoted Greek examples. Two authors also wrote contrastive studies. Ambrosius Theodosius Macrobius (ca. 400 AD) analyzed differences and similarities between the verb in Latin and Greek, focusing on verb morphology, while Dositheus (fourth century AD) wrote a bilingual *Ars grammatica*.

3. Priscian

Priscian (ca. 500 AD) represents both the culmination and the end of Roman linguistics. Writing at a time when Christianity had taken over and medieval linguistics was well on its way, he collected and systematized the results of centuries of grammatical studies in the Roman world.

Born in Mauritania in North Africa and working in the largely Greek-speaking Constantinople, he was destined to become one of the most influential grammarians in history,- and much of linguistics in the Middle Ages was based on his works. His main and most impressive work, the *Institutiones grammaticae* in 18 books, goes far beyond what other Roman grammarians had aimed at or achieved. The syntactic part of his work is to a large extent inspired by and based upon the works of the leading Alexandrian grammarian Apollonius Dyscolus (see *Apollonius Dyscolus and Herodian*), the only Greek linguist who had written about syntax.

Priscian's treatment of Latin morphology, which covers most of the first 16 books (*Priscianus Major*), is one of the most thorough and well-documented morphological descriptions we have of any language, and his fascinating and complicated set of rules for word-formation within an inflectional paradigm still has important theoretical interest for morphological theory today. Priscian operates with a system of chains of rules where he starts with one basic form (e.g., nominative) and from that form derives another (e.g., genitive) which then forms the basis for the formation of the dative, and so on. But in this as in most other respects Priscian is not a theoretical innovator, since the basis of this theoretical approach to morphological analysis is well-documented in some of the sources quoted by Charisius. His two last books (*Priscianus Minor*), which treat syntax, lay the foundation for syntactic studies in the Middle Ages. No other extant work by a Roman linguist is devoted to syntax, although some of Varro's lost works (see *Varro and Early Latin Language Science*) may have focused on syntax. But we must not forget that the chapters on syntactic errors (*soloecismus*) in some of the grammars contained a multitude of observations on syntax.

Priscian is clearly 'data-oriented' in his approach. Even in morphology he constantly seeks attested examples from Latin literature for the forms (especially rare ones) he gives in his paradigms. On the other hand, he is much more open than are many of his predecessors to taking semantic considerations into account in arguing for a certain classification or arrangement of data. Furthermore, he articulates new basic problems for linguistic research like, for instance, the reason behind the order of elements, e.g., why *a* precedes *b* in the alphabet, or why we treat the noun before the verb in our description of the parts of speech. In the syntactic part of Priscian's work the two points that may have had the strongest impact on subsequent syntactic studies are his manner of analyzing complex syntactic structures with subordination as equivalent to synonymous coordinating structures and his way of analyzing elliptical constructions by tracing them back to complete constructions.

4. The Roman *Ars Grammatica*—An Attempt at a Synopsis

Contrary to what has been generally assumed, Roman linguistics was not characterized by any lack of originality and innovation, or by stability and conformity. The Roman grammatical tradition was a very versatile and multifaceted one characterized by continuity and development.

On the one hand, there is the formally oriented elementary school grammar tradition exemplified by Donatus's two grammars and by numerous similar grammars, mostly by unknown authors (e.g., the *Ars* of Cledonius (fifth century AD) and sometimes spuriously attributed to Remmius Palaemon, Probus, and Asper). This tradition is undoubtedly very uniform, and the differences between the various grammars are relatively small. With the collapse of the Roman empire there was a general decline in higher education and centers of learning in western Europe. Donatus's elementary textbooks and Christianized (largely by replacing the names of Roman gods with Christian names) versions of it become the basis for the elementary teaching of Latin in western Europe (Holtz 1981).

In a situation in which the language of the pupils was either very divergent from the norms of classical Latin or another language altogether, these books may also have been the most suitable ones available. But in the classical Roman educational system, in which the language of the pupils was quite close to the written language and where the main purpose of grammar teaching was to help the pupils to acquire a necessary background and basic metalanguage for reading poetical literary texts, grammars like those of Victorinus and Fortunatianus must have been much more instrumental. Among other things that characterize the Donatus-tradition is the lack of use of examples from literary texts, the lack of references to Greek and of Greek examples, and the lack of references to semantic criteria in the morphological classification.

Other grammars (e.g., those of Sacerdos, Charisius, Diomedes, and Priscian), and the commentaries on Donatus cover a number of different genres, topics, and theoretical approaches. Usually they include, besides the basic morphological part, a treatment of metrical matters, phonology (especially syllable quantity), orthography, and a comparison of Latin and Greek.

A characteristic aspect of the Roman grammatical tradition is the extensive treatment of stylistic matters, including statements concerning 'correct' and 'incorrect' Latin. Much space was devoted to establishing principles for correctness of language and to asking whether structural uniformity of paradigms, language usage, and/or the authority of the best authors should be the decisive criterion in cases of doubt.

While in the beginning the grammarians used a mixture of semantic and formal morphological criteria in their analysis and classification of Latin morphology, Donatus established a purely nonsemantic approach which became dominant in the elementary *ars grammatica*. Among other grammarians, however, a more semantically oriented approach emerged, culminating in Pompeius, Phocas, and Priscian, who laid the foundation for the philosophical approach to language analysis in the Middle Ages (Hovdhaugen 1987).

Most authors have their favorite theme; for instance, the *Instituta artium* spuriously attributed to Probus concentrates on the comparison of adjectives. Another popular topic (dating back to Quintilian; see *Roman Language Science in the Early Empire*) was the analysis of the Latin case system. Not only had Latin one more case than Greek (namely, the ablative), but also the semantic and partly morphological heterogeneity of the ablative (originating from three Indo–European cases, viz., instrumental, locative, and ablative) led some grammarians (e.g., Sacerdos and Diomedes) to discuss extensively the position of the ablative and to ask whether the ablative was, in effect, one or two cases.

While the phonology (i.e., letters and their pronunciation and syllable quantity) and the morphology with its numerous paradigms and lists of examples are based in most instances on data without sources and probably to a large extent on the authors' introspection (an exception is Priscian, cf. above), stylistic and metrical matters are usually well-documented with quotations from the main Latin poets (very rarely prose writers), especially Virgil and Horace.

The most important aspect of the Roman *ars grammatica* is that it formed the grammatical metalanguage and above all the structural arrangement for elementary and advanced grammars and textbooks for language teaching in western Europe for more than 1,000 years. Even in the late twentieth century many grammars have clear echoes of Donatus.

See also: Varro, Marcus Terentius; Varro and Early Latin Language Science.

Bibliography

Barwick K 1922 *Remmius Palaemon und die römische ars grammatica.* Dieterich, Leipzig

Holtz L 1981 *Donat et la tradition de l'enseignement grammatical: Étude sur l'Ars Donati et sa diffusion (IVe–IXe siècle et édition critique.* Centre National de la Recherche Scientifique, Paris

Hovdhaugen E 1982 *Foundations of Western Linguistics: From the Beginning to the End of the First Millennium* AD. Oslo University Press, Oslo

Hovdhaugen E 1987 *Genera verborum quot sunt*: Observations on the Roman grammatical tradition. *HL* XIII(2/3): 307–21

Kaster R A 1988 *Guardians of Language: The Grammarian and Society in Late Antiquity.* University of California Press, Berkeley, CA

Keil H (ed.) 1855–80 *Grammatici Latini*, 7 vols. and supplement. Teubner, Leipzig

Taylor D J (ed.) 1987 *The History of Linguistics in the Classical Period.* Benjamins, Amsterdam

E. Hovdhaugen

Roman Language Science in the Early Empire

During the early Roman Empire, roughly 27 BC–200 AD, grammatical activity becomes ubiquitous, providing employment for its professionals and attracting attention from the educated elite, poets, men of letters, and even emperors themselves. The period witnesses the publication of the first Latin lexicon and the first *ars grammatica* in its technical sense of 'grammatical manual' as well as works on more traditional topics like orthography. Etymology becomes a common resource to be employed wherever appropriate, e.g., in definitions, rather than a self-contained area of expertise, but language science expands to include the virtues and vices of speech.

This, then, is the period when the Roman grammarians do what Romans do best, namely, organize, but it is also a period from which precious little grammatical literature has survived. Quintilian, the master rhetorician and holder of the first scholarly chair in Western education, is arguably the leading intellect of the time. In his monumental tome on the art of rhetoric Quintilian includes a sketch of the grammatical curriculum as he either knows it or thinks it ought to be structured, and this text provides the best evidence for the nature and extent of early imperial grammatical inquiry. With the advent of the third century AD, Roman grammar is a *fait accompli*, both a well-defined scholarly discipline and the heart and soul of the educational system, and it was destined to remain as such throughout history.

1. The Status of Grammar

By attending publicly to grammatical details in his own speaking and writing, the emperor Augustus affirms the value of such technical matters, and by dedicating the temple of Palatine Apollo along with its attached library (28 BC), he likewise validates both literature and the study of literature. The emperor's actions also testify to the two special provinces of the Roman *ars grammatica*: the *ratio loquendi* 'art of speaking correctly' and the *enarratio auctorum* 'interpretation of authors.' Both these endeavors had been practiced by Greek grammarians, but the Romans formalize them. Moreover, although some Roman grammarians specialize in one or the other, most claim both technical and exegetical expertise.

In the middle of the first century AD grammar commands the attention of Pliny the Elder and garners the opprobrium of the philosopher Seneca. Pliny's *Dubius Sermo* examines irregular word forms from the perspective of prescriptive analogy. Seneca inveighs mightily against grammar, which he reductively refers to as the analysis of syllables, attentiveness to words, accounts of myths, and principles of versification, and thereby unwittingly verifies that grammar has become a decidedly influential component of the Roman intellectual scene. At the end of the century grammar and grammarians earn a degree of literary eminence, at least of a sort. Martial enjoins his third book of epigrams not to fear Probus, the foremost grammarian of contemporary Rome, and piously hopes that his poems may prove pleasing to grammarians without, however, requiring their professional scrutiny. Juvenal satirizes women who display their grammatical erudition at dinner parties (*Sat.* VI. 434–56). The women and, it may be inferred, their grammatical sources discuss literature and compare Latin and Greek poetry. They indulge themselves in logical syllogisms and *historiae*, the often obscure details, especially mythological, embedded in literary texts and the stuff of which pedantry consists. They consult Palaemon's grammatical manual (see below), cite its rules and prescriptions, quote antiquarian verses, and chastise solecisms. All of this is too much for Juvenal, but it is instructive for historians of linguistics. Martial's testimony avers that contemporary as well as antiquarian poetry is at the mercy of the grammarians' strictures, and although some grammarians are said to receive extravagant salaries or honoraria, Juvenal goes out of his way to commiserate with their financial woes.

Attention to grammar and grammarians continues unabated in the second century AD. Twenty-four chapters or paragraphs of Suetonius' *De grammaticis* remain. These biographical sketches of famous grammarians feature gossip and anecdotes, beginning with Crates of Mallos, whose visit to Rome in 168(?) BC commences grammatical scholarship in the eternal city, and concluding with Probus and

Palaemon, who, judging from contemporary literary references and citations in the later grammatical tradition (see *Roman ars grammatica, including Priscian*), are the two most important grammarians of the early empire. More than 60 percent of the topics addressed by Aulus Gellius in his *Noctes Atticae*, a miscellany of contemporary lore and learning, have to do with grammar. Etymologies abound, as do references to parts of speech, *Formenlehre*, analogy, orthography, literary and textual criticism, *Latinitas*, and so forth. Gellius' rambling ruminations on grammatical topics offer a vivid picture of grammar's status as the science of sciences.

2. Grammarians and their Texts

Grammatical texts dating from the early empire are few and far between, and so their contents must be inferred from titles, fragments, and citations in later texts. Inspired by Rome's new library and the immediately recognized brilliance of Augustan poetry, Hyginus and Modestus produce commentaries, while Pomponius Marcellus, a captious critic of the worst sort, upbraids even Tiberius' speech, arguing that the emperor is capable of granting citizenship to men but not to a word. The first major linguistic treatise of the period is Verrius Flaccus' *De verborum significatu*, which seems to have been as much encyclopedia as lexicon, and its loss is especially regrettable. The same author's *De orthographia* serves as the primary source for later treatments of orthography.

The major scholar of the age and its most famous grammarian is Quintus Remmius Palaemon. Despite his depraved sexual appetites, which according to the emperors Tiberius and Claudius made him morally unfit for educating the youth of Rome, Palaemon is as popular (cf. his role in Juvenal's satire as discussed in Sect. 1) as he is influential (he is the first grammarian to have grammatical treatises spuriously ascribed to him). Our knowledge of Palaemon's version of Roman language science, however, is indirect only and extremely limited at best; this is particularly vexing because Palaemon has traditionally been credited with (a) authorship of the first *ars grammatica* in and for Latin; (b) substituting the interjection for the article, which Latin lacks, in the *partes orationis* 'parts of speech'; (c) discovering the Latin declensions and conjugations; and (d) organizing Latin grammar into the form in which it is found several centuries later. Our meager evidence for these claims derives from various sources, including extant fragments, Juvenal's testimony, and most notably Quintilian's grammatical sketch, which is thought to be based to some degree on Palaemon's *ars grammatica*.

Palaemon's *ars* is certainly the first known of, and since it is his definition of the interjection which predominates in subsequent grammatical literature, he is most probably the one who substitutes the interjection for the article. The extant fragments of Palaemon's *ars* also suggest that its major contributions to progress in language science are concentrated within the sphere of the uninflected parts of speech, for they deal almost exclusively with the adverb, preposition, conjunction, and interjection. Palaemon's role in determining declensional and conjugational affiliations is less obvious. If he was Quintilian's teacher, as one source claims, his student seems never to have understood the significance of assigning nouns to declensions and verbs to conjugations, for Quintilian is uniformly silent about such affiliations even though he has ample opportunity—and, given some of the linguistic problems he addresses, he needs but is apparently not able—to refer nouns and verbs to declensions and conjugations respectively. Moreover, the later tradition manifests little uniformity either in the enumeration of declensions or in the basis of assigning nouns to declensions, and vacillates between recognizing three or four conjugations. Thus Palaemon's role, if any, in this endeavor seems ineffectual at best, and in any case the declensions and conjugations are already present, at least in theory, in Varro's *De Lingua Latina* (see *Varro and Early Latin Language Science*).

The grammatical vignette in Juvenal (see Sect. 1) states that Palaemon's *ars* dealt with linguistic rules, antiquarian verses, barbarisms, and solecisms, and implies that it was both rational and prescriptive. None of this is especially surprising except for the references to barbarisms and solecisms, topics which figure prominently in the later *ars grammatica* under the rubric of *vitia virtutesque orationis* 'vices and virtues of speech' but which have not previously been addressed by Roman grammarians in any formal sense. Such matters are often referred to as the third part (after phonology and morphology) of ancient Latin grammar, and Palaemon may be the first grammarian to have treated them systematically. Exactly what other topics Palaemon essays in his *ars* are not known for certain, but Juvenal's micro-account of Palaemon's *ars* does accord well with Quintilian's more extensive grammatical sketch (see Sect. 3). If Quintilian is dependent upon Palaemon's *ars*, then it would seem to be the model for other *artes* to follow, but the evidence, however tantalizing, is too slim to allow certainty.

Marcus Valerius Probus is the other celebrated grammarian of the first century AD, but the extant works attributed to him are manifestly not by his hand. He is a textual critic and philologist par excellence, and later grammarians frequently cite him as a source when dealing with verbs. The next century witnesses the publication of several treatises on orthography by Terentianus Scaurus, Velius Longus, and Flavius Caper; Terentianus Maurus' manual on metrics is but another indication that literary and linguistic scholarship go hand in hand; and Porphyrion's extant commentary on Horace contains grammatical and lexical information still useful to students and scholars alike. Festus abridges Verrius Flaccus' lexicon, but only the sections on the letters M through V have survived. The trend for ensuing centuries has been set, and later grammarians continue to mine the works of their predecessors. Presumably the nature and scope of Roman language science have also been established by the grammarians of the early empire, but since almost all texts are now missing, twentieth-century scholars are at a loss to specify exactly how that process of organization and formalization actually occurred.

3. Quintilian and Grammar in Roman Education

Given the dearth of specifically linguistic texts, Quintilian's account of the grammatical curriculum in first century AD Roman education looms larger in the history of linguistics than would otherwise be expected. The *Institutio Oratoria* describes Quintilian's ideal of the education required to produce a master orator. As soon as the child has learned to read and write, he begins the formal study of grammar, which Quintilian divides into two parts: *recte loquendi scientia* 'knowledge of speaking (to which he adds writing and reading) correctly' and *enarratio poetarum* 'interpretation of poets.' Quintilian refers to grammar as both a profession (*professio*) and an art (*ars*), and his sketch (I. 4–9) provides the best extant account of what grammarians and their students are doing in the first century AD. The following survey scrupulously adheres to the sequence and general linguistic contents of Quintilian's account but does not indicate the extent to which Quintilian pursues any given topic.

The grammarian first distinguishes between vowels and consonants, dividing the latter into semivowels and stops, and examines the alphabet phonetically. He then examines derivation, especially by prefixes, treating both synchronic alternations in verb roots and diachronic changes, e.g., rhotacism. Next he addresses the number and nature of the parts of speech. Quintilian refers to several competing schemes of enumeration, to which he attaches no significance whatsoever, but it is here that he names Palaemon for the first and only time, classing him and Aristarchus among those who do not differentiate between common and proper nouns. Students must then learn how to decline (*declinare*) nouns and verbs (but note that Quintilian has no word meaning 'to conjugate'), paying special attention to matters of gender, origin of names, and the function of the ablative (which, according to Quintilian, in its instrumental usage is neither a true Latin ablative nor a true Greek dative) in the case of nouns, and in verbs to matters of accidence, ambiguous forms (those which may be either a noun or a verb—Pliny's *Dubius Sermo* may be lurking behind this topic), impersonal passives, and defective verbs (suppletive forms and active impersonals).

Quintilian then turns to style and its virtues and vices, which he treats in terms of words, not sentences. The single virtue is euphony, and the two vices are barbarisms and solecisms. The former are mistakes in individual words and may be classified, in the case of writing, as either addition, subtraction, substitution, or transposition (i.e., the *quadripertita ratio*), and as separation, combination, aspiration, and sound in the case of speaking. Quintilian pointedly remarks that some grammarians may be incompetent to deal with such topics, since they have only entered the *vestibulum artis huius* 'forecourt of this art,' and must therefore restrict themselves to the contents of commonly available *commentariola* 'elementary textbooks.' The art, i.e., grammar, therefore either already encompasses or in Quintilian's opinion should encompass, one is compelled to conclude, the *vitia virtutesque orationis*, and the phonological and morphological matters adduced heretofore do not in themselves constitute a full-fledged *ars* but only a *commentariolum*. Quintilian then addresses a variety of barbarisms committed in writing and speaking; the latter include errors in vocalic quantity and in accent.

Solecisms are errors involving more than one word and may also be classified according to the *quadripertita ratio* with but one exception: substitution is always an error, whereas addition, subtraction, and transposition may be viewed positively as pleonasm, ellipse, and anastrophe or hyperbaton, respectively. Verb usages are especially subject to solecisms, but to how many depends on how one arranges the taxonomy of verbal accidence; thus Quintilian

implies that verbal accidence is not a fixed inventory. Solecistic errors involve number, both verbal and nominal, gender, comparatives and superlatives, patronymics and possessives, and diminutives, and occur frequently in the parts of speech, though these latter faults are often, in the case of poets and orators, treated as figures. Quintilian then returns to a threefold binary classification of words originally articulated at the outset of his account of stylistic matters but so far unused: words may be native or foreign, simple or compound, proper or metaphorical. The major question is whether foreign words, particularly Greek nouns, should retain their inflection or should be adapted to Latin. Quintilian's analysis of compounds is nowhere near as sophisticated as that found in ancient Sanskrit grammar, but it is a potentially profitable topic. Neologisms and onomatopoeia obfuscate the distinction between proper and metaphorical usage.

Quintilian then analyzes principled or rule-governed linguistic behavior in speech. Language consists of *ratio* 'reason,' which is a matter of *analogia* especially and sometimes of *etymologia*; *vetustas* 'antiquity,' which adds majesty; *auctoritas* 'authority,' which mainly deals with precedents from oratorical and historical prose because poetic license invalidates much of poetry's *auctoritas* (Quintilian may be uniquely biased on this point); and *consuetudo* 'usage,' which is the surest guide. Analogy is comparison of the unknown with the certain and focuses on final syllables, i.e., endings, and diminutives in order to reveal declension and/or gender. Analogy is useful for determining the quantity of vowels in verb forms, e.g., the infinitive, and for discovering the correct present indicative on the basis of other tenses. Analogy is sometimes inconsistent and in any case is not a divinely ordained phenomenon but a humanly discovered one and therefore, ultimately, a product of usage. Some grammarians go too far, actually altering attested forms in favor of artificially, i.e., analogically, created ones. Since some forms are clearly doubtful, Quintilian concludes that it is one thing to speak Latin, another to speak grammar. Etymology inquires into the origin of words and is useful in definitions and in identifying barbarisms. Archaic words add majesty and charm but should be used sparingly, and despite their textual authority, not all words receive sanctioning. Usage is a tricky issue, for it involves idiosyncratic as well as uneducated habits; Quintilian defines it as the agreed practice of educated men. Rules of writing, i.e., orthography, are discussed next. Difficult cases, diachronic changes, and discrepancies between spelling and pronunciation all require critical judgment on the part of grammarians. Quintilian concludes with a caveat to his readers: such trivial matters are no hindrance to excellence, but grammatical superfluities can become pedantry.

Despite appearances to the contrary Quintilian's account has been remarkably well organized, but he gives no clue as to whether that organization has been imposed by himself or is a product of some unnamed source. That issue is still sub iudice. Apart from the matter of organization, Quintilian would appear to be indebted to Varro for much of his discussion of analogy and etymology, to Verrius Flaccus for his account of orthography, and to Pliny vis-à-vis dubious grammatical forms, but he does not say so. At this point Quintilian has finished his sketch of the *recte loquendi scientia* and now turns to *enarratio poetarum*, and the moving rhetoric of his presentation suggests that the passage, at least that part on *lectio* 'reading,' is his own.

Reading is a matter of pausing and breathing, inter alia— it should be remembered that the ancients invariably read aloud (exceptions are noteworthy)—and takes the student into the realm of literature. After the student parses and scans a verse, the professor identifies barbarisms, instances of poetic license, *glossemata* 'uncommon words,' and literary figures. *Historiae* are the next topic, and here Quintilian echoes Seneca's and Juvenal's scorn of such minutiae, concluding that not to know some things is to the teacher's credit. Finally, Quintilian enumerates several additional exercises in composition for those students not yet ready to progress onward and upward in their studies: paraphrases of Aesop's fables, aphorisms, character sketches, and moral essays; such matters are not, however, inherent in grammar proper. Quintilian is now by his own admission done with his sketch of grammar, a topic on which he has not tried to say everything, for it is infinite.

Nonetheless, Quintilian has, in fact, authored the only extant text of its kind datable to the early imperial period. Through him has come the knowledge of what language scientists were doing at the time, and they continue to do much the same thing throughout the next half-millenium. They may elaborate any given topic almost to excess and may vary their organization of the material, but generally speaking, the tripartite table of contents addressed by the later monumental Roman *ars grammatica* tradition— phonology, morphology, vices and virtues of speech—is also grammar as constituted in the *Institutio Oratoria*. To be sure, in time, the grammarians flesh out Varro's embryonic declensions and conjugations and add them to their morphological sections. They even create a new genre of grammatical literature, namely, the grammatical commentary, i.e., commentaries on grammars, and Priscian ultimately incorporates syntax into the *ars grammatica*. But otherwise the form and contents of the Roman *ars* are established in the first century AD, and the result is a discipline and a profession central to Roman life and letters in late antiquity and equally central to those of the late twentieth century.

Bibliography

Barwick K 1922 *Remmius Palaemon und die römische ars grammatica*. Dieterich, Leipzig
Bonner S F 1977 *Education in Ancient Rome: From the Elder Cato to the Younger Pliny*. Methuen, London
Mazzarino A 1955 *Grammaticae Romanae Fragmenta Aetatis Caesareae*. Loescher, Turin
Taylor D J (ed.) 1987 *The History of Linguistics in the Classical Period*. Benjamins, Amsterdam

D. J. Taylor

Roman Religion

The religion of ancient Rome, a highly ritualistic polytheism, was traditionally supposed to have been codified by Numa Pompilius, the successor of Romulus as king of Rome. Religious law (*ius divinum*) regulated the relations of men with the gods, as civil law regulated their dealings with one another. Public sacrifices and festivals, celebrated by the magistrates, maintained the *pax deorum* or 'peace of the gods,' while the divine will was manifested through divination, prophecies, and omens. The state ritual was principally supervised by the College of Pontifices headed by the *Pontifex Maximus*. The science of divination (from the flight of birds, the entrails of sacrificed animals, meteorological phenomena, etc.) was greatly elaborated under Etruscan influence. The Romans saw the kinship between their religion and that of the Greeks, and syncretistic identifications of Roman and Greek gods were easily made. Sometimes these were supported by an etymological connection (Jupiter = Zeus) but more often a Roman divinity was assimilated to the Greek god or goddess whose sphere of influence was most nearly equivalent; thus Mars = Ares, Minerva = Athena, etc. Some had no equivalent in Greek religion or mythology, e.g., Janus (god of doorways and of beginnings—hence January). The Romans perhaps derived from the Greeks a tendency to deify abstractions; thus there were temples and public cults of Victory, Concord, Fortune, etc. A host of minor spirits (*numina*) were invoked in specific contexts. Elaborate rituals surrounded birth, marriage, and death, and private cults (*sacra*) were handed down in the family or attached to particular localities. Every individual Roman had a tutelary spirit (*genius* if a man, *Juno* if a woman) and every Roman family had its *Lares* (gods of the household) and its *Penates* (gods of the storecupboard); household worship was in the hands of the head of the family (*paterfamilias*). During the Principate, divine honors were paid to present and past emperors.

Roman ritual was an elaborate discipline with its own technical terminology. Accurate enunciation of ritual formulae (*carmina* or *verba concepta*) in prayers, vows, sacrifices, oaths, and other ceremonial acts was considered most important. If a sacrificing magistrate made a slip of the tongue, it was considered a bad omen; the whole sacrifice might have to be repeated (*instauratio*) and the fault expiated with a further sacrifice (*piaculum*). The language of ritual was often old-fashioned (as was the language of Roman law). Some extant items of religious Latin, such as the Saliar and Arval Hymns, are so archaic as to be largely unintelligible even with the help of philological research, and it is doubtful whether the Romans of the classical period understood them any better than modern scholars do. Latin prayers, such as those preserved by Cato the Elder in *De Agricultura* (139–41), show a standard pattern: first the god or gods concerned are invoked by name, then the petition is made, and finally the sacrifice (i.e., the payment for the granting of the request) is offered, with the formula *macte esto* (possibly meaning 'be thou increased'). Alliteration, isocolon, rhyme, and collocations of synonyms are all common in Latin ritual formulas, and these features combine with archaism in vocabulary and accidence to form a distinctive register of Latin, touches of which could be employed to good literary effect by authors such as Virgil and Livy.

Verbal prophecies were accepted as a potentially valid communication from the gods. The Roman state kept a collection of oracles (apparently written in Greek) known as the Sibylline Books, which were consulted on occasions of national emergency. Prophets (*vates*), diviners, and (later, under Graeco–Oriental influence) astrologers were taken seriously; an accidental utterance by an ordinary person could be regarded as an omen in certain circumstances. The verbal declaration of a god's will was called *fatum* (from *fari* 'to speak'), whence the use of this word to mean 'destiny' or 'fate.'

In general, Rome was receptive to foreign religious influences, although cults which threatened public order were from time to time officially suppressed. Cults of various origins were transported around the Empire by soldiers, tradesmen, and others; among these were the so-called mystery religions (Greek *mysteria* 'initiatory rites' from *myeo* 'initiate,' *myo* 'shut the eyes'), of Greek or Near Eastern origin, whose devotees progressed through various stages of initiation of a more or less secret nature. Temples of the Egyptian deities Isis and Serapis were established at Rome by the end of the Republic, while the religion of Mithras, 'the Unconquered Sun'—who probably bore an extremely tenuous relationship to the ancient Iranian god Mithra—was particularly congenial to the military classes. Owing to the secrecy of Isiac and Mithraic ritual, very little is known about its language; some Egyptian or Iranian formulas may have been preserved in it (as in contemporary magical documents), but it is likely that the main language was originally Greek, the lingua franca of the Eastern Mediterranean since the time of Alexander the Great, while Mithraists in the West probably used Latin.

Some central items of Christian Latin vocabulary derive directly from Roman paganism, though their meaning was altered (often consciously) by the influence of the Greek and Hebrew words which they were used to translate. Examples are *sacer, sanctus, sacramentum, sacrificium*; *pius, pietas*; *votum, devotio*; and of course *religio* itself. However, some other pagan terms, such as *pontifex*, were imported into ecclesiastical usage as a result of classicizing revival in the Renaissance.

Bibliography

Liebeschuetz J H W G 1979 *Continuity and Change in Roman Religion*. Clarendon Press, Oxford
Ogilvie R M 1969 *The Romans and Their Gods in the Age of Augustus*. Chatto and Windus, London
Palmer L R 1954 *The Latin Language*. Faber, London
Scullard H H 1981 *Festivals and Ceremonies of the Roman Republic*. Thames and Hudson, London
Warde Fowler W 1922 *The Religious Experience of the Roman People*. Macmillan, London
Wardman A 1982 *Religion and Statecraft among the Romans*. Granada, London
Wissowa G 1912 *Religion und Kultus der Römer*. Beck, Munich

J. G. F. Powell

Romance Languages

The Romance Languages are those which have developed from the spoken Latin of the early Middle Ages. In this sense one can claim that Latin is not dead; about a quarter of the world's population still speak it; but it has acquired several new geographically based names (Spanish, Portuguese, French, Italian, Romanian, Catalan, Occitan, Sardinian, Galician, Rhaeto-romanic, here listed roughly in descending order of number of speakers). These are for political reasons considered to be separate 'Romance' languages, but there is still essentially one dialect continuum overlaid by the several artificially extended standards. Apart perhaps from Romanian, the location and history of whose earliest speakers is still controversial, the definitive divergence into separately identifiable languages should be dated to no earlier than the ninth century, and in several cases later.

1. Reconstruction

There are two main kinds of evidence for the Romance (spoken Latin) that existed before the separate languages diverged: surviving written texts and the results of 'reconstruction.' Hall and others have reconstructed a hypothetical 'Proto-Romance' on the basis of the later Romance languages; features they have in common are taken to have existed in their ancestor. As compared with 'classical' Latin, this Proto-Romance contains, for example, no neuter nouns, no ablative cases, no datives and genitives outside pronouns, no synthetic passives or futures, no adverbs in -*iter*, no phonemic length distinctions in vowels, no originally final consonants other than alveolars, and no velar consonants before front vowels other than those that were originally labiovelar. On the other hand, the evidence of modern Romance languages suggests that their base included extended uses of prepositions (particularly *ad* and *de* to replace inflectional nominal suffixes); analytic passives with auxiliary *esse* + tense-indeterminate participles; extended use of grammatically reflexive *se* with passive meaning; analytic futures (and 'conditionals') formed with the infinitive + *habeo*; new analytic perfects (including future perfects and pluperfects) formed with activized participles + *habeo*; extensive use of *ille* and *ipse* with the functions of the definite article; many diminutives in -*iculum* and other affixed forms (such as *adiutare*, rather than *iuvare*, as the base of Port *ajudar*, Sp *ayudar*, Cat *ajudar*, Fre *aider*, Italian *aiutare*, Romanian *ajuta*, etc.); the use of preposed *magis* or *plus* instead of comparative -*ior*; palatal affricates and semivowels; and much new vocabulary from, in particular, Germanic sources.

2. Texts

This reconstructed language is not very like that of the surviving written texts of the time. Janson described reconstruction and textual analysis as being two different keyholes through which one can look into the same one large room. For the rules of correct writing did not change, and 'mistakes' are rarely attested. Most texts were written on perishable wax tablets or papyruses; the extant versions are usually later manuscript copies prepared by scribes who had specific instructions to 'correct' their originals according to the arcane and eventually archaic rigidities of the Imperial grammarians. Texts without such distortions are few; Adams has published some letters and drafts, and Väänänen's study of the Pompeii *Graffiti* revolutionized the discipline by showing how 'incorrectly' nonscholars wrote in 79 AD. Even these texts, however, are obviously not phonetic transcriptions of actual speech. From painstaking statistical analyses of surviving inscriptions (mostly on tombstones), whose textual details cannot be 'corrected,' Herman has concluded that Imperial spoken Latin was evolving but also converging, with new features starting in one place becoming eventually attested anywhere. Some further progress is made by studying borrowings from spoken Latin into, for example, Irish, Welsh, Berber, Albanian, and Greek.

3. Divergence

Wide variation arose, but this need not imply mutual unintelligibility. Many historians, textual critics, philologists, sociolinguists, and historical linguists currently view early Medieval Romance Europe as a single lively speech community, where almost everyone could understand old-fashioned written texts when read aloud (McKitterick 1990; Wright 1991). These were not 'Dark' Ages. Early Medieval speakers rarely made metalinguistic distinctions which we take for granted now, neither diatopic (between French, Spanish, etc.) nor diastratic (between Romance and Medieval Latin). The latter distinction was probably imported from Germanic-speaking areas, where vernacular Germanic and official Latin *grammatica* were unrelated and self-evidently different languages; conscious distinctions between separate Romance languages only became widespread after the fashion for inventing distinctive writing systems in different areas, which began experimentally in ninth-century eastern France but only generalized in the twelfth and thirteenth centuries. Indeed, to some extent the speech of the central Romance area is still mutually intelligible, given goodwill and clarity from those in the conversation; peripheral languages, such as Romanian, Portuguese, and French, are rarely intelligible elsewhere.

See also: Spanish; Portuguese; French; Italian; Romanian; Catalan; Occitan; Sardinian; Rhaeto–Romance.

Bibliography

Adams J N 1977 *The Vulgar Latin of the Letters of Claudius Terentianus.* Manchester University Press, Manchester
Hall R A 1976 *Proto-Romance Phonology.* Elsevier, New York
Harris M, Vincent N 1987 *The Romance Languages.* Croom Helm, London
Herman J 1990 *Du Latin aux langues romanes: Etudes de linguistique historique.* Niemeyer, Tübingen
Janson T 1979 *Mechanisms of Language Change in Latin.* Almqvist and Wiksell, Stockholm
McKitterick R (ed.) 1990 *The Uses of Literacy in Early Mediaeval Europe.* Cambridge University Press, Cambridge
Posner R, Green J N 1980–93 *Trends in Romance Linguistics,* 5 vols. Mouton, The Hague
Väänänen V 1937 *Le latin vulgaire des inscriptions pompéiennes.* Academy, Helsinki
Varvaro A 1968 *Storia, problemi e metodi della linguistica romanza.* Liguori, Naples
Wright R 1982 *Late Latin and Early Romance in Spain and Carolingian France.* Cairns, Liverpool
Wright R (ed.) 1991 *Latin and the Romance Languages in the Early Middle Ages.* Routledge, London

Roger Wright

Romani

Romani (Romany, Romanes, Gypsy) is a collective name which refers to 60 or more widely diverging dialects, spoken throughout Europe and the former Soviet Union, and in European postcolonial territories overseas. Some Romanologists treat these as distinct languages rather than as dialects of a single language.

Romani is spoken by the descendants of a population which left India at the end of the first millennium AD and which made its way into Europe, via Persia and the Byzantine Empire, arriving there some time during the thirteenth century. The identity of that first population, and the circumstances of their exodus, have been the subject of scholarly debate since the 1780s. Late twentieth-century research, some of it being undertaken in India, suggests strongly that the original population consisted of different Indo–Aryan-speaking peoples of non-Aryan descent (in particular Dravidians and the Prātihārā, migrant populations who had settled in India from the north), out of whom were created Rājpūt armies to resist the Islamic incursions into India led by Mohammed Ghaznavid. As these armies moved further west, they were again caught up in, and displaced by, the spread of Islam as it overtook the Byzantine Empire. It was this westward movement which pushed the Romani population up into Europe. The common name *Gypsy* (like *Gitano* in Spanish) originates in the misassumption that the population had come from Egypt. Other common exonyms such as *Zigeuner* (German), *Tsigane* (French), and *Cigan* (Slavic) are likewise based on the mistaken association of the population, probably with a Manichean sect, the *Athinganoi*, in the Byzantine Empire. The self-designation is *Rom* or (plural) *Roma* (< Sanskrit *ḍoma*).

A major division occurred during the first century after arrival in Europe, the population separating into those who were kept as slaves in the principalities of Moldavia and Wallachia (= Romania), and those who were able to move on through the Balkans and fan out into northern and western Europe. Those held in bondage by the Romanian clergy and landowners were not fully emancipated until the mid-nineteenth century, at which time the freed slaves moved rapidly into the rest of Europe and some thence to the Americas.

Arriving in Europe at the time of the Islamic threat, being the first nonwhite, non-Christian foreign population to settle permanently in western Europe, and having no economic, territorial, political, or military strength, the Roma were soon subjected to the cruelest of repressive measures. With the advent of colonial expansion overseas, western European nations began to ship Roma to their colonies as a means of disposing of them; they were being transported to North America, for instance, by the Spanish, the French, the Dutch, the Germans, and the English. Even the Swedish government had such a policy. The biggest transatlantic migrations, however, occurred in the nineteenth and early twentieth centuries, following the abolition of slavery in Romania.

Romani falls into a number of distinct dialect groups. These have been classified as Vlax (i.e., Vlach or Wallachian) and non-Vlax, the latter consisting of Northern, Central, Balkan, and Iberian. Their classification, however, has been very unevenly treated (for a summary, see Hancock

1988). The most widespread geographically, as well as the largest numerically, are dialects belonging to the Vlax group.

The first known record of the language dates from 1542 and consists of 13 sentences in a variety of northern Romani collected in a tavern in England by Andrew Boorde. These were identified as '*Egipt speche*' and were accompanied by a description of the land of Egypt. Two other early samples, both published in The Netherlands, were Johan van Ewsum's 53 words and sentences in '*Clene Gijpta sprake*' (ca. 1565) and Antoine Morillon's vocabulary of 71 Romani words in 'Nubian' published by Bonaventura Vulcanius in 1597. The first attestation from eastern Europe was Evliya Çelebi's short discussion of the language from what is now Greece in 1668, where once again the Roma are linked with the Egyptians. The first extended attempts to write the language were not made until the nineteenth century. There has not been ready access to literacy skills for most Romani groups, and some have consciously maintained a functional nonliteracy (in the coexisting non-Gypsy language, and as a result in Romani as well) as a means of insulating the Romani culture from outside influences. Since the increased participation of the Romani people in international affairs (for example, since gaining representation in the Council of Europe in 1972 and the UN Economic and Social Council in 1979), issues of orthographic and language standardization have become a central concern, and a language planning commission exists within the framework of the International Romani Union to address these tasks. The compilation of a multivolume *Great Romani Encyclopedia*, a general work of reference in the Romani language, is also a major ongoing project.

Vlax Romani (as a randomly selected dialect for discussion here) has a typically neo-Indic SVO or SOV structure, with two genders, two numbers, and three cases (subject, oblique, and vocative); it is also characterized by a set of postpositions which are enclitic to the oblique noun or pronoun. In some grammatical descriptions, these postposed forms are treated as separate nominal cases.

Perhaps the most distinctive feature of Romani is its division into two distinct grammatical paradigms, which operate separately for thematic and for athematic lexical items. The thematic lexicon includes items of Indic (both central and northwestern) origin and adoptions from all languages with which contact was made prior to entry into Europe, including Persian, Kurdish, Ossete, Georgian, Armenian, and Byzantine Greek; athematic items include later Greek, South Slavic, Romanian, East Slavic, Hungarian, German, and so on. Athematic morphology, mainly of Greek and Romanian derivation, is found in the nominal, adjectival, verbal, and adverbial systems:

	Thematic	Athematic	
Verb:	kam-áv	vol-ív	'I love'
	kam-l-ém	vol-i-sar-d-ém	'I loved'
	kam-l-ó/í	vol-i-mé	'loved' PT PPL
Noun:	kam-i-pé(n)	vol-i-mós	'love, desire'
	rakl-ó	beját-o	'boys, boys' SUBJ
	rakl-é	bejéci	
	rakl-és	beját-os	'boy, boys' OBL
	rakl-én	beját-on	
Adjective:	lošen-ó	vésol-o	'happy' masc/fem SG SUBJ
	lošen-i		
	lošen-é	vésol-i	'happy' masc/fem PL SUBJ
	lošen-é	vesol-on-é	'happy' masc/fem
	lošen-á	vesol-on-já	SG OBL
	lošen-é	vesol-on-é	'happy' masc/fem PL OBL
Adverb:	lošen-és	vesel-on-és	'happily'

Dialects of Romani are spoken by perhaps 70 percent of the world's 9–12,000,000 Roma. For some groups, these have become restructured through contact with coexisting non-Gypsy languages, in Britain, Spain, Scandinavia, Serbia, and Greece, for example, and can no longer be typologically classified with Romani. The language supports a growing literature, and in some places (e.g., in Australia and the former Yugoslavia) is used in radio broadcasting.

The two best available grammatical treatments, in the traditional framework, are Sampson (1926) for a Northern dialect, and Gjerdman and Ljungberg (1963) for one variety of Vlax. Hancock (1988; 1989) presents an overview of research on the language, and a history of the people respectively, while Uhlik (1983), Barthélémy (1988), and Demeter and Demeter (1990) are useful dictionaries.

Bibliography

Barthélémy Y 1988 *Dictionnaire du Tsigane Kalderash*. Chez l'Auteur, Abbeville

Dankoff R 1989 The languages of the world according to Erliyá Çelebi. *Journal of Turkish Studies* 13: 23–32

Demeter R S, Demeter P S 1990 *Gypsy–Russian and Russian–Gypsy Dictionary*. Russky Yazyk Publishers, Moscow

Ewsum J van ca. 1565 *Clene Gijpta Sprake*. Leiden

Gjerdman O, Ljungberg E 1963 *The Language of the Swedish Coppersmith Gipsy Johan Dimitri Taikon*. Lundeqvistska Bokhandeln, Uppsala

Friedman V, Dankoff R 1991 The earliest known text in Balkan (Rumelian) Romani: A passage from Evliya Çelebi's *Seyāhat-nāme*. *Journal of the Gypsy Lore Society* 5(1)

Hancock I 1988 The development of Romani linguistics. In: Jazayery M A, Winter W (eds.) *Languages and Cultures: Studies in Honor of Edgar C. Polomé*. Mouton de Gruyter, Amsterdam

Hancock I 1989 The Romani diaspora. *The World and I*: March: 613–23; April: 644–55

Sampson J 1926 *The Dialect of the Gypsies of Wales*. Oxford University Press, Oxford

Uhlik R 1983 *Srpskohrvatsko–Romsko–Engelski rečnik*. Svjetlost Publishers, Sarajevo

I. Hancock

Romania: Language Situation

The central feature of the language situation in Romania, as in certain other countries of eastern Europe (e.g., Bulgaria, Poland), is the existence of stable minority-language communities within the geographical confines of what would otherwise be a relatively homogeneous nation state. Any description of the situation must take into account the historical tensions between the various ethnic or national groups and the postwar communist government's efforts to create a strong, centralized administration.

The broad outlines of the situation are straightforward. The only official language is Romanian, spoken as a first language by approximately 88 percent of the population

(1977 census figures). The standard language is essentially uniform throughout the country, having been established as a standard only in the nineteenth century, though there is a fair amount of variation in nonstandard rural speech. Standard Romanian is the language of administration and virtually all higher education. Members of the national minorities (*popoarele conlocuitoare*, literally 'coinhabiting peoples') are expected to learn Romanian in school, and, with the exception of elderly rural people, most speak it well. However, there are provisions for the extensive use of minority languages in primary and secondary education, publishing, broadcasting, and the arts. These provisions are comparable to those made by other communist governments in postwar eastern Europe: wherever the ethnic composition of the population warrants it, newspapers and books are published in minority languages, and schools and state-supported theaters in minority languages are established.

Romania's twentieth-century territory is traditionally divided into three provinces: Wallachia (Romanian *Ţara Românească*) to the south, Moldavia (Romanian *Moldova*) to the east, and Transylvania (Romanian *Transilvania* or *Ardeal*, Hungarian *Erdély*, German *Siebenbürgen*) to the north and west on the continental side of the Carpathian Mountains. The two main groups of minority language speakers, Hungarians and Germans, are concentrated in Transylvania, which has a long history as a semi-independent feudal state. As early as the fourteenth century, the Transylvanian nobility was almost exclusively Hungarian, while the military and merchant classes in the developing cities were in many cases German. The peasantry was by no means entirely Romanian, but most Romanians were peasants. Romanian nationalist movements were active during the late eighteenth and nineteenth centuries, when Transylvania was part of the Austro–Hungarian Empire, and in 1920 the province was awarded to Romania under the Treaty of Trianon. The catalogue of wrongs arising from this complex history is both substantial and carefully tended by all the groups concerned.

There are Hungarians throughout Transylvania. They represent some 8 percent of the population of Romania as a whole, but in certain areas of the province they constitute a substantial majority. They do not regard themselves as Romanian. Hungarian remains in active use almost everywhere, in the officially supported contexts discussed above, and in shops and on unofficial (but not official) signs. The Germans, by contrast, are restricted to scattered settlements in and around the cities in the south of the province (e.g., Sibiu, German *Hermannstadt*) and various rural communities, especially in the Banat (the far western area around Timişoara). At the time of the 1977 census, the Germans made up 1.2 percent of the population of Romania as a whole, but under the terms of an agreement with the then Federal Republic of Germany, at least a third of the German population emigrated during the 1980s.

Throughout the country, there are small populations of speakers of other languages, including Serbs, Ukrainians, and Gypsies. Together they constituted 2.8 percent of the population in 1977. There is a large population of Romanian ('Moldavian') speakers to the east of the country in the Republic of Moldavia.

During the Ceauşescu regime, many of the provisions for minority languages were dismantled, in what members of the minority communities saw as deliberate Romanianization. It is difficult to be entirely objective about this: Ceauşescu's policies (in particular the destruction of villages and the 'systematization' of their displaced inhabitants in 'agroindustrial complexes') often affected ethnic Romanians as well. However, while some of Ceauşescu's policies have been repudiated, there is little doubt that ethnic and linguistic tensions remain a serious problem, and that the postcommunist regime has a strong Romanian nationalist bent. It is difficult to predict how the situation will evolve during the 1990s and beyond.

See also: Romanian; Moldavia.

D. R. Ladd

Romanian

Romanian is a Romance language spoken in Romania, in the former Soviet Republic of Moldova, and in parts of Hungary and the former Yugoslavia bordering on Romania. Almost 90 percent of Romania's population of 23,000,000 have Romanian as their mother tongue, and in addition there are 2,800,000 native Romanian speakers who represent 65 percent of the population of Moldova.

Romanian, or Daco–Romanian, so named because its development is associated with the Roman province of Dacia, is one of four varieties of the Romance subgroup known as Balkan Romance. The other three are: Aromanian or Macedo–Romanian, spoken in a number of communities in northern Greece, Albania, and the south of the former Yugoslavia; Megleno–Romanian, spoken in a small area to the north of Thessaloniki; and Istro–Romanian, spoken in a very small number of villages in the Istrian peninsula on the Adriatic. All four varieties are considered to have developed from the Latin spoken in the area of the Balkans covered by the Roman provinces of Dacia, Moesia, and Illyricum, with their separation being caused by the intrusion of the Slavs in the sixth and seventh centuries. Thereafter, any reference to, or trace of, the Romance-speaking population of this area is extremely rare. Two seventh-century chroniclers, writing in Greek and both using the same original text, mention a soldier in the Byzantine army who spoke these words in his native language: *Torna, torna, fratre*. The phrase, connected with an event during a campaign in Thrace in 587, is believed to be the earliest evidence of Balkan Romance. There follows, in the history of Romanian, a silence of almost 1,000 years.

The earliest text in Romanian to have been dated is a letter of 1521. Contacts in the fourteenth century with the Slavs south of the Danube resulted in the first durable cultural links, and, via them, in a Slavonic garb, the Romanians received from the Byzantine Empire its religion, art, literature, and, in the revised Cyrillic form, its alphabet. The language of the Romanians' literary culture was, until the seventeenth century, Church Slavonic. Romanian, when used, was written in the Cyrillic alphabet. At the end of the eighteenth century, a Latinist movement among the educated Romanian clergy of the Greek Catholic (Uniate) Church in Transylvania encouraged the use of the Roman in place of the Cyrillic alphabet, and at the same time attempted to 're-Latinize' the vocabulary by introducing an etymological spelling system that rendered *soare*/soare/ 'sun' by *sole*. The system made little impact on the Romanian writers of Muntenia and Moldavia, who, aware of their linguistic ties with the western Romance languages, in particular with French and Italian, sought during the second and third decades of the nineteenth century to 'modernize' the language by importing neologisms from French and Italian and by adapting them to the contemporary phonological and morphological structures of Romanian. The practical problem of matching the phonemes of Romanian with the Cyrillic alphabet led, via the stages of transitional alphabets in the first half of the century, to the abandonment of the Cyrillic in favor of the Roman alphabet in the 1860s.

Romanian in the 1990s is written and printed in the Roman alphabet with three diacritics; until 1989, the Romanian used in Moldova was written and printed in a form of the Russian Cyrillic alphabet. In view of the adoption of the new Romanian alphabet, there has been little time for the written and spoken languages to diverge. Romanian can be divided into a number of (sub)dialects. The principal forms are Muntenian and Moldavian, spoken in the former principalities of Muntenia or Wallachia (southeast) and Moldavia (northeast). Other dialects are found in northern and central Transylvania. During the nineteenth century, a convergence of factors led to the adoption of Muntenian as the literary standard. The most prolific of the language reformers was Wallachian who owned his own printing press to propagate his ideas, and it was the Wallachian town of Bucharest which became the capital of the modern Romanian state in 1859.

The isolation of Romanian has led to a number of features that distinguish it from the other Romance languages. The vowel system is notable for the presence of *ă* and *î*, both central vowels, the origins of which have given rise to much controversy, one school claiming that they derive from the Daco–Thracian substratum, the other that they result from a system of accentuation common to several Balkan languages. The first vowel, *ă* /ə/, most frequently derives from an unstressed Latin /a/ but may also appear in words of Slavonic and Hungarian origin: Latin *laudam > laudă* 'praise'; Slavonic *gradino > grădină* 'garden'; Hungarian *lakat > lacăt* 'padlock.' The second vowel, *î* /ɨ/, often derives from /a/ before nasals in closed syllables: Latin *campum > cîmp* 'plain,' but not in open syllables: Latin *annum > an* 'year.' Another feature that is attributed to the influence of the substratum is the fact that Romanian, unlike the other Romance languages, does not confuse Latin *ŭ* with Latin *ō*, but with Latin *ū*: Latin *gŭlam > gură* 'throat' but *gola* in Italian, Spanish, and Portuguese.

Extensive palatalization is a characteristic of the Romanian consonantal system. Unlike the other Romance languages, /t/, /d/, and /s/ are palatalized before a front vowel: Latin *terram > ţară* 'country'; Latin *septem > şapte* 'seven'; Latin *dicit > zice* (cf. French *terre, sept, dit*). Curiously, however, where western Romance turned many of the consonantal clusters inherited from Latin into palatals,

Romanian has substituted a labial: Latin *lactem > lapte* 'milk'; Latin *coxam > coapsă* 'thigh'; Latin *factum > fapt* 'fact' (cf. French *lait, cuisse, fait*). The lateral /l/ is regularly rhotacized, giving Romanian another of its features: Latin *solem > soare* 'sun' (cf. French *soleil*).

Romanian alone has preserved three distinct case forms: vocative, nominative/accusative, and genitive/dative. Like Italian, Romanian inherits vowel-final plurals from the Latin nominative: *domini > domni* (final -*i* represents palatalization of the final consonant). It has also reconstructed a neuter gender. Uniquely among the Romance languages, Romanian has a suffixed definite article—Latin *dominam illam > doamna* 'the lady' (cf. the western Romance pattern from *illa domina*)—and in this respect resembles Bulgarian and Albanian, but indefinites follow the normal Romance practice: *o doamnă* 'a lady.' Adjectives follow the morphological pattern of the nouns and agree in number, gender, and case. There are four verb conjugations, closely related to those of classical Latin. The present subjunctive shares the forms of the indicative, except in the third person, and is always introduced by the subordinating particle *să*. The verb *a fi* 'to be' is, however, irregular in both indicative and subjunctive. The future tense is periphrastic, the literary form being derived from the Vulgar Latin forms of *volere* 'to wish' (*voi, vei, va, vom, veţi, vor*) + infinitive. The choice of 'wish,' as opposed to 'have,' and the sequence auxiliary + infinitive compared with infinitive + auxiliary, as in western Romance, is a solution that Romanian shares with Albanian. The conditional, too, is periphrastic, based on forms of Latin *habere* 'to have' (*aş, ai, ar, am, aţi, ar*) + infinitive. The numbers are derived from Latin, with the exception of *sută* 'hundred' from Church Slavonic *suto*. For the teens and multiples of ten, the model of Slavonic has been calqued: *tres super decem > treisprezece* 'thirteen'; *tres + decem > treizeci* 'thirty.' The Latin conjunction *et* 'and' has not survived, being replaced by *sic > şi*.

The basic word order is: subject–verb–object (SVO). Yes/no questions are usually indicated by a change in intonation, but inversion of subject and verb is an option. Pronouns can be used in different positions as clitics of their full forms, and thus complicate word order: *fata a dat biletul controlorului* 'the girl gave the ticket to the ticket inspector,' but (*ea*) *i l-a dat* literally '(she) to him it gave.' The ability to distinguish morphologically subject from object increases the frequency of the order OVS, as does the use of the preposition *pe* (usually 'on'), which acts as an accusative marker for all pronouns and for nouns denoting persons. In these latter cases, the clitic forms of the pronouns are normally used reduplicatively: *Maria l-a văzut pe Radu* 'Maria saw Radu'; *pe Radu l-a văzut Maria* 'As for Radu, Maria saw him.'

Băiatul este englez şi a venit în România să viziteze doi prieteni români. /bəjatul jeste englez ʃi a venit ɨn romɨnija sə viziteze doi prijeteni romɨni/
'The boy is English and he has come to Romania to visit two Romanian friends.'

(a) -*ul* is the nominative masculine singular definite article;
(b) *a venit* is the third person singular of the compound perfect formed with an auxiliary from *habere* plus past participle;
(c) *să viziteze* is an example of the third person singular present subjunctive;
(d) *români* is a masculine accusative plural adjective agreeing with and following the noun.

Bibliography

Agard F B 1958 *Structural Sketch of Rumanian.* Linguistic Society of America, Baltimore, MD
Close E 1974 *The Development of Modern Rumanian: Linguistic Theory and Practice in Muntenia 1821–1838.* Oxford University Press, Oxford
Deletant D 1983 *Colloquial Romanian.* Routledge and Kegan Paul, London
Graur A, et al. 1963 *Gramatica limbii romîne*, 2 vols. Academy of Sciences, Bucharest
Lombard A 1974 *La Langue Roumaine: Une présentation.* Klincksieck, Paris
Mallinson G 1987 Rumanian. In: Comrie B (ed.) *The World's Major Languages.* Croom Helm, London
Rosetti A 1968 *Istoria limbii române de la origini pînă în secolul al XVII–lea.* Editura ştiinţifică, Bucharest
Rosetti A 1973 *Brève histoire de la langue roumaine des origines à nos jours.* Mouton, The Hague
Sandfeld K, Olsen H 1936–62 *Syntaxe roumaine*, 3 vols. Droz, Paris

D. J. Deletant

Romansch

SEE Rhaeto-Romance

Ronjat, Jules (1864–1925)

Jules Ronjat, a native of Dauphiné, was an amateur scholar who in his later years lectured as a *privat-docent* at the University of Geneva. He is mainly remembered for his posthumously published four-volume historical syntax of modern 'Provençal' dialects ('historical' here meaning 'post-medieval' and 'Provençal' meaning 'Occitan'), which began life as a thesis published in 1913. Also in 1913, he had published a second thesis, undertaken at the suggestion of Maurice Grammont, in which he studied the linguistic development of his bilingual child, Louis, whose mother was German and who also had the company of other German-speakers. Following his mentor, Grammont, he adopted a hostile attitude (expressed in his reviews of works on dialectology in the *Revue des langues romanes*) to linguistic geography as practiced by Gilliéron and his followers (see *Gilliéron, Jules*). He espoused the cause of spelling reform and applied his principles throughout his historical syntax (adopting, for example, such forms as *fonétique* and *istorique*).

See also: Occitan.

Bibliography

Ronjat J 1913 *Le Développement du langage observé chez un enfant bilingue.* Champion, Paris
Ronjat J 1930–41 *Grammaire istorique* (sic) *des parlers provençaux modernes*, 4 vols. Société des langues romanes, Montpellier

G. Price

Root Compounds and Synthetic Compounds

Languages frequently have ways of creating a new lexical item by putting together two freestanding stems or words. These new items are called 'compounds.' The literature of linguistics distinguishes two types of compounds: root (or primary) compounds and synthetic (also called 'verbal' or 'verbal nexus') compounds; the distinction seems to be one of structure and semantic interpretation, although there has been some debate over this in recent years.

1. Introduction

1.1 What Constitutes a Compound?

Both root and synthetic compounds are distinguished from phrases by a number of phonological, morphological, syntactic, and semantic criteria which may vary from language to language. Phonological criteria for determining compounds include stress and tone sandhi. It is well known that most compounds in English can be distinguished from phrases by their characteristic left-hand stress (*a gréenhouse* vs. *a green hóuse*). In Turkish as well compounds can be distinguished from phrases by their characteristic stress patterns. Most words in Turkish receive stress on the final syllable. Compounds are stressed on the final syllable of the first stem, so that *ilk okul* is a compound meaning 'elementary school,' while *ilk okúl* is a phrase meaning '(the) first school' (Yükseker 1987: 87). The Wu dialects of Chinese are reported to distinguish compounds from phrases via differing rules of tone sandhi (Anderson 1985: 41).

A typical morphological criterion for distinguishing compounds from phrases is that the nonhead element of the compound may not be inflected. For example, the initial element of an English compound must (usually) not be plural: **dogsbowl*, **filescabinet*. Similarly, the first verb in a Japanese verb–noun compound may not bear tense inflection: *tabe-mono* 'eat (stem)-thing = food' is a compound, whereas *tabe-ru mono* 'eat + PRESENT thing' is a phrase meaning 'something to eat' (Kageyama 1989: 76).

Syntactic criteria for distinguishing compounds from phrases typically include insertion (modifiers may not be inserted into compounds)—**bird metal cage* in English; anaphora (in Breton the nonhead element in the compound may not have a reference independent of that of the compound as a whole (Stump 1987: 15)); gapping (in Japanese, gapping cannot elide one element of a V–V compound and leave behind the other (Kageyama 1989: 76)); and lack of syntactic particles (in Chinese compounds a modifier is not separated from the modified element by the particle *de*, which must be present in phrases (Anderson 1985: 41)).

Finally, compounds are sometimes, but not always, distinguished from corresponding phrases by a semantic criterion: whereas phrases are typically compositional in meaning, compounds sometimes have undergone semantic drift so that their meanings no longer follow entirely from the meanings of their component parts. Of these criteria, the semantic criterion is perhaps the least reliable, since the most productive of compounding processes generally result in forms which are perfectly compositional in meaning.

1.2 Distinction between Root and Synthetic Compounds

Synthetic compounds are most often defined as those whose heads are deverbal, that is, derived from a verb, such as *truck driver* or *handmade* in English, *initiatiefnemer* 'initiative taker' in Dutch, or *Autobahnbefahrer* 'highway-driver' in German. Root compounds are all others, that is, all compounds whose heads are not derived from verbs, for example, in English such compounds as *file cabinet, sky blue, greenhouse,* or *icy cold.* In synthetic compounds the nonhead element is almost always interpreted as an argument of the deverbal head—so *truck driver* is 'someone who drives trucks.' Root compounds frequently have modifier-modified interpretations (*file cabinet*), or coordinate interpretations (*producer-director*) (see Sect. 2.3 for further discussion of the semantics of compounds). An alternative definition of synthetic compounds can be found in Botha (1984: 2), where it is suggested that a synthetic compound is a compound based on any word group or syntactic construction. Botha thus includes compounds like *long-legged* and *hard-hearted* as synthetic compounds.

Although the distinction between synthetic and root compounds is clear enough in principle, in practice it is difficult in some instances to decide whether particular compounds are synthetic or root compounds. For example, by definition *speech synthesizer* is a synthetic compound, since it has a second element which is deverbal, but *speech synthesis* is a root compound. Yet both display the same head–complement relation. Furthermore, are English compounds like *air traffic control* or French compounds like *essuie glace* 'wipe-windshield' = 'windshield wiper' to be classed as root or synthetic? Under an analysis in which *control* or *essuie* are converted from verbs to nouns with a zero affix, they might arguably fit the definition of synthetic compounds.

The distinction between root and synthetic compounds is one that may be applied to any language. In practice, it seems primarily to have been used in discussions of Germanic compounding. But compounds in Tagalog such as *pamatid-uhaw* 'thirst quencher,' (*pamatid* 'used for cutting,' *uhaw* 'thirst'), and *panawag-pansin* 'attention getter' (*panawag* 'used for calling,' *pansin* 'attention'), seem to be good candidates for synthetic compounds outside of Germanic.

1.3 Productivity

Synthetic compounds are typically completely productive; that is, new synthetic compounds such as *sushi-eater* and *driveway-washing* in English may be coined freely and are rarely noticed by native speakers as new formations. Root compounds may also be completely productive, but typically there is variability in productivity depending on the category of the base words. For example, in English and Dutch, noun–noun (N–N) root compounds are completely productive, but noun–verb (N–V) and verb–noun (V–N) compounding occurs only sporadically, and cannot be performed freely. Other sorts of compounding may fall somewhere in between the full productivity of synthetic and N–N root compounding in English and the near unproductivity of V–N compounding; native speakers of English are more likely to notice and to find peculiar new noun–adjective (N–A) compounds of the sort *stone-hard* than new N–N compounds. Some languages such as West Greenlandic and Turkana are reported to have no productive process of compounding at all, although why languages might lack compounding is not clear.

2. Theoretical Issues

Much of the theoretical discussion of root and synthetic compounds has revolved around the issue of distinctness: are root and synthetic compounds to be treated differently or are they to be generated and interpreted by a single set of mechanisms in the grammar? Basic structural issues and issues of derivation and interpretation are examined in turn.

2.1 Headedness, Inflection, and Internal Structure

A basic difference between root and synthetic compounds is the structural one. Root compounds have a relatively straightforward internal structure since, at least in the simplest case, there are only two morphemes, whereas the internal structure of synthetic compounds is somewhat more controversial. The fact that synthetic compounds consist of at least three morphemes leaves open two structural possibilities.

For categories X and Y, endocentric root compounds exhibit either structure (1a) or structure (1b).

$$\text{(a)} \quad \underset{Y \quad X}{\overset{X}{\diagdown}} \qquad \text{(b)} \quad \underset{X \quad Y}{\overset{X}{\diagdown}} \qquad\qquad (1)$$

(1a) is a right-headed structure, that is, one where the compound as a whole exhibits the categorial and morphosyntactic properties (e.g., gender and declension class) of its right-hand member. Semantically in a right-headed root compound the compound as a whole typically is a subset of the item or idea denoted by the right-hand member; so a *towel rack* is a kind of *rack*, and *sky blue* is a sort of *blue*. English, Dutch, German, and Turkish all have right-headed compounds. Less well-known are the languages which exhibit compounds with the left-headed structure (1b). Among them are Vietnamese (*nhà thuong* 'establishment-be wounded' = 'hospital'), Tagalog (*isip-lamok* 'mind-mosquito' = 'weak mind'), French (*timbre poste* 'stamp-postage' = 'postage stamp'), Spanish (*hombre-rana* 'man-frog' = 'frogman'), and Breton (*gavr-venez* 'goat-mountain' = 'chamois').

Root compounds may be inflected either by adding an affix to the compound as a whole, or by adding the affix to the head. Languages differ in the strategy they choose. In English, where root compounds are right-headed and inflections suffixal, it is unclear how to determine which of the two structures in (2) is correct; the literature is silent on this issue.

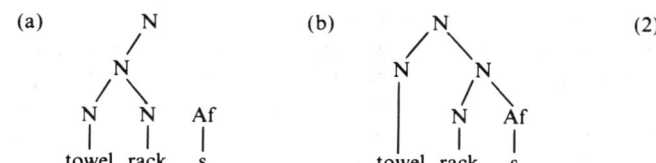

But for left-headed compounds with suffixal inflections, the difference is easily visible: both possible sites for inflection exist in Breton for different classes of compounds, according to Stump (1987). Example (3a) illustrates the structure with inflection on the head, (3b) the structure with inflection outside the compound.

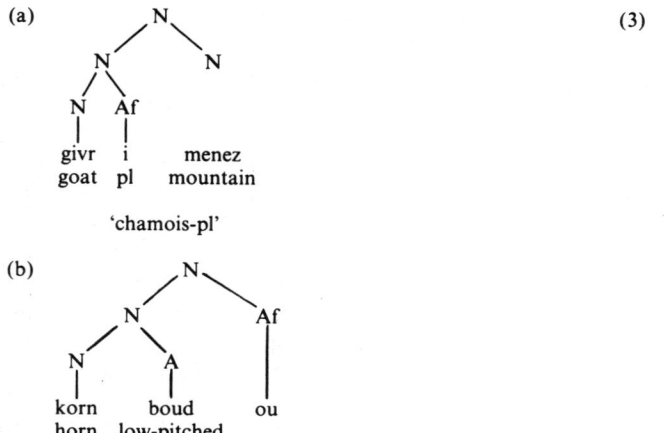

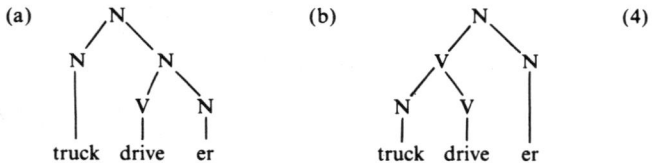

(a)

givr i   menez
goat pl mountain

'chamois-pl'

(b)

korn boud ou
horn low-pitched

'low-pitched horns'

(3)

Italian, French, and Hebrew have left-headed compounds that inflect on the head (Italian: *navi traghetto* 'boat-pl ferry' = 'ferryboats'; French: *timbres poste* 'stamp-pl post-age' = 'postage stamps'; Hebrew: *bat-ey sefer* 'house-pl book' = 'schools').

The internal structure of synthetic compounds, at least of right-headed ones, has been a subject of some dispute; the issue is whether the deverbalizing affix is structurally sister to the right-hand stem of the compound, as in (4a), or to the compound as a whole, as in (4b).

(a)   (b)   (4)

truck drive er   truck drive er

Although (4b) more directly illustrates the intimate connection between the verb on which the compound is based and its argument, and has been argued for in Lieber (1983) and Roeper (1988), (4a) is the more widely agreed upon structure (Selkirk 1982; Booij 1988; among others), at least for English and other Germanic languages. English and the Germanic languages in general do not have a productive class of N–V root compounds; since (4b) implies that the highly productive synthetic compounds are based on N–V root compounds which do not exist independently, it is less plausible as the structure of synthetic compounds for these languages. This of course does not rule out (4b) as a possible structure for some languages. Similar structural ambiguity could arise in languages with left-headed synthetic compounds where the deverbalizing morpheme is a prefix, as is the case, for example in Tagalog compounds like *pamatid uhaw* 'used for cutting-thirst' = 'thirst quencher,' where the deverbalizing prefix is *pang-*.

2.2 Derivation of Compounds in Generative Theory

An issue of primary concern in linguistic theory since the 1960s has been the derivation of root and synthetic compounds. Analyses can be divided roughly into three periods: (a) early transformational, (b) lexicalist, and (c) post-lexicalist, following major developments in syntactic theory.

Lees (1960) proposed the earliest transformational treatment of compounding, one in which a nominal compound is derived by reduction from a full sentence. He observes that the relationship between the two elements of a compound is very similar to the relationship among constituents in a full sentence. For example, the N–N compound *marrow bone* is generated from the sentence *The bone has marrow* which is reduced by successive transformations as follows: *the bone has marrow→bone which has marrow→bone with marrow→marrow bone* (Lees 1960: 133). Interestingly, Lees does not distinguish root and synthetic compounds, but creates certain sorts of synthetic compounds as a stage in the generation of root compounds. The N–N compound *oil well*, for example, is generated from *well yielding oil* via *oil-yielding well* (Lees 1960: 145). *Oil-yielding* is of course a synthetic compound. Lees realizes that a large number of transformations would be necessary for deriving all possible nominal compounds, the chief fault for which his analysis has been criticized.

Levi (1977) follows in the tradition of Lees, attempting to generate compounds as reductions of relative clauses and NP complements. Her claim, however, is that the range of underlying base structures, and therefore the number of reduction transformations can be strictly limited (1977: 6); compounds are derived either by deletion of a small set of predicates or by nominalization of the predicate of the underlying structure. Again, Levi does not distinguish between root and synthetic compounds.

Starting in the mid-1970s, theories of word formation eschewed the use of transformations in deriving compounds of all sorts, following the general trend of the lexicalist era to restrict the power of transformations. Consequently, lexicalist morphologists such as Allen and Selkirk derived compounds with the use of word-formation rules of various sorts. Allen's (1979) compound formation rule is one of simple adjunction: $N_1 + N_2 \rightarrow [N_1 + N_2]_{N_3}$. This rule accounts only for N–N compounds, but does not distinguish between root and synthetic N–N compounds; Allen assumes that rules of word formation cannot in fact distinguish those N_2s which are deverbal from those which are not. Selkirk (1982) uses rules of the sort N→NN or N→NA to generate compounds. Analogous to the phrase structure rules of standard generative syntax, these rules put together new compounds within a separate morphological component of the grammar. Again, a single set of rewrite rules produces root and synthetic compounds (see Botha (1984) for a thorough critique of lexicalist analyses of compounding).

The third period in the derivation of compounds in fact echoes the first. Following Baker's (1987) analysis of noun incorporation, Roeper (1988) again proposes to analyze synthetic compounds via a movement transformation. Baker argues that an Onandaga sentence like *Pet waʔ-ha-hwist-ahtu-ʔt-aʔ* ('Pat PAST-3MascSg-money-lost-CAUS-ASP' = 'Pat money-lost') derives from *Pet waʔ-ha-htu-ʔt-aʔ neʔ o-hwist-aʔ* ('Pat PAST-3MascSg/3Neut-lost-CAUS-ASP the PRE-money-SUF' = 'Pat lost the money') by incorporation of the object noun into the lexical verb form. Roeper (1988) adapts a similar analysis to English synthetic compounding. An object noun in English incorporates into a lexical verb form by moving leftward and adjoining to

3609

that verb; movement of the affix -*ing* into the verb triggers a change of category to N: roughly,

-ing ᵥ[throw] ₙₚ[ₙ[rock]]→-ing ᵥ[ₙ[rock]ᵥ[throw]]

→ₙ[ₙ[rock]ᵥ[throw] ing]

(Roeper 1988: 190). Although neither Baker nor Roeper discusses the issue explicitly, it is clear that root compounds must be derived differently in this postlexicalist analysis.

2.3 Interpretation of Root and Synthetic Compounds

Whereas the majority of analyses of compounding in the three decades since the 1960s derive root and synthetic compounds using the same mechanisms, many analysts assume that different principles of interpretation are at work in root and synthetic compounds. Root compounds, especially N–N root compounds, are relatively free in interpretation. Although, as Allen (1979: 94) points out, a compound like *water mill* has an institutionalized meaning 'mill powered by water,' it could conceivably also mean 'mill which produces water' (like *steel mill*), 'mill which contains water' (like *water jug*), 'mill where people drink water' (like *water hole*), or even 'mill which floats on water' (like *water lily*). Indeed any meaning consistent with the semantic features (for example, animacy or concreteness) of *water* and *mill* is conceivable. The position of the head on the right in English compounds determines the one fundamental semantic constraint on the interpretation of root compounds, that a *water mill* is a kind of *mill*, and not a kind of *water*.

The interpretation of synthetic compounds is much more closely constrained, however. Specifically, the first element of a synthetic compound must be interpretable as the internal (roughly nonsubject) argument of the verbal base of the second element; thus an *apple polisher* is 'someone or something which polishes apples.' This principle is formulated by Roeper and Siegel (1978: 208) as the First Sister Principle (FSP). When the second element of the synthetic compound lacks an internal argument, as is the case with passive participles, a nonargument noun can be the first element, as, for example, in *homemade*. The first element in a synthetic compound cannot be interpreted as a subject argument; Selkirk points out (1982: 34) that compounds like *girl-swimming are impossible. Furthermore, if a verb has more than one obligatory argument, all arguments must be satisfied within the synthetic compound; that is, synthetic compounds based on a verb like *put* which requires an object and a locative argument are impossible (*bookputter on shelves, *shelfputter of books). Selkirk calls this the First Order Projection Condition (FOPC).

Still, there is some evidence that the principles of interpretation at work in synthetic compounds may be at work in root compounds as well. Lieber (1983) argues that the possibility of coining new N–V and V–N root compounds in English is limited by the fact that verbs must be able to assign all of their obligatory arguments within the compound. Root compounds like *shelf put or *put shelf are ruled out for the same reason that the synthetic compound *shelfputter is. On the other hand, N–N root compounds are not ruled out by the FSP or FOPC since nouns typically do not have argument structures that must be fulfilled (this will be the case unless a noun is itself derived from a verb). Boase-Beier and Toman (1987) suggest that assignment of arguments goes on within German root compounds as well,

for example, in *Eßapfel* 'eating apple,' and *menschenähnlich* 'man similar,' among others. Much remains to be done however in assessing the extent to which the argument structures of argument-taking categories can or must be fulfilled within root compounds in other languages.

Bibliography

Allen M 1979 *Morphological investigations*. Unpublished PhD diss, University of Connecticut, Storrs, CT

Anderson S R 1985 Typological distinctions in word formation. In: Shopen T (ed.) *Language Typology and Syntactic Description*, vol. III. Cambridge University Press, Cambridge

Baker M C 1987 *Incorporation: A Theory of Grammatical Function Changing*. University of Chicago Press, Chicago, IL

Boase-Beier J, Toman J 1987 On θ-role assignment in German compounds. In: Asbach-Schnitker B, Roggenhofer J (eds.) *Neuere Forschungen zur Wortbildung und Historiographie der Linguistik*. Gunter Narr Verlag, Tübingen

Booij G 1988 The relation between inheritance and argument linking: Deverbal nouns in Dutch. In: Everaert M, Evers A, Huybregts R, Trommelen M (eds.) *Morphology and Modularity: In Honour of Henk Schultink*. Foris, Dordrecht

Botha R 1984 *Morphological Mechanisms: Lexicalist Analyses of Synthetic Compounding*. Pergamon Press, Oxford

Kageyama T 1989 The place of morphology in the grammar: Verb–verb compounds in Japanese. *Yearbook of Morphology* 2: 73–94

Lees R B 1960 *The Grammar of English Nominalizations*. Indiana University, Bloomington, IN

Levi J N 1977 *The Syntax and Semantics of Complex Nominals*. Academic Press, New York

Lieber R 1983 Argument linking and compounds in English. *LIn* 14: 251–85

Roeper T 1988 Compound syntax and head movement. *Yearbook of Morphology* 1: 187–228

Roeper T, Siegel M E A 1978 A lexical transformation for verbal compounds. *LIn* 9: 199–260

Selkirk E O 1982 *The Syntax of Words*. MIT Press, Cambridge, MA

Stump G 1987 Headedness and inflection of compounds in Breton. Unpublished MS, University of Kentucky, Lexington, KY

Yükseker, H 1987 Turkish nominal compounds. *Toronto Working Papers in Linguistics* 7: 83–102

R. Lieber

Rosetta Stone

The Rosetta Stone is the key to ancient Egyptian civilization (see *Egyptian Hieroglyphs*). It was discovered, built into a fortress at the Rosetta mouth of the Nile, in July 1799 by officers of Napoleon's expedition to Egypt, and it was quickly realized that the text, written in Egyptian hieroglyphics and demotic, but also in Greek—a known language—might provide the long-lost clue to the decipherment of Egyptian. After the surrender of French forces in Egypt to the British in 1801, the black basalt Stone was given, along with other antiquities, to the British Museum, where it is now exhibited. A translation of the Greek text of the Stone was soon in circulation throughout Europe, and it attracted the attention of Orientalists such as Åkerblad and Silvestre de Sacy. In England, the problems of the Rosetta Stone were tackled by Thomas Young, physicist,

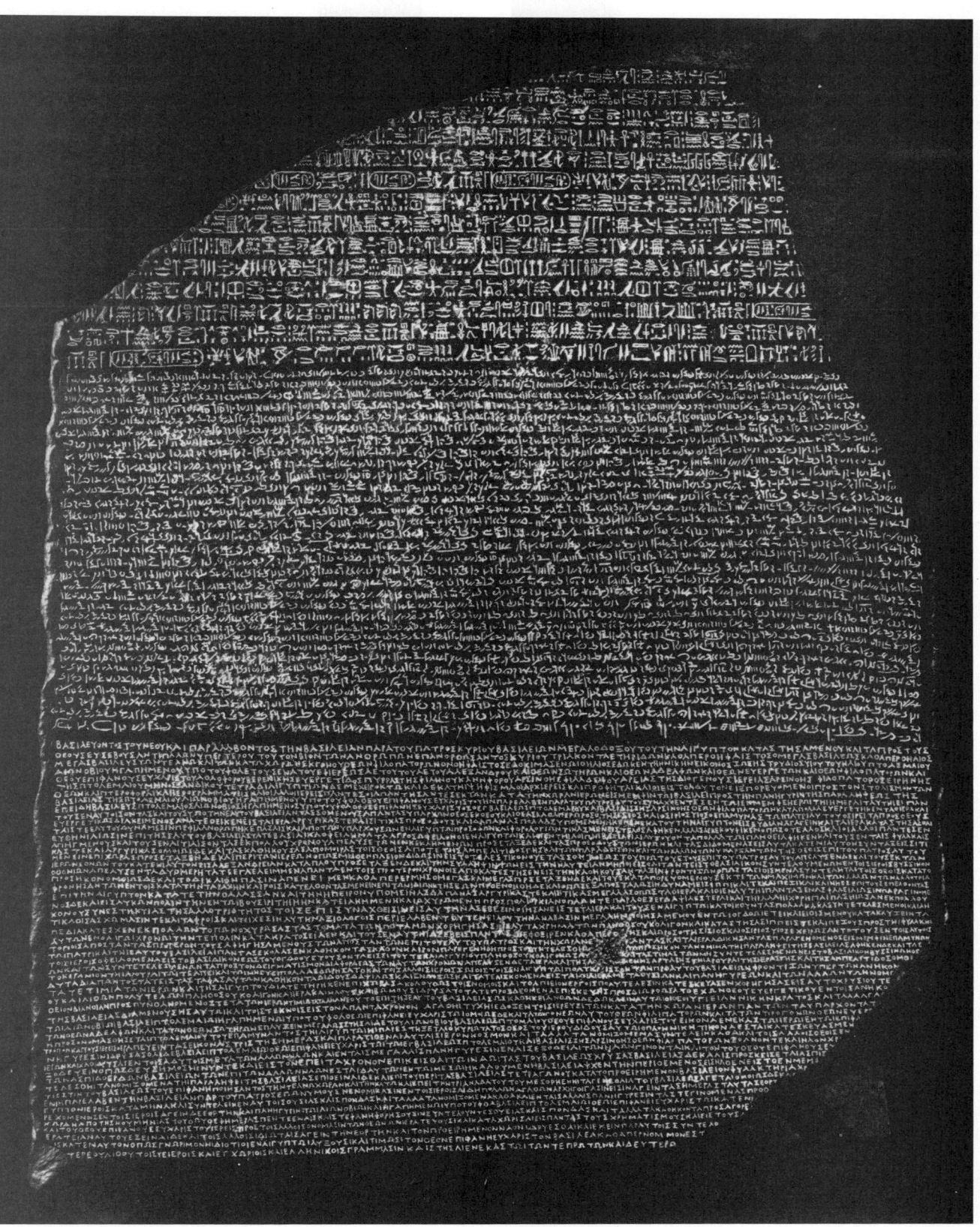

Figure 1. The Rosetta Stone. By courtesy of the British Museum, London.

linguist, and optician. Young made important contributions to the study of the hieroglyphic text, and achieved even more progress with the central (demotic) section of the Stone, which is the best preserved; however, the decipherment of the hieroglyphic was essentially the work of the French scholar, Jean-François Champollion (1790–1832). Champollion's method was outlined in his *Lettre à M. Dacier*, which was completed in September, 1822. He began by reading Greek names such as Ptolemy and Cleopatra, which he knew from the Stone and from another, shorter, bilingual text. The fortunate fact that these names contained the same sounds in different positions helped Champollion to draw up a hieroglyphic alphabet, on the lines already suggested by Young. However, the French Egyptologist went far beyond this, proceeding rapidly to decipher the names of earlier Pharaohs discovered on other monuments. A knowledge of Coptic grammar and vocabulary, and a list of kings' names preserved in classical sources, greatly aided his efforts (see *Ancient Egyptian and Coptic*). By the end of his short life, Champollion was able to read ancient Egyptian, and was well on the way to reconstructing Pharaonic history, religion, and civilization.

The text of the Rosetta Stone records a decree set up in the temples of Egypt in 196 BC, during the reign of the Greek Pharaoh, Ptolemy V Epiphanes. The generosity of the ruler toward the Egyptian temples is emphasized, and the best possible light put on the fact that he had just suppressed an Egyptian revolt. In return, the Egyptian priesthood agree to celebrate the royal cult with renewed splendor. The concessions made by the crown are far greater than the cosmetic actions of the native priesthood, and the whole text gives a valuable insight into the realities of Hellenistic politics. Other copies of this inscription are now known.

Ancient Egyptian would have been deciphered sooner or later, as the number of texts on stone or papyrus constantly increased throughout the nineteenth century, but the Rosetta Stone gave a dramatic birth to the new science of Egyptology. It is certainly a major landmark in the history of linguistics, and it is also an important symbol of the modern world's need to understand its origins (see Fig. 1).

See also: Silvestre de Sacy, Baron Antoine-Isaac; Young, Thomas; Champollion, Jean-François.

Bibliography

Andrews C A R 1981 *The Rosetta Stone*. British Museum Publications, London
Pope M 1975 *The Story of Decipherment*. Thames and Hudson, London
Quirke S, Andrews C A R 1988 *The Rosetta Stone; Facsimile Drawing, with an Introduction and Translations*. British Museum Publications, London

J. D. Ray

Rosetti, Alexandru (1895–1990)

Alexandru Rosetti was born in Bucharest on October 23, 1895. After graduating in 1920 at the University of Bucharest he spent eight years in Paris where he studied under Meillet, Rousselot, and Gilliéron (see *Meillet, Antoine (Paul Jules)*; *Rousselot, Pierre Jean, Abbé*; *Gilliéron, Jules*)

among others and obtained his doctorate in 1926 for a thesis on Romanian historical phonetics. He returned to Romania in 1928 to take up a post at the University of Bucharest and in 1932 was promoted to the rank of professor. In 1938 he succeeded his former teacher, Ovid Densusianu, in the chair of the Romanian language which he was to occupy until his retirement in 1965. He maintained throughout his long life his preoccupation with phonetics, both historical and theoretical, and directed (1963–69) the Center for Phonetic and Dialectal Research in Bucharest. His authoritative history of the Romanian language up to the sixteenth century, which was first published in six parts (1938–66), was revised in one volume, taking it up to the seventeenth century, in 1968 (3rd edn., 1986). He also made important contributions to general linguistic theory, in particular with his book (1943) tackling the problem of defining the 'word' as a linguistic entity. He founded and edited the periodical *Bulletin linguistique* (1933–48) and later, when existing journals were discontinued and replaced by others after the communist regime took full control of the country in 1948, edited at various times the periodicals *Studii şi cercetări lingvistice*; *Fonetică şi dialectologie*; *Revue roumaine de linguistique*; and *Cahiers de linguistique théorique et appliquée*. In the 1930s he was closely associated with King Carol II and was editorial director (1933–45) of the Royal Foundation for Literature and Art. He succeeded, however, in coexisting with the post-1948 communist regime (he was, indeed, one of the foundation members of the Academy of the Romanian People's Republic which replaced the Romanian Academy in that year), but (unlike some others) without compromising his intellectual probity. He outlived the regime by two months and one of his last acts, after the overthrow of Nicolae Ceauşescu in December 1989, was to call for the full restoration of the Institute of Phonetics which, like various other institutions, had been downgraded. This was done and, after his death in Bucharest on February 27, 1990, the Institute was renamed after him. (Bibliographies of his writings up to 1965, 1975, and 1980 respectively may be found in Rosetti 1965, 1975, 1980.)

Bibliography

Rosetti A 1926 *Recherches sur la phonétique du roumain au XVIe siècle*. Champion, Paris
Rosetti A 1947 *Le Mot: Esquisse d'une théorie générale*. Munksgaard, Copenhagen
Rosetti A, Cazacu B, Onu L 1961 *Istoria limbii romîne literare: De la origini pînă la începutul secolului al XIX-lea*. Editura ştiinţifică, Bucharest
Rosetti A 1965 *Omagiu lu: Alexandru Rosetti la 70 de ani*. Editura Academiei, Bucharest
Rosetti A 1968 *Istoria limbii române: De la origini pînă în secolul al XVII-lea*. Editura ştiinţifică, Bucharest
Rosetti A 1975 Bibliography. *Revue Roumaine de Linguistique* 20: 445–49
Rosetti A 1980 Bibliography. *Revue Roumaine de Linguistique* 25: 457–60

G. Price

Rousseau, Jean-Jacques (1712–78)

Rousseau's *Essai sur l'origine des langues* mixes in a paradoxical way favorite topics of the eighteenth century and passionate—but also hesitating—intuitions about the politics of language.

The *Discours sur l'origine de l'inégalité* (1755) stresses the *embarrassments* of the question of the origin of language (see *Origin of Language Debate*), in a manner reminiscent of Frain du Tremblay (*Traité des langues*, 1703). Two types of conclusions were deduced: (a) this question is unsolvable and the efforts of such a great mind are typically vain (Kant; see *Kant, Immanuel*; Nietzsche, etc); (b) there is an absolute solidarity between language and society, from which some authors will infer a sort of linguistic revelation related to a fixed political order.

According to Rousseau, the *Essai sur l'origine des langues* was 'a fragment of the *Discours sur l'inégalité*, cut out for being too long and irrelevant.' In so far as the chapters of the *Essai* dealing with the 'politics of language' offer ideas differing from the *Discours*, it has been supposed that they give an earlier, immature state of Rousseau's thinking. The contrary was also argued: the passage 'cut out' would in fact be dealing with the polemic which opposed to Rameau's theory of harmony Rousseau's ideas about the 'melodic' musicality of Italian, supposedly lost by French and more suitable to opera.

Rousseau's complexities or contradictions about language can be traced back to the picture of the origins given in the *Discours*. Speech arises amid 'singing and dancing—true children of love and leisure.' 'The best singer or dancer, the one who was the most beautiful, strong, skilful, or eloquent became the most esteemed; and it was the first step towards inequality, and towards vice at the same time.' An idealistic, sentimental conception of language is combined—at least in a dialectic tension—with a critical and materialistic approach associating language with the rise of social damage. Words appear in an 'order radically heterogeneous to the natural one,' endowed with an 'irreducible autonomy and originality.' Modern criticism has stressed the fact that the birth of a real language is described as it took place in historical times, and then seems to be separated from the very principle of 'origin' (Starobinski 1990).

The link between speech, passion, and singing, based on a climatology opposing the 'northern languages' to the south, is partly borrowed from Condillac's genesis of human arts and polemically directed against his giving a prominent part to material needs (see *Condillac, Etienne Bonnot de*). Any paradisiac beginnings of man are revoked in the *Essai*, as well as a linear development of language, which seems to have more complex origins. The ages of the 'hunters' ('bloodthirsty barbarians') and of the 'shepherds' are characterized by social division and they are supposed to prepare the rise of a real civil language appearing with agriculture. On one side, the experiment of mutual help—which required some communication—seems to participate at each level in the transcending of animal selfishness towards the accomplishment of man's social nature. On the other, the *Essai* puts a critical emphasis on the depravation of urbane language, which became a cold and courteous instrument of oppression.

The first signs were 'primitive metaphors' (see *Metaphor*). This 'preromantic' topic, perhaps stemming from Vico, found its full rationality in sensualist philosophy, which sees words as dynamic and culturally signifying 'images' of the world, working on reality to give it some sense, just as metaphors transform things and designations by adding new meanings. This paved the way for Humboldtian relativism.

The *Discours de l'inégalité* had the provocative sharpness of a reference pattern opposing ideal to reality. The *Essai* produced a more complex picture which introduced violence and economical rationality of history into the origins of language, lost some of its critical power and left the genetic problem unsolved. It is understandable that Rousseau did not publish his 'scribble' (edited posthumously in 1781), while he was personally experimenting with the failures and ambiguous nature of language, always oscillating between individual and community (*Emile*), and the regeneration of a style challenging the heat of natural communication.

Bibliography

Porset C 1976 'L'inquiétante étrangeté' de L'Essai sur l'origine des langues: Rousseau et ses interprètes. *Studies on Voltaire and the Eighteenth Century*.
Starobinski J 1990 Présentation. In: Rousseau J J *Essai sur l'origine des langues*. Gallimard, Paris

D. Droixhe

Rousselot, Pierre Jean, Abbé (1846–1924)

Rousselot, known to his close friends simply as 'l'Abbé,' is one of the major figures in the development of that branch of phonetics known as 'experimental'; that is to say the study of speech by means of techniques devised to examine its physical characteristics more closely, and to make analogical records of speech events. It is so widely accepted today that it is hard to imagine phonetics without it, but at the end of the nineteenth century it was still in its infancy, and many phoneticians, including Sweet (see *Sweet, Henry*) and Jespersen (see *Jespersen, Otto*) were far from convinced of its relevance to the study of speech. There was a need for someone who could at the same time command both scientific techniques of investigation and an expertise in the observation of speech by more traditional means.

Rousselot was born in St Claud, a country town in Charente, France. He became a teacher and acquired some knowledge of Romance languages, becoming interested in the study of dialects, and he undertook a major survey of French dialects, though illness prevented its completion. He came to Paris in 1885 and was influenced by the teaching of Gaston Paris and Paul Meyer, among others. He came to realize that in studying the sounds of speech the ear on its own is not a sufficient guide.

In 1887 he founded, with Gilliéron (see *Gilliéron, Jules*) the *Revue des patois gallo-romans* and was already a distinguished scholar when he presented his thesis (Rousselot 1891), a work which exemplified the scrupulous attention to detail that characterized all his subsequent research into phonetics, and made use of his newly developed experimental techniques.

By this time there existed a number of instruments for the investigation of the speech mechanism, but Rousselot describes them as 'analytic' rather than 'synthetic' in nature, looking at isolated aspects rather than '*la parole elle-même*.'

He tried for many years to develop an instrument which would respond directly to the speech wave—what he called an '*oreille inscriptrice*.' His research included acoustic investigations into the nature of vowel sounds.

Although he did not invent it, and was not the first to use it, he developed and made extensive use of the technique of palatography. The insertion into the mouth of a thin artificial palate coated with talc allowed one to observe where the tongue had touched the palate in the course of a simple articulation.

The work for which he is chiefly known is *Principes de phonétique expérimentale*, which occupied him for 13 years, containing 1,250 pages and 751 figures. Rousselot regarded this work rather as illustrating the evolution of a new experimental science than constituting a carefully organized survey. While writing it he had been provided with an experimental phonetics laboratory by the Collège de France, and a Chair of Experimental Phonetics was created there for him. His informants represented a variety of different languages, and provide a mine of information. He edited the *Revue de Phonétique* with H. Pernod from 1911 to 1922.

Bibliography

Pernod H 1928 L'Abbé Rousselot (1846–1924). *Revue de Phonétique* **5**: 10–23

Rousselot P-J 1891 *Les modifications phonétiques du langage étudiées dans le patois d'une famille de Cellefrouin (Charente)*. Welter, Paris

Rousselot P-J 1897–1908 *Principes de phonétique expérimentale*, 2 vols. Welter, Paris

Rousselot P-J, Laclotte F 1902 *Précis de prononciation française*. Welter, Paris

J. A. Kemp

Rule Application

In general, the question of whether a particular rule may be applied to some phonological representation is answered by comparing the 'structural description' or 'structural analysis' of the rule with the feature content of the representation. If the representation 'satisfies' the rule's structural description, i.e., properly includes it, and if in the sequencing it is that rule's turn to be scanned, then its 'structural change' will be imposed. But the rule will not be applied if there is no such match between its structural description and the representation being scanned, or if it is some other rule's turn in the applicational sequence.

1. The Direct Mapping and Free Reapplication Hypotheses

The idea that phonological rules should be applied in a (single) linear sequence is of course not the only logical possibility (see *Rule Ordering*). Under the 'direct mapping hypothesis,' for example, there would be only one step in derivation between underlying and surface representation. Rules whose structural descriptions are satisfied by underlying representations would then be applied directly, but those whose requirements on some occasions are met only through the action of other rules would not be applied in these instances at all. As it turns out, the direct mapping

hypothesis is adequate to account for a great many required rule applications, for it is commonplace that the operation of one rule has nothing at all to do with that of another (see *Rule Ordering*). For example, the specification in English that voiceless stops must be aspirated at the beginning of the word or syllable has no bearing on the additional requirement that tautosyllabic sequences of nasal consonant plus stop must be homorganic. The initial consonant in *camp* is aspirated, and the nasal shares its place of articulation with the following consonant, but as neither of these requirements bears in any way on the other, the rules which impose them can both be applied directly to the underlying representation, presumably /kæNp/ ($\to$ [kʰæmp]).

Such one-step, 'simultaneous application' also suffices to accommodate derivations in which the operation of one rule might affect another, but in fact does not (see *Rule Ordering*). In cases where the application of one rule actually causes an increase in the number of forms to which another applies, however, the rules must be subject to 'sequential application,' for otherwise the required feeding interaction will not take place. Thus it is necessary that in Yawelmani Yokuts the rule of epenthesis precede rounding harmony, because the vowel introduced by epenthesis (e.g., /hubs + hin/ $\to$ /hubis + hin/) itself undergoes rounding harmony ($\to$ /hubus + hin/, ultimately [hubushun] 'choose' ACT AOR). If harmony could not be applied after—i.e., could be scanned only at the same time as—epenthesis, then of course epenthetic vowels could not harmonize (*[hubishin]). On the other hand, the correct feeding results would obtain if the otherwise unordered rules were subject to 'free reapplication' so that even after a single-step, direct mapping of underlying into derived representations the rules were free to apply again to any string which satisfied their structural requirements. All things being equal, this mode of application would, whenever possible, result in feeding rule interaction. It would also result in consistently counterbleeding rather than bleeding interaction, since the initial round of simultaneous application would not allow for one rule to eliminate some of the inputs to another. In order for Yawelmani epenthesis to bleed the shortening of long vowels in closed syllables, for example (/mo:xl + hin/ $\to$ [mo:xilhin] 'grow old' ACT AOR, not *[moxilhin]), it is necessary that epenthesis precede closed syllable shortening, not be applied with it at the same time. Under the conventional theory of generative phonology, bleeding interaction (as well as all other types) is accommodated through sequential, extrinsic ordering of the rules rather than through appeal to general principles which predict the required sequencing of rules (see *Rule Ordering*).

The strongest argument against direct mapping/free reapplication (and in support of extrinsic ordering) comes from cases in the study of language change and dialect variation where it would appear that the same rules must be applied in a particular sequence in one dialect but in the reverse sequence in another. It has often been observed that a certain diversity among dialects of Canadian English can be characterized in this way, for example. Vowel raising affects the diphthongs /ay/ and /aw/, centralizing them to [əy] and [əw] before voiceless consonants, as in *write* [rəyt] versus *ride* [rayd]. Voicing (actually, tapping) of /t/ also takes place intervocalically, so that /t/ merges with /d/ in *writer* and *rider*. But whether these words emerge as homophonous depends on the applicational interaction of the rules as just described. If raising takes place before (counterbleeds) medial voicing, then, as characterizes one variety of Canadian English, the diphthong in *writer* will be centralized in comparison to that in *rider*: [rəydəʳ] versus [raydəʳ]. But if voicing is applied before raising, and hence bleeds it by eliminating the voicelessness which raising requires, then the two words will be pronounced the same, i.e., both as [raydəʳ], which represents the speech of another dialect. As Kiparsky and Menn (1977: 48) observe, however, this variation can also be characterized in rather more 'concrete' terms, with, they suggest, /ay/ and /əy/ as separate phonemes and in the second dialect an additional rule (which the first one has lost) lowering /əy/ to /ay/ before voiced segments. Under this kind of interpretation, which easily extends to analogous cases, the rules are not identical, and the variation between the dialects is due to a difference in the rules themselves rather than in their mode of interaction.

2. Directionality and Iteration

In *The Sound Pattern of English*, Chomsky and Halle (1968: 344) propose that:

> To apply a rule, the entire string is first scanned for segments that satisfy the environmental constraints of the rule. After all such segments have been identified in the string, the changes required by the rule are applied simultaneously.

Since the program of phonology developed in that work also held that rules were not to apply to their own outputs (so that a rule of consonant apocope, for example, would remove only the last in a cluster of word-final consonants, not the entire cluster), the structural description of rules like Yawelmani rounding harmony as discussed above (Sect. 1) had to be complicated considerably in order to allow for multiple application. As developed subsequently, however, the theory of 'directional rule application' allows a simple distinction to be drawn between rules which do and do not apply to their own outputs. The former category of rules has been termed 'iterative,' exemplified earlier by the multiple, self-feeding applications of rounding harmony in the derivation of Yawelmani /hubs+hin/→ /hubis+hin/ via epenthesis, then /hubis+hin/→/hubus+ hin/→[hubushun] via two applications of rounding harmony.

The part of the structural description which undergoes a rule can be called its 'focus,' and the part which serves as the environmental trigger can be called its 'determinant.' In a rule of the form, A → B/C__ whose structural description then consists of the sequence CA, A is the focus, B is the structural change, and C is the determinant. Rounding harmony in Yawelmani would be a rule of this form, whose focus identifies a vowel with the same value for the feature [high] as that of the rounded vowel determinant:

$$\text{Rounding harmony:} \begin{bmatrix} +\text{syllabic} \\ \alpha\text{high} \end{bmatrix} \rightarrow [+\text{round}] / \begin{bmatrix} +\text{syllabic} \\ \alpha\text{high} \\ +\text{round} \end{bmatrix} C_0 \text{\_\_}$$

In order to feed itself, this rule must exhibit 'left-to-right application,' that is, first the /i/ in /hubis+hin/ (</hubs+hin/) undergoes the rule (→/hubus+hin/), then the syllable to its right is scanned so that the next instance of /i/ can be changed to /u/ (→[hubushun]). If the rule instead were subject to 'right-to-left application,' only the epenthetic /i/ would become rounded, and the rule would counterfeed itself by virtue of not scanning the string in a direction which creates new determinants for its application.

The fact that Yawelmani rounding harmony actually feeds rather than counterfeeds itself follows the natural or unmarked mode of rule application (see *Rule Ordering*), and with respect to iterative rules correlates with the observation that direction of application proceeds from the determinant to the focus. As the rule 'eats' its way through the string, in other words, its expected direction of application is toward rather than away from the focus. This principle of directionality gives rise to an alternating pattern when the result of iterative rule application is potentially self-bleeding. In the Micronesian language Woleaian, for example, the vowel /a/ dissimilates to [e] when followed in the next syllable by another instance of /a/, as in /mata+j/ (</mata+ji/) → [metaj] 'my eye.' When a longer series of syllables with the underlying vowel /a/ comes about, left-to-right application of the rule, a → e /__C₀ a, would proceed in a direction away from its focus and result in incorrect counterbleeding application; but right-to-left application toward the focus produces the observed alternating pattern that derives from bleeding: /xa+tapa+tap/ (</xa+tapaN+tapaN/) → [xetapetap], not *[xetepetap]. (In the few cases of marked rule self-interaction that have been discussed in the literature, special reversal of directionality would have to be specified.)

3. Other Aspects of Rule Application

If the structural change of a rule is already met by a form that satisfies its structural description, application of the rule is said to be 'vacuous.' An application of the rounding harmony rule presented above, for example, would be vacuous if it 'affected' a vowel which was already rounded. Rounding /u/ to [u] is certainly redundant, but it makes for a simpler rule than one which excludes already rounded vowels from its focus, and it allows for the further interpretation of the rule as an 'if-then' constraint on phonotactics, e.g., 'if in Yawelmani a vowel follows a rounded vowel with the same value for the feature [high], then it too must be rounded' (see *Conspiracies*).

Though the structural change of the rounding harmony rule is itself silent on this matter, it is a further fact about Yawelmani that rounded vowels are always back, i.e., the language has no front rounded vowels. Strictly speaking, then, rounding harmony must produce not only vowels which are [+round], but ones which are also [+back]. Since cooccurrence of the feature [+back] with [+round] is an independent generalization about the language, however, it would be misleading to include [+back] in the structural change of the rounding harmony rule, because this would suggest that it actually could be otherwise, i.e., that the rounding rule could have the effect of simply rounding vowels without also backing them—indeed, the rule would be one feature simpler if it did so. But under the 'linking convention,' the output of phonological rules is 'linked' to the universal marking conventions which provide the unmarked or expected values of features in their various segmental configurations (see *Redundancy Rules in Phonology*; *Generative Phonology*). One of these specifies that the unmarked value of [back] is [+back] for vowels which are [+round], as in the output of rounding harmony, and so this feature value is provided automatically, and separately from, the phonological rule which imposes the feature [+round]. In fact, under this conception of redundancy and markedness, a vowel rounding rule whose output remained [−back] would be more complex than the actual Yawelmani rule, for it would require that this feature be specified in its structural change in order to block the automatic provision of [+back] due to linking.

Sometimes separately expressable rules may be collapsed into 'rule schemata,' illustrated by the pair of linear stress rules affecting English verbs which can be conflated to the generalization, $V \rightarrow [+stress]/\_C_0(VC)\#$. The larger expansion of this rule, i.e., the rule as given but without parentheses, applies to stress the penultimate syllable in verbs which end in a short vowel followed by single consonant (*édit*); the smaller expansion, or the part of the rule remaining after the entire parenthetical expression has been removed, applies to stress the ultimate syllable in all other cases, as when the verb ends in a consonant cluster (*evíct*). The precedence of the larger, more specific expansion over the smaller, more general one then derives from a principle of rule application to the effect that the general rule is blocked just in case the specific one actually is applied (see *Rule Ordering*).

Finally, as expressed particularly in the theory of lexical phonology developed by Paul Kiparsky, a useful distinction may be drawn between 'cyclic' and 'postcyclic' application. Within the lexicon itself, rule application is cyclic. This means that lexical phonological rules obey the 'strict cycle condition,' which holds that phonological structure built up through the word formation process constitutes a 'derived environment' and that this is the only kind of environment in which lexical rules may apply. For example, application of the rule trisyllabic shortening in English accounts for the shortness of the stressed vowel in a composite form like *divin + ity* (the stressed vowel in *divine* is basically long), but the rule applies here only because the bracketed morphological structure [[*divin*]*ity*] is crucially derived with respect to the trisyllabic environment. In monomorphemic *nightingale*, by contrast, there is no morphological compositionality, hence no derived environment and no application either of trisyllabic shortening. As a cyclic, lexical rule, then, shortening is sensitive to the derived environment requirement imposed by the strict cycle condition (see also *Lexical Phonology and Morphology*). Postcyclic rules, on the other hand, are not sensitive to this limitation, but rather are free to apply 'across-the-board,' i.e., irrespective of whether a relevant derived environment has been created by the rules of word formation. The postcyclic, postlexical voicing of Canadian English /t/ to [d], therefore, takes place both in a polymorphemic word like *fatter* ([fædəʳ]), whose morphological compositionality constitutes a derived environment, and in monomorphemic *matter* ([mædəʳ]), a word which does not.

Bibliography

Anderson S R 1974 *The Organization of Phonology*. Academic Press, New York

Chomsky N, Halle M 1968 *The Sound Pattern of English*. Harper and Row, New York

Howard I J 1972 A directional theory of rule application in phonology (Doctoral dissertation, Massachusetts Institute of Technology)

Kenstowicz M, Kisseberth C 1977 *Topics in Phonological Theory*. Academic Press, New York

Kiparsky P 1982 Lexical morphology and phonology. In: Linguistic Society of Korea *Linguistics in the Morning Calm*. Hanshin, Seoul

Kiparsky P, Menn L 1977 On the acquisition of phonology. In: Ioup G, Weinberger S H (eds.) *Interlanguage Phonology*. Newbury House, Cambridge, MA

G. K. Iverson

Rule Ordering

Within the generative phonological system (see *Generative Phonology*), individual rules are not applied independently, but rather interact with others in the language according to their placement in a sequential list. Though often it makes no difference at all just where in this list a rule is specified to appear—in which case 'linear ordering' of the rules is quite arbitrary—at other times the sequencing of a rule's application with respect to one or more other rules is significant in that a different derivational sequencing would produce incorrect phonetic results. This article surveys the kinds of rule interactions that may be found in phonology, and describes the 'adjacency' relations that are expressed in terms of rule ordering.

1. Rule Interactions

The relationship one rule bears to another depends on the linguistic forms to which it applies (or would apply if not preempted by some other rule). In the conventional theory of generative phonology developed by Chomsky and Halle (1968), rules are 'extrinsically ordered,' i.e., their particular sequencing is a language-specific property determined only by consideration of what interaction is required in order to produce the correct phonetic forms. If a rule A is applied before a rule B in such a system, then A will bear one of the following three relations to B:

(a) A 'feeds' B if and only if the application of A increases the number of forms to which B can apply.

(b) A 'bleeds' B if and only if the application of A decreases the number of forms to which B can apply.

(c) A 'does not affect' B if and only if A neither feeds nor bleeds B.

1.1 Feeding

The feeding relation can be illustrated by a pair of rules from the frequently cited Yawelmani dialect of Yokuts. In this American Indian language, epenthesis serves to break up clusters of three consonants, which come about in word formation through the juxtaposition of a morpheme ending in two consonants with one that begins with a consonant, as when the active aorist suffix /-hin/ is appended to the stem /logw-/ 'pulverize': /logw + hin/ → [logiwhin]. (Before a vowel-initial suffix, however, such as the passive aorist /-it/, the stem's diconsonantal cluster remains intact: /logw + it/ → [logwit].) There is also in Yawelmani a general phenomenon of rounding harmony, according to which a vowel becomes rounded if preceded in the previous syllable by a rounded vowel with the same height value, e.g., the active aorist of 'eat' is [xathin] (</xat+hin/), but of 'swear,' which has a high rounded stem vowel, it is [muthun] (</mut+hin/). Both rules may apply to representations in which a triconsonantal cluster is immediately preceded by a high rounded vowel, for the consonant cluster configuration meets the structural requirements of epenthesis, and the high vowel produced by epenthesis in turn is crucial to meeting the structural description of rounding harmony. Epenthesis thus 'feeds' rounding harmony. For example, the stem /hubs-/ 'choose' when followed by the suffix /-hin/ first undergoes epenthesis (/hubs+hin/ → /hubis+hin/) to interrupt the triconsonantal cluster, then, because the epenthetic vowel is of the same height as the preceding rounded stem vowel, it also undergoes rounding harmony (/hubis+hin/ → /hubus+hin/, ultimately [hubushun] by yet another application of rounding harmony).

Epenthesis feeds rounding harmony in this derivation because it actively creates a vowel—the intermediate /i/—which otherwise would not exist and so could not undergo rounding harmony. It is in this quite literal sense that epenthesis increases the number of forms to which rounding harmony can apply, for if the former were not in the grammar (and triconsonantal clusters accordingly were acceptable, as in a hypothetical *[hubshun]), the latter would exhibit as many fewer applications as epenthesis would have provided vowels to interrupt consonant clusters following /u/. Just as epenthesis feeds rounding harmony, moreover, rounding harmony also feeds itself in the final step of the derivation /hubs+hin/ → /hubis+hin/ → /hubus+hin/ → [hubushun] (see *Rule Application*). Here an application of rounding harmony affecting the epenthetic vowel happens also to create the vocalic configuration required to induce rounding of the suffix vowel, too, which is to say that the rule of rounding harmony in this kind of derivation is 'self-feeding.'

In the phonology of English, to illustrate further, derivations involving both copula contraction and progressive voice assimilation also exhibit feeding interaction. When *is* contracts after (and cliticizes onto) a noun ending in a voiced segment, as in *Bill is here* → *Bill's* ([z]) *here*, the underlying voicing of the fricative /z/ does not change; but if contraction takes place after a noun ending in a voiceless segment, as in *Jack is here* → *Jack's* ([s]) *here*, the same devoicing takes place as affects the inflectional ending /z/ (cf. *boys, girls, dogs*, all with final [z], but *cats, sacks* with final [s]). Contraction thus feeds voice assimilation because it increases the number of forms—contractions following voiceless segments—to which voice assimilation may apply.

1.2 Bleeding

Another general property of Yawelmani phonology is that long vowels must be short when in a closed syllable (syllable division will be indicated by '.'). In open syllables a vowel may be either long ([goː.bit], from the stem /goːb-/ 'take in') or short ([go.pit], from the stem /gop-/ 'take care of an infant'); but in closed syllables a vowel is invariably short ([gob.hin], [gop.hin]). In long vowel stems with final consonant clusters, such as /moːxl-/ 'grow old' (the vowel of which appears as short in the closed syllable of passive

aorist [mox.lit]), it is possible for both epenthesis and closed syllable shortening to apply if a consonant-initial suffix is appended. The effect of these rules on /moːxl+hin/ is not *[mo.xil.hin], however, which would result from application of both rules, but rather [moː.xil.hin], showing application only of epenthesis. This result can be made to obtain by ordering the epenthesis rule before closed syllable shortening, because the application of epenthesis (/...xl+h.../ → [...xilh...]) eliminates the consonant cluster environment (/xl/) which is required for the application of closed syllable shortening. Since it decreases the number of forms to which the shortening rule applies, epenthesis is said to 'bleed' closed syllable shortening.

It is also possible for a rule to bleed itself, as would be the case with respect to epenthesis if clusters of four consonants were to arise in the course of derivation. The first three consonants in a string of four (/...CCCC.../) constitute one reading of the structural description of epenthesis (→/...CiCCC.../), and the last three another (→/...CCiCC.../), so it is logically possible that both applications could take place to yield [...CiCiCC...]. Though Yawelmani presents no morpheme combinations which produce intermediate quadriconsonantal clusters, Iraqi Arabic does, and epenthesis in this language operates essentially the same as in Yawelmani. Thus, clusters are interrupted by the introduction of /i/ between the first two of three consonants, as in /triid ktaab/ → [triidiktaab] 'you want a book.' In quadriconsonantal clusters, however, the epenthetic vowel appears only once, between the middle two consonants: /triid-l-ktaab/ → [triidliktaab] 'you want the book,' not *[triidiliktaab]. The application of epenthesis in Iraqi is therefore 'self-bleeding' since interruption of the second triconsonantal cluster (/l-kt/ in /...d-l-kt.../) happens also to interrupt the first such cluster (/d-l-k/), hence preempting the rule's reapplication.

There is also an epenthesis process at work in the phonology of English, one which interacts with other rules much as in Yawelmani. In English, consonantal inflections are separated from the stems to which they attach by an inserted vowel whenever the consonant cluster that would otherwise result consists of (nearly) identical segments. Thus, sibilant clusters are interrupted in plurals such as *garages, buzzes, judges*, but there is no epenthetic vowel in *boys, girls, dogs, cats*, etc. If the noun stem ends in a voiceless segment, the sibilant suffix also becomes voiceless whenever epenthesis cannot apply (*cats, caps, sacks*, etc.); but if the stem-final voiceless segment is itself a sibilant, and epenthesis therefore does apply, progressive voice assimilation is bled by the vocalic interruption of the obstruent cluster (*dishes, buses, witches*, etc., all with final [z], not [s]).

Bleeding rule interaction can be seen to be a consequence of the grammar's effort to bring phonological structures into conformity with the phonotactics of the language in as parsimonious a way as possible (see *Syllable*; *Word, Phonological*). If a rule's structural description is read as identifying phonological configurations which are impermissible in the language, and its structural change is considered the 'default' means by which they are brought into phonotactic conformity, then bleeding emerges as a natural mechanism for achieving that objective without actually having to apply the rule. Application of closed syllable shortening in Yawelmani, for example, is made unnecessary whenever epenthesis (which has to apply anyway to break up triconsonantal clusters) can serve also to remove instances of a long vowel in a closed syllable (but by opening the syllable rather than shortening the vowel). Satisfaction of the phonotactic constraint underlying the rule of closed syllable shortening comes for free, in other words, in just those cases where epenthesis has to apply in order to satisfy its own phonotactic requirement (see *Conspiracies*).

Feeding rule interaction can be viewed in the same light, moreover, though here no one rule can do the work of two. For example, the feeding of rounding harmony by epenthesis is necessary if, as can be presumed to motivate the rule, it is a phonotactically valid generalization at some level that a vowel in Yawelmani must be rounded if the preceding syllable contains a rounded vowel with the same height value. For epenthesis to feed rounding harmony is thus simply to conform to the phonotactic constraint that precludes unrounded vowels from following rounded ones of the same height.

1.3 Nonaffecting

The perhaps most common effect a rule A may have on a rule B, where A is ordered before B, is no effect at all. If closed syllable shortening is ordered before rounding harmony in Yawelmani, for example, rounding harmony applies to neither more nor fewer forms than if closed syllable shortening did not even exist in the grammar, because the harmony rule, defined on a rounded vowel followed by a vowel of the same height in the next syllable, is not sensitive at all to whether the syllables it scans are open or closed, or their vowels long or short. Hence, shortening will take place in the derivation of the stem /ʔuːt-/ 'steal' when it is suffixed by /-hin/, and /-hin/ following /ʔuːt-/ will undergo rounding harmony irrespective of closed syllable shortening: [ʔothun] (the lowering of the stem vowel to [o] is due to the operation of a later rule). The ordering of shortening before harmony would thus be entirely arbitrary, and represents a 'nonaffecting' type of rule interaction, or simply no interaction at all (see *Generative Phonology: Abstractness Controversy*; also Sect. 2.2 below).

It is possible, however, for a rule A applied before B to neither increase (feed) nor decrease (bleed) the number of forms to which B applies, by definition a nonaffecting interaction, and yet have an influence on the output of B. Say that in some language stress is regularly assigned to the penultimate syllable, and that final short vowels in trisyllabic or longer words are apocopated. A representation like /bane + ka/ would then emerge as [banék] if stress assignment preceded apocope, but as [bánek] if apocope preceded stress assignment. Under either ordering, both rules apply, i.e., variation in order would not correlate with either an increase or a decrease in the number of forms which undergo one rule or the other. But despite their technically nonaffecting type of interaction, it makes a phonetic difference as to what sequence these rules are applied in. The order which produces [banék], with superficial penultimate stress, contributes to the 'transparency' of the stress assignment rule since the surface form of the word conforms to the rule's output; the order which produces [bánek], on the other hand, contributes to the 'opacity' of stress assignment

inasmuch as stress appears superficially on the ultima rather than the penult.

Transparent nonaffecting rule interaction shares with both feeding and bleeding interaction the property that the environmental conditions which invoked the rule's application in the first place are recoverable even after the application of other rules. Just as forms like [bánek] assure transparency of penultimate stress assignment (despite the prior, technically nonaffecting application of apocope), the nonapplication of progressive voice assimilation in English derivations where it is bled by epenthesis (*dishes*, etc.) makes voice assimilation transparent as well, because that rule will not have applied in an environment which—due to epenthesis—no longer satisfies its structural description. When *is* contracts in the derivation of an English sentence like *Jack's here*, moreover, it feeds voice assimilation, whose application cannot be circumvented since its structural requirements are still satisfied; but as the rule then actually does apply to devoice the reduced copula, it remains transparent.

2. Rule Counterinteractions

When a rule A is applied before a rule B in a system of extrinsic ordering, A bears one of the three relations to B that have just been discussed, either feeding, bleeding, or nonaffecting. But B will also bear an applicational relation to A, definable as one of three counterinteractions:

(d) B 'counterfeeds' A if and only if the application of B would increase the number of forms to which A could apply if B were to apply before A.

(e) B 'counterbleeds' A if and only if the application of B would decrease the number of forms to which A could apply if B were to apply before A.

(f) B 'does not affect' A if and only if B neither counterfeeds nor counterbleeds A.

2.1 Counterfeeding

Illustrating once again from the rich phonology of Yawelmani, one observes that this language exhibits phonetic occurrences of high vowels only if they are short; yet there is good reason to suppose that some phonemically long vowels are high underlyingly. In particular, rounding harmony applies as if the long stem vowel in some forms were high even though it actually is not, as in the word [ʔothun], in which the suffix /-hin/ has undergone rounding even though the rounded vowel preceding it is not of the same value for the feature [high]. The equal height restriction is necessary in order to understand why suffix vowels do not round in representations like /gop + hin/ (→ [gophin]) or /goːb + hin/ (→ [gobhin] via closed syllable shortening), but do round in /mut + hin/ (→ [muthun]) and /hubs + hin/ (→ [hubushun] via epenthesis and multiple applications of rounding harmony). If the representation underlying [ʔothun] were considered to be /ʔuːt + hin/, then rounding harmony could apply to its suffix vowel under the same equal height conditions as in other forms; what would then be required in order to produce the correct surface form, in addition to the closed syllable shortening rule already established, is a rule lowering long high vowels in all contexts.

Once lowered, however, underlyingly long high vowels do not serve as the context for rounding harmony even when the following suffix vowel bears the same value for the feature [high]. Although the nonhigh vowel of the dubitative suffix /-al/, for example, does undergo rounding when preceded by a basically nonhigh rounded vowel, as in /gop + al/ → [gopol], /goːb + al/ → [goːbol], it is not subject to rounding when preceded by a basically high rounded vowel, as in /mut + al/ → [mutal], /hubs + al/ → [hubsal], or, especially, /ʔuːt + al/ → [ʔoːtal]. Thus, despite the fact that when lowered to [oː] the stem vowel of /ʔuːt + al/ has the same value for [high] as the suffix vowel, rounding harmony does not apply. This result can be assured by extrinsically ordering rounding harmony before vowel lowering, which will have the effect that lowering 'counterfeeds' harmony in derivations with an underlying long high rounded stem vowel followed by a nonhigh suffix vowel, viz. /ʔuːt + al/ → [ʔoːtal], /wuːwl + al/ → [wowlal] 'might stand up,' etc. If lowering were to have applied before harmony, of course, it would have fed it, but this interaction of the rules yields phonetically incorrect results (*[ʔoːtol], *[wowlol]); instead, the rules fail to interact at all, or rather exhibit the special kind of noninteraction known as 'counterfeeding,' in which one rule fails to feed the other when it in principle could have.

2.2 Counterbleeding

Since it is only long vowels that lower in Yawelmani (cf. [mutal], [hubushun], etc.), there is the potential for bleeding interaction between the rules of closed syllable shortening and long vowel lowering. Forms like [ʔothun] (< /ʔuːt + hin/) and [wowlal] (< /wuːwl + al/) illustrate, however, that lowering actually takes place as if shortening did not exist in the grammar, i.e., the potential for shortening to bleed lowering (and so produce *[ʔuthun], *[wuwlal]) is not realized. This failure of shortening to bleed lowering when in principle it could have also represents a special kind of rule noninteraction, known as 'counterbleeding.' Under assumptions of extrinsic ordering, the counterbleeding of lowering by shortening can be assured by ordering shortening after lowering.

Though the interaction between the rules of lowering and rounding harmony was characterized above as a counterfeeding one because an [oː] lowered from /uː/ did not induce rounding of a following nonhigh vowel, it is also counterbleeding with respect to high suffix vowels. Thus, rounding does take place in /ʔuːt + it/ → /ʔoːtut/ (and /wuːwl + hin/ → [woːwulhun], etc.) despite the fact that lowering causes the stem vowel to have a value for [high] which is opposite that of the suffix vowel. Lowering could have bled rounding harmony (*[ʔoːtit], *[woːwilhin]), in other words, but, since it did not, its relation to harmony in derivations involving high suffix vowels is counterbleeding, whereas it is counterfeeding with respect to derivations involving nonhigh suffix vowels. This shows that the ordering relation in a pair of rules is dependent on the forms they apply to, for it is quite possible for one relation to obtain between two rules in some forms, another in others.

The noninteractional, counterbleeding/counterfeeding effect of lowering in the phonology of Yawelmani is tantamount to its not being there at all except as a late, surface generalization (indeed, the rule is missing altogether from other dialects of Yokuts in which surface long high vowels do occur freely). By its failure to interact significantly with rounding harmony, however, long vowel lowering contributes heavily to that rule's opacity since various surface forms either stand in clear contravention of it (when counterfed by lowering) or require its application even in the superficial absence of proper conditioning environment (when counterbled by lowering). Although transparent rule interaction is by far preferred in languages, ordinarily calling for feeding and bleeding when possible, the opacity resulting from late application of long vowel lowering in Yawelmani is in fact quite necessary in view of its special status as a rule of 'absolute neutralization.' Since lowering merges /uː/ with /oː/ in all environments, the resulting loss of contrast between these two phonemes is total, and recoverable only from the effects of other phonological rules (as opposed to 'contextual neutralization,' which is recoverable from allomorphy that the neutralization itself creates). More specifically, the only reason a contrast between /uː/ and /oː/ would be proposed for Yawelmani in the first place is that effects of this underlying distinction can be observed among rules other than the one that merges the contrast. In the case at hand, if lowering did not counterfeed and counterbleed rounding harmony, then there would be no relevant difference between resulting forms like *[ʔoːtol], *[ʔothin] (which are actually [ʔoːtal], [ʔothun]), with underlying /uː/, and [goːbol], [gobhin], with underlying /oː/. The mere fact that the posited contrast between /uː/ and /oː/ is absolutely neutralized assures that the rule which accomplishes this must be delayed in the applicational sequencing until rules whose effect is to give evidence of the contrast have had an opportunity to apply—otherwise, there would be no grammatical function to be served by a phonemic distinction which is everywhere neutralized. It is a property of any synchronically retained absolute neutralization rule, in other words, that it will contribute to the opacity of other rules in the system, that it necessarily will fail to either feed or bleed them.

2.3 Nonaffecting

When a rule A is applied before a rule B, it is also possible—indeed, common—for B to have not even a potential effect on A. In the earlier illustration from English of feeding interaction, for example, it was noted that contraction of *is* created new input to progressive voice assimilation (*Jack's here*); but the relation that voice assimilation bears to contraction, which it potentially neither feeds nor bleeds, is strictly 'nonaffecting.'

If an earlier applied rule A does not affect B, and B does not affect A, their compound (lack of) interaction can be termed 'mutually nonaffecting.' It obviously makes no difference in which order (A > B or B > A) such rules are applied if transparency plays no role, as, for example, with respect to Yawelmani rounding harmony and closed syllable shortening, neither of which, either actually or potentially, feeds or bleeds the other. On the other hand, shortening must follow (counterbleed) long vowel lowering in the list of ordered rules, since long high vowels lower as well as shorten, and lowering must follow (counterfeed/-counterbleed) rounding harmony, since lowered vowels harmonize as if they were still high (cf. [ʔothun]). Thus, despite the fact that rounding harmony and closed syllable shortening do not interact, their relationship to long vowel lowering, whose own application must be sandwiched between them, does establish a unique order: rounding harmony > long vowel lowering > closed syllable shortening. Finally, since epenthesis must precede (feed) rounding harmony as well as (bleed) closed syllable shortening, the full set of ordered rules discussed here for Yawelmani places epenthesis at the top, to apply before any of the others.

3. Other Aspects of Rule Interaction

A not infrequent type of complex rule interaction is one that has been characterized as 'mutually bleeding,' actually a compound relation in which A bleeds B and B counterbleeds A. In a common analysis of standard German, for example, the voiced stop /g/ deletes after a tautosyllabic homorganic nasal (i.e., in words like *lang* 'long,' *sing.bar* 'singable,' but not in *un.ge.fähr* 'approximately'); obstruents are also made voiceless when in syllable-final position (so that /g/ is articulated as [k] in *Tag* 'day,' *un.sag.bar* 'unsayable,' but not in *Ta.ge* 'days,' *sa.gen* 'to say'). Velar stop deletion bleeds final obstruent devoicing, because deleted /g/ cannot devoice, and final obstruent devoicing counterbleeds velar stop deletion, because although postnasal /g/ deletes, /k/ does not (cf. *Bank* 'bank,' *sink.bar* 'sinkable'). Thus, the required sequencing of the rules is velar stop deletion > final obstruent devoicing, an ordering relation that results in both bleeding and counterbleeding interaction.

Pairs of rules in a mutual bleeding relation, as well occasionally as others, typically interact according to a general principle of rule application known as 'proper inclusion precedence,' often referred to as the 'elsewhere condition.' Interacting with one of the rules discussed in the preceding paragraph, for example, a common variety of standard German spirantizes /g/ at the end of a word when it is preceded by unstressed /ɪ/, as in *ruhig* 'quiet' or *König* 'king,' both with final fricatives (as opposed to plosive articulation in *ruhiger* 'quieter,' *Königin* 'queen'). The structural description of the spirantization rule, which affects the particular final obstruent /g/ just when after unstressed /ɪ/, is more specific than—and properly includes—that of the general devoicing rule, which affects any final obstruent whatever. Under these formal set inclusion conditions, the specific rule is predicted to take precedence over the general, and, indeed, spirantization must apply before devoicing in German lest the latter bleed the former, for /k/ is not subject to spirantization.

The ordering among all of the rules discussed so far is 'conjunctive,' moreover, because the output of one freely serves as input to the next in sequence if it satisfies its structural description. In the present case, where the counterbleeding precedence of German spirantization over devoicing is derivable from the independent principle of proper inclusion precedence, the fricative output of the specific rule (/g/ → /ɣ/) also serves as input to the more general devoicing rule (producing /x/, which palatalizes to [ç] after front vowels). For rules standing in the inclusion relation whose structural changes are either incompatible or identical, however, the observed ordering is 'disjunctive,' i.e., the output of the earlier rule does not serve as input to the next one. In linear accounts of stress (which nowadays is handled metrically; see *Metrical Phonology*), for example, the rule which stresses the penultimate syllable of English

verbs ending in a single consonant (V → [+stress]/__C₀ V C #), as in *édit*, properly includes the (sub)rule which stresses the last syllable in verbs ending with a consonant cluster (V → [+stress]/__C₀ #), as in *evíct*. But as their structural changes are the same, the specific rule must be applied disjunctively with respect to the general one, which will have the correct effect that main stress appears only once in a word that satisfies the structural descriptions of both rules (*édit*, not **édít*).

The sense in which the required ordering between rules can be determined from consideration of the grammar as a whole and from general principles of rule function, rather than from inspection of any particular language's phonetic forms, is often termed 'intrinsic ordering.' In a phonological system where word stress is completely predictable, for instance, any rule which crucially refers to stress (say, to lengthen stressed vowels in open syllables) obviously cannot apply until after stress assignment has taken place. This kind of necessary interaction may be called 'absolute intrinsic ordering' (here, absolute feeding) since it is impossible in principle for the rules to interact in any other way if indeed they are to remain rules of the grammar. This is the motivation as well behind the 'survival constraint,' which holds simply that a rule may not so interact with another as to result in its elimination from the grammar (if counterfed absolutely, for example, a rule would never have anything to apply to). Related to this, one can identify various approaches that have been taken to derive 'natural' or 'unmarked order' between rules, specifically, the view that rule interaction should result in transparency unless overridden, in the case of 'universally determined rule application,' by general formal or functional principles like proper inclusion precedence and the survival constraint, or, in the case of 'local ordering,' by language-specific stipulations. Thus, to return to Yawelmani, one version of local ordering would hold that the transparent feeding and bleeding interaction obtaining between epenthesis and the rules of rounding harmony and closed syllable shortening, respectively, need not be specified in the grammar at all since, whenever feeding or bleeding is possible, that is the expected, 'natural' mode of interaction between rules. The fact that long vowel lowering both counterfeeds and counterbleeds rounding harmony, however—the 'unnatural' mode of interaction—would have to be encoded arbitrarily in the grammar of Yawelmani. The universalist position, by contrast, would seek to establish a general account of why natural order is overridden just in the case of long vowel lowering, and would make particular reference to the consistently similar pattern of (non)interaction exhibited by rules of absolute neutralization in other languages (see *Generative Phonology: Abstractness Controversy*; also Sect. 2.2 above).

Freeing rules to apply according to their mode of interaction rather than to the dictates of a linear list removes an 'ordering paradox' that sometimes otherwise ensues. In Icelandic, for example, it can be shown that a rule of syncope operates to relate forms in the inflectional morphology, e.g., *hamar* NOM SG, *hamri* DAT SG 'hammer,' and that a rule of *u*-umlaut, which rounds *a* to *ö* before *u* in the next syllable, functions to relate paradigmatically associated forms like *barn* NOM SG, *börnum* DAT PL 'child.' When possible, syncope feeds—hence must precede—*u*-umlaut, as in the derivation of *kötlum* 'kettle' DAT PL from /katil + um/. But syncope also counterbleeds—hence must not precede—*u*-umlaut in derivational morphology, as in the sourcing of *böggull* 'package' NOM SG from /bagg + ul + r/. Because the required order for feeding interaction is syncope > *u*-umlaut, but for counterbleeding it is *u*-umlaut > syncope, a paradox emerges under the standard system of linear order, which must establish one and only one rule applicational sequence. Under the assumption that rules are not ordered in a single list, however, but rather apply (whether idiosyncratically or predictably) according to whatever interactional mode is called for (see *Lexical Phonology and Morphology*), it is entirely possible and nonparadoxical that a particular sequencing should obtain in certain derivations but not in others.

Bibliography

Anderson S R 1974 *The Organization of Phonology*. Academic Press, New York

Chomsky N 1967 Some general properties of phonological rules. *Lg* **43**: 102–28

Chomsky N, Halle M 1968 *The Sound Pattern of English*. Harper and Row, New York

Itô J 1989 A prosodic theory of epenthesis. *NLLT* **7**: 217–59

Kenstowicz M, Kisseberth C 1979 *Generative Phonology: Description and Theory*. Academic Press, New York

Kiparsky P 1968 Linguistic universals and linguistic change. In: Bach E, Harms R T (eds.) *Universals in Linguistic Theory*. Holt, Rinehart and Winston, New York

Kiparsky P 1973 'Elsewhere' in phonology. In: Kiparsky P, Anderson S R (eds.) *A Festschrift for Morris Halle*. Holt, Rinehart and Winston, New York

Koutsoudas A (ed.) 1976 *The Application and Ordering of Grammatical Rules*. Mouton, The Hague

Koutsoudas A, Sanders G, Noll C 1974 The application of phonological rules. *Lg* **50**: 1–28

Sanders G 1974 Precedence relations in language. *Foundations of Language* **11**: 361–400

G. K. Iverson

Rules

The idea that linguistic practice is essentially rule-governed has found widespread acceptance, especially among those engaged in constructive work in grammar or semantics, and has been regarded by some as almost self-evident. Nonetheless it is highly controversial within the philosophy of language. Proponents have suggested a great number of kinds of linguistic rule, and serious attempts at demarcating and explicating the concept of a rule have been made, whereas opponents have concentrated on more general epistemological issues particularly regarding what it is to know a language and the place that rules might have in such knowledge. (For further discussion, see *Convention*.)

1. The Concept of a Rule

1.1 General Characterization

The term 'rule' belongs to a group of terms, including 'norm,' 'convention,' 'standard,' 'regulation,' 'directive,' 'instruction,' 'law' (in the prescriptive sense), many of which frequently occur together in dictionary explanations,

sometimes presented as synonyms. Ordinary linguistic usage does not provide clear-cut distinctions and no taxonomic consensus has been established among theorists.

Nevertheless, there are differences between the use of the term 'rule' and uses of its cognates which to some degree explain why it is often preferred in theories of language.

(a) 'Rule' is less tied to the notion of an authority, for example with power to issue rules, than 'law' and 'regulation.'

(b) 'Rule' is more closely tied to the notion of guiding persons in action than are 'norm' and 'standard.'

(c) 'Rule' is more closely tied to the notion of evaluating actions as right or wrong than, for example, 'convention' and 'direction.'

(d) 'Rule' is more closely tied (than, for example, 'norm' and 'standard') to direct evaluation of action as opposed to indirect evaluation, in which someone is judged responsible for defects in a product. There is, however, a traditional distinction between on the one hand so-called rules of action, or ought-to-do rules (Tunsollen) and on the other hand so-called ideal rules, or ought-to-be rules (Seinsollen), such as standards for chemicals.

(e) 'Rule' has a stronger suggestion of arbitrariness than, for instance, 'norm.' It often refers to items that can be introduced, adopted, and replaced by decision, whereas 'norm' is typically used for standards perceived as not being subject to choice. Connected with this is the tendency, again marking a difference, to use 'norm' so that being in force, in a community, say, is built into the concept of being a norm.

(f) 'Rule,' more than related terms, is used with respect to special procedures (rules of inference) and institutionally created activities, such as games. The modern tradition distinguishes between regulative rules, serving to regulate preexisting activities (traffic regulations), and so-called constitutive rules, which define institutions and create new types of action (like checkmating).

(g) 'Rule' is tied to a notion of generality in a way which, for instance, 'instruction' is not and which is often taken to exclude overlap with the use of 'command.' Two kinds of generality are usually seen as characteristic of rules. On the one hand a rule concerns a type of action; it can be violated or complied with indefinitely many times. On the other hand it concerns agents generally, or agents in a type of situation; it can be violated or complied with by an indefinite number of people. Although this characterization is not without problems it points at a feature which can be claimed to be essential to the concept.

(h) There is a use of 'rule,' as in 'strategic rule' and 'rule of thumb,' such that an item of this more factual kind (sometimes called technical) is subject to direct justification: does complying with it generally lead to desired results? It is essential here that what counts as a desired result is well-determined; stating the purpose may be part of stating the rule (If you want to . . .) or else the purpose may be clear from the area of application of the rule (as in strategic rules of chess). This double usage is convenient, since something may be called a rule whether it imposes or just registers a regularity (such as a grammatical one).

In explicating the concept of a rule some writers are content to elaborate on features such as those already listed. Some proceed to analyze the structure of rules. Von Wright (1963), by using 'norm' as the most general term, distinguishes between 'character' (obligation, permission, prohibition), 'content' (type of action or activity; that which is obligatory, permitted, prohibited) and 'condition of application' (a condition that is met in a situation where someone can act in accordance with or against the rule). He also distinguishes between categorical and conditional rules, and between positive, negative, and mixed rules, depending on whether the content is a type of doing something, forbearing to do something, or a mixed complex of these. This analysis is then fitted into a so-called deontic logic, that is, a logic of rules (norms, or better, norm-statements).

Explications or analyses more or less similar to that of von Wright have been given within ethics and philosophy of law. What is generally missing in such treatments are distinctions between kinds of correctness: an utterance may be semantically correct and yet a violation of etiquette. That is, the particular respect in which actions are evaluated with respect to a rule is not perceived as corresponding to an ingredient in the rule itself.

1.2 What Rules Are

The question of what rules really are has received much less attention. It is common to think of rules as abstract entities. Some, however, take them to be linguistic, while others take them to be nonlinguistic. Ross, for instance (1968), takes rules to be a species of directives, themselves intrinsically normative entities that are meanings of prescriptive sentences, like propositions are of descriptive sentences. Although rules have even been thought to be particular inscriptions of rule-sentences, the concept of a rule is normally distinguished from that of a formulation of a rule, as described by Max Black (1962). Black, however, denies that rule-formulations designate, describe, or even express rules (as their meanings). Instead, to understand what a rule is we must look to the use of rule-formulations. This is in line with Wittgenstein's later philosophy (see *Wittgenstein, Ludwig*).

To Wittgenstein (1958) the concept of a rule is a family resemblance concept (see *Family Resemblance*): members of the family of rules have various features in common with other members, but it is misguided to look for any defining feature common to all members, an essence of rules. To understand the concept of a rule, consideration should be given not only to what is called a rule, but also to all that is involved in a rule-following practice, including training, explaining (how to proceed), justification (and limits thereof), and evaluation of actions by means of reference to rules.

Many other theorists insist on social function or social acceptance as part of what it is to be a rule. Ross, for instance (1968), takes a rule to be a rule of some community, a (general) directive corresponding to social facts, being generally complied with in the community. Bartsch (1987) characterizes norms, social rules, as the social reality

of correctness notions. This feature is particularly prominent in Shwayder's attempt at a truly informative explication (Shwayder 1965). Roughly, a rule (in the primary, communal sense) is a system of expectations in a community concerning behavior of its members, such that (a) members believe other members to have the same expectation, (b) the expectations of others constitute the reason for a member to act in accordance with them, and (c) members expect that other members conform for this reason. This idea has been developed and refined by David Lewis for the notion of a convention (regarded by Lewis as a kind of rule) and has, via Lewis, given rise to a whole tradition of varieties of the approach (see *Convention*).

2. Linguistic Rules

The notion of a linguistic rule is perhaps most immediately associated with very general rules of traditional school grammars; rules of spelling (e.g., *nn* never occurs before *t*), phonological rules (e.g., voiced endings turning voiceless in certain contexts), morphological rules (e.g., endings of regular verbs in various tenses), and simple syntactic rules (e.g., noun and verb must agree in number). Rules of this kind are explicitly stated, used in language teaching, applied as standards of correct linguistic usage, and, usually in contradistinction to much else included in grammars, called rules.

What should properly be called a linguistic rule, however, is another matter. To the extent that the required generality of a rule concerns its relation to behavior, the statement that *killed* is the past tense form of the verb *kill* is a statement of a rule, since it is general with respect to agents and highly general with respect to particular speech acts governed by it. Seen in this light the general rule about past tense forms of regular verbs appears to be a more factual or technical rule, a general guide or recipe for speaking in accordance with the more particular rules (governing individual verbs) that may be regarded as normative. In this way normativity, or the degree thereof, may be inversely related to the degree of generality.

Stating that in English *gold* is a noun, or a mass noun, is not generally considered as stating a rule, but rather as stating a fact. To the extent that the property of being a mass noun in English is a conventional one, however, this is a fact about a convention, and the statement may then also be regarded as a statement of the convention, or rule, itself. Together with, say, the rule that mass nouns do not take the indefinite article, the rule (about *gold*) so stated also has a share in syntactic standards of linguistic behavior. Indeed, from a formal point of view it may be regarded as a rule of higher order, implicitly laying down what other (lower order) rules apply to *gold* (namely the rules governing mass nouns).

On the other hand, however, the statement that *gold* is a mass noun may also be regarded in a number of other ways. The situation is quite unlike that with respect to formal languages. The class of sentences of a language for predicate logic is determined by a few simple clauses, stating on the one hand the basic vocabulary of signs of various categories, and on the other hand the formation rules, which comprise rules for forming atomic sentences (by way of joining terms and predicate letters) and for forming complex sentences out of these and the logical symbols (for example, if *A* and *B* are sentences, then *A&B* is a sentence). These rules are easily stated, and learned, and define the language in question (see *Propositional Calculus*; *Predicate Calculus*; *First Order Logic*).

2.1 Syntactic Rules in Generative Grammar

Specifying the class of sentences of a natural language, like English, on the other hand, is the task of modern generative grammars. The syntactic part of such a grammar may consist of a set of phrase structure rules, a set of lexical insertion rules, and a set of transformation rules. Rules of the first kind produce so-called deep structures of sentences (the most basic being S → NP VP, which, roughly stated, produces the category structure NOUN PHRASE–VERB PHRASE out of the category SENTENCE). Rules of the second kind provide for inserting linguistic expressions (lexical items) into structures, at appropriate places, depending on their respective categories (such as NOUN). Rules of the third kind are rules for transforming results of applying rules of the former kinds by way of operations such as reordering and deletion (as with the rule of equi NP deletion, for removing a repeated occurrence of a particular noun phrase).

Such systems are readily understood as systems of rules for producing sentences. They are stated and can be followed. It is another question in what sense, if any, they are rules of a particular natural language. On the one hand the grammar may be incorrect in the sense of producing sentences which are not recognized as well-formed by speakers of the language. Even if correct its rules are clearly not, in any strict sense, followed by the speakers. Neither is it generally claimed by linguists that such rules are subconsciously operative in actual practice. It is, on the other hand, claimed, for example, by Chomsky (1976, 1980), that a grammar which is adequate in a stronger sense represents the linguistic competence of the speakers, their knowledge of the language. If this claim is good there is a sense in which the rules of such a grammar are rules of the language, but in that sense they can hardly be said to define it (see *Cognitive Grammar*; *Chomsky's Philosophy of Language*).

2.2 Semantic Rules

With respect to formal languages semantic rules, concerning meaning, can be stated and regarded as just as normative/defining as formation rules. Carnap (1956; see *Carnap, Rudolf*) distinguishes between rules of designation for simple expressions (predicates—'H' designates Human—and individual constants—'s' designates Walter Scott) and rules of truth (e.g., *A&B* is true if and only if *A* is true and *B* is true). In addition to rules of this kind he also proposes so-called meaning postulates, such as a rule to the effect that the formal counterpart of *Bachelors are not married* is true, in order to capture nonlogical conceptual (analytical) truths (see *Analyticity*). In Montague semantics (Montague and Thomason 1974; see *Montague Grammar*) there are meaning postulates as well as semantic rules corresponding to Carnap's rules of truth (and also for other operators and functions of higher types), but they belong to a grammar for (a fragment of) natural English. Thus, they are presented as in some sense being rules of English.

So-called truth theories of natural languages, according to Davidson's conception (1984; see *Davidson, Donald*), are to contain statements of virtually the same kind as Carnap's statements of rules of designation and rules of truth. However, to the extent that they are rule statements the rules are just rules of the theory; the claim that they govern the practice of the speakers is not part of the theory and it is also rejected by Davidson. In the conception of Lewis, on the other hand, the connection between a set of abstract syntactic and semantic rules, thought of as defining a particular natural language, itself regarded as an abstract entity, is forged by means of a highly general rule, or convention (in Lewis's sense), which the speakers actually follow (see *Convention*).

2.3 Semantic Rules in Generative Grammar

In a grammar of modern linguistic theory the semantic component may look like this: on the one hand there is a so-called dictionary, the entries of which consist of lexical rules for primitive expressions, providing meaning (where possible by means of verbal meaning explanations) and grammatical category. On the other hand there are so-called projection rules for arriving at the meaning of complex expressions, and ultimately sentences, by way of selecting the readings of ambiguous simpler expressions that fit together within the more complex ones. In grammars of other kinds, however, what are thought of as semantic structures (doubling as phrase structures) are generated directly, providing the basis for transformations and insertion of lexical items. Such generating rules are not semantic in the sense of (directly and overtly) providing interpretations of linguistic expressions. Within modern linguistic theory the notion of a syntactic rule is clearer than that of a semantic rule, but for several reasons, in part connected with the existence of various constraints imposed on syntax by semantics or vice versa, the two notions are not sharply separated.

2.4 Semantic Rules and Language-games

In Hintikka's game-theoretic semantics (Hintikka and Kulas 1983; see *Game-theoretical Semantics*), developed for both formal and natural languages, a different conception of semantic rules concerning truth can be found. A sentence *S* is true in case there is a winning strategy, for the player Myself against the player Nature, in the semantical game associated with *S*. Such a game is defined by a number of rules, such as: the first move in a game associated with a conjunction *A&B* is Nature's choice of either *A* or *B*, whereupon the rest of the game is that associated with Nature's choice (that is, *A* or *B*; since Nature makes the choice, Myself must have a winning strategy for *A* as well as for *B*). Hintikka connects this approach with Wittgenstein's notion of a language-game (see *Language-game, Wittgenstein's Concept*), claiming that a speaker's understanding of a sentence actually consists of his mastery of the rules associated with it and that semantic (word–world) relations are established in linguistic activity as governed by such rules.

In Sellars's writings (1963, 1974) a more abstract conception of the nature of semantic rules can be found. Sellars, too, employs the notion of a language-game, and makes the analogy with (some) ordinary games rather close. In using a linguistic expression one takes a position in the language-game. A move in the game is a transition from one position to another. Rules of inference, material as well as formal (logical), govern such moves. One example (material) is the move from calling something *red* to calling it *extended* (the rule of which corresponds to a meaning postulate in Carnap's sense). Other rules, however, govern transitions which are not moves proper but transitions into (language entry) and out of (language departure) the game. The transition from observing a red patch to calling it *red* is of the former kind, and the transition from uttering *I am going out* to going out is of the latter kind. Rules of these three kinds determine the meaning of expressions, but for epistemological reasons (compare Sect. 3) they are primarily to be thought of as ought-to-be rules, that is, as rules providing standards for linguistic behavior, not as rules to be directly obeyed. Corresponding to these rules, however, there are ought-to-do rules for mature language users, requiring them to see to it that those standards are met, by training, teaching, and criticism (including self-criticism). Sellars's picture of linguistic practice as rule-governed is, of course, highly speculative, and it is doubtful that it can be borne out by more detailed considerations.

The notion of a language-game is originally Wittgenstein's (1958). The analogy with games strongly suggests a view of linguistic practice as rule-governed, and although it often arises in connection with other points, Wittgenstein repeatedly speaks of rules of language-games. It is open to debate, however, to what extent he acknowledges the existence of semantic rules as determining the meaning of linguistic expressions (see *Vagueness*).

On the one hand there are in Wittgenstein references to grammatical rules, though 'grammar' is not here used in the ordinary sense but rather in the sense of a set of standards of description, which themselves give rise to rules of inference. Such standards can be expressed in so-called grammatical statements, such as *White is lighter than black*, or *An order orders its own execution*. These rules provide for inferences from *A is white* and *B is black* to *A is lighter than B*, and from *A was ordered to V* and *A didn't V* to *A didn't execute the order*. They also exclude descriptions which are inconsistent with such inferences as nonsensical, counter to grammar. These grammatical statements are normative; they do not flow from the meanings of the words involved but are part of the determination of meaning.

On the other hand it is not fully clear whether Wittgenstein's view was that there is, for example, a meaning-determining rule governing the use of *red*, or just something closely analogous, namely (institutional) standards of correctness of that use. The difference, if there is one, would be that if there were such a rule, then that rule would concern a certain transition, namely that from recognizing something as red to calling it *red*, and at least, so Wittgenstein argues, there is no rule of that kind. It may be, however, that the point is not to insist on a distinction, but to correct an erroneous conception of (semantic) rules. This is suggested in other passages, where it is stressed that the determination of the use of a word by rules is not complete; new situations can always arise which are not covered by the rules (so-called open-texture).

2.5 Pragmatic Rules

The notion of pragmatic rules is one of rules governing linguistic activity in respects other than those of syntax and

semantics, in respects peculiar to communication. This is an area where it is difficult to distinguish features characteristic of linguistic practice as such from other factors, such as (everyday) human psychology, cultural or social norms, and contexts; indeed the desirability of employing that distinction is also questionable. Nonetheless, elaborate pragmatic analyses in terms of linguistic rules have been carried out, above all concerning individual speech acts and features of conversational interaction.

Austin (1976; see *Austin, John Langshaw*) introduced the notion of illocutionary acts, speech acts such as asserting, promising, commanding, congratulating. A speech act belongs to one of these categories by virtue of intrinsic properties, as opposed to properties depending on further reactions of the hearer, by virtue of which the act can be characterized as an act of scaring, amusing, or persuading. In contradistinction to acts of these kinds, called perlocutionary, illocutionary acts were held by Austin to involve conventions, but he did not develop this idea. It was later developed by Searle (1969), who extracted a number of rules for various kinds of illocutionary act. As regards promising, Searle's main example, there are five rules, understood as governing the use of expressions such as *I promise* and other linguistic devices indicating the illocutionary type of promising (and in virtue of this Searle characterizes these rules as semantic). The first of these requires that such an expression be uttered only in the context of predicating a future action of the speaker (the propositional content rule), the second that it be uttered only if the hearer prefers performance of that action to nonperformance and the speaker also believes this of the hearer, the third that it be uttered only if that action would not obviously be performed anyway (preparatory rules), the fourth that it be uttered only if the speaker intends to perform the action (the sincerity rule). These four rules are held to regulate the practice of promising. The fifth, on the other hand, the so-called essential rule, is seen by Searle as constitutive of that practice, as a rule which makes promising possible. This is the rule which (provided that the requirements of the first three rules are met) holds that such an utterance counts as undertaking an obligation to perform the action in question. These rule statements no doubt capture standard features of promisory utterances, even though Searle's conception of the rules themselves, especially the fifth, has been subject to discussion.

A different kind of pragmatic rule is the one which Grice (1989) has labeled conversational maxims. It includes rules such as: Make your contribution as informative as required (for the current purposes of the exchange)! Do not say that for which you lack adequate evidence! Be relevant! By means of reference to such rules Grice explains varieties of so-called conversational implicature, as in the phenomenon of deliberately conveying or implying something else than one is literally saying. (For more on this see *Conversational Maxims*; *Pragmatics*.)

3. Is Linguistic Practice Rule-governed?

The idea that linguistic practice is essentially rule-governed, that the meaning of linguistic expressions is determined by rules, is intimately connected with a conception of linguistic capacity as a kind of knowledge. On this conception a speaker stands in a cognitive relation to his own mother tongue; his ability to use it is a way of knowing the meaning of its expressions. Given the further idea that the meaning of a linguistic expression is arbitrary, the speaker's knowledge must be a knowledge of rules. These two tenets, about determination of meaning by rules and about knowledge of one's language, are almost invariably discussed together.

3.1 Language as Conventional

The most basic conception of meaning as determined by rules is that of meaning as conventional. One argument against this (Davidson 1984) is that we can give an account of what a speaker means by his words without requiring that the speaker *knows* the meaning of his words, and hence without requiring that he knows conventions. The basic point of another well-known argument (Quine 1976) is that, since proponents of the view must ultimately appeal to *unstated* conventions, the claim that speakers go by conventions runs the risk of becoming empty (for more on this, see *Convention*).

Sellars, too (1974), stresses that only antecedently stated rules can be said to be obeyed. His conclusion, however, is that for this reason rules which determine meaning must be so-called ought-to-be rules (compare Sect. 2.4). In this way Sellars hopes to avoid a regress: knowledge of language requires knowledge of rules, which is knowledge of rule formulations, which in turn requires knowledge of language, and so on. However, since just conforming to ought-to-be linguistic rules, in Sellars's view, falls short of constituting understanding, it is not clear that the regress is really avoided.

3.2 Wittgenstein on Normative Linguistic Practice

In Wittgenstein's view (1958) there are other ways of stating rules than that of providing full-fledged verbal formulations. The word *elephant* can be explained (partially, at least) by pointing at one, saying that that is an elephant. The point is that in doing so it is not just giving one example of how the word is applied, not just giving a hint for guessing at how to apply it in other cases. It is an explanation in its own right, a way of specifying the standards governing the use of the word, a way of expressing a rule. The tendency to think otherwise, that is, to think that no number of mere examples of using a word, or applying a rule, could determine future applications, presupposes that understanding of an expression, grasp of a rule, is something essentially private, something which cannot be fully conveyed to others. But, so Wittgenstein argues, nothing mental could determine the correctness or incorrectness of future applications, since anything mental could at most be contingently related to them. Hence, understanding cannot be essentially private, a hidden mental phenomenon; if a word is understood, then it can also be explained to others (see *Private Language*).

Wittgenstein's point of departure is the practice of speaking a common language. Such a practice stands out as normative, involving training, explaining, and correcting. Accordingly, a speaker taking part in the practice is pictured as one who has acquired knowledge of the practice, a great number of interrelated abilities. Such an ability is not only in conformance with communal standards, but is an ability to specify and independently apply those standards.

Only within such a practice does a rule-formulation have meaning. The rule, however, is no more precise than the interpretation of the expression of the rule. Therefore, what is determined by, or is a consequence of, a rule, is nothing other than that which is determined within the practice of applying that rule (and related rules). This has consequences within the philosophy of mathematics (Wittgenstein 1978). It is a necessary outcome of rules of mathematics that $2 + 3 = 5$ only insofar as this is regarded as a necessary outcome within mathematical practice. Saying that it is a necessary outcome is a legitimate way of expressing a normative attitude, the attitude of treating $2 + 3 = 5$ as unshakable, immune to revision, as a rule of grammar, in Wittgenstein's sense, but humans are inclined to misconceive themselves as having observed a logical or metaphysical fact, independent of any human activity, as if the rules could grind out consequences on their own.

On Wittgenstein's view there must be something intermediary between finding out the consequences of a rule and just adding to the explanation, or definition, of the rule itself. The notion of such an intermediary is, however, problematic (see *Wittgenstein, Ludwig*).

3.3 Deep Linguistic Competence

In Chomsky's view (1976, 1980), if there are two grammars for a given language, both of which correctly specify the class of sentences of that language, then there is a basis for claiming that only one of them is the correct one, that it specifies the class of sentences in the right way.

What the right way is depends on the linguistic knowledge of the speakers. That knowledge is knowledge of the rules of the language. It is not knowledge of any ordinary kind, but a special kind of competence, consisting in having the rules of the language internally represented, in the mind, or in the brain. That grammar is correct which provides the rules which are so represented. This conception is shared by many other linguists. Linguistics is, accordingly, regarded as a branch of psychology.

According to Chomsky, the correct grammar is the one which conforms to general grammatical principles, together making out the so-called 'universal grammar.' These principles are common to all humanly possible languages. On the one hand these principles specify grammatical categories and category structures, like the noun phrase–verb phrase structure, which are common to all possible languages, and on the other hand they impose restrictions on further rules; some transformations, for instance, are acceptable, while others are not.

The universal grammar is thought by Chomsky to play the decisive role in the explanation of language acquisition. The problem is to explain how the child, being exposed to only a comparatively small number of grammatically well-formed sentences, can develop the competence to produce an indefinite number of well-formed sentences himself. The reason why this is a problem is that the fragment of sentence examples which the child has encountered can be described by infinitely many different grammars, most of which do not correctly describe the whole language. Somehow the child learns to conform to rules that are correct, not only for the initial fragment, but for the entire language.

This is explained as follows. Given a sufficiently large and diverse finite set of sentences of a language, the universal grammar, in virtue of the restrictions it imposes on acceptable rules, selects the correct grammar of the language. Assuming that the child's development is somehow guided, or determined, by the principles of the universal grammar, the set of sentence examples which the child encounters will yield internal representations of the rules of the correct grammar. Thus, the acquisition of linguistic competence can be explained by assuming that the universal grammar, or knowledge of it, is innate, perhaps in virtue of the structure of the brain (see *Competence and Performance; Sentence Types and Clause Subordination; Innate Ideas*).

3.4 Criticism of the Idea of Deep Linguistic Competence

This theory has met with much criticism, only some of which, however, focuses on the nature of rules. Quine (1976) has rejected the idea that there is anything intermediary between, on the one hand, merely conforming to rules and, on the other hand, being guided by explicitly stated rules. You can learn a foreign language by way of learning to follow rules, as explicitly stated, but you do not learn your mother tongue that way. Since there is nothing intermediary, learning a mother tongue is not a matter of acquiring rules at all. Consequently there is no basis for claiming that a grammar which correctly specifies the class of sentences of a language may still be incorrect. The student can only choose between equally good grammars on the basis of preference for elegance and simplicity.

An extensive criticism, based on interpretation of Wittgenstein, directed at Chomsky and other linguists as well as at several modern philosophers of language, has been provided by Baker and Hacker (1984). First of all, they stress that to the extent that there are rules of a language, these rules have normative force. Only rules which speakers of the language in fact express, apply, and appeal to in teaching, justification, and criticism can have normative force. Rules which are only discovered by the linguist and thought to operate unconsciously, by way of being internally represented, cannot have any normative force and are not, therefore, rules which govern the linguistic practice.

Another, even more basic, point concerns the very notion of a set of rules which determine the whole class of well-formed, meaningful sentences, and also provide interpretations of them. According to Baker and Hacker, this conception belongs to the mistaken picture of rules grinding out consequences on their own. The correct view is that the meaning of an expression is determined by nothing else than its actual use. This holds for complex expressions as much as for individual words. It is a mistake to think that the meaning of a sentence is determined in advance. It is again a mistake to think that a line can be drawn, once and for all, between what is a sentence and what is not a sentence, and between expressions that make sense and expressions that do not. Something which does not make sense in one context of use may make perfectly good sense in another.

Above all, so Baker and Hacker claim, it is a mistake to think that there is any particular problem about producing and understanding new sentences, something which needs to be explained and which is to be explained by appeal to rules. Only if it is assumed that the meaning of a new sentence is determined in advance does the question arise as to how one can know what it is. Thus, rules of a particular kind are appealed to for explaining certain alleged facts about understanding, but the assumption that there are such facts itself depends on the assumption that there are rules of that kind in the first place.

3.5 Concluding Remarks

A person can be said to have an ability only if what counts as success, in exercising that ability, is sufficiently well determined. In the case of linguistic abilities, however, it can only be speakers of the language who decide what is to count as success. So it seems that what counts as successful exercise of linguistic abilities is determined precisely by exercise of linguistic abilities. This makes the notion of rules of language problematic.

On the other hand that notion clearly seems to require, if the idea of a common language is to be retained, something in which members of a speech community have competence. If that idea is given up, then it will be hard to make sense of notions such as mutual understanding and speaker's responsibility.

See also: Convention; Wittgenstein, Ludwig; Private Language.

Bibliography

Austin J L 1976 *How to Do Things with Words*, 2nd edn. Oxford University Press, Oxford
Baker G P, Hacker P M S 1984 *Language, Sense & Nonsense*. Basil Blackwell, Oxford
Baker G P, Hacker P M S 1985 *Wittgenstein, Rules, Grammar and Necessity*. Basil Blackwell, Oxford
Bartsch R 1987 *Norms of Language*. Longman, London
Black M 1962 The analysis of rules. In: *Models and Metaphors*. Cornell University Press, Ithaca, NY
Carnap R 1956 *Meaning and Necessity*, 2nd edn. University of Chicago Press, Chicago, IL
Chomsky N 1976 *Reflections on Language*. Temple Smith, London
Chomsky N 1980 *Rules and Representations*. Basil Blackwell, Oxford
Davidson D 1984 *Inquiries into Truth and Interpretation*. Clarendon Press, Oxford
Grice P 1989 *Studies in the Ways of Words*. Harvard University Press, Cambridge, MA
Gumb R D 1972 *Rule-governed Linguistic Behavior*. Mouton, The Hague
Hintikka J, Kulas J 1983 *The Game of Language*. Reidel, Dordrecht
Kripke S A 1982 *Wittgenstein on Rules and Private Language*. Basil Blackwell, Oxford
Lewis D K 1969 *Convention: A Philosophical Study*. Harvard University Press, Cambridge, MA
Montague R, Thomason R H (eds.) 1974 *Formal Philosophy*. Yale University Press, New Haven, CT
Quine W V O 1976 *The Ways of Paradox and Other Essays*, 2nd edn. Harvard University Press, Cambridge, MA
Ross A 1968 *Directives and Norms*. Routledge and Kegan Paul, London
Searle J 1969 *Speech Acts*. Cambridge University Press, London
Sellars W 1963 Some reflections on language games. In: *Science, Perception and Reality*. Routledge and Kegan Paul, London
Sellars W 1974 Language as thought and as communication. In: *Essays in Philosophy and its History*. Reidel, Dordrecht
Shwayder D 1965 *The Stratification of Behavior*. Routledge and Kegan Paul, London

Wright G H von 1963 *Norm and Action*. Routledge and Kegan Paul, London

Wittgenstein L 1958 *Philosophical Investigations*, 2nd edn. Basil Blackwell, Oxford

Wittgenstein L 1978 *Remarks on the Foundations of Mathematics*, 3rd edn. Basil Blackwell, Oxford

P. Pagin

Runes

Runes are the letters of the first alphabet or script used by the Germanic peoples which, over time, developed several variant types. The script was used primarily for epigraphic purposes. Extant, known runic inscriptions, the earliest of which date from about the second century AD, number 5,000 or so in total. The great majority of objects (portable and nonportable) inscribed with runes by Germanic-speaking people originated and survive in Sweden; the remainder are to be found in Norway, Denmark, Iceland, England, Lowland Scotland, the Orkney and Shetland Islands, the Western Isles, Greenland, the Faroes, Ireland, and the Isle of Man. There are also a few from Germany, Poland, Hungary, and the former Soviet Union. By the twelfth century, runes had been more or less superseded by Roman letters everywhere except in the Scandinavian countries where runes continued to be used occasionally until about the seventeenth century. Though runic inscriptions are generally brief, those predating the twelfth century are of immense value since they constitute the earliest, and sometimes only, linguistic evidence of several of the Germanic languages.

1. The Origins and Uses of Runes

1.1 Origins

It is not known for certain when, where, and by whom runes were invented. Three theories exist (see Page 1987: 9). Moltke (1985) holds that runes were created by one of the Germanic tribes of Denmark, probably of southern Jutland. For several reasons, this is credible. Many of the earliest known inscriptions come from there. Two scripts: the Etruscan (from southern Switzerland and northern Italy) and the Roman-letter (itself influenced by the Etruscan and Greek scripts) seem, from a comparison of character shapes, to have formed the basis of the runic one. Of Nordic Germanic areas, southern Jutland was geographically closest to Switzerland and Rome. Also, Denmark, though independent of Imperial Rome, traded with its trading posts and military camps on the Rhine—circumstances facilitating adoption and adaptation of the mixed-origin Roman-letter script. The maturity of epigraphic and rune-using skills apparent in the earliest inscriptions supports an invention date of around the beginning of the Christian era.

1.2 Uses

Runes were incised on free-standing boulders, living rock, stone crosses, and a variety of moveable objects like brooches, buckles, neck-rings, and medallions in precious or semiprecious metals, bone combs, spearheads, scabbards, boxes made of wood, ivory, or whalebone, urns, coins, and even tweezers. The inscriptions most often name owners or makers, e.g., the famous one on the fabulous golden horn, made ca. 400 AD and known as the 'Gallehus Horn' after the place in Denmark where it was found: (tr. = transliterated) *ekhlewagastiR | holtijaR | horna | tawido* 'I, Hlewagastir, son of Holti, made the horn.' Sometimes they merely name the object they are carved on. Many are memorial inscriptions. A few give the complete runic alphabet; fewer still are verse texts like that on the 'Ruthwell Cross.'

It is often claimed that runes had ritualistic or magical significance in Germanic society. Their mention in this connection in later Germanic literature, together with the existence of largely uninterpretable inscriptions, such as (tr.) *aaaaaaaRRRnnn?bmuttt:alu* where only the last three characters read as a recognizable word (reputed to mean 'good luck'), as well as the historical definition of the word 'rune' itself ('secret/mystery/whispering') do point to this conclusion. It should, however, be borne in mind that the ability to write and read any script, runic or not, would seem secret and mysterious anyway to the majority of the Germanic population who would be unable to do either. Additionally, the runic script was the only one known to Germanic peoples, except the Goths, until into the seventh century; consequently it had, perforce, to be used for all writing purposes—magic ones as well as everyday ones.

2. The Runic Script and its Development

2.1. Characteristics

The angular shape of the runes in the original Common Germanic alphabet, along with their vertical and slanting, not horizontal, strokes, attest their original epigraphic purpose and the material—wood—on which they were cut at first. The direction of writing of runes is variable; sometimes they read from left to right, sometimes vice versa and sometimes boustrophedon (left to right, and right to left, with the runes reversed, in alternate lines). Runic script is always what one would think of as upper case. Mirror image and upside-down runes sometimes occur and the rune shapes themselves can show some minor variation in form within each alphabet.

Spelling characteristics include: the ligaturing of runes, i.e., two or more of them could be combined, for example OE ᛗ where ᚾ, ᛗ and ᚱ have been combined into one bind-rune; the representation by only one rune of double consonants or the same consonant ending one word and beginning the next, e.g. Proto-Germanic (tr.) *wihailag* for *wih hailag* 'holy' 'inviolate'—here the *h* rune does double duty. Long vowels usually are not marked as such and word division and punctuation (dots, dashes, or vertical strokes) are often absent or inconsistently employed. Finally, the omission of the runes for the nasal stop consonants /n/ and /m/ before those for homorganic stop consonants is a feature of Scandinavian inscriptions, i.e., that for /m/ before those for /p/ or /b/ and that for /n/ before those for /t/, /d/, /k/ or /g/, so for example, (tr.) *kabu* appears instead of **kambu* 'comb.'

2.2 Runic Alphabets

The Common Germanic runic alphabet had 24 letters arranged in the order depicted in Fig. 1(a). It is known, from the first six letters of this traditional sequence, as the *fuþark*. From ca. 800 AD this fuþark was reduced in number from 24 to 16 runes in Scandinavian (especially Swedish) usage and some of the rune shapes changed quite significantly (Fig. 1(b)). These two fuþarks are normally referred to respectively as the older and the younger. The younger fuþark had a major—short-twig—variant type in which the runes were slightly more cursive as shown in Fig. 1(c). Some inscriptions mixed both younger fuþark types. Several other minor Scandinavian variants developed, for instance, the dotted fuþark (after ca. 1000 AD), in which a system of dots was used to point up some of the vowel and consonant distinctions missing since the ninth century, or the Hälsinge runes, which lack vertical strokes and were in use from the tenth to the twelfth century in the Hälsingland region of Sweden. The runes used in Anglo-Saxon England resemble fairly closely those of the older fuþark, but some rune shapes were changed (becoming diagnostic of source) and new ones were invented (bringing the final total to 34) thus reflecting diachronic phonological differences between the two branches of Germanic (Fig. 1(d)).

3. Deciphering Runes

Each rune symbol had a name, usually a common noun of the language. The runic system worked on an acrophonic principle whereby each rune represented a broad phonetic value derived from the initial sound segment of its name. These sound values can be reconstructed, for Proto-Germanic and its individual offshoots, with the help of the rune names and the alliterative schemes given in the 'Rune Poem' which survives in Old Norwegian, Old Norse, and Old English manuscript versions. So, for instance, the rune ᛚ has the name *lagu* 'water' in Old English and, with the same meaning, *lǫgr* in Old Norse. The defining line accompanying the rune in the Old English 'Rune Poem': *Lagu byð leodum langsum geðuht* 'water (ocean) to people interminable seems' has the initial letter of *lagu* alliterating with those of *leodum* and *langsum* and so the sound value /l/ can be assigned to this rune.

Conventionally, runes are transliterated into Roman letters or, for Old English ones, a mixed system of Roman letters, untransliterated runes and IPA symbols devised by Bruce Dickins (1932). For the purposes of obtaining adequate, unambiguous linguistic information, both systems are unsatisfactory. It would be a truer, more accurate, and more consistent reflection of the admirable phonetic sophistication, variation, and diachrony of runic usage simply to transliterate runic inscriptions directly into the letters of the IPA, as suggested in King (1986), at least where the reader's interest in runes is primarily phonological.

4. Runes as Linguistic Evidence for Germanic

4.1 Drawbacks

These consist of the peculiarities described in Sect. 3 above. These may sometimes be put down to carvers, who cannot be assumed in all cases to have composed the inscriptions, being semiliterate or not literate, and might be increased if an unsatisfactory transliteration system is employed to present the linguistic information contained in the inscriptions. Other drawbacks center on the shortness of inscriptions generally and the fact that only a small proportion of what must have been a sizable corpus of them survives. Among other things, many inscriptions on materials like wood will have perished, ones on nonprecious metals are subject to corrosion and become unreadable, and precious metal objects whether or not they have runes on them are likely to be melted down (as was the 'Gallehus Horn') as bullion. The extant corpus may, too, be only partially representative of the whole. Nothing can be done about these latter problems, except for respecting the existing runic data as they stand. The first ones, however, can be considerably lessened with knowledge of the spelling characteristics of runic usage, combined with use of a good transliterating system.

4.2 Advantages

Rune names were predominantly common nouns so they, like the nouns, were subject to diachronic and diatopic linguistic developments (i.e., changes over time and according to geographical situation). Rune names were changed in accord with these developments, so through the name changes the linguistic developments themselves can be traced. For example, the twelfth rune in the fuþark, had the name **jára* in Primitive Norse. By the Old Norse period, the rune name is changed to *ár* and so it can be deduced from this evidence and that of the inscriptions' data that some time around 600 AD, word initial /j/ was lost in Norse. Of similar value in evidencing diachronic sound changes, but this time also diatopic ones, is the change in the vowel of the rune name meaning 'riding' from PrGmc **raiðō* to ON *reið* and OE *rād*. This provides evidence of the evolution of Gmc /ai/ to /ɑ:/ in Old English, but to /ei/ in Old Norse. (For more, detailed information on this and further phonological developments in the Pre-Old English and Old English periods, see King 1986.)

Not only the rune names, but also the data of the inscriptions themselves are useful in this respect. The runic spellings on Old English coins of the personal names of moneyers and kings (whose reign dates are known) can, for instance, be of especial value in dating Old English sound changes fairly precisely. The data themselves record the very earliest known details of Proto-Germanic phonology, inflectional morphology, syntax, lexis (both lexical stock and information on derivational morphology), and onomastics—otherwise there would be no evidence of these until the fourth century when the first manuscript in Gothic was written. Developments affecting inflectional morphology, etc. from Proto-Germanic and into the individual Germanic languages can be traced by comparing the earlier with later runic inscriptions (see Antonsen 1975; Haugen 1982). This information is precious with regard to the Scandinavian languages—were it not for inscriptions in runes, no record of Old Norse, for instance, would exist until the eleventh century when Roman-letter writing was introduced.

See also: Germanic Languages; Writing: Overview of History; Writing Materials: Influence on Writing; Writing Systems: Principles and Typology; Old English; Gothic.

Bibliography

Antonsen E H 1975 *A Concise Grammar of the Older Runic Inscriptions*. Niemeyer, Tübingen

Dickins B 1932 A system of transliteration for Old English runic inscriptions. *Leeds Studies in English* **I**: 15–9

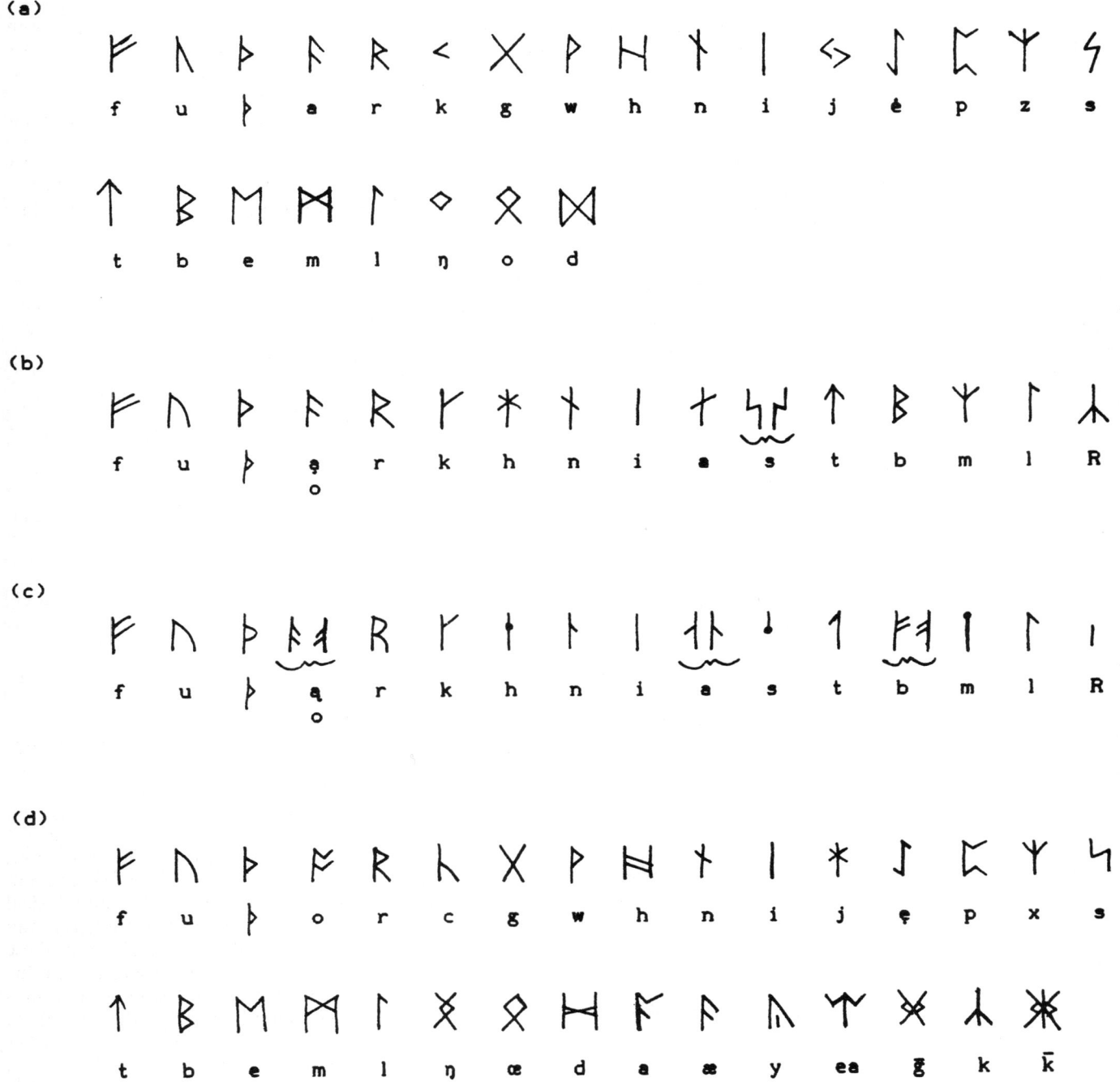

Figure 1. Runic alphabets.

Elliott R W V 1959 *Runes: An Introduction.* Manchester University Press, Manchester

Haugen E 1982 *Scandinavian Language Structures.* University of Minnesota Press, Minneapolis, MN

King A 1986 The Ruthwell Cross: A linguistic monument (Runes as evidence for Old English). *FoLH* **VII(1)**: 43–79

Moltke E 1985 *Runes and their Origin: Denmark and Elsewhere.* Nationalmuseets Forlag, Copenhagen

Page R I 1973 *An Introduction to English Runes.* Methuen, London

Page R I 1987 *Runes.* British Museum Publications, London

A. King

Russell, Bertrand (1872–1970)

Russell's most famous contributions to philosophy of language are his theories of names and definite descriptions, developed in the first decade of the twentieth century (see *Names and Descriptions*). Both theories exclude from the category of 'referring expressions' words that might naively have been taken as paradigms of the category, for example 'Bismarck' and 'the first man to walk on the moon' (see *Names and Descriptions*). In this early period, Russell also produced an account of propositional attitudes, which has been taken as a model in recent work (see *Propositional Attitudes*). In his later philosophy, starting from the end of World War I, Russell sketched causal theories of meaning that are not dissimilar in approach to some accounts formulated over half a century later (see *Meaning: Philosophical Theories*).

1. Life and Influence

Bertrand Russell (1872–1970), third Earl Russell, was a prolific writer not only on specialist topics in mathematical logic, epistemology, philosophy of mind, and philosophy of language, but also on a wide range of more popular social and political issues. He was awarded the Nobel Prize for Literature in 1950. His father, Viscount Amberley, was the son of Lord John Russell, the Whig politician who introduced the 1832 Reform Bill; his mother was the daughter of Lord Stanley of Alderley, his godfather John Stuart Mill. For many years, though by no means all his working life, he held a fellowship at Trinity College, Cambridge, where he worked closely with both G. E. Moore and Ludwig Wittgenstein (see *Wittgenstein, Ludwig*). He collaborated with A. N. Whitehead in the monumental three-volume *Principia Mathematica* (1910–13), an attempted reduction of mathematics to logic, and like Gottlob Frege (see *Frege, Gottlob*) played a major role in the development and philosophical consolidation of first-order logic (see *First Order Logic*; *Logic: Historical Survey*). He was the first modern philosopher to see the significance, and potential damage, of logical paradoxes (see *Paradoxes, Semantic*), both in the foundations of mathematics and, more generally, for any systematic, logical theory of language (see *Truth and Paradox*). The main concerns here are his philosophy of language, in particular his accounts of reference, mental content, and meaning.

2. Reference

In his *Principles of Mathematics* (1903), his earliest discussion of semantic questions, Russell was simply unaware of a distinction between meaning and reference, and as a result had trouble with what he called 'denoting phrases' (e.g., 'a man,' 'all men,' 'the man'). Shortly afterwards, and certainly before he wrote the famous 'On Denoting' (1905), he became aware of Frege's distinction between Sinn ('sense') and Bedeutung ('reference' or 'meaning'), but argued that it was untenable (see *Frege, Gottlob*; *Sense*). His agenda was thus to provide a semantic theory that did not make a Frege-like distinction, and yet which did not founder on the problem of denoting phrases.

To lack a distinction between sense and reference is to confront at least two conspicuous problems: there are apparently meaningful terms that do not refer; and there are coreferential but apparently nonsynonymous expressions. In his 1903 work, Russell disposes of a range of apparent examples of the first problem by in effect denying that they do not refer. The fundamental semantic relation is that of indicating. Expressions indicate 'terms' (1903: 44), and a proposition is *about* its terms. The expression *Vulcan* indicates the term 'Vulcan'; there is such a thing (term) as Vulcan but, like many terms, it does not exist (1903: 45). There are more things to refer to than there are things that exist.

In this early work, there is no sign of awareness of the second problem. Rather, what mainly concerned Russell was the difficulty of accommodating denoting phrases within the framework based on the notion of indicating. For example, in the sentence 'I met a man,' the expression 'a man' ought to indicate a concept (a kind of term), but the sentence is not *about* the concept 'a man' (1903: 53). A proper account of denoting is thus a crucial difficulty for Russell's aim of basing semantics upon the single notion of reference (indication).

2.1 The Theory of Descriptions

The key part of the solution to the problem is provided by the famous 'theory of descriptions.' Russell argues that denoting phrases are quantifier phrases, and are to be identified not by their actually denoting something, but by their form. In particular, 'the,' applied to a predicate in the singular, functions as a uniqueness quantifier, and sentences of the form 'The F is G' are equivalent to 'There is exactly one F and it is G.' The upshot is that denoting phrases like 'The present King of France' no longer need to refer to, denote, or indicate anything in order to have their proper semantic role. As Russell puts it, they are 'incomplete symbols' and 'have no meaning in isolation' (1905: 42). The last phrase may mislead, as it condenses two thoughts. One is that, whether in isolation or in context, these phrases do not have the semantic role of referring, so that a failure of reference is not a failure of semantic role. The other thought is that the right way to explain their semantic role is to say how they contribute to the meaning (not here equated with reference) of whole sentences in which they occur. His 'On Denoting' (1905) contains a rather creaking attempt to provide standard disquotational clauses for quantifiers (see *Quantifiers*; *First Order Logic*).

Russell allows that some denoting phrases denote. For example, a definite description 'the F' denotes if and only if something is uniquely *F*. However, a phrase may be a denoting one without denoting: it is not an expression whose semantic role is to denote. If 'referring expression' means an expression whose semantic role is to refer, Russell's theory of descriptions places definite descriptions outside the category of referring expressions.

The theory is a major step towards permitting the identification of meaning and reference, subject to two restrictions: it is to apply only to genuinely semantically simple expressions, and it is not to apply to the logical constants. This provides solutions to the two problems mentioned earlier. Since the semantic complexity of definite descriptions ensures that they acquire their semantic role derivatively, they are not to be thought of as expressions whose role is to refer to or indicate entities, so there is no problem about meaningful but nonreferring descriptions. Moreover, since definite descriptions are no longer classifiable as referring expressions, there cannot be 'coreferential' definite descriptions, in the way that seemed to ensure synonymy. Of course, there can be codenoting descriptions, but their different semantic structure explains their nonsynonymy (see *Names and Descriptions*; *Determiners*).

2.2 The Theory of Names

Both the original problems resurface in connection with apparently simple expressions. Some, like 'Vulcan,' are meaningful yet do not refer; and some pairs, like 'Hesperus' and 'Phosphorus,' are apparently coreferential while apparently nonsynonymous (see *Frege, Gottlob*). Russell's solution is to deny that these expressions really are semantically simple. Rather, they are 'truncated' or 'abbreviated' definite descriptions, and the two problems disappear.

However, questions arise about what could it mean to say that a name like 'Vulcan' is 'really' complex and about how could it be settled, given the idiosyncratic nature of the information that people possess about individuals, which description a name abbreviates. Russell gives clear answers to these questions, answers which involve a modification of one standard interpretation of his views.

In his *Problems of Philosophy* (1912), his discussion of names is guided by the 'principle of acquaintance,' according to which one can understand an expression whose semantic role is to refer only if one is acquainted with its referent. Since he held that the only things with which we can be acquainted are sense data and (perhaps) ourselves, this principle places severe limitations, derived from a source quite different from the two problems mentioned, upon which expressions can be counted as genuine names.

Russell takes the example of the name 'Bismarck,' which Bismarck himself can use as a genuinely semantically simple expression, but which his friends and anyone else cannot, since he is not a sense-datum. When people 'make a judgment about him, the description in our minds will probably be some more or less vague mass of historical knowledge . . . for the sake of illustration . . . "the first Chancellor of the German Empire."' The problem is that intuitively we want a stable role for 'Bismarck,' common to speakers and hearers in successful acts of communication, yet this cannot be provided by the idiosyncratic and variable descriptions we associate with a name. Russell's solution is to stress that the story about associated descriptions is intended only to give a correct account of what is in the mind of an individual speaker or hearer. In order to achieve a correct account of communication, one must see Bismarck himself as the common object of the judgments at which speakers are aiming:

> What enables us to communicate in spite of the varying descriptions we employ is that we know there is a true proposition concerning the actual Bismarck, and that however we may vary the description (so long as the description is correct) the proposition described is still the same.
>
> (1912: 31)

A major question in the philosophy of language is how to relate a notion of meaning appropriate to individuating units of communication (what is shared by a speaker and a hearer when they understand one another) and a notion of meaning appropriate to describing the states of mind of individuals when they think, speak, and understand. Russell's theory that many names are really truncated descriptions is clearly located by him as belonging to the latter enterprise and as unsuited to the former. So the many contemporary criticisms of Russell (e.g., Kripke 1972; see *Names and Descriptions*) which take him to hold that for each proper name there is a definite description that specifies the name's invariant contribution to communicative acts have not correctly identified their target. The most with which one could credit Russell is the view that on each occasion a proper name is used, there is a description that accurately represents what is going on in the mind of the user of the name on that occasion.

The difficulty with this weaker view is that it is unclear whether or not it speaks to the original problems of apparently meaningful yet bearerless names, and of apparently coreferential yet nonsynonymous ones. Perhaps the tendency to think of Russell's view as stronger than the texts justify is to be explained by the thought that only a stronger view could hope to resolve these problems.

3. Mental Content

If no distinction is made between meaning and reference, it is natural to see thoughts as involving direct or immediate relations to objects, mirroring the way that the words which can express thoughts relate directly to objects. Thus Russell (1912) analyzes the belief ascription 'Othello believes that Desdemona loves Cassio' as an extensional four-place relation (the belief relation), said to hold between Othello, Desdemona, love and Cassio. (It is necessary to pretend that Shakespeare's story is factual.) Russell insists that judging or believing does not involve ideas. In believing what he does, Othello is directly related to various particulars and universals in the world; the relation is not mediated by ideas, which are dangerous in that they lead to idealism. This explains why Russell was happy to equate meaning and reference: there is no room, in his philosophy at this time, for more than one way of thinking about a single thing. Thought involves an unmediated relation to its object. (This view led in turn to the restriction on the possible objects of thought to sense data.)

The account, which has been an inspiration to many contemporary philosophers (e.g., Salmon 1986; David Kaplan; see also Almog, et al. (eds.) 1989), faces two main problems. First, it apparently runs foul of Frege's puzzle. As stated above, Russell would try to avoid this by saying that if the substitution of, for example, 'Phosphorus' for 'Hesperus' really fails to preserve truth value, then the substituted expressions must be descriptions, and not really names.

The other problem is that it is unclear how Russell's theory could be extended to sentences containing logical constants, and this is a problem that he did not address (see *Intentionality*; *Propositional Attitudes*).

4. Later Views on Meaning

In *My Philosophical Development* (1959), Russell says that it was not until 1918 that he 'first became interested in the definition of "meaning" and in the relation of language to fact' (1959: 145). This raises questions, given that the problems of descriptions and names, to which he contributed so much before 1918, seem to be precisely such issues.

In the earlier period, he was content to identify the meaning of a genuinely simple name with its bearer, and leave the matter there. In *The Analysis of Mind* (1921), however, the question is 'not who is the individual meant, but what is the relation of the word to the individual which makes the one mean the other' (1921: 191). What he provides is an account of the conditions under which a speaker has internalized a name–object relation. An example of a sufficient condition for one to understand a word is that one be caused by the impact of that word to do what one would have been caused to do by the impact of what it stands for (1921: 199; 1940: 25). He is right to say that this is a topic, bringing as it does a causal element into meaning, to which he made no attempt to contribute before 1918.

The second way in which Russell's classification of his early work can be understood as not relating to linguistics is that in the early period he often writes as though what matters above all is what is going on in the mind of the thinker, rather than the words which may be used to express this. Hence his willingness to say that ordinary names are 'really' descriptions: as an account of language, thought of as a public vehicle of communication, this would be nonsensical, and, as seen above in connection with 'Bismarck,' Russell would not accept it. However, the view has a chance of being true if it is an account of nonlinguistic entities (Russell often speaks of 'propositions') which are the vehicles of thought.

See also: Linguistic Philosophy; Philosophy of Language; Names and Decriptions; Indexicals; Quine, Willard van Orman.

Bibliography

Almog J, Perry J, Wettstein H (eds.) 1989 *Themes from Kaplan*. Oxford University Press, Oxford
Frege G 1892 Über Sinn und Bedeutung. *Zeitschrift für Philosophie und Philosophische Kritik* **100**: 25–50 [1952 On sense and reference. In: Geach P, Black M (eds.) *Translations from the Philosophical Writings of Gottlob Frege*. Basicl Blackwell, Oxford]
Kripke S 1972 Naming and necessity. In: Davidson D, Harman G (eds.) *Semantics of Natural Language*. Reidel, Dordrecht
Russell B 1903 *Principles of Mathematics*. Allen and Unwin, London
Russell B 1905 On denoting. In: Marsh R C (ed.) 1956 *Logic and Knowledge*. Allen and Unwin, London
Russell B 1910 Knowledge by acquaintance and knowledge by description. In: Russell B 1963 *Mysticism and Logic*. Allen and Unwin, London
Russell B 1912 *Problems of Philosophy*. Oxford University Press, Oxford
Russell B 1921 *The Analysis of Mind*. Allen and Unwin, London
Russell B 1940 *An Inquiry into Meaning and Truth*. Allen and Unwin, London
Russell B 1959 *My Philosophical Development*. Allen and Unwin, London
Sainsbury R M 1979 *Russell*. Routledge, London
Salmon N 1986 *Frege's Puzzle*. MIT Press, Cambridge, MA

R. M. Sainsbury

Russian

Russian is the native language of some 134 million of a total population of the former Soviet Union of 286.7 million (figures approximate, 1989). With Ukrainian (some 36 million speakers) and Belorussian (some 7.9 million speakers) Russian forms the East Slavonic group of the Slavonic languages, all three being descended from Old East Slavonic or Old Russian.

1. The Written Language

1.1 Diglossia

The adoption of Eastern Christianity in the tenth century brought to the East Slavs the religious language of the Slavs, Old Church Slavonic (OCS), written in Cyrillic.

Syntax, phraseology, and much of the word-formation of OCS owed much to Byzantine Greek. In a russified form, OCS served for centuries as the language of 'culture' of the Russians. The earliest extant text is an aprakos Gospel compiled in 1056–57 by Deacon Grigorij for Prince Ostromir ('Ostromir Gospel'). Secular works—writs, treaties, codes of law (e.g., *Russkaja Pravda* 'Russian Law,' mid-eleventh century, earliest extant copy 1282), etc.,—were written in vernacular Russian.

1.2 Eighteenth Century

Church Slavonic (CS) and Russian now merged to provide the foundation for the modern literary language. Though the everyday language which V. K. Trediakovskij (1703–69) advocated as a literary language cannot be found in his own writings, he amply demonstrated the word-forming capabilities of CS elements and processes. M. V. Lomonosov (1711–65) wrote the first complete grammar of Russian as Russian (1757), distinguishing 'high style' forms (i.e., of CS origin) from the rest and insisting elsewhere that CS words were an ineradicable part of Russian.

Writers of the late eighteenth and early nineteenth centuries, e.g., N. M. Karamzin (1766–1826) and others, created a 'new style' (*novyj slog*), in which clarity and straightforwardness were fundamental criteria, eradicating the ponderous, convoluted earlier eighteenth-century prose style. French provided a model for sentence-structure and element-order. Karamzin himself produced many new words—straight loans, calques (many based on French) and new creations using the resources of Russian.

Thus, modern literary Russian may be said to be at base a blend of a Graecized Church Slavonic, vernacular Russian and French syntax and order.

2. Church Slavonic Features

Almost any printed page of modern Russian reveals numerous elements of CS origin. Such are the nominative singular masculine ending of the adjective *-yj/-ij*, the present active participle in *-ushchij*, etc., (and in general the use of participles), suffixes such as *-ie*, *-stvo/-estvo*, *-tel'* and compound suffixes such as *-enie/-anie/-janie*, etc.

Some morphophonemic alternations show CS origin. For example, CS are $d \sim zhd$, $t \sim shch$ against Russian $d \sim zh$, $t \sim ch$. Compare *pobedit'* (PRFV) $\sim$ *pobezhdat'* (IMPFV) 'to conquer' with *brodit'* 'to ferment' $\sim$ *brozhenie* 'fermentation,' and *obet* 'promise' $\sim$ *obeshchat'* 'to promise' with *otvetit'* (PRFV) $\sim$ *otvechat'* (IMPFV) 'to answer.' In the striking alternation of pleophonic (*polnoglasnyj*) forms, of Russian origin, and apleophonic (*nepolnoglasnyj*) forms, of CS origin, a vowel *o* or *e* flanks both sides of *l* or *r* in pleophonic forms, whereas a single vowel *a* or *e* follows *l* or *r* in apleophonic forms. Thus: *moloko* 'milk'—*mlekopitajushchij* 'mammalian,' *Mlechnyj put'* 'Milky Way'; *korotkij* 'short,' *ukorotit'* 'to shorten'—*kratkij* 'brief,' *prekratit'* 'to curtail'; *golos* 'voice,' *golosovye svjazki* 'vocal cords'—*glasnyj* 'vowel,' *soglasnyj* 'consonant'; *bereg* 'bank'—*bregoukreplenie* 'reinforcement of banks,' *bezbrezhnyj* 'boundless.' Pleophonic forms are 'concrete,' mundane, apleophonic forms are 'abstract,' 'learned,' 'technical.'

3. Phonetics

Old Russian had twelve vowel phonemes and some two dozen consonant phonemes, with open syllables and few clusters. The lapse, from the twelfth century, of two ultra-short vowels in certain positions initiated the development towards a language with five vowel phonemes, many more consonant phonemes, many clusters and closed syllables, and a system in which palatalization is largely independent of the following vowel, i.e., is largely phonemic.

The vowels /i, e, a, o, u/ have several allophones each, depending on location of stress, consonantal environment or the two combined. For example, /a/—*dast* [dast] 'he will give,' *dal* [dɑ + l] 'gave' MASC, *pjat'* [pæt̪] 'five,' *dala* [dɐ'la] 'gave' FEM, *vydat'* ['vɨdət̪] 'to give out.'

The accent is not fixed and is mobile, shifting in regular patterns both in declension and conjugation, e.g., *storoná* 'side,' ACC *stóronu*, GEN *storoný*, NOM PL *stórony*, GEN PL *storón*, DAT PL *storonám*, etc.

Except as described below, /o/ is replaced in unstressed syllables by /a/, in a system known as *akan'e* 'a-saying' (operating also in southern dialects and Belorussian but not in northern dialects or Ukrainian). Thus 'town' appears as *gorod* /'gorat/ NOM SING, *goroda* /gara'da/ NOM PL, *mezhdugorodnyj* /m̪iʒduga'rodnij/ 'interurban.' The last example also illustrates *ikan'e* 'i-saying,' in which /e/ is replaced in unstressed positions by /i/ (cf. *mezhdu* /'m̪eʒdu/ 'among, between'). *Ikan'e* also affects, in pretonic positions, /a/ after palatalized consonants and /j/, and /o/ after palatalized consonants, /j/ and the palatals /ʃ/ and /ʒ/. Thus: *pjat'* /p at̪/ 'five' ~ *pjati* /pi't̪i/ GEN, *let* /l ot/ 'flight' ~ *letat'* /l̪i'tat̪/ 'to fly,' *zheny* /'ʒoni/ 'wives' ~ *zhena* /ʒi'na/ 'wife.' The orthography ignores both *akan'e* and *ikan'e*.

There are thirteen pairs of distinctively non-palatalized/palatalized consonants: /p–p̪/, /b–b̪/, /m–m̪/, /f–f̪/, /v–v̪/, /t–t̪/, /d–d̪/, /s–s̪/, /z–z̪/, /n–n̪/, /l–l̪/, /r–r̪/, /k–k̪/. Consonants /g/ and /x/ have palatalized allophones, /tʃ/ and /ʎ/ (realized as [ʎʎ]) are nondistinctively palatalized. In addition there are /ts/, /ʃ/, /ʒ/ and /j/.

Voiced consonants except sonants are devoiced word-finally and before voiceless consonants. Conversely, voiceless consonants are voiced before voiced consonants except sonants, /v/ and /v̪/. Nonpalatalized consonants are frequently replaced by corresponding palatalized consonants before palatalized consonants, especially homorganic ones. Apart from a very few items and the devoicing of /z/ in prefixes, (e.g., *raz-* ~ *ras-*, *iz-* ~ *is-*), the orthography entirely ignores the various consonant assimilations and final devoicing. Thus: *otdat'* /ad'dat̪/ 'to give back,' *sdelat'* /'z d̪elat̪/ 'to do,' *gorod* /'gorat/.

4. Grammar

4.1 Nouns

The Old Russian system of eight declensions, three numbers and seven cases has been simplified into a system of three principal declensions and a vestigial consonant-stem declension, two numbers and six cases, the dual number and the vocative case having been discarded.

The 'feminine' declension in *-a/-ja* declines in the singular thus: NOM *komnata* 'room,' GEN *komnaty*, DAT *komnate*, ACC *komnatu*, INSTR *komnatoj*, PREP (*v*) *komnate*. A few masculine nouns are found in this declension. A typical noun of the 'masculine' declension is: *stol* 'table,' *stola*, *stolu*, *stol*, *stolom*, (*na*) *stole*. Neuters decline as masculines except for nominative and accusative, e.g., *okno* 'window,' PL *okna* (cf. *stoly*) and, usually, GEN PL—cf. *stolov*—*okon*. One masculine noun is still found in the declension which is now otherwise feminine, illustrated by *chast'* 'part,' *chasti*, *chasti*, *chast'*, *chast'ju*, (*o*) *chasti*.

Nouns of the masculine declension denoting animate beings use the genitive as an accusative, thus *muzh* 'husband,' GEN and ACC *muzha*. The genitive-accusative also applies to all nouns denoting animate beings in the plural, of whatever gender: *zhena*—GEN ACC PL *zhen* (/ʒon/).

Remnants of old declensions include an additional genitive in *-u* of some masculine nouns (usually partitive in function): *kilo sakharu* 'a kilo of sugar,' cf. *vkus sakhara* 'taste of sugar'; and an extra PREP case in *-ú* of some masculine nouns, having purely locative function: *v lesu* 'in the wood' (cf. *o lese* 'about the wood').

A vestige of the dual probably explains the NOM PL MASC in *-á* instead of *-y*, e.g., *goroda*, cf. *stoly*. The graphic identity of the old NOM MASC in *-a* with the GEN SING in *-a* of the same declension has led to the use of the GEN SING of a noun of any gender with the numerals *dva* 'two,' *tri* 'three,' *chetyre* 'four' and higher numerals ending in these elements. Numeral syntax is further complicated by the use of NOM SING with all numerals ending in *odin* 'one' and GEN PL with all other numerals: *dva stola* 'two tables,' *tridtsat' tri stola* '33 tables,' *sorok chetyre stola* '44 tables,' *sto odin stol* '101 tables,' *pjat' stolov* 'five tables.'

The genitive is not only obligatory in negative partitive expressions—*Net otveta* (GEN SING) 'There is no reply,' *Deneg* (GEN PL) *ne khvataet* 'There isn't enough money,' but is more frequent than the accusative with negated transitive verbs—*Shkoly* (GEN SING) *ona ne brosit* / *Shkolu* (ACC SING) *ona ne brosit* 'She will not give up school.'

Syntactically interesting too is the predicative instrumental, standard with certain copula-like verbs and the future of *byt'* 'to be': *Ona okazalas'/stala/budet sirotoj* 'She turned out to be/became/will be an orphan.' With the past tense of *byt'* both the instrumental and the nominative are found: *V to vremja ja byl student(om)* 'At that time I was a student,' the nominative being more colloquial. *Byt'* has no present tense: *Ona sirota* 'She (is) an orphan.'

There is no article, definite or indefinite. The 'long' form of the adjective, with a declension different from that of nouns, originally expressed 'definiteness' but is now simply the basic form of the adjective and the only attributive form. The 'short' form no longer declines and is restricted to predicative function, where it simply assigns a property to a subject—*Solntse velika, a Zemlja mala* 'The Sun is big but the Earth is small.' The long form is also used predicatively, assigning the subject to a class of like entities. Compare: *Vera ochen' umna* (short form) 'Vera is very clever' and *Vera ochen' umnaja* (long form) 'Vera is (a) very clever (person).' This distinction, while still active, is being eroded, especially in colloquial Russian, in favor of the long form.

4.2 Verbs

The aspect system of imperfective versus perfective, already active in Old Russian, has led to the reduction of the multiple tenses of Old Russian to just three: past, IMPFV or PRFV, present, IMPFV. only, and future, IMPFV or PRFV. The past, originally a periphrastic participial form, is now reduced to what was the participle and so changes according to gender and number, while present and future have 'true' conjugations of three persons and two numbers, the future imperfective being periphrastic. Thus: 'to infringe'—IMPFV *narushat'*, PRFV *narushit'*: past MASC *narushal/narushil*, FEM *narushala/narushila*, NEUT *narushalo/narushilo*, PL *narushali/ narushili*; present *narushaju, narushaesh', narushaet, narushaem, narushaete, narushajut*; FUT IMPFV *budu/ budesh'/ budet/ budem/ budete/ budut narushat'*, FUT PRFV *narushu, narushish', narushit, narushim, narushite, narushat*. The two aspects are differentiated formally by prefixation, suffixal changes or a combination of the two and occasionally by suppletion. A complication is the existence of many verbs which are not members of minimal pairs, distinguished only by aspect. These form the groups known as *sposoby dejstvija*, Aktionsarten, 'modes of action.' While associated with a base verb, each Aktionsart, appearing in one aspect only, adds a nuance to the base verb, without forming a plain aspectual counterpart. For instance, *stuchat'* 'to knock' is IMPFV and has no plain PRFV counterpart: *postuchat'* PRFV is diminutive or attenuative—'to knock a little / for a short time' and may have to serve in lieu of a plain PRFV; *stuknut'* PRFV is semelfactive—'to give a single knock'; *zastuchat'* PRFV is inceptive—'to start to knock'; *prostuchat'* PRFV is perdurative—'to knock for a certain period of time'; *postukivat'* IMPFV is intermittent(-diminutive)—'to knock (a little) from time to time.'

The dozen or so pairs of 'verbs of motion,' while participating in the aspect system, also distinguish between determinate (motion in a single direction) and indeterminate (motion not restricted so): *On letel v Moskvu* 'He was flying to Moscow'—*On letal v Moskvu* 'He flew to Moscow (and back, or several times).'

There are five participles: PRES ACT *narushajushchij* 'infringing,' PRES PASS *narushaemyj* 'being infringed,' PAST ACT IMPFV *narushavshij* 'were infringing' and PRFV *narushivshij* 'having infringed' and PAST PASS PRFV *narushennyj* 'infringed.' They decline as adjectives and the two passive ones have short forms, the PRFV PASS short form being an indispensible component of the passive voice: *Zakon byl narushen* 'The law was infringed.' The two indeclinable adverbial participles, often called gerunds, are, for example, IMPFV *narushaja* 'infringing' and PRFV *narushiv (shi)* 'having infringed.' Subordination by means of participles and gerunds, instead of relative and adverbial clauses, is common.

5. Lexis

While the bulk of the lexis is Slavonic, Russian has not been averse to borrowing at all periods. From Western European languages Dutch has provided nautical terminology: *botsman* 'bosun,' *kil'vater* 'wake'; German—military and other terminology: *lager'* 'camp,' *landshaft* 'landscape,' *buterbrod* 'sandwich'; French—military, mundane and cultural vocabulary: *batal'on* 'batallion,' *pal'to* 'overcoat,' *rezhisser* 'producer'; English—nautical terms: *michman* 'midshipman,' mundane: *bifshteks* 'steak,' industrial: *rel'sy* 'railway lines,' sociopolitical: *bojkot* 'boycott,' *khuligan* 'hooligan,' and in the twentieth century, sport: *futbol* 'football,' *vindsorfing* 'windsurfing' and technical: *bul'dozer* 'bulldozer,' *komp'juter* 'computer.'

Naturally, Russian has in the twentieth century gone on exploiting its historically established word-forming processes but it has also exploited less traditional ones. In this respect notable are appositional compounds such as *raketanositel'* 'carrier rocket,' *dom-muzej* 'home (which is also a) museum' and above all acronyms and various other accreted abbreviations—*vuz* (*vysshee uchebnoe zavedenie*) 'higher educational institution,' *GUM* (*Gosudarstvennyj Universal'nyj Magazin*) 'State Department Store,' *ROSTA* (*Rossijskoe Telegrafnoe Agentstvo*) 'Russian Telegraph Agency,' *kolkhoz* (*kollektivnoe khozjajstvo*) 'collective farm,' *univermag* (*universal'nyj magazin*) 'department store,' *zarplata* (*zarabotnaja plata*) 'wages,' *fizkul'tura* (*fizicheskaja kul'tura*) 'physical training.'

6. Influence of Russian

In varying degrees, Russian has provided loanwords, especially relating to twentieth century life, of technological and cultural significance, for many non-Slavonic languages of the former Soviet Union. An extreme case of such borrowing from Russian is provided by Chukchi. In Altaic, North Caucasian and easterly Uralic languages subordinating constructions on the Russian model have become common. The languages of many small speech-communities (Ingrian, Veps, Vot, Mordvinian, Siberian languages, etc.) have retreated or are retreating in the face of Russian.

Bibliography

Comrie B, Stone G 1978 *The Russian Language Since the Revolution*. Oxford University Press, Oxford
Isačenko A V 1962 *Die russische Sprache der Gegenwart, Teil I—Formenlehre*. Niemeyer, Halle
Issatschenko A 1980–83 *Geschichte der russischen Sprache*. Carl Winter, Heidelberg
Unbegaun B 1960 *Russian Grammar*. Oxford University Press, Oxford
Ward D 1981 Loan-words in Russian. *Journal of Russian Studies* **41**: 3–14, **42**: 5–14

D. Ward

Russian Federation: Language Situation

Following the collapse of the USSR in 1991 the Russian Federation, consisting of Russia and 16 autonomous republics, became a component of the Commonwealth of Independent States. The vast majority of the population of Russia (approximately 130 million in 1992) are speakers of Russian. At the time of the 1979 census, the main ethnic groups in the other republics, with percentages of the total population of each, were as shown in Table 1. Even apart from the fact that the figures are not recent, they can be taken to give only an approximate indication of the numbers of speakers of the languages. In the former USSR the percentage of speakers of the language associated with a given ethnic group varied from 99.8 percent for Russian to about 70 percent for some other languages, with Karelian at 47.8 percent being exceptionally low.

Table 1. Ethnic groups in republics of the Russian Federation (1979 figures).

Republic	Population (000s)	Main ethnic groups	%
Bashkir	3,849	Russian	40.3
		Tatar	24.5
		Bashkir	24.3
Buryat	900	Russian	72.0
		Buryat	23.0
Chechen–Ingushia	1,154	Chechen	52.9
		Russian	29.1
		Ingush	11.7
Chuvash	1,292	Chuvash	68.4
		Russian	26.0
Dagestan	1,628	Avar	25.7
		Dargva	15.2
		Kumyk	12.4
		Russian	11.6
		Lezgi	11.6
		Lak	5.1
Kabardino–Balkaria	674	Kabard	45.6
		Russian	35.1
		Balkar	9.0
Kalmyk	294	Russian	42.6
		Kalmyk	41.5
Karelia	736	Russian	71.3
		Karelian	11.1
		Belorussian	8.1
Komi	1,119	Russian	56.7
		Komi	25.3
Mari	703	Russian	47.5
		Mari	43.5
		Tatar	5.8
Mordvinia	991	Russian	59.7
		Mordva	34.2
North Ossetia	597	Ossete	50.5
		Russian	33.9
Tataria	3,436	Tatar	47.7
		Russian	44.0
Tuva	267	Tuva	60.5
		Russian	36.2
Udmurt	1,494	Russian	58.3
		Udmurt	32.2
		Tatar	6.6
Yakut (now Sakha)	839	Russian	50.4
		Yakut	36.9

See also: Commonwealth of Independent States (CIS).

Bibliography

Comrie B 1981 *The Languages of the Soviet Union*. Cambridge University Press, Cambridge

Rwanda

This Bantu language, more accurately called Runya-Rwanda, and also known as KinyaRwanda, is spoken in Rwanda, extreme south-west Uganda, and the north-west corner of Tanzania by a total of approximately 7.5 million. Guthrie's J.61, it is one of a number of languages grouped together as so-called Interlacustrine Bantu.

1. Typology

KinyaRwanda is a head-initial SVO inflectional language, with prepositions, auxiliary preceding the main verb, and a typically Bantu noun class system.

2. Phonology

It has a five vowel system, with contrastive length. Its consonant inventory is complex; in addition to plain stops and affricates, it includes palatalized (C + y) and labialized (C + w) prealveolar stops, prenasalized (N + C), prenasalized-palatalized (N + C + y), prenasalized-labialized (N + C + w) stops.

It is a two-tone language, of comparable complexity to other Bantu languages.

3. Morphology

Rwanda has a system of sixteen noun classes, in which paired CV prefixes mark singular/plural, and with an augment (preprefix) vowel whose presence or absence marks indefinite/definite respectively.

The verb has a typically Bantu morphology, with subject and object agreement proforms, and tense (and negative) markers prefixed to the root, which can also carry one or more suffixed extensions, a tense-aspect-mood element and the verb-final vowel.

As in other Bantu languages, there are five basic tenses, marking present ($\emptyset \sim$ -*a*-), and recent and remote past (-*a*-, -*a*-' - respectively) and future (-*ra*-, -*zaa*- respectively) tenses, with typical semantic/pragmatic fluidity between the recent/remote distinction. The verbal extension includes -*w*- (passive), -*ir*- (applicative, which introduces a new object argument to the verb) -*iiš*- (causative/instrumental), -*an*- reciprocal, -*ik*- neutral, -*uuk*-/-*uur*- reversive, -*y*- causative/instrumental.

4. Syntax

Except for demonstratives, noun phrase modifiers follow the head-word. Compound tenses occur, formed with auxiliaries which carry important temporal and aspectual information. Normally the grammatical subject preceeds the verb, but KinyaRwanda can undergo Subject/Object reversal for emphasis. The alternation in present tense marking noted above is explained by noting that $\emptyset$ occurs when a complement follows, and -*a*- when there is none. Infinitival, subjunctive, and tensed sentential complements introduced by a complementizer, occur.

```
u-mu-gabo  y-aanz-e      ko    u-mu-huûngu a-roóngor-a
man        he-refuse-ASP COMP  boy         he-marry-ASP

u-mu-koôbwa we
girl        his
```

'The man refused that the boy marry his daughter.'

(adapted from Kimenyi 1980)

Bibliography

Kimenyi A 1980 *A Relational Grammar of Kinyarwanda*. University of California Publications in Linguistics 91. University of California Press, Berkeley, CA

Kimenyi A 1986 Review of Jouannet F (ed.) *Le kinyarwanda, langue* du Rwanda: Etudes linguistiques. *JALL* **8(2)**: 177–89

R. J. Sim

Rwanda: Language Situation

Rwanda (population 6,300,000 in 1986) has one of the highest population densities in Africa (238 people/km^2). High population growth (3.7 percent) and levels of soil erosion make for major pressure on land distribution. The rural population is over 95 percent (World Bank 1984), the capital, Kigali, having a population of 118,000 (1978 census). As with Burundi, an existing Rwanda kingdom was absorbed into German East Africa in 1899, and mandated to Belgium from 1916 to 1962, after which Rwanda became independent.

1. Linguistic Relationships

KinyaRwanda (or RunyaRwanda) is a Lacustrine Bantu language of Guthrie's zone J, closely related to (Ru)Rundi; the differences have been said to be more psychological than linguistic. The tiny Hima community on the Ugandan border speaks a closely related zone-J Bantu language.

2. Language Policy, Education, and Literacy

Both KinyaRwanda and French are official languages, and the former is the medium of instruction in lower primary. Only 2 percent of the eligible population are enrolled in secondary school. The official literacy rate is 25 percent.

3. Language Shift, Use, and Attitudes

KinyaRwanda is mother tongue to 90 percent and second language to 8 percent of the population (World Bank), with its first-language community extending into Uganda (870,000 speakers), Zaire (250,000), and Tanzania (88,000). In Rwanda, it is the first language of the Hutu (89 percent), Tutsi (10 percent), and Twa (1 percent) ethnic communities. The Hutu (agriculturalist Bantu), moved into the area in the times of the major Bantu expansions. The non-Bantu pastoralist Tutsi, Nilotic people originating from the direction of Ethiopia, at some point shifted their language to KinyaRwanda.

As in Burundi, a feudal situation developed from the fifteenth or sixteenth century, in which the Tutsi were the dominant class, ruling through a *mwami* 'king.' A Hutu elite, which emerged in the 1960s, took power and forced many Tutsi to seek refuge in Burundi and Uganda.

The stratification resulted in social variation, in which the Tutsi speech variety was regarded as prestigious and the Hutu variety as common. The Christian Bible (1954/57) was published in the latter.

The Twa are KinyaRwanda-speaking pygmies with a hunter, potter, ironworker, and busker lifestyle. They speak a distinct variety of the language.

4. Minority Languages

(Ki)Swahili is mother tongue to 10 percent of the people (World Bank).

The Hima community consists of some 4,000 speakers, and is a surviving dialect of a formerly widespread community.

Bibliography

1991 *Africa South of the Sahara*, 20th edn. Europa, London

R. J. Sim

Ryukyuan

The Ryukyuan language comprises a group of dialects, some of them mutually unintelligible, spoken throughout a group of islands located at the southwestern tip of Japan.

The earliest systematic description of 'Luchuan' was likely that of the English linguist Chamberlain in his study of 1895. Hattori (1976) hypothesized that Ryukyuan diverged from Japanese around the sixth century AD. Ryukyuan displays many of the grammatical and phonological features, as well as lexical features, of Old Japanese. Thus, whereas the particle *ga* is used only nominatively in modern Japanese, it also appears in a genitive form in Ryukyuan reflecting an earlier usage. Also, whereas the Old Japanese consonant *p* eventually became *h*, as in modern Japanese *hana* 'flower,' *ha* 'leaf,' and *hi* 'fire,' the original sound is retained in Ryukyuan as *pana, pa,* and *pi*. Systematic sound correspondences such as the raising of mid-vowels *e* and *o* to *i* and *u* occur as seen in the following equivalents for 'rain,' 'wine,' 'sash,' and 'bone': [Tokyo] *ame, sake, obi, hone*; [Shuri dialect] *ami, saki, ubi, funi*. Chamberlain observed that the sequence vowel plus laryngeal phoneme /'/ plus vowel corresponded to the single vowel syllable in modern Japanese.

Ryukyuan is regarded by most Japanese dialectologists as a collection of Japanese dialects rather than an autonomous language. The view is held on the basis of genetic relation, the presence of linguistic similarities between Ryukyuan and Japanese, and the underlying political fact of the islands' assimilation by Japan. Conversely, it is pointed out that the two are mutually unintelligible, possess a distinctive sociohistorical development and display different cultural and sociolinguistic characteristics. Established in the early fifteenth century as an independent Ryukyuan kingdom, Okinawa became *Okinawa-ken* or 'prefecture' following the Meiji Restoration of 1867, after which the use of the Ryukyuan language was discouraged. The return of the islands to Japan in 1972 continued pressure on Ryukyuan, accelerating its decline. School instruction throughout the Okinawan islands is conducted in standard Japanese. Recent years have shown increasing local interest in the language and its ethnolinguistic maintenance.

Based on shared phonological and morphological features, Ryukyuan can be divided into three main groups. The Amami–Okinawa group comprise the Amami dialects (Amami, Kikaijima, Tokunoshima) and the Okinawan dialect of Shuri, although the political location of the Amami group is now Kyushu (Kagoshima prefecture) and not Okinawa. The Miyako–Yaeyama dialects (Hirara, Miyako, Ishigaki-jima, Hateruma) comprise the second group and the southernmost Yonaguni dialect comprises the third group. Shuri is generally regarded as the 'Standard Ryukyuan' dialect, and as well as being used on the island of Okinawa has traditionally been the lingua franca of the Ryukyus. Two sociolinguistic varieties of Shuri speech are noteworthy: the form spoken by the former aristocracy (*yukatcu*) and the 'popular' form of the common people (*hyakusoo*).

See also: Japanese; Dialect and Dialectology; Sociolinguistics.

Bibliography

Chamberlain B 1895 *Essay in Aid of a Grammar and Dictionary of the Luchuan Language*. Trubner, London

Hattori S 1976 Ryukyu hogen to hondo hogen. In: *Okinawagaku no Reimei*. Okinawa Bunka Kyokai, Tokyo

Kokuritsu Kokugo Kenkyujo 1963 *Okinawago Jiten*. Okura-sho, Tokyo

Uemura Y 1965 Okinawa no hogen. *Bungaku* **33**: 7

J. C. Maher

S

Saadya Gaon (882–942AD)

Saadya Gaon, son of Joseph Gaon, was born in Upper Egypt and became the religious leader (Gaon) in Babylon. He was a polymath and innovator in many disciplines including Hebrew grammar, and is generally regarded as the first Hebrew grammarian. His linguistic writings show familiarity with contemporary Arabic philology. He was the author of the first Hebrew lexicon, *Ha-'Egron*, which is only partially extant. Its purpose was to assist poets in constructing acrostics and finding rhymes. To this end, he arranged the dictionary in two lists alphabetically; one according to the initial letters, the other according to the final letters of words. Each word is illustrated with quotations from biblical and rabbinic texts. Under the influence of Arab philologists, he later reissued the dictionary with a new title *Book of Poetics: Books of Languages* in a revised form, adding an Arabic preface, translating the Hebrew terms into Arabic, and including a section on the consonants. In an extract from this last section quoted in his commentary to the mystical work *Sēpher Yĕṣirā* (*Book of Creation*), he discusses the 'guttural' letters—Aleph, He, Heth, Ayin. In this commentary, he also suggests the distinction between the eleven unchanging consonants and the other eleven and discusses the pronunciation of the letter Resh in Babylon and Palestine.

His work entitled *Book of Elegance of the Language of the Hebrews* (also known as the *Books on the Language* or simply *Twelve Parts*), which has not been preserved in its entirety, constitutes the first study of Hebrew grammar as a separate discipline independent of Massoretic studies. The first part of the work appears to have included a study of the permutation of the twenty-two consonants according to phonetics and lists the precluded combinations of letters. The extant fragments cover the following subjects: augmentation and contraction of Hebrew stems (i.e., when root letters are doubled or elided—he did not recognize the tri-literality of the Hebrew stem); inflection of nouns, verbs, and particles; the *dagesh* (a *dagesh* is a dot in the letter indicating either that the consonant is doubled or the plosive pronunciation of the letters *bgdkpt*); vowels and phonetics; the quiescent and vocal *shewa*; laryngeal (or 'guttural') letters and the changes in their vocalization; interchangeable letters. This work, despite its rudimentary nature, laid the foundation of the scientific treatment of Hebrew grammar.

Saadya Gaon also wrote a glossary of ninety *hapax legomena* in the Hebrew Bible, bringing analogies from postbiblical Hebrew, as well as a treatise on the obscure words in the *Mishnah*.

See also: Grammarians, Hebrew.

Bibliography

(For a full list of publications of fragments of Saadya Gaon's works, see Tene D 1971.)
Allony N (ed.) 1969 Saadya Gaon *Ha-'Egrōn Kitāb 'Uṣūl 'Al-Shi'r 'al-'Ibrānī*. The Academy of the Hebrew Language, Jerusalem
Hirschfeld H 1920 *Literary History of Hebrew Grammarians and Lexicographers*. Oxford University Press, Oxford
Malter H 1921 *Life and Works of Saadia Gaon*. Jewish Publication Society of America, Philadelphia, PA
Skoss S L 1955 *Saadiah Gaon, the Earliest Hebrew Grammarian*. Dropsie College Press, Philadelphia, PA
Tene D 1971 Linguistic literature, Hebrew. In: *Encyclopaedia Judaica*, XVI, pp. 1364–65; 1367–69. Keter, Jerusalem

J. Weinberg

Sabellian

SEE Italic Languages

Sacks, Harvey (1935–75)

Sacks was an original scholar, a profound genius whose thought spanned traditional disciplines and founded a new one, conversation analysis, thereby contributing to the systematic study of language in interaction. His efforts were oriented to the study of the organization or orderliness of language use. The sociological, linguistic, and philosophical foundations of his thought are rooted in those whose work he studied or worked with: Garfinkel and ethnomethodology, Erving Goffman and interaction analysis (see *Goffman, Erving*), Chomskyan linguistics (see *Chomsky's Philosophy of Language*), and Wittgenstein's ordinary language philosophy (see *Wittgenstein, Ludwig*).

Sacks earned his doctorate in sociology at the University of California, Berkeley, USA (1966) an LLB at Yale Law School (1959), and a BA at Columbia College (1955). For a period of approximately 11 years, 1964–75, he lectured at the University of California, Los Angeles and Irvine. His lectures were recorded, transcribed, and then duplicated and made available to those who requested them. The tapes were not saved. His colleagues and collaborators, primarily Gail Jefferson and Emanuel Schegloff, have since been responsible for editing and preparing his lectures for publication. Sacks's lectures achieved a worldwide circulation during his lifetime and influenced many scholars and researchers in sociology and linguistics.

He treated such topics as: the organization of person-reference; adjacency-pairs; topic organization in conversation; pronouns as transformational operations in conversation; speaker selection preferences; sequential tyings; the pre-sequence; preference for recipient-design or 'orientation to co-participant' in talk; 'pro'-verbs and performatives in conversation; the organization of turn-taking; turn-allocation constraints on turn-construction; conversational openings and closings; and puns, jokes, stories, and repairs in conversation.

Two volumes now contain the bulk of his lectures (Jefferson 1989; Sacks 1992). He never published a book during his lifetime though he had planned one and written an introduction to it.

Bibliography

Coulter J 1976 Harvey Sacks: A preliminary appreciation. *Sociology* **10**: 507–12

Garfinkel H, Sacks H 1970 On formal structures of practical actions. In: McKinney J M, Tiryakian E A (eds.) *Theoretical Sociology: Perspectives and Developments*. Appleton Century Crofts, New York

Jefferson G (ed.) 1989 Harvey Sacks—Lectures 1964–1965 with an Introduction/Memoir by Schegloff E A. *Human Studies* **12**: 211–393

Sacks H 1963 Sociological description. *Berkeley Journal of Sociology* **8**: 1–16

Sacks H 1967 The search for help: No one to turn to. In: Schneidman E S (ed.) *Essays in Self Destruction*. Science House, New York

Sacks H 1972 An initial investigation of the usability of conversational data for doing sociology. In: Sudnow D N (ed.) *Studies in Social Interaction*. Free Press, New York

Sacks H 1972 On the analyzability of stories by children. In: Gumperz J J, Hymes D (eds.) *Directions in Sociolinguistics: The Ethnography of Communication*. Holt, Reinhart and Winston, New York

Sacks H 1972 Notes on police assessment of moral character. In: Sudnow D N (ed.) *Studies in Social Interaction*. Free Press, New York

Sacks H 1973 On some puns with some intimations. In: Shuy R W (ed.) *Report of the 32nd Annual Round Table on Linguistics and Language Studies*. Georgetown University Press, Washington, DC

Sacks H 1974 An analysis of the course of a joke's telling in conversation. In: Bauman R, Sherzer J F (eds.) *Explorations in the Ethnography of Speaking*. Cambridge University Press, Cambridge

Sacks H, Schegloff E A, Jefferson G 1974 A simplest systematics for the organization of turn-taking in conversation. *Language* **50**: 696–735

Sacks H 1975 Everyone has to lie. In: Blount B, Sanches M (eds.) *Sociocultural Dimensions of Language Use*. Academic Press, New York

Schegloff E A, Jefferson G, Sacks H 1977 The preference for self-correction in the organization of repair in conversation. *Language* **53**: 361–82

Sacks H 1978 Some technical considerations of a dirty joke. In: Schenkein J (ed.) *Studies in the Organization of Conversational Interaction*. Academic Press, New York

Sacks H 1979 Hotrodder: A revolutionary category. In: Psathas G (ed.) *Everyday Language: Studies in Ethnomethodology*. Irvington, New York

Sacks H, Schegloff E A 1979 Two preferences in the organization of reference to persons in conversation and their interaction. In: Psathas G (ed.) *Everyday Language: Studies in Ethnomethodology*. Irvington, New York

Sacks H 1992 (ed. Jefferson G) *Lectures on Conversation*, 2 vols. Blackwell, Oxford

Schegloff E A, Sacks H 1973 Opening up closings. *Semiotica* **7**: 289–327

Schegloff E A 1989 Harvey Sacks—Lectures 1964–1965. Introduction/Memoir. *Human Studies* **12**: 185–209

G. Psathas

Sainliens, Claude de (Claudius Hollyband, Claudio a Sancto Vinculo) (?–1597)

Claude de Sainliens was the most popular and most prolific of the French instructors in England in the second half of the sixteenth century, writing a number of instructional texts for French and Italian, along with at least two major French–English dictionaries.

A native of Moulins, France, de Sainliens fled the Wars of Religion early in the 1560s. He may be the M. Claudius who helped John Baret prepare the French part of his trilingual dictionary (*Alvearie*, 1573/74), and some attribute to him the *Dictionarie French and English* (1570).

His general French textbooks were the *French Schoolemaister* (1573) and the *Frenche Littelton* (1576). They represent slightly different philosophies of language instruction, the former presenting grammar and pronunciation rules first, the latter relegating those to reference status at the end. In 1580 de Sainliens published three texts meant to supplement the *Littelton*: *De pronuntiatione linguae gallicae* (in which he attacked efforts for orthographic reform); *A Treatise for the declining of verbs*; and a bilingual dictionary, *A Treasurie of the French tong*. In 1593 he considerably expanded the dictionary, retitling it *A Dictionarie French and English*. This dictionary was an important source for Cotgrave's dictionary of 1611. Both schoolbooks remained popular well into the seventeenth century, with many posthumous editions.

See also: Dictionaries, English, before Johnson.

Bibliography

Eccles M 1986 Claudius Hollyband and the earliest French–English dictionaries. *Studies in Philology* **83**: 51–61

Farrer L 1908 *Un devancier de Cotgrave: La vie et les oeuvres de Claude de Sainliens*. Presses universitaires, Paris

Kibbee D A 1991 *For to Speke Frenche Trewely. The French Language in England, 1000–1600: Its Status, Description and Instruction*. Benjamins, Amsterdam

D. A. Kibbee

St Christopher and Nevis: Language Situation

The official language of the two islands which make up this country (also known as St Kitts–Nevis), lying at the northern end of the Leeward Islands, is English. Most of the 41,870 inhabitants (1990) speak Kittitian Creole (Lesser Antillean Creole English). There are radio broadcasts in Spanish in addition to English.

St Helena: Language Situation

The population of the British colony of St Helena, which apart from the island of St Helena itself, includes the island groups of Ascension and Tristan da Cunha, totals approximately 8,500, all of whom are speakers of English.

St Lucia: Language Situation

Though the official language is English, the vast majority of the 153,000 inhabitants (1991) of St Lucia, one of the Windward Islands, speak Lesser Antillean Creole French (also known as Patwa). Radio stations broadcast in English, French, and Creole.

St Pierre and Miquelon: Language Situation

The French overseas *collectivité territoriale* of the Iles Saint-Pierre-et-Miquelon consists of a number of small islands lying some 25 kilometers to the south of Newfoundland. Almost all the 6,392 inhabitants (1990) are speakers of French.

St Vincent and the Grenadines: Language Situation

The official language of the 107,598 inhabitants (1991) of St Vincent and the Grenadines, a small group of islands forming part of the Windward Islands, is English, but Lesser Antillean Creole English is the most widely used spoken language. A small number speak a French-based creole. Education is not compulsory. Literacy is at 82 percent.

Sajnovics, János (1735–85)

Sajnovics, astronomer and linguist, was born on May 12, 1735, in Tordas, Hungary, the younger son of a well-to-do noble family. He entered the Jesuit Order in 1748, studied philosophy and mathematics at the Universities of Nagyszombat (Czech: Trnava; German: Tyrnau) and Vienna, and astronomy at the Vienna Imperial Observatory (1766). As a member of a team of Austro–Hungarian astronomers he traveled, in 1769, to the Arctic island of Vardø, there to record the passage of Venus and to measure the earth–sun distance. Sajnovics, having observed a number of similarities between the words used by the indigenous Lapps and Hungarian words, went to study written sources in Copenhagen, which confirmed his theory that the two languages are related. He reported this to the Danish Royal Society, which published his account (Sajnovics 1770). Unfavorable reaction to his theory in his native country turned Sajnovics away from further language studies, but he continued distinguished research and teaching in astronomy until his death in Buda (now Budapest) on May 4, 1785. He was a member of the Royal Societies of Denmark and Norway.

By comparing words in the two languages as well as some grammatical structures, such as markers for plural, comparison, and diminution, Sajnovics confirmed in systematic detail earlier adumbrations of the existence of the Finno–Ugric family of languages, providing a prototype for an improved approach to the study of language filiation, one requiring both lexical and grammatical evidence. His model was fully developed and extended to the entire Finno–Ugric family by Sámuel Gyarmathi (see *Gyarmathi, Sámuel (1751–1830)*.

Bibliography

Erdödi J 1970 Sajnovics, der Mensch und der Gelehrte. *Acta Linguistica Academiae Scientiarum Hungaricae* **20**: 291–322
Gulya J, Szathmári I 1974 *Sajnovics János*. Magyar Nyelvtudományi Társaság, Budapest
Lakó G 1970 J Sajnovics und seine Demonstratio. *Acta Linguistica Academiae Scientiarum Hungaricae* **20**: 269–89
Sajnovics J 1770 *Demonstratio, idioma Ungarorum et Lapponum idem esse.* Salicath, Copenhagen; 2nd edn. 1771 Soc. Jesu, Nagyszombat; German transl. by Ehlers M 1972 *Beweis, dass die Sprache der Ungarn und Lappen dieselbe ist.* Harrassowitz, Wiesbaden

V. E. Hanzeli

Samar-Leyte

This West Malayo-Polynesian language of the Philippines is widely spoken as a first language by an estimated 2,180,000. According to the 1980 census, it is employed in 4 percent of Filipino homes. Also known variously as 'Waray,' 'Waray–Waray,' 'Samareno,' 'Samaran,' or 'Binisaya,' it is spoken on Samar and Leyte islands. In 1909, a regional association was formed to promote the language, the 'Academy of the Leyte-Samar Bisayan Dialects.'

See also: Philippines; Tagalog; Cebuano; Ilocano; Kapampangan; Bikol; Pangasinan.

Bibliography

Mintz M W 1971a *Bikol Grammar Notes*. University of Hawaii Press, Honolulu, HI
Mintz M W 1971b *Bikol Dictionary*. University of Hawaii Press, Honolulu, HI

J. C. Maher

Samāsa

Samāsa is a 'nominal compound' in Pāṇini's grammar. Each consists of a main part (*pradhāna*) and a subordinate part (*upasarjana*).

See also: Avyayibhāva; Bahuvrīhi; Dvandva; Karmadhāraya; Tatpuruṣa; Pāṇinian Linguistics.

Bibliography

Staal J F 1966 Room at the Top in Sanskrit: Ancient and modern descriptions of nominal composition. *Indo–Iranian Journal* **9**: 165–98

Samoyed

SEE Uralic Languages

Sampling

Linguistic surveys have become progressively more sophisticated in their use of research methodology, but there is still much that sociolinguists can learn from the sampling techniques employed by sociologists and political scientists. Gone are the days when it could be believed that any competent speakers could give adequate data about a language. It is realized that every aspect of language varies across individuals and subgroups in a population, and thus that care must be taken to obtain data from a representative sample.

1. The Purpose of Sampling

The aim of social research is to arrive at justified conclusions—descriptive and explanatory—about human populations. Usually the focus of such conclusions is some subset of the human family: e.g., Americans, teenagers, Catholics. To draw conclusions that apply to all members of such populations, it might seem appropriate and necessary to observe the entire population. Such studies are called *censuses* or *total enumerations*. Often, however, it is simply not possible to observe all members of the populations that interest social scientists. Therefore, numerous techniques have been developed that allow conclusions to be drawn about a specified population on the basis of observing only some of its members. The selection of the members to be observed for this purpose is called *sampling*.

Political polling offers evidence of the power of modern sampling techniques. Samples of only a few thousand voters can predict what tens of millions of voters will do on election day. Indeed, pollsters are often criticized for taking the suspense or the fun out of political campaigns and are sometimes blamed for low voter turnout—by convincing voters the election outcome is already determined. Political sample surveys have not always been so accurate, however.

In 1920, the *Literary Digest* newsmagazine, published from 1890 to 1938, broke new ground in political polling by mailing postcard ballots to around 600,000 voters in six major states, asking them how they planned to vote on election day. Names had been selected from lists of automobile owners and telephone subscribers. The answers of those who responded to the poll encouraged the *Digest* to predict Warren Harding the winner over James Cox—and they were right. The 1920 success led the *Digest* to repeat their pre-election poll in 1924, 1928, and 1932. Each time, they increased the size of the mailing, and they correctly predicted the winner in each election.

In 1936, the *Digest* mailed ten million postcard ballots, two million of which were returned. On the basis of poll results and cautioning 'We make no claim to infallibility,' the *Digest* nonetheless confidently predicted victory for Kansas senator Alf Landon in a landslide over incumbent president Franklin Delano Roosevelt. The *Digest* was correct only in predicting a landslide. Two weeks later, Roosevelt's 61 percent of the popular vote represented the largest presidential landslide in American history.

The *Literary Digest's* downfall lay with their choice of respondents: they were not representative of all American voters. It is important to recognize that the USA in 1936 was just recovering from the Great Depression, and many citizens were still quite poor. Those who had automobiles and telephones, therefore, were wealthier than the average. Finally, the poor are traditionally more likely to vote for Democratic candidates in American politics, and they were especially supportive of Roosevelt, whose New Deal had

offered them the beginnings of economic recovery. As a consequence, those voters most likely to vote for Roosevelt were never polled by the *Digest*.

In 1936, a young opinion pollster, George Gallup, correctly predicted that Roosevelt would be reelected. In contrast to the *Digest's* two million respondents, Gallup's prediction rested on the responses of a few thousand voters. His success was due to his system of selecting respondents.

Gallup began with a demographic description of the American electorate: the numbers of men and women, young and old, rich and poor, rural and urban, etc. He then selected his respondents so as to insure that the distribution of such characteristics in his sample matched those of the larger population of voters: the same percentage of young-rich-urban-males, old-rich-rural-females, young-poor-rural-males, etc.

Whereas the *Literary Digest* underrepresented poor voters, Gallup's *quotas sampling* method took that variable into account. As a consequence, Gallup correctly predicted FDR as the winner in 1936. He was similarly successful in the 1940 and 1944 elections, using his same quota sampling technique. In 1948, however, Gallup predicted New York governor, Thomas Dewey, the winner over incumbent president Harry Truman.

Gallup's 1948 downfall lay largely in the same problem the *Literary Digest* suffered in 1936: the poll respondents were not adequately representative of the population they were intended to reflect. In 1948, Gallup's description of the national electorate was primarily based on the 1940 US Census.

The country's population and its voters had changed dramatically during the 8 years following the census, however. For example, the war years saw a massive migration from the country to the city and an expansion of the assembly-line work force. Traditionally, city-dwellers and assembly-line workers have voted Democratic more than the average. As a consequence, Gallup predicted how 1940 America would have voted, which was quite different from 1948 America.

Unlike the *Literary Digest*, the Gallup Poll stayed in business, largely due to their adoption of newly developed sampling techniques. In 1948, a number of academic researchers experimented with *probability sampling* methods, and they called the election correctly. Probability sampling has subsequently become the standard for social research.

2. The Logic of Probability Sampling

Probability sampling is based on the fundamental principal—taken from probability theory—that a sample of elements will be generally representative of the population from which it is selected if every element in that population had the same chance of being selected into the sample. Thus, if all members of a community are given the same probability of selection for a survey of foreign language ability, then the sample so selected will be representative of the whole community: with the proper numbers of men, women, rich, poor, and so forth. This is called an *EPSEM* (equal probability of selection method) sample.

The term *random sampling* is often used interchangeably with probability sampling, since random selection is the prototypic method for assuring equal probability to elements being considered for a sample. Flipping coins, rolling dice, and computer-generated tables of random numbers are all examples of random selection.

In practice, probability sampling rests on a somewhat broader principle than the EPSEM model just described, since it is often impossible or impractical to give every element in a large, complex population the same chance of being selected. If each element in a population has a *known*, *non-zero* probability of selection, and each element selected is given a *weight* equal to the inverse of that probability, then the resulting, weighted sample will be representative of the total population. An illustration follows of that logic in practice.

For example, suppose that a community of 1,000,000 has only 1,000 residents of Chinese descent. A random sample of 1,000 respondents from that community should contain only one of the Chinese residents since the overall *sampling ratio* would be 1/1,000. Suppose, however, that the analytical aims of the study of foreign language made it desirable to have at least 100 Chinese respondents. It would be necessary to select a one-tenth sample, totalling 100,000 respondents, in order to accomplish that with an EPSEM sample. The larger study would cost 100 times as much as the smaller one.

If it were possible to identify the residents of Chinese descent prior to sampling, however, it would be possible to select one-tenth of them at random, producing the desired 100. For the rest of the population, a 1/1,100 sampling ratio would be used, producing approximately 900 more respondents, for a total of 1,000. Notice that the resulting sample would not be representative of the whole community, however. The sample would overrepresent those of Chinese descent, just as the *Literary Digest* poll underrepresented poor voters.

The misrepresentation could be accommodated statistically, however. In all calculations from the sample, suppose that every Chinese respondent was counted ten times and every non-Chinese respondent was counted 1,100 times. This procedure would provide a statistical re-creation of the whole population of one million—with the proper proportion of Chinese and non-Chinese members.

If the analysis of the weighted sample indicated that 3,100 residents (900 of Chinese descent and 2,200 of the others) could speak Mandarin, that should provide a fairly close estimate of the corresponding numbers of Mandarin-speakers within the total community.

3. Sampling Error

Probability sampling does not guarantee that samples will represent their parent populations *exactly*, but probability theory permits the *calculation of how close* a sample will come in its representation of a population. The following formula estimates the *sampling error* (*se*) of percentages, such as the percentage favoring a particular political candidate.

$$se = \sqrt{\frac{p \times q}{n}}$$

In this formula, p represents the percentage of the sample taking some position: favoring Candidate X, for example; q represents the rest of the sample: those who do not favor Candidate X. (Notice that $q = 1.00 - p$.) Finally, n is the size of the sample.

With a sample of 100 respondents, in which 50 percent favored Candidate X—thus $n = 100$, $p = 0.5$, $q = 0.5$—the sampling error, *se*, would be 0.05 or five percentage points.

Probability theory, which will not be explicated here, warrants assertions regarding the likelihood that the percentage favoring Candidate X in the whole population falls within a certain interval around the sample percentage of 50 percent. Specifically, there is a 95 percent likelihood that the population figure lies within ±2 *se* of the sample percentage: between 40 percent and 60 percent in the present example. Put differently, there is a five-in-a-hundred chance that the true figure lies outside that interval.

Probability theory also indicates there is a 99.9 percent likelihood that the population figure lies within ±3 *se* of the sample percentage. Or, there is only one chance in a thousand that the percentage favoring Candidate X in the whole population is outside the interval from 35 percent to 65 percent.

To review, if 50 percent of a probability sample say they favor Candidate X, the best estimate of the percentage favoring X in the larger population is 50 percent. It is unlikely, however, that *exactly* 50 percent favor X. Notice that it could be said with one hundred percent confidence that X's support in the whole population lies somewhere between 0 percent and 100 percent—since there are no other possibilities. This is not a useful assertion, however. But, probability sampling warrants somewhat more useful assertions: it is said, for example, that 'we are 95 percent *confident* that the percentage favoring X in the population is between 40 and 60 percent.' In this statement, the interval from 40 to 60 is called the *95 percent confidence interval*.

Notice in the above formula that the sampling error is inversely proportional to the sample size: the larger the sample, the smaller the sampling error. Specifically, quadrupling the sample size cuts the sampling error in half. Thus, if a sample had been selected of 400 in which 50 percent favored Candidate X, it would be 95 percent certain that 45 percent to 55 percent of the total population favored X. Had the sample been 1,600 (common in national samples), there would have been a 95 percent certainty that the percentage found in the sample would be within 2.5 percentage points of the percentage favoring X in the population.

Sampling error is also affected by p and q in the formula. Specifically, it is reduced as the percentage split observed in the sample moves away from half-and-half. Thus, if 90 percent were found to favor Candidate X in a sample of 400, it would be estimated (with 95 percent confidence) that X's population support would fall between 87 percent and 93 percent: ±3 percentage points, as contrasted to ±5 percentage points in the case of a 50/50 split.

4. Probability Sampling Techniques

In this section are examined some of the concrete techniques employed in probability sampling, beginning with a discussion of *sampling frames*: the lists or quasi-lists from which samples are selected.

4.1 Sampling Frames

The theoretical discussion of sampling above speaks of selecting a sample from a population. This assumes implicitly that there exists some way of identifying the members of that larger population, so that a sample can be selected. Ideally, there would be a list of the members by name. In practice, such lists are not always available and compromises need to be made.

Finding no list of all the residents of a city, researchers have at times selected their samples from telephone directory listings (as did the *Literary Digest*). The fundamental principle to be recognized here is that probability samples are representative of the sampling frames from which they are selected. Thus a sample taken from a telephone directory will be representative of those listed in the directory. Persons without telephones or with unlisted numbers will not be represented by such a sample.

Even sampling frames that seem perfectly suited to the research aims may be flawed. A list of students enrolled in a specific college may, in fact, be missing some names or may include names of students who have subsequently dropped out. By the same token, the list of registered voters will not have the names of people who will subsequently register and vote on election day.

Since it is seldom possible to obtain or create a list that contains the entire target population and no one else, it is always important to bear in mind any mismatches when generalizing from a sample to a population.

4.2 Simple Random Sampling

The introductory discussion of probability sampling earlier described *simple random sampling*. To determine the extent of foreign language ability at a college of 10,000 students, a list of the student body could be numbered from 1 to 10,000. Then, if a sample of, for example, 1,000 was desired, a simple computer program could be written to generate 1,000 random numbers between 1 and 10,000. The students whose numbers were selected would comprise the sample.

Simple random sampling, while it illustrates the logic of probability sampling, is seldom used in practice. Other techniques are more practical and/or produce more accurate results.

4.3 Systematic Sampling

Systematic sampling is a commonly used form of probability sampling. It is very straightforward and usually produces results comparable to simple random sampling.

In the college of 10,000 students, a sample of 1,000 could be selected by simply taking every tenth student in the list. One of the first 10 students would be chosen at random, plus every tenth student thereafter. If the random number selected were 6, for example, the sample would consist of students 6, 16, 26, 36, etc. The sampling interval (10 in this case) is calculated by dividing the total population (10,000) by the sample size desired (1,000).

Notice that if the list of students was in a random order, then a systematic sample from that list would essentially be a random sample. Typically, however, such lists are not in random order, but this usually works to the sampler's advantage. The list of college students, for example, might very well have all the freshmen first, then sophomores, and so forth. A simple random sample from such a list would come close to the proper percentage from each class, within the range of sampling error discussed above. A systematic sample from such a list, however, would have exactly the right numbers from each class, since one-tenth of each class

would be selected. This is the principle of *stratification* to be discussed in Sect. 5.4 below.

The only danger in systematic sampling is the rare possibility that a list will have been organized in a periodic fashion that corresponds to the sampling interval. In one survey of soldiers during World War II, a systematic one-tenth sample was selected from a list organized by squads. Every squad contained ten men, one of whom was the squad sergeant. The sample contained only sergeants. A similar problem could arise in sampling apartments in a large building with the same number of apartments on each floor or sampling houses in a subdivision having the same number of houses on each block. In practice, however, the problem of *periodicity* seldom arises.

4.4 Stratified Sampling

Sampling error can be reduced by sampling from within homogeneous subsets of the population. In the case of the college example, it may be possible to select separate samples (of the appropriate size) from among freshmen, sophomores, etc. Thus, there would be no sampling error for the variable of school class. Moreover the sampling error for variables related to school class (such as age) would be reduced as well. It might also be possible to stratify the sample on gender, major, or any other variable contained in the data file being sampled.

Stratification can be accomplished by selecting a separate, simple random sample from within each stratum (e.g., female-freshman-Art majors) or by grouping students in subsets along one continuous list and selecting a systematic sample throughout the list.

4.5 Multi-stage Cluster Sampling

Each of the sampling techniques discussed so far has involved a *single stage* of sampling from a list containing all the members of the population in question. Often, however, it is impossible or impractical to find or create such a list. While individual colleges have lists of their students, for example, there is no list of all college students, nor would it be feasible to collect all the lists from individual colleges and combine them. However, it *is* often desirable to study a sample representative of all college students.

Multi-stage cluster sampling is possible when the elements to be studied (e.g., college students) can be located within natural clusters or groupings (e.g., colleges). Thus, for example, it would be possible to obtain a list of all colleges and select a sample of colleges. Each of the selected colleges would be contacted and asked for a list of its student body. All the student lists would then be sampled, providing a national sample of college students.

A national sample of the national household population could be selected in a slightly more complex manner. The procedure would begin with the selection of a sample of cities. Second, cities are organized in census blocks, which could be sampled next. Research workers would be sent to visit each of the selected blocks, compiling lists of all the households they discovered. Samples of households would be selected from the several lists. Interviewers would be sent to the selected households, and the interviews would begin with an enumeration of everyone living at that household. Interviewers would be provided with instructions on how to select a household member at random for the main interview. Thus, a four-stage sampling design would produce a representative probability sample of the individuals living in the nation's households. Of course, such a sampling procedure would require considerable time and money.

4.6 Probability Proportionate to Size (PPS)

The above comments imply that each of the samples would be selected on the basis of *equal* probabilities. Each of the census blocks, for example, would have the same chance of being selected. Sometimes, this is not the preferred technique.

Since census blocks differ greatly in the number of households they contain, equal probability sampling presents two problems. First, there is a danger that some very large blocks might be missed altogether and the large number of households contained on them would not be represented in the final sample at all. Second, if a large block was selected, then taking a fixed percentage of the households contained thereon would mean that a rather large number of households in the final sample would come from that single block.

If the block(s) in question comprised several large, low-rent apartment houses, then the final sample would either contain too many of such households or too few, depending solely on whether the block happened to be selected. If the block(s) comprised several large luxury-condominiums, then the overall sample would have too many or too few of that type of household. Both situations would undercut the aim of representing the different kinds of households in the city—in their proper proportions.

Notice that the central element in the problem is that the households to be found on a given block are relatively homogeneous, at least in comparison with households across the city. This homogeneity offers the key to a solution, however.

Survey practice shows that a sample of around five households typically offers a representative picture of all the households on a given block. Selecting more than five households tends to produce diminishing returns as far as representativeness is concerned. The most representative sample is one in which a large number of blocks is selected, with relatively few households (for example, five) chosen from each of the selected blocks.

In probability proportionate to size (PPS) sampling, then, each block is given a chance of selection proportionate to the number of households contained on it. (Note that the number of households on individual blocks can usually be obtained from census data.) Thus, a block containing 100 households would be given twice the chance of selection as one containing 50 houses. This can be accomplished by creating a list of blocks similar to that shown in Table 1.

Table 1.

Block	Number of Households	Cumulative Households
Block 1	200	1–200
Block 2	400	201–600
Block 3	20	601–620
Block 4	100	621–720
Block 5	10	721–730
Block 6	50	731–780
Block 7	100	781–880
Block 8	600	881–1480
Block 9	10	1481–1490
Block 10	40	1491–1530

To select a block with a probability proportionate to size, a random number between 1 and 1,530 would be selected (the total number of households contained on all the blocks). If the random number were 567, for example, then Block 2 would be selected, since 567 falls within its range of numbers (201–600). Notice that this procedure gives each block a chance of selection that is literally 'proportionate to size.'

By selecting the same number of households from each selected block, however, this design gives each household the same overall probability of selection. This can be verified by calculating the probability of selection enjoyed by households on different blocks.

Block 1, with 200 households, has a chance of selection equal to 200/1,530. Block 2, with 400 households, has twice the chance of selection: 400/1,530. If Block 1 were selected each household would have a probability of 5/200 of selection in the next stage of sampling. On Block 2, however, individual households would have a probability of 5/400 of selection, only half as good. The overall probability of selection for a given household is the product of the two individual probabilities. Thus, households on Block 1 have an overall probability of selection equal to:

$$\frac{200}{1,530} \times \frac{5}{200} = \frac{5}{1,530}$$

Block 2 households have an overall probability of selection equal to:

$$\frac{400}{1,530} \times \frac{5}{400} = \frac{5}{1,530}$$

A quick inspection of these two calculations make it clear that every household will have the same probability (5/1,530) of selection, regardless of the size of its block. The PPS design, however, reduces the danger of either over-representing or underrepresenting the households on very large blocks.

4.7 Random-digit Dialing

Survey research has turned increasingly to the use of the telephone surveys instead of face-to-face, household interviews—due largely to the high cost of household interviews. Whereas telephone interviewing was initially regarded as a poor-quality technique, it has been improved greatly. In part, the improvements have to do with the achievement of representative samples.

When they were first employed, telephone samples suffered from three defects. First, a minority of the population did not have telephones and would not, therefore, be represented by a sample selected from the telephone directory. Second, another minority of the population had unlisted telephone numbers. Finally, samples drawn from telephone directories would often select inappropriate numbers: stores, offices, government agencies, etc.

In the 1990s, with virtually all households in the USA having telephones, the first defect is less significant. The development of *random digit dialing* systems has solved the second problem and reduced the third. In its most primitive form, this technique consists of instructing a computer to generate a series of seven-digit random numbers. These could be dialed as a simple random sample of telephone numbers, whether listed in directories or not.

Unfortunately, most of the randomly generated seven-digit numbers would not turn out to be active telephone numbers. However, it is possible to determine which exchanges (the first three digits) are operational in a given locale, and the telephone company may also be able to specify the range of numbers in service within each exchange. Finally, certain exchanges or ranges of numbers are reserved for commercial or government use. Thus, a somewhat more sophisticated sampling system would instruct the computer to select random numbers having a high probability of being appropriate to the survey.

5. Nonprobability Sampling Techniques

While probability sampling techniques are the preferred choice in most survey situations, there are times when rigorous sampling may be impossible or not feasible. Thus, the research literature still presents surveys conducted with nonprobability samples. Typically, such studies are to be regarded with caution, particularly in matters of statistical description.

5.1 Available Subjects

The easiest 'sampling' technique involves the study of convenient respondents. The students in a college class, persons passing a busy intersection, etc., are typical examples of 'available subjects' sampling.

Such samples can be used profitably in exploratory studies, seeking initial insights into a subject or in the development of questionnaire items. They cannot be taken as the basis for definitive findings, however.

5.2 Snowball Sampling

When a research design calls for the study of a subpopulation not easily located for rigorous sampling, it may be possible to develop a body of subjects through referral. A study of Marxist investment counselors, for example, would face such a difficulty. The researcher, in such a case, would begin by interviewing the handful of Marxist investment counselors he or she was aware of, asking each of those respondents for the names of other Marxist investment counselors known to them. Each subsequent interview would ask for referrals, generating an ever-growing, 'snowball sample.'

Once again, such a technique can be useful in exploratory research, but it would never be possible to know for sure that the Marxist investment counselors identified and interviewed in this fashion would be representative of all Marxist investment counselors.

5.3 Quota Sampling

This technique was discussed earlier in connection with the Gallup Poll's success in predicting the 1936 presidential election and their failure in the 1948 election.

Quota sampling is based on the development of a 'quota matrix' that describes a target population in terms of several relevant variables: e.g., the percentage of that population who are rich, young, urban, white, males; the percentage who are rich, young, urban, white, females; etc.

Interviewers are instructed to locate and interview respondents who fit into the various cells in the quota matrix. Either numbers of each cell-type are selected for study in proportion to their share of the whole population, or equal numbers might be selected to represent the several cells, with weights assigned to reflect their share of the population.

As Gallup discovered in 1948, however, the representativeness of quota sample depends heavily on the accuracy of the quota matrix in describing the population.

See also: Reliability/Validity; Scaling; Sociology Language.

Bibliography

Kish L 1965 *Survey Sampling*. John Wiley, New York
Scheaffer R L, Mendenhall W, Ott L 1986 *Elementary Survey Sampling*. Duxbury Press, Boston
Sudman S 1976 *Applied Sampling*. Academic Press, New York

E. Babbie

San Marino: Language Situation

The Republic of San Marino has some 23,000 inhabitants (1991), all of whom speak Italian.

Sanctius, Franciscus (1523–1600)

Sanctius was called the father of general grammar. He was born in the small town of Brozas in the Spanish province of Cáceres, and he studied at the University of Salamanca, where he subsequently obtained the Chairs of Rhetoric, Greek, and Latin. Little is known about the nonacademic life of Sanctius. The dearth of information was due to his own or his immediate family's attempts to hide their possible non-Christian ancestry from the Inquisition. Sanctius composed didactic grammars of Greek and Latin: *Verae brevesque grammatices Latinae institutiones* (1562), *Arte para en breve saber latín* (1576), and *Grammatica Graeca* (1581). He also wrote several works which extended over a range of topics such as dialectic, rhetoric, philosophy, astronomy, literature, and translation. In 1562, at Lyons, Sanctius published his first *Minerva*, which he entitled *Minerva seu de Latinae linguae causis & elegantia*. This early work was a succinct but good prefiguration of various aspects of Sanctius's grammatical doctrine. His main theoretical treatise was *Minerva seu de causis linguae Latinae* (1587).

The sources of Sanctius's linguistic ideas can be traced back to Greece and Rome. Plato's *Sophist* (see *Plato*) already included a definition of the logical sentence. In his *Institutio oratoria*, Quintilian distinguished between 'natural' and figurative speech; figures of speech were liable to change in accordance with *consuetudo* or the linguistic habits of speakers. Like Sanctius later, Quintilian equated the 'natural' or logical level with a former historical stage of language. In his *Institutiones* (Books 17 and 18), Priscian attempted to recover the logical structure of sentences. This syntactic approach had a bearing on Sanctius and his predecessors. Sanctius's grammatical views were also influenced by Judaeo–Arabic scholarship, Thomas Linacre, Julius Caesar Scaliger (see *Scaliger, Julius Caesar*), and Petrus Ramus (see *Ramus, Petrus*).

The purpose of the *Minerva* was to uncover the origins and logical structures (*causae*) as well as the internal rules (*vera principia*) of the Latin language. Sanctius's logical structures were an integration of both a historical and a logical level, as may be seen in his statement on ellipsis to the effect that solely those elements supplied by the Ancients must be assumed, or those without which the system of grammar (*grammaticae ratio*) cannot be established. His logical structures reconstructed from usage or figurative speech were posited on the basis of several criteria: 'naturalness,' comparison among languages, semantics, philosophy, and grammar. The *ratio* or rules that allow passage from the logical level to the level of speech, following the rhetorical tradition, were addition, deletion, permutation, and substitution. Out of these, deletion or ellipsis was the most common in his grammar. His natural level helped in the description of the grammar of language and accounted for the simplicity of its rules. Sanctius's theoretical grammar had a practical bent. The simplicity of its rules in keeping with the Renaissance language-teaching tradition had didactic implications. In addition, logical structures assisted in the interpretation of difficult passages found in the writings of classical authors.

Gasparus Scioppius and especially Jacobus Perizonius added extensive notes to the *Minerva*, contributing to its popularity in Italy, the Netherlands, Portugal, France, and Germany, in the seventeenth and eighteenth centuries. Scioppius's *Grammatica philosophica* was the practical application of Sanctius's views to the field of language teaching. Claude Lancelot (see *Lancelot, Claude*) was instrumental in the dissemination of Sanctius's doctrines in France. According to Lancelot, Sanctius explained syntax in a simple way by reducing it to its first principles and by referring to the old usage of Latin authors. Sanctius's ideas came into the *Grammaire générale et raisonnée* of Port-Royal through Lancelot. César Chesneau du Marsais followed, in part, Sanctius's and Port-Royal's views to delineate a methodology for teaching grammar. Nicolas Beauzée's *Grammaire générale* (see *Beauzée, Nicolas*) fell within the Sanctius and Port-Royal tradition (see *Port-Royal Tradition of Grammar*). Beauzée continued the critical trend on Sanctius for by neglecting, at times, to correlate his linguistic principles with the observation of usage, but his overall views reflected Sanctius's theoretical framework. In the nineteenth and twentieth centuries, a certain lack of interest in general grammar was noticeable. However, with the advent of the Chomskyan model in the late 1950s, there has been a renewed curiosity in Sanctius's grammatical work; the *Minerva* has been viewed by a number of scholars as prefiguring certain aspects of transformational grammar.

Bibliography

Breva-Claramonte M 1983 *Sanctius' Theory of Language: A Contribution to the History of Renaissance Linguistics.* John Benjamins, Amsterdam
González de la Calle P U 1922 *Vida profesional y académica de Francisco Sánchez de las Brozas.* V. Suárez, Madrid
Lakoff R 1969 Review of Herbert E. Brekle 1966. *Language* **45**: 343–64
Mayans y Siscar G (ed.) 1766 *Francisci Sanctii Brocensis opera omnia,* 4 vols. Apud Fratres de Tourmes, Geneva
Sanctius F 1587 *Minerva seu de causis linguae Latinae.* Apud Joannem & Andraeam Renaut, fratres, Salmanticae (Facsimile reprinted 1986. Friedrich Frommann, Stuttgart-Bad Cannstatt)

M. Breva-Claramonte

Sandhi

That words and morphemes, when they are combined with each other, may undergo phonological modifications, was discovered by the ancient Indians and referred to as *saṃdhi* or *sandhi* 'putting together.' Insight in these modifications and a considerable amount of information about them was contained in the Padapāṭha and in the Prātiśākhyas and was brought to perfection by Pāṇini.

The Padapāṭha and the Prātiśākhyas, with their philological approach, were mainly interested in sandhi between particular words occurring in the Vedic school to which they were attached. The linguist Pāṇini generalized and systematized the discovery that many phonological rules apply both inside and across words ('internal sandhi' and 'external sandhi'). His grammar puts these rules together in several groups following the rule *saṃhitāyām* 'in close contact, continuously' (6.1.72) which uses the term *saṃhitā* that denoted the *continuous* form in which the Vedas were handed down orally.

In formulating sandhi rules, the Prātiśākhyas adopted the *corpus*-oriented approach whereas the analysis of Pāṇini and the schools of the grammarians recognized the infinity of language. Later Prātiśākhyas, or Prātiśākhyas which are known only in a later version, were influenced by the Pāṇinian school and exhibit, therefore, mixed features: one sandhi rule is purely enumerative and confined to the words of a particular Vedic composition, and the next one is formulated in general linguistic terms, for example, Taittirīya Prātiśākhya 10.14 and 15:

10.14: 'When followed by *eṣṭaḥ, etana, eman, odman, oṣṭha* or *evaḥ,* an *a*-vowel is elided.'

Pāṇini does not mention these special cases but formulates a series of rules for -*a* including 6.1.88: '*vṛddhi* is substituted when *ec* (the class of diphthongs) follows,' which corresponds to Taittirīya Prātiśākhya 10.6 ('when *e* or *ai* follow, substitute *ai*') and 10.7 ('when *o* or *au* follow, substitute *au*').

Taittirīya Prātiśākhya 10.15: 'An *i*-vowel and *u* become respectively *y* and *v*.'

Pāṇini generalizes this so as to apply to the replacement of the class of four vowels *i, u, ṛ, ḷ* by their nonsyllabic counterparts, respectively the semivowels *y, v, r, l.*

Pāṇini's sandhi rules use artificial expressions (such as *ec*) that derive from his enumeration and classification of the sounds of the language through systematic abbreviations. The rules of vowel sandhi make use of the definitions of *guṇa* and *vṛddhi* that occur at the outset of the grammar (see *Guṇa*).

Of all the Sanskrit linguistic terms which have been taken over by modern western linguistics, it is *sandhi* which has been the most widely used and which is the most fully assimilated into European languages, following what appears to be the first instance of its adoption in general linguistics in the west in the nineteenth century by Georg von der Gabelentz (1891). Four decades later it made frequent appearances in the published work of one of the greatest of twentieth-century Pāṇinians, Leonard Bloomfield (see Rogers 1987). The use of *sandhi* rather than already existing lexemes such as *juncture* and *junction*, which are commonly taken to be synonymous with it, may seem surprising, for it has rarely, except in the context of descriptions of Sanskrit, been used in any manner which clearly distinguishes it from these terms. It has been suggested that the reason lies in the very 'notoriety' of the alternation between variant forms of the same morpheme in Sanskrit, such alternations being both 'extensive and graphically transparent' (Allen 1962: 15–16). This graphemic transparency lies in the fact that as contrasted with, for instance, English, which makes no orthographic distinction between the word-final /t/ of *clocked* and the /d/ of *clogged*, the rules of Sanskrit orthography require that such differences are always indicated by the script in the written form of a word. If the same position obtained in English, the difference (in some styles of utterance at least) between the *is* of *is he* (/ɪz/) and the *is* of *is she* (/ɪʃ/) would have to be indicated.

The rules of sandhi in Sanskrit as generally understood are, in the case of external sandhi, concerned essentially, though not exclusively, with variations in the final segment of a word as determined by the nature of the initial segment of the following word (initial segments being mostly invariable). In internal sandhi the relevant segments are, of course, the corresponding ones in two juxtaposed morphemes within a single word. When used in modern times with relation to languages other than Sanskrit, the scope of the term is broader than this. Bloomfield (1933: 186–89), for example, uses it with reference to a range of '[f]eatures of modulation and of phonetic modification [which] play a great part in many syntactic constructions.' A sandhi-form is described as a variant from an absolute form, the latter being the form of a word or phrase when uttered in isolation. Examples cited by Bloomfield include the atonic forms of English, such as the unstressed variants of determiners, pronouns, and auxiliary verbs; a range of phenomena in French (which 'has a great deal of sandhi'), such as the elision of vowels and the occurrence of liaison consonants; initial consonantal mutations in Irish, e.g., [an 'voː] 'the cow,' as compared with the 'absolute' form ['boː] 'cow' (the example is Bloomfield's and does not take account of the possible assimilation of the nasal consonant of /an/ to the following [v]); and modifications of pitch in Chinese.

Many of these points, not necessarily with reference to Bloomfield, were taken up in the 1980s, when sandhi as a technical term seems really to have come into its own. There are a number of examples in Andersen 1986: M Herslund on 'French External Sandhi: The Case of Liaison' (pp. 85–92), G E Booij on 'Two Cases of External Sandhi in French: Enchaînement and Liaison' (pp. 93–102), and B Ó Cuív on 'Sandhi Phenomena in Irish' (pp. 395–414). Bloomfield's 'modifications of pitch' in Chinese are now discussed in terms of 'tone sandhi,' but the treatment is entirely compatible with his very brief presentation. A word in standard Chinese (Putonghua) will in isolation be pronounced with one of four distinctive tones, sometimes called 'lexical'

tones. Within a sentence, however, when there is a sequence of words each with the same lexical tone, there will be dissimilation of a sort that has the effect of one or more of the words being pronounced with a pitch contour associated with a different lexical tone. Examples given by Kaisse (1985: 170–78, based on a paper by Liu Feng-hsi) include the following:

```
lao li [mai [hao jui]]_VP
old Li buy  good wine
3    3    3     3    3      lexical tone
2    3    3     2    3      surface tone
'Old Li buys good wine.'
```

It is evident that such presentations go somewhat beyond the use of *sandhi* in Pāṇinian linguistics, partly no doubt because the phonological rules needed for the languages concerned are different from those needed for Sanskrit. Suprasegmentals are nevertheless not ignored in the Indian tradition. The accent sandhi of Vedic, for instance, is described both by the Prātiśākhyas and by Pāṇini. One important refinement in the development of Pāṇinian ideas has been in the concept of phonological domains within which a given sandhi rule will apply (see, for example, J Gvozdanović in Andersen 1986: 27–54). In an elegant discussion of what might constitute a universal set Selkirk (1980) proposes 'four progressively larger sorts of prosodic domain: the word, ... the phonological phrase, ... the intonational phrase, ... and the utterance.'

A further point hinted at by Bloomfield and developed subsequently by others is a distinction between optional and compulsory sandhi, a distinction not commonly associated with Sanskrit linguistics, since most external sandhi rules in Sanskrit are presented as applying without lexical or syntactic restrictions, apart from not applying across a pause. However, many of the rules of Pāṇini's *Aṣṭādhyāyī* are in fact stated as applying optionally. More than this, it has been shown that the three terms used by Pāṇini to indicate optionality (*vā*, *vibhāṣā*, and *anyatarasyām*) can be seen as indicating three different types (see Kiparsky 1979). English and other European languages provide numerous examples of optional sandhi forms both within words and across word boundaries. Thus for *invite*, both [ɪnvaɪt] and [ɪmvaɪt] are possible. Similarly, [ɪn frʌnt] and [ɪm frʌnt] for *in front*. In Italian a rule belonging to the utterance domain, that of syntactic doubling (*raddopiamento sintattico*), in terms of which the initial consonant of a word will be doubled if certain syntactic conditions are satisfied (e.g., *piu caldo* [pju kkaldo] 'hotter'), is also optional in some regional varieties (see Napoli and Nespor 1979).

Modern discussions of sandhi (again outwith the context of Sanskrit) also commonly take account of such factors as register and speed of utterance. French, for good reason, has been a favorite source of material for such discussions; compare the relatively formal [mɛ zil nã vø pa] (*Mais il n'en veut pas*) with the more familiar [me i nã vø pa] in respect of the liaison consonant potentially linking *Mais* and *il*. Such factors have, of course, long been taken account of, for example by Paul Passy (see *Passy, Paul Edouard*) at the end of the nineteenth century and by Lilias Armstrong (see *Armstrong, Lilias Eveline*) in the 1930s, but rigorous formalization is much more recent. Consideration of phenomena of this kind was not foreign to linguistic thought in ancient India. Both register and speed of utterance were referred to even prior to the grammarians in the śrauta sūtras of vedic ritual. Pāṇini himself refers to shouting from afar and in ritual exclamations, among other situations.

It is clear, without the further multiplication of examples, that twentieth-century use of the borrowed term sandhi extends uses of the term sandhi that were in many cases already suggested by Pāṇini, his predecessors, or his successors within the Indian linguistic tradition. On the basis of a claim that this extremely broad usage has led to conceptual confusion, there have been proposals to restrict, and to define clearly, the use of the term. Given the existence of a range of approximate synonyms—sandhi, juncture, junction, joining—such proposals would seem to have some merit. There are, however, no clear signs of agreement on whether terminological clarity should be sought by restricting the use of *sandhi* approximately to its use in Pāṇinian linguistics and using other terms for other types of joining (cf. E Ternes, 'A Grammatical Hierarchy of Joining' in Andersen 1986: 11–21), or by the establishment of clearer subdivisions within *sandhi* as an overarching term. The evidence in the early 1990s is that the second tendency will win the day.

See also: Bhartṛhari; Pāṇinian Linguistics; Padapāṭha; Prātiśākhya.

Bibliography

Allen W S 1962 *Sandhi: The Theoretical, Phonetic, and Historical Bases of Word-Junction in Sanskrit*, Janua Linguarum, XVII. Mouton, 'S-Gravenhage
Andersen H (ed.) 1986 *Sandhi Phenomena in the Languages of Europe*, Trends in Linguistics: Studies and Monographs, 33. Mouton de Gruyter, Berlin
Bloomfield L 1933 *Language*. Holt, New York
Gabelentz G von der 1891 *Die Sprachwissenschaft: Ihre Aufgaben, Methoden und bisherigen Ergebnisse*. Tauchnitz, Leipzig
Kaisse E M 1985 *Connected Speech: The Interaction of Syntax and Phonology*. Academic Press, Orlando, FL
Kiparsky P 1979 *Pāṇini as a Variationist*. Poona University Press, Poona
Napoli D J, Nespor M 1979 The syntax of word-initial consonant gemination in Italian. *Lg* **55**: 812–41
Rogers D E 1987 The influence of Pāṇini on Leonard Bloomfield. In: Hall R A (ed.) *Leonard Bloomfield: Essays on his Life and Work*, Studies in the History of the Language Sciences **47**; Historiographia Linguistica **14**. Benjamins, Amsterdam
Selkirk E O 1980 Prosodic domains in phonology: Sanskrit revisited. In: Aronoff M, Kean M-L (eds.) *Juncture. A Collection of Original Papers*, Studia Linguistica et Philologica, vol. 7. Anma Libri, Saratoga, CA
Selkirk E O 1984 *Phonology and Syntax: The Relation between Sound and Structure*. MIT Press, Cambridge, MA

F. Staal

R. E. Asher

Sanskrit

The Sanskrit language—one of the oldest of the Indo–European group to possess a substantial literature—has particular interest for linguists from the circumstances of its becoming known to western scholars and the stimulus so given to historical linguistics. It has also been of enormous and continuing importance as the classical language of Indian culture and the sacred language of Hinduism.

1. Origin and History

Sanskrit, in its older form of Vedic Sanskrit (or simply Vedic), was brought into the northwest of India by the Āryans some time in the second half of the second millennium BC and was at that period relatively little differentiated from its nearest relation within the Indo–European group, Avestan in the Iranian family of languages (these two being the oldest recorded within the Indo–Iranian branch of Indo–European). From there, it spread to the rest of North India as the Āryans enlarged the area that they occupied, developing into the classical form of the language, which subsequently became fixed as the learned language of culture and religion throughout the subcontinent, while the spoken language developed into the various Prākrits. There is ample evidence of rapid evolution during the Vedic period, with the language of the latest phase, attested for example in the Upaniṣads, showing considerable grammatical simplification from that of the earliest hymns. The later Vedic is, in broad terms, the form of the language that Pāṇini described with such exactness in his grammar around the fourth century BC, thereby creating—no doubt unintentionally—an absolute standard for the language thereafter; his work is clearly the culmination of a long grammatical tradition, based on concern to preserve the Vedas unaltered (hence the stress on phonetics), and is itself intended for memorization and oral transmission, as its brevity indicates.

This standardization was not as universal as has sometimes been represented (nor was the preceding Vedic a unified language, for it exhibits features only explicable as coming from slightly differing dialects, while classical Sanskrit is based on a more eastern dialect than the one attested in the *Ṛgveda*) and it has come to be recognized that, for example, the two Sanskrit epics exhibit systematic divergences from the language described by Pāṇini and represent a distinct epic dialect. However, with the growth of classical Sanskrit literature (mainly within the period from the fourth to the tenth centuries AD, when Sanskrit was clearly no longer a natural language), Pāṇini's description was regarded as prescriptive and followed to the letter, although the spirit was less closely observed (as shown by the tendency to longer and longer compounds, to nominal constructions and the like).

The earliest record of the language is contained in the hymns of the *Ṛgveda*, which belong to around 1200–1000 BC, but they were not committed to writing until a much later period because of their sacred character, for the Indian tradition has always placed greater emphasis on oral tradition than on written texts. In fact the earliest dated record in Sanskrit is an inscription of 150 AD, significantly later than the use of Prākrit by the Buddhist ruler Aśoka for his inscriptions in the third century BC. Early inscriptions used one of two scripts: the Kharoṣṭhī, deriving from the Aramaic script used in Achaemenid Iran, and the Brāhmī, less certainly deriving from a North Semitic script. The latter evolved into the Nāgarī family of scripts, to which the Devanāgarī script now usually used for Sanskrit belongs, although before the twentieth century manuscripts were normally written in the local script.

2. Characteristics

Any analysis of Sanskrit syntax must take account of the shift from the natural language of the Vedic and epic forms of Sanskrit to the learned language of the classical literature, which selectively exploits certain features of Pāṇini's description. Whereas the older forms of the language show frequent use of nominal compounds of two or three members and Pāṇini's grammar describes their formation in great detail (but in terms of their analysis into types: *dvandva*, *bahuvrīhi*, *tatpuruṣa*), classical literature is marked by a predilection for longer compounds, consisting in some styles of writing of twenty or more members. Another common feature, inherited from the Indo–European background but found much more extensively in the classical language, is the use of nominal sentences involving the juxtaposition of the subject and a nonverbal predicate. The frequent use of the past participle passive as a verbal equivalent leads to a preference for passive constructions, in a way typical of the Prākrits. Use of the absolutive becomes in the classical language a common means to form complex sentences by indicating actions occurring prior to that of the main verb; again the effect is a reduction in finite verbal forms. The usual sentence order is subject, object, verb; however, this is so commonly modified for emphasis (with initial and final positions in the sentence or verse-line carrying most emphasis) that Sanskrit word order is often regarded as being free. In vocabulary, the freeing from the affective connotations of a natural language brought a striking enlargement of the range of synonyms, skillfully exploited in much of the classical literature to produce rich sound effects.

In its morphology, Sanskrit is broadly comparable to Greek or Latin, though somewhat more complex. In both the nominal and verbal systems the dual is obligatory for all twos, not just pairs. The nominal system employs eight cases (seven according to the Indian reckoning, which regards the vocative as a form of the stem), three numbers and three genders (masculine, feminine, neuter). Unlike other Indo–European languages, Sanskrit lacks a developed series of prepositions and the relatively few adverbial formations used to define case relationships more exactly tend to be placed after the noun. The use of *vṛddhi* (IE strengthened grade) to form derivatives from nominal stems is a notable feature. The verb has two voices, active and middle, their functions well distinguished by the Sanskrit terms for them: *parasmaipada* 'word for another' and *ātmanepada* 'word for oneself'; it also has five moods (injunctive, imperative, subjunctive, optative, and precative) in the Vedic, somewhat simplified in the classical language. Prepositional affixes to the verb may in Vedic be separated from the verb but in the classical language must be prefixed to it (there is a comparable development between Homeric and classical Greek). There is both an ordinary sigmatic future and a periphrastic future (formed through a specialized use of the agent noun), several aorist formations (principally a sigmatic aorist and a root aorist), and a perfect normally formed with a reduplicated stem; these are comparable to the equivalent tenses in Greek or Latin. The augment is prefixed to several past tenses: imperfect, aorist, pluperfect,

and conditional. Verbal roots are divided by the Sanskrit grammarians into ten classes: six athematic and four thematic. A distinctive feature of the verbal system is the employment of secondary conjugations with specific meanings: causative, intensive, and desiderative. Historically, the passive is also such a secondary conjugation, formed by adding the middle endings to a modified root. The Vedic language is marked by rather greater grammatical complexity with, most notably, a whole range of case forms from nouns functioning as infinitives, which are reduced to a single infinitive in the classical language. It also possessed a pitch accent which had died out by the time of the classical language.

Phonetically Sanskrit is marked by a number of innovations by comparison with other Indo–European languages of comparable age. It is also notable for the concern with phonetics of its own grammarians (exemplified by the fact that the alphabet is arranged according to the organ of articulation, with vowels preceding consonants) and the precision of their descriptions. On the one hand Sanskrit has collapsed the three Indo–European vowels *a*, *e*, and *o* into *a*, and on the other it has introduced a complete new class of consonants, that of the retroflex consonants, mainly under the influence of one of the other language groups already present in India, either Dravidian or Munda, although in some instances the retroflex consonants probably arose through internal phonetic developments in relation to *s* and *r*. The most widely known feature is that of *saṃdhi* 'junction,' the process of phonetic assimilation of contiguous sounds at the junctures between both words and their component parts (external and internal *saṃdhi*).

3. Sample Sentence

teṣām   khalv eṣām bhūtānāṃ   trīṇy eva bījāni bhavanty
/teṣaːŋ   khəlv eṣaːŋ bhuːtaːnaːŋ   triːŋy evə biːjaːni bhəvənty*
aṇḍajaṃ   jīvajam   udbhijjam   iti‖
əṇḍəjəŋ   jiːvəjəm   udbhijəŋ   iti/

'Living beings here have just three origins [literally 'Assuredly of these living beings are/come into being indeed three seeds']: being born from an egg or live-born or produced from a sprout.'

This simple sentence (from *Chāndogya Upaniṣad* 6.3.1) nonetheless exemplifies already several of the features which are taken to extremes in the classical language. There is the avoidance of a transitive construction (although here the verb, *bhavanti*, is expressed, whereas later such a copula is normally suppressed), the employment of compounds and the liking for etymological figures (the latter two combined in the three compounds ending in the adjectival form *-ja*, coming from √*jan* 'to be born,' while the use of cognates is exemplified by *bhavanti* 3rd pl present indicative and *bhūta* past participle passive from √*bhū* 'to become'). The use of *iti* may also be noted—here to function as the equivalent of the colon in the translation, more usually to perform the function of quotation marks, to mark off a passage in direct speech from the sentence in which it is embedded (an idiom probably calqued on the Dravidian); Sanskrit has no method of indicating indirect speech.

4. Role and Influence in Indian Culture

As is implicit in some of the statements above, it is clear that throughout the main period of its use as a literary language Sanskrit was not the first language of its users, who in North India would have been native speakers of one of the Prākrits deriving from Sanskrit (used here in its widest sense of the group of OIA dialects) or even of the next stage of MIA, the Apabhraṃśas, and in South India were speakers of one of the Dravidian languages (which have been influenced to varying degrees in their vocabulary by Sanskrit). The prestige attaching to its use for the Vedas, the authoritative scriptures for Hindus, resulted in its being regarded as the only language fit for use in the major rituals of brahmanical Hinduism, a role that to a limited extent it retains to the present day. This was undoubtedly the reason why the Purāṇas and the many popular texts related to them were composed (from the fourth century to as late as the nineteenth century) in a form of Sanskrit which is greatly indebted to the epics for its linguistic and metrical expression, while similarly Mahāyāna Buddhism employed the so-called Buddhist Hybrid Sanskrit (essentially a Sanskritization of MIA). Sanskrit has therefore been a dominant influence on the development of the languages in both the MIA and NIA phases, supplying much of the religious vocabulary in the form of direct loans, over and above the large proportion of the vocabulary descended from Sanskrit.

5. Sanskrit and the West

First acquaintance with Sanskrit by Western scholars came even before the period of British rule. Sir William Jones's famous discourse in 1786 to the Asiatick Society in Calcutta on the affinity of Sanskrit with Greek, Latin, and the other languages now known as Indo–European was not the first notice of such connection, which had been proposed two centuries earlier by Thomas Stevens (in 1583) and Fillipo Sassetti (in 1585). However, his eminence ensured it a much wider audience than before and this was in a significant sense the start of the discipline of comparative philology, while the appreciation before long of the achievements of the early Indian grammarians was an important stimulant to the development of modern linguistics, which has paid them the compliment of borrowing a number of their terms, such as *saṃdhi*.

See also: Sanskrit: Discovery by Europeans; Sanskrit Grammatical Terms.

Bibliography

Burrow T 1973 *The Sanskrit Language*, 3rd edn. Faber and Faber, London
Cardona G 1988 *Pāṇini: His Work and its Traditions*, vol. 1. Motilal Banarsidass, Delhi
Coulson M 1992 *Sanskrit: An Introduction to the Classical Language*, 2nd edn. Hodder and Stoughton, London
Gonda J 1971 *Old Indian*, Handbuch der Orientalistik, 2. Abt., 1. Bd., 1. Abschnitt. E J Brill, Leiden-Cologne
Scharfe H 1977 *Grammatical Literature*, History of Indian Literature, vol. V, fasc. 2. Harrassowitz, Wiesbaden

J. L. Brockington

Sanskrit: Discovery by Europeans

The discovery of Sanskrit by Europeans played a determinant role in the development of comparative Indo–European linguistics. Yet, this process was neither rapid nor linear. The observation, recording, and transmission of data, the methods according to which they were analyzed and interpreted within existing theories of language, and the purposes which they were made to serve, were largely independent variables. This complex history has been further muddied by the tendency of later generations to read their predecessors' statements anachronistically.

1. Pioneers: Missionaries and Travelers in India (1583–1768)

Though the ancient Greeks have left records, some accurate, most fantastic, of their travels to India, their linguistic slate is blank. Mercantile contacts between Rome and India also failed to prompt linguistic observations. The first-known linguistic comment was made in a letter of 1583 by an English Jesuit in Goa, Thomas Stephens (Stevens), who does not mention Sanskrit, but points to a structural similarity between Indian languages and Greek and Latin. It remained unpublished until 1957. In 1586, the Florentine litterateur and merchant Filippo Sassetti wrote from Cochin of Sanskrit's status as the learned language of India, of its high antiquity and complexity, and of lexical similarities with Italian, notably in numerals 6 to 9 and words for 'God' and 'snake.' His letters were only published in 1855.

Europeans began to study Indian languages in a sustained manner in the seventeenth century, with evangelical efforts primarily in South India. Jesuits played a leading role in the discovery of Sanskrit. Since, following Roberto (de) Nobili (1577–1656), they targeted the upper castes and accommodated existing cultural and social norms—the controversial issue of the Malabar rites—they tended to devote great attention to the language of the high Brahmanical tradition. Nobili's works attest to his knowledge of Sanskrit, yet contain no linguistic observations. The first-known European grammar of Sanskrit was composed in Agra between 1660 and 1662 by Heinrich Roth. Written in Latin and on a Western pattern, it followed traditional Indian terminology and analysis. Brought to Rome and long thought lost, it was only published in 1988. Roth also contributed the tables of Devanāgarī script and the transliterations of the Latin texts of the Lord's Prayer and of the Hail Mary for Athanasius Kircher's *China Illustrata* (1667). The transliteration of the Lord's Prayer entered polyglot compilations from Andreas Müller (1680) to John Chamberlayne (1715). A grammar written in Kerala in the first third of the eighteenth century by Johann Ernst Hanxleden, and later brought to Rome, described, and used by Paulinus a Sancto Bartholomaeo, appears to have been lost since.

Protestant missionaries in Danish Tranquebar, reports from whom were published in Germany from 1718 on, also contributed information on Sanskrit. In 1717, Bartholomaeus Ziegenbalg, primarily a scholar of Tamil, provided Christian Benedict Michaelis with a syllabary for Sanskrit. In a letter of 1725, published in 1729, Benjamin Schul(t)ze, provoked by a remark by Veyssière de La Croze to the effect that numerals in Malabar are 'pure Latin,' listed the Sanskrit numerals 1 to 20, 30, and 40, with equivalents in Latin for all, and in other European languages for some. He also offered in the *Orientalisch- und Occidentalischer Sprachmeister* (1748), translations of the Lord's Prayer in

Sanskrit and other Indian languages, which still recur in Adelung's *Mithridates* (1, 1806).

French Jesuits had the greatest impact on scholarship with the publication of their *Lettres Edifiantes et Curieuses* (1707–) in multiple editions and translations. Most important was a survey of Sanskrit literature by Jean François Pons (1740), which described Sanskrit as 'admirable for its harmony, copiousness, and energy' and reported on the analysis by which native grammarians had reduced 'the richest language in the world' to a small number of primitive elements to which derivational suffixes and inflectional endings are added according to rules the application of which generates 'several thousand correct Sanskrit words.' Published in 1743, it informed the works of de Brosses, Dow, Sinner, Voltaire, Monboddo, Halhed, Beauzée, and Hervás, and was plagiarized by John Cleland (1778). Of less immediate, yet momentous, impact was a request issued by the Abbé Bignon upon assuming the direction of the French Royal Library in 1718, that French missionaries in Asia send manuscripts according to a list of desiderata drawn up by the orientalist Etienne Fourmont. In 1732–33, Pons sent from Bengal 168 Sanskrit manuscripts which included the first five chapters of a grammar in Latin with Sanskrit words in Bengali script. A sixth chapter on syntax, completed in South India, in French with Sanskrit words partly in Telugu, partly in Roman script, was forwarded in 1772 by Gaston-Laurent Coeurdoux. Pons's grammar was the source of the table of Bengali script in the *Encyclopédie* and the primer used by the first students of Sanskrit in Europe, which Anquetil-Duperron came close to publishing in 1804. Coeurdoux was the author of a memoir that included, besides a basic Sanskrit vocabulary, lists of Sanskrit words that have equivalents in Latin, Greek, or both, notably the numerals 1 to 21, 30, 40, and 100, pronouns, and a partial paradigm of *as-* 'to be.' Solicited in 1767 by the Abbé Barthélemy of the Académie des Inscriptions et Belles-Lettres, who gave it to Anquetil-Duperron, it was only read in 1786 and published in 1808, the same year as Schlegel's *Ueber die Sprache und Weisheit der Indier*, which rendered it obsolete.

These pioneers' sometimes faulty data—muddled by erratic transliterations that reflected different local pronunciations and the recorders' various native tongues, and subject to misreadings—were interpreted according to, or used to bolster, divergent linguistic theories. Gottfried Siegfried Bayer (1738) explained similarities by contact and borrowing, pointing to the Indo–Greek kingdoms after Alexander's campaigns as the source of commonalities between Greek, Persian, and Sanskrit, yet the memoir of the Tranquebar missionary Christian Theodor Walther (1733) that he appended attributed them to the common 'Scythian' origin propounded by Boxhorn (see *Boxhorn, Marcus Zuerius*), Saumaise, Jäger, Leibniz (see *Leibniz, G. W.*), and others. La Flotte (1768) also posited a 'North Asian' origin for the Brahmans, while Sinner (1771) thought exclusively in terms of borrowing from Greek and Latin into Sanskrit, yet wondered how it could have taken place. The emphasis on numerals and other basic vocabulary, i.e., vocabulary unlikely to have been borrowed, which De Laet, Grotius, Leibniz, and others had pioneered, did not necessarily lead to the conclusion of a common origin. Schul(t)ze was inclined to credit similarities between Latin and Sanskrit to

borrowing from Portuguese, yet wondered how Brahmans could have done without counting for so long, while Coeurdoux favored the biblical myth of Babel, making of Sanskrit one of the primitive languages which preserved elements that antedated separation. Scholars in Europe eagerly awaited more information, which they hoped would further their particular lines of enquiry, from the 'language mechanics' of de Brosses (1765), fascinated by Pons's report of Sanskrit's derivation from a handful of primitive elements, to the Celtomania of Le Brigant (1767).

2. Breakthrough: British Colonials in Bengal (1768–94)

When, in 1765, the East India Company obtained the administrative rights to Bengal, Bihar, and Orissa, knowledge of India's culture became a colonial necessity. The reluctance of pandits to instruct foreigners in their sacred language and Sanskrit's reputation for being 'amazingly copious' and for showing a 'regularity of etymology and grammatical order,' induced Alexander Dow (1768) to suspect that it had been invented by Brahmans 'upon rational principles' to be 'a mysterious repository for their religion and philosophy.' This led Christoph Meiners (1780) to explain similarities by assuming that the Brahmans had patterned their artificial language after Greek, a notion Dugald Stewart and Charles William Wall still held in the nineteenth century.

Governor Warren Hastings' decision in 1772 to apply native laws in courts and his patronage of both pandits and orientalists caused a breakthrough. In the introduction to the translation (1776) of the code of Hindu law commissioned by Hastings, which underwent several editions and translations, Nathaniel Brassey Halhed gave an account of Sanskrit that interested Beauzée and Monboddo among others. In his grammar of Bengali (1778) he digressed on features of Sanskrit, spelling out the importance of similarities in basic vocabulary, i.e., 'not in technical and metaphorical terms, which the mutuation of refined arts and improved manners might have occasionally introduced; but in the main groundwork of language, in monosyllables, in the names of numbers, and the appellation of such things as would be first discriminated on the immediate dawn of civilization,' and noting similarities in morphology, such as the conjugation in -*mi* in Sanskrit and Greek. In an unpublished letter of 1779, he articulated a method built on Monboddo's view that Latin was a dialect more ancient than Greek: Sanskrit, closer to Latin than to Greek, had to be even more ancient, yet, what of 'the existence of the dual number and the middle voice in this tongue and in the Greek, which are totally absent from the Latin'? Holding, after Monboddo, that 'it is one of the last gradations of art to simplify a complex machine,' he mentioned 'in favour of the pretensions to priority of original in the Shanscrit [sic] language, that it contains every part of speech, and every distinction which is to be found in Greek or in Latin, and that in some particulars it is more copious than either.'

Sanskrit's 'copiousness,' noted by Pons, Dow, and Halhed, was emphasized again in a statement (1786) by Sir William Jones, a scholar of Persian and one of the most accomplished men of his day, who, as a judge of the Supreme Court in Calcutta, began to study Sanskrit to check the authenticity of legal opinions given by pandit assistants to the courts:

The Sanskrit language, whatever be its antiquity, is of a wonderful structure; more perfect than the Greek, more copious than the Latin, and more exquisitely refined than either, yet bearing to both of them a stronger affinity, both in the roots of verbs and in the forms of grammar, than could possibly have been produced by accident; so strong indeed, that no philologer could examine them all three, without believing them to have sprung from some common source, which, perhaps, no longer exists: there is a similar reason, though not quite so forcible, for supposing that both the Gothic and the Celtic, though blended with a very different idiom, had the same origin with the Sanskrit; and that the old Persian might be added to the same family.

Taken out of context, this was elevated later to the rank of a charter of comparative Indo–European linguistics. For Jones, and in keeping with the monogeneticism of his times, it was part of a search for the cradle of civilization from which arts, letters, science, religion, and philosophy might have spread, and which linked the Indians not only to the Persians, Goths, and Celts, but also to the Ethiopians, Egyptians, Chinese, Japanese, and even Peruvians. Less famous, yet of lasting importance, was Jones's 'Dissertation on the Orthography of Asiatick Words in Roman Letters' (1786), informed by the Indian tradition of phonetics, which set a standard for the transliteration of Sanskrit in Roman script.

Most noticed was the unveiling in rapid succession of Sanskrit literary masterpieces with translations by Charles Wilkins of the religiophilosophical poem *Bhagavadgītā* and the moral fables *Hitopadeśa* (1785, 1787), and by Jones of the play *Śakuntalā*, the erotic-mystical songs *Gītagovinda*, and the 'Laws of Manu' (1789, 1792, 1794). These underwent multiple editions and translations and drew enthusiastic comments: the *Bhagavadgītā* from Schopenhauer, *Śakuntalā* from Herder and Goethe. By founding the Asiatic Society in Calcutta (1784) and its organ, the *Asiatick Researches* (1788–), Jones provided a forum for further advances and a channel to broadcast them to Europe, where they were republished and translated into French and German.

3. Taking Stock in Europe (1780–1806)

European curiosity about Sanskrit was piqued, yet interpretations remained scattered. Summing up the evidence provided by Pons, Dow, and Halhed, Michael Hissmann (1780) still attributed similarities to borrowing into Sanskrit. Drawing from the same sources, Beauzée's five-page article in the *Encyclopédie méthodique* (1786)—up from a few lines in Diderot's original *Encyclopédie* (1765)—sought to provide a model for an international scholarly language.

The discalced Carmelite, Paulinus a Sancto Bartholomaeo (born Philip(p) Wessdin (Vesdin)), returned in 1789 from Malabar and undertook to catalogue oriental collections in Rome and to publish in Latin for the use of future missionaries encyclopedic, if polemical, works that incorporated the sum of current knowledge on India. These included a description of Indian scripts (1791) based on the *Alphabetum Brammhanicum* and the *Alphabetum Grandonico-Malabaricum* edited by Amaduzzi (1771, 1772); two grammars—the first grammars of Sanskrit to be printed (1790, 1804)—based on manuscripts of Hanxleden; an edition of the first section of Amarasimha's dictionary (1798); and dissertations on the relationship of Zend (Avestan), Sanskrit, and German, and of Latin, Zend, and Sanskrit (1798, 1802). They encapsulate traits of the eighteenth century: the authority still granted to testimonies of classical antiquity; an emphasis on basic vocabulary presented in tabular form for comparison; and, particularly for clerics, a wish to match linguistic evidence with biblical accounts. Explanations by contact and borrowing, however, were discarded, and common origin affirmed. The connection of German and Iranian was accepted, yet, with Sanskrit added, a northern, Scythian origin was rejected in favor of an oriental cradle. Puzzlement persisted on whether to consider Sanskrit closer to Latin or to Greek, with preference for the former, yet with an acknowledgment that morphological similarities, such as the augment and the reduplicated perfect, point to the latter. Franz Carl Alter (1799) published the Sanskrit words in the St. Petersburg vocabularies corrected by Paulinus, and Paulinus's and his comparisons of these with other oriental languages. Hervás (1801) and Adelung (1, 1806) drew heavily on Paulinus's work.

4. A New Beginning: Sanskrit in Paris (1802–08)

Paulinus's first printed grammar provided a means to learn Sanskrit, which the publications from Calcutta made a subject of literary, philosophical, and linguistic interest, not just of evangelical or colonial necessity. In 1802 the Paris collections, the richest in Europe, attracted at the same time European scholars eager to learn Sanskrit and a member of the Asiatic Society returned from Calcutta eager to teach it. Detained in Paris by war between Britain and France, Alexander Hamilton cataloged anew the Sanskrit manuscripts in the French National/Imperial Library with their keeper, Louis-Matthieu Langlès, and introduced all those who were interested to Sanskrit. Of the first consequence was his daily tutoring of Friedrich Schlegel, which provided a foundation for Schlegel's *Ueber die Sprache und Weisheit der Indier* (1808). In this complex, sometimes paradoxical book, which blends linguistic, literary, historical, philosophical, and theological themes, Schlegel was already retreating from the first enthusiasm that had him exclaim that Sanskrit is 'the actual source of all languages, of all thoughts and poetry of the human spirit; everything, everything without exception stems from India,' yet he still viewed Sanskrit as the most perfect, spiritual, quasidivine language, the oldest, and possibly the parent of, 'organic' inflectional languages, which he considered superior to the 'mechanical' agglutinative languages. Deeming lexical similarities inherently inconclusive, he focused on morphological similarities as the determining criterion for establishing genealogy.

5. Mainstream (1808–)

Schlegel's example demonstrated that Sanskrit could be learned in Europe. It inspired Antoine-Léonard de Chézy, who, self-taught with the grammars of Paulinus and Pons and other manuscripts in the French National/Imperial Library, became in 1814 the first incumbent of a chair of Sanskrit, at the Collège de France. August Wilhelm Schlegel followed in the footsteps of his younger brother, learning Sanskrit in Paris before initiating its teaching in Germany (Bonn 1818). Franz Bopp (see *Bopp, Franz*), Othmar Frank, and others went on from Paris to London to consult manuscripts in the East India Company Library founded in 1801 according to a plan proposed by Charles Wilkins, who became its first librarian. Thanks to collections made in India by the likes of Colin Mackenzie and Henry Thomas Colebrooke (the first author of a Sanskrit grammar in English, which remained incomplete, and the first Sanskrit scholar some of whose works are still read for other than antiquarian purposes), the London holdings soon eclipsed those in Paris; however, Britain was slow in recognizing Sanskrit as more than a colonial necessity. Hamilton, upon his release from France in 1806, taught Sanskrit at the East India College, but no mainstream British university offered it until 1832, when the Boden chair was created at Oxford thanks to a bequest by a former military officer of the East India Company. The chair's first incumbent, Horace Hayman Wilson, who had learned Sanskrit from pandits in India, was embroiled in a dispute with A. W. Schlegel, who had learned Sanskrit in Europe, about the qualifications required of a Sanskrit scholar, so epitomizing the extent to which Sanskrit had become appropriated by Europeans, particularly on the Continent.

More than joining the academic mainstream, Sanskrit took pride of place in the development of comparative Indo–European grammar. Though, unlike Friedrich Schlegel, Bopp never referred to Sanskrit as the parent language, he made it the centerpiece of his comparative studies of conjugational and other grammatical systems, and, although he did not share Schlegel's Romantic enthusiasm but bore down on matters purely linguistic, he likewise appended translations of Sanskrit texts to his *Conjugationssystem* (1816). Sanskritocentrism remained the norm for generations of comparatists. So significant was the discovery of Sanskrit in the development of comparative Indo–European linguistics that it has been felt necessary of late to voice reminders that it was not a prerequisite—as the works of Rask, Grimm, and others demonstrate (see *Rask, Rasmus Kristian*; *Grimm, Jacob Ludwig Carl*). Accounting in part for the magnitude of this impact are the quality, quantity, antiquity, and longevity of Sanskrit literature, yet more important was the fact that Sanskrit was first taught to Europeans—directly or mediately—according to the enduring tradition of rigorous analysis by Pāṇini and other Indian grammarians and phoneticians. The identification of the root as the smallest common denominator of derived forms, vocalic alternation, derivational and inflectional suffixes, substitution rules, zeroing, etc., and the description of articulatory processes were the procedures according to which Europeans learned Sanskrit from pandits. While this created an illusion that Sanskrit is more regular and transparent than other languages, the fact that the same procedures could serve to analyze cognate languages provided a framework that facilitated comparison.

Bibliography

Benfey T 1869 *Geschichte der Sprachwissenschaft und orientalischen Philologie in Deutschland*. Cotta, Munich.

Camps A, Muller J-C 1988 *The Sanskrit Grammar and Manuscripts of Father Heinrich Roth S J (1620–68)*. Brill, Leiden

Koerner E F K 1977 *Friedrich Schlegel: Ueber die Sprache und Weisheit der Indier*, new edn. Benjamins, Amsterdam

Mayrhofer M 1983 Sanskrit und die Sprachen Alteuropas: Zwei Jahrhunderte von Entdeckungen und Irrtümern. *Nachrichten der Akademie der Wissenschaften in Göttingen 5*

Muller J-C 1985 Recherches sur les premières grammaires manuscrites du sanskrit. *Bulletin d'Études Indiennes* **3**: 125–44

Rocher L 1977 *Paulinus a S Bartholomaeo: Dissertation on the Sanskrit Language*. Benjamins, Amsterdam

Rocher R 1968 *Alexander Hamilton (1762–1824): A Chapter in the Early History of Sanskrit Philology*. American Oriental Society, New Haven, CT

Rocher R 1983 *Orientalism, Poetry, and the Millennium: The Checkered Life of Nathaniel Brassey Halhed 1751–1830*. Motilal Banarsidass, Delhi

Schwab R 1984 *Oriental Renaissance: Europe's Rediscovery of India and the East, 1680–1880*. Columbia University Press, New York

Windisch E W O 1917 *Geschichte der Sanskrit-Philologie und indischen Altertumskunde*. Trübner, Strasbourg

Wüst W 1929 Indisch. In: Streitburg W A (ed.) *Die Erforschung der indogermanischen Sprachen: Indisch, Iranisch, Armenisch*. de Gruyter, Leipzig

R. J. Rocher

Sanskrit Grammatical Terms

The discovery of Sanskrit by western scholars, many of whom, as missionaries, traders, administrators, or soldiers, had other occupations as their prime duties, had an impact on linguistics in Europe and later in America that has never been paralleled by the discovery of another language, however 'exotic.' The impact was mainly of two sorts. There was first of all the flowering of comparative Indo–European linguistics in the nineteenth century and the direction which this took. The story of this is often told in such a way as to suggest that there was a sudden burst of activity in this sphere following Sir William Jones's famous address to the Asiatick Society of Bengal in 1786, where there had been nothing before, though in fact there had been speculation by Europeans on the interest that Sanskrit held as much as two centuries earlier. Similarly, there were comparativists in language study as early as the sixteenth century. The year 1786 nevertheless remains one of the most important dates in the history of western linguistics.

The second development was of rather later date and came after the antiquity, breadth, and profundity of speculation about language in India had become apparent. One effect of the study of the ancient Indian phonetic, grammatical, and linguistico–philosophical texts has been that many Sanskrit technical terms in linguistics have become at least partly familiar in the west even to scholars who know no Sanskrit, and a few of them have become fully assimilated into English and other European languages. The most widely known among these terms are the subjects of separate short articles. They are: anubandha (see *Anubandha*); anuvṛtti (see *Anuvṛtti*); avyayībhāva (see *Avyayībhāva*); bahuvrīhi (see *Bahuvrīhi*); dvandva (see *Dvandva*); guṇa (see *Guṇa*); kāraka (see *Kāraka*); karmadhāraya (see *Karmadhāraya*); lopa (see *Lopa*); paribhāṣā (see *Paribhāṣā*); samāsa (see *Samāsa*); sandhi (*Sandhi*); sphoṭa (see *Sphoṭa*); sūtra (see *Sūtra*); tatpuruṣa (see *Tatpuruṣa*); vṛddhi (see *Guṇa*).

See also: Sanskrit; Sanskrit: Discovery by Europeans; Pāṇinian Linguistics.

R. E. Asher

São Tomé and Príncipe: Language Situation

The official language of the Democratic Republic of Sao Tomé and Príncipe is Portuguese, and this is the medium of education, but varieties of a Portuguese-based creole are widely used among about half of the 140,000 population (1991). Two of these varieties, Santomese (*lungwa san tomé*) and Angolar (*lungwa angola*) are spoken on Sao Tomé, and Principense (*lungwa iyé*) on Príncipe. A related creole, Annobomese (*fa d-ambo*) is spoken on the small island of Ano Bom, lying 200 km to the south and forming part of Equatorial Guinea. Adult literacy is 45 percent.

Bibliography

Hodges T, Newitt M 1988 *Sao Tomé and Príncipe: From Plantation Colony to Microstate*. Westview Press, Boulder, CO

Sapir, Edward (1884–1939)

Edward Sapir, unquestionably the most distinguished student of Native American languages trained by Franz Boas (see *Boas, Franz*) and cofounder with Leonard Bloomfield (see *Bloomfield, Leonard*) of an autonomous discipline of linguistics in the USA, distinguished himself in such diverse fields of anthropology as linguistics, sociolinguistics, ethnology, folklore, and culture-and-personality; he wrote poetry and literary reviews and composed music. He remains the exemplary proponent of the humanistic roots of anthropology and linguistics as well as of the inseparability of their subject matters and points of view.

Sapir was born in Lauenberg, Pomerania on January 26, 1884. His parents, Eva Siegel and Jacob David Sapir, a Jewish cantor, emigrated to New York City in 1889. While still in high school, he won a prestigious Pulitzer scholarship to Columbia University. He received a BA in 1904 and an MA in 1905 in Germanic philology. His PhD in 1909 was in anthropology and reflected the program of urgent ethnology and linguistics of Franz Boas. Sapir was the only one of Boas's students to specialize in linguistics and rapidly came to set the standards for linguistic description and theory for all of Boasian anthropology, including the work of his former teacher and mentor.

Sapir held research fellowships at the University of California in 1907–08 and at the University of Pennsylvania in 1908–10, and headed the new Division of Anthropology of the Geological Survey of Canada from 1910–25. He taught at the University of Chicago from 1925–31 and at Yale University from 1931 until his premature death on February 4, 1939.

His major linguistic fieldwork was with Wishram Chinook (1905), Takelma and Chasta Costa (1906), Yana (1907–08, 1915), Ute (1909), Southern Paiute (1910), Nootka (1910, 1913–14), Sarcee (1922), Kutchin and Ingalik (1923), Hupa (1927), and Navajo (1929). He attempted to follow the Boasian ideal of a grammar, texts, and a dictionary for each language studied. As early as 1911, in relation to the publication of his extensive grammar of Takelma in the *Handbook of American Indian Languages*, Sapir challenged the standards for linguistic description in aboriginal America set by Boas so as to include work by individuals without professional training. This was, in retrospect, Sapir's first move toward the separation of North American linguistics from its basis in anthropology and the study of the American Indian.

Time Perspective in Aboriginal America: A Study in Method (1916) set forth the theoretical foundations of historical reasoning in anthropology, using language as a model to distinguish genetic from areal change. North American archaeology was not yet useful for even relative dating. Sapir's contention was that language was different from other parts of culture in that sound changes preserved the history of language development and culture contact so that the two could be disambiguated. Linguistics, therefore, could answer ethnological questions.

Between 1911 and 1921, Sapir turned to questions of genetic relationship in native North America, consolidating the 55 independent linguistic families of the Bureau of American Ethnology classification of 1892 into six superstocks having implications for migration and culture history. Language was to be the guide to ethnological interpretation. The six-unit classification dominated North American linguistics until the 1960s and is still widely discussed.

In 1921, Sapir published *Language: An Introduction to the Study of Speech* which was geared to the educated layman. It remains a classic for its citation of non-Indo–European languages, appreciation of the relationship between language and culture, inclusion of humanities perspectives on language, and insistence on the beauty and elegance of linguistic form.

Independently of parallel developments in Europe, Sapir developed the concept of the phoneme, emphasizing the psychological reality of sounds for the speakers of a language (see *Phoneme*). He moved toward morphophonemics, pioneered in the study of English semantics, emphasized a process model for the writing of grammar, dabbled in the construction of an international language, and returned at the end of his life to Indo–European philology with reference to the definition of the circum-Mediterranean cultural and linguistic area.

Much of his later work moved away from linguistics in the narrow sense. After his appointment at the University of Chicago in 1925, Sapir rapidly became the anthropological spokesman for the interdisciplinary social science emerging around the Chicago School of Sociology in the 1930s, particularly through his collaboration with interactional psychoanalyst Harry Stack Sullivan and political scientist Harold D. Lasswell. Sapir's theoretical writing in the period after his Rockefeller Foundation-funded move to Yale in 1931 emphasized the impact of culture on the development of personality and the creative role of the individual in culture. His Yale student, Benjamin Lee Whorf (see *Whorf, Benjamin Lee*), developed Sapir's ideas about the relationship of language and culture (see also *Sapir–Whorf Hypothesis*).

Sapir's years at Yale were not entirely happy ones. He was particularly plagued by anti-Semitism and ill-health. At Chicago and Yale, however, Sapir trained a coterie of American Indian linguists. Among his most distinguished linguistic students were F. K. Li (see *Li, Fang-Kuei*), Morris Swadesh (see *Swadesh, Morris*), Stanley Newman, Mary Haas (see *Haas, Mary Rosamond*), George Trager (see *Trager, George L.*), Benjamin Whorf (see *Wharf, Benjamin Lee*), Zellig Harris (see *Harris, Zellig S.*), and Charles Hockett (see *Hockett, Charles Francis*). Sapir was a cofounder of the Linguistic Society of America in 1925 and taught at its Linguistic Institute in 1937.

Bibliography

Darnell R 1990 *Edward Sapir: Linguist, Anthropologist, Humanist*. University of California, Berkeley, CA

Koerner K (ed.) 1984 *Edward Sapir: Appraisals of his Life and Work*. Benjamins, Amsterdam

Mandelbaum D (ed.) 1949 *Selected Writings of Edward Sapir*. University of California, Berkeley, CA

Sapir E 1921 *Language: An Introduction to the Study of Speech*. Harcourt Brace, New York

R. Darnell

Sapir–Whorf Hypothesis

1. Statement of the Hypothesis

The relationship between language and culture, or language and world view, has been noted at least since Wilhelm von Humboldt (1836; see *Humboldt, Wilhelm von*). But discussion remained relatively dormant until the 'Golden Age of Native American Indian Linguistics' in the first half of the twentieth century.

Although everyone calls it the Sapir–Whorf hypothesis, its most persistent proponent was Whorf (Carroll 1956; see also *Whorf, Benjamin Lee*). And yet, perhaps surprisingly, the most popular formulation comes from Sapir (see *Sapir, Edward*).

1.1 Sapir's, or the Lexical, Version

Sapir never sought the interface between language and culture anywhere but in the lexicon. The quote below is used most commonly to characterize the Sapir–Whorf hypothesis:

> Human beings do not live in the objective world alone . . . but are very much at the mercy of the particular language which has become the medium of expression for their society. The worlds in which different societies live are distinct worlds, not merely the same world with different *labels* attached.
>
> (Sapir in Mandelbaum 1963: 162, emphasis added)

A similar statement stressing the classificatory or categorizing nature of language is expressed in even stronger terms by Whorf (though this quote is seldom used to characterize the hypothesis):

> We dissect nature along lines laid down by our native languages. The categories and types that we isolate from the world of phenomena we do not find there because they stare every observer in the face. . .
>
> (Whorf in Carroll 1956: 213)

Both quotes emphasize the words or lexical resources of a language. That is, both stress that while nature is continuous human beings cut nature into discrete categories and each culture does this cutting somewhat differently. People make up words or concepts in order to talk about their world or cultural universe.

This version of the Sapir–Whorf hypothesis is one of two alternatives. It is called the lexical version in this article.

While one could ascribe the 'anomaly' that the hypothesis is usually characterized by the first, or Sapir's, quote to some historical accident, there seem to exist deeper reasons that will soon become apparent.

1.2 Whorf's, or the Grammatical, Version

The view expressed by Whorf in the second quote (above) is relatively unusual. He searched for the interface between language and culture beyond the vocabulary (or the lexicon) and sought to discover the roots of cultural regularities in a language's grammar:

> . . . the grammar of Hopi bore a relation to Hopi culture, and the grammar of European tongues to our own 'Western' or 'European' culture.
>
> (Whorf 1939: 73)

(The Hopi Indians live in villages in Arizona and speak a language of the Uto–Aztecan language family), and:

> By 'habitual thought' and 'thought world' I mean more than simply language, i.e., than the language patterns themselves.
>
> (Whorf in Carroll 1956: 147)

(following the usage of the times one can equate 'language patterns' with grammar), and again:

> . . . the background linguistic system (in other words the grammar) of each language is not merely a reproducing instrument for voicing ideas but rather is itself the shaper of ideas, the program and guide for the individual's mental activity, for his analysis of impression, for his synthesis of his mental stock in trade.
>
> (Whorf in Carroll 1956: 212)

Finally, in the statements in which Whorf gives the Sapir–Whorf hypothesis its alternate name, he again sees the relationship of language and culture in grammar:

> . . . the 'linguistic relativity principle,' which means, in informal terms, that users of markedly different grammars are pointed in different evaluations of externally similar acts of observations, and hence are not equivalent as observers but must arrive at somewhat different views of the world.
>
> (Whorf in Carroll 1956: 221)

These quotes represent the second way of interpreting the Sapir–Whorf hypothesis—the grammatical version.

1.3 Discussion

The two versions of the Sapir–Whorf hypothesis, or the 'linguistic relativity principle,' namely, the lexical version, espoused by Edward Sapir, and the grammatical, the predominant view of Benjamin Lee Whorf, have created considerable mischief in the profession. The reasons for the confusion lie in the different definitions of language used by anthropologists and linguists.

To anthropologists it was self-evident that the lexical resources of a language are part of that language. Therefore, the anthropological definition of language, at least implicitly, consists of phonology, grammar (syntax), *and* the lexicon.

The definition of language used by linguists explicitly excludes the lexicon. To this day linguists tend to give the lexicon short shrift. The science of linguistics considers only the structured parts of language amenable to analysis. One can easily detect pattern (i.e., structure) in phonology and in grammar (syntax). The lexicon was perceived as a 'collection of idiosyncratic features' (Gleason 1962), therefore not amenable to scientific analysis, and therefore outside of linguistics proper and, in the end, outside of what linguists considered to be language (perhaps best stated as 'language is what linguists do'). H. A. Gleason summarizes this view: 'lexicography is something that cannot be done but must be done.'

Several conferences about the hypothesis in the 1950s (Hoijer 1954; Hymes 1960; McQuown 1960) remained strangely inconclusive, largely because participating anthropologists and linguists operated with a basic misunderstanding about the nature of language. These conferences demonstrated vividly Kuhn's (1962) notion that discussions between members subscribing to two different scientific paradigms (views of the world) are always inconclusive. The irony of these discussions is that they are about language and world view, though Kuhn (ibid.) demonstrates that all world view disputes are hampered by the same sounding words used with different senses (e.g., 'language' as used by linguists versus anthropologists).

The Sapirean formulation of the hypothesis gained wide acceptance. The influence of grammar on world view was difficult to demonstrate. Whorf's exotic interpretations of Hopi thought were often attributed to his imaginative native consultant (Carl F. Voegelin, personal communication). (Most of Voegelin's later work, with Florence M. Voegelin, dealt with the Hopi Indian language and culture, e.g., Voegelin and Voegelin 1957.)

Meanwhile the basic linguistic attitude changed from an orientation that 'every language must be described in its own terms' (the structuralist paradigm) to a preoccupation with language universals ushered in by Chomsky's transformational/generative revolution in linguistics (see *Chomsky's Philosophy of Language*). Suddenly all languages looked very similar.

Many more or less serious statements were made to this effect. Robert E. Lees is credited with asserting that 'all languages are dialects of English.' A few years later James McCauley 'corrected' Lees's assertion by declaring that 'all languages are dialects of Japanese.' McCauley's remark was prompted by the surface structure of Japanese which appeared to be very close to a universal, hypothetical deep structure valid for all languages.

The interdependence of a culture and the lexicon that speakers associate with that culture to talk about their experiences seems almost obvious—especially to anthropologists. The validity of the hypothesis was, of course, of much greater interest to anthropologists than to linguists and found, concurrent with the Chomskyan revolution but independent of it, expression in the New Ethnography (Sect. 3).

In 1970 Oswald Werner demonstrated that the contribution of grammar to world view can only take place through grammatical categories. However, grammatical categories are, in the prevailing theories of linguistics, inherently part of the lexicon—specifically of lexical entries. In transformationalist theories of language these lexical entries are in the semantic component of the grammar of specific languages.

Each entry of the form (C, P) has a conceptual part C—a representation of the 'meaning'—and a phonological part P—representing directions for pronouncing the entry. Therefore, the 'linguistic relativity principle' becomes an investigation of the relationship between a culture and its associated lexicon—including grammatical categories.

It may be useful to recapitulate briefly Werner's argument. His demonstration starts with the Chomskyan assumption that the parts of a grammar are known and can be represented by the formula (1):

$$G (\#, \frown, \rightarrow, S, V_{nt}, V_t) \tag{1}$$

where the $\#$ symbol represents the boundary conditions of a sentence (or utterance). This is the silence (absence of speech) that precedes and follows every sentence. The $\frown$ symbol stands for the operation of concatenation. The rewrite symbol $\rightarrow$ (right arrow) stands for the rewrite operation that specifies structure, for example, the formula (2):

$$S \rightarrow NP \frown VP \tag{2}$$

(read: 'rewrite sentence as consisting of a noun phrase followed by a verb phrase') specifies the structure of S, the sentence, that consists of a noun phrase followed by a verb phrase. Thus, S in (1) stands for sentence, V_{nt} for the nonterminal vocabulary of the grammar, such as NP and VP in (2), and V_t for the terminal vocabulary. These lowest level units of a grammar or grammatical categories have no further structure (no rewrite rules can be applied and therefore these symbols never appear on the left side of any rewrite rules). In the process of sentence generation or production, actual lexical entries replace terminal vocabulary items in each language in question. (For details on the rules governing lexical insertion into terminal grammatical categories see the publications of Noam Chomsky.) Typical terminal categories are 'mass noun,' 'count noun,' 'performative verb,' 'manner adverbial,' 'definite article,' etc.

Obviously, $\#$, $\frown$, and $\rightarrow$ are part of the formalism of all grammars, hence language universals, and cannot therefore contribute to meaning and world view.

The high level nonterminal vocabulary V_{nt} are assumed by linguists to be also universal, that is, they occur in every language and cannot therefore influence language specific world views. Languages such as Nootka (one of a large number of languages spoken on the northwest coast of the USA) which consists almost entirely of verbs, and Sierra Miwok (one of a large number of languages spoken in the state of California), which consists almost entirely of nouns, can be made to conform naturally to the structure of noun phrases and verb phrases. In Nootka nouns are formed by nominalizing verbs (English analogue: to walk—to take a walk) and in Sierra Miwok verbs are formed by verbalizing nouns (English analogue: table—to table, e.g., a motion).

The above argument leaves only the low level nonterminal (V_{nt}) and the terminal (V_t)—the lowest level of grammatical categories of a given language—as potential contributors to language specific aspects of world view.

If M. A. K. Halliday's principle of 'delicacy' is now added, that states that when the limit of linguistic analysis (the ultimate delicacy) is reached, then every lexical item in every language represents its very own unique grammatical category.

The parts of grammar that could contribute to world view are therefore the low level nonterminal and the terminal grammatical categories. But since these are part of the lexicon, in any language, the interaction of language and culture must be seen as firmly rooted in the lexicon.

Ultimately, therefore, the Sapirean definitions and the definition of the hypothesis in Whorf's first quote of this article prevail. In the other, the Whorfian formulation, every time he mentions 'grammar,' or 'pattern,' these terms should be read as standing for 'low level grammatical categories,' or 'language specific grammatical categories.'

2. The Contribution of Grammatical and Lexical Categories

Before examining the issue of how these language specific categories contribute to world view, two additional notions require discussion: the strong version of the Sapir–Whorf hypothesis, according to which language *determines* thought, and the weak version, which asserts that language has a tendency to influence thought. Whorf is often viewed as representing the strong version. However, a review of his quotes (for example, in Sect. 1.2) reveals that he always qualifies his assertions.

While Whorf does say that speakers of different languages 'must arrive' at different interpretations of the world, these interpretations are not totally different only 'somewhat different' (Whorf in Carroll 1956: 221). Hopi grammar does not determine Hopi culture only 'bore a relation to [it]' (Whorf 1939: 73). And the 'background linguistic system' is not a determiner of ideas but merely a 'shaper of ideas.' He talks about 'habitual thought' rather than thought fully determined by the language of the speakers. It is thus difficult to find representatives of the strong version of the hypothesis.

All other points of view, including Whorf's, represent relatively stronger or relatively weaker versions of the weak version of the cultural relativity principle. The Sapir–Whorf hypothesis can therefore be paraphrased as follows:

> The categorial system of every language, including lower level grammatical and all lexical categories, points its speakers toward somewhat different evaluations of externally similar observations. Hence speakers of different languages have somewhat different views of the world, somewhat different habitual thought, and consequently their language and cultural knowledge are in a somewhat different relationship to each other. They don't live in the same world with different labels attached but in somewhat different worlds. The more dissimilar two languages are, in their lexicon—that is, in conceptual and grammatical categories—the greater their tendency to embody different world views.

Finally, Whorf's search for traces of world view in grammar, or in grammatical categories, is not without merit considering that different parts of language tend to change at different rates. Thus lexical items referring to objects change fastest as technology and customs change. For example, in Anglo–American culture new words like 'jeep,' 'radar,' 'laser,' 'napalm,' 'frozen yogurt,' 'yuppie,' and many others are quickly adopted into everyday use.

Verbs change more slowly. For example, until 1957 only planets, comets, and meteorites could orbit. Since Sputnik, the Soviet Union's first artificial satellite, an assortment of objects propelled into space are in orbit. A few years ago a telescope could not be thought of as orbiting. However, with the Hubble Deep Space Telescope in orbit, the range of the verb has been extended even to human beings. For example almost everyone understands the sentence *The astronauts are orbiting the earth.* There are other verbs introduced or extended by the rapid changes in Anglo–American culture. For example, *I word processed all morning*; *This program is good at error trapping*, etc. Not too surprisingly, new verbs are harder to think of than new nouns.

Still rarer are examples of changes in low level grammatical categories. These aspects of language change slowest and have therefore a much more lasting influence on 'habitual thought.'

In the following sections the amended definition of the Sapir–Whorf hypothesis (above) is used to explain a number of anomalies in the relationship between language and culture.

2.1 The Role of Different Symbol Systems

This amended definition still contains some mystification, for example, the dilemma of how it is that different categorial systems, that is, different languages, lead to somewhat different world views.

The insight that the choice of a symbol system is crucial to the solution of a mathematical problem is attributed to the Hungarian mathematician George Polya. A solution may be easy, difficult, or impossible depending on how a problem solver symbolizes the problem. Though mathematical problems are hardly identical with human problems for which language may provide a symbolization, mathematical problems display many similarities to such problems. Language provides human beings with categories of thought (see Lucy and Shweder 1979, below); these may or may not facilitate thinking in a given cultural domain.

It is clear from the Ethnoscience movement of the 1960s and 70s that speakers of different languages often do classify things very differently (see *Ethnoscience*). For example, the Navajo Indians classify the plant world as in Fig. 1.

It is clear from Fig. 1 that Navajos use different criteria for classifying plants than do speakers of English. Strangely, in Navajo—with about 500 named plants—no further subdivisions of even the largest class of flexible plants seem to exist.

However, alternate classifications do exist. One Navajo medicine man classified all plants according to their use. The surprise was a subclass of dangerous plants that were poisonous. However an even greater surprise was that each

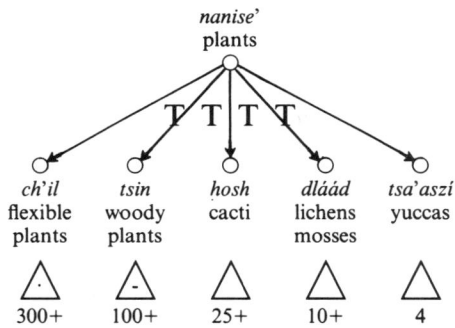

Figure 1. Navajo classification of plants. The T's symbolize the taxonomic relationship, e.g., *hosh nanise' át'é,* or 'A cactus is a (kind of) plant.'

dangerous plant has an antidote plant that can undo the effect of the poison.

One more unusual example showing that a language can facilitate talk (and solutions?) on some topics: the Navajo language has a rich vocabulary for describing the 'behavior' of lines. I list half a dozen examples from a growing corpus of about one hundred:

dzígai	a white line running off into distance (infinity)
adziisgai	a group of parallel white lines running off into distance
hadziisgai	a white line running vertically upward from the bottom to the top of an object
ahééhesgai	more than two white lines form concentric circles
ałch'inidzígai	two white lines coming together to a point
áłnánágah	a white line zigzagging back and forth

The ease with which Navajos talk about the behavior of white and other colored lines is amazing. This facility with 'geometry' is perhaps explainable by Navajo names or descriptions of features of the landscape that rarely utilize similarities to everyday objects (e.g., Hat Rock). Instead Navajos use geometrical description of verticals, horizontals, lines, and points. For example, a rock formation near Tuba City, Arizona, called by Navajos *Tsé Áhé'ii'áhá*, 'two rocks standing vertically parallel in a reciprocal relationship to each other' was named by English speakers 'Elephant's Feet.'

2.2 Language and Culture do not Covary

The *perfect* correlation of different cultures speaking different languages was an artifact of the biases of early cultural anthropology. In the formative years of the profession each ethnographer selected his or her own tribe with a distinct language. Nevertheless, anomalies to language/culture homogeneity were soon noted.

Three small tribes in Northern California represent the paradigm case. The Yurok, Karok, and Hupa Indians (the Yurok language is distantly related to the Algonquian, Karok to the Siouxan, and Hupa to the Na-Dene (Athabascan) language family) in the Klamath and Trinity river valleys near the California–Oregon border speak three different languages belonging to three different language families, yet their cultures are almost identical.

The linguistic record is incomplete, but there is evidence that many lexical categories (and possibly grammatical categories) were converging in the three languages. For example, all three use the phrase 'fish eater' for naming the sea otter.

There is growing evidence that extensive language and cultural leveling appears in areas where speakers of very different languages live in close proximity and in intimate contact with each other. For example, on the border of the Indo–European and Dravidian languages of India there are communities where vocabulary and grammar of the two languages (Marathi, Indo–European and Kannada, Dravidian) converge to such a high degree that people do seem to live in an almost identical world with different labels attached (Gumperz 1971).

In other words, very different languages can, over time, under the influence of their converging cultures, level many of their differences, while similar languages may diverge over time if their cultures are developing in different directions.

Examples of the latter case are the Apachean languages of the southwest USA. The Navajo Indian language, in the Apachean group, accommodates a culture that incorporates many Puebloan traits into its world view. None of the Apachean-speaking tribes live in villages. The Puebloan villagers have relatively homogeneous cultures but speak a diversity of languages. The other Apacheans did not assimilate Puebloan elements into their culture. Navajo and the other Apachean languages do remain similar, but the Navajos use extensive specialized vocabularies (and folk theories) appropriate to their world view that is alien to the other Apacheans.

2.3 Language Mixing

Bilinguals when in each other's company tend to mix languages. The reasons seem obvious. There are many things that can be said better, more efficiently, in an aesthetically more pleasing manner, in one language than in another. Language purity is usually maintained only in the presence of (especially) high status monolinguals who would consider mixing the discourse with an unknown language offensive.

Language mixing, a universal occurrence when bilinguals converse, provides a good indicator of the utility of the idioms or technical vocabulary of one language over another. That is, different languages offer different (more or less elegant?) solutions to speech about the same or similar 'cultural things.'

2.4 Language Acquisition

Since all definitions of culture stress that culture includes all things '... acquired [learned] by man as a member of society' (Tylor 1958), any language learned by children belongs therefore within culture. This fact underlies the formulation of the relationship as 'language *in* culture.'

However, many scholars became concerned that language is not just 'in culture' or 'part of culture,' but is also the major vehicle for the acquisition of culture. The confusion of culture with its chief vehicle of transmission proved troublesome, particularly since language is held responsible for the cumulativeness of culture. That is, language makes possible not only the transmission of culture, but also the increase of culture from generation to generation. This cumulativeness through language is the major mechanism of cultural evolution.

The solution, while 'obvious' in light of the developments of cognitive anthropology (Ethnoscience and New Ethnography are near synonyms) was nevertheless never clearly formulated (see *Ethnoscience*; *Ethnography of Speaking*).

Only one additional assumption need be made: the acquisition of language by a child has a natural history and in the course of this development language changes its function. At first the child learns its native language 'as a member of society' and therefore following the standard definitions of culture, language is part of culture.

However, there is more to it. Language acquisition specialists agree that language learning is complete by the age of 4–6 years. Formal education, the institutionalized commencement of the acquisition of culture through language, begins after the child fully masters its native language. This happens universally at the age of 5 or 6 years.

The child has now completed learning those aspects of culture that do not require language and begins to learn the accumulated wisdom and technology of the social group in which it is growing up, and that is encoded in language. Through language the child learns the verbalizable aspects of his or her culture. The function of language has shifted, now culture is in language, or it is acquired through language.

3. Cognitive Anthropology and the Sapir-Whorf Hypothesis

The New Ethnography or Ethnoscience entered anthropology with two papers published in *Language* by Floyd Lounsbury (1956) and his student Ward Goodenough (1956). The topic was a componential analysis of the Pawnee (which belongs to the Cadoan language family and was spoken in the southern Great Plains) and the Trukese (Austronesian-speaking Micronesians) kinship systems.

The point of componential analysis, in the context of the Sapir-Whorf hypothesis, is that kinship terminology or the kinship lexicon of every language/culture combination views the same kinship space, but tends to subdivide it differently. The examples of kinship terminologies confirm the 'linguistic relativity principle.' Speakers of languages in different cultures experience the same 'objective reality' but assign different terminology to it. The speakers of different languages lexicalize (set to words) the universal kinship space very differently.

For example, the Yankee kinship system used by English-speaking North Americans merges all cousins: most Americans no longer fully understand the terminology that classifies cousins by degree (first, second, . . . cousin) based on the distance from a common ancestor (first cousin = two generations, i.e., shared grandparents, etc.) and by generational distance (once, twice, . . . removed).

For example, Tagalog (see *Tagalog*), the main language of the Philippines, makes no distinction between grandparents and grandparents' brothers and sisters. Crow and Omaha, both Siouxan languages spoken in the Great Plains, merge some of the terms for cousins with certain aunts or uncles. Since the Crow reckon descent through the maternal line (they are matrilineal) and the Omaha through the paternal line (they are patrilineal) the two systems are mirror images of each other. Navajo and Hungarian, a Finno–Ugric language of central Europe, on the other hand, make a careful distinction between the relative age of brothers and sisters. The list of culturally prescribed differences in kinship terminologies is virtually endless.

Componential analysis was soon followed by the discovery of folk taxonomies. Folk classifications had been noted before (e.g., Mauss 1964) but this was the first time that anthropologists/ethnographers collected folk taxonomies systematically. The seminal monograph was Conklin's *Hanuno'o Agriculture* (1954; the Hanuno'o are Austronesian speakers living on the island of Mindanao in the Philippines). A flurry of activity followed taxonomizing everything from ethno-anatomies to folk zoologies. Werner (1983) even presented the taxonomic aspects of the entire traditional Navajo universe.

In this lively debate the Sapir–Whorf hypothesis was mentioned only rarely and often outside the context of the New Ethnography. The participants in this ferment tacitly assumed that componential analysis and folk taxonomies clearly demonstrate the weak lexical version of the hypothesis.

Out of these developments arose cognitive anthropology that took as its goal the investigation of human cognition, especially cultural knowledge. It soon developed two branches. One is ethnoscience ethnography, which tacitly assumes the validity of the weak lexical form of linguistic relativity but does not elaborate this link to the past. The more pressing task is seen as the perfection and systematization of ethnography.

The second branch moved closer to cognitive psychology and by that route to cognitive science. Berlin and Kay (1969) soon emerged as the leaders in this field with their work on color terminology. That different language/culture groups have different color terminologies was considered in the debates of the 1950s and early 1960s the prime example of the lexical version of the Sapir–Whorf hypothesis. Obviously, the color spectrum is a continuum of colors from red to purple, but human beings in different parts of the world partition this continuum differently.

Berlin and Kay's first important discovery was that the color spectrum is not a good example for the hypothesis. '[C]olor categorization is not random and the foci of basic color terms are similar in all languages' (Berlin and Kay 1969: 10) and '. . . the eleven (see Fig. 2.) basic color categories are panhuman perceptual universals' (Berlin and Kay 1969: 109).

However, Berlin and Kay (1969: 160 n.2) stress that their work should not be confused with a thorough study of the ethnographic ramifications of color terminology. That is, '. . . to appreciate the full cultural significance of color words it is necessary to appreciate the full range of meanings, both referential and connotative . . .' or the lexical/semantic fields in which individual color terms are embedded.

Their second discovery was that color terminology evolves in a very lawful sequence. Although their formula has been 'fine tuned' following new cross-cultural data, it can be represented as shown in Fig. 2. (their original formulation, 1969: 4).

Lucy and Shweder (1979) revived the controversy by showing in several well-designed experiments that color memory is highly sensitive to the lexical resources of a language and culture. They conclude that the universality of color categories is overstated by Berlin and Kay and that the weak Sapir–Whorfian lexical formulation corresponds more closely to the facts.

Willet Kempton extended the methodology of cognitive anthropology to the shapes of objects, thus exploring the

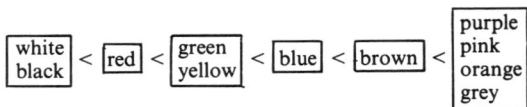

Figure 2. The cultural evolution of color terminology. If a language has the term 'red,' then it also has 'black' and 'white'; if a language has the term 'green' and 'yellow,' then it also has 'red,' 'white,' and 'black,' etc. The more technologically developed a given culture, the more of the 11 basic color terms are in use. (In the third box either order of [green < yellow] or [yellow < green] is possible).

boundary between categories. Cecil Brown applied the evolutionary idea in Fig. 2. to other aspects of human vocabularies, especially botanical and zoological terminologies.

Ethnographers soon expanded their view beyond componential analysis after it was shown by a number of anthropologists and linguists that components are also lexical items and hence most often language specific rather than universal. John Lyons's critique of componential analysis as a universal theory for cultural knowledge (and semantics) is devastating. Nevertheless, componential analysis remains a superb tool for understanding exotic kinship terminologies.

In 1970 Casagrande and Hale, who had collected a large number of folk definitions in Papago (an Uto–Aztecan language of southern Arizona) published 13 lexical/semantic relations. They failed to find examples of a postulated 14th, the part/whole relation. A close analysis of their data shows that the part/whole relation did appear in its inverse form: that is, instead of 'A is a part of B' they found and classified as a spatial relation the inverse 'B has an A.'

Casagrande and Hale's work was seminal for a number of researchers (see the summary in Evens et al. 1980). Through these scholars their work was linked to the cognitive sciences. However, this link did not develop into strong ties.

The major insight of field theory can again be framed in terms of the linguistic relativity principle: the weak lexical version is accepted as self-evident. The lexical/semantic fields of the languages used in different cultural contexts look very different. However, there is unity because the lexical/semantic fields are held together by *universal* lexical-/semantic relations.

Unfortunately there is no agreement on the basic set of lexical/semantic relations which range from Werner's (Werner and Schoepfle 1987) two to the over 50 lexical relations of Apresyian et al. (1970). Werner's two relations are 'taxonomy' and 'modification' plus several derived complex relations, a relation for sequential phenomena, and logical relations, including modal logic. Apresyian et al.'s relations are derived from practical lexicography or the construction of more systematic dictionaries. For example, their relation EQUIP is the relation in 'ship' EQUIP 'crew' ('A crew operates a ship'). The folk taxonomic model can be applied to whole cultures. Closely related encyclopedic works display the lexical and cultural knowledge dimensions of a culture. That is, a background document fully exploring the lexical resources of a language represents an important aspect of the culture as a whole.

Ethnography is seen by many scholars as translation *par excellence*. Ethnographic translation fundamentally encourages translator's notes (definitions), which explain cultural ramifications of lexical items (or phrases) in native texts. Therefore, a carefully documented encyclopedic lexicon may represent an extensive set of translator's notes prepared in advance of the analysis of any future ethnographic texts.

An extension of these ideas is the recent focus on cultural schemata (Casson 1983). Schemata, recast into the lexical version of the Sapir–Whorf hypothesis, are folk theories often labeled by words (especially verbs) or phrases that usually require complex (e.g., up to monograph length and beyond) explanations or folk definitions.

4. Summary and Conclusions

The choice of the symbol system (e.g., language) affects the ease or difficulty with which one can talk about particular domains of cultural reality and solve problems in them. Thus the lexicon of language does provide a loosely laced straitjacket for thinking because it limits individuals to customary categories of thought. Only in this sense does it constrain thought.

At the same time language allows the inventive human mind to create alternative categorizations for solving new problems. The history of science and the rich diversity of thousands of human languages and cultures attests to the inventiveness of the human spirit.

True, the combinatorial possibilities in human language are enormous. Thus the very use of language results in a drift of meanings and with it inadvertent changes in world view. This process is analogous to genetic drift. But in addition there are analogues and historical examples of meaning mutations: conceptual revolutions and conversions.

However, these escapes from the mold of one's habitual language patterns are never easy—'. . . anomaly is recognized only with difficulty' (Kuhn 1970). It usually takes genius to show the rest of humanity how to see the world in a new light, that is in new categories. In such conversion experiences the language is affected 'to the core' (Kuhn 1970)—specifically, most grammatical categories remain the same but geniuses revamp lexical categories in ways that facilitate new thought which the rest of humanity may in time follow.

Bibliography

Apresyian Y D, Mel'čuk I A, Žolkovsky A K 1970 Semantics and lexicography: Toward a new type of unilingual dictionary. In: Kiefer F (ed.) *Studies in Syntax and Semantics*. Reidel, Dordrecht

Berlin B, Kay P 1969 *Basic Color Terms: Their Universality and Evolution*. University of California Press, Berkeley, CA

Carroll J B (ed.) 1956 *Language, Thought, and Reality: Selected Writings of Benjamin Lee Whorf*. MIT, New York

Casagrande J B, Hale K L 1967 Semantic relationships in Papago folk definitions. In: Hymes D H, Bittle W E (eds.) *Studies in Southwestern Ethnolinguistics*. Mouton, The Hague

Casson R 1983 Schemata in cognitive anthropology. *Annual Review of Anthropology*: 429-62

Conklin H C 1954 The relation of Hanuno'o culture to the plant world (Doctoral dissertation, Yale University)

Evens M W, Litowitz B E, Markowitz J A, Smith R N, Werner O 1980 *Lexical/Semantic Relations: A Comparative Survey*. Linguistic Research, Edmonton

Gleason H A 1962 The relation of lexicon and grammar. In: Householder F W, Saporta S (eds.) *Problems in Lexicography*. Indiana Research Center in Anthropology, Bloomington, IN

Goodenough W H 1956 Componential analysis and the study of meaning. *Lg* **32**: 195–216

Gumperz J J 1971 Dialect differences and social stratification in a North Indian village. In: Gumperz J J, Dill A (eds.) *Language in Social Groups*. Stanford University Press, Stanford, CA

Hoijer H (ed.) 1954 *Language in Culture*. University of Chicago Press, Chicago, IL

Humboldt W von 1836 (1960) *Über die Verschiedenheit des menschlichen Sprachbaues*. Dümmler, Bonn

Hymes D H 1960 Discussion of the symposium on the translation between language and culture. *AnL* **2**(2): 81–84

Kuhn T S 1970 *The Structure of Scientific Revolutions*, 2nd edn. University of Chicago Press, Chicago, IL

Lounsbury F G 1956 A semantic analysis of the Pawnee kinship usage. *Lg* **32**: 158–94

Lucy A J, Shweder R A 1979 Whorf and his critics: Linguistic and nonlinguistic influences on color memory. *AmA* **81**: 581–615

Mandelbaum D G (ed.) 1963 *Selected Writings of Edward Sapir in Language, Culture, and Personality*. University of California Press, Berkeley, CA

Mauss M 1964 On language and primitive forms of classification. In Hymes E (ed.) *Language in Culture and Society*. Harper Row, New York

McQuown N A 1960 Discussion of the symposium on the translation between language and culture. *AnL* **2(2)**: 79–80

Tylor E B 1958 *Primitive Culture*, new edn. Harper, New York

Voegelin C F, Voegelin F M 1957 Hopi domains: A lexical approach to the problem of selection. *IJAL* **23(2)**1: Memoir 14

Werner O, Manning A, Begishe K Y 1983 A taxonomic view of the traditional Navajo universe. In: Sturdevant W C, Ortiz A (eds.) *Handbook of North American Indians. Vol. 10: Southwest*. Smithsonian Institution, Washington, DC

Werner O, Schoepfle G M 1987 *Systematic Fieldwork, vol. 1: Foundations of Ethnography and Interviewing*, vol. 2: Ethnographic Analysis and Data Management. Sage Publications, London

Whorf B L 1939 The relation of habitual thought and behavior to language. In: Spier L (ed.) *Language, Culture, and Personality*. Sapir Memorial Publication Fund, Menasha, WI

O. Werner

Saramaccan

SEE Pidgins and Creoles

Saudi Arabia: Language Situation

The official language of Saudi Arabia is Arabic, which is also the native language of all of the country's approximately 11 million inhabitants. English and a number of languages of the Indian subcontinent are spoken by the large, transient, multinational workforce. To some extent, English functions as a lingua franca between the Saudis and this latter group.

Arabic is the language of government, politics, religion, the media, and public education: indeed, even English-medium private schools are legally bound to teach Arabic to their pupils. However, in some faculties of Saudi Arabia's universities (Medicine and the Applied Sciences in general) the medium of instruction is English. The main foreign language taught is English.

Literacy levels in Arabic vary with age and sex. Literacy is virtually universal among the under-20s, but decreases with age, so that of those aged 40–50, no more than perhaps 50 percent are literate. This figure drops to less than 20 percent among the over-70s. The rate for women is lower than for men in every age-group, falling to virtually nil among the over-60s.

The language situation in Saudi Arabia, like that in every other Arab country, is characterized by diglossia: a pan-Arab, nonnatively spoken variety of Arabic is used in all written communication (Modern Standard Arabic = MSA), and in speech in most public, official, and pedagogical contexts, whereas dialectal Arabic is universal in domestic, everyday usage. However, increasing education is causing the dialect to move closer in vocabulary and syntax to MSA.

See also: Arabic; Diglossia.

C. Holes

Saurashtri

This Indo–Aryan language is spoken in the heart of the Tamil country by some 200,000 members of a weaver community domiciled for the past 1,000 years in the environs of the city of Madurai in Tamil Nadu, south India.

See also : Gujarati.

Bibliography

Dave I R 1976 *The Saurashtrians in South India*. Saurashtra University, Rajkot

Randle H N 1943–4 An Indo–Aryan language of south India. *BSOS* **11**: 104–21, 310–21

Saussure, Ferdinand(-Mongin) de (1857–1913)

Saussure was born on November 26, 1857 in Geneva, and died on February 22, 1913, at Château Vufflens near Geneva. He is best known for the posthumous compilation of his lecture notes on general linguistics, the *Cours de linguistique générale*, edited by his former students and first published in 1916 (since translated into more than a dozen languages, including—in order of their first appearance since 1928—Japanese, German, Russian, Spanish, English, Polish, Italian, Hungarian). However, during his lifetime, Saussure was most widely known for his masterly *Mémoire* of 1879, devoted to an audacious reconstruction of the Proto-Indo–European vowel system. It is generally agreed that his *Cours* ushered in a revolution in linguistic thinking during the 1920s and 1930s which is still felt in the 1990s in many quarters, even beyond linguistics proper. He is universally regarded as 'the father of structuralism.'

Although from a distinguished Geneva family which—beginning with Horace Bénédict de Saussure, whose portrait adorns the Swiss twenty franc note—can boast of several generations of natural scientists, Ferdinand de Saussure was early drawn to language study, producing an '*Essai pour réduire les mots du grec, du latin et de l'allemand à un petit nombre de racines*' at the age of 14 or 15 (published in *Cahiers Ferdinand de Saussure* 32: 77–101 [1978]). Following his parents' wishes, he attended classes in chemistry, physics, and mathematics at the University of Geneva during 1875–76, before being allowed to join his slightly older classmates who had left for Leipzig the year before. So in the fall of 1876 Saussure arrived at the university where a number of important works in the field of Indo–European phonology and morphology, including Karl Verner's (see *Verner, Karl Adolf*) epoch-making paper on a series of exceptions to 'Grimm's Law,' had just been published. Saussure took courses with Georg Curtius (see *Curtius, Georg*), the mentor of the '*Junggrammatiker*,' and a number of the younger professors, such as August Leskien (see *Leskien, August*), Ernst Windisch, Heinrich Hübschmann, Hermann Osthoff (see *Osthoff, Hermann*), and others in the fields of Indic studies, Slavic, Baltic, Celtic, and Germanic. During 1878–79 Saussure spent two semesters at the University of Berlin, enrolling in courses with Heinrich Zimmer and Hermann Oldenberg. After barely six semesters of formal study, when just 21, he published the major work of his lifetime (Saussure 1879). In this 300-page work he assumed the existence, on purely theoretical grounds, of an early Proto-Indo–European sound of unknown phonetic value (designated *A) which would develop into various phonemes of the Indo–European vocalic system depending on its combination with various 'sonantal coefficients.' Saussure was thus able to explain a number of puzzling questions of Indo–European ablaut. But the real proof of Saussure's hypotheses came many years later, after his death, following the decipherment of Hittite and its identification as an Indo–European language, and after the Polish scholar Kuryłowicz (see *Kuryłowicz, Jerzy*) in 1927 had pointed to Hittite cognates that contained the sound corresponding to Saussure's *A. These were identified as laryngeals, sounds previously not found in any of the other Indo–European languages.

Having returned to Leipzig, Saussure defended his dissertation on the use of the genitive absolute in Sanskrit in February 1880, leaving for Geneva soon thereafter. Before he arrived in Paris in September of that year, he appears to have conducted fieldwork on Lithuanian, like Schleicher and others before him. In Paris Saussure found a number of receptive students, among them Antoine Meillet, Maurice Grammont, and Paul Passy, but also congenial colleagues such as Gaston Paris, Louis Havet, who had previously written the most detailed review of his *Mémoire*, and Arsène Darmesteter. Michel Bréal (see *Bréal, Michel Jules Alfred*), the doyen of French linguistics, secured him a position as Maître de Conférences at the École des Hautes Études in 1881, a post he held until his departure for Geneva ten years later.

During his lifetime, Saussure was best known for his *Mémoire* and the paper on Lithuanian accentuation (1896). Since the 1920s, however, his influence and fame have been almost exclusively connected with the book he never wrote, the *Cours de linguistique générale*. This was largely based on notes carefully taken down by a number of his students during a series of lectures on the subject that he had given from 1907–11 at the University of Geneva (to which he had returned as a professor of Sanskrit and Comparative Grammar in 1891). One of them was Albert Riedlinger, whose name appears on the title page of the *Cours*, which was put together by Saussure's successors, Charles Bally and Albert Sechehaye (see *Geneva School of Linguistics after Saussure*), neither of whom had attended these lectures themselves (though it is frequently, but erroneously, stated in the literature that they had). The *Cours* was in fact never published in Geneva and was not published in 1915 but in Lausanne and Paris in 1916, that is, exactly 100 years after Franz Bopp's (see *Bopp, Franz*) *Conjugationssystem*, which is usually regarded as the beginning of comparative–historical Indo–European linguistics.

The ideas advanced in the *Cours* produced a veritable revolution in linguistic science; historical–comparative grammar which had dominated linguistic research since the early nineteenth century was soon relegated to a mere province of the field. At least in the manner the *Cours* had been presented by the editors, Saussure's general theory of language was seen as assigning pride of place to the non-historical, descriptive, and 'structural' approach (Saussure himself did not use the last-mentioned term in a technical sense). This led to a tremendous body of work concerned with the analysis of the linguistic system of language and its function, and a neglect of questions of language change and linguistic evolution in general—a situation which remains characteristic of the linguistic scene in the 1990s, in particular the framework associated with the name of Noam Chomsky. From the 1920s onwards a variety of important schools of linguistic thought developed in Europe that can be traced back to proposals made in the *Cours*. These are usually identified with the respective centers from which they emanated, such as Geneva, Prague, Copenhagen, and Paris. In North America too, through the work of Leonard Bloomfield (see *Bloomfield, Leonard*), Saussure's ideas became stock-in-trade among linguists, descriptivists, structuralists, and generativists.

At the core of Saussure's linguistic theory is the assumption that language is a system of interrelated terms which he called 'langue' (in contradistinction to 'parole,' the individual speech act or speaking in general). This 'langue' is the underlying code which ensures that people can speak and understand each other; it has social underpinning and is an operative system embedded in the brain of everyone who has learned a given language. The analysis of this system, Saussure maintains, is the true object of linguistics. The system is a network of relationships which he characterized as being of two kinds: syntagmatic (i.e., items are arranged in a consecutive, linear order) and associative, later termed 'paradigmatic' (i.e., the organization of units in a deeper fashion dealing with grammatical and semantic relations). Saussure's emphasis on language as 'a system of (arbitrary) signs' and his proposal that linguistics is the central part of an overall science of sign relations or 'sémiologie' have led to the development of a field of inquiry more frequently called 'semiotics' (following C. S. Peirce's terminology), which deals with sign systems in literature and other forms of art, including music and architecture.

Many of the ingredients of Saussure's general theory of language have often been taken out of their original context and incorporated into theories outside of linguistics, at times quite arbitrarily, especially in works by French writers engaged in 'structuralist' anthropology (e.g., Claude Lévi-Strauss, see *Lévi-Strauss, Claude*) and philosophy (e.g., Louis Althusser), literary theory (e.g., Jacques Derrida), psychoanalysis (e.g., Jacques Lacan, see *Lacan, Jacques*), and semiotics (e.g., Roland Barthes, see *Barthes, Roland*), and their various associates and followers. The trichotomies (usually reduced to dichotomies) which have become current in twentieth-century thought, far beyond their original application, are: langage–langue–parole (i.e., language in all its manifestations or 'speech'; language as the underlying system; and 'speaking'), signe–signifié–signifiant (sign, signified, and signifier), synchrony versus diachrony ('panchrony' would be a combination of these two perspectives), and syntagmatic versus paradigmatic relations.

Bibliography

(For a full bibliography of Saussure's writings see Koerner 1972a.)

Engler R 1975 European structuralism: Saussure. In: Sebeok T A (ed.) *Current Trends in Linguistics. Vol. XIII: Historiography of Linguistics*. Mouton, The Hague

Engler R 1976– Bibliographie saussurienne. *Cahiers Ferdinand de Saussure* **30**: 99–138; **31**: 279–306; **33**: 79–145; **40**: 131–200

Godel R 1957 *Les sources du Cours de linguistique générale de F. de Saussure*. Droz, Geneva

Koerner E F K 1972a *Bibliographia Saussureana, 1870–1970: An Annotated, Classified Bibliography on the Background, Development and Actual Relevance of Ferdinand de Saussure's General Theory of Language*. Scarecrow Press, Metuchen, NJ

Koerner E F K 1972b *Contribution au débat post-saussurien sur le signe linguistique: Introduction générale et bibliographie annotée*. Mouton, The Hague

Koerner E F K 1973 *Ferdinand de Saussure: Origin and Development of his Linguistic Thought in Western Studies of Language*. Friedrich Vieweg Sohn, Braunschweig

Koerner E F K 1988 *Saussurean Studies/Études saussuriennes*. Slatkine, Geneva

Saussure F de 1879 *Mémoire sur le système primitif des voyelles dans les langues indo–européennes*. B. G. Teubner, Leipzig

Saussure F de 1896 Accentuation lituanienne. *Anzeiger* of *Indogermanische Forschungen* **6**: 157–66

Saussure F de 1916 *Cours de linguistique générale*. Lausanne. (Harris R 1983 *Course in General Linguistics*. Duckworth, London)

Saussure F de 1922 *Recueil des publications scientifiques* . C. Winter, Heidelberg.

E. F. K. Koerner

Saussurean Tradition in Twentieth-century Linguistics

The Swiss linguist Ferdinand de Saussure (1857–1913) established his reputation at an early age, with his 1878 monograph *Mémoire sur le système primitif des voyelles dans les langues indo–européennes* ('the original vowel system of the Indo–European languages'). The *Mémoire* posited the existence of two Proto-Indo–European 'sonant coefficients' which appeared in no attested forms of the daughter languages, but could account for certain vowel developments which had previously appeared irregular. Fifty years later an *H* with exactly the distribution of Saussure's sonant coefficients was discovered in Hittite, confirming his hypothesis.) After his 1881 doctoral thesis on the absolute genitive in Sanskrit, Saussure published no more books, only articles on specific topics in historical linguistics.

But in 1907, 1908–09, and 1910–11, he gave at the University of Geneva three courses in general linguistics, a topic on which he never published anything. Soon after his death in 1913, his colleagues Charles Bally (1865–1947) and Albert Sechehaye (1870–1946), appreciating the extraordinary nature of the courses Saussure had given, began gathering what manuscript notes they could find, together with the careful and detailed notebooks of students who had taken one or more of the three courses, especially Albert Riedlinger (1883–1978). From these they fashioned the *Cours de linguistique générale*, published at Lausanne

and Paris in 1916. It would become one of the most influential books of the twentieth century, not just for linguistics, but for virtually every realm of intellectual endeavor.

In order to trace the Saussurean tradition in twentieth-century linguistics, this article considers nine key elements of Saussure's view of language. For each a summary is given of the condition prior to Saussure, of Saussure's own view, and of how his view has shaped linguistic inquiry in the years since the publication of the *Cours*.

1. The Establishment of Synchronic Linguistics

At the time of Saussure's lectures, the study of language had been dominated for over 30 years by (a) historical work on the language of written texts (work which had only gradually come to be distinguished from 'philology,' inquiry aimed not at the language but at better understanding of the text itself); (b) dialectological work based on field investigation of local dialects; (c) phonetics, which demanded increasingly minute observation in strong adherence to the positivistic spirit; and (d) psychology, the principal domain of a global perspective on language, dominated by the ideas of Wilhelm von Humboldt (1767–1835) and his followers, notably Heymann Steinthal (1823–99) and Wilhelm Wundt (1832–1920) (see *Twentieth-century Linguistics: Overview of Trends*; *Steinthal, Heymann*; *Wundt, Wilhelm (1832–1920)*).

A fifth approach existed—the study of language as a general phenomenon independent of historical or psychological considerations—but it had made little progress since the death of its principal exponent, the American scholar William Dwight Whitney (1827–94; see *Whitney, William Dwight*). Furthermore, the publication of a major study of language in 1900 by the Leipzig psychologist Wundt appeared to signal that the new century would give the 'general' study of language over fully to that discipline.

Saussure's problem was to delineate a study of language that would be neither historical nor ahistorical, neither psychological nor apsychological; yet more systematic than Whitneyan general linguistics, so as to be at least the equal in intellectual and methodological rigor to the historical, psychological, and phonetic approaches. His solution was to make a strong distinction between the study of language as a static system, which he called 'synchronic' linguistics, and the study of language change, which he called 'diachronic' linguistics (or, until 1908, 'evolutive'). Saussure's rejection of the traditional term 'historical' seems to have been based in part on a disdain for the reliance it suggested upon extralinguistic factors and written texts, and in part on a desire for terminological symmetry with 'synchronic.' Synchronic linguistics would henceforth designate the study of language systems in and of themselves, divorced from external considerations of a historical or psychological sort, or any factor having to do with actual speech production.

This is the single most sweeping of Saussurean traditions: for insofar as twentieth-century linguists have focused their efforts neither on simple description of languages, nor on their evolution, nor on their connection to 'national psychology,' they have realized Saussure's program of synchronic linguistics. Furthermore, historical linguistics has largely become the diachronic enterprise envisioned by Saussure (though the term 'historical' continues in general usage), and even the purely 'descriptive' approaches have been profoundly marked by the Saussurean concept of language as a system where *tout se tient* ('everything holds together'), a phrase often associated with Saussure, though there is no record of his using it in his Geneva lectures. It may be that its first use was in a lecture delivered by Antoine Meillet in 1906 (see Meillet 1921: 16; see also *Meillet, Antoine (Paul Jules)*).

In establishing synchronic linguistics, Saussure was not engaging in an exercise of scholarly exactitude, but serving notice upon psychologists and others that the general study of language should fall to persons with historically based training in specific languages and language families, rather than to experts in the functioning of the mind. Many of Saussure's statements about language can best be understood in conjunction with this need for establishing the autonomy of linguistic inquiry vis-à-vis adjoining fields.

2. The Primacy of Spoken Language

The idea that speech is the original and primal form of language, and writing a secondary imitation of speech, runs counter to the general popular accordance of greater prestige to writing. Yet the primacy of spoken over written language became embedded in linguistics in the early nineteenth century, doubtless in connection with the Romantic belief that folk traditions embodied the national spirit more deeply than urban practices like writing, which were more subject to external influences. The trend continued over the course of the nineteenth century as linguistics moved away from philology and became increasingly concerned with the gathering of spoken forms from living dialects. By the turn of the twentieth century few linguists would have disputed that the best source for determining the original form of anything in any language was to reconstruct it from its living descendant dialects, and not from written records surviving from intermediate stages.

Saussure formalized the marginalization of written language as well as anyone, and if its survival is often viewed as a Saussurean tradition, it is because he has borne the brunt of the 1967 attack on this marginalization by Jacques Derrida (1930–). For Saussure, writing is not language, but a separate entity whose only 'mission' is to represent real (spoken) language. The 'danger' of writing is that it creates the illusion of being more real and more stable than speech, and therefore gains ascendancy over speech in the popular mind. Derrida demonstrated the irrationality and internal inconsistency of this extreme phonocentrism; in his deconstructionist wordplay, all language is a kind of 'writing' (in a sense that is unique to Derrida).

But so deeply ingrained is this tradition in twentieth-century linguistics that few linguists saw the need to respond to Derrida, whose critique was summarily dismissed. Well over 10 years passed before linguists began to admit that the marginalization of writing had been carried to an irrational extreme; and despite some tentative steps toward a linguistics of writing in various quarters, this tradition of privileging spoken language—shared though not founded by Saussure—is in no danger of passing away.

3. The Object of Linguistics: *Langue* versus *Parole*

The role of the human will in language production has constituted a problem for linguistic thought at least since

Plato's *Cratylus*: humans are constrained by the conventions of language, yet it is through language that will and individuality are shaped and realized. Since modern science is predicated upon the elimination of the will from any object of inquiry, human desire, action, and creation came to be excluded from the 'scientific' study of language. This has necessitated a considerable abstraction of language away from its role in human affairs, treating it as if it existed independently of speakers and speech acts. But here two problems arose: (a) the metaphor of language as organism (which qua metaphor had been fruitfully employed by early nineteenth-century linguists) became extremely attractive as a way of talking about language independently of speakers, and as Michel Bréal (1832–1915; see also *Bréal, Michel Jules Alfred*) complained in the introduction to his *Essai de sémantique* (1897), the metaphor was taken literally by many people, giving rise to gross misunderstandings; (b) Wundt's *Völkerpsychologie* ('national psychology') seemed to offer a more sophisticated way of dealing with linguistic phenomena: it eliminated the metaphysical abstraction of 'language,' but replaced it with still less satisfactory explanations that revolved around the 'spirit of peoples,' were untestable, and could not sustain any approach to language that was detailed or systematic.

Saussure's contribution was to dissect the total phenomenon of language (*langage*) into (a) actual speech production (*parole*), including the role of the individual will, and (b) the socially shared system of signs (*langue*) that makes production and comprehension possible. Although he spoke of a linguistics of *parole* that would cover the phonetic side of language and the products of individual will, Saussure made it clear that the linguistics of *langue* is the essential, real linguistics. *Langue* is beyond the direct reach of the individual will. Saussure's formulation is both a defense and a refinement of the procedures of traditional grammar and historical linguistics, yet at the same time it stakes out an autonomous realm for general linguistic inquiry.

Despite much debate among scholars as to just what Saussure meant by *langage*, *langue*, and *parole*, the distinction has held firm throughout twentieth-century linguistics. It has been suggested that certain work in stylistics (e.g., by Saussure's disciple Bally) and in discourse pragmatics constitutes an attempt at a linguistics of *parole*, but it is not yet clear how any aspect of language, once it is systematized, fails to enter the sphere of *langue* (see *Geneva School of Linguistics after Saussure*). The human will remains in exile from linguistics, and *langue* (naturally somewhat evolved from Saussure's original conception of it) continues to be the object of study of virtually every approach to which the name 'linguistics' is accorded (see Sect. 4).

4. *Langue* as a Social Fact

Saussure's insistence upon the social nature of *langue* grew during the years in which he lectured on general linguistics, largely at the expense of psychologically based considerations. Again, this may be tied in part to the need to establish synchronic linguistics independently of the dominant post-Humboldtian psychological establishment. The young science of sociology embodied the spirit of positivism, with which it shared the same recognized founder, Auguste Comte (1798–1857). Positivism was coming to be equated with scientificness in general thought, making classical psychology appear old-fashioned and metaphysical. For the sociologists, Wundt's *Völkerpsychologie*, based on non-empirical generalizations (and more akin to what today would pass as philosophy of mind, not psychology) was already unacceptably passé.

Much ink has been spilled regarding the degree to which Saussure's conception of language was directly influenced by work in sociology, particularly by Emile Durkheim (1858–1917) and Gabriel Tarde (1843–1904). Saussure's former student and lifelong intimate Antoine Meillet (1866–1936; see also *Meillet, Antoine (Paul Jules)*) was closely allied with Durkheim and his journal *L'Année sociologique*; and there is often a close correspondence between Saussure's and Durkheim's use of terms like 'social fact' and 'collective consciousness.' But since Saussure never cites Durkheim or Tarde (he was after all teaching a course, not writing a book), support for any claim of direct influence is lacking.

In Saussure's view, *langue* is a 'treasury' or 'collection of impressions' that is 'deposited' in identical form in the brain of each member of a given speech community. He uses the metaphor of a dictionary, of which every individual possesses an identical copy. What the individual does with this socially-shared system falls entirely into the realm of *parole*. This distinction (which was not yet clear to Saussure at the time of his first course in general linguistics of 1907) differentiates Saussure's dichotomy from that between 'competence' and 'performance' established in the 1960s by Noam Chomsky (1928–) (see *Generative Grammar: Principles*). Chomsky explicitly related competence with *langue* and performance with *parole*, though in actual fact the analogy was only partial: for Chomsky, competence (derived from innate universal grammar) is mental and individual, and performance the locus of its social actuation. Furthermore the considerable differences between Saussure's orientation toward language as a semiotic system and Chomsky's toward competence as a mental faculty make any such equations difficult.

Saussure's views on the social nature of language have had a great resonance in linguistics and many other fields. By the mid-1930s it was commonplace to equate 'synchronic linguistics' (indeed, 'scientific linguistics') with 'social linguistics,' and to include under this heading the work of Meillet and his many European disciples, including Alf Sommerfelt (1892–1965; see *Sommerfelt, Alf*) and Joseph Vendryès (1875–1960; see *Vendryes, Joseph-Jean-Baptiste-Marie*); the American structuralists Leonard Bloomfield (1887–1949; see *Bloomfield, Leonard*) and Edward Sapir (1884–1939; see *Sapir, Edward*); and even the 'social behaviorists' (or 'pragmatists') John Dewey (1859–1952) and George Herbert Mead (1863–1931; see *Mead, George Herbert*). Bloomfield in particular exploited the power of the social as an antidote to the psychological (or 'mentalist') approach at the time of his conversion from Wundtian social psychology to empirical behaviorism (see *American Structuralism*). Beginning in the 1940s dialect geographers such as Raven McDavid (1911–1984; see also *McDavid, Raven I., Jr*) began to realize the crucial importance of social factors in linguistic production; around the same time, the sociologist Paul Hanly Furfey (1896–1992) began training students jointly in the techniques of social

class measurement and descriptive linguistics. By the early 1950s inquiry combining empirical sociological and linguistic techniques was underway, to be refined significantly by William Labov (1927– ; see *Labov, William*) and others in the 1960s.

In terms of Saussurean traditions, sociolinguistics pursues the Saussurean view of the social nature of *langue*, while Chomskyan generative linguistics (to which sociolinguistics has stood in irreconcilable contrast for a generation) pursues the Saussurean view of the mental and abstract nature of *langue*. An eventual reconciliation of this split—to which a deeper understanding of Saussure's thought may provide a clue—would certainly constitute a major breakthrough in the understanding of language.

5. *Langue* as a System of Signs: Semiology

The semiological conception of language as a collection of signs (a sign being understood as the collation of a signifying word and a signified concept) was anticipated in the philosophy of Aristotle (384–322 BC; see *Aristotle*), elaborated by the Stoics, and reached its summit in the 'speculative grammar' of the twelfth century. But starting in the fourteenth century, the view of language as a sign system began to cede pride of place to that of language as a social institution, an approach more characteristic of Plato (ca. 429–347 BC; see also *Plato*), the diffusion of whose works defines the new era of humanism that led to the Renaissance. The semiological perspective was never entirely lost, and would resurface notably among the seventeenth-century British empiricists. But the 'conventional' perspective with which it coexisted periodically overshadowed it, and the early nineteenth century was one such period, when abstract systems disembodied from human activity ceased to be of central interest (see *Aristotle and the Stoics on Language*; *Linguistic Theory in the Later Middle Ages*; *Plato and His Predecessors*; *Renaissance Linguistics: General Survey*; *Universal Language Schemes in Seventeenth-century Britain*).

As noted in Sect. 3, abstraction and disembodiment would reemerge as part of the 'scientific' spirit of the later nineteenth century; and it is thus no great coincidence that the 'semiotic' perspective on language was reopened independently by Charles Sanders Peirce (1839–1914; see *Peirce, Charles Sanders*) in the USA. Peirce's work in this area, like Saussure's, went unpublished during his lifetime, and was not seriously revived by philosophers until the 1930s. Only in the 1950s and 1960s were attempts made at unifying Saussurean 'semiology' (practiced mostly by European linguists) and Peircean 'semiotics' (practiced mostly by American philosophers) into a single paradigm, under the organizational leadership of Thomas A. Sebeok (1921– ; see also *Sebeok, Thomas Albert*).

For Saussure, the network of linguistic signs which constitute *langue* is made up of the conjunction of a *signifiant* ('signifier'), understood as a sound pattern deposited in the mind, and a *signifié* ('signified'), a concept that is also deposited in the mind. Saussure compares them to the front and back of a single sheet of paper. It is important to note that the signifier is wholly distinct from the actual uttered word, as is the signified from the actual physical thing conceived of (if one exists). Although the distinction between concept and object has existed since antiquity, that between sound pattern and actual sound is Saussure's own contribution, of which some have seen a foreshadowing in the hypothetical 'sonant coefficients' of his early *Mémoire*.

Saussure predicted that *sémiologie*—the study of signs both within and outside of language—would have linguistics as its 'pilot science' (a further challenge to psychology, for the semiological domain is precisely where language is most explicitly mental), and indeed this came to pass in the founding of modern semiotics discussed above. But while linguistics has furnished the paradigmatic model for semiotics, the impact of semiotic inquiry upon linguistics has been slow in coming, with a certain acceleration perceptible in the last decade.

The one place where linguistics has been profoundly affected is in the nearly universal acceptance of Saussure's concept of the signifier as an abstract sound pattern. This view became the cornerstone of the concept of the phoneme as elaborated by Jan Baudouin de Courtenay (1846–1929; see *Baudouin de Courtenay, Jan Ignacy Niecislaw*) and Mikolai Kruszewski (1851–87; see *Kruszewski, M. H.*) in Russia, and subsequently by N. S. Trubetzkoy (1890–1938; see *Trubetzkoy, Nikolai Sergeyevic*) in Vienna and Roman Jakobson (1896–1982; see *Jakobson, Roman*) in Brno and Prague; Daniel Jones (1891–1967; see *Jones, Daniel*) in the UK; and Kenneth L. Pike (1912– ; see *Pike, Kenneth Lee*) in the USA, to name only the most prominent figures (see *American Structuralism; Firth and the London School; Prague School Phonology; Prague School Syntax and Semantics*). It resulted in the banishment of experimental phonetics from linguistic inquiry in favor of more abstract phonology, based not upon physical differences of sound, but on the ability to distinguish between concepts (see Sect. 8). The distinction between a physical 'etic' level (from phon*etic*) and an abstract 'emic' level (from phon*emic*) would be extended to every level of linguistic structure, and would become a hallmark in particular of postwar American linguistics.

6. The Arbitrariness of Linguistic Signs

As with the semiological nature of language, the arbitrariness of language—the fact that a signifier like the series of sounds /p a j/ has no internal connection with the concept of a 'pie' which it signifies—reflects an ancient doctrine that had never fallen very far from the center of debate about the nature of language up through the end of the eighteenth century. Though not a direct concern for most of the historical linguists of the nineteenth century, the ancient debate between *physis* 'nature' and *nomos* 'convention' in the establishment and operation of language had been revived by Whitney and the Humboldtian psychologists, with Whitney's views of language positioned on the side of *nomos* and the Humboldtians' on the side of *physis*. Saussure, who at age 21 had met Whitney and greatly admired his work, doubtless encountered the debate there.

Saussure's precise formulation of the linguistic sign allows him to situate arbitrariness—which he called the 'first primary concept' of linguistics—precisely at the conjunction of signified and signifier, just as presented in the first sentence of the preceding paragraph. This represented an advance over most earlier formulations of arbitrariness, which (despite Aristotle) focused upon the relationship between the sign as a whole and the real-world objects

conceptualized in the signified. Unfortunately, the *Cours* is not consistent in its presentation of arbitrariness, and quickly falls back into the older schema. Another problem with the presentation in the *Cours* is that the arbitrariness doctrine is first encountered in radical form in a very tense, strongly worded, and memorable section; then only later is this tempered with a section on relative arbitrariness that is often ignored, but without which Saussure's conception of language is inaccurately understood. Saussure's point in the later section is that while signifiers are always arbitrary relative to signifieds, they can be motivated relative to other signifiers. Thus, for example, the French numbers *dix-neuf* '19' and *vingt* '20' both show arbitrariness between signifier and signified, yet *dix-neuf* is motivated relative to the numerals *dix* '10' and *neuf* '9' which compose it, hence *dix-neuf* is relatively arbitrary while *vingt* is radically so. (This is connected to Saussure's distinction between syntagmatic and associative relations, discussed in Sect. 8.) Cases of onomatopoeia, where there seems to be a motivated relationship between signifier and real-world analog, are dismissed as not really part of linguistic systems.

The fact that the *Cours* presents the radical version of arbitrariness first and most forcefully led to its assuming the status of dogma in twentieth-century linguistics (though undoubtedly it also appealed to something deeper in the Zeitgeist). It is one of the first views of language to which budding linguists are exposed in introductory courses and textbooks, often as one of the design features of language identified in 1958 by Charles Hockett (1916– ; see *Hockett, Charles Francis*). Like most dogmata, the radical form of arbitrariness is counterintuitive and requires a certain faith beyond what reason can sustain. Also, it is not always observable in the practice of those who preach it, particularly because of the influence of Jakobson, who beginning in the early 1930s mounted a sustained attack on radical arbitrariness through his work on markedness, child language acquisition, and aphasia, which suggested that linguistic elements differ in naturalness. Jakobson was to have a significant impact upon Chomsky, Joseph Greenberg (1915– ; see *Greenberg, Joseph H.*), and many others, with the result that language is not treated as exhibiting anything like the radical arbitrariness of the dogma. Besides Jakobson, arbitrariness was problematized by Louis Hjelmslev (1899–1965; see *Hjelmslev, Louis Trolle*), Émile Benveniste (1902–76; see *Benveniste, Emile*), and numerous others in a series of attacks on and defenses of the Saussurean view (often poorly represented) appearing from 1939 to about 1947 (see *Greenberg Universals; Glossematics; Twentieth-century Linguistics: Overview of Trends*).

7. The Linearity of Signifiers

After arbitrariness, the second primary principle of linguistics for Saussure is that linguistic signifiers are 'linear,' in the sense that, because they have a temporal existence, they represent a dimension that is measurable only as a line. This is one of the more mysterious of Saussure's ideas, in that he never made clear to what he was opposing it (he notes that it is obvious to everyone, but that its implications have not been appreciated). Linearity is part of what distinguishes spoken language as 'real' language, as opposed to writing, a secondary representation that is not necessarily linear (see Sect. 2); and it is what allows us to analyze connected discourse into meaningful units. One also detects a hedging on the inherent psychologism of the semiological view of language as consisting of perfectly juxtaposed signifiers and signifieds: Saussure here insists that signifiers exist in a completely separate dimension.

This principle has given rise to many interpretations. Jakobson formulated his doctrine of distinctive features in phonology—the idea that phonemes are not monoliths, but consist of bundles of features existing simultaneously—as part of a critique of the linearity of the signifier. Others have argued that Saussure's principle is not in disharmony with the concept of constituent features, but rather was intended (a) to deny the accumulation of signifiers, not their decomposition (a distinction which depends upon what one classifies as a signifier), (b) to insist that, however constituted, signifiers cannot be conceived apart from the dimension of time, and (c) to prepare the ground for the introduction of syntagmatic relations (see Sect. 8).

8. Syntagmatic and Paradigmatic Relations: *Langue* as Form, not Substance

Saussure distinguished between the 'syntagmatic' relations a linguistic element has with the elements preceding and following it in an utterance, and 'associative' (now usually called paradigmatic) relations it has to other elements with which it shares partial identity, but which do not occur in the particular utterance at hand. For example, in the sentence *Crime pays* the element *crime* has a syntagmatic relationship with *pays* that determines, among other things, their order relative to one another and the fact that *pays* has the inflectional *-s*. At the same time, *crime* has paradigmatic relations with countless other elements, including the inflectionally related *crimes*, the derivationally related *criminal*, the conceptually related *misdemeanor* (and the conceptually opposite *legality*), and the phonetically related *grime*. As the last example suggests, each sound of the word *crime* /kraim/ has paradigmatic and syntagmatic relations with at least the sounds around it: /k/ is paradigmatically related to the /g/ that could in principle replace it; and syntagmatically related to the following /r/, since in English the presence of /k/ as the initial element of the word immediately restricts the following sound to /l r w/ or a vowel.

Saussure notes that the two types of relations, which correspond to different types of mental activity, contribute in different ways to the 'value' of the sign. In particular, the paradigmatic relations generate a negative value: the identity of the /r/ in /kraim/ is essentially that it could be, but is not, /l w/ or a vowel. This is important because the actual sound that represents /r/ can differ dramatically from one English dialect to another (being rolled, flapped, retroflex, etc.); but the actual sound content does not matter, so long as /r/ is kept distinct from the other sounds to which it is associatively related. *Langue*, Saussure insisted, is form, not substance.

Before Saussure, the syntagmatic relations of morphemes within a given utterance were certainly recognized as a matter of linguistic concern, though relatively neglected. But there was little or no precedent for the idea suggested by the *Cours* (implicitly if not explicitly) that there exists a syntax not only of words, but of sounds, meanings, and the relations uniting them; or that every time a sound, word, or meaning is chosen, a vast network of related elements is summoned up in absentia. The latter concept in particular set the study of language on a new course of abstraction that did not rely on psychological theorizing, but remained internal to language.

In many ways, the Saussurean notion of paradigmatic and syntagmatic relations would become the hallmark of twentieth-century linguistics: first, because it proposed that a single principle of structure unites all the levels at which language functions—sound, forms, and meaning; second, because it suggested a way of analyzing language that would not depend on a simple listing of elements with their 'translation' into either another language or some sort of philosophical interpretation. Elements could henceforth be analyzed according to the relations they maintained with other elements, and the language could be understood as the vast system—not of these elements—but of these relations. This was the point of departure for structuralism (see Sect. 9).

To a large extent, the distributional method developed by Bloomfield is a working out of this Saussurean notion, with special emphasis on the paradigmatic relations. With the work of Bloomfield's student Zellig S. Harris (1909–1992; see *Harris, Zellig S.*) the syntagmatic relations assumed a status of equal importance, and with Harris's student Chomsky, overriding importance. (Regarding word order, Saussure's view is that the syntagmatic relations constitute that part of syntax which is predetermined—like the use of a 3rd person singular verb form after the singular subject *crime*—and so a part of *langue*; while the rest of syntax, being subject to free combination, is relegated to *parole*.)

9. The Systematicity of *Langue:* Structuralism

Certainly the most wide-reaching Saussurean intellectual tradition, both within and outside of linguistics, derived from Saussure's characterization of *langue* as a wholly self-contained network of relationships among elements which, as discussed above, have no positive content or value, but only the negative value generated by their differing from one another. Like most of his contemporaries, when Saussure thought of language he thought first of sounds and their combinations, and extrapolated outward from that level. The study of sounds had for several decades been a battleground between those who, later in the twentieth century, would be called the 'phoneticians,' proponents of an extreme form of positivism who believed that the key to understanding language lay in ever more precise measurement of sound waves and vocal apertures; and those who would now be called 'phonologists,' who preferred to operate on a more abstract (and traditional) plane, dealing with classes of sounds rather than the minute differences within classes. But the phoneticians were steadily gaining prestige, since their positivistic approach had the characteristic look of modern science.

As noted in Sect. 4, Saussure was attracted to positivism, but within limits. If psychology represented the Scylla of hyperrationalism, experimental phonetics was the Charybdis of hyperempiricism, equally to be avoided. Perhaps more so: whereas Saussure never attempted a complete divorce of language from the domain of the mind, his characterization of *langue* as a network of pure relations, of form and not substance, succeeded in marginalizing phonetics to the point that within a few decades it would retreat to the position of an auxiliary discipline to linguistics. The term *phonème*, used by Saussure as early as 1878 (five years after its coinage by A. Dufriche-Desgenettes, 1804–79) to denote an abstract unit representing sound, but never actually defined by him, was taken up by Baudouin de Courtenay and Kruszewski and joined to an essentially Saussurean conception: 'phoneme' became the name for Saussure's abstract mental sound pattern, identifiable as the minimal unit of sound capable of changing the meaning of a signifier in a language. It eventually became the basis for further, related new concepts: the morpheme (coined by Baudouin de Courtenay) or moneme (minimal unit of meaning), tagmeme (minimal meaningful unit of syntax), toneme, and so on.

The full implications of Saussure's view of *langue* were realized in Prague, principally by Trubetzkoy, who elaborated complete phonological schemata for a panoply of languages from all over the world; and Jakobson, who extended the implications of 'functional' phonology to other domains of linguistic (and literary) inquiry. But strikingly similar projects were underway in other quarters: in the USA with Bloomfield, who saw himself as at least partly under the influence of Saussure (in a 1945 letter he described his major work *Language* as showing Saussure's influence 'on every page'); in Denmark, with the overtly Saussurean glossematics of Hjelmslev; in France, where Meillet had transmitted the Saussurean perspective to a whole generation of students, including André Martinet (1908–); Gustave Guillaume (1883–1960); and Benveniste (see *American Structuralism*; *Guillaumean Linguistics*; *Glossematics*; *Functional Grammar: Martinet's Model*). All the lines of affiliation among these 'schools' are not yet clear. But their work came to define the mainstream of linguistics in the twentieth century, and all of it assumes the conception of *langue* set out in the *Cours*.

The idea that language forms a self-contained system justified the autonomy of linguistic study not only vis-à-vis phonetics, but every other discipline as well, including psychology, anthropology, and sociology (the latter, again, was never deemed a threat). The only discipline under whose aegis it hypothetically fell was semiology, but even had semiology existed, the status of linguistics as its pilot science meant that it yielded its autonomy to no other field. Indeed, between the 1940s and the 1960s most fields of human knowledge came under the domination of 'structuralism' (a term first used in linguistics around 1928), understood in this context as the extrapolation out of linguistics of Saussure's concept of *langue* as a self-contained system of syntagmatic and paradigmatic relations among elements of negative content (see *Twentieth-century Linguistics: Overview of Trends*). Its most widely heralded application was in the field of anthropology, by Claude Lévi-Strauss (1908– ; see *Lévi-Strauss, Claude*), who discovered Saussure in 1942 in a course taught by Jakobson. Other areas and their most prominent structuralist practitioners include: biology, Ludwig von Bertalanffy (1901–72) and C. H. Waddington (1905–75); literary theory, Roland Barthes (1915–80); Marxist theory, Louis Althusser (1918–90); mathematics, 'Nicholas Bourbaki' (the pseudonym of a group of French mathematicians); psychoanalysis, Jacques Lacan (1901–79; see *Lacan, Jacques*); and psychology (where the groundwork for it had

already been laid by the concept of *Gestalt*), Jean Piaget (1896–1980; see *Piaget, Jean*). The rejection of structuralism by such figures as Jacques Derrida and Michel Foucault (1926–84; see *Foucault, Michel*), which became widespread as part of the French student revolts of 1968, launched the 'poststructuralist' era, whose very name indicates that the Saussurean tradition remains an active force even when shaping the direction of reactions against it.

Within linguistics, the effects of poststructuralist thought are only beginning to be felt; the field in which structuralism began is the last to let it go. Precisely at midcentury the great British linguist J. R. Firth (1890–1960) was able to state that 'Nowadays, professional linguists can almost be classified by using the name of de Saussure. There are various possible groupings: Saussureans, anti-Saussureans, post-Saussureans, or non-Saussureans.' As we approach the twentieth-century's end, the only change one is tempted to make to Firth's statement is to remove 'non-Saussureans,' as it is doubtful that any survive. All work on or against language as an autonomous, self-contained system—and this includes work in generative grammar, universal–typological linguistics, discourse pragmatics, and sociolinguistics—falls squarely within the most important Saussurean traditions.

See also: Saussure, Ferdinand(-Mongin) de; Generative Grammar; Generative Grammar: Principles; Sociolinguistics.

Bibliography

Aarsleff H 1982 *From Locke to Saussure*. Athlone, London
Culler J 1986 *Ferdinand de Saussure*, 2nd edn. Cornell University Press, Ithaca, NY
Engler R 1989–90 *Édition critique du Cours de linguistique générale de F. de Saussure*. Harrassowitz, Wiesbaden
Gadet F 1989 *Saussure and Contemporary Culture*. Hutchinson Radius, London
Harris R 1987 *Reading Saussure*. Duckworth, London
Holdcroft D 1991 *Saussure: Sign, Systems and Arbitrariness*. Cambridge University Press, Cambridge
Joseph J E 1988 Saussure's meeting with Whitney, Berlin, 1879. *Cahiers F. de Saussure* **42**: 205–13
Koerner E F K 1973 *Ferdinand de Saussure: Origin and Development of his Linguistic Thought in Western Studies of Language*. Vieweg, Braunschweig
Koerner E F K 1987 *Saussurean Studies/Études saussuriennes*. Slatkine, Geneva
Meillet A 1921 *Linguistique historique et linguistique générale*. Champion, Paris
Saussure F de 1916 *Cours de linguistique générale*. Payot, Paris
Saussure F de 1922 *Recueil de publications scientifiques*. Sonor, Geneva
Saussure F de 1972 *Cours de linguistique générale*. Payot, Paris
Saussure F de 1983 (trans. Harris R) *Course in General Linguistics*. Duckworth, London

J. E. Joseph

Sayce, (Rev.) Archibald Henry (1845–1933)

An English scholar of the Near East, Sayce was born at Shirehampton, September 25, 1845. He was educated at Bath and Oxford, most of his career being associated with the latter place, where he became the first Professor of Assyriology in 1891. He followed his father into the Church, at a period when the discoveries of Darwin had brought about a crisis; it is no accident that he spent 10 years as a member of the Old Testament Revision Company, charged with modernizing the text of scripture in the light of archaeology and of linguistic research. He also played an important role in the Society for Biblical Archaeology, which was also a product of this movement. His interest in the scripts and languages of the ancient Near East was in evidence even in the early 1870s, when he published a series of articles on the Carian alphabet. He attempted to read this undeciphered language by comparison with the Greek alphabet and with the syllabic script used on Cyprus, which had recently been deciphered by George Smith. Sayce then turned his attention to the cuneiform script of Mesopotamia, which was used to write a language akin to Hebrew. This period saw the earliest discoveries in Turkey of the remains of the Hittite Empire, and Sayce, in a paper read to the Society for Biblical Archaeology in July 1880, was the first to recognize the true identity of this civilization. He also made substantial progress with a bilingual text written in hieroglyphic Hittite; although this was not a complete decipherment, Sayce deserves to be known as the father of Hittite. Here, his great comparative knowledge of the Near East served him well.

Sayce took up the civilized habit of spending his winters on a houseboat in Egypt, and he made many contributions to Egyptology from this comfortable base. His autobiography, *Reminiscences*, shows him to have been a person of great breadth of vision and sympathetic wit, although his complex racial theories seem dated and unhelpful. The study of the Near East has moved on, and the branches which he covered with such ease are now independent. Nevertheless, the influence which he had on such a range of studies is probably unique. His long career serves as a reminder that the ancient Near East was not an assortment of competing disciplines, but an interconnected world.

Bibliography

Dictionary of National Biography 1931–1940, 1949 (ed. Legg L G W). Oxford University Press, London, pp. 786–8

Pope M 1975 *The History of Decipherment*. Thames & Hudson, London

Sayce A H 1923 *Reminiscences*. Macmillan, London

J. D. Ray

Scale and Category Grammar

Scale and Category Grammar was developed by M. A. K. Halliday in the period around 1960, and arose out of an attempt to build a linguistic theory based on the somewhat programmatic ideas of the British linguist J. R. Firth. (For a more detailed review than can be given here, see Butler, 1985.) A clear, simplified account of the main features of the model can be found in Halliday, et al. (1964), and a more complete and technical statement in the collection of Halliday's writings edited by Kress (1976: 52–72).

1. Scale and Category Grammar in an Overall Model of Language

Scale and Category Grammar was developed as the grammatical component of a tristratal linguistic model. The level of *form* consists of the two demi levels of *grammar* and *lexis*; the level of *substance* is concerned with the manifestation of language in sound or written symbols; the level of *context* relates linguistic form to features of the situations in which language is used.

2. Scales and Categories

The model operates with the three scales of *rank*, *delicacy*, and *exponence*, and the four categories of *unit*, *structure*, *class*, and *system*.

2.1 Unit and Rank

Units are the stretches of language which carry grammatical patterns. For English, the units originally proposed were: sentence, clause, group, word, and morpheme. These units are arranged hierarchically, in a 'consists-of' relationship, on the scale of rank, such that in the simplest cases, a sentence consists of one or more clauses, a clause of one or more groups, a group of one or more words, and a word of one or more morphemes. The theory also allows for downward *rankshift*, in which a unit at a particular position on the rank scale can occur within the structure of a unit of the same or lower rank. For instance, in the sentence (1)

The boy who is sitting in the corner is my brother (1)

the group *the boy who is sitting in the corner* consists of two words (*the* and *boy*), but also of a (relative) clause *who is sitting in the corner*. A unit may not, however, be rankshifted to behave as if it were a unit of higher rank. An important principle is that of 'total accountability,' which requires that every item must be accounted for at all ranks. The simple reply *Yes* would therefore be treated as a sentence consisting of one clause, which in turn consists of one group, consisting of one word, consisting of a single morpheme.

2.2 Structure and Delicacy

Structure is the category set up to reflect likeness between stretches of language on the syntagmatic axis, or *axis of chain*. Consider the following sentences (2):

Jim	*drove*	*the car*	*into the village.*
The farmer	*led*	*his cows*	*out of the field.*
My cat	*chased*	*a tiny mouse*	*in the garden.*
We	*saw*	*a rainbow*	*this morning.* (2)

The similarity in syntagmatic patterning here is captured by postulating a structure for the clause consisting of four types of element, namely S(ubject), P(redicator), C(omplement), and A(djunct), where the C element subsumes the direct and indirect objects and predicative complements of traditional grammars. These elements are defined in terms of the groupings of units at the next lower rank which can operate there: for instance, P is that element at which the class (see Sect. 2.3) of groups known as verbal groups operates. Some elements may appear more than once (e.g., C and A in clause structure). Structures are also recognized for sentences, for various kinds of group, and for words.

The scale of delicacy is connected with the concept of structure (and also with class: see Sect. 2.3, and refers to the degree of detail to which a structural description is pursued. Consider, for example, the following nominal group (3):

all the old books on that shelf (3)

The least delicate structural analysis of this group would specify that *all*, *the*, and *old* each occupy a structural element named 'modifier,' while *books* is the 'head' and *on that shelf* a 'qualifier' (equivalent to *postmodifier* in many other accounts). A more delicate analysis would specify that *all* and *the* are 'determiners,' whereas *old* is an 'epithet'; and at tertiary delicacy the 'predeterminer all' would be distinguished from the 'central determiner' *the*. Later versions of Scale and Category Grammar also apply the scale of delicacy to systems (see Sect. 2.4).

The kinds of structures reviewed above are *multivariate*: that is, the relationships between the elements are different (the relationship between S and P is different from that between P and C, and so on). Also of importance are *univariate* structures, in which the relationships between elements are of the same kind. Examples are to be found in coordinated, *paratactic* structures of the type exemplified in (4) below:

Bill is a teacher, Sue is a doctor and Harriet is a lawyer.
Bill, Sue, and Harriet are teachers. (4)

and also in (*hypotactic*) subordination relations:

I'll call you if I'm still in when the postman arrives. (5)

In example (5), the clause *if I'm still in* is dependent on the main clause *I'll call you*, and *when the postman arrives* is in the same kind of dependency relation with *I'm still in*. Later versions of Scale and Category Grammar introduce the concept of unit complex to account for univariate structuring: *Bill, Sue, and Harriet* in example (4) would then be a nominal group complex, and a sentence consisting of more than one clause can be treated as a clause complex, so removing the need for a separate unit of sentence at the top of the rank scale.

2.3 Class

Class is defined as the grouping of members of a given unit which can operate at a particular element in the structure of the next higher unit. For instance, verbal groups operate at P, and adverbial groups at A. The nominal group is what was later called a 'cross-class,' able to occur at both S and C. Note that classes are not defined in relation to the internal constituency of the units concerned: thus, for example, groups which can operate at A, and are therefore classified as adverbial, can have adverbs as heads (e.g., *very slowly*), or can be prepositional (*in the city*), or noun-headed (*this morning*). The grouping of units by internal structure is referred to in some later accounts of Scale and Category Grammar as *type*.

The scale of delicacy can be extended to class in that, for example, within the primary class of nominal group singular and plural nominal secondary groups can be recognized. Secondary classes can also arise in other ways: for example, the 'deictics' *all* and *the* can be differentiated more finely in terms of their position in the nominal group.

2.4. System

System is the category set up to account for patterning on the paradigmatic axis, or 'axis of choice.' A system is defined as a closed, finite set of terms, each of which excludes the others, and one of which must be selected if the entry conditions for that system are satisfied. For instance, any nominal group in present-day English selects between the two terms, or features, [singular] and [plural], and these terms form a simple system acting at the nominal group. A further example would be the choice of indicative or imperative mood for a main clause. In early versions of Scale and Category Grammar system was seen as equal in importance to the other three categories. In later versions, however, system is increasingly seen as the central category: that is, it is claimed that the underlying patterning of language is paradigmatic, and that the syntagmatic patterns captured in the concept of structure are derived from systemic choices by means of the scale of exponence.

2.5 Exponence

Exponence is the scale which links the four categories to each other, and to the data under description. Consider the group *the little boy* in the following sentence (6):

The little boy was sitting in the corner. (6)

This group acts as the S element of structure in the clause which constitutes the whole sentence. The *chain of exponence* leading from the category S to the ultimate grammatical structure consisting of a deictic acting as determiner, an adjective acting as epithet, and a noun acting as head, is as follows. The element S of the clause unit is expounded by a group unit of the nominal class, which selects the term [singular] from the system of number. This group has a structure consisting of the elements *m*(odifier), *m*(odifier), and *h*(ead), the modifiers being more delicately specified as determiner and epithet respectively. The determiner element is *realized* by a word of the deictic class, more delicately classified as an article, the epithet by a word of the adjective class, and the head by a word of the noun class, more delicately specified as a count noun. The term 'exponence' was replaced, at a late stage in the development of the model, by the term *realization*, under the influence of Lamb's stratificational linguistics.

Bibliography

Butler C S 1985 *Systemic Linguistics*: Theory and Applications. Batsford, London
Halliday M A K, McIntosh A, Strevens P 1964 *The Linguistic Sciences and Language Teaching*. Longmans, London
Kress G R (ed.) 1976 *Halliday: System and Function in Language*. Oxford University Press, London

C. Butler

Scaliger, Joseph Justus (1540–1609)

Joseph Scaliger has entered history as one of the greatest Renaissance philologists, especially in the field of the Classical languages.

Born in Agen, Lot-et-Garonne (Southern France) in 1540, a son of the renowned humanist Julius Caesar

Scaliger, Scaliger received his Latin training mainly from his much-demanding father. In 1559 he went to Paris where he read Greek and various Semitic languages. In 1562 he embraced the Protestant faith and in the following years he traveled widely. Scaliger actively participated in the religious wars in France and in 1572 he fled from the country to Geneva where he lectured in philosophy at the Calvinist academy. In 1574 he returned to France and lived there until 1593, when he moved to Leiden where the University had offered him an attractive post free from lecturing duties. He remained in Leiden until his death in 1609, and bequeathed his books and invaluable manuscript collection to the University of Leiden.

Scaliger's first book, an edition of Varro's (see *Varro, Marcus Terentius*) *De lingua Latina* (1565) (included in Varro 1573), was an immediate success. In it he displays the philological methods to which he would thenceforth adhere and which were to exercise a lasting influence on contemporary and later scholars. He brought the method of presenting critical text editions to perfection by insisting on the consultation of as many manuscript versions of a text as possible. Many of his conjectures and emendations still stand in the early 1990s. Scaliger was a very prolific scholar, especially during his period at Leiden. There he also stimulated fellow scholars to explore the disciplines of history, epigraphy, Semitic, Slavonic, and Old Germanic studies, among others.

In the late twentieth century Scaliger is esteemed for his insightful criticism of the many texts he edited, as well as for his major achievement in creating order in the chronology of world history (see Scaliger 1583). Finally, he must be counted as one of the founding fathers of comparative linguistics.

Bibliography

Bremmer Jr R H 1993 Joseph Justus Scaliger. In: Stammerjohann H (ed.) *Lexicon grammaticorum*. Niemeyer, Tübingen
Hamilton A 1990 Franciscus Raphelengius: The Hebraist and his manuscripts. *De Gulden Passer* 68: 105–17
Scaliger J J 1583 *Opus novum de emendatione temporum*. M. Patissonius, Paris
Varro M T 1573 *M. Terentii Varronis opera . . . In lib. de ling. Lat. conjecteana J. Scaligeri recognita*. H. Stephanus, Geneva

R. H. Bremmer Jr

Scaliger, Julius Caesar (1484–1558)

Julius Caesar Scaliger is known for his philosophical grammar—in fact, rather a work of reflection about grammar—which sets up a link between medieval speculative thought and general grammar.

Giulio, son of the Paduan miniaturist Benedetto Bordon, was born in April 1484 and studied at the University of Padua (Italy). Once qualified as a physician, he accompanied (1524) Bishop A. della Rovere to Agen (France), where, under the name of Scaliger, he became a naturalized Frenchman (1528) and got married (1529). He stayed in Agen until his death (October 21, 1558), practicing as a physician and holding municipal posts.

The author of numerous humanistic works, some of which are lost (in particular a treatise on etymology, *De originibus*), translations and commentaries, he claimed the direct authority of Aristotle, and carried on sharp polemics with his contemporaries (e.g., Erasmus, Cardano). His most important linguistic work is the *De causis linguae Latinae*, in which he set out to analyze the earlier grammatical tradition in a critical way (he spotted 627 'mistakes' in his predecessors' writings). His Aristotelianism, often more rhetorical than rigorously technical (Jensen 1990), is evinced by the way he used the four Aristotelian causes, and he stressed the arbitrary character of language. Organizing his development according to the Classical sequence 'voice/letter/syllable/word,' he proposed a thorough analysis of the sounds of the language, and often had accurate intuitions about their evolution (Stéfanini 1976). The major remaining part of the work is devoted to the signifying units, called 'species dictionis' (and not 'partes orationis') and considered to be reflections of the mind and the real world: his critical study of their semantic foundations and of their characteristics makes up for the almost total absence of syntax. Conscious of the evolution of tongues, Scaliger sided with the analogists against the anomalists, and thought that 'reason' (ratio) organizes the language, even if it may have to bow to the tyranny of usage.

As a theoretician of literature, in his *Poetices libri VII*, Scaliger was a champion of Ciceronianism and promoted poetics founded on the imitation of Virgil.

Thanks to its systematic criticism of linguistic concepts and its search for universality, the *De causis* exercised a deep influence on Classical linguistic theories, in particular on Sanctius and Port-Royal (see *Sanctius, Franciscus*; *Port-Royal Tradition of Grammar*).

Bibliography

Billanovich M 1968 Benedetto Bordon e Giulio Cesare Scaligero. *Italia Medioevale e Umanistica* 11: 187–256
Chevalier J-C 1968 *Histoire de la syntaxe*. Droz, Geneva
Cubelier de Beynac J, Magnien M (eds.) 1986 *Acta Scaligeriana*. Société Académique, Agen
Jensen K 1990 *Rhetorical Philosophy and Philosophical Grammar: Julius Caesar Scaliger's Theory of Language*. Fink, Munich
Lardet P 1988 Scaliger lecteur de Linacre. In: Rosier I (ed.) *L'héritage des grammairiens latins*. BIG, Paris
Padley G A 1976 & 1985 *Grammatical Theory in Western Europe 1500–1700 (The Latin Tradition & Trends in Vernacular Grammar I)*. Cambridge University Press, Cambridge
Scaliger J C 1540 *De causis linguae Latinae libri XIII*. S. Gryphius, Lyon
Scaliger J C 1561 *Poetices libri VII*. A. Vincentius, Lyon/J
Stéfanini J 1976 Jules-César Scaliger et son *De causis* [...]. In: Parret H (ed.) *History of Linguistic Thought and Contemporary Linguistics*. W de Gruyter, Berlin

B. L. Colombat

Scaling

Throughout the social sciences, it often becomes necessary to measure a variable through a combination of several pieces of information, and a variety of techniques developed outside linguistics that can be employed profitably in language studies. First, sociolinguists need scaling techniques in order to measure the social variables they correlate with variations in language. Second, language variations themselves may often be measured most accurately through scales, rather than by relying upon single bits of data or upon intuitive summary judgments. Finally, scaling techniques rest on the linguistically interesting observation that people can seldom if ever express their attitudes validly and reliably in a single utterance, but need several utterances such as the answers to an entire set of survey questions.

1. The Logic of Composite Measures

It could be said that all social research is about the description and interrelating of variables. For example, Basil Bernstein's famous research related the variable of social class to speech codes; and other researchers have compared the speech of women with that of men. In either case, *measurement* is a fundamental element in social research: the classification of individuals (or other units of analysis) in terms of the relevant variables. Sometimes, measurement is relatively simple and straightforward, as in the case of gender, which can be determined readily through a single question. Many of the variables that interest social researchers, such as social class, authoritarianism, alienation, prejudice are not so simply measured. Such variables call for a more sophisticated measurement strategy.

In those cases where no single piece of information will represent the meaning of a complex variable *reliably* and *validly*, the solution is to construct a measure from several independent pieces of information. This is especially appropriate when the purpose is to measure a variable comprised of several attributes, representing different levels of intensity of degree. Thus, prejudice might be represented by the attributes: Extremely Prejudiced, Very Prejudiced, Somewhat Prejudiced, Slightly Prejudiced, Unprejudiced. Or, intelligence, is sometimes represented by the scores of an IQ test: 100, 101, 102, 103, etc.

The construction of composite measures is based on two assumptions: (a) that the theoretical variable under study actually represents a dimension of variation among people and (b) that there are numerous indicators of that variation. In the case of prejudice, for example, it is assumed that some people are more prejudiced, in general, than others and that there are several pieces of information attainable about people that offer clues as to how prejudiced they are.

The first assumption should not be accepted as obvious. It is not necessarily the case that those prejudiced against Jews, for example, would also be prejudiced against Blacks, against women, or, particularly, prejudiced against Arabs. Variations in prejudice against Jews, then, may occur more consistently than variations in prejudice in general. Thus, if it can be said with greater certainty that Person X is more prejudiced than Person Y then one can say that Person X is more prejudiced than Person Y in general.

Once the assumption is made that people do vary on the variable under study, it can be assumed further that there are several indicators of that variation. Agreeing with the statement that 'Jews tend to cheat in business' would be one indicator of antisemitism. Similarly, agreeing with the statement that 'Jews are clannish' would be another. Another possible indicator would be agreement with the

statement that 'The Jews are God's Chosen People,' in this case, representing the *opposite* of antisemitism. Both positive and negative indicators of variables can be appropriate to composite measures.

There are several techniques for combining indicators into composite measures.

2. Simple Cumulative Indexes

The simplest method for creating a composite measure of a variable is to identify some list of indicators of that variable and give each subject a score equal to the number of those indicators that apply to them.

To measure levels of political activity among a sample of people possible indicators might include answers to the questions, asked in a survey questionnaire:

'Did you vote in the last election?'
'Have you ever contributed money to a political campaign?'
'Have you ever volunteered to work on a political campaign?'

Primarily, such indicators are selected on a prima facie basis, though it is often a good idea to test the empirical relationships among indicators. If voting and contributing money are both indicators of political activism, for example, it would be reasonable to expect that voters would be more likely to give money than would the nonvoters— and vice versa.

Having asked these three questions, subjects could be given one point for each 'yes' answer. The result would be a simple index ranging in scores from 0 (said 'no' to all three questions) to 3 (said 'yes' to all three).

In creating a measure such as this, the resulting index will be assumed to have the quality of *ordinality*: that those with scores of 3 are more politically active than those with scores of 2, who are more politically active than those with scores of 1, who, in turn, are more politically active than those with scores of 0.

Index scores could then be used for purposes of determining the relationship between political activism and other variables. To determine whether men or women were the more politically active, the average index scores for men and women could be calculated: if men had an average score of 2.5 and women had average scores of 1.0, it would be concluded that men were more active than women. (In lieu of such an index, comparison could be made of the percentages of men and women who vote, who have contributed money, and who have volunteered.)

Similarly, a composite index would allow the exploration of the conseqences of political activism. Table 1 would suggest that politically active people are less likely to attend church than the politically less active.

Table 1.

	Index of Political Activism			
	0	1	2	3
% who attended church during week . . .	60	52	43	35

Simple indexes like this one have two major weaknesses. First, the several indicators of a given variable often represent different levels of intensity. For example, volunteering to work on a political campaign seems a stronger indicator of political activism than simply voting. Yet in the simple index described above, all three indicators are treated equally. The scaling techniques to be discussed below take account of the differing intensities of indicators.

Second, while simple indexes usually represent *ordinal* measures of variables, some of the scales which will be examined seek to create *interval* measures: with equal increases of intensity separating the categories on the scale. In the political activism index above, for example, it is assumed that those with a score of 3 are more active than those scored 2; it cannot be assumed, however, that the *degree* of activism separating 3s from 2s is the same as that separating 2s from 1s and 1s from 0s. Some of the scaling techniques examined below seek to create equal-interval measures.

3. Bogardus Social Distance Scaling

E. S. Bogardus provides an excellent illustration of the different intensities represented by various indicators of a variable. Suppose, that the degree to which people are willing to associate with ex-convicts is to be measured. Presumably some people would generally welcome ex-convicts back into society, feeling they had paid their debt to society, perhaps, while others would be less forgiving and/or less trusting. This phenomenon is commonly referred to as the 'social distance' people desire with regard to ex-convicts.

A simple index of the social distance in this instance might be created by asking about relationships people would be willing to have with ex-convicts: buying shoes from them; sitting beside them on the subway, etc. We would simply add the number of such relationships a person would willingly accept.

It is possible, however, to create a list of relationships which, in themselves, represent differing social distances. Consider the following.

Would you be willing to have a convicted child-molester, who had served his time in prison and been released:

... live in your country?
... live in your city?
... live in your neighborhood?
... live on your block?
... live next door to you?
... marry into your immediate family?

Take a minute to answer these questions for yourself. How many did you answer 'yes.' If you answered 'yes' to at least one and fewer than all six, then you should be able to see an interesting pattern in your responses. If you said yes to only one, for example, it probably was the first one: letting the child-molester live in your country; if you said 'yes' to two, they were probably the first two items in the list. If you agreed to five of the six, on the other hand, you probably only objected to the last: marriage into your immediate family.

Imagine that these questions were asked among a sample of a thousand respondents. If each of them was assigned a score, representing the *number* of relationships agreed to, those numbers would also—in most if not all cases—reveal the answers given to each of the six questions. For example, the person with a score of 3 probably answered: yes, yes, yes, no, no, no. Such summary *scale scores*, then represent the relative *social distance* our respondents are willing to tolerate with convicted child-molesters. The same technique, of course, could be used to determine social distance with regard to groups based on religion, race, social class, nationality, etc.

The general principle illustrated in the Bogardus Social Distance Scale is that a set of attitudes may have a logical and/or empirical structure, which can be represented by a single number. This is the fundamental logic involved in all scaling.

The role of *pattern* is seen in the scoring of response patterns that seem illogical on their face. Suppose, a respondent was unwilling to let a convicted child-molester live in his or her country, city, neighborhood, block, and even next door—but agreed to have let one marry into the family. In terms of all but one of the indicators, the respondent appears to have extremely low tolerance for convicted child-molesters. Perhaps the respondent in question, however, has such an ideological commitment to letting one's children marry who they want that he or she would grimace and agree to letting the child-molester marry into the family. That response, then, would not represent tolerance toward child-molesters as much as commitment to freedom in mate-selection. In such a case, scoring the person 0 points—for no tolerance—rather than one point would seem a more accurate portrayal of their level of tolerance.

The Bogardus Social Distance scale has the quality of *ordinality*: a score of 2 represents more tolerance than a score of 1, and a score of 3 represents more tolerance than a score of 2. Ordinality is one goal of any index or scale, and the Bogardus Social Distance scale virtually assures the quality of ordinality.

Another goal—more difficult to achieve—is the creation of *equal intervals*—between the scale positions. Thus it cannot be said that the distance between 0 and 1 on the Bogardus Social Distance scale is the same as the distance between 1 and 2. The achievement of equal intervals was addressed by L. L. Thurstone and his colleagues.

4. Thurstone Scaling

As seen in the case of the Bogardus Social Distance Scale, the indicators of a given variable can differ from one another in terms of *intensity*: some indicate a stronger degree than others. This phenomenon is not limited to social distance. For just about any variable, there are mild and extreme indicators of it. For example, the view that 'A woman should only be permitted to have an abortion in the case of rape or incest' represents a mild degree of anti-abortion sentiment in comparison with the view that, 'Physicians who perform abortions should be given the death penalty.'

L. L. Thurstone (1931) developed a technique for systematizing the differences in intensity that exist among the several indicators of a variable. His procedure began with the creation of a great many indicators (for example, a hundred), such as the two presented above. These were then presented to a panel of experts (e.g., PhD researchers specializing in studies of the variable in question) with instructions to score each item on a scale of, for example, 1 to 11.

Once each panelist had scored each item, Thurstone then reviewed their scoring to identify items they had agreed on. Those items that produced disagreement among the panelists were discarded. Among those the panelists scored consistently, some were picked to represent each step on the scale: one or more items the panelists had agreed were

1s, items agreed to be 2s, etc. The resulting set of items were then administered to respondents.

Assume respondents were given a set of 11 items, one for each step in the intensity scale. Assume further that Respondent A agreed with all 11 items. In the creation of a simple index, such a person would receive a score of 11, representing an extreme case of whatever was being measured. If Respondent B disagreed with all 11, that person should receive a score of 0. Both respondents would receive those same scores on a Thurstone scale.

However, consider Respondent C, who agreed with 10 of the items, disagreeing only with the rather mild item rated 2 by the experts. In the creation of a simple index, such a respondent would receive a score of 10, representing the number of items agreed to. In Thurstone scaling, however, it would be reasoned that such a person must have idiosyncratic reasons for disagreeing with item 2, reasons that did not really reflect how they stood on the variable being measured, including misreading the item or checking the wrong box. In Thurstone scaling, Respondent C would be scored 11, based on the overall pattern of responses.

Or consider Respondent D, who agreed with only the most extreme item. Such a person would be judged to have reasons for that response that did not really reflect the variable in question—warranting a score of 0, based on the overall pattern of responses. Notice that this scoring procedure follows the same logic as discussed earlier in terms of Bogardus Social Distance scaling.

Thurstone scaling, like Bogardus scaling, results in the creation of *ordinal* scales: respondents scored 4 on the scale have a more extreme degree of the variable in question than those scored 3. In addition, however, Thurstone scales may also qualify, arguably, as *interval* scales. A simple ruler illustrates this quality of equal intervals. The *difference* in length between an object two inches long and an object three inches long is the same (one inch) as the difference between an object thirteen inches long and one that is fourteen inches long.

An interval scale, then, is one which has a standard distance between adjacent positions on the scale. On an ordinal scale of prejudice, for example, a person scored 3 would be *more* prejudiced than one scored 2 and one scored 4 would be *more* prejudiced than one scored 3. On an interval scale, the prejudice of the person scored 3 would exceed that of the one scored 2 by the same *amount* as the prejudice of the person scored 4 would exceed that of the person scored 3. Because of the manner in which they were generated—asking expert judges to rate items along an interval scale and accepting only those items the judges agreed on—Thurstone scales are sometimes described as being comprised of 'equal-appearing intervals.'

Although Thurstone scaling nicely illustrates the logical purpose of scaling in general, it is seldom used. The reason for its disuse is logistical: it is too difficult and expensive to hire a large team of expert panelists to undertake the task of scoring hundreds of potential items. Moreover, once the task has been completed and items have been selected for a scale, the passage of time will cause a change in how certain of the items are regarded by people—and, hence, what agreement or disagreement with them implies. Thus, it is necessary to repeat the difficult and expensive procedure from time to time.

5. Likert Scaling

Rensis Likert is best known for creating a questionnaire format that remains very popular among survey researchers: illustrated most commonly by the response categories 'Strongly agree,' 'Agree,' 'Disagree,' and 'Strongly disagree.' There are three main appeals to such a format. First, it is convenient to present respondents with a number of statements on a variety of topics, following each with a set of boxes to check, labeling each column of boxes with one of the response categories listed above. Second, the set of responses can be remembered easily by respondents and they can easily understand how to record their responses to specific statements.

Finally, the Likert response categories have an undeniable *ordinality* 'strongly agreeing' clearly represents more agreement than simple 'agreeing,' which represents more agreement than 'disagreeing' which, in turn, contains at least more agreement than 'strongly disagreeing.' Notice, by contrast, that responses such as 'kind of agree,' 'more or less agree,' and 'agree to some extent' are ambiguous as to the relative degree of agreement they represent. It would not be possible to arrange them in order of magnitude. And even if *you* have a clear view of how they differ, there is no assurance that all respondents in a survey would regard and use the terms in that same fashion.

Likert was interested in something more than just ordinality among response categories, however. Like Thurstone, he wanted to create *interval* measures. Rather than using expert judges, however, Likert looked for evidence of an interval quality among the patterns of responses given by respondents in a study.

Likert's *item-analysis* began in a similar fashion as the creation of a simple index. Items would be selected on the basis of face validity. Then respondents were given scores based on how they answered *all* those items. For simplicity's sake, assume that all the items were worded in the same direction: agreement meant prejudice and disagreement meant tolerance, for example. Respondents would be given 3 points for every 'strongly agree,' 2 points for each 'agree,' 1 point for each 'disagree,' and no points for 'strongly disagree.' If there were 10 items under consideration, this procedure would produce an index with scores ranging from 0 to 30.

The potential interval quality of each item was assessed by calculating the average scores (on the large index) for those who strongly agreed with the item in question, those who agreed, and so forth. Consider the case in Table 2.

Table 2.

| | Responses to Item 1 | | | |
	Strongly Agree	Agree	Disagree	Strongly Disagree
Average scores on the large index . . .	25	20	15	10

In this example, the 'distance' between 'strongly agree' and 'agree' would appear—at least in terms of the simple index scores—to be the same as between 'agree' and 'disagree' and so forth.

By contrast, consider the possibility in Table 3. Here, there does not appear to be much difference in the overall views of those who strongly agreed and those who agreed, nor between those who disagreed or strongly disagreed—

Table 3.

	Responses to Item 2			
	Strongly Agree	Agree	Disagree	Strongly Disagree
Average scores on the large index ...	30	28	17	13

but there is a substantial difference between agreeing and disagreeing overall. Given the fact that responses to Item 2 do not correlate well with scores on the index overall, the conclusion must be that Item 2, despite its face validity, does not provide a good measure of the variable in question.

Following a Likert item analysis, a scale might be constructed from among those items which appeared to have the quality of equal-appearing intervals. There are a number of specific techniques that might be used in the actual construction of such a scale.

6. Guttman Scaling

Guttman scaling, created by Louis Guttman, is probably the most common scaling technique used at the beginning of the 1990s. Like Likert scaling, it is based on an analysis of the empirical patterns to be observed in responses to items. It is more general than Likert scaling, since it can be applied to a variety of item formats—including Likert-type items.

To begin, the items considered for a Guttman scale are evaluated for intensity on the basis of how people responded. Consider two indicators of prejudice toward child-molesters: 'Do you think that child-molesters are different from other people?' and 'Do you think that all child-molesters should be executed?' Surely, more people would say yes to the first item than to the second. This is due to the fact that the first statement would have to be regarded as representing a very low level (if any) of prejudice, whereas the second is pretty extreme. Anyone who agreed to the second item would surely agree to the first as well, hence more would agree to the first one overall than to the second.

Guttman scaling would begin by examining the apparent degree of prejudice, for example, represented by each item—based only on the number who would be judged prejudiced by responses to that item. Next, responses to *pairs* of items are examined to determine whether those who agree to the harder one always (or almost always) agree to the easier one. In this fashion, a set of items would be selected appropriate to the creation of the scale.

A key to Guttman scaling lies in the scoring of response patterns. Scale scores are assigned in such a fashion as to permit the most faithful reproduction of original responses, called the *coefficient of reproducibility*. Table 4 illustrates.

Table 4.

Item 1	Item 2	Item 3	Item 4	Pattern	Score
+	+	+	+	1	4
−	+	+	+	2	3
−	−	+	+	3	2
−	−	−	+	4	1
−	−	−	−	5	0
+	−	−	−	6	0
+	+	+	−	7	4
+	+	−	+	8	4
−	+	+	−	9	3
−	−	+	−	10	0 or 2

Notice that patterns 1 through 5 are scored just as they would be in a simple cumulative index: one point for each indicator of the variable. More important, by knowing the scale score, all the specific responses could be faithfully reproduced. Knowing that a person was scored 3 for example, a '−' on Item 1 and a '+' on Items 2–4 could be predicted.

Look at Pattern 6, however. The only '+' is for Item 1, presumably the *hardest* item. In a simple index, such people would be scored 1, leading to the assumption that such people were '+' on Item 4 and '−' on the rest. In each such case, then, two errors (Items 1 and 4) would arise if an attempt were made to reproduce the specific responses given by such people. By assigning a scale score of 0 in this instance, only one error would arise in reproducing the responses: guessing a '−' for Item 1.

A similar situation applies to Pattern 7. If such people were scored as 3, two errors would be made in reproducing the responses of each. Instead, by scoring them 4, only one error would be made for each such person. Patterns 8, 9, and 10 present other response patterns, indicating how each might be scored, so as to produce the fewest errors in reproducing the specific responses. Notice that in Pattern 10, either a score of 0 or 2 would produce the same number of errors (1), whereas an index score of 1 would produce two errors.

The *scalability* of a set of items is determined by calculating the *coefficient of reproducibility*. The total number of predictions that would be made (the number of cases times the number of items) is divided into the number of correct predictions that could be made on the basis of the scale scores. As a rough rule of thumb, a coefficient of 80 percent or higher is generally considered sufficient to justify the use of Guttman scale scoring instead of simple index scores.

There are numerous other techniques for creating composite measures, such as scales based on factor analysis or other such multivariate techniques. The foregoing examples should illustrate the logic of scaling techniques, however.

See also: Multidimensional Scaling; Reliability/Validity; Sampling; Social Psychology; Sociology in Language.

Bibliography

Bogardus E S 1933 A social distance scale. *Sociology and Social Research* 17: 265–71

Guttman L 1944 A basis for scaling qualitative data. *American Sociological Review* 9: 139–50

Likert R 1974 A method of constructing an attitude scale. In: Maranell G M (ed.) *Scaling: A Sourcebook for Behavioral Scientists*. Aldine, Chicago, IL

McIver J P, Carmines E G 1981 *Unidimensional Scaling*. Sage, Beverly Hills, CA

Thurstone L L 1931 The measurement of social attitudes. *Journal of Abnormal and Social Psychology* 26: 249–69

E. Babbie

Scenes-and-frames Semantics

Charles Fillmore's *scenes-and-frames* approach to semantics takes its starting-point in the assumption that the human conceptual apparatus does not consist of isolated concepts, but is organized into larger, internally structured wholes. These larger chunks of knowledge, comprising coherent sets of human beliefs, actions, experiences, or imaginations, are called *scenes*. *Frames*, on the other hand, are the linguistic means available to refer to (aspects of) the scene. An example is the 'scene of commercial transaction,' prototypically involving the selling and buying of goods. (Because a scene is a flexible entity, there may also be peripheral instantiations of the scene that deviate from the prototypical case.) The frame correlated with the commercial transaction scene comprises verbs such as *buy*, *sell*, *charge*, and *pay*, but also nouns such as *price*, *cost*, and *money*, and grammatical constructions such as the fact that the buyer is identified by a *to*-phrase with the verb *sell*, but appears as the subject of the sentence when the verb *buy* is used. The semantic description of various expressions thus refers to a single conceptual scene. As such, the scenes-and-frames approach is clearly related to the older *word field* approach (see *Lexical Field*). At the same time, it is related to the frame approach to knowledge representation in Artificial Intelligence, as introduced by Minsky (1975) (compare the article *Knowledge Representation*).

Bibliography

Fillmore C J 1977 Scenes-and-frames semantics. In: Zampolli A (ed.) *Linguistic Structures Processing*. North Holland Publishing Company, Amsterdam
Minsky M 1975 A framework for representing knowledge. In: Winston P H (ed.) *The Psychology of Computer Vision*. McGraw-Hill, New York

D. Geeraerts

Scherer, Wilhelm (1841–86)

Wilhelm Scherer was born in Schönborn, Lower Austria, on April 26, 1841, the son of the High Bailiff. In 1858 he entered the University of Vienna, and in 1860 he went to Berlin, where Franz Bopp was one of his teachers (see *Bopp, Franz*). He also became personally acquainted with Jacob Grimm (see *Grimm, Jacob Ludwig Carl*). Scherer died on August 6, 1886.

In 1868 Scherer wrote his only major philological work, *Zur Geschichte der deutschen Sprache*. This was built on the foundation of Jacob Grimm's *Deutsche Grammatik*, hitherto the standard work on Old Germanic philology. The first part of Scherer's book is devoted to the sounds of Germanic, which he describes from a physiological point of view. He maintained that the phonological development of speech followed unvarying rules, introducing the concept of analogy to explain some apparent exceptions. The second part of the book, on morphology, includes an attempt to establish the origin of Indo-European forms. The book was much admired by Scherer's contemporaries, but his attempt to connect the development of the languages with the character and spiritual nature of the various races, and his imaginative explanations of the origin of the inflections, do not find sympathy with modern scholars.

Later in his life Scherer turned his attention to literature, and published a number of works in this field. His *History of German Literature* of 1883 was translated into English in 1886.

Scherer's writings were much influenced by his enthusiasm for all things German. They appeared at a time of great nationalist feelings in Germany.

Scherer reacted against earlier theories that language could be treated as a natural organism apart from man; changes in languages were caused by man. His insistence on the fact that sound laws could have no exceptions, helped by the new concept of analogical change, paved the way for the work of the Neogrammarians (see *Comparative Linguistics: History*). Although the imaginative and patriotic aspect of Scherer's philological work is alien to our modern ideas, many new concepts introduced by him helped to further the study of language. Not the least of these was his conviction that the development of a language should not be divided into a prehistoric period of creation followed by a historical period of decay, but should be regarded as a continuous period of development.

Bibliography

Basch B 1889 *Wilhelm Scherer et la philologie allemande*. Nauch, Paris
Scherer W 1868 *Zur Geschichte der deutschen Sprache*. Weidmann, Berlin
Scherer W 1883 *Geschichte der deutschen Litteratur*. Weidmann, Berlin; 1886 3rd edn. 1906, *A History of German Literature* Conybeare F C (transl.), Müller F M (ed.). Clarendon Press, Oxford
Schmidt J 1887 Gedächtnissrede auf Wilhelm Scherer, *Abhandlungen der königlichen Akademie der Wissenschaften zu Berlin* 1.1–19. Repr. Sebeok T (ed.) 1966 *Portraits of Linguists*, vol. I. Indiana University Press, Bloomington, IN
Schröder E 1890 Wilhelm E. Scherer. In: *Allgemeine deutsche Biographie*; 2nd edn. 67–71, vol. 31, pp. 104–14, 1970. Duncker and Humblot, Berlin

E. C. Dove

Schizophrenia: Language Dysfunction

The term 'schizophrenia' is used for a group of disorders that share the common features of psychotic symptoms and a partial response to neuroleptic treatment. Both language disturbance and thought disorder have been proposed as a characteristic of schizophrenia since early descriptions of the illness by the late nineteenth-century psychiatrist, Kraepelin.

1. Language Changes and Symptomatology

The main issue concerning the symptomatology of schizophrenia has been whether, following Kraepelin, language changes represent a disorder in the processing of language per se, or whether, as proposed by Bleuler in 1911, they can be regarded as a reflection of an underlying thought disorder. Schizophrenic speech has been analyzed extensively and found to contain more speech errors and to be less syntactically complex, textually cohesive, and interpersonally appropriate than normal speech. It is characterized by chaining, glossomania, inappropriate rhyming, neologisms, and word salads. The pattern of language disturbance has been used to contribute to the diagnosis of schizophrenia, and to distinguish between the positive and negative symptomatology. In particular, there is evidence that schizophrenic patients with negative symptomatology are distinguished by poverty of speech and that the content is less syntactically complex.

2. Studies of Language Changes in Schizophrenia

The predominant strategy of studies of language changes in schizophrenia has been a statistical analysis of language utterances. One example is the use of the type token ratio (TTR) (Fairbanks 1944), a means of determining the efficiency of language developed by Zipf through statistical means. The TTR represents the frequency of word use as a function of the types of words used by a person. The TTR tends to be reduced in schizophrenic patients, indicating an increase in the repetition of the same words in passages of utterances.

Schizophrenic language has also been shown to be more prone to disruption by irrelevant associations. For example, one of Bleuler's (1911) patients when listing the members of her family started with 'father' and 'son' and then added 'and the Holy Ghost.' One explanation for this phenomenon is that the pattern of associations between words is abnormal. In support of this, many studies indicate idiosyncratic responses to test words on word association tasks. However, another reason is that competing associations may more easily achieve access to consciousness and interfere with the patient's response. In support of this, schizophrenic patients are more prone to 'punning' confusions in language usage without apparent awareness and less able to use the context of a word to disambiguate the meaning. Maher (1972) has advanced the notion of a deficit in attentional focusing which underlies the associative intrusional speech utterances.

Linguistic analysis of schizophrenic language has also revealed changes in the cohesion between sentences or phrases. 'Linguistic cohesion' occurs when a speaker uses the same root, synonym, or superordinate to create a semantic link between elements in a text. Schizophrenics appear to rely to a greater extent on lexical cohesion and, in particular, within-clause lexical cohesion, as illustrated by the example of the following phrase recorded by Rochester and Martin (1979): 'Each life you, know you can't always remember your past lives.' In this case the word 'lives' is tied to the word 'life' earlier in the clause. This type of utterance is also found more frequently in patients with manic-depressive psychosis.

More recent studies have focused on the syntax of schizophrenic language and fluency of speech. Schizophrenics have been found to use less complex syntax, but also be more prone to errors when complex syntax is employed. Likewise, the fluency of speech is decreased when measured by the relative frequency of repeat words and part words. Again, dysfluencies tend to increase with the structural complexity of the utterances. The changes in syntax and fluency appear to discriminate schizophrenics from patients with manic-depressive psychosis.

See also: Pathology, Acquired: Causes; Disorders of Fluency; Language Dysfunction in Dementia; Pathology: Evaluation; Pathology: Intervention.

Bibliography

Bleuler E 1911 (transl. Zinkin J 1950) *Dementia Praecox: Or the Group of Schizophrenias*. Trans. International University Press, New York

Fairbanks H 1944 The quantification differentiation of samples of spoken language. *Psychological Monographs* **56**: 19–38

Maher B 1972 The language of schizophrenia: A review and interpretation. *British Journal Psychiatry* **120**: 3–17

Morice R, McNicol D 1986 Language changes in schizophrenia: A limited replication. *Schizophrenia Bulletin* **12(2)**: 239–51

Pavy D 1968 Verbal behavior in schizophrenia: A review of recent studies. *Psychological Bulletin* **70**: 164–78

Rochester S, Martin J R 1979 *Crazy talk: A study of the discourse of schizophrenic speakers*. Plenum Press, New York

Thomas P, King K, Fraser W I 1987 Positive and negative symptoms of schizophrenia and linguistic performance. *Acta Psychiatrica Scandinavica* **76(2)**: 144–51

R. Morris

Schlegel, August Wilhelm von (1767–1845)

Schlegel, August Wilhelm [from 1815:] von, writer, literary critic, translator, philologist, and student of the Sanskrit language and its literature, elder brother of Friedrich Schlegel (see *Schlegel, (Carl Wilhelm) Friedrich von*), was born in Hanover (Germany) on September 5, 1767. He studied theology and philosophy at the University of Göttingen, where he was mainly influenced by the philologist C. G. Heyne and the poet G. A. Bürger. Between 1791 and 1795 he was a tutor in Amsterdam. From 1798 he was associate professor at the University of Jena. He moved to Berlin where he delivered courses of private lectures on literary history (1801–04). From 1804 till her death in 1817 he was secretary, traveling companion, and literary adviser to Madame de Staël (Anne Louise Germaine de Staël-Holstein, 1766–1817). In 1818 he was appointed professor of the history of art and literature at the University of Bonn, where he established Indic studies, thus becoming the founder of Indic philology in Germany. He died in Bonn on May 12, 1845.

Schlegel was a prominent member of the Romantic movement in Germany and succeeded in transforming the genuine romantic interest in foreign cultures, languages, and literatures, into a systematic scientific approach. He produced excellent translations of Italian and Spanish authors and of the dramas of Shakespeare (in a project later continued by L. Tieck and Tieck's daughter Dorothea). His most influential contributions to the study of language lay in the fields of language typology and reflections on method. As early as 1798 he pointed out the difference between analytical and synthetic languages (Schlegel 1798: 60ff.; cf. Schlegel 1818: 16). By coining the term *'vergleichende Grammatik'* (Schlegel 1803: 203) he paved the way for the linguistic theories of his brother Friedrich (e.g., Schlegel 1808: 28) and significantly contributed to the theoretical evolution of comparative linguistics. He took up and refined Friedrich's theory of language classification (outlined in Schlegel 1808: 44ff. and elsewhere) by proposing three types of languages: those without any grammatical structure, languages using affixes, and inflectional languages (Schlegel 1818: 14ff.). This theory was much discussed throughout the nineteenth century. With his severe criticism of J. Grimm's early etymologies (Schlegel 1815) he gave a decisive impulse to strict methodological rigor in the study of the history of the Germanic languages. He also set the standards for the study of the Sanskrit language by applying the methods of classical philology to the analysis of its literature and the publication of Sanskrit texts (e.g., in his editions of the Bhagavad-Gītā 1823 and parts of the Rāmāyaṇa 1829–38).

Bibliography

Muncker F 1890 Schlegel. *Allgemeine Deutsche Biographie* **31**: 354–68
Schlegel A W 1798 Die Sprachen; Ein Gespräch über Klopstocks grammatische Gespräche. In: Schlegel A W, Schlegel F (eds.) 1798–1800 *Athenaeum: Eine Zeitschrift 1–3*. Vieweg/Frölich, Berlin
Schlegel A W 1803 Ankündigung: Sprachlehre von A. F. Bernhardi. *Europa: Eine Zeitschrift* **2**: 193–204
Schlegel A W 1815 Altdeutsche Wälder. *Heidelbergische Jahrbücher der Literatur* **8**: 721–66
Schlegel A W 1818 *Observations sur la langue et la littérature provençales*. Librairie grecque-latine-allemande, Paris
Schlegel A W (ed.) 1820–30 *Indische Bibliothek 1–2.1*. Weber, Bonn
Schlegel F 1808 *Ueber die Sprache und Weisheit der Indier: Ein Beitrag zur Begründung der Alterthumskunde*. Mohr und Zimmer, Heidelberg

K. Grotsch

Schlegel, (Carl Wilhelm) Friedrich von (1772–1829)

Schlegel was born in Hanover, March 10, 1772, and died in Dresden, January 12, 1829. In the annals of linguistic science he is usually accorded a minor role only. His strong involvement in the Romantic movement and his literary production may explain why he is usually seen as a poet and literary critic, and hardly ever as a linguist. It is true that his interest in Oriental studies had originally been aroused by translations from Sanskrit and Persian literature. The book he wrote during 1805 and 1807 and for which he became famous, *Ueber die Sprache und Weisheit der Indier*, contains chapters of approximately equal length on the philosophy and theology (Schlegel 1808: 89–153) and on the '*historische Ideen*' concerning India (ibid. 157–230), with translations of Indian poetry into German (ibid. 231–324). Yet there is no doubt that the first part on language ('*Von der Sprache*,' 1–86) attracted the most enduring interest among his contemporaries. The fact that the King of Bavaria granted two of his subjects, Othmar Frank and Franz Bopp (see *Bopp, Franz*), scholarships to pursue the study of Persian and Sanskrit in Paris a few years later, may serve as an indication of the importance that was soon attached to Oriental studies, and this largely as a result of Schlegel's book. His importance in the history of linguistic science rests on this one work; it appears, however, that once the year 1816, the date of Bopp's *Conjugationssystem*, had been chosen by historians as marking the beginning of linguistics, Schlegel's book was only mentioned as precursory. It was no longer read, although the

so-called founding fathers of comparative–historical philology, Bopp (see *Bopp, Franz*), Rask (see *Rask, Rasmus Kristian*), and Grimm (see *Grimm, Jacob Ludwig Carl*), acknowledged their indebtedness to his work. Schlegel is traditionally credited with the first use of the term '*vergleichende Grammatik*.' However, others, like J. S. Vater, had used it in 1801 and the elder Schlegel, August Wilhelm (see *Schlegel, August Wilhelm von*), used it in 1803 before his brother. But it is clear from Friedrich Schlegel's book (p. 28) that he had been inspired by the example of Blumenbach and Cuvier's Comparative Anatomy. By today's standards, Schlegel had a checkered career; following the study of law in Göttingen and Leipzig, he soon turned to literature as his main occupation, circulating among the Romantics as well as the people at the Court of Weimar, notably Goethe, Schiller, and Herder (see *Herder, Johann Gottfried*), who was largely responsible for creating the general climate of the time that expected new and profound ideas to come from the East ('*ex Oriente lux*'). Schlegel's exposure to the writings of Sir William Jones (see *Jones, Sir William*) led him to travel to Paris, where Persian, Arabic, and other Oriental languages were taught. He was introduced to Persian by Antoine Léonard de Chézy soon after his arrival in 1802, and familiarized himself with the ancient language of India through Alexander Hamilton, from whom he took private lessons during 1803 and 1804. He copied Sanskrit manuscripts and translated literary texts; for a living, he gave lectures on German literature and philosophy.

Ueber die Sprache und Weisheit der Indier was important for the development of comparative–historical as well as typological linguistics in the nineteenth century. Schlegel's suggestion of comparing grammatical features in order to establish genetic relationships, though not entirely new, was influential. For instance, his suggestion of investigating the conjugation system of Sanskrit in comparison with all the languages thought to be related to it led Bopp to his first work; his evolutionary view of language paved the way for Grimm's emphasis on the historical treatment of language, and his classification of languages according to morphological structure initiated an entire research program. This went from Wilhelm von Humboldt (see *Humboldt, Wilhelm von*) to Steinthal (see *Steinthal, Heymann*) to Sapir (see *Sapir, Edward*), to Greenberg (see *Greenberg, Joseph H.*), and beyond, especially after his brother August had introduced the synthetic/analytic distinction in his 1818 essay on the history of the Romance languages. Timpanaro (1972: 77) has pointed out that, when Schlegel discussed at length questions of change and language mixture, he anticipated substratum theory, usually associated with Ascoli (see *Ascoli, Graziadio Isaia*), Schuchardt (see *Schuchardt, Hugo*), and others at the end of the nineteenth century. Schlegel maintained that language contact and the resulting borrowings made it difficult at times to identify all 'Sanskritic' languages, making it necessary to consider what we may call the external history of a given language, in addition to submitting it to close morphological analysis. In discussing linguistic contamination and the question of language descent, Schlegel drew particular attention to Armenian, in which he found many similarities with Latin, Greek, Persian and German roots, and to agreements in grammatical structure. He was not quite ready to include

Armenian among those belonging to the Indo–European language family, but in view of the material he had at his disposal, he made a great number of important observations which were borne out by subsequent generations of historical linguists. Schlegel undoubtedly deserves a place among the 'founding fathers' of comparative Indo–European grammar, and not only as an interesting 'philological instigator' (see Klin 1967).

Bibliography

Klin E 1967 Friedrich Schlegel als philologischer Anreger (1802–08). *Germanica Wratislaviensia* **11**: 83–103

Koerner E F K 1987 Friedrich Schlegel and the emergence of historical–comparative grammar. *Lingua e Stile* **22**: 341–65

Nüsse H 1962 *Die Sprachtheorie Friedrich Schlegels.* C Winter, Heidelberg

Oppenberg U 1965 *Quellenstudien zu Friedrich Schlegels Übersetzun-gen aus dem Sanskrit.* N G Elwert, Marburg

Plank F 1987a The Smith–Schlegel connection in linguistic typology: Forgotten fact or fiction? *ZPhon* **40**: 198–216

Plank F 1987b What Schlegel could have learned from Alexander ('Sanscrit') Hamilton besides Sanscrit. *Lingua e Stile* **22**: 367–84

Schlegel F von 1808 *Ueber die Sprache und Weisheit der Indier.* Mohr and Zimmer, Heidelberg

Schlegel F von 1849 (trans. Millington E J, Bohn H G) *The Aesthetic and Miscellaneous Works of Frederick von Schlegel.*

Schlegel F von 1975 (eds. Behler E, Struc-Oppenberrg U) *Studien zur Philosophie und Theologie,* Schöningh, München–Paderborn–Wien

Struc-Oppenberg U 1980 Friedrich Schlegel and the history of Sanskrit philology and comparative studies. *Canadian Review of Comparative Literature* **7**: 411–37

Timpanaro S 1972 Friedrich Schlegel e gli inizi della linguistica indo–europea in Germania. *Critica Storica* **9**: 72–105

Timpanaro S 1977 Friedrich Schlegel and the beginnings of Indo–European linguistics in Germany. In: Schlegel F von 1977

Twaddell W F 1943 Fr. Schlegel's criteria of linguistic relation. *Monatshefte für deutschen Unterricht* **35**: 151–55

E. F. K. Koerner

Schleicher, August (1821–68)

Schleicher, Indo–Europeanist and Slavist, was born on February 19, 1821 in Meiningen, Germany, and died on December 6, 1868 in Jena. He enrolled in the fall of 1840 at the University of Leipzig to study theology, but moved in spring 1841 to Tübingen to study theology, philosophy, and Semitic languages with Heinrich Ewald. He abandoned theology two years later to enroll at the University of Bonn where he studied, among other things, classics with Friedrich Ritschl, oriental languages with Christian Lassen, and German dialects with Friedrich Diez (see *Diez, Friedrich*). He completed his studies with a dissertation on Latin syntax, an examination for high school teaching, and a *venia legendi* for 'Indic language and literature and comparative grammar,' all between January and March 1846. From summer 1846 to early 1848 he taught at Bonn as a *Privatdozent*, adding Slavic to his research interests. He involved himself in the revolutionary movements of 1848–49, acting as a journalist in various European capitals, especially in Prague, where he learned Czech from a young

native, Alois Vaniček, who later became one of his students. He returned to Bonn late in 1849, where his continued work on Slavic languages led, in March 1850, to the offer of an extraordinary professorship, first for classical philology, subsequently for comparative linguistics and Sanskrit, at the University of Prague, where, in 1853, he became a full professor, with German linguistics added to his subjects. There Georg Curtius (see *Curtius, Georg*) was his colleague. In 1857, after difficult years (Schleicher, a foreigner, a Protestant, and a man of integrity and honesty engaged in matters concerning political freedom and justice, was subjected to various indignities at the hand of the Austrian authorities and misguided Czech nationalists) he was glad to accept a lesser position at the University in Jena, where he remained as an *ordentlicher Honorarprofessor* for comparative linguistics and German philology, despite offers from Warsaw and the Academy of St Petersburg (both in 1862) and Dorpat (in 1863), until his premature death at the age of 47 years.

Contrary to widespread belief, Schleicher's views on language and linguistics were fixed early in his career. Shortly after the publication of his first book, *Zur vergleichenden Sprachengeschichte* (1848), Schleicher worked out a naturalistic conception of language and a research program inspired by Hegelian philosophy and the exact analytical methods of the natural sciences, in particular botany and geology. His second book (Schleicher 1850) documents this turn to a natural science conception of linguistics very well. In his *Die Deutsche Sprache* (1860) and several other subsequent publications, he repeated almost verbatim what he had first pronounced in the 1850 book. Significantly, he published his first *Stammbäume* (genealogical trees) in 1853, six years before the publication of Darwin's *Origin of Species*, and in 1859 he introduced the term '*Morphologie*' into linguistic nomenclature.

Schleicher was the most distinguished Indo–Europeanist of his generation and an accomplished synthesizer of the accumulated linguistic knowledge of his time, as may be gathered from the various editions of his *Compendium* (1861–62). Although he did not introduce the asterisk into scholarly practice, it was he who developed the method of reconstruction in comparative linguistics on which subsequent generations built. His famous story written in Indo–European was not 'a joke' (as Delbrück held in 1880; see also *Delbrück, Berthold*) but a demonstration of the comparative method. In the fields of Baltic and Slavic as well as dialectology and the study of child language (1861) he was innovative; his synthesis of Indo–European phonology and morphology in the *Compendium* served as a model for subsequent research, especially Brugmann and Delbrück's *Grundriss* (1886–1916). Schleicher is nowadays best known for his Darwinian essays (e.g., 1863), although these are in fact his weakest works. His most distinguished students were Jan Baudouin de Courtenay (see *Baudouin de Courtenay, Jan Ignacy Niecislaw*), August Leskien (see *Leskien, August*), Johannes Schmidt (see *Schmidt, Johannes*), and Hugo Schuchardt (*Schuchardt, Hugo*).

Bibliography

For a full bibliography, see Dietze J 1966.

Bynon T 1986 August Schleicher: Indo–Europeanist and general linguist. In: Bynon T, Palmer F R (eds.) *Studies in the History of Western Linguistics: In Honour of R. H. Robins*. Cambridge University Press, Cambridge

Dietze J 1966 *August Schleicher als Slawist: Sein Leben und Werk aus der Sicht der Indogermanistik*. Akademie-Verlag, Berlin

Koerner E F K 1975 European structuralism—early beginnings. In: Sebeok T A (ed.) *Current Trends in Linguistics. Vol. XIII: Historiography of Linguistics*. Mouton, The Hague

Koerner E F K (ed.) 1983 *Linguistics and Evolutionary Theory: Three Essays by August Schleicher, Ernst Haeckel, and Wilhelm Bleek*. Benjamins, Amsterdam

Koerner E F K 1989 *Practicing Linguistic Historiography*. Benjamins, Amsterdam

Maher J P 1966 More on the history of the comparative method: The tradition of Darwinism in August Schleicher's work. *AnL* **8(3)** 2: 1–12

Priestly T M S 1975 Schleicher, Čelakovský, and the family-tree diagram: A puzzle in the history of linguistics. **HL** 2: 299–333

Schleicher A 1850 *Die Sprachen Europas in systematischer Uebersicht*, Linguistische Untersuchungen, 2. H B König, Bonn

Schleicher A 1853 Die ersten Spaltungen des indogermanischen Urvolkes (Kieler). *Allgemeine Monatsschrift für Wissenschaft und Literatur* **Sept. 1853**: 786–87

Schleicher A 1859 *Zur Morphologie der Sprache*, VIIe série, tome I, No. 7. Eggers, St Petersburg

Schleicher A 1860 *Die Deutsche Sprache*. Cotta, Stuttgart.

Schleicher A 1861, 1865 Einige Beobachtungen an Kindern. *Beiträge zur vergleichenden Sprachforschung* **2**: 497–98, **4**: 128

Schleicher A 1861–62 *Compendium der vergleichenden Grammatik der indogermanischen Sprachen*. H. Böhlau, Weimar

Schleicher A 1863 *Die Darwinsche Theorie und die Sprachwissenschaft*. Böhlau, Weimar (1983 Linguistics and Evolutionary Theory. Benjamins, Amsterdam)

Tort P 1980 *Evolutionnisme et linguistique; suivi de August Schleicher, La théorie de Darwin et la science du langage; De l'importance du langage pour l'histoire naturelle de l'homme*. J. Vrin, Paris

Trnka B 1952 Zur Erinnerung an August Schleicher. *ZPhon* **6**: 134–42

E. F. K. Koerner

Schmeller, Johann Andreas (1785–1852)

The Germanist Johann Andreas Schmeller, born in the north of Bavaria, was a notable pioneer of German dialectology, whose academic career was preceded by ten years' soldiering in various countries during the Napoleonic wars. In the course of these travels, apparently, he came to the then unfashionable view that dialects have intrinsic value and also philological importance, and began to collect material. After leaving the army he became Librarian of the Royal Bavarian State Library, and professor in Munich University.

At the request and with the support of the Bavarian Academy of Sciences, Schmeller undertook a survey of the dialects of the Kingdom of Bavaria. As its boundaries embraced Bavarian, Alemanic, and Franconian speakers (Schmeller was one of these last), the task constituted the first comparative study of different German dialects—in which he latterly included Austrian material also. Schmeller collected all his data personally in 15 years of fieldwork, making some important innovations. He devised a simple historically based transcription, adequate to the phonology

of the dialects; and in each district collected data systematically from both rural and urban dialect speakers, and from educated persons who used the local standard German. Unlike some of his successors, he did not pursue the mirage of tribal dialect boundaries, but simply set out to establish a boundary for each item collected. When J. Grimm's (see *Grimm, Jacob Ludwig Carl*) historical German grammar appeared (1819), it confirmed Schmeller's perception that dialects are regular developments from the older language, showing him how to combine the study of dialect and of older documentary sources, and this he did exhaustively in his survey.

The material collected was embodied in two publications, the first being a phonological and morphological study *Die Mundarten Bayerns* (1821), which also included the considerable mass of textual and cultural matter collected; followed by the *Bayerisches Wörterbuch* (1827–37), in which the entries, arranged by word stems, included full morphological information (another innovation) and documentary data.

During the 1830s, Schmeller was also prominent as an editor of medieval German texts, in some cases the first editor: Heliand, Muspilli, Tatian, and Carmina Burana. Further lexical works were a glossary of the Saxon dialect, and one of 'Cimbrisch,' an isolated Bavarian dialect in northern Italy (both 1840).

Bibliography

Schmeller J A 1821 *Die Mundarten Bayerns*. K. Thienemann, Munich

Schmeller J A 1827–37 *Bayerisches Wörterbuch mit urkündlichen Belegen*, 4 vols. Stuttgart and Tübingen

Schmeller J A 1827 *Ueber das Studium der altdeutschen Sprache und ihrer Denkmäler*. J J Lentner, Munich

T. Hill

Schmidt, Johannes (1843–1901)

Born on July 4, 1843, Schmidt spent his boyhood in Stettin (Szczecin, H. G. Grassmann's home; see *Grassmann, Hermann Günther*). His undergraduate career was in Classics at Bonn, where he returned for his final graduation in 1868. But his linguistic career was decided by his pupillage under August Schleicher (see *Schleicher, August*) at Jena in 1862–66. Not only did Schmidt remain committed to historical comparativism and Indo–European issues, but he was the passionate defender of Schleicher's own reputation against all detractors.

After a professorial appointment in Graz (from 1873) he was chosen in 1876 for the chief philological chair in Berlin, and held that office till his death on July 29, 1901. Pedersen was among his pupils (see *Pedersen, Holger*). From 1880 he was coeditor of the influential *Kuhn's Zeitschrift*—the 1877 issue's title page is misleading—and in 1884 he was elected to the Berlin Academy.

Unlike fellow Jena students Leskien and Baudouin de Courtenay (see *Leskien, August*; *Baudouin de Courtenay, Jan Ignacy Niecislaw*), Schmidt concentrated on the study of the Indo–European languages (especially Sanskrit, Greek, French, and the Slavic group) and of their vowel systems and morphology, and also of their original home-land (which he placed in Asia). He became the standard-bearer of the Berlin faction in the academic war with Leipzig which enlivened the later nineteenth century, and even credited Schleicher, with originating the central Neo-grammarian tenet of exceptionless change. Hence he was skeptical on such matters as 'sonant liquids and nasals.' But when the 'law of the palatals' surfaced in Leipzig he altered his whole stance to accept this new truth (in 1877—even half-claiming the discovery), and he was always an enemy of doctrinaire attitudes, being a cautious and essentially nonintuitive scholar.

In 1870 he revised, with Leskien, the famous *Compendium* of Schleicher. His own two-volume history of Indo-European vowels followed (1871–75) and was rightly prized in his day; and in 1889 he propounded the usually accepted identity of Indo-European neuter plural and collective feminine singular formants.

But his outstanding contribution was his replacement (1872) of the concept of cognate language evolution as a 'family tree' by the 'wave theory,' which pictures innovations as spreading outwards like the concentric ripples from a disturbance on a pond. This analogy avoids the problem that the actual distribution of various shifts makes it hard to draw a tree with incontrovertible consistent branching. But it can itself explain the absence of a change in a given language only by the influence of competing waves and/or unstable positions of languages in the 'pond.' However, the model retains some attraction (it was the harbinger of isogloss study) and Schmidt's fame abides.

Bibliography

Kretschmer P 1905 Obituary notice. *Zeitschrift für Vergleichende Sprachforschung* **38**: V–XIV

Pedersen H 1924 (transl. 1931 Spargo J W) *Sprogsvidenskaben i det nittende Aarhundrede*. Gyldendal, Copenhagen; reissued 1962 as *The Discovery of Language*. Indiana University Press, Bloomington, IN

Schmidt J 1871–75 *Zur Geschichte des indogermanischen Vocalismus*, 2 vols. Böhlau, Weimar

Schmidt J 1872 *Die Verwandtschaftsverhältnisse der indogermanischen Sprachen*. Böhlau, Weimar

Schmidt J 1889 *Die Pluralbildungen der indogermanischen Neutra*. Böhlau, Weimar

Schmidt J 1890 Die Urheimat der Indogermanen und das europäische Zahlsystem. In: *Proceedings of the Königliche Akademie der Wissenschaften*

N. E. Collinge

School Language Policies

School language policies are viewed by many in education as an integral and necessary part of the administration and the curriculum practice of modern schools. A language policy is a document compiled by the staff of a school, often assisted by other members of the school community, to which the staff give their assent and commitment. It identifies areas in the school's scope of operations and program where language problems exist that need the commonly agreed approach that is offered by a policy. A policy sets out what the school intends to do about these areas of concern; it is an action statement.

1. Origin and Early Developments

In 1966 members of the London Association for the Teaching of English began to develop and extend their interest in the concept of 'language across the curriculum' (see *Language across the Curriculum*) by preparing a discussion document entitled 'Towards a Language Policy Across the Curriculum' (Rosen in Barnes, et al. 1971). This discussion document provided the catalyst for action that its authors had intended. Schools in various places within Britain, in other countries of the British Commonwealth, and in the United States began to develop their own language policies, using the original document as a reference point. In 1975 the point and value of language policies for British schools received official endorsement in *A Language for Life* (The Bullock Report): Each school should have an organized policy for language across the curriculum, establishing every teacher's involvement in language and reading development throughout the years of schooling (see *English Teaching in England and Wales: Key Reports*.)

Subsequently several influential texts (e.g., Torbe 1980) addressed the need for a whole-school language policy, especially at secondary level, and discussed the implementation of such a policy. As the idea of having school language policies spread, practitioners and theorists began to see potential in them for small-scale but important educational reform: for example Knott (1985) presents novel ideas for researching pupil language use and discovering the attitudes of secondary school staff to language issues; and Maybin (1985) provides practical approaches for working towards a primary school policy for implementation in a culturally pluralist school setting.

2. Language Planning, National Language Policies, and School Language Policies

'Language planning' is another name for the evaluative approach to the sociology of language (see *Sociology of Language*). Broadly conceived, language planning is concerned with any problem area in which language plays some role: it is the organized pursuit of solutions to language problems. Following in the language planning tradition as they do, national language policies are comprehensive and coherent documents that enable national decision makers to make choices about language issues in a rational and balanced way. Australia's 'National Policy on Languages' released in 1987 is an example of a policy of this kind (see *English Teaching in Australia: Key Reports*; also *English Teaching in Canada: Key Reports*; *Wales: Language Education Policy*; *Ireland: Language Education Policy*).

In spite of great advances in language planning, researchers in the area have paid very little attention to the school as the basic context for language change. Even those rare texts that have linked language planning with education (Kennedy 1983) tend to address education as a macro phenomenon. However official documents have begun to suggest the need for formal school-level planning. In 1985 *Education for All* (The Swann Report) responded to the growing pluralism in British schools by warning that 'unless there is a school language and learning policy across the curriculum there will be a wastage of effort and often confusion' (see *Black English in Education: UK*). The micro setting of the school as a site for language planning is now receiving more attention, beginning with research studies in New Zealand that address the role of the school as the key agency in language planning. These studies borrow the model of 'language policies across the curriculum' developed for London schools and extend its original focus on mother-tongue concerns to include second language, bilingual, foreign language, and social justice issues (Corson 1989) (see *New Zealand: Minority Languages in Education*). The studies argue that the social institutions needed to translate the visions of national policies into strategies capable of enhancing individual lives already exist throughout pluralist societies in the form of their schools. It seems a very reasonable thing to ask schools to be responsible for much of the working end of language planning and of national policies that deal with language issues.

3. Administration, Policy Studies, and Research in Education

The design and implementation of a school language policy are ultimately the responsibility of the school's administration, acting through a policy-making group, departmental subcommittees or possibly through the participation of the whole school's staff and community. As a result the applied value of the ideas in school language policies will depend on how well the concept is integrated into the training and professional development of school administrators and curriculum planners. Moreover many types of small-scale and large-scale research will be necessary in schools if policies are to provide adequate and implementable solutions to local language problems. The training of teachers in basic language research methods will need to become more common. A beginning has been made in all these areas (Corson 1989, 1990a).

The rise in interest in school language policies coincides with moves in Canada, Britain, the United States, Australia and New Zealand to devolve most educational decision making away from central bureaucracies and down to school level. A groundswell of interest in school policy making of all kinds has resulted (Corson 1990b). Perhaps much of the impetus for further development will come from the growing need in modern societies to improve the quality of the solutions offered to the problems of large-scale cultural pluralism. Increasing tolerance worldwide in the treatment of linguistic minorities should hasten this development. Encouraging evidence for these conclusions is to be found in recommendations about 'language policies across the curriculum' that are sensitive to local cultural situations, made in Britain's *English for Ages 5–16* (The Cox Report; see *National Curriculum: English (England and Wales)*) and in a Special Issue of UNESCO's *International Review of Education* in 1991 devoted to school language policies.

Bibliography

Barnes D, Britton J, Rosen H 1971 *Language, the Learner and the School*. Penguin, Harmondsworth

Corson D 1989 *Language Policy Across the Curriculum*. Multilingual Matters, Clevedon

Corson D 1990a Three curriculum and organisational responses to cultural pluralism in New Zealand schooling. *Language, Culture and Curriculum* 3: 213–25

Corson D 1990b Applying the stages of a social epistemology to school policy making. *British Journal of Educational Studies* 38: 259–76

Kennedy C (ed.) 1984 *Language Planning and Language Education*. Allen and Unwin, London

Knott R 1985 *The English Department in a Changing World*. Open University Press, Milton Keynes

Maybin J 1985 *Every Child's Language: An In-Service Pack for Primary Teachers*. Open University Press/Multilingual Matters, Clevedon

Torbe M (ed.) 1980 *Language Policies in Action: Language Across the Curriculum in Some Secondary Schools*. Ward Lock, London

D. J. Corson

Schools Council (UK): English Teaching Program

By the mid-1960s any formal linguistic content had largely disappeared from English teaching in secondary schools in England, in favor of largely literary work (see *English Grammar in British Schools* 1960–1990; *Grammar Teaching and Language Skill*). Concern over this has been evident ever since. An early response was a request from the Nuffield Foundation to Professor M. A. K. Halliday, then at University College London, to oversee a broad-spectrum curriculum development project. This began in 1964 and from 1967 to its end in 1971 was funded by the Schools Council. A handful of linguists and a team of teachers worked in three unrelated sections.

David Mackay led a team developing *Breakthrough to Literacy*, a body of practical literacy learning materials for children aged 5–8. Having rapidly become a staple approach to early reading in the UK, it is still also widely used for developing writing. Published from 1969 onwards, its linguistic component has never been prominent (see *Reading Teaching: Materials*).

A second group addressed the need to reshape conventional notions of knowledge about language studied in the 8–14 age range. It published three textbooks, *Language and Communication*, in 1977–80 when numerous competitors were appearing, but their popularity with pupils served them well. Publication as a separate series, however, reinforced the peripheral status of its content in British schools; continental European practice is much more systematic and informative, notably in the Italian *scuola media* (see, e.g., Pittano 1983).

A third group focused on post-16-year-old students, for whom materials on the study of language scarcely existed. Full-scale trials led to publication of plans for sets of lesson sequences, on topics that explored social and linguistic facts in disciplined ways. Examples included exploring levels of formality in news-reading, studying the use of marked and unmarked forms in everyday life, and relating styles of naming to social distance. The 110 units in *Language in Use* (Doughty, et al., 1971, 1972) were widely but selectively used. They exerted much influence and widened the agenda for English teaching across the whole 11–18 range. *Language in Use* sold well for two decades and made its way into the consciousness of generations of English teachers.

The near-missionary function of the project was sustained for some 12 years through the intensive writing and editorial work of the *Language in Use* team, which proved particularly effective in post-16-year-old vocational education and in teacher training. A key premise was that older pupils needed a developed language awareness in place of doubtfully linked fragments of linguistic information (see *Language Awareness*). The later 1980s brought a wide recognition that the need is for both: awareness must derive in part from knowledge; it has to be acknowledged that the project's inability to count on teachers' own linguistic knowledge weakened its impact.

See also: English Teaching in England and Wales: Key Reports; National Curriculum: English (England and Wales).

Bibliography

Doughty P S, Thornton G M, Pearce J J 1971 *Language in Use*. Edward Arnold, London
Doughty P S, Thornton G M, Pearce J J 1972 *Exploring Language*. Edward Arnold, London
Forsyth I, Wood K 1977–80 *Language and Communication* One, Two, Three. Longman, Harlow
Mackay D, Thomson B, Schaub P 1970 *Breakthrough to Literacy*. Longman, Harlow
Pittano G 1983 *Lingua/Espressione/Communicazione*. Mondadori, Milan

J. J. Pearce

Schuchardt, Hugo (1842–1927)

Schuchardt was born in Gotha, Germany, and died in Graz, Austria. His father was a jurist (*Staatsassessor*) in Gotha; his mother, of noble extraction, was from a family closely connected with the court of the Duke of Sachsen Gotha-Altenburg. Schuchardt studied under Diez at Bonn (see *Diez, Friedrich*), was *privatdozent* at Leipzig (1870), and professor at Halle (1873) and at Graz (1876–1900). A man of independent means, he remained in retirement in Graz for the last 27 years of his life, choosing to stay in the isolated southern Austrian city rather than to return to his native Germany. By all appearances, he was a hypochondriac, believing he was suffering from neurasthenia—but nevertheless living into his eighties. He never married. His house, the Villa Malvina (named after his mother), was bequeathed to the university and subsequently became the home of the Department of Romance Languages. His papers, still largely uncataloged, form an important collection in the rare book section of the university library.

Schuchardt was the first professional linguist to turn serious and detailed attention of a general and comparative nature to the topic of pidgin and creole languages as a typological genre within linguistics. Accordingly, many consider him the father of creolistics. Throughout much of his long life, he was keenly interested in geography, anthropology, and travel descriptions of all kinds. Because of real or imagined problems with his health, and his general disinclination to undergo the rigors of travel outside Europe, he was destined never to see those creole areas he studied so passionately, and was thus denied the opportunity to experience the 'trade and slave languages' at firsthand. Instead, starting about 1880, he came to rely

> on a vast network of correspondents who relayed texts and sociological background information to him in Graz. The correspondents ranged from trained professional ethnologists and linguists, to missionaries, diplomats, military men, adventurers, and travellers generally.
> (Gilbert 1980: 4)

The 1880s saw the publication of the bulk of his work on creoles, above all the *Kreolische Studien*, in nine parts, dealing with '*Kreolisch*' in its Portuguese, French, or English guise. An insightful manuscript, the tenth creole study 'On the Negro English of West Africa' discovered among his papers in 1983 (Gilbert 1985), was found to anticipate the creole-origin hypothesis of the genesis and development of US Black English, as it was formulated a half-century later by Melville Herskovits, T. Earl Pardoe, John Reinecke (see *Reinecke, John E.*), and Lorenzo Dow Turner (see *Turner, Lorenzo Dow*), working independently. Early in his career, Schuchardt was inclined not to go along with the extreme universalist position (as represented, for example, by the Portuguese Creolist, Adolpho Coelho; see *Coelho, Francisco Adolpho*) that universal psychological or physiological laws were at work in the formation of creole languages. He tried to account for them on a case by case basis, citing substrate influences, common (chiefly societal) conditions of development, and so forth.

> Nevertheless, time and again he was struck by grammatical similarities in geographically widely separated pidgins and creoles, especially in the verb system.
> (Gilbert 1980: 7)

In the first fifteen years of the twentieth century, two additional and highly insightful works on creole appeared: a detailed description of all that was then known about the Lingua Franca (1909) and an important essay (1914) modestly entitled '*Vorbericht*' ('*Preface*') introducing his edition (the first published) of C. L. Schumann's (1778) *Saramaccan Dictionary* and other texts. In these works, Schuchardt shows the increasing influence of Wilhelm von Humboldt (see *Humboldt, Wilhelm von*) on his thinking, especially the notion of inner and outer form. Language simplification by individuals or by speech communities is now seen to involve the automatic stripping away of the superficial to arrive at the essential, the inner form. The increased emphasis on psychological processes in the last years of Schuchardt's life indicates the narrowing of the gap between him and Coelho's speculations of the 1880s, on the one hand, and—on the other hand—Bickerton's Language Bioprogram Hypothesis (see *Bickerton, Derek*); which lay 65 years in the future.

See also: Pidgins and Creoles; Pidgins and Creoles: Morphology; Pidgins, Creoles and Change.

Bibliography

Gilbert G G 1980a Introduction. In: Gilbert G G (ed.) 1980b
Gilbert G G (ed. and transl.) 1980b *Pidgin and Creole Languages: Selected Essays by Hugo Schuchardt*. Cambridge University Press, Cambridge
Gilbert G G 1985 Hugo Schuchardt and the Atlantic Creoles: A newly discovered manuscript 'On the Negro English of West Africa.' *AS* **60**: 31–63

Schuchardt H 1882 Kreolische Studien I. Über das Negerportugiesche von S. Thomé. *Sitzungsberichte der kaiserlichen Akademie der Wissenschaften zu Wien (philosophisch–historische Klasse)* 101(2): 889–917

Schuchardt H ca.1891 Kreolische Studien X: *Über das Negerenglische von Westafrika*, ms.

Schuchardt H 1909 Die Lingua Franca. *Zeitschrift für romanische Philologie* 33: 441–61

Schuchardt H 1914 *Die Sprache der Saramakkaneger in Surinam.* Müller, Amsterdam

G. G. Gilbert

Schütz, Alfred (1899–1959)

Alfred Schütz, a phenomenologist, philosopher, and sociologist, was born in Vienna in 1899 and died in New York in 1959. He studied law and the social sciences at the University of Vienna and early became interested in the work of Max Weber (see *Weber, Max*), the influential German sociologist, especially in Weber's effort to establish a methodological foundation for the social sciences. Schütz was influenced by phenomenology, particularly by the work of the philosopher Edmund Husserl (see *Husserl, Edmund*) to whom he dedicated his first major work in 1932, *Der Sinnhafte Aufbau der Sozialen Welt* (translated in 1967 as *The Phenomenology of the Social World* but literally, the 'meaningful construction of the social world').

Schütz left Austria prior to the arrival of the Nazis, went to Paris for one year and then emigrated to the United States in 1939 where he later became lecturer and professor at the New School for Social Research in New York. He continued to publish articles and papers throughout his life, all of which were assembled posthumously in three volumes of *Collected Papers* published in 1962, 1964, and 1966. His major work, incomplete at his death, has subsequently been completed by Thomas Luckmann, his former student, in two volumes titled *The Structures of the Life-World* (1974, 1989).

Schütz used phenomenological methods and insights to ground, for example, a theory of ideal types, to develop a philosophy of the social sciences and also to undertake studies of the world of everyday life. He took as the fundamental problem of the social sciences the study of the world of everyday life and of the commonsense reality that is shared by members of society in a taken-for-granted manner.

His various essays dealt with such topics as: concept and theory formation in the social sciences; the relation of phenomenology to the social sciences; the analysis of intersubjectivity, multiple realities, language in society, symbols and reality; the problem of rationality; the description and analysis of such social phenomena and situations as the stranger, the homecomer, the well-informed citizen, and making music together; and the structures of the life-world including such topics as the natural attitude, idealities of 'and so forth' and 'I can do it again,' of relevance structures, of spatio–temporal stratifications of the life-world, of the social distribution of knowledge and of language and communication. His analyses provide a strong foundation for a sociology of knowledge and for a philosophy of the social sciences which takes seriously the exploration of the role of knowledge at the level of everyday discourse in the constitution of the social world.

Specifically with regard to language, his focus on types and typifications developed and utilized in society led him to emphasize how language incorporates 'relative natural conceptions of the world approved by respective linguistic groups' and that 'what is worthwhile and . . . necessary to communicate depends on the typical, practical, and theoretical problems which have to be solved and that these will be different for men and women, for the young and for the old . . . and in general, for the various social roles assumed by the members of the group' (Schütz 1962: 349).

Schütz saw language as 'a system of typifying schemata of experience, which rests on idealizations and anonymizations of immediate subjective experience' (Schütz and Luckmann 1974: 233). This view would necessarily lead to studies of terms and categories and of types and typifications of all manner of social experiences as these are embedded and incorporated in linguistic usages. Although he himself did not pursue such studies, his perspective is compatible with those who study the development, usage, and social distribution of formulations of everyday knowledge in language.

See also: Ethnomethodology; Ideal Types; Phenomenology; Sociology of Language; Weber, Max.

Bibliography

Schütz A 1932 *Der Sinnhafte Aufbau der Sozialen Welt.* Springer, Vienna; 2nd edn., 1960 (Walsh G, Lehnert F 1967 *The Phenomenology of the Social World.* Northwestern University Press, Evanston, IL)

Schütz A 1962–1966 *Collected Papers*, vols. I, II, III. Nijhoff, The Hague

Schütz A, Luckmann T 1973 *The Structures of the Life-World*, vols. I, II. Northwestern University Press, Evanston, IL

Wagner H R (ed.) 1970 *Alfred Schütz on Phenomenology and Social Relations: Selected Writings.* University of Chicago Press, Chicago, IL

Wagner H R 1983 *Alfred Schütz: An Intellectual Biography.* University of Chicago Press, Chicago, IL

G. Psathas

Scientific Nomenclature

Our understanding of the world is powerfully shaped by science, and science expresses itself through distinctive terminology. Although science has the most modern vocabulary, it draws heavily upon dead languages. Intended to provide an unambiguous, exact picture of reality, it may at times inhibit insight and distort communications through its choice of words. Each science has its own linguistic character, and the division between the natural and social sciences is as great as any that separates language families.

1. Word Origins

Scientific nomenclature is in many respects more disciplined than ordinary vocabularies. International organizations make it their business to standardize usage, and every term receives a formal definition almost the minute it is born. Yet the sources of scientific terminology are many, and the complex processes by which new words emerge are worthy of linguistic study.

1.1 Classical Languages

Classicist John Hough was not far from the mark when he said that nearly 100 percent of scientific terminology is Latin or Latinized Greek. But this is true because biology and chemistry have huge vocabularies and both draw heavily upon Classical roots, while some other sciences primarily take their words from non-Classical sources. As recently as the eighteenth century, scientific essays were commonly written in Latin, which still served as the international language. When Guyton de Morveau published his influential memoir on chemical terminology in the 1780s, he urged readers to employ the generally known dead languages so that a word's meaning would be suggested by its roots.

German science draws less heavily upon classical languages than do French or English (Pinchuck 1977), often translating Classical roots into German equivalents, as in the case of *Wasserstoff* 'hydrogen,' both *Wasser-* and *hydro-* meaning water. Lancelot Hogben suggested that modern Latin-based chemical language spread from French to English far more readily than to German because the latter lacked many important suffixes, derived from Latin and Greek, already possessed by French and English, such as *-ic* and *-ous*. However, equivalent suffixes do exist in German, and the German tendency to use its own roots, rather than Classical roots, extends to all aspects of vocabulary. Subsequently, of course, chemical nomenclature has evolved considerably, including the substantial abandonment of these suffixes to indicate valence state, but many of the roots employed today to create new terms are still Classical in origin.

Some Classical words have been taken from Latin or Greek without significant changes of meaning: *tibia* 'shin bone,' *edema* or *oidema* 'swelling.' Others have been adapted through often inventive metaphors, as when Galen called the human tail bone the *coccyx* 'cuckoo' because it resembled a bird's beak. But most scientific concepts have no parallel in Classical languages, so terminology has been constructed out of general-purpose roots. Consider the modern instrument called the *electron microscope*. *Electron*, and all related words, are drawn from the Greek word for amber, because one traditional way of generating static electricity was to stroke fur or cloth with amber. *Micro-* 'small' and *-scope* 'look at' or 'see into' are Greek roots used in many combinations.

A wealth of standard prefixes and suffixes makes it easy to produce many words from a few roots. Practically every organ of the body can become diseased, inflamed, or cut out, producing a technical term ending in *-osis*, *-itis*, or *-ectomy*. John Hough notes that suffixes take different spellings, depending on the route by which they made their way to English. The Greek suffix *-sia* appears in words like *apepsia* taken directly into English, or like *magnesia* brought through Latin, while transit through French modifies it, as in *epilepsy*.

Although the wealth of meaning that can be garnered from Classical languages makes scientific word coinage easy, errors arise if one tries to deduce an unfamiliar term's meaning by translating Latin or Greek roots into English. Perhaps the best example is *schizophrenia* 'split mind' or

'split personality.' Popular writers and the general public persist in believing that the term denotes the existence of multiple personalities within a single person, but this is wrong. The split is between different aspects of a single personality, as when thought and emotion become detached from each other causing radically inappropriate reactions to events.

Great confusion centers on the pronunciation of Classically derived scientific words. Theodore Savory noted eight different ways the word *epigyne*, which refers to an organ of female spiders, could be pronounced. Speakers disagree as to whether it has three syllables or four, a hard *g* or a soft one, a long or short initial *e*. In part, such confusion stems from lack of training in Classical languages and from competing official systems of pronouncing Latin and Greek. But Savory believes another important cause is the fact that scientific communication relies so heavily upon the printed rather than the spoken word.

1.2 Personal Names

For more than a century scientific associations have named units of measurement after famous scientists and engineers, and today practically every such unit possesses a former proper name. At its first meeting in 1881 the International Electrotechnical Commission approved the words *volt*, *ampere*, *ohm*, and *watt*. The first commemorates the Italian electrical pioneer, Alessandro Volta. André Marie Ampère and Georg Simon Ohm were scientists from France and Germany, while James Watt was a British steam engine inventor. Neither English nor German uses the accent applied by the French to *ampère*, and the colloquial American version is simply *amp*. *Ohm* is frequently abbreviated as the Greek letter Omega (ω or Ω). It is said that the international acceptance of *watt* was impeded for a few years by the difficulty of using the letter 'w' in French.

Aside from the honor bestowed upon the eponymous scientists, the purpose of this practice is to create an internationally recognized scientific terminology that is not bound to any one language. The cost, often, is the loss of transparency of meaning. The standard unit of vibration, whether in acoustics or radio, is the *hertz*, adopted in 1933 by the International Electrical Commission, defined as a frequency of one cycle per second. However, Americans have spoken of *cycles per second* (or *cps*), and the adoption of *hertz* may have obscured the meaning of the unit, especially for people who were not professionally involved in one of the related sciences.

Complete international uniformity has not yet been achieved. A year after telephone inventor Alexander Graham Bell died, the Bell telephone company in the USA adopted the name *bel* to measure the ratio of two powers as a logarithm to the base ten, which gave rise to the popular unit, the *decibel*. In Europe, the *neper* is more commonly used, defined as the ratio of two powers expressed as a natural logarithm and derived from the Latinized version (Nepero) of the name of the great Scottish mathematician and inventor of logarithms, John Napier.

A person's name may be attached to many different kinds of scientific concept. Edwin Hubble discovered that the light from distant galaxies appears shifted toward the red end of the spectrum, a phenomenon now called the *Hubble effect*. It is usually interpreted to mean that they are moving away from us and that the universe is expanding. In 1929 he proposed that a galaxy's recession velocity equals a constant times its distance. This conjecture became known as *Hubble's law*, and the constant as *Hubble's constant* (notated by H). Its reciprocal is the time elapsed since the expansion began, the *Hubble time*, and this is usually taken to be the age of the universe. After Hubble's death, his name was proposed for a unit of vast distance, 1,000,000,000 light years; it has also been given to a large space telescope launched in 1990.

1.3 Other Origins

In paleontology and archaeology, scientific concepts are often given the names of places where the first or most prominent example was found, sometimes called the 'type site.' *Neanderthal* man is named after the Neander valley in Germany. Place names may be transformed when they are assigned to scientific concepts, as when the Jura mountains of Switzerland gave their name to the *Jurassic* geological period; and the names used are not always the vernacular, as with the *Cambrian* period from the Latin *Cambria* 'Wales.' Astronomers frequently name general categories of objects after a particular example. *Cepheid* variable stars get their name from the first one discovered, Delta Cephei. Victims can also be commemorated, as in the case of *Legionnaires' Disease* named after participants at an American Legion convention whose sickness led to its discovery. Thus, both a distant star and a disease victim can be conceptualized as the site where the type was discovered.

Mathematicians and physicists enjoy adapting common words for exotic purposes, sometimes with confusing results for their students. In physics the word *work* is defined in terms of force exerted over a distance, while the ordinary person might feel that pushing against a heavy object was work even if the object did not move. What the English-speaking mathematician calls *a set* the German calls *eine Menge*, a term that is often translated into English as 'a great quantity or crowd.' The ordinary meanings of the words may color their technical meanings in different ways: the English word implies that a fixed ordering principle unites the members of the set, while the German word hints that a large number of members belong to it. One wonders if students learning mathematics through the two languages have different sets (or Mengen) of difficulties in understanding the concept.

Analogies are common. In computer science, a *bit* is the smallest possible piece of data, a contraction of 'binary digit.' The physical architecture of computers and programming practice generally work with eight-bit units, called *bytes*, and four-bit units are occasionally called *nibbles*. Here an apt pun on the word 'bit' evokes the imagery of the human jaw biting off various sizes of data unit. The *spin* of an electron is similar to the rotation of a large object, but not precisely the same, and users of the word may differ in the extent to which they are aware they are using an analogy.

Also common are terms like *bit* that are abbreviations of their definitions. A *light year* is the distance light travels in a year, and a *parsec* the distance that produces a PARalax of one SECond of arc. Acronyms are most common in scientific language drawn from technology, but may arise whenever

a long standard phrase is used often. Names may consist of a string of letters that are meant to be spelled out, rather than pronounced: astronomers frequently refer to nebulae and galaxies whose names consist of *NGC* 'New General Catalogue' followed by a number. Subcategories of a phenomenon are often designated by letters of the alphabet, not always in alphabetical order; the spectral classes of stars can be remembered from the initial letters of: 'Oh Be A Fine Girl, Kiss Me.' Nationwide contests have failed to find a popular alternative to this sexist mnemonic.

2. The System of Paleontology

Every natural science illustrates the development of systematic nomenclature, with all its advantages and disadvantages, but paleontology is an especially rich example. Like other branches of biology, paleontology employs a system for naming organisms derived from the work of Carl von Linné, known also by the Latin form of his name, Linnaeus. The heart of the terminology is the *binomen*, a name stating both genus and species, the former being invariably capitalized and often abbreviated, the latter not. We belong to *Homo sapiens* 'thinking man.' Our generic name is *Homo*, and our specific name is *sapiens*. *H. erectus* is an earlier, extinct member of the same genus.

2.1 Principles of Zoological Nomenclature

The concept of species takes note of the fact that living forms exist in separate breeding communities that cannot reproduce with each other. The concept of genus notes that some species are very similar in form. Linnaeus apparently conceived of each genus as an association of species grouped around a type, and he selected a type species to describe it. In addition, genera are grouped together into orders, and orders into classes. The Linnaean system was devised 250 years ago, under intellectual influences that might seem antiquated or irrelevant today, the philosophies of Plato and Aristotle and the Christian belief that God created each species separately according to a coherent plan. Yet in large measure, the system remains in force in the late twentieth century.

Each species discovered by paleontologists must be named in accordance with a strict set of rules. In 1985, the General Assembly of the International Union of Biological Sciences issued a new edition of the international code of zoological nomenclature, in a book published with alternate pages in English and French. Collectively, all taxonomic categories are known as *taxa*, the plural of *taxon*. To be valid a name must be spelled in Latin letters (including j, k, w, and y—with j and v commonly used for i and u when they are consonants), with no diacritic or other marks. If not Latin in origin, it must be Latinized by giving it a Latin termination. Kangaroo, from the Kokoimudji language, became *Kangurus*. Because many names are drawn from Greek, the code includes detailed instructions for Latinizing Greek words, based greatly on how the Classical Romans used to do it.

The generic name is a noun, and the specific name may be a noun or adjective. Under a somewhat complex set of circumstances a specific name must agree in gender with its generic name, according to the rules of Latin. This means that attention must be given to determining the gender of the nouns, not always an easy task. Authors are asked to explain the origins of names they propose and may state their gender as well, not necessarily identical with the gender that the Romans would have assumed. *Dendrocygna* is feminine, despite the fact that it derives from *cygnus*, which is masculine. Endings of variable gender are usually taken to be masculine, as in the case of *Sylvicola*; although most Latin nouns ending in -*a* are feminine, exceptions include *agricola* 'farmer.' Latinized Greek terms with -*us* ending are masculine, regardless of the gender of the original Greek word. Words from other European languages possessing gender generally take the gender they had in that language, and words of non-European origin are masculine unless the author who first employs the word announces otherwise.

Tradition has ascribed one or the other gender to entire categories of animals and plants, but the discoverer of a species is free to innovate. 'Dinosaurs' (not a scientific taxon) whose names end in -*saurus* have masculine gender because the suffix is the masculine Latinized form of the Greek *sauros* 'lizard'—for example, *Tyrannosaurus rex* 'tyrant lizard king.' But when paleontologist John R. Horner discovered a genus of dinosaurs whose mothers apparently gave tender loving care to their children, he stressed its maternal quality by naming it *Maisaura* 'good mother lizard' with feminine gender.

According to the principle of priority, the oldest appropriate name given to a taxon is the valid name, and the purpose of this rule is to preserve stability in terminology. In particular cases the Commission may decide to overturn this rule in favor of a widely used name, but this is seldom done. Because priority of publishing is so important, the code found it necessary to define at length what 'publishing' was, excluding, for example, distribution of xeroxed handouts to a group of students, and to offer instructions on how to establish the exact date on which a publication occurred. If two synonymous appropriate names have been used, the senior synonym is valid and the junior synonym is invalid. Thus, in a sense, one of the most popular dinosaurs, *brontosaurus*, and the dawn-horse, *eohippus*, do not exist. These names are junior synonyms for *apatosaurus* and *hyracotherium.*

Among the central concepts of the system is the principle of name-bearing types. As in the work of Linnaeus himself, each genus is defined in terms of a type species, and each higher-level taxon also possesses a defining type, such as a type genus. Species are defined in two ways, through systematic verbal descriptions in scientific publications and through representative specimens placed in museum collections. A *holotype* is the single specimen upon which a taxon is based in the original publication. If a taxon is based on a collection of specimens, they constitute the *type series*, and one may be subsequently singled out as the representative *lectotype*, or the entire series may be considered *syntypes*.

2.2 Problems with the Nomenclature

The Linnaean system has served science well for a quarter of a millennium, and the insight that species can be grouped into genera and higher-level taxa has been tremendously productive. But in a number of ways, the nomenclature may be at variance with objective reality and retard scientific advance. For example, if evolution is a process of gradual change in the gene pool of a breeding population, then the concept of species becomes ambiguous when applied to different points in the development of a single lineage. A person is the same species as his or her grandparents, but if someone's family were to be traced back half a million years or so, their ancestors were members of *H. erectus*, not *H. sapiens*. Where does one draw the line between these two species, if one gradually evolved out of the other? The term *chronospecies* is sometimes applied to such cases, to indicate that the assignment of specimens to separate taxa is somewhat arbitrary.

During the 1980s, a number of paleontologists became dissatisfied with gradualistic models of evolution and argued that change is saltational (jumpy), long periods of equilibrium being punctuated by relatively brief periods in which one species suddenly emerges from another. These paleontologists take the concept of species very seriously, and many of this group belong to a school of analysis called *cladism* or *cladistics* whose main business is the comparison of species (Cracraft 1981). Thus the definition of species is inextricably tied up with competing conceptions of evolutionary process, and the nomenclature of a field is saturated with its major theoretical assumptions (Gingerich 1985).

Quantitative studies frequently attempt to chart changing rates of evolution and biological diversity based on counts of taxa. If paleontologists have been overzealous in splitting specimens into many taxa, then the rate of evolution will appear high. Among the factors that cause names to proliferate unnecessarily is the competition for honor between paleontologists, because a species is permanently connected in the literature with the name of its discoverer. The chief practical use of paleontology is as a tool for dating strata of rock, and paleontologists may focus on every tiny detail of fossils that are used for this purpose, such as ammonites, thus splitting them into far more species than was done for other fossils. There may also be a tendency to give different names to very similar specimens in the same lineage found in adjacent strata which have already been given different names.

Published data seldom permit statistical analysis of numbers of species, but of genera and families, and these higher-level taxa are largely human constructs (Culver, et al. 1987). To be sure, species are objectively related in varying degrees, and paleontologists may share a general sense of how different two specimens have to be to be assigned to different classes rather than orders. But for each category of fossils, the particular pattern of distinctions used to establish higher-level taxa is the result of tradition developed by the particular people who have worked on it over the years. Thus, terms like 'class' may not be comparable in meaning when applied to different kinds of organism.

Since the 1960s, paleontology like many other sciences has begun to employ numerical taxonomy, a variety of quantitative methods for categorizing. In principle, an approach based on objective measurement would be superior to the Linnaean system, dispensing with names for genera, families, orders, and classes in favor of precise numbers expressing how closely species or specimens were related. The results have been quite mixed, however. For one thing, one often has to rely upon human judgment concerning which features of an organism are important and which trivial. Overall size is easy to measure, but often is not considered to be defining; an ant and a spider may be of identical size, but the different number of legs is seen as decisive. In addition, different statistical techniques often give different results.

Thus, for the foreseeable future, paleontology will continue to use a system of nomenclature developed long ago and based on a very different set of assumptions about the world than held by paleontologists working in the late twentiety century. A number of potential problems with the system have been noted, but it is impossible in the early 1990s to evaluate the extent to which the words used to categorize fossils may inhibit or channel scientific progress.

3. Nomenclature and the Social Sciences

The social sciences are frequently accused of pretending expertise by giving obscure names to perfectly ordinary things (*consociate* 'friend'), and they clearly have not achieved the intellectual coherence or terminological stability of the natural sciences. Indeed, debates still rage over what Karl Marx meant by *alienation*, and terminological consensus does not exist outside narrow, well-disciplined schools of thought. Yet sociologists and social historians have begun to study language use among natural scientists, with sometimes interesting results.

3.1 Social Scientific Terminology

The social sciences tend to lack units of measurement altogether, and this may be a sign of their immaturity. One can imagine a sociological measure of anomie called the *durkheim*, after the French sociologist, Emile Durkheim, who wrote much on this concept at the end of the nineteenth century. But subsequent scholars have disagreed greatly over what anomie is, and a unit of measurement cannot be defined until the phenomenon in question has been unambiguously identified. For Durkheim, anomie was a crisis of meaning that could beset societies, reflected in the suicide rate. Thus, a durkheim could be a rate of one suicide per million population per year. But suicide has many causes, and there even remains some question whether anomie is among them. Many sociologists have defined anomie as social disorganization or personal disorientation, and others have employed the term in novel ways without even offering a definition.

George Homans has seriously questioned whether most terms used to describe features of human societies are defined adequately for scientific purposes. He calls definitions that unambiguously state how to measure the phenomenon 'operating definitions,' because they tell one how the terms operate in scientific propositions and permit one to work with them. In contrast, he says, many central concepts in sociology and anthropology, such as *role* and *culture*, are 'nonoperating definitions' because they fail to define variables that can appear in testable propositions. At best, they can serve to orient a discussion toward certain vague topics. Homans doubts that coherent societal-level phenomena actually exist, and thus that real sciences of sociology and anthropology are possible, and he suggests we may have to be content to analyze social behavior in terms of concepts about individuals, for example, reducing sociology to psychology.

Max Weber (see *Weber, Max*) advocated a method of defining sociological concepts called 'Ideal Types' (see *Ideal Types*), but it has been widely ignored outside his circle of disciples and has drawn criticism for building definitions that are too ornate to describe reality adequately. For example, the ideal type of religious sect is separated from the secular world, is exclusive in attitude and social structure, emphasizes a conversion experience, has voluntary membership, seeks regeneration, and practices ethical austerity. Real religious organizations may possess any combination of these qualities and cannot be ranked unambiguously in degrees of sectarianism. Many social scientists prefer to work with narrowly defined variables, but the influential theories generally employ global concepts that are very difficult to define and measure, such as 'alienation,' 'modernity,' and 'solidarity.' Frequently, terms are taken out of their intellectual context and the result is pseudoscientific verbiage of uncertain meaning. 'Capitalism,' for example, loses precise meaning outside Marxist analysis, and the word is bandied about quite irresponsibly.

3.2 The Social Construction of Science

Natural scientists generally believe that their work discovers objective facts about reality, and that scientific nomenclature merely assigns names to entities that already exist. Many social scientists take a very different position, contending that reality is not merely described but 'socially constructed' by scientific subcultures. When the science in question is a social science, natural scientists might be quick to agree, since everybody agrees that the social sciences are saturated with political doctrines and other ideologies that color markedly how various phenomena are seen.

Erich Goode argued that naming has political implications and cited the vocabular controversy over mind-altering drugs that raged in the 1960s. The prodrug social movement called the substances *psychedelic* 'consciousness expanding.' Opponents of the movement called them *hallucinogenic* 'hallucination producing' or *psychotomimetic* 'madness mimicking.' Medical doctors railed against *drug abuse*, by which they meant the taking of drugs without paying them to supervise it. Goode noted that such pejorative terms claimed clinical objectivity yet merely expressed the vested interests of the physicians (see *Medicalization*). Different groups in society vary in their conceptions of what is real and they also vary in their access to power and legitimacy. Thus, the scientific status of one or another version of reality becomes a political issue, partly fought out through the names used to identify the terms in the debate.

In the eighteenth century, scientists widely believed in the existence of *phlogiston*, a hypothetical fire substance. In 1774, Joseph Priestley discovered a gas that supported fire exceedingly well, and he called it *dephlogisticated air*, under the theory that it lacked phlogiston and thus was capable of absorbing great quantities of this fire substance. Not long afterwards, Antoine Lavoisier became convinced that Priestley had misunderstood this gas, saying that it was a constituent of ordinary air rather than air from which something had been removed. He first called it *la principe oxygine*, later shortened to *oxygène* 'oxygen.' The name is from the Greek, referring to something that generates things that are sharp to the taste, that is, acids, because Lavoisier believed that the gas produced acids when it combined with other substances. In fact, not all oxides are acids, and not acids are oxides. When German chemists added the concept to their lexicon, they expressed the same incorrect idea in their own language: *Sauerstoff* 'sour stuff.' In working out his own theory Lavoisier had great difficulty shaking off Priestley's assumptions. Yet it cannot be said with certainty that the term 'dephlogisticated air' caused him any special trouble beyond that created by Priestley's scientific reports, and certainly the inappropriate meaning of oxygen and *Sauerstoff* do not seem to give modern chemists any trouble.

These two examples suggest the limits of the social constructionist approach. No scientist uses the word 'phlogiston,' and 'psychedelic' has practically dropped from the lexicon as well, although some scholars continue to claim that the defeat of the psychedelic ideology was political rather than scientific. Research on the social processes that establish facts and give them names in neuroendocrinology (Latour and Woolgar 1979) and particle physics (Pickering 1984) reveal complex social negotiations over what phenomena are to be considered real and how they are to be named. However, in the natural sciences such questions seem to get resolved, sooner or later, and the importance of socially shaped definitions after the initial period of uncertainty and dispute remains to be demonstrated.

See also: Sociology of Knowledge; Sociology of Language; Technological Nomenclature.

Bibliography

Asimov A 1959 *Words of Science and the History Behind Them.* Houghton Mifflin, Boston, MA

Ballentyne D W G, Lovett D R 1980 *A Dictionary of Named Effects and Laws in Chemistry, Physics, and Mathematics*, 4th edn. Chapman and Hall, London

Cahn R S, Dermer O C 1979 *Introduction to Chemical Nomenclature*, 5th edn. Butterworths, London

Cracraft J 1981 Pattern and process in paleobiology: The role of cladistic analysis in systematic paleontology. *Paleobiology* **7**: 456–68.

Culver S J, Buzas M A, Collins L S 1987 On the value of taxonomic standardization in evolutionary studies. *Paleobiology* **13**: 169–76

Flood W E 1960 *Scientific Words: Their Structure and Meaning.* Duell, Sloan, and Pearce, New York

Gingerich P G 1985 Species in the fossil record: Concepts, trends, and transitions. *Paleobiology* **11**: 27–41

Goode E 1972 *Drugs in American Society.* Knopf, New York

Hogben L 1970 *The Vocabulary of Science.* Stein and Day, New York

Holmes F L 1985 *Lavoisier and the Chemistry of Life.* University of Wisconsin Press, Madison, WI

Homans G C 1967 *The Nature of Social Science.* Harcourt, Brace and World, New York

Hough J N 1953 *Scientific Terminology.* Rinehart, New York

Jerrard H G, McNeill D B 1986 *A Dictionary of Scientific Units, including Dimensionless Numbers and Scales.* Chapman and Hall, London

Larson J L 1971 *Reason and Experience: The Representation of Natural Order in the Work of Carl von Linné.* University of California Press, Berkeley, CA

Latour B, Woolgar S 1979 *Laboratory Life: The Social Construction of Scientific Facts.* Sage, Beverley Hills, CA

Mandell A 1974 *The Language of Science.* National Science Teachers Association, Washington, DC

Pickering A 1984 *Constructing Quarks: A Sociological History of Particle Physics.* University of Chicago Press, Chicago, IL

Pinchuck I 1977 *Scientific and Technical Translation.* Andre Deutsch, London

Ride W D L, Sabrosky C W, Bernardi G, Melville R V (eds.) 1985 *International Code of Zoological Nomenclature.* University of California Press, Berkeley, CA

Savory T H 1967 *The Language of Science.* Andre Deutsch, London

Sneath P H A, Sokal R R 1973 *Numerical Taxonomy: The Principles and Practice of Numerical Classification.* W. H. Freeman, San Francisco, CA

W. S. Bainbridge

Scope and Binding

The notions of scope and binding arise in the context of the syntax of formal languages. Those languages typically contain operators O which combine with an expression E to form a compound expression: $O.E$. E is called the 'scope' of O. Variable binding operators are operators which combine with a variable v and an expression E (in which v may have free occurrences) to form the compound expression $Ov.E$. These operators are said to 'bind' the free occurrences of v in E (if any). Well-known examples of variable binding operators are the existential and universal quantifier in first order logic and the lambda operator in typed logic. Interestingly, scope and binding have also been claimed to be relevant notions for the semantic and syntactic analysis of natural languages. Within various formal semantic theories so-called 'scope ambiguities' are analyzed in terms of the scope of certain operators. For example, *A Mac adorns every desktop* can be assigned two readings: 'There is a Mac that adorns every desktop' and 'Every desktop is adorned by a Mac.' These readings can be characterized in terms of the relative scope of the operators *a Mac* and *every desktop*. Moreover, binding of variables by operators is often invoked in representing the relation between anaphoric pronouns and their antecedents. A sentence like *Every Mac says that it has unexpectedly quit* can be represented as: *For every Mac x: x says that x has unexpectedly quit*. Here, *for every Mac x:* is a variable binding operator which binds two free occurrences of x in the expression *x says that x has unexpectedly quit*.

1. Scope and Binding in Formal Languages

In the language of first order logic, a simple English sentence with a transitive verb such as *Tulip admires Apple* corresponds to an atomic formula ADMIRE(*tulip*, *apple*), which is made up of a binary relation, ADMIRE, and two arguments, *tulip* and *apple*. The symbols *tulip* and *apple* are argument-symbols that fill the slots . . . and - - - in the expression ADMIRE(. . . , - - -). First order logic uses *variables* $x, y, z, \ldots$ to mark those slots. So, instead of ADMIRE(. . . , - - -), the atomic formula is written ADMIRE(*x*, *y*) which contains the free variables x and y. There are various operators for forming compound formulas. Thus, the unary negation operator $\neg$ forms a compound formula $\neg\phi$ out of one formula ϕ; and the binary conjunction, disjunction, and implication operators &, $\vee$ and $\rightarrow$ form compound formulas (ϕ & ψ), ($\phi \vee \psi$), and ($\phi \rightarrow \psi$) out of two formulas ϕ and ψ. Moreover, the expressions $\forall$ and $\exists$ can combine with any variable v to yield universal and existential quantifiers $\forall v$ and $\exists v$, respectively.

Like the negation operator, the unary *variable binding operators* $\forall v$ *and* $\exists v$ form compound formulas $\forall v.\phi$ and $\exists v.\phi$ out of one formula ϕ. But the quantifiers also exploit the possible presence of slot-filling variables. For example, the sentence *Everyone admires Apple* is analyzed as $\forall x.ADMIRE(x, apple)$, a compound formula consisting of the operator $\forall x$ and the atomic formula $ADMIRE(x, apple)$. The latter contains a free variable x. In the compound formula $\forall x.ADMIRE(x, apple)$ this variable is said to be in the *scope* of the quantifier $\forall x$, and hence to be 'bound' by it. A formula without free variables is called a 'sentence.' Note that it is occurrences of quantifiers which have scope, and occurrences of quantifiers which bind occurrences of variables, since there are formulas like $(\forall x.PRINT(x)$ & $\forall x.QUIT(x))$ ('Everyone prints and everyone quits'), where the scope of the first occurrence of $\forall x$ is the subformula $PRINT(x)$ and the scope of the second occurrence of $\forall x$ is the subformula $QUIT(x)$. So, the first occurrence of $\forall x$ binds the first occurrence of x, whereas the second occurrence of $\forall x$ binds the second occurrence of x. This is reflected in the following definitions:

(a) If $\forall x.\psi$ (or $\exists x.\psi$) is a subformula of ϕ, then ψ is the *scope* of the indicated occurrence of $\forall x$ (or $\exists x$) in ϕ.
(b) A slot-occurrence of a variable x in the formula ϕ is *free in* ϕ if it does not occur in the scope of a quantifier $\forall x$ or $\exists x$ in ϕ.
(c) If $\forall x.\psi$ (or $\exists x.\psi$) is a subformula of ϕ and an occurrence of x is free in ψ, then that occurrence of x is *bound by* the indicated occurrence of $\forall x$ (or $\exists x$).

The treatment of several quantifying expressions in one sentence is unproblematic in first order logic: the representation of *Everyone admires someone*, $\forall x.\exists y.ADMIRE(x, y)$, can be constructed by universally quantifying over x in $\exists y.ADMIRE(x, y)$, which represents x *admires someone* (itself the result of existential quantification over y in $ADMIRE(x, y)$, the representation of x *admires* y). Notice that whereas $\forall x.\exists y.ADMIRE(x, y)$ is a sentence, its subformulas contain free variables. A stronger reading of *Everyone admires someone*, $\exists y.\forall x.ADMIRE(x, y)$, according to which there is someone who is admired by everyone, can be formed by reversing the order in which the quantifiers are introduced. In the latter sentence, the existential quantifier has scope over the universal quantifier, while in the former sentence the existential quantifier is within the scope of the universal quantifier.

Typed logical languages contain another variable binding operator, the lambda operator λ. The expressions of typed logic are called 'terms.' Every term has a unique type. The set of 'types' consists of primitive types, usually e (the type of entities) and t (the type of truth values), and function types (a, b) formed out of types a and b. A *frame* $\mathbf{D}$ is a set of domains D_a, one for each type a, such that D_e is the set of individuals; D_t is the set of truth values $\{1, 0\}$ (where 1 and 0 represent 'true' and 'false,' respectively); and $D_{(a,b)}$ is the set of functions from objects in D_a to objects in D_b (normally written as $D_b^{D_a}$).

The formal 'language' to refer to objects in such structures consists of the following terms: infinitely many variables x_a of each type a; some typed constants c_a; and the following compound terms: if $\sigma_{(a,b)}$ and τ_a are terms, then $(\sigma)(\tau)$ is a term of type b (*application*); if σ_b is a term and

x_a is a variable, then $\lambda x.\sigma$ is a term of type (a,b) (*abstraction*); and if σ_a and τ_a are terms, then $\sigma = \tau$ is a term of type t (*identity*). A term of type t is called a 'formula.' Syntactically, λx is just a unary variable binding operator, and the above definitions of 'scope,' 'free,' and 'bound' can be extended to it in a straightforward way.

A *model* M is an ordered pair $\langle \mathbf{D}, \mathbf{I} \rangle$, where $\mathbf{D}$ is a frame, and $\mathbf{I}$ is an *interpretation function*: a function such that $\mathbf{I}(c_a) \in D_a$ for each constant c_a. $|\sigma|^{M,g}$, the *extension* or *interpretation* of a term σ in a model $\mathbf{M}$ under a *variable assignment* g (i.e., a function such that $g(x_a) \in D_a$ for each variable x_a; $g[d/x]$ is the assignment g' such that $g'(x) = d$ and $g'(y) = g(y)$ if $x \neq y$) is defined as follows: $|c|^{M,g} = \mathbf{I}(c)$; $|x|^{M,g} = g(x)$; $|(\sigma)(\tau)|^{M,g} = |\sigma|^{M,g}(|\tau|^{M,g})$; $|\lambda x.\sigma|^{M,g} = f \in D_b^{D_a}$ such that for all d: $f(d) = |\sigma|^{M,g[d/x]}$; and $|\sigma = \tau|^{M,g} = 1$ iff $|\sigma|^{M,g} = |\tau|^{M,g}$. Within typed logic, all operators of first order logic are definable in terms of application, abstraction, and identity.

An example: let $P_{(e, t)}$ and x_e be variables which (due to their type) range over (characteristic functions of) sets of individuals and individuals, respectively. Let $PC_{(e,t)}$ and MAL-$FUNCTION_{(e,t)}$ be constants interpreted as (the characteristic function of) the set of personal computers and the set of malfunctioning entities. So, $\lambda P.\exists x.(PC(x)$ & $P(x))$ is a complex term of type $((e, t), t)$ which denotes the function from sets of entities to truth values such that a set is assigned the value 1 if there is a personal computer in that set: a plausible interpretation for the noun phrase *a personal computer*. Next, consider the term $(\lambda P.\exists x.(PC(x)$ & $P(x)))(MALFUNCTION)$ of type t. The value of this term is the above function applied to the set of things that malfunction. It equals 1 if there is a personal computer which malfunctions. In fact, the term is equivalent to the first order formula $\exists x.(PC(x)$ & $MALFUNCTION(x))$. This is an instance of a general equivalence: $(\lambda x.\alpha)(\beta) \Leftrightarrow \alpha[x := \beta]$. Here, $\alpha[x := \beta]$ denotes the result of substituting β for all free occurrences of x in α, and the condition is that the substitution causes no free variable in β to become bound in the result $\alpha[x := \beta]$. The reduction of $(\lambda x.\alpha)(\beta)$ to $\alpha[x := \beta]$ is called 'lambda conversion.'

2. Scope and Binding in Natural Languages

Montague (1974) includes the first explicit truth-conditional semantics for a fragment of English which observes the principle of compositionality: the meaning of an expression is a function of the meanings of its parts and of the way they are syntactically combined. The syntactically minimal parts of the sentence *Everyone admires someone*, for example, are *everyone*, *someone*, and *admires*. Somewhat simplified, the noun phrases are interpreted as the generalized quantifiers $\lambda P.\forall x.(P(x))$ and $\lambda P.\exists y.(P(y))$, typed logic terms of type $((e, t), t)$, while the verb is interpreted as $\lambda T.\lambda v.T(\lambda w.ADMIRE(v, w))$ of type $(((e, t), t), (e, t))$. A rule which constructs verb phrases says that their interpretation is obtained by applying the interpretation of the transitive verb to the interpretation of the direct object. In the case of [$_{VP}$admires someone] this results in the term $(\lambda T.\lambda v.T(\lambda w.ADMIRE(v, w)))(\lambda P.\exists y.(P(y)))$ of type (e, t), which reduces to $\lambda v.\exists y.ADMIRE(v, y)$ after three lambda conversions. A rule building up sentences interprets them as the result of applying the interpretation of the subject to the interpretation of the verb phrase. For [$_S$everyone

$[_{VP}$admires someone$]]$, $(\lambda v.\exists y.\text{ADMIRE}(v, y))(\lambda P.\forall x.(P(x)))$ of type t is the outcome, which reduces to $\forall x.\exists y.\text{ADMIRE}(x, y)$ after two lambda conversions. This way of constructing sentences always yields readings in which the subject takes scope over the direct object.

As illustrated above, the sentence *Everyone admires someone* is assumed to have a stronger reading as well, $\exists y.\forall x.\text{ADMIRE}(x, y)$, in which the direct object noun phrase has wide scope. Notice that this 'scope ambiguity' is not obviously of a lexical or structural nature; the lexical meanings and the syntactic structure involved do not seem to be different. Hence, a second way of constructing the same syntactic structure is needed. For that purpose, Montague introduces an infinite number of so-called 'syntactic variables' PRO_0, PRO_1 ... (noun phrases which are interpreted as $\lambda P.(P(x_0)), \lambda P.(P(x_1)), \ldots)$ plus 'quantifying-in' rules Q_i (for every $i \in N$) that combine noun phrases and sentences. Syntactically, the Q_i are rules of substitution: roughly, if α is a noun phrase, and β is a sentence, then $Q_i(\alpha, \beta)$ is a sentence, and $Q_i(\alpha, \beta)$ results from β by replacing the first occurrence of PRO_i by α, and the remaining occurrences by appropriate anaphoric pronouns. The semantic interpretation of $Q_i(\alpha, \beta)$ is obtained by applying α', the interpretation of α, to $\lambda x_i.\beta'$, where β' is the interpretation of β: $(\alpha')(\lambda x_i.\beta')$. With these devices *Everyone admires* PRO_{17} can be constructed, which is interpreted as $\forall x.\text{ADMIRE}(x, x_{17})$. Applying Q_{17} to that 'sentence' and the noun phrase *someone* gets us *Everyone admires someone*, this time interpreted as $(\lambda P.\exists y.(P(y))\,(\lambda x_{17}.\forall x.\text{ADMIRE}(x, x_{17}))$, which reduces to $\exists y.\forall x.\text{ADMIRE}(x, y)$ after two lambda conversions.

It can be argued that in this particular case the 'wide scope object' interpretation needs no separate representation, since it is stronger than the 'wide scope subject' interpretation. But there are sentences like *A Mac adorns every desktop*, where the situation is the other way round. Moreover, quantifying-in can also take care of logically independent readings. For example, if *seek* is interpreted as SEEK of type $(((e, t), t), (e, t))$, then *FIND FILE seeks a document* gets the '*de dicto*-reading' $\text{SEEK}(FF, \lambda P.\exists x.(\text{DOCUMENT}(x)$ & $P(x)))$. Using quantifying-in, however, produces the '*de re*-reading' $\exists x.(\text{DOCUMENT}(x)$ & $\text{SEEK}(FF, \lambda P.P(x)))$.

In addition to the representation of scope, quantifying-in is used for an analysis of anaphoric pronouns in terms of binding. Thus, PRO_4 *says that* PRO_4 *has unexpectedly quit* is interpreted as $\text{SAY}(x_4, H.U.QUIT(x_4))$. If Q_4 is used to combine this with *every Mac* $(\lambda P.\forall x.(\text{MAC}(x) \to P(x)))$, the sentence *Every Mac says that it has unexpectedly quit* is achieved. Its interpretation reduces to $\forall x.(\text{MAC}(x) \to \text{SAY}(x, H.U.QUIT(x)))$.

There exist, of course, alternatives to Montague's treatment of quantification and bound anaphora. Within the framework of formal semantics, Robin Cooper (1983) has proposed a mechanism for semantically storing quantifiers and pronouns. His approach avoids the 'unintuitive' syntactic features of quantifying-in, but this is accomplished at the price of complicating the semantic component. Hintikka (1974) shows that scope ambiguities may be 'analyzed away' in second order logic by using Skolem functions. More recent semantic proposals concerning quantifier scope (Emms 1990, Hendriks 1993) do without stores, due

to the adoption of flexible interpretation. Syntactically oriented theorists in Generative Grammar and Government Binding (GB) theory have postulated a separate component of the grammatical framework which they call Logical Form (LF). Structures in LF derive from syntactic surface structures by a series of structure-transforming rules such as 'quantifier raising' (see May 1985), which deals with the scope behavior of quantified noun phrases. This rule adjoins a quantified noun phrase to a sentence, which is coindexed with the trace it leaves behind. The trace is 'interpreted' as a variable, so that the resulting structures closely resemble formulas of first order logic.

All mentioned proposals analyze the ambiguities in terms of linearly ordered scope relations between quantified noun phrases, which saddles them with two kinds of problems. First, they predict too much. There are clear cases where wide scope object readings are simply absent: *Zero laser-writers print zero documents* has the reading 'Every laser-writer prints at least one document,' but it does not mean that every document is printed by at least one laserwriter. Second, they predict too little. The sentence *600 Dutch firms own 5000 American computers* has a so-called, cumulative reading, (Scha 1984) in which the noun phrases have 'equally wide' scope: 'The number of Dutch firms owning an American computer is 600, and the number of American computers owned by a Dutch firm is 5000.' (An analogous interpretation is available for *Zero laserwriters print zero documents*.) Whereas the above informal paraphrase shows that this reading can be represented using 'standard' $((e, t), t)$-type quantifiers, the representation has no obvious (i.e., straightforwardly compositional) relationship with the 'standard' syntactic structure of the sentence $([_S NP[_{VP} V\ NP]])$. Finally, Keenan (1987) has shown that the context independent reading of *Every firm owns a different computer* ('The own-relation restricted to firms on its first argument and to computers on its second, is one-to-one') cannot be expressed in terms of $((e, t), t)$-quantifiers at all (see Van Benthem 1989).

The second aspect of quantifying-in, the semantic representation of anaphoric pronouns in terms of bound variables, also has its problems. Its syntax ('replace [...] by appropriate anaphoric pronouns') is hardly explicit, for example, it does not discriminate between pronouns and reflexives: *Everyone admires him* is assigned the reading $\forall x.\text{ADMIRE}(x, x)$ that 'belongs to' *Everyone admires himself*. Some syntactic 'binding theory' *à la* GB is needed (see Landman and Moerdijk 1983). And in its present format (replace 'the *first* occurrence of PRO_i by α, and the remaining occurrences by [...] pronouns'), the mechanism of quantifying-in is unable to account for 'cataphoric pronouns' such as the word *its* in the present sentence. Moreover, anaphoric connection is not always possible, witness the contrast between *No Mac says that it has unexpectedly quit* and *Every programmer who bought no Mac replaced it*. In the latter type of sentences it appears to depend on the nature of the antecedent whether an anaphoric link is permitted or not, whereas quantifying-in will apply indiscriminately in all cases. Besides, anaphoric pronouns cannot without exception be treated as bound variables (Evans 1980, Reinhart 1983). Thus, if a link *is* permitted in a 'donkey sentence' (they owe their name to the particular examples in Geach 1968) like *Every programmer who owns a Mac uses it*, the desired reading $\forall x.\forall y.((PROGRAMMER(x)$ & $MAC(y)$ & $OWN(x, y)) \rightarrow USE(x, y))$ is not obtained; using quantifying-in the only interpretation one gets is $\exists x.(MAC(x)$ & $\forall y.((PROGRAMMER(x)$ & $OWN(x, y))$ $\rightarrow USE(x, y)))$.

This phenomenon has been studied intensively (see Heim 1983, Kamp 1984), and it led to the development of Discourse Representation Theory (DRT). DRT draws a sharp distinction between definite (*the Mac*) and indefinite (*a Mac*) noun phrases on the one hand, and quantified noun phrases (*every Mac, no Mac*) on the other, which enables it to account for 'donkey pronouns' and intersentential anaphora: *A/the/*every/*no man walks in the park. He whistles.* Groenendijk and Stokhof (1990, 1991) show that, contrary to what has been claimed, phenomena like these do not undermine the principle of compositionality. The insights of DRT may very well be incorporated into a compositional theory of dynamic Montague grammar.

Bibliography

Cooper R 1983 *Quantification and Syntactic Theory*. Reidel, Dordrecht

Emms M 1990 Polymorphic quantifiers. In: Barry G, Morrill M (eds.) *Studies in Categorial Grammar*. Centre for Cognitive Science, University of Edinburgh, Edinburgh

Evans G 1980 Pronouns. *LIn* **11**: 337–62

Gamut L T F 1991a *Logic, Language and Meaning. Volume I: Introduction to Logic*. University of Chicago Press, Chicago, IL

Gamut L T F 1991b *Logic, Language and Meaning. Volume II: Intensional Logic and Logical Grammar*. University of Chicago Press, Chicago, IL

Geach P T 1968 *Reference and Generality: An Examination of Some Medieval and Modern Theories*. Cornell University Press, Ithaca, NY

Groenendijk J A G, Janssen T M V, Stokhof M (eds.) 1984 *Truth, Interpretation and Information. Selected Papers from the Third Amsterdam Colloquium*. Foris, Dordrecht

Groenendijk J A G, Stokhof M 1991 Dynamic predicate logic. Institute for Language, Logic, and Information, University of Amsterdam, Amsterdam

Groenendijk J A G, Stokhof M 1990 Dynamic Montague Grammar. In: Kálmán L, Pólos L (eds.) *Papers from the Second Symposium on Logic and Language*. Akadémiai Kiadó, Budapest

Heim I R 1983 *The Semantics of Definite and Indefinite Noun Phrases*. University Microfilms International, Ann Arbor, MI

Hendriks H 1990 *Flexible Montague Grammar*. Institute for Language, Logic, and Information, University of Amsterdam, Amsterdam

Hintikka J 1974 Quantifiers versus quantification theory. *LI* **6**: 153–77

Kamp H 1984 A theory of truth and semantic representation. In: Groenendijk J, Janssen T, Stokhof M (eds.) *Truth, Interpretation and Information*. Foris, Dordrecht

Keenan E L 1987 Unreducible n-ary quantifiers in natural language. In: Gärdenfors P (ed.) *Generalized Quantifiers: Linguistic and Logical Approaches,* Studies in Linguistics and Philosophy No 31. Reidel, Dordrecht

Landman F, Moerdijk I 1983 Compositionality and the analysis of anaphora. *LaPh* **6**: 89–114

May R 1985 *Logical Form: Its Structure and Derivation*. MIT Press, Cambridge, MA

Montague R 1974 *Formal Philosophy*. Yale University Press, New Haven, CT

Reinhart T 1983 Coreference and bound anaphora: A restatement of the anaphora questions. *LaPh* **6**: 47–88

Scha R J H 1984 Distributive, collective and cumulative quantification. In: Groenendijk J A G, Janssen T M V, Stokhof M (eds.) *Truth, Interpretation and Information*. Foris, Dordrecht

Van Benthem J 1989 Polyadic quantifiers. *LaPh* **12**: 437–64

H. L. W. Hendriks

Scots

Scots is a group of dialects spoken in Lowland Scotland, in Orkney and Shetland, and in parts of Ulster. These dialects form a continuum with those of the north of England.

A standard based on the dialect of Edinburgh (then the capital of an independent kingdom) was emerging when Scots was replaced in formal use by Standard English, in the late sixteenth century. The Reformation of 1560 led to the dissemination of the Bible in English and its establishment as the basis of mass literacy. Standard English became the spoken language of the ruling class following the Union of the Crowns in 1603. After the Union of the Parliaments in 1707, this spread to the professional classes, especially in Edinburgh. Attempts to make teachers speak only Standard English in the classroom began with the institution of a national inspectorate in 1845.

The Scots dialects are nowadays perceived by their speakers partly as nonstandard English and partly as the (humble) descendants of what was once a national language. There is no accepted name. 'Scots' or 'Lowland Scots' is favored by academics, 'Lallans' (literally 'Lowlands') by language revivalists, and 'the Doric' in the northeast, where the vernacular is particularly strong. The name 'Scotch,' which was normal amongst an older generation, has been rejected by the educated as an anglicization of 'Scots.'

Nowadays the speakers of Scots are mainly working-class, though it reaches further up the social scale outside central Scotland. Class rather than ethnicity has been the main force in Scottish politics, and this is rather infertile ground for language revivalism. However, this does exist in the Scots Language Society, and in the work of twentieth-century writers such as Hugh MacDiarmid (Christopher Grieve).

Scots is in a sociolinguistic continuum with Scottish Standard English, and is often intermingled with it in practice. As a language variety it is unfocused, and it is therefore impossible to define or enumerate the speakers of Scots.

The separateness of Scots is clearest in the written language. The record is very thin between Old English and Older Scots. The first substantial text in Early Scots (1375–1450) is John Barbour's epic poem *The Brus*, written ca. 1375. The earliest manuscripts are letters and Acts of Parliament from the 1380s. The Middle Scots period (1450–1700) produced such *makars* (poets) as Gavin Douglas, Robert Henryson, and William Dunbar.

The language continued to be written by poets such as Robert Burns and novelists such as Walter Scott and John Galt. Burns and Scott were also amongst the collectors who gave written form to Scots folksong. Singer–songwriters such as Hamish Henderson and the late Matt McGinn continue this popular tradition.

There are many minor differences in grammar from English dialects. Scots preserves a double system of concord in the present tense of verbs. If the subject is a personal pronoun adjacent to the verb, the verb is inflected only in the third person singular. Otherwise the inflection is added in all persons and numbers.

Only the dialects of Orkney and Shetland preserve the second person singular pronoun, in the form *du* 'thou.' A new second person plural form *youse*, introduced from Ulster into Glasgow, is spreading in Central Scots. There is a third term in the demonstrative system: *this*, *that* and *yon* (or *thon*), expressing a further degree of distance from both speaker and hearer.

In Scots, as in English dialects north of the River Humber, Old English *ū* remains /u/ in, for example, 'about, house.' Old English *ā* did not become rounded, but gives modern /e/, for example, *hame*, *stane* corresponding to Standard English 'home, stone.' Old English *ō* was fronted to /ø/, which remains in Orkney and Shetland and Southern Scots, e.g., *do*, *mune* 'moon,' *use*. In the Northeast, this unrounds to /i/, thus *dee*, *meen*, *eese*. In Central Scots, the vowel unrounds to /e/ before voiced fricatives and /r/ and morpheme-finally, thus *dae*, *yaise* (verb), and to /ɪ/ otherwise, thus /mɪn/, /jɪs/ (noun).

Old English *ī* splits into /aɪ/, in the same environments as /e/ from /ø/, e.g., 'five, why'; and /əi/ otherwise, e.g., 'Fife,' 'line'. This /əi/ merges with the reflex of Anglo–Norman *ui* as in *bile* 'boil,' *jine* 'join,' and of *ai* word-finally, e.g., *cley* 'clay,' *hey* 'hey.' Scots influence is seen in a similar [aɪ] ~ [əi] allophony in Canadian English.

The unrounding of *ŭ* to /ʌ/ is complete: there is no /ʊ/ phoneme in Scots, thus 'push, bull,' etc. have /ʌ/.

The phoneme /l/ vocalizes after *ă* and *ŏ* and less regularly after *ŭ*, e.g., *baw* /bɔ/ 'ball,' *gowd* /gʌud/ 'gold,' *fu* /fu/ or *full* /fʌl/ 'full.'

Some of these points can be illustrated thus in Central Scots: *Wirkin fairmers weirs nickie tams o strae rape aroun thir trousers whan they gang out tae dae aw the mucky wark*, i.e., 'Working farmers wear bands of straw rope around their trousers when they go out to do all the dirty work.' /wɪrkɪn fermɪrz wirz nɪke tamz ʌ stre rep ʌrun ðir truzirz ʍʌn ðe gaŋ ut te de ɔ ði mʌke wark/

Scots vocabulary draws on the same sources as English generally. Old Norse is more important than in Standard English, giving, for example, *kirk* 'church,' *brig* 'bridge,' *skellie* 'squint.' The dialects of Orkney, Shetland, and Caithness are particularly heavily influenced by the extinct Scandinavian language, Norn. Middle Dutch gives, for example, *craig* 'the neck,' *redd* 'clear up.' Anglo–Norman gives, for example, *leal* 'loyal,' *hurcheon* 'hedgehog,' and later colloquial French gives, for example, *Hogmanay* 'New Year's Eve.' Literary French and Latin loans were numerous in Older Scots but survive mainly in the terminology of the Scottish legal system, which remains separate under the terms of the Act of Union, e.g., *feu duty* a kind of ground rent, *dispone* 'convey (land).' Gaelic loans are more significant in local dialects north of the River Forth, but examples in general use include *car-* or *corrie-(fistit)* 'left-(handed),' *sonse* 'prosperity' (see *Scottish Lexicography*).

Bibliography

Grant W, Dixon J M 1921 *A Manual of Modern Scots*. Cambridge University Press, Cambridge

Macleod I, et al. (eds.) 1990 *The Scots Thesaurus*. Aberdeen University Press, Aberdeen
Mather J Y, Speitel H-H (eds.) 1975–86 *The Linguistic Atlas of Scotland*, 3 vols. Croom Helm, London
Murison D D 1977 *The Guid Scots Tongue*. Blackwood, Edinburgh
Robinson M, et al. (eds.) 1985 *The Concise Scots Dictionary*. Aberdeen University Press, Aberdeen

C. Macafee

Scots Gaelic

SEE Goidelic Languages

Scottish Lexicography

Scots have been indulging in lexicography since the early seventeenth century; indeed, there appears to be an instinct for it in their psyche. Perhaps because many are brought up as dialect speakers, or speakers of Anglo–Scots, there is an awareness of language differences and deeper observations of the spoken word. But not all go as far as James B. Lindsay of Dundee, who, after graduating from St Andrews in the 1820s, set about compiling a dictionary embracing 50 languages, the design of which was to determine the origin and history of man. When he gave up 20 years later, he turned his mind to a 'Telegraphic Dictionary for the Submarine Telegraph.' This never appeared, though he did publish in 1846 his *Pentecostal Paternoster; or the Lord's Prayer in Fifty Languages*. Such linguistic enterprise and persistence has marked Scottish lexicographers, among whom must be numbered some of the greatest the world has known.

1. The Earlier Contributions

The lexicographical instinct was at first expressed largely in the form of glossaries to other works (cf. Aitken 1989) at the end of the sixteenth century, when Modern Scots had emerged from Middle Scots. Their appearance from this period must relate to a perceived need, flowing either from language changes or pressures from English itself, or simply from the need to explain technical vocabularies. The earliest was one of about 600 words appended to Andrew Duncan's Latin grammar of 1595 (Skeat 1874). The next, a major work, had a legal context. It was by Sir John Skene (ca. 1543–1617), advocate, Clerk Register, and Lord of Session. In preparing a revision of the laws of Scotland, he found it necessary to compile his *De verborum significatione* (Skene 1599). The 1599 edition differs very little from that of 1597; however, it does have at least one additional entry, '*Hebdomas* . . . quhilk signifies sevin.' This 132-page work is an early and notable contribution to Scottish lexicography, with careful reference to the source from which the words come, and an attempt at etymology ('*Infangthefe*, . . . ane Dutch word'—though in fact the word is Old English). The often lengthy definitions, or rather disquisitions, contain much of cultural as well as linguistic interest.

2. The Eighteenth Century

There followed a gap until 1710, when a major glossary appeared, considered since 1770 to be by Thomas Ruddiman. It is a 3,000-word, 88-page glossary to the first modern edition of Gavin Douglas's translation of Virgil's *Æneid*. Ruddiman (1674–1757), born at Boyndie in Banffshire, worked after 1706 with the printer and bookseller Robert Freebairn in Edinburgh. Though he later set up his own printing and publishing business, it was with Freebairn that his Glossary appeared ('Printed by Mr Andrew Symson, and Mr Robert Freebairn, and sold at their Shops, MDCCX'). He was well aware of words 'to this Day used in some parts of Scotland by the Common People,' and gave them a specific indicator. He also added 'a great Number of Scottish Words, Phrases and Proverbs, which are not to be found in our author,' claiming that the Glossary would therefore help with the reading of any book written in Scots. He even carried out field research: 'It was found necessary also to converse with people of the several Shires and Places, where some of the old Words are as yet used. This seem'd the best Method for discovering their true Meaning.' Examples of words so gathered are *brodemell* 'brood, offspring'; *maik* 'a mate, match, equal'; *smure* 'to smother'; *wangrace* 'wickedness'; *reistis* 'door hinges.'

In terms of the shaping of the method of lexicography, Ruddiman not only took into account contemporary and past usages, but also referred to English vernacular usage, employed textual references, provided etymologies, and offered full definitions for the most part (Aitken 1989: 236–37).

For the rest of the eighteenth century, literature and lexicography went hand in hand through glossaries prepared by poets like Allan Ramsay and Robert Burns for their own works. Another fertile source was the publication of lists of 'Scotticisms,' of which speakers and writers were expected to beware (cf. Murison 1987: 18–19; Aitken 1989: 240–41).

3. The Nineteenth and Twentieth Centuries

The early nineteenth century brought the first comprehensive Scottish dictionary, by the Reverend John Jamieson (1759–1838). An Anti-Burgher minister, Jamieson produced not only religious works but also editions of Scottish classics like Barbour's *Brus* and Blind Harry's *Wallace*. These no doubt sparked off an interest in words, but he was further stimulated by a meeting with the Icelander Grim Thorkelin, Professor of Antiquities in Copenhagen. Jamieson, who had regarded Scots as a corrupt form of English, became aware of the many links between Scots and Scandinavian words, and for the next 20 years he collected words from oral and printed sources. By 1802, he was circulating a prospectus for his Scottish dictionary.

Jamieson was not alone, however. An Edinburgh surgeon, Robert Allan, brought out the first part of his *Dictionary of the Ancient Language of Scotland, with the etymons in Anglo–Saxon, Gothic, Danish, Swedish, Islandic, Belgic, Irish, British, Gaelic, Latin, and French* in 1807, basically a compilation of eighteenth-century Scots words collected by his father. His definitions were good, and he clearly understood the origins of Scots to lie in Old English (unlike Jamieson, who saw Scots as Norse-derived). But the first part was the last part, and the field was left open for Jamieson.

Jamieson's *An Etymological Dictionary of the Scottish Language* appeared in two volumes in 1808 and a further two in 1825. There were abridged editions in 1818 and 1867. J. Johnstone edited an 1841 edition, J. Longmuir and D. Donaldson an edition in 1879–82, and Donaldson a Supplement in 1887. Yet it is not fully published; of the 12 MS volumes in the National Library of Scotland, volumes X–XII have not seen the light of day yet in the early 1990s. The material, however, is incorporated in the *Scottish National Dictionary*. Jamieson's was a massive personal achievement, influenced in its method and treatment by the later editions of Samuel Johnson's *Dictionary of the English Language* (see *Johnson, Samuel*), and was a treasure trove of ethnological information, even if it fell short in terms of etymologies, indications of pronunciation, forms of headwords (spelling), and the like.

It sparked off a series of smaller dictionaries, some derivative, some independent (e.g., Picken 1818; Motherby 1828; Brown 1845; 'Cleishbotham' 1851), and the first technical dictionary in Scots (Barrowman 1886). Also to be noted are the dictionaries or glossaries of local speech or dialect. The earliest is Mactaggart's (1824) *Gallovidian Encyclopedia* (he includes an entry on himself under *Mactaggart*). Others appeared in the 1860s (e.g., Edmondston 1866: Shetland and Orkney; Gregor 1866: Banffshire), and several others followed in the twentieth century (e.g., Angus 1914: Shetland; Watson 1923: Roxburghshire; Marwick 1929: Orkney; Jakobsen 1928–32: Shetland; Graham 1979, 1984: Shetland; Lamb 1988: Orkney). Some of these, such as Marwick and Jakobsen, showed outstanding scholarship.

In the meantime, the Philological Society of England had been gathering material for a dictionary of English. James Murray (knighted in 1908) became involved in editing the *New English Dictionary* (later *Oxford English Dictionary*) in 1878 (see *Oxford English Dictionary*). The tribulations of this enormous task were many, but Murray played a leading role in the work until his death in 1915. The *OED* was completed in 1928 (Murray 1979). Murray was a Scot, a Borderer from Denholm; because of his knowledge of Scots and because Scottish literature is also part of the heritage of English, the *OED* includes much Scots material. The *OED* must also be considered in association with Scots lexicography in itself, and because of its influence on the two great Scottish dictionaries, the *Scottish National Dictionary* and the *Dictionary of the Older Scottish Tongue*, and on their editors. All of these share the system of using extracted literary quotations, first used by Johnson. They make use of teams of helpers, largely voluntary, as readers and extractors, following the method of the *Deutsches Wörterbuch* of the brothers Jacob and Wilhelm Grimm (Murray 1979: 134, 136; see also *Grimm, Jacob Ludwig Carl*). In the days before computers, the editors sorted material on slips of paper arranged in pigeonholes or boxes, attempting to find illustrative quotations for the senses and gradations of meanings in simple and compound words over the full range of the period covered.

To the *OED* editorial team was added in 1901, after a period of apprenticeship begun in 1897, another Scot, the Dundonian (Sir) William Alexander Craigie (1867–1957).

He is important for Scottish lexicography in particular and English lexicography in general. In 1907, the Scottish Branch of the English Association adopted his suggestion to collect words, and William Grant, later the first editor of the *SND*, was put in charge. In 1919, Craigie further proposed a series of period dictionaries of English, to include the classical period of Scots up to 1700, and modern Scots from 1700 onwards. The outcome was the *DOST*, edited by Craigie, and the *SND*, edited by Grant, in 1929.

Grant died in 1946, and David Donald Murison (1913–) took over as editor. By 1976, when the *SND* was complete in 10 volumes, including a supplement which is a revision of the earlier volumes, Murison had personally edited seven-eighths of the whole work, with the help of a small group of assistant editors (for example, Alexander Fenton edited the 275 pages of the letters K, N, and O) overseeing every entry as the work proceeded (for details, see Aitken 1983: viii ff.). The *SND* totals 4,676 pages containing about 150,000 illustrative quotations (Aitken 1987: 92–3).

In 1956, after Craigie had relinquished his interest in the *DOST* to Edinburgh University, Professor Adam Jack Aitken (1921–) became editor, having been assistant to Craigie from 1948–56. He held the post for 30 years until 1986, when he retired. His successors were the late Dr James Stevenson, and Harry Watson.

The *DOST* is bigger than the *SND*, since it aims at a complete record for the period which it covers (ca. 1100–1700). It is compiled from around 1,500,000 quotation slips containing over 200,000,000 words. The *SND*, on the other hand, records the dialects that are all that remain of the Older Scots of Stewart Scotland; it treats only distinctively Scots words and distinctively Scots senses of otherwise English words. For each dictionary, coverage of individual words is deliberately encyclopedic, with much cross referencing. They are indices not only to the language, but also to the entire culture that they represent for a period of over 800 years, thanks especially to the intensive programs of excerpting undertaken by Murison, Aitken, and their helpers (cf. Aitken 1980: 33–56). The *DOST* is in print up to Part XLII, *Ru* to *Sanct*, giving a total so far of seven complete volumes, one part of volume 8, and 5,151 pages to date (1992).

The *DOST* and the *SND* have become the fundamental dictionaries on which other, smaller dictionaries must depend, for between them they deal with over 50,000 words peculiar to Scots in form or meaning. An earlier exception was Alexander Warrack's *Chambers Scots Dialect Dictionary* (1911). Warrack had excerpted much post-1700 Scottish material for Joseph Wright's *English Dialect Dictionary*, and later extracted the Scottish words in the *EDD* for his own dictionary, including English literary words which had a Scottish sense. Jamieson was also a major source. He did not attempt to localize words, or to give etymologies, as the *DOST* and especially the *SND* do.

Other dictionaries relating to regional forms of Scots have already been mentioned. An attempt to cover Scots as a whole is William Graham's *The Scots Word Book*, with 4,000–5,000 entries for Scots into English and about 6,000 for English into Scots. The major influential piece of Scottish lexicography of the late twentieth century, however, is Mairi Robinson's *Concise Scots Dictionary*. Published in

1985, it takes into account the source material from the *DOST*, the *SND*, and also the *OED*. Its 815 pages hold about 25,000 main entries. It indicates time-spans and the location or distribution of every word and every meaning. It gives etymologies and indicates pronunciations. For one-volume dictionaries, it is a unique and pioneering work, made possible by the exact scholarship of its parent volumes.

In turn, the *CSD* has spawned two further works through the Scottish National Dictionary Association (SNDA). One is *The Pocket Scots Dictionary*, inexpensive and widely usable for educational purposes. The second is *The Scots Thesaurus*, which categorizes 15 major themes within the word-hoard of Lowland Scots. Room remains for another volume, and the *SNDA* has plans for this, as for other material, using a computerized database.

Scottish lexicography is alive and well, and is also being aided by the Scottish Office, which in the early 1990s has given financial support to the SNDA and to the *DOST* (for the latter through The Friends of the *DOST*).

Bibliography

Aitken A J 1983 Foreword. In: McClure J D (ed.) *Scotland and the Lowland Tongue: Studies in the Language and Literature of Lowland Scotland in Honour of David D Murison*. Aberdeen University Press, Aberdeen

Aitken A J 1987 The lexicography of Scots: The current position. *Review of Scottish Culture* 3: 91–6

Aitken A J 1989 The lexicography of Scots 200 years since: Ruddiman and his successors. In: *In Other Words: Transcultural Studies in Philology, Translation, and Lexicology Presented to Hans Heinrich Meier on the Occasion of his 65th Birthday*. Foris Publications, Dordrecht

Angus J S 1914 *A Glossary of the Shetland Dialect*. Alexander Gardner, Paisley

Barrowman J 1866 *Glossary of Scottish Mining Terms*. W. Naismith, Hamilton

Brown T 1845 *A Dictionary of the Scottish Language*. Simpkin and Marshall, London

Cleishbotham the Younger 1851 *A Handbook of the Scottish Language*. David Bryce, Glasgow

Edmondston T 1866 *An Etymological Glossary of the Shetland and Orkney Dialect*. Asher, London

Graham J G 1979 *The Shetland Dictionary*. The Thule Press, Stornoway

Graham W 1980 *The Scots Word Book*. The Ramsay Head Press, Edinburgh .

Gregor W 1866 *The Dialect of Banffshire*. Asher, London

Jakobsen J 1928–32 *An Etymological Dictionary of the Norn Language in Shetland*. David Nott, London

Jamieson J 1808 *An Etymological Dictionary of the Scottish Language*. W Greech, A Constable, and W Blackwood, Edinburgh

Jamieson J 1825 *An Etymological Dictionary of the Scottish Language*. W and C Tart, Edinburgh

Lamb G 1988 *Orkney Wordbook: A Dictionary of the Dialect of Orkney*. Byrgisey, Birsay

Macleod I, Cairns P, Martin M A R 1988 *The Pocket Scots Dictionary*. Aberdeen University Press, Aberdeen

Macleod I, Cairns P, Martin M A R, Macafee C 1990 *The Scots Thesaurus*. Aberdeen University Press, Aberdeen

Mactaggart J 1824, 1876 *The Scottish Gallovidian Encyclopedia*. Hamilton, Adams and Co., London

Marwick H 1929 *The Orkney Norn*. Oxford University Press, London

Motherby R 1828 *Taschen-Wörterbuch des Schottischen Dialekts.* Königsberg

Murison E 1987 Scottish lexicography. In: Macafee C, Macleod I *The Nuttis Schell: Essays on the Scots Language.* Aberdeen University Press, Aberdeen

Murray E K M 1979 *Caught in the Web of Words: James A H Murray and the Oxford English Dictionary*, 2nd edn. Yale University Press, New Haven, CT

Picken E 1818 *A Dictionary of the Scottish Language.* Edinburgh

Robinson M 1985 *The Concise Scots Dictionary.* Aberdeen University Press, Aberdeen

Ruddiman T 1710 *Virgil's Æneis, Translated into Scottish Verse, by the Famous Gawin Douglas, Bishop of Dunkeld . . . To Which is Added a Large Glossary, Explaining the Difficult Words: Which May Serve as a Dictionary to the Old Scottish Language.* A Symson and R Freebairn, Edinburgh

Skeat W W (ed.) 1874 *A[ndrew] Duncan, Appendix Etymologiae.* English Dialect Society

Skene Sir J 1597 *De Verborum Significatione. The Exposition of the Termes and Difficill Wordes, Conteined in the Fovre Bvikes of Regiam Majestatem, and vthers in the Actes of Parliament, Infeftments, and vsed in Practicque of this Realme, with Diuerse Rules, and Commoun Places, or Principalles of the Lawes.* Robert Waldegrave, Edinburgh

Warrack A 1911 *A Scots Dialect Dictionary Comprising the Words in Use from the Latter Part of the Seventeenth Century to the Present Day.* Chambers, London

Watson G 1923 *The Roxburghshire Word-Book, Being a Record of the Special Vernacular Vocabulary of the County of Roxburgh, with an Appendix of Specimens.* Cambridge University Press, Cambridge

Wright J 1898–1905 *The English Dialect Dictionary.* Henry Frowde, London

A. Fenton

Scripts, Indian, Northern

In no modern country are so many parallel writing systems in use as in India, where since the nineteenth century scripts have become very powerful cultural symbols of religious and regional linguistic identity. This is graphically exemplified by the use of the right-to-left Perso–Arabic script to write those modern Indo–Aryan languages predominantly spoken by Muslims, notably Urdu and Kashmiri, as well as other languages of Pakistan. It is still more remarkably to be seen in the continuing and full contemporary vitality of no less than five visually distinctive scripts of the indigenous north Indian group, written from left to right. The most widely diffused is the Nagari script, historically and culturally closely associated with Sanskrit, and in the twentieth century used to write two national languages, Hindi and Nepali, also Marathi. North-eastern India and Bangladesh are dominated by the Bengali script, also used to write Assamese. Oriya has its own script, as does Gujarati, while the sacred associations to Sikhism of the Gurmukhi script underlie its use to write Panjabi in India. The extraordinary variety of the north Indian group becomes still more apparent if account is taken of a comparable number of barely obsolete members, in addition to these five modern standard scripts. With the partial exception of abbreviated commercial shorthands, the accuracy and economy of the north Indian scripts in indicating such typical features as retroflex articulation and consonantal aspiration makes them far superior as writing media for Indo–Aryan languages to both the Perso–Arabic and Roman scripts.

1. Origin and Development

As a consequence of the primacy of oral transmission in the Hindu tradition, the details of script development are less clearly attested in India than in the Middle East or Europe. The essential characteristics of all north Indian scripts (Diringer 1968(1): 257–97) are nevertheless already clearly present in their phonetically highly sophisticated common ancestor, the classical Indian Brahmi script (Dani 1963) used to write the Prakrits of the Ashokan inscriptions of the third century BC, above all the principle of syllabic writing with the distinctive feature that vowels following a consonant are differentiated by the use of subsidiary signs (called *mātrā*) graphically subordinate to it. Typologically, this places both them and the closely related South Indian scripts between the consonantal-syllabic Semitic scripts and the fully alphabetical Greco–Roman systems.

The more immediate ancestor of the north Indian scripts is the imperial Gupta script of the fourth to sixth centuries AD (from which the Khotanese and the modern Tibetan scripts derive, and from whose numerals the Arabic numerals are borrowed). By the eleventh century AD this had developed into the script whose standard status in northern India is indicated by the name Nagari ('City Script'), and whose characteristic square-shaped syllabary reflects its writing by pen or brush with Indian ink. The alternative name Devanagari ('Script of the City of the Gods') indicates a particular association with Sanskrit which has important implications for its organization. The design of the Brahmi script reflects the characteristic syllabic structure of Middle Indo–Aryan, with its prevalence of open V or CV syllables. Sanskrit, however, has many closed CVC or CCVC syllables. In order to accommodate the resulting sequences of two (or rarely three) consonants, Nagari developed a quite elaborate inventory of some 170 conjunct clusters, in which a part of the first consonant is typically joined to the second, a short subscript stroke being used for the very common combinations with *-r-*. A special convention denotes closed syllables ending in *-r* by a superscript hook (*repha*) written above the following consonant. The difficulty of reading Sanskrit is considerably increased by the conventions of word sandhi, the final letter of one word in a verse or sentence being combined with the initial letter of the next, resulting in long graphic sequences joined by a continuous horizontal line from which the letters appear to hang.

With the introduction of printing to India and the concomitant development of Hindi (H) and the other new Indo–Aryan languages in the early nineteenth century, this convention was abandoned in favor of word division, and the indigenous vertical stroke used as an equivalent of the full stop was amplified by the borrowing of English punctuation marks (along with such graphic devices as bold styles, although not of italics or the Roman script's distinction of capital letters). In writing the numerous *tatsama* loans from Sanskrit (Sk), all the modern scripts other than Gurmukhi do, however, continue to employ the conjunct consonants, in spite of their considerable awkwardness for printing or typing (though they are more easily computer-generated). Further conventions have evolved for writing consonant

The Nāgarī script

Vowels:

अ a   आ ā   इ i   ई ī

उ u   ऊ ū   ऋ (ri)

ए e   ऐ ai   ओ o   औ au

Consonants (+ -a):

क ka	ख kha	ग ga	घ gha	ङ ṅa
च ca	छ cha	ज ja	झ jha	ञ ña
ट ṭa	ठ ṭha	ड ḍa	ढ ḍha	ण ṇa
त ta	थ tha	द da	ध dha	न na
प pa	फ pha	ब ba	भ bha	म ma
य ya	र ra	व va	ल la	
श śa	ष ṣa	स sa	ह ha	

Consonants + vowels:

कः (kaḥ)	कं kaṃ	क ka	कां kāṃ	का kā	
किं kiṃ	कि ki	कीं kīṃ	की kī	कुं kuṃ	कु ku
कूं kūṃ	कू kū	कृ (kri)	कें keṃ	के ke	
कैं kaiṃ	कै kai	कों koṃ	को ko	कौं kauṃ	कौ kau

Dotted consonants:

क़ qa	ख़ <u>kh</u>a	ग़ <u>g</u>a	ज़ za

ड़ ṛa	ढ़ ṛha	फ़ fa

Illustrative conjunct consonants:

क्क kka	क्ख kkha	क्त kta	क्य kya	क्र kra	क्ष kṣa
ज्ञ jña	त्त tta	त्त्व ttva	त्य tya	त्र tra	न्द्र ndra

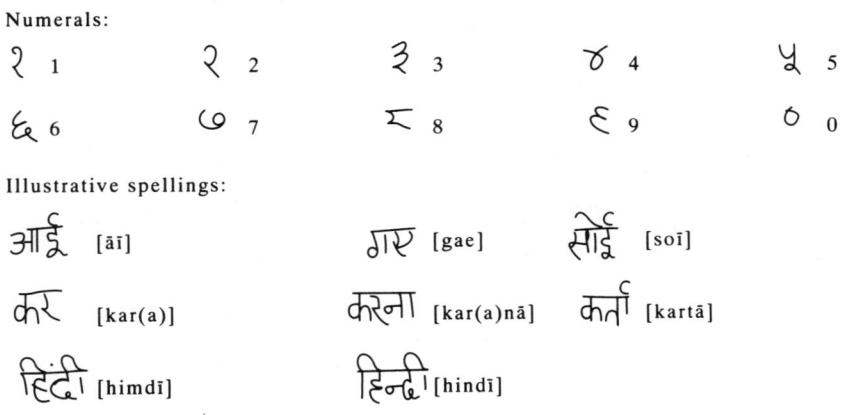

Numerals:

२ 1   २ 2   ३ 3   ४ 4   ५ 5

६ 6   ७ 7   ८ 8   ९ 9   ० 0

Illustrative spellings:

आई [āī]   गए [gae]   सोई [soī]

कर [kar(a)]   करना [kar(a)nā]   कर्ता [kartā]

हिंदी [himdī]   हिन्दी [hindī]

John 3:16 in Hindi:

क्योंकि परमेश्वर ने संसार से ऐसा प्रेम रखा कि अपना एकलौता
पुत्र दे दिया, कि जो कोई उस पर विश्वास करे, नष्ट न हो, परंतु शाश्वत
जीवन पाए ।

[kyomki parameśvara ne samsāra se aisā prema rakhā ki apanā]
kyomke parmeśvar ne sansār se aisā prem rakhā ke apnā
[ekalautā putra de diyā, ki jo koī usa para viśvāsa kare,]
eklautā putr de diyā, ke jo koī us par viśvās kare,
[nasta na ho, paramtu śāśvata jīvana pāya.]
nast na ho, parantu śāśvat jīvan pāe.

Figure 1

sequences in non-Sanskritic words, as described here for
the contemporary Nagari orthography of modern Hindi
(Lambert 1953; McGregor 1977: 22–30; Shackle and Snell
1990: 26, 35–7).

2. The Nagari Script

Of the 43 letters of the alphabet, the first 11 denote open
V syllables containing one of the 10 Hindi vowel-phonemes,
plus Sk *r* (=H *ri*). Letter names are formed from their
sounds plus—*kār*, i.e., *akār, ākār*, etc. The alphabetical
arrangement of the following 33 consonantal letters according to position, aspiration, and voicing, reflects the sophistication of the Sanskrit phoneticians, although some are
now subphonemic in Hindi. They are all regarded as containing the inherent vowel *a*, other vowels in CV syllables
being variously indicated by a preceding stroke (-*i*), following strokes (-*ā*,-*ī*,-*o*,-*au*), subscripts (-*u*,-*ū*,-*r*) or superscripts
(-*e*,-*ai*). Simple vowels are alphabetically preceded by nasalized vowels, indicated by either a superscript dot (*anusvār*)
or a dot within a half moon (*candrabindu*), the distinction
between the two not being entirely logical or consistent.
These are in turn preceded by *tatsama* words containing
vowel plus *h*, called *visarga*. While additional consonants
(mostly subphonemic in Hindi) are straightforwardly distinguished by a subscript dot, e.g., [q z ṛ] from [k j ḍ], the
graphic system makes it harder to mark additional vowels,
though a semi-circle above [-ā] may be used to indicate /ɔ/
in such English loanwords as H *ḍākṭar* 'doctor.' Like the
other north Indian scripts, Nagari has a distinctive set of
numerals, though Western numerals are also employed.

Both the most ambiguous and the most cumbrous
features of Hindi orthography concern the writing of consonants in non-CV contexts. In addition to special conventions for writing certain vowels, e.g., [-i] or [-ya] for final

e, the absence of the inherent vowel *a* must be indicated in
Sanskrit by a short subscript stroke (*virāma*, H *halant*), a
resource often employed in printed Hindi to indicate the
first member of graphically awkward consonant combinations. As a consequence of postmedieval phonetic change,
Hindi has lost *a* in nearly all final and many medial positions, rendering the use of *halant* redundant if at the cost
of ambiguity. Thus in native words written [kara], [karanā]
correspond to *kar* 'do!' and *karnā* 'to do.' But in loans from
Perso–Arabic and English, the *tatsama* system of conjunct
clusters, including the superscript *repha* (H *reph*) is generally employed, for example, so *farz* 'duty,' *vārḍ* 'ward,'
kartā 'creator' are spelt [farja, vārḍa, kartā]. A double system of orthography also prevails in the writing of noninitial
clusters composed of nasal + homorganic plosive, for which
two conventions are in simultaneous use, either that already
established in Brahmi of using a superscript mark of nasalization or the alternative use of a conjunct consonant, hence
for *hindī* 'Hindi' alongside the preferred [himdī], the
spelling [hindī] is also possible.

Although Marathi and Nepali share the Nagari script,
their autonomy from Hindi is jealously preserved. A distinctive typeface is used in printed Marathi, which employs
numerous orthographic conventions not found in Hindi,
including an additional letter for retroflex *ḷa*, added to the
end of the alphabet (as also in the Oriya and Gujarati
scripts). The separate status of Nepali as a national language is symbolically demonstrated by extensive use of the
halant and conjunct consonants to indicate the absence of *a*,
and by deliberate preference for conjuncts in nasal clusters.

3. Other North Indian Scripts

Sharing with Nagari the tendency for handwriting to be
closely linked to printed forms, i.e., only semicursive in

Other North Indian scripts A

John 3:16 in Bengali:

কারণ ঈশ্বর জগৎকে এমন প্রেম করিলেন যে, আপনার
একজাত পুত্রকে দান করিলেন, যেন, যে কেহ তাঁহাতে
বিশ্বাস করে, সে বিনষ্ট না হয়, কিন্তু অনন্ত জীবন পায়।

John 3:16 in Oriya:

କାରଣ ଈଶ୍ୱର
ଜଗତକୁ ଏତେ ପ୍ରେମ କଲେ ଯେ ସେ ଆପଣା
ଅଦ୍ୱିତୀୟ ପୁତ୍ରଙ୍କୁ ଦାନ କଲେ, ଯେପରି ଯେ କେହି
ତାହାଙ୍କଠାରେ ବିଶ୍ୱାସ କରେ, ସେ ବିନଷ୍ଟ ନ
ହୋଇ ଅନନ୍ତ ଜୀବନ ପ୍ରାପ୍ତ ହେବ ।

John 3:16 in Gujarati:

કેમ કે દેવે જગત પર એટલી પ્રીતિ કરી
કે તેણે પોતાનો એકાકીજનિત દીકરો આપ્યો,
એ સારુ કે જે કોઈ તેના પર વિશ્વાસ કરે તેનો
નાશ ન થાય, પણ તે અનંતજીવન પામે.

John 3:16 in Panjabi (Gurmukhi)

ਕਿਉਂਕਿ
ਪਰਮੇਸ਼ੁਰ ਨੇ ਜਗਤ ਨੂੰ ਅਜਿਹਾ ਪਿਆਰ ਕੀਤਾ ਜੋ
ਉਹ ਨੇ ਆਪਣਾ ਇਕਲੌਤਾ ਪੁੱਤ੍ਰ ਬਖ਼ਸ਼ ਦਿੱਤਾ ਤਾਂ ਜੋ
ਹਰੇਕ ਜੋ ਉਸ ਉੱਤੇ ਨਿਹਚਾ ਕਰੇ ਹਲਾਕ ਨਾ ਹੋਵੇ
ਪਰ ਸਦੀਪਕ ਜੀਉਣ ਪਾਵੇ

Figure 2

nature, the autonomy of the other modern scripts (Masica 1991: 137–51; Zograph 1982: 197–205) is guaranteed by a visual appearance so distinctive as to prevent mutual comprehension. The separate status of the proto-Bengali script is attested from at least ca. 1000 AD, although the standardization of spikily elegant modern Bengali script dates, as with Nagari, from the nineteenth century. The Oriya script is a separate offshoot from proto-Bengali, in which the letter shapes are dwarfed by large circular flourishes. As in the case of the south Indian scripts which the Oriya script superficially resembles, these are thought to originate from the need to avoid horizontal lines in the traditional method of writing by incising with a stylus on palm leaves. The modern Gujarati script is a more recent offshoot from Nagari (still employed for printing Old Gujarati texts), being a nineteenth-century standardization of the local semicursive hand, hence its distinctive lack of the Nagari horizontal word stroke. Rules for word division follow Marathi rather than Hindi norms, e.g., the practice of writing postpositions together with their preceding noun.

The fundamental structural features described for Nagari govern these three scripts also, besides others surviving until

Other North Indian scripts B

	Nagari	Bengali	Oriya	Gujarati	Gurmukhi
a	अ	অ	ଅ	અ	ਅ
ā	आ	আ	ଆ	આ	ਆ
kā	का	কা	କା	કા	ਕਾ
i	इ	ই	ଇ	ઇ	ਇ
ki	कि	কি	କି	કિ	ਕਿ
ī	ई	ঈ	ଈ	ઈ	ਈ
kī	की	কী	କୀ	કી	ਕੀ
u	उ	উ	ଉ	ઉ	ਉ
ku	कु	কু	କୁ	કુ	ਕੁ
ū	ऊ	ঊ	ଊ	ઊ	ਊ
kū	कू	কূ	କୂ	કૂ	
r̥	ऋ	ঋ	ଋ	ઋ	
kr̥	कृ	কৃ	କୃ	કૃ	
ē	ए	এ	ଏ	એ	ਏ
kē	के	কে	କେ	કે	ਕੇ
ai	ऐ	ঐ	ଐ	ઐ	ਐ
kai	कै	কৈ	କୈ	કૈ	ਕੈ
ō	ओ	ও	ଓ	ઓ	ਓ
kō	को	কো	କୋ	કો	ਕੋ
au	औ	ঔ	ଔ	ઔ	ਔ
kau	कौ	কৌ	କୌ	કૌ	ਕੌ
ka	क	ক	କ	ક	ਕ
kha	ख	খ	ଖ	ખ	ਖ
ga	ग	গ	ଗ	ગ	ਗ
gha	घ	ঘ	ଘ	ઘ	ਘ
ṅa	ङ	ঙ	ଙ	ઙ	ਙ
ca	च	চ	ଚ	ચ	ਚ
cha	छ	ছ	ଛ	છ	ਛ
ja	ज	জ	ଜ	જ	ਜ
jha	झ	ঝ	ଝ	ઝ	ਝ
ña	ञ	ঞ	ଞ	ઞ	ਞ
ṭa	ट	ট	ଟ	ટ	ਟ
ṭha	ठ	ঠ	ଠ	ઠ	ਠ
ḍa	ड	ড	ଡ	ડ	ਡ
ḍha	ढ	ঢ	ଢ	ઢ	ਢ
ṇa	ण	ণ	ଣ	ણ	ਣ
ta	त	ত	ତ	ત	ਤ
tha	थ	থ	ଥ	થ	ਥ
da	द	দ	ଦ	દ	ਦ
dha	ध	ধ	ଧ	ધ	ਧ
na	न	ন	ନ	ન	ਨ
pa	प	প	ପ	પ	ਪ
pha	फ	ফ	ଫ	ફ	ਫ
ba	ब	ব	ବ	બ	ਬ
bha	भ	ভ	ଭ	ભ	ਭ
ma	म	ম	ମ	મ	ਮ
ya	य	য	ଯ	ય	ਯ
ra	र	র	ର	ર	ਰ
la	ल	ল	ଲ	લ	ਲ
va	व	ব	ଵ	વ	ਵ
śa	श	শ	ଶ	શ	ਸ਼
ṣa	ष	ষ	ଷ	ષ	
sa	स	স	ସ	સ	ਸ
ha	ह	হ	ହ	હ	ਹ
ṛa	ड़	ড়	ଡ଼		ੜ

Figure 3

the twentieth century, like the Sharada script formerly used to write Sanskrit by the Brahmins of Kashmir. All, for instance, share the rules of historical spelling for Sanskrit *tatsamas* and, while the phonemic structures of Bengali, Assamese, Oriya, and Gujarati naturally determine particular local orthographic conventions, rules for the phonetic realization of the graphically inherent *a* are also very similar.

Although it is visually the closest to Nagari, the Gurmukhi script used by the Sikhs for writing Panjabi is typologically the most individual. It has proved the sturdiest survivor of a formerly very widespread subgroup which might be termed 'semilearned' in view of its intermediate position between learned scripts of the Nagari type on the one hand and the commercial shorthands on the other. Other members at different stages of obsolescence include the Kaithi script associated with the scribal Kayasth caste of northern India, the Khojki script of the Ismaili Muslims of western India, the Hindu–Sindhi script abortively promulgated by the British in the late nineteenth century, and the Modi script formerly very widely used as an everyday and administrative script for Marathi.

These semilearned scripts contrast with the Nagari type in having a reduced syllabary, e.g., 35 for Gurmukhi against the Nagari 43, often eliminating some distinctive vowel graphemes as well as signs for consonants found only in Sanskrit. They also represent a reversion to the Brahmi model in largely eliminating the conjunct consonants of the learned scripts, besides such precise marks as the *halant*. Thus in place of conjuncts, Gurmukhi has only subscripts to indicate -*r*- and -*h*- (and a rarely used *v*-). The awkward Nagari dichotomy between native and *tatsama* spellings is thus avoided, if at the consequence of extending the ambiguity of inherent *a*, e.g., the Gurmukhi spelling of Sk *kartā* 'creator' as [karatā]. The doubled consonants so generally retained in Panjabi from Middle Indo–Aryan are indicated as in Brahmi by writing a single consonant, versus the conjunct obligatory in Nagari, e.g., Panjabi [makhan] = *makkhan* 'butter' versus H [makkhan]. A modern Gurmukhi refinement, doubtless inspired by the Arabic *tashdīd*, indicates such doubling by a superscript semicircle (*addhik*), but its use remains erratic.

Extremes of simplification are reached in the commercial shorthands proper, used in a great variety of regional forms for many centuries as business and revenue scripts. The Mahajani script of northern India still has some currency among shopkeepers, though it is tellingly now generally taught through Nagari. Dispensing not merely with consonant clusters, but also with most vowel signs (though vowel letters are sometimes erratically inserted as *matres lectionis*), Mahajani is famously easier to write than to read, given that, for example, [krt] may represent not simply *kartā* but also *karte*, *kīrti*, *kr̥t*, etc.

Bibliography

Dani A H 1963 *Indian Palaeography*. Oxford University Press, Oxford

Diringer D 1968 *The Alphabet*, 2 vols, 3rd edn. Hutchinson, London

Lambert H M 1953 *Introduction to the Devanagari Script*. Oxford University Press, London

Masica C P 1991 *The Indo–Aryan Languages*. Cambridge University Press, Cambridge

McGregor R S 1977 *Outline of Hindi Grammar*, 2nd edn. Oxford University Press, Delhi

Shackle C, Snell R 1990 *Hindi and Urdu since 1800*. School of Oriental and African Studies, London

Zograph G A 1982 *Languages of South Asia*. Routledge and Kegan Paul, London

C. Shackle

Scripts, Indian, Southern

Dravidian languages like Tamil, Kannada, Telugu and Malayalam which have some of the longest histories in the world have had their own scripts from very ancient times. The scripts used for these languages are derived from Brāhmi which is the mother of all the scripts used for the languages of Hinduistic origin and the non-Muslim languages of the surrounding countries. The earliest inscriptions in Brāhmi date to third century BC. According to some scholars a few can also be assigned to about the fourth century BC on paleographical grounds.

Among the scripts used for the Dravidian languages, which are of immense linguistic and literary value, the Tamil–Brāhmi script which can be assigned to about the fourth–third century BC is the earliest. Of the other scripts used for Dravidian languages, Kannada and Telugu had a common script for about one thousand years from about the fifth–sixth century AD, after which they got separated. Even to this day most of the letters in these two scripts are similar. The Grantha and Vaṭṭeḻuttu scripts which were in use in the Malayalam speaking area gave birth to the Malayalam script during the thirteenth century AD. A few of the Dravidian languages spoken in small regions in South India have their own scripts which are based on the major scripts of the area. For example some inscriptions in the Tulu language predominantly spoken in the South Kanara district of Karnataka are engraved in a script which is a modified form of Malayalam. Nowadays, however, the regional language of the State, Kannada, is used for printing works in Tulu.

1. Kannada-Telugu Script

This script, known as Kannada-Telugu or Telugu-Kannada, took shape in about the 5th century AD and continued for about one thousand years as a common script, after which it branched into the Telugu and Kannada scripts. The southern Brāhmi script prevalent in the Karnātaka-Andhra region came to be used for Kannada and Telugu inscriptions respectively during the middle of the fifth and early part of the sixth century AD. The western and the central Indian varieties of the southern alphabet also influenced the formation of this script. The serif above the consonantal letters is a legacy of the Bhaṭṭiprōlu (Guntur District, Andhra Pradesh) script of about third century BC, which influenced the scripts of the Andhra-Karnataka region throughout the early centuries of the Christian era.

From the fifth century onwards the script developed during the reign of the Kadambas, Western Gaṅgas, Chalukyas of Vātāpi, Rāṣṭrakūṭas, Chālukyas of Kalyāna, Kalachuryas (of Karnataka), Hoysaḷas, Yādavas, and their

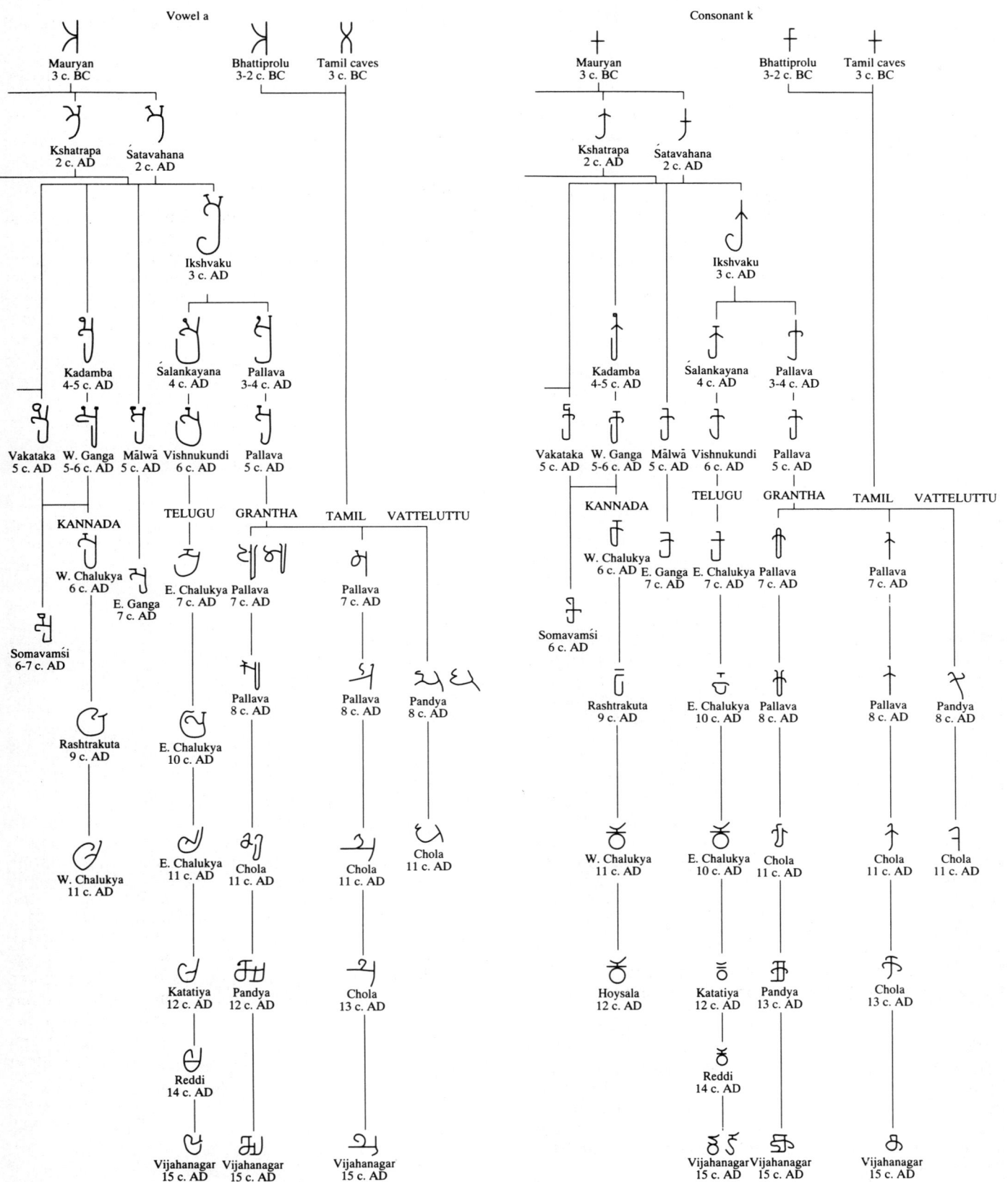

Figure 1. Development of Dravidian Scripts

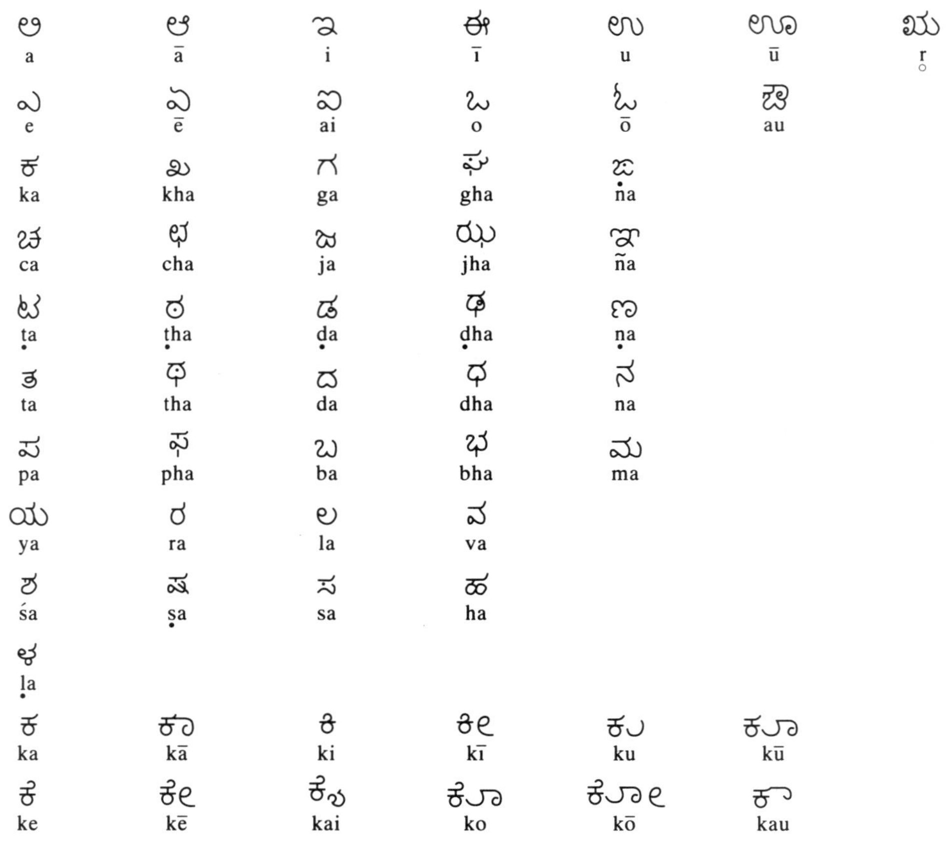

a	ā	i	ī	u	ū	ṛ
e	ē	ai	o	ō	au	
ka	kha	ga	gha	ṅa		
ca	cha	ja	jha	ña		
ṭa	ṭha	ḍa	ḍha	ṇa		
ta	tha	da	dha	na		
pa	pha	ba	bha	ma		
ya	ra	la	va			
śa	ṣa	sa	ha			
ḷa						
ka	kā	ki	kī	ku	kū	
ke	kē	kai	ko	kō	kau	

Figure 2. Kannada Script

feudatories in Karnataka and the Telugu-Chōḍas, Eastern Chālukyas, Kākatiyas, Reddys and other regional families in the Andhra region. It continued as a common script up to about the fifteenth century AD when the Vijayanagara dynasty was in power in South India. Subsequently, a few letters like *ka* (ₔ, ₔ), *chha* (ₔ), *sha* (ₔ), *ha* (ₔ) etc. underwent slight modification and appear as slightly different shapes in the present day Kannada and Telugu scripts. The two scripts contain the following vowels *a, ā, i, ī, u, ū, ṛi, e, ē, ai, o, ō, au* (the vocalic symbols *ṛī, ḷi, ḷī*, theoretically part of the script, are not used); the *anuswāra* (*aṁ*) and *visarga* (*aḥ*); the 25 *vargīya-vyañjanas* (classified consonants) and *anunāsikas* (class nasals) like *k, kh, g, gh, ṅ; c, ch, j, jh, ñ; ṭ, ṭh, ḍ, ḍh, ṇ; t, th, d, dh, n; p, ph, b, bh, m* and the other consonants like *y, r, l, v, ś, ṣ, s, h, ḷ, ḷ,* and *ṛ*. Thus both the Kannada and Telugu scripts have 54 letters. The conjunct consonants *kṣ* and *jñ* also are regarded as regular parts of the script.

The Dravidian letters *viz. ḷ* and *ṛ* form part of the alphabetic system from the earliest stage. The script contains resources for expressing practically all the sounds of any Dravidian and Sanskrit language. There is also a facility to combine any vowel with any consonant. Most of the medial vowel signs are attached at the top. The sign for *ā* attached to the top of the letter has a downward curve on its right side and the sign of *u* is attached below the letter. There are separate signs for subscripts in a few cases, while in the rest the consonants in their original form (without the serif) are used as sub-scripts. From about the fifteenth

century AD, a separate sign (ₔ) was introduced in Kannada for indicating the long medial vowels *ī, ē* and *ō*. In Telugu an additional curve (*c*) was attached at the top of such letters. A vertical lines was attached to the bottom of the letter *b* to make it aspirate (ₔ).

About the numerical system it can be noted that in the initial stage modified forms of some letters were used as numerals, but they gradually developed into distinct numerical symbols which are retained to this day.

From the point of view of the development of these two scripts it can be noticed here that the letters appear longish during the fifth to about seventh century AD, while during the eighth–ninth centuries AD, their length is slightly reduced and the letters look wider. From tenth century onwards they attain a fairly roundish form. The script between eleventh–thirteenth centuries AD appears very beautiful and at times the letters are embellished with ornamentation. For example the Kannada script during the Hoysaḷa period can be quoted here. Other noteworthy features are as follows: The *anuswāra* was placed at the top of the letter up to about the eighth century AD and subsequently immediately after the letter. The standard script which was in use during the fifth–sixth centuries AD popularly known as the Kadamba script is known as the box-headed variety of the Southern alphabet, where the boxes were squarish, the space within them being completely blank. This can be classified as the urban variety of the script. There was another variety which did not have box-heads but ordinary serifs, which (as reflected in the

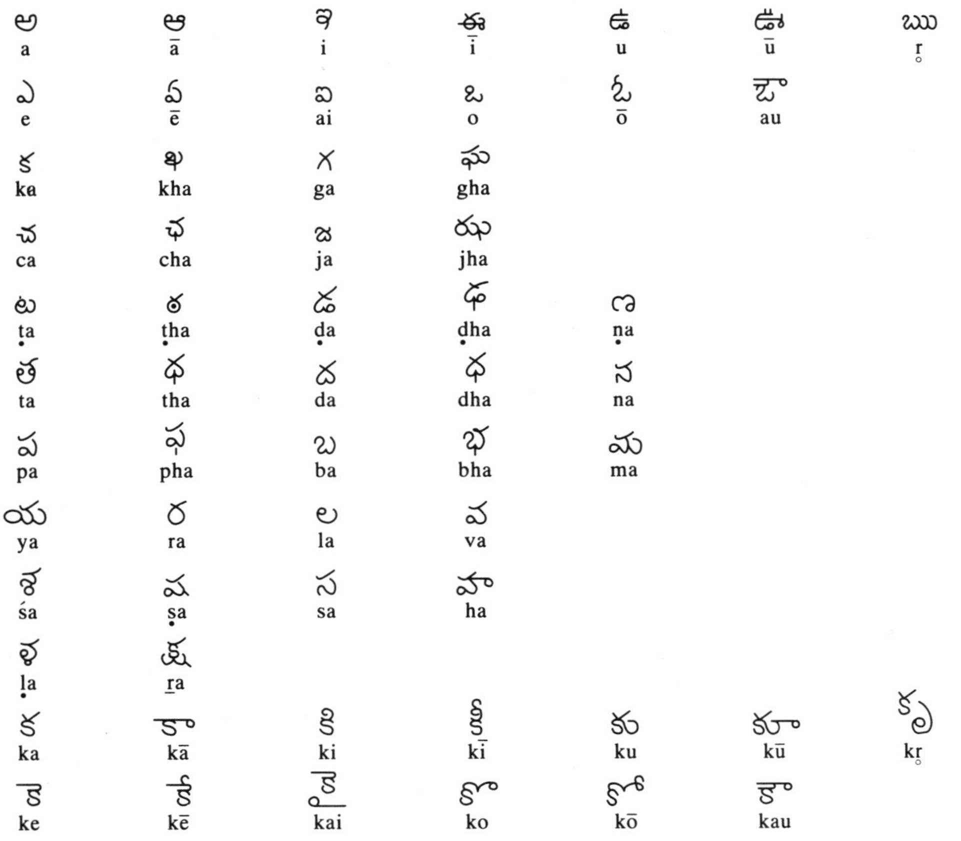

a	ā	i	ī	u	ū	ṛ
e	ē	ai	o	ō	au	
ka	kha	ga	gha			
ca	cha	ja	jha			
ṭa	ṭha	ḍa	ḍha	ṇa		
ta	tha	da	dha	na		
pa	pha	ba	bha	ma		
ya	ra	la	va			
śa	ṣa	sa	ha			
ḷa	ṟa					
ka	kā	ki	kī	ku	kū	kṛ
ke	kē	kai	ko	kō	kau	

Figure 3. Telugu Script

earliest Kannada Inscription from Halmidi, Hassan District, Karnataka) can be regarded as its rural variety. It can also be noted that though from the paleographical points of view the script during any particular century showed a standard form of letters, there were always some regional stylistic variations (like the Rāshṭrakūta, Vaidumba, Nolamba and Bāna styles of writing during the eighth–ninth centuries AD). Between eighth and fourteenth century AD the letters *ma*, *ya* and *va* had also cursive forms which were alternately used in the inscriptions. It may also be mentioned that most of the letters in the present day Kannada and Telugu scripts appear completely different from their original forms while letters like *ga* and *sa* retain their original shapes significantly. (See Figs. 1, 2, and 3).

2. Tamil, Vaṭṭeluttu, Grantha, and Malayālam scripts:

2.1 Tamil

The earliest Tamil inscriptions found in different caves in Tamil Nadu can be assigned to the fourth–third century BC on palaeographical grounds. The script has many similarities with the Asōkan Brāhmi. The most important aspect of the script is that while it contains all the vowels, amongst the consonants belonging to the five groups (*vargīya-vyañjanas*) it has only the first and the last letter of each *varga* i.e., the voiceless unaspirated consonants and homorganic nasals like *k*, *ṅ*; *c*, *ñ*; *ṭ*, *ṇ*; *t*, *n* and *pa*, *ma*. There are no separate letters for voiced consonants and aspirates (like *g*, *j*, *ḍ*, *d*, *b*; *kh*, *ch*, *ṭh*, *th*, *ph* and *gh*, *jh*, *ḍh*, *dh*, *bh*). The other letters *y*, *r*, *l*, *v*, *ḷ*, *ḻ*, *ṟ* are also found in the script.

There is an additional letter *ṉ*, which is palatal alveolar. It is also interesting to note that letters are used as numerals in this script.

The script developed significantly during the reign of the Pallavas, Chōḷas and Vijayanagara rulers between sixth and fifteenth centuries AD. The present script predominantly resembles the Vijayanagara script. In attaching the medial vowels *e* and *o*, the signs are separately placed by the side of the main letters.

The other noteworthy features of this script are: the basic consonants do not have the *a* vowel as found in the other Dravidian scripts in the initial stage, but their later development is similar to the contemporary Dravidian scripts. In the earliest centuries of the Christian era, a *puḷḷi* (a dot above the letter) was used to indicate the mute consonants, which has continued to this day. For forming conjuct consonants the original letters are placed side by side with a *puḷḷi*. This script does not have ligatures and signs for the aspirates, sibilants, *anusvāra* and *visarga* (Fig. 4).

2.2 Vaṭṭeluttu

This script was widely prevalent in many districts of Tamil Nadu and Kerala from about the sixth to fourteenth century AD. Basically this is a cursive form of writing and reflects a roundish character of letters. Noteworthy of the letters of this script are, the vowels *a*, *ā*, *u* and *e* which undergo considerable change by about the eleventh century AD; the consonant n and class nasals *ñ*, *ṅ* and *m*. Amongst

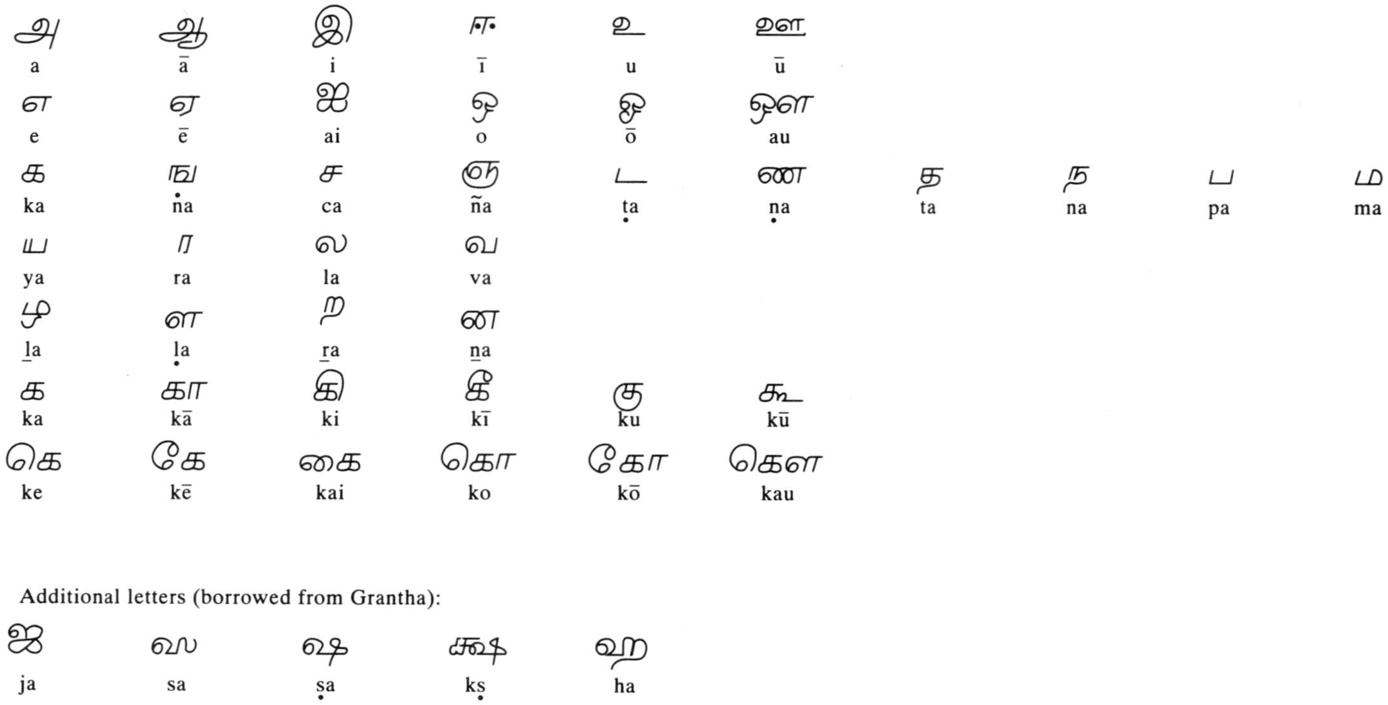

அ	ஆ	இ	ஈ	உ	ஊ				
a	ā	i	ī	u	ū				
எ	ஏ	ஐ	ஒ	ஓ	ஒள				
e	ē	ai	o	ō	au				
க	ங	ச	ஞ	ட	ண	த	ந	ப	ம
ka	ṅa	ca	ña	ṭa	ṇa	ta	na	pa	ma
ய	ர	ல	வ						
ya	ra	la	va						
ழ	ள	ற	ன						
ḻa	ḷa	ṟa	ṉa						
க	கா	கி	கீ	கு	கூ				
ka	kā	ki	kī	ku	kū				
கெ	கே	கை	கொ	கோ	கௌ				
ke	kē	kai	ko	kō	kau				

Additional letters (borrowed from Grantha):

ஜ	ஸ	ஷ	க்ஷ	ஹ
ja	sa	ṣa	kṣ	ha

Figure 4. Tamil Script

the other letters the letters *y* and *v*, which are very roundish, call for a special attention.

2.3 Grantha

As the name of the script itself indicates, this script was invented during the Pallava period to write the Sanskrit texts and is also popularly known as Pallava–Grantha. Since in the Tamil script only the first and last letters of each *varga* are in use, this script was introduced in order to fecilitate incorporation of other letters for writing Sanskrit texts. Basically, the southern Brāmi script prevalent during the fourth–fifth centuries AD was adopted for this script with a few modifications. This script contains all the vowels and conconants used in the Nāgari script. Many of the letters resemble Kannada-Telugu letters of that period, noteworthy among them being the vowels *a* (ఆ, ఆ), *ā* (ఆ), the consonants *k* (ఈ), *g* (ఠ, వ), *r* (ఐ), *ś* (ఠ, వ) etc. While the vertical line is doubled in respect of letters like *k* (ఈ) and *r* (ఐ), an upward curve is added to the left wing of the letter *g* (వ) and *ś* (వ). The horizontal line of the letter *ś* found in other parts of South India changes into a curl on the inner side in this script. A leftward horizontal line is added at the bottom of letter *r* from about the thirteenth century onwards. Some of the letters are very ornamental during the Pallava period. The medial vowels like *ā*, *ī*, *ē*, *ō* and *au* are attached to the side of letters. Even to this date for writing Sanskrit texts Grantha letters are interspersed with Tamil wherever necessary.

This script underwent significant changes during the seventh, eleventh, and thirteenth centuries AD. Amongst the other noteworthy features, opening of the top of letters *b* (ౘ) from the eighth century AD, adoption of northern variety of *bh* (ౘ) in this script, the letter *s* (ౘ) turning into a combination of a loop and two curves may be noted here. The script has not incorporated the Dravidian letters *ḻ* and *ṟ*, but the cerebral variety of *ḷ* is found in this script. Tamil numerals are also used in the Grantha script.

2.4 Malayālam

The Malayālam script can be traced from about the thirteenth century AD in parts of Kerala and occasionally in the adjoining areas. This script owes its origin to the Grantha script and shows the influence of Vaṭṭeluttu. The vowels *a*, *ā*, *o*, *ō*, and consonants *g* (which is more roundish than the Grantha letter ౘ), *ṭ* (ఠ), *t* (ౘ) which is formed by two curves interlocked in the middle), class nasal *ñ* (ౘ), which develops an inward curve on the right side), *m* (ౘ the lower end of which is triangular instead of roundish) are noteworthy. The cerebral letter *ḷ* resembles the corresponding Tamil letter. The numerical symbols used in the script are very much stylised and cursive and in some cases recall the letters in their background as in case of the Tamil script. Medial vowels *ā*, *ī*, *ē*, *ō* and *au* are attached to the side instead of the top. (See Fig. 5.)

The southern scripts had considerable impact not only in the region of their origin where they are in use to the present day, but also in the adjoining countries of South and South East Asia due to politico-social, commercial and religious contacts with these countries during the early centuries of the Christian era up to about the eleventh century

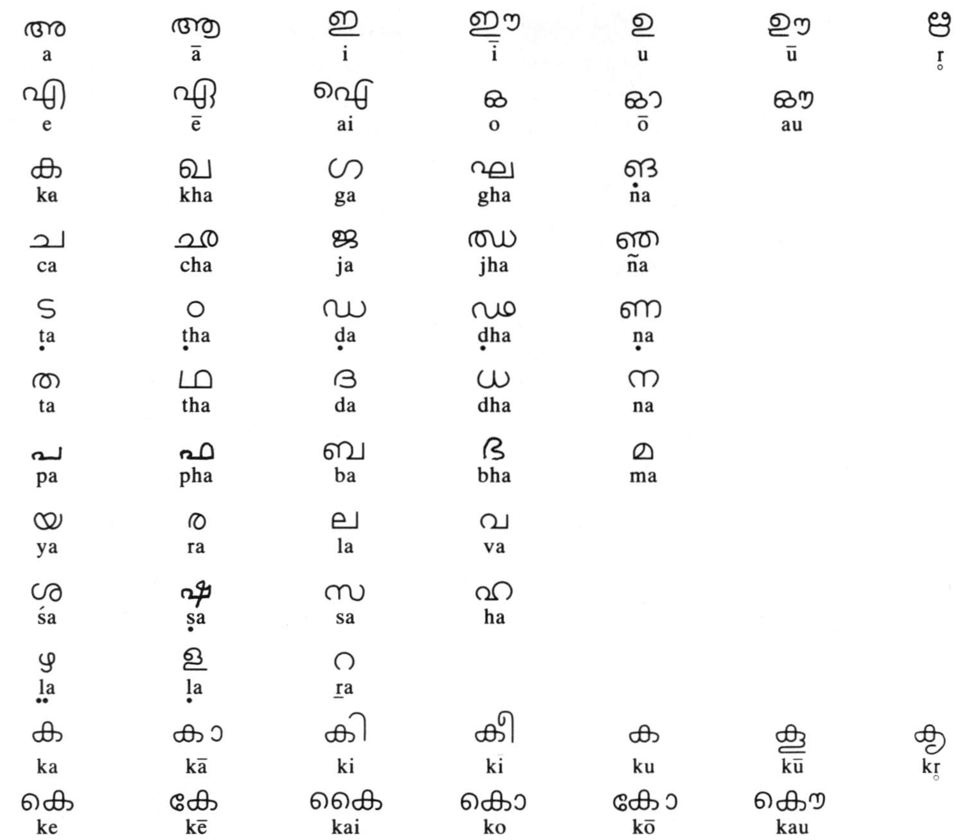

a	ā	i	ī	u	ū	ṛ
e	ē	ai	o	ō	au	
ka	kha	ga	gha	ṅa		
ca	cha	ja	jha	ña		
ṭa	ṭha	ḍa	ḍha	ṇa		
ta	tha	da	dha	na		
pa	pha	ba	bha	ma		
ya	ra	la	va			
śa	ṣa	sa	ha			
ḷa	ḻa	ṟa				
ka	kā	ki	kī	ku	kū	kṛ
ke	kē	kai	ko	kō	kau	

Figure 5. Malayālam Script.

AD. The scripts of these countries reflect a stage of development comparable to that of the land of their origin, India, during the same period. Specific mention may be made of the impact of the Kadamba, Chalukya, Rāshtrakūṭa, Pallava and Chōḷa dynasties in this respect.

Bibliography

Bühler G *Indian Palaeography*. New Age Publishers, Calcutta

Dani A H 1963 *Indian Palaeography*. Clarendon Press, Oxford

Katti Madhav N 1972 *Lipiśāstra Pravēśa* (*Kannaḍa*). Mysore

Ojha G H 1918 *The Palaeography of India*. Scottish Mission Industries Company, Ajmer

Ramesh K V 1984 *Indian Epigraphy*, vol. I. Sundeep Prakashan, New Delhi

Sivaramamurthy C 1952 *Indian Epigraphy & South Indian Scripts*. Madras (*Bulletin of the Madras Government Museum*, n.s., General Sect., Vol. 3, No. 4)

M. N. Katti

Scripts, Javanese and Related

This article outlines the systematics and history of the scripts used to write Javanese (central and east Java) and a number of neighboring languages: Malay (Malaysia, east Sumatra, coastal regions of Borneo), Sundanese (west Java), Madurese (Madura and east Java), Balinese (Bali and western Lombok), and Sasak (central and eastern Lombok). The scripts to be discussed are Indic, Arabic, and Roman.

1. Indic Scripts

The scripts of Indian origin that are used for writing Modern Javanese, Sundanese, Madurese, Balinese, and Sasak are very similar. They are syllabaries. Writing is from left to right, without spaces between words. On the basis of form, function, and indigenous graphology, five major classes of characters may be distinguished:

(a) A main character represents a sequence of a consonant and a vowel. The inherent, unmarked vowel is /a/.

(b) Vowels other than /a/ are marked by means of vowel diacritics placed above, underneath, preceding, following, or preceding and following the main characters.

(c) Supplementary characters, placed underneath or following main characters, represent the second consonants of consonant clusters. They usually resemble the corresponding main characters in form.

(d) A number of special diacritics represent additional pre- and postvocalic consonants. In Modern Javanese script these include the *wignyan* for syllable-final /h/ (descended from the Indian *visarga*) and the *cecak* for syllable-final /ŋ/ (descended from the marker of the Sanskrit *anusvāra*). The 'vowel killer' (*patèn*, descended from the Indian *virāma*), nullifies the vowel inherent in a main character. Generally it is only used preceding punctuation, or it doubles as a punctuation mark itself.

(e) Finally there are characters representing vowels not preceded by a consonant, and numerals.

There are many varieties of the Indic scripts. At any one time different regional, local, and institutional varieties are used. The earliest examples in Indonesia are found in Sanskrit inscriptions of east Borneo (ca. 400 AD). Their script has been identified as that of the south Indian Pallava dynasty. Varieties of Pallava script were used in Sanskrit and Old Malay inscriptions in Java, Sumatra, and the Malay peninsula until the early eighth century, when they were superseded by scripts known collectively as *Kawi*. These were used until the fifteenth century for Sanskrit, Old Javanese, Old Malay, Old Balinese, and Old Sundanese inscriptions (de Casaros 1975), and up to the eighteenth century in Old Javanese palm-leaf manuscripts written in mountain hermitages (van der Molen 1983: 95–98). With the exception of Malay (see Sect. 2), inscriptions and most manuscripts from the seventeenth century onwards utilize modern varieties of Indic script, whose precise relation to the *Kawi* scripts is still unknown.

Before the nineteenth century the Indic scripts were exclusively hand-written or inscribed on stone or bronze. The first printing font was created in the 1820s for Javanese. Indic scripts are still used in Bali and in the courts of central Java, but on the whole they have been superseded by Arabic and especially Roman script.

Finally mention should be made of scripts such as Batak (northern Sumatra), Lampung (south Sumatra), and Buginese (south Celebes), which are also Indic.

2. Arabic Script

Arabic script (see *Arabic script: Adaptation for Other Languages*) is also used to write Modern Javanese, Malay, Sundanese, Madurese, and a number of other languages of Indonesia. It reached maritime southeast Asia via India, where it had absorbed several new characters. By means of the addition of dots underneath or above the characters, Austronesian consonants without Arabic and Persian parallels were incorporated.

The Arabic script as used for the writing of Malay is known as *huruf Jawi* 'Jawi letters.' *Jawi* derives from the Arabic designation of maritime southeast Asia. In reference to Javanese, what is essentially the same script is called *pégon*, from a Javanese word meaning 'outlandish.'

Malay texts in Arabic script tend to be unvocalized. The Arabic character *yā'* (transliterated as *ī* and *y* in Arabic) represents /i, e, j/, while *wāw* (*ū* and *w* in Arabic) represents /u, o, w/, but not all vowels are written. As a consequence, context plays an important role in the reading of Malay in Arabic script. Unvocalized Arabic script (called *gundhil* 'bald' in Javanese) is also found in the case of Javanese, Madurese, and Sundanese, but texts in these languages are usually vocalized. The vowel diacritics (*sakal* in Javanese, from Arabic *shakl*, vocalization) are the same as those in Arabic, with one addition for *shwa* /ə/. Here /e/ is represented by means of a combination of the vowel diacritic marking /a/ (*fatha* in Arabic) followed by *yā'*, and /o/ by means of the *fatha* followed by *wāw*.

The oldest instance of Arabic script in Indonesia is found in an Arabic inscription on a tombstone in East Java. It is probably dated 1082 AD and seems to have been imported. From at least the fourteenth century Arabic script was used for writing Old Malay, as evidenced by an inscription found in Trengganu on the Malay peninsula. During the same period Indic scripts, too, were in use for Old Malay, but in later times Arabic script completely superseded Indic scripts for the writing of Malay. The same did not apply to Javanese and neighboring languages. Here functional differentiation occurred: Arabic script was primarily used for texts of an explicitly Islamic character.

Arabic script is still used in the twentieth century in lithographed publications of Islamic treatises and in literary manuscripts in some rural traditions in Sumatra, Java, Madura, and Lombok. Its use is more widespread in Malaysia.

3. Roman Script

In Indonesia, Roman script spread gradually after the arrival of European traders in the late sixteenth century. In the course of the nineteenth and early twentieth centuries it largely superseded the Indic and Arabic scripts. This was due to Western-style education and to the relative cheapness of its use in printing. Since Indonesian independence (1945) very little has been published in scripts other than Roman. Handwriting, too, is largely in the Roman alphabet.

Bibliography

Casparis J J de 1975 *Indonesian Palaeography: A History of Writing in Indonesia from the Beginnings to c. AD 1500*. E. J. Brill, Leiden

Molen W van der 1983 *Javaanse tekstkritiek: Een overzicht en een nieuwe benadering geïllustreerd aan de Kunjarakarna*. Foris, Dordrecht

Pigeaud T G T 1967 *Literature of Java, vol. I: Synopsis of Javanese Literature, 900–1900 AD*. Martinus Nyhoff, The Hague

B. Arps

Search Problems

Many problems in computational linguistics and artificial intelligence (see *Artificial Intelligence*) can be thought of as 'state space search problems'—problems that can be characterized in the following way:

(a) generating a solution requires going through a sequence of states;
(b) the initial state is provided by the problem definition;
(c) given a state, there are a number of possible next states;
(d) a solution is obtained by reaching a particular kind of final state.

For instance, bottom-up recognition given a context free grammar (see *Parsing Techniques*) can be regarded as a process of progressively rewriting a string to the start symbol S, at each stage using a rule of the grammar to replace an instance of the right-hand side of the rule with the left-hand side of the rule:

(1) we teach advanced courses		(1–9)
(2) PRON teach advanced courses	(using PRON → we)	
(3) NP teach advanced courses	(using NP → PRON)	
(4) NP VERB advanced courses	(using VERB → teach)	
(5) NP VERB ADJ courses	(using ADJ → advanced)	
(6) NP VERB ADJ NOUN	(using NOUN → courses)	
(7) NP VERB NP	(using NP → ADJ NOUN)	

(8) NP VP   (using VP → VERB NP)
(9) S   (using S → NP VP)

Here a state is simply a string of terminal and nonterminal symbols, the initial state being simply the string to be recognized and the final state of a successful recognition being the string S. Although the sequence (1–9) is successful, it represents only one of many possible sequences that could be explored—at each stage there may be a number of ways of rewriting the current state to give a new one. For instance, going from state (4) one could, assuming an appropriate grammar, just as well have rewritten VERB to VP (though that would not have led to a successful recognition). The fact that at each stage it is necessary to make a choice with no clear indication of which possibilities will lead to solutions is what makes this a search problem.

Other examples of search problems are plan generation and recognition (see *Natural Language Processing: Planning and Plan Recognition*) and logical inference (see *Inference*). A task like speech recognition (see *Speech Technology: Overview*) similarly involves a search among combinations of possible hypotheses accounting for parts of the input waveform. A typical feature of search problems is that they are 'combinatoric,' that is, from a given state there are a number of possible next states, from each of these there are a number of possible next states, and so on, which means that the actual number of states to be considered multiplies rapidly. For instance, in a problem where each state introduces exactly two possible next states there will be 2^n possible states reachable after n moves.

There are a number of standard state–space search techniques that have been developed. In principle, any of these could be used on any search problem, although in practice there is a certain amount of skill involved in selecting the technique that best fits the problem (i.e., that generates solutions as efficiently as possible).

1. Terminology

A state–space search problem involves a set of possible states, of which some are distinguished as 'success states' (possibly by there being some goal test that can be applied to a state, to determine whether it represents success or not). The search starts off with a set of 'initial states.' Given a state, a number of 'operators' can be applied, each yielding a possible next state. Some states have no possible next states and are nevertheless not success states—these are often called 'failure states.' The space of possible states, the search space, can be displayed as a 'search tree' (Fig. 1)

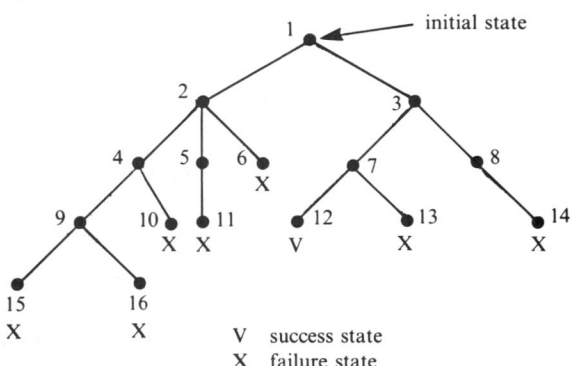

V   success state
X   failure state

Figure 1. Search tree.

with each state linked below to its next states. In fact, if duplicate states can be generated in several ways, it is more appropriate to regard the search space as a graph. For simplicity, however, this article will continue to regard search spaces as trees.

2. A Generic Search 'Algorithm'

With a standard sequential computing device, in a search problem only one of the possible states can be investigated at a time (though parallel computer systems provide other models). There needs to be a systematic exploration of the whole search tree, and so there has to be a representation of the branches of the tree that remain to be looked at. One way of organizing the search is to keep an 'agenda' of alternative states to be investigated. At each stage in the traversal, one of these alternatives is selected. The valid next states from this state are worked out and added to the agenda. Then another alternative is selected from the agenda, and so on. The starting point is an agenda containing the set of initial states provided by the problem at hand. Here is an informal description of this 'algorithm' (10–11):

> Set the agenda to be the set of initial states.   (10)
>
> Do the following repeatedly: (11)
> If the agenda is empty, stop and announce failure. Otherwise:
> (i) Select a state from the agenda (removing it).
> (ii) If it is a success state, stop and announce success.
>   Otherwise:
>   (a) Calculate the next states that could follow from it.
>   (b) Add these to the agenda.

This is not a complete description of what to do (and hence not an algorithm in the technical sense—see *Algorithms*), because it does not specify how to decide which alternative to select at each stage. It is through varying this particular aspect that one obtains the various different search algorithms used in AI and computational linguistics.

3. Depth-first and Breadth-first Approaches to Search

Two basic approaches to searching are 'depth-first' and 'breadth-first' search. In terms of the search tree, depth-first search follows a path deeper and deeper in the search tree and only moves up the tree to consider an alternative if all the possibilities below its current state have been tried. In the above tree (Fig. 1), this would involve the following sequence of states being selected in order (12):

1, 2, 4, 9, 15, 16, 10, 5, 11, 6, 3, 7, 12.   (12)

Depth-first search is also known as 'backtracking search,' and it is the basis of the search mechanism of the programing language PROLOG (see *Prolog*). It is very efficient to implement, because the set of remaining choices can be derived from a simple representation of the path through the search tree from the initial state to the current state. Depth-first search will not always find a solution that is present in the search space (that is, it suffers from a lack of 'completeness'). This is because it might be possible to continue infinitely down a branch to the left of the tree and hence never reach a state on the right of this branch. Breadth-first search, on the other hand, investigates states in order of their depth in the tree. Intuitively, depth-first search involves preferring to investigate alternatives that have been added to the agenda recently, whereas breadth-first search attempts to be fair by avoiding any alternative remaining too long in the agenda before being investigated. The sequence of states selected in a breadth-first search of the above search tree would be (13):

$$1, 2, 3, 4, 5, 6, 7, 8, 9, 10, 11, 12. \qquad (13)$$

4. Heuristic Methods

Pure depth-first and breadth-first search strategies are blind, in that they select a state from the agenda without regard to how promising that state is. Often in a search problem one can construct a heuristic scoring function that determines approximately how 'close' a state is to a success state. For instance, in the recognition task, one could construct a closeness-to-success score that depends inversely on the number of symbols in the string or the number of terminal symbols in the string, or one that depends on the number of S symbols in the string, or some combination of these. This score can be used to select from a set of alternative states one which is likely to be the most promising to investigate (the one which seems 'closest'). A heuristic score is justified almost entirely by its effectiveness in hastening the search for a solution in practice—it does not need to be accurate or theoretically motivated.

'Hillclimbing' is a modified version of depth-first search. In this scheme, the next states of a state being investigated are tried in order of their promise, as suggested by the heuristic score. If the search below the apparently most promising state fails to find a solution, then the next most promising one is tried, and so on.

'Best-first search' is more like a varient of breadth-first search. In this scheme the whole agenda is ordered according to the heuristic score and new items are spliced into positions according to their scores. At each stage one of the states that is closest to a solution is selected for investigation. This may not be related in any simple way in the search tree to whatever state was selected last.

Bibliography

Winston P H 1984 *Artificial Intelligence*, 2nd edn. Addison-Wesley, Reading, MA

Woods W A 1982 Optimal search strategies for speech understanding control. *Artificial Intelligence* **18**/3: 295–326

C. S. Mellish

Sebeok, Thomas Albert (1920–   )

Sebeok is among the world's leading scholars and prognosticators of semiotics, the doctrine of signs. Born in Budapest, Hungary, on November 9, 1920, he emigrated to the USA in 1937 and became a naturalized citizen in 1944. He received his BA degree (1941) from the University of Chicago where, he suggests, 'my early linguistic attitudes had essentially been molded by two men, neither of whom was at Chicago any longer: Manuel Andrade, who died prematurely, and Leonard Bloomfield, who reluctantly accepted a call to Yale in 1940' (Sebeok 1979: 223). It is worth noting that Andrade was a student of Franz Boas (see *Boas, Franz*), perhaps suggesting an early source of Sebeok's expansion of linguistic interests into semiotic connections with anthropology, biology, communicology, and other human sciences (Lanigan 1992). As Claude Lévi-Strauss (see *Lévi-Strauss, Claude*) notes:

> In reading Sebeok's work, one is confounded by his familiarity with the languages and cultures of the world, by the ease with which he moves across the research on psychology, on the specialities of cerebral neurophysiology, cellular biology, or those ethnologists doing work on certain aspects of zoological species ranging from unicellular organisms to high order mammals, passing through insects, fish, and birds.
>
> (Bouissac, et al. 1986: 3)

While still at the University of Chicago, Sebeok's semiotic orientation was stimulated by his teacher, Charles Morris, second only to Charles Sanders Peirce (see *Peirce, Charles Sanders*) in the history of American semiotics (Sebeok 1991a: 75). However, the early behavioral influences of Bloomfield (see *Bloomfield, Leonard*) and Morris at Chicago were to take on a modification as Sebeok moved to Princeton University, where he received MA (1943) and his PhD (1945). While at Princeton during World War II, he came under the guiding semiotic and phenomenological influence of the renowned communicologist and linguist Roman Jakobson (1972; see Holenstein 1976; see also *Jakobson, Roman*) at the Ecole Libre des Hautes Etudes, housed at the New School for Social Research, in New York City. 'Although my PhD degree was from Princeton, Jakobson served, to all intents and purposes—and with the enthusiastic concurrence of my chairman, Harold H. Bender—as my thesis supervisor; it was thus, and in this sense, that I chanced to become his "first American student" ' (Sebeok 1979: 226). From 1943, Sebeok was a member of the faculty at Indiana University in Bloomington, Indiana, USA. On his retirement from teaching in 1991, he completed the local part of an academic career as colorful and diverse as any, recounted with pleasure in his speech 'Into the Rose-garden' (Sebeok 1992). He remained the interim Director of the Research Center for Language and Semiotic Studies, which he founded in 1956, holding the coterminous emeritus appointments of Distinguished Professor of Linguistics and Semiotics, Professor of Anthropology, Professor of Uralic and Altaic Studies, Fellow of the Folklore Institute and Professor of Folklore, and chairman of the Graduate Program in Semiotic Studies. His international reputation as a scholar and researcher, reflected in these academic titles, is founded on the approximately 454 books and articles which he published between 1942 and 1991; the list through 1985 is published in Bouissac, et al. (1986: 575–621). A biographical and intellectual summary of the milieu surrounding this prodigious research accomplishment occurs in Sebeok (1991a). Perhaps best known for his continuing work on animal communication (Sebeok 1977), for which his designation of *zoosemiotics* is widely acknowledged, Sebeok is in fact a Renaissance person whose writings authoritatively cover the full range of subject matters belonging to the arts, humanities, and sciences. A modest sampling may be found in several collections of essays, including his most-cited work (Sebeok 1976; 1979), his sense of playful work (Sebeok 1981), and his most recent work (Sebeok 1991b). Sebeok's many honors include the PhD *honoris causa* from the University of Budapest, the DSc *honoris causa* from Southern Illinois University, and the presidency of the Linguistics Society of America (1975) and the Semiotic Society of America (1984). A founding member of the International

Association for Semiotic Studies, Sebeok has continued to serve as the editor-in-chief of the association's journal *Semiotica*.

See also: Animal Communication; Semiotics.

Bibliography

Bouissac P, Herzfeld M, Posner R (eds.) 1986 *Iconicity: Essays on the Nature of Culture; Festschrift for Thomas A. Sebeok on his 65th Birthday*. Stauffenburg Verlag, Tübingen

Holenstein E 1976 *Roman Jakobson's Approach to Language: Phenomenological Structuralism*. Indiana University Press, Bloomington, IN

Jakobson R 1972 Verbal communication. In: *Communication: A Scientific American Book*. W. H. Freeman, San Francisco

Lanigan R L 1992 *The Human Science of Communicology*. Duquesne University Press, Pittsburgh, PA

Sebeok T A 1976 *Contributions to the Doctrine of Signs*. Indiana University Press, Bloomington, IN

Sebeok T A (ed.) 1977 *How Animals Communicate*. Indiana University Press, Bloomington, IN

Sebeok T A 1979 *The Sign and its Masters*. University of Texas Press, Austin, TX

Sebeok T A 1981 *The Play of Musement*. Indiana University Press, Bloomington, IN

Sebeok T A 1991a *Semiotics in the United States*. Indiana University Press, Bloomington, IN

Sebeok T A 1991b *A Sign Is Just a Sign*. Indiana University Press, Bloomington, IN

Sebeok T A 1992 Into the rose-garden. *Ural–Altaic Yearbook* **64**: 1–12

R. L. Lanigan

Second/Foreign Language Pedagogy: Vocabulary

In considering vocabulary pedagogy the focus is on the contribution of the course writer and classroom teacher to the development of a language learner's vocabulary, rather than on what is known about the learner's own part in the process (see *Second Language Acquisition: Lexis*). However, effective pedagogy will be that which takes account of the learner, and there are various ways in which modern vocabulary teaching can do this.

Though teachers in the field have always been aware of the importance of vocabulary, it was for a long time neglected in professional discussion of language teaching. In the early 1990s it has become a focus of attention once more, and the vocabulary element in a language course—the 'lexical syllabus'—is now widely regarded as crucial. Yet there do remain differences of opinion about how far it is possible or desirable to handle vocabulary as a component in a language course separate from grammar, and so on.

In the following account the discussion on vocabulary will necessarily be somewhat divorced from other aspects of language teaching. The main phases in its pedagogical treatment will be reviewed, using English as the example target language.

1. What is Vocabulary?

Teachers typically include under this term words that belong to the major parts of speech: nouns like *book*, *decision*; verbs like *eat*, *understand*; adjectives like *red*, *interesting*; and adverbs like *sadly*. Other words like *the*, *should*, *in*, and *more* are usually regarded as not 'vocabulary words,' but rather as belonging with the treatment of grammar.

Second, though teaching vocabulary is often thought of as teaching 'words,' what is usually meant, for pedagogical purposes, is a unit that is in some ways less and in some ways more than a word. Most words have more than one meaning, and many also occur in set/idiomatic phrases, etc: for example, *break* occurs in a basic physical meaning (as in *I broke my leg*) but also in less tangible senses like that in *Let's break for lunch*; further it occurs with distinct meanings in phrases like *break down* (verb and noun). Typically these would not all be scheduled to be taught at once, but come up at separate times in a course—that is, the useful teaching units are each sense/phrase separately, not the word *break* considered as a whole.

Third, if a word, even thought of in terms of one sense/phrase at a time, is to become part of the 'active' vocabulary of learners (i.e., actually used, not just 'passively' understood when it happens to occur), then there is rather more to know than just a spelling linked to a meaning. To be fully equipped to use *break* just in its basic sense learners need to know its pronunciation, irregular inflected forms (*broke*, etc.), that it is applied to objects like *cup* and *leg* but not *paper*, that it is stylistically neutral (unlike *fracture*), and so forth. The term 'word' shall be used in this article to mean a vocabulary item in the way just outlined (see also *Applied Linguistics: Lexicology*).

2. Selecting What Vocabulary to Teach

Before any vocabulary teaching occurs, some principled choice is commonly made (usually by the course writer) of which words should be dealt with at any given point in a course, which should be left till later, and which left out entirely. This issue looms particularly large in vocabulary teaching since languages contain so many words that even native speakers do not know them all.

Over the years many criteria have been proposed as the bases for vocabulary selection. Mostly they relate to one or other of two aspects of words which may be characterized as their 'price' and their 'value.' Price here refers to ease/difficulty of teaching or learning and value to importance or utility for the learner. Though it has been argued that the teacher should seek bargains wherever possible (words that are both important and easy to learn), it is apparent that often one cannot have both at once (e.g., *go* and *woman* would on any criteria be important, useful English words for a learner, but come at some cost as they both have irregular inflected forms—*went* and *women*).

Ease is often a criterion relied on in a beginners' course, where it can be argued that learners are faced with so many new things at once in the area of sounds, grammar, and perhaps orthography that simplifying the vocabulary element is a valuable relief. Thus the words introduced may be short, regular in spelling and inflection, and with concrete meaning easily demonstrable in the class (e.g., *dog*, *desk*, *red*, proper names of students and countries).

Another way in which words can be easy is where they resemble in a helpful way words that the learners already know in other languages. For example, for the German learner of English *man* is easier than *child* because the German for the former is *Mann* but for the latter is *Kind* (which if anything is confusing as it does not mean the same as English *kind*). For many learners whose native languages (unlike German) are not connected with English, 'international' words like *taxi* and *burger* may already be familiar. Ease can also be realized in a more general way by choosing for a course situations and topics which are familiar to learners by virtue of their age, cultural background, etc., so that although the words will be new, the concepts they label will be known.

After initial teaching, though the teacher's handling of vocabulary will always need to be informed by an understanding of factors that make particular words easy or difficult for particular learners, most often the basic selection decision will be made on some other criterion. Commonly an effort is made to identify vocabulary that is important for particular target learners in some way, and the leading considerations are discussed below.

Where learners have definable language needs (see *Needs Analysis*), the teacher can immediately limit the area of vocabulary that may be relevant. An example would be Arabic learners of English destined to be air traffic controllers (see *Languages for Specific Purposes: Pedagogy*), though for many learners the main need will be less well-defined 'survival' in common situations, for example, visiting countries where the target language is spoken. If the teacher wishes to maximize use of the target language in class, then the vocabulary of classroom management and textbook instructions is a clear need (e.g., *repeat*, *page*, and *exercise*). A definable need for most learners is the ability to cope with standard examinations that have to be taken. If these are based on published lists of words (as, for example, GCSE French for English schoolchildren), then the selection is ready made for the teacher. If they are not (as, for example, the Cambridge examinations for foreign learners of English), then the teacher must attempt to gauge the kind of vocabulary required. Ideally, learners will be able to judge such needs for themselves, and so contribute to the selection of what words to learn on a continuing basis.

The other commonest 'importance' criterion is frequency, particularly where precise learner needs are unclear: the most important words of a language are deemed to be those that the learner will meet most often. Often 'range' is invoked as well—more important words are those that occur in more different contexts and varieties of English. Word frequency counts exist for most major languages and many language courses make use of them. However, it has come to be realized that frequency is no substitute for learner need. Whatever collection of language material frequency lists are based on, they tend to agree on the words that are most frequent, and so are relevant for the first few years of second/foreign language teaching. However, they disagree on the frequencies of mid- and low-frequency words, where it seems to matter very much what sort of language material made up the corpus in which the word frequencies were counted. In fact it has proved difficult to find any reliable guide to the most important vocabulary at intermediate and advanced level where learners are studying another language with 'no particular purpose.'

Though other criteria (such as the 'coverage,' 'availability,' and 'familiarity' of words) have been put forward, what often happens in the situation just described is that courses fall back more on topics and consequent vocabulary that they think will interest the learner. For example, for

teenagers, units might be based round pop music or a spy story, and to an extent learners can be invited to choose their own vocabulary to learn, on the basis of individual interest.

3. How Much Vocabulary to Teach

The number of words that learners can reasonably be expected to learn varies tremendously in relation to variables such as age, level, and motivation of learners, whether the learners meet and use the target language in the community or only in language lessons in school, the nature of the words (e.g., their ease again), etc. Thus it makes no sense to lay down a dogmatic universal figure. Nevertheless, a figure of around 8–10 new words per class lesson is often quoted as a crude average, based on teachers' collective experience.

What is more important is that teachers often find that course materials or other sources of target-language input to the learner overestimate the number of new words they can cope with. An important part the teacher can play here is to filter the words, or indeed teach learners to filter them themselves, using some of the selection criteria described above. Already some courses distinguish between new words in a lesson that are to be learnt for future productive use, and so should attract more effort, and those that it is only worth remembering for when they will be met passively. Teachers can reflect this distinction in the elaborateness with which they present and practice the words (Sects. 4 and 5). In addition the concept of 'throwaway vocabulary' is useful—words not worth the learner trying to remember at all. These may have to be summarily glossed if they are of local importance for a particular reading passage or lesson, but need not be bothered with further.

4. Initial Teaching of New Vocabulary

A key moment in vocabulary teaching is when a new word is introduced to learners for the first time. At the very least one meaning of a word and its spelling and/or sound shape must come across. Spelling is readily given, but sound shape may present difficulties. For example, for English it may need to be decided whether a British or US pronunciation should be offered, or some other standard (e.g., Indian English) (see *Accent*). Teachers or coursebooks may employ phonemic transcription to convey sound, but often an audible model is desirable as well (on tape if the teacher is not a native speaker). However, the biggest problem usually is how to convey the meaning.

There are three broad ways of explaining the meaning of a word—by nonlinguistic means, via translation, and via the target language. All have their pros and cons, and teachers need to check carefully that the meaning has been conveyed, whichever combination of means they use. The nonlinguistic, 'ostensive' approach (pointing at objects, miming, using pictures, etc.) is valuable in initial teaching, especially where the teacher does not speak the learners' native language. However, it tends to take more time than a translation, and is not suitable for the many words that do not have a concrete meaning.

Translation has always been popular with many teachers, though for a time language-teaching methodologies such as the 'Direct Method' strove to outlaw it (see *Language*

Teaching Methods). It has the advantage of speed and likelihood of being more definitely understood by the learner than the other approaches. Also such translation need only be done once when the word first occurs—it does not necessarily entail extended memorization and practice of translation equivalents. Often teachers, struggling to mime or construct a simple target-language explanation, find learners interpreting their efforts in terms of a translation anyway. However, there are opportunities for misunderstanding arising from the fact that many words do not translate one-to-one between languages.

Explanation via the target language itself takes a multitude of forms. It can be done via synonyms, opposites, or by putting the word in a linguistic context that defines it in some periphrastic way. The last may take the form of a conventional dictionary-like definitional paraphrase (e.g., *favorite means 'most loved'*) or it may come in one of a variety of more colloquial forms (e.g., *If something is your favorite that means you like it the best* or *My favorite color is one I like the best* or *There's nothing I like better than apples. They are my favorite fruit*). The conventional form is briefer, and ostensibly presents a phrase that substitutes for the word defined, but it often seems harder for learners to decode than the unconventional forms, which, though wordier, offer the unknown word and its explanation in a fuller context showing how it is used. Obviously none of these can be used until learners have acquired a modicum of the target language.

New words may crop up in a variety of circumstances in teaching—in passages for reading comprehension, in taped listening material, in thematic tables or arbitrary lists in course materials, and so forth. Teachers may wish to impose other groupings through practice later (Sect. 5). A further issue is when to explain new words—before or after the learner meets them in such lesson material? Preteaching some key words may make a subsequent task more amenable, but if it is uncertain which words are going to be unknown, it might be better to wait until problems arise. Connected with this issue is the point that if all new words are always pretaught, the learner is robbed of the chance to develop the self-help substitutes for having word-meaning explained (see Sect. 7 below). The teacher can decide not to explain some new words at all, and perhaps instead supply extra examples of the word in use, or helpful pictures, if the basis for guessing is thin in the original context.

Finally, there is very much more to knowing a word in the full sense than just the three aspects so far mentioned (Sect. 1). Often these more detailed aspects will not be dealt with on first meeting a word, but will be introduced by the teacher when the word recurs, or left to be soaked up by learners from repeated exposure to the word in use or discovered by being corrected when they try to use the word and get something wrong.

5. Follow-up Practice of Vocabulary

Good initial presentation is only a first step in the teaching of vocabulary. The readiness with which new words are forgotten is only too well-known, and there is much that the teacher and course writer can do to prevent this.

It is clear from research on memory that one essential for the effective retention of vocabulary by learners (but by no means the only requirement) is that the words must recur. Too often course materials fail to do this 'recycling' beyond the unit in which the new word first arises. Here the teacher can step in by keeping track of the important vocabulary from past lessons and ensuring that it comes up again in a variety of ways in language activities not just a week later, but months later.

The range of activities that teacher or coursebook can use as media for the recycling of vocabulary is vast. At one end of the scale are games and exercises that focus on words overtly separated from other aspects of language, and often practice specific aspects of words only. For example, an anagram game ('Spot the word hidden in *tofo*') focuses just on the spelling of words in isolation, whereas a crossword puzzle involves both meaning and spelling, and a synonym discrimination task ('What's the difference between *He deceived her* and *He put one over on her*?') focuses on the finer connotational and stylistic overtones of words. Many games/exercises have been devised to practice vocabulary in semantically related groups (e.g., opposites or thematic sets like 'means of transport'), as there is evidence from learning research that native speakers store words in the mind linked in these ways: for example, 'Spot the odd word out' requires identification of words as members of a set or not, and a task like 'Disagree with the statement *I love dancing*' evokes opposites.

At the other extreme are tasks which closely simulate real-life use of language to communicate, and in which words connected with a common situation are practiced entirely coincidentally, in naturalistic contexts—for example, where learners role-play visiting the doctor, or search for accommodation for a hypothetical visit to the target country, using authentic advertisements.

A new addition to the teacher's armory for vocabulary practice is the computer (see *Language Teaching: Computer Technology*). Many vocabulary-related activities are computerized versions of games and exercises like those described above—for example, Hangman and gap-filling. They have the advantage that many can be used by the learner in self-access mode outside the class, and so be an additional rather than replacement source of practice.

Many of the activities described above are ones that the teacher can encourage learners to do for themselves. This is all the more important since in many teaching situations there is limited time in class to spend on vocabulary, and much of the follow-up learning has to be left to the learner outside the class. Essential guidance here can include showing learners how to keep a useful record of new words in a booklet or on cards, with examples of their use, not just the word and a translation, and perhaps with words of related meaning grouped together. They can also be shown how to develop effective mnemonic techniques and strategies to help themselves memorize and retain vocabulary.

6. Checking on Learners' Vocabulary

Teachers want to check on learners' vocabulary from time to time for a variety of reasons. They may want to identify what recently taught words they have misunderstood or failed to retain, so that remedial work can be done, or they may be interested in how many words learners know, as a feature of their general proficiency, so they can be placed in a class of a suitable level. Vocabulary is also tested in standard examinations for certification purposes. The means by which vocabulary is formally tested often resemble the sort of practice materials outlined above, though multiple-choice gap-filling items are particularly popular—for example, *The sea is very thick/deep/profound* (see also *Language Testing*).

Another way in which all teachers check on learners is informally, by their errors, as they occur in whatever the learner writes or says. Such errors may reveal problems with any of the aspects of words (Sect. 1), and may or may not be explicable as due to first language interference. For example, *This watch does not walk well* shows *walk* clearly used in the wrong meaning—either because the learner is French and the word *marcher* in French, properly translated in this context as *function* or *work*, would be translated in others as *walk*, or because *walk* and *work* sound similar within English. The handling of errors like this should not necessarily be judgmental. Making errors and being corrected is an essential part of vocabulary learning, and in some cases learners realize they may be wrong but are determined to try and express a message nevertheless, something that the teacher would often approve of.

A rather different sort of check focuses not on error but use: for instance the number of different words used by learners per 100 words written in compositions on the same topic gives an idea of the richness of the vocabulary they each have at their disposal. Aspects of vocabulary error and use like these can be explicitly brought to the attention of learners, so that they become more aware, and can 'monitor' their own output better.

7. Teaching Vocabulary Survival

Teaching often goes on in situations where the precise vocabulary needs of learners are uncertain (Sect. 2), so it is impossible for the teacher to ensure that learners are introduced to all the words they will ever need in any future use of the language (whether in exams or 'real' communication). This unpredictability is deliberately heightened where the teacher wants learners to read and hear 'authentic,' unsimplified language and to convey what they themselves really want to say when they speak or write, rather than stay within the confines of course material. Further, learners may be unable to recall a word, or some crucial aspect of it, when needed, even though they have at some time been taught it (e.g., the learner may realize the word he/she needs is *stop*, but may not be sure of the correct complement construction it takes—whether one says *He stopped to run* or *He stopped running*).

Hence attention, in the 1990s, is often paid not only to teaching actual words 'directly,' but also to teaching the skills that enable learners to manage successfully when they find themselves *lacking* the vocabulary they need. Study of learner behavior reveals a number of strategies that learners use spontaneously in these situations, of which some are more successful than others, and hence should be encouraged selectively by the teacher (see *Communication Strategies in a Second Language*).

To help with this problem in reading, the teacher can make learners more aware of *when* it is a good idea just to skip unknown words, when to try and guess (or 'infer') the meaning, and when to resort to a dictionary or ask someone; this is dependent on the apparent importance of the word for the message, the availability of clues to guess from, purpose of reading, etc. It is known, for example, that overuse of the dictionary can totally fracture the flow of the reading process.

Further, learners' actual guessing skills can be developed. One way is by making sure they know common morphological elements and structures of words of the target language. For example, learners of English will benefit from being familiar with the *-ness* suffix, as it makes regular derived nouns from many adjectives. If learners have some knowledge of simple adjectives, they will then decode on their own (and go on to learn) nouns such as *happiness, redness,* and *greatness* whenever they crop up for the first time. Another way is by work on exploiting contextual clues. For example, suppose *collapse* were the unknown word in the sentence *The wind grew stronger and the huts began to shake and collapse*: to be able to get close to the meaning of *collapse* from this context, the learner has to be made alive to the factual clue in the first subject of the sentence (What do we know wind does to huts?) and to the fact that *and* often links two events that follow each other, and are not just coordinate. This will not be so easy if learners are forced to read material where the density of new words is excessively high.

In speaking or writing, again the teacher can point to the advantages and disadvantages in different circumstances of learners simply 'avoiding' a topic where they do not know the word, or are uncertain about some aspect of how to use it, as against attempting a paraphrase, using a better-known simpler word, or resorting to the dictionary/asking someone. It is known, for example, that in a situation where the dictionary and personal appeal are ruled out and accuracy is at a premium, avoidance can actually be the best policy (If in doubt, leave it out); but if getting the message across is the main thing, then a paraphrase will be better, even though it may sound odd. There is scope for developing learners' paraphrasing abilities, both by making sure they know the useful general words round which paraphrases can be built (e.g., *thing, way, kind of*), and by giving them tasks where avoidance would be sure to be detected (e.g., telling a story from pictures).

In both reception and production the most accurate information will be obtained if the learner either appeals to a better speaker of the language, or refers to a dictionary. Teachers can help with the former by making sure learners are equipped with the language needed to elicit the information they may want: for example, *How do you spell . . . ?, What does . . . mean?* They can help with the latter by making sure good learners' dictionaries are available and showing learners how to get the most out of them. Learners have to be able to use the target language alphabetical order fluently, and to be made alive (e.g., via targeted exercises) both to the shortcomings of pocket bilingual dictionaries and the wealth of valuable information in good monolingual dictionaries for learners, which often is not sufficiently used.

Bibliography

Carter R 1987 *Vocabulary: Applied Linguistic Perspectives*. Allen and Unwin, London
Carter R, McCarthy M 1988 *Vocabulary and Language Teaching*. Longman, London

Gairns R, Redman S 1986 *Working with Words: A Guide to Teaching and Learning Vocabulary*. Cambridge University Press, Cambridge

McCarthy M 1990 *Vocabulary*. Oxford University Press, Oxford

Meara P M (ed.) 1983, 1987 *Vocabulary in a Second Language*, vol. 2. Centre for Information on Language Teaching and Research, London

Nation I S P 1990 *Teaching and Learning Vocabulary*. Newbury House, NY

Rivers W M, Temperley M S 1978 *A Practical Guide to the Teacher of English as a Second or Foreign Language*. Oxford University Press, New York

P. J. Scholfield

Second and Foreign Language Teaching

A language may be termed a 'second' or 'foreign' language according to its status either for the individual who speaks that language or for the society in which that language is spoken. In both cases that status may change in the course of time. It is therefore inevitable that the classification of a language as second or foreign is frequently neither clear-cut nor stable. In this article the relation between a first and a second language will be considered, then the distinction between a second and a foreign language for the individual will be examined, and finally the social status of languages and notions of second or foreign language teaching, in particular, will be reviewed.

1. First and Second Language

There is no strict definition of what it means to speak of an individual's first language. The language may be first in the sense of either first-learned or dominant among the person's several languages. This dominance in turn may be psycholinguistic, if competence in one language is more extensive and the language processing more efficient than in others, or social, if one language is required more extensively for communicative use. Although the stereotype may be of a person whose first-learned language remains the psycholinguistically and socially dominant language, in practice there are many people in whom a language has become dominant which was not their first-learned language. Infant bilinguals may also constitute a special case in that by developing two languages simultaneously, they may be said to have either two first languages or no first language at all.

The term second language is used in contrast to first language in any of its senses above. However by far its most widespread use is in contrast to first-learned to refer to any language learned subsequently to the first(-learned), whatever the circumstances of the learning. In this sense it is commonly encountered in such phrases as second-language learning or second-language teaching and is used where the user does not necessarily wish to differentiate second from foreign-language learning or teaching.

2. Second and Foreign Language in the Individual

The difference between a second and a foreign language for an individual depends entirely on the circumstances in which the language was learned. Someone who is learning a language wholly in a classroom or self-instructional environment is said to be learning a foreign language, whereas someone who additionally has contact with at least some communicative use of the language outside the classroom or indeed is learning wholly from contact with such uses of the language is said to be learning a second language. The latter is often perceived as the most natural way to learn a language and is frequently referred to as second-language acquisition. Once an individual's language system has reached stability and scarcely develops any further, whether the system is complete or not, the distinction between foreign and second language becomes largely irrelevant. Although in ordinary use of language it is common to speak of someone who has reached this stage as having a certain proficiency in a foreign language, in the academic literature it is more common to speak of an individual's second language.

3. Second and Foreign Languages in Society

Whether a person is learning a language as a second or foreign language will depend substantially but not entirely on the status of the languages in the society as a whole. At one extreme, though such examples are difficult to find, there are states where only one language is spoken and where all other languages are therefore foreign languages. Japan is commonly cited as coming close to this state. At the other extreme are the many kinds of multilingual state within which what is a second language for one person may be a first language for someone else. One example would be Switzerland where multilingualism is institutionalized and has long historical roots. Another would be countries like the USA and, particularly in recent years, many European countries where immigration has created important linguistic minorities. Between the two extremes come the numerous countries where an external language (often a language like English or French and designated as a 'language of wider communication') has functions in, for example, the media, the courts, and in government administration and may indeed be used as the medium of education at some levels in spite of the fact that there is no significant number of native speakers of that language in the community. This is the case of many of the postcolonial states of Africa and elsewhere.

The need to distinguish between teaching a language as a foreign language and teaching it as a second language originates in the belief that a different pedagogy is required if the target language is simultaneously being used as the medium of instruction for other parts of the curriculum. In this case the rest of the curriculum provides valuable language learning experience and language teaching as such can be dedicated to language education of the kind normally associated with the first language. Where the target language is clearly a foreign language and no experience of the language outside the language class is available, a pedagogy has to be adopted which ensures that the language is made accessible to the learner under conditions that optimize learning. This has usually been taken to mean that the learner should be exposed to the language system in some structured way (see *Language Teaching Methods*).

The factors at work in multilingual societies are so diverse that the simple opposition of foreign and second language rarely proves more than a starting-point for discussion of an appropriate approach. French may be a second language both for a Wolof-speaking child in Senegal and for a similar child living in a major French city, but far more linguistic support is available through normal communicative uses of language in France and one would expect this to be clearly reflected in the child's progress in learning the language and in the role of that language subsequently. To contrast two other cases, Switzerland may be a multilingual state but nonetheless German may be a foreign language for many French-speaking children in Switzerland because, in spite of its status as an official language, it is not used as a medium of instruction in the French-speaking part of Switzerland and children may have no occasion to use it or come into contact with it socially. On the other hand English has no status as a second language in Holland, but the availability of English through the media in particular is such that there is substantial extracurricular support for the learning of the language and in some respects the conditions are more favorable for language learning than in some more obviously second-language situations.

It is clearly necessary to look closely at the linguistic environment of a language learner in order to understand to what extent and in what ways the situation is one of foreign or of second-language learning. It is unlikely that the bald use of these labels would survive such a close examination. In any case it should be noted that the methodological trend in foreign-language teaching in recent years has been to try and introduce more features of natural language use into the foreign-language classroom, thereby blurring the opposition of second- and foreign-language teaching.

See also: Individual Bilingualism; Bilingualism, Societal; Multilingualism.

Bibliography

Christophersen P 1968 *Second Language Learning*. Penguin, London

Davies A 1991 *The Native Speaker in Applied Linguistics*. Edinburgh University Press, Edinburgh

Grosjean F 1982 *Life with Two Languages: An Introduction to Bilingualism*. Harvard University Press, Cambridge, MA

D. A. Wilkins

Second Language Acquisition: Conversation

Learning a second language involves the learning of the grammar rules of that language, along with vocabulary items and correct rules of pronunciation. It is commonly assumed that putting those rules to use in the context of conversation is a natural extension of grammar acquisition. Such a view implicitly assumes that language use, including the way a 'good conversation' progresses, does not vary from a first language situation to a second language situation. It further assumes that all that would be needed to successfully converse in a second language would be to plug in the correct forms to say the same thing as one does in one's native language.

This article deals with characteristics of second language conversations, focusing on ways in which native language use differs from second language use in conversations.

There are two possible ways in which non-native speakers may act differently from native speakers in a conversation. First, because of their lack of competence, conversations involving non-native speakers may be similar to those which occur in distorted communication (those situations in which normal message transmission and/or reception is obstructed, e.g., by loud noise, static on the telephone). Second, they may incorrectly apply conversational rules which are valid in their native language to conversation in a second language. This article only considers the first type of difference. In the discussion, attention is paid to the interrelationship of second language use (conversation) and language learning.

1. Native Language Use versus Second Language Use

In most conversations the discourse progresses in a smooth fashion, with each person responding to what was just said, or, less commonly, to what was said slightly further back in the conversation. When participants in a conversation share a common background (social/cultural) and/or language, turn-taking among participants proceeds smoothly. Barring loud noises, inattentiveness, etc., participants in a conversation have full understanding of what has been said and of how their contribution to the conversation fits in with previous contributions (theirs or others).

The following example illustrates a typical native speaker conversation:

Ben:	You have to . . . uh . . . uh—Hey, this is the best herring you ever tasted. I'll tell you that right now.
Ethel:	Bring some out so that Max could have some too.
Ben:	Oh, boy.
Max:	I don't want any.
Ben:	They don't have this at Mayfair, but this is delicious.
Ethel:	What's the name of it?
Ben:	It's the Lasko but there's herring snack bits and there's reasons why—the guy told me once before that it was the best. It's Nova Scotia herring.
Bill:	Why is it the best?
Ben:	'Cause it comes from cold water. 'Cause cold-water fish is always . . .
Max:	[?] when they . . . uh . . . can it.
Ethel:	Mmmm.
Ben:	Cold-water fish is—
Ethel:	Oooo, Max, have a piece
Ben:	This is the best you ever tasted.

(From Tannen 1986: 106)

In the preceding example, each person takes a conversational turn fully understanding what has preceded. Ben, Bill, Max, and Ethel all know that they are talking about the particular herring they are eating and that the comments refer to how good it is. Had Max not commented on the canning of the fish, but about a movie he had seen, the others would perhaps have perceived this apparent change of topic as somewhat out of place, and therefore, odd. In fact, it is likely that the conversation in such a case would have come to a halt until the participants were able to sort out what is happening. This is not to say that all parts of native speaker conversation are grammatical, or complete, but it does suggest that the norm is for participants to be fully aware of where their contribution fits in to the emerging conversation.

In conversations in which there is not shared background, or in which there is some acknowledged 'incompetence' (e.g., incomplete knowledge of the language being spoken, or lack of knowledge of the topic—as in a doctor speaking with a patient), the conversational flow is marred by numerous interruptions, as in the following example, in which the effect of conversing with a non-native speaker is seen primarily in the speech of the native speaker.

(NS = native speaker; NNS = non-native speaker)

NNS: There has been a lot of talk lately about additives and preservatives in food. How—
NS: —a a a lot, a lot of talk about what?
NNS: uh. There has been a lot of talk lately about additives and preservatives in food.
NS: Now just a minute. I can hear you—everything except the important words. You say there's been a lot of talk lately about what [inaudible]
NNS: —additive, additive, and preservative, in food—
NS: Could you spell one of those words for me, please
NNS: A-D-D-I-T-I-V-E
NS: Just a minute. This is strange to me.
NNS: h h
NS: -uh-
NNS: 'in other word is P-R-E-S-E-R-V-A-
NS: —oh, preserves
NNS: preservative and additive
NS: -preservatives, yes, okay. And what was that—what was that first word I didn't understand?
NNS: OKAY in—
NS: —additives?
NNS: OKAY.
NS: —additives and preservatives
NNS: yes
NS: ooh right . . .

(from Gass and Varonis 1985: 41)

When participants lose their 'conversational footing,' as in the above example, they often compensate by questioning particular utterances (*you say there's been a lot of talk lately about what?*) and/or requesting conversational help (*could you spell one of those words for me?*). In other words, they 'negotiate' that which was not understood. Negotiation of meaning of this sort allows participants to maintain, as well as possible, equal footing in the conversation and provides the means for participants to respond appropriately to one another's utterance and to regain their places in a conversation after one or both have 'slipped.'

1.1 Negotiation of Meaning

Reference was made above to 'negotiation of meaning.' This refers to those instances in conversation in which participants need to interrupt the flow of the conversation in order for both parties to have full understanding of what the conversation is about, as in the preceding example. In conversations involving non-native speakers of a language, particularly those with low proficiency, negotiations of meaning are frequent, at times occupying a major portion of the conversation. The example below is an illustration.

J = native speaker of Japanese
S = native speaker of Spanish

J: And your what is your mm father's job?
S: My father now is retire
J: retire?
S: yes
J: oh yeah
S: But he work with uh uh institution
J: institution
S: Do you know that? The name is . . . some thin like eh control of the state.
J: aaaaaaaah
S: Do you understand more or less?

J: State is uh . . . what what kind of state?
S: It is uhm
J: Michigan State?
S: No, the all nation
J: No, government?
S: all the nation, all the nation. Do you know for example is a the the institution mmm of the state mm of Venezuela
J: ah ah
S: had to declare declare? her ingress
J: English?
S: No. English no (laugh) . . . ingress, her ingress
J: Ingress?
S: Ingress. yes. I-N-G-R-E-S-S more or less
J: Ingless
S: Yes. If for example, if you, when you work you had an ingress, you know?
J: uh huh an ingless?
S: yes
J: uh huh OK
S: yes, if for example, your homna, husband works, when finish, when end the month his job, his boss pay—mm—him something
J: aaaah
S: and your family have some ingress
J: yes ah, OK OK
S: more or less OK? and in this in this institution take care of all ingress of the company and review the accounts
J: OK I got, I see
S: OK my father work there, but now he is old

(from Varonis and Gass 1985a: 78–79)

In the preceding lengthy conversation, the speakers spend the majority of their time in straightening out the meaning of words, specifically the words 'retire,' 'institution,' 'state,' and 'ingress' (income). In conversations involving nonproficient non-native speakers, exchanges of the sort exemplified above are frequent, with a considerable effort going into resolving nonunderstanding as opposed to exchanging ideas or opinions (the typical material of conversation).

1.2 Miscommunication

Miscommunication differs from nonunderstandings. It occurs when the speaker and hearer do not interpret the spoken message in the same way. In fact, when non-native speakers do not negotiate, the result is often confusion and/or miscommunication. In the following conversation that situation can be seen exactly. A native speaker of Spanish, studying English in the USA, called a store to inquire about the price of a TV set. However, he did not realize that when he looked up the telephone number in the telephone book, he had looked up numbers for TV repair shops.

(NS = native speaker; NNS = non-native speaker)

NS: Hello
NNS: Hello could you tell me about the price and size of Sylvania color TV
NS: Pardon?
NNS: Could you tell me about price and size of Sylvania TV color

PAUSE

NS: What did you want? A service call?
NNS: uh 17-inch huh?
NS: What did you want a service call? or how much to repair a TV?
NNS: yeah TV color
NS: 17-inch
NNS: OK

SILENCE

NS: Is it a portable?
NNS: uh huh

NS:	What width is it? What is the brand name of the TV?
NNS:	ah Sony please
NS:	We don't work on Sonys.
NNS:	or Sylvania
NS:	Sylvania?
NNS:	uh huh
NS:	Oh, Sylvania OK. That's American made.
NNS:	OK
NS:	All right. Portables have to be brought in
NNS:	hm hm
NS:	And there's no way I can tell you how much it'll cost until *he* looks at it.
NNS:	hm hm
NS:	and it's a $12.50 deposit
NNS:	OK
NS:	and if he can fix it that applies to labor and if he can't he keeps the $12.50 for his time and effort.
NNS:	hm hm
NS:	How old of a TV is it? Do you know off hand?
NNS:	19-inch
NS:	How old of a TV is it? Is it a very old one or only a couple years old?
NNS:	oh, so so
NS:	The only thing you can do is bring it in and let him look at it and go from there.
NNS:	new television please
NS:	Oh you want to know
	SILENCE
	how much a new television is?
NNS:	yeah I want buy one television.
NS:	Do we want to buy one?
NNS:	yeah
NS:	Is it a Sylvania?
NNS:	Sylvania TV color
NS:	Well, you know even, even if we buy 'em, we don't give much more than $25 for 'em. By the time we fix 'em up and sell 'em, we can't get more than
NNS:	hm hm
NS:	$100 out of 'em time we put our time and parts in it
NNS:	Is it 17-inch?
NS:	Well, I don't . . . the only thing I can tell you to do is you'd have to come have to come to the shop. I'm on the extension at home. The shop's closed
	SILENCE
NNS:	19-inch? you don't have?
NS:	Do we have a 19-inch?
NNS:	yeah
NS:	No, I've got a 17-inch new RCA
NNS:	OK. Thank you. Bye
NS:	Bye.

(from Varonis and Gass 1985b: 332–33)

This conversation differs markedly from the previous example in that here there was no negotiation, although there are indications throughout (pauses, silence) that the native speaker realizes that there is some confusion. The non-native speaker replies with appropriate English forms (*uh huh*, *OK*) leading the native speaker to believe, at least initially, that they were both discussing the same topic (according to the non-native speaker, the purchase of a TV set and according to the native speaker, the repair of a TV set). Because speakers did not spend conversational time negotiating, the result was a conversation which consisted of exchanges involving miscommunication from beginning to end.

1.3 Foreigner Talk

When native speakers of a language speak to a non-native speaker of that language, speech adjustments are commonly made. These adjustments reveal speech patterns that would not ordinarily be used in conversations with native speakers. A change from the norm when speaking with nonnative speakers is known as 'foreigner talk.' It shares features in common with what is known as 'caretaker speech,' the language spoken to young children. Some of the most salient features of foreigner talk are: slow speech rate, simple vocabulary, repetitions and elaborations, paucity of slang and idioms. Below are two examples:

NNS:	How have increasing food costs changed your eating habits?
NS:	Well, we don't eat as much beef as we used to. We eat more chicken and uh, pork, and uh, fish, things like that?
NNS:	Pardon me?
NS:	We don't eat as much beef as we used to. We eat more chicken and uh, uh pork and fish . . . We don't eat beef very often. We don't have steak like we used to.

(from Gass and Varonis, 1985: 48)

In this example, taken from a survey on food and nutrition, as a result of the non-native speaker's indication of nonunderstanding (*Pardon me?*), the native speaker reassesses the non-native speaker's ability to understand. The changes made reveal a restatement (the first two sentences) following by repetition (*We don't eat beef very often*) and an elaboration (*We don't have steak like we used to*). From the same survey comes the following example:

NNS:	How have increasing food costs changed your eating habits?
NS:	Uh well that would I don't think they've changed 'em much right now, but the pressure's on.
NNS:	Pardon me?
NS:	I don't think they've changed our eating habits much as of now . . .

(from Gass and Varonis, 1985: 51)

As in the previous example, the native speaker attempts to clarify the original statement by making the utterance more explicit as a result of the nonnative speaker's indication of nonunderstanding (changing *'em* to *our eating habits*).

1.4 Modification of the Conversational Structure

Not only is the form of the speech produced by native speakers modified, but also the structure of the conversation itself shows differences. Michael Long was the first to point out that conversations involving non-native speakers exhibited forms which did not appear to any significant degree when only native speakers were involved in nondistorted conversations. For example, confirmation checks (*is this what you mean?*) or comprehension checks (*do you understand? do you follow me?*) are peppered throughout conversations in which there is a nonproficient non-native speaker participant. Furthermore, different kinds of questions are asked.

The examples below come respectively from two native speakers of English and from a native speaker and a non-native speaker of English.

(NS = native speaker; NNS = non-native speaker)

NS1:	What do you think of Michigan?
NS2:	It's nice, but I haven't gotten used to the cold weather yet.
NS:	Do you like California?
NNS:	Huh?
NS:	Do you like Los Angeles?
NNS:	Uhm . . .

NS: Do you like California?
NNS: Yeah, I like it.
(from Larsen-Freeman and Long 1991: 120–21)

In the first example, the conversation proceeds in step-wise fashion; in the second, there is an indication of non-understanding (*Huh?*), with the result being a narrowing down of the topic (California > Los Angeles) followed by a final repetition of the original question. These conversational tactics provide the nonnative speaker with as much information as possible as she attempts to ascribe meaning to the native speaker's stream of sounds.

Yet another frequent modification in the discourse of native speakers has to do with the types of questions native speakers ask. In the following example the native speaker asks an 'or-choice' question. That is, the native speaker not only asks a question but also provides the non-native speaker with a range of possible answers.

(NS = native speaker; NNS = non-native speaker)

NS: Well, what are you doing in the United States? Are you just studying or do you have a job? Or . . .
NNS: No. I have job
(from Larsen-Freeman and Long 1991: 122)

In all of the examples discussed in this section, the effect of modifications (whether intentional or not) is to aid the non-native speaker in understanding. This reduces the burden for the non-native speaker in that he or she is assisted by others in understanding and in producing language appropriate to the situation.

1.5 Discourse Differences

Besides the obvious differences of grammar, pronunciation, and vocabulary, there is yet another dimension which differentiates native speaker from non-native speaker speech in conversation. Even when native speaker speech is entirely grammatical, there are subtle features which may mark a speaker as non-native.

Non-native speakers and native speakers of a language often select different material to describe. For example, work conducted by Tomlin (1984) showed that when asked to describe a segment of a movie, native speakers usually provide a description of the main events of the story-line and then supplement their descriptions with events which are not central to the story-line. On the other hand, non-native speakers only reported significant events and omitted mention of the nonsignificant ones. Thus, the descriptive content differs depending on whether descriptions are given in the native or the second language.

In terms of actual language forms selected, when providing a description of a visual scene, native speakers differentiate between expressions using the future tense, such as *you will see* or *you will find* and those without the future tense, such as *you see*. The former type of expression is used when giving specific instructions (*On the board, you will find two girls playing. Move one to the bottom*), whereas the latter is used when attempting to determine whether the other person's attention is focused on the relevant object (*You see where the two sides intersect?*). In non-native speaker speech, this distinction is frequently blurred. Both future tense and non-future tense are used for both functions.

2. Second Language Conversation and Learning Outcomes

An important aspect of language learning is what is known as 'metalinguistic awareness.' This refers to the ability to consider language not just as a means of expressing ideas or communicating with others, but as an object of inquiry. Thus, making puns suggests an ability to think *about* language as opposed to only using it for expressive purposes. Similarly, judging whether a given sentence is a grammatical one in one's language or translating from one language to another requires a person to think about language as opposed to engaging in pure use.

The ability to think about language is often associated with increased ability to learn a language. In fact, bilingual children have been shown to have greater metalinguistic awareness than monolingual children (see, for example, Bialystok 1987).

Non-native speakers in a classroom setting often spend more time on metalinguistic activities than on activities of pure use. This takes place, for example, when studying rules of grammar or memorizing vocabulary words. Much classroom activity in earlier language teaching methodologies engaged learners in just this type of 'consciousness raising.' However, there are other ways in which increased metalinguistic awareness can take place. To relate this specifically to the earlier discussion of negotiation, learners are made aware of errors in their speech (whether in grammar, pronunciation, content or discourse) through the questioning that often goes on in negotiation. In other words, negotiation is what makes learners aware that there is incongruity between the forms they are using and the forms used by the native speaking community. In order to respond to an inquiry of nonunderstanding, the non-native speaker must modify his/her output. For this to take place, the learner must become aware of a problem and seek to resolve it. Hence, the extent to which second language learners are able to think about the language they are producing and the language they hear, the greater the possibility they will be able to make appropriate modifications to their speech. While there is limited evidence as to the long-range effects of these modifications, one can presume that negotiation, because it leads to heightened awareness, ultimately leads to increased knowledge of the second language. For example, in the following exchange, the non-native speaker never produces the correct form, but is made aware of a pronunciation problem.

(NS = native speaker; NNS = non-native speaker)

NNS: and they have the chwach there
NS: the what?
NNS: the chwach—I know someone that—
NS: What does it mean?
NNS: like um like American people they always go there every Sunday
NS: yes?
NNS: you know—every morning that there pr-that -the American people get dressed up to got to um chwach
NS: oh to church—I see
(from Pica 1987: 6)

As a first step to learning, a learner must be aware of a need to learn. Negotiation of the sort which takes place in conversation is a means to focus a learner's attention on just those areas of language which do not 'match' with those of the language being learned. This allows learners to begin the long process of internal modification of the structure of their second language.

See also: Second Language Processing: Speaking; Discourse in Cross-Linguistic Contexts; Phatic Communion; Communication Strategies in a Second Language.

Bibliography

Bialystok E 1987 Words as things: Development of word concept by bilingual children. *Studies in Second Language Acquisition* **9**(3): 133–40

Day R R 1986 *Talking to Learn: Conversation in Second Language Acquisition*. Newbury House, Rowley, MA

Gass S M, Madden C (eds.) 1985 *Input in Second Language Acquisition*. Newbury House, Rowley, MA

Gass S M, Varonis E M 1985 Variation in native speaker speech modification to non-native speakers. *Studies in Second Language Acquisition* **7**(1): 37–57

Larsen-Freeman D, Long M H 1991 *An Introduction to Second Language Acquisition Research*. Longman, London

Long M 1980 Input, interaction and second language acquisition. (Doctoral dissertation, University of California, Los Angeles, CA)

Long M 1981 Input, interaction and second language acquisition. In: Winitz H (ed.) *Native Language and Foreign Language Acquisition*. New York Academy of Sciences, New York

Long M H 1983a Native speaker/non-native speaker conversation and the negotiation of comprehensible input. *Applied Linguistics* **4**(2): 126–141

Long M H 1983b Linguistic and conversational adjustments to non-native speakers. *Studies in Second Language Acquisition* **5**: 177–93

Pica T 1987 Second-language acquisition, social interaction, and the classroom. *Applied Linguistics* **8**(1): 3–21

Sharwood Smith M 1988 Consciousness raising and the second language learner. In: Rutherford W, Sharwood Smith M (eds.) *Grammar and Second Language Teaching*. Newbury House, New York

Tannen D 1986 *That's Not What I Meant*. Morrow, New York

Tomlin R 1984 The treatment of foreground–background information in the on-line descriptive discourse of second language learners. *Studies in Second Language Acquisition* **6**: 115–42

Varonis E M, Gass S 1985a Non-native/non-native conversations: a model for negotiation of meaning. *Applied Linguistics* **6**(1): 71–90

Varonis E M, Gass S 1985b Miscommunication in native/non-native conversation. *Language in Society* **14**: 327–43

S. M. Gass

Second Language Acquisition: History and Theory

Any normal human being acquires a language, with ease, unconsciously, and without instruction. Yet it is very difficult for many adults to acquire a second language, even with painstaking effort and expert instruction. Only the lucky few attain sufficient proficiency to pass for natives. The task of a second language acquisition (SLA) theory is to explain why this is so; to provide an accurate description and explanation of the process of second language acquisition. The task has barely been begun, and there is as yet no such thing as a theory of second language acquisition. It will be the burden of this article, then, not to present a

theory or theories, but rather to discuss the conceptual and empirical problems facing theory construction in this field, and to introduce current approaches to the construction of an adequate theory. (For more detailed accounts of empirical research in specific areas of SLA, see *Second Language Acquisition: Syntax*; *Second Language Acquisition: Phonology*; *Second Language Acquisition: Lexis*; *Second Language Acquisition: Conversation*; and *Second Language Acquisition: Semantics*.)

1. Historical Background

Although interest in second languages goes back to Babel, it is not necessary to trace the roots of SLA research as a scientific discipline further back than World War II, and the wartime and postwar interests in foreign language teaching. From the 1940s to well into the 1960s, the dominant theoretical position on language learning reflected the dominance of behaviorism in psychology, and of structuralism in linguistics. Briefly put, it held that language learning, whether of a first or second language, is a form of habit formation. In this sense there was no theory of SLA as such, given that no reason was seen for anything other than a general learning theory for all types of learning. SLA research concentrated on identifying the sources of difficulty of habit formation for a learner of a second language; 'difficulty,' of course, being defined in terms of degree of success or failure in producing native-like utterances in the second language.

The orthodoxy for this period is usually summed up in the term 'contrastive analysis (CA) hypothesis' (see *Contrastive Analysis*). This hypothesis held that insofar as the native language (L1) and the second language (L2) were similar in their surface syntax or phonology, the L2 would be easily acquired—given appropriate training and reinforcement—and where there were differences acquisition would be difficult. Efforts were, of course, made to refine the hypothesis, but by and large CA was really more of a central assumption than a hypothesis, and research was geared more to illuminating it than to testing it.

CA was seriously challenged once the implications of Chomsky's critique of behaviorism and structuralist grammar came to be felt within the field of SLA. Following similar work in first language acquisition, a number of SLA researchers began investigating the acquisition of English grammatical morphemes, and found what appeared to be a regular acquisition order irrespective of L1. This suggested the operation of some sort of universal process of language acquisition, and cast doubt on the CA hypothesis. In opposition to CA, the 'creative construction (CC) hypothesis' was put forward, claiming that SLA was a process not of habit formation but of grammar construction mediated by an internalized language acquisition device (LAD), and that the effects of the L1 on SLA were minimal. (For a classic expression of CA, see Lado 1957; for a comprehensive CC position see Dulay, *et al.* 1982.)

The best articulated and most ambitious CC position was developed by Krashen, in what was often referred to as the Monitor Theory. The Monitor Theory claimed that SLA is essentially the same as first language acquisition, in that the same LAD operates in the same way in both children and adults; that given sufficient comprehensible input, the LAD operates to acquire an L2 step by step in a universal natural order of acquisition; and that failure to achieve native-like competence in an L2 is attributable to affective factors such as motivation (see *Variables, Individual, in Language Learning: Classroom Implications*). Although extremely influential at first, the Monitor Theory was soon shown to suffer from major theoretical and empirical shortcomings, and the theory was generally abandoned by the mid-1980s.

One of the main failings of the Monitor Theory was that it did not take into account current linguistic theory as a component of SLA theory. It is only since the mid-1980s that SLA researchers have begun to apply systematically the insights of linguistic theory, especially theories of generative grammar, to the question of SLA, and it is at this point that SLA research can be said to have matured to a degree where it is possible to talk about serious attempts to construct a viable SLA theory. These attempts are discussed below in Sect. 2, but first it is necessary to clarify just what is at stake in constructing a theory of second language acquisition.

2. SLA Theory: Goals and Problems

A theory is a set of statements intended to provide an explanation for some phenomenon; it is an attempt to answer a 'why' or a 'how' question. A successful theory gives a satisfying answer; an unsuccessful one gives a less than satisfying answer. The question of what criteria of satisfaction are to be used is an extremely vexed one, on which there is very little agreement. Nonetheless it is necessary here to make a few rough preliminary distinctions in order to assess proposed SLA theories.

First of all, it is necessary to distinguish between explanation, description, and prediction. Accurate description of a phenomenon is of course a desideratum; but it leaves the phenomenon unexplained. A complete description of the stages of acquisition, if there were one, would not be an explanation of the process of acquisition, although it would make clear what it is that is to be explained. However, there are cases where the distinction between description and explanation blurs: for instance, it can be argued that the ungrammaticality of a given sentence type is explained by appealing to a principle of 'universal grammar,' which just *is* a description of the appropriate constraint (see Sect. 2.2).

Again, it is possible to predict a given phenomenon without being able to explain it correctly (as with pre-Copernican astronomy), or to explain it without being able to predict it (as with earthquakes). In SLA, for instance, there is a well-attested series of stages of negation through which L2 learners of English pass. The stages have been carefully described, and one can predict what a given learner's negative utterances will look like at any given stage, but there is still no satisfactory explanation of these stages. A good deal of current SLA research is, necessarily, descriptive work devoted to clarifying the nature of the phenomena to be explained, without necessarily proffering explanations of what is described.

2.1 The Domain of an SLA Theory

Given that an SLA theory should be explanatory, not just descriptive, what should it explain? What is the proper domain of an SLA theory? The acquisition of a second language, presumably, but there's the rub: it is not clear to what extent, if any, second languages are acquired. In first

language acquisition theory, one starts with the fact that acquisition is complete and universal; to all intents and purposes every human acquires a first language. This fact, formulated as the 'learnability condition' (see *Learnability Theory*), is a fundamental constraint on theory construction, a constraint that is of great benefit to theorists, since it drastically limits the kinds of theories to be entertained. For instance, a theory that appeals to imitation or instruction can be eliminated out of hand for, even if examples of both can be found, it is clear that neither imitation nor instruction is universal; for that reason alone such a theory can be rejected outright. In SLA theory, however, the learnability condition manifestly does not obtain, which makes the SLA theorist's job much more difficult. It might be claimed, for example, that instruction is necessary, and that it is precisely only those learners who had sufficient instruction who reach native-like proficiency.

But not only does the inapplicability to SLA theory of the learnability condition complicate theory construction by increasing the number of possible explanations, it also complicates the question of just what is to be explained. Where L1 acquisition theory has to explain acquisition, it would seem that SLA theory has to explain both acquisition and failure to acquire, or else it has to deny the existence of any successes (the failures seem to be undeniable).

The domain problem does not stop there, however. Even granting that the domain of SLA theory is the acquisition of an L2, it is not clear what is involved in the term 'acquisition.' Older, CA-style explanations would not even have spoken of acquisition, but rather of learning or habit formation, and they would have limited themselves to the utterances produced by L2 learners: what is now referred to as *performance*. The shortcomings of this approach to delimiting a domain have been clear since Chomsky (1965): even if an L2 learner's acquisition is totally different from that of an L1 learner, SLA involves the acquisition of knowledge, or competence. An L2 learner does not acquire utterances, but rather the (often incomplete) knowledge of structure and meaning underlying utterances. Accordingly, an SLA theory should explain what it is L2 learners know about the L2, and how they come to know it.

2.2 Explanation in SLA Theory—Performance versus Competence

The consequences of adopting L2 competence as the domain of an SLA theory are profound. For one thing, defining the domain to include competence increases the explanatory burden of the theory, and thus raises the standards for evaluating the theory's adequacy. The explanation of the acquisition of linguistic knowledge is dependent on a theory of linguistic knowledge; which is to say that an acquisition theory depends essentially on a linguistic theory. But this means that in part the explanation offered by the SLA theory will not be the type of causal explanation usually taken to be typical of theories, but rather something more like a functional explanation (or functional analysis) wherein a learner's complex knowledge of language is explained by being described; that is, by being broken down into simpler components (such as principles and parameters of universal grammar) and their interactions.

On the other hand, while an acquisition theory is a theory of the acquisition of *knowledge*, it is also a theory of the *acquisition* of knowledge. In explaining acquisition, it must appeal to some sort of causal explanation. In other words an SLA theory must detail the mechanism by which a learner moves from a state of not knowing x to a state of knowing x, where x is some aspect of an L2. Where the commitment to explaining competence entails a description, not of the types of utterances produced at different stages by a learner, but rather of the linguistic knowledge imperfectly and partially reflected by such utterances, the commitment to explaining the acquisition of that knowledge requires a description of the mechanism that moves the learner from stage to stage, if there are stages, or along the learning continuum if there are not.

This dual commitment—to explaining both competence and its acquisition—acts as a severe constraint on the types of SLA theory that can reasonably be entertained. It forces the theorist to go beyond elaborating the conditions under which SLA takes place. A few examples of SLA research will illustrate the insufficiency of many of the most common approaches to second language acquisition. For instance, a number of SLA researchers, influenced in part by trends in sociolinguistics, are interested in the problem of how and why a given learner's synchronic production varies according to task or situation: a learner may say *he speak English* or *he speaks English*, and the variability may or may not be systematic. The problem is simply that there is no reason to believe that the causes of variation in production—such variables as attention, interlocutor, discourse function, and linguistic context have been suggested—have any connection with the causes of acquisition. Insofar as production can be taken as evidence for acquisition (see Sect. 5), variable production of a given form only indicates that more than one variant has been acquired; and determining the causes of variation in the learner's output presupposes, rather than explains, the acquisition itself.

Again, many SLA researchers stress the importance of the communicative context of most L2 learning, and try to establish the discourse characteristics of successful SLA (see *Discourse in the Language Classroom*; *Discourse in Cross-Linguistic Contexts*; *Communication Strategies in a Second Language*). In some cases, the claim seems to be that, for instance, certain forms of input or feedback from a native-speaker interlocutor are in some way causes of SLA. However, no concrete proposals have been put forward to explain how modified input would lead to the internalization of an L2 grammar. In other cases, however, the goal is explicitly not explanatory, but rather descriptive and predictive; the reasoning behind such research is that given the need for comprehensible input, it is worth trying to find out what discourse or input factors contribute to comprehensibility. Such research is not only useful but for many practical purposes sufficient; nonetheless it does not explain how an L2 is acquired.

Still another major field of L2 research centers on the relation between SLA and linguistic universals, or language typology (see *Universals, Linguistic*). In particular, there is a good deal of SLA research that makes appeal to the concept of markedness, as defined within a system of language typology. Marked forms or structures are those that are rarer in the world's languages, or in some intuitive sense more complex, than their unmarked counterparts. So, for instance, of the six logically possible orders of Subject (S),

Object (O), and Verb (V) in a simple declarative sentence, OVS would be a marked order, while the SVO of English or the SOV of Japanese would be unmarked. Preposition-stranding (as in English *Who are you talking to?*) is quite rare among the world's languages, hence marked, while piedpiping (*To whom are you talking?*) is unmarked.

The concept of markedness has enabled SLA researchers to make highly specific predictions about acquisition, although these predictions have not necessarily been confirmed. For instance, it is often claimed that marked forms will be harder to acquire than unmarked forms, at least *ceteris paribus*, and consequently where both forms appear in the L2, the unmarked will be acquired first. Or, where structures form a so-called implicational hierarchy—where if a language has x it will have y, but not necessarily the reverse—it is often claimed that the L2 learner will acquire those structures in the hierarchical order, from unmarked (y) to most marked (x).

To take one interesting example, there evidently is a hierarchy of noun-phrase positions that can be relativized: if a language can relativize indirect objects (*the woman who(m) I sent the message to*) it can also relativize direct objects (*the man I love*) and subjects (*the dog that bit me*); if it can relativize genitives (*the man whose wife you met*) it can relativize the other three, and so on. It has been predicted that L2 learners of English would have increasing difficulty in producing relative clauses as one moves down the hierarchy from unmarked to marked. The claim has been largely, although not perfectly, borne out, but regardless of the experimental results the question is, what does this explain about SLA? Noun phrases corresponding to English *the man than whom I'm taller* are not possible in most of the world's languages, which is to say that such a relative noun phrase is marked; but the fact that a structure does not exist in most of the world's languages is hardly likely to cause difficulty for someone acquiring the structure in a language where it does exist, any more than acquisition of a given structure in a given language should be facilitated by the frequency of that structure's occurrence in other languages.

Since marked forms are generally less common than unmarked, an acquisition order that parallels the markedness order might be attributable simply to, say, comparative frequency in input. But in such a case 'markedness' has very little explanatory value; it is simply another term for 'infrequency.' On the other hand it is sometimes the case, as with English preposition-stranding, that the marked form is overwhelmingly the most common form in the input. If typological markedness were itself a causal variable in SLA, greater difficulty in acquiring preposition-stranding would be expected, despite the wealth of input, than in acquiring piedpiping, which, however unmarked it may be in the world, is extremely rare in English. Empirical research suggests that this is not in fact the case; but even if it were, the acquisition of English preposition-stranding would not be explained—only the conditions for acquisition would be partially described. In order to make markedness an explanatory concept in an SLA theory, it is necessary to define markedness in such a way as to connect it with learning mechanisms within the individual learner. Typological markedness is basically a statistical concept, defined across individuals and across languages; it is not at all clear what causal role it could play in an acquisition mechanism.

2.3 A Learnability Approach to SLA Theory Construction

If the goal of an SLA theory is to describe and explain the acquisition of L2 knowledge (as well as the failure to acquire such knowledge), such learner-external approaches as outlined above can only play a secondary role in theory construction. An SLA theory is a psycholinguistic theory, one that focuses on the individual learner. Learnability theory is one way of focusing on the internal workings of the language learner (see *Learnability Theory*), by manipulating the four basic components that play a role in acquisition: (a) the target language (TL); (b) the input that the learner actually receives in the course of acquisition; (c) the linguistic or other relevant knowledge the learner brings to the learning task; and (d) the learning mechanism(s) that the learner is equipped with.

There are of course differences in the nature of these four variables between first and second language acquisition. For instance there are likely to be differences (b) between the nature and amount of input received by a one-year-old child and an adult, and these differences may have an effect on the acquisition outcome. Perhaps the most important input difference may be that so-called negative evidence—that is, explicit evidence as to the ungrammaticality in the TL of a given structure—is essentially absent from L1 input, whereas it is often available in L2 input, especially in the case of formal L2 instruction. Whether this difference is important or not is a subject of some disagreement. More interesting perhaps is the difference in (c); an adult begins the acquisition of a second language already equipped with a great deal of knowledge—of the world, of languages, and preeminently, of the L1—and it is hard to imagine how this knowledge could not have some effect on acquisition. As for (d), there is controversy within L1 acquisition theory as to whether these mechanisms mature over the course of childhood acquisition, and within SLA theory as to whether they degenerate or even disappear afterwards.

There are various ways a theorist can manipulate the relative importance of these parameters; for instance, the mechanism in (d) may be assumed to be dedicated to language acquisition, as it is by theorists who employ some concept of universal grammar, or to be general-purpose, as perhaps most other SLA theorists would claim. If the TL is thought to be sufficiently simple, which was probably the case for most early acquisition theorists, the learning mechanisms can be that much simpler. Or if the input is taken to be highly rich and explicit—as seems to be the position of many discourse-oriented SLA researchers—it can be posited that the initial knowledge state of the learner is correspondingly less complex. There are limits, however, to the freedom one has in weighting these variables: there is overwhelming evidence, for instance, of the extreme complexity of natural languages, which calls into question any acquisition theory that relies on overly simple learning mechanisms or puts too much faith in input as a teaching device.

This learnability approach is utilized by a number of SLA researchers who, while working within the same framework and sharing many of the same assumptions, nonetheless differ among each other sharply in interesting ways. The common ground may be outlined as follows:

(a) The TL (L2) is highly complex. Further, it can best be represented by a generative grammar, of the sort provided by, say, Government Binding Theory, or lexical functional grammar (see *Generative Grammar: Principles* and *Lexical Functional Grammar (LFG)*).

(b) The input vastly underdetermines the TL grammar, which is to say that the linguistic knowledge represented by the grammar transcends the input.

(c) Therefore the learner must bring to bear on the input internalized knowledge of a highly abstract and subtle sort; simply extrapolating from input will not do.

The differences among the various proponents of learnability-oriented SLA theories are outlined below, along with discussion of the problems facing the various positions.

3. Universal Grammar in SLA: Theists and Deists

Most SLA theorists working within the learnability framework agree that some form of universal grammar (UG) is an essential element of language acquisition. UG consists of a set of universal principles which drastically constrain the set of possible hypotheses that can be entertained by the (L1) language acquirer. Some of these principles are universal in the strictest sense, in that they are necessarily instantiated by any human language. Some principles are universal in the sense that gender-specific biological functions are universal in the human species; they are universal across all languages that instantiate them, but irrelevant to languages that do not. Languages that do not instantiate the principle also do not violate it.

Finally, and perhaps most interestingly for SLA theory, some principles, known as parameters, vary in specific limited ways, for instance the order of head and complement. Parametric variation accounts for the major type of variation across languages. A principles and parameters theory also provides a more useful, psycholinguistic definition of markedness: a marked parameter setting is one that requires input to be chosen. Not all parameters have markedness values, but for those that do, the unmarked value is the default value, the one that will be chosen by the learner in the absence of evidence in the input that that value is inappropriate.

The question for SLA theory is, what is the role of UG in SLA? Clearly, at least two neatly contrasting positions are conceivable, and indeed held: UG functions in SLA just as it does in L1 acquisition; or, UG ceases to function once an L1 is acquired in childhood. The latter claim accords to UG the sort of role Enlightenment deism gave to God, that of the *deus abscondidus*, who having once created the universe, lets it run on its own without any interference. UG, in this view, having produced the individual grammar of the learner, retires from the scene to let that grammar do its work. The former position sees UG in a more traditional not-a-sparrow-falls theistic light; UG itself is still active in the adult, both in constraining the adult's knowledge and use of his L1 and also in guiding the acquisition of an L2. Despite the theological terminology introduced here, these are empirical claims, susceptible of empirical testing. Sects.

3.1 and 3.2 explain how they have been tested; it may be that both positions are too extreme, and that middle ground will have to be found.

3.1 Theism: L2 Acquisition = L1 Acquisition

The claim that SLA is mediated by UG would at first glance seem to have certain points in its favor. For instance, it is often claimed in support of the theist position that in the absence of UG, which constrains the learner's hypotheses, the L2 learner would be expected to violate UG. It has often been either claimed or taken as a working assumption that the language of the L2 learner—what is known as the learner's interlanguage—is itself a natural language. In terms of late twentieth-century linguistic theory, this is to say that interlanguages do not violate UG. (UG of course does not cover everything in language; errors like *he speak English* or *I have a book blue* are not UG violations.) And indeed it would seem that interlanguage grammars are never 'crazy' grammars; learners do not seem to use rules calling for movement of the nth word in a sentence, for example, or for mirror-reversal of word order. To this extent at least there seems to be support for the idea of UG actively mediating SLA.

On the other hand, once the explanatory role of theory is taken into consideration, there is a major problem with SLA theism: if UG is at work in SLA, why does it do such a poor job? If the learnability condition applied to SLA—that is, if all adults acquired an L2 with the ease, rapidity, and completeness of children acquiring an L1—the theist claim would be much more convincing. Indeed, the burden of proof would clearly be on the deists. But in fact perfect L2 acquisition is the exception not the rule. At a minimum the theist is obliged to provide an explanation for the widespread failure of L2 learners to acquire. One explanation that has been offered (as seen above with Krashen) is that affective factors such as motivation or attitude toward the L2 either reduce input or reduce the effectiveness with which input is processed. A rather interesting different proposal is that, while UG is indeed active, other more general learning mechanisms are also at work in the adult, and these conflict with UG, whereas in the child UG works unimpeded. So far there has been no detailed proposal made to substantiate either of these suggestions, so it is hard to evaluate them empirically at present.

Assuming for the moment that there was a satisfactory explanation of failure to acquire, how much weight does the mere absence of UG violations in interlanguage have? Practically speaking, of course, the absence of 'crazy' grammars would offer cold comfort to the learner: since no natural language violates UG, and yet most natural languages are mutually incomprehensible, it should theoretically be possible to acquire an interlanguage while at the same time being totally incomprehensible and uncomprehending when using it. More specifically in terms of SLA theory, it is open to the deist to respond to the theist that the conformity of the interlanguage to UG is solely a result of the L1, not of UG. It appears that one is entitled to expect stronger claims from the theists, and one way of framing such stronger claims is provided by the concept of parameters.

For example, given an L1 and an L2 that differ with respect to a given parameter—in other words, the L1 and the L2 have different parameter settings—there are different possible claims a theist might wish to make. For instance:

(a) Strong theism: The learner starts at zero, with UG in its initial state; the L1 has no influence. Thus the L2 learner fixes the parameter setting in the same way as a native speaker of the L2 would.

(b) Weak theism: The learner starts with the L1 grammar, but is able to make the appropriate adjustments in parameter settings thanks to the operation of UG.

With respect to (a), it might be thought that given such clear evidence as foreign accents or those L1-related syntactic errors that textbooks warn against, such a position would be an obvious nonstarter. It must be remembered, however, that the theist claim is not that there is no L1 influence, or transfer as it is often called, but only that the L1 parameter value will not influence the learner's setting of the parameter in the L2. In any case it can be said that there is no empirical support for strong theism. It might be added that (a) presents conceptual problems, in that it is not clear how learners could ignore their L1 knowledge when first encountering L2 input.

The similarities and differences between strong and weak theism can be summed up as follows:

(a) any truly universal principle should be evident in the interlanguage, either because of the direct influence of UG (strong theism) or perhaps because of transfer from L1 (weak theism);

(b) any principle instantiated only in the L2 should be acquired (given sufficient appropriate input);

(c) there either may be (weak theism) or will not be (strong theism) a sequence (from inappropriate to appropriate) in the acquisition of parameter values that differ between the L1 and L2;

(d) negative evidence, such as explicit instruction, should not be necessary.

3.2 Deism: The Fundamental Difference Hypothesis

The theist position is based on the claim that even if L2 acquirers do not attain the level of native speakers, they nonetheless do (often) acquire a sufficiently complex and subtle knowledge of the L2 to require, as in L1 acquisition, appeal to UG for a source of explanation. To this the deist replies that in so far as such knowledge is attained, it can be explained by the effects of UG through the L1 (see Bley-Vroman 1989 for a deist position).

The essential argument is that in order to explain the noticeable differences between L1 acquisition and L2 acquisition, the most important being the inapplicability of the learnability condition in the latter, it makes sense to assume that UG does not directly operate in SLA. (Deists often appeal to the claim that there is a critical period, usually thought to end roughly at the onset of puberty, after which L1-like language learning is biologically impossible.) Where L1 acquisition involves UG on the one hand and a language-specific learning mechanism on the other, the deist claim is that in SLA, UG survives only as specifically instantiated in the L1, and that in the place of a language-specific learning mechanism the L2 acquirer must rely on general learning mechanisms, such as hypothesis-testing, inductive and deductive reasoning, analogy, and so on. Such mechanisms are not capable of producing the kind of competence found among all native speakers; but that very insufficiency can be used in SLA theory to account for failure to acquire an L2. It can also be used to explain the variation in L2 proficiency, since humans do vary widely in, say, their hypothesis-forming abilities. On the other hand, since UG is still in an indirect sense available, there is a possible explanation for those SLA successes that seem to transcend the capabilities of general learning mechanisms.

4. Testing Hypotheses in SLA Theory

Of course, phrased this loosely, the appeal of the deist position can easily appear to be undermined by its apparent lack of falsifiability: if a learner is successful it is because of UG via the L1, if unsuccessful it is because UG is not available. This danger is avoidable, however, once the deist claims are made more specific.

4.1 Refining Predictions

Deists and theists make conflicting claims about the function of UG in SLA; these claims can be made more explicit by phrasing them as testable predictions about the L2 knowledge acquired by learners. Both sides would agree that any truly universal principles (such as structure dependence) will be manifest in the learner's interlanguage, as will any principles that obtain in both the L1 and the L2 (such as subjacency in English and French). Thus in order to distinguish between theism and deism empirically, one of the following two situations needs to be investigated: (a) a given principle is instantiated in the L2 but not the L1, and hence the L1 can be eliminated as a source of L2 knowledge of this principle; (b) a given parameter is set differently in the L1 and the L2. (Logically, a third possible case is where a principle is instantiated in the L1 but not the L2. A theist would claim of course that the principle would not manifest itself in the interlanguage; but on the other hand the deist is not committed to claiming that the learner would carry over the principle in a situation where it is totally irrelevant. There is no need for a deist to claim, for example, that an English-speaker learning Korean will try to observe the constraints imposed by subjacency on *wh*-movement, despite the fact that there is no *wh*-movement in Korean.)

Actually, these claims need to be refined even further. Given that input is also one of the factors affecting the learnability of an L2, input must also be eliminated as a potential source of information about the principle or parameter. The head-position parameter, for instance, governs the order of head and complement, and has two values, head-initial and head-final. Even where the L1 and L2 differ in values (as in Japanese and English), it should be immediately evident from very simple input what the order is, and hence the successful acquisition of English head positions by a Japanese learner can hardly be telling evidence against deism. Similarly, the so-called prodrop parameter distinguishes inter alia between languages which permit and forbid deletion of pronoun subjects (for instance, Spanish and French, respectively). A French speaker learning Spanish will soon encounter large numbers of subjectless sentences, which should enable him to set the parameter to the L2 value (at least with respect to this aspect of the parameter).

Thus what is necessary is a situation where the four elements of the learnability approach (see Sect. 2.3) can be applied in such a way that both the input and the learner's

L1 (and extralinguistic) knowledge can be eliminated as sufficient causes of acquisition of a given L2 form, as defined by linguistic theory, leaving UG as the only logical source of explanation. The difference here is that the element of preexisting knowledge is further refined, and divided into L1 knowledge and knowledge of UG. It may be worth noting that one effect of this approach is the formulation of a highly precise CA hypothesis, one anchored firmly in linguistic theory.

4.2 Controlling for Input; the Subset Principle

What does it mean to say that one has eliminated input as an explanation of the acquisition of a principle or parameter setting? Obviously SLA cannot proceed without L2 input, and thus in this sense input cannot be eliminated. What input itself cannot do, however, is tell the learner what is *not* possible in the target language. For instance, both Spanish and English permit sentences with pronoun subjects. Nothing in the input of sentences with overt subjects, however, tells the learner that pronoun deletion is forbidden in English, or permitted in Spanish. Of course the Spanish learner (L1 or L2) will hear subjectless sentences, and the English learner will not (or not in those situations where they are permitted in Spanish). But absence from the input (even assuming that the learner can notice such an absence) is not a sufficient condition for a learner to exclude a rule or structure from the developing grammar; if it were, no generalizations would be possible. The question is, how does the English learner (L1 or L2) know what generalizations are overgeneralizations?

The problem can be posed in this way: There are countless situations where two grammars stand in a subset/superset relation to each other, whether those grammars are of two different languages or two possible versions of one language. (Properly speaking, it is the sets of sentences generated by the two grammars that are in such a relation.) For instance, a grammar that permits both overt and deleted pronoun subjects is a superset of one that permits only overt pronouns; a grammar that permits both preposition-stranding and piedpiping is a superset of one that permits only piedpiping; a grammar that permits relative pronoun deletion is a superset of one that forbids it. If a learner starts with the subset hypothesis—for example, the assumption that subject pronouns are not deletable—and the target grammar is actually the superset, there should be no problem, since superset sentences should be in the input. But if the learner incorrectly hypothesizes the superset grammar, nothing in the input itself should lead to a revision of that hypothesis.

This problem does not seem to arise in L1 acquisition, a fact which has led to the claim that children in the course of acquisition follow some sort of 'subset principle' that keeps them from overgeneralizing. In SLA theory, it would seem that a strong theist would have to claim that the principle works for adults too; the evidence is clearly against that claim. For instance, Spanish-speaking learners of English quite often have an extremely difficult time avoiding pronoun deletion, and Japanese learners of English often interpret reflexive pronouns much more widely than English in fact permits (so that, for example, they would take *John wants Bill to abase himself* as ambiguous). This evidence does not, however, necessarily vindicate deism against weak theism; after all, both the subset language and the superset language conform to the constraints of UG. Rather, as White suggests, the difference between L1 acquisition and SLA may lie not in the nonavailability of UG in SLA, but in the failure of learning mechanisms like the subset principle to operate.

Needless to say, the question of the role of UG in SLA is still open, and much work still needs to be done (for detailed discussion see White 1989). But it is clear that the existence of a well-articulated linguistic theory developed with an eye to learnability offers the hope of finally constructing a cogent SLA theory.

5. A Note on Method

There is no direct way to observe or measure L2 knowledge. This fact has led some SLA researchers to conclude that L2 competence theories are unempirical, and to restrict themselves to observable behavior, or performance. Such a conclusion is unwarranted, and such a restriction is self-defeating. It is true that knowledge itself cannot be observed, but it is just as true that energy or mass or evolution cannot be observed. What can be done is observe linguistic performance, under both natural and experimental conditions, and infer from performance to competence, precisely where inference can be made to nothing else.

This is simply to say that performance is evidence for a theory, not the object of the theory. The evidence for an SLA theory may come from any of a wide variety of experimental tasks and observational situations. Not all methods are appropriate at all times, and not all have the same utility; what they have in common is that the data they produce are all performance data. But just as the behavior of a falling feather does not refute a theory of gravitation, so no given performance data are necessarily a refutation of a hypothesis about competence. This does not make SLA theory unempirical, but it does make theory construction harder than mere observation and classification.

6. SLA outside of UG

This article has concentrated on the role of UG in SLA, and the role of UG in a theory of SLA, for two related reasons. First, although one's linguistic competence, L1 or L2, is not only complex but wide-ranging, the kind of knowledge that UG theories of language try to account for is certainly central and indispensable. Second, it is only in the area where UG is relevant that rich and detailed theories (that is, theories of UG) are currently available. Consequently, it is much clearer what is at stake in this area with regard to a potential SLA theory.

Still it should not be forgotten that L2 knowledge includes a great many areas that are either unrelated or only indirectly related to UG. UG-oriented SLA theorists do not (or do not yet) make claims about the acquisition order or difficulty of English grammatical morphemes, or about the acquisition of indirect request forms. The price one pays for the more accurate focus gained by a UG theory is that the domain of inquiry is necessarily narrowed. It may very well turn out that no unified theory of SLA is possible; for instance, it may turn out that there is no essential difference between learning the Japanese word for *cockroach* and learning the population of Chicago, which if true would mean that at least part of L2 learning is subsumed under a general theory of learning. The future development of SLA theory is not yet clear, and indeed one of the major tasks facing theorists is the delimitation of the domain of the theory that awaits construction.

Bibliography

Bley-Vroman R 1989 What is the logical problem of foreign language learning? In: Gass S M, Schachter J (eds.) *Linguistic Perspectives on Second Language Acquisition.* Cambridge University Press, Cambridge
Chomsky N 1965 *Aspects of the Theory of Syntax.* MIT Press, Cambridge, MA
Dulay H, Burt M, Krashen S 1982 *Language Two.* Oxford University Press, New York, NY
Ellis R 1985 *Understanding Second Language Acquisition.* Oxford University Press, Oxford
Flynn S, O'Neil W (eds.) 1985 *Linguistic Theory in Second Language Acquisition.* Kluwer, Dordrecht
Gregg K R 1989 Second language acquisition theory: The case for a generative perspective. In: Gass S M, Schachter J (eds.) *Linguistic Perspectives on Second Language Acquisition.* Cambridge University Press, Cambridge
Krashen S D 1982 *Principles and Practice in Second Language Acquisition.* Pergamon Press, Oxford
Lado R 1957 *Linguistics Across Cultures.* University of Michigan Press, Ann Arbor, MI
Larsen-Freeman D, Long M H 1991 *Introduction to Second Language Acquisition Research.* Longman, London
McLaughlin B 1987 *Theories of Second-Language Learning.* Edward Arnold, London
White L 1989 *Universal Grammar and Second Language Acquisition.* John Benjamins, Amsterdam

K. R. Gregg

Second Language Acquisition: Lexis

The acquisition of lexis has only become a question of interest to applied linguists since the early 1980s. The position in the early 1990s is that lexis has been unduly neglected in the past, and is due for a reevaluation, but as yet, this reevaluation has not got very far.

Two basic questions about the acquisition of lexis will be addressed in this article. The first is: what strategies do learners use to acquire words, and which of these strategies are efficient? The second question changes the focus of enquiry from the learner's acquisition of words, and asks instead: what happens to a word once it is acquired? How is it integrated into a learner's existing stock of words? Almost all the extant applied linguistic research has dealt with the first of these questions.

1. How Do Learners Acquire Words?

Research on the strategies that learners use to acquire new words suggests that in any group of learners, a wide variety of strategies will be found. On the whole, however, better learners adopt a wider range of strategies for learning than less successful learners. Good language learners tend to take responsibility for improving their own vocabulary, while less successful learners do not. Within this general framework, there are two main types of acquisition strategy: conscious learning and incidental learning.

The bulk of the research that has looked at vocabulary acquisition has concentrated on the conscious acquisition of words. There are obvious reasons for this: in general, it is easier to compare methodologies if one can control the variables easily, and this has led to a large number of studies which have compared various methods of learning foreign language vocabularies. The basic research method is for two groups of students to learn a list of words; one group uses an experimental method, while the other uses what is generally referred to as a 'traditional' method, but in practice, usually consists of scanning a list of L2 words and their translation equivalents. The scores of the two groups are then compared. A large number of studies of this type have been published, and almost all of them are very unsatisfactory. The two exceptions to this criticism are an outstandingly good, but apparently little-known study by Lado, et al. (1976), and a large group of studies run by Levin and Pressley (see Meara 1983 and 1987 for summaries of this work). Lado, et al.'s work is a series of detailed experiments on the effects of different presentation methods on vocabulary acquisition, and Levin and Pressley's work consists of a large number of experiments on the applications of mnemonic imagery techniques to the acquisition of vocabulary. The essence of this work is that the more a learner interacts with a word s/he is trying to learn, the more likely it is that the word will be acquired. Levin and Pressley's work in particular suggests that it is possible to learn very large vocabularies very quickly by constructing vivid visual images that link the L2 target word with an L1 equivalent via an L1 word resembling the L2 target word in sound. There is some considerable disagreement among language teachers about what to do with this finding, and how to integrate it into a syllabus, but there is no serious disagreement about the effectiveness of the method in its own terms.

One of the main shortcomings of the type of research outlined in the preceding paragraph is that it has focused attention on the acquisition of vocabulary divorced from use or from real context. Many of the subjects tested in the methodological comparisons were not real language learners, the time-scale studied was short compared to the time it takes to learn a language, and the vocabularies learned were actually quite small in comparison to what a real language learner has to acquire to become fluent. There is a serious shortage of good research that has looked at the behavior of real language learners acquiring vocabularies over a long time-scale.

A rather different approach to the acquisition of lexis, which avoids some of these problems is to study the way real language learners acquire the meanings of new words in context. The preferred method for studying this process is the use of think-aloud techniques, where learners, usually in pairs, discuss the possible meanings of unknown words that they have found in texts. These discussions are tape-recorded and transcribed, and then analyzed for evidence of inferencing. In general, the best work in this area shows that learners *are* able to infer the meaning of a sizeable proportion of the unknown words they meet in texts. Good learners are able to use a wide range of contextual clues to work out what an unknown word must mean. Less adept learners tend to stick with surface phonological or orthographical clues, and are less able to use clues provided by discourse structure, sentence structure, and so on. I. S. P. Nation has argued that it is possible to teach learners good guessing strategies which can improve the number of words they can guess correctly. Teaching this kind of strategy is important because it is now recognized that no language course can cover all the vocabulary that a learner needs to know by overt instruction, and that some method other than overt instruction must account for most of the words a learner acquires in an L2.

This leads on to the question of whether lexis can be acquired incidentally rather than consciously. Research on this question is almost nonexistent in an L2. There is, however, some very good L1 research that is relevant. Nation reports research showing that there is a fairly high probability of L1 learners picking up new words after hearing them read aloud in stories. The pick-up rate was even higher if the reader was able to gloss new words as they occurred. Nagy and Herman (in McKeown and Curtis 1987) suggest that passive exposure to L1 via reading is able to account for almost all the new words acquired in the teens. Their argument goes as follows: given the available information about the amount of material that typical teenagers read in the course of a year, and the proportion of words in this material that they are not likely to know, it is possible to estimate how many unknown words a typical reader is likely to meet in the course of a year's reading. It is also possible to determine empirically the likelihood of a reader being able to infer the meaning of one of these unknown words, and the likelihood of this meaning being retained beyond the immediate context. When all these figures are put together the prediction is that an average reader will acquire about 1,000 new words each year—a figure that is broadly in line with empirical work on vocabulary growth in teenage L1 speakers. It would be relatively easy to replicate this work in an L2, and to do a systematic study of the factors that affect the take-up rate of L2 words encountered in meaningful contexts. One would perhaps expect learners to be less good at inferring word meanings, but better at retaining those that were inferred successfully. It is not known how this prediction agrees with what actually happens. There are no normative data on vocabulary growth in L2 speakers, and this makes comparisons with L1 speakers impossible. Some of Nation's recent (1990) work on estimating vocabulary size looks as though it might provide standard tools for assessing vocabulary growth in the not too distant future.

2. Acquired Words: Their Integration and Use

So far, the learner has been the focus of attention of the research reviewed: what the learner did to acquire words; the effectiveness of the method. It is possible to shift the focus of the question, however, and to concentrate instead on the thing that is learned. This shift produces a completely different set of questions—questions that have typically been asked by psychologists rather than by language teachers and applied linguists. These questions concern the structure of the lexicon, and they have typically been investigated by comparing the way bilinguals and monolinguals behave on simple psychological tasks involving word skills. This research enables the development of tentative answers to questions such as: do bilinguals have a single, integrated lexicon, or two more or less separate ones?; and, more generally, how is the L2 speaker's lexicon structured relative to that of his L1?

Many applied linguists will be familiar with a distinction that used to be made between compound bilinguals and coordinate bilinguals. Compound bilinguals were typically learners, often children, who had acquired two languages in a single situation. Coordinate bilinguals were learners, usually adults, who had acquired their two languages at different times, and in different settings. It was sometimes argued that compound bilinguals had a single, integrated lexicon, while coordinate bilinguals had two largely separate lexicons. This distinction is not now widely used, but still informs the way some applied linguists think about lexis.

During the late twentieth century, psychologists have become interested in the relationship between bilingualism and the structure of the brain. There is now a very large body of experimental research on this topic, much of it based on analyses of bilingual aphasics, and much of it attempting to show that the lexicon of the L2 is more strongly supported by the right hemisphere of the brain than by the left. Most of this research is inconclusive, though there is some evidence that cognate words, and other items where transfer is possible from L1 to L2, may be stored rather differently from L2 words which are completely unrelated to L1 items. However, a lot of this work is based on people's ability to recognize individual printed words, and because of this, it is not seen as addressing problems of immediate practical interest to language teachers. It is, furthermore, difficult to interpret these data because the experiments are generally closely tied to particular models of the mental lexicon, and the implications of these models are often not well-understood even by experts, let alone by the interested general reader. It is probably safe to assume that the structure of the lexicon in one's L1 does affect the way that one acquires words in an L2, and that, insofar as the lexicon is concerned, at least, being bilingual in English and French, or English and Dutch, is not the same thing as being bilingual in English and Arabic or English and Japanese. It follows from this, that the lexical tasks facing an Arab learning English, for instance, will be very different from the tasks that face a Chinese speaker learning French, or a German speaker learning Quechua.

A second reason why this literature is difficult to generalize to L2 learners is that most of it has been concerned with the performance of high-level bilinguals, whose lexical skills are well-developed, and whose lexicons are very large. The lexical problems experienced by less advanced non-native speakers, particularly beginners, are often very severe, but at the same time, performance on some well-known words can be almost as good as that produced by native speakers. This suggests that it is a mistake to look at the learner's L2 lexicon as a single undifferentiated whole. Instead, researchers need to think about L2 lexicons as containing many different types of words—some fully integrated into the learner's verbal repertoire, others more marginal.

Much of the literature on vocabulary acquisition assumes that there are basically two types of words—active vocabulary and passive vocabulary. In practice, this classification is probably too crude to be of much real use. Most learners will readily classify words in their L2 into half a dozen or

so categories, ranging from words they are completely sure about, through words they are less sure about and words they know they once knew, but have now forgotten, to words they are sure they have never met. Words seem to move around fairly freely between these different states—an L2 learner may be able to use a word easily today, but next week it may have retreated to the edge of competence, and three weeks later, for no apparent reason, it may come readily to mind when required. In as much as applied linguists use explicit models of lexical development at all, the models which are in use in the early 1990s do not take account of this fluctuation: they tend to assume that the learner's lexicon is a rather static thing, and that learning new words simply involves activating passive vocabulary, and adding new items to the stock of active words. This widely accepted view of the L2 lexicon is clearly an oversimplification, but at the moment it is not clear what sort of model could profitably replace it.

3. Conclusion

Corder once said that applied linguistics was rather like gardening: if one provided the right conditions the flowers would grow, and the applied linguist's job was to specify the right conditions for the growth to take place. A great deal of research in the early 1990s on the lexicon is rather like this. It is fine as far as it goes, but rather limited in the sorts of questions it asks. What is really needed is the equivalent of a biochemistry of vocabularies: a framework that will allow questions to be asked about how vocabularies grow, what makes stable structures in lexicons, how these structures vary from one individual learner to another, and how they interact with other aspects of second language competence.

See also: Applied Linguistics: Lexicology; Second/Foreign Language Pedagogy: Vocabulary.

Bibliography

Carter R, Nation I S P (eds.) 1989 AILA Review **6**: whole volume
McKeown M G, Curtis M E (eds.) 1987 *The Nature of Vocabulary Acquisition*. Erlbaum, Hillsdale, NJ
Meara P M (ed.) 1983 *Vocabulary in a Second Language*, vol. 1. Centre for Information on Language Teaching and Research, London
Meara P M 1987 *Vocabulary in a Second Language*, vol. 2. Centre for Information on Language Teaching and Research, London
Nation I S P 1990 *Teaching and Learning Vocabulary*. Newbury House, New York

P. Meara

Second Language Acquisition: Phonology

Mastering the sounds of a new language is by common consent one of the most difficult tasks facing the foreign language learner. Popular opinion has it that getting rid of an 'accent' in the second language is almost impossible, at least for adults. Having 'a foreign accent' is for most people a matter of speaking the new language using the *pronunciation* patterns of the native language. Some of the central issues raised in the field of second language phonology will be addressed in this article. These include whether learning a new set of pronunciation patterns is all that is involved in acquiring the *sound system*, that is, the *phonology*, of a second language; whether adults can indeed learn the sound system of a second language; and exactly *which* factors (including the first language) impede or facilitate the learning of the new phonology.

1. What Is Learnt in a Second Language Phonology

1.1 Articulatory (and Perceptual) Patterns

The most obvious task facing the learner is to develop a new mode of pronunciation. This involves gradual mastery of a different set of *articulatory* and *perceptual* patterns from that used in the native language. Although certain sounds as such may be familiar from the native language or other languages, other sounds are likely to be quite different. For example, an English-speaking learner of French comes across the sounds [p t k f v s z l m n], [ʃ] (*sh* in English *ship*), and [ʒ] (*s* in English *measure*) in the foreign language, similar versions of which are present in the learner's own language. However, sounds like [y] (Fre *u* in *lune*), [ø] (Fre *eu* in *feu*), and [ɔ̃] (Fre *on* in *bon*) are also met, which are not familiar from English. Even so, *all* sounds of the second language (L2), whether familiar or not, in all their combinations have to be realized via a new set of articulatory patterns (and their associated perceptual representations).

The articulatory patterns of the L2 are of course not just a matter of displacing the tongue, lips, soft palate, etc. from one sound to the next, but are themselves subject to the stress, rhythm, and intonation characteristics of the new language. Thus, for the English-speaking learner of French, 'getting the pronunciation right' equally involves making sure that the stress on words, phrases, and sentences is on the last syllable in each case, that the rhythmic and intonational focus of the language is also on the last syllable of phrases and sentences, and that individual syllables are produced with far fewer length distinctions than they are in English.

In other words, the pronunciation 'skill' part of learning the phonology of a second language requires the gradual development of a new and complex set of sensorimotor patterns of the speech organs and control over their displacement in time and space.

1.2 A Phonological System

Perhaps contrary to popular belief, learning new articulatory movements is not all that is involved in acquiring the sound system of a second language. The learner also has to develop some systematicity in the sounds acquired, over and above their actual physical realization. In order to learn a new language *system*, it is also necessary to discover its underlying sound regularities, or *phonology*, in the narrower sense of the term. This means learning, for instance, which are the distinctive sounds or *phonemes* of the new language, which *features* characterize and distinguish them, how their forms vary according to context (i.e., as *allophones*), and in which combinations they can occur (i.e., the *phonotactics* of the language; see *Phoneme*). In addition, the learner must acquire knowledge of word-stress rules and of those stress and intonational features which distinguish phrase and sentence units of the L2.

Thus, the Dutch learner of English has to learn that /g/ is a *phoneme* in the L2 (which it is not in the L1, although [g] *does* occur as an *allophone* in the language), that is, that it can distinguish words, as in /g/ versus /k/ in *game* versus *came*, and *dog* versus *dock*, and that the features which distinguish /g/ from other phonemes in English involve the properties [voiced] and [velar], etc. He also has to learn, for example, that /g/ can occur in syllable-initial combinations only with following /w/, /j/, /r/, and /l/ as in *Gwen*, *argue*, *grey*, and *glow*, and that the phonemic distinction between /g/ and /k/ is effectively neutralized in initial three-consonant clusters such as /skr/ in *screw*, etc (see *Neutralization*).

1.3 A Phonetic Representation

These two aspects of sound structure, the purely physical or 'skill' element and the abstract or 'knowledge' element, are related in the learning task by the *phonetic* values of sounds. Developing a *phonetic representation* means establishing a set of values which express the phonological features of the sound system in such a way that they can be directly related to physical substance, that is, enable the more abstract properties of sounds to be converted into actual articulatory (and perceptual) realization. Again, each language encodes its phonological substance differently: whereas in French the distinctive feature [voiceless] for /p t k/ is *phonetically* realized as [unaspirated/short-lag voice onset time (VOT)], in English the same distinctive feature for /p t k/ is realized variably as [aspirated/long-lag VOT] when these sounds occur syllable-initially; [unaspirated/short-lag VOT] when following /s/ initially, as in *spear*, *steer*, *skier*; and [glottalized] in syllable-final position, as in *sip*, *sit*, *sick*.

The third task facing the L2 learner is, then, to construct phonetic representations for the sounds and sound patterns of the new language via which the articulatory (motor) and perceptual (sensory) patterns necessary for the actual pronunciation of the language can be related to the more underlying systematic relations obtaining between them.

2. Adult Acquisition of a Second Language Phonology

2.1 Biological Influences

It is widely believed that children can acquire the sounds of a foreign language more readily than adults, and indeed there is research which supports this, at least as far as the development of articulatory and perceptual abilities is concerned. Concerning the development of knowledge of an L2 phonological *system*, however, it might be argued that adults share an advantage over children, since they are able to apply maturer cognitive capacities to the establishing of underlying relations between sounds. But even with articulatory and perceptual abilities, adult learners are not always at a disadvantage. It has been shown, for instance, that in early stages of L2 pronunciation learning, adults make more rapid progress than children.

The argument which supports the 'Joseph Conrad syndrome,' that is, that postpubertal learners can rarely, if ever, achieve a nativelike pronunciation in the second language, rests largely on the 'critical period hypothesis' (Lenneberg 1967). Lateralization of cortex function occurring around puberty inhibits subsequent attempts at mastery of the sound patterns of a new language (Scovel 1989). However, at least as far as sound *discrimination* abilities in the L2 are concerned, it would seem that poorer performance by adults as opposed to children is to be ascribed to the fact that older learners tend to process the L2 signal *linguistically* in terms of their L1 auditory/acoustic patterns, whereas younger learners are more capable of *auditory* processing of the signal without reference to already developed L1 linguistic patterns. Whether this may be interpreted as evidence for an absolute loss or deterioration of perceptual abilities with postpubertal learners is a matter of debate.

2.2 Social–Psychological Factors

It is a commonly shared feeling among learners of new languages that pronunciation is somehow a more sensitive area socially and psychologically than other levels of language structure such as syntax and vocabulary. Developing a set of new sound patterns involves taking on another 'language ego' to an extent not experienced in developing a new syntax or a new lexicon, for example. Individual and social pressure may variously inhibit or facilitate this L2 pronunciation proficiency (see *Accent*).

Attitudes to pronunciation in both the native culture and the foreign culture play an important role in the learning process by partly determining the level of proficiency wished to be attained. Cultures vary in the extent to which a 'good' pronunciation of both native languages and foreign languages is valued. For example, Japanese and French cultures in general lay greater value on a near-native pronunciation by foreigners of their languages than Dutch culture, whereas the latter lays greater value on the 'correct' pronunciation of foreign languages than the former. These cultural differences influence the acquisition behavior of the native learners of foreign languages and the foreign learners of the native language. Equally, the learners' own attitudes to the society and culture of the people whose language is concerned have been shown to be highly significant in determining L2 pronunciation success.

Type and degree of motivation for learning the second language are as much an important determinant in pronunciation acquisition as with other areas of language development, perhaps even more so. The greater the desire to immerse oneself in the foreign society and culture, the greater the pronunciation level likely to be reached.

Personality variables such as empathy, intuition, self-esteem, and the 'flexibility of ego boundaries' have been shown to correlate positively with a learner's ability to acquire accurate L2 pronunciation.

3. Perception and Production

Mention has been made in Sect. 1.1 above of the fact that learning 'the phonology' of a second language includes, most obviously, the development of new sensorimotor (articulatory and perceptual) speech patterns. However, this raises the questions of how production and perception abilities are related in L2 speech acquisition and of whether it is indeed the case, as is generally assumed, that perception is always ahead of production in development, that the accuracy of the latter *presupposes* accuracy of the former, and that the two skills are closely interrelated.

Research on the developmental relation between perception and production in L2 learning presents an inconclusive picture. While perception and discrimination abilities are shown to be ahead of production capacity on certain tasks, the opposite is true on other tasks in the L2. Studies of a wide range of adult second language learners with differing L1s and L2s show varying results as to the relative predominance of perception versus production attainment. One conclusion, therefore, to be drawn from the research is that perception and production abilities in the foreign language are certainly *not* inextricably related, but rather develop as quasi-independent linguistic skills.

However, the one way in which perception and production abilities *are* related is via the phonetic representation (see Sect. 1.3) of the sounds of the new language. The phonetic representation of sounds mediates not only between their properties as abstract entities of an underlying phonological system and as concrete instances of articulated and perceived 'sound,' but also between their realization in production and perception modalities. Developing perception and production skills in a foreign language, then, involves gradually refining control over the sensory and motor interpretation of an L2 phonetic model sound or 'prototype.' The extent to which perceptual and production accuracy diverges is not so much a product of any inherent relation between these skills, but rather of other factors, such as the extent to which the L2 phonetic prototype coincides with equivalents in the L1. The learner, in other words, develops perception and production abilities relative to a particular processing-neutral L2 phonetic norm.

4. Structural Influences on Second Language Phonology

4.1 The Role of the First Language

In the popular view, the influence of the native language is omnipresent in second language sound learning. Indeed, the learner's task is seen by some as the systematic elimination of L1 influences over time. While it is true that the sound structure of the L1 manifests itself in the learning of the L2 in a more immediately obvious way than, for example, the syntactic structure of the L1, it is certainly not the case that the influence is random. Research has shown that L1 structure affects the developing L2 sound structure *under certain conditions*.

However, only some sound entities are subject to this selective L1 influence. Whereas patterns of articulation and perception, sound sequencing (phonotactics), and stress and intonation inevitably carry over from the native to the foreign language, certainly in early stages of learning, what *has* been shown to be subject to differential influence from the L1 is the establishment of the phone types of the L2. All things being equal, it seems that those sound types of the L2 which are phonetically *similar* to those of the L1, that is, which share major characteristics but differ in minor ones, will be subject to a greater amount of L1 influence than those which are either identical to or completely different from sound types of the L1. To give an example, the influence of L1 Dutch on L2 English will be greater in the case of [e] as in *well* (a similar, but not identical, phone type in the two languages) than with L2 [æ] as in *cat* (different) or L2 [ɪ] as in *bit* (identical). It has also been generally shown that L1 influence is relatively greater with 'lower' (i.e., phonetic/articulatory-perceptual) levels of sound structure than with 'higher' (i.e., purely phonological) levels.

4.2 The Mechanisms Relating L1 and L2 Sound Structure in Acquisition

Saying that degrees of similarity between L2 and L1 phones are criterial in establishing the degree of L1 influence on the developing L2 sound structure presupposes a means and mechanism by which the structures are compared in learning.

In common with the study of other areas of L2 acquisition, theories of second language phonology attribute to the learner a selective capacity to employ the resources of his L1 in acquisition. However, while the physical substance of the speech signal inevitably constrains the hypotheses which a learner makes as to the nature and comparability of L2 phone types encountered, the learner nonetheless 'chooses' to transfer his L2 sound type or not. In other words, 'transfer' of L1 structure in sound learning is as much a *cognitive* mechanism of acquisition as a *behavioral* one. With reference to the above, degrees of similarity and difference between sound types of the L2 and L1 are significantly a matter of learner judgment and of change in this judgment as the learner's own L2 sound system evolves.

However, the learning processes employed in second language phonological acquisition are not necessarily the same as those attributed to the child mastering the sounds of his mother tongue. What the child has in terms of vocal versatility, the adult to a large extent compensates in terms of cognitive skill. However, by and large, the learning model remains the same, that is, acquisition proceeds by testing hypotheses as to the nature of the target sound structure, constrained on the one hand by the physical substance involved, but informed on the other by the linguistic resources available in what has been learnt already, namely the L1, *and* in the developing L2 itself. An example of 'generalization' of L2 knowledge in phonological acquisition, that is, of using the linguistic resources already established in the foreign language to 'solve' a particular L2 sound 'problem,' would be the L1 French speaker's assumption in English that *all* instances of [p], [t], and [k] in initial (cluster) position are aspirated, leading to the well-attested mispronunciations of *speak* as [spʰiːk], *stand* as [stʰænd], *skin* as [skʰɪn], etc. L1-based transfer and L2-based generalization are considered, then, to be the two main learning processes or strategies in sound acquisition, as much as they are assumed to be present in other areas of second language acquisition.

4.3 The Developmental Dimension

The degree of structural influence, and with it the role of transfer as a processing strategy, varies in the course of L2 speech acquisition. As at the syntactic or lexical level, the effects of transfer seem to be more obviously present at earlier rather than later stages of acquisition, at least as far as phone realization is concerned. As acquisition proceeds, the influence of the L1 and the mechanism of transfer give way gradually to other influences that shape the developing L2 phonology, such as the mechanisms ('developmental processes') associated with the acquisition of the mother tongue. Developmental processes are those presumably inherent phonological strategies which one finds operating in earlier child language, such as devoicing of word- and syllable-final obstruents, consonant cluster simplification, nonweakening of unstressed syllables, etc.

However, the relative influence over time of transfer and developmental processes remains very much subject to the compatibility of L2 and L1 sound structures as assessed by the learner. For instance, as far as phone types are concerned, the closer a particular L2 sound is judged to be to an L1 'equivalent,' the more likely it will be open to transfer effects and the less to developmental effects—bearing in mind that compatibility judgments themselves will change over time.

4.4 Contextual Influences

A number of generalities may be observed concerning the influence of context on the acquisition of L2 sounds. For example, all things being equal, stressed syllables are produced more accurately than unstressed syllables and initial consonants more accurately than final consonants. This itself may be evidence for the earlier acquisition of the former elements in question. However, studies have shown that virtually *any* L2 phone which does not have an L1 equivalent is acquired in a particular contextual order. By and large, consonants in the L2 are acquired first in a prevocalic environment and last in an environment in which they cooccur with consonants similar to them in 'place' and 'manner of articulation' (see *Phonetics, Articulatory*). Extrapolating from these findings to the acquisition of L2 English [θ] (*th* as in *thank*) by learners who have no [θ] in their L1, one expects that [θ] in *thank* will be acquired before [θ] in *bath* before [θ] in *through* before [θ] in *months*.

Furthermore, context in the sense of the activity engaged in when producing L2 speech has been shown to be a significant determinant of the realization of L2 phones. Comparisons of the degree of accuracy produced for various 'new' L2 sounds in different speech activities demonstrate that the more 'formal' the task (e.g., word-list reading as opposed to free speech), the more targetlike is the realization.

4.5 Typological Factors

The role of structural influences on second language phonology, as will be clear from the discussion, is a matter of the interplay of L1–L2 compatibilities and 'general' preferences in sound structure realization. These 'general' or *typological* characteristics of sound systems influence L2 phonological acquisition to varying extents.

Sound types which occur less frequently in the languages of the world, that is, which are typologically 'marked,' are indeed likely to present more difficulty in the L2 and/or be acquired later (than those sounds which are not thus 'marked'). For example, as with children learning English as their mother tongue, foreign speakers of English will, all things being equal, have greater problems with typologically marked sound types such as [θ] and [ð], that is, *th* as in *thing* and *that*, than, for example, [t] and [d] as in *ten* and *den*.

However, not only particular sound types, but also sound contrasts, sound combinations, and syllable types have been shown to be subject to markedness considerations in second language phonological acquisition. For instance, those sound contrasts which are positionally marked in the L2 are more 'difficult' to acquire than those which are unmarked, *on condition that they are not present in the L1*. Thus, the voicing contrast between obstruents in word–final position in English as an L2 (e.g., /p/ versus /b/ in *cap* versus *cab*, or /s/ versus /z/ in *loose* versus *lose*) will be more difficult to acquire for learners than the same contrast word-medially or word-initially, because typologically the contrast at final position is most marked. Similarly, if reduction of consonant clusters is a feature of L2 learning, then such reduction will not violate typological markedness relations: Mandarin Chinese-speaking learners may reduce final consonant clusters in English since the L1 has none, but they will never produce combinations such as fricative + fricative or stop + stop, since these combinations are typologically marked. Thus, for the final cluster [lst] in *whilst*, if reduction occurs, say from three to two consonants, it will be to [ls], [lt], or [st] or similar combinations, but never to [tt], [dt], [ss], or [zs], for example. Concerning syllable types, however, there is little evidence to show that typological markedness is *overall* a dominant factor in L2 acquisition. In cases where a second language has a more complex syllable structure than the L1, for example, allowing syllable-final consonants and consonant clusters as opposed to a simple consonant + vowel (CV) combination, learners' renderings of the new structures are more influenced by L1 transfer than by any general preference for a CV, that is, typologically unmarked syllable type.

In conclusion, then, it seems that the influence of typological factors on second language phonology is very much subject to similarity measures between the L2 and L1, and that the compatibility of the sound structures of the two languages in contact is in fact the most important determinant in shaping the developing L2.

See also: Accent; Second Language Pedagogy: Pronunciation.

Bibliography

Flege J E 1988 The production and perception of foreign language speech sounds. In: Winitz H (ed.) *Human Communication and Its Disorders*. Ablex, Norwood, NJ

Hammarberg B 1988 Acquisition of phonology. *Annual Review of Applied Linguistics* **9**: 23–41

Ioup G, Weinberger S (eds.) 1987 *Interlanguage Phonology*. Newbury House, Rowley, MA

James A 1988 *The Acquisition of a Second Language Phonology*. Narr, Tübingen

James A, Leather J (eds.) 1986 *Sound Patterns in Second Language Acquisition*. Foris, Dordrecht

Leather J, James A (eds.) 1990 *New Sounds 90: Proceedings of the Amsterdam Symposium on the Acquisition of Second-language Speech*. University of Amsterdam, Amsterdam

Leather J, James A 1991 The acquisition of second-language speech. *Studies in Second Language Acquisition* **13**: 305–41

Lenneberg E 1967 *Biological Foundations of Language*. Wiley, New York

Scovel T 1989 *A Time to Speak*. Newbury House, Rowley, MA

A. R. James

Second Language Acquisition: Semantics

'Semantics' is the study of word-internal, referential, and compositional meaning of verbal expressions. Whether they are children or adults, the linguistic and communicative tasks of learning are quite similar for all second language learners:

(a) They need content words in order to communicate, and they need to communicate in order to get access to content words and grammatical meaning; this can be called the 'learning paradox.'

(b) In order to satisfy the fundamental 'referential,' 'communicative,' and 'personal' functions of language use, the learner needs the expressions for semantic concepts like *time*, *space*, *modality*, *quality*, *specificity*, *causes*, *conditions*, etc. S/he needs a 'functional semantic framework for schematizing experience'. This is partly cognitive work, since some of the concepts exist in the second language (L1), but not in the first language (L2), and vice versa.

(c) In order to use language economically and efficiently, learners have to stabilize the expressibility of basic communicative functions by 'grammaticalization'; this implies in an elementary stage of learning that the learner finds out appropriate, polyfunctional candidates for the expression of his/her intentions that have to be elaborated and differentiated by semantic functions and grammatical form, e.g., 'come' or 'go' for the semantic field of locomotion without any further verbal differentiation, the negator 'no' and/or the connective 'but' for the semantic field of 'adversativity', and so on (see Skiba and Dittmar 1992).

Whether learners acquire an L2 in a natural context ('SLA [second language acquisition] without explicit teaching') or in a classroom setting ('tutored SLA'), the acquisition of semantics proceeds *on-line* by the *application* of verbal knowledge in 'real' interaction. The dynamics of the acquisition of semantic concepts involves the supply of words (lexical items) to semantic fields, the constraining of competing words and phrases to their 'conventional' meaning, and the organization of recurrent semantic representations by stable grammatical devices. A learner using the invariant form *come* as a covering form ('candidate') for the list of expressions for 'movement' in a language or as a marker of requests (performative use) in combination with other verbs (*come take . . .*), *overgeneralizes* the meaning of this verb applying it in polyfunctional ways for 'go,' 'take,' 'make,' 'drive,' etc. Constraining overgeneralized forms to their habitual meaning and developing grammatical devices for specific semantic functions is the essential semantic challenge for the learner.

1. 'Semantics' and First Language Acquisition (FLA)

Based on cross-sectional and longitudinal studies, the acquisition of meaning has been described in most detail for FLA (Clark and Clark 1977: 407–514; Wode 1988: 134–78, 217–25). Semantic aspects of FLA deal with the world of experience that is organized by the mind 'in categories such as persons, objects, events, actions, states, times, places, directions, and manners. Propositional structures are composed of elements representing entities of these sorts . . .' (Levelt 1989: 74). FLA starts with single words and their global, context-specific ('protosemantic') meaning in a wide range of primarily pragmatic functions. In developing words within 'semantic fields,' their meaning components (shape, color, form, quality, quantity, etc.) are acquired to establish cognitive boundaries and contrasts between them. The first 'holophrastic' stages (chunks of words, ritual expressions) are followed by two-word utterances, so-called 'pivot' constructions that show the fixed position of an element P in S (a small stock of items), where other elements (X) vary freely and appear in a wide range of different words (three basic patterns: $P_1 + X$, $X + P_2$, $X + X$). In this 'pivot' stage, the following semantic functions are acquired: presence versus absence, existence versus nonexistence, reappearance, agent and action, object and action, possessor and possession, localization and attribution. The stage of three and more word utterances is dominated by processes of 'grammaticalization' (morpho-syntactic elaboration of the verbal and nominal groups).

2. 'Semantics' and Second Language Acquisition (SLA)

Most of the studies in SLA have focused on the acquisition of verbal means to represent semantic fields. Other research has given preference to a 'cognitive approach' to meaning which is concerned with the conceptual side of grammar. This mapping of form onto function will be considered below in more detail.

2.1 Focus on 'Interlanguage'

The standard paradigm in SLA is the description of learner varieties 'outside the classroom' with a focus on 'learning under natural conditions' of communication (without explicit teaching), with an emphasis on cross-sectional studies in the 1970s (cf. Klein and Dittmar 1979) and on longitudinal research in the 1980s (cf. Perdue 1982; Dittmar and Terborg 1991). Instead of errors being perceived as derivable and predictable from static structural contrasts between two 'a priori grammar' descriptions (term coined by Hopper 1987), they came to be seen as creative learner constructions and as part of natural transitions from one stage of learning to the next in approximating the 'target language' (TL) via a continuum of forms and functions constrained by psycho- and sociolinguistic factors (cf. Klein 1986). Studies in 'contrastive semantics' (numerous in Eastern countries) are thus excluded from this article because they do not take acquisitional *processes* into account.

2.2 Form versus Function

Words and forms are not 'autonomous' as some linguists seem to suggest, but they have communicative functions (cf. Pfaff 1987). Studying the semantics of learner varieties means describing the mapping of forms/expressions onto semantic concepts that have particular communicative functions in the course of the learning process. The distinction between 'form' and 'function' is necessary because many forms can be found in SLA that do *not* have the meaning of the corresponding target language and thus are 'overgeneralized,' or simply are 'different' or 'deviant' (see for empirical evidence Dittmar 1981, 1984; Stutterheim and Klein 1987). The basic questions within this framework are, then, these: What are the verbal candidates for expressing a certain 'semantic concept'? What are the formal and grammatical devices that are developed within these 'semantic concepts' in the course of the learning process (see *Grammaticalization and Lexicalization*)?

2.3 Bilingual Lexicon

Do bilinguals have two different semantic representations, one for *table* and another for *tarabeeza*, or do they have only *one* single underlying representation for two words? Or do they add to a representation of *table* a phonological variant which leads to *tarabeeza* in Egyptian Arabic? The second perspective is supported by some observational studies of children learning two languages simultaneously, which were made in the first decades of the twentieth century. Ronjat reports that Louie, a French and German bilingual, began giving word pairs at 20 months (*oeil—Auge*; *oui—ja*). In his process of acquiring two languages, Louie continued—at the stage of 36 months—to elicit equivalents: having learned *gefüllte Tomaten* 'stuffed tomatoes' in German, he asked his father in French *Comment tu dis, toi*? 'how do you say' in order to elicit *tomates farcies*.

Leopold's child, Hildegard, also elicited word pairs, but from time to time she adapted the pronunciation to that of the other language, or she created a parallel form, for example, *Butterfliege* from 'butterfly' for German *Schmetterling* (see Hatch 1983: 64–74 for an account of Ronjat, Leopold and other investigations in the lexicon). These examples suggest that the children learned one semantic representation with two phonological shapes. However, there is also a good deal of evidence against this explanation (see Hatch 1983: 66–7). For the time being, no clear conclusion is possible from these results. The findings need further study.

Whereas bilingual *children* learning two languages simultaneously manifest many 'overextensions' of meaning along semantic feature lines, *adult* L2-learners seem to be more cautious. Kellerman holds that transfer from L1 to L2 is a basic, systematic mechanism and that it relates to the psychological reality of 'coreness' for lexical items. In several studies on the learning of French, English, and German by Dutch students, Kellermann found a strong correlation between 'coreness' and transferability. 'However, when searching for the attributes of coreness, he found that concrete meanings are not necessarily all more transferable than abstract meanings, so coreness is not simply concrete versus abstract. High imagery also might be an attribute of coreness, since it correlated with judgments of coreness ... Kellermann found no *simple* relationship between linear distance away from core and transferability' (see Hatch 1983: 73, where the reader will also find an overview of Kellermann's studies).

Further research is needed to evaluate these hypotheses.

2.4 'Operating Principles': The Semantic Strategies Model

SLA learners seem to acquire some structures before others because of the 'operating principles' they apply to L2. Starting to talk in a 'pragmatic mode' (characterized by 'polysemy' and 'parataxis' of content words, avoidance of grammatical codification) learners pass through a stage where they organize semantic coherence in utterances by strategies of information processing (given information precedes new information, expect the first N–V–N sequence to be agent, action, and object, etc.); there is evidence that semantic insecurity (caused, for example, by the competition between two verbs) impedes the process of grammaticalization (cf. Skiba and Dittmar 1992). The passage from the 'pragmatic mode' to the 'syntactic mode' (grammaticalization) seems to be 'operated' by semantic strategies.

Some basic organizational principles of 'polyfunctional' meaning which learners apply are the following:
   (a) Give preference to that expression which is semantically marked over one that is less marked.
   (b) Approximate as closely as possible the relevant features of the target item.
   (c) Select from among the appropriate expressions those
      (i) relating to your native language;
      (ii) occurring most frequently in everyday communication;
      (iii) with a broad rather than narrow semantic field;
      (iv) that can fulfill many communicative functions (cf. Dittmar 1981: 151; Pfaff 1987: 84 uses the term 'principles of plurifunctionality').
Klein (1986) adds 'principles of semantic coherence':
   (d) Place elements that belong together semantically as close as possible together ('principle of semantic connectedness').
   (e) Place orienting elements (information as to place, time, and modality) at the beginning of the utterance ('principle of orientation', see Klein (1986: 94) for these and other principles).
Many researchers in SLA are concerned with the intriguing question of how the learner progresses from the linguistic product of an elementary utterance to that of a more elaborated utterance. 'Semantic' and 'cognitive strategies' seem to explain the *process* of this progress. The learner's task in overcoming semantic (lexical) gaps in communication constitutes a special case of 'semantic processing.' 'The gaps can take many forms—a word, a structure, a phrase, a tense marker, an idiom. Our attempts to overcome these gaps have been called "communication strategies"' (Bialystok 1990: 1). 'Communication strategies' (in opposition to 'learning strategies') have been investigated in numerous empirical studies in the 1970s and 1980s. Bialystok (1990) examines the current definitions and research findings.

2.5 Semantic Concepts: Longitudinal Studies

Longitudinal studies of semantics in SLA are the most advanced investigations:
   (a) Huebner (1983) studied the 'natural' acquisition of English by an adult Hmong speaker for one year recording his 'interlanguage' every three weeks.
   (b) The European Science Foundation (ESF) project 'Second Language Acquisition by Adult Immigrants' (cf. Perdue 1982) investigated undirected SLA of four informants each of two different source languages learning one of the following target languages: Dutch, English, French, German, and Swedish for 30 months (one source language (SL) was shared by a pair of target languages (TL)):

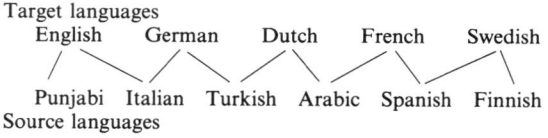

Target languages
English   German   Dutch   French   Swedish

Punjabi Italian Turkish Arabic Spanish Finnish
Source languages

   (c) Kuhberg studied the SLA of an 11-year-old Turkish boy and an 11-year-old Polish girl for 18 months (see Dittmar and Kuhberg 1988).

   (d) The Berlin project 'The Grammatical Elaboration of Elementary Learner Varieties' investigates the 'natural' acquisition of German as L2 by Polish migrants over a period of 24 months (five male and three female subjects).
Among other aims, detailed observations were made in these three studies concerning the acquisition of semantic concepts like 'temporality,' 'locality,' and 'modality.'

2.5.1 Temporality

The referential areas 'time' and 'space' are two domains which are very basic to success and failure in communication. SLA studies benefited from excellent theoretical frameworks for their empirical descriptions.

The most advanced studies in semantics of SLA have been done on temporality. The Heidelberg data gathered in the 1970s (cf. Klein and Dittmar 1979; Dittmar 1981) showed that a morphologically based tense analysis of elementary and elaborated learner varieties of German does not adequately describe the semantic emergence of temporality in the lexicon and in discourse. Changes over time were not only expressed by verb morphology, but also by the discourse principle of the natural order of events and specific lexical items like calendaric expressions, prepositional phrases, etc.

The acquisition of verbal expressions within the semantic concept 'temporality' has been described in depth by the ESF project (Bhardwaj, Dietrich, and Noyau, = BDN, 1988). The comparison of the temporal acquisition sequences of five target languages by learners of six source languages is based on an explicit, theoretical frame of analysis distinguishing 'types of temporality' (tense, aspect, aktionsart), 'temporal reference' ('theme,' 'relatum,' 'relation'), 'embedding in time-aspect,' and 'discourse structure.' Based on the categories of this outline, the learning of temporality has been described at the elementary, intermediate, and advanced level of the learners' proficiency. From this rich body of research the answers to three basic questions are selected for consideration here:

(a) How are temporal relations expressed?
'The time of utterance is the basic relation in locating matters in time' (BDN 1988: 505). The first expressions are adverbials (*now, today*) expressing partial or total simultaneity. The first grammaticalized tense distinctions are past versus nonpast (differences in the morphological marking according to source language). 'Anaphoric relations' appear very early and are mostly indicated by indirect means (principle of natural order). It seems that the earliest anaphoric means express the relation AFTER, expressions of BEFORE follow. Linguistic means for the relation SIMULTANEOUS are learned very late.

At least temporal verb morphology is developed by all learners, but some do not develop tense contrasts. Bound morphemes occur first as tense markers, auxiliaries come later (p. 506). It is true for all target languages that tense markers occur with particular classes of verbs under specific 'favorable semantic and formal conditions' (p. 506).

(b) Embedding in time
'The organization of temporality in early L2 does not entail explicit indication of temporal referentiality, let alone aspect differentiation ... referentiality proceeds from

implicit to lexical and from there to grammatical devices' (BDN 1988: 507–08). It is interesting that learners with an L1 which has aspect acquire the corresponding target language means before learners where this is not the case.

(c) Internal temporal features as typical of L2 acquisition by children

Are these observations also valid for children who acquire temporal relations in a second language? Similar developmental stages have been found by Dittmar and Kuhberg (1988), but there are the following striking differences:

   (i) Both children acquire inchoative, durative, iterative, and continuative actionality very early.

   (ii) Both children learn within a time span of 8–12 months complex morphological markings of the verbal tense system (the Turkish boy starts with striking 'aspectual' features).

   (iii) Discourse organizational principles do not play such an important role as in adult SLA.

Dittmar and Kuhberg (1988) isolate four functional–semantic phases in the learning process: lexical and implicit-pragmatic; grammaticalization; lexical and grammatical elaboration; close approximation to the target language.

2.5.2 Spatial Relations

How learners organize 'spatial meaning' has been described by the ESF project in various publications. The overall results of the study are presented in Becker, Carroll, and Kelly (= BCK 1988).

The 'frame of analysis' is inspired by the work of Piaget and made concrete by the following categories of spatial reference which cover all linguistic means found in the learner varieties:

  (a) reference to the locomotion of movers (persons/vehicles);

  (b) reference to the relocation of objects (causative movements);

  (c) reference to the path of a movement;

  (d) reference to the spatial relations existing between theme and relatum at source/goal; to name a few examples:

    – topological relations (containment, interiority, neighboring, contact, distant, exteriority);

    – projective relations (verticality, left/right, in front of/behind).

One important result of the study is that learners fall into two groups with respect to 'reference to locomotion': learners of French on the one hand and learners of Dutch, English, and German on the other. 'While the former group applies a number of verbs of locomotion at the earliest stage of acquisition, the latter starts with one form which is not even systematically realized in all appropriate contexts' (BCK 1988: 367). The group learning German, Dutch, English starts with a simple verb for *move*, without differentiation of 'motion' and 'direction'; more specific expressions have to be encoded by combinations of verb and spatial deictic particles (prefixes of the verb). These particles occur late because they have a complex formal structure (word order rules, etc.). 'In opposition to this, learners of French encode both MOTION and PATH/DIRECTION incorporated in the verb' (BCK 1988: 367). Learners of German, for example, begin the acquisition of

expressions for MOTION and DIRECTION by *raus* 'out of,' *weg, fort* 'away,' *auf, oben* 'up,' *unten* 'down,' *zurück* 'back,' and combine these spatial particles (later) with simple verbs of motion like *gehen* 'go,' *kommen* 'come,' or *machen* 'make.' The following examples show the differences between the target languages German and French for:

S/HE IS GETTING ONTO A BUS/TRAIN   (1)

Source language Moroccan–Arabic	Source language Italian
Target language French	Target language German

Zahra:
le garçon entre le bus
'the boy enters the bus'

Gina:
Kommen auch der Mädchen und oben dies *camion*
'come also the girl and up this truck'

Tino:
Sie geh schnell oben der Zug
'she go fast up the train'

S/HE IS CLIMBING ON A CHAIR   (2)

Zahra:
monter avec la chaise
'climb with the chair'

Gina:
geh oben de stuhl
'go up the chair'

Tino:
er geh oben eine stuhl
'he go up a chair'

'To sum up, one can say that the learner's access to reference to locomotion is guided by characteristic encoding procedures of the target languages. At a semantic micro-level, L1-influence could well intervene in the semantic organization of the repertoire' (BCK 1988: 369).

Another area that was compared cross-linguistically concerned 'reference to causative motion' which is encoded in verb stems; therefore, learning processes cannot be divided up into a 'path of lexicalization' and a 'path of morphological verb coding.' That is to say that morphological information and meaning of the verbs cannot be separated. 'It is rather the intransparency of causative verbs in context that provides the biggest stumbling block ... A goal-oriented causative expression may leave the motion implicit or very unspecifically encoded and still be successful' (pp. 370–71). The learners of the target languages German and Dutch had specific difficulties with the causative verbs *stellen, setzen, legen* 'put, set, lay down.'

It is still a matter of debate whether the German utterance *Der Schlüssel steckt in der Tür* and its French version *la clé est sur la porte* mean the same thing ('the key is in the door'), although the local relations are expressed by quite different verbal means (German *in* = CONTAINMENT, INTERIORITY; French *sur* = CONTACT). Does learning a second language involve cognitive differences? Slobin (1991: 23) holds that the languages that 'we learn in childhood are not neutral coding systems of an objective reality' and agrees with Wilhelm von Humboldt who wrote in 1836 (quoted in 1988: 60):

To learn a foreign language should therefore be to acquire a new standpoint in the world-view hitherto possessed, and in fact to a certain extent this is so, since every language contains the whole conceptual fabric and mode of presentation of a portion of mankind. But because we always carry over, more or less, our own world-view, and even our own language-view, this outcome is not purely and completely experienced.

Early-1990s research using a similar methodological approach as for the description of the learning of 'temporal' and 'spatial relations' is being conducted into the acquisition of verbal means for the concept of 'modality.' The discovery of sequences in the acquisition of lexical and grammatical means in the field of modality is a challenge in identifying appropriate fieldwork techniques (the marking of 'propositional attitudes' by modal expressions is not necessarily obligatory in utterances and is often very subjective), and for identifying an explicit description (there is no unified theory of the basic modal categories). A good overview of the descriptive problems and the acquisitional sequences in learning the means for 'deontic' and 'epistemic' modality is found in Dittmar and Terborg (1991) and Skiba and Dittmar (1992).

3. Conclusion

Important progress has been made in SLA descriptions of semantics. The preferred areas of analysis are those which are well elaborated in linguistic theory and widely explored in FLA. There has been a fundamental change in research from cross-sectional to longitudinal types of developmental studies. This change in paradigm was only made possible by leaving the classroom as the privileged research area and looking at learning within natural contexts. Indeed, SLA has adopted similar methods to FLA. It should not be feared that these trends diminish attention to improvements in foreign language learning under controlled conditions. So much can be learnt from deeper insights into learning and communication strategies and into factors that affect successful learning (input, data processing, the role of the structure of source language and target language, etc.) that, in the long run, teachers in applied linguistics will profit from these detailed studies.

A number of issues in SLA semantics may be suggested as requiring further work:

(a) How do the particular semantic domains work together in order to accomplish *coherence* in utterances? There is intensive research on temporality and locality; more should be done on 'reference to persons,' 'modality,' and the semantics of 'verbal predicates.' How do these domains interact with each other in learner varieties at different stages?

(b) How do semantic processes interact with discourse principles? The systematic work on semantics reported in this article should be combined with the detailed pragmatic and interactive microanalyses of 'exolingual communication' (the discovery of communication and learning strategies in the process of on-line interaction between native and nonnative).

(c) How does the construction of semantic fields interrelate with individual and social experience? In what respect do 'cognitive processing' and 'cultural norms' filter the learning process? Do they have 'additive' or 'subtractive' effects on the learning product?

Bibliography

Becker A M, Carroll M, Kelly A (= BCK) (eds.) 1988 *Reference to Space*. European Science Foundation (ESF), Strasbourg

Bhardwaj M, Dietrich R, Noyau C (= BDN) (eds.) 1988 *Temporality*. European Science Foundation (ESF), Strasbourg

Bialystok E 1990 *Communication Strategies: A Psychological Analysis of Second-language Use*. Basil Blackwell, Oxford

Clark E V, Clark H H 1977 *Psychology and Language*. Harcourt Brace Jovanovich, New York

Dittmar N 1981 On the verbal organisation of L2 tense marking in an elicited translation task by Spanish immigrants in Germany. *Studies in Second Language Acquisition* 3(2): 136–64

Dittmar N 1984 Semantic features of pidginized learner varieties of German. In: Andersen R W (ed.) *Second Languages: A Cross-Linguistic Perspective*. Newbury House, Rowley, MA

Dittmar N, Kuhberg H 1988 Der Vergleich temporaler Ausdrucksmittel in der Zweitsprache Deutsch in Lernervarietäten zweier elfjähriger Kinder mit den Ausgangssprachen Polnisch und Türkisch anhand von Longitudinaldaten. In: Ullmer-Ehrich V, Vater H (eds.) *Temporalsemantik*. Niemeyer, Tübingen

Dittmar N, Terborg H 1991 Modality and second language learning: A challenge for linguistic theory. In: Ferguson Ch, Huebner T (eds.) *Second Language Acquisition and Linguistic Theory*. Benjamins, Amsterdam

Ellis R 1985 *Understanding Second Language Acquisition*. Oxford University Press, Oxford

Gutfleisch I, Rieck B O, Dittmar N 1979 Interimsprachen- und Fehleranalyse: Teilkommentierte Bibliographie zur Zweitspracherwerbsforschung 1967–1978. *Linguistische Berichte* 64: 105–42 and 65: 51–81

Hatch E M 1983 *Psycholinguistics*. Newbury House, Rowley, MA

Hopper P 1987 Emergent grammar and the a priori grammar postulate. In: Tannen D (ed.) *Linguistics in Context: Connecting Observation and Understanding. Vol. XXIX, Series Advances in Discourse Processes*. Ablex, Norwood, NJ

Huebner T 1983 *The Acquisition of English: A Longitudinal Analysis*. Karoma Publishers, Ann Arbor, MI

Humboldt W von 1988 (trans. Heath P) *On Language: The Diversity of Human Language-structure and its Influence on the Mental Development of Mankind*. Cambridge University Press, Cambridge

Klein W 1986 *Second Language Acquisition*. Cambridge University Press, Cambridge

Klein W, Dittmar N 1979 *Developing Grammars: The Acquisition of German by Foreign Workers*. Springer-Verlag, Berlin

Levelt W J M 1989 *Speaking: From Intention to Articulation*. MIT Press, Cambridge, MA

Perdue C (ed.) 1982 *Second Language Acquisition by Adult Immigrants: A Field Manual*. European Science Foundation, Strasbourg

Pfaff C W (ed.) 1987 *First and Second Language Acquisition Processes*, Cross-Linguistic Series on Second Language Research. Newbury House, Cambridge, MA

Skiba R, Dittmar N 1992 Pragmatic, semantic and syntactic constraints and grammaticalisation: A longitudinal perspective. *Studies in Second Language Acquisition*

Slobin D 1991 Learning to think for speaking: Native language, cognition, and rhetorical style. *Pragmatics* 1(1): 7–25

Stutterheim C von, Klein W 1987 A concept-oriented approach to second language studies. In: Pfaff C W (ed.) 1987

Tarone E, Frauenfelder U, Selinker L 1976 Systematicity/variability and stability/instability in interlanguage systems. In: Brown H D (ed.) *Papers in Second Language Acquisition*, Proc. 6th Annual Conf. on Applied Linguistics, University of Michigan, January 30–February 1, 1975. Research Club in Language Learning, Ann Arbor, MI

Wode H 1988 *Einführung in die Psycholinguistik: Theorien, Methoden, Ergebnisse*. Max Hueber Verlag, Ismaning/Munich

N. Dittmar

Second Language Acquisition: Syntax

Research into the syntactic development of second language learners had a slow start but is now a fast developing area. In the 1970s, when second language acquisition studies really got under way, the emphasis was first laid on morphological phenomena. This obviated the need for sophisticated linguistic analysis and, in particular, allowed comparisons between second language behavior and the linguistic patterns already documented and discussed in current *first* language (mother tongue) studies. Now, work on syntax has become a growth area and linguistic theory as well as psycholinguistic principles are being applied to the problem of learner development and learner performance in second language (L2) syntax. Key issues include (a) the feasibility of particular linguistic and psychological theories to explain L2 phenomena and, more specifically; (b) the way in which learners pass through given stages of syntactic development; (c) to what extent correction and explicit knowledge or rules can affect that development; and finally, (d) whether hypotheses that are based on L2 research involving a small number of world languages are still relevant when applied to the learning of a much greater range of structurally diverse grammatical systems.

1. Early Research

Early L2 studies based on behaviorist psychological principles embraced all areas of the language, including syntax. The theory predicted in a straightforward way that, where the learner mother tongue and target languages syntax differed, mother-tongue syntactic habits would show up in the form of 'interference.' Just as a particular accent would characterize a speaker whose mother tongue was, say, German, so that same learner's syntax would betray German characteristics where it diverged from the L2 norm. Hence if German learners of English attempt to form a question with, say, 'who' then they will initially follow their German syntactic habit and say 'Who likes chocolates?' This habit, when carried over to English, should result in an English sentence which is, as it were 'by accident,' perfectly correct. However, in other questions, the German habit will lead to interference as, for example, where English requires the auxiliary 'do' as in 'Where *does* the woman go?' In this case, Germans should follow the German pattern and produce the incorrect *'Where goes the woman?' To some degree, these predictions were borne out but actual error analyses generally showed that somewhat less than half the errors could be accounted for in this way. 'Somewhat less than half' is, of course, far from being a satisfactory result for this particular theory. The problem is how to account for the other systematic errors, that is, where a simple mother-tongue interference explanation will not do. Clearly, despite its common-sense appeal, the current theory of the time was not enabling researchers to predict the majority of syntactic errors. Research on learner syntax has since focused on what stages learners go through and on how to interpret as much of their systematic syntactic behavior, native-like or nonnative-like, as is possible.

In the course of the 1970s, attention was turned to the development of interrogation and negation. Although the effects of first language influence could not be ruled out, stages of development were discovered for L2 learners which were strongly reminiscent of stages found for the development of the same structure in mother-tongue acquisition, again chiefly with reference to English. For example, learners typically begin with intonational questions retaining a statement order ('You are happy?'). *Wh*-words, when they appear in initial position do not, at first, force an inversion of subject and verb ('What you want?' as opposed to 'What do you want?'). Again, negators tend to occur outside the main sentence structure ('*No* Mike want it') or at least prior to the verb phrase ('I *no* can see him') only later moving inside the auxiliary-plus-main verb complex ('Mike does *not* want it,' 'I can*not* see him'). Preverbal negation was also noted by Hyltenstam in the early Swedish of migrant workers whether or not their mother tongue allowed this construction (Hyltenstam 1977).

This research, that is, investigations into interim stages of acquisition, fuelled speculation that the course of L2 development was much more like mother-tongue development than had hitherto been suspected, and despite the apparent absence of guaranteed uniform success as far as L2 development was concerned. At the same time, findings show that the kind of stages learners go through suggests that it is still important to talk separately of *second* language learner development. This is because the patterns of development are not necessarily identical to those recorded in first language acquisition. The influence of the mother tongue does seem to play some role in L2 acquisition, either trapping learners for a delayed period in some interim stage (Zobl 1978) or helping to shape some particular interim structure in the learner's performance. It often happens in L2 research that some results are shown to be misleading or at least ambiguous. For example, Jansen, et al. (1981) showed that Turkish learners of Dutch used a 'Turkish' verb-final order in their Dutch (main clauses). A potential explanation based on solely mother-tongue influence was undermined by the finding that Moroccans also followed this order. If they had followed their own Arabic (non verb-final) order, they would have produced a correct construction. Nevertheless, the patterns of relative speed or delay in given stages suggested, for example, by Zobl were also manifest in this study indicating an interaction between mother tongue influence and a developmental order common to all L2 learners.

2. Current Developments

Today, work is proceeding into various aspects of L2 syntax using different linguistic and psychological models that are more sophisticated than the early model derived from habit formation theory. As far as linguistic theories are concerned, more recent versions of Chomskyan grammar have attracted much attention (Cook 1988). The two most obvious advantages provided by this theory are the degree of linguistic precision it offers and, more especially, the explicit link with the phenomenon of language acquisition. Here, linguists try to solve the riddle of how children who are trying to build up a mental grammar of the language around them are guided to the correct solutions without the benefit of instruction. This implies, in particular, the nonavailability of constant correction of error (see *Applied Linguistics: Lexicology*). Researchers pursuing this line of investigation have been encouraged to consider whether the innate language acquisition capacities that Chomsky claims to underlie the processing of language data by the young mother-tongue learner are also available to the L2 learner. In other words, if the child is helped by a narrowing down of the vast range of logically possible options for making sense of the linguistic data (input), it is possible that L2 learners might be similarly limited and helped. To the extent that this might be so, the expectation is that the developing grammars of second language learners will show just those typical features that characterize the grammars of natural languages (according to the aforementioned theory). It would also be expected that certain logically possible rules and principles would not underlie these developing grammars. These would be rules which, according to the theory, natural languages could not contain. For example, one would not expect structure-independent rules (rules that make no reference to the structural elements like 'noun phrase' within the sentence): for instance, one would find no learners following a rule which went 'questions are formed by inverting the third and fourth word,' i.e., simply involving counting elements irrespective of what grammatical function was performed by those elements. In this way, L2 learners, like children, would not make sense of new languages by making just any kind of generalization. Also, it is to be expected that older learners would be insensitive to evidence showing them what was not possible in the target language, for example, correction by the teacher. If they were building mental syntax like children they could not rely on an outside agency telling them that some rule they had devised was not in fact a correct one. In this way, L2 learners, like young children, would not only manage without correction when working out the basic makeup of the target grammar, they would not even be able to make proper use of the information correction provides. This also goes for explicit knowledge about how the grammar works. Knowing the rules for forming a passive from the evidence provided by correction and by consciously studying the grammar would be as useless as, say, knowing the principles of bicycle riding as far as instructing the rider's balance mechanisms to keep the bicycle on a straight course are concerned. In this way, the possibility that there are two types of grammatical knowledge has become generally recognized, namely intuitive knowledge *of* the grammar and explicit, theoretical, or 'metalinguistic' knowledge *about* the grammar (see contributions to Rutherford and Sharwood Smith 1988). Whether these two types of knowledge can somehow interact or whether they remain totally separate, whatever area of grammar is in question, is still the object of lively debate.

Parameter-setting (see *Generative Grammar: Principles*; *Learnability Theory*), in Chomsky's model, provides one way of limiting the creative generalizations which the child, and, by hypothesis, the L2 learner might make and which, without sensitivity to correction, would lead to all kinds of permanent error. Part of syntax can be reduced to particular choices to be made with regard to specific sets of options. For example, the learner must decide whether the target language places its heads initially or finally in phrases. It will help the learner if the automatic expectation is that the position of the head is consistently initial or consistently final. This expectation will be useful both in learning languages which conform to it and languages which do not. A language which places head nouns second in the noun phrase as in, for example, '. . . red *mill*' as opposed to '. . . *mill* red' might be expected to place relative clauses modifying a head noun like 'mill' before the noun as in: '. . . *which we know* mill' as opposed to '. . . mill *which we know*' (see Flynn 1986). English, here, goes completely against these expectations as these examples show. Except for a small set of adjectives, French is more typical, that is, more consistently head-initial. The translation equivalents of the above examples conform neatly to expectations '. . . moulin *rouge*' (initial head NOUN + ADJ) and '. . . moulin *que nous connaissons*' (initial head NOUN + relative clause). If a learner, instead of running through a large range of possibilities could, on encountering and noticing a particular single example like 'moulin rouge,' more simply set a given parameter, then they could work out in one go a range of syntactic facts tied to that particular parameter (e.g., position of adjectives versus nouns, relative clauses, and nouns). Where the language was inconsistent, English being one example, the counterevidence would show up clearly in the data. Learners, exposed to examples defying their expectations, would be able to fine-tune their grammar accordingly. They would, in principle, need no correction beyond what the input itself provides. Researchers have asked themselves the question whether L2 learners approach the evidence provided by the target language input as young mother-tongue learners would, i.e., with an open mind, or whether their own mother tongue plays some role in delaying or otherwise inhibiting the acquisition of the L2. The L2 learner might logically, where possible, assume that the particular parameter-setting selected for the L1 also obtains for the new language being acquired. If so, this might cause special problems.

Hilles, using proposals by Hyams regarding the prodrop or 'null subject' parameter (see *Null Subject Languages*), noted that learners of a language which allowed empty subject positions where the identity of the subject is easily understood ('Is a dog here,' 'Is good,' 'Comes today') have difficulty acquiring a language where the subject position, under most circumstances, *must* be filled ('There is a dog here,' 'She is good,' 'He comes today'). Her research suggests that such learners have to 'reset' the prodrop parameter which, according to the theory in question, lies behind this particular phenomenon. The intriguing feature of such a theory is that it links up syntactic phenomena which would normally appear quite unconnected. For example, languages where the specific setting of this parameter creates the possibility of missing subject noun phrases also lack auxiliary verbs. The pro-drop parameter, it has been claimed, links these apparently unrelated features of the grammar (missing subjects and auxiliary verbs). If evidence of one feature is noticed, then the learner ought to be able to grasp the implications and reset the parameter accordingly. Changes would then be expected in the other associated area of the learner's syntax. Hilles's evidence indeed suggests that when learners with a prodrop language like Spanish and who are learning non-prodrop English, begin to show evidence of grasping the obligatory nature of NP in subject position, they also show a growth in the acquisition of the verbal auxiliary system. The evidence that triggers this insight appears to be the acquisition of such subject position fillers as the expletive 'there': ('*There* is a dog'), forms which exist in the 'subject-filling' English system but not in the Spanish system which has no problem with empty subjects. This trigger is the crucial evidence that alerts the Spanish learners (subconsciously) to the dangers of leaving subject position empty even where the meaning is absolutely clear with such a filled subject. And, as they begin to use expletives, they also begin to develop a verbal auxiliary system (more properly 'lexically filled *aux*') which the theory in question links with the null-subject phenomenon.

The question of whether second language learners have access to the principles of universal grammar (UG) may be most effectively tested by seeing if learners who have had no use for a particular parameter when building a grammar for their mother tongue later encounter a language where such a parameter is indeed relevant and necessary. One example would be Korean. Korean learners do not have to take syntactic movement into account when building a mental grammar of their mother tongue: Korean word order does not, for example, signal basic syntactic distinctions such as the difference between questions and statements. This means that general principles limiting movement that are part of UG will not be drawn on in the acquisition of Korean. Korean learners will consequently encounter an entirely new situation in English. The issue is whether they will automatically be able to limit the scope of moved elements in the syntax of English and thereby exhibit a sensitivity to limitations on movement which are deemed to be part of UG and as such crucial guidelines for the child learner of English as a mother tongue. Or, alternatively, whether they will show insensitivity and make all kinds of wild guesses about how movement works in English. Work by Flynn using Japanese and English has already raised this question with regard to head direction (see, for example, Flynn 1986). This topic has been investigated more recently by Schachter who claims to show that Koreans do not show such sensitivity and therefore do not give evidence of being like mother tongue learners of English (see Schachter 1990). The accessibility of second language learners to UG and the right way of investigating developing syntactic competence within this framework remains a hotly debated issue.

3. Different Ways of Viewing the Relevance of Linguistic Markedness

Although Chomskyan-based research has attracted a great deal of attention recently, it would be a grave error to conclude that it completely characterizes current findings in SLA syntax. Indeed, since UG related questions by no means determine the whole of syntactic acquisition, it is important that other approaches are tried out. Apart from earlier work done using other models, especially Greenbergian universals (see *Greenberg Universals*), there is much available to readers of the literature of a more fact-finding nature, i.e., less theoretical in nature but nonetheless valuable for future research (Greenberg 1974).

Linguistic markedness has been widely used to investigate ease and difficulty in second language syntactic development. Using principles proposed based on an analysis of many world languages, it has been suggested that linguistic phenomena may be divided up into more marked and less marked such that the more marked and less frequently found features could be less frequent precisely because they posed extra learning difficulties. Marked features are supposed to be less learnable because their structural properties and their comparative rarity suggest it (see *Markedness*). Some features are implicational so that if a language has prepositions, for example, and also has movement, then prepositional phrases will be able to move together as in, for example, wh-questions ('*To whom* am I talking?'). Some but all languages of this type allow the separation or 'stranding' of the preposition ('*Who* am I talking *to*?'). By this reasoning, stranding in a language implies the presence of the nonstranded option, and stranding is therefore more marked. This notion of learnability is based on an analysis of many existing languages and is different from Chomskyan learnability which is based on the presumed insensitivity of young mother tongue learners to correction: here unmarked means 'in the evidence provided by native speakers,' i.e., 'learnable from the input' (see discussion in Comrie 1981). Hence, depending on the theoretical linguistic model adopted, a given syntactic phenomenon might, in principle, be interpreted as marked or unmarked. And even where two different markedness theories both classify some phenomenon in the same way, the reasons given will be totally different.

Eckman proposed a 'markedness differential hypothesis' in which interference from the mother tongue would depend on whether or not the learner had to learn a more marked version of some area of the language (Eckman 1977). It would not simply depend on the L1 and the L2 being different. To give a concrete example from syntax, if the most dominant basic (main declarative clause) word order evident in the world's languages was SVO (Subject Verb Object), this would define the unmarked variant. This would mean that learners of SOV languages acquiring, say, English, an unmarked (SVO) language would have less difficulty than their counterparts, i.e., those English learners of an SOV language who would be trying to learn a language whose syntax was more marked.

Researchers (e.g., Eckman 1977; Gass 1979) have used the 'noun phrase accessibility hierarchy' proposed by Keenan and Comrie (1977) as a basis for investigating markedness in L2 learning (see *Nouns and Noun Phrases*). The 'accessibility hierarchy' hypothesis suggested that there were different degrees of learning difficulty possessed by the various ways of forming relative clauses. Keenan and Comrie proposed that certain options automatically implied other options such that, for example, if a language allowed the relativization of a direct object ('The *dog* [DIRECT OBJECT of "love"] that I loved'), it would allow relativization of a subject noun phrase ('The dog [SUBJECT of "loved"] who loved you') but not vice versa. In the same way, the relativization of a indirect object ('the door on which you painted a picture') implies, then, that the language also allows the previously two mentioned options. There was, then, some L2 researchers suggested, a hierarchy of difficulty to be associated with such implicational chains of possibilities: if Y exists in a language, therefore possibility X exists. If X exists, then possibility Y does not necessarily have to exist. For L2 researchers like Gass, this suggested that a learner might have difficulty in going from a language that allowed fewer marked possibilities to a language that allowed more. This is another example of how linguistic theory may be used to modify the original interference (or 'contrastive analysis' theory of the behaviorists; see *Contrastive Analysis*), where straight difference between the two languages of the learner (source and target) would imply learning difficulty. In this case just mentioned, the target language may be different in that it allows fewer possibilities in the hierarchy but would in fact be quite easy to learn. Research on the implicational hierarchy has yielded suggestive results but nothing definite.

One obstacle faced by researchers applying linguistic theory is that the theory itself changes. Hence opinions differ about the validity of the prodrop parameter as originally stated by Hyams, or the adjacency parameter or Keenan and Comrie's NP accessibility hierarchy. Upsets in the theory force a reconsideration of research based on that theory. Nevertheless, L2 researchers have followed the changes and later studies may (and certainly have) used later versions of the particular model or hypotheses in question. Also, syntactic studies which lead to results that are undermined by new interpretations of theory still provide useful database for future research. White and others investigating the prodrop parameter have had to consider the theoretical question of which option (if any) is marked. Markedness in UG research crucially depends on evidence in the input. By hypothesis, the learner assumes the unmarked option until evidence in the input forces a reconsideration. If the learner assumes prodrop in advance, it is important that there is evidence in the input that alerts him or her to the fact that the target language disallows empty subjects in the grammar. Under this scenario, prodrop is assumed to be unmarked. But not all researchers agree: the opposite claim has been made. More recently researchers have seen null-subject as a part of a different parameter entirely (Jaeggli and Safir 1989). Again, White in her study of the interruption of verbs and direct objects allowed in French grammar but disallowed in English ('He loves *now* the cat') first applied the notion of adjacency. Later on, she adopted a different approach to the question and a different relevant parameter (White 1989).

4. Processing Models

Research on L2 syntax has also proceeded without specific reference to complex linguistic models although these have later been used to examine the results. Typical of this approach is the ZISA project carried out in Germany looking at the acquisition of German by immigrants from various language backgrounds. Much focus has been laid on findings regarding word order acquisition. The data shows an apparent steady move through various word order stages beginning with the default or 'canonical' SVO pattern. It should be stated clearly that word order here refers to surface word order and not the underlying order typical of Chomskyan theory. Here, an apparently stable order was discovered in the acquisition of German word order whereby learners irrespective of language background seemed to begin with the canonical order placing adverbial outside this SVO complex and then moved on to later stages where this canonical order could be manipulated. The first explanations of this L2 order of development were in terms of assumed ease of processing. The learner first develops the ability to manipulate elements in the syntax using simple operations before being able to go on to more complex

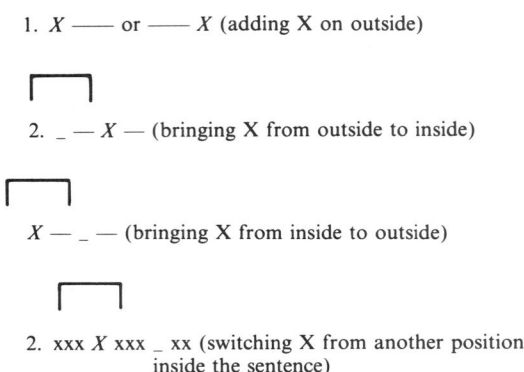

1. X —— or —— X (adding X on outside)

2. _ — X — (bringing X from outside to inside)

X — _ — (bringing X from inside to outside)

2. xxx X xxx _ xx (switching X from another position inside the sentence)

Figure 1. Processing complexity and stages of acquisition.

operations (see below). This language processing explanation competes with arguments on some facets of linguistic theory.

The processing approach has been advanced, for L2, by Pienemann (1987). The explanation is that it is processing complexity which determines the order of development. It would appear that, given the canonical order as the starting point, when manipulation of the order takes place, it is first easiest to place new elements, typically adverbial, externally, in initial or final position ('*Today* I see John,' 'I see John *today*'), harder to move elements from the outside in (or vice versa) and harder still to move around internal elements, i.e., inside the sentence. These processing laws, it is claimed, dictate the fixed order of acquisition schematically represented below, X being the element that is added or manipulated and '__' being a space abandoned by X__ the reader may care to think of X as, for example, a time adverbial like 'often' and the rest of the utterance as 'John may miss his train' (see Fig. 1).

Pienemann has been particularly concerned to explore the implications of this processing approach for teaching. In one study (Pienemann 1987), he asks the question whether natural learning processes in L2 acquisition (which are seen to operate in an immigrant situation, for instance) will also show up in the classroom and indeed can be affected by formal instruction. Pienemann's claim is that, where certain fixed stages have been established by research, you can teach a structure only when the learner is developmentally ready, i.e., has gone through the appropriate stages *en route* to the target structure in question and has therefore acquired the processing prerequisites. The effect of teaching can only be to speed up acquisition at specific points in the learner's acquisitional career and not to enable the learner to jump stages or go through them in a different order.

In a copula-inclusion experiment with immigrants, teaching was shown by Pienemann to be successful in promoting a decline in nonnative omission of the copula, the point being that when the learner has shown s/he can produce the copula sometimes, s/he is ready for instruction. Even in this situation there is some doubt: one subject, Monica, interviewed 9 months after the copula experiment showed a rise in omission to 34 percent (backsliding). It seems that instruction cannot disrupt the natural acquisitional order but it can speed up full command of a structure given the learner is naturally ready for it. With regard to the role of grammar teaching with those learners not continually exposed to the language of native speakers, Pienemann found that formal instruction also seemed to make no inroads into a natural order which emerged in his Australian learners of German as a foreign language.

5. Elicitation Methods

Methods for investigating L2 syntax depend very much on the theoretical approach adopted. Much use has been made of grammaticality judgment tests of various kinds following the Chomskyan line, the aim being to investigate the learner's underlying intuitions and tap as directly as is possible his or her underlying 'competence.' Other methods look more at production on the basis that what the learner actually produces is what counts, not so much what he or she recognizes or perceives. There is a general recognition that all methods are flawed in one way or other. Linguistic judgments are beset with various kinds of problems such as what exactly is being judged (which linguistic features of a test sentence) and what the subject is counting as a criterion (probability of cooccurrence, stylistic elegance, prestige versus nonprestige forms, formal versus informal style). Judgments of this kind are as much a matter of performance as production tests. The claim is, nonetheless, that production places more demands on the learner and is thus likely to give a possibly over conservative picture of their real intuitions about the target language. Again, if no distinction is made between competence and performance, then production tests where the learner is focused on getting the message across rather than on sounding correct emerge as being more reliable since they are not beset by problems such as the ones mentioned above. It also means that syntactic variation that occurs in syntactic behavior of L2 learners may be interpreted without reference to a failure to let a less variable competence shine through in performance. Production tests involving translation are useful for controlling for meaning but are suspected by some for artificially provoking transfer from the learner's mother tongue.

6. Future Perspectives

A vast amount remains to be done in the study of L2 syntax. This should involve developments in theory and an increase in the coverage of what is generally felt to be syntax. Even if UG as currently understood were shown conclusively to be directly relevant to the acquisition of nonnative syntax, it only covers certain areas of the grammar. It can therefore never hope to serve to explain all acquisitional grammatical phenomena. Also, future work seems bound to continue to investigate other languages than English to gain more generality for theoretical claims postulated on the basis of one or two languages alone. For example, with the general European interest in migrant worker language development, detailed work has started on the acquisition of a number of languages, the Nijmegen-based European Science Foundation project being a prime example of this. Changes in linguistic theory will most certainly be reflected in new approaches to old problems such as interrogation and negation. The research on null-subjects provides an excellent example of how a given linguistic theory can be applied to L2 development, how changes in the theory can

affect the approach to a given problem and how controversy may arise on to whether such a phenomenon can really be explained as a matter of syntax, or whether it is really more a problem of pragmatics. In cases where the particular linguistic approach in use allows for it, L2 findings in syntax may even affect linguistic theory itself. Finally, advances in theories of language processing will certainly affect the advance of the new trend in L2 research which involves looking more specifically at the processing aspects of L2 syntactic behavior. In this connection, it is likely that computer modelling will become a useful technique to show how L2s are processed both in the making of more precise claims about how the current mental grammars of given learners are accessed in real time as well as in making claims about how those grammars are structured and restructured over time. In particular, theoretical advances in other fields such as linguistics and psychology should help researchers to analyze systematic variability in performance, already a well-established topic of debate in the literature (Gass, et al. 1989). If research has now conclusively shown that L2 syntactic acquisition is a complex process controlled in part by deep-seated processes which are hard to manipulate, every theory so far proposed to account for such processes remains highly controversial.

Bibliography

Comrie B 1981 *Language Universals and Linguistic Typology.* Blackwell, Oxford

Cook V 1988 *Chomsky's Universal Grammar.* Blackwell, Oxford

Eckman F 1977 Markedness and the contrastive analysis hypothesis. *Language Learning* 27: 115–330

Flynn S 1986 *A Parameter-Setting Model of Second Language Acquisition.* Reidel, Dordrecht

Gass S 1979 Language transfer and language universals. *Language Learning* 29: 327–44

Gass S, Madden C, Preston D, Selinker L 1989 *Variation in Second Language Acquisition.* Multilingual Matters, Clevedon, OH

Greenberg J 1974 *Language Universals: A Historical and Analytic Overview.* Mouton, The Hague

Hilles S 1986 Interlanguage and the pro-drop parameter. *Second Language Research* 2: 33–52

Hyams N 1986 *Language Acquisition and the Theory of Parameters.* Dordrecht, Reidel

Hyltenstam K 1977 Implicational patterns in interlanguage syntax variation. *Language Learning* 27: 383–411

Jaeggli O, Safirk 1989 *The Null Subject Parameter.* Kluwer, Dordrecht

Jansen B, Lalleman J, Muysken P 1981 The alternation hypothesis: The acquisition of Dutch word order by Turkish and Moroccan foreign workers. *Language Learning* 31: 315–36

Keenan E, Comrie B 1977 Noun phrase accessibility and universal grammar. *LIn* 8: 63–99

Pienemann M 1987 Determining the influence of instruction on L2 speech process, (Unpublished manuscript, University of Sydney)

Rutherford W, Sharwood Smith M 1988 *Grammar and Second Language Teaching.* Newbury House, Rowley

Schachter J 1990 On the issue of incompleteness in second language acquisition. *Second Language Research* 6: 94–124

White L 1989 *Universal Grammar and Second Language Acquisition.* Benjamins, Amsterdam

Zobl H 1978 The formal and developmental selectivity of L1 influence on L2 acquisition. *Language Learning* 30: 43–57

M. A. Sharwood Smith

Second Language Learning and Teaching, Theory of

Learning a second language has been important to human beings from earliest historical times. The Sumerians of the third millennium BC used bilingual tablets in Sumerian and Akkadian to educate their children, and compiled the world's oldest known bilingual dictionaries. Bilingual tablets were used in ancient Egypt, and, in the Ptolemaic period, the upper classes in Egypt received their education in Greek. In the Hellenistic period, the majority of people in Asia Minor who could read and write did so in Greek, their second language. Until the fourth century BC, bilingual education in Greek and Latin was an important part of the curriculum for Roman children.

At the beginning of the third century BC, the Romans developed bilingual manuals called *Hermeneumata Pseudodositheans*, which were comparable to modern conversational handbooks. They contained a Greek–Latin vocabulary and a series of simple texts of a narrative or conversational character. The text included Aesop's fables, an elementary book on mythology, and an account of the Trojan war. These handbooks attempted to introduce grammatical features in a systematic order, beginning with simple structures and advancing to more complex ones.

In medieval Europe, Latin was considered an international language of communication and culture. It was a living language taught for oral communication. By the Renaissance, however, emphasis had shifted from learning Latin as a practical tool for communication to learning Latin (and Greek) to develop the mind. Emphasis was placed on grammatical training with little or no attention to oral skills.

This grammaticalism predominated into the twentieth century. Languages were taught in the same way as Latin and Greek: through the systematic learning of paradigms, tables, declensions, and conjugations. Like Latin and Greek, modern languages were taught as dead languages, divorced from communicative context. Students spent their time translating written texts line by line. This approach, now generally rejected, is usually referred to as the 'grammar-translation method.'

Instead of this method, much late twentieth-century language teaching uses what is often called the 'direct method.' Although a number of other prominent educators made the same arguments, the best-known advocate of this method is Maximilian Berlitz, whose schools now exist in all parts of the world. Berlitz maintained that the learner must be taught as quickly as possible to think in the second language and for that reason must use that language constantly, without reverting to the first language. Exclusive stress is placed in the 'Berlitz method' on the oral aspects of the language. Teachers must be native speakers, and classes must be small (never more than 10 pupils) so that instruction is as individual as possible. Grammatical rules are not taught explicitly; instead, grammar is conveyed to the student by example and by visual demonstration. Reading and writing are taught only after the spoken language has been mastered.

Like Berlitz, other advocates of the direct method took a similar point of view. According to Jespersen (1904), the pupil should be steeped in the target language and should learn grammar inductively. Because listening, practice, and repetition are the means by which children learn their *first language*, these processes should be employed in second-language learning as well (Palmer 1940). Linguistic principles, especially phonetics, were emphasized in an effort to insure that the speaker's oral pronunciation approximated, as closely as possible, that of native speakers in the target language.

Linguistic principles and phonological accuracy are especially important in the 'audiolingual method.' The linguistic principles come from 'structural linguistics,' with its emphasis on the 'contrastive analysis' of linguistic structures of the first and second languages. This was linked to behavior notions of the learning process, which viewed language learning as involving the *formation of habits* via pattern practice. The goal of phonological accuracy is to be achieved through repetitive drills with audio-feedback in language learning laboratories. Like the direct method, the audiolingual approach stresses the learning of second languages in a manner that simulates first-language learning. Children do not learn their first language through translating and learning rules of grammar by rote; they learn by hearing and speaking.

There has been a strong reaction against the audiolingual method in many quarters on the grounds that its theoretical foundations are suspect. As will be seen, the behaviorist assumption that language learning comes about merely through repetitive drills and pattern practice has been sharply attacked. Contrastive analysis has also been shown to be of limited practical use for language teaching because learners do not make the predicted errors. Finally, structural linguistics has been put to rout by revolutionary changes in linguistic theory.

One criticism of the audiolingual technique is that it is dehumanizing, that it treats language learning as a mechanical process rather than as learning experience that involves the whole person. A number of pedagogical developments have occurred that can be grouped under the rubric of a 'humanistic approach' to second-language teaching. Examples include 'Counseling-Learning' (Curran 1976), the 'Silent Way' (Gattegno 1972), and 'Suggestopedia' (Lozanov 1979). What these techniques have in common is an emphasis on individualized instruction through an eclectic assortment of methods.

Table 1 summarizes the four approaches to the teaching of second languages that have been sketched here. There are many other ways of categorizing developments in language teaching, and this division is proposed merely to orient the reader to what follows. There is a great deal of overlap between approaches and it is difficult to trace the contribution of specific theories to specific pedagogical approaches.

1. Theory in Second-language Research

This article began by examining theories that are used to justify contemporary pedagogical practice in second-language learning and teaching. Three mainstreams: *learning theory*, *linguistic theory*, and *cognitive theory* will be given consideration. Then the extent to which these theories have had an impact on pedagogical practice will be considered.

1.1 Learning Theory

Several assumptions underlie the classic learning theory approach to language learning. First, language is learned

Table 1. Four approaches to second-language teaching.

Grammar-Translation:

> Emphasis on systematic learning of rules of morphology and syntax; rote memorization of vocabulary; line-by-line translation of target-language texts into the learner's first language; oral proficiency minimized; little training in pronunciation.

Direct Method:

> Rejection of translation and emphasis on speech; grammar learned inductively; reading and writing learned after spoken language is mastered; phonetics stressed so that pronunciation approximates that of a native speaker.

Audiolingual Method:

> Stress is on repetitive drills and pattern practice; spoken language is primary; translation rejected; contrastive analysis guides instruction; grammar learned inductively; phonological accuracy sought through repetitive drills in language-learning laboratories.

Humanistic Approaches:

> Individual instruction and focus on learner needs and attitudes; eclectic orientation to method; focus on oral communication; rejection of drill and practice focus of the audiolingual method.

just like anything else; the principles of general learning account for language learning. Second, language learning is habit formation involving imitation, reinforcement, and repetition as means of controlling behavior. Old habits get in the way of new habits. When learning a second language, the learner must acquire a new system of habits in addition to the pre-existing habits that constitute first-language competence. If old habits are similar to, or the same as, the new habits that must be learned, 'positive transfer' will occur and the result can be beneficial; if old habits are different from the new habits, 'negative transfer' occurs and learning is hindered.

1.1.1 Contrastive Analysis

In the field of second-language acquisition, contrastive analysis has developed as a 'theory of transfer' that attempts to predict when and where learner errors will occur and adjust language instruction to prevent those errors. Psychologically, contrastive analysis is based on classic learning theory and the notion of habits. Linguistically, contrastive analysis is based on the work of structuralist linguists such as Bloomfield and Fries. It is pedagogically oriented and motivated, as a method of teaching second languages more efficiently.

In its strong form, contrastive analysis claims that all errors are the result of negative transfer and can be predicted by comparing the first language with the second and identifying differences between the two. In its *weak form*, contrastive analysis is a diagnostic tool that can be used to identify or explain the errors found in second-language learning that are the result of negative transfer.

In practice, contrastive analysis involves a comparison of the learner's first language with the language to be acquired so as to specify constructions that will give the learner difficulty. Areas of difference are assumed to lead to difficulties for the learner because they lead to negative transfer and 'interference.' These differences can then be targeted in instruction with special drills and repetitions in an effort to prevent error and overcome the consequences of interference.

1.1.2 The Critique

The implications of the learning theory perspective are most obvious in the audiolingual method, as will be seen. However, there have been serious criticisms raised against the classic approach, especially as embodied in the notion of habit formation and articulated in the contrastive analysis hypothesis. The strong version of the contrastive analysis hypothesis cannot be maintained in the face of empirical research that indicates that the majority of learners' errors are not the result of negative transfer. The weak version of the hypothesis, which states that contrastive analysis is a diagnostic tool that helps identify or explain errors, is not useful unless predictions can be made as to when, where, and why interference between languages occurs.

To be useful, contrastive analyses of languages must be based on underlying linguistic universals, rather than on surface characteristics. This argument reflects the basic reorientation in thinking about language that has occurred as a result of the 'Chomskyan revolution in linguistics,' which we shall consider shortly. However, these theoretical developments do not necessarily mean that practices based on classic learning theory have been abandoned. Many contemporary classrooms continue to employ drill-and-practice exercises, and many teachers would justify their pedagogical practices by invoking the principles of classic learning theory.

1.2 Linguistic Theory

Contemporary linguistic theory makes a fundamental distinction between 'competence' (the speaker's underlying knowledge and intuitions about language) and 'performance' (how language is actually produced and comprehended). Under the influence of generative linguistics, language competence has come to be seen as an abstract system of rules that 'generate' all of the grammatical utterances of a language. Language acquisition, then, is the process of learning the abstract rules that comprise the native speaker's competence. However, because language learners are only exposed to performance, in the form of actual speech, language acquisition must involve the extraction of abstract knowledge about language from concrete examples.

To explain the nature of this abstract knowledge, generative linguistics introduces the notion of 'deep and surface structure representations' of language. 'Transformational grammar' posits a number of movement/deletion rules (transformations) that operate on deep structures to produce some structural change, which is then reflected in the surface structures. Identical surface structures, however, do not necessarily share the same deep structure. For example, *John is eager to please* and *John is easy to please*. In the first example, *John* is the one doing the pleasing, and thus *John* would be the deep structure subject of *please*. In the second example, however, *John* is the one being pleased, and therefore should be the deep structure object of *please*.

1.2.1 The Innateness of Linguistic Knowledge

A number of considerations have led linguists to the conclusion that language acquisition is more than simple habit formation and involves some sort of *innate capacity*. First, there is the argument that children learn a first language at a very young age despite the obvious difficulty of extracting abstract linguistic rules from performance data alone. Second, language learners within a language community can be exposed to very different data and yet arrive at the same abstract rules.

Similar arguments can be made for second-language learning. To the extent that second-language learners attain native-like competence, their competence approximates that of other members of the speech community, although clearly based on different performance input/data. In addition, some evidence indicates that second-language learners pass through acquisition stages that are not only similar to those of other second-language learners but also to those first-language learners of the target language pass through (Lightbown 1985). This suggests that some sort of innate mechanism is guiding second-language learners as well.

Furthermore, second-language learners, like first-language learners face a difficult 'projection problem.' Like children learning a first language, they have to work out abstract rules on the basis of 'deficient' data (White 1989). Several examples may make this clearer. A French speaker, learning English, must learn that in English, unlike French, an adverb cannot come between a verb and a direct object. In English we do not say *The dog bit viciously the boy*. Yet adverbial placement in English is relatively free, so that sentences such as *The dog bit the boy viciously*, *The dog viciously bit the boy*, and *Viciously, the dog bit the boy* are all allowed. A native speaker of French who assumes that English is like French in adverbial placement will not receive positive input indicating that this is not the case. Nor will this information come from extra-linguistic sources. Therefore, the argument runs, it is unclear how such constructions are learned unless certain forms of linguistic knowledge are innate.

1.2.2 Universal Grammar

Advocates of the Chomskyan generative grammar approach assume that the first-language learner comes to the acquisition task with innate, linguistically specific knowledge, or 'universal grammar.' It is generally assumed in universal grammar theory that the child starts with all the principles of universal grammar available and furthermore, that all human languages conform to these principles. The child builds the best grammar available on the basis of what is cognitively possible at a particular maturational point.

According to Chomsky, universal grammar provides the only way of accounting for how children are able to acquire their native language. If one assumes that children *form hypotheses* about their language that they then test in practice, the question of how they reject incorrect hypotheses needs to be answered. Chomsky and his followers argue that the child does not meet enough *negative evidence* to reject incorrect hypotheses. Nor do children produce enough incorrect sentences to test out hypotheses adequately. Hence, it is necessary to assume that children are in some way constrained in the hypotheses they form.

If there are constraints on the range of hypotheses children form, it becomes possible to explain how acquisition occurs. Rather than working from inductive principles alone, the child is restricted by the constraints of universal grammar in forming hypotheses about the input. The child's task is to test the options available against input from the environment. Thus the claim is that hypothesis

testing is a possible explanation once it is accepted that the child's hypotheses are limited in number and that the environment contributes triggering rather than negative evidence.

Chomsky's theory sees the environment to play both a negative and a positive role. Negatively, the theory denies that the environment provides sufficient evidence for learning particular aspects of syntax without the aid of a powerful built-in grammar. Positively, the theory claims that the environment provides positive evidence to help the learner fix the ways in which universal grammar is realized in the target language. Consequently, the theory does not deny that external factors influence the course of language acquisition; the right environmental input at the right time furthers the acquisition process.

1.2.3 Parameter Setting

In universal grammar theory, there is involved a set of principles with certain parameters. These parameters remain 'open' until they are set by experience with the environment. For Chomsky, language acquisition is not so much a problem of acquiring grammatical rules, but rather a process whereby the learner sets the values of the parameters of the principles of universal grammar. The grammar of a language is the set of values it assigns to the various parameters. As Chomsky put it, 'Experience is required to set the switches. Once they are set, the system functions' (cited in Flynn 1985).

An oft-cited example of such a parameter is the 'prodrop parameter,' which specifies that languages vary with regard to whether they allow the deletion of pronouns in subject positions, together with related phenomena such as inversion of subject and verb. English does not have prodrop because a subject is required for every sentence and the subject cannot be inverted with the verb in declarative sentences. This is not true of Spanish, however, which, as a language that allows prodrop, allows empty subjects and subject–verb inversion in declarative sentences. For example, while Spanish allows the equivalent of *Is very busy* for *She is very busy*, English does not.

Another example is the principle of 'adjacency,' according to which noun phrases must be next to the verb or preposition that gives them case. This accounts for the adverbial placement rule cited previously. In English an adverb cannot intervene between a verb and its direct object. Sentences such as *Mary ate quickly her dinner* are not allowed, whereas in French such sentences are permitted: *Marie a mangé rapidement le dîner*. The French option is assumed to be 'set' for the child learning French as a first language on the basis of *positive evidence* in the form of such sentences. Thus the theory claims that the parameters that have been set in the first language will need to be reset or readjusted for the second language.

1.2.4 Core Versus Peripheral Grammar

Universal grammar theory maintains a distinction between 'core' and 'peripheral' grammar. Core grammar refers to those parts of the language that have 'grown' in the learner through the interaction of the universal grammar with the relevant language environment. In addition, however, it is assumed that every language also contains elements that are not constrained by universal grammar. These elements comprise the peripheral grammar and include elements that are derived from the history of the language, have been borrowed from other languages, or have arisen accidentally.

Although it is thought that learners prefer to adopt rules based on universal grammar, they must also learn peripheral aspects of language. These peripheral aspects fall outside the learner's preprogramed instructions and hence are more difficult to acquire. This is not to say, however, that peripheral aspects of language are learned later developmentally. Chomsky was careful to point out that the order in which structures are learned may be influenced by the learner's 'channel capacity.' Aspects of the core grammar may be learned later than peripheral aspects because of maturational processes or because of 'frequency effects.'

1.2.5 Creativity

The approach to language learning that developed in the wake of the Chomskyan revolution and the advent of generative linguistics relies heavily on the view of language learning as a 'creative process.' According to this viewpoint, language learning is not determined by external forces alone, as had been suggested by learning theory. Instead, language acquisition is 'creatively constructed' within the learner through interaction with members of the speech community.

Presumably, the same principles apply to second-language learning. universal grammar theory postulates that second-language learning occurs as learners encounter more evidence from the second language, and set or reset the parameters of the new grammar. Universal grammar serves to constrain the hypotheses that learners make and helps them creatively construct their new knowledge of the target language through interaction with native speakers.

1.3 Cognitive Theory

We turn now to a somewhat different theoretical perspective. Cognitive theory is based on the work of psychologists and psycholinguists, who have applied the principles and findings of *contemporary cognitive psychology* to the domain of second-language learning. The intent is to determine whether such a perspective casts light on second-language phenomena.

Contemporary cognitive psychology is quite different from the behaviorism of the past. Contemporary cognitive psychology emphasizes 'knowing,' rather than 'responding.' Cognitive psychologists are concerned with finding scientific means for studying the *mental processes* involved in the acquisition and application of knowledge. The focus is not 'stimulus-response bonds,' but 'mental events.'

A second characteristic of the cognitive approach is that it emphasizes mental structure or organization. The argument is that human knowledge is organized and that new input is interpreted in the light of this organization. Here the field is especially indebted to Jean Piaget, the Swiss scholar who maintained that all living creatures are born with an invariant tendency to organize experience, and that this tendency provides the impetus for cognitive development.

Finally, the cognitive approach, in contrast to behaviorism, stresses the notion that the individual is active, constructive, and planful, rather than a passive recipient of environmental stimulation. For cognitive psychology, any complete account of human cognition must include an analysis of the plans or strategies people use for thinking, remembering, and understanding and producing language.

Within this framework, second-language learning is viewed as the acquisition of a complex cognitive skill. To learn a second language is to learn a *skill*. Because various aspects of the task must be practiced and integrated into fluent performance, language learning requires the automatization of component sub-skills. Learning is a *cognitive* process, because it is thought to involve internal representations that regulate and guide performance. In the case of language learning, these representations are based on the language system and include procedures for selecting appropriate vocabulary, grammatical rules, and pragmatic conventions governing language use. As performance improves, there is constant restructuring as learners simplify, unify, and gain increasing control over their internal representations. These two notions —'automatization' and 'restructuring'—are central to cognitive theory.

1.3.1 The Routinization of Skills

The acquisition of the skills involved in any communication task requires the assessment and coordination of information from a multitude of perceptual, cognitive, and social domains. The speaker must communicate the intended message unambiguously and must learn to obey a large number of conversational conventions. Because humans are limited-capacity processors, such a task requires the integration of a number of different skills, each of which has been practiced and routinized.

Several researchers (e.g., Schneider and Shiffrin 1977, Shiffrin and Schneider 1977) have conceived of the differences in the processing capacity necessary for various mental operations in a dichotomous way: either a task requires a relatively large amount of processing capacity, or it proceeds automatically and demands little processing energy. Furthermore, a task that once taxed processing capacity may become, through practice, so automatic that it demands relatively little processing energy.

In their discussion of human information processing, Shiffrin and Schneider conceived of *memory* as a large collection of nodes that become *associated through learning*. Each node is a grouping or set of informational elements. Most of the nodes are inactive and passive and, when in this state, the interconnected system of nodes is called 'long-term store.' When, because of some kind of external stimulus, a small number of these nodes are activated, the activated nodes constitute 'short-term store.'

There are two ways in which these nodes may become activated: Shiffrin and Schneider called these the automatic and the controlled modes of information processing. 'Automatic processing' involves the activation of certain nodes in memory each time the appropriate inputs are present. This activation is a learned response that has been built up through the consistent mapping of the same input to the same pattern of activation over many trials. Since an automatic process utilizes a relatively permanent set of associative connections in long-term storage, most automatic processes require an appreciable amount of training to develop fully. Once learned, however, automatic processes occur rapidly and are difficult to suppress or alter.

The second mode of information processing, 'controlled processing,' is not a learned response, but instead a temporary activation of nodes in a sequence. This activation is under the attentional control of the subject and, because attention is required, only one such sequence can normally be controlled at a time without interference. Controlled processes are thus tightly capacity-limited, and require more time for their activation. But controlled processes have the advantage of being relatively easy to set up, alter, and apply to novel situations.

1.3.2 Automaticity and Learning

In this framework, learning involves the transfer of information to long-term memory and is regulated by controlled processes. That is, skills are learned and routinized (i.e., become automatic) only after the earlier use of controlled processes. It is controlled processes that regulate the flow of information from short-term to long-term memory. Learning occurs over time, but once automatic processes are set up at one stage in the development of a complex information-processing skill, controlled processes are free to be allocated to higher levels of processing. Thus controlled processing can be said to lay down the 'stepping stones' for automatic processing as the learner gradually moves to more and more difficult levels.

In this conceptualization, complex tasks are characterized by a 'hierarchical structure.' That is, such tasks consist of sub-tasks and their components. The execution of one part of the task requires the completion of various smaller components. As Levelt (1978) noted, speaking is an excellent example of a hierarchical task structure (Table 2). The first-order goal is to express a particular intention.

Table 2. The hierarchical task structure of speaking.

First-order goal:	to express particular intention
Second-order goal:	to decide on topic
Third-order goal:	to formulate a series of phrases
Lower-order goals:	to retrieve lexicon needed
	to activate articulatory patterns
	to utilize appropriate syntactic rules
	to meet pragmatic conventions

(Based on Levelt 1978.)

To do this, the speaker must first decide on a topic and select a certain syntactic schema. In turn, the realization of this schema requires additional subactivities, such as formulating a series of phrases to express different aspects of the intention. But in order actually to utter the phrase there is also the need for lexical retrieval, the activation of articulatory patterns, utilization of appropriate syntactic rules, etc. Each of these component skills must be executed before the higher-order goal can be realized, although there may be some parallel processing in real time.

In order to function effectively, humans develop ways of organizing information. Some tasks require more attention; others that have been well practiced require less. The development of any complex cognitive skill involves building up a set of well-learned, automatic procedures so that controlled processes are freed up for new tasks. In this way limited resources can be spread to cover a wide range of task demands. The notion of 'capacity-free (automatic) processes' provides an explanation for improvement in learner performance. Because human learners are limited in their information-processing abilities, only so much

attention can be given to the various components of complex tasks at one time. When one component of a task becomes automatized, attention can be devoted to other components of the task and what was previously a difficult or impossible task becomes possible.

1.3.3 Restructuring

The integration of hierarchically ordered skills requires practice. Repeated performance of the components of the task through controlled processing leads to the availability of automatized routines. But there is more involved in learning a complex cognitive skill than automatizing sub-skills. The learner must also impose organization and structure the information that has been acquired. As more learning occurs, internalized, cognitive representations change and are restructured. This restructuring process involves operations that are different from, but complementary to, those involved in gaining automaticity.

In acquiring complex skills, such as second languages, learners devise new structures for interpreting new information and for imposing a new organization on information already stored. Cheng (1985) described this process as the result of a restructuring of the components of a task so that they are coordinated, integrated, or reorganized into new units, thereby allowing a procedure involving old components to be replaced by a more efficient procedure involving new components.

Cheng gave the example of two alternative procedures for solving arithmetic problems, such as finding the sum of ten 2s. One can solve this problem by nine addition operations; or one can learn the multiplication table and solve the problem by simply looking up the entry 2×10. A single multiplication operation would thus be equivalent to nine addition operations. Cheng argued that the gain in efficiency thus achieved is not the result of performing nine additions operations in an automatic manner. Nor is the gain in efficiency the result of an automatic multiplication operation. Rather the limitations in performance have been overcome by restructuring the task procedure.

Another example Cheng gave is piano-playing. Why is it that learners have difficulty in coordinating two tasks, each of which has been automatized—such as coordinating the two hands in playing the piano? For players with some experience, combining four even notes to a measure with eight even notes to a measure is relatively easy, as is combining three even notes to a measure with six or nine even notes. But although these tasks are automatic, combining three even notes against four even notes is extremely difficult. That this task is learnable indicated for Cheng that the difficulty does not stem from any physiological incompatibility, but rather from lack of a suitably structured skill.

Because of the possibility of restructuring, learning inevitably goes beyond mere automaticity. Learning involves the constant modification of organizational structures. Rumelhart and Norman (1978) identified restructuring as a process that occurs 'when new structures are devised for interpreting new information and imposing a new organization on that already stored' (p. 39). They contrasted this process of learning with (a) 'accretion,' whereby information is incremented by a new piece of data or a new set of facts, and (b) 'tuning,' whereby there is a change in the categories used for interpreting new information. In tuning, categories, or schemata, are modified; in restructuring, new structures are added that allow for new interpretation of facts.

Rumelhart and Norman argued that learning is not a unitary process, but that there are different kinds of learning, one of which is restructuring. Whereas some learning is thought to occur continuously by accretion, as is true of the development of automaticity through practice, other learning is thought to occur in a discontinuous fashion, by restructuring. This discontinuity accounts for the second-language learner's perception of sudden movements of insight or 'clicks of comprehension.' At such moments, presumably, the learner can be said to understand the material in a new way, to be looking at it differently. Often learners report that this experience is followed by rapid progress, as old linguistic information and skills are fitted into this new way of understanding.

Whether it is necessary to postulate different *kinds* of learning, as Rumelhart and Norman suggested, or whether automaticity and restructuring can be seen as different *phases* of a single learning process, cognitive theorists agree that there is more to learning a complex cognitive skill than developing automaticity through practice. Learning involves a reassembly and refinement of procedures of the mind. Acquisition of cognitive skills involves consolidation, refinement, and restructuring, as the learner gains increasing control.

1.3.4 Second-language Learning as a Complex Cognitive Skill

According to cognitive theory, second-language learning, like any other complex cognitive skill, involves the gradual integration of subskills, as controlled processes initially predominate and later become automatic. Thus the initial stages of learning involve the slow development of skills and the gradual elimination of errors as the learner attempts to automatize aspects of performance. In later phases, there is continual restructuring as learners shift their internal representations. Although both processes occur throughout the learning of any complex cognitive skill, gains in automaticity are thought to be more characteristic of early stages of learning and restructuring of later stages. For the most part, second-language researchers have been more concerned with the development of automaticity than with restructuring, though there has been some recognition of the role restructuring plays in second-language acquisition.

A number of authors have commented on discontinuities in the second-language learning process Lightbown (1985) pointed out that second-language acquisition is not simply linear and cumulative, but is characterized by 'backsliding' and loss of forms that seemingly were mastered. She attributed this decline in performance to a process whereby learners have mastered some forms and then encounter new ones that cause a restructuring of the whole system.

> [Restructuring] occurs because language is a complex hierarchical system whose components interact in non-linear ways. Seen in these terms, an increase in error rate in one area may reflect an increase in complexity or accuracy in another, followed by overgeneralization of a newly acquired structure, or simply by a sort of overload of complexity which forces a restructuring, or at least a simplification, in another part of the system.
>
> (Lightbrown 1985: 177)

This provides an explanation for examples of 'U-shaped developmental functions,' where performance declines as more complex internal representations replace less complex ones, and increases again as skill becomes expertise. There are many examples of such U-shaped functions in the literature on first-and second-language learning (see McLaughlin 1990). The explanation for such U-shaped functions is that integrating large subtasks makes heavy demands on working memory, and hence performance is actually worse in subsequent stages than it is initially. Thus it is possible for increased practice to create conditions for restructuring with attendant decrements in performance as learners reorganize their internal representational framework.

2. The Impact of Theory on Second-language Pedagogy

What connections can be made between theoretical developments and the practice of language teaching as it occurs in classroom settings? There are some cases where a direct link is possible; in other cases, there are similarities between assumptions and tenets in theory and language teaching, but a direct link between theory and practice would be difficult to establish.

2.1 Learning Theory and the Audiolingual Approach

During and after World War II, the deployment of armed forces personnel in many countries of the world resulted in the need for intensive language programs for the US military. These programs were for essentially pragmatic reasons directed at the spoken word. New techniques were developed, and modern linguistic knowledge was applied to the practical problem of language training. In time, the method used by the military spread to universities and to the public school system.

This method, which was sometimes referred to as the 'army method,' became known more widely as the audiolingual method. It stresses the use of repetitive drill as a means of teaching new language habits. Grammar is taught inductively once oral mastery of syntactic structures is acquired. Translation is proscribed and contrastive linguistics is seen as a tool for the teacher.

The audiolingual method won the blessing of psychologists because the then prevalent learning theory approach regarded language learning as a process of habit development to be inculcated by various contingencies of reinforcement. Hullian and Skinnerian theories were invoked to justify increasing automatization of language instruction. Even more flexible advocates were fond of speaking of sequential control of the learning process, specification of learning goals, and the effectiveness of immediate reinforcement.

But the audiolingual method appealed to linguists as well. As the field of linguistics swung around to a Chomskyan perspective and transformational grammar dominated the field, a number of researchers saw the possibility of a rapprochement between audiolingual methods and transformational grammar.

In time, however, it became increasingly apparent that the audiolingual approach and generative linguistics were strange bedfellows. The Chomskyan revolt against structuralist linguistics had attacked the fundamental assumption of the audiolingual approach—namely that language learning involved the acquisition of new habits. Instead, the now dominant paradigm viewed language as a creative process, and language competence was regarded as underlying knowledge of abstract principles and rules.

2.2 The Implications of the Chomskyan Revolt

'Generative linguistics' provided a formal and fundamental distinction between deep and surface structure representations of language. It developed a complex and elegant system of rules and conventions to describe language. It was not clear, however, how transformational grammar could be applied to classroom language instruction. The focus of generative linguistics is on describing the abstract system of rules that comprises a native speaker's linguistic competence. Not only is generative theory unconcerned with actual performance, it is also unconcerned with the psychological reality of this system of rules.

Chomsky and his followers have been engaged in an enterprise aimed at describing linguistic rules designed to generate all and only the grammatical utterances of a language and to offer a principled account of the relationships between these rules. These rules were never assumed by linguists to be the rules used in real-life production and comprehension. In an often cited passage, Chomsky wrote:

> I am frankly rather skeptical about the significance, for the teaching of languages, of such insights and understanding as have been attained in linguistics and psychology... It is difficult to believe that either linguistics or psychology has achieved a level of theoretical understanding that might enable it to support a 'technology' of language teaching.
> (1966 p. 37)

Linguistic theory could, however, provide the language teacher with insights into the nature of language, though it could not be used to justify particular teaching methods. Some suggested that what current linguistic theory has to offer the language teaching profession are not applications but implications. Indeed, the concept of language as a creative, generative competence has profound implications for techniques of second-language teaching. If language is creative and generative, pattern-practice drills are counterproductive. The most significant development that typifies this movement away from language learning as habit formation to language acquisition as a creative construction process is the so-called 'natural approach' (Krashen and Terrell 1983).

2.2.1 The Natural Approach

The natural approach is predicated on the belief that *communicative competence*, or functional ability in a language, arises from exposure to the language in meaningful settings where the communicative intent expressed by the language is understood. Rules, patterns, vocabulary, and other language forms are not learned as they are presented or encountered, but are gradually established in the learner's repertory on the basis of exposure to comprehensible input. As in other instances of the direct method discussed earlier, rule isolation and error correction are explicitly eschewed in the natural approach. If the teacher uses a grammatical syllabus, she is likely to be teaching structures that some learners know already and that are too far beyond other learners. If the teacher corrects errors, her students are not free to experiment creatively with the language.

'Creative construction' is the result of the role system-internal factors play in the acquisition process. Like early Chomskyan theorists, Krashen and Terrell posit an innate capacity for acquiring language, referred to as the 'Language acquisition device' (LAD). The LAD is assumed to aid humans in processing speech in order to be able to construct the system that underlies it. The LAD is also assumed to contain some 'universal' features of language, such as the role of word order in signaling meaning and basic grammatical relationships between items such as subject and object, so as to facilitate and speed up language acquisition. It is assumed that adults can access the same natural LAD that children use (Krashen 1982).

However, as Gregg (1984) has pointed out, Krashen appears to be giving the LAD a scope of operation much wider than is normally the case in linguistic theory. Krashen seemed to equate LAD with unconscious 'acquisition' of any sort; in contrast, Chomsky—who first developed the notion of a LAD—saw the mind as modular, with the LAD as but one of various 'mental organs' that interact with each other and with the input to produce linguistic competence.

According to Chomsky, the LAD is a construct that describes the child's initial state, before the child receives linguistic input from the environment. The LAD is constrained by innate linguistic universals to generate grammars that account for the input. It is not clear how the concept of LAD can be applied to an adult learner (Gregg 1984). The adult is no longer in an initial state with respect to language and is also endowed with more fully developed cognitive structures.

In fact, Chomsky stated at one point that he believed that whereas first-language acquisition takes place through the essential language faculty, which atrophies at a certain age, it is still possible to learn a language after that age by using other mental faculties such as the logical or the mathematical. This suggests that for Chomsky, the ability to use LAD declines with age and that adult second-language learners must rely on other 'mental organs.'

More recently, however, Chomsky has made some statements about second-language performance that seem compatible with Krashen's argument that adults and children have access to the same language acquisition device. Chomsky maintained that 'people learn language from pedagogical grammars by the use of their unconscious universal grammar' (1975: 249). If one assumes that the LAD is constrained by an innate universal grammar that enables the child or adult second-language learner to project grammars that account for the input from speakers of the target language, then universal grammar theory appears to be compatible with Krashen's notions.

On closer examination, however, it is difficult to fit Krashen's notions within contemporary universal grammar theory. As Flynn (1985) noted, Universal Grammar theory is focused on abstract and linguistically significant principles that are assumed to underlie all natural languages. These principles are argued to comprise the essential language faculty with which all individuals are in general uniformly and equally endowed. Language acquisition is seen as a process of setting the values of the parameters of these universal principles, and not as a problem of acquiring grammatical rules. This is a very different enterprise from the one that concerns Krashen. Other than its recourse to the notion of LAD, the natural approach shows little direct relationship to current Chomskyan theory.

Nonetheless, in spite of these differences, it can be argued that the Krashen–Terrell natural approach does reflect Chomskyan thinking about language as a generative and creative process. Generative linguists might have a different agenda, but they would certainly applaud the basic assumptions of the natural approach—that language teaching needs to move from a grammar-oriented curriculum that focuses on the correction of erroneous habits to a more communicatively-oriented curriculum that allows learners to discover the underlying rules creatively.

2.2.2 Interlanguage and Developmental Sequences

The term 'interlanguage' was coined by Selinker (1972) to refer to the 'interim grammars' constructed by second-language learners on their way to the target language. Since the early 1970s inter-language has come to characterize a major approach to second-language research and theory, and some authors use it as synonymous with second-language learning generally.

In Selinker's original use of the term, interlanguage means two things: (a) *the learner's system* at a single point in time; and (b) the range of interlocking systems that characterizes the development of learners over time. The interlanguage is thought to be distinct from both the learner's first language and from the target language. It evolves over time as learners employ various internal strategies to make sense of the input and to control their own output. These cognitive strategies include 'transfer,' 'overgeneralization,' and 'simplification.'

In contrast to Selinker's cognitive emphasis, Adjemian (1976) argued that the systematicity of the interlanguage should be analyzed linguistically as rule-governed behavior. In this view, the internal organization of the interlanguage can be idealized linguistically, just like any natural language. Like any language system, interlanguage grammars are seen to obey universal linguistic constraints and evidence internal consistency. We may not be able to generate the interlanguage—or any language—through linguistic constructs, but we can learn something about the second-language learner's speech by making a series of descriptions of the learner's interlanguage.

Adjemian cited Corder's (1973) suggestion that research be directed at the learner's 'transitional competence'—that is, at the set of grammatical intuitions about the interlanguage that the learner possesses at a given point in time. Once knowledge is obtained about transitional competence, Adjemian saw the researcher to be in a much better position to infer the psychological mechanisms involved. For this reason Adjemian argued that analysis of the systematicity of the interlanguage should begin with the regularities observed in a large body of data and should be directed at determining the properties of the learner's grammar.

This enterprise is compatible with UG thinking, but it is not clear how it relates to pedagogy. One possible application comes from recent work on 'developmental sequences' in the interlanguage. For example, Zobl (1986), assuming a UG-based approach, accounted for the relative difficulty of several second-language parameters e.g., word order, subject-vs-object prominence, in terms of available processing resources. He argued that the acquisition of the target parameter is constrained by relative processing difficulty, with structure requiring fewer processing resources being acquired at an earlier stage.

In a similar manner, Pienemann and Johnston (1987), invoke general, perceptually-based processing strategies to explain acquisitional stages based on *implicationally-scaled data* obtained from German and English second-language learners. The interesting claim is made that these hierarchically-ordered processing strategies constitute necessary—but not sufficient—constraints on the appearance of specific surface forms—e.g., the appearance of the 3rd person singular.

If there are psychologically constrained developmental sequences in the interlanguage, what can be learned in the language classroom may be subject to some of the constraints that determine the course of natural acquisition. Pienemann (1989) has argued that this is in fact the case, and that instruction can only promote language acquisition if the interlanguage is close to the point when the structure to be taught is acquired in a natural setting. The learner must be ready to acquire given items—ready in the sense that he or she has already passed through the necessary preliminary developmental sequences.

Pienemann's argument has important implications for language syllabus construction. Research on *developmental sequences* found in learners' interlanguage could be used as a guide for the ordering of the language syllabus. Unfortunately, there is little consensus on what developmental sequences exist in the interlanguage, and there is also evidence that instruction can produce deviations from the 'natural' order, even when instruction is directed at meaningful communication in natural contexts.

2.2.3 Current UG Theory

As was pointed out earlier, Chomsky's is a theory of grammatical competence, not of grammatical performance. The theory is based on abstraction:

> To discover the properties of Universal Grammar and core grammar we must attempt to abstract away from complicating factors of various sorts, a course that has its hazards but is inescapable in serious inquiry...
>
> (Chomsky 1981: 39).

The theory separates competence from performance, acquisition from development, and the core from the periphery. Each of these operations takes the inquiry further from actual language as it is used by its speakers.

Furthermore, there is the question of how to make the connection from a linguistic theory of language competence to a theory of second-language learning. Chomsky is not concerned in his writings with second-language learning. The burden rests on those who would apply his ideas to second language to show how the connection is to be made. What has happened to this point is that researchers have used universal grammar theory as a source of hypotheses about second-language learning. This enterprise has yielded interesting information about interlanguage development, but attention has been restricted to a relatively small set of syntactic phenomena.

There is even debate about the issue of whether UG is accessible to adult second-language learners. Some theorists take the position that UG is not accessible to adult learners and that second-language learning in adulthood involves *problem-solving* or general *learning strategies*.

Even those who believe that UG is accessible in adult second-language acquisition are extremely cautious when it comes to drawing applications to language teaching. Principles of UG, such as 'Subjacency,' 'Pro Drop,' or the 'Theta Criterion,' are highly abstract and are not the kinds of properties of language that language teachers currently teach—nor is it clear that they should (White 1989). The UG claim is that such properties cannot be learned; they are highly abstract universal principles that are part of the learner's competence. They are not principles to be taught; they are presupposed for learning to occur.

But this does not mean that UG has nothing to say. There are potential implications for language teaching with respect to the question of what kind of evidence can be used to reset parameters (White 1989). Certain types of grammar lessons and correction in the language classroom can sometimes fill a gap not covered by positive evidence from the input to which learners are exposed. The example mentioned earlier was adverbial placement: French learners of English may need to be told that English does not allow adverbs to intervene between verb and object. Japanese learners of English may need to be told that English reflexives always require a local antecedent. In this sense, UG may lead to a revised 'contrastive analysis,' one based not on the structural comparison of rules, but rather on the ways that the rules exploit the same underlying principles. The UG argument is that surface properties of English stem from deeper principles and parameters, and as we learn more about these principles and parameters, it may be possible to identify surface features that will cause learners from a specific first-language background certain difficulties with a specific second-language.

2.3 The Impact of Cognitive Theory

According to contemporary cognitive psychology, the learning of a complex skill, such as a second language, involves the gradual integration of lower-level skills and their accumulation as automatic processes in long-term storage. In the learning process component skills that require more mental work become routinized and thereby free up controlled processes for other functions. As automaticity develops, controlled processing is bypassed and attentional limitations are overcome. This transition from controlled to automatic processing is central to learning.

2.3.1 Top-down and Bottom-up Processes

There are several ways that this transition can be achieved. In the jargon of cognitive psychology one can distinguish 'top-down' and 'bottom-up' processes. A top-down, or knowledge-driven system is thought to use higher-level information to facilitate the processing of incoming data. A bottom-up, or inductive system relies principally on the information carried by the input. In contrast to children, who usually do not seek out abstract, higher-level information about language, adult learners can use higher-level abstract knowledge of linguistic structure to shortcut the learning process, saving them from the trouble of generating false hypotheses about underlying rules.

This does not mean that the application of cognitive theory leads to grammar-based instruction. Many adult learners can profit from bottom-up techniques that ignore explicit considerations of form and focus instead on communication. What cognitive theory provides is a way of thinking about the learning process, not prescriptions for pedagogy. There are various strategies learners can use in tackling a second language, that require differing degrees of focal attention to formal rules.

Learner Strategies. A significant recent development inspired by cognitive psychology is work on learner strategies. A body of evidence in the cognitive psychology literature suggests that 'experts' use different information-processing strategies than do more 'novice' learners. Differences between experts and novices have been found in research on learning mechanisms in physics, arithmetic, algebra, geometry, computer programing, and chess. For the most part, research indicates that experts restructure the elements of a learning task into abstract schemata that are not available to novices, who focus principally on the surface elements of a task. Thus experts replace complex subelements with a single schema that allows more abstract processing.

In second-language research within an 'expert systems' framework (e.g., Oxford 1986; O'Malley and Chamot 1989), the attempt has been made to specify strategies that good language learners use. The goals have been to identify strategies used by good learners and to teach them to less experienced learners. The intent has been to expand and refine the repertoire of strategies of poor learners so that they may benefit from the strategies used by 'expert' learners. It has been noted that intervention research in the training of cognitive strategies to learners in other skill areas has demonstrated that the continued choice and appropriate use of strategies in a variety of situations requires 'metacognition.' It is not enough for learners to be trained to use a particular strategy, they must also understand the significance of the strategy and be able to monitor and evaluate its use.

The Role of Practice. It is often assumed that the focus of cognitive theory on the integration of skills invariably leads to the promotion of routine drills in language teaching. Indeed, the cognitive description of the learning process stresses the notion that repeated performance of the components of a task through controlled processing leads to the availability of automatized routines. However, these automatized routines should be conceptualized as higher-order *plans*, thought to be flexible entities that allow for integrated execution of various complex tasks. As Levelt (1978) noted, while an essential object of training is automatization of lower-level components, it is incorrect to conclude that this should be done exclusively by frequent repetition of one and the same activity. Training should involve the frequent use of a particular sentence structure in varied lexical settings, not the frequent use of particular sentences in isolation. Once automaticity is developed and controlled processing bypassed, the learner should be able to call up different lexical items and syntactic subcomponents, depending on the task. Thus the same plan can generate different realizations, depending on the lexical setting.

It is also clear from the experience of researchers in the second-language field that practice does not make perfect. Even though there are acquisition sequences, acquisition is not simply linear or cumulative, and having practiced a particular form or pattern does not mean that the form or pattern is permanently established. Learners appear to forget forms and structures which they had seemed previously to master and which they had extensively practiced (Lightbown 1985).

In this view, practice can have two very different effects. It can lead to improvement in performance as subskills become automated, but it is also possible for increased practice to lead to restructuring and attendant decrements in performance as learners reorganize their 'internal representational framework.' It seems that the effects of practice do not accrue directly or automatically to a skilled action, but rather cumulate as learners develop more efficient procedures. Performance may follow a U-shaped curve, declining as more complex internal representations replace less complex ones, and increasing again as skill becomes expertise (McLaughlin 1990).

3. Conclusion

Did behaviorism or structural linguistics lead to the audiolingual approach? Did the concern with interlanguage grammars result from generative linguistics? Is the current focus on learner strategies a direct result of contemporary cognitive psychology? Did developments in humanistic psychology spawn methods of language teaching that emphasize the whole person and affective processes?

The answer to these questions may be indeterminate because of the difficulties inherent in tracing intellectual genealogies. In some idealized epistemological realm, theories are developed, their predictions are tested, and the results of this empirical research are incorporated into practice. In the real world, it is more likely that practice evolves independently of theory, but uses theory as its justification. Theory and practice are typically the products of some vague and ill-defined *Zeitgeist*. Both reflect common intellectual currents that affect the thinking of individuals with different agendas.

It should be clear from the emphasis placed on them in this article that the most intellectually dynamic theories presently are those based on work in generative linguistics and cognitive psychology. They reflect two different approaches to the language-learning process. Many researchers and theorists adopt the linguistic perspective with its focus on the 'creative construction process,' and on the mechanisms and principles whereby the learner constructs an understanding of the target-language system.

Many teachers, however, follow a more psychological model, and assume that if learners are required to produce predetermined pieces of language (through drills or questions-and-answers), this productive activity will lead them to internalize the system underlying the language, to the point where the system operates without conscious reflection (Littlewood 1984). This model is closest to the cognitive–psychological perspective that sees the use of a second language as a cognitive skill involving the internalization, through practice, of various information-handling techniques to overcome capacity limitations. Skill acquisition is seen to involve the accumulation of automatic processing through initial controlled operations that require more workload and attention. Internalized rules are restructured as learners adjust their internal representations to match the target language. This restructuring process involves the use of learning, production, and communication strategies.

The difficulty with a skill model of language learning is that teaching can easily lapse into drill-and-practice exercises. The critique of the traditional approach to language teaching made by Krashen and others is that such an approach leaves little room for creative construction and places too great an emphasis on the conscious learning of rules.

There is an obvious need to incorporate both the more creative aspects of language learning and the more cognitive aspects that are susceptible to guidance and training. This is likely to be the next phase in the theory of language pedagogy, and to some extent it is already happening in practice as individual teachers develop their own eclectic techniques.

Bibliography

Adjemian C 1976 On the nature of interlanguage systems. *Language Learning* **26**: 297–320

Cheng P W 1985 Restructuring versus automaticity: Alternative accounts of skill acquisition. *Psychological Review* **92**(3): 414–423

Chomsky N 1966 Linguistic theory. In: Mead R C (ed.) *Reports of the Working Committee*. Northeast Conference on the Teaching of Foreign Languages, New York

Chomsky N 1975 *Reflections on Language*. Pantheon, New York

Chomsky N 1981 *Lectures on Government and Binding*. Foris, Dordrecht

Corder S P 1973 The elicitation of interlanguage. In: Svartvik J (ed.) *Errata: Papers in Error Analysis*. CWK Gleerup, Lund

Curran C 1976 *Counselling–Learning in Second Language*. Apple River Press, Apple River, IL

Flynn S 1985 Principled theories of L2 acquisition. *Studies in Second Language Acquisition* **7**: 99–107

Gattegno C 1972 *Teaching Foreign Languages in Schools: The Silent Way*. Educational Solutions Inc., New York

Gregg K R 1984 Krashen's monitor and Occam's razor. *Applied Linguistics* **5**: 79–100

Jespersen O 1904 *How To Teach a Foreign Language*. Allen and Unwin, London

Krashen S 1982 *Principles and Practice of Second Language Acquisition*. Pergamon Press, Oxford

Krashen S D, Terrell T D 1983 *The Natural Approach: Language Acquisition in the Classroom*. Pergamon Press, Oxford

Levelt W J M 1978 Skill theory and language teaching. *Studies in Second Language Acquisition* **1**: 53–70

Lightbown P M 1985 Great expectations: Second-language acquisition research and classroom teaching. *Applied Linguistics* **6**: 173–89

Littlewood W T 1984 *Foreign and Second Language Learning: Language-Acquisition Research and Its Implications for the Classroom*. Cambridge University Press, Cambridge

Lozanov G 1979 *Suggestology and Outlines of Suggestopedy*. Gordon and Breach, New York

McLaughlin B 1990 Restructuring. *Applied Linguistics* **11**: 113–28

O'Malley J M, Chamot A U 1989 *Learning Strategies in Second Language Acquisition*. Cambridge University Press, Cambridge

Oxford R L 1986 *Second Language Learning Strategies: Current Research and Implications for Practice*, Technical Report 3. University of California, Los Angeles, CA

Palmer H E 1940 *The Teaching of Oral English*. Longmans, London

Pienemann M 1989 Is language teachable? Psycholinguistic experiments and hypotheses. *Applied Linguistics* 10: 52–79

Pienemann M, Johnston M 1987 A predictive framework of SLA (Unpublished manuscript, University of Sydney)

Rumelhart D E, Norman D A 1978 Accretion, tuning, and restructuring: Three modes of learning. In: Cotton J W, Klatzky R (eds.) *Semantic Factors in Cognition.* Lawrence Erlbaum, Hillsdale, NJ

Schneider W, Shiffrin R M 1977 Controlled and automatic human information processing, vol. I: Detection, search, and attention. *Psychological Review* 84: 1–66

Selinker L 1972 Interlanguage. *IRAL* 10: 209–31

Shiffrin R M, Schneider W 1977 Controlled and automatic human information processing. Vol. II: Perceptual learning, automatic attending, and a general theory. *Psychological Review* 84: 127–90

White L 1989 *Universal Grammar and Second Language Acquisition.* Benjamins, Amsterdam

Zobl H 1986 A functional approach to the attainability of typological targets in L2 acquisition. *Second Language Research* 2: 16–32

B. McLaughlin
S. Robbins

Second Language Pedagogy: Grammar

Over the years, second language educators have alternately favored pedagogical approaches to grammar which begin by focusing on grammatical structures, and those which initially emphasize communication. In the former, students systematically encounter more and more complex structures, building up or synthesizing their knowledge of the target language grammar as they proceed. In the latter approaches, structural complexity is not strictly controlled. Instead, grammatical structures are isolated and dealt with as they arise in the service of communication. These days it is the approaches which start with communication which are preferred.

It is worth noting that some modern applied linguists question whether explicit attention should be given to grammar at all. Rather, they expect second language learners to absorb the rules of grammar unconsciously while they are engaged in communication, much as children absorb the rules of their native language. Most educators, however, agree that second language learning is facilitated by directing student attention to specific grammatical features of the target language. This view is reinforced by language students themselves, who are often eager to study grammar because they perceive its acquisition as necessary to language mastery.

Above all, it should be understood that whether or not one begins with students communicating, the ultimate goal of second language teaching is to have students be able to use the language for communicative purposes. Thus, the teaching of grammar is a means to an end, not an end in itself. If students could recite all the grammar rules but fail to deploy them when communicating, grammar teaching would be considered a failure.

Teachers of grammar must be concerned with the content of what they teach and the process, i.e., the way they teach it. Consequently, grammar pedagogy needs to be informed by what is known about the nature of language (linguistics) and about how languages are acquired (psycholinguistics). Linguistic and psycholinguistic considerations will be treated in turn below.

1. Linguistic Description

Developers of grammar teaching materials draw on different schools of linguistic thought to arrive at the most comprehensive description of the target language possible. Thus, from a linguistics standpoint, pedagogical grammar materials are eclectic. And, as the goal of language teaching is not to teach abstract rules of competence but to get students to comprehend and produce language meaningfully, the materials are more performance-based. Due to learnability requirements, they are also simplified. Such materials typically do not reflect the full complexity of native language behavior. Yet, while they are not as complex as theoretical linguistic descriptions, they often exhibit a broader scope. Grammar teaching cannot be restricted to presenting the formal properties of structures if learners are to be able to use grammar to achieve meaningful communication. Grammar teaching would be less than successful if students could produce, say, the present participle form of the verb but not know what it means or when to use it. Thus, the goal of grammar teaching must be to enable students to produce grammatical structures accurately, meaningfully and appropriately. In order to foster accuracy, meaningfulness, and appropriateness in the use of grammar structures, linguistic descriptions of form, meaning, and use are needed. The pie chart below (Fig. 1) depicts these three dimensions present in all languages, with the arrows suggesting their interconnectedness:

1.1 How is a Grammar Structure Formed?

The form of a structure in a pedagogical grammar is first described in terms of its constituents: the morphemes and words which comprise it. For example, it can be said that the English present progressive 'tense' consists of some present tense form of the verb BE and the present participle, the bound morpheme -*ing*. Second, the description of the form is extended to its syntax or where it fits in a sentence. As an SVO language, English places verbs following subjects and before objects. The *BE* verb, which is an auxiliary verb, would follow all other auxiliary verbs, save the passive *BE*. The -*ing* participle is discontinuous; that is, it exists apart from the *BE* verb and in the active voice is attached to the main verb, as in:

She *is* read*ing* a book.

In a question form, the *BE* verb and subject are inverted:

Is she reading a book?

and in the negative, the *not* is placed after the *BE*, often in contracted form:

She isn't reading a book.

A final fact relevant to the form of a grammatical structure has to do with its distribution, or the total set of contexts in which it can occur. The present progressive, for instance, can generally only be used with dynamic verbs, not stative verbs such as *know, like,* or *own.* A common

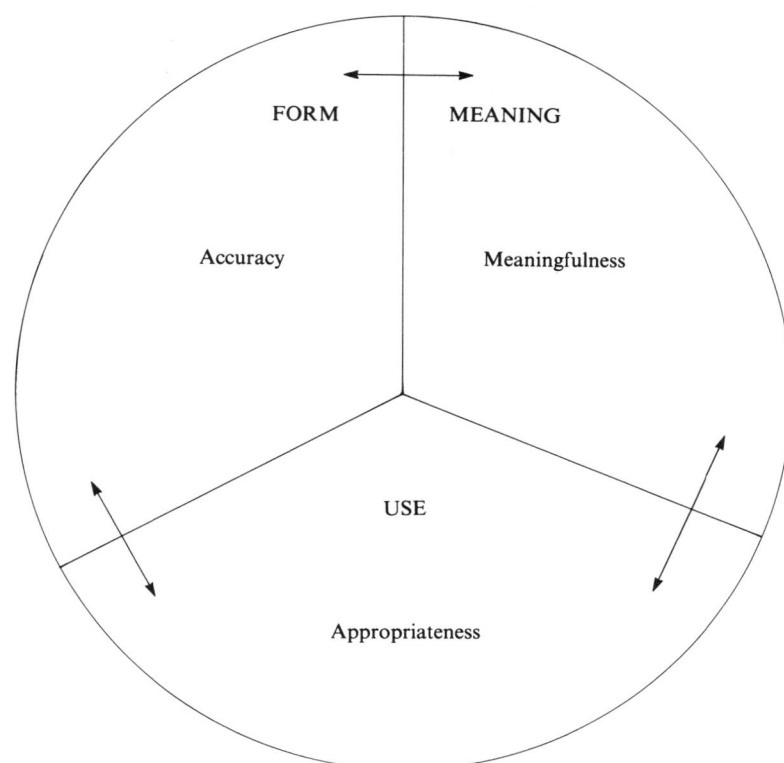

Figure 1. The three dimensions of language.

error made by English learners is to overgeneralize the *-ing* form and apply it to stative verbs, as in:

*He is knowing the answer.

1.2 What Does a Grammar Structure Mean?

The meaning of a structure in a pedagogical grammar may be of two types: lexical or grammatical. Lexical meanings are found in dictionary definitions for members of certain grammatical categories such as prepositions (on, in, by), phrasal verbs (look up, run across, give up), or modal verbs (should, might, will). Single grammar structures do not have lexical meanings as such, but instead have grammatical meaning: a conditional states a condition and a result, for example. In the case of a present participle, a structure we have already examined, it may be said that it ascribes to an action the meaning that it is in process and therefore incomplete. The incompleteness is manifest in different ways, depending upon the semantic category of the verb. With punctual verbs, the present participle signals iteration (The wind is banging the shutter); with durative verbs, duration (They are studying linguistics), or it can signal a temporary, as opposed to an enduring, state of affairs (cf. Steven is living with his parents; Steven lives with his parents). Thus, the grammatical meaning of the present participle varies somewhat depending upon the verb to which it is attached but, in general, conveys that the activity is in progress and therefore incomplete. This is its grammatical meaning, regardless of the tense of the *BE* verb.

1.3 When is the Grammar Structure Used?

The use of a structure as described in a pedagogical grammar refers to its appropriateness either to a social context or to a linguistic discourse context. Often a number of grammatical structures will convey roughly the same meaning but will not all be equally appropriate to the context. For example, when a host is trying to be especially courteous, it is more polite in English to make an offer using the past tense form of the verb and *something* rather than *anything* (cf. Did you want something to eat? Do you want anything to eat?). Phrasal verbs are considered more appropriate in an informal context than their single-word counterparts (cf. The man got up before dawn; The man rose before dawn). Sometimes even one form of the same structure is more appropriate than another on a given occasion. Thus, for example, the fronting of the preposition in a relative clause is considered more appropriate in a formal context (cf. The person with whom I am speaking is a former colleague; The person whom I am speaking with is a former colleague). Students must be made aware of the necessity for choosing among grammatical structures in order to satisfy the appropriateness demands of the context.

The same criterion of appropriateness applies when choosing grammar structures to use in linguistic discourse. The passive voice is preferred over the active in a particular discourse framework when the theme, as opposed to an agent, is in focus (cf. The statue of David was disfigured; A man disfigured the statue of David); and the use of the definite article *the* (as opposed to the indefinite articles *a* or *an*) is appropriate when a noun phrase has already been introduced (cf. I took the book (i.e., the one you recommended) out of the library yesterday; I took a book out of the library yesterday). To continue with our example of the present participle, one consideration of use would specify when it is appropriate to use the present progressive, as compared with the simple present, to report future events (cf. The train leaves tomorrow; The train is leaving tomorrow).

In short, in order for language students to be able to use grammar structures accurately, meaningfully, and appropriately, the content of grammar teaching must not only deal with the form of grammar structures but also their meaning and use. How this content is imparted needs to be informed by psycholinguistic considerations. It is to these we turn next.

2. Psycholinguistic Considerations

As time and student attention are limited in the classroom, considerations of a psycholinguistic nature must be drawn upon in order to use the allotted time most effectively. Grammar teachers may be unable to deal comprehensively with all that is known about the target language grammar; therefore, they must select what is most important for students to assimilate. An aid in this endeavor is the recognition that typically one of the three dimensions of form, meaning, and use for any given structure affords groups of students the greatest challenge.

2.1 Defining the Challenge

What is likely to be difficult for a given group of language students is that aspect of the target language which is most inherently complex. The difficulty is compounded if the grammar of the students' native language is likely to interfere with the learning of the target language structure. For example, for most learners of English, the forms and meanings of the English tense–aspect system are fairly easy to learn. What is problematic, however, is to learn when it is appropriate to use each. Distinctions between the past tense and present perfect or *going to* future and *will* future are but two notorious examples of the many which cause much perplexity among students learning English as a second language. The fact that the distinctions themselves are not always clearcut (with some overlapping functions and inconsistencies) is not helped by the fact that there is no one-to-one functional correspondence between English tenses and those of other languages. How the target language and native language conceptualize reality can be fundamentally different and, of course, the grammatical devices used to instantiate the conceptualizations can be divergent as well. The experienced teacher of English grammar then knows that the students' long-term challenge in mastering the English tense–aspect system will be in their learning when to use each tense.

With English phrasal verbs, it is a different matter. Here the fact that each verb and particle combination yields a unique, often unpredictable, meaning will lead even the most observant student awry. How is the hapless student to know that *slow down* and *slow up* are virtually synonymous? Then, too, few languages in the world have structures comparable to two-word or phrasal verbs. Thus, the learning challenge of the tense–aspect system lies in its overlaps and inconsistencies, whereas the learning challenge of phrasal verbs resides in the fact that little generalizing is possible and prior knowledge (of the meaning of the verb and particle when they are not used in combination) is often misleading. These factors which contribute to difficulty in learning are not unique to the learning of English. It is the responsibility of teachers of all languages to be sensitive to the areas of a grammar structure which create obstacles to learning.

It is also important to recognize that the three dimensions of language (form, meaning, and use) are not learned in the same way and should, therefore, not be taught in the same way. Getting students to produce grammatical forms accurately, for instance, is likely to require a great deal of meaningful repetition before the pattern is internalized. When the meaning dimension is being taught, it is crucial that students have an opportunity to forge a bond between a particular structure and its real-world representation or a native language equivalent. With use as the challenge, it is important that students work with language at the discourse level, i.e., with oral or written text: dialogues, paragraphs, riddles, songs, etc. Students should be presented with a choice between two structures for a given context, where they can receive feedback on the appropriateness of their choice. (Specific examples of techniques which address the three different dimensions will be offered in Sect. 2.3 below.)

2.2 Selection and Sequencing

At a more global level, grammar teachers must be concerned with the selection and sequencing of grammatical structures. What is selected will be determined by the purpose for which the language learning is undertaken. The grammar structures taught in a basic language survival course, for example, would differ in principled ways from those included in a course preparing students to deal with academic subject matter.

In addition to selection, the matter of sequencing is also of concern. Even if teachers are not approaching grammar teaching with a preordained grammatical syllabus, certain of the structures which arise in communication will be designated to be taught before others. Typically the grading of linguistic structures has been accomplished by adhering to certain principles, among which are relative linguistic simplicity, frequency of occurrence, communicative utility, and contrastive difficulty for speakers of a particular native language.

While pedagogical sequences are still often based on such principles, an additional factor has received attention of late. This consideration has to do with psycholinguistic evidence that learners apparently must learn to perform certain grammatical operations before they can be expected to acquire others. Evidence adduced from studies of the acquisition of German and English, for instance, has revealed that students will first learn to move sentence internal elements to initial or final position in the sentence (e.g., She is reading a book → Is she reading a book?) before they learn sentence internal permutations (e.g., We handed in our term papers last week → We handed our term papers in last week). Such observations have led to the conclusion that natural processing constraints restrict what is learnable at any one time, and hence efforts to teach structures beyond which learners are capable of processing will prove futile. This is a strong claim and one that requires further empirical validation. If the findings are corroborated, the implications for the sequencing of grammatical structures are enormous. At this point, all that can be said with any degree of certainty is that pedagogical sequences are at best superfluous and at worst obstructionist if they do not coincide with any natural learning order which may exist.

One final point that should be made with regard to sequencing is that although learners may develop certain grammatical operations before others, it is not the case that learners tackle one grammatical structure, practice it until it is fully acquired and then proceed to begin anew with another structure. The learning of grammar structures does not take place by aggregation. Rather, the process can be characterized as a gradual one, involving the mapping of form, meaning, and use. Even when learners appear to have acquired a particular structure, it is not unusual to find backsliding occurring as new structures are introduced.

The implication of this awareness is that a grammatical syllabus must follow a cyclic, rather than linear, sequence. Students must contend with the same structure, albeit with a focus on different aspects, again and again. Moreover, teachers often find an advantage in not sticking rigidly to the sequence of grammar structures in a syllabus, but rather in being sensitive to student needs at the time and attempting to meet them by providing instruction on structures which students appear ready to learn.

2.3 Manner of Instruction

A standard grammar lesson is divided into three phases: presentation, practice, and communication. One of two strategies is adopted during the presentation phase: deductive or inductive. In accord with a deductive strategy, the grammar teacher presents a pattern or a rule to students and then provides sufficient examples until satisfied that it is understood. In an inductive approach, students are first given examples of a given structure, typically embedded within a text, be it a specially constructed dialog or some sample of authentic text such as an excerpt from a newspaper. Students are then encouraged to induce the target language rule or generalization. Sometimes the rule is never formally articulated, remaining implicit, a tactic in keeping with the previously stated goal of not teaching the grammar rules themselves but rather using them to encourage students to bring their linguistic behavior in increasing conformity with the target language.

Psycholinguistic evidence has not demonstrated the superiority of one of these strategies over the other; however, in general, deductive strategies are thought to be more effective when the rules are convoluted, and probably not especially useful when learners are young. For children, in particular, the formal explication of the rule would probably obfuscate more than elucidate. Furthermore, an inductive strategy has the advantage of allowing a teacher to determine what it is that students already know about a given structure and what remains to be clarified and reinforced. For these reasons and because students possess different learning styles, most teachers will make use of both strategies during the course of instruction.

Once the grammar structure has been introduced, the practice phase ensues. Students practice the new rule or pattern with exercises which are first tightly controlled and later of a freer nature. Vocabulary diversity and situational complexity are limited in controlled exercises so that the students can focus upon the grammatical challenge. Controlled exercises such as grammar drills are used for working on the form of a grammar structure. Question and answer drills might be employed, for example, in order for students to practice the form of short answers:

Teacher: Is this a box?
Student: No, it isn't. It's a book.
Teacher: Is this a pen?
Student: Yes, it is.

While such drills are highly restrictive, they do allow for abundant repetition of the target structure.

For freer practice which would address the formal challenge, grammar games are useful. With games, the vocabulary and information load are much less constrained, but production of the target structure is still necessary. An example of a game which teachers use to practice question formation is 'twenty questions,' wherein students must guess something the teacher or a classmate is thinking of by posing a series of up to twenty yes/no questions.

When dealing with a meaning challenge, an example of a controlled exercise is one in which students are asked to perform some simple action in response to a command. For instance, after the teacher models the actions, students would be asked to carry out a routine such as 'stand up, sit down, turn around,' etc. in order to associate a meaningful action with a phrasal verb. A freer practice exercise that would work to reinforce a meaningful bond is a problem-solving task. A typical task is one containing an information gap. Each student in a pair receives one-half of the information necessary to solve a problem. Only by pooling the information they have been given can the problem be solved. Students might, for example, be charged with the task of identifying the buildings on a town map. One student in the pair has a map in which one-half of the buildings are labeled; the other student has an identical map, except for the fact that the other half of the buildings are labeled. By asking and answering each other's questions, the students should be able to complete the maps, while practicing the meaningful use of spatial prepositions (next to, behind, across from, etc.).

A common controlled exercise designed to work on the dimension of use is one in which students are asked to make a choice which depends on contextual factors. Students might be asked, for example, to fill in the blanks in a text where they would need to supply the appropriate verb tense. A freer practice exercise that would work well on appropriateness in social situations is the use of structured role plays. In a role play students are asked to act as if they had taken on someone else's identity and to do so in accordance with the appropriate degree of politeness or formality. A role play where one student is asked to give advice to another student, initially as if the other student is the first's employer and then as if a spouse, would give students practice in using modal verbs appropriately.

When students have demonstrated some dexterity with the target structure, the final or communicative phase of a grammar lesson takes place. In this phase, learners engage in more open-ended, less controlled activities. The aim during this phase is to have students use the structures they have been practicing in as natural and fluent a manner as possible. Because there are relatively few constraints, however, there is no guarantee that students will choose to use the target structures at all.

Examples of communicative activities which would permit the students to work on one of the three dimensions of grammar would be interviewing one's fellow students about their hobbies (to practice the *form* of questions), giving one's fellow students recipe directions (to practice using certain connectors—e.g., first, then, after that—*meaningfully*) and to ask students to write a paragraph about an invention (to practice the *use* of the passive voice).

2.4 Learner Feedback

An extremely important component of any approach to teaching grammar is that students receive feedback on the accuracy, meaningfulness, and appropriateness of the language they produce. Psycholinguistic evidence has shown that when students initially grapple with target structures, the forms that they produce are nontarget-like at first (and many persist in this manner for some time). The nontarget-like productions of learners are due to many factors, two common ones being the influence of similar, but not identical, structures in the native language and forms which result from students' applying a rule beyond what the language allows, as in the example we cited earlier of the use of the present participle with stative verbs (*I am knowing the answer). It is widely acknowledged that teacher feedback is invaluable in providing students with negative evidence that will allow them to revise their hypotheses about the target language rules and ultimately to bring their performance into alignment with the target language.

Further, it is recognized that error correction by the teacher is most helpful when the error the student is committing is systematic (i.e., results from a misunderstanding of a rule and is pervasive, not merely a slip) and when the correction is judicious. With regard to the latter, it is better for a teacher to call attention to selected errors during the practice phase of a lesson, for instance, rather than the communicative phase. It is also thought that teacher prompts at student self-correction will be more successful in the long run than if the teacher simply offers the correct form.

3. Future Investigation

What has been presented here is a fairly conventional view of grammar pedagogy. The presentation will conclude with three recent proposals which could have a significant impact in the future on the way second language grammar is taught.

The first proposal stems from the concern that traditional grammatical sequences do not reflect what is known about language acquisition. Recall the earlier point that language acquisition does not take place through linear aggregation but is more of a metamorphic process which is represented in students' production by increasing grammaticization (Rutherford 1987). It has been suggested that an approach to grammar teaching more in keeping with the acquisition process would be one where grammar teachers would help students achieve an understanding of general principles of grammar (e.g., how to modify basic word order) rather than concentrating on their remembering structure-specific rules in the target language. Investigation into the nature of the grammaticization which takes place and further identification of the general principles will be necessary in order to evaluate the efficacy of this approach.

The second proposal relates to the fact that what is crucial for language learners to know is how grammar functions in alliance with words and contexts to create meaning (Widdowson 1990). The objection to current practice is, therefore, that grammatical structures are given primacy over lexis, with words being introduced merely to exemplify a grammar structure. What has been suggested instead is that a reverse order may be more beneficial—that is, that learners start by being taught target language words and then be shown how they need to be modified grammatically to be communicatively effective.

The third on the list is less a proposal and more an awareness. It has been increasingly apparent that much of what contributes to (at least) initial fluency in a second language is not mastery of grammar rules but rather the learner's control over a number of prefabricated or formulaic chunks of language. For example, when a learner of English first uses 'How are you?' it is not likely that the question is the result of the application of English question formation rules. It is much more likely that the learner has memorized it as a whole phrase. Whether later these chunks are analyzed from patterns to creative language use or whether they remain in a learner's repertoire as holophrases forever is a matter of current debate. Future investigation is clearly needed in this area, not only for the light it will shed on the acquisition process but also for the potentially challenging implications it will have for second language grammar pedagogy.

Bibliography

Celce-Murcia M, Hilles S 1988 *Techniques and Resources in Teaching Grammar*. Oxford University Press, Oxford
Celce-Murcia M, Larsen-Freeman D 1983 *The Grammar Book*. Newbury House, Rowley, MA
Larsen-Freeman D 1991 Teaching grammar. In: Celce-Murcia M (ed.) *Teaching English as a Second or Foreign Language*, 2nd edn. Newbury House, New York
Rutherford W 1987 *Second Language Grammar: Learning and Teaching*. Longman, London
Rutherford W, Sharwood-Smith M (eds.) 1988 *Grammar and Second Language Teaching*. Newbury House, New York
Ur P 1988 *Grammar Practice Activities*. Cambridge University Press, Cambridge
Widdowson H G 1990 *Aspects of Language Teaching*. Oxford University Press, Oxford
Wilkins D A 1976 *Notional Syllabuses*. Oxford University Press, London

D. Larsen-Freeman

Second Language Pedagogy: Listening

Since the early 1960s, rapid developments in understanding the nature of listening and its role in second language learning have helped to revolutionize teaching materials and methods. Yet it is worth remembering that listening has been a feature of language learning and teaching for a very long time. When children are learning their first language, the ability first to hear and then to listen to what is being said is vital. The same is true of learners of a second or foreign language. For example, it is clear that very young children who are learning a second or foreign language, either informally at home or more formally at school, typically have to depend on their ability to listen well before they are able to exploit their capacity to speak, read, and write.

For older learners too, the role of listening is equally well established. Adult second language learners have always been obliged to listen to their teachers' instructions and explanations, even if they are not always given in the language being taught. And learners of all ages have always depended on listening to their teachers in order to get some idea of what the language being taught actually sounds like, or is supposed to sound like.

1. Listening as a Skill

Listening is important in second language pedagogy not only because it is something that learners inevitably do, but also because it is considered to be a skill in its own right. In the 1960s, teachers were taught to think in terms of there being four language skills: listening, speaking, reading, and writing. They were traditionally thought of as the two 'active' skills (speaking and writing), and the two 'passive' skills (listening and reading).

The proposition that there are four separate language skills which can be divided into active and passive skills has been very influential. It has helped teachers to understand why, for example, some students seem to be better at speaking than reading. It has helped teachers to organize their teaching units in different ways, and to think of language learning and teaching not just as one monolithic, almost mysterious, process, but as a series of separately identifiable components. And as far as listening is concerned, its status as a separate skill has gradually given teachers the opportunity to focus on particular activities which before had been either taken for granted or hardly developed at all.

Researchers' understanding of listening as a skill has been largely influenced by two fields of inquiry: research into second language acquisition and theories of comprehension. Since the 1980s, there has been an increasing interest in experiments which simulate the comprehension of language, though much of the research work involving listening has focused on the comprehension strategies of native speakers of English, and not of people for whom English is a second or foreign language. In all events, experimental work on listening has tended to conclude that central to any definition of listening as a skill is the notion that listening involves learners understanding units larger than the sentence; using knowledge of the world; using their experience of what typical 'listening texts' sound like and contain; and exploiting a variety of inferencing and other strategies that help them to interpret what is heard.

Listening strategies have in their turn been described as processes, or subskills which may involve, for example, remembering, guessing, anticipating, predicting, and while listening, revising and updating one's understanding in the light of personal experiences and of new information being heard. Rost (1990) identifies 22 skills involved in the listening process. His list—there are many others—includes perceiving and discriminating sounds in isolated words; deducing the meaning of unfamiliar words; identifying the speaker's intention; transferring information from a spoken source to some other form, for example, to written notes; and providing appropriate feedback to a speaker.

So, contrary to the characterization in the 1960s of listening as a separate, indivisible, passive skill, the tendency in the 1990s is to think of listening as something that is bound to occur in combination with reading, writing, and speaking; that itself consists of a series of describable subskills; and that requires real effort and active participation from the learner. Therefore, as even the simple example in Fig. 1 illustrates, the vast majority of listening activities are not confined to teaching or testing the listening skill in isolation, and they may require a great degree of concentration and attention to detail.

2. Traditional Listening Texts and Exercises

In the 1950s and 1960s, before the identification of listening as an apparently separate skill, there was a general assumption that the main purpose of listening was to develop the students' 'perception' of the language being learned. To that end, listening *texts* were often regarded as an opportunity to provide specially crafted, model instances of the language being taught, while listening *exercises*, where they existed at all, were not required to be very different from the sorts of activities that students were doing in the other, nonlistening parts of their courses. In many respects, the choice of texts and exercises used for listening were at that time not so different from those used in the teaching of reading comprehension, and typically included blank-filling exercises, true/false exercises, and multiple choice questions.

In traditionally designed listening materials, there is another implicit assumption that if students can improve their perception of the second language by listening to it, then their ability to speak the language will also improve. In the 1960s, the role of listening as an aid to pronunciation was greatly supported by the fashionable structuralist linguistic theories of the time. Contrastive analysis was very popular, and a great deal of attention was given to comparing and contrasting the meaningful sound segments (phonemes) in different languages. So, taking their cue from linguistic theory, early listening activities required students to listen very carefully indeed to sound segments and their variations (e.g., [p] in *pie* versus [b] in *buy*; but also aspirated [p^h] in *pie* versus unaspirated [p] in *spy*). All the taped material was specially written, and carefully delivered by speakers—invariably male—chosen for the clarity of their diction and their suitability as model speakers of the language.

In traditional listening activities (which remain very common in the 1990s), listening texts are typically short, and exercises are limited in range. The listening script—the text—frequently consists of little more than groups of words and phrases designed to improve the perception and pronunciation of individual sounds and, as Fig. 2 illustrates, sometimes also to help students appreciate the relationships between sound and spelling. The most common instruction to students is to 'Listen and repeat,' after which they might be asked to match what they hear with a written version of the spoken material; or to perform some simple discrimination task, also with reference to written material. For example, they might be asked to listen to (and often at the same time to read) word groups such as *sea leaf pear tea leap*, and then be instructed to identify the odd one out

Recipes

Activity 1

You will hear the ingredients for three recipes. Listen and write down the amounts needed. Use these abbreviations:

g = grams
kg = kilograms
l = litre(s)
tsp = teaspoon(s)
tbsp = tablespoon(s)

Figure 1. This listening activity also involves reading and writing. The exercise calls for active concentration and attention to detail on the part of the learner (Richards 1990: 15, 68).

(*pear*). Clearly, this kind of listening activity is closely allied to the teaching of pronunciation. Materials such as *Ship or Sheep?* (Baker 1982) and *Tree or Three?* (Baker 1982), much of which focuses on the learner's ability to discriminate between utterances which are only minimally different from each other, remain very popular in the 1990s.

Students may also be presented with material in which the focus is not on individual sounds, but on stress, rhythm, and intonation. Thus, generations of students who are learning British English have been asked to listen to and to discriminate between question tag sentences such as *She's a teacher, isn't she!* ↘, said with falling intonation, and confidently expecting agreement; and *She's a teacher, isn't she?* ↗, said with rising intonation, and indicating relative uncertainty. In the UK, the continuing need to record this kind of listening material for secondary school courses, where question tags and intonation often figure largely on syllabuses, has meant that all the major publishers tend to use the same small number of actors who have learned to reproduce such sentences and intonation patterns on demand.

6 **Say these words after the recording or your teacher.**

1. am   cat   back   hand   bad
2. came   late   wake   rain   made
3. car   last   glasses   bath   half
4. saw   tall   walk   talk   all

Figure 2. The very simplest kind of traditional listening exercises often focus on the student's ability to perceive and then to say sounds. In addition, this exercise deals with the complex relationships between sounds and spelling (Swan and Walter 1984: 59).

Even the longest of traditional listening texts rarely consists of much more than one or two specially *written* paragraphs, the main point of which is usually to provide further examples of a grammatical point, usually a verb tense, that is being taught. Such listening texts include an artificially high incidence of any particular grammatical point, for example, the present perfect tense: *she has been; he has not seen; they have taken*, and are frequently used by the teacher as an opportunity for some simple comprehension work, or as a prompt for a class dictation.

3. A Demand for Authenticity, and for Tasks

In the mid- and late 1970s, traditional approaches to the teaching of listening were greatly influenced by a shift of emphasis in the theory and practice of second language pedagogy, by advances in technology, and by commercial pressures.

The publication of David Wilkins's *Notional Syllabuses* (1976) and the work on language functions promoted by, among many others, the Council of Europe, created an immediate demand for language materials that focused not only on linguistic forms, but also on *why* people use language, for example, to apologize, to explain, to describe. This gave rise to an increased demand for real instances of such language uses. Teachers increasingly expressed a preference for recordings of real and especially *authentic* language which, ideally, had been recorded live, or at least with real people.

Fully scripted listening materials were suddenly out of fashion. Semiscripted or rehearsed scripts were allowable only if, like lectures or speeches, they would be designed and delivered that way in real life. To be fully authentic, listening materials, it was felt, should be unscripted, spontaneous, and natural. The argument was that students should be exposed to real conversations and to everyday speech in the target language, taken from a variety of real-life contexts, and uttered by real people of different ages and speaking with different accents. Furthermore, the exercises for students should themselves reflect real-life *tasks*. These might involve, for example, identifying a speaker's purpose (*to explain, to describe, to apologize,* and so on), listening for gist, distinguishing a point of view, following instructions, completing a form, giving or taking advice, or taking notes. As the example in Fig. 3 shows, the emphasis on such listening materials is less on language forms and more on the *information* carried by texts: that is, on their content.

The impetus provided by the shift from structurally based pedagogy toward functionally based pedagogy gave listening a tremendous boost. Within a very short time, listening

12 Hiring a car

Listening

Write down the answers to the customer's questions.

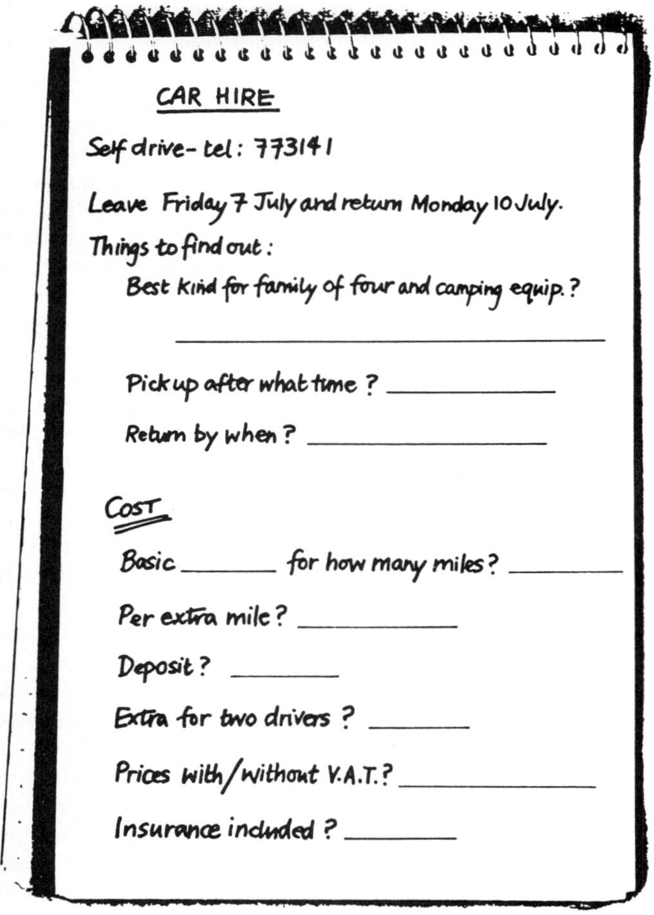

Figure 3. A good example of a task-based listening and note-taking activity. Both the text and the exercise reflect aspects of the real world. Having been assigned a role, in this case that of someone enquiring about car hire details, the student's focus is on understanding the content and not the form of what is being said (Blundell and Stokes 1981: 24).

materials were freed from the constraints of having to be closely tied to the language forms of general language courses. Materials specifically devoted to listening began to appear (e.g., Underwood 1975, 1976, 1979). A listening component was felt to be an essential ingredient of any general language course, and in the 1980s, publishers began to produce 'skills series,' which typically consisted of separate materials for each of the four language skills, at four levels. Although many of the exercises in listening materials were still essentially traditional in design, the listening texts themselves were often fresh, original, interesting in their own right, and not spoken by professional actors. The situations depicted in materials resembled those of real life, and learners could identify with them.

4. A Compromise

In practice, however, the goals of authenticity and task-based activities have proved harder to achieve than many teachers (and especially full-time teacher-trainers) at first realized. In the first place, it is extremely difficult to record fully authentic material, and there are ethical problems involved in using material which has been secretly recorded. Second, although radio would seem to be an ideal source for listening material, it is often difficult to get permission to use such material in classes. Third, genuine tasks are not all that easy to come by, if only because in most classroom situations involving listening, the students are not participants in the original context: more typically, they are listening in, or overhearing, or acting as silent witnesses. To that extent, the second language learner's role as a 'genuine' listener is invariably a restricted one.

Also, fully authentic material often includes phenomena (pauses, hesitations, interruptions, periods where several voices speak at once, difficult accents, impenetrable idioms, rapid changes of direction in the topics being discussed, intrusive background noise) which in practice create problems for both teachers and learners. Traditional listening materials usually dealt with these issues by ignoring them altogether, with the result that in such materials, very little of the text is redundant: students have to listen very carefully to *everything*, in order to prove that they have understood what they have heard. Functional or communicative listening materials tend to operate the other way. In their attempt to be realistic and authentic, those recordings often include a lot of material that is not pertinent to the tasks in hand, or that deliberately misleads or distracts the careless listener: in such cases, students must grasp only the *relevant* information, and discard the rest.

Both approaches have their advantages and disadvantages. Having to listen to everything and to catch every detail helps learners to concentrate, but it also imposes a great strain on them, and does not really reflect how people listen in real life. Traditional listening materials do not always acknowledge the fact that in real-life listening situations, people constantly select from what they hear the things that they need or want to know. At the other end of the scale, having to listen to relatively long stretches of unscripted material can reflect some real-life situations, but it can also be tiresome, especially if the learner has not been given a very active listening role, or is just not interested in the topic or the task in question. So, although the case for students being required to listen to authentic texts seems unassailable, the reality is that they often find such material difficult to hear well or to understand, and they stop listening. Unfortunately, some teachers interpret the learner's impatience and refusal to listen as an inability to understand.

One response to the difficulties presented by authenticity has been the slogan: 'grade the task and not the text.' The argument is that the naturalness and complexity of the original authentic text can be retained, but that in order to make the material accessible to teachers and learners, the tasks should be relatively straightforward. It is for that reason that some materials consist of relatively elaborate texts and transcripts, linguistically far beyond the range of students, but tempered by allegedly easy questions such as 'How many people are speaking?' or 'Does the speaker sound angry?' The difficulty with this approach is that though such tasks may be considered relatively simple, they are often not very useful or interesting, or directly concerned with the content of the text.

Another response, and one favored by most commercial textbook writers, has been to compromise. Most contemporary listening activities, especially those to be found in general language courses, strike a balance between the highly controlled texts and exercises of traditional materials on the one hand, and the open-endedness of authentic materials and tasks on the other. There is still a tendency to claim that listening materials are 'authentic': the pressure to make such claims is very great. But in many cases, the listening work is either fully or semiscripted, and the speakers are more often than not specially briefed, or professional actors. That is particularly true of the increasing range of materials for primary and secondary school foreign language students, most of whom greatly prefer their listening work to be combined with watching videos.

In practice, therefore, most people who prepare listening materials have realized that it is not just the format or the structure of the text and task that counts, but also the level of interest that their content actually generates among learners. In other words, although listening material can be well designed and theoretically sound, unless its subject matter engages the interest of the learners, it will not work. Students find it more difficult to tolerate poorly constructed or uninteresting listening activities than they do poorly constructed or uninteresting reading activities.

5. Factors Affecting the Evaluation of Materials and Methods

Teachers know to their cost that it is impossible to evaluate listening materials on sight. They have to be used, and that takes time. In her survey review of listening materials, Kellerman (1992) considers the technical quality of recordings, the themes developed in materials, the transparency and appropriateness of accompanying exercises, the inclusion or otherwise of helpful teacher's notes (which should include a readable transcription of all listening material and suggestions for further activities), and any special claims made by materials. Kellerman notes correctly that, of all the claims made about contemporary listening material, the most common is that the recordings are authentic. But, as she points out, this is not always the case.

Another comment frequently made about listening materials is that they tend to test rather than to teach. It is

true that a comparison of so-called teaching material, with explicitly designed testing material such as that produced for the TOEFL examination (taken by foreign students who wish to study at American universities) or the Cambridge First Certificate intermediate level examination (e.g., Field 1983) shows that there are more similarities than differences between the two sorts of product. There are some listening materials which do try to 'teach' students to listen, and to do well in listening tests (e.g., Rixon 1988). But on the whole, the differences between materials that allegedly teach and those that actually test listening are often slight. For most practical purposes, the most important differences involve the degree of attention paid to the learner's responses: in tests, the responses really do count.

It is also said that listening materials often focus too much on the 'product' and not the 'process' of listening. In the late 1980s, it was fashionable to make a clear distinction between product and process, and to argue that of the two, the language learning *process* was the more important, and the one to be developed. To some extent, listening materials which deal explicitly with subskills such as listening for gist, or which ask students to explain how they completed particular tasks, may be said to be dealing more with the process of listening (i.e., what goes on in the student's head) than with the product (i.e., the learner's visible or audible response to listening tasks, or, more prosaically, the answers to exercises). But more than that, it is difficult to see how, in practical terms, listening materials, teachers, and learners can get much closer to what is essentially hidden from view. The truth is that the mechanism of the listening process is not yet fully understood.

For teachers and learners, one of the greatest difficulties with listening materials is that the design of listening exercises is not always fully thought through. Kellerman (1992) gives several instances: of grids whose layout does not coincide with the sequencing of information on the recording; of gap-filling exercises that seem to perform no purpose; and of activities which are far beyond the range of the student. Good materials, on the other hand, are those in which it is perfectly clear to both the student and the teacher what is expected of them, and in which the prelistening, listening, and postlistening activities can be completed *in reasonable time*.

6. Teacher Competence and Listening

Another problem is that many teachers have not been specially trained to handle listening activities. There are some very good theoretical books about listening (e.g., Brown and Yule 1983; Anderson and Lynch 1988), and some very helpful practical books (e.g., Ur 1984; Underwood 1989) which try to compensate for that lack of training.

But in most cases, teachers learn to teach listening by a process of trial and error, and experimentation. The best advice for teachers is to allow plenty of preparation time both for themselves and their students, and to practice dealing with the combination of the students' book, the teachers' notes, and the cassette. For the teacher's preparation time to be fully effective, a clear transcript of the listening material is needed, and the teacher needs to be able to juggle with the student's materials, a teacher's guide, a cassette, an answer guide, and the class itself. To do that well requires a lot of practice, a good deal of confidence, and reliable material.

Teachers and learners also need to know how long the different phases of a listening activity are likely to take, because in practice it turns out that many listening activities take up much more time than anyone (including, it would seem, the materials writer) had allowed for. Most second language lessons in the world are quite short, and conducted by nonnative-speaking teachers working in difficult circumstances. Whereas native speakers of a language (who dominate the thinking behind nearly all listening material, and who produce nearly all of it) can tolerate so-called natural language spoken at normal speed, some nonnative-speaking teachers and their students are threatened by recorded material which is too fast and too complex.

So, for listening activities to be built into many lessons, they need to be clearly defined, carefully managed, interesting, and not too long. Unfortunately, not all listening materials take full account of these constraints, with the inevitable result that, notwithstanding many teachers' best efforts, a great deal of listening work done in second language work is probably less effective than it might be.

Bibliography

Anderson A, Lynch T 1988 *Listening*. Oxford University Press, Oxford

Baker A 1982a *Ship or Sheep?* Cambridge University Press, Cambridge

Baker A 1982b *Tree or Three?* Cambridge University Press, Cambridge

Blundell L, Stokes S 1981 *Task Listening*. Cambridge University Press, Cambridge

Brown G, Yule G 1983 *Teaching the Spoken Language*. Cambridge University Press, Cambridge

Field J 1983 *Cambridge First Certificate English Practice: Listening Comprehension*. Macmillan, London

Kellerman S 1992 Survey review: Recent materials for the teaching of listening. *English Language Teaching Journal* **46**(1): 100–12

Richards J 1990 *Listen Carefully*. Oxford University Press, Oxford

Rixon S 1988 *Successful Listening for First Certificate*. Oxford University Press, Oxford

Rost M 1990 *Listening in Language Learning*. Longman, London

Swan M, Walter C 1984 *The Cambridge English Course*, Book 1. Cambridge University Press, Cambridge

Underwood M 1975 *Listen to This*. Oxford University Press, Oxford

Underwood M 1976 *What a Story!* Oxford University Press, Oxford

Underwood M 1979 *Have you Heard?* Oxford University Press, Oxford

Underwood M 1989 *Teaching Listening*. Longman, London

Ur P 1984 *Teaching Listening Comprehension*. Cambridge University Press, Cambridge

Wilkins D 1976 *Notional Syllabuses*. Oxford University Press, Oxford

N. F. Whitney

Second Language Pedagogy: Pronunciation

While it is a commonplace for writers in the field of second or foreign language (henceforth L2) teaching to describe their chosen topic as 'a neglected area,' there is no topic which better fits this description than the teaching of pronunciation. Not only has it received very little attention in pedagogical theory since the heyday of behaviorism in language teaching, but many materials writers and language teachers either make only the most cursory gesture in the direction of pronunciation teaching, or—in contrast to other aspects of language—do not deal with it at all. This may be because of low expectations of achievement, views on poor return for effort expended, views on the equal validity of different accents, views on the low priority of pronunciation in a communicative approach to language teaching, fear of a complex and little-understood area of language—or any combination of these. This survey will consider the scope of pronunciation as it appears in second language teaching, views on the appropriacy of teaching it, objectives of pronunciation teaching, and methodological issues. Through this account of the way things are, it is to be hoped that suggestions will emerge for the way things might be. Examples are given from English (as a foreign language), but the arguments are applicable to all languages.

1. The Appropriacy of Pronunciation Teaching

While language teachers will usually accept that it will be necessary for most learners to acquire a new pronunciation—to some extent at least—for the L2, the view is regularly expressed by a minority of language teachers that it is actually ethically wrong, linguistically misconceived, socially undesirable or politically undesirable for L2 pronunciation to be taught beyond the bare minimum necessary for intelligibility. These views are rarely to be found in print, but may be strongly held, and account for the reluctance of some teachers to involve themselves in pronunciation teaching.

Arguments about unethicality center on assertions that pronunciation, more than any other aspect of language, is a sensitive and intimate expression of a speaker's self-image. Any attempt to modify a person's pronunciation—even when that pronunciation is in a new language—will, it is felt, imply a value judgment of the speaker him- or herself, and such judgments are unethical, as well as being unconducive to effective language learning.

A rather different view is that it is unnecessary, and possibly undesirable, to teach an L2 pronunciation, in just the same way as some would consider it to be unnecessary and possibly undesirable to teach an alternative pronunciation of the mother tongue. It is in the nature of language that there will be a variety of different accents for any single language: different accents have equal validity, regardless of whether they are determined socially, regionally—or, it is argued, by reason of different mother tongues. In this view, then, to require learners to change or modify their accents when speaking either L1 or L2 is to ignore the natural variability inherent in language, and so is linguistically misconceived.

The use of a particular accent will frequently be laden with sets of cultural values associated with those who normally use that accent. In a society where a second language is widely used, one or more second-language accents specific to that society will usually develop. In such circumstances, the use of an accent normally associated with mother-tongue speakers of that language may imply—or be taken as implying—a rejection of the society and culture of those who use second-language accents. Thus a Sri Lankan teacher might propose to take British English 'received pronunciation' as a model for her learners, but if that (in Sri Lanka) essentially alien accent were perfectly acquired by her learners, they might run the risk of being ostracized by the society around them: 'Who do they think they are?' In these circumstances it would be reasonable to regard attempts to change a second-language accent into a mother-tongue-user accent as socially undesirable.

On an individual level, particular learners might not wish to lose an L1 accent which instantly characterizes them in a way that they are proud of, e.g., 'When I speak English, I want people to notice that I am Greek!' So long as the speaker is easily intelligible, should the teacher urge this learner to lose all linguistic trace of her Greekness when speaking English?

Such assertions of cultural identity and independence may have political significance: while the English 'language' may be a practical necessity, a British or American 'accent' may call up unfortunate overtones of present or past political subservience. For this reason, some teachers in some countries actively discourage learners from attempting to acquire a native-like L2 accent (see *Accent*).

2. The Scope of Pronunciation Teaching

Perhaps the most widely held assumption in pronunciation-teaching materials and related pedagogical discussion is that the acquisition of an appropriate L2 pronunciation consists in the acquisition of a productive proficiency in the L2 phonological system or systems. Attention is focused on the ability to perceive and produce the segmental (individual sound) and suprasegmental (stress and intonation) contrasts deployed by the language, and to do this in ways which in some degree approximate to native-speaker practice, or which are in some other way recognized as acceptable or correct. Acceptability or correctness in pronunciation is thus concerned with articulation and sound production (physiological and acoustic matters) on the one hand, and on the other hand with the realization of individual contrastive units through the various articulations and sounds appropriate in a given language to the pronunciation contexts in which the units occur (matters of conceptual organization). Pronunciation difficulties may be of either type, and either type may impair intelligibility, but the great weight of effort in pronunciation teaching is currently placed on the physiological and acoustic aspects of pronunciation. This leaves the undeniably important aspect of the conceptual organization of sounds relatively neglected.

In the case of intonation, efforts are normally made to relate contrastive patterns of pitch and pitch movement to various types of meaning. Difficulties in the systematic relation of intonation to meaning have led many (see Crystal and Quirk 1964) to include much more than systematic variation in pitch in accounts of the ways in which meaning is conveyed by suprasegmental means. Features such as loudness, huskiness, breathiness, pause, rhythmicality, variation in pitch range, etc., in total generally characterizable as 'tone of voice,' are also involved. Indeed, it has frequently been remarked that native speakers have a particular, distinctive physiological 'set' which characterizes their speech as a whole and goes well beyond the production of particular sounds and contrasts. Tone of voice and physiological set have however been largely neglected in pronunciation pedagogy, perhaps largely because of the great range and variety of features involved, and because of the difficulty in accounting for their systematic use.

Finally, and going beyond questions of phonological systems, most—but not all—L2 learners are already literate in another language, usually their mother tongue (L1). As the L2 is usually taught in its written form from an early stage, it is to be expected that the L2 pronunciation will to some extent be affected by the sound–spelling relationships to which the learner is accustomed in the other language—as also by a growing awareness of patterns in sound–spelling relationships in the L2. Teaching materials frequently relate pronunciation to spelling patterns in the L2, but the effect on L2 pronunciation of L1 patterns, though clearly important, is rarely taken into account.

3. Phonology and Phonetics in Pronunciation Teaching

Overwhelmingly, pronunciation teaching materials are based on a 'phonemic' (or 'tonemic,' in the case of intonation) account of the phonology of spoken language. What is to be acquired is understood and presented in terms of contrastive units of sound (the phonemes, indicated by letters between sloping brackets—e.g., /i/—and the tonemes), and sequences of these units. The fact that these phonemes are essentially abstract, while a given unit is actually pronounced in different ways in various specifiable contexts, tends not to be thoroughly or systematically dealt with. However it is often precisely this detail—the phonetics of the language—which distinguishes native from nonnative pronunciation. Thus the RP pronunciation of the vowel in the word *school* and of the vowel in the word *scoop* are not the same, but they do not contrast. Both are realizations of the same phoneme /u/; one type of realization occurs before 'dark l'—the kind of 'l' sound that comes at the end of the word *school*—while the other occurs in any other context. A learner with only one type of sound for /u/ in the L1 is likely to produce that sound in English in both *school* and *scoop*—after all, both have the same vowel phoneme—and consequently will sound nonnative-like, because of lack of attention to phonetic detail.

4. Which Pronunciation?

While there are many native-speaker accents of English, very few appear in teaching materials. Thus for British English it is only the accent known as 'received pronunciation,' or 'RP,' which is taught, underpinned by such authoritative works as Gimson (1962) or the perhaps more accessible Roach (1983). Moreover, one among the many curious features of RP is that, although it is the only British accent regularly taught in EFL/ESL, only a small minority of British native speakers actually speak it in a pure form (although far more speak an approximation to it). As an unfortunate side effect of this, people who arrive in Britain having learned English in other countries often find that although they are readily understood when they speak, they cannot themselves understand what is said to them in reply.

5. The Goal of Pronunciation Teaching

While the goal in other aspects of L2 learning will usually be to approximate as closely as possible to native-speaker proficiency, most language teachers are satisfied with the lesser goal of 'comfortable intelligibility' (Kenworthy 1987) for the acquisition of pronunciation, i.e., just that level of proficiency in pronunciation which will allow the learner to be understood without difficulty in those situations where there is likely to be a need or wish to use the L2. This utilitarian satisfaction with a lesser goal may derive from the kinds of view of appropriacy described above, from a communicative focus on the message rather than on the vehicle for its expression, or simply from a conviction born of experience that it is simply not cost-effective in the classroom to aim to achieve anything more. It should be noted that this is a teacher-held view which is not necessarily held by the learners themselves—at least not when they begin their language-learning career. What evidence does exist about what the learners themselves want suggests that many may begin with considerably higher aspirations, although teacher expectations eventually take their inevitable toll on learner achievement.

6. Methodological Issues

6.1 Learning versus Practice

It is important in any discussion of language learning to distinguish between learning and practicing. Learning is concerned with moving from a state of not knowing something, or how to do something, to a new state of knowing something, or knowing how to do it, however tentative and shaky the new knowledge might be. Practice, however, is concerned with exercising the newly acquired knowledge in order to strengthen it and to make it more readily and effectively deployable. Clearly both learning and practice will be necessary in the acquisition of an L2. It has to be admitted, however, that many pronunciation-teaching materials and activities confuse learning with practice, focusing heavily on repetitive practice activities in the implicit or explicit belief that learning will result. Thus an exercise that requires the learner to tick words which have a particular stress pattern can only be done if the stress patterns have already been learned; such an exercise is concerned with practice, and it should not be expected that it will result in learning.

6.2 Modeling and Imitation

It would seem to be a *sine qua non* for successful pronunciation learning that the learner should be exposed to examples of correct pronunciation of the target sounds or sequences. Not surprisingly, then, by far the commonest pronunciation-teaching procedure consists in a teacher—or tape recording—speaking the target sounds or sequences as models for the learners to imitate. Where the typical sequences of phonemes in the L2 are similar to those in the mother tongue, and where particular phonemes are realized in the same way in both languages, a learner proceeding on the hypothesis that the two languages are pronounced in the same way will achieve satisfactory results. However, where the L2 has sounds which do not exist in the mother tongue, simple exposure to those sounds may not be sufficient to achieve the desired results; the learner may simply not know how to articulate the target sounds, or may even not recognize that these sounds are distinct from ones with which he is familiar in his mother tongue. Alternatively, the problem may be not so much one of articulation, but more of understanding the different types of sequences of sounds in the L2. For example, 'l' and 'r' sounds exist both in English and in Japanese, but whereas in English these sounds represent separate phonemes, distinguishing between otherwise identical words (*read* and *lead*, *Henley* and *Henry*), in Japanese they are contextual variants of a single contrastive unit. Under these circumstances, given the right phonetic context, a Japanese learner of English is likely to pronounce an /l/ where an /r/ would have been expected. It will clearly be insufficient to simply model the 'correct sounds' for the Japanese learner, as the learner is already producing reasonable approximations to the target sounds. It is rather the 'contrastive nature' of the two sounds in English which needs to be learned and operationalized; the learner will presumably not acquire such an abstract concept simply through imitating models of the target sounds in isolation or in sequences.

6.3 Diagrams

Modeling and imitation will often not be enough in themselves; other teaching strategies will need to be deployed. It will often be the case that a learner will be able to hear the distinctive nature of the sound which he has to produce, but will be at a loss when it comes to knowing how actually to produce it. In an attempt to help the learner with this problem, many materials offer diagrammatic displays of the necessary articulation—showing the positioning of the vocal organs as a whole, the shape of the lips, the contour of the surface of the tongue in the oral cavity, patterns of pitch-movement, etc. While such diagrams are undoubtedly of some help to some learners in the production of some sounds—particularly sounds involving visible contacts and movements involving the lips and teeth—it will not always be easy for the learner to translate readily such visual information into actual positions and movements of the appropriate vocal organs. Most difficult are articulations which involve different characteristic tongue shapes, e.g., the vowels or clear versus dark /l/. A diagram will show clearly how the articulations of typical realizations of /e/ and /æ/ differ, but such knowledge 'about' pronunciation will not necessarily translate into the necessary production ability.

6.4 Explanations

Verbal explanations such as:

> In /i/ the tongue is pulled up a little closer to the roof of the mouth, and is a little more fronted, than in /ɪ/

or:

> In British English 'RP,' the sound /r/ is only made before a vowel

serve the same function as diagrams; they seek to help the learner to internalize the psychokinetic processes involved in the production of target sounds, or the new way in which the L2 organizes sounds, by presenting those processes, etc., in another medium—this time verbal. Here again, such explanations can be very helpful in some cases for some learners. This is particularly true where the articulation concerned or the processes involved are quite unlike anything in the learner's previous experience (e.g., the /h/ sound in *house* or *unhappy*, or the dropping of the underlined /t/ sound in '*mashed potatoes*' or '*postman*'). Nevertheless the problem remains that such explanations 'about' pronunciation phenomena will not necessarily be readily converted to productive ability in the learner. It may be that verbal explanations tend to be more useful with older and more academically inclined learners.

6.5 Elicitation from the Learner

In order to side-step the problems with diagrams and explanations noted above, and recognizing that presenting a model pronunciation for the learner to imitate will not necessarily lead to successful imitation, practitioners of the method known as 'silent way' attempt to elicit the desired sounds directly from the learner. This is done through a process first of encouraging the production of sounds which have something in common with the target sound, and then getting the learner gradually to 'shape' these sounds until they reach acceptability. Where this method works, it has the additional advantage that the new sound is first encountered by the learner in his own production, so that there is no debilitating feeling that 'I can't make that sound.' Of course, such a procedure is suitable only for the achievement of particular articulations and consequent sound qualities; thus while it could be used to develop an awareness of the difference between a clear /l/ and a dark /l/, it will not in itself help the learner to understand that both are representations of the same phoneme.

6.6 Reception and Production

It is generally felt that before a learner can be expected to 'produce' acceptable pronunciation, he must be able to 'recognize' it. Teaching materials will commonly introduce a new pronunciation target through various forms of recognition task, e.g.:

Read the two short conversations below, and listen to the recording.

1. '*Hertford 31453.*' '*Adam?*' '*No, this is George.*'
2. '*What's your name?*' '*Adam.*'

Adam is a question in the first short conversation.
The voice rises. *Adam?*
In the second short conversation, *Adam* is a statement.
The voice falls. *Adam.*

Now listen to the remaining words and expressions, and decide whether they are questions or statements. Write a question-mark after the words if they are questions, or underline them if they are statements.

While this might seem a logical arrangement, it is not inevitable. The reader will note that the 'silent way' procedure described above reverses the procedure, placing production first.

6.7 Sounds in Isolation versus the Flow of Speech

Many teachers and materials initially present sounds—particularly vowels—in isolation. It may be that this is done as a means of avoiding the distraction of surrounding sounds, some of which may themselves pose problems for the learner. There are two major areas of objection to this practice, one practical and one principled. As regards practicality, the learner may simply not hear the characteristic quality of some consonantal sounds unless they are embedded in a context—the most extreme case being a glottal stop—while vowels and other continuants are frequently distorted when pronounced in isolation. Then in principle there seems little point in presenting in isolation sounds which hardly ever occur isolated, particularly as these sounds are frequently modified according to their phonetic context. In fact the presentation of sounds in isolation may encourage the erroneous view in the learner that each contrastive unit—each phoneme—is realized by only one sound, regardless of context. On grounds therefore both of practicality and of phonological principle it would seem essential that sounds should be presented and practiced in contexts at least one word long. Where the concern is with phenomena affected by longer sequences, such as weak forms, assimilation, elision, rhythm or intonation, then longer contexts should be presented.

6.8 Updating Methodology in Pronunciation Teaching

It is a striking feature of current pronunciation teaching that while methodology for teaching the rest of language has undergone many revolutions over recent years, with the ramified implications of 'functional,' 'humanistic,' 'learner-centered,' 'skill theory,' and 'communicative,' etc. approaches being worked out in a myriad teaching applications, methodology for teaching pronunciation has remained with a few partial exceptions largely uninfluenced. Whether for the development of receptive or productive abilities, it continues to rely heavily on drills and other repetition exercises involving words, phrases, sentences or dialogues, with the normally unspoken assumption that productive facility and mastery will emerge from frequent repetition.

One side effect of this reliance on repetition for pronunciation purposes is that the learner is often required to produce totally abnormal utterances—frequently uncontextualized—containing excessively frequent occurrence of the—presumably problematic—target sounds, e.g.:

'Paula saw her naughty daughter fall in the water.'
'The trainer tried to trick Tracy!'

These are in essence tongue twisters and, as is well-known, tongue twisters cause problems with the repeated sounds rather than helping the speaker to pronounce them more accurately or fluently; the teaching material here is more difficult to deal with than natural language!

The possibilities for methodological exploration and creativity offered by an attempt at thoroughgoing application to pronunciation teaching of any of the approaches mentioned above, however defined, are immense. This is not the place for a thorough exploration of these possibilities, or for a definitive account of these approaches. It could nevertheless be nothing less than provocative and fruitful to consider the implications in this respect of such notions—commonly occurring in other domains of language teaching—as focus on meaning, using language for a purpose, learner-centeredness, learner-independence, appropriacy in language and language use, plentiful exposure to authentic language use, motivation, learning as an ongoing process beyond the confines of the classroom, taking account of students' wants and needs, and finally, and very importantly, learning to use language rather than learning about language.

6.9 The Teaching/Learning Sequence

In the very limited literature written with a thoughtful interest in the pedagogic aspects of pronunciation teaching (e.g.,

Kenworthy 1987; most of the articles in Morley 1987) one can recognize a repeatedly expressed concern with a number of distinct phases in the teaching–learning process. The distinction between learning and practice has already been noted. Whatever form the practice takes, it may itself be divided into an earlier phase in which the learner pays careful conscious attention to (monitors) the pronunciation aspect of spoken language production, and a later more lightly monitored phase, shading eventually into free unmonitored language use. Then the point at which the mysterious alchemy of actual learning occurs may be seen as preceded by various activities designed to help it happen. Thus there might be an initial phase of sensitization to features of pronunciation in general together with measures designed to build the learner's confidence in his own ability to produce different accents, followed by activities raising awareness of the existence and nature of specific areas selected for attention. This breakdown could thus be seen as offering something like a seven-phase pedagogic sequence:

(a) Sensitization to pronunciation in general, and confidence-building;
(b) Raising awareness of the existence of specific problems;
(c) Raising awareness of the nature of the specific problems;
(d) The specific pronunciation feature is learned;
(e) Close monitoring;
(f) Light monitoring;
(g) Free unmonitored speech.

The opportunities for methodological innovation which such a sequence of prelearning, learning, and postlearning phases offers, particularly when married to the concepts mentioned in the previous section, remain to be developed. Of course, not all teachers would in any case wish to work through the full sequence for all learners and all learning targets. Many teachers, for many learners, would wish to work on specific pronunciation problems only as they occurred, and only to the extent that comfortable intelligibility was achieved. This might require working through only a part of such a sequence. But the awareness which the sequence embodies of pronunciation teaching and learning as strategy and developmental process represents, in the opinion of the writer, an important step in bringing pronunciation teaching into line with the rest of modern language teaching.

7. The Future

There is some evidence of increasing interest among teachers, methodologists and materials writers in L2 pronunciation and its teaching. The state of the art is however so underdeveloped that no new coherent approach is to be expected for some time. Nevertheless it is to be hoped that an awareness of the current problems and potential areas for development outlined in this article will serve to initiate productive new thinking in this field.

See also: Accent; Second Language Acquisition: Phonology.

Bibliography

Crystal D, Quirk R 1964 *Systems of Prosodic and Paralinguistic Features in English*. Mouton, The Hague
Gimson A C 1962 *An Introduction to the Pronunciation of English*. Arnold, London
Kenworthy J 1987 *Teaching English Pronunciation*. Longman, Harlow
Morley J (ed.) 1987 *Current Perspectives on Pronunciation: Practices Anchored in Theory*. TESOL, Washington, DC
Roach P 1983 *English Phonetics and Phonology: A Practical Course*. Cambridge University Press, Cambridge

D. Porter

Second Language Pedagogy: Reading

Since there is no universally approved method of teaching a second language, and since even the teaching of first language reading is a matter of contention, there is inevitably a lack of consensus on the teaching of reading in a second language. Furthermore, the phrase 'the teaching of reading' is itself ambiguous in the context of second-language pedagogy. On the one hand, it may refer to the teaching of initial reading in the second language. On the other hand it may refer to teaching aimed at improving the reading comprehension and general reading skills in the second language of those who have already learned to read in that language. As far as English as a second language is concerned, most attention, in terms of research effort and material production, has been devoted to the latter concern, namely improving the second language reading of those already able to read in it.

1. The Teaching of Initial Reading in a Second Language

There are a variety of approaches to the teaching of initial reading in a second language, which largely derive from first language approaches. Thus in countries where English is used as a medium of initial education the methods of teaching reading will generally involve any, or a combination of phonic, whole word, whole sentence, or 'language experience' approaches. (A brief characterization of these approaches follows. For more detailed treatment, see *Reading Teaching: Methods*.)

The phonic method proceeds from the conventionalized 'sound values' of letters—the letter *c* being given the value 'kuh' /kə/ for example, and the word *cot* being analyzed to the pronunciation 'kuh' 'oh' 'tuh' /kə/, /ɒ/, /tə/ and then synthesized to *cot* /kɒt/. The main advantage of this approach is that it enables learners to 'build up' by saying aloud, and hopefully recognizing, words that they know but have not previously met in printed form. It is sometimes referred to as the 'phonetic' method, although it makes no use of phonetic symbols. One obvious disadvantage is the lack of consistent letter-sound relationship in English (see *English from the Introduction of Printing*).

In the whole word or whole sentence methods learners are presented with whole words, phrases or sentences, which they are expected to memorize through repetition, and recognize as wholes. The claimed advantage of this is that it facilitates rapid recognition of whole units, rather than depending on a laborious letter-by-letter strategy, and, as such, that it approximates more closely to fluent proficient reading. The disadvantage of the method is that it does not help learners to work out for themselves words that they have not already met in print. The method is sometimes referred to as the 'look-and-say' method, or the 'global' method.

In first language initial reading, learners are often able to use their own knowledge of syntax and vocabulary to help them decode. Thus native English beginner readers would be able to recognize *about* in the sentence *This rabbit is fussy about his food*, although they might have difficulty in decoding the word *about* if it were presented in isolation. That native speakers have this knowledge of their language has been incorporated into the pedagogy of first language reading, where it is sometimes called the 'language awareness' or 'linguistic' method.

In practice most initial teaching of reading in English as a first language employs a combination of the above methods, this often being referred to as the 'eclectic' method or approach.

In second language pedagogy the selection of a particular approach to initial reading is complicated by the fact that learners may be:

(a) nonreaders in any language;
(b) readers in their own language which has the same script as the second language (e.g., English learners of French; Pakistani learners of Arabic);
(c) readers in their own language which has a different script from the second language (e.g., Chinese or Arab learners of English).

(a) Despite doubts as to the efficacy of the procedure, there are many situations where children who cannot read in their first language are taught a second language, and how to read in that language, simultaneously. Such is the case of many excolonial countries in Africa, and of minority groups generally. In such cases, the teaching methods are generally taken from the first language procedures used by the excolonial power, or those used by the majority group. Such learners have to learn to read in the fundamental sense of appreciating that the marks on paper represent language, and the conventions by which this is achieved.

(b) In the case of learners who are already literate in their own language, and where it has the same script as the second language, then many teachers assume that the reading skills will transfer from the first language to the second, with some ad hoc attention normally given to letter–sound relationships that differ markedly from those of the L1 (the pronunciation of the letter *r* as /R/ for English learners of French, for example, or the pronunciation of the letters *th* as /θ/ or /ð/ for those learning to read in English). Such concerns are not strictly speaking to do with reading (if 'reading' involves a concern with understanding) but with attributing sounds to letters. The fact that many learners of English who are literate in a Roman script (e.g., French, Spanish, German) learn to read in English with little or no overt attention given to initial reading as such is evidence for a degree of transfer at this level.

(c) In those instances where the learners are literate, but in a script that differs from that of the second language there is generally a systematic attempt to teach the conventional sound–letter relationships of the target language (assuming the script attempts to represent segments—other types of writing may present difficulties (see *Writing Systems: Principles and Typology*)). This is typically followed by the reading aloud of words and simple sentences.

A further variable in second language initial reading is the degree of proficiency of the initial readers in that language. Clearly, in this context, methods of initial reading that depend on the learner having prior language knowledge (such as a native speaker child could be expected to possess) would have to be very cautiously adapted, for the obvious reason that beginner language learners, by definition, have only limited familiarity with the second language.

If reading is defined as a process of perceiving and deriving meaning from what has been written, then it is obviously an activity that can be, and normally is, carried out silently. In first language pedagogy, reading aloud is primarily a means of checking that the learner knows how to read, and of assessing progress at the early stages. In second language pedagogy however, even when it has been established that learners know how to read, they are often required to read aloud as a means of practicing pronunciation, although this is a questionable method because of the 'interference effect' of the written forms.

2. Improving Second Language Reading

While recognizing that reading is a highly integrated task, this section will, for ease of reference, deal with the following areas: text, reader, interaction between text and reader, and teaching approaches.

2.1 Text

The principal sources of texts for second language learners are: texts in the language course book, which are generally intended to improve the learner's language by exemplifying particular structures or vocabulary items; texts in reading comprehension books, often aimed at improving both language and reading skills; longer texts such as short stories, intended to provide opportunities for extensive reading, usually done out of class. The latter texts will be referred to as Readers (capitalization denoting reference to texts, rather than persons).

As far as language difficulties are concerned (bearing in mind that they are not the only difficulties readers face) research into text difficulty has looked at the contribution of both structure and vocabulary. To pose the question of whether vocabulary is a greater problem to learner readers than structure, in an absolute sense, is misguided. The answer will depend upon the relationship between texts and readers, and vary from case to case. There are broadly speaking three ways of tackling readers' language difficulties. One is to teach more language, the other is to teach strategies to cope with language difficulties. The first may be impractical and also uneconomical of time and effort, if the learner does not need to know the whole of the language. On the other hand the strategies for coping with difficulties (for example, using dictionaries, analyzing the morphology of words, or attempting to guess words from context) may be time consuming and unsuccessful in given instances. In practice, most second language pedagogy attempts both to teach language and to teach 'coping strategies.'

The third procedure, which attempts to avoid rather than remedy the problem of poor comprehension arising from language difficulties, is to select texts where language is controlled according to putative notions of simplicity. Vocabulary for such simple (or simplified) texts is usually selected according to a vocabulary list (e.g., West 1953), where the frequency of words is provided from the most common to the least common. Many publishers have produced series of Readers graded according to such word counts, with the lowest grade using only the most common 1,000 words, the second grade the most common 2,000 words, etc. (see Hedge 1985). Of course, there is no reason to suppose that high frequency words will be conceptually easier than low frequency words; the argument is that they will be more useful, since a fairly consistent research finding is that approximately 80% of the total number of words in most written texts in English come from the 2,000 most common words.

The syntax of such simple texts is graded according to notional criteria of simplicity, with much attention given to the verb phrase. The present tense, for example, will appear before the past, the nonprogressive before the progressive, etc. Thus *They spend a lot of money* will appear before *A lot of money was being spent* (see *Language Teaching Methods*). Despite the fact that the psycholinguistic validity of such graded progression has been questioned, and indeed that the relative complexity of certain structures is difficult to assess, graded text is the norm for most coursebooks, and the use of graded Readers is widespread.

Some specialists in English as a second language, however, eschew simplified text, and insist upon 'authentic text' which usually refers to texts not specially produced for language learners. Proponents of authentic texts (e.g., Grellet 1981) argue that they are more motivating, and that language difficulties can be overcome by grading the task rather than simplifying the text. It is also suggested that simplifying a text may actually make it more difficult to understand if the number of linguistic and extralinguistic clues are reduced, and further that learners are best taught to cope with 'real world' texts by having experience of them in the classroom.

In an alternative, less frequent interpretation, authentic text is defined not by the writer's intention, but solely by reference to the reader's response. Here any text, whether written for language teaching purposes or not, that readers find appropriate to their purpose—which may or may not correspond to the writer's intention—is 'authentic' for that reader. This interpretation is pedagogically useful to the extent that it highlights that the reader's response is more important than the provenance of the text.

It is widely accepted that the way in which a text is organized will affect the quantity and the ordering of what is recalled. Urquhart (1984) found that narrative text organized in chronological sequence, and descriptive text organized in a unidirectional sequence, were more readily recalled than text not so sequenced. Whether discourse structures are culture bound, such that readers from certain cultures are conditioned to expect certain text organizations, with consequent problems if their expectations are not met, is a much-vexed question for which there is no decisive evidence.

2.2 The Reader

The commonsense notion that the more linguistically difficult the text, the more linguistically competent the reader needs to be finds general support. However, the reader's prior nonlinguistic knowledge is also regarded as an important element in understanding a text. The role of prior knowledge in L2 reading has been investigated using the notion of 'schema' (a schema is an abstract structure representing concepts stored in memory—more simply, it refers to what a reader already knows about a given topic). Research upon the effect of schemata on reading suggests that given adequate language ability, a reader with appropriate background knowledge (e.g., on an academic topic, or a cultural issue) is generally a more effective reader (see Alderson and Urquhart 1984; Carrell et al 1988).

2.3 Interaction of Reader and Text

The term reading style is now reasonably well established as a descriptive label for the reader's behavioral response to text. The reading style is motivated by the reader's purpose, and mediated by the accessibility of the text to the reader. The styles most commonly identified in current work in second language reading are skimming (rapid reading to establish the general content of a text), scanning (rapid reading to locate a specific point), intensive reading (slow reading directed at complete understanding), and extensive reading (relatively rapid reading, typically carried out for pleasure). These are low level constructs, established on the basis of observable behavior (notably speed of reading, degree of re-reading, 'skipping' of text).

Observable responses to reading which are characteristic of extremely intensive reading include regressive eye movement, an excessive number of eye fixations per line, very long fixations, and various forms of subvocalization (from silent 'mouthing' of words to outright reading aloud). These were once regarded as obstacles to comprehension but are now increasingly accepted as symptoms, rather than causes, of poor comprehension (cf. Alderson and Urquhart 1984). Further, it has been claimed that, although subvocalization increases when subjects read in a second language, any attempt to suppress subvocalization leads to loss of comprehension (Gibson and Levin 1975). It would therefore appear reasonable to suggest that subvocalization and other manifestations of an extremely intensive style, may be not only symptoms of difficulty, but also means of overcoming difficulty. They should therefore not be prematurely suppressed, but should disappear as the learner becomes a more fluent reader—and at the same time more proficient in the language—through practice. One cannot therefore speak of 'good' reading speeds in second language reading in an absolute sense. There is, however, a widespread belief that second language readers read more slowly than they need to, this being possibly the effect of too much reading aloud, or of too much intensive reading. A further cause may be insufficient practice of reading (in the first as well as the second language) especially if the learner comes from a cultural background where reading is nonexistent or unusual.

With respect to the terms *skill* and *strategy*, both research literature and teaching material display considerable terminological inconsistency. In principle, one may distinguish the terms by defining a skill as an acquired ability, carried out largely subconsciously (e.g., rapid, automatic word recognition), whereas a strategy is a conscious procedure carried out in order to solve a problem (e.g., phonic 'sounding out' when faced with an unfamiliar word). In practice however, the distinction is often difficult to make.

In second language pedagogy, as in first, much of the debate concerning reading skills arises from whether reading is to be regarded as a holistic ('unitary') process, or a process made up of discrete and therefore separately teachable skills. Further, if the discrete skills view is accepted, then what are the relevant skills, and what is the relationship between them?

Many different lists of the reading skills of L1 readers have been drawn up, some based on empirical work, others on armchair speculation. The oft-cited taxonomy of Barrett lists 5 reading skills: (a) literal comprehension; (b) reorganization of the ideas in the text; (c) inferential ability; (d) evaluation; and (e) appreciation. Although the notion of discrete reading skills has always been attractive to educationalists, there has been considerable doubt as to their psychological validity. No two lists of reading skills are identical, but casual inspection suggests that the skills which feature in them might be grouped roughly into 'language related' skills, and 'reason related' skills. The former relate to knowledge of orthographic conventions, vocabulary and syntax, and the latter primarily to inferences made on the basis of information from the text, or from the reader's general knowledge.

The product of the reading process, in terms of the reader's comprehension whether in first or second language, has also been a source of some disagreement. Neville and Pugh (1982: 9) make the point that 'the output of reading is . . . difficult to capture, since what is achieved from (real life) reading with comprehension is often a modification of the conceptual system.' At the more superficial level of the reader's immediate understanding, the question is whether a text is best regarded as having a single immanent meaning, or as consisting of a set of cues from which different readers will draw different meanings. That different readers will create different meanings from the same text is beyond dispute. This raises the question of whether all meanings are to be regarded as equally valid, as opposed to equally justifiable. In short, the debate is between those for whom the text's meaning is an 'ideal' interpretation (which is not necessarily every reader's objective, and with which every reader may not agree), and those for whom the text's meaning is a personally satisfying interpretation (see Urquhart 1984). The debate has practical implications for reading in second language pedagogy, in that current techniques of assessing reading comprehension are based on the notion of 'correct interpretation.'

2.4 Teaching Approaches

An enduring distinction in second language pedagogy is that between intensive reading and extensive reading. Extensive reading refers to a relatively rapid style of reading, typically of longer texts which are judged to be within the language proficiency of the reader. There are only a few tasks or comprehension exercises associated with the texts, and there may be none at all. Extensive reading is typically, though not necessarily, associated with graded Readers. An important factor in extensive reading is that, as few or no tasks are set, then the motivation for reading—in terms of interest or enjoyment—should come from the reader. In order to maximize such motivation, extensive reading is often organized in self-access mode with a classroom library. Although for logistic reasons extensive reading may not be consistently practiced in second language pedagogy, it is agreed to be an important activity, not only because of general acceptance of the dictum that one becomes a good reader through reading, but also because it is claimed to improve language proficiency generally.

Intensive reading refers to extremely careful reading, where the aim is complete comprehension of the text. Texts for intensive reading are generally short (often around 500 words), at a language level judged to be slightly above the readers' proficiency, and with a high proportion of task items. In order to complete the tasks the reader may have to resort to word-by-word reading or frequent re-reading. The principal aims of intensive reading are to provide input and practice in the second language and also practice in reading skills and styles. Materials for intensive reading often advocate a three stage approach with a prereading preparatory stage, a second reading stage, and a third post-reading stage.

The majority of current reading comprehension books in English as a second language contain both traditional and innovative approaches, traditional here referring to comprehension questions based upon a text. The purpose of such comprehension questions has been queried in recent years. They can only check comprehension selectively, and there is no evidence that they directly help comprehension. In fact, their true function seems to be to ensure that the readers actually read the text (although it is often possible to arrive at correct answers either by repeating, without understanding, the relevant section of text, or by using appropriate knowledge of the world).

One of the most frequent features of recent second language reading comprehension books is the prereading activity. Some books suggest elaborate activities involving group work, discussion, or writing, while others simply suggest predicting the content of the text from the title. In theoretical terms such activities constitute attempts to activate the students' schemata; they may also provide language preparation, motivation and variety in the classroom activity. Research suggests that activation of prior knowledge does tend to improve comprehension.

Despite the inconsistency of the evidence for distinct reading skills, they too figure prominently in reading materials. Materials writers now regularly incorporate such exercises as guessing the meaning of unknown words, recovering pronoun reference, inference, and prediction. The emphasis on guessing word meaning is supported by research which claims that a willingness to guess is characteristic of good learners and readers. However, there is evidence that skilled readers in their first and second language find it impossible to guess more than a small proportion of words, and obviously inaccurate guessing can have negative effects on comprehension. Some reading comprehension books stress the importance of ignoring certain unknown words, a procedure supported by research suggesting that fluent readers typically ignore rather than guess unknown lexis—again, there is clearly a limit to which words and how many words may be ignored.

Inferring is another skill which receives attention in many books. The term generally refers to the reader coming to conclusions that are not explicitly stated in the text, but for which the text provides evidence. Tasks requiring the identifying of reference are again very common, usually practiced through a question such as *What does this refer to?*

As far as second language reading programs are concerned, most specialists favor a combination of intensive and extensive reading components. It should be remembered, however, that while intensive and extensive are convenient terms for referring to opposite ends of a reading-style continuum, and to materials intended to promote those styles, the fact is that in reality, and irrespective of how the materials are labeled, readers adopt their style to suit their immediate purposes (for example, reading intensively whenever they have difficulty in understanding).

A notable feature of reading in second language pedagogy is that the theoretical positions embodied in the texts and tasks of reading have tended to come from outside the classroom—from psychology (behaviorism, cognitivism), from linguistics (structuralism), or from applied linguistics (functionalism, discourse analysis). Reading pedagogy has not in general been grounded in the observation of classroom practice. The role of the teacher, apart from that of managing the activities provided in the material, has received little attention. There has been little published research into longitudinal studies of initial reading in a second language (but see Wallace 1988) and few published evaluations of classroom-based attempts to improve reading comprehension.

Bibliography

Alderson J C, Urquhart A H (eds.) 1984 *Reading in a Foreign Language*. Longman, London

Clymer T 1968 What is 'reading'? In: Robinson H M (ed.) *Innovation and Change in Reading Instruction*. University of Chicago Press, Chicago, IL

Carrell P L, Devine J, Eskey D E (eds.) 1988 *Interactive Approaches to Second Language Reading*. Cambridge University Press, Cambridge

Gibson E J, Levin H 1975 *The Psychology of Reading*. MIT Press, Cambridge, MA

Grellet F 1981 *Developing Reading Skills*. Cambridge University Press, Cambridge

Hedge T 1985 *Using Readers in Language Teaching*. Macmillan, London

Neville M H, Pugh A K 1982 *Towards Independent Reading*. Heinemann, London

Nuttall C 1982 *Teaching Reading Skills in a Foreign Language*. Heinemann Educational, London

Urquhart A H 1984 The effect of rhetorical ordering on readability. In: Alderson J C, Urquhart A H (eds.) 1984

Wallace C 1988 *Learning to Read in a Multicultural Society*. Pergamon Press, Oxford

West M P 1953 (ed.) *A General Service List of English Words*. Longman, London

Williams E, Moran C 1989 Reading in a foreign language at intermediate and advanced levels with particular reference to English. *Language Teaching* **22(4)**: 217–28

E. Williams

Second Language Pedagogy: Speaking

Paradoxically, proficiency in speaking is often assumed to be the central aim of foreign language courses, and yet the methodology for teaching oral proficiency is not always clearly distinguished from more general aspects of language pedagogy. This article first briefly considers this paradox; it then looks at the nature of the pedagogy of oral language processing, the pedagogy of oral discourse, and concludes with a discussion of the role of the teacher.

1. Oral Proficiency in Foreign Language Teaching

The many methods that have been devised for teaching foreign languages have generally concentrated on oral proficiency as a means of learning language forms, rather than as a particular type of language proficiency to be learnt in its own right. Some methodologies use oral processing to promote repetition and memorization, while others use it as a medium for eliciting and comprehending new language items presented by the teacher. Some methodologies concentrate on the language for use in different situations, while others concentrate on the language of politeness and interaction. Few have elaborated detailed syllabuses for the development and assessment of oral skills, comparable, say, to those developed for teaching reading and writing.

In spite of the tendency to confuse oral activities with general pedagogical aims, most methodologies nonetheless generally contain activities which in fact lead learners to practice different oral skills, albeit often without explicit organization. The methodologies that have been used, however, have differed in focus in terms of their view of the nature of language and of language learning. The first major difference has been as to whether language courses in general—and oral skills in particular—should aim to conform to the target language in terms of grammatical rules and lexico–grammatical expressions, or whether language is essentially a tool for creative self-expression, in which the rules of grammar are seen as a reference point rather than a straitjacket. Directly related to this controversy has been the debate over whether language learning is principally a matter of learning to conform via a process of repetition, familiarization, and routinization, or whether it is largely a process of learner-directed exploration. This article takes the view that both elements are necessary—the routinization of foreign norms as a target for language use, and the exploration of individual preferences for modes of expression: routinization and exploration, conformity and creativity are inevitable features of language learning and language use.

The problem of oral language pedagogy is how to promote fluency and accuracy across these fundamental dimensions. The focus, then, is on the question: what types of exercises can be used to develop oral fluency and oral accuracy, first of all as distinct from written proficiency, and then, in terms of developing a mastery of oral discourse skills?

2. Exercises for Oral Language Processing

Oral language processing involves the formation of communicative intentions, in the form of plans, and their subsequent realization through speech (Levelt 1978). The plans include the message content to be communicated, and the language needed to convey it. Since this process is unscripted, the speaker is mainly involved in piecemeal elaboration of messages, and their eventual execution. In this, spoken language differs from written language in two key ways: first, it is fragmented; and second, it is contextualized. The pedagogy of spoken language first needs to provide practice in these two dimensions if the mastery of spoken language skills is an objective of the course.

2.1 Fragmentation

Whereas written language usually consists of fully formed, and possibly quite elaborate sentences, spoken language characteristically uses a wider variety of syntactic units, often much smaller than the sentence. Short phrases are frequently employed. In addition, editing is overt in speech, in contrast to writing, where such processes are covert as far as the finished product is concerned. Thus, repetition, reformulation, self-correction, false starts, pauses, and hesitations are all present. Speakers are not expected to perform without such features even in their first language: dysfluent speech should not be discouraged in the second language classroom either. Such features occur naturally precisely because speech is improvised. Planning time is limited, plans change during execution, and so time needs to be gained through these devices if the flow of speech is to be maintained. For the same reason, phrases (as opposed to full syntactic sentences) are often used where they are communicatively adequate.

Thus, exercises for oral language development need to allow for the presence of such features. A basic requirement therefore is for such exercises to require the unscripted use of oral language. Authentic features of speech which arise through lack of planning time will only occur if speech has to be planned afresh during the activity. Drill exercises therefore are not appropriate activities for providing practice in this dimension of speech production. Task exercises (drill exercises and task exercises are further described under Sect. 3 below) on the other hand tend to involve the use of unscripted speech, and thus are more likely to encourage the occurrence of fragmentation features.

2.2 Contextualization

The second basic feature of spoken language is that it is generally to some extent contextualized. Generally, speakers have the opportunity to refer directly to all participants in the discourse, as well as to physical and temporal features of the situation. Thus speakers will require the use of first and second person pronouns, demonstrative pronouns and adjectives, and deictic adverbs. Contextualization is also a reason why spoken language tolerates far more ellipsis than written language: the context, and the presence of the interlocutors, make it possible for speakers to achieve greater economy, given that misunderstandings can always be clarified if understanding has been compromised. Finally, context also tends to have an effect on the occurrence of a number of verb forms, notably the present progressive and present perfect aspects. Task exercises will typically encourage the use of such forms, along with the use of future constructions and the imperative, in language used to organize and monitor the progress of assigned tasks.

2.3 Drills and Speech Production

Whereas drills can practice the production of particular language forms and patterns, and the formulation of specific linguistic contrasts in the target language, they are nonetheless clearly insufficient in terms of providing adequate practice of the use of these features within the context of normal communicative speech production. It is worth reviewing the reasons for these shortcomings:

(a) It is in the nature of drills that they require the use of a cued form, rather than the formulation of a particular message. The learner is given a model sentence, and then required to produce sentences with similar patterns given a new cue word. The result is that the learner can quite easily produce a formally correct required response without actually thinking about the meaning, or any of the other things that speakers have to attend to during normal speech. The response is cued by the model plus a new stimulus, shortcutting the need for attention to meaning.

(b) In most drills the message is also preselected: the learner is not being required to select a message and then to find a way of expressing it. Instead, the message is predetermined by the cues which indicate the required response.

(c) The syntactic form of the message is also predetermined by the cues, so that the speaker does not necessarily have to choose the appropriate structure and elaborate it during speech.

(d) During drills the speaker is not having to respond to an interlocutor, nor ensure that an interlocutor is understanding.

(e) The point of a drill is to emphasize speed of response. The pausing of natural speech is thus discouraged by the rhythm of the exercise.

The limitations of drills are thus multiple, and indicate why teachers and students are frequently frustrated by the artificiality and lack of transfer of drill practice. On the other hand, the very limitations of drills are their strength: drills permit the controlled practice of certain aspects of oral proficiency, by relieving the learner of a number of decisions which might overwhelm him and impede performance. Nonetheless, natural language processing is not to be found in the context of controlled drills, nor for that matter in other similarly controlled exercises such as reading aloud, or the production of memorized dialogues. Normal speech involves the improvised use of language in real time to communicate the speaker's own messages, as they are planned, for sharing with a specific interlocutor. Whereas drills can be useful to help the automation of lower level lexico–grammatical and phonological skills, their use does not extend to the practice of lower level skills in the context of higher level decisions. It is this realization which has considerably altered the pedagogy of spoken language in recent years.

2.4 Oral Language Proficiency: An Integrated View

The teaching of oral proficiency has come to be seen as the development of a skill in which two fundamental elements need to be integrated—relative accuracy in the use of features, and relative fluency in their deployment.

2.4.1 Accuracy

Accuracy can be defined as the dimension relating to the clarity, appropriacy, and correctness of a particular message in relation to the interlocutors involved and a given linguistic norm (this definition differs from that proposed by Brumfit 1984). The success of a message is affected by its selection, formulation, and comprehensibility of execution, always bearing in mind the age and background of the interlocutor(s).

This dimension then covers the use of grammar, pronunciation, as well as the use of vocabulary and the selection of appropriate expressions, discourse markers, and register. For pedagogical purposes, it is important to bear in mind that undue emphasis on grammatical and phonological accuracy can have two effects: first, it can divert attention from the selection of lexical or idiomatic expressions. And second, if it results in a disproportionate amount of criticism, it can discourage learners, since grammatical features are often the parts of languages which are at one and the same time the hardest to learn, and offer the least obvious return for effort expended, due to their relative redundancy (George 1972). A broader emphasis is thus generally favored amongst methodologists and teacher educators.

2.4.2 Fluency

Fluency is the ability to choose, formulate, and execute the expression of messages in reasonable time. What is reasonable in terms of time can vary according to context, intention, preparation, and level of proficiency of the learner. In any case, even in first language situations the speed of delivery can vary according to conditions or contexts: in an important interview, technical debate, or presentation, speakers may well speak at a more measured pace than during casual conversation in the lunch queue. Practice will also often give rise to improved fluency, even where performance is routine rather than verbatim (Fillmore 1979).

There is therefore a possible trade-off between fluency and accuracy: slower performance may be more accurate in various ways than quicker production of speech. Teaching and assessment therefore need to consider fluency under different conditions to develop and assess a learner's proficiency.

Thus, speech, like all use of language, is to a large extent a type of skilled behavior. This means that typically accuracy and fluency increase in direct proportion to the simplicity and/or familiarity of a given task. Scripted tasks are thus simpler to perform than unscripted tasks. Cued tasks are likely to be simpler than uncued tasks. Patterned tasks are likely to be easier than unpatterned ones. Closed tasks, involving a single pathway or approach, with a single unambiguous goal, are simpler than open tasks, offering a range of possible pathways, and a range of possible solutions. Tasks involving several interlocutors are likely to be more complicated than tasks involving few participants. Short tasks are likely to be easier than long ones. And prepared, rehearsed, or otherwise familiar tasks are likely to be simpler to perform than unfamiliar ones.

This view lends support to the widespread notion that practice activities can be usefully organized to help learners by providing support in various ways (such as cuing, patterning, scripting, repetition, and chorus work) in the early stages. Littlewood (1981) stresses the value of precommunicative activities. Rivers and Temperley (1978) suggest the need for 'skill-getting' as well as 'skill-using' activities. And Harmer (1983) distinguishes between 'practice' and 'communication' activities, while Brumfit (1984) argues for the use of accuracy activities and fluency activities—any activity being a potential focus for either dimension.

The provision of various kinds of support for learners still leaves plenty of scope for learners to practice on more complex activities, which is the theme of the next section.

3. Pedagogy of Oral Discourse

In the preceding section, it was shown that oral language pedagogy needs to take into consideration the conditions of oral language production, so that exercises provide practice in the kinds of language processing typical of speech. The skill of oral language production can be roughly represented by the diagram in Fig. 1:

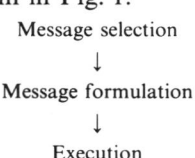

Figure 1. A basic model of speech production.

In addition to this, however, clearly an oral syllabus needs to involve learners in the exercise of this skill in a range of different contexts and for a multitude of different purposes in which they are likely to have to use speech: oral discourse can vary considerably in structure and content, showing characteristics quite distinct from those of written language, and the pedagogy of oral language needs to take this potential range into consideration when attempting to meet the needs of different learners.

The characteristics of oral discourse have been usefully separated into two main dimensions: transactional features, and interactional features (Brown and Yule 1983).

3.1 Transactional and Interactional Features

The term 'transaction' refers to the information focus of the discourse. Transactional discourse typically includes macrodiscourse types, such as description, narration, instruction, and explanation. These discourse types can characteristically form extended chunks of discourse, although they may also make up quite short passages of speech, indeed short turns.

The 'interactional' dimension, on the other hand, relates to the aspects of the discourse which are negotiated by the interlocutors. Negotiation can be overt, or covert, and can cover a number of features, such as the participation and understanding of the interlocutors, and the topic of the discourse. These two dimensions will be looked at more closely. (The term 'interaction' is being used slightly differently here from the way it was employed by Brown and Yule 1983.)

3.1.1 Transactional Features of Oral Discourse

Transactional language, the language of information content, focuses on the communication of information. Descriptions, for example, may present information about people, places, objects, buildings, institutions, works of art, food, etc. Instructions will explain how to follow recipes, rules, directions, administrative procedures, laws and regulations. They may include instructions for use of appliances, and the highway code. Narrations may involve stories, historical accounts of events and journeys, accidents, diary reports, and news reports. Process descriptions, another form of transactional discourse, tend to report experiments or describe processes of production. Comparisons, a further type of transactional discourse, will often relate two descriptions or narrations or sets of instructions in order to identify similarities and differences, advantages and disadvantages.

Transactional language will tend to involve repeated use of particular verb forms, especially simple verb forms. Noun group reference—the use of definite articles, often combined with adjectives and postmodifying clauses or phrases—often needs to be managed clearly and unambiguously. Time or sequence markers in the form of adverbial adjuncts or conjuncts, will also often be important.

Transactional language is conveniently practiced by the use of factual prompts—genuine or fictitious, pictorial or verbal. Pictures or diagrams are often used to give rise to story telling, descriptions, comparisons, historical narratives, and instructions. Indeed, the use of diagrams and pictures to cue speech (or indeed to prompt written language) is one of the simplest and most far-reaching developments in language teaching generally since the invention of drills.

A key element of transactional discourse is that it is of importance to the listener. Oral exercises therefore commonly create an 'information gap': the listener needs to listen to the speaker in order to obtain some information which has been deliberately omitted from the listener's materials. Simple examples of information gap activities can be found in Matthews and Reid (1981), and Littlewood (1981). The use of materials for more extended transactional discourse is demonstrated in Brown and Yule (1983), and in Bygate (1987).

3.1.2 Interactional Features of Oral Discourse

Interactional features of discourse are always present in speech—just as speech is impossible without some information content. Interactional features, however, are those which arise from a need to negotiate the development and success of the discourse with the interlocutors.

The participation of the interlocutors is an essential aspect of oral interaction, and this includes turntaking (who speaks for how long and when), which is often straightforward, but can often involve interruptions, politeness markers, and the use of backchannels. A second aspect of speech participation is the adoption and distribution of different speech roles. In teacher–class interaction one danger is that the teacher always adopts the same central role in the interaction, while the students always have to act in a different, more peripheral role. In real life, speakers need to be able to act in a range of roles—as active listener, as main raconteur, as seeker of information, as explainer and guide. These different aspects of oral interaction may not need to be explicitly taught, but they may need to be practiced in different exercises (McCarthy 1991).

In addition to participation in the interaction, speakers need to be able to negotiate the selection of topics and ensure mutual understanding. Topic selection involves the use of the ability to change or develop a topic of discourse. Negotiation of understanding, on the other hand, involves the ability and skill of checking that one has understood the message, or checking that one's interlocutor has understood, and clarifying where necessary.

Finally, interactive features include interpersonal speech acts, such as agreeing, disagreeing, greeting, questioning,

apologizing, and the ability to handle different degrees of formality. Activities which are likely to provide practice in the interactive dimensions of oral discourse clearly need to involve students in activities requiring clarification of information; varying kinds of formality; the need to cooperate on tasks, and to exchange opinions as well as information; and participation in interaction with differing numbers of interactants in a range of different roles. Transaction-based activities can clearly provide practice in a number of these features. However, some activities, perhaps at more advanced levels of proficiency, may need to involve participants in discussions, debates, and a variety of activities using different formats, but allowing a wide range of choice of topic and opinion.

3.1.3 Summary

Identification of transactional and interactional dimensions of language enables course providers to identify a range of potential needs that courses might hope to meet. In recent years a number of different types of oral exercises have been developed to meet these needs. Such exercises can be used systematically to vary the amount of support that learners receive on tasks, and to provide a range of different discourse types which learners can be required to practice and explore. The following section provides a brief outline of the principal types of exercises that have been produced, together with an indication of how they can contribute to developing some of the different aspects of oral proficiency that have been identified above.

3.2 Exercise Types for Oral Discourse

Oral exercises can conveniently be grouped into four kinds: drill exercises; task exercises; dramatizations; and project exercises. Each kind of exercise can be used at any level of proficiency, and can be used to develop transactional and interactional skills, as needed. Since the complexity of an exercise is a function of the number of decisions and amount of information to be processed by the speaker, drill exercises are by definition the least complex, all other things being equal, while projects are potentially the most complex. Drill and task exercises are cued at the time of performance, whereas dramatizations are not. Projects are essentially cued by the speakers themselves. In the case of drills, the cue is at the level of the sentence, whereas in task exercises the cue is at the level of task. The following subsections will look at each of these exercise types in turn.

3.2.1 Drill Exercises

Drills can be used to practice the production of transactional language in particular, since they typically provide the opportunity to manipulate minimally distinctive elements of the language. This frequently means practicing features of verb tense, aspect, and concord; clause and sentence structure; and noun inflections and modifications. These features are commonly associated with the notional base (Wilkins 1976) of the language.

Drills can also be used however to practice the production and formulation of a range of speech acts of an interactional nature, as well as a number of turntaking gambits, and exchange patterns and adjacency pairs (such as greetings, invitations and responses, apologies and responses).

Drills can be scripted or unscripted. Scripted drills are most common, and are generally published in the form of prerecorded tapes. Unscripted drills can also be found. These can be information gap drills (such as Matthews and Reid 1981, in which several of the exercises are utterance-focused rather than task-focused) or noninformation gap drills, in which pictures are used as a stimulus for a series of utterances of a given type (e.g., Harkess and Eastwood 1976 and 1981).

3.2.2 Task Exercises

Task exercises are cued activities using either nonverbal or verbal support. They are by definition unscripted, and set a task which learners complete by a sequence of exchanges. An example of a task exercise would be a 'picture differences' activity in which speakers have to identify the differences between two pictures, of which each speaker can only see one. Information has to be pooled orally.

Such tasks can be more or less controlled. At the least they involve selection of an appropriate message to carry out the task (e.g., a question or a statement), and an appropriate formulation (selection of effective vocabulary items), and judgment of whether the selections have been successful. Simple task exercises involve a minimum of different utterance types repeated throughout the task: a 'picture differences' task might involve a repeated series of questions and answers, or a series of parallel descriptive utterances, all in the simple present. More complex task exercises will involve a wider range of utterance types. For example, a prioritizing task, in which participants have to select their preferred candidate for a post, will involve the elicitation and expression of opinions, and the coordination of the overall task to ensure that it has been properly completed.

In all cases, task exercises can encourage the development of routines, as speakers increase their familiarity with the requirement of the task and of useful language for completing it. With increasing familiarity, speakers can improve their efficiency in selecting and formulating messages, so that accuracy and fluency can increase in turn.

Typical examples of task exercises are the following:

Games:	Guessing games
	Association games
Tasks:	Comparison and contrast tasks
	Instruction tasks (directions; describe and draw, etc.)
	Combining tasks
	Sequencing tasks (picture stories)
	Organizing tasks
	Prioritizing and selecting tasks

Examples of tasks can be found in Ur (1981).

The main feature of game tasks is their emphasis on formulation skills (notably lexical accessing). Association games tend not to impose turntaking restrictions, or restrictions in the selection or sequencing of particular ideas. In addition they tend not to involve information transfer, and thus tend to leave the distribution of speech roles and exchange patterns very free. However, some attention to preceding utterances may be necessary if any line of coherence is built into the task.

In contrast, guessing games generally function within a rule system (e.g., '20 questions') which imposes some kind of exchange structure and speech role on the participants. In other respects guessing games are similar to association games in imposing relatively few restrictions on propositional sequencing.

Whereas games generally define the nature of individual turns, tasks define a problem and leave the participants to talk their way toward a solution. For this reason tasks require the speakers to adopt speech roles in order to set up a series of exchanges. The kinds of exchanges selected may be a function of the proficiency of the learners, which can affect the length of turns that they are able to handle productively and receptively. A further feature of tasks is that they will tend to require more use of metadiscoursal language than games—that is, language for organizing who should do what; to check on progress; and to decide whether the task is being done correctly, and whether it is completed. Constraints on topic selection and turntaking are largely imposed by the task, in particular by the way information is distributed to the participants. This only becomes an area for active decision-making in the more complex tasks, and in projects.

3.2.3 Dramatizations

The possible scope of dramatizations is considerable, and it is not the purpose of this article to explore the pedagogical use of dramatizations in any detail. They are, however, commonly used, and it is therefore appropriate to briefly review the justifications for their employment.

Dramatizations involve the representation of a situation, with the students adopting roles other than themselves. Dramatizations are cued replications of a situation, either improvised or carefully rehearsed. The cue may be the mention of a prototypical scene from daily life; it may be a video or audio-taped extract; it may be a picture or a series of sound effects; it may be a news report or short story, or it may involve the improvisation of variations on a simple theme.

The purpose is to enable the students to rehearse language, or to explore linguistic variants—either for a common social situation, or else to help understanding of culturally unusual situations.

The more elementary the learners, the less they are expected to say, and the greater the likely emphasis on rehearsal prior to performance. More advanced learners, on the other hand, are more likely to use dramatization to explore linguistic variations in humanly more complex situations. With advanced learners, the emphasis may be more on performance than on rehearsal, and may lay more stress on the range of improvisations by different participants.

The cultural rationale behind the use of dramatizations is the notion that the use of a foreign language can for some learners resemble a form of impersonation or character-acting. By the same token, methodologists who argue that foreign language teaching should avoid leading learners towards 'acculturation' (i.e., membership of the target language community) or encouraging them to resemble speakers of the target language, tend not to favor the use of dramatizations, and prefer to encourage the use of other exercise types (e.g., Brumfit 1984). At the very least, dramatizations can be seen as a useful way of combining rehearsal and performance around a single theme.

3.2.4 Projects

Projects, the fourth kind of oral exercise, are real or simulated tasks involving some factfinding and some form of oral report and discussion. They often involve the use of writing, and are used to encourage the integration of spoken and written activities. Simulated projects will involve the settling of some problem in a fictitious place or imagined community. Participants are themselves with their own personalities but will usually adopt some social role, such as social worker, businessman, shopkeeper, bank manager, headmaster, reporter, parent, and so on. The task may be to solve a planning problem involving local amenities—traffic, leisure, business development, the environment.

Nonfictitious projects are similar but involve real-world problems in the learner's community. Learners will adopt roles which are discourse-related—e.g., chairperson, presenter, secretary, audience, discussant, interviewer, questioner, rapporteur.

The use of language in project exercises includes the language of planning and organizing of roles and tasks; the organization and preparation of information and opinions; the organization and running of small and large group sessions; and the communication of information and negotiation of meaning that this involves. Thus projects naturally engage the use of interactional and transactional language, the handling of all kinds of referential language, and the use of interactive conventions. In so doing, learners practice the strategic use of language for a wide range of purposes.

As with task exercises, projects can be seen as requiring learners to develop their own language routines for carrying out a range of different but recurring purposes. The fact that similar needs recur in the context of different exercises provides a systematic basis for the two principles of learning outlined earlier—that of repetition and exploration—to occur meaningfully under conditions of normal communication.

The open nature of such tasks, their unscripted nature and the freedom learners have in deciding what language to use to get the tasks completed, does not imply a lack of overall control or sense of direction on the part of the teacher. Although unscripted tasks require a lack of teacher control while students carry out the tasks, they can nonetheless be selected for particular language purposes; students can be monitored during performance by the teacher; and many tasks can be repeated by groups once they have been completed—either in whole or in part—to enable teacher and students to evaluate the use of the target language. Tasks can also be carried out under the evaluative eye of a member of the group: evaluation should be built into the use of such tasks so that students carry them out with a purpose, and develop their own ability to monitor their language while using it.

4. Conclusion

The pedagogy of language always requires an outline of objectives, in the form of a syllabus, and the selection of a range of exercises and activities which will help to achieve those objectives. The unscripted use of speech for transactional and interactional purposes forms the nub of any oral language course. The specific objectives for any given course can be selected from a wide range of possible purposes and conventions. And the methods available for implementing them have been outlined. The key to oral language pedagogy, however, is the recognition of the possibilities of balancing repetition and exploration, not just in scripted exercises, but also in unscripted tasks.

See also: Second Language Processing: Speaking.

Bibliography

Brown G, Yule G 1983 *Teaching the Spoken Language*. Cambridge University Press, Cambridge
Brumfit C J 1984 *Communicative Methodology in Language Teaching*. Cambridge University Press, Cambridge
Bygate M 1987 *Speaking*. Oxford University Press, Oxford
Fillmore C J 1979 On fluency. In: Fillmore C J, Kempler D, Wang W S-Y (eds.) *Individual Differences in Language Ability and Language Behaviour*. Academic Press, New York
George H V 1972 *Common Errors in Language Learning*. Newbury House, Rowley, MA
Harkness J, Eastwood J 1976 *Cue for a Drill*. Oxford University Press, Oxford
Harkess J, Eastwood J 1981 *Cue for Communication*. Oxford University Press, Oxford
Harmer J 1983 *The Practice of English Language Teaching*. Longman, London
Levelt W J M 1978 Skill theory and language teaching. *Studies in Second Language Acquisition* 1(1): 53–70
Littlewood W T 1981 *Communicative Language Teaching*. Cambridge University Press, Cambridge
Matthews A, Reid C 1981 *Tandem*. Evans Brothers, London
McCarthy M 1991 *Discourse Analysis for Language Teachers*. Cambridge University Press, Cambridge
Rivers W M, Temperley M S 1978 *A Practical Guide to the Teaching of English as a Second or Foreign Language*. Oxford University Press, New York
Ur P 1981 *Discussions that Work*. Cambridge University Press, Cambridge
Wilkins D A 1976 *Notional Syllabuses*. Oxford University Press, London

M. Bygate

Second Language Pedagogy: Writing

The amount of literature produced since the 1970s on the pedagogy of second language writing has been substantial and is testament to renewed interest in a hitherto taken-for-granted area of language use and language development. Such interest is indicative of the value accorded to this activity, both for learning purposes in educational spheres and for transactional purposes in social and professional spheres. It is also acknowledgment of the difficulty experienced by writers in expressing themselves accurately and appropriately in a second language.

The concern to develop an effective pedagogy for second language writing has been particularly strong in educational contexts where the second language is the language of the classroom and of examinations and where it thereby performs a gate-keeping function. Students able to manipulate the written language effectively are those who pass through the gate to greater opportunities in learning and in life.

There is also a strong body of opinion that writing in education is a major means of learning. It is a problem-solving activity in which students generate and organize their own arguments and clarify ideas to themselves as they try to communicate them clearly to their readers. Alternatively, writing may involve the assimilation, interpretation, and reformulation of other people's ideas and the formation of individual opinions. Writing can therefore be viewed as an instrument in the process of learning, and effective writing pedagogy may have the crucial function of facilitating learning.

This view of writing as thinking, as discovery, as more than recording, is termed the 'process' view. Its focus is on the writer and the types of strategy used during the process of composing. It has provided an important addition to the more traditional 'product' view, in which focus has been on the written product and its characteristics.

It is possible, then, to build a framework for writing pedagogy by distinguishing two areas of interest: the writer and the writing. Research has provided insights into the composing processes of writers. It has also provided models for the analysis of written products. Current pedagogy seeks to integrate these two aspects of writing, process and product. It is an integrated pedagogy which is applicable in principle to all groups of learners, though the particular focus may vary according to age, language proficiency, stage of writing development, and purposes for writing in a second language.

1. The Process View of Writing

The process view is that writing is the result of employing cognitive strategies to manage the composing process, which is a process of exploration and gradually developing organization. It involves setting goals, generating ideas, organizing information, selecting appropriate language, drafting, reviewing, revising, and editing. It is a complex activity which for many second language writers is difficult. The issue for pedagogy, in fact, is whether composing strategies can be taught, and the process approach strives precisely to do this. It focuses on providing support during the process of writing. The exact nature of that support depends on the nature of the students and their reasons for writing.

The primary aim of the process approach is to help students to gain greater control over the cognitive strategies involved in composing. Research yields useful insights into the strategies used by a 'successful' writer in producing a text of good quality and can thereby inform the design of supportive pedagogic activity. There appear to be a number of activities engaged in by a good writer.

1.1 Planning Activities

First, good writers concentrate primarily on overall meaning and organization of a text and engage in planning activities. The amount of planning varies from relatively spontaneous writing, for example, a postcard or an informal letter, to carefully planned writing, for example, an academic essay for assessment or a difficult memorandum. The process of planning varies from the formulation of a brief mental checklist to detailed note-making. However, planning is subject to review at any point during writing as writers critically evaluate the emerging text and generate new ideas and plans.

If pedagogic procedures are to support planning, a primary requisite is to involve students in the writing of whole, contextualized pieces of communication, essays, letters, reports, or, with younger learners, short descriptions, stories, and so on. Practice in writing clear, correct sentences,

the aim of many traditional classroom exercises, is only one aspect of writing. Current pedagogy also places emphasis on practice in developing and linking information, ideas, and arguments through a longer text.

Another perceived need is to give students support in developing effective planning strategies. Take an example from a college-level second language classroom, in which students of economic geography have been given the title:

> What are the factors which would be taken into account by a manufacturing company when deciding whether to use rail haulage or road transport?

A first step in pedagogy could be to encourage students to work in pairs and arrive at an understanding of the task by questioning and clarifying the meaning of key expressions and deciding on the exact nature of the information needed to fulfill the task. A second step could be elicitation from the class by the teacher of points for content, and collation of these on the blackboard. As a third step, before students begin drafting, individuals could prepare a logical organization of points to compare with a partner.

Take a second example from the second language syllabus of a school classroom. Students have the task of preparing a description for a tourist brochure of a local festival. The pedagogic sequence below would support the composing process in the ways suggested in the diagram:

Step 1	Ask students to brainstorm for 4 minutes individually, jotting down ideas for the content of the brochure.	← *clarifying aims* ← *generating ideas*
Step 2	Elicit suggestions from the class and write them on the board, demonstrating how to group randomly suggested items into topics	← *grouping ideas* ← *structuring them into an initial plan*
Step 3	Discuss labels with the class for the topics as they have emerged, e.g., origins of festival, public celebrations, family customs, etc.	← *identifying categories for the overall organization*
Step 4	Ask students in pairs to add information to each identified topic.	← *adding detail to the emerging structure*
Step 5	Pool ideas in a class plenary session and build appropriate vocabulary for the task.	← *selecting appropriate language*
Step 6	Ask students to suggest a logical sequence for the topics.	← *planning a coherent sequence*

In this way, classroom activities take students through an effective planning process and the strategies of brainstorming ideas, imposing a structure, making notes, ordering information, etc. It gives initial support in what will eventually be an individually undertaken process.

1.2 Awareness of Audience

A second characteristic of successful writers is that they are aware of their readers. Most of the writing undertaken in the real world is done with a particular reader in mind: a tutor, a friend, or someone occupying a role in an institution, for example, an editor, a public relations officer, an examiner. Knowing who the reader is provides us with a context for the writing which determines what is appropriate content and style in the writing. In order to produce an appropriate text, a student writer needs to answer the following questions:

Who am I writing to?
What do I need to say?
How can I make my writing accessible to my reader?

Helping student writers to develop this sense of audience is another task for the teacher. In educational writing the audience is the tutor and the student's task is to learn the appropriate style, to learn the correct conventions for essays, abstracts, and bibliographies, and to learn how much knowledge to assume in the reader and how much information to make explicit in the text. These are all points for instruction and practice.

With less mature writers, who may not have developed a sense of audience in their first language, writing teachers can create audiences and build an awareness of the reader. Sometimes the teacher can become a more personal audience as a reader of student journals or as correspondent in an exchange of letters. Sometimes the teacher can set up roles in class in which students, for example, exchange letters of invitation and replies. Sometimes students can write to real audiences, both inside the school, with stories for younger students or class magazines for publication among peers, or outside the school, with letters of enquiry to organizations in which the second language is spoken. Collaborative writing also provides students with readers and critics of their work among their peers. This can be set up informally by encouraging students to work in groups, sharing and exchanging drafts for comment, or it can be formally structured by asking students to write different parts of a text within a group and then to make the result a coherent whole. Of primary importance, however, in any writing task, is that an audience is specified and that the task fulfills a communicative purpose, whether real or simulated.

1.3 Reviewing and Revising

A third characteristic of successful writers is that they move from thinking to writing to revision but also move backwards and forwards between these processes. Drafting is often interrupted as writers stop to review, to see how the text is emerging, to revise plans, to develop new ideas, and to restructure. It also seems to be the case that successful writers concentrate first on getting the meaning clear and leave details of accuracy in spelling, word order, and grammar until the final editing process.

Teachers are now concerned to find ways of encouraging students to improve their own work through self-monitoring, exchanging work for peer review, conferencing with the teacher, class revision of selected drafts, proofreading exercises and reformulation procedures. Conferencing, for example, has become a popular technique. As students work on their writing, the teacher can engage in conversation with individuals about work in progress. Through questioning and elicitation the teacher can support the student writer in organizing ideas, can extend the student's thinking about the theme, and can assist with selection of appropriate language. Conferencing, as with the other activities mentioned, aims to encourage students to see writing as something that can be improved and to view revision as an integral part of the process of writing.

2. The Product View of Writing

The process approach has emerged from recent research into strategies used by writers during the process of composing. The product approach has its origins in the traditions of rhetoric and has been characterized in several ways. It has involved the study of model texts in order to raise students' awareness of the features of texts. It has often involved practice of these features, such as the use of passives in the description of a process, in sentence level exercises or in the development of a paragraph. And it has involved a pedagogy which analyzes student writing after the text has been produced in order to diagnose and assess strengths and weaknesses. Traditional marking systems for the 'product' have also tended to focus on accuracy as the primary criterion for 'good' writing.

This traditional product-oriented approach has evolved more recently into a pedagogy in which insights from the study of text still have substantial significance but with a rather different application, one which integrates with the process approach. Analysis of written discourse cannot reveal the processes involved in composition. However, it can produce possibilities for description and evaluation, and both of these have their place in second language pedagogy.

2.1 Describing the Product

Analyzing the products of writing can contribute to pedagogy in a number of ways.

2.1.1 Defining the Range

One can observe the range of writing products particular groups of students need to produce and the ways in which one form differs from another. For example, the conventions and style of a formal letter differ from those of an informal letter, and both may differ from similar texts in the student writer's first language. The issue for teachers is to define the writing purposes of the student group. To do this, one can consider the language environment of the learners: whether they are learning a second language in order to live, study, and work in the second language context; or whether they are learning a foreign language with little current need for it in their home context and thus a restricted set of writing needs. Teachers can then decide on relevant goals for classroom writing in relation to types of personal and professional writing, selecting among:

(a) personal writing, e.g., diaries;
(b) study writing, e.g., notes and summaries;
(c) public writing, e.g., letters of enquiry, application, etc.;
(d) creative writing, e.g., poems, stories;
(e) social writing, e.g., invitations, personal letters;
(f) institutional writing, e.g., academic essays, professional reports.

In this way teachers can design a relevant writing program specific to the needs of student writers.

2.1.2 Describing Discourse Organization

One can observe the ways in which the overall organization of texts differ according to the purpose for which they were written. Patterns can be clearly defined within written discourse in which smaller units of meaning combine to form longer stretches of discourse. The smaller units, rhetorical functions, perform identifiable functions such as defining, narrating, explaining. These smaller units combine to form rhetorical patterns as can be seen in the extract below. Here a definition is followed by a classification which provides us with information on the basis of classification and the members of each class. The latter are then described and examples are given:

> Plastics are a group of materials which consist of a combination of oxygen, carbon, hydrogen, nitrogen and other elements. The basis for distinction between the two main classes available to engineers is their behavior when heated. Those which soften when heated and become rigid when cooled again are called thermoplastics. Examples are nylon, PVC and . . .

The issues are whether such sequences are relatively predictable and whether a range of consistent patterns exists and is available for exploitation as teaching devices.

Certainly patterns are not rigid. Within certain conventions it is possible to be flexible and create patterns according to the purpose of the writing. For example, a description of a person involving physical appearance, character, and social background, might begin with any one of these according to which is more important or interesting to the writer, to the readers, or to the purpose for writing the description, for example, to describe a new friend, to introduce a new character in a story. This raises the issue of whether we take a reductionist approach and present basic patterns to learners, raising awareness at the same time of how and why the patterns might vary.

Second language pedagogy has moved in various directions. First, there is an attempt to draw the student writer's attention to different patterns through class analysis of texts. Second, there is an attempt to build awareness of discourse organization appropriate to the task in hand while supporting students through the planning process. To take an example, the task given earlier to compare road haulage and rail transport must be organized in a logical way to highlight effectively contrasts and comparisons. In thinking about the topic, points for content will occur randomly to students and will need to be structured. Fig. 1 could usefully be presented as a possible framework to elaborate.

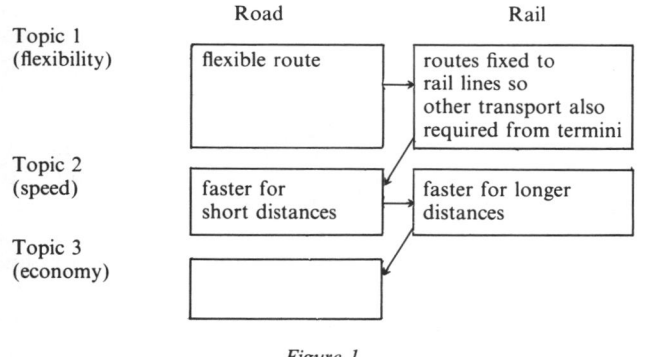

Figure 1

While the suggested plan should not be seen as a straitjacket but something to be reviewed and revised as content develops, a task of this type can consciously develop students' understanding of how ideas can be structured to fulfill a particular communicative purpose. It is common now to find teaching materials which follow a syllabus through which students explore various discourse types in turn, for example, process description, cause and effect, problem-solution, contrast and comparison, and classification.

Third, students can be encouraged to improve their plans through a question and answer technique. For example, students can be asked to write a report of an accident. After they have produced initial drafts, they work in pairs. One student presents his draft while the other challenges with questions, obliging his partner to omit or add detail. The questions, suggested by the teacher, or elicited from the class, derive from the schema for a report, for example: Who was involved? What exactly happened? What was the cause? Who was responsible? What was the outcome? The questioning leads to clarification of what a reader would want to know, would help to determine the inclusion and order of information, and generate a clearer discourse organization.

2.1.3 Describing Features of Coherence

A third area of study from which pedagogy draws insights is that concerned with explaining coherence in a text by analyzing the linguistic features which link meaning across sentences and paragraphs within an overall structure. Cohesive devices are the means by which parts of a text are linked as logically related sequences. Pronouns, for example, can be used for reference back to a previous noun phrase as in *On the contrary, they could not decide what to do.* Conjunctions and conjunctive adverbs have logical functions as well as grammatical ones, making clear the meaning relation of the connection. For example, *however* in *However, they went on to make some criticisms* signals a contrary or concessionary statement to follow.

Such devices clarify the developing thread of meaning which the writer is trying to communicate. Different types of text require different degrees of complexity in sentence structure. An informal letter might use sentences loosely coordinated with *and* and *but*. An academic essay might use subordinate clauses and link meanings with conjunctive adverbs such as *nevertheless* and *despite*. Direct instructions may take the form of simple sentences as in *Do not forget to cancel the newspapers.* Instructional information may use more complex structure as in *If you forget to cancel the newspapers, their build-up on the porch might signal your absence and could result in a break-in during your absence.*

Students need to exploit cohesive devices and use appropriate degrees of complexity in their writing. A survey of current pedagogy would suggest that teachers help students in the following ways.

First, extensive reading provides students with language tools for the effective drafting of their own texts. As they observe the use of cohesive ties in published texts and texts produced by their peers, they may begin to acquire and use them in their own writing.

Second, controlled writing tasks, with a focus on specific linguistic features, may be useful for some students, but not necessarily all. The kind of accuracy-based class exercises which ask students to combine sentences by creating subordinate clauses or by using certain cohesive ties, can raise awareness but not all students will be able to transfer from this type of practice to their own writing.

Current pedagogy prefers practice within the fluency context of writing a whole text. For example, in the task discussed in Sect. 1.1 to compare road and rail transport, teachers can present ties such as *while*, *whereas*, and *on the other hand*, during prewriting activities, explaining their functions and the grammatical restrictions on their use. Then, as students read each other's drafts, they can be encouraged to ring around cohesive ties to assess whether partners are using them appropriately and accurately.

2.2 Evaluating the Product

An approach which attempts to build awareness in student writers that discourse organization should be appropriate to the communicative function of the writing, and that a range of cohesive devices should link meaning in a syntactically appropriate text implies that appropriateness, range, and complexity might be useful criteria for the assessment of writing.

Earlier pedagogic approaches placed value on accuracy as the primary criterion of good writing and it was not uncommon to find marking strategies among teachers for simply indicating or correcting errors of spelling, punctuation, and grammar. However, if student texts are viewed as functionally and linguistically meaningful within the context of the task set, then criteria for evaluation must be based on more than accuracy. The following task might serve as an example:

> You see an advertisement about a sponsored walk for charity. Write a letter to a friend, persuading him/her to take part with you and make arrangements to train together.

Here it would be possible to apply any or all of the following criteria in evaluating the letter: adherence to the conventions of the letter format; completion of all parts of the task; an appropriate range of rhetorical functions; coherence; range of vocabulary; appropriate complexity of syntax; and accuracy in grammar, spelling, and punctuation.

Such criteria are the focus of current professional debate. For the classroom teacher the issues are to select criteria relevant to the age, conceptual development, and language development of their students; also to find ways in which to apply the criteria in feedback which will indicate to students how they are developing in their writing ability.

3. An Integrated Pedagogy for the Future

Pedagogy attempts to exploit aspects of both process and product approaches. The degree to which these are integrated depends partly on the goals of writing and partly on the intellectual and developmental needs of learners. For example, teachers of commercial correspondence may find the use of models and a focus on the linguistic features of these specialized texts most effective. With younger learners, on the other hand, an approach which emphasizes awareness of audience and the need to develop a range of styles might be preferred, while learners at secondary school may need a carefully integrated approach which both refines their composing strategies and raises awareness of discourse features and organization.

There is much lively debate among educators on the many issues relating to process and product approaches and examples in the literature of creative pedagogic procedures.

These will undoubtedly develop in accordance with available resources. For example, the use of computers for drafting and revising will undoubtedly progress to the wider use of electronic mail systems to encourage student communication across the world. Most significantly, there is clear evidence of teachers using insights from research to evolve a more effective pedagogy for supporting the writing development of their learners.

Bibliography

Brookes A, Grundy P 1990 *Writing for Study Purposes*. Cambridge University Press, Cambridge
Hamp-Lyons L, Heasley B 1987 *Study Writing*. Cambridge University Press, Cambridge
Hedge T 1988 *Writing*. Oxford University Press, Oxford
Hudelston S 1988 Writing in a second language. *Annual Review of Applied Linguistics* 9: 210–22.
Pery-Woodley M-P 1991 Writing in L1 and L2: Analysing and evaluating learners' texts. *Language Teaching* 24(2): 69–83
White R V, Arndt V 1991 *Process Writing*. Longman, London

T. Hedge

Second Language Processing: Listening

Listening is commonly referred to in discussions of language, generally to denote the process of deriving meaning from sound. 'Language processing,' which is a more specialized term, is used in the cognitive sciences, including linguistics, to refer to a wide range of interactions between sensory perception (hearing and seeing) and memory systems when spoken or written language is used. 'Listening' is a term used in language studies and language education to refer, more narrowly, to a set of cognitive interactions involved in oral language processing. As a critical element in oral language development, listening has received considerable attention in second language acquisition studies and also in second language pedagogy.

1. Listening as a Process

Listening is accomplished through overlapping and interdependent cognitive operations of phonological perception, word recognition, grammatical parsing, and contextual inferencing. These processes are largely automatic, occurring efficiently and without conscious awareness, except in cases where problems of comprehension and interpretation arise. Both first language (L1) listening and second language or foreign language (L2) listening are assumed to entail the same cognitive operations. However, both efficiency of processing and cognitive affect (the user's sense of ease in processing) differ in L1 and L2 listening. The main paradigms for the description and examination of L2 listening are drawn from L1 psycholinguistics, including the development of L1 competence with spoken language.

1.1 Comprehension, Interpretation, and Understanding

A key distinction when characterizing listener goals in normal (nonpedagogical) language use is that between comprehension and interpretation. It is now generally accepted that the goal of deriving relevant meaning from spoken language cannot be defined solely in terms of objective, measurable information content of the language spoken to the listener, as was commonly supposed in early information processing paradigms of communication. It is now accepted that the goal must be referenced to the listener's transactional (information seeking) requirements and interpersonal (relationship maintaining) goals in the language-use situation. Both transactional and interpersonal objectives will guide the listener's attention to the input and to other salient features of the situational context.

In most L1 and L2 settings, the listener's goal involves a degree of comprehension, driven by the purpose of perceiving accurately the sense and 'illocutionary force' (communicative intentions) of the speaker and also a degree of interpretation, driven by the purpose of constructing a plausible arrangement of information in the event which is consistent with the listener's world knowledge and expectations. 'Understanding' denotes an optimal interaction between comprehension of the oral input and interpretation of that input in the situational context. An additional term, 'intake,' is often used in second language acquisition research to refer to input which is understood.

2. Parallels between First Language and Second Language Listening

L2 listening is assumed to parallel L1 listening in terms of processing procedures, strategies (plans for understanding), and heuristics (problem-solving routines), except to the extent that it is influenced by processes of knowledge transfer from the L1 or by developmental capacity limitations.

The chief sources of knowledge transfer in L2 listening will be phonological, lexical, grammatical, and pragmatic. Phonological transfer occurs when the listener utilizes his or her L1 knowledge of identical or similar sounds to identify sounds from the L2. Lexical transfer occurs when the listener utilizes his or her L1 knowledge (for example, of cognates, of similar sounding words, or of L2 words mentally associated with L1 words) to identify word references. Grammatical transfer occurs when the listener utilizes knowledge of L1 grammatical rules (for example, word order) to derive meaning from L2 input. Pragmatic transfer occurs when the listener utilizes experience with speakers in L1 speech situations (for example, how shop attendants treat customers) to infer meanings in L2 settings. Transfer of all types is likely to occur to some degree in any instance of L2 listening; this transfer may be termed 'positive' to the extent that it promotes efficiency of comprehension and ease of interpretation, or 'negative,' to the extent that it detracts from such efficiency or ease.

Capacity limitations may occur in any of the cognitive processes involved in listening: sound perception, word recognition, grammatical parsing, or inferencing, thus leading to instances of 'nonunderstanding,' in which the listener does not possess sufficient knowledge to construct a viable meaning. Instances of second language nonunderstanding are persistent among most L2 users, but are often relative, rather than absolute, and can typically be repaired either through compensatory strategies to infer a plausible meaning, by way of clarification requests to the speaker to simplify the input, or through subsequent learning of linguistic information.

3. Listening in L2 Acquisition

In virtually all theoretical perspectives of L2 development, listening plays a crucial role, and often a leading one, given the apparent causal relationship between intake of spoken language and language acquisition. These perspectives are divided into complementary psycholinguistic and sociolinguistic orientations.

3.1 Psycholinguistic Orientations

One line of second language acquisition (SLA) research has suggested a causative link between amount and type of spoken language intake to L2 development. The focus on this research, which is best summarized in the work of Diane Larsen-Freeman and Michael H. Long (1991), was initially a description of the features of language input that tended to make language comprehensible, and therefore available to a language acquisition mechanism. The central tenet is that comprehensible input triggers a language acquisition mechanism which allows the L2 learner to understand (and therefore acquire) increasingly complex (and more authentic, native-like) spoken language. The tangible outcomes of this research were largely in detailing aspects of linguistic, paralinguistic (intonational), and nonlinguistic (contextual) simplification which led to measurable comprehension of language by the L2 user.

A critical theoretical development in this line of research has been in isolating interactional routines initiated by the listener in trying to understand spoken language that was not understood initially. This development has highlighted the role of learner strategy (e.g., requesting clarification, rephrasing the speaker's contribution) in making the speaker's language more understandable, as well as on the role of speaker adjustments in interactional features (e.g., asking for confirmation, building upon the listener's question). This approach aims to identify key interactional features which lead to efficient language acquisition. The fundamental reasoning behind this approach to research was that: if it can be shown that in general comprehensible language and manageable interaction promotes language acquisition, then it can be deduced that those specific linguistic and conversational (interactional) adjustments promote language acquisition. The pedagogic implications are immediate: language instruction should focus on engaging learners in tasks which allow for and encourage such interactional and linguistic adjustment (see *Learning Strategies*; *Second Language Acquisition: Conversation*).

A related development is the increasing focus on what the learner (the L2 user) 'notices' of the formal features of language structure (phonological, lexical, and syntactic) in the spoken language input, once the language is understood. While to some extent the order of the features of language that can be noticed is determined by universal cognitive 'developmental constraints,' to some extent the order of features that will be noticed is variational and will be subject to individual motivation, interest, and access to appropriate input (see *Variables, Individual, in Language Learning: Classroom Implications*).

Thus, while the underlying theme in the psycholinguistic orientations is an emphasis on exposure to spoken input as a required condition for acquisition, they differ in how they view the means by which input is understood, and thereby converted to 'intake' in order to trigger language development. The developmental paradigm used in a psycholinguistic approach is one of gaining 'receptive competence' to process increasingly complex language. This competence entails combined abilities in phonological perception, word recognition, grammatical parsing, and contextual inferencing (see *Second Language Pedagogy: Listening*).

3.2 Sociolinguistic Orientations

A second line of SLA research has posited a causative link between a listener's social performance in L2 settings and L2 development. This type of SLA research, which provides a critical focus on the role of the listener in language understanding, is known as the 'interpretive' or sociolinguistic approach. Listening research derived from this approach has focused on how the user's knowledge (or lack of knowledge) of social norms and conventions for language use influences comprehension and interpretation.

Sociolinguistically oriented acquisition research, best typified by the work of the European Science Foundation's project on 'language understanding,' under the direction of Clive Perdue and Christopher Candlin, has helped define specific listener strategies and behaviors that are developed in the course of language development. Chief among these listener behaviors are: participating in turn taking; providing back-channeling comprehension cues to the speaker; providing queries and initiating repairs; and checking one's own understanding. This line of research has also focused on cognitive strategies (sometimes called 'interpretive procedures') used by listeners to help them to comprehend the speaker's intent, through the use of visual and vocal cues and the activation and utilization of relevant background assumptions.

The pedagogical implications here are immediate as well: language instruction should focus on authentic discourse and language contact experiences which allow the learners to investigate these listener activities and to develop a suitable repertoire of their own. The developmental paradigm used in sociolinguistic approaches is one of gaining pragmatic competence: the learner comes to respond to salience in speech situations; utilize speech input to complete a socially-motivated task; seek repair and clarification when necessary; and employ compensatory strategies when listening skills are insufficient for understanding (see *Second Language Acquisition: Conversation*).

4. Phonological Perception and Word Recognition

Phonological perception and word recognition are closely interrelated in listening. Phonological perception begins with the reception of sound waves (produced by speech signals) in the inner ear (delicate hair-like fibers inside the cochlea which are highly specialized to hear speech wave frequencies), where physical sound waves are differentiated in terms of minute variations in quality (for example, friction or stridency), loudness (intensity), pitch (frequency), and duration (time). (These latter three dimensions can be displayed visually on a spectrogram, which is often used to demonstrate these variations between speech sounds.) There is no known physical limitation in humans to prevent our learning to perceive hundreds of phonemic sounds in human languages, many times more than those of any one language.

The goal of phonological perception is word recognition. The process of lexical search leading to word recognition begins once incoming speech sounds are separated auditorily and passed along, instantaneously, to the auditory cortex of the brain, where they are available to be converted to a code. Various models of word recognition have been proposed in psycholinguistics, but all consist of a central operation of matching incoming sound to 'lexical templates,' which are idealized forms of words the user knows.

4.1 Word Recognition in L2

Word recognition is a memory retrieval process which is achieved when the listener has located a suitable reference in his or her mental lexicon, one which suitably matches the speaker's signal. There is some evidence that bilingual listeners utilize a kind of 'switch mechanism' which allows them to suppress phonological and lexical knowledge of the L1 when the L2 is in use, although the more prevalent view is that the bilingual listener must analyze all features of the input regardless of the language being used.

If the bilingual cannot 'switch off' L1 knowledge during L2 listening, then disambiguating sounds and words (which may be similar in the L1 and L2) must be part of a more general inferencing process in which context, both phonological and pragmatic (situational), assists the listener in comprehension of the speech signal. In either case, whether by use of a switch mechanism or through use of contextual inferencing, the L2 listener must accomplish matching of sound to correct code. This matching process is fundamentally 'bottom up,' that is, dependent on accurate coding of the input. But, as with other cognitive processes, it depends critically on 'top down' predictive processes as well, in order to make sense of distorted signals and to compensate for the inability of the perceptual mechanism to detect distinctly the large number of phonemic segments given in normal, fluent speech.

4.2 Processing Speed

Specifically, in fluent speech there may be up to 25 mechanically distinguishable speech segments per second. (One syllable, for example [*bam*], may consist of only three phonemes, but each phoneme may consist of more than one segment.) Since the human hearing mechanism cannot reliably differentiate this many segments in real time, auditory perception must also be an inferential process based on samples of the speech signal, rather than on a continuous decoding.

It is assumed that, as a heuristic (problem-solving) device to compensate for this perceptual limitation, successful listeners depend on accurate perception of stable segments in the speech stream—those most clearly articulated, typically (in the case of most varieties of English) the stressed syllables—and infer the presence of the less clearly articulated forms (weak forms) and less certainly perceived signals. L2 listeners commonly report L2 speech as being 'too fast,' which is a reflection of affective discomfort in managing the uncertainty of phonological perception.

4.3 Mishearings

L2 auditory perception will tend to be additionally problematical because of L1 transfer, leading to numerous auditory mistakes, or 'mishearings.' Mishearings may have one or more origins: phonemic segment confusions (e.g., *over the gate* for *over to Kate*); stress pattern misassignments (e.g., *that snow doll* for *that's not all*); or pitch misplacements (e.g., *You're not going?* for *You're not going*).

Many such mishearings occur when the L2 listener is not familiar with the speech simplification patterns that occur in the target language. Specifically, in all varieties of English, several phonological phenomena are problem-posing to L2 users: consonant assimilation (*handbag* becomes *ham-bag*); vowel reduction (unstressed vowels tend toward a central schwa sound, as in *the*); elision (omission of a sound, as in the elision of /h/ in *give it to him*); and free variation (/t/ in *butter* may be flapped, to sound more like /d/). In addition, for L2 listeners who have learned one variety of English (e.g., general American English), there may be additional problem-posing phonological changes when they are first exposed to other varieties of English (e.g., a regional British English).

Such mishearings are brought about by lexical effects and schematic effects of language processing known to operate in both L1 and L2 listening. Influenced by 'lexical effects,' the listener tends to 'hear' words that he or she already knows, even if the input contains unknown words. Influenced by 'schematic effects,' the listener tends to 'hear' words that are more common or expected in a given context, even when less common or less expected words are actually spoken.

5. Grammatical Parsing

Grammatical parsing is the process of assigning recognized words to grammatical classes (noun, verb, adjective), representing the semantic interrelationship between words (agents of actions, objects of actions, attributes of objects, etc.), and, further, linking this new interrelationship to already understood parts of the discourse. The goal of grammatical parsing is to construct a 'propositional representation' of incoming discourse which can be used for making inferences and for constructing a relevant meaning. As with other listening processes, grammatical parsing is interdependent in its functioning. Just as word recognition (lexical search) provides top-down (predictive) information needed in phonological processing, grammatical knowledge provides top-down information to assist in word recognition.

As an illustration of the first component of grammatical parsing, suppose a listener hears: *We need to rent a room. Rent* is to be understood as a verb meaning 'take financial action to secure use of the room' versus a noun meaning 'the money required.' As a first step in grammatical parsing, such assignments for all content words are necessary, or at least, promote efficiency in processing.

As an illustration of the second component process, suppose a listener hears: *She's holding a club.* The listener may assign 'club' to the appropriate grammatical category, but would further need to know the semantic relationship between *she*, *hold*, and *club*. If *club* is an instrument which she intends to use to beat something, the representation the listener forms is different than if *club* is the name of a suit in a card game which she is now playing.

As an illustration of the third component step, suppose a listener hears: *I saw Tom and his 3-year old son. He had ice cream all over his face.* The listener must decide whether *he* refers to Tom or Tom's son in order to understand the utterance and form a mental representation of what was heard.

5.1 Lexis First Principle

In many cases, grammatical parsing is not dependent on syntactic information from the speaker; syntactic processing can often be bypassed and propositional representation can be constructed from recognized words alone. This is known as the 'lexis first principle.' This principle is particularly evident in discourse which is marked by ellipsis, in which already known elements are not reiterated:

Speaker 1: *Are we going to the party on Friday?*
Speaker 2: *Yes. My car?*

In this excerpt, Speaker 1 most probably will understand *my car?* to be an ellipted form of 'Are we going to the party on Friday in my car?' While it is unnecessary to assume that speakers reconstruct full propositional representations as they parse incoming speech, it is evident that some type of linking of new information to given information is required.

5.2 Understanding 'Given' and 'New' Information

Understanding spoken language in large part requires integrating 'new' information with 'old' (and often unstated) information at a rapid pace. A commonly reported difficulty in L2 listening (particularly in native speaker/nonnative speaker conversation) is managing the large amount of new information. In the following extract, there is evidence that the nonnative speaker (NNS) has difficulty separating 'new' information from what the native speaker (NS) assumes to be 'given':

NS: *So when I was living in Australia,*
      I had a very nice flat.
NNS: *Live?*
NS: *Yes, when I was living in Australia.*
NNS: *Australia?*

The L2 listener in this case needs more processing time, in part due to difficulties with word recognition, in order to integrate new information. The speaker's assumptions about what the listener already knows and can recognize, as evidenced by the rapid pace of the speaker, are unwarranted. As a result, the conversation takes on a disjointed pace, with the listener not able to process the language at the 'normal' speed of the speaker.

5.3 Misunderstandings

Misunderstandings can occur during grammatical parsing, if words are assigned to the wrong grammatical class, if insufficient syntactic information is given or recognized, if semantic relationships between lexical items are not properly computed, or if the underlying representation of the discourse is inaccurate.

At present, there is no clearly defined system for predicting or interpreting misunderstandings due to grammatical parsing errors, as there is with phonological perception and word recognition, since grammatical parsing is closely informed by the more 'open' cognitive systems involved in contextual inferencing.

6. Contextual Inferencing

Sound perception, word recognition, and grammatical parsing of speech are fundamental operations in listening which are often considered bottom-up processes in that they depend upon the speech signal as a primary information source. By themselves, however, these operations form only the basis of listening. They must be supplemented with inferential processes derived from the listener's background knowledge. These inferential processes are sometimes referred to as top-down processes since they impose order on the incoming speech signal.

Once incoming speech has undergone word recognition and grammatical parsing, the propositional representation is available for contextual inferencing. Contextual inferencing is a goal-driven cognitive process of utilizing speech (linguistic) representations, other paralinguistic information (intonation, pausing, loudness), nonlinguistic information (facial gestures, physical setting), and crucially, relevant background knowledge to make sense of an event. For example, if someone walks into a shop and the shop-keeper says, *Good morning. What can I do for you?*, the customer can utilize paralinguistic information to understand the intention of the speaker (cheerful, welcoming, helpful?), nonlinguistic information to understand the appropriacy of the utterance (specifically, there is one person [*I*] asking the question to an addressee [*you*]; the time of day [*morning*]), and background information (it is customary and expected for shopkeepers to make some kind of greeting and query to customers). This same linguistic input (*Good morning. What can I do for you?*') would, by contrast, be rather difficult to process if uttered by a stranger, in the evening, in a crowded elevator.

Contextual inferencing may be usefully divided into two types of interrelated reasoning processes: deductive inferencing and inductive inferencing.

6.1 Deductive Inferencing

Deductive inferencing is the process of recalling a known information paradigm, sometimes called a 'schema' or 'schematic frame,' in order to supply missing information points when forming a mental representation of a text. For instance, upon hearing an utterance *He cut himself shaving*, the listener may infer some specific information, though it is technically missing: that the actor (*he*) cut himself with a razor blade (rather than a knife) and that he cut part of his face (rather than his chest). This deduced information then becomes part of the listener's discourse representation, and cannot be readily separated from the listener's memory of the text (what was actually said).

It is obvious that language understanding depends upon deductive inferencing of this kind, the success of which in turn depends both on the listener's having previously acquired (learned) the relevant schemata and on the listener's ability to bring the relevant schema or schemata into working memory. The L2 listener is faced with the added difficulty of knowing which schemata are universal (for example, the face-shaving routine apparently is universal) and which are culture-specific (for example, the steps in making a purchase in a shop apparently vary from culture to culture).

6.2 Inductive Inferencing

Inductive inferencing refers to the process of supplying relational links (for example, causal links) for features of events and supplying implications (entailments) of events. For instance, when hearing *He cut himself shaving*, the listener

can infer a causative link (the actor may have been careless, in a hurry, etc.) and an unlimited number of logical entailments (there probably was not much bleeding, the actor probably did something to take care of it, and probably did not need emergency treatment). The actual inferences that the listener does form depend in part upon his or her intellectual capacity, but more critically on the listener's determination of relevance: the listener will make all and only the inferences necessary to achieve understanding in a given context.

Contextual inferencing, both deductive and inductive, is of importance in L2 listening for two main reasons. First, as a linguistic understanding process, contextual inferencing draws upon general cognitive reasoning, and hence is subject to influence from the L2 user's nonlinguistic knowledge. As a result, any utterance to an L2 listener, whether a presumably simple and unambiguous utterance (*This food is good*) or an assertion obviously laden with cultural overtones (*The people in this country are free*), may receive a different interpretation from the expected or normal L1 interpretations. Indeed, part of L2 competence is said to consist of a sociolinguistic dimension, in which L1 cultural interpretations are learned and applied in listening.

Research on schematic understanding processes, dating back to Bartlett's seminal recall studies in the 1930s, have verified this point. Frames for virtually every commonly occurring event in a society (from restaurant going to tribal initiation rites) are schematized in memory in order to become readily available for interpretation of new events. All of these schemata can be said to be culturally specific, and in that sense arbitrary (see *Discourse in Cross-Linguistic Contexts*).

The second reason that inferencing is important in L2 listening is related to information availability. Because all inferencing is generally based on incomplete information (or on information that is judged to be less than fully reliable), the efficiency of this process is based upon one's sense of certainty of the information that is available. In L2 listening, the listener is often basing inferences on linguistic information which itself is incomplete or uncertain: unclearly perceived sounds, unfamiliar words, and approximate grammatical parsings will be part of the information base. As a result, the L2 listener must seemingly depend more (than the L1 listener) on inductive inferencing in order to understand spoken language.

See also: Second Language Processing: Reading; Second Language Pedagogy: Listening.

Bibliography

Anderson A, Lynch T 1988 *Listening*. Oxford University Press, Oxford

Bremer K, Broeder P, Roberts C, Simonot M, Vasseur M 1988 *Procedures Used to Achieve Understanding in a Second Language*. European Science Foundation, Strasbourg

Brown G 1990 *Listening to Spoken English*, 2nd edn. Longman, London

Faerch C, Kasper G 1986 The role of comprehension in second language learning. *Applied Linguistics* **7**(3): 257–74

Hamers J F, Blanc M H A 1989 *Bilinguality and Bilingualism*. Cambridge University Press, Cambridge

Kellerman E, Sharwood-Smith M (eds.) 1986 *Crosslinguistic Influences in Second Language Acquisition*. Pergamon, Oxford

Larsen-Freeman D, Long M H 1991 *An Introduction to Second Language Acquisition Research.* Longman, London
Rost M 1990 *Listening in Language Learning.* Longman, London

M. Rost

Second Language Processing: Reading

A commonsense view of the process of reading in a second language (L2) could be stated as follows: first the would-be readers must learn the language, its vocabulary, and grammar. Then, given that they are already literate in their first language (L1), and given that both L1 and L2 are written in the same or similar scripts, the reading process can proceed with very little hindrance.

Thus reading is seen as a skill separate from, though to some extent parasitical on, language. It is seen as more or less the same activity regardless of the language being read, and is independent of any particular language.

If one accepts this view, then reading in an L2 can be seen as a process of *transfer* of reading skills from the L1. There are really only two variables to take into account: the readers' knowledge of the L2, and their reading skill, initially in the L1. For this reason, the transfer approach to L2 reading has seen the problem as one of distinguishing between these variables, reading as either a reading problem or a language problem (Alderson 1984).

The commonsense view outlined above is not the only approach to reading in an L2. It is possible, indeed legitimate, to view reading as one manifestation of language in use, similar to listening. From this point of view, L2 reading is likely, at least in part, to be language specific, and can no more be considered as independent of the language in question than listening. Seen from this point of view, L2 readers are likely to come across features of the L2 in their reading which conflict with expectations based on their experience with the L1. This approach to L2 reading looks at different components of texts, and examines the effect of such variables on the reading process. Both approaches involve the notion of transfer between the L1 and L2 situations. But whereas in the first approach, there are only two variables, in the second there are likely to be many— some language specific, some relating to particular groups of readers.

1. Reading as a Language Activity

In all societies, people begin to acquire their mother tongue (L1) orally, by speaking and listening. However, in modern literate societies, children are taught to read, starting from about the age of five, and from then on have access to the language in two mediums, the oral and the written one. Because of the typical sequence of events, it is easy to think of reading as a skill, or set of skills, 'added on' to an already complete grasp of the L1, and hence to view reading as somehow separate from language use, written texts as representations of spoken language. This view, carried over into L2 pedagogy, is probably responsible for the quite widespread belief that before one can read in a foreign language, it is necessary first to acquire a grasp of the spoken form.

However, the view is, at least in part, a misconception. To begin with, it is very unlikely that a child's command of the L1 is complete in any sense at the age of five. It has long been recognized that vocabulary is built up gradually, and that much of one's store of lexical items has been acquired through the written medium. According to Menyuk, it is increasingly being recognized that one's grasp of the more complex syntax of L1 is acquired much later than the opening years of primary education. Menyuk appears to believe that structures must still be encountered orally before they can be recognized in the written medium, but there seems little reason for this belief. It is quite likely that one acquires a significant amount of structural knowledge by means of reading. And the same is probably true of familiarity with the conventions of more extended texts, narrative, exposition, etc., and their organization. Thus reading is not a skill acquired once L1 has been mastered; it is likely that a great deal of knowledge of the L1 is acquired through reading. As far as L2 pedagogy is concerned, since written texts are as much a manifestation of the language as oral ones, there is no absolute requirement for the learner to go through an oral stage: learners for centuries have been learning languages by means of reading.

The point is being stressed here because of a tendency in the L2 reading research discussed below to view reading as separate from language knowledge. In estimating learners' knowledge of an L2, tests of grammar, for example, are taken as valid measures, while learners' ability to deal with written texts are viewed as evidence of something else, a transferable reading skill. But while it is perfectly legitimate to describe reading skills which may be independent of any particular language, it should be kept in mind that at certain levels, reading the language involves knowing and using the language. The dichotomy between L2 reading as a language problem or a reading problem is in part a false one.

2. Who is the Typical L2 Reader?

Reference has been made above to variables in the L2 reading process. It is worthwhile at this point stressing how many variables may have to be taken into account, some related to specific languages and scripts, others not. It is at least arguable that any one of the following variables may affect the L2 reading process:

(a) The relationship between L1 and L2. English and French, for example, are comparatively similar in many respects: English and Kiswahili seem markedly less so.

(b) The script of L1 and L2. English and Kiswahili are both written using the same alphabet; English and Greek are both written in alphabetic scripts, but the alphabets are different; Chinese is not usually written in an alphabetic script at all, but in a script in which symbols represent morphemes, with no attempt to 'spell' sounds alphabetically.

(c) The presence of previously acquired L2s. Some L1 speakers of Arabic may approach English as an L2; others may already be highly literate in another language, e.g., French, so that English becomes the L3.

(d) Literacy in the L1. Some readers of English as a foreign or second language may be illiterate in their L1.

(e) Proficiency in the L2. L2 readers are not all at the same level of proficiency; some may be beginners, others very advanced. It is often asserted in the literature that advanced L2 readers behave in more or less the same way as literate natives, though this assumption may not always be safe.

If reading is assumed to be more or less the same activity in all languages, then it might seem that the differences listed above will not matter much. If, however, the view is taken that reading is a language process, which in any particular situation will involve the processing of a large number of elements specific to one language, then these differences will seem to be very important indeed. Their existence should at least make one cautious about generalizing about 'L2 reading processes.'

3. Approaches to the Reading Process

Approaches to describing the reading process, initially in the L1, have been characterized as 'bottom-up,' 'top-down,' and 'interactive.' In 'bottom-up' approaches, the reader is seen as moving from the smallest textual elements, letters, sequentially upwards to higher elements. In 'top-down' approaches, readers are seen as approaching texts with their own preconceptions, motivations, and as sampling the text to confirm predictions. In 'interactive' approaches, the reader is seen as moving between 'levels,' not always in the same direction, e.g., moving from words to syntax then back to words again.

The last two approaches are complicated by the fact that they may or may not incorporate 'schema' theory, in which knowledge is seen as 'packaged' into structures (schemata) with components and interrelationships between components. For most of the 1980s, L2 reading research was dominated by top-down approaches incorporating, at least to some extent, schema theory. Such approaches, emphasizing psycholinguistic aspects of the reading process, tend to focus on the transfer of reading skills from one language to another.

4. L2 Research: Reading Skill versus Language Proficiency

Considerable research has been devoted to examining whether such transfer does, in fact, occur. The research can be seen as a debate about the relative importance of language-independent reading skills as opposed to language skills. Alderson (1984) provides a critical review, and there is another discussion in Devine (1988).

Some of the research has been carried out with bilinguals, or presumed bilinguals, where it might be assumed that language proficiency was not a factor, and where a reading improvement in one language could be expected to be transferred to reading in the other language. The data reviewed by Alderson suggests that this is sometimes the case but by no means always. However, as Alderson makes clear, bilingualism is a very complex phenomenon, and it is often very difficult to compare one bilingual group with another.

Other research has investigated subjects reading English as an L2. Here the hypothesis is that, given comparable proficiency in the L2, those subjects who are good readers in their L1 will perform better on L2 reading tasks than subjects whose reading proficiency in the L1 is inferior. Alderson himself investigated Spanish speakers learning English, but the results suggested that proficiency in the L2, measured by general language tests, was a better predictor of L2 reading success than reading proficiency in the L1. In other words, reading proficiency did not seem to transfer.

Clarke (1979) also investigated Spanish speakers, again divided into good and poor readers in Spanish. He found that the good readers did perform better on an English reading test than the poor readers, although the English language proficiency of the two groups was considered to be the same. However, an analysis of some of the data led Clarke to believe that limited language proficiency prevented the good readers from transferring their reading skills. He presented this as the 'short circuit hypothesis,' which suggests that potentially transferable reading skills are blocked because of inadequate mastery of the L2. This suggestion, also known as the 'threshold limit' has received wide acceptance, and can be seen as a compromise between the two extreme positions. Eskey and Grabe (1988) refer to a critical mass point which must be reached in the acquisition of the L2 before 'effective' L2 reading can begin (the reader may note the suspiciously large number of metaphors used in this research area). Alderson has pointed out that the threshold will vary depending on reader and task, and it may be doubted whether the concept has any practical value in research.

Interactive approaches to reading are likely to incorporate both generalizable reading skills and specific language knowledge, and therefore do not present the issues in the same confrontational form as some of the suggestions from researchers or teachers devoted to top-down approaches. The extreme form of the transfer view, that language skills could be transferred regardless of L2 language proficiency is totally implausible; as one writer has said, if you know no Chinese, not even the script, it is unlikely that you will initially be able to read a Chinese text. However, the notion that someone literate in their L1 will transfer some 'skills' or even attitudes to written language in the L2 is an attractive one. In order to be examined empirically, issues perhaps should be defined more precisely than they have been in the past.

4.1 Flaws in the Research

The question as to whether transfer of skills does or does not occur is still in many ways unresolved, partly as a result of flaws in the research.

(a) Few of the studies define what they mean by 'reading,' although the tasks or activities subsumed under the term vary widely. Nor is there much discussion as to what defines the 'good reader.' In the absence of definition, 'good reading' is defined by default in terms of the tasks employed in experiments, e.g., the ability to fill in missing words in texts.

(b) Related to this, there is little realization that reading is task-driven, and that performance may depend on the particular task being attempted. Alderson rightly points out that the 'threshold level' will vary, not just with different individuals but also with the reading tasks they are attempting. 'Find all the proper names in the following passage' would seem to require far less L2 proficiency than 'Provide a summary of the following text.'

(c) 'Language proficiency' is often described separately from reading ability (in fact the transfer approach requires this to be done). But it cannot be assumed that performance on a multiple-choice grammar test is necessarily a better indicator of language ability than performance on a reading test. If someone performs poorly on the first, and well on the second, this cannot be taken as evidence that, for example, it is possible to read well in the L2 without 'knowing the language'; it merely indicates that the reader is successful on at least one occasion in using the written language, but not very proficient at a different language-related task.

(d) When researchers investigate the transfer of skills from the L1 to the L2, there is little precision as to precisely what skills are being transferred. There is even a lot of variation in the terms used: 'skills,' 'strategies,' 'processes,' even 'knowledge.'

(e) Few writers distinguish between reading skills and reading acquisition skills. The discussion often seems to assume that there must be a period of 'language acquisition' before the reading begins. This, as has already been argued, is not necessary: the acquisition of the L2 can take place at least partly through the reading process. But it is highly likely that the processes dominant during the acquisition phase may differ markedly from those of the linguistically more advanced reader, and this may complicate any transfer of skills. It is even possible that language acquisition skills may have to be relearned: for example, guessing unfamiliar vocabulary is often mentioned as a reading skill, but it is one that skilled adult readers probably use fairly rarely in their L1 reading.

In later research some of these flaws have been avoided. Sarig analyzed four types of reading 'move' exhibited by her subjects reading in Hebrew and English. The moves she identified, which can be considered as reading 'skills,' are 'using technical aids,' 'clarification and simplification,' 'coherence detecting,' and 'monitoring.' She concludes that subjects used similar moves in both the L1 (Hebrew) and the L2 (English); in other words, transfer of reading skills was taking place. Sarig also defined reading in terms of different tasks, e.g., 'selecting main ideas.' Of three such tasks, she concluded that 'higher level' reading tasks were tackled in similar ways in both languages. Her work can be taken as evidence that, once one has defined terms, it is possible to detect some transfer of skills taking place.

5. Research into Components of the L2 Reading Process

Another line of research lays less emphasis on transfer between L1 and L2, and concentrates on the effect of different variables, often linguistic, in the L2 reading situation. From the point of view of an interactive model of the reading process, this can be seen as investigation of the effects of different components of a model of the L2 reading process. What now follows is a brief account of research into some areas, mainly linguistic, widely thought to be relevant.

5.1 Background Knowledge

Background knowledge is often discussed in terms of schema theory. However, in much of the L2 research, the schemata involved are seldom described with sufficient precision to justify the use of the term. In consequence, the more neutral term 'background knowledge' is used here.

In studies done by Alderson and Urquhart (1983), it seemed clear that students with a low level of proficiency in English but a background in engineering were able to read engineering texts at least as well as liberal arts students with a higher level of English proficiency. That is, the engineers appeared to be able to compensate for their gaps in linguistic knowledge by referring the text to their existing knowledge. A similar situation seems to have been found by Mohammed and Swales (1984). Faced with the task of reading instructions in order to set the time on a digital alarm clock, subjects performed in the following order of proficiency: (1) native speakers (NS) scientists; (2) non-NS scientists; (3) NS arts; and (4) non-NS arts. In other words, background knowledge was more important than linguistic ability.

In neither of the above cases does it seem useful to refer to schema theory, since the 'schemata' involved may be both very general and very particular, and possibly very large in number. However, this is not the case in the well-known experiment conducted by Steffensen, et al. (1979). Here subjects, North American and Asian Indian, read texts relating to American and Indian weddings. Both groups showed by their recalls that they had operated by relating the texts to their different schemata for weddings, as the theory would predict. In this case the schemata involved were particular enough for individual cases of recall to be related to them.

5.2 Text Organization

There have been two areas of activity here. One has investigated whether orthodox organization of English texts has an effect on L2 readers, e.g., by making the text easier, in contrast to a text where the organization has been 'mutilated' in some way. Studies tend to show that relatively advanced readers behave the same as L1 readers in response to organization. The interaction of organization with, for example, lower linguistic proficiency and greater content knowledge, has not yet been investigated. There has also for some time been an interest in 'contrastive rhetorics,' the notion that different languages display typical and contrasting rhetorical organizations of text, and that this should have an effect on L2 readers and writers. There are a number of indications that this is the case, although it is difficult to establish. If true, the effect on L2 readers would be similar to the postulated effect of L2 syntax, but at a 'higher' level (see *Text/Rhetoric*).

5.3 Intersentential Relationships

Comparatively little empirical work has been done on the effect of implicit relationships between sentences, termed 'intersentential' or 'interclausal.' Cooper (1984) studied two groups of Malaysian readers of English as an L2, a 'practiced' group and an 'unpracticed' group. He correlated the scores of the groups on various language tasks with a test of reading comprehension to see which skills contributed most to reading success. A test in which the subjects read one sentence, then chose from alternatives the sentence which best completed the text, correlated very highly with the comprehension test and discriminated very well between the two groups. Presumably this indicates that the good readers were using a top-down approach; success with intersentential relations will also involve the readers using their background knowledge.

5.4 Cohesion

Rather more attention has been given to cohesion, overt signaling of relationships across sentence boundaries, and sometimes, by extension, to the same or similar relationships across clause boundaries. Cohesion is a cover term for a number of language systems, each of which is best treated separately.

Writers may choose to repeat lexical items, or use lexical variations such as synonyms, across sentences. This repetition produces what Berman (1984) refers to as 'transparent' texts. On the other hand they may use pronominal reference, grammatical substitution and ellipsis, producing 'opaque' texts. Berman reports a study where substituting lexical repetition for reference and ellipsis had the effect of making an English text more accessible than the original for Hebrew-speaking readers. This may be because of one or other of two factors: first, lexical repetition may be more acceptable in Hebrew than in English; hence, the reliance of English on referential pronouns, ellipsis, etc., may run counter to the Hebrew readers' textual expectations. Second, in the L2, the presence of ellipsis, etc., may simply put more strain on a system already struggling with an unfamiliar syntax.

Cooper's subjects had little problem with reference and ellipsis. The difference in the findings may be due to a method effect; Cooper used short texts with multiple-choice alternatives. Such a method may reduce readers' difficulties by focusing their attention on the cohesive referents.

5.4.1 Conjunctives

Conjunctives, or 'logical connectors' such as *for example*, and *moreover*, by signaling intersentential relationships, might be expected to make recognition of the relationships easier. Cooper's findings provide no support for this; his practiced group were at least as successful with the implicit relationships. On the other hand, Cohen, et al. (1988) found that with a reasonable extended text, native speakers of English structured their understanding in part by depending on conjunctives, whereas the nonnatives failed to appreciate the relationships signaled by the conjunctives. Cohen, et al. suggest that this is because the nonnatives were processing the text 'locally,' not seeing wider relationships. In other words, they may have been operating more of a bottom-up approach. Cohen, et al. report that in some cases their subjects simply did not know the meaning of conjunctives such as 'thus.'

5.5 Syntactic Processing

One view of the effect of syntax is that it is comparatively unimportant. Ulijn and Kempen (1976) conducted an experiment in which the L2 was Dutch or French, and the subjects French or Dutch L1 speakers. Strother and Ulijn (1987) experimented with speakers of Dutch and other languages reading English, and compared them with L1 readers. Ulijn and his associates concluded that syntax had little or no effect on L2 reading, and that lexical knowledge and knowledge of the world were much more important.

This does not seem altogether plausible as a general statement. In the experiment by Ulijn and Kempen, the texts seem to have been fairly simple and French and Dutch, the two languages involved, are both western European languages and both relatively closely related. In the later experiment, the focus was on simplification, i.e., whether some syntactic forms are easier than others. The fact that altering the syntactic forms in very limited parts of a text had little or no effect on readers, most of whom were linguistically very proficient in English, hardly seems enough evidence for the claim that readers adopted 'a conceptual strategy aiming at content words,' and that 'a thorough syntactic analysis is unnecessary.'

In studies conducted by Berman (1984) and by Cohen, et al. (1988), Hebrew-speaking subjects with a relatively high level of proficiency in English reported difficulties in comprehending sentences like:

> Thus, it was conjectured that such treatments as holding cells in buffer after irradiation before placing them on nutrient agar plates might function by inhibiting normal growth processes while repair systems completed their task.

Here the syntax is undeniably complex. Also Hebrew (the students' L1) and English are syntactically very dissimilar languages and this may have had an effect. Finally, one of the major study methods of both Berman and Cohen and his associates involved the students in reporting on their problems in reading, and it is possible that this form of self-monitoring may have been more successful in detecting syntactic problems than conventional testing devices like yes/no questions.

The study conducted by Cooper in Malaysia seems to throw doubt again on the importance of syntax, and support the position of Ulijn and his associates. Cooper's syntax subtest correlated very poorly with the comprehension test, and also failed to distinguish between good (practiced) and poor readers.

There are, however, two problems with Cooper's study. It seems likely that the kind of syntactic processing activities required in reading may be very different from the activities involved in completing multiple-choice, discrete point, grammar items. The readers interviewed by Berman and by Cohen, et al. reported difficulty in 'parsing' sentences, i.e., in finding major syntactic constituents such as subjects and verb phrases. Secondly, the actual grammar features selected by Cooper for testing, e.g., modality and tense, may not have been relevant for reading.

5.6 Vocabulary

Vocabulary is one of the features which the lay person and the learner would probably mention in connection with reading in an L2. However, though the literature is full of pedagogical advice on what to do about unknown vocabulary, there is comparatively little empirical evidence as to what L2 readers actually do.

Research has generally found that good readers operate with bigger stores of vocabulary than poor readers. Also that they decode items too fast for predicting strategies to be involved. Eskey in fact remarks that frequent use of top-down strategies at word level suggests a simple failure to decode properly (Eskey 1988). However, Cooper's practiced readers did significantly better on tests of guessing the meaning of nonsense words, or selecting the correct meaning for a multiple-meaning word than his unpracticed group. The poor readers tended to be too influenced by irrelevant previous knowledge and by known collocations.

What is not clear is *how* good readers acquire and store their larger stocks of vocabulary. It would seem reasonable to suggest that they have found ways of grouping words and word relationships in some organized way in their lexicon. The subjects studied by Cohen, et al. reported problems with nontechnical or semitechnical terms, apparently because they had stored only one meaning of the item. They also had difficulty with recognizing contextual paraphrases, forcing them, as Cohen, et al. suggest, to store items separately.

5.7 The Effect of Orthography

It has already been suggested that orthography of the L1 may have an effect on processing of the L2. Some orthographies, i.e., English, are sound-based; others, i.e., Chinese, are not. If readers carry over to the L2 strategies developed for handling the L1 orthography, one might expect this to have an effect.

Koda (1987) found that in the case of Japanese reading English script, a group faced with a text containing phonologically unpronounceable words (e.g., 'pnotdu') actually read the text faster than an equivalent group faced with pronounceable words (e.g., 'pontdud'). The behavior of these subjects contrasted with a group of L1 English speakers in an earlier experiment, who performed better with the pronounceable items.

Randall and Meara (1988) compared the strategies of English and Arabic speakers. Faced with recognizing previously seen target letters in a word-like array of letters, Arabic speakers behaved in identical fashion with both Arabic and roman script, being fastest at recognizing the target when in the middle of the array. English readers performed similarly with letter-like shapes. However, with arrays of roman letters, they behaved differently, being fastest with targets at the beginnings and ends of 'words.' Suarez and Meara hypothesized that speakers of Spanish, which has a highly regular orthography, will operate with a phonological word recognition strategy, as opposed to English readers, who, it is suggested, operate with a phonological approach together with a direct visual approach. The experimental evidence, however, was inconclusive.

Finally, Ryan and Meara (1992) conducted experiments which suggest that the lexical structure of Arabic, in which roots are typically composed of three consonants, plus the Arabic orthography, which represents consonants and only occasionally vowels, should make Arabic speakers reliant on consonant structure when recognizing English words. Ryan and Meara conclude that Arab learners of English may be faced with particular word-processing problems, and speculate as to whether other L1 orthographies produce similar psycholinguistic difficulties.

6. Conclusion

The literature is scattered with pleas for further research, and in this case this is no mere academic convention. The question is where research can most profitably be focused. It has been suggested that highly proficient L2 readers are likely to behave like L1 readers. Their problems can then be left to those people working in the L1 area. It has also been suggested, by Grabe and others, that it is at the lower levels of the reading model (word recognition, syntax, etc.) that interesting differences between readers with different L1s are likely to emerge. Certainly there is scope for research here. Another interesting research focus is on the way that an otherwise nonproficient reader may compensate for weaknesses, e.g., by using superior topic knowledge to make up for lack of syntactic expertise. Interactive models allow for this, but so far little empirical evidence has been obtained to support it.

Many of the reported findings from empirical research in this article appear to be contradictory. Some of this seems to be the result of the differences among L2 readers described earlier, and will thus have to be accepted. Researchers would help if they were very explicit about the nature of the readers being investigated—the relevant characteristics of the L1, the readers' level of L2 proficiency, etc. But valid comparison across groups is often prevented by experimenters using radically different methods. There is now wide acceptance of an interactive model. If researchers could agree informally to use similar methodologies, and even repeat previous experiments with different L2 groups, then we should begin to gather some really worthwhile knowledge about L2 reading processes.

See also: Second Language Pedagogy: Reading.

Bibliography

Alderson J C, Urquhart A H 1983 The effect of student background discipline on comprehension: A pilot study. In: Hughes A, Porter D (eds.) *Current Developments in Language Testing.* Academic Press, London

Alderson, J C 1984 Reading in a foreign language: A reading problem or a language problem? In: Alderson J C, Urquhart A H (eds.) *Reading in a Foreign Language.* Longman, London

Berman R A 1984 Syntactic components of the foreign language reading process. In: Alderson J C, Urquhart A H (eds.) *Reading in a Foreign Language.* Longman, London

Carrell P L, Devine J, Eskey D E 1988 *Interactive Approaches to Second Language Reading.* Cambridge University Press, Cambridge

Clarke M A 1979 Reading in Spanish and English: Evidence from adult ESL students. *Language Learning* 29: 121–50

Cohen A, Glasman H, Rosenbaum-Cohen P R, Ferrara J, Fine J 1988 Reading English for specialized purposes: Discourse analysis and the use of student informants. In: Carrell P L, Devine J, Eskey D E (eds.) 1988

Cooper M 1984 Linguistic competence of practised and unpractised non-native readers of English. In: Alderson J C, Urquhart A H (eds.) *Reading in a Foreign Language.* Longman, London

Devine J 1988 The relationship between general language competence and second language reading proficiency: Implications for teaching. In: Carrell P L, Devine J, Eskey D E (eds.) 1988

Eskey D E, Grabe W 1988 Interactive models for second language reading: Perspectives on instruction. In: Carrell P L, Devine J, Eskey D E (eds.) 1988

Grabe W 1988 Reassessing the term 'interactive.' In: Carrell P L, Devine J, Eskey D E (eds.) 1988

Koda K 1987 Cognitive strategy transfer in second language reading. In: Devine J, Carrell P L, Eskey D (eds.) *Research in Reading in a Foreign Language.* TESOL, Washington, DC

Mohammed M, Swales J 1984 Factors affecting the successful reading of technical instructions. *Reading in a Foreign Language* 2(2): 206–17

Randall M, Meara P 1988 How Arabs read Roman letters. *Reading in a Foreign Language* **4(2)**: 133–45

Ryan A, Meara P 1992 The case of the invisible vowels: Arabs reading English words. *Reading in a Foreign Language* **7**: 1

Steffensen M S, Joag-Dev C, Anderson R C 1979 A cross-cultural perspective on reading comprehension. *Reading Research Quarterly* **15**: 10–29

Strother J B, Ulijn J M 1987 Does syntactic rewriting affect EST text comprehension. In: Devine J, Carrell P L, Eskey D (eds.) *Research in Reading in a Foreign Language*. TESOL, Washington, DC

Ulijn J M, Kempen G A M 1976 The role of the first language in second language reading comprehension: Some experimental evidence. In: Nickel G (ed.) *Proceedings of the 4th International Congress of Applied Linguistics,* vol. 1. Hochschulverlag, Stuttgart

A. H. Urquhart

Second Language Processing: Speaking

Speech processing at a normal rate is only possible if virtually all the necessary procedures function automatically. For most people speaking a second language, those procedures seem to require more conscious effort and attention and, in general, the more attention devoted to the task, the less fluent the performance. The key to fluent second-language speech seems to be the conversion of attended or consciously controlled procedures into unconscious, automatic processes. How that is accomplished remains largely a mystery, but there are a few clues.

1. Basic Characteristics

In a consideration of the special properties of speech processing in a second language, the operating features of the basic human speech production system have to be assumed. Anyone attempting to speak, with communicative intent, must have a general conceptualization of what is to be communicated, a means of converting that conceptualization into a message structure suitable to the recipient and the social context, then into a linguistic form which can be articulated, all subject to some general monitoring and repair procedures. However, the unconscious ease with which that basic system functions in the normal production of utterances in the first language is not typically matched in second-language speech production. Even in the speech of highly proficient second-language speakers, there inevitably remain traces of foreign accent, occasional difficulties with precise vocabulary, some unusual ordering of constituents, and phrasings which seem inappropriate to the general context of the utterance. For the less proficient second-language speaker, and typically for those still in the process of learning the second language in an instructional setting, the number and frequency of nonnative-like features in their speech is much more noticeable. In order to understand how some of the characteristic features of second-language speech come about, a number of constraining influences on the basic psycholinguistic processing model of human speech production must be taken into account. Since the most generally recognized characteristics of second-language speaking are typically identified in pronunciation, an obvious starting point is the effect of articulatory constraints on second-language speech processing (see *Language Production*).

2. Pronunciation

It is generally believed that for an adult to achieve native-like pronunciation in a second language is the rare exception rather than the rule. This general fact has been labeled the 'Joseph Conrad phenomenon' after the renowned author whose literary ability in the English language was beyond question, but whose spoken English retained the strong Polish accent of his first language. If adults find second-language pronunciation so difficult, what specific processes are to blame? One answer is that the key to second-language pronunciation is not initially a production issue at all, it is a matter of perception. Sound distinctions that are important in the pronunciation of the second language may not have an important function in the first language and, because of the powerful influence of the first language system, those second-language sound distinctions may not even be perceived by the learner. The inability of Arabic speakers, in the early stages of learning English, to perceive the distinction between a pair of English words like *pack* and *back* can be traced to the fact that the English distinction between the /p/ and /b/ sounds is simply not a distinction made in Arabic and hence relatively difficult for Arabic speakers to perceive.

In terms of perception, this process essentially leads to an inaccurate categorization of new phonemes in the second language as varieties of familiar phonemes in the first language, and is described by some as 'phonemic false evaluation' and, by others, as 'equivalence classification.' In terms of production, if the speaker uses the first-language sounds as equivalents for the second-language sounds, the process is described as 'transfer' (see *Second Language Acquisition: Phonology*).

3. Transfer

When there is a close match between the transferred first-language sounds and their perceived second-language equivalents, the speaker will typically benefit from 'positive transfer' and be able to produce accurate pronunciation features with little processing effort. The obvious problems arise through 'negative transfer,' when the equivalence is misperceived, and inaccurate second-language sounds are produced. For many Japanese speakers in the early stages of learning English, the English sounds /l/ and /r/ are identified as equivalent to a single sound in Japanese and the pronunciation of that single sound is transferred into English. The effect is one of processing ease for the speaker, yet substantial processing difficulty for the English-speaking listener who does not recognize the unfamiliar sound.

Making matters more complex is the fact that some second-language sound distinctions may be misperceived by learners in some linguistic contexts, but not in others. The most obvious basis for this effect is the availability of a sound type in the first language that seems close enough to what is heard as the second-language sound and hence can be used in certain word positions requiring that sound. The tendency of German speakers of English to pronounce *back* and *bag* as virtually identical is not a result of the Germans failing to perceive a distinction between /k/ and /g/. Such a distinction, between a voiceless (/k/) and a voiced (/g/) sound, is common in German. However, this distinction is never made in word-final position and so, among German speakers, English word-final voiced consonants tend to be pronounced as voiceless. This process is technically known as 'devoicing.'

For other second-language speakers of English, this type of pronunciation problem may have a different solution. If a voiced consonant sound is required at the end of a word like *bag*, the tendency to devoicing can be limited by the inclusion of a final vowel sound such as schwa /ə/. This solution is a common feature among Chinese speakers of English and produces the appropriate voiced consonant, yet followed by an inappropriate schwa sound /bægə/. Mandarin speakers learning English will also use this final schwa sound to cope with the unfamiliar articulation problems of final consonant clusters. Instead of being pronounced as a single syllable ending in two consonants (i.e., a cluster), a word like *test* may be converted to two syllables *tes + te* by the addition of a final schwa sound. Indeed, if this process interacts with a very general simplification process in second-language speech toward 'open syllables' (i.e., one consonant plus one vowel), the resulting pronunciation may be closer to *te + se + te*. When the vowel sound is added at the end of a word, it is technically known as 'schwa paragoge' and, more generally, when it is inserted within the word to create an open syllable, it is described as 'epenthesis.'

A similar process used to cope with initial consonant clusters can be observed among those Spanish speakers of English who, using a pattern more familiar in their first language, pronounce words like *skill* and *state* with an initial /ɛ/ sound or, sometimes, with that sound inserted between the first two consonants (see *Contrastive Analysis*).

4. Temporal Variables

Second-language speaking also exhibits a number of features which affect fluency and which are often taken to be evidence of planning and processing difficulties. These features are collectively known as 'temporal variables' because they have to do with the timing, particularly the rhythm, of utterances. As second-language speakers implement their speaking plans, they have a tendency to make greater use of pauses, filled pauses (e.g., *er*, *em*), lengthened vowels, and the repetition of words or parts of phrases. Such features are typically associated with processing difficulty and represent attempts to gain more time while trying to find appropriate forms and structures. The general effect is that the 'speaking rate' (i.e., syllables per minute) becomes measurably different, typically slower than the native-speaking norm. This description seems to fit lower proficiency speakers and also those whose learning experiences have led them to devote processing time to achieving accuracy in the form of second-language utterances (see *Learning Strategies*). It does capture the speaking style of many Korean learners of English, for example, who often exhibit a slow speaking rate and substantial repetition and self-correction. Some Spanish learners of English, however, exhibit quite different features, with substantially fewer repetitions, corrections, and pauses, and many more 'lexical substitutions' (words from Spanish), so that the actual speaking rate may seem faster than the native speaker norm. One source of that impression is the effect of length of 'speaking runs' (i.e., number of syllables between pauses) which can, on average, be substantially different from one language to the next.

It has been noted that first-language characteristics of speaking rate, such as the length and placement of pauses, can actually become more noticeable in second-language speaking when the learner becomes more proficient, because that proficiency may obviate the need to manipulate temporal variables to gain additional processing time (see *Applied Linguistics: Sociolinguistics*).

5. Interlanguage Processes

In the preceding discussion, some attention has been given to the transfer of features from the first language into second-language speaking as a means of increasing fluency through already existing automatic processes. While the first language exists as an obvious influence on second-language processing, that influence may be quite indirect or even subverted by more powerful forces. If, for example, there is a sound in the second language which is perceived to be particularly difficult, learners may simply avoid using words containing that sound. Alternatively, the learner may produce a version of some targetted second-language sound, particularly a vowel sound, and overgeneralize the use of that same vowel to other contexts where a qualitatively different vowel would be required in the second language. The resulting phenomenon is a sound regularly and generally used by the learner in speaking the second language which is neither an identifiable first-language sound nor an appropriate second-language sound in that context. These two processes of 'avoidance' and 'overgeneralization' are often appealed to in discussions of an underlying system of second-language processing known as the speaker's 'interlanguage.' This system certainly has some features transferred from the first language and also has some identifiable features of the target language, but it is quite distinct from both.

As a processing system, an interlanguage is typically subject to a great deal of variability, both internally, as some aspects of pronunciation accommodate to new patterns, and externally, according to the communicative demands of the situation. When an individual second-language speaker fixes on a particular interlanguage pronunciation pattern and does not exhibit any further variability, the result is described as 'fossilization.' In processing terms, fossilization would represent a fixed, nontarget-like routine for producing second-language sounds and combinations of sounds. This would enable the second-language speaker to make certain processes automatic and potentially increase speaking rate, thereby achieving greater fluency. Such fluency will be purchased at the expense of accuracy in the second language and, although the speaking rate may increase, the communication rate (i.e., being easily understood by native speakers) may show no increase at all. While fossilized pronunciation is often attributed to adult second-language speakers, there is, in fact, more evidence to support the concepts of instability and variability as typical characteristics of second-language speaking, rather than the fixed invariant properties associated with fossilization (see *Communication Strategies in a Second Language*).

6. Variability

There are two main sources which interact to create variability in the process of second-language speaking. Most of the features described so far will give rise to variability in the speaker's performance as a result of processes internal to the speaker. Moreover, as speakers develop greater proficiency in using the second language, or perhaps lose some of their proficiency through periods in which there are no opportunities to use the second language, their level of performance will change. These observable differences give rise to what is called 'intraspeaker variability' and they can occur independently of the speaking context.

The second main source of variability is the nature of the speaking task which can change the processing demands on the speaker's second-language resources and result in different levels of speaking performance. Accuracy in second-language pronunciation, for example, is generally better in reading a text aloud than in free conversation and even better when reading single words aloud from a list. One reason for these differences may be that there is a substantially reduced processing load when the message structure is already organized, with syntactic and lexical choices determined, as in the read-aloud task, and hence processing energy can be more fully devoted to articulation. In free-speaking tasks, with a larger number of processing decisions to be made, less attention can be devoted to pronunciation alone and hence the speaker may appear less accurate and potentially less fluent (see *Applied Linguistics: Sociolinguistics*).

7. Communicative Stress

The speaking task can also become more demanding because of factors external to the speaker within the speaking context, particularly in interaction with other speakers, where messages have to be constructed and articulated on-line and in response to immediately preceding utterances by other speakers. Variation in this respect can be tied to levels of 'communicative stress.'

Second-language speaking may not be very stressful in a comfortable situation, for example, talking to friends on a familiar topic. It is more stressful for a second-language speaker to attempt to talk on an unfamiliar topic, in new surroundings, to strangers. Unfamiliar topics make it less likely that the speaker can rely on some of the more automatic message structures, and the 'prefabricated patterns' of syntax and vocabulary used to encode them, that have been used in the past with familiar topics. New surroundings and unfamiliar interlocutors also make it difficult for the speaker to decide what is known information and what is new for a particular occasion and hence make the organization of message structure problematic. Decisions about the degree of formality versus informality, the relative status relationship between interlocutors, and a variety of other social factors will all serve to create additional stress on the processing capacity of the speaker (see *Applied Linguistics: Sociolinguistics*). In some cases this will give rise to more hesitations, more repairs, and a general disfluency in performance as the speaker experiences difficulty executing all complex processing plans simultaneously within the limited time constraints of interactive speaking. In other cases, it may lead to topic abandonment and an unwillingness to use the second language at all in situations associated with communicative stress (see *Discourse in Cross-Linguistic Contexts*).

8. Strategies

Faced with processing difficulties in the second language, many speakers will employ a range of strategies which either reduce the processing load in some way or make use of other available resources to make the communicative task more manageable for the available processing capacity. The first type of solution has generally been described in terms of 'message adjustment' and is characterized by second-language speakers replacing the message they want to communicate with another message that they feel they have the means to communicate. It may be this process that occasions the frequent number of topic shifts observed in interactions involving lower proficiency second-language speakers. This may also provide an explanation for the higher incidence of planning pauses, hesitation markers, and self-repairs which characterize some second-language speech and give it a very disrupted rhythm.

The second general solution has been described as 'resource expansion' and is realized in a number of different ways. The second-language speaker, wanting to refer to an object, but not knowing or not remembering an appropriate second-language expression, may use gestures or mime, a term borrowed from the first language, a made-up word, or a paraphrase, and various other strategies that essentially invite the listeners to add their active processing abilities to help the speaker overcome some temporary processing difficulty. Clearly, such strategies depend on a cooperative interlocutor and are more likely to be used by a second-language speaker who is willing to take more risks in an attempt to communicate than one who avoids or abandons topics when difficulties are encountered. Risky or not, any strategy that seeks to involve the interlocutor in the joint construction of meaning is likely to be more beneficial for the second-language speaker, both in terms of the immediate interaction and in terms of developing better second-language skills in the longer term (see *Communication Strategies in a Second Language*).

9. Communicative Effectiveness

The role of the interlocutor in studies of second-language speaking has generally been neglected. As much of the preceding discussion has indicated, second-language speakers experience a substantial processing challenge, and much of the training that is normally provided in instructional environments tends to focus on the production processes and how to increase fluency and accuracy. There is some evidence, however, that an overemphasis on the linguistic features of speaking, particularly in terms of formal accuracy, will lead to an excess of self-monitoring and a corresponding reduction in both fluency and attention to the interactive expectations of the interlocutor. Moreover, an emphasis on fluency, or just developing the speaking rate in the second language, will tend to reduce the level of accuracy, without necessarily proving beneficial for the communicative demands of the interaction.

Emphasizing either accuracy or fluency, or even both, will tend to create second-language speakers who concentrate most of their processing energy on their own spoken performance. They become more proficient monologue speakers in the second language. When faced with an interactive speaking situation in which their interlocutor indicates a communication problem, such speakers will tend to concentrate on themselves, their perspective, and their expression of that perspective, rather than attempt to take the other's perspective into account. In most interactive communication, however, there is an inherent requirement that communicative problems are to be negotiated and resolved jointly, with each speaker accommodating to the other's expressed perspective. When second-language speakers are sensitized to the nature of an interlocutor's requirements, they tend to develop more effective spoken communication skills and can use their fluency, not just to express their own perspectives, but to discover their interlocutors' perspectives. The development of such skills is usually marked by an increase in a number of interactive moves, such as monitoring the other's world of reference, checking for comprehension, anticipating potential problems, and seeking confirmation whether some basic information is shared or not. These aspects of speaking are typically identified as 'clarification requests,' 'confirmation checks,' and 'confirmation responses.'

What these aspects of second-language processing appear to indicate is that, as the interaction proceeds, the second-language speaker is jointly constructing, with the interlocutor, a mutually understood world of reference. Operating in this way, the second-language speaker will be concentrating processing energy at the conceptualization and message structure levels in order to tailor spoken contributions to what is known, or needs to be known, about the interlocutor's world, rather than focusing on structuring and articulating a message that is already formulated in terms of the speaker's world alone.

In general, previous work on second-language speech processing, both in research and teaching, has tended to pay most attention to formal aspects of the speaker's articulation and little attention to ways in which interactive language use demands that spoken contributions should be 'recipient designed.' As the goal of second-language speaking becomes less tied to the articulatory level, dominated by concepts such as fluency and accuracy, and begins to be more closely associated with communicative effectiveness in particular contexts, involving concepts like negotiated meanings and information exchange, there will likely be a change in the amount of attention devoted to the different components in the standard model of speech production. Instead of a linear progression from speaker's conceptualization through message structuring to an instantiation in linguistic form, there will be a more elaborate role for checking and monitoring procedures which interact between speaker's conceptualizations and perceived listener's conceptualizations before message structures are formulated.

See also: Second Language Acquisition: Phonology; Second Language Acquisition: Conversation; Second Language Processing: Listening; Discourse in Cross-Linguistic Contexts; Communication Strategies in a Second Language.

Bibliography

Brown G, Yule G 1983 *Teaching the Spoken Language*. Cambridge University Press, Cambridge
Dechert H W, Raupach M (eds.) 1987 *Psycholinguistic Models of Production*. Ablex, Norwood, NJ
Dechert H W, Raupach M (eds.) 1989 *Transfer in Language Production*. Ablex, Norwood, NJ
Faerch C, Kasper G (eds.) 1983 *Strategies in Interlanguage Communication*. Longman, London
Gass S, et al. (eds.) 1989 *Variation in Second Language Acquisition*, vol. 2, Psycholinguistic Issues Series. Multilingual Matters, Clevedon, OH
Ioup G, Weinberger S H (eds.) 1987 *Interlanguage Phonology: The acquisition of a second-language sound system*. Newbury House, Cambridge, MA
Levelt W J M 1989 *Speaking: From Intention to Articulation*. MIT Press, Cambridge, MA
Tarone E 1988 *Variation in Interlanguage*. Edward Arnold, London

G. Yule

Second Language Processing: Writing

Writing in a second language is a complex phenomenon obviously involving an interaction between writer and reader that is less obviously a cognitive activity. The resulting process of composition has been the focus of students of contrastive rhetoric and, more recently, students of cultural and cross-cultural second-language processing. This survey of the field begins with what second-language (L2) writers bring into the writing situation: cultural models of what 'good' coherent writing is. Such models are formed from semantic and syntactic knowledge, and include as well knowledge of text structures, of acceptable topics, and of appropriate compositional procedures. Although these L1 cultural models can often be transferred successfully into L2 writing, the potential for negative transfer is obvious. To study L1 and L2 writing, researchers—applied linguists and rhetoricians—examine both writing processes and the written products using a variety of communicative, cognitive, and linguistic analyses.

1. Current Theories of Writing

1.1 Writing as Communication

In current theories of writing, writing is considered an act of communication between writer and reader(s). It is recognized that in a genuinely communicative social interaction, a writer pays careful attention to the audience and its needs in order to make sure that the text is comprehensible, persuasive, or memorable—that is, fulfils whatever demands the specific writing situation requires. Therefore, texts are not seen as overt, concretely describable entities. Instead, linguists admit that 'the interpretability [of texts] is the dependence of situational context and the knowledge of the world shared by the producer and the receptor of discourse' (Enkvist 1990: 26).

Many models of writing which address this mutual dependence have been developed by rhetoricians interested in considering the purposes of writing (e.g., Britton 1975; Kinneavy 1971). As has frequently been noted, these models resemble Jakobson's (1960) well-known schema of the functions of language. Jakobson identifies six factors: addresser, addressee, context, message, contact, and code. Each determines a different function of language: 'emotive' or 'expressive' (expressing the addresser's feelings and experiences); 'conative' (focusing on changing the addressee's behavior, thinking, or action); 'referential' or 'epistemic' (focusing on the context and informing the addressee of topics outside the addresser and the addressee); 'poetic' (focusing on the self-referentiality of the message); 'phatic' or 'associational' (emphasizing the relationship between the addresser and the addressee); and 'metalingual' (focusing on the lexical or syntactic code of language).

The similarity with Jakobson's model of the functions of language and the rhetorical models of writing is illustrated by Kinneavy's widely accepted 'theory of discourse.' Kinneavy's theory is based on four components as contrasted to Jakobson's six: encoder, decoder, reality, and signal. Depending on the situation, language (the signal) stresses the persons (encoder or decoder), or the reality to which the reference is made, or the product (the text produced). Consequently, discourse can be 'expressive' (focused on the encoder, Jakobson's addresser), 'persuasive' (focused on the decoder, the addressee), 'informative' (focused on reality or the context), and 'literary' (focused on the text—Jakobson's 'poetic' function). Kinneavy's model has been useful in explicating reader–audience relationships in writing because, more clearly than the Jakobsonean model, it distinguishes the aims or purposes of discourse from the modes or means of discourse, for example, classification and description.

1.2 Writing as a Cognitive Activity

Clearly, as an act of communication between the reader and the writer, writing is a complex cognitive skill requiring appropriate processes and strategies. In the 1970s and 1980s, a great deal was learned about these processes. Both L1 and L2 researchers have examined the mental states of writers, their problem-solving strategies and decisions about focus, audience, and language use, and their stylistic decisions and composing processes—planning, decisions during writing, and revising—in order to determine what is involved in the act of writing and what skills are required.

For example, researchers have studied *student* writers at work. In first-language writing, Emig's (1971) pioneering research, *The Composing Processes of Twelfth Graders*, was the first to shift emphasis from product to process and to establish a case study approach using audiotaped think-aloud protocols of writers as data. Emig analyzed the writing processes of eight high school seniors, audiotaping their composing aloud, observing the students while they wrote, and interviewing them afterwards.

One of the most powerful models of composing is that developed by Flower and Hayes (1981), from their studies of thinking-aloud protocols collected from mature, college-level writers while in the act of writing. Flower and Hayes's cognitive process model represents writing as consisting of four interactive components—task, environment, the writer's long-term memory, and the composing processes themselves. The task environment consists of the writing topic, the audience, the degree of urgency of the task, and the text produced *so far*. The writer's long-term memory retains definitions of the topic, identity of the audience, and possible writing plans. The writing processes include planning, translating, and reviewing. Planning involves generating ideas, goals, and procedures. Translating

involves expressing ideas and goals in verbal forms, while reviewing includes evaluating and revising.

Using this theoretical model to explain data from numerous empirical studies, Flower and Hayes have identified composing as an exceedingly complex problem-solving activity responding to a rhetorical situation in a form of a text. Most importantly, their research has determined that writing ordinarily is not a linear process where a writer moves from planning to translating and to reviewing in an orderly sequence. Instead, writers have been found to write recursively, not knowing what the written outcome will be when they start.

Research on writers' composing processes shows that composing involves a variety of plans and processes which the writer brings to bear throughout the writing process. Research on the composing process contradicts previous composition pedagogy which has required that students find a topic, construct an outline, and then write in an orderly, linear sequence. It has also discovered differences between the strategies of skilled and novice writers. Skilled writers pay greater attention to matters of content and organization while weaker writers are preoccupied with mechanics (see Hillocks 1986 for a comprehensive review of L1 writing process research).

2. Theories of Writing and Composing in L2

2.1 Research on Composing Processes

Second-language writing research reflects a keen awareness of L1 writing process research (see Krapels 1990 for a review of the ESL writing process research). Raimes's (1987) case study is a good example; it includes only one writing task, and data are gathered from both process- and product-oriented sources. Think-alouds are analyzed with regard to processing model components: students' planning, translating, and reviewing are charted; strategies to address the audience are assessed; and procedures to address the writing task in general are explained. With regard to product-oriented data, students' written essays are analyzed and evaluated according to their length, use of various syntactic measures, coherence, development, and other features contributing to essay quality.

However, the findings from the 100 or so studies on L2 composing are contradictory. In a review of these studies, Krapels (1990) found that the findings *tend* to show the following:

(a) Composing competence is more important in ESL writing than language competence.
(b) The composing processes of expert L2 writers are similar to the composing processes of expert L1 writers; likewise the composing processes of novice L2 writers are similar to the composing processes of novice L1 writers.
(c) Composing processes in L1 are transferable to L2.
(d) Composing processes in L2 are somewhat different from those in L1 (a contradiction of (b), Krapels points out).

At this time, it seems too early to generalize about L2 writing processes because the studies have been conducted with few students in different settings. Students have typically written an essay on a prescribed topic. The research has focused on one aspect—composing processes—and has not considered other variables that enter into the writing situation according to the communicative model, for example, knowledge of the audience, the context, and the purpose.

2.2 Contrastive Rhetoric: Cross-cultural Differences in the Organization of Texts

Since the 1960s, after observing problems in L2 writing of international students, second-language acquisition researchers have tested theories about differing writing patterns in students' L1 cultures and their effect on L2 writing. Kaplan's (1966) research was the first major study that analyzed how L1 thinking and discourse structures are manifested in L2 writing. His research was influenced by the work of sociologists and anthropologists who believed that logic is a cultural phenomenon, and who were influenced by the Sapir–Whorf hypothesis, which holds that the structure of one's native language strongly influences one's view of the world. Kaplan's major thesis was that different linguistic and cultural interpretations lead to different rhetorics, or modes of communication. This causes difficulties for nonnative speakers writing in the target language. Such students need to be taught the appropriate target language patterns and their associated logics.

Kaplan's was the first attempt in ESL to consider the rhetoric of writing rather than the purely linguistic features emphasized by traditional sentence-based analyses such as 'transformational generative grammar.' In order to contrast English rhetorical patterns with other rhetorics, Kaplan analyzed some 500 essays written by ESL students with heterogeneous L1 backgrounds. He found that Arabic students' essays were characterized by the use of repetitions and parallel expressions; Chinese students' writing was marked by what Kaplan called an approach of indirection—writing in a circular pattern which takes a long time to come to the point; while students with Romance and Russian backgrounds frequently tended to digress.

Coined as 'contrastive rhetoric,' Kaplan's research has encouraged numerous other ESL researchers to account for certain patterns in the writing of ESL students as interference from L1. (Contrastive discourse analyses between English and several languages—American Indian languages, German, Hindi, Japanese, Korean, Mandarin, and Marathi—are included in the 1983 volume of the *Annual Review of Applied Linguistics* (Kaplan 1983).) However, the emphasis of other ESL researchers has been on the development of contrastive rhetoric as a more comprehensive discipline that draws on theories of cultural and linguistic relativity, discourse analysis, translation theory, rhetoric studies, and teaching and learning theory. Two recent anthologies (Connor and Kaplan 1987; Purves 1988), for example, focus on the contributions of discourse analysis alone in contrastive rhetoric.

Because of the growing emphasis on processes of writing, contrastive rhetoric has come under intense criticism during the 1980s and early 1990s. It has been criticized for focusing on products or finished essays rather than on the processes involved in writing. Based on some process theories, the claim has been made that since all student writers, both in L1 and L2, have similar problems in composing and revising their writing, little influence should be expected from L1 interference, as has been asserted by Kaplan.

Despite this criticism, interest in contrastive rhetoric has been renewed because of an increased awareness that, for a comprehensive theory and for effective instruction, both product and process need to be considered. For example, it has been pointed out (Connor 1987) that descriptions of writing processes have been achieved by analyzing different kinds of products—transcripts of processes, analyses of student revisions of their own writing, and studies of teacher comments on student writing. Further, the role of text analysis is important; as Raimes (1987) shows, ESL writers concentrate on the challenge of finding the right words and sentences to express meaning instead of focusing on the development of ideas in their essays. In addition, contrastive rhetoric has expanded its scope from a narrow interest in organizational patterns in student writing to viewing student writing from a contrastive point of view in a larger instructional and sociolinguistic context. It now includes comparing stages in writing activity cross-culturally as well as examining cross-cultural differences in writing due to different expectations of audience.

2.3 Writing as a Cultural Activity

Important contributions to knowledge about language, writing, and culture have emerged from the International Study of Written Composition as part of the International Association for the Evaluation of Educational Achievement (IEA) (Gorman, et al. 1988). The IEA study has examined the written achievement of students and instructional practices of writing in 14 different countries: Chile, England, Finland, the Federal Republic of Germany, Hungary, Indonesia, Italy, the Netherlands, New Zealand, Nigeria, Sweden, Thailand, the United States, and Wales. Thousands of school-age students have written essays on a variety of topics ranging from reflection to persuasion.

Working from the vast empirical data resulting from this project, Purves (1988) has proposed that there are both an 'international interpretative community' and 'national communities.' Although the countries were able to agree on common tasks and scoring procedures, differences were found in the style, content, and pragmatics of the essays across cultures. Purves concluded that good writing is culturally determined.

In addition to evaluating the quality and characteristics of student essays across languages and cultures, the IEA study revealed cultural differences in 'writing activity.' It was observed that in some cultures greater emphasis appears to be placed on criteria for editing while in others there appears to be a greater emphasis on criteria for planning and drafting. Purves and Hawisher (1990: 190), for example, comment that 'there are strong national differences in perception . . . such as the relatively low emphasis on "organization" in Chile and on "style and tone" in the Netherlands. In New Zealand and Sweden, teachers appear to emphasize "process" more than in other countries, but in Sweden more of this emphasis concerns choice of topic than is the case in New Zealand.'

In another landmark article describing the IEA study, Purves and Purves (1986) claim that guidelines or rules for 'good' or 'appropriate' writing determine cultural models for finished texts as well as cultural models for good writing in specific contexts. They list three basic forms of required knowledge: 'semantic knowledge,' 'knowledge of text models,' and 'knowledge of social and cultural rules governing both when it is appropriate to write and when it is obligatory to write as well as knowledge of the appropriate procedures to use in the activity of writing' (1986: 179).

The work conducted in the IEA study and the theoretical implications discussed by Purves and his colleagues are significant in expanding contrastive rhetoric in three directions. First, the sample writing in the IEA study was in the students' mother tongues, allowing for a more direct discussion of cross-cultural differences. Second, the sample sizes were large enough to allow statistical inferences and generalizations. Third, the study recognized the importance of going beyond static linguistic and discourse analyses for learning about cross-cultural conventions of writing.

It should be noted that the IEA study examined writing solely in L1 and in L1 cultural contexts, a limitation which does not directly lend itself to generalizing for L2 contexts. But when the study is considered in light of what is known through contrastive rhetoric studies about the transfer of L1 writing patterns into L2 writing, one can easily speculate that cultural models learned in L1 context—related to purposes of writing, audience, topics, and discourse genres—transfer into L2 situations to some degree.

2.4 Cross-cultural Differences in Text Coherence

Coherence is the most important aspect in the interpretability and comprehensibility of a text. L2 researchers around the world have examined features that make texts coherent. Two competing theories have dominated: one that emphasizes the reader's interaction with the text, and the other that focuses on the text itself. Although the latter is important in that a certain number of surface signals in discourse are necessary for ease of processing (e.g., overt cohesive links like transitional conjunctions), more researchers now consider coherence as part of a process of comprehension that is 'sensitive to situation and context including the world knowledge of the communication partners' (Enkvist 1990: 26)—in other words, cross-culturally intelligible. Accepting the view of coherence that emphasizes the situation, context, and the world knowledge of the encoder and the decoder, helps one to understand the inherent difficulties of L2 writers. Thus, for example, it is not enough to know the covert textual signals of cohesion in the target language—itself a formidable task. In addition, L2 writers have to structure their discourse so that their L2 readers are able to make the right inferences.

Clearly, to use text structures that in the target language are viewed as achieving coherence helps the reader make the right inference. But textual patterns used to express coherence vary among languages and across cultures. Hinds, for example, has shown that writing in Japanese, Chinese, Thai, and Korean favors an inductive rather than a deductive style of presentation, or what Hinds calls 'delayed introduction of purpose' (1990: 98). The specifics lead up to what appears to be, and often is, the conclusion. This delayed introduction of purposes makes the writing appear incoherent to the English-speaking reader (although not to the native reader), especially since the concluding paragraph does not always constitute a conclusion in the English sense. English-speaking readers expect most essays to be organized deductively, from the general to the particular, at least in appearance.

In addition to achieving coherence through textual structures such as the inductive, writers need to be sensitive to the different expectations of reader/writer responsibilities across cultures. In proposing a new typology of language based on 'speaker and/or writer responsibility as opposed to listener and/or reader responsibility,' Hinds has shown that, with respect to coherence, for example, Japanese writing demands more of the reader, while the inference-based rhetorical form preferred in the West places the expository burden chiefly on the writer (1987: 143, 146).

Hinds's extensive research on English and Japanese expository prose shows that English readers expect and require landmarks of coherence and unity as they read. The writer needs to provide the transitional statements. In Japanese, on the other hand, transitions may be lacking. The reader is expected to piece together sections to make a coherent text. Hinds's findings are consistent with analyses of persuasive essays written for the IEA study, which show that the Western tradition favors the rational, logical aspects of argument. The burden in the Western tradition is clearly on the writer, for the writer is expected to make obvious the steps in the argument and the pertinence of the evidence.

2.5 Directions for Future Research in L2 Writing

Acknowledging that writing is a cognitive and communicative activity embedded in a culture, L2 research continues to explore processes in L2 writing as well as to examine products in order to learn more about the transfer—both positive and negative—of L1 linguistic and cultural orientations. Studies of processes need to move beyond examining processes of planning, translating, and reviewing to considering setting, context, audience, and effect of L1 background. Product-based research, on the other hand, continues to establish rhetorical and linguistic norms and conventions of writing in students' L1 cultures as well as to examine the development of culture-specific communication and writing styles.

Bibliography

Britton J 1975 *The Development of Writing Abilities*. Macmillan Education, London

Connor U 1987 Research frontiers in writing analysis. *TESOL Quarterly* **21**: 677–96

Connor U, Johns A M (eds.) 1990 *Coherence in Writing: Research and Pedagogical Perspectives*. TESOL Publications, Arlington, VA

Connor U, Kaplan R B 1987 *Writing Across Languages: Analysis of L2 Text*. Addison-Wesley, Reading, MA

Emig J 1971 *The Composing Processes of Twelfth Graders*. National Council of Teachers of English, Urbana, IL

Enkvist N E 1990 Seven problems in the study of coherence and interpretability. In: Connor U, Johns A (eds.) *Coherence in Writing: Research and Pedagogical Perspectives*. TESOL Publications, Arlington, VA

Flower L S, Hayes J R 1981 A cognitive process theory of writing. *College Composition and Communication* **32**: 365–87

Gorman T P, Purves A C, Degenhart R E 1988 *The IEA Study of Written Composition Vol. I: The International Writing Tasks and Scoring Scales*. Pergamon Press, New York

Hillocks G Jr 1986 *Research on Written Composition: New Directions for Teaching*. ERIC Clearinghouse on Reading and Communication Skills and the National Conference on Research in English, Urbana, IL

Hinds J 1987 Reader versus writer responsibility: A new typology. In: Connor U, Kaplan R B (eds.) *Writing Across Languages: Analysis of L2 Text*. Addison-Wesley, Reading, MA

Hinds J 1990 Inductive, deductive, quasi-inductive: Expository writing in Japanese, Korean, Chinese, and Thai. In: Connor U, Johns A M (eds.) *Coherence: Research and Pedagogical Perspectives*. TESOL Publications, Alexandria, VA

Jakobson R 1960 Linguistics and poetics. In: Sebeok T A (ed.) *Style in Language*. Wiley, New York

Kaplan R B 1966 Cultural thought patterns in intercultural education. *Language Learning* **16**: 1–20

Kaplan R B (ed.) 1983 *Annual Review of Applied Linguistics*, vol. 3. Newbury House, Rowley, MA

Kinneavy J 1971 *A Theory of Discourse*. Prentice-Hall, Englewood Cliffs, NJ

Krapels A R 1990 An overview of second language writing process research. In: Kroll B (ed.) *Second Language Writing: Research Insights for the Classroom*. Cambridge University Press, New York

Purves A C (ed.) 1988 *Writing Across Languages and Cultures*. Sage, Beverly Hills, CA

Purves A C, Hawisher G 1990 Writers, judges, and text models. In: Beach R, Hynds S (eds.) *Developing Discourse Practices in Adolescence and Adulthood*. Ablex, Norwood

Purves A C, Purves W C 1986 Viewpoints: Cultures, text models, and the activity of writing. *Research in the Teaching of English* **20**: 175–97

Raimes A 1987 Language proficiency, writing ability, and composing strategies: A study of ESL college student writers. *Language Learning* **37**: 439–67

U. Connor

Selectional Restrictions

A selectional restriction is a restriction on the ways in which a lexical item may combine with others. The notion played a rather important role in the early development of generative grammar. In the semantic theory developed by Jerrold Katz and his collaborators, selectional restrictions were properties of readings of lexical items, and determined how these could be combined with readings of other constituents. One possible consequence of violating a selectional restriction was a semantically anomalous sentence, such as *Sincerity admires John*, where *admire* would be restricted to human subjects. In Chomsky (1965), a different approach to selectional restrictions was taken in that they were seen as basically syntactic, on the grounds that they involve features (such as 'Human') that also show up in rules of a clearly syntactic character. An influential critique of Chomsky's position is found in McCawley (1973), who maintains that selectional restrictions are predictable from the meanings of lexical items and can be seen as restrictions on 'possible messages.' Possible counterexamples to the predictability thesis are words such as *addled*, which can be combined only with words like *eggs* and *brains*, although its apparent synonym *rotten* is not restricted in this way.

An alternative treatment of selectional restrictions is given in presupposition theory (Seuren 1985), where they are seen as conditions on the referents of arguments of predicates (see *Categorial Presupposition*). (Notice the difference to Katzian semantics, where a selectional restriction constrains the sense of the arguments rather than their reference.)

Bibliography

Chomsky N 1965 *Aspects of the Theory of Syntax*. MIT Press, Cambridge, MA

Katz J, Postal P 1964 *An Integrated Theory of Linguistic Description*. MIT Press, Cambridge, MA

McCawley J D 1973 *Grammar and Meaning: Papers on Syntactic and Semantic Topics*. Taishukan, Tokyo

Seuren P A M 1985 *Discourse Semantics*. Basil Blackwell, Oxford

Ö. Dahl

Self, Definition of

In philosophical, sociological, social psychological, and psychological discourse, few terms have been so contested as the concept of self. Theorists from Plato to Descartes, James to Freud and Mead, Sartre and Heidegger to Goffman and Althusser have debated its meanings, origins, and importance for the understanding of human experience. This article will briefly review the many meanings that have been brought to this concept from philosophy, psychology, psychoanalysis, and social psychology. It will then present the symbolic interactionist theory of the self, its origins, and development.

1. Definition of the Self

In its broadest sense *self* is synonymous with the broadest usage of ego; that is it references the core of the personality system organized around the person's conscious and unconscious (or out-of-awareness) conception of himself, including his interests, values, identities, commitments, and desires. In this sense, as Manford Kuhn notes, the self is what it is to the 'objective' observer. The reflexive character of the self (it can be an object to itself) has led some social psychologists to narrow the definition so that the self denotes the individual as viewed by the person (Manford Kuhn).

A more phenomenological view (Heidegger, Sartre, Denzin) defines the self as that process that unifies the stream of thought and experiences which the person has about himself around a single pole or point of reference. Here the self is not a thing, but a process. It is consciousness conscious of itself, referring always to the sameness and steadiness of something always present to the person in his thoughts, as in 'I am here, now, in the world, present before and to myself.' The self, under this view, involves moral feelings for the self, including all the subject calls his at a particular moment in time, such as material possessions, self-feelings, and relations to others. It also includes the meanings the person gives to himself as a distinct object and subject at any given moment, involving the meaning of the person to himself as he turns back on himself in reflection. The self is not in consciousness, but in the world of social interaction. Its presence and meaning haunt the subject.

An intermediate position defines the self as a process of internal and interpersonal communication. It is seen as arising in and through the situations of interaction, or circuits of selfness (Sartre) that the individual addresses, and that anchor him into the world (Mead, Sullivan, Goffman, Strauss, Stone).

2. Multiple Meanings of Self

As these three positions or usages indicate, multiple meanings surround this term. In Classical and contemporary thought, the self has meant any of the following: (a) ego, subject, I, me, as opposed to the 'not-me' (W. James); (b) the self as knower versus the self as known (James); (c) the self as subject or 'I' versus the self as object or 'me' (Mead); (d) the self is the quality of uniqueness and persistence through changes by virtue of which any person calls himself or herself 'I,' leading to the distinction among selves, as implied in such words as 'myself,' 'yourself,' 'himself,' etc.; (e) the self is the metaphysical principle of unity underlying subjective experience, sometimes called the soul; (f) the self is the bearer of subjective experience; (g) the self references those meanings that are applied to the content of that experience, sometimes called the psychological self; (h) the self is that form of subjectivity created by bourgeois, humanistic ideology (Althusser; Foucault); (i) the self is the rational side of consciousness (Freud); (j) the self is a form of self-awareness where the self is the object and subject of experience (Sartre); (k) the self is a mask that is worn in public (Goffman); (l) the self is nothing apart from the bundle of successive perceptions that make up experience: there is nothing that justifies the concept of self that can be given by introspection (Hume); (m) the self is the subject known to itself through thinking—'I think, therefore I am' (Descartes); (n) the self is self-consciousness, or the knowledge by the self of itself; (o) the self is selfhood, or the unique individuality possessed by a self or person; (p) the self is the empirical ego, or the individual self conceived as a series of conscious acts and contents which the mind is capable of knowing by direct introspection; (q) the self is pure ego, inferred from introspection, but inaccessible to direct knowledge (e.g., soul theory, and Kant's transcendental theory which considers the self an inscrutable subject presupposed by the unity of empirical self-consciousness).

2.1 Psychological Formulations

Contemporary psychologists and social psychologists, drawing upon many of William James's formulations, have also contributed to the discussions of the self. For Manford Kuhn the *self-conception* may be defined as the person's view of himself. He argued that the self-conception (like the self) is derived from taking the role of significant others in social interaction. A self-conception (for Kuhn) consists of one's identity (how I am known by others and how I know myself), one's interests, worldview, goals, and some sense of self-evaluation. Here self-conception is equivalent to the self. Theorists such as Carl Rogers and Ruth Wylie have extended this relationship between the self and self-conception. They have suggested a distinction between the 'personal self-concept,' or self-attributes seen from the person's perspective, the 'social self-concept' (how one thinks others see them), and the self-ideal, or conceptions of what one would personally wish to be like. 'Self-ideals' are then applied to the personal and social self-concept. 'Self-esteem' (also a James term), refers to the overall or global level of self-evaluation of self-regard the person holds about himself. For some (Maslow), self-esteem is directly related to 'self-actualization', or the process of becoming a self-actualized person. For Maslow a hierarchy of needs is central to self-esteem. There are two categories of esteem needs: the need for strength and mastery, and the need for prestige, status, and recognition. When these needs converge and are met the person experiences self-actualization. For Horney (the psychoanalyst) and Coopersmith (the social psychologist), self-esteem is directly affected by the approval the person receives from parents. Positive parental attention is regarded as an antecedent to one's self-esteem. 'Self-acceptance' refers to liking or respecting one's self. Persons who self-actualize like themselves. 'Self-disclosure' (the process by which the person reveals private information to another) is seen as being central to an understanding of interpersonal relationships. Such relationships are based on the mutual sharing of personal information about the self. There is no clear-cut evidence concerning what kind of person is more likely to self-disclose. Self-disclosure appears to be a situational phenomenon.

2.2 Psychoanalytic Formulations

In psychoanalytic thought (Freud, Erikson, Sullivan, Kohut) the concept of identity is regarded as a critical component of ego strength and ego development. For theorists like Erikson, personal identity refers to the continuity of self despite developmental or environmental changes. For Erikson, one's identity is an integration of all previous identifications and self-images. In his eight-stage theory of ego (psychosocial) development, specific identity crises throughout the life cycle are experienced. These involve identity change, achievement, and diffusion around the following areas: trust and mistrust, autonomy and doubt, initiative versus guilt, industry versus inferiority, intimacy versus isolation, generativity versus self-absorption, integrity versus despair, and purpose versus meaninglessness. In Erikson's theory identity crises are built into the life cycle, but they are especially critical during adolescence.

2.3 Social Psychological Formulations

In this book on stigma Erving Goffman offers a slightly different view of identity. He distnguishes 'self-identity' (how the person establishes a personal identity through documentation) from 'social' and 'personal identity,' which he contrasts to Erikson's concepts of 'ego' or 'felt' identity. For Goffman 'ego identity' is a subjective, reflexive matter, that must be felt by the individual. 'Social identity' refers to how the person is defined by others (e.g., alcoholic). The 'personal identity' describes how the individual handles these definitions that come from others.

The symbolic interactionist social psychologists Gregory P. Stone and Anselm L. Strauss take a less complicated view of identity. For them (like Kuhn) identities are social categories (e.g., male, female, professor, etc.), through which people may be located and given meaning in some situation. When one has an identity he is situated—that is cast in the shape of a social object by the acknowledgment of his participation in a social relationship. Identities are created in social situations, by interacting individuals who are in some relationship with one another. According to Gregory P. Stone, these relationships are of two types: structural and interpersonal. A structural relationship is anchored in an institution where a person exchanges a name for a title and a position. In interpersonal relations persons exchange only names, or nicknames.

3. The Symbolic Interactionist Conception of Self

The concept of self has a long tradition within the school of thought known as symbolic interactionism (see *Symbolic Interactionism*), starting with William James, and moving through the works of Charles Horton Cooley, George Herbert Mead (see *Mead, George Herbert*), Herbert Blumer (see *Blumer, Herbert*), Manford Kuhn, Erving Goffman (see *Goffman, Erving*), Anselm Strauss, and Gregory P. Stone.

3.1 William James (1842–1910)

As noted above James distinguished between the 'empirical self,' or the 'self as known,' and the 'self as knower,' otherwise called the '*me*,' and the '*I*.' The '*I*,' or self as knower, is given in consciousness. It is always changing. However, for James, it is connected to my personal identity, so that my thoughts about myself have a constant reference back to me. For James a person is the sum total of all he can call his, not only his body and his psychic powers, but his clothes, and his house, his wife and his children, his ancestors and friends, and his reputation. The social me is the recognition which the person gets from others. Persons have as many social selves as there are individuals who recognize them and carry an image of them in their mind. Persons have as many different social selves as there are distinct groups of persons about whose opinion they care. Self-feeling and self-esteem depend on the ratio of our successes over our pretensions.

3.2 Charles Horton Cooley (1864–1929)

The looking-glass concept of the self is commonly attributed to Charles Horton Cooley who, in elaborating on William James's discussion of the social self, suggested that a reflected self arises when individuals appropriate a self-feeling on the basis of how they think they appear in the eye of the other. Cooley stated that 'A social self of this sort might be called the reflected or looking-glass self: 'Each to each a looking-glass, reflects the other that doth pass' (Cooley 1956: 184).

While Cooley is credited with the looking-glass conception of the self, its appearance in the literature may be traced to the works of Adam Smith, who, in the *Theory of Moral Sentiments* (1792) stated: 'We examine our persons limb by limb, and by placing ourselves before a looking-glass, or by some expedient, endeavor, as much as possible to view ourselves at the distance and with the eyes of the other' (1792: 162).

The metaphor of the looking-glass carries a double meaning in Smith's and Cooley's formulations. In everyday life, persons see their faces, figures and dress in the glass, and are, as Cooley argues, 'interested in them because they are ours, and pleased or otherwise with them according as they do or do not answer to what we should like them to be.' The other becomes the mirror to the self. Their interpretation of us is given in their gestures, their facial expressions, and their statements. Anselm Strauss has captured this relationship in the title of his essay on identity, *Mirrors and Masks*.

The self-idea that incorporates self-feeling, according to Smith and Cooley, has three principal components: the imagination of the person's appearance to other persons, the imagination of the other's judgment of that appearance, and some sort of self-feeling, such as pride or mortification.

This self-feeling is appropriated on the basis of the imagined judgment of the other. This imputed or internalized sentiment, taken from the other, and directed inward to the self, moves the individual to action.

The basic structure of this self-feeling is threefold, involving (a) a feeling for one's self, (b) a feeling of this feeling, and (c) a revealing of the moral self through this feeling. The feeling person feels the self in emotion. Self-feeling thus becomes central to an understanding of the empirical social self (the self as known), as well as the self as knower.

Cooley elaborated the looking-glass self comment in a brief comment on 'On a remark of Dr. Holmes.' He suggested that 'six persons take part in every conversation between John and Thomas.' There is the real John, John's ideal John (never the real John), and Thomas's ideal John, and there are three Thomasses. In everyday life the matter is more complicated. Twelve persons participate in every interaction, six on each side. For example, Alice, who has a new hat, meets Angela, who has a new dress. In this situation, there is the real Alice, Alice's idea of herself in her new hat, her idea of Angela's judgment of her new hat, her idea of what Angela thinks she thinks of her new hat. Also, there is Angela's actual idea of Alice, Angela's idea of what Alice thinks of herself, and six analogous phases of Angela and her dress.

Self-feelings move through these imputed and imagined reactions of each interactant to the other's real and imagined judgments of their social selves. Every interaction is thus peopled by many selves, and there are always more persons (selves) present in a situation than there are real bodies. The strength of Cooley's formulation lies in its emphasis on the multiplicity of definitions, feelings, and meanings that arise in any situation when two persons come together for interaction.

The looking-glass self-concept is basic to the symbolic interactionist theory of interaction and remains central to current social psychological theorizing on the social self and emotion. The centrality of the self and of self-processes in the study of emotional feeling and emotional expressions is pivotal in current neuropsychological formulations of emotion. Cooley's concepts of self-feeling and the looking-glass self warrant reexamination in light of this fact.

3.3 George Herbert Mead (1863–1931)

Mead's theory of the self builds on, yet rejects, the formulations of Cooley and James. He argued that their versions of the self were solipsistic, subjective and based on an introspective model of inquiry that was not scientific. Mead regarded the self as dependent on language for its development. He saw it as arising in the context of social experience and social interaction. The word *self*, for Mead, is a reflexive, indicating that which is both subject and object. The self is that 'which can be an object to itself, and it is essentially a social structure.' A key to Mead's self is the process of self-consciousness, or the self carrying on an internal conversation with itself. In this conversation the self comes to direct its own behavior, thoughts and feelings through the reflected appraisals of others (the 'me'), and the more spontaneous responses of the self to these internalized responses (the 'I').

3.4 Gregory P. Stone (1921–80)

In *Appearance and the Self* Gregory P. Stone has offered perhaps the most sophisticated, if not the most inclusive interactionist conception of the self. His framework incorporates the formulations of James, Cooley, Mead, Blumer, Sullivan, Goffman, and Strauss. For Stone our appearance before others commands their gaze and produces reciprocal identification. The self, that is, is established, maintained, and altered in and through communication. Stone contends that every social transaction must be broken down into two analytic components, appearance and discourse. For him appearance is at least as important as discourse for the establishment of the self. In every interaction the person's appearance is reviewed by others, and judged by the person being evaluated in terms of a program. When programs and reviews coincide, the self is validated. When programs and reviews conflict, the self is challenged. Stone thus merges Mead, Cooley, and Sullivan. From Mead he argues that the self is a social object established by appearance. From Cooley and Sullivan, who underscore the importance of value ('reflected appraisals of others,' the good and bad me) and self-feeling, he takes the argument that the meaning of appearance consists of the establishment of identity, value, and mood. Value and mood are two key terms which qualify and define how identities (one's situated meaning) are established.

Stone fitted his model to the origins and development of the self in early childhood, building on Mead's play, game, generalized other theory (see *Mead, George Herbert*). The processes of discourse and appearance which structure the emergence of the self involve the following stages: preplay, play, and game. These three phases are organized by different discursive processes, and different types of conversation, dressing processes, and types of appearance. For example, the pre-play phase of selfhood involves: parental representations of infant babbling, Mead's conversation of gestures, Sullivan's prototaxic mode of communication, investiture as a dressing process, and modes of appearance that stress representations of the infant as a gendered being (e.g., blue and pink clothing). In the game phase, the child takes the attitude of the generalized other, speaks in socialized speech, dresses in and wears clothing shaped by peer-group influences.

The self, for Stone, is a multiclothed thing, a product of appearance and discourse. It is created and changed in and through communication, which involves discourse about appearance, as well as about talk itself.

3.5 Goffman's Gendered Self

In an article entitled 'The arrangement between the sexes' (1977), Erving Goffman (1922–82) offered a gendered theory of the self, which examined how the courtesy and courtship systems of modern societies produced gendered selves. Arguing that the gender identity is the deepest identity the person can hold, seeing it as the core of the self, Goffman described how genderisms (ways of doing gender) and the male and female gender subcultures of American society reproduce a sexual division of labor that makes women second-class citizens in public and private life. A system of reflexive institutional arrangements reproduces these gendered identities. These arrangements include toilet practices, differential job placement for men and women, gendered socialization functions in the household, the norms that govern attractive appearance for women,

and the courtship, marriage and courtesy rituals that underlie the interaction order (see *Goffman, Erving*).

4. Reflections on the Interactionist Self

There are three basic problems with the interactionist conception of the self. The first involves the 'I'–'me' formulation which extends from James through Stone. This may be termed the fallacy of the self as the center of interaction. The second problem points to the tendency of some interactionists to conceptualize the verbal person and the self as products of language. This is the linguistic fallacy. The third problem concerns the asexual nature of the interactionist self.

4.1 The Centering ('I'–'me') and Linguistic Fallacies

Interactionists have taken two basic views of the self. The first follows from James and Mead, who borrowed the concepts of the 'I' and the 'me' from Kant. These two concepts are simply posited, argued into existence, without empirical evidence. For Kant they functioned as a lever against the 'bundle of perceptions' theory of Hume. For Mead, who argued against James's theory of the stream of consciousness, the self became a structure that organized the flow of experience in terms of the social act. This conception of the self has been maintained, more or less without change, in all ineractionist theories of the self.

The second conception that is contained within the interactionist tradition is given by Perinbanayagam in his 1985 Book *Signifying Acts*. Here the self is a linguistic structure and the 'I' and the 'me' are seen as linguistic terms that are given in the language of the subject.

These two views of the self are incompatible. The self and its component structures are either in linguistic structures, in which case language speaks for the subject; or the 'I' and the 'me' have to be assumed to exist along side language, as primordial, deep structures of a struc ture called the self. The two views cannot be held simultaneously.

4.2 The Asexual Bias

This bias, or fallacy, charges that interactionists do not offer a fully gendered theory of the self. It builds on Lacan's observation that the individual enters language, in the 'mirror stage' as a sexed individual. The interactionist self in the theories of Mead, Blumer, Strauss, and Perinbanayagam are sexually neutral. Even Stone's gestures in the direction of appearance and gender fail to fully ground selfhood in the gendered meanings brought to sexuality and identity. Goffman's threefold theory of identity is genderless, but his essays on the gender stratification system do take into account how the courtesy and courtship systems of contemporary cultures produce gendered, sexual beings.

What is absent, is a fundamental rethinking of the linguistic and interactional structures of the self and their connections to language. If males and females enter language as gendered beings, as Lacan claims, then the origins of gender, which is basic to selfhood, lie in language. This is a fertile area for interactionist research.

5. The Future of the Self

The interactionist view of the self, despite its problems, remains the most fruitful theory of human agency. How to make sense of the human reflexive ability to be both a subject and an object to itself remains a problem which no theory can afford to ignore. A concept of self will always be present in social theory, even when it is negated.

See also: Social Psychology; Sociology in Language; Symbolic Interactionism.

Bibliography

Cooley C H 1956 *Human Nature and the Social Order*. The Free Press, Glencoe, IL
Goffman E 1959 *The Presentation of Self in Everyday Life*. Doubleday, Garden City, NY
James W 1890 *The Principles of Psychology*. Holt, New York
Mead G H 1934 *Mind, Self, and Society*. University of Chicago Press, Chicago, IL
Perinbanayagam R 1985 *Signifying Acts*. Southern Illinois University Press, Carbondale, IL
Sartre J-P 1956 *Being and Nothingness*. Philosophical Library, New York
Stone G P 1981 Appearance and the self: A slightly revised version. In: *Social Psychology Through Symbolic Interaction*, 2nd edn. John Wiley, New York

N. K. Denzin

Semantic Categories: Morphological Encoding

There seem to be scarcely any limits to the semantic categories that can be encoded morphologically. At the same time it is clearly the case that some categories are more frequently encoded morphologically than others. It can never be assumed, however, that any particular category will be encoded at all in a given language, far less that it will be encoded morphologically. All of the categories discussed below may be encoded lexically (by the use of a different word) or syntactically in other languages.

Categories of aspect, case, mood, number, person, tense, etc., which are very general in their application, are frequently encoded in inflectional morphology. But even if such categories are encoded morphologically, it cannot be assumed that they will be encoded inflectionally: Diyari, for instance, is reported as a language in which plurality is a derivational category (see *Inflection and Derivation*).

Typical derivational categories are those which derive one part of speech from another: nouns from verbs and adjectives, verbs from nouns and adjectives, adjectives from nouns and verbs or, less commonly, other parts of speech from one of these three. It is normally the case that there is not just one possible derivative in all of these categories, and not all languages will necessarily have formal means of changing part of speech in this way. Consider, for example, the nouns that can be derived from the verb *admit*: *admitter, admittee, admission, admittance*. (For cases where there is no formal marker of change of status, see *Conversion*; and the case of isolating languages is discussed in *Morphology, Categorial*.) It is also normal to be able to derive one class of adjective, noun, or verb from another; consider English *blu+ish*, *king+dom* and French *mord+ill+er* 'nibble' from *mord+re* 'to bite.' Where verbs are concerned, causatives, reflexives, frequentatives, and affixes which make transitive verbs intransitive and vice

versa are frequent categories across languages. These categories may be represented inflectionally rather than derivationally.

The boundaries between inflection and derivation are not clear, nor constant over time (see *Inflection and Derivation*). For example, affective categories such as diminutives and augmentatives are interesting in that they are frequently coded on the borderline between inflection and derivation. They are derivational in some languages, inflectional in others, and in some languages, like older German, the affixes marking them are ordered in unexpected ways, so that in *Kind+er+chen* child+PL+DIM, 'small children' inflectional plurality is marked closer to the root than derivational diminutive.

If the categories discussed as typically inflectional and typically derivational above provide the kernel of morphological categories, the periphery is far less clear. A few examples should make the point. Mangarayi has suffixes to denote the focal member of a group, to denote the place of death of specified relatives, and to denote that the object suffixed is the unique member of its class. Imbabura Quechua has a suffix which is deprecative, and another which is limitative (i.e., equivalent to English *only*). It also has a verbal suffix which indicates that the action is carried out to excess. While speakers of Indo–European languages are familiar with markers for feminine gender, as in *tigr+ess*, Abkhaz has a marker of masculine gender as in *à+c°+aγ* 'bull' (literally: 'male cow'). Kusaiean has an affix which means 'to wear the object in the base,' so that *susu+yang* 'to wear a hat' is derived from *susu* 'a hat,' and another suffix to mean 'to become infested with the object in the base.' In Turkana there is a suffix to mark whether the motion expressed in the verb is towards the speaker or away from the speaker. In Kiowa it is obligatory to mark by a prefix whether or not the object of the verb is a dual (as in *to clap hands*, for example). West Greenlandic, which is a polysynthetic language, has over 400 affixes the meanings of a few of which are given here: previous/discarded; smell of; previously owned; the sound of (some action); mutual or in a converse relation (as in *they are friends*). A number of languages have affixes for marking the degree of responsibility the speaker takes for the accuracy of the events reported, equivalent to 'I saw it with my own eyes,' 'someone once told me,' and so on.

In summary, then, what is viewed as a nameable category in any language, or what is viewed as a category which is general enough to require an affix to denote it, is a culturally determined feature, not a linguistically determined one. Language simply provides the means of denoting the culturally determined categories, and, while some generalizations can be made, these vary enormously from language to language.

See also: Sapir–Whorf Hypothesis; Morphological Universals.

Bibliography

Bybee, J L 1985 *Morphology: A Study of the Relation between Meaning and Form*. John Benjamins, Amsterdam

L. Bauer

Semantic Change, Laws of

Regular patterns in the semantic development of natural language expressions are sometimes called 'laws of semantic change.' Although the term 'law' calls up associations with the 'laws' of sound change, the notion of exceptionlessness as applied to the latter plays no role in diachronic semantics: it is standard knowledge that the laws of semantic change are mere tendencies that allow for exceptions, rather than strict rules. Research into the laws of semantic change involves showing that groups of words having a particular (set of) feature(s) in common undergo parallel semantic developments. The more specific the set of words that a particular type of change applies to, the less general is the type of change itself. A rough classification of three types of regular patterns of change can then be made on the basis of the specificity of the change involved.

At one extreme are the highly general mechanisms of change that are the traditional focus of diachronic semantics. Mechanisms of semantic change such as metaphor, metonymy, specialization, and generalization rate low on the specificity scale, in the sense that they would seem to be applicable to any word whatsoever. They are not, however, without imposing restrictions on possible changes: postulating a particular set of mechanisms embodies the prediction that semantic changes will predominantly take the form of one of the mechanisms (or, conversely, that semantic changes not conforming to the mechanisms are implausible). Moreover, the general mechanisms can be made more specific (and hence, more restrictive) by identifying subtypes (see, for example, *Metonymy*, where the subclassification of metonymical transfers is discussed).

At the other extreme are changes that apply to the members of restricted lexical fields. The most famous illustration of the hypothesis that semantically related words may undergo parallel changes is Gustav Stern's study of words meaning 'rapidly' in Old and Middle English (1931). Although there are clear chronological differences between the moments when the various words enter the next stage of their semantic development, all words exhibit the same developmental pattern: starting from the phase in which they mean 'rapidly,' they shift towards the meaning 'immediately' through an intermediate stage in which both senses are simultaneously present. (Words meaning 'rapidly' that are incorporated into English after 1400 do not exhibit the shift.) Other examples of parallel developments in relatively specific lexical fields will be found in Lehrer (1985).

Somewhere in between general mechanisms such as metaphor and metonymy, and very specific developments such as those illustrated by Stern, those developmental patterns should be situated that affect the members of large lexical sets. (The distinction between the degrees of specificity of developmental patterns is obviously a gradable one.) At stake here are longitudinal developments within broadly defined lexical sets such as spatial terms, temporal expressions, or words denoting sense experiences. It has been shown, for example, that words denoting tactile sensory experiences regularly develop a meaning connected with tasting rather than touching (*sharp*, *crisp*); they may further extend towards emotions, as in the word *feeling* itself (Williams 1976; Sweetser 1990). Similarly, spatial terms may become temporal terms (*before*, *after*), grammatical relation markers (*by* as a passive marker), connectives (*anyway*,

thereby), and speech act verbs (*to put forward*) (see Traugott 1985).

It is on this third, intermediate type of semantic regularity that late twentieth-century research on the laws of semantic change focuses. As can be inferred from the spatial examples, this kind of research overlaps with the research on grammaticalization (i.e., the development of grammatical morphemes from open class words).

See also: Historical Semantics; Metonymy; Metaphor; Semantic Specialization and Generalization; Non-denotational Semantic Change; Lexicon Grammar: Application to French.

Bibliography

Lehrer A 1985 The influence of semantic fields on semantic change. In: Fisiak J (ed.) *Historical Semantics—Historical Word-formation*. Mouton, Berlin

Stern G 1931 *Meaning and Change of Meaning*. Elanders Boktrycker, Aktiebolag, Gothenburg

Sweetser E 1990 *From Etymology to Pragmatics*. Cambridge University Press, Cambridge

Traugott E C 1985 On regularity in semantic change. *Journal of Literary Semantics* **14**: 155–73

Williams J M 1976 Synaesthetic adjectives: A possible law of semantic change. *Lg* **52**: 461–78

D. Geeraerts

Semantic Differential

A widely used survey research technique, developed at the University of Illinois by Charles Osgood and his associates, the semantic differential asks respondents to judge words or other stimuli along a number of scales between paired-opposite concepts. Statistical analysis of the data reveals underlying dimensions of meaning, each reflected in several of the scales. When the stimuli are words, the resultant quantitative measurements can be said to provide valid definitions of their meanings, even though they do not at all resemble the definitions found in dictionaries.

1. The Measurement of Meaning

For example, if one were trying to determine the meaning linguistics, as a scholarly field, held for university students. A questionnaire would be made up, including a section where students were instructed to judge 'linguistics' against a number of bipolar scales, such as the following:

happy	1	2	3	4	5	6	7	sad
hard	1	2	3	4	5	6	7	soft
slow	1	2	3	4	5	6	7	fast

The respondent would circle a number, 1 through 7, for each of the pairs of opposites, to indicate where linguistics seemed to lie between them, even though many of the terms seem to have little to do with the scholarly discipline of language research. The questionnaire would include similar sections, using the same set of bipolar scales, for which the stimuli might be other academic fields. Once data from a few dozen university students was obtained, mathematical techniques like factor analysis would be used to identify the dimensions of meaning in the concept *linguistics* and to compare them with similar analyses of the other academic fields in the survey.

When this technique was first described, it was said to achieve 'the measurement of meaning.' Criticism from scholars in linguistics and other fields led Osgood to narrow the claimed scope of the semantic differential to measurement of 'connotation' or 'affective meaning.' Indeed, the same three dimensions seemed to emerge again and again, regardless of what concepts were being judged or who was doing the judging, so the technique clearly misses many aspects of word meaning.

The first dimension revealed by the semantic differential was 'evaluation,' represented by such scales as *good–bad*, *beautiful–ugly*, *true–false*, and *kind–cruel*. A 'potency' dimension emerged in such distinctions as *hard–soft*, *strong–weak*, *heavy–light*, and *masculine–feminine*. And an '*activity*' factor revealed itself in scales like *fast–slow*, *active–passive*, and *excitable–calm*. Although Osgood's team was able to find other dimensions, using statistical techniques like partial correlations to remove the influence of the first three dimensions, this triad of general concepts dominates semantic differential analysis. Despite this limitation, the technique can achieve very fine discriminations between stimulus concepts, mapping them as points in a three-dimensional semantic space.

Clearly, much depends on the set of polar opposites chosen as the measuring scales, and Osgood went to great lengths to develop methods of creating linguistically unbiased scales. Early in the research, his team extracted 289 adjective pairs from Roget's *Thesaurus*, considering this reference work to be an objective source of the major concepts used in English. Research on clarity and conceptual overlap employed students in writing classes to winnow this excessively long list down to 76, the largest number that could be handled by the computers of the time. Next, 100 college undergraduates judged 20 concepts in terms of these 76 scales, a laborious task in which each respondent made 1,520 judgments. Finally, statistical factor analysis of this huge mass of data found the three dimensions of affective meaning and identified a subset of scales that measured them most efficiently.

2. Theory and Research

Osgood argues that biological evolution may have shaped human beings to judge phenomena in terms of the three dimensions of evaluation, potency, and activity (Osgood 1976: 89). When confronted with something, the primitive human first needed to decide if it was good or bad. If an antelope jumps out, that is good. But if a saber-toothed tiger leaps out, that is bad. The second question is whether the thing is strong or weak, compared to the protohuman, for example, a tiger or a mosquito. Finally, it benefits the individual to know whether the thing is active or passive, such as a leaping tiger or a stagnant pool of quicksand. Once these three questions have been answered, the human can act quickly—escaping, attacking, ignoring, or doing whatever else is appropriate. Thus, the three semantic dimensions may be wired into our brains and built into our languages.

Among the research projects of greatest interest to linguistics was a study of the semantic effects of word combination (Osgood 1976: 60). Eight nouns were selected to cover a range of classes of persons (nurse, scientist, thug, prostitute, husband, comedian, imp, and secretary), and eight highly varied adjectives were picked to go with them (artistic, hairy, listless, average, sincere, shy, treacherous, and breezy). Semantic differential questionnaires were given to eight groups of subjects, with about 25 persons in each, varying the combinations of nouns and adjectives. On the same set of bipolar scales, respondents judged each of these 16 words and all 64 possible combinations of noun and adjective. The point was to determine the semantic distances separating an adjective–noun combination from each of its component words.

The theory employed by Osgood for this particular study held that one could predict the location of an adjective–noun combination in semantic space from knowledge of the locations of adjective and noun when they were given to respondents as separate stimuli. To be precise, the coordinates of the adjective–noun combination should be the average of the coordinates of the adjective and those of the noun. However, Osgood found that the adjective–noun pair was generally displaced in the direction of the adjective, suggesting that adjectives have more affective–semantic power than do nouns.

The grandest research project based on the semantic differential was a vast cross-cultural study performed in two dozen languages, from Arabic to Yoruba. Rather than merely translate Osgood's survey instrument from English into the various languages, an international team constructed fresh instruments in each language, following a lengthy and systematic procedure. First, scholars of all the languages developed a diverse list of 100 translation-equivalent substantives, nouns that seemed to have very similar meanings across languages. Then native speakers of each language suggested adjectives that might describe these nouns. Finally, sophisticated judges derived 50 pairs of opposites for each language from this material. The resultant semantic differential scales were believed to be unbiased and to describe a wide range of nouns of significance in human language. The three dimensions of affective meaning emerged in every language, although the scales measuring them differed significantly, and a vast body of semantic data was archived for analysis by scholars interested in cross-cultural research.

See also: Multidimensional Scaling; Social Psychology.

Bibliography

Osgood C E 1976 *Explorations in Semantic Space*. Mouton, The Hague
Osgood C E, Suci G J, Tannenbaum P H 1957 *The Measurement of Meaning*. University of Illinois Press, Urbana, IL
Osgood C E, May W H, Miron M S 1975 *Cross-Cultural Universals of Affective Meaning*. University of Illinois Press, Urbana, IL

W. S. Bainbridge

Semantic Interpretation in Natural Language Processing

Most computer applications in natural language processing, such as natural language interfaces to databases and knowledge bases, and systems that summarize texts, require the computer to act on the *meaning* of its input. 'Semantic interpretation' (sometimes called 'conceptual analysis') is the process of computationally determining the meaning of a text and constructing a representation of that meaning for use by the application program. This includes finding the meaning of individual words and phrases and determining the relationships between them. If there is ambiguity in any aspect of the utterance, the computer must decide which reading is the one that the speaker or writer intended. A 'semantic interpreter' is the part of a computer system for processing natural language that, in conjunction with a parser and other components, performs the task of constructing a representation of the meaning of its input.

1. Computational Representations of Meaning

Most theories of meaning (see *Meaning: Philosophical Theories*), if not all, ultimately take meanings or semantic objects to be nonlinguistic entities. But a computer can manipulate only symbols or numbers. However, such symbols can be regarded as a *representation* of meaning if they are related, implicitly or explicitly, to some theory of semantics; and, as most semantic theories include a notation for the entities that they posit, this notation can be used by the computer. For example, if Montague semantics were chosen (see *Montague Grammar*), the computer symbols could be thought of as equivalent to the textual notations that this theory uses to represent the semantic objects which it reifies, such as entities in the world and mathematical functions upon them. Thus, the symbol *g87* might serve to represent the set of cars in the world, and thus as an interpretation of the words *car, automobile, voiture*, etc. Alternatively, *g87* may be thought of as representing the *concept* of cars. (In practice, one would use a mnemonic symbol such as *car* rather than *g87*; but it must be remembered that it is purely a symbol, and it gains nothing from the English word to which it is similar.) The grounding of the symbol in the actual set of cars occurs initially through the understanding of the programmer of the system, and, ultimately, through the operation of the system itself in its ability to respond correctly to utterances whose semantic representations make use of the symbol.

Viewed in this way, a computational representation of meaning can be seen to be effectively the same as a knowledge representation, as used in artificial intelligence (see *Knowledge Representation*). Knowledge representation formalisms, which are often first-order or higher-order logics, can express facts and propositions about concepts such as *g87* above, and are designed to permit various kinds of inference to be carried out on these propositions; the importance of this is that a computer system can therefore interpret natural language input into expressions in such a formalism and then reason about what it has been told by manipulating the expressions according to the rules of inference. However, not all knowledge representation formalisms are equally amenable to use in semantic interpretation (see Sect. 4). Moreover, no knowledge representation has yet been developed that has the full expressive power of natural language—that can express all the ideas that natural languages can; consequently, many sentences defy interpretation in any natural language computer system developed by the late twentieth century.

There are two main exceptions to this view that semantic formalisms can (or should) be reduced to knowledge representations for computational purposes. The first is in a method of semantic interpretation known as 'procedural semantics,' which is suitable primarily for systems in which a database is interrogated in natural language (see *Semantics, Procedural*). A knowledge representation per se is not used; rather, semantic interpretation is carried out by a series of rules that convert syntactic structures of the sentence directly into calls on procedures that interrogate the database; the substantive words of the input sentence are regarded as direct or indirect reflections of uninterpreted relations or values in the database. The second exception is in natural language computer systems that are based on artificial neural networks—a variety of connectionism in which representations are 'distributed' (see *Connectionist Approaches to Language Processing*). In such systems, meaning representations are implicit in the exact connections in the system, their relative strengths, and the state of the system at any given moment. In effect, meaning is stored 'holographically,' and no single element of the system represents a single meaning.

Thus, the 'meaning' that a semantic interpreter derives for a sentence is generally an expression in a logic or other kind of knowledge representation formalism. For example, in a very simple system, sentence (1) might be represented as the expression shown:

Nadia smeared honey on her cat.   (1)

```
(smear
(time = past)
(agent = Nadia)
(patient = honey indefinite)
(location = (surface (cat definite (owner = Nadia))))))
```

This expression, which uses mnemonic symbols for ease of exposition, may be glossed thus: 'There is a smearing that happened in the past, and the thing that did it was Nadia, the thing that got smeared was some unspecified honey, and the surface on which it was smeared was that of some particular cat that she owned.'

Such expressions, or semantic structures, are often called the 'logical form' of a sentence (see *Logical Form*). Exactly what is meant by that term varies widely, but the central idea is that the expression represents only a very literal interpretation of the sentence: the pragmatic effects of the context in which the sentence was uttered are not accounted for. These include: determining the presuppositions of the utterance; possibly interpreting it as an indirect speech act; anaphor resolution; comprehending any metaphor; and inferring the speaker or writer's larger goal or intent. (These tasks would normally be performed by subsequent processes; see *Reference and Anaphor Resolution in Natural Language Processing*; *Natural Language Processing: Planning and Plan Recognition*.)

2. Ambiguity Resolution in Semantic Interpretation

An integral part of semantic interpretation is the resolution of ambiguity (see *Ambiguity*) in the sentence, the assumption being that (except in the special case of word play or deliberate ambiguity) the utterer intended a single meaning. Kinds of ambiguity that must be considered include ambiguity of word sense, of sentence structure, of thematic relations, of quantifier scope, and of type of reference (i.e., whether a reference is intensional, extensional, or generic—see *Intensionality*; *Extensionality*; *Genericity*). Usually, the first three of these are resolved as an initial logical form is constructed; this form is then used and modified in the resolution of the other two.

Generally, each type of ambiguity requires a different method of resolution. Each, therefore, is handled by a separate process that works in conjunction with the semantic interpreter. Often, however, the ambiguities are interdependent, and so the semantic interpreter must coordinate the flow of information. For example, in the simple sentence *Fans cheer at rock stars*, each word is highly ambiguous, but each constrains the others to yield a single sensible reading (for a more detailed treatment of methods of ambiguity resolution, see *Disambiguation: Role of Knowledge*).

3. The Relationship between Semantic Interpretation and Parsing

It should be clear that semantic interpretation is quite different from parsing (see *Parsing Techniques*), which is the structural analysis of a sentence without regard to its meaning. Except in a few applications, such as authorship attribution (see *Stylometry*), where linguistic structure is the primary object of study, the goal of natural language processing is to use the meaning of the input, and parsing need take place only to the extent that it serves that goal. Some early systems, therefore, performed only a minimal structural analysis of their input (e.g., Riesbeck 1975). However, it has come to be recognized that an adequate semantic interpretation does require the information provided by a complete parse of the input (Marcus 1984). This is because, first, word order and syntactic relations contain much semantic information, and, second, syntactic relations often constrain the allowable semantic interpretations of a sentence, for example, by restricting the permissible attachment points for a modifying phrase or clause. (For that matter, syntactic relations also constrain the allowable pragmatic interpretations of a sentence, for example, the constraints placed by c-command on the antecedent of an anaphor; see *Reference and Anaphor Resolution in Natural Language Processing*.)

If parsing is to take place in support of semantic interpretation, the two activities must be coordinated. In some early systems, a complete parse was produced before any semantic analysis took place. This proved to be unsatisfactory. First, it is contrary to human methods of understanding, where it is clear that people begin semantic analysis of the first part of an utterance without waiting for its end. Second, most sentences admit more than one parse, and determining the one intended by the speaker requires consideration of the meaning of the sentence (see *Disambiguation: Role of Knowledge*). But to consider the meaning, one must determine the parse! To resolve this stand-off, most systems perform the two activities simultaneously, coordinating the flow of information between them. The exact nature of the coordination varies widely, but the general idea is that the parser will determine various analyses of the sentence that are consistent with the grammar of the language, and the semantic interpreter will then choose among them.

4. Methods of Semantic Interpretation

Most theories of semantics are by and large 'compositional'; that is, the meanings of individual words are used in a systematic way to build the meanings of phrases and, eventually, that of the complete sentence (see *Compositionality of Meaning*). Computational systems mostly follow this general approach.

This requires that the system have a lexicon (see *Lexicon*) that lists, as expressions in the knowledge representation formalism that it uses, the meaning or meanings of each word that the system knows. The representation of a word may be a single symbol, as in the *g87* example above, or it may be a more complex structure into which the meaning of other words is to be fitted. The latter case may occur in particular with verbs; for example, *smear* in example (1) above might have the entry shown in (2), in which each '?' represents a slot into which the meanings of other parts of the sentence will go (see *Case Grammar*).

$$(smear \qquad\qquad (2)$$
$$(time = ?)$$
$$(agent = ?)$$
$$(patient = ?)$$
$$(location = ?))$$

Under the direction of the parser, the semantic interpreter combines the representations of meanings of individual words to create those for phrases, which, in turn, are combined eventually to create that of the sentence. For example, suppose that the parser has determined that the group of words *her cat* is a noun phrase consisting of a determiner and a noun. The meaning representations for each word are found in the lexicon; suppose that they are respectively '(? definite (owner = ?))' and 'cat.' They are then combined in the manner appropriate to their forms, yielding the representation of the meaning of the noun phrase, '(cat definite (owner = ?)).' This representation can then be used in forming that for the prepositional phrase *on her cat*. (Anaphor resolution would subsequently determine the referent of *her*, and replace the '?'; see *Reference and Anaphor Resolution in Natural Language Processing*.)

In some systems, such as that of Hirst (1987) and most unification-based NLU systems, the relationship between the parser and the semantic interpreter is a strict lockstep: the parser decides which rule of grammar it will follow, and the semantic interpreter follows the corresponding semantic rule. Such systems are thus consistent with the 'rule-to-rule hypothesis' of semantic theories. A tacit assumption is that the semantic formalism chosen, the knowledge representation, is 'compositional'—that a representation of the meaning of a sentence can, in fact, be built in a systematic way from the representations of the meanings of the parts.

It is this process of construction of semantic expressions that is complicated by ambiguity. If the parser does not know which of several grammar rules to choose from, it may ask the semantic interpreter to decide by inspecting the semantic expressions built so far and determining which possibility is most plausible as the next move. If a word is ambiguous, the semantic interpreter will have to decide which of the several representations associated with the word is the most plausible in the context (for the techniques that a semantic interpreter may use to resolve each of these situations, see *Disambiguation: Role of Knowledge*).

See also: Natural Language Analysis; Semantics, Procedural; Disambiguation: Role of Knowledge.

Bibliography

Hirst G 1987 *Semantic Interpretation and the Resolution of Ambiguity*. Cambridge University Press, Cambridge

Marcus M P 1984 Some inadequate theories of human sentence processing. In: Bever T G, Carroll J M, Miller L A (eds.) *Talking Minds: The Study of Language in the Cognitive Sciences*. MIT Press, Cambridge, MA

Pollard C, Sag I A 1987 *Information-based Syntax and Semantics. Vol. 1: Fundamentals*. Center for the Study of Language and Information, Stanford, CA

Riesbeck C K 1975 Conceptual analysis. In: Schank R C (ed.) *Conceptual Information Processing*. North-Holland, Amsterdam

G. Hirst

Semantic Primitives

The semantic features used in componential definitions of meaning (see the article *Componential Analysis*) are sometimes called 'semantic primitives.' The background of this terminology is the reductionist character of componential definitions: word meanings are defined in terms of more simple and more basic semantic elements. Features, then, are the elementary building-blocks of definitions. They are not themselves words (in spite of the fact that they may be represented by means of forms like 'human' and 'male' that are quasi-identical with English words), but they belong to a 'definitional metalanguage' that does not coincide with the language to be defined. In that sense, the definitional features are not themselves defined, but they are given in the definitional metalanguage. Componential features, in short, are considered to be primitive in two ways: they are intuitively primitive in the sense that they are more basic than the concepts in the definition of which they occur; and they are primitive in the technical sense in which scientific theories contain undefined elements as a part of the formal language in which the theory is formulated.

1. The Motivation for Semantic Primitives

The advantage of having definitional elements that themselves remain undefined resides in the possibility of avoiding circularity: if the definitional language and the defined language are identical, words are ultimately defined in terms of themselves, in which case the explanatory value of definitions seems to disappear as a whole. More particularly, definitional circularity would seem to imply that it is impossible to step outside the realm of language and to explain how language is related to the world.

This motivation for having undefined primitive elements imposes an important restriction on the set of primitive features. In fact, if achieving noncircularity is the point, the set of primitives should be smaller than the set of words to be defined: there is no reductive or explanatory value in a set of undefined defining elements that is as large as the set of concepts to be defined. Furthermore, the idea was put forward that the restricted set of primitive features might be universal, just like in phonology. (As explained in the article *Componential Analysis*, the featural approach in semantics was inspired by phonological feature analysis.) This universality is not, however, a necessary consequence

of the primitive nature of features: the definitional set of features could well be language-specific.

2. The Elusiveness of Semantic Primitives

Except in the work of Anna Wierzbicka, there have been few systematic attempts in linguistics to define a restricted set of features (in Wierzbicka 1980, no more than 13 primitive concepts are used). Still, the primitive nature of features did play an important role in the discussion between a componential and an axiomatic, nondecompositional conception of semantic representation.

The debate then shifted towards the psychological question whether there was any evidence for the psychological reality of semantic decomposition (see *Lexical Semantics*; *Meaning Postulate*). In the course of the same process, the a priori justification of decomposition in terms of noncircularity lost its importance when it was realized that featural noncircularity did not really solve the question of how language could be related to the world. The appeal of noncircular definitions seemed to be that they could explain how the gap between linguistic meaning and extralinguistic reality is bridged: if determining whether a concept A applies to thing B entails checking whether the features that make up the definition of A apply to B as an extralinguistic entity, words are related to the world through the intermediary of primitive features. But obviously, this does not explain how the basic features themselves bridge the gap. More generally, the 'referential connection' problem for words remains unsolved as long as it is not solved for the primitives, and conversely, if the 'referential connection' problem could be solved for primitive features, the same solution might very well be applicable to words as a whole. So, if noncircularity does not as such solve the referential problem, decomposition is not a priori to be preferred over nondecompositional approaches, and psychological evidence for one or the other can be taken into account. The outcome of the psychological search, however, is that primitive semantic components are not likely to exist in the mental lexicon (see Aitchison 1987 for an overview of the discussion).

Bibliography

Aitchison J 1987 *Words in the Mind: An Introduction to the Mental Lexicon*. Blackwell, Oxford

Wierzbicka A 1980 *Lingua Mentalis: The Semantics of Natural Language*. Academic Press, New York, NY

D. Geeraerts

Semantic Specialization and Generalization

Semantic specialization and generalization are types of lexical–semantic change by means of which a lexical item develops a new meaning that stands in a relationship of, respectively, subordination or superordination to the older meaning (see *Hyponymy and Hyperonymy* for background of these terms). If the semantic range of application of an item is conceived of in set-theoretical terms, specialization implies that the range of application of the new meaning is a subset of the range of the old meaning. In the case of generalization, the new range includes the old one. Terminologically, 'restriction' and 'narrowing' mean 'specialization'; and 'expansion,' 'extension,' and 'broadening' mean 'generalization.'

Examples of specialization are *corn* (originally a coverterm for all kinds of grain, now specialized to 'wheat' in England, to 'oats' in Scotland, and to 'maize' in the USA) and *queen* (originally 'wife, woman,' now restricted to 'king's wife or female sovereign'). Examples of generalization are *moon* (primarily the earth's satellite, but extended to any planet's satellite), and French *arriver* (which etymologically means 'to reach the river's shore, to come to the bank,' but which now signifies 'to reach a destination' in general). A comparison of the *moon* example and the *corn* example shows that the original meaning may either remain present or may disappear after the development of the new meaning.

It is quite common for specialization and generalization to go hand in hand with social factors. For instance, specialization regularly originates in specific social or professional circles. Thus, the Dutch word *drukken* 'to press, to push hard' acquired the specialized meaning 'to print' in the context of the (older) printing office. Conversely, generalization may signal the spreading of a term outside of its original, technically restricted domain. For instance, the generalization of *arriver* is said to have involved its spread from the language of boatmen and sailors to the general vocabulary. Other social factors than the relationship between technical and general vocabulary may also play a role. When, for instance, *to drink* specializes to 'to drink alcohol habitually and excessively,' the crucial factor is euphemism.

See also: Historical Semantics.

Bibliography

Sappan R 1987 *The Rhetorical–Logical Classification of Semantic Changes*. Merlin Books, Braunton
Ullmann S 1962 *Semantics: An introduction to the science of meaning*. Blackwell, Oxford

D. Geeraerts

Semantics, Procedural

Since ancient times, philosophers have grappled with the concept of meaning in language. With the advent of language-processing computer programs, these issues have taken on a new perspective that has both enlightened age-old philosophical questions and given them a new, practical relevance. The term 'procedural semantics' refers to a theory in which the meanings of sentences are grounded in abstract procedures that combine symbolic reasoning operations with a potential for direct sensory–motor interaction with the physical world. This theory not only suggests a way to address the philosophical dilemma of the mind–body problem, but also provides some practical and sound engineering techniques for constructing systems that reason about the contents of computer databases.

The term 'procedural semantics' was first used by Woods (1968) to describe a general method for characterizing sentence meanings for computer systems that understand and answer natural-language questions. The method consists of interpreting the meanings of sentences in terms of abstract procedures for determining referents, verifying facts, computing values, and carrying out actions. In this methodology, procedures are used both for characterizing the truth conditions of statements and for procedurally answering questions and carrying out actions. Previous approaches to natural-language question-answering had treated the meanings of sentences primarily as structures to be matched against a database.

This engineering use of procedural semantics permits a computer to understand, in a single, uniform way, the 'meanings' of conditions to be tested, questions to be answered, and actions to be carried out. By identifying the meanings of sentences with procedures that might be carried out, rather than with structures to be matched, procedural semantics permits a general-purpose language-understanding system to be used with different databases that may have different representational conventions and different data structures. The procedural framework can handle questions whose answers require coordinated use of several databases at once, and can even accommodate questions whose answers would involve testing physical parameters in the real world. For example, a question such as *How many bolts are left?* might be answered by counting bolts in a bin using physical sensors and manipulators.

The first major demonstration of procedural semantics, in this engineering sense, was the LUNAR system (Woods 1973; Woods, et al. 1972), developed for NASA to answer natural-language questions about the Apollo 11 moon rocks. In LUNAR, an English question is translated into an expression in a formal meaning-representation language that is a procedural extension of a predicate calculus with typed quantifiers. In this system, quantifiers are treated as abstract procedures that can successively bind variables to members of a class and then evaluate conditions and carry out actions in the context of those bindings. For example, the sentence *Which samples contain silicon?* translates into an abstract procedure expressed roughly as:

```
(FOR EVERY X15 / (SEQ SAMPLES) SUCH-THAT
  (CONTAIN X15 (QUOTE SIO2) (QUOTE NIL));
  (PRINTOUT! X15))
```

where (SEQ SAMPLES) represents a class over which the quantified variable X15 is to range and is defined by a procedure that will enumerate the lunar samples known to the system. The database access is defined by a procedure CONTAIN that tests whether a sample contains a chemical in a specified part of the sample—in this case, whether X15 contains SIO2 (silicon dioxide) in any part. The action (PRINTOUT! X15) is a procedure that will print out the result. More complex examples include procedures for computing averages, ratios, and unions of sets.

The general format for LUNAR's quantifiers is:

```
(FOR: ⟨quant⟩⟨variable⟩ / ⟨class⟩
  SUCH-THAT ⟨condition⟩; ⟨expression⟩)
```

where ⟨quant⟩ is a quantifier such as EVERY, SOME, or THE; ⟨variable⟩ is the variable to be quantified; ⟨class⟩ is the class over which quantification is to range; ⟨condition⟩ is a further restriction on the range of quantification; and ⟨expression⟩ is the expression being quantified, which may be either a condition to be tested or an action to be carried out. This notation, while procedurally defined, is also a direct extension to traditional predicate calculus notations of formal logic and, as such, can be manipulated by formal reasoning systems such as deductive theorem-provers (see *Predicate Calculus*). This gives rise to two distinct kinds of inference in systems such as LUNAR: extensional inference, in which the elements of a class are enumerated and tested individually; and intensional inference, in which symbolic expressions are manipulated by formal reasoning techniques to see if, for example, some axiom implies that all samples contain silicon.

In a somewhat different sense of the term, Winograd (1971, 1973) used the term 'procedural' to describe a methodology for parsing and interpreting natural-language sentences using procedures. Winograd advocated the use of procedures written in a backtracking programming language as an alternative to formal grammars and semantic interpretation rules. This goal is in contrast to that of Woods, whose objective was to provide a semantics for the notation in which semantic interpretations are expressed. These two uses of the term 'procedural semantics' are quite different and have each generated their own controversies. A third use of the term that combines elements of the two objectives was used by Levesque and Mylopoulos (1979) in specifying a semantics for a semantic network.

Shortly after Winograd's thesis, a controversy arose about the use of notations that are overtly procedural (like Winograd's) as opposed to using so-called 'declarative' representations which have their basis in formal logic. Winograd (1975) provides an overview of some of the debate. A fundamental issue in this debate, although not generally explicit, is an attempt to articulate the advantages of having an abstraction in which the essence of a phenomenon can be expressed without an unnecessary commitment to nonessential details of an implementation. This debate is ongoing in the early 1990s, and the term 'declarative' is still used to describe representations that can be viewed in terms of what they say or assert rather than in terms of the details of the computations that they will cause.

While the advocates of declarative semantics were opposed to Winograd's overtly procedural specifications, Woods argued that the meanings of even declarative representations are fundamentally procedural. For example, the semantic representations used in the LUNAR system are formal extensions of the predicate calculus that could easily qualify as declarative representations. However, in characterizing their meanings, Woods pointed out that the traditional mechanisms of formal logic all derive their meaning from a kind of abstract computation. For example, the logical operations of AND, OR, and IF-THEN derive their meanings from rules for assigning truth values to complex sentences as a function of the truth values of their constituents. Similarly, the operations FOR-EACH and THERE-IS derive their meanings from rules for assigning truth values to universally and existentially quantified sentences. Thus, one can interpret expressions in a formal logic as expressing a kind of abstract procedure for determining truth values.

Woods made the point that from a procedural perspective, traditional logical notations can be generalized to account for a more diverse range of phenomena. In particular, procedures can formalize the meanings of actions that have causal interaction with the physical world (such as controlling a robot vehicle). Viewed as abstract procedures, the mechanisms of formal logic can be extended to deal with interrogative and imperative sentences, while traditional logic deals only with declarative propositions. Moreover, generalizations of the traditional universal and existential quantification can be defined as abstract procedures, allowing appropriate interpretations for such things as the definite determiner *the* and quantifiers such as *most* and *many*. Within this framework, a powerful range of quantificational operators has been developed, including operators for finding antecedents of pronouns and general counting, filtering, and averaging operators (Woods 1978).

From this overall perspective, work in procedural semantics splits into two distinct areas of focus: (a) a body of engineering techniques for efficient implementation of computer systems that understand natural language; and (b) a philosophical search for a theory of meaning capable of accounting for the way in which meaning is embodied in language and thought. The former has produced powerful techniques for building natural-language interfaces (Woods 1968–78; Woods, et al. 1972) and has stimulated related research such as the query optimization work of Reiter (1977), and the theory of anaphoric reference of Webber (1979). The philosophical perspective is embodied in a series of articles (Woods 1979–87) that address the more subtle problems of developing an adequate theory of meaning.

As a semantic theory, procedural semantics attempts to provide a foundation for the concept of meaning that deals adequately with the causal connections that relate internal representations and logical formalisms to objective situations in the world. It postulates that the meanings of representations reside in abstract procedures that could in principle be invoked to manipulate combinations of internal representations and (through the sensory motor system) physical objects in the external world. This requires procedures that are abstract in the sense that they do not express undesired commitment to implementation details (Woods 1981, 1986), but which, unlike arbitrary mappings from possible worlds into truth values, can be finitely represented and used by a person or a computer system. Procedural semantics builds on the insight from the theory of computation that infinite classes of objects can be finitely characterized by abstract automata that recognize or generate instances of the class.

Procedural semantics as a theory of meaning (as opposed to a computational technique) has produced its own controversies—most notably a colorful broadside by Fodor (1978), apparently aimed at all proponents of anything 'procedural,' and an equally entertaining riposte by Johnson-Laird (1978). Hadley (1989), provides a reasoned argument against Fodor's position, demonstrating the necessity for a procedural foundation for logical representations, and he extends the theory to incorporate default reasoning. In a series of refinements to the basic theory, Woods (1981, 1986, 1987) makes a distinction between the external language that one uses to communicate and the internal language/notation/representation with which one reasons and within which one interprets the meanings of utterances. The internal language needs a semantic foundation, and it is this problem that Woods addresses through the use of a concept of abstract procedure.

Woods (1987) distinguishes between two kinds of semantics for expressions, both of which can be characterized by abstract procedures: an operational semantics, in which an expression means what it causes to happen; and a criterial semantics, in which an expression means what it claims about the world. Some expressions may have an operational meaning while other expressions must have a criterial meaning. For example, an explicitly mental action such as *remember that red things are hot* might be defined by an operational semantics that determines how the memory is to be modified. On the other hand, the embedded claim that *red things are hot* should have a criterial semantics that can be used to test whether the claim is valid and/or to recognize violations of the claim when they are encountered.

A somewhat similar distinction is made in the PROLOG community (Kowalski 1979; Przymusinski 1989); between 'declarative' and 'procedural' interpretations of PROLOG programs, where the 'declarative' interpretation is effectively a rule (i.e., a criterion) for deciding when a proposition is true, while the 'procedural' interpretation represents a specification of behavior to be carried out. Both interpretations are highly procedural, however, so the 'criterial'/ 'operational' terminology introduced above seems to express the important issue more directly.

For expressions used to record hypotheses about the world, criterial semantics are of fundamental importance. Without distinguishing the operational procedures that draw conclusions and record facts from the procedures that define the meaning criteria for those conclusions, it is not possible to interpret conclusions as making claims or predictions about the world beyond the data actually examined to deduce them. Without such a distinction, it is not possible to learn improved models of reality by making predictions, detecting counter examples, and altering one's models accordingly.

Bibliography

Fodor J A 1978 Tom Swift and his procedural grandmother. *Cognition* 6: 229–47

Hadley R F 1989 A default-oriented theory of procedural semantics. *Cognitive Science* 13(1): 107–37

Johnson-Laird P N 1978 What's wrong with Grandma's guide to procedural semantics: A reply to Jerry Fodor. *Cognition* 6: 249–61

Kowalski R 1979 *Logic for Problem Solving*. North-Holland, New York

Levesque H J, Mylopoulos J 1979 A procedural semantics for semantic networks. In: Findler N V (ed.) *Associative Networks*. Academic Press, New York

Przymusinski T S 1989 On the declarative and procedural semantics of logic programs. *Journal of Automated Reasoning* 5(2): 167–206

Reiter R 1977 *An Approach to Deductive Question-Answering*, Report 36499. Bolt Beranek and Newman, Cambridge, MA

Webber B L 1979 *A Formal Approach to Discourse Anaphora*. Garland, New York

Winograd T 1971 Procedures as a representation for data in a computer program for understanding natural language (Doctoral dissertation, Massachusetts Institute of Technology)

Winograd T 1973 A procedural model of language understanding. In: Schank R C, Colby K M (eds.) *Computer Models of Thought and Language*. Freeman, San Francisco, CA

Winograd T 1975 Frame representations and the declarative procedural controversy. In: Bobrow D G, Collins A M (eds.)

Representation and Understanding: Studies in Cognitive Science. Academic Press, New York

Woods W A 1968 Procedural semantics for a question-answering machine. In: *AFIPS Conference Proceedings, Fall Joint Computer Conference*. ARFIPS Press, Montvale, NJ

Woods W A 1973 Progress in natural language understanding: An application to lunar geology. In: *AFIPS Conference Proceedings 42, 1973 National Computer Conference*. AFIPS Press, Montvale, NJ

Woods W A 1978 Semantics and quantification in natural language question-answering. In: *Advances in Computers*, vol. 17. Academic Press, New York

Woods W A 1979 *Semantics for a Question-Answering System*. Garland, New York

Woods W A 1981 Procedural semantics as a theory of meaning. In: Joshi A K, Webber B L, Sag I A (eds.) *Elements of Discourse Understanding*. Cambridge University Press, Cambridge

Woods W A 1983 Under what conditions can a machine use symbols with meaning? In: *Proceedings of the Eighth International Joint Conference on Artificial Intelligence (IJCAI83)*. William Kaufmann, Los Altos, CA

Woods W A 1986 Problems in procedural semantics. In: Pylyshyn Z, Demopoulos W (eds.) *Meaning and Cognitive Structure*. Ablex, Norwood, NJ

Woods W A 1987 Don't blame the tool. *Computational Intelligence* 3(3): 228–37

Woods W A, Kaplan R M, Nash-Webber B L 1972 *The Lunar Sciences Natural Language Information System: Final Report*, BBN Report 2378. Bolt Beranek and Newman, Cambridge, MA

W.A. Woods

Semantics versus Syntax: Shifting Perspectives on Natural Language Content

The period between 1972 and 1992 has been a period of an assumed dichotomy between syntactic and semantic forms of explanation. However, at the end of this period, the sharpness of the division is being questioned as problems of interpretation emerge that need structural solutions. As will be demonstrated, the resolution of this dichotomy involves an accompanying shift in assumptions about the language faculty itself.

In 1972, the battlelines between syntactic and semantic investigations into properties definitive of natural language were drawn up by Lewis (1972): semantics was announced to be the articulation of truth-theoretic content, and representational approaches to content were dismissed as 'markerese' with the comment that 'one might just as well translate into Latin.' These antimarkerese arguments were addressed against Katz's theory of semantic markers (cf. Katz 1972), but were taken as applying to any characterization of meaning which advocated meaning representations intermediate between syntactic explications of structure and the semantic objects which constitute the interpretation of that structure. Chomsky responded to this challenge with the retort (articulated in most detail in Chomsky 1986) that semantics was not part of any natural language grammar, hence *a fortiori* not definitive of the language faculty. These two positions became ideological stances, the Lewis approach to natural language understanding developed by those working in the Montague paradigm (Thomason

1974; Dowty 1979; Dowty, et al. 1981; Chierchia and McConnell-Ginet 1990), while the Chomskian concept of natural language developed into the 'government and binding paradigm' (Chomsky 1982; May 1985; Chomsky 1986).

A phenomenon which poses both sides of the divide with problems of equal severity (though recognized only within semantics, cf. Partee 1984b) is the phenomenon of context dependence. The information conveyed by natural language expressions varies from context to context, and the process whereby we as hearers establish such values involves processes of general reasoning. The simplest examples involve pronouns indexically used. Example (1) can be an assertion about Tom, Dick or Harry, depending on who is being talked about:

He is sick. (1)

By model-theoretic criteria, the sentence is ambiguous, having different interpretations as the referent varies. The phenomenon of multiple ambiguity is by no means restricted to such indexical uses. There is an array of different kinds of interpretation assigned to pronominal expressions, labeled variously as bound-variable pronouns, discourse coreference (Reinhart 1983, 1986), E-type pronouns (Evans 1980; Heim 1982), donkey-type pronouns (Kamp 1981; Heim 1982), and lazy pronouns (Karttunen 1968; Cooper 1979). All share the property that the interpretation of the pronoun is determined by some form of linkage with an antecedent, but the type of linkage varies, as does the type of model-theoretic content):

John came in. He was sick. (2)

Every student worries that she is going to fail. (3)

Joan worries that she's going to fail. (4)

Only a few students entered the exam, but they were confident they would pass. (5)

Every student who entered for an exam, passed it. (6)

Every student who puts her cheque in the building society is more sensible than the student who puts it in her current account. (7)

With model-theoretic assumptions underpinning the concept of linguistic content, the full set of pronominal uses is nonunitary. Such assumptions thus fail to provide a semantic basis for characterizing the information conveyed by a pronoun qua pronoun (there is a voluminous literature on the degree to which the heterogeneity of this phenomenon can be reduced, cf. Cooper 1979; Hausser 1979; Kamp 1981; Heim 1982; Kempson 1988; Heim 1990).

This proliferation of ambiguities is across the board. All anaphoric expressions depend for their interpretation on some concept of context of utterance giving rise to a range of truth-theoretically discrete types of meaning. Examples (8)–(17) display an array of VP, nominal, and demonstrative anaphoric dependencies, having in common only this property of dependency on their immediate surrounding context for assignment of some interpretation:

John likes Mary, but I don't. (8)

Everyone worries about their logic paper, except Marcelo, who never does. (9)

John kissed everyone that Sue didn't. (10)

Don't. (11)

Most students like Maths, but I know at least one who does not (12)

One will do. (13)

Jo telephoned a journalist every time Sue interviewed one. (14)

That man is a nuisance. (15)

She made a cake for John and that bastard never thanked her. (16)

Every time she had a coke, she knew that later that week, she'd have a headache. (17)

The phenomenon is not even restricted to explicitly anaphoric processes. It can apply to tense construal (Partee 1984b), to the interpretation of adjectives (Klein 1980), adverbs (Stump 1985), and so on. Indeed natural-language expressions, both simple and complex, are invariably construed relative to some unfolding concept of context. We seem faced with a multiplicity of ambiguities far beyond what any lexical sources of ambiguity would lead us to expect.

This phenomenon is additionally problematic for the Montague program, because it conflicts with a central cornerstone of the program—the compositionality principle. According to this principle, the meaning of any compound expression is recursively defined as a function of the meaning of its elementary parts. Indeed the force of model-theoretic semantics lies in large measure in the substance it provides to the claim that the truth-theoretic content for sentence-sized expressions is a function of the way in which the content of lexical elements combines together to yield a truth-evaluable whole. But as Kamp pointed out in 1981, it is not obvious in what sense the sentence *He was sick* in (2) has a truth-evaluable content as a sentence—rather the truth-evaluable content that it has is dependent on the evaluation of the previous sentence *John came in* and the relation between the two.

The solution Kamp proposed to these problems became the first model to blur the syntax–semantics dichotomy, and this analysis was the first dynamic model of semantic evaluation (Kamp 1981). He defined an intermediate level of characterization called 'discourse representation structure' (DRS), a structure defined by an algorithm whose role was to assign values to anaphoric expressions as part of the mapping from syntactic construct to DRS. The DRS so assigned to a sentence was then subject to model-theoretic evaluation. So rather than interpreting the sentence *John came in*, and only then, independently interpreting *He was sick*, the algorithm projects a DRS for the first sentence (I), and extends this by the information provided by the second sentence to create the new DRS II:

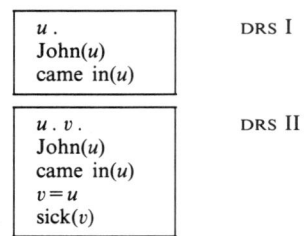

A DRS is a partial model containing some nonempty set of entities called discourse referents, and predicates on those entities. Truth is then defined for a DRS in terms of its embeddability in some total model, and not as a property of sentences directly. Despite the model-theoretic status of these mini-models, the internal structure of such DRS's has played an important role in the way the theory has developed. There is for example a stated locality condition on the identification of a discourse referent for pronouns that they be identified from some 'higher' DRS. This structural condition on pronominal identification led in its turn to a rule moving elements from some subordinate box to some higher DRS. For example the two readings of (18) according as the indefinite is or is not internal to the conditional are distinguished as the discourse referent for the indefinite is or is not moved to the 'top box':

If a friend of mine comes to see me, let her in. (18)

Such locality conditions and/or movement processes critically invoke properties of the DRS qua representation in ways not naturally reducible to some model-theoretic image. Thus we get the first blurring of semantic and syntactic constructs—constructs defined in semantic terms but manipulated in terms of their configurational properties. There is also unclarity in the status of such intermediate representations. Are they a set of representations internal to the natural-language grammar, or are they rather part of some general model structure onto which natural-language strings are mapped. A formal algorithm is defined from natural language expressions onto DR structures, suggesting that they are envisaged as being part of natural-language grammars. Yet they are defined for entities for which those grammars do not provide input—viz., sequences of sentences. This is the problem which lies at the heart of the context-dependency phenomenon: the articulation of truth-evaluable vehicles is not defined over sentence-strings as determined by principles internal to the grammar alone, but by such principles in combination with something else. If we are to isolate a concept of natural language content attributable to natural language expressions independent of context, then we have to model two related phenomena: (a) the underdeterminacy displayed by many natural language expressions, simple and complex, vis a vis the truth-theoretic content attributable to them; and (b) the process whereby the lexically-assigned natural-language content is enriched to yield some such complete specification. DRT was one of the first theories of semantic modeling to seriously grapple with this problem (cf. also Heim 1982; Barwise and Perry 1984).

The context-dependency of truth-theoretic content is no less problematic for standard syntactic assumptions, for the recognition that grammar-internal specification of anaphoric expressions very considerably underdetermines interpretation conflicts with familiar syntactic distinctions. There is claimed to be a distinction between discourse coreference and bound variable anaphora, the latter (but not the former) being subject to a c-command restriction between it and the operator on which it is dependent (Reinhart 1983, 1986). Hence the widely adopted grammar-internal characterization of bound-variable anaphora. This assumption that some anaphoric dependencies are determined exclusively by grammar-internal principles cannot be sustained. The reason is this: for every anaphoric linkage, howsoever established, there is a corresponding bound-variable analogue. In particular there are anaphoric linkages demonstrating two major central cognitive activities:

(a) logical deduction

Joan isn't so anti-private practice as not to have any private (19)
patients, but she's always complaining that they
treat her as a servant.

(b) retrieval from memory of contingently known information associated with specified objects

The fridge is broken. The door needs mending. (20)

Establishing the anaphoric linkage in (19) involves a step of 'double negation elimination': establishing the anaphoric linkage in (20) involves making a link in virtue of the knowledge that fridges have doors. Both processes are central to any account of human reasoning of the most general sort, and are not properties of the language faculty itself. But these examples have straightforward analogues in which the pronominal linkage involves central cognitive processes while yet licensing a bound-variable interpretation:

Every one of my friends who isn't so anti-private practice as (21)
not to have any private patients is complaining that they treat
her as a servant.

Every fridge needs the door mending. (22)

These data pose us with a number of alternatives, only one of which is free of inconsistency. They display an interaction precluded by all standard theories of syntax, that between general cognitive processes and constraints said to be subject to grammar-internal explication. It appears that the output of such general cognitive processes has to be checked against a syntactic restriction on interpretation. We could take these data as evidence that the encapsulation of the language faculty should simply be abandoned and free interaction of processes internal to the language faculty and central cognitive processes should be allowed. Since this would involve jettisoning all possibility of characterizing properties specific to language, this alternative is not acceptable. Notice however that the alternative of invoking the ambiguity of bound-variable anaphora and discourse coreference as a means of dividing off grammar-internal processes from general cognitive processes is not a viable option. To postulate ambiguity here is no help—the grammar-internal phenomenon still involves interaction with the relevant central cognitive processes. And to stipulate double negation elimination or bridging cross-reference as a grammar-internal phenomenon is to incorporate central cognitive processes into the grammar, and this too involves reneging on the language-encapsulation view. Our only recourse is to grant the underdeterminacy of all anaphoric expressions, allow the phenomenon of anaphoric dependence to be characterized as part of the pragmatic process of assigning interpretation to utterances, and characterize the constraint on bound-variable interpretations in like manner to the disjointness requirement on pronominal anaphora (principle B) as a filter on licit choices of anaphoric dependence made as part of this pragmatic process.

Exploring this last route gives us a much more syntactic view of content. We need to define concepts of locality, c-command, etc., over configurations licensed both by grammar-internal processes and by general cognitive processes. There is evidence that this is the right direction in which to look for a solution. Elliptical processes display the underdeterminacy of natural-language expressions vis-à-vis the interpretation assigned to them even more dramatically than anaphora, but are yet subject to familiar grammar-internal constraints such as the so-called 'island' constraints precluding dependency into a relative clause for example (cf. Morgan 1973). Thus bare argument fragments can be interpreted in context as expressing whole propositions, reconstructing complex propositional structure from some antecedent source:

> Joan wants Sue to visit Bill in hospital. And Mary too.   (23)

The elliptical *And Mary too*, which can be uttered by some other speaker, can be reconstructed either as (a) 'Mary wants Sue to visit Bill in hospital,' or (b) 'Joan wants Mary to visit Bill in hospital,' or as (c) 'Joan wants Sue to visit Mary in hospital.' However, just as *wh-* questions cannot license binding of the *wh-* expression into a relative clause, so these fragments cannot be reconstructed as replacing some expression inside a relative clause:

> Joan visited the woman who likes Bill, in hospital.   (24)
> And Mary too.

The fragment in (24) can be construed as 'Mary visited the woman who likes Bill in hospital,' and as 'Joan visited Mary in hospital.' But it cannot be interpreted as 'Joan visited the woman who likes Mary, in hospital.' This island-constraint phenomenon is generally taken as definitive of a grammatical phenomenon. But there is independent reason to consider that the interpretation of fragments is a pragmatic process, sensitive to general on-line constraints on utterance interpretation—just as is anaphora. If we are not to abandon all hope of retaining the concept of grammar as some encapsulated language-specific faculty, we have to state grammar-internal processes in such a way that they are able to be implemented over pragmatically induced configurations. We need to define utterance interpretation as a structure-building process from the under-determining input provided by grammar-internal principles, and construe all configurational constraints on interpretation as constraints on that structure-building process. We thus arrive at the conclusion that processes of interpretation need to be just as syntactic as the configurations familiar from syntactic theory. The boundaries between syntax and interpretation need to be blurred yet further.

The exploration of such processes of interpretation is taking several routes. There is Discourse Representation Theory, with its intermediate hybrid representations, part semantic, part syntactic. There is so-called 'structured semantics,' in which structure is superimposed on the model itself (cf. Cresswell 1985). And there is a proof-theoretic route whereby utterance interpretation is characterized as an inferential process of syntactically building a proof structure. This was first proposed by Sperber and Wilson (1986) as one aspect of their overall theory of utterance interpretation. Here a formal model of this option is outlined (Gabbay and Kempson 1992), showing how it predicts directly the interaction between familiar syntactic constraints and processes of general reasoning without abandoning the encapsulation of the language faculty as an independent input to processes of general reasoning.

Suppose we assume that stored in the lexicon for each lexical item is a specification of its contribution to utterance interpretation. In the simple cases, this takes the form of a pair—a conceptual expression, and a specification of its logical type (expressed as in Montague semantics in terms of the two primitives: *e*, an individual denoting expression; and *t*, a truth-bearing entity; and combinatorial functions on these). A verb such as *swim* for example, expresses the two-place relation swim', an expression of logical type $\langle e, \langle e, t \rangle \rangle$. Expressing types as propositions and taking the corresponding logical expression as a matching label for its twinned type, we can view this lexically stored information as labeled premises in a logic—premises which will combine together to deduce the proposition expressed by an uttered sentence, as conclusion. Thus in a sentence such as *John loves Mary*, we have three words:

> *John, loves, Mary*

yielding from the lexicon three premises:

> John' : e
> love' : $e \rightarrow (e \rightarrow t)$
> Mary' : e

Assuming here concepts of subject and tense, information from the lexicon will lead by two steps of modus ponens to the proposition:

> love' (Mary') (John') : t

For every step of modus ponens taken, the information in the labels builds up, recording the assumptions used and their mode of combination, the resulting conclusion a well-formed formula of a predicate logic labeling the logical type t (the logic assumed is the labeled natural deduction system of Gabbay 1992 forthcoming).

Such a sentence as this displays no obvious underdeterminacy, but the phenomenon of anaphora can be reconstructed, with its under-determining input, and dependency established in context, as a process of natural deduction. An initiating assumption of some metavariable over labels is entered as the premise lexically associated with the pronoun, an assumption which is discharged by identification with some information independently recoverable from the inference-structure already presented—in effect, the natural deduction moves of the Rule of Assumptions, reiteration of a premise from one inference-structure to another, and assumption discharge:

John loves Mary. She loves him.

John'	: e	
love'	: $e \rightarrow (e \rightarrow t)$	
Mary'	: e	
love' (Mary')	: $e \rightarrow t$	Modus Ponens
love' (Mary') (John')	: t	Modus Ponens

u	: e	condition: $\Theta u \notin$ local proof-structure
		female(Θu)
		[Θ an instantiation function]
Mary' : e		Reiteration
CHOOSE $\Theta u = $ Mary'		
love'	: $e \rightarrow (e \rightarrow t)$	
v	: e	condition: $\Theta v \notin$ local proof-structure
		male(Θv)
John'	: e	Reiteration
CHOOSE $\theta v = $ John'		
love' (John')	: $e \rightarrow t$	Modus Ponens
love' (John') (Mary')	: t	Modus Ponens

Reconstructed this way, anaphoric linkage is a relation

established across structure—proof-theoretic structure. Locality restrictions on this process, whether to some non-local domain as with pronominals, or to some local domain as with anaphors, are naturally expressible as side conditions on the process of instantiating the initiating assumed variable. We have principle A and principle B of the binding theory stated directly as a specification given in the lexicon as definitional of anaphors/pronominals but implemented on proof structures as part of the process of arriving at some labeled conclusion, here:

love' (John') (Mary') : *t*.

Utterance interpretation can now be defined as a process of natural deduction from some initiating set of premises to some conclusion *a* : *t*, *a* being the proposition expressed, with some of the words presented as premises to that conclusion, others determining how the conclusion is reached. With this mode of explanation the concept of interpretation is essentially structural: linguistic content is characterized in various ways according as the lexical item contributes to this process of proof-unfolding. Lexical items such as *love* contribute labeled premises:

love   love' : *e → t*.

Items such as pronouns and anaphors contribute premises labeled by a metavariable with some associated side condition determining how that variable is to be identified:

he   u : e   CONDITION $\Theta u \notin$ local proof structure
male(Θu)
(Θ an instantiating function)

And some expressions contribute solely by providing some constraint on the proof process. Relative clause markers, for example, are a means of linking one local piece of reasoning with another—through some unifying variable. Suppose, for example, we wish to link together two pieces of information, that a man fainted and that that man smiled. We can do so through the relative clause structure:

A man who smiled fainted.   (25)

The relative marker provides a means of constructing such linked pieces of information, through common use of some unifying variable. Reflecting this, *wh-* can be characterized as initiating, from the lexicon, a database to be so linked. The logic defines a concept of linked databases, two databases being linked if and only if some free variable in each is replaced by some common unifier. And we assign to *wh-* the lexical specification that it impose the requirement that its containing proof structure lead to a conclusion of type *t* labeled by some open formula containing a variable, a structure which can then be linked through some associated determiner:

wh- { . . . . . .} $\vdash \alpha$(u) : *t*

The lexical content of *wh-* does not itself constitute a premise to be manipulated in any proof structure—rather it provides a restriction on the form of conclusion that must be established.

We now have a new construal of the nature of interpretation—lexical items contain specifications which constrain the building of a proof-structure from which the more orthodox concept of truth-content will be derivable. The essence of linguistic content so defined is that it is meta to any such level and hence essentially syntactic. Furthermore, the building of this configurational structure is not charac-

terized as a grammar-internal process but as a process of central cognitive reasoning. We have arrived at a conclusion which not only blurs syntactic and semantic distinctions but sets a different boundary between grammar-internal and central cognitive processes. Yet despite the apparent merging of syntax and logical deduction, the language faculty itself remains as a discrete construct. The input information, characterized as the lexicon, is the necessary input to the deduction process, its own internal statements encapsulated from and not affected by any subsequent processes of deduction. We abandon the concept of the language faculty as a body of knowledge entirely divorced from our faculty for reasoning, but we retain the concept of encapsulation vis a vis its a priori nature, the essential input to any cognitive processing of linguistic stimuli. The apparent interaction of syntactic and cognitive constraints is now unproblematic. The linguistic input severely underdetermines the output structure constituting its interpretation, and the entire process of actually building that structure is a process of reasoning. Many so-called syntactic phenomena emerge as consequences of the proof discipline itself. One such is the island constraint phenomenon displayed in the interpretation of elliptical fragments.

Recall first (23) (repeated here):

Joan wants Sue to visit Bill in hospital. And Mary too.   (23)

We have in the interpretation of the first sentence some complex database leading to the conclusion:

want' (visit' (Bill') (Sue')) (Joan')) : *t*.

With the fragment *and Mary too*, the hearer faces the goal-directed task of reaching some conclusion α : *t* but here he has only *Mary* provided as input. In order to arrive at some conclusion, he must create the necessary propositional structure. To do this, he reuses the entire previous clause, creates a one-place predicate out of it, and reapplies this result to the new argument *Mary*. This step of building a lambda-abstract is licensed because it is a move from some premise of the form α : *t* to a premise of the form $\lambda x(a)$: e → t, a perfectly licit step of conditional-introduction. Depending upon which position is abstracted over, we can create for (23) any of the interpretations (a)–(c) above. Relative clauses being two such local reasoning structures linked together through a common variable, the relative-clause island phenomenon follows directly:

Joan visited the woman who likes Bill in hospital.   (24)
And Mary too.

We build for an interpretation of the first sentence of (24) the linked database:

Joan' : *e*
visited' : *e → (e → t)*
u : *e*
in-hospital' : *(e → t) → (e → t)*

↑

u : *e*
woman' : *e → t*

↑

u : *e*
likes' : *e → (e → t)*
Bill' : *e*

To reconstruct the fragment we need to take one step of conditional introduction, but on which local structure should we carry out this step? In order to create the complex reading substituting Mary in place of Bill in the relative clause, we would need to carry out conditional introduction on the first of these local structures (corresponding to the matrix clause). But the premise which we wish to withdraw is not there—it is only in some separate, albeit linked, structure. But conditional introduction is a local step of reasoning—it cannot be vacuously carried out in one structure as a record of some such step in another structure. The logic itself precludes any such interpretation. Hence the island constraint phenomena are a direct consequence of the logic discipline adopted. The apparent puzzle of interaction between grammar-internal constraints and the pragmatic process of utterance interpretation is resolved. Syntactic phenomena are explained not by properties definitional of a discrete encapsulated language faculty but by the logic discipline in which the language faculty is embedded. But to do so, we have had to abandon Lewis's stricture and set up a syntactic concept of interpretation, manipulating semantic constructs (such as the type vocabulary) as expressions in a calculus for which inference is syntactically defined.

Within this new perspective, we are able to retain both the concept of a universal human capacity for constructing and manipulating structural configurations through the medium of language; and the concept of parametric variation between languages. Each language is a logic, with its own internal constraints on how the building up of proof-theoretic structures is controled—with idiosyncratic locality restrictions (parametric variation in anaphor binding, for example), with idiosyncratic specification of how one structure is linked online to another (parametric variation in the value of *wh-* dependencies), and so on. But any one such logic falls within the general family of logics defined by the 'labeled deductive system': all such logics are natural deduction systems which model our ability to take elementary concepts, progressively build them up to form complex structured concepts, and then reason with those complex structures as wholes. Our innate language capacity is, that is to say, firmly embedded in our capacity for reasoning.

Bibliography

Barwise J, Perry J 1984 *Situations and Attitudes.* MIT Press, Cambridge, MA

Chierchia G, McConnell-Ginet S 1990 *Meaning and Grammar: An Introduction to Semantics.* MIT Press, Cambridge, MA

Chomsky N 1982 *Lectures on Government and Binding.* Foris, Dordrecht

Chomsky N 1986 *Knowledge of Language.* Praeger, New York

Cooper R 1979 The interpretation of pronouns. In: Heny F, Schnelle H (eds.) *Syntax and Semantics,* vol. 10. Academic Press, London

Cresswell M J 1985 *Structured Meanings.* MIT Press, Cambridge, MA

Dowty D R 1979 *Word Meaning and Montague Grammar.* Reidel, Dordrecht

Dowty D R, Wall R E, Peters S 1981 *Introduction to Montague Semantics.* Reidel, Dordrecht

Evans G 1980 Pronouns. *Linguistic Inquiry* 11: 337–62

Gabbay D 1992 *Labelled Deductive Systems.* Blackwell, Oxford

Gabbay D, Kempson R 1992 Natural-language content: A truth-theoretic perspective. In: *Proceedings of the 8th Amsterdam Formal Semantics Colloquium,* Amsterdam

Hausser R R 1979 How do pronouns denote? In: Heny F, Schnelle H (eds.) *Syntax and Semantics,* vol. 10. Academic Press, London

Heim I 1982 The semantics of definite and indefinite noun phrases (Doctoral thesis, University of Massachusetts)

Heim I 1990 E-type pronouns and donkey anaphora. *Linguistics and Philosophy* 13: 137–78

Kamp H 1981 A theory of truth and discourse representation. In: Groenendijk J A G, Janssen T M V, Stokhof M B J (eds.) *Formal Methods in the Study of Language.* Mathematisch Centrum, Amsterdam

Karttunen L 1968 *What do Referential Indices Refer to?* Santa Monica publication no. P-3554

Katz J J 1972 *Semantic Theory.* Harper and Row, New York

Kempson R 1988 Logical form: The grammar's cognition interface. *Journal of Linguistics* 24(2): 393–431

Klein E 1980 A semantics for positive and comparative adjectives. *Linguistics and Philosophy* 4: 1–45

Lewis D 1972 General semantics. In: Davidson D, Harman G *Semantics of Natural Languages.* Reidel, Dordrecht

May R 1985 *Logical Form: Its Structure and Derivation.* MIT Press, Cambridge, MA

Morgan J 1973 Sentence fragments and the notion 'sentence.' In: Kachru B B, Lees R B, Malkiel Y, Pietrangeli A, Saporta S (eds.) *Issues in Linguistics: Papers in Honor of Henry and Renee Kahane.* University of Illinois Press, Urbana, IL

Partee B H 1984a Nominal and temporal anaphora. *Linguistics and Philosophy* 13: 243–86

Partee B 1984b Compositionality. In: Landman F, Veltman F (eds.) *Varieties of Formal Semantics.* Foris, Dordrecht

Reinhart T 1983 Coreference and bound anaphora: A restatement of the anaphora question. *Linguistics and Philosophy* 6: 47–88

Reinhart T 1986 Center and periphery in the grammar of anaphora. In: Lust B (ed.) *Studies in the Acquisition of Anaphora,* vol. 1. Reidel, Dordrecht

Sperber D, Wilson D 1986 *Relevance: Communication and Cognition.* Blackwell, Oxford

Stump G T 1985 *The Semantic Variability of Absolute Constructions.* Reidel, Dordrecht

Thomason R H (ed.) 1974 *Formal Philosophy: Selected Papers of Richard Montague.* Yale University Press, New Haven, CT

R. M. Kempson

Semilingualism

Considerable debate has focused on the question of whether some students from linguistic minority backgrounds can be characterized as 'semilingual' (sometimes termed 'doubly semilingual'), a condition that implies inadequate development of both first and second languages (L1 and L2). A related question concerns the extent to which such linguistic and/or cognitive deficits may be regarded as causal factors in explaining the poor academic performance of some minority students (Cummins and Swain 1983; Edelsky, et al. 1983; Hansegard 1972; Kalantzis, et al. 1989; Martin-Jones and Romaine 1986; Paulston 1982; Skutnabb-Kangas 1984; Stroud 1978). In many respects the controversy parallels the issue of whether working-class children are characterized by language deficits that contribute to their difficulties in schools (Bernstein 1971; Labov 1970).

Hansegard (1972) has provided the most elaborated description of the construct of 'double semilingualism' based on his observations among Finnish and Saami communities in Northern Sweden. Six characteristics are outlined by Hansegard:

(a) size of the repertoire of words, phrases, etc., understood or actively available in speech;
(b) correctness with respect to syntactic, phonemic, and discoursal aspects of language use;
(c) degree of automatism in use of the language;
(d) ability to create or neologize in the language;
(e) mastery of the cognitive, emotive, and volitional function of language;
(f) degree of richness in the semantic networks available to the individual through the language.

Edelsky, et al. (1983) characterize this description of the construct as 'a confused grab-bag of prescriptive and descriptive components' and argue that to attribute minority students' academic difficulties to 'semilingualism' even as one link in a causal chain constitutes a deficit theory that 'blames the victim.' Paulston (1982) similarly argues that there is no empirical evidence for the construct and deplores its use (primarily by Skutnabb-Kangas) in the Swedish debate as an argument for Finnish home-language classes. Martin-Jones and Romaine (1986) also dispute the existence of 'semilingualism.' They attribute apparent inadequacies of linguistic competence among bilinguals to the normal processes of language contact and language shift.

Skutnabb-Kangas (1984), in response to criticism, makes the point that most of the studies that claim not to have found evidence for inadequate command of two languages have focused on *syntax*, whereas many of those that support the construct have focused on range of vocabulary. She furthermore argues that semilingualism cannot be regarded as a deficiency inherent in the individual but should be treated as one result of the societal and educational discrimination to which minority groups are subjected. In other words, it is a political as much as an educational construct. Semilingualism can be avoided when minority children receive intensive L1 instruction through 'language shelter' (i.e., L1 immersion) programs.

Several authors have adopted an intermediate position with respect to this debate. McLaughlin for example, suggests that:

> Semilingualism may be a useful way of describing those cases where, through extreme social deprivation, bilingual children do not learn to function well in either language. At issue here, however, is whether it is a useful concept when talking about bilingual children in general. If the concept of semilingualism is defined as meaning that bilingual children do not perform as well as native speakers in either language, then there is some agreement that in fact this may be the case at certain points in the development of their languages.
>
> (McLaughlin 1985: 33)

Kalantzis, et al., similarly point to the situation 'in which the home language is not continued with growing sophistication past entry to formal schooling either at home or at school, and in which the initial experience of formal schooling does not adequately prepare students for proficiency in their second language' (1989: 30). They suggest that the consequence of this situation can be what they have termed a 'cognitive void' (or what Hansegard has termed 'semilingualism') in which 'children's ability to express themselves and manipulate the world around them through language is hampered' (1989: 31).

Appel and Muysken (1986) make the point that the bilingual's verbal repertoire can be viewed as different and not deficient even though at some point in their development they may know less of each of their languages than monolingual children. For example, bilinguals' code-switching abilities give them the opportunity to convey messages in subtle and sophisticated ways not available to monolinguals. Appel and Muysken also point out that comparisons with monolinguals may not be justified since bilinguals use their two languages in different domains and for different purposes. In other words, from a sociolinguistic perspective, the two languages of the bilingual can be viewed as one linguistic repertoire that is adequate in a wide variety of situations.

The issues in this debate appear to be less complex than might be indicated by the heated controversy that surrounds the use of the term. In the first place, virtually all theorists on both sides of this issue agree that the major causal factors in minority students' underachievement are sociopolitical in nature; specifically, the pattern of dominant–subordinated group relations in the wider society and the interactional manifestations of these relations in the school context. Second, if one admits that variations in language and literacy abilities exist among monolingual populations, then there is no reason to deny the existence of such variations among bilingual populations in their two languages. It is clear that there are major individual differences in literacy skills and in certain aspects of oral language skills among the general population in their L1s (or first languages). Not everybody is capable of reading and writing at the same level nor does everybody have identical oral repertoires (e.g., oratorical skills). In the same way, bilingual children and adults vary in their degree of mastery of different aspects of their two languages. Even Edelsky, et al., admit that 'semilingualism might mean something more substantial (e.g., an inability to use language in its ideational or representational function . . .)' (1983: 11).

If it is allowed that variation exists, then it appears that certain bilinguals will have relatively low levels of literacy in both their L1 and L2 (or second language), while others will have relatively high levels of literacy in both languages. Certainly some minority children born in the host country who do not receive sufficient L1 instruction at school develop L1 oral and literacy skills only to a very limited extent (Wong Fillmore 1990). These children will also vary in the degree of formal L2 academic skills that they develop at school. The extent of mastery of these formal language skills is directly linked to future educational and economic opportunities. As Kalantzis, et al. (1989: 31) point out, 'in the modern world, formal language skills of speaking, reading and writing are the means to certain sorts of futures and power.' They suggest that all children should have the opportunity to develop mastery of these formal language skills and academic researchers 'who have mastered the pinnacle of mainstream language' should not view as unproblematic the fact that a disproportionate number of minority students fail to realize the full range of options in their two languages.

In short, the issue does not seem to revolve around the existence of variation in language and literacy skills among bilingual (and monolingual) populations. The issue is rather whether it is appropriate or theoretically useful to label some of these bilingual children 'semilingual' or 'doubly semilingual' or 'deficient' as a means of characterizing their relatively limited repertoires in certain aspects of their two languages.

There appear to be compelling scientific and sociopolitical reasons to avoid using such labels. First, as the debate clearly shows, there has been no precise linguistic or cognitive operationalization of the term 'semilingualism.' In other words, there is no scientific rationale for choosing one arbitrary cut-off point over another as the level below which it is appropriate to label an individual 'semilingual.' Thus, the term has no explanatory or predictive value but is rather a restatement of the vague notion of 'limited proficiency in two languages.' At a sociopolitical level the term has assumed pejorative connotations and may be misinterpreted as suggesting that linguistic deficits are a primary cause of minority students' academic difficulties, despite denials to the contrary. Furthermore, the futile debates to which use of the term has given rise suggest that its continued use is counterproductive.

There appears to be little justification for continued use of the term 'semilingualism' in that it has no theoretical value and confuses rather than clarifies the issues. However, those who claim that 'semilingualism does not exist,' appear to be endorsing the untenable positions that (a) variation in educationally-relevant aspects of language does not exist, and that (b) there are no bilinguals whose formal language skills are developed only to a relatively limited level in both L1 and L2. Just as there are monolinguals whose formal language skills are developed only to a limited degree, so too there are bilinguals whose formal language skills are developed only to a limited degree.

Bibliography

Appel R, Muysken P 1987 *Language Contact and Bilingualism.* Edward Arnold, London

Bernstein B (ed.) 1971 *Class, Codes, and Control*, vol. 1. Routledge and Kegan Paul, London

Cummins J, Swain M 1983 Analysis-by-rhetoric: Reading the text or the reader's own projections? A reply to Edelsky, et al. *Applied Linguistics* **4**: 23–41

Edelsky C, et al. 1983 Semilingualism and language deficit. *Applied Linguistics* **4**: 1–22

Hansegard N E 1972 *Tvåspråkighet eller Halvspråkighet?* Aldus Bonnier, Stockholm

Kalantzis M, Cope B, Slade D 1989 *Minority Languages and Dominant Culture: Issues of Education, Assessment and Social Equity.* Falmer Press, London

Labov W 1970 *The Study of Non-Standard English.* National Council of Teachers of English, Champaign, IL

Martin-Jones M, Romaine S 1986 Semilingualism: A half-baked theory of communicative competence. *Applied Linguistics* **7**: 26–38

McLaughlin B 1985 *Second-language Acquisition in Childhood. Vol. 2: School-age children*, 2nd edn. Lawrence Erlbaum, Hillsdale, NJ

Paulston C B 1982 *Swedish Research and Debate about Bilingualism.* National Swedish Board of Education, Stockholm

Skutnabb-Kangas T 1984 *Bilingualism or Not: The Education of Minorities.* Multilingual Matters, Clevedon

Stroud C 1978 The concept of semilingualism. *Lund University Working Papers* **16**: 153–72.

Wong Fillmore L 1990 Now or later? Issues related to the early education of minority group children. In: Harris C (ed.) *Children at Risk.* Harcourt Brace Jovanovich, New York

J. Cummins

Semiotic Anthropology

The designation 'semiotic anthropology' (Silverstein 1975) refers to a branch of anthropology which applies Charles S. Peirce's theory of signs and their meanings to illuminate anthropological research. It is roughly coextensive with 'structural' and 'semiological anthropology' (Lévi-Strauss 1967, 1976), 'interpretive anthropology' (Geertz 1973), 'comparative symbology' (Turner 1974), 'semantic anthropology' (Crick 1976), 'symbolic anthropology' (Schneider 1969), 'semiotics of culture' (Umiker-Sebeok 1977; Winner, Umiker-Sebeok 1979), 'ethnosemiotics' (Hertzfeld 1983), 'ethnography of communication' (Gumperz and Hymes 1972). 'Semiotic anthropology' differs from these other designations by emphasizing Peirce's classification of signs and his doctrine of semiotics.

Thomas Sebeok's *Semiotics in the United States* (1991) mentions some of those designations, but prefers 'semiotics without any qualifiers' (1991: 50–51). If considered as a branch of semiotics, that may be the best usage. Considered, however, as a branch of anthropology, the qualifiers help to differentiate semiotic anthropology from all the other hyphenated anthropologies.

Margaret Mead popularized the unqualified 'semiotics' when she suggested that it be used to refer to patterned communication in all sensory modalities. Another compromise was introduced by Jean Umiker-Sebeok and Irene Portis Winner in the *Semiotics of Culture* (1977, 1979).

If Peirce's own practice is to serve as a model, his principle of 'the ethics of terminology and notation,' which honors the chronological priority of the innovative usage, should be taken seriously. This, in any case, is the reason for preferring 'semiotic anthropology.' There is also the additional consideration that Peirce had a strong interest in comparative and historical linguistics, archeology, and ethnology. His frequent recourse to colloquial formulations and illustrations, such as 'my language is the sum total of my self' or 'all thought is in signs' teased his and the reader's imagination to look for observations, classifications, and generalizations about how the doctrine of signs could be applied to the problems and materials of anthropology and linguistics.

Edmund Leach's review of Singer's *Man's Glassy Essence: Explorations in Semiotic Anthropology* (1984) did not see much value in returning to Peirce's difficult theory of signs and, besides, he saw in the book the expression of a Chicago dogma, that cultures are systems of symbols and meanings.

The important feature of Leach's review was not its negative and critical character, which was balanced by other preponderantly favorable reviews of the book, but its reference to 'a Chicago dogma.' It so happens that in the late 1960s and early 1970s there was an unusual convergence of interests among the faculty in Chicago's anthropology department on theories of cultural symbolism. Clifford

Geertz and David Schneider, Stanley Tambiah and Nur Yalman, Victor Turner and Terence Turner, Leslie Freeman, Norman McQuown, Paul Friedrich and Michael Silverstein come to mind. So this much of Leach's impression was well founded. The independent testimony of Raymond Firth, who visited the department in 1970 and gave a series of lectures on symbolism, acknowledged this convergence of interest on theories of symbolism (Firth 1973: 10). There was not, however, a department consensus on any single theory of cultural symbolism. Except for Silverstein and Singer, and probably Tambiah and Friedrich, there was little interest in Peirce's semiotics. More importantly, the diversity of backgrounds, fieldwork, and previous training did not add up to anything that could be called a 'Chicago dogma.' Geertz and Schneider acknowledged Talcott Parsons at Harvard as an important influence, Tambiah and Yalman the Cambridge School, Victor Turner paid his respects to Max Gluckman and Van Gennep, Friedrich to Jakobson at Harvard and Goodenough in Philadelphia, McQuown to Sapir at Yale, Silverstein to Jakobson, Benveniste, Kurylowicz, Putnam and Quine at Harvard. If there was a dogmatic theory about cultural symbolism, it was as much a Harvard, Cambridge, Manchester, Philadelphia, Yale 'dogma' as a Chicago 'dogma.' As different members moved around, the convergence was dispersed. In this milieu it is no wonder that Peirce's semiotics should have appealed to some, as Saussure's structural linguistics appealed to other members of an earlier generation.

Even during the period of convergence at Chicago, the most influential source of stimulation was located in Paris, not in Chicago, or any American University—in Claude Lévi-Strauss's structural anthropology. Lévi-Strauss acknowledged Saussure's semiology for an analysis and interpretation of North and South American myths, and a structural theory of 'totemism' and the 'savage mind.' The obvious contrast between Saussure's dyadic relation of 'signifier' and 'signified' and Peirce's triadic relation of 'sign,' 'object,' and 'interpretant' provided an opportunity to distinguish the two theories of signs, at least as ideal types. Lévi-Strauss was not prevented by his adoption of Saussure's semiology from considering triadic relations, as well as dyadic oppositions among some of the peoples he studied. On the other hand, Peirce's triadic relation of iconic, indexical, and symbolic signs already contained within it the dyadic relation of an indexical sign and its object, as well as the more general signifier–signified relations (cf. Singer 1978).

Lévi-Strauss's acknowledgment of Roman Jakobson's lectures on Saussure in 1942 as a source of structuralism was not Jakobson's only connection with semiotics. In addition to many incidental references to Peirce, Jakobson included Peirce and Saussure in a brief history of semiotics (Jakobson 1975). How Jakobson's classification of linguistic functions could be applied to social anthropology was explained by Silverstein in *L'Arc* (1975). In this article Silverstein referred to *anthropologie sémiotique*.

A widely influential social anthropologist who contributed a distinctive emphasis to the 'Chicago dogma' was Victor Turner. Beginning with his Morgan lectures in 1969, *The Ritual Process*, Turner elaborated a theory of cultural symbolism rooted in British social anthropology and his interest in poetry and theater. He added some novel features which brought his position fairly close to American semiotic anthropology. Acknowledging Van Gennep's classic *Rites of Passage* and Freud as his point of departure for a theory of ritual, Turner emphasized, not static social and cultural structures, but the dynamic processes whose functions were often antistructural. The place of 'liminality' ('betwixt and between') in the rituals became for him opportunities for expressing alternative structures, and achieving 'communitas.' He not only applied this innovative analysis to the Ndembu he observed in Africa, but extended it to a more general analysis of religious pilgrimage, celebrations, festivals and other cultural performances (Turner 1974, 1982, 1986). Breaking with a predominantly antipsychological and antibiological orientation among British social anthropologists, Turner declared his interest in this psychobiological pole of the ritual process by citing Freud, Dilthey, and Dewey, among others (Turner 1986). In one of his later papers, referring to his analysis of cultural symbolism as 'comparative symbology,' Turner noted an explicit correspondence between his own triadic analysis to interpret symbols ('positional meaning,' 'exegetical meaning,' and 'operational meaning') and the division of semiotics into 'syntactics,' 'semantics,' and 'pragmatics' (Turner 1974: 11–12).

Far from regarding Victor Turner as a renegade deviant from British social anthropology, Adam Kuper's history of British Anthropology and Anthropologists locates him in 'the direct line of descent' from Radcliffe-Brown, by way of Max Gluckman and Monica Wilson. And as one of his students, M. N. Srinivas, reminds us, Radcliffe-Brown introduced a theory of 'ritual idiom' based on the idea of ritual as a language, probably as early as the second edition of *The Andaman Islanders* (1932).

Victor Turner's revival and extension of Van Gennep's schemes for the rites of passage to Ndembu in Africa and to a general theory of the ritual process attracted a lot of attention among anthropologists and stimulated a new interest in ritual, and its symbolic analysis. A more or less simultaneous renewal of interest in the ritual process was sparked by the studies and publications of a Sanskritist and symbolic logician, Frits Staal. Staal investigated the survival of Vedic chants and recitations and the Vedic fire ceremony in Kerala. His combination of textual Sanskritic scholarship with thorough observations of the rites as still practiced and reenacted produced an impressive new kind of ethnographic monograph on the vedic symbolism in the contexts of the textually prescribed rituals (Staal 1989). The most provocative features of this research, however, were the theoretical implications which Staal drew from it. One implication was that his research provided a foundation for a more general 'science of ritual' which exceeded anything yet attempted by anthropologists. A second and more provocative implication, he suggested, is that rituals, at least in their early stages, are meaningless. Invoking his knowledge of modern logic and linguistics, Staal formulated a structuralist theory of ritual in which the symbols and acts may be meaningless and uninterpreted. Applying this theory to an evolutionary time perspective, he speculated that animal rituals, like bird songs, and also some human rituals, precede the emergence of meaningful language and culture. He did not claim that the vedic rituals in his monograph were meaningless, except for some non-sense syllables. They obviously appeared at a stage of human evolution already pervaded by language and culture. He seems to believe, however, that it is possible to extrapolate backward in time to when the rituals were completely meaningless. An anthropologist would question Staal's identification of structuralism with meaninglessness, and ask for evidence of a paleo–anthropological record that indicated the existence of structural perception and thought before the appearance of culture and language.

1. Emblems of Personal and Social Identity

The violence and destruction of World War II overwhelmed and transformed the anthropologist's assumptions about personality and human nature. After the Nazi Holocaust, the massive bombing raids on London, the Allied bombing of Hamburg, and the dropping of atomic bombs on Hiroshima and Nagasaki, it was difficult and utopian to cling to an optimistic view of human nature. Even Malinowski's acceptance of the 'moderate behaviorism' of Dewey, G. H. Mead, and Grace de Laguna, as well as his neo-Freudian 'matrilineal complex' began to arouse opposition among anthropologists.

Freud's more pessimistic views about human aggressiveness and destructiveness, especially as expressed in his answer to Einstein's question 'Why war?' (1931), and in *Civilization and its Discontents* (1927), were reconsidered and reassessed by some anthropologists as well as by psychologists and other scholars. Robert Redfield, suffering a terminal illness from lymphatic leukemia, talked with a stranger and quoted Camus in what must be interpreted as a desperate expression of hope for the survival of the human spirit (Redfield 1953). In such an atmosphere, it is not surprising that Singer's lecture to the American Anthropological Association in 1978 ('Signs of the Self') urging a return to Peirce's concept of a semiotic self should have received an interested, if somewhat puzzled, response. One colleague later wrote that the audience believed that they heard something important but were not exactly sure what it meant. In retrospect, it could be suggested that the message of that lecture challenged professional anthropologists to reconsider their received conceptions of personality as individualistic, subjectively introspective, split between mind and body, emotion and cognition, thought and action. Peirce's conception of a semiotic self, expressed in linguistic and other signs, within both internal and external dialogues, with an 'outreaching identity' that embraced other people, was presented as an alternative anti-Cartesian conception of the self. At least two people who heard that lecture raised the question whether Peirce did not remain Cartesian since he retained a phenomenological 'immediate consciousness' in his theory. Perhaps the reply did not satisfy them—that for Peirce 'phenomenology' included whatever was immediately present to the mind, without respect to its truth value, and did not assume its indubitability as it did for Descartes's '*cogito, ergo sum*.'

This 1978 recommendation of a return to an earlier conception of a self was also made in a joint volume which returned to Marcel Mauss's 1938 essay on The 'Category of the Person.' Although not as anti-Cartesian as Peirce, the group of anthropologists, philosophers, and historians also questioned and clarified the going assumptions about the relations between individual persons and their social and cultural contexts. Mauss's contribution to the discussion has been reevaluated, not so much as a reaffirmation of Durkheim's position, but as a more refined analysis of the linguistic differences in French and English, and the influence of Hinduism and Buddhism on conceptions of self.

Simultaneously with this reconsideration and reevaluation of older theories of the self, there has been an increasing number of ethnographic field studies of 'person' and 'self' in different cultures which have been moving away from the Benedict-Mead 'culture and personality' approach of the 1930s and 1940s, and toward a more semiotic, semiological, and symbolic approach.

To illustrate how the recent ethnographic studies of persons and selves have made use of semiotic, semiological, and symbolic analyses, several examples will be cited. It has been noted elsewhere that Lévi-Strauss's discovery of a genuine structuralist analysis of totemism in Radcliffe-Brown's second lecture on totemism led him to construct a kind of algebraic formula, a postulate of homologies between two sets of differences; Eaglehawk moiety is to Crow moiety, as eaglehawk totem is to crow totem. As is well known, Durkheim interpreted the concrete totems as clan symbols and emblems. 'A totem is the flag of the clan,' said Durkheim, and he went on to suggest that totems constitute a sort of language. Lévi-Strauss's interpretation of the totemic language as a Saussurean *langue* led him directly to a structuralist analysis. However, the individual totem as a concrete physical object also needed attention. For this purpose, Lévi-Strauss seems to have accepted Durkheim's idea that a totem is an emblem like a flag and Radcliffe-Brown's Australian idea of dual opposition. The rather elaborate discussion and diagrams in *The Savage Mind* are intended to clarify the relations of an individual totem to the social groups. Whether this is a purely structural relation, or also a causal relation as in Durkheim and Mauss, remains ambiguous in *The Savage Mind*. The diagrams and some of the associated discussion include references to the individual level of the classifications. On the other hand, Lévi-Strauss's desire to clear an intellectual space for a structural analysis of relations without a commitment to a particular empirical 'infrastructure' probably explains this ambiguity.

Lloyd Warner, who observed and analyzed the Murngin system in Australia under Radcliffe-Brown's guidance, interpreted the relation between totems and social groups in more causal terms without abandoning a structuralist analysis. An interesting feature of Warner's analysis is that he uses it, in reverse, as an analogy in his later study of 'Yankee City.' Flags in Yankee City, used to decorate graves and parades, are like totemic animals among the Murngin (Singer 1984: 110–14, 153–54). The implication of this analogy is not that nationalism is a focus of tribalism, but that emblems of a national identity in relation to their social groups behave like emblems of tribal identity in relation to their corresponding social groups.

2. Art and Icon

Robert Redfield's article 'Art and Icon' was probably the last he wrote before his death in 1958. It marked his further move toward a humanistic model for anthropology, and away from the social science model of anthropology as a natural science of society. His use and quotation of Peirce on an iconic sign to formulate criteria for distinguishing between an esthetic and an ethnographic object marked an increasing interest in symbolic analysis, an interest which he had already declared in his 1952 Wenner-Gren paper. The side-by-side synchronic comparison of communities in Yucatan and Guatemala was to be replaced by historical studies of the 'worldviews' and 'great traditions' of different cultures and civilizations, as well as of the folk traditions of 'little communities.' Although it was not prominently noted at the time, Redfield's reorientation of anthropology in the 1950s brought his position closer to the Benedict and Kroeber 'configurational' analysis. Kroeber's interest in cultural symbolism extended as far back as his Arapaho study. His calling classificatory kinship terms 'little systems of semantics' was invoked as a point of departure for the development of componential analysis by Goodenough and Lounsbury. Kroeber's comparative histories of cultures and civilizations were recognized as early as 1944 with the publication of his massive empirical testing of Spengler. While acknowledging Kroeber's priority in comparative civilization studies, Redfield wished to develop 'a social anthropology of civilizations.' Kroeber was skeptical and suggested that a 'comparative morphology' of civilizations was a more feasible objective because cultural causality was too complex and intricate to unravel, and the gap between the study of little communities and total culture patterns was too wide to bridge.

Redfield personally preferred to enter another civilization via the little community of a village, but he encouraged exploration of other modes of entry into a civilization, including the cultural role of cities, and of systems of signs and social functions which represent these different kinds of knowledge and cosmology.

Peirce's definition of an icon did not appeal to Redfield because he thought that it encapsulated a world view or a cosmology. He did not think the carving of the twins did that; rather to an ethnographer the meaning of the carving was to be found in the contexts of worship, ceremony, customs, of crafts and craftsmen, as well as in the direct image of the figures portrayed by the carving. The connection between the interpretations which transcend the context and cosmology of the carving and the 'system of forms' which constituted the art object is not absolutely sharp and cannot be ignored, according to Redfield. Some effort to abstract the esthetic object from the ethnographic object is obviously required in order to apply Redfield's analysis in 'Art and Icon.'

Redfield's 'Art and Icon' does not of course filter esthetic appreciation through iconic signs. By emphasizing the contextual and transcendent meanings of an object, he is able to take advantage of the 'dream-like' radiating meanings of the object which cannot be encapsulated in any particular set of iconic signs. In Peirce, the ever-widening circles of interpretations of a given sign meet their boundaries in the habits of interpreters (the logical interpretants), or in the cybernetic systems which recycle and replicate them (for Peirce on iconicity, see Zellweger 1990).

3. City as Symbol

At his inaugural lecture, 'City as Symbol,' delivered at University College London, 20 November 1967, Paul Wheatley pointed out that the history of cities in the non-Western world has been neglected in urban studies, which are 'based on the Euro–American experience and have comparatively seldom been tested in the conditions of the traditional world' (Wheatley 1969). Without much ado, he then proceeded to make amends for this neglect with a magnificently erudite discussion of traditional ceremonial cities in China, South and Southeast Asia, Japan, and the Middle East. Nor did his lecture neglect the theoretical concepts of urbanism and the process of urbanization which have been discussed in Urban's studies. The Chicago schools of sociology, anthropology, archeology, and theology are all cited. And as the lecture's title promises, the discussion focused on the symbolism of the traditional city, as well as of the modern city.

Wheatley's inaugural lecture of 1967 was but a prelude to a whole series of studies he was soon to publish on traditional cities in the non-Western world. A notable feature of these studies was the symbolism of the 'astrobiological principles.' Wheatley suggested in his inaugural lecture that these principles, formulated by René Berthelot, provided a set of symbols characteristic of traditional cities, and proceeded to identify them in his empirical studies as an *axis mundi*, the symbols of cardinal orientation, and micro–macro cosmo–magical symbolism. When Wheatley invited Singer to present a paper to his 1984 conference on 'meanings of the city,' the latter used the occasion to apply the three astrobiological principles as a test of the distinction between traditional and modern cities in India (Chandigarh, Madras, and Madurai). The fact that several historical studies had been published on Madras and Madurai, where Singer had also made some personal observations, and that Norma Evenson had published a richly documented study on Le Corbusier's Chandigarh, made it quite feasible for Singer to draft a paper on 'Purusha and Modulor as Architectural Symbols.' The availability of Frits Staal's thorough ethnographic study of the Vedic fire sacrifice added important comparative data. Singer's paper was then extended and published in *The Semiotics of Cities, Selves and Cultures: Explorations in Semiotic Anthropology* (Singer 1991). This paper, 'A semiotic of the city: Purusha and Le Corbusier's Modulor as Architectural Symbols,' and the two papers on 'Yankee City,' also in the book on *The Semiotics of Cities*, contain important evidence that the author's visits to India and to 'Yankee City' showed how the problem of the relation between traditional and modern cities could lead to an emergence of a 'semiotic anthropology.' In Madras, the relationship appeared as a case of modernization through 'traditionalization,' but in 'Yankee City' it appeared that restoration was 'a path to progress.' Mrs. Warner's biography of Lloyd Warner explains that his interest in 'the symbolic life of Americans,' so well described in his monograph *The Living and the Dead* (1959), was already a strong interest at the beginning of his 'Yankee City' research in the early 1930s; this enabled Singer to understand why the relation of tradition and innovation in 'Yankee City' was the mirror image of the relationship in Madras. His paper 'The Symbolism of the Center, the Middle and the Periphery' traces how the Chicago school of symbolic interactionism was taken to Yucatan by Robert Redfield, then to 'Yankee City' by Lloyd Warner, and finally to Madras and 'Yankee City' by himself.

4. Configurationism, Structuralism, and Semiotics

In his introduction to a collection of lectures, 'Local Knowledge: Fact and Law in Comparative Perspective' delivered at the Yale Law School in 1981, Clifford Geertz explained his resistance to the identification of semiotics and structuralism, and to structuralism in particular. Apropos his essay 'Art as a Cultural System,' delivered as a part of 'a wildly multidisciplinary symposium' on 'semiotics' to commemorate Charles Peirce, Geertz suggested that art was neither a universal transcendent category nor a completely culture-bound category. He concluded that it was more useful to talk about the social contexts of particular works 'than to force them into schematic paradigms, or stripping them down to abstract rule systems that supposedly "generate" them.'

These options do seem incomplete and unsatisfactory, and Geertz does avoid being imprisoned by them when he points out that 'anthropological translation' reshapes categories, so that they can reach beyond the contexts in which they originally arose and took their meaning so as to locate affinities and mark differences. Geertz's thick description of 'Person, Time and Conduct in Bali' and 'Deep Play in a Balinese cockfight' remain persuasive examples of 'interpretive anthropology.'

Although Morris's iconic theory of esthetics was not widely influential among literary critics and philosophers, his pragmatic interpretation of Peirce's semiotics gained some followers among some linguists (e.g., Bloomfield, Jakobson, Sebeok), philosophers, and social scientists. His lucid style of exposition and his genial and tolerant personality were chiefly responsible for the short-lived synthesis of American pragmatism, the Vienna circle, and British empiricism in the late 1930s that was called 'scientific empiricism' and 'logical empiricism.' His monograph *Foundations of the Theory of Signs* (1938) for the *Encyclopedia of Unified Science*, which he coedited with Rudolf Carnap and Otto Neurath, stimulated a revival of interest in Peirce's semiotics that is still very much alive in the 1990s (see Sebeok 1991). Because Morris's later book *Signs, Language and Behavior* (1946) emphasized a behavioristic interpretation of semiotics, he was discounted as an interpreter of Peirce. Yet Peirce's leaning toward behaviorism should not be overlooked, as Morris pointed out in his controversy with Dewey about 'interpreters,' and in his quotation from Peirce on habit as the 'logical interpretant.' As a student and successor of G. H. Mead at Chicago, and an editor of Mead's published lectures, Morris was probably the last link between the 'Chicago School' of pragmatism and 'symbolic interactionism,' and the updated Peircean semiotics which reemerged in Carnap's 'logical syntax of language,' Tarski's 'semantics,' and Morris's 'pragmatics.' While none of these developments was linguistic in a strict sense, they provided a vocabulary and method of analysis which took 'a linguistic turn' in philosophy, anthropology, and the social sciences. 'Semiotic anthropology' was just one of the by-products of these interdisciplinary interactions.

A brief sketch of how American configurational anthropology became affiliated with French structural anthropology with a little help from German *gestalt* psychology would explain the emergence at Chicago of symbolic, interpretative, and semiotic anthropology. A confluence of anthropological streams from Cambridge and Oxford and Manchester, Harvard and Philadelphia, Berkeley and Paris met at Chicago. At least one scholar noticed this emerging confluence as early as 1961, when Arnold Toynbee acknowledged that his theory of the encounters of civilizations owed something to Kroeber's configurationism, the Frankforts' and Braidwood's work on the beginnings of civilization in the Near East, and Redfield on the transformations of the primitive world and worldview. It was not, however, until the early 1970s that Raymond Firth could point to Chicago's anthropology department as a place where interest in cultural symbolism was high and wide (Firth 1973: 10).

After Firth's lectures on *Symbols, Private and Public*, the confluent streams of interest in cultural symbolism continued to flow at Chicago and elsewhere. Collections of essays by several generations of scholars have appeared. To name some of these with Chicago connections is not intended to be invidious (Dolgin, Kemnitzer, and Schneider (eds.) 1977; Lee and Urban (eds.) 1989; Maquet 1982; Marriott 1990; Mertz and Parmentier (ed.) 1985; Varenne 1986). In addition, individual monographs and articles are equally in evidence (Boon 1972; Cohn 1987; Daniel 1984; Friedrich 1986; Gold 1989; Herzfeld (ed.) 1983; Munn 1973; Parmentier 1987; T. Turner 1980; Urban 1991; Witherspoon 1987).

Not all of these authors and editors describe their works as 'semiotic anthropology' but a family resemblance can be traced. Authors without Chicago connections and crossing over from other disciplines to apply a semiotic also appeared.

At the annual meeting of the American Anthropological Association held in Chicago in 1987, a colloquium on the theory of tropes in anthropology attracted a good deal of attention. Five of the nine participants belonged to Chicago's department of anthropology (Fernandez, Friedrich, Presman, Silverstein, and Turner). While Lévi-Strauss, Peirce, and Radcliffe-Brown receive only marginal mentions in the published book of the colloquium (Fernandez (ed.) *Beyond Metaphor* 1991), the social and cultural matrix of the discussion overlaps the matrix which provided the context for the emergence of symbolic anthropology, structuralism, and semiotic anthropology. Peirce's definition of a metaphor in terms of iconic signs whose relational structures are similar to the relational structures of the sign's object already implicates the semiotics that goes beyond metaphor (Singer 1984: 55, 108). Fernandez's distinction of 'signal,' 'sign,' and 'symbol' approximates Peirce's 'index,' 'icon,' and 'symbol.'

Edward Sapir's perspectival epistemology which distinguished individual from social behavior by analytic point of view and not by its empirical content, made it possible for him to publish almost simultaneously a paper on speech as an individual personality trait and on the symbolic emblems on a university building (cf. Singer 1961). This bifocal perspective also enabled him to reverse Ruth Benedict's metaphor of cultural configurations as personality 'writ large' by turning the individual personality into a locus of cultural configurations 'writ small.' Michael Silverstein's paper on 'Sapir's Psychological and Psychiatric Perspectives on Culture' illustrates with quotations from some of Sapir's letters and articles how the bifocal perspective enabled Sapir to take account of the 'consciousness or . . .

subconsciousness in native speakers of the organic (differentially significant) phonetic elements of their language' (Silverstein 1992: 13). Yet Sapir's individualization of cultural configurations did not prevent him from accepting the language of mathematics and science as an asymptotic normative model for the design and construction of an auxiliary international language.

5. Peirce's Continuing Relevance for Semiotic Anthropology

Surveying the fields 'in which Peirce's relevance is now recognized,' Max Fisch cited in his *Monist* article of 1982 contemporary works in linguistics, anthropology, sociology, social psychology, psychiatry, and philosophy. The 'range of Peirce's relevance' is impressive. A question which remains to be answered is why Peirce's theory of signs is relevant to all of these fields and when that relevance was first recognized. To answer this question adequately would require a short monograph, but a brief chronology of the recognition of the relevance of Peirce's semiotics for anthropology will not be out of place in the conclusion of this memoir. Margaret Mead's suggestion at the 1962 Bloomington conference that 'semiotics' be adopted as the name for the field which studies 'all patterns of communication in all modalities' was probably one of the first recognitions by an American anthropologist of Peirce's relevance. The context of discussion there was multidisciplinary—linguistics, anthropology, and psychology. A more distinctly anthropological context was described by Lévi-Strauss in his inaugural lecture of 1960 at the Collège de France, where he proposed that anthropology study 'all signs at the heart of social life not already preempted by linguistics.' He also acknowledged the study Saussure called 'semiology' (Lévi-Strauss 1976). In Lévi-Strauss's classification, 'mythic language, the oral and gestural signs of ritual, marriage rules, kinship systems, customary laws, economic exchange' would constitute some of the signs and symbols anthropology can study. 'Everything is symbol and sign, when it acts as an intermediary between two subjects' (Lévi-Strauss 1976). Peirce's semiotic conception of signification as a triadic relation of sign, object, and interpretant encompasses the Saussurean dyadic relation of signifier–signified, as Jakobson recognized (Singer 1984: 70, 78).

After Lévi-Strauss's inaugural lecture in 1960 the idea that anthropologists study societies and cultures as systems of symbols and meanings became fairly widespread. Firth noticed it at Chicago in 1970; Eco attributed it to Schneider (Eco 1976: 67); and Leach called it a 'Chicago dogma.' As Schneider, Geertz, and other Chicago faculty members have acknowledged, Chicago did not have a monopoly on the idea that cultures are systems of symbols and meanings. And only two or three members turned to Peirce's theory of signs and symbols for a general theory of signs.

Firth's book on *Symbols* identified Leach as the first anthropologist to mention Peirce (Firth 1973: 62). This reference, however, carries a stinger with it, for Leach claimed it was not Peirce who influenced Malinowski, but James (Leach in Firth 1957: 121–22). Firth is entirely justified for not agreeing with Leach, for a case can be made for the argument that the first anthropologist to make use of Peirce's theory of signs was Malinowski in his 1923 essay on 'Problem of Meaning in Primitive Languages' (Singer 1991: 260–308).

Peirce's general theory of signs and symbols, or 'semiotics,' is so comprehensive, philosophically sophisticated, and historically informed that it is puzzling to find anthropologists and other empirical scholars resisting its obviously relevant applications to their respective fields. One common explanation for this resistance is Peirce's disposition to use technical terms and original coinages. He defended this practice as a 'principle of the ethics of terminology,' which he claimed was followed in chemistry, philosophy, mathematics, and exact science to acknowledge chronological priority. In addition, another of his mitigating dispositions is often overlooked, namely, his habit of citing colloquial glosses for practically every technical term and formulation. Sometimes he may refer to one of these colloquial translations as 'a sop to Cerberus,' as in the explanation of an 'interpretant' as 'the effect of a sign on a person.' This practice, however, is entirely consistent with his taking a colloquial conversation between two persons as his model for 'semiosis'—a communication between an utterer and interpreter of signs in a particular context (Singer 1984: 68, 75). In fact, Peirce's recourse to the language analogy is so frequent that his dictum that 'my language is the sum total of my self' may strike the reader as a colorful metaphor until Peirce begins to spell it out in terms of the pronouns 'I,' 'it,' and 'thou' (Singer and Urban in Lee and Urban 1989).

Closely related to the resistance to Peirce's use of technical terms is the impression that Peirce's theoretical analysis is very formal and abstract from ordinary empirical contexts. Clifford Geertz has objected to 'a semiotics of esthetics' on these grounds. Peirce, however, tried to protect semiotic analysis from this kind of abstractness and formalism by introducing a principle of 'collateral information and observation' which presupposed some acquaintance of the utterers and interpreters with the objects of the signs.

Another source of resistance to Peirce's theory of signs is its apparent relation to an idealistic metaphysics and ontology. The three categories of firstness, secondness, and thirdness are most often interpreted as the ultimate categories of Peirce's metaphysics and ontology, which, it is argued, are out of step with modern science and modern logic. Overlooked in this criticism is Peirce's insistence that his categories are based on his logic and on his more than thirty years experience with the United States Geodetic Survey, practicing 'the laboratory habit of mind.' Careful observations, exact measurements, rigorous logical reasoning and mathematical analysis were essential ingredients, for Peirce, in 'the laboratory habit of mind.' That science was fallible and self-corrective, and dependent on operationalist criteria of meaning and truth was part and parcel of this laboratory habit of mind. Even mathematics turns out to be an observational science by these criteria, and pragmatism a method for clarifying the meaning of obscure concepts. As a general theory of signs, semiotics encompasses logic and mathematics, and is as much a phenomenological, pragmatic, and social science as it is a branch of philosophy. If signs pervade the universe, and human beings are signs, as Peirce said, we cannot escape the obligation to interpret these signs, including ourselves, as Royce added (Royce in Singer 1984: 94).

Peirce defended himself against the charge of 'triadomania' by pointing out that useful classifications in the history of science were often trichotomies. Perhaps the most famous of his trichotomies was his acceptance of his first wife's feminist interpretation of the trinity, and his theory of evolution as including evolution by necessity, by chance, and *agape* or love. In his theory of signs the ultimate trichotomy was the triadic relation of signification as a relation of sign, object, and interpretant. If one adds the utterer and interpreter to this relation, as Peirce did, then the triad becomes a pentad. Bertrand Russell once questioned whether four-term relations and greater should not also be included. Peirce replied by demonstrating that only triadic relations were irreducible.

Roman Jakobson's retrospective observation in 1952 of 100 years' parallel development of concepts in mathematics, structural linguistics, and anthropology suggests the possibility that such a parallelism may continue for another 100 years with the developments of 'semiotic anthropology,' 'structural anthropology,' and 'symbolic anthropology.'

In archival research Shea Zellweger has discovered that Frederick Augustus Rauch published a book on psychology in 1840, when Peirce was about one year old, which uses *semeiotic* as both a noun and an adjective, and distinguishes three kinds of signs along the lines of Peirce's icon, index, and symbol. Rauch also used symbolical, emblematic, and semiotical. Perhaps Jakobson's 100 years of parallel development of mathematics, linguistics, and anthropology should begin in 1840 rather than in 1850 (Zellweger 1990).

Bibliography

Not all titles cited in the text are included in the following bibliography. Those which are not included will be found in the more comprehensive bibliographies included in Singer's papers and in Thomas A. Sebeok's *Semiotics in the United States* (1991). The present bibliography emphasizes late-twentieth-century publications, and especially those with anthropological applications of semiotic analysis. No attempt has been made to cover independent national developments in France, Italy, Russia, or other countries.

The most accessible introduction to Charles S. Peirce's writings on semiotics can be found in Justus Buchler's *Philosophical Writings of Peirce* (1940), Max H. Fisch's 'Introduction to Writings of Charles S. Peirce' in *A Chronological Edition*, vol. 1 (1982) and his *Peirce, Semeiotic and Pragmatism*, edited by K. L. Ketner and C. J. W. Kloese (1986). Volume 2 of the Charles Hartshorne and Paul Weiss's edition of Peirce's *Collected Papers* contains many of Peirce's original writings on semiotics.

The titles selected for inclusion in this bibliography represent either important compilations of diverse formulations, or have a claim to chronological priority for introducing a particular kind of symbolic analysis, or are a recent ethnographic contribution.

Barthes R 1982 *Empire of Signs*. Hill and Wang, New York

Bateson G, Mead M 1942 *Balinese Character: A Photographic Analysis*. New York Academy of Sciences, New York

Boon J A 1972 *From Symbolism to Structuralism: Lévi-Strauss in a Literary Tradition*. Blackwell, Oxford

Boon J A 1982 *Other Tribes, Other Scribes: Symbolic Anthropology in the Comparative Study of Cultures*. Cambridge University Press, Cambridge

Cohn B S 1987 *An Anthropologist Among the Historians and other Essays*. Oxford University Press, Delhi

Crick M 1976 *Explorations in Language and Meaning: Towards a Semantic Anthropology*. John Wiley/Halsted, New York

Daniel E V 1984 *Fluid Signs: Being a Person the Tamil Way*. University of California Press, Berkeley, CA

Dolgin J D, Kemnitzer D S, Schneider D M 1977 *Symbolic Anthropology: A Reader*. Columbia University Press, New York

Douglas M 1970 *Natural Symbols*. Cresset Press, London

Eco U 1976 *A Theory of Semiotics*. Indiana University Press, Bloomington, IN

Errington J L 1988 *Structure and Style in Javanese: A Semiotic View of Linguistic Etiquette*. University of Pennsylvania Press, Philadelphia, PA

Fernandez J W 1965 Symbolic Consensus in a Fang Reformative Cult. *AmA* 67: 902–29

Fernandez J W 1986 The argument of images and the experience of returning to the whole. In: Turner V, Bruner E M (eds.) 1986

Fernandez J W (ed.) 1991 *Beyond Metaphor: The Theory of Tropes in Anthropology*. Stanford University Press, Stanford, CA

Firth R 1973 *Symbols: Public and Private*. Cornell, Ithaca, NY

Firth R (ed.) 1957 *Man and Culture: An Evaluation of the work of Bronislaw Malinowski*. Routledge and Kegan Paul, London

Fisch M H 1982 *Introduction to Writings of Charles S Peirce: A Chronological Edition*, vol. 1. Indiana University Press, Bloomington, IN

Fisch M H 1982 The relevance of Charles Peirce. *The Monist* 65: 123–41

Fisch M H 1986 *Peirce, Semeiotic, and Pragmatism*. Indiana University Press, Bloomington, IN

Friedrich P 1986 *The Language Parallax: Linguistic Relativism and Poetic Indeterminacy*. University of Texas Press, Austin, TX

Geertz C 1973 *The Interpretation of Cultures*. Basic Books, New York

Geertz C 1983 *Local Knowledge*. Basic Books, New York

Gold A 1989 The once and future Yogi: Sentiments and signs in the Tale of a Renouncer King. *Journal of Asian Studies* 48(4)

Griaule M 1965 *Conversations with Ogotemmeli: An Introduction to Dogon Religious Ideas*. International African Institute, Oxford

Gumperz J J, Hymes D (eds.) 1972 *Directions in Sociolinguistics: The Ethnography of Communication*. Holt, Rinehurst and Winston, New York

Herzfeld M (ed.) 1983 Signs in the field: Semiotics/Perspectives on ethnography. *Semiotica* 46: 99–330

Jakobson R 1978 *Six lectures on Sound and Meaning*. MIT Press, Cambridge

Jakobson R 1953 Comments. In: Tax S, et al. *An Appraisal of Anthropology Today*. Chicago University Press, Chicago, IL

Jakobson R 1975 *Coup d'oeil sur le dévelopement de la sémiotique*. Indiana University Publications, Bloomington, IN

Kroeber A L 1901 Decorative symbolism of the Arapaho. *AmA* 3(2): 308–36

Leach E 1976 *Culture and Communication: The Logic by which Symbols are connected*. Cambridge University Press, Cambridge

Lee B, Urban G (eds.) 1989 *Semiotics, Self, and Society*. Mouton de Gruyter, Berlin

Lévi-Strauss C 1963 *Totemism*. Beacon, Boston, MA

Lévi-Strauss C 1966 *The Savage Mind*. Weidenfeld and Nicholson, London

Lévi-Strauss C 1967 *Structural Anthropology*. Doubleday, New York

Lévi-Strauss C 1970 *The Raw and the Cooked*. Harper and Row, New York

Lévi-Strauss C 1976 *Structural Anthropology*, vol II. Basic Books, New York

Malinowski B 1923 The problems of meaning in primitive languages. In: Ogden C K, Richards I A (eds.) *The Meaning of Meaning*. Kegan Paul, London

Malinowski B 1963 *Coral Gardens and their Magic*, vol II. Indiana University Press, Bloomington, IN

Maquet J (ed.) 1982 *On Symbols in Anthropology*. Undena Publications, Malibu

Marriott M (ed.) 1990 *India through Hindu Categories*. Sage, Newbury Park, CA

Mertz E, Parmentier R (eds.) 1985 *Semiotic Mediation*. Academic Press, London

Morris B The rise and fall of the human subject. *Man* **20**: 722–42

Munn N D 1973 *Walbiri Iconography*. Cornell University Press, Ithaca, MN

Parmentier R J 1987 *The Sacred Remains: Myth, History, and Polity in Belau*. The University of Chicago Press, Chicago, IL

Piatigorsky A B, Zilberman D B 1976 The emergence of semiotics in India. *Semiotica* **17(3)**: 255–65

Radcliffe-Brown A R 1957 *A Natural Science of Society*. University of Chicago, Chicago

Radcliffe-Brown A R 1958 The comparative method in social anthropology. In: Srinivas M N (ed.) *Method in Social Anthropology*. University of Chicago Press, Chicago, IL

Ramanujan A K 1988 Is there an Indian way of Thinking? In: Marriott M (ed.) 1990

Redfield R 1953 Relation of anthropology to the social sciences and the humanities. In: Kroeber A L (ed.) *Anthropology Today*. University of Chicago Press, Chicago, IL

Redfield R 1959 Art and icon. In: *Aspects of Primitive Art*. The Museum of Primitive Art, New York

Sapir E 1949 *Selected Writings of Edward Sapir*. University of California Press, Berkeley, CA

Schneider D M 1969 Kinship, nationality and religion in American culture. In: Spencer R I *Forms of Symbolic Action*. Proc. American Ethnological Society. University of Washington Press, Seattle, WA

Sebeok T A 1991 *Semiotics in the United States*. Indiana University Press, Bloomington, IN

Silverstein M 1975 La sémiotique Jakobsonienne et l'anthropologie sociale. *L'Arc* **60**: 45–49

Silverstein M 1992 Sapir's psychological and psychiatric perspectives on culture. *California Linguistic Notes* **23(2)**: 11–16

Singer M B 1961 A survey of personality and culture theory and research. In: Kaplan B (ed.) *Studying Personality Cross-Culturally*. Row and Peterson, Evanston, IL

Singer M B (ed.) 1968 *Krishna, Myths, Rites and Attitudes*. University of Chicago Press, Chicago, IL

Singer M B 1978 For a semiotic anthropology. In: Sebeok T A (ed.) *Sight, Sound and Sense*. Indiana University Press, Bloomington, IN

Singer M B 1980 *When a Great Tradition Modernizes: An Anthropological Approach to Indian Civilization*. University of Chicago Press, Chicago, IL

Singer M B 1984 *Man's Glassy Essence: Explorations in Social Anthropology*. Indiana University Press, Bloomington, IN

Singer M B 1989 Pronouns, persons and the semiotic self. In: Lee B, Urban G (eds.) 1989

Singer M B 1991 *Semiotics of Cities, Selves and Cultures: Explorations in Semiotic Anthropology*. Mouton de Gruyter, Berlin

Staal F 1989 *Rules without Meaning*. Peter Lang, New York

Stanner W E H 1965 Religion, Totemism and Symbolism. In: Berndt R M and C G (eds.) *Aboriginal Man in Australia*. Angus and Robertson, Sydney

Tambiah S J 1985 The magical power of words. In: *Culture, Thought and Social Action*. Harvard University Press, Cambridge, MA

Tambiah S J 1979 A performative approach to ritual. In: *Culture, Thought, and Social Action*. Harvard University Press, Cambridge, MA

Turner T 1980 The social skin. In: Cherfas J, Lewin R (eds.) *Not Work Alone*. Temple Smith, London

Turner V 1974 *Dramas, Fields, Metaphors: Symbolic Action in Human Society*. Cornell, Ithaca, MN

Turner V 1982 *From Ritual to Theatre*. Performing Arts Journal, New York

Turner V, Bruner E M (eds.) 1986 *The Anthropology of Experience*. University of Illinois Press, Urbana, IL

Umiker-Sebeok J 1977 Semiotics of culture: Great Britain and North America. *Annual Review of Anthropology* **6**: 121–35

Urban G 1991 *A Discourse-Centred Approach to Culture*. University of Texas Press, Austin, TX

Varenne H (ed.) 1986 *Symbolizing America*. University of Nebraska Press, Lincoln, NB

Warner W L 1959 *The Living and the Dead: A Study of the Symbolic Life of Americans*. Yale University Press, New Haven, CT

Wheatley P 1969 *City as Symbol*. University College, London

Wheatley P 1971 *The Pivot of the Four Quarters*. Aldine, Chicago, IL

Winner I P, Umiker-Sebeok J 1979 *Semiotics of Culture*. Mouton, The Hague

Witherspoon G 1987 *Navajo Weaving: Art in its cultural context*. Museum of Northern Arizona, Flagstaff, AZ

Wolf E 1958 The Virgin of Guadalupe: A Mexican national symbol. *Journal of American Folklore* **LXXI**: 34–39

Zellweger S 1990a Before Peirce and icon/index/symbol. *The Semiotic Scene* **2(1)**.

Zellweger S 1990b John James Van Nostrand and semantology. *Semiotics* 229–40

M. Singer

Semiotics

As human beings, we may decide not to eat or drink, not to talk or communicate, or perhaps not even to live, but as long as we do live we cannot choose not to convey 'meaning' to the surrounding world. 'Semiotics,' in the broadest sense, is the study of the basic human activity of creating meaning. 'Signs' are all types of elements—verbal, nonverbal, natural, artificial, etc.—which carry meaning. Thus, semiotics is the study of sign structures and sign processes. In certain research traditions, the name of this study has been 'semiology'; the distinction between semiology and semiotics has often been interpreted conceptually, and not just terminologically, whereas today this superficial distinction has been abandoned: 'semiotics' is the generally accepted ecumenical term, which will also be adopted here.

As a specific discipline, semiotics is most developed as the study of the signs which function in the world of human activity. Here, semiotics investigates three fundamental problems. First, how the world which surrounds us is 'constituted' as a human environment because of our perception and apprehension of it through signs; second, how this world is coded and decoded, and thus made into a 'specific cultural domain' consisting of networks of signs; third, how we 'communicate' and 'act' through signs in order to make this domain a collectively shared cultural universe.

Semiotics may deal with the basic and general aspects of such a study; in this case neighboring areas, covered by specialized disciplines such as linguistics, psychology, anthropology, sociology, or aesthetics, will to a certain extent be subsumed by semiotics.

Semiotics also carries out investigations of concrete sign processes. In this case, semiotics will have to take into account signs of different 'types' which are simultaneously engaged in the process, such as signals, multileveled meaning structures, unintended manifestations of meaning, etc., and their different systems of expression or 'media' (visual, verbal, gestural, tactile, etc.).

As a discipline in its own right, albeit a not too sharply delimited one, or as an integrated part of other disciplines, semiotics is involved whenever the production and exchange of information and meaning is studied. Such studies range from animal communication, through stimulus and response processes occurring throughout the biosphere, to the processing of information in machines. In these contexts, while semiotics does not define the fundamental research questions, it contributes methodologically or conceptually to the actual investigations (see *Communication; Meaning: Philosophical Theories*).

1. Basic Semiotic Notions

The key notions of semiotics are generated in a variety of disciplines, and semiotic research is carried out by different semiotic schools. This situation produces a different terminology and different specific research interests inside the entire field of semiotics, but five notions are recurrent 'attractors' for the semiotic enterprise through the modern history of semiotics to the late-twentieth-century state of affairs, and will remain so in the future of semiotics. These five notions are 'code,' 'structure,' 'sign,' 'discourse,' and 'text.'

The following presentation of the notions opens with the most abstract ones, 'code' and 'structure.' They are modified by semiotics in order to serve its purpose: the study of the production of 'meaning.' The following notions, 'sign' and 'discourse,' bring out the increasing complexity of the process of creating meaning. The final notion 'text,' encompasses the whole field of semiotics.

1.1 Code

Imagine a painter at work. He chooses different colors at the palette, mixes them, and, through repeated strokes of the brush, he combines the colors on the canvas. When he is finished, he adds his signature. A process of selection and combination of colors and letters has taken place, and a complex cultural sign, a work of art, has come into being.

This process is a rule-governed activity. The rules governing the combination and selection are called codes. Not all the coding mechanisms involved in the process are semiotically relevant, and the study of codes in general is broader than semiotics. From a simple definition of code, the discussion now moves to a more complex one of genuine semiotic character.

Assume that there are two elements which can be distinguished from each other. If a rule for their interrelation can be set up, the minimal requirement for the existence of a code will be fulfilled. The rule is a code. If the elements are characterized by one feature, say a straight line and a curved line, and if the rule dictates size, distance, iteration, vertical and horizontal order, it would be possible to produce most of the letters of the Latin alphabet through a

coded process of 'combination' of the elements according to the rule. That is what the painter actually did when he signed the painting with his name.

If the elements are characterized by more than one feature, for instance if color is added to the straightness and curvedness of the lines, the rule must also be capable of 'selecting' among the different features, for instance shape 'or' color, or shape *and* color, in order to convey a 'specific identity' to the element in relation to other elements. Thus, the relevance of the selected features, and hence the identity of the element, is context-dependent, i.e., dependent on the context in which the rule-governed combination is to be realized.

If color and not shape is selected as the relevant feature, the rule of combination may produce an aesthetic object and not the letters. The elements are placed in an aesthetic context. If color is irrelevant and only shape is relevant, letters may be produced. One's signature on a contract is valid whether it is signed with blue, black, or green ink. But the two features, color and shape, may interact, as is most often the case, and create the signature of a painter on canvas, for example.

So far no specific semiotic codes, but only the code in general, has been dealt with: a rule for the selection and combination of relevant features in given elements. But when the painter has finished his picture through the coded combinations of (at least) color and shape, ending with a signature, an object with a content has emerged. The codes have been creating 'meaning.' Only codes such as these are 'semiotic codes.'

The minimal requirements for the existence of semiotic codes and of the process they initiate are more complex than for the code in general. In semiotics, two elements and a combination rule will not suffice: the elements 0 and 1 combined through a rule creating the series 0101010101 . . . do not necessarily produce meaning. At least two sets of elements are required, each of them combined by using one or more rules according to selected features, e.g., clothing as fashion as one set and a more or less closed system of perceptual categories or social values as another. If one then has a rule for the combination of the two systems, so that one system can refer to or represent the other, it can be said that 'meaning' is produced.

In semiotics two levels of coding are at work simultaneously: at one level a code unites a set of elements as a well-defined, but not necessarily closed system, and at another a code combines at least two such systems. Here it can be said that the code transforms or translates one system into the other.

In agreement with Umberto Eco (1984: 164–88), the codes working at the first level could be called code systems or 's-codes,' and the codes working at the second level could be called transformation codes or simply codes. In language for example, the s-codes organize the semantic system and the expression system, while the codes bring about the combination of these systems into meaningful language signs. Semiotics works on the assumption that s-coded systems from which features relevant for the production of meaning can be selected already exist. The way these systems are built up in detail is not the subject of semiotics (but may be an area for linguistics, perceptual psychology, etc.).

When the painter puts his name on the canvas, the s-coded expression system of colored letters and the s-coded system of the more or less institutionalized social activity of creating art are combined through the coded process of signing, and the meaning 'Picasso did this painting' occurs.

If a more complex case like a theater performance is looked into, then a whole series of s-coded systems is met (dress, verbal dialog, hairdo, body movements, lighting, etc.) and a tight network of codes combining them in different ways and perhaps ways which change during the performance. The result is a highly complex and often, as in most works of art, ambiguous meaning. The two-level semiotic coding process does not normally give rise to propositions which are clearly true or false as in logic, but to a complex meaning which functions on all levels of our culture.

1.2 Structure

Semiotics has often been seen as totally absorbed by the structuralist wave. According to structuralist thought, the structure is an immanent relational network of elements constituting an object. The network is the specific identity of the object. So, the notion of structure and the notion of s-code is the same. As the s-code is only of semiotic interest when connected with the code proper, it is necessary to modify the general and rigid definition of the structure, in order to make it a semiotic prerequisite for the understanding of the occurrence of signs. However, the notion of structure has played an important role in semiotics as an 'epistemological' and 'methodological' entity.

In an epistemological perspective, the focus is on the ontological status of a structure. A structure is considered either as an immanent constitutive organization of the object itself, or as a theoretical construct. According to the first conception, the structure is the 'idea' of the object, a structure *an sich* which defines the object as a whole. The second interpretation results in considering a structure as a construction, based on specific aspects of a given object and in accordance with explicit theoretical criteria. The structure has to be related to a set of methodological procedures so that the constructed structure can be tested in relation to the object.

Raymond Boudon (1968) characterizes the first conception as an 'intentional' context for a definition of structure, the second as an 'effective' context. The basic presupposition in the first case is this: any object has an essential form which can be revealed. In the second case the assumption is weaker: there are phenomena which, to a certain extent, contain aspects which can be systematized. A 'structure' is one of several possible 'specifications' of this generally presupposed structurability which Boudon calls the 'object-system.' Although both conceptions have been part of semiotics, the latter is the more predominant.

In the effective context, four different types of object-systems can be specified as structures. First, there are systems constituted by interrelated elements with finite definitions, such as the elements of the Indo–European vowel system, or of the system of possible marriages in a South American Indian tribe, depending on kinship relations. The construction of a specific structure of vowels or of marriages can be tested directly or empirically in the linguistic and social reality.

A second type of object-system contains elements defined by an infinite number of features only delimited ad hoc. This is the case when, for example, a structure is ascribed to a population in an opinion poll during an election campaign, or to the semantic reservoir of a language. But still the structure can be empirically tested.

The traditional literary genres exemplify a third type of object-system. Like the first type, this one has a finite number of distinctive features. However, a structure of genres in a given historical period will be subject to an indirect test, because the absence of a given genre or subgenre or the occurrence of literary works which do not belong to any genre, will not falsify the structural analysis, which is concerned with the predominant tendency or possible trends of literature.

Finally, if the psychoanalytical specification of the structure of the human mind is taken into account, for example, we will meet the result of an analysis of a fourth type of object-system. It is defined by an infinite number of distinctive features and is only liable to indirect proof.

The classical notion of structure as a closed network of interdependent elements only covers the first type, and cannot, in semiotics, be identified with structure as such. However, it has been the basis of a widespread 'methodological' approach in semiotics: given one basic semiotic system, e.g., verbal language, others, like film, kinship relations, architecture, etc., will be conceived of as being 'analogous' to this system. This analogy permits the methods of structural linguistics in particular to be applied directly to the other systems in question.

However, when semiotics investigates all four types of object-systems, it cuts across epistemological as well as methodological borderlines. With the existence of an object-system, and thus of an s-coded phenomenon, as a basic assumption for the construction of structural specifications, semiotics is based on a 'soft' epistemology: semiotics argues neither for a pure nominalism (there is a radically arbitrary relation between structure and object), nor for a pure realism (the identity of the structure is derived from the identity of the object); neither does semiotics adopt a purely extensional view of the object (through the structure the object is identified as a member of a class of objects, the extension of the structure), nor a purely intensional view (the structure characterizes the object through the organization of its supposedly relevant features). Semiotics will assume a *predominantly* realistic and intensional attitude, because certain properties are presupposed as real, and because they are taken to be relevant for the production of meaning.

With regard to methods, semiotics often has to face objects which manifest several of the four types of object-systems at the same time, e.g., a theater performance or aspects of urban culture. Hence, semiotics will have to work with a plurality of methods in an interdisciplinary perspective without giving absolute priority to one single semiotic system as a master system or to the methods connected with that system. On the other hand, structures in which the 'sign' is essential will play the leading role.

1.3 Sign

According to the Scholastic definition of the sign, a sign occurs when *aliquid stat pro aliquo*. This statement was valid before the Middle Ages and it still is in the late twentieth century (Rey 1973: 76): a sign is any object which represents another object. Meaning is the representation of an object in or by another object. The sign or the representing object can have any material manifestation as long as it can fulfill the representational function: a word, a novel, a gesture, a reaction in the brain, a city, etc. On the status of the represented object nothing is made explicit by this definition. It may be material or mental, fictitious or factual, fantasized or real, natural or artificial. From this it follows that something which is a sign in one context may be an object in another and vice versa. Signs do not constitute a class of objects. A sign is a 'functional' unit.

Consequently, no object can be pointed out as a sign unless it is integrated in a concrete process, in which more than the sign itself will have to be included in order to actually produce meaning. Only here a concrete distinction and relation between sign and object is established. So, a sign in itself is a 'virtual' unit which is 'realized' in a process creating meaning. This *real* and coded process is called a 'semiosis.'

In a semiosis, one infers something from a phenomenon one thus considers as a sign, concerning something else, the object. Through this inference, the relation between sign and object is specified according to a code on the basis of certain presuppositions. Some of these presuppositions are derived from the notions of code and structure: there must be distinguishable elements at hand which show systematically organized features. Semiotics never starts *ab nihilo*, but from already existing experience, investigating how it works and how it can be reworked through semiosis. Here the inferential specification manifests itself in new signs, referring to already existing sign–object relations. The semiosis is a continuous process of sign production.

In the history of semiotics, two strategies have been followed in order to define this process. In agreement with the first one, the representational relation is conceived of as secondary to the sign itself. This is the *formal* tradition which emphasizes the role of the formal properties of the sign itself. In this tradition, the main purpose is to produce an immanent analysis of the manifestations of specific sign systems, e.g., verbal texts, in an attempt to *generalize* the formal properties of the particular sign system to be valid for semiotic structures as such.

The second strategy, in contrast to the formal one, stresses the representational function as constitutive for the sign. This is the *pragmatic* tradition which focuses on the sign–object relation without paying much attention to the specificity of particular sign systems. Here the semiotic theory is a 'general' theory of signs, trying to reach an understanding of the concrete functioning of any particular sign system.

1.3.1 The Formal Tradition

The origin of the formal tradition is, first of all, structural linguistics, especially as laid out by Ferdinand de Saussure (1857–1913) in particular (see *Saussurean Tradition in Twentieth-Century Linguistics*). Here the linguistic sign is the point of departure for the semiotic generalization. The basic quality of a sign as a semiotic entity is its relative autonomy or arbitrariness vis-à-vis the object and the immanent dichotomization of the sign in expression and

content. Each of the two sign components is built up by clusters of features, through the combination of which the phonetic and the semantic units respectively are coded as formal units. The identity of the units of the expression component is exclusively defined by the mutual relations between them. The specific totality of these relations is the structure of the component. The same goes for the identity of the units and for the structure of the content component. A sign is created through the relation between the two components.

According to this definition, a chess piece which is only used in order to play chess is not a sign, because there is no difference between expression and content: the content is the coded moves and the expression is the same coded moves. According to André Martinet (1908–) such an element is said to have only one articulation. A linguistic sign, however, has a double articulation: in a chain of signs there is a first articulation to articulate them according to their content; the separate signs have a second articulation according to the specific system of expression used. In a semiotic perspective, any sign is defined, totally or partially, through a double articulation which produces an asymmetry between the two levels of articulation. A one-to-one relation between all units of the two components, as with the chess piece, will never occur.

Following the formal tradition it is the double articulation that gives rise to representation. The chess piece, in the context referred to above, does not represent anything except itself. In a genuine sign, however, the double articulation forces us to unite expression and content through a specific mental act, an inference or interpretation, by Saussure called an association. As the associative inference cannot be located exclusively in the expression or in the content, representation is a derived effect of the double articulation of the sign which *creates* an object relation. Meaning is the representational effect produced and conditioned exclusively by the immanent properties of the sign. The order of things and the structure of experience is an effect of the sign structure.

The claim of this tradition is that the s-codes and the codes of the immanent structure of the sign are generally valid irrespective of the specific system of expression used. When two components are united through a double articulation, that is a sign which may be manifested in any medium such as the visual, the gestural, or the architectonic. The analysis of such sign systems that are formally identical with verbal language is carried out using the same methods as are applied in linguistics. Thus, the strategy for the semiotic generalization of the properties of the basic sign system is a methodological analogy.

1.3.2 The Pragmatic Tradition

In contrast to this tradition, the 'pragmatic' tradition is not concerned with the internal structure of the sign itself, and is therefore indifferent as to the specific medium of the sign. The sign is never seen in abstraction from the sign–object relation which is assumed to constitute the sign. In the pragmatic perspective, the main focus of interest is the way this relation is incorporated into the semiosis. The theoretical background of this tradition is, first and foremost, philosophy and logic with Charles Sanders Peirce (1839–1914) in particular, but also Karl Bühler (1879–1963) among the leading figures.

For pragmatic semioticians, the formal properties of the sign will not suffice to define it. The definition of the sign must include elements necessary to explain the *use* of the sign with regard to the object: the status of the object will have to be taken into account (real, fictitious, etc.) as well as the purposiveness of the sign process; the assumed properties of the sign in relation to the object (similarity, copresence, difference, etc.) as well as the types of code involved (mental, material, strategical, etc.) must be dealt with.

From the pragmatic point of view, the semiosis is the 'integration' of an object into a sign process in such a way that new knowledge concerning the object can be manifested in a new sign, which may be a word, an act, an image, etc. In the formal tradition the goal is different. Here the construction of an autonomous sign or structure of signs conveys an 'arbitrary layout' to the object.

If the object is the history of Europe, a sign may be a book, an exhibition, or a movie giving a specific version of this history which, in turn, makes us produce a new sign, e.g., the participation in a peace demonstration, the writing of a new book, the establishing of a new political party or just a psychological reaction of joy or frustration. As an effect of the first sign, each of these new signs establishes a relation to the same object on a new basis.

From a formal point of view the most important question which arises from this example is how the structure of the original sign, as it occurs in a specific system or systems of expression, creates a specific object. If any new sign is produced, the next question will be how the structure of this sign, related to its system of expression, forms an object. The pragmatic approach, on the other hand, looks for how the new sign comes into being as an effect of the manifestation of the first one. Here the transformation or translation between signs and sign systems, irrespective of their material specificity, is the pivotal point of the analysis. Meaning in the pragmatic context is this effect as embedded in a continuous sign production creating new object relations.

The two traditions have different problems to face in an application outside linguistics and philosophy, but they both attempt to cooperate with other disciplines. The formal tradition is anchored in the analysis of a specific sign system and thus it possesses strong methodological and applicative resources, which in fact have given this tradition a great deal of impact. But the strategy of seeing other sign systems as analogous to verbal language may underestimate the particular semiotic capacities of nonverbal sign systems.

Guided by the pragmatic tradition, the overall general logic of the semiosis forces us to concentrate on how different sign systems work together. This interest has broadened the scope of semiotics. But being neutral to the specific medium of the sign, this tradition sees no necessary link between the general structure of semiosis and the particular sign systems engaged in the semiosis. Hence, there are no precise analytical tools left for the understanding of specific sign processes.

A common focal point for the two traditions is the conception of the semiotic inference from sign to object or from expression to content as more comprehensive than logical inference. The goal of any semiotic process is meaning and not logical truth value, which is only one specific type of meaning, integrated in more important and multidimensional effects of meaning produced by the semiotic activity of everyday life. This being the case, the inferential process can never be reduced to a formal structure alone, but contains necessarily nonformal elements which define it as a 'discourse.'

1.4 Discourse

Through the notion of discourse, the semiotic inference is comprehended as an act, implying first of all a specific 'orientation' and a mark of 'subjectivity.'

'Intentionality' in general is defined by phenomenology as the capacity of any consciousness to be a consciousness about something. The mind is constituted by its always being oriented towards an object, which is totally unspecified except for being positioned in relation to the mind. In the discourse, consciousness, abstractly comprehended as intentionality, is embedded in a concrete sign process which is the starting point for the semiotic analysis of intentionality.

In order to be realized as a unity creating meaning, any sign has to be a link in a chain of signs, organized in an irreversible order which is oriented toward an object. From a semiotic point of view, even an anaphoric reference to a previous sign in a syntagmatic chain will contribute to the general irreversibility of the chain, because the anaphora takes place as a production of a new sign, thus basically a movement ahead. This irreversible intentional order is the discourse.

In this perspective, intentionality acquires a more differentiated definition than in philosophy or in descriptions of explicitly purposive instrumental acts. First, there is the 'general' intentionality, because any process of creating meaning is directed towards an object in order to be meaning productive at all. This goes for animals and machines as well as for human beings. Second, there is the 'subjective' intentionality, giving the fact that there is consciousness or human subjectivity involved. Third, we orient ourselves in accordance with the 'ontological' status of the object, the specific type of reality it presumably belongs to (dream, reality, etc.). Fourth, we have a 'specifying' intentionality which is inherent in the fact that a semiosis is aiming at identifying or giving a specific meaning to the intended object, e.g., in the semantic structure of a given sign system. Fifth, a discourse carries an instrumental purposiveness, a 'strategic' intentionality. In the discourse, all these types of intentionality work together so that virtual signs are realized in an 'act.'

The turning point is subjectivity. In the discourse the communicating subject is located in relation to other subjects and in relation to the referential dimension. This situating function is brought about by specific elements in the sign system which carry out this situational function, viz. the 'deictic' elements. Through these elements, e.g., a blast of a horn, a twitch of the eye, subjects and objects are located in time and space in relation to the semiosis. In verbal language, for example, pronouns, certain adverbs, forms of conjugation, are deictic elements; in a film, camera angle or perspective may carry this function; in gestural language, nodding and pointing may exercise deictic functions, etc. No system of elements can be a sign system without deictic elements, and each system is characterized by its particular deictic devices. Systems without deictic elements, like a set of chess pieces, will have to be embedded into semiotic sign systems, like language or gestures, in order to function in a process which creates meaning, e.g., a game one practices to win.

In this way the discourse is framed by a 'discursive universe' for the semiosis. The discursive universe is the set of 'presuppositions' which situates the semiosis in relation to subjects and objects in such a way that a semiosis can take place 'concerning these subjects and objects.' To put it in a less abstract way: the discursive universe is a shared cultural knowledge and experience which is involved in the semiosis, but which we do not need to make explicit. It is the context necessary for the understanding of the outcome of a semiosis.

All the five aspects of intentionality are not listed explicitly when signs are used in a discursive process. But whenever one says 'Look!,' any understanding of this utterance implies that we agree that we have an object outside the speaker; that we communicate to other subjects; that we are looking for something real we want to identify, unless we are explicitly informed otherwise. On the basis of these presuppositions we may want to make certain intentional aspects explicit, e.g., the purpose for the outcry, and ask 'Why?'

The discursive universe is a 'shared' and thus social universe of already existing and accepted knowledge about what we consider a 'possible' world which we make 'real' in producing 'collective' or 'intersubjectively' 'valid' signs about it. The discourse makes the semiosis a 'communicative' act: the semiosis becomes a sign process between subjects about their world. This act is realized in 'texts' (see *Presupposition*; *Deixis*; *Discourse*).

1.5 Text

The compound of actually realized signs, filtered through the discursive logic of intentionality, is a 'text.' The text might seem the most self-evident of the semiotic key notions: the material manifestation of signs, especially verbal signs. But it has in fact received different definitions and has been used on different levels of argumentation.

In Louis Hjelmslev's (1899–1965) linguistic version of the formal tradition, the text is the infinite chain of realized signs. The signs themselves are entities defined by elements in finite structures which are realized in the text. From the point of view of text 'production,' the text is the result of a code engendering an endless number of sign combinations based on a selection among a limited repertoire of sign components. From the 'reception' perspective, the text requires segmentation in delimited individual texts, according to certain methodological criteria which can separate textual features which are pertinent for the sign system in itself, from other features, e.g., genres or rhetorical elements. In this perspective, the discursive intentionality and the problem of contextualization are not taken into account. But on the other hand, the sign system as a stock of possibilities for an infinite sign production is important for semiotics.

When this conception is generalized in semiotics, other sign systems are dealt with as analogous with language.

This means that other semiotic systems produce an endless text in the same material space as language, and that they have to be *received* according to the same analytical linguistic procedures. In this way, the entire world of human activity is turned into one global text or intertextual compound of texts. The globalization of the text removes it from the position as a material object which is accessible through specific methods, and turns it into a general notion concerning the status of objects in the world of human activity: they are all texts. Hence, on the methodological level the formal tradition can only make prescientific distinctions between texts according to the immediately perceived differences between expression systems: visual texts, verbal texts, gestural texts, etc.

The pragmatic tradition, too, also has its problems with the apparently simple notion of text. Here the notion of sign is not bound to a specific system of expression, so there is no distinction between sign and text on the empirical level: a book can be a sign in itself or be looked upon as being built by signs; a city can be regarded as one single sign or it can be seen as a text constituted by a complex networks of signs. So, in this tradition distinctions also have to be made ad hoc between signs and texts and between texts according to the context and to the goal of the analysis.

But as signs in the pragmatic tradition are defined according to the inferential semiotic process, the whole range of discursive elements are also part of the sign definition. So, we will have at our disposal concepts outside the sign system, but inside the semiosis, to operate a distinction between texts.

Seen in this light, everything is a possible text or sign, but not everything has the status of text or sign at the same time, i.e., not everything serves the concrete production of meaning in the actual semiosis. In any concrete semiosis we have a text: a delimited material manifestation of signs containing elements (a) which are necessary to operate a distinction between text and nontext, and (b) which are necessary to draw the line between presupposed elements and explicit elements in the text in order to produce an understanding of its meaning.

In a theater performance, everything on stage is part of a text in a complex network of individual sign systems. In everyday communication, words, gestures, facial expression, etc. as a whole make up a text. In both cases we have neutral elements which do not partake in the semiosis: they are not coded by the s-codes involved in the text in question. The architectural construction of the room or the clothing worn during the communication is irrelevant to the text, not because they do not belong to the sign systems in question, as a partisan of the formal tradition would have stated, but because they do not contribute to the semiosis. On the other hand, they *can* be integrated in the semiosis: the director can use the auditorium as part of the theatrical space of the performance and the limits between text and nontext may even change during the performance; the interlocutors can dress in a way which improves or deliberately interrupts the communication.

Certain elements *can never* be part of the text: parts of the body of the actor will never be coded as signs (illness, sexual dispositions, etc.) and will impose definite limits on the text; during the conversation the telephone may ring or a third person may turn on the radio so that the interlocutors cannot hear one word. These are all elements which are not part of the text as an 'intentional discursive phenomenon,' but they may be components of other texts, and they definitely mark the limits of a text.

No text can ever be infinite from this point of view, but the text itself will contain a level of presupposed elements which are necessary for the existence of the text as a discursive phenomenon. The presupposed elements which can be made explicit by the text, belong to the text, e.g., a theatrical metafiction with an autoreferential dimension may integrate auditorium, audience, technical staff, etc. in the text. Other presupposed aspects, like the actors' salaries, the state of the buildings, the budget of the house, etc. belong to other texts. This means that no text is self-sufficient in a kind of immanent infinity. When one cannot express oneself well enough in an oral verbal text, one can use gestures to compensate. This new verbal–gestural text as a whole now produces one meaning in an intersemiotic textual totality.

In this way, signs and texts necessarily partake in a continuous semiosis through which the limits between texts and between presupposed and explicit elements are constantly moving. Signs are always meant to be transformed into other signs of similar or different types. The text is the materialization of this transformation (see *Text Linguistics*).

2. Semiotic Schools

Semiotics has been institutionalized worldwide in many national associations, which communicate in journals and newsletters of more or less limited distribution. All of them are united under the umbrella of the International Association of Semiotic Studies, with *Semiotica* as its official journal. There are a number of centers and departments at institutions of higher education around the world offering semiotics programs on all levels, mostly integrated in more extensive programs. Apart from this administrative institutionalization, semiotics is guided by the concepts and ideas developed in four major schools.

2.1 Structuralist Semiotics

Structuralist semiotics was inaugurated by Ferdinand de Saussure's *Cours de linguistique générale* (1916) and further developed especially by Louis Hjelmslev's glossematic theory and Algirdas Julien Greimas's (1917–) structural semantics in particular.

Saussure sets out to define linguistics as a specific science by assigning a specific object to it, the particular aspect of language which can only be dealt with by linguistics. The genuine object of linguistics is the language 'system,' the closely interrelated structure of elements that are different from the individual *use* of language, which it determines in such a way that it becomes an understandable chain of meaning carrying verbal unities, signs, and not just a series of sound waves. Although they are parts of language as a global phenomenon, the sociological, physiological, psychological, or aesthetic aspects of language can be left to other disciplines: they are not the *differentia specifica* of verbal production of meaning.

The aim of this project is not to isolate linguistics from other sciences and its object from other sign systems, but to give a precise outline of linguistics and its object in such a way that, from the particularity of language and linguistics, the general aspects of sign systems and the general guidelines for the study of such systems can be developed. Language has to be seen as a particular sign system and linguistics has to be seen as a branch of semiotics, which Saussure himself calls 'semiology.'

With the notion of sign as the heart of linguistics, and with 'dichotomization' as the basic analytical device, Saussure sorts out the conceptual framework of linguistics in order to make the semiotic perspective possible. In a series of dichotomies, the opposition between *system* and *use* being the basic one, he defines a number of dimensions and elements of the language system, so that its internal structure of elements is constitutive for the sign. From a semiotic point of view, the most important among these dichotomies are those immediately connected with the sign, i.e., the distinction between the sign components, 'signifier' and 'signified,' the sign levels, 'form' and 'substance,' the distinction between the principles for the linkage of signs, 'paradigmatic' and 'syntagmatic' order, and, finally, the opposition between the two methodological viewpoints, 'synchrony' and 'diachrony.'

The identity of a signifier or of a signified is its relation, i.e., its simultaneous difference and similarity, to other signifiers and signifieds. This relational identity is the 'value' of the signifying and signified unit. The identity of the signifiers is not bound to the material character of the expression, and the identity of the signifieds does not depend on the quality of the signified objects. Through the value of the sign components, a sign as a whole is then defined as a 'formal' and not as a 'substantial' entity: its identity depends on its relation to other signs in the same system of expression. Thus, a radical or epistemological arbitrariness between sign and object is manifested in the sign as an internal arbitrariness between signifier and signified.

There are two kinds of arbitrariness working in cooperation in the sign system according to two rules of combination. A combination of signs or sign components can be 'syntagmatic,' i.e., bound to a sequential determination or relative arbitrariness, e.g., *str-* at the beginning of an English syllable must be followed by a vowel. If the combination of signs or sign components indicates simultaneous but alternating possibilities (as does the nominal case system), we have a 'paradigmatic' organization, based upon absolute arbitrariness.

Any system built upon arbitrarily combined signs or sign components can be studied from two viewpoints, the historical or 'diachronical,' or the 'synchronical,' i.e., that of a certain frozen situation.

With the notion of value as the key to the whole theory as a semiotic theory, Saussure succeeds in defining language both as a specific structure in its own right, depending on the specificity of the relations involved, and as an example of a general sign structure. This is due to the fact that value is a formal notion, indifferent to how it is materialized and to the character of the objects it represents, so that any system that acts like language in any medium and referring to any object, can be studied as a quasi-linguistic sign system.

With an extension of one of Saussure's own examples: the 8.45 pm train from Paris to Geneva is defined in relation to other trains as listed in the timetable, not with regard to the specific carriages used at any specific moment. The timetable is the paradigmatic order, the organization of carriages with the engine in front is the syntagmatic chain. Changes in the timetable or in the position of the engine, depending on technological developments for example, will be a diachronical study of the Paris–Geneva transportation system, while the analysis of what is going on with regard to rail traffic between the two cities in the 1970s will constitute a synchronical investigation.

In Louis Hjelmslev's glossematics, the semiotic key notions are 'form' and 'hierarchy.' Saussure regards form, *grosso modo*, as equivalent to independence of substance, while Hjelmslev takes form to mean what can be formalized according to formal logic. Formal elements are elements which are exclusively defined by their reciprocal or unilateral relation to other elements. The sign is also a type of reciprocal relation, called the 'sign function,' between two units, the 'expression plane' and the 'content plane.' Elements which are related by concurrence alone have no formal definition. In this way, the formal structure is defined only by these two types of formal relation.

This formalistic or algebraic interpretation of Saussure puts further constraints on the basic analytical principle of dichotomization, in order to set up the final object description. The analysis is carried out as a division of the object in units which can be related and thus defined and only defined by the formal relations. This will lead to a noncontradictory object description. The analysis is exhaustive when all elements which are only characterized as concurrent are left out. They do not belong to the formal description even if they can be repeated, e.g., the quality of Humphrey Bogart's voice, which is always concurrent with the verbal signs he utters. If more than one exhaustive description is possible, the simplest is to be preferred. With this notion of form, Hjelmslev has contributed considerably to the methodological development of semiotics.

Even if the concurrent elements are excluded from one sign system, they may acquire a formal definition by the description of another sign system. Thus, the rigid formalism opens a hierarchy of interrelated semiotic levels. Hjelmslev's vision is a complete structure of sign systems referring to each other in order to create form out of substance on a global scale.

The basic molecule of the hierarchy consists of several sign systems: first, we have a 'denotative' language, constituted by the sign function and thus having an expression plane and a content plane, e.g., the language used by Humphrey Bogart when he orders a scotch on the rocks in a bar. Second, we have a 'metalanguage' which contains an exhaustive formal description of this language as English, thus having the entire denotative language as its content plane and the glossematic description as the expression plane. Also, glossematics will contain nonformal elements, i.e., certain indefinable elements which can be integrated in a 'meta-metalanguage' and there be given a formal definition, i.e., in a nonlinguistic science (philosophy, logic, mathematics, etc.). This language will constitute a third step.

Now, if the metalanguage has left out what is only concurrent in the denotative language, there will be the possibility that another type of metalanguage, called the 'connotative' language, will deal with those formal leftovers. Such a language will have the entire denotative language as its expression plane and also comprise, for example, the quality of Humphrey Bogart's almost mythological voice as a condition for a specific content which is more comprehensive than the whisky as such ordered by the movie star, it is the-scotch-ordered-by-Humphrey-Bogart. This additional creation of meaning can roughly be characterized as 'symbolic' and allows for a new metalanguage that can provide us with a formal description *ad modum glossematicum* of this enlarged meaning, i.e., an analysis of aesthetic, ideological, or mythological effects. The connotative language is parallel to the metalanguage. The hierarchical relation between the denotative language, the metalanguage, and the connotative language with its progress to higher levels has enlarged the possibilities in structural semiotics to take into account a multileveled production of meaning.

After the publication of A. J. Greimas's *Sémantique structurale* (1966), the ideas of structuralist semiotics have had an impact on a variety of subdisciplines of semiotics: literary studies, film studies, anthropology, art history, architecture, etc. Especially in France, Denmark, Spain, Italy, Canada, Brazil (and now also in the USA), an ongoing application and reworking of notions are taking place (see *Hjelmslev, Louis Trolle*; *Paradigms*; *Saussure, Ferdinand(-Mongin) de*; *Values*).

2.2 Phenomenological Semiotics

Semioticians inspired by phenomenology can hardly be said to form a school. What they have in common is the application of notions and ideas from Edmund Husserl's (1859–1938) phenomenology, particularly as expounded in his *Logische Untersuchungen* (1900–01). They belong to a great variety of disciplines, and except for the activities of the Prague School between the two wars, they never formed a group. In the Prague group, influential personalities were Jan Mukařovský (1891–1975), Karl Bühler (1879–1963) and Roman Jakobson (1896–1982).

Husserl himself was not primarily preoccupied with semiotic questions, but with the traditional philosophical problem of how to obtain true knowledge. In order to reach that goal, we have to direct our consciousness toward the objects; we have to express this relation in signs; and, finally, we have to acknowledge that objectivity is based on certain structural principles. This argument leads to the introduction of three semiotically relevant key notions: 'intentionality,' 'sign,' and 'foundation.'

Husserl wants to use these notions to go beyond the realm of the sign to the truth of the object. The purpose of semiotics, on the other hand, is to study the domain of the sign with the sign as its object, to see how the sign is founded, and to see how intentionality works in a sign process to create meaning. As this endeavor is only an intermediary step in Husserl's research, the reference to Husserl in phenomenological semiotics is always selective and often indirect. He indicates a horizon for the semiotic research interest.

Husserl introduces two types of signs: first, the 'indication,' which is a sign that points to a *de facto* presence of the object, without attributing any content to it—the noise from an unidentified thing approaching you; second, the 'expression' in which a mind makes clear that it has been oriented towards an object—a shout like 'Watch out!' accompanied by a nodding head and a pointing finger. Here, the sign–object relation is rooted in a subjectivity, or to put it less phenomenologically: somebody wants to say something to somebody.

Now, the point is that this combination of sign and intentionality as a communicative intersubjectivity is not in the first place an act of deliberate will. It is made possible by the fact that the sign is 'founded,' i.e., it belongs to a structure of relations, called a pure logical grammar, through which it is constituted as a specific type of object, namely as capable of carrying intentionality in intersubjective communication. The notion of foundation is adapted by the Prague School as the notion of structure.

When Husserl's discussion of the sign is transferred to linguistics or other disciplines with a semiotic perspective, it is obvious that a sign structure can never be interpreted as an immanent formal structure. In the structure, the sign occupies the position of an intermediary instance in a communicative and referential structure, and the grammar of any sign system will have to pay special attention to elements which articulate the communicative functions, such as deictic elements.

This is what happens in Karl Bühler's so-called organon model (*Sprachtheorie* 1934). Here the sign is the 'organon' or medium through which an expressive relation to the sender, an appellative relation to the receiver, and a representative relation to an object are present 'simultaneously' in order to create meaning.

The precondition for the transformation of a material object into a sign is the 'abstractive relevance': Any sign–object, e.g., a gesture, has to be structured in such a way that we are able to retain only the features that are relevant for its meaning-creating function. This capacity of the subject and these objectively manifested features must be part of a collectively shared consensus, i.e., be founded in a formal grammar. From this argument Bühler is led to the seminal idea of phonology as an independent study of the structure of such features, which are formal in the sense that they are conditions for the function of sounds as differentiating meaning, but which are not formalistic in the sense that they are defined only through their internal organization.

Roman Jakobson develops Bühler's simple, phenomenologically based communication model into a more differentiated structure with more than three functional relations. One of these relations is of special semiotic interest: the so-called 'poetic' function. This is the function through which the sign is related to itself, the sign represents itself as an object within the communicative structure as a whole. In verbal language, this function can be specified as a transformation of syntagmatic relations into paradigmatic ones. As soon as a work of art is apprehended, it is in a way frozen as one set of simultaneously interrelated elements, in spite of the fact that it is perceived as a sequential order. In a novel the beginning and the end are directly connected once the reading is over.

This idea emerged among the Russian formalists, a group of linguists, literary scholars, poets, and artists, who worked together just before World War I. Parallel to Saussure, they tried to define the study of art as a specific scholarly activity based on the specific artistic character of its object, especially its 'literarity.' This phenomenon was seen as the specific set of devices (rhyme, narrative structure, genre structures, etc.) through which the material aspect of the artistic object is given its specific artistic character as opposed to the ordinary use of the same material, e.g., artistic language as opposed to everyday language. Hence, taken as art, a given object becomes autoreferential. Because the same material is also used outside the artistic context, the effect of the autoreferentiality is not an isolation of the arts, but it is a way of introducing new meaning in the ordinary context. The artistic function always works together with other communicative functions and with other sign systems. The specificity of the artistic object, and of any other object as a sign, is the devices it provides us with to carry out this intersemiotic relation.

This conception of aesthetics was taken up in Prague by Mukarovsky, among others, and a semiotics of the arts (literature, theater, folklore, film, etc.) was created with ideas which are still active in semiotics. Jakobson's contribution was to combine the ideas of Russian formalism and the Prague School with essential aspects of structuralist semiotics, without being taken in by its hard-core formalism.

Another link between phenomenology and structural semiotics is established on a philosophical level in the grammatological analysis of the sign as inaugurated by Jacques Derrida (1930–) in his *De la grammatologie* (1967) and in the hermeneutics of Paul Ricœur (1913–) in *Le Conflit des Interprétations* (1969).

Ricœur criticizes the rigid notion of structure behind the structuralist sign notion. It produces a biased view on the concrete sign process, which in his work is seen as a concrete event where several interpretations of the world meet, e.g., in metaphors and symbols, and not simply as a manifestation of a transindividual structure.

Derrida is more oriented toward the epistemological aspects of the structuralist sign notion: according to him, this notion implies the existence of a transcendental meaning that can be reached through the sign which is regarded as transparent vis-à-vis the virtual structure. But he also points out that this transcendental meaning has to be expressed in signs. The only mode of existence of what is beyond the sign, is the signs in which this beyond is expressed. This paradox is the creative dynamics of all texts. No text will ever express a conclusive meaning, but will always produce a continuous dissolution or 'deconstruction' of stable meanings.

While Ricœur anchors structuralist semiotics in the hermeneutical tradition, Derrida's work has inspired a philosophical relativism characterized as postmodern, deconstructionist, or poststructuralist. But as a whole, phenomenological semiotics is a broadly and *culturally* oriented movement which is still developing and focusing on how human beings are determined by signs (see *Bühler, Karl; Husserl, Edmund; Jakobson, Roman; Prague School Syntax and Semantics*).

2.3 American Semiotics

North American semiotics as a school is identical with Peircean semiotics, rooted in the works of Charles Sanders Peirce. Other types of semiotic activities in the USA are of non-American origin, being of structuralist or postmodern inspiration.

Peirce is a polyhistorian with logic as the center of his thought; logic considered as the way of reasoning about the world through the manipulation of signs which represent this world. So, for Peirce, logic is semiotics. Like Husserl, he is inspired by the medieval schoolmen and he adopts a phenomenological point of departure for his semiotics.

In Peirce, the core of semiotics is the 'semiosis' or the structured process in which the 'sign' imposes a 'coded relation' to an 'object' on a mind. Behind this triadic notion of semiosis are three basic phenomenologically conceived 'modes of being' of objects in relation to the mind. There is the mode of 'firstness,' the object as it is in itself as a virtuality; there is the mode of 'secondness' or the actually existing object as different from and opposed to the mind and to other objects; finally, there is the mode of 'thirdness' where the object is presented according to a law which makes it accessible to recognition. Semiosis is the process governed by thirdness.

The constitutive triad of the semiosis is the sign, the 'interpretant' or the coded relation, and the object. So, all signs are objects which function as instances of thirdness; they are liable to abstractive relevance, as Bühler would say.

The particularity of the sign in the semiosis depends on the sign–object relation inside the triadic relation. If this relation is based on 'similarity' between sign and object, i.e., expresses firstness, we have an 'iconic' sign. As the sign is part of a triadic structure, the similarity is not immediate, but coded as a specific similarity (spatial, oral, visual, olfactory, etc.). When the foundation of a sign–object relation is 'copresence,' the sign manifests 'secondness' and is called an 'indexical' sign (a pointing finger, the smoke of a fire, an outcry caused by pain, etc.). Finally, a sign–object relation may be established according to 'convention' and thus express 'thirdness,' which produces a 'symbolic' sign (a linguistic sign, gestures of politeness, etc.). Being an instance of thirdness in the semiosis, which is thirdness as a process, the symbolic sign is the most complete sign of the three types of signs.

The symbolic sign is similar to the arbitrary sign in Saussure and is also bound to a collectively shared structure of understanding. But it can never be isolated in the semiosis from manifestations of the other types of sign. Any semiosis is a compound of iconic, indexical, and symbolic signs: the indexical sign aspects establish a relation to an object, the iconic sign aspects open for analogies which are essential to our everyday behavior when we imitate former experience, and the symbolic sign aspects produce coded knowledge on which we can agree or disagree and reach new knowledge. No sign aspects can be disposed of. So, Peirce's semiotics is close to the phenomenological insistance on the whole dialogical structure of semiosis.

In being object-related, Peirce's sign is also close to the expression in Husserl's theory. Like Husserl, Peirce introduces a differentiation of 'objects': first, the 'dynamical' object, which is the object outside the semiosis towards which this process is directed, posed by the semiosis as its goal, but neither formed nor determined by it. Second, the 'immediate' object which is the object as represented in the semiosis, e.g., as expressed in the semantic structure of a language. The demarcation line between the two dimensions of the object is the result of the semiosis and it is constantly replaced by the semiotic activity when knowledge is created.

The 'interpretant' is the cornerstone of Peirce's semiotics. It is the code or law through which sign and object are related so that an effect of the semiosis can occur. It is not an imitation of an immanent structure of the sign or of the object, and it is not an arbitrary structure imposed on the object from the outside. The interpretant is the law which is made necessary by the sign–object relation in order to give this relation a generally valid character. The interpretant is an 'effect' of the sign–object relation, determined by it and, in turn, specifying it. That the relation is generally valid means that it can be subsumed under a law which can be agreed upon and repeated. So, the mode of being of an interpretant will be the 'habits' according to which we actually deal with the object. These habits will be manifested as signs in other semioses and reinterpreted and perhaps changed. The interpretant creates new signs and thus a continuous semiosis.

The interpretant as an effect has three aspects: the 'immediate' interpretant is the presupposed organized character of the object which make the application of a law possible, what Boudon calls the object-system. The 'dynamical' interpretant is the delimited effect, a concrete physical or mental act performed by somebody or something as the result of the sign–object relation. The 'final' interpretant will be this act regarded as the general truth about the object, such as a law which is a universally valid guideline for a habitual act, i.e., a way of reasoning in mathematics, independently of any individual subject. The connection between semiosis and habits made Peirce call his semiotics 'pragmatism.'

The dynamical interpretant is of particular semiotic interest, because it is this effect which is the motor of the semiosis. If a driver is waiting in a lane in front of a traffic light, ready to continue when the light is green, the traffic light will be the sign and the traffic the dynamical object. The immediate object will be the representation of the traffic in the sign systems known by the driver (urban phenomenon, regulated by law, dangerous, etc.). The rules which regulate the traffic through the traffic light (stop, go, wait, etc.) will be the interpretant. The object has presumably a certain order which makes it reasonable to learn and to obey the traffic light. This preconception of the object as structurable will be the immediate interpretant. The final interpretant, i.e., the ideal and universal organization of traffic is of mainly theoretical interest, but it is a working concept in functionalist urban planning, for example.

From this perspective, the dynamical interpretant will be the act which incorporates the code: as soon as the light turns green, the driver manipulates his car and off he goes. This interpretant is manifested in the semiosis as a new sign, the moving car, which in turn may be interpreted in relation to the same object by the drivers further down the lane who cannot see the traffic light: they turn on their engines, ready to go. If a driver had started while the light was red, his act would still have been a dynamical interpretant, but a police officer might have stopped him, taking it as a sign related to the same dynamical object but representing another immediate object. In this case, the traffic would no longer be a practical affair but a legal complex.

Because of the generality of Peirce's thought and its comprehensive character, bridging the gap between profound epistemological viewpoints, cultural and historical problems, and particular types of signs and sign processes in different disciplines, it has had an immense influence in all semiotic domains.

The tripartition of signs has been the emblem of his semiotics and has been used to characterize sign processes of all types and in all kinds of expression systems. And his emphasis on the dialogical structure of the semiosis and of the shared knowledge presupposed by the semiosis, has led to penetrating studies in philosophical and literary hermeneutics or in anthropology and the social sciences (e.g., Singer 1984). But in most cases the generality also means a lack of specific analytical devices, so that the application of Peirce's notions is normally integrated as specifying guidelines for a methodological pluralism. In this capacity, Peirce's semiotics has a global influence as well as a growing one.

2.4 The Moscow–Tartu School

With the Moscow–Tartu School, a school in the literal sense of the word was established. Founded in 1962, it continues the cooperation between the Slavic countries and the other countries on the European continent which dates back to Saussure and his foundation of structural linguistics, to Russian formalism, and to the Prague School. Among the leading figures are Jurij Lotman (1922–) from Tartu and Vjaceslav Ivanov (1929–) from Moscow.

Although the activities of the school have several sources of inspiration, structuralist semiotics is the most decisive: the Saussurean sign and the Hjelmslevian hierarchy (see Grzybek 1989). On the basis of these fundamentals, the ambition is to focus on more complex sign structures than verbal language and to transform the basic notions and methods of the linguistically based structural semiotics beyond a mere analogy. Hence, the main interest of the school is the study of 'culture' as a semiotic system. The basic notions are 'text' and 'model.'

Culture is based on a process of creation, exchange, and storage of information, and the specific 'unity' of this process is the object of cultural semiotics. The material for this study is the 'text' in which this process materializes, and the 'invariants' which can be found in the texts constitute the ultimate object of cultural semiotics. The text is a megasign, as it were, and is built up of binary signs. In the structuralist sign conception, the invariants are the relationally defined elements which constitute the signifier-component and the signified-component. But in the cultural flow of information, the invariants are neither located in the sign itself nor in the text in itself. Therefore, the signifier of the sign is seen as a material unit, not as a formal unit. Furthermore, when the text is seen in analogy with the sign, it is regarded as any delimited material unit with a content that can be divided in smaller units of the same kind.

Following this idea, the formal definition of the invariants requires another notion, the notion of 'model.' First of all, the notion of model implies a 'hierarchy' between two levels, a model being a model of something. The invariants are the elements which remain stable when meaning from one level in a hierarchy is transformed to another. Second, the notion of model is necessarily linked to the assumption of a basic 'code' or structure which reworks an object, duplicating or replacing it by a model. In culture the basic object is always a text, dealing with our world of experience, e.g., a linguistic or visual text. The model is another text which uses the first one as expression and which contains the rules by which this expression takes place. This is an application of the connotative hierarchy in Hjelmslev.

The point is that any text, also the basic one, in order to be text must be placed in a modeling hierarchy, either as the so-called 'primary modeling system,' e.g., the verbal text which functions as a model of our experience of the world, or as a 'secondary modeling system' which reconstructs the first modeling system's way of systematizing our experience. So, a 'model' is a text considered as an organizing system in relation to another text.

From this point of view, the cultural invariants are attached to the text-as-model, functioning in an irreducible double structure consisting of at least two modeling systems. The two systems will never be identical, neither by being identical repetitions nor by being infinite, because texts as models impose limits on the infinite flow of information from the surrounding world. They will be different and often in opposition.

The advantage of this approach is that the basic text, the primary modeling system, will be delimited according to the purpose of the analysis, i.e., the relation to another modeling system. Furthermore, in a cultural perspective the text is always linked to a hierarchy which cannot be reduced to a homogeneous whole where the two modeling systems function as one. Thus, culture is always seen as a dynamic intersection or a continuous process of unifying heterogeneous texts.

In an analogy to the notion of biosphere, this cultural space is called the 'semiosphere' by Jurij Lotman. With this notion he wants to draw our attention to the fact that the domain of texts, in order to be texts, is always opposed to a domain of phenomena which are not texts. The heterogeneous character of the semiosphere is a result of the continuous replacement of its limits by the production of texts confronting the nontextual sphere in a ongoing cultural attempt to integrate it into the world of human activity, producing an interior reorganization of this world of activity (see *Model*).

3. Semiotic Domains

A survey of the different fields of research in semiotics is given in the general semiotic encyclopedias (Nöth 1985; Sebeok (ed.) 1986; Posner (ed.) 1992). Contributions from the humanities (literary studies, epistemology, logic, hermeneutics, aesthetics, architecture, design, linguistics, film studies, musicology, theater studies) are abundant, but the social sciences (mass media studies, communication studies, studies of urban culture and popular culture, cultural anthropology, ideology studies, women's studies, pedagogics, marketing) and psychology (psychoanalysis, cognitive science) are also richly represented, as are theology and law. Less numerous are works in the sciences and medicine (animal communication studies, biology, computer sciences, pathological studies of body signs), but a growing interest is shown in these fields. Many of the separate domains organize the research in special associations with journals and congress activities.

4. Future of Semiotics

The late-twentieth-century activities of semiotics in an international perspective indicate at least four main roads for the future progress of semiotics, which will run parallel to a continuous activity in the particular fields of research.

4.1 Cooperation of Schools

The historical differences between two basic traditions and between the main semiotic schools will tend to disappear in the years to come: the formal tradition needs the global perspective of the pragmatic tradition which will, in turn, need the detailed knowledge of specific sign systems presented by the formal tradition. The turning point will be the elements in the specific sign systems, which define their particular pragmatic capacity, namely the elements through which any sign system is anchored in a discursive process in relation to other sign systems and to situational conditions. These are the elements carrying the 'indexical or deictic functions,' which will attract increasing attention also inside the specific branches of semiotics.

4.2 Cultural Semiotics

There is a growing interest in 'cultural semiotics.' This will encompass the study of whole cultures, such as European culture, or larger segments of culture, like youth culture, as complex sign systems, with a special emphasis on the intercultural dynamic exchange of signs. The endeavor of this study is to cover all cultural activities, from the basic establishment of time and space relations and structures of subjectivity to specific cultural phenomena such as political rhetoric or the arrangement of pedestrian zones, seen in the perspective of meaning production through signs. In this way, semiotics tries to integrate the more specific semiotic studies from recent years in a global perspective. But in the field of cultural studies, semiotics is at the same time constantly confronted with nonsemiotic approaches which are necessary to delimit the texts to be investigated, so that semiotics has now been forced into an open interdisciplinarity, breaking down the walls around semiotics itself.

4.3 Human and Nonhuman Signs

Another trend will be the 'combination of human and nonhuman sign production,' be it animal communication or the computerized processing of information. This orientation leads to a reevaluation of the notion of sign and will focus on other types of units which create meaning, like signals, units with one articulation, etc., and it will open to a stronger interest in communicative and informational acts which are not, like the more traditionally conceived interpretation, exclusively bound to doubly articulated signs and complex sign systems. Here an interest in studying the cooperation between signs and nonsigns will emerge.

4.4 Possible Worlds

An important aspect of our modern culture which has been permeated by the effects of computer technology, is the way the logical problem of 'possible worlds,' dating back to Leibniz, becomes part of the meaning production, not only in different types of fiction or of logical constructs, but in the process of the planning of the future. We have to be able to construct scenarios for the long-term consequences of things such as the depositing of nuclear waste, of huge climatic changes, of computerized communication processes and their influence on local cultures, etc. We are able to construct such scenarios in great detail, but none of us will live long enough to see if they will ever be real or true.

But despite the fact that these possible worlds (or virtual realities) only exist in sign systems, we have, nevertheless, to respond to them in terms of practical actions here and now, and in doing so we inevitably take a stand as to their reality. Semiotics will be of increasing importance in the construction of possible futures as cultural and not only technological universes.

See also: Language; Philosophy of Language; Pragmatics; Structuralism and Semiotics, Literary.

Bibliography

Boudon R 1968 *A quoi sert la notion de structure?* Gallimard, Paris
Bühler K 1982 *Sprachtheorie*. Fischer, Stuttgart
Eco U 1984 *Semiotics and the Philosophy of Language*. Indiana University Press, Bloomington, IN
Greimas A J 1966 *Sémantique structurale*. Larousse, Paris
Greimas A J, Courtés J 1979–86 *Sémiotique: Dictionnaire raisonné de la théorie du langage*, 2 vols. Hachette, Paris
Grzybek P 1989 *Studien zum Zeichenbegriff der sowjetischen Semiotik*. Brockmeyer, Bochum
Hjelmslev L 1969 *Prolegomena to a Theory of Language*. University of Wisconsin Press, Madison, WI
Husserl E 1968 *Logische Untersuchungen*. Niemeyer, Tübingen
Innis R E 1985 *Semiotics: An Introductory Anthology*. Hutchinson, London
Lotman I U M 1990 *Universe of the Mind: A Semiotic Theory of Culture*. Tauris, London
Nöth W 1985 *Handbuch der Semiotik*. Metzler, Stuttgart
Peirce C S 1958 *Collected Papers*, 8 vols. Harvard University Press, Cambridge, MA
Posner R, et al. 1992 *Semiotik: Ein Handbuch zu den zeichentheoretischen Grundlagen von Natur und Kultur*. Walter de Gruyter, Berlin and New York
Rey A 1973 *Théories du signe et du sens*, 2 vols. Klincksieck, Paris
Saussure F de 1972 *Cours de linguistique générale*. Payot, Paris
Sebeok T A, et al. 1986 *Encyclopedic Dictionary of Semiotics*, 3 vols. Mouton de Gruyter, Berlin and New York
Singer M 1984 *Man's Glassy Essence*. Indiana University Press, Bloomington, IN
Tobin Y (ed.) 1988 *The Prague School and Its Legacy in Linguistics, Literature, Semiotics, Folklore and the Arts*. John Benjamins, Amsterdam

S. E. Larsen

Semitic Languages

The term 'Semitic,' derived from the Hebrew name Shem (Genesis 10: 21–31; 11: 10–26) and originally applied to Arabic, Aramaic, and Hebrew by A. L. Schlözer in 1781, now also includes several other languages, some only discovered in the late twentieth century. Although inaccurate it is a convenient label for a set of languages sharing common features within the larger family of Hamito–Semitic, or Afroasiatic as it is now commonly called. General issues such as dialect geography, connections with very early non-Semitic languages and the defining characteristics of a Semitic language are now to the fore in scholarly debate. The tendency for scholars to study better known and better attested languages to the neglect of others considered less important or peripheral has contributed to the difficulty in making statements of general application to the Semitic language group.

1. The Semitic Language Group

Among the two dozen or so languages or dialects which can be identified as Semitic are Akkadian, Amharic (see *Amharic*), Arabic (see *Arabic*), Aramaic, Assyrian, Babylonian (see *Babyonian Grammatical Texts*), Eblaic (see *Eblaic (Eblaite)*), Epigraphic South Arabian, Ethiopic (see *Ethiopian Semitic Languages*), Ge'ez (see *Ge'ez*), Hebrew (see *Hebrew*), Maltese (see *Maltese*), Mandaic, Nabataean, Palmyrene, Phoenician (see *Phoenician/Punic*), Punic, Syriac, Ugaritic (see *Ugaritic*), and Ya'udic. For some of these languages the evidence is very meagre. For example, Amorite is known almost entirely from personal names in texts from Mari on the Upper Euphrates and the glosses to the El-Amarna Letters (written predominantly in Babylonian) are the only vestiges of the Canaanite dialect used by the scribes. Others, such as Linear A (from Crete), have been classed as Semitic but may not be and the Proto-Sinaitic and Proto-Canaanite inscriptions remain difficult to read. For yet other languages, such as Hebrew and Arabic, there exist relatively large written corpuses developed over a very long and continuous time span and a wide range of geographical locations, which display clear differences connected with historical period, region, and register.

2. Contact with Non-Semitic Languages

The area covered by Semitic languages includes Mesopotamia (modern Iraq), parts of Turkey, Syria and the Levant, the Arabian Peninsula as well as coastlands and islands of the Mediterranean. Not only was there influence on the Semitic-speaking world from outside but even within the same area speakers of Semitic and non-Semitic languages coexisted. Thus, in Mesopotamia, both Sumerian and Akkadian were used and in the kingdom of Ugarit, Anatolian influence, particularly from Hurrian and Hittite, was strong. Similarly, Cushitic influenced Ethiopic, and the European languages have affected modern Arabic and Hebrew. To take a concrete example, it has been suggested that although other Semitic languages developed from SOV (Subject-Object-Verb) to VSO, Akkadian remained an SOV language. The determining factor was interference from Sumerian which prevented this evolution. There was also mutual influence between languages within the Semitic family. For example, the verb forms of the Akkadian used at ancient Ugarit (Ras Shamra) were subject to Ugaritic grammar and Aramaic words were borrowed into Akkadian and Hebrew.

3. The Characteristics of Semitic

Typical of the Semitic languages are verbless clauses, in which no verb equivalent to 'to be' is expressed, for example, Akkadian *awâtum dannâ* 'affairs are pressing.' The verbal system, which appears historically to have expressed 'aspect' more than 'tense,' employs an extensive series of inflections of a consonantal 'root' (typically comprising three consonants) in order to express in a regular and productive manner modalities such as passive, causative, intensive, reflexive, passive-reflexive, etc. for example, (from the root *SBT* in Akkadian) *iṣbat* 'he will seize,' *iṣṣabit* 'he was seized,' *taṣṣabbata* 'you will grasp one another,' *tiṣbut* 'it is joined to,' *uṣabbit* 'he captured,' *ušaṣbit* 'he caused to seize,' *ittaṣbatā* 'they were gripped together.' Lists of common lexical items or isoglosses have also been compiled, e.g., Akkadian *bītu*, Arabic *bayt*, Aramaic *baytā*, Ethiopic *bēt*, Hebrew *bāyit*, Phoenician and Ugaritic *bt* (vocalization uncertain) all meaning 'house,' and the verb *bky* 'to weep,' found in all these languages and also in Eblaic. Only two genders are well-attested, masculine and feminine, although there are also traces of a common gender. In general there are extremely few compound nouns in Semitic.

Other features are sometimes claimed to be typical of, although not necessarily exclusive to, the Semitic languages.

  (a) Emphatic consonants (often held to be velarized) are used in phonemic opposition to nonemphatic (nonvelarized ones) and the pharyngeal consonants are common.

  (b) Typically, a triconsonantal lexical root/or a lexical root comprising three consonants/ (or 'archilexeme') is employed from which words are derived by incorporating vowels and affixes (e.g., from Arabic *ʕLN* 'evident,' *ʕalana* 'to become known,' *ʕalin* 'overt' *muʕlin* 'announcer' *ʕalāniya* 'publicity'); however, many roots are apparently biconsonantal or appear to have only two consonants (e.g., *ʔḫ* 'brother'), others have just one consonant (e.g., *p* 'mouth'), and a few four or even five consonants (e.g., *ʕqrb* 'scorpion,' *sprdʕ* 'frog'). In fact, it is now generally accepted that many verbal roots were originally biconsonantal, later expanded by the affixing of another consonant or the insertion of a root vowel.

  (c) Following on from (b) it has been asserted that the root meaning is carried by the (three) consonants with the vowels as modifiers. However, the same phenomenon of grammatical inflexion by vowel change is attested in non-Semitic languages, e.g., 'fall,' 'fell.' Further, as just mentioned, not all roots comprise three consonants and even where that is the case words can have identical consonants but distinct meanings, e.g., *RGM* 'to call' in Akkadian (and Ugaritic) but 'to stone' in Hebrew (and Arabic).

  (d) In syntax, coordinated main clauses predominate over the use of subordinate clauses.

4. Proto-Semitic

The fact that Semitic languages share so many characteristics has led historically to the search for a common ancestor usually termed 'Proto-Semitic.' Although scholars now would hesitate to posit development from an unattested proto-language, the clear existence of elements common to many recorded Semitic languages makes the concept of Proto-Semitic, or at least of 'Common Semitic,' a useful one. Various theories have been put forward concerning the alleged homeland of the earliest Semites and their spread over the area where Semitic is found. A series of migrations in waves, all stemming from the Arabian desert, notably an Amorite migration in the second millennium followed by a migration of Aramaeans in the first, has long been the accepted explanation. A refinement of this thesis prefers to speak of 'infiltration' rather than 'invasion.' The use of a lingua franca, for example, Akkadian in the second millennium BC or Aramaic in the first may have played a part in the spread of different dialects.

Geographical linguistics has also been employed to help explain the evolution of the Semitic languages. Generally one can speak of a 'center' producing linguistic innovations which spread out to 'marginal' areas. In this case, the central area, the Arabian Peninsula, underwent less change than the two marginal regions, which comprised Syria to Mesopotamia to the north and Ethiopia to the south. In fact, the first of these 'peripheral' regions, especially in the northwest corner, itself became a major center of innovation through its special contacts with the non-Semitic world and with other Semitic-speaking areas. Examples of innovation are broken plurals and both the passive and the causative in the verbal system. It is also possible that instead of a single origin, there was a convergence of the various Semitic languages followed by a later divergence.

5. Semitic within Afroasiatic

The Hamito–Semitic phylum, now commonly referred to as Afrasian or Afroasiatic (see *Afroasiatic Languages*), has six branches: Berbero–Libyan (or Libyan–Guanche), Chadic, Cushitic, Egyptian, Omotic, and Semitic. After Egyptian, Semitic is the oldest recorded language group. These languages cover a very wide area (for maps see Diakonoff 1965) and their origin is very ancient. Broadly speaking they fall into two groups: the northern group, more open to change, with the great civilizations of Egypt, Syria, and Mesopotamia as its center, and the southern group, far removed from the center and therefore more traditional in character.

6. Subdivisions within Semitic

Although no overall consensus exists regarding allocation of languages within the family tree, it is generally accepted that there are two main branches: East Semitic (i.e., Akkadian, from about 3000 BC) and West Semitic (ca. 2000 BC). Further subdivision is into northwest (Ugaritic, Hebrew, Aramaic) and southwest (Arabic and South Arabic with Ethiopic). Diakonoff groups these languages as follows: northern peripheral (Akkadian), northern central (Eblaic, Canaanite, Amorite, Ugaritic, Hebrew, Phoenician–Punic, Aramaic, etc.), south central (Arabic), south peripheral (Early South Arabic), and Ethiosemitic both north and south (see *Ethiopian Semitic Languages*). The disagreements involve the subbranches due, in part, to the discovery of languages such as Eblaic and Ugaritic. A new subbranch of the western branch, called 'Central Semitic' embracing Aramaic, Canaanite and, unexpectedly, Arabic has been proposed. The morphology of the verb, though, seems to suggest, instead, that Central Semitic has two further

branches: Northwest Semitic (Ugaritic and the El-Amarna glosses; Arabic, Aramaic, and Canaanite) and Southwest Semitic (Epigraphic South Arabian). The different Semitic languages use a variety of scripts but this is of no significance for classification (see *Writing: Overview of History*).

7. Modern Semitic Languages

The following languages survive among speakers in the early 1990s: Amharic, Tigre, etc. in Ethiopia; Arabic in the Arabic-speaking world; Modern Western Aramaic dialects in Syria (notably the village of MaꞆlūla), and Eastern Aramaic dialects (in the mountains of Kurdistan, the shores of Lake Urmia and elsewhere), and Modern Israeli Hebrew. Syriac is still in liturgical use.

8. Future Work

Future research needs to take into account languages only discovered in the late twentieth century (e.g., Eblaic, Ugaritic), and dialects (e.g., the Akkadian dialect used at Emar), and integrate them within the larger group of Afroasiatic languages. Certain languages or dialects such as Ya'udic (used in Northern Syria) remain unclassified. Detailed syntactic, as opposed to morphological analyses are rather sparse in certain of the Semitic languages. Onomastics, reflecting to some degree the correlation between a population and its language(s) is a further important area of future study. A synchronic approach, which examines a Semitic language or a group of related languages as it presents itself at a particular period needs to be complemented by a diachronic approach which takes account of the historical evolution of the language or languages. Furthermore, scholars usually stress similarities (for example, between Ugaritic and Phoenician) but it is equally important to determine the individual characteristics of each language and establish, for instance, what makes Hebrew different from Akkadian. It also remains to be determined whether some languages are really dialects (e.g., Moabite may be a dialect of ancient Hebrew) or even pidgins (e.g., the glosses to the El-Amarna Letters). The interactions between such dialects and standard languages also require study.

Bibliography

Bergsträsser G 1983 *Introduction to the Semitic Languages: Text Specimens and Grammatical Sketches*. Eisenbrauns, Winona Lake, MN

Blau J 1970 *On Pseudo-Corrections in Some Semitic Languages*. Israel Academy of Sciences and Humanities, Jerusalem

Diakonoff I M 1965 *Semito–Hamitic Languages: An Essay in Classification*. Nauka, Moscow

Garr W R 1985 *Dialect Geography of Syria–Palestine, 100-586 BC*. University of Pennsylvania, Philadelphia, PA

Haayer G 1986 Languages in contact: The case of Sumerian and Akkadian. In: Vanstiphout H L J, Jongeling K, Leemhuis F, Reinink G J (eds.) *Scripta Signa Vocis: Studies about Scripts, Scriptures, Scribes and Languages in the Near East, presented to J. H. Hospers by his pupils, colleagues and friends*. Egbert Gorsten, Groningen

Hospers J H 1973 *A Basic Bibliography for the Study of the Semitic Languages*. Brill, Leiden

Khan G 1988 *Studies in Semitic Syntax*. Oxford University Press, Oxford

Moscati S, et al. (eds.) 1964 *An Introduction to the Comparative Grammar of the Semitic Languages: Phonology and Morphology*. Harrassowitz, Wiesbaden

Rabin C 1963 The origin of the subdivisions of Semitic. In: Winton T D, McHardy W D (eds.) *Hebrew and Semitic Studies: Presented to Godfrey Rolles Driver*. Clarendon, Oxford

Retsö J 1989 *Diathesis in the Semitic Languages: A Comparative Morphological Study*, Studies in Semitic Languages and Linguistics, 14. Brill, Leiden

Sáenz-Badillos A 1993 *History of the Hebrew Language*. Cambridge University Press, Cambridge

Sekine M 1973 The subdivisions of the north-west Semitic languages. *Journal of Semitic Studies* **18**: 205–21

Ullendorff E 1958 What is a Semitic language? *Orientalia* **27**: 66–75

Voigt R M 1987 The classification of Central Semitic. *Journal of Semitic Studies* **32**: 1–21

W. Watson

Semitic Scripts: Dissemination and Influence

All contemporary writing systems, with the exception of those based on the Chinese script (see *Japanese Writing System*; *Korean Writing System*) can be traced back to Semitic prototypes which developed in the near Middle East between 1800–1500 BC. Semitic scripts are consonantal in character; this means that words are primarily represented by their consonants which carry the root meaning (see *Semitic Scripts, North and South*; and for all modern forms *Hebrew* and *Arabic*). One of the advantages of Semitic scripts over previous systems (see *Egyptian Hieroglyphs*; *Sumerian Writing*) is the small number of signs required which in turn promotes greater flexibility. When adapted for the use of non-Semitic languages Semitic scripts developed into alphabets in Europe (see *Alphabet: Development*), and into syllabic scripts in south and southeast Asia (see *Scripts, Indian, Northern*; *Akkadian*; *South East Asian Scripts*); with variants along the old trade routes which

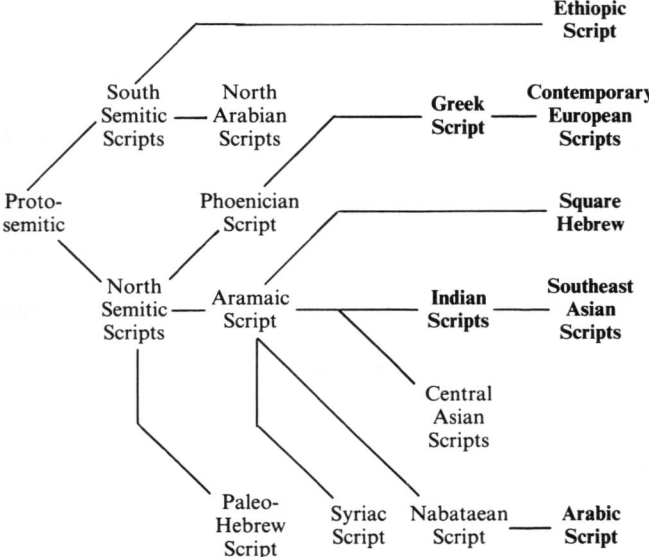

Figure 1. (After A. Gaur *A History of Writing*, reproduced with permission.)

connected Central Asia and China to the west (see also *Writing: Overview of History*).

1. Europe and the Alphabet

Around 1000 BC the Greeks came into contact with the Phoenician form of writing and by using some of the Semitic consonant signs to represent vowels, they adapted it successfully to the use of their own (Indo–European) language. In the eighth century Greek settlers took the Greek alphabet to Italy where it was used, first by the Etruscans, and from around the seventh and sixth century BC on, by the Romans (see *Alphabet: Development*; *Runes*; *Ogam*).

2. Iranian and Central Asian Scripts

Semitic traders and Christian (Manichaean and Nestorian) missionaries brought writing to Iran and Central Asia. The scripts which consequently evolved to serve, with varying degrees of success, a large number of local languages go directly or indirectly (via Syriac) back to Aramaic (see *Semitic Scripts, North and South*).

Decisive for the development of writing in Central Asia was the script used from 500 AD for Sogdian (a Middle Iranian language). It was a basically consonantal script, consisting of seventeen letters plus two special signs. At first letters were written separately but in the seventh century a more cursive hand developed which linked individual signs by a continuous baseline. In the eighth century the Uighur script evolved from a later form of Sogdian among the Buddhists in Turkestan. It was not a good instrument for writing Turkish, especially when the dots meant to distinguish certain letters were omitted. In 1206 Genghis Khan chose the Uighur script (and language) for the Mongol chancellery. Efforts to use the Mongolian vernacular as the official language led to a remodeling of Uighur; in 1272 the so-called Passepa script, an adaptation of the Tibetan seal script added some (Indian) syllabic elements (see *Scripts, Indian, Northern*); a hybrid and still cumbersome script called Kalika developed to become the forerunner of modern Mongolian.

3. Syllabic Scripts in Asia and Ethiopia

3.1 The Indian Subcontinent

Around the seventh century BC Semitic traders and Persian administrators brought Aramaic to the northwestern part of India. Two scripts developed: Kharoshthi (third century BC–seventh century AD), a short-lived and historically less important cursive business script, and Brahmi, first documented in the inscriptions of the Emperor Asoka (272–31 BC); both of them syllabic. Since the correct pronunciation of the Vedic hymns had always been an essential aspect of ceremonial Hinduism, an orally transmitted knowledge of phonetics existed prior to the use of writing, and Brahmi was perfectly adapted to the sounds of Indian languages. All contemporary Indian scripts (see *Scripts, Indian, Northern*; *Scripts, Indian, Southern*) including those used in the Himalayan countries and in Sri Lanka, can be traced back to Brahmi. They consist basically of about 48 to 54 signs with vowels written in their full form only if used on their own or in an initial position; in conjunction with a consonant they are abbreviated to auxiliary signs before, after, below, or above the consonant sign.

3.2 Southeast Asia

During the first Christian millennium Indian traders, colonists, military adventurers, and Buddhist missionaries brought their scripts (mostly a South Indian grantha variation of Brahmi) to Southeast Asia. Designed to fit the linguistic peculiarities of Indian languages they now had to accommodate four entirely different language groups: Sino–Tibetan, Malayo–Polynesian, Austro–Asiatic, and Thai. This was achieved by a number of compromises (some more, some less effective), mostly restricted to the usage and the number of characters; sometimes diacritical marks were added for the representation of the tonal range. The basic internal structure of the script, the arrangement and construction of the syllabic unit, the way in which vowels were represented (either initial or auxiliary), and the phonetic arrangement of the characters remained however largely the same (for details see *South East Asian Scripts*; *Scripts, Javanese and Related*).

3.3 Ethiopia

The Ethiopic script, first documented in the fourth century AD, goes back to a South Semitic prototype (see *Semitic Scripts, North and South*). It consists of 27 consonant and seven vowel signs which are manipulated in a manner similar to Indian syllabic scripts (for details see *Ethiopian Syllabaries*).

Bibliography

Diringer D 1968 *The Alphabet—A Key to the History of Mankind*. Hutchinson, London

Gaur A 1987 *A History of Writing*, 2nd edn. British Library, London

Healey J F 1980 *The Early Alphabet*. British Museum Publication, London

A. Gaur

Semitic Scripts, North and South

Semitic scripts go back to a purely phonetic form of writing which originated in the Near Middle East between 1800–1500 BC. They are generally divided into two, considerably different main branches, a northern and a southern one, with the latter being of less importance. In the course of time Semitic scripts became the most powerful instruments for the storage and dissemination of knowledge, stimulating the development and growth of a large number of new and highly effective writing systems in Europe and Asia—some extinct, some still in use (see *Semitic Scripts: Dissemination and Influence*; *Alphabet: Development*; *Scripts, Indian, Northern*; *Scripts, Indian, Southern*; *South East Asian Scripts*).

1. What are Semitic Scripts?

1.1 Characteristics

The term 'Semitic' was first used in the eighteenth century in relation to a group of languages of which Hebrew and Arabic were the most prominent constituents, and referred to an imaginary connection with Shem, the son of Noah. The characteristics of Semitic scripts are that of the Semitic language: the root meaning of a word is born by the consonants (usually three in number), vowels serve mainly to fashion grammatical forms. Thus the Arabic root k-t-b, depending on the interpolated vowels, can stand for *kātib*

'writer,' *kataba* 'he wrote,' *kitāb* 'book,' *kutub* 'books' *kutubī* 'bookseller,' *kitāba* 'writing,' *maktab* 'office,' and *maktaba* 'library, book shop'; which vowels have to be interpolated depends on the context and on the grammatical construction of the sentence. This absence of vowel signs was to some extent remitted, at quite an early stage, by the use of consonant signs, such as *j* and *w*, for the representation of long vowels ī (ē) and ū (ō), and by using the sign for the glottal stop (*aleph*) for ā. Though this convention has been retained up to the present, it was never used consistently. Only relatively late, by the middle of the first millennium AD, languages such as Arabic, Hebrew, and Syriac developed additional systems by which vowels could be indicated through the use of diacritical marks, but such conventions were always strictly optional.

One of the advantages Semitic scripts offer is the small number of characters necessary for writing: twenty-two for North Semitic, twenty-nine in the case of South Semitic scripts. Compared to the large amount of signs used by other pre-Christian scripts of the Near Middle East (see *Egyptian Hieroglyphs*; *Sumerian Writing*), and the even larger number of characters required for writing some of the contemporary scripts of the Far East (see *Chinese Writing System*; *Japanese Writing System*), Semitic scripts are more economic, more easily accessible, and in consequence more flexible. The reason for this lies in the fact that Semitic scripts are purely phonetic in character: individual signs are meant to represent, not ideas or concepts, but the smallest possible sound unit (phoneme) of a particular language, and though phonetic elements played an important role in almost all ancient writing systems (see *Memory Aids and the Origin of Writing*; *Writing: Overview of History*) in the case of Semitic scripts this element was for the first time used in an exclusive and consistent manner.

Other characteristics Semitic scripts share are the names given to many (though not all) individual letters, and (except for Arabic) the basic order in which those letters are represented; the direction of writing, somewhat ambivalent at first, has since c.1100 BC been consistently from right to left.

1.2 Origin

The question of the origin of the Semitic script is one of the most debated subjects in the history of writing and has occupied scholars and amateurs from antiquity to the present day. Was it an independent, unique invention of the Semitic people, an adapted borrowing from one of the prevailing scripts of antiquity—Egyptian, Cuneiform, Cretan, Cypriote, or Hittite (see *Writing: Overview of History*); or did it originate in Crete from a set of prehistoric geometric signs (Evans 1909)? The theory still most widely accepted is that of an, at least tentative, connection with Egyptian role models which is to a large extent based on a series of short inscriptions found in Sinai and subsequently also in Palestine, which have (roughly) been dated to a period between ca. 1730–1580. this proto–Sinaitic script is thought to use Semitic words for pictorial signs which some scholars (Gardiner and Peet 1955) equate with carelessly executed Egyptian hieroglyphs (see *Egyptian Hieroglyphs*); the Semitic word used provides, by the acrophonic principle, the new value for this particular sign; e.g., the Egyptian sign for 'house' (p-r) stands, when translated into Western

Semitic, for *bet*; the first letter of this word can then be used to represent the consonant *b*, and so forth. Adherent to this theory point out that to this day languages like for example, Greek or Hebrew name some of their letters in a fashion which seems to hark back to the object depicted by an original (Egyptian?) pictorial sign (hieroglyph?); despite the fact that those words are meaningless in either language. This theory is not universally accepted and much does indeed rest on guesswork. Some scholars (Sethe 1917), while agreeing to Egyptian influence, see this influence less in the outward appearance of the characters (see also *Writing Materials: Influence on Writing*) but in the concept of single consonant signs which indeed formed part of the Egyptian system (see *Egyptian Hieroglyphs*). It has been argued that the letters may just be conventional signs with no direct relation to original pictorial signs, and the names given to them nothing but mnemonic devices.

Another question still under discussion is: who invented the Semitic script? One single inventor (Schmitt 1938) or a group of people? The latter theory, which has generally more credence, has again been answered differently by different scholars, one theory naming the Hyskos, a Semitic pastoral people who used a Canaanite language (Sethe 1917) and conquered lower Egypt in about 1670 BC. Another possibility is that of a series of parallel developments in the Syro–Palestinian area which does, however, not exclude variations of mutual influence (Jensen 1970).

Attempts at cuneiform phonetic scripts were made, at around the same time, in northern Syria and Palestine. Inscribed clay tablets found at the site of the ancient city of Ugarit (ca. 1400–1200 BC) document a system which uses some thirty different cuneiform signs (twenty-seven for consonants and three for vowels). The order of the letters is more or less the same as that used in the Phoenician and the Hebrew system. Various theories have been put forward as to the relationship between the cuneiform and the linear forms of phonetic writing. In the opinion of some scholars (Diringer 1968) cuneiform phonetic scripts presuppose the existence of North Semitic (see *Cuneiform, Non-Sumerian*); but much is still speculative.

2. North Semitic Scripts

North Semitic scripts are generally thought to have emerged from the above proto–Sinaitic/proto–Semitic/proto–Canaanite. They are divided into various branches; the two most important ones, which are directly or indirectly responsible for the development of most contemporary forms of writing, are Phoenician and Aramaic.

2.1 The Phoenician Script

The Phoenician script, which became stabilized ca. 1050 BC, can claim the distinction of being the direct ancestor of the Greek alphabet (see *Alphabet: Development*); it seems to have evolved in a direct line of descent from early North Semitic consonantal script forms. During the long period of its existence (thirteenth/eleventh–third centuries BC) it remained remarkably consistent, any development, even in its many colonial subdivisions—Cypro–Phoenician (ca. tenth–second centuries BC) and the Catharginian orpunic script with its secondary branches (the last discovered Punic inscription dates from the third century AD)—being purely external. The number of letters (twenty-two) and their

phonetic value stayed unchanged, as did the direction of writing which remained horizontal, with the script running from right to left.

2.2 The Aramaic Script

The most vigorous offshoot of the Phoenician script was Aramaic, which came into existence around the eleventh/tenth century BC. Whereas the Phoenician script, despite its wide use among trading communities, had basically been a national script, Aramaic soon acquired a truly international character. In the seventh century BC, after the Aramaic city states had lost their independence to the Assyrians, the Aramaic language, written in the Aramaic script, became the lingua franca of the Assyrian empire. In the period of the Persian Empire (ca. 550–323 BC) Aramaic was the official language and the principal script of diplomats and traders between Egypt and northern India; its introduction to India had far-reaching consequences and led to the development of a large number of scripts in South and Southeast Asia (see *Semitic Scripts: Dissemination and Influence*; *Scripts, Indian, Northern*). From the eighth century BC onward Aramaic became progressively more cursive and simplified: the tops of certain letters such as *b*, *d*, and *r* (originally closed) became open, a tendency toward a reduction of strokes in certain letters appeared, final angles became more rounded, and ligature were introduced. After the collapse of the Persian empire the Aramaic language, and the Aramaic script, both up to then fairly homogenous, split into several local dialects, and corresponding scripts developed. The main variants being Jewish (Square Hebrew), Palmyrene, Nabataean (Arabic), and Syriac; there was in addition also the Mandaic script used by the Mandaeans, a gnostic Jewish–Christian sect. The continued tendency toward cursiveness in some of those scripts (notably Syriac and Nabataean) led to the emergence of final forms of letters, and of definite conventions about how individual letters should be joined.

2.3 Hebrew, Syriac, and Arabic

At first the Hebrews simply used the Phoenician script unaltered but by the ninth century BC a distinct script form

א ב ג ד ה ו ז ח ט י כ ל מ נ ס ע פ צ ק ר ש ת
' b g d h w z ḥ ṭ y k l m n s ' p ṣ q r š t

Figure 1. The Hebrew script (order of letters from right to left).

appeared in an inscription found in the Moab. This early (paleo)–Hebrew script was however a purely national form of writing, more or less restricted to the people of Judea; in the course of time it was also favored by certain Jewish sects such as the Samaritans who retained it for their (hand-written) literature.

After the sixth century BC this script was abandoned in favor of Aramaic. To give legitimacy to the new convention, its introduction was ascribed to Ezra, who is supposed to have brought it back from the Babylonian exile, and by the second century BC a somewhat modified form of Aramaic was used by most Jewish communities. This script, which became known as Square Hebrew, spread eventually throughout the Jewish Diaspora and is still the standard

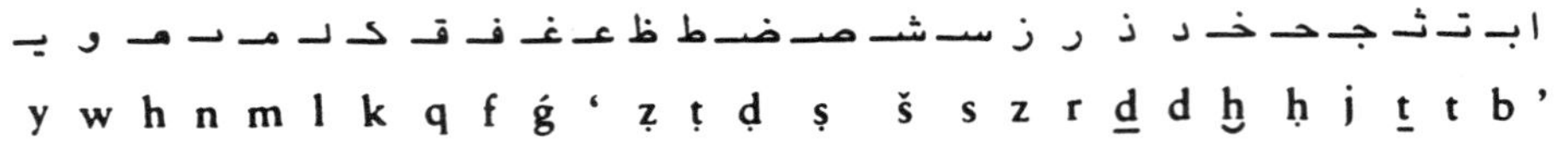

ا ب ت ث ج ح خ د ذ ر ز س ش ص ض ط ظ ع غ ف ق ك ل م ن و ي

y w h n m l k q f ġ ʻ ẓ ṭ ḍ ṣ š s z r ḏ d ḫ ḥ j ṯ t b ʼ

Figure 2. The Arabic script (order of letters from right to left).

Jewish book hand. Square Hebrew letters are bold and well proportioned, nearly all of them have a top bar or head, some have a base as well. Out of the twenty-two Hebrew letters five (*kaf, mem, nun, pe, tzade*) have dual form, one when standing initially or medially, and another in the final position. During the Middle Ages two cursive hands developed alongside Square Hebrew: the rabbinical (after the scholar Rashi d. 1105) used by medieval Jewish savants, and another cursive script which became responsible for the creation of many local variations in the Levant, Morocco, Spain, and Italy.

Like all Semitic scripts, Hebrew is purely consonantal, though some letters (*āleph, hē, vāv,* and *yodh*), generally referred to as *matres lectiones*, can be used for the representation of long vowels. But with Hebrew being replaced by Aramaic as the language of daily use, and the knowledge of Biblical Hebrew in decline, the need arose for a system of vocalization which would ensure the correct pronunciation of the Biblical texts. Vocalization by means of punctuation marks, consisting of little dots and dashes placed above or below a consonant, was probably introduced in the fifth or sixth century AD, with the older Syrian vowel indication system acting as model. The three main systems of vocalization are the Palestinian and the Babylonian (both supralinear) and (after the eighth/ninth century) the Tiberian (sublinear) which eventually superseded the others and is still in use today.

Syriac, another offshoot of Aramaic, developed in Edessa in the first century AD. In its early stage, it showed a strong resemblance to Palmyrene; both scripts have a tendency to join letters together, and most letters are written differently according to whether they stand alone, at the beginning of a word, at the end of it, or whether they are joined on both sides to another letter. An important event, which encouraged the maturing of the Syriac script, was the fact that Edessa became the focus for the spread of Christianity to Semitic-speaking countries. When in the third century the Bible was translated from Greek into Syriac (the local Aramaic dialect) the difficulty of transcribing Greek words written in the alphabet into Semitic consonant script encouraged moves toward a reasonably consistent and effective vocalization. The three main systems eventually used are: Nestorian, the earliest, which consists of a combination of the consonants *w* and *y* and a dot placed above or below them, and of one or two dots placed above below or above the consonant to be vocalized; the Jacobite system created c. 700 AD, which uses small Greek letters placed below or above the line, and the later Syriac system consisting of a combination of diacritical vowel marks and small Greek letters.

Over the centuries variations of Syriac, mainly based on the choice of the vocalization system, came into being.

The three most important ones being Estrangela (the earliest extant manuscript is dated 411 AD), Nestorian, and Jacobite; the two latter scripts developed as a result of a heretical split between Syrian Christians. As the Nestorian church grew in importance, Nestorian missionary monks traveled westward along the old trading routes and brought the knowledge of their script to central Asia and India (see *Semitic Scripts: Dissemination and Influence*).

Arabic, the final offshoot from Aramaic, is today the most prominent Semitic script, and, after the Latin alphabet, more widely used than any other form of writing. It is generally accepted that it originated in the fourth/fifth century AD from the script of the Nabataeans, the people of the first well-defined (northern) Arab kingdom around Petra (now Jordan). The Nabataeans employed two script variations, one monumental for inscriptions, and another, more cursive, which developed into a cursive forerunner of modern Arabic. Before the coming of Islam in the seventh century, the Arabs relied to a large extent on oral traditions for the transmission of their rich literature, but the revelation of the Qu'rān created the need for more widespread literacy.

The Arabic script consists of twenty-nine letters made up of the original twenty-two Semitic consonant signs, plus seven additional characters designed to represent the finer shades of pronunciation required by the Arabic language. Graphically those letters are made up of seventeen basic outlines plus diacritical points to distinguish otherwise identical character signs. Short vowels can be indicated by vowel marks written above or below the consonant preceding the vowel. Some Arab traditions name al-Khalil (d. 786?) the inventor of this vocalization system which gained prominence in the eighth century, but its roots go back to much earlier, probably Syriac models. Vocalization is to some extent less important since Arabic has remained a living language. But the sacred nature of the Qu'rān requires exactness of transmission and to this day vocalization is employed consistently in Qu'rānic texts.

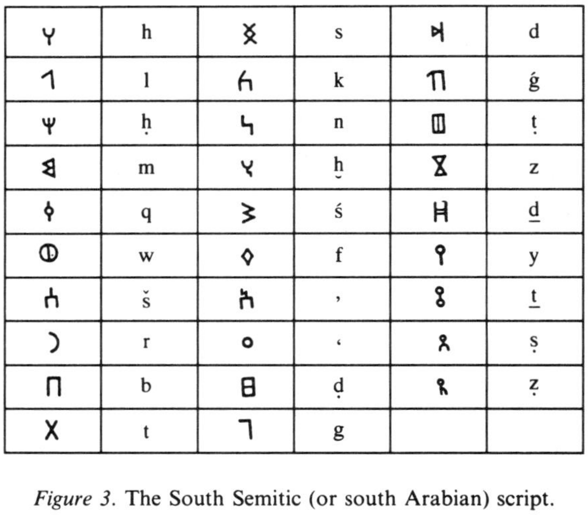

౪	h	౾	s	⋈	d
౧	l	ჩ	k	⊓	ġ
Ψ	ḥ	ㄴ	n	Ⅲ	ṭ
౩	m	Ɣ	ẖ	ⴟ	z
φ	q	⋝	ś	Ħ	ḍ
⏚	w	◇	f	ꝑ	y
҄	š	ㄏ	ʼ	౪	ṯ
)	r	◦	ʻ	⋊	ṣ
⊓	b	⊟	ḍ	⋊	ẓ
✕	t	౧	g		

Figure 3. The South Semitic (or south Arabian) script.

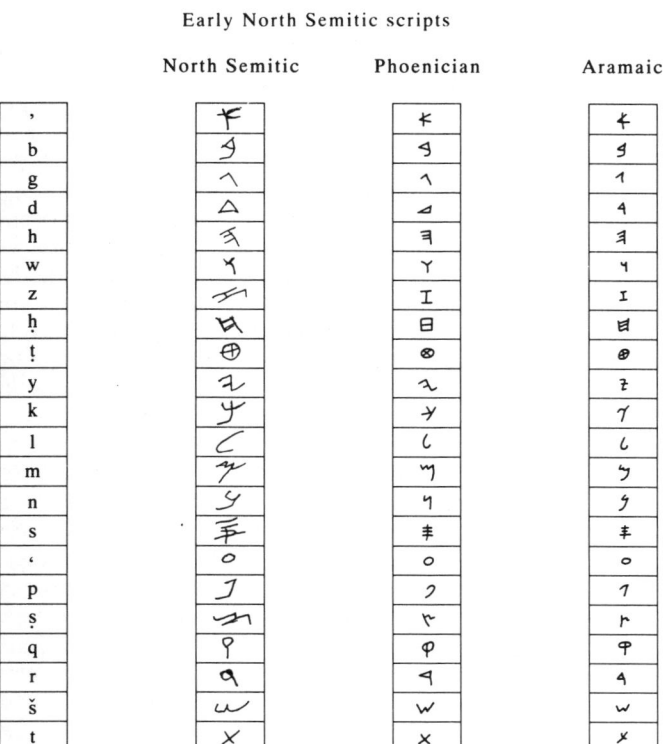

Figure 4. Early North Semitic scripts.

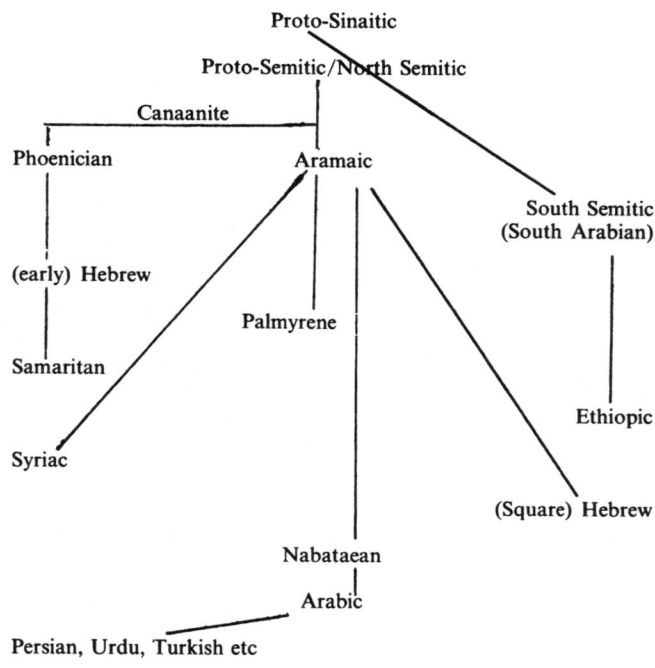

Figure 5. Relationship between main scripts.

Already in the early Islamic period two distinct styles of writing existed: Kufic, a bold monumental script which became the favored script for the writing of the Qu'rān; and Naskhi, a more rounded and cursive form which served as model for a number of different styles that developed at the courts of non-Arab rules—it is also the parent of modern Arabic.

3. South Semitic Scripts

South Semitic scripts remained confined within Arabia where they were used by the Minaens and Sabaens; there are also some inscriptions written in Himyaritic, Qatabanic, and Hadhramautic. Despite much effort, those inscriptions are still difficult to date, the earliest is thought to ge back to c. 500 BC and the script(s) became extinct at around 600 AD; with the exception of Sabaen which spread into Africa and became the direct ancestor of the classical Ethiopic and the modern Amharic scripts (see *Ethiopian Syllabaries*). Sabaean (or south Arabian) inscriptions are written in a beautifully proportioned, elegant scrit, individual letters are carefully arranged and executed, often—especially after 300 BC—in hollow relief. During the same period related forms of writing were used in northern Arabia for Thalmudene, Liyanite, and Safaitic. Inscriptions in those scripts are mostly irregular, cursive, stone graffiti; they too are difficult to date and may have existed down to the Islamic period.

The question of the origin of the South Semitic scripts, and their exact connection with North Semitic, is still under discussion. Some seventh/eighth century BC inscriptions seem to indicate a line between proto–Canaanite and South Arabian (Healey 1990), but on the whole it is doubtful that South Semitic descended directly from North Semitic; e.g., the South Arabian/Sabaen *b*, *d*, *h*, and *p* have a more archaic appearance and are closer to Sinaitic; also, like Ugaritic, South Semitic, with its twenty-nine letters employs symbols for phonemes no longer presented in North Semitic languages. One view (Diringer 1968) sees in proto–Sinaitic a possible link between proto–Semitic/Canaanite and South Semitic.

4. Summing up

The revolutionary achievement of Semitic scripts lie less in their (linear) appearance than in the applied ability to isolate individual basic sounds of a particular language and represent each sound by one distinct sign. The question about their exact origin will probably remain speculative. The reasons for their emergence, however, were geographical and historical: the cosmopolitan nature of the coastal towns, and changes in the old hieratic/theocratic Egyptian and Mesopotamian order which created the need for a more 'democratic' (Diringer 1968) form of writing.

Bibliography

Diringer D 1968 *The alphabet—a key to the history of mankind*, 3rd edn. Thames and Hudson, London

Driver G R 1948 *Semitic writing: from pictography to alphabet.* Oxford University Press, London

Evans A J 1909 *Scripta Minoa.* Clarendon Press, Oxford

Gardiner A H, Peet T E 1955 *The inscriptions of Sinai.* Egypt Exploration Fund Memoirs, London

Gaur A 1992 *The history of writing*, 3rd enlarged edn. Abbeville Press, New York/London

Gelb I J 1952 *A study of writing: The foundations of grammatology.* Routledge and Kegan Paul, London

Harris R 1986 *The origin of writing.* Duckworth, London

Healey J F 1990 *The early alphabet.* British Museum Publication, London

Jensen H 1970 *Signs, symbols and cripts: An account of man's effort to write.* Hutchinson, London

Mercer S A B 1959 *The origin of writing and our alphabet.* Luzac, London

Naveh J 1982 *Early history of the alphabet.* Magnes Press, Jerusalem

Petrie W F W 1908 *The formation of the alphabet.* British School of Archaeology in Egypt, London

Sampson G 1985 *Writing systems.* Hutchinson, London

Schmitt A 1938 *Die Erfindung der Schrift.* Academia Fridericiana, Erlangen

Sethe K 1917 *Die neuentdeckte Sinaischrift und die Entstehung der Semitischen Schrift.* Nachrichten der Goettingen Gesellschaft der Wissenschaften, Goettingen

A. Gaur

Sen, Sukumar (1900–92)

Sukumar Sen was born on January 15, 1900 and died on March 3, 1992. He is probably the last major linguist in India to work within the historical-comparative framework and one of the best. He was the most famous student of Suniti Kumar Chatterji (see *Chatterji, Suniti Kumar*), and the one also on closest terms with his illustrious teacher. Chatterji and Sen first worked together, and then Sen took over the former's mantle to give the department of comparative philology (now department of linguistics) at the University of Calcutta a dignity and distinction that attracted many scholars from India and abroad to study and carry on research there. This eventually led to many excellent works on the histories of various languages of this subcontinent, appropriately modeled after Chatterji's magnum opus *The Origin and Development of the Bengali Language* (or *ODBL* 1926).

Sen's school career was replete with medals and prizes. He was awarded the Asutosh Gold Medal, the University Gold Medal, the Premchand and Roychand Scholarship, the Girish Memorial Prize (three times) and the Sarojini Medal—all from his own alma mater—the University of Calcutta. The Asiatic Society, Calcutta, awarded him the Jadunath Sircar Medal and, in 1984, the Gold Medal of the Royal Asiatic Society of London was bestowed on him as a fitting acknowledgment of his lifelong contribution to linguistics.

His tenure as a teacher was long and distinguished. He served the same department for about 34 years. Early on he was appointed the Khaira scholar attached to the department of comparative philology at the University of Calcutta where he served as an honorary lecturer. He then became a full-time member of faculty and promotions followed naturally and deservedly. He became the chairman of his department in 1953, when he was already a professor, and held the position till he retired in 1964. During his long career as a teacher, he not only did excellent research himself, but also supervized some 100 scholars, including several foreign students, who produced celebrated research works.

Sen's early interest was historical syntax, and he was the first to explore the Old Indo–Aryan morphosyntax (see *Indo–Aryan*) in his *Use of Cases in Vedic Prose* (1928) and *Buddhist Hybrid Sanskrit* (1928). This preoccupation with syntax continued when he proceeded to analyze Middle Indo–Aryan in *An Outline of Syntax of Middle Indo–Aryan* (1950). His *Old Persian Inscriptions* (1941) and *A Comparative Grammar of Middle Indo–Aryan* (1960), displayed his strong command of historical-comparative methodology and his meticulous concern for details in which etymological insights came to figure prominently. His *Bhāshāra Itivṛtta* (1939) is the first book in Bengali on the historical evolution of the language. Although he acknowledges his debt to Chatterji's *ODBL*, his *Itivṛtta* is not merely a condensed restatement of his teacher's book. Sen ventured beyond what his teacher had covered at several points, for example, in postulating the fifth dialect, i.e., Jharkhandi, for Bengali against Chatterji's four and also in suggesting various alternative etymologies for several lexical items. It is interesting to note that, by publishing the above books, and a number of others, he covered about 3500 years of the history of the Aryan languages.

He also produced some descriptive studies, the most notable among which are *Women's Dialect in Bengali* (1923) and a description of standard colloquial Bengali published in *Language Handbook* (Census of India 1971). His history of Bengali Prose (1934) began and still remains the only example of a systematic stylistic description of the literary prose dialect of his language. Etymology, however, became his preferred area in the later years and his *Etymological Dictionary of Bengali* (2 vols, 1971), probably the largest work on historical etymology of any Indian language, and *Bānglār Sthāna Nāma* ('Place-names of Bengal' 1981) are works that show this concern. He also wrote a large number of English and Bengali articles on linguistic subjects bearing both a historical and descriptive orientation.

Apart from the above, Sen published some 70 books on other subjects showing his wide and varied interests, ranging from the pop literature of Calcutta to an analytical history of crime fiction. He himself wrote five collections of crime stories and an autobiography in two volumes, but the work in Bengali that towers above all his other publications is his four-volume history of Bengali literature, *Bāngālā Sāhityera Itihāsa* (1941–58; now issued in five volumes) which has made him the premier historian of this literature. It probably represents a desire to match his teacher's celebrated work of reconstruction of the history of the language, by a parallel and equally meticulous survey of that of the literature. His eminent success in this area has, however, pushed his excellence as a linguist into the background, at least for his compatriots in Bengal.

Pabitra Sarkar

Senegal: Language Situation

Wolof is the dominant language, but this state of affairs tends to hide the linguistic heterogeneity of Senegal which it is difficult to describe briefly. In the current state of research, it is impossible to be precise as to the exact number of languages and/or dialects. Senegalese multilingualism is to be seen in terms of complementarity, of cultural enrichment, and of peaceful coexistence. However, the latter is resulting in the decline of minority languages and the probable elimination, over a period of time, of the weakest amongst them.

1. Languages Spoken

1.1 First Languages

More than a score of African languages are spoken as first languages in Senegal. They can be divided into the Atlantic group (with some 90 percent of speakers, see Doneux 1977) and the Mande group. The first group includes the following (dialects or local forms of the language are listed in parentheses):

Northern
  (a) Wolof (Lebu, Saalum, Ndar), Serer (Siin, Fajut, Ñominka), Pulaar (Fuuta, Fuladu, Jeeri, Bawol);
  (b) Cangin languages: Lehaar, Safeen (=Saafi-saafi), Noon, Ndut-paloor.

Bak
  (a) Joola (=Diola) languages: Fonyi, Buluf, Kombo, Karon, Bayot, Huluf, Esulaluur, Kasa, Her, Gusilaay, and Kwatay;
  (b) Manjaku languages: Manjaku dialects, Pepel, and Mankanya;
  (c) Balante languages represented in Senegal by Fca (other members of the group being spoken in Guinea–Bissau).

Tenda-nyun
  Bedik, Basari, Konyagi, Jaad (=Bajaranke, Pajade) and Nyun (=Baynuk).

The following belong in the Mande group: Manding (=Malinke), Bambara, Jaxanke, Jalonke, and Soninke (=Sarakole).

Portuguese creole is the first language of the descendants of Cape-Verde islanders, who are now integrated into the population of Senegal, whilst Arabic is the mother tongue of the Syrians, Lebanese, and Mauritanians, some of whom have Senegalese nationality.

French is also the first language of a not inconsiderable number of families.

1.2 Second Languages

The main second languages are Wolof (see Sect. 3.1), French, Portuguese creole, and Arabic.

2. Languages: Status and Contexts

2.1 Status

French is the official language. Six of the African languages mentioned above have been declared national languages. These are Wolof, Serer, Pulaar, Joola, Manding, and Soninke.

2.2 Contexts of Use

  (a) *Administration*: French.
  (b) *Education*: French at all levels; Wolof in state-run nursery schools; French and Arabic in 'Franco-Arabic Schools'; Wolof, Pulaar, Serer, and Joola at the University of Dakar. These four languages are not used as mediums of instruction: they are however subjects which are taught.

Experiments aiming to integrate the national languages into the school system were carried out between 1978 and 1981.

The percentage of adults literate in the national languages is estimated at 11 percent (see UNESCO 1985).

  (c) *International relations*: French

  (d) *Radio, television, and literacy programs*: French and the six national languages.
  (e) *Press*: French, Pulaar, and Wolof.
  (f) *Written literature, theatre, and cinema*: French and Wolof.
  (g) *Music*: French and the six national languages.
  (h) *Parliament*: French and Wolof.
  (i) *Religion*: Preaching is of course carried out in the language understood by the majority of the congregation. Religious instruction is given in Arabic in Koranic schools.
  There are several cassettes in Wolof on religious themes, available commercially, which are widely distributed.

3. Languages: Relative Position

3.1 Wolof

Wolof is used as lingua franca by more than 70 percent of the population. In verbal exchanges, Wolof may be used at any time and in any context, even in cases where the exclusive use of French is expected.

3.2 National Languages

Table 1 contains the consolidated figures for speakers' first and second languages (see DPS 1991). The population was estimated at 7,000,000 in 1988.

Table 1.

Language	No. of speakers	Percentage
Wolof	4,801,080	70.9
Pulaar	1,634,570	21.1
Serer	929,360	13.7
Manding	420,880	6.2
Joola	384,800	5.7
Soninke	93,070	1.4

It should be noted that the survey makes no distinction between Serer and the Cangin languages. The latter are only spoken in the southeast Kajoor region and the northwest Bawol region.

See also: Mande Languages.

Bibliography

Direction de la prévision de la statistique (DPS) 1991 *Recensement général de la population de l'habitat du Sénégal*
Doneux J L 1977 Les groupes linguistiques. In: Van chi-Bonnardel (ed.) *Atlas national du Sénégal*. IGN, Paris
Dumont P 1983 *Le Français et les langues africaines au Sénégal*. A.C.C.T. and Karthala, Paris
Grimes B F 1988 *Ethnologue*. Summer Institute of Linguistics, Dallas, TX
Martin V, Becker C 1977 Les groupes ethniques. In: Van chi-Bonnardel (ed.) *Atlas national du Sénégal*. IGN, Paris
Ndiaye-Corréard G, Schmidt J 1978 *Le Sénégal: Inventaire des études linguistiques sur les pays d'Afrique noire d'expression française*. CILF-SELAF, Paris
UNESCO 1985 *African Community Languages and their Use in Literacy and Education*. Unesco-Breda, Dakar

C. Mbodj

Sense

There is a perfectly ordinary use of 'sense' which is roughly equivalent to 'meaning' and opposed to 'nonsense.' We say that a sentence is true 'in a sense,' that we 'grasp its sense,' that a word 'has two senses,' and so on. One might hope that we could detail a single notion of the meaning of an expression that would unite these nontechnical uses of 'sense': meaningful expressions have 'meanings,' ambiguous expressions have multiple meanings, the meanings of sentences are things that can be true, that can be grasped, believed, and so on.

1. The Complexity of Meaning

However, Gottlob Frege argued persuasively that no single notion of meaning can play all these roles in a coherent theory (see *Frege, Gottlob*). Frege held that an adequate theory of meaning must distinguish two aspects of the meaning of an expression. On the one hand there is the expression's 'referent' (*Bedeutung*), the entity the expression stands for. On the other there is the expression's 'sense' (*Sinn*), the way the expression presents the referent, or the aspect of the referent captured by the expression. Variants of this distinction have proved popular in philosophy of language, but have all been quite controversial (see *Reference, Philosophical Issues concerning*).

2. Sense and Reference

The distinction is easiest to make with respect to singular terms (expressions designating objects). The two expressions 'the morning star' and 'the evening star' both stand for the planet Venus (so they have the same referent), but the first picks out Venus *as* the brightest star in the morning, while the second picks it out as the brightest star in the evening (so the expressions have different senses). According to Frege (though this interpretation of him is controversial; see Dummett 1981), the sense of an expression *determines* its referent, in that its referent is simply whatever entity has the features constituting its sense. This helps explain the fact that 'the morning star is the evening star' can be found informative, and is not a trivial truth concerning Venus's self-identity; the explanation is that informativeness is a matter of sense, not reference. The distinction also helps explain how someone might believe that the morning star is visible in the morning, without believing that the evening star is visible in the morning. Statements like these ascribe senses, not merely referents, as the objects of belief.

Frege's distinction forms the centerpiece of his two-level, doubly compositional semantics. The referent of a complex expression (truth value in the case of a sentence, (roughly) a set in the case of a predicate) is determined by only the referents of its component expressions, and the sense of a complex expression (an abstract 'thought' in the case of a sentence) is determined by only the senses of its parts. The truth values of 'propositional attitude' statements like belief reports depend on the senses and not on the referents of the embedded sentences. This forms no exception to the compositionality of reference, since on Frege's view the referents of embedded sentences in such statements are what normally would be their senses. However, this is an exception to the rule that the referent of an expression is determined independently of facts about which other expressions surround it.

The resulting systematic semantics is impressively powerful and strikes many as intuitively plausible. Unfortunately,

the key notion of sense was left obscure by Frege, and later attempts to fill in the details have met with trouble.

3. Troubles with Sense

One difficulty facing accounts of sense with respect to proper names, is that it seems unlikely that there is a single definite aspect, feature, or group of features of an object universally associated with a given name for it. Frege mentioned that it is a defect of actual languages that the sense of a name can vary from person to person. As one of his chief concerns was with designing a formal language, the tactic of chiding natural language may have seemed adequate, but if Fregean semantics is to be seriously directed at natural languages, the interpersonal variation of sense presents an imposing obstacle. If different persons assign different senses to an expression, it is difficult to explain in what sense they can understand each other's statements. Similarly, it is difficult to explain (what ought to be easy on a Fregean account) how one person can report what another believes or says. This is not only because the two can assign different senses to the same words, but in some cases also because the two might not speak the same language, and so would not attach the same sense to any expression whatever.

Even if the difficulties about interpersonal differences can be handled, there remains a deeper problem. The notion that the referent of a term is whatever entity has the features constituting its sense (for a given person), has met with serious, possibly unanswerable challenges from several philosophers, notably Saul Kripke (see *Kripke: Philosophy of Language*). Kripke argues that which individual one refers to with the name 'Einstein' does not hinge on what prominent features one attaches to the bearer of the name. If the only feature you attach to 'Einstein' is that he invented the light bulb, then your belief is about *Einstein*, and you have a false belief about him, not a true belief about Edison (the actual inventor of the light bulb). Your use of 'Einstein' refers to Einstein, Kripke proposes, because of the causal chain leading to your acquisition of the name: you got the name from someone who got the name from someone else who got the name, ultimately, from someone who dubbed Einstein with it. The features you attach to 'Einstein' do not come into determining reference (see *Reference, Philosophical Issues concerning*; *Proper Names: Linguistic Aspects*).

In the face of these difficulties, some philosophers have recently pursued amended versions of Fregean semantics. These views give up one or another of the central features of traditional Fregeanism, such as that sense determines reference, or that sense is given by the important features one believes an object to possess (see Peacocke 1983; Forbes 1990).

See also: Frege, Gottlob; Proposition; Reference, Philosophical Issues concerning; Proper Names: Linguistic Aspects.

Bibliography

Dummett M 1981 *The Interpretation of Frege's Philosophy*. Duckworth, London
Forbes G 1990 The indispensibility of *sinn. Philosophical Review* **99**

Frege G 1952 *Translations from the Philosophical Writings of Gottlob Frege*. Basil Blackwell, Oxford
Kripke S A 1980 *Naming and Necessity*. Blackwell, Oxford
Peacocke C 1983 *Sense and Content*. Clarendon Press, Oxford

M. Crimmins

Sentence Stress

The phenomenon which is variously called 'sentence stress,' 'sentence accent,' 'nuclear stress,' 'nuclear accent,' 'nucleus,' 'focal accent,' and 'tonic' is remarkably difficult to define. It might be defined for a start as 'that which distinguishes the most stressed syllable in a sentence.'

1. Problems of Predicting Placement of Sentence Stresses

Consider the following, which can all be said to be sentences:

> Get out! (1)

> Birds fly. (2)

> Don't tell me the Green Party are running another candidate! (3)

> Melvin, the garage door opener sales rep and my sister's second husband (the man I told you about over the phone last week, just before your washing machine exploded), expects to visit the ruins of Knossos in a few months, if he gets his expenses paid by the company. (4)

While considerable agreement might be reached about the unmarked stress pattern of (1) and (2), even here there is room for choice among native speakers of English. The first two sentences could easily be equally stressed on both words, though it is probably more common to stress the end. In the more complex sentences, the decision as to which item is most stressed is correspondingly more complicated: stress in (3) will obviously be related to the environment in which it is being said. In a political environment where the Green Party had a superfluity of candidates, it might well be stressed on *another*. In a situation where the Labour Party has just announced ten new candidates, the word *Green* might receive the main stress. Other conditions could be imagined where *me* would be stressed. One might feel reluctant to stress *candidate* (even though the rules discussed below would predict that the stress falls here), since what else would a political party run? If the final word were *raffle*, final stress would seem more appropriate.

Linguists frequently distinguish between normal sentence stress, which is placed on a sentence under neutral conditions, and contrastive sentence stress, which is used to emphasize a word with reference to something which is said elsewhere. For example:

> You ought to hear the NEW one if you think their first recording was bad. (5)

or

> I said 'GLAZED FRUIT,' not 'grazed flute.' (6)

It is hard to imagine a neutral situation for the articulation of sentence (3), so perhaps all of the interpretations outlined above involve contrastive stress.

Work on stress in units larger than the word has *not* tended to use sentences as its point of departure, most focusing on the phrase or clause. For example, sentence (4) might be divided up as follows:

> MELvin
> the garage DOOR opener sales rep
> and my sister's second HUSband
> the man I TOLD you about
> over the PHONE last week
> just before your WASHing machine exploded
> expects to visit the ruins of KNOssos in a few months
> if he gets his expenses paid by the COMpany.

Which of these counts as the sentence stress is not at all obvious, though many linguists will say that in English the final stress in a sentence is the strongest.

2. Analyses of Sentence Stress

Sentence stress, then, is an imprecise way to refer to the fact that, in many if not most languages, when words are used in phrases or other syntactic collocations, the stress of one word is normally superordinated to that of other words in order to achieve highlighting, focus, or contrast, to mark new information, or to comment on a topic.

This superordination is very closely tied to intonation. One view is that *accent* is a way of dividing an utterance into a succession of shorter phrases and to signal relationships among these patterns which organize them into larger groupings. *Stress* is a type of accent in which the tune of the accentual pattern cannot be specified in the lexicon but rather is chosen for a specific utterance from an inventory of tunes provided by the intonation system.

Linguistic opinions differ widely as to the factors determining the placement of the major stress in utterances larger than the word. The schools of thought do not fall into neat categories: the major dichotomy seems to be between those who believe it is determined by syntactic and morphological structure (Sect. 2.1) and those who think it is determined by discourse structure and pragmatic considerations such as degree of interest (Sect. 2.3). There are also hybrid positions (Sect. 2.2).

2.1 The 'Stress by Structure' Position

In *The Sound Pattern of English* (1968), Chomsky and Halle suggest that the stress pattern of linguistic constructions larger than the foot is determined by (a) word stress, (b) type of construction, and (c) the stress cycle. Word stress processes allow the assignment of primary stress to a single vowel in each word. When the words are put together in larger constructions, one stress will become dominant. The stress rules apply first in the most embedded construction, assigning primary stress to the (already) primary-stressed vowel of the rightmost item in verb, noun, and adjective phrases and of the previous-to-rightmost item in compound nouns. When a vowel is assigned primary stress, all others in the unit under consideration are demoted by one level. (See *Generative Phonology*; *Word Stress*).

Sentence stress in this case falls on the syllable which ends up with primary stress at the end of the derivation. This approach has been criticized because it can generate a very large number of stress levels in long utterances, most of which are presumably auditorily indistinguishable and linguistically irrelevant, and because it leads one to suppose that stress relations between items at a great distance are significant, while they almost certainly are not. It has also been pointed out that the stress cycle as described above is fundamentally different from other phonological rules, and the necessity for a completely different mechanism for assigning stress has been questioned.

More recent approaches which developed as a reaction against the Sound Pattern of English framework also start with a base of knowing the segmental structure and grammatical function of the sequence to be assigned stress, but the rules work on a much more local basis: the utterance is assigned a binary-branching tree structure and each branch assigned a label 'strong' or 'weak,' depending on its metrical properties. Principles much like those described above determine this assignment: the right branch is labeled 'strong' in case the unit is a phrase or if it is a lexical category and branches. Otherwise, the right node is 'weak' and the left 'strong.' This approach does not call upon the stress cycle except in some cases of morphological derivation, though it allows for as many levels of structure as necessary.

Further refinements include the creating of a foot level. This makes it possible to distinguish between the stress patterns of sequences like *rabbi* (s−w; two feet) and *rabbit* (s−w; one foot). The sentence stress in this case falls on the syllable totally dominated by strong markers (see *Metrical Phonology*).

2.2 The 'Stress by Structure and Function' Position

Other linguists have suggested that aspects of linguistic structure determine sentence stress, but give more importance to pragmatics and discourse features than those mentioned previously. They hold that stress or accent placement within the unit in question is not a mechanical selection of the rightmost content word (i.e., for English and similar languages) but that it depends somehow on the interaction of the position in the constituent and a hierarchy of parts of speech: a noun or noun phrase is most favored for stress placement, then an adjective, then a verb. If the rightmost item is not, however, new information, it can be demoted, causing the major stress to pass to another element in the utterance. For example, whereas *Victoria* would normally receive the principal stress in:

I'd take the green bus to Victoria. (7)

In a case where the destination was assumed, *bus* would be emphasized. If the destination and means of transport were predetermined, *green* would receive the stress.

2.3 The Case for Interest or Focus

Still others largely discount the syntactic structure of the utterance as a determinant of sentence stress, instead assuming that semantics and pragmatics are most important. A typical stance here is that a sentence has (or may have) a theme (subject, topic, old information) and a rheme (predicate, comment, new information), both of which are marked by special emphasis. Rhematic stress is stronger than thematic stress, and since the rheme tends to come last in an English sentence, the stronger stress will also occur at or near the end. This may be called an 'unmarked' stress pattern, but the speaker is still free to add more

accents or even to put the 'more important' accent first. Accent is thus an active part of an individual message.

In this framework, focus of *interest* is more important than focus of information (despite the recognition of the theme/rheme opposition). Information structure, truth value, and syntax are seen as secondary to the momentary need to focus attention on some aspect of the utterance.

3. The Descriptive Tradition

As mentioned above, stress is known to have several possible phonetic correlates, among them increased syllable duration, increased amplitude, and higher fundamental frequency. Many British linguists have focused their attention on the fundamental frequency of phrases, under the assumption that where there is a major peak or trough (i.e., a turning point) in fundamental frequency, the most stressed syllable in the unit under investigation will be found. Any unit which has a noticeable intonation peak is separated out as a phrase or 'tone group,' and analysis takes place in terms of these groups, which are assumed to be on the order of a clause or sentence. The units are described as ending in a 'nuclear tone,' though this tone may be followed by one or more unimportant, unstressed syllables which can bear part of the tonal pattern. Most linguists of this persuasion think that a limited number of these patterns can be found, though categorization of real speech into these patterns necessarily involves some degree of abstraction and generalization. The patterns are, therefore, more phonological than phonetic. Later attempts in the same tradition have tried to provide a wider range of options, thus aiming at a more phonetic characterization of patterns. However, on a phonetic basis, the conflation of stress and intonation still makes this system difficult to use in describing abnormal patterns and/or languages which differ markedly from English.

These linguists acknowledge that the place and type of nuclear tone found in a tone group conveys something about the speaker's attitude toward what is said and/or the propositional content of the utterance, but no invariable mapping is assumed between intention and nuclear tone: the goal is straightforwardly descriptive rather than generative. It is assumed that any type of tonal pattern can occur on any grammatical structure, depending on the speaker's meaning. This stance can be traced to the original motivation for this approach, which was practical rather than theoretical: it was invented as a tool for teaching the suprasegmental aspects of English to speakers of other languages.

Some members of this school recognize but question the traditional assumption that the domain of the intonation contour of the tone unit is either the clause or sentence. Although they allow that there may be a tendency for tone units to be coextensive with clauses, they point out that in spontaneous speech, one cannot find a significant correlation between clause and tone unit. One suggestion is that the domain of the tone unit should be units smaller than the clauses or *elements* of structures, such as subject, nominal group, vocative, and so on (see *Tone-Group*).

A similar descriptive position was taken by American structuralists in the first half of the twentieth century, though their approach separated stress from intonation. They were primarily concerned with phonemic stress at the word level, but also observed that the primary stress of a phonemic phrase will come as near to the end as possible (in English). Some allowed for 'expressive stress,' which made it possible for a nonfinal item to bear primary stress.

In summary, though it is largely agreed that where there is identifiable stress in some unspecified unit longer than a single word there will be one syllable which is more stressed than the others (in English and related languages and probably in most others) and that the primary cue for this stress is fundamental frequency, there is still considerable discussion about how this observation can be usefully integrated into linguistic theory. The term 'sentence stress' is not an especially good label for this phenomenon: constituents bearing a recognizable main stress are often smaller than a sentence, and a sentence can contain several recognizable main stresses.

4. Further Reading

For the 'stress by structure' position, see Chomsky and Halle, 1968, Chapters 2 and 3 and the Liberman and Prince article. For 'stress by structure and function,' see Ladd. For 'stress by focus,' see Bolinger. O'Connor and Arnold and Crystal both discuss the discovery and annotation of nuclear tone groups.

Bibliography

Beckman M 1986 *Stress and Non-Stress Accent*. Foris, Dordrecht
Bolinger D 1985 *Intonation and its Parts*. Edward Arnold, London
Chomsky N, Halle M 1968 *The Sound Pattern of English*. Harper & Row, New York
Cruttenden A 1986 *Intonation*. Cambridge University Press, Cambridge
Crystal D 1980 The analysis of nuclear tones. In: Waugh L R, van Schooneveld C H (eds.) *The Melody of Language*. University Park Press, Baltimore, MD
Ladd D R 1979 Light and shadow: A study of the syntax and semantics of sentence accent in English. In: Waugh L R, van Coetsem F (eds.) *Contributions to Grammatical Studies: Semantics and Syntax*. Brill, Leiden
Liberman M, Prince A 1977 On stress and linguistic rhythm. *Linguistic Inquiry* **8**: 249–336
O'Connor J D, Arnold G F 1961 *Intonation of Colloquial English*. Academic Press, London

L. R. Shockey

Sentence Types and Clause Subordination

There are numerous dimensions on which sentences can be classified, but as a technical term of grammar 'type' is used specifically for that dimension which correlates with the use of sentences for the performance of different kinds of speech act—of acts with different illocutionary force. The three types which recur most frequently in the world's languages are declarative, interrogative, and imperative, which correlate respectively with the speech act categories statement, inquiry, and directive (a cover term for requests, commands, orders, instructions, and the like). Examples from English are given in (1):

	Sentence type	Characteristic use	(1)
(a) It is raining again.	Declarative	Statement	
(b) What do you want?	Interrogative	Inquiry	
(c) Stand still.	Imperative	Directive	

The correlation between the sentence types and the speech act categories is, however, by no means one-to-one. For example, the declarative *Passengers are requested to remain seated until the plane has come to a complete standstill* would typically be used as a directive (a request), and so would the interrogative *Would you be good enough to pass me my towel?*; on the other hand, the imperative *Sleep well* would generally be used not to issue a directive but to express a wish (for there are many other kinds of speech act than statement, inquiry, and directive). It is for this reason that the heading in the third column of (1) above is 'characteristic use': declaratives are not invariably used as statements, but generally, characteristically, they are—and analogously for the other types.

When a clause is subordinated it ceases—again, characteristically but not invariably—to carry its own illocutionary force. Compare (1a), for example, with:

Kim says it is raining again.　　　　　　　　　　(2)

If I utter (1a) on its own I state (normally) that it is raining again, but when I subordinate it within a larger clause, as in (2), I do not: what I state in uttering (2) is that Kim says it is raining again, not that it is raining again. Nevertheless, some at least of the type contrasts, e.g., that between declaratives and interrogatives, are also found in subordinate clauses, as in (3) (where material in square brackets is relevant context but not part of the expression being analyzed):

(a) [She doesn't know] that it is raining again.	Declarative	(3)
(b) [She doesn't know] what you want.	Interrogative	

There are thus significant links between the two major topics covered in this article, and the treatment of clause subordination will examine the correlation between subordination and loss of illocutionary force and the applicability of the type categories to subordinate constructions.

1. Sentence Types

1.1 Sentence Type as the Grammaticalization of Illocutionary Force

It was noted above that the correlation between sentence type and speech act (illocutionary force) is complex, rather than one-to-one, and precisely for this reason it is important to keep the two sets of categories conceptually and terminologically distinct. Traditional grammars often fail to do this, so that the terms 'statement,' 'question,' and 'command' are commonly used as the names of the major sentence types; modern grammars generally use distinct terms for sentence type and speech act in the case of the pairs declarative/statement and imperative/directive, but it is still very common to find question applied instead of interrogative (or as an alternative to it) to a sentence type as well as to a speech act category, a usage with the potential for considerable confusion. This article will maintain a sharp distinction between the terms for sentence types (categories of grammar) and the terms for illocutionary acts (categories of use, pragmatic categories). It will, moreover, prefer 'inquiry' to question as a label for the most characteristic use of interrogatives: an inquiry involves asking the addressee a question, but this is not the only thing one can do in expressing a question (cf. Lyons 1977: ch. 16). This usage will free the term question for the semantic level, for a category defined by its logical relation to a set of answers. Question in this sense is relevant to the interpretation of subordinate interrogatives such as [*She inadvertently revealed*] *where he was* (i.e., the answer to the question 'Where was he?'), where there is no implication that any act of inquiry took place.

The sentence types, like other grammatical categories found in more than one language, need to be defined at two levels: the language-particular level and the general level (see Lyons 1966 for the origin of this distinction, and Palmer 1986: 2–7, 23–33 for its application to the present topic). At the former level the concern is with the grammatical properties—matters of form—which distinguish one category from another in the particular language being described, English, French, Urdu or whatever it might be. Thus as a first approximation for English one may note that (1a) and (b) are distinguished by the order of the subject and the first verb, while (c) differs from both of them in having no subject. At the general level the concern is with what is common to a given category across different languages, and it is here that the correlation with the speech act categories is invoked. Thus a general definition of the term declarative is that it applies to a grammatically distinct class of sentence (or clause) whose members are characteristically used to make statements—and analogously for interrogative and imperative. *Sleep well* belongs by virtue of its form, its structure, to the same grammatical category as *Stand still*, *Open the door*, *Go away*, etc., and this category satisfies the general definition of imperative because the majority of its members would typically be used as directives.

Although the general definitions are based, unlike the language-particular ones, on properties of use, they nevertheless incorporate a condition of 'grammaticalization', i.e., of grammatical distinctiveness. The speech act or illocutionary force categories of statement, inquiry, and directive are grammaticalized in English precisely because there are distinct grammatical constructions associated with them, but the category of offer, say, is not. Such examples as *Would you like another sherry?* (interrogative), *Have another sherry* (imperative), *There's some more sherry here if you'd like some* (declarative) could all naturally be used in an appropriate context with the illocutionary force of an offer, but the interpretation as offers arises principally from the 'lexical' content (notably *sherry*, *have/like*): one does not find any special grammatical features associated with offers in contrast to other speech acts, and there will accordingly be no question of recognizing 'offerative' as a sentence type in English. This is an uncontroversial example, but there are places where it is less clear whether the condition of grammaticalization is satisfied, and consequently differences among grammarians concerning the precise set of sentence types in a given language.

1.2 'Type' as a Category of the Clause rather than the Sentence

Before further investigation of the relation between grammatical type and illocutionary force, it will be helpful to clarify the domain of the type category. The distinction that is commonly drawn between sentence and clause may be explained by reference to the following example:

(a) Kim had written the letter. (4)
(b) Kim had written the letter, but she had not posted it.
(c) He didn't know Kim had written the letter.

In all three *Kim had written the letter* is a clause—by virtue of having a clausal structure (*Kim* is subject, *had written* is predicator, and *the letter* is object, these being three of the major elements of clause structure). In (a) the clause is also a sentence—because it is not part of any larger syntactic construction; in (b) and (c), by contrast, *Kim had written the letter* is not a sentence, precisely because it *is* part of a larger syntactic construction (in (b) it is coordinated, in (c) subordinated). Within this framework it is to the clause rather than the sentence that the type dimension applies. *Kim had written the letter* is a declarative clause, because it has the structure of one—it lacks the special feature of inverted order in interrogative *Had Kim written the letter?* (or the special interrogative conjunction in the subordinate interrogative *whether Kim had written the letter*). Example (4b) is not appropriately classified as a declarative sentence because it is the separate clauses that select for type, not the sentence as a whole. This is evident from the fact that different types can be coordinated in a single sentence: *Kim had written the letter but had she posted it?* (declarative + interrogative), *Come around six or is that too early?* (imperative + interrogative), *It's your fault and don't try to deny it* (declarative + imperative), and so on. In (4c) one can replace the subordinate declarative *Kim had written the letter* by the interrogative *whether Kim had written the letter* but this would not produce an interrogative sentence: the resulting sentence (*He didn't know whether Kim had written the letter*) has the form of a declarative clause. For these reasons, this article will henceforth speak of 'clause type' rather than 'sentence type.'

Notice in this connection that the domain for the type categories may differ from that for the illocutionary ones. It has already been seen that type may apply to subordinate clauses whereas illocutionary force normally does not, but there may also be differences in coordinative constructions, as in (5):

Have you moved or are you about to move? (5)

This is taken from a bank statement, where it is followed by *If so, please phone the number below*: in this context it is clearly a single inquiry (asking a question whose answer is 'yes' if you either have moved or are about to move), although it consists grammatically of two interrogatives. It differs from such examples as *When is she going or can't you say?*, where there are two questions asked: this contrast in domain reinforces the need to distinguish grammatical interrogative from semantic question or pragmatic inquiry.

1.3 Markers of Clause Type and of Illocutionary Force

It has been emphasized that clause type does not fully determine illocutionary force, for there is not a one-to-one relation between them. Clause type is nevertheless the primary factor determining illocutionary force in that, other things being equal, a declarative will be used to make a statement, an imperative to issue a directive, and so on. The point is, however, that other things are not always equal—that other factors may cause the utterance to have an illocutionary force different from that which its clause type would initially lead one to expect.

Two somewhat different cases where this occurs are illustrated in (6) and (7):

Must you have the radio on so loud? (6)

I promise not to tell anyone what you have just done. (7)

In uttering (6) in an appropriate context I might well be telling you to turn the radio down, i.e., issuing a directive, even though the type is interrogative rather than imperative. The literal meaning is that of a question concerning the necessity for the radio to be on so loud, but with the readily available assumption that the answer is 'no' and that I am asking because I do not like it so loud the utterance will convey, indirectly, that I want you to turn it down: it is accordingly a clear instance of what is known as an 'indirect speech act.'

An utterance of (7) is most likely to be intended and construed as a promise, but it is not desirable to say that it belongs to a special corresponding clause type ('promissive,' say): it is simply declarative. This example differs from the last in that the conveyed force here derives from the literal meaning. The promise force comes from the fact that it contains the verb *promise* used 'performatively,' i.e., in the performance of the illocutionary act it denotes. (Contrast the nonperformative use of the same verb in such examples as *It was wrong of you to promise to go; I don't make a promise by saying this.*) The reason why nevertheless it is not desirable to postulate a promissive clause type here is that the promise force is signaled by quite different linguistic means than the inquiry force of *What do you want?*, the directive force of *Stand still*, and so on. This is evident from such correspondences as one finds in (8) and (9):

(a) I try to help. (8)
(b) Do you try to help?
(c) Try to help.

(a) I promise to help. (9)
(b) Do you promise to help?
(c) Promise to help.

The relation of (a) to (b) to (c) is the same in both sets, and it is for this reason that one can say that in both of them (a) is declarative, (b) interrogative, (c) imperative; the fact that (9a) could be used to make a promise whereas (8a) would normally be simply a statement follows from the lexical–semantic properties of the verb *promise* (vs. *try*), not from any difference in grammatical construction.

It is not always easy to draw a sharp distinction between direct and indirect speech acts, and indeed some writers define indirect speech act in such a way as to cover (7) as well as (6). Explication of the concept indirect speech act is, however, a task for pragmatic theory rather than grammatical theory: for present purposes (6) and (7) can be treated together as cases where various factors override clause type in the determination of illocutionary force. The issue here is thus the distinction between those linguistic features which are markers of clause type and those which, although relevant to illocutionary force, are not. This distinction too is not always easy to draw, and significant differences in the description of clause type in different grammars of the same language are attributable to differences in the way it is drawn. The major guiding principle will be that the clause types constitute a grammatical system

(cf. Sadock and Zwicky 1985: 148–49). This is to say that the various types are mutually exclusive: no (unambiguous) clause can belong to more than one type. This criterion has already been used to argue that (8a) and (9a) do not belong to different clause types: the presence of *promise* does not mark a distinct clause type because it can occur in any of the three major types, as shown in (9). The criterion can likewise be used to show that in the following set (11) belongs to a different clause type than the declarative (10), whereas (12) does not:

She gave a great performance. Declarative (10)

What a great performance she gave! Exclamative (11)

She did give a great performance. Declarative (12)

Example (11) differs from (10) by virtue of the special exclamative phrase *What a great performance*, and such phrases cannot occur in the other major types recognized, imperative and interrogative. Thus *give what a great performance* is not a well-formed imperative, and (the rather marginal) *What a great performance did she give* is simply a variant of (11), not an interrogative clause. The initial phrase therefore puts (11) in a category that is mutually exclusive with imperatives, interrogatives, and declaratives, and accordingly (11) is assigned to a distinct clause type, exclamative. The difference between (12) and (10) is not like this. Example (12) contains the emphatic marker *do*, but the contrast between unmarked and emphatic is found also in imperatives (*give a great performance* vs. *do give a great performance*) and in interrogatives (*Who gave a great performance?* vs. *Who did give a great performance?*). Emphatic *do* is therefore not to be regarded as a marker of clause type: it belongs on a different dimension of clause structure. Another example is provided by *please*: although it serves to signal request force, it is not a clause type marker as it occurs not just in imperatives but also in interrogatives (*Could you please pass the salt?*) and declaratives (*You will please ensure that this does not happen again*).

The major markers of clause type that are found in English and/or other languages are:

(a) verb-form—contrast the different inflectional forms of the verb *be* in declarative *You are generous* and imperative *Be generous*;

(b) order—contrast the linear order of subject and verb in declarative *She is ill* and interrogative *Is she ill?*;

(c) special words or classes of word, for example, interrogative *Who has finished?* is distinguished from declarative *Someone has finished* by the interrogative word *who*;

(d) omission of elements—*Leave after lunch*, for example, is marked as imperative by the absence of the subject, an element that is normally obligatory in declarative and interrogative clauses.

One further linguistic feature that is commonly included in the set of clause type markers is intonation, but the view taken here (following, for example, Lyons 1981: 137–38; Palmer 1986: 6, 30–31) is that intonation is better regarded as one of the features that can override clause type in the determination of illocutionary force than as itself a marker of clause type. The issue arises particularly in the case of inquiries—the area where the single term question is widely used for both form and meaning. In many languages inquiries are characterized by rising intonation, and this may be the only feature distinguishing them from statements. Thus *You have seen it* could be spoken with rising intonation to ask the question 'Have you seen it?' There are nevertheless good reasons for saying that the clause is declarative, not interrogative.

It has been emphasized that clause types are grammatical categories and hence the basis for grouping items together in the same category must be shared grammatical properties, not likeness of illocutionary force. Yet there are no grammatical grounds for regarding rising intonation as comparable to the inverted order that marks *Have you seen it?* as interrogative. Consider, for example, the distribution of various items such as *ever* (in the sense 'at any time'). Such items are restricted to 'nonaffirmative' contexts, mainly negatives, conditionals—and interrogatives. Thus one can say *None of you have ever been to Paris; if you have ever been to Paris; Have you ever been to Paris?*, but not affirmative **You have ever been to Paris*. *You have been to Paris* can be spoken with rising intonation conveying inquiry force, but it is still not possible to insert *ever*: the intonation, unlike inverted order, does not create a grammatically nonaffirmative context. A further point is that rising intonation and inverted order may differ in the scope or domain of the inquiry they signal. This can be illustrated with examples like *I don't suppose you've seen my keys↑* or *Surely you're not going to agree↑* (where ↑ indicates rising intonation). The scope of the inquiry in the first is simply the subordinate clause: one understands it as 'Have you seen my keys?' not 'Don't I suppose you have seen my keys?' And similarly in the second the initial adverb is outside the scope of the inquiry: *surely* reinforces the 'conducive' nature of the inquiry (indicating a belief that the answer should *surely* be negative); the inverted-order construction *Are/Aren't you going to agree?* would not accept *surely* with this function. It should also be noted that empirical studies show that the correlation between rising intonation and inquiries is not nearly as close as one might expect on the basis of intuitions about constructed examples taken out of context (see Geluykens 1988).

A final argument against treating rising intonation as a marker of interrogative clause type is that the inquiry it signals can be of the 'echo' kind, and echo-inquiries can combine with any of the grammatical clause types. Suppose, for example, you utter the declarative *She hadn't enough money*: I might repeat your words with an intonation conveying something like 'Are you really telling me she hadn't enough money?' Or I might echo your imperative *Be patient?*, with rising intonation conveying 'Are you really telling me to be patient?' Similarly interrogative *Is it ready?* might be echoed so as to convey 'Are you really asking me whether it is ready?' and so on. By the guiding principle the echo thus cannot itself be a clause type: it is not in contrast with the clause types declarative, imperative, interrogative, but combines with any. It provides a very general instance of the situation where clause type is overridden in the determination of illocutionary force: the echo *Be patient?*, for example, is not a directive. The echo inquiry is certainly a rather special kind of inquiry, but it is nevertheless an inquiry: it therefore provides strong grounds for the insistence on the distinction between categories of form and categories of meaning/use, as it shows that a noninterrogative can be used with inquiry force. It is, moreover,

extremely doubtful whether an echo inquiry can always be distinguished simply by its prosody from an ordinary inquiry.

With this distinction between markers of clause type and (other) marks of illocutionary force established, the clause types found in main clauses can now be reviewed. The primary focus will be on English; remarks on other languages will draw heavily on the admirable survey in Sadock and Zwicky 1985 (see also Schneider, et al. 1982; Ultan 1978; and—for both sections—Comrie 1987). Attention will be confined to the four major types, leaving aside such minor constructions as are illustrated in *Would I had never set eyes on him!; if only I had more time!; God bless you*, etc.

1.4 Declaratives

In English declarative is the unmarked term in the system: a clause is declarative if it lacks the special features which mark the other terms. Except where there are overriding factors of form, prosody, or context, an utterance of a declarative main clause will have the force of a statement. Several such factors have already been mentioned: the performative use of an illocutionary verb, as in (9a), to signal whatever illocutionary act is denoted by that verb, *please* to convey directive force, rising intonation to signal an inquiry.

It is not always the case that the declarative is unmarked in the sense of simply lacking the special features of other types: in some languages it has special features of its own. This arises particularly where clause types are distinguished by verb-forms (as in Greenlandic or Blackfoot) or contrasting particles (as in Hidatsa, where in fact there is not a single declarative particle, but a set of five, yielding distinct subtypes).

1.5 Imperatives

The major distinctive features of English imperatives are: (a) the verb appears in the base form (e.g., *be* in *You be careful* in contrast to present tense *are* in declarative *You are careful*); (b) the subject is an optional element, usually omitted, being recoverable from the context (as in *Be careful*); (c) *do* is required in negatives and emphatic positives before any verb, whereas in declaratives it does not occur with *be* or certain uses of *have* (compare declarative *You aren't late* with imperative *Don't be late*). The subject (overt or covert) is usually 2nd person, but a 3rd person subject is also possible, as in *Somebody open the window*; pragmatically, however, such subjects are normally understood as applying within the domain of the addressees, so that one understands 'somebody among you.'

One special subtype is the *let*-imperative, as in (13):

Let's be generous.   (13)

The traditional name for (13) is '1st person (plural) imperative,' but this reflects the meaning rather than the grammatical form: the *let* has lost the 'allow' meaning of the ordinary imperative (*Please*) *let us come with you*, but it still behaves as a verb (as is evident from its occurrence with *do* in emphatic *Do let's be generous* or negative *Don't let's go*), and clearly *'s* is not its subject. A genuine 1st person imperative is found in such a language as French, where (13) translates as *soyons généreux*, with *soyons* a 1st person plural imperative verb-form, contrasting with 2nd person *soyez*.

It seems that all languages have an imperative category. Typically the grammatical markers are similar to those given for English. The subject is commonly missing (in some languages obligatorily so). The verb-form is often different from, and morphologically simpler than, that used in declaratives and interrogatives. Many languages indeed (e.g., French, as noted above) have a specifically imperative verb-form. The term 'imperative' is thus standardly used both for a verbal category and for a clausal category. As a verbal category, it is a term in the system of mood, typically contrasting with such other moods as indicative and subjunctive; as a clausal category, it is a term in the system of type, typically contrasting with declarative and interrogative. This dual usage requires that the term be applied with some caution, for it is important to emphasize that imperative clauses are not necessarily marked as such by an imperative verb-form. Traditional grammars of English analyze the *be* of an imperative clause like *Be careful* as an imperative verb-form (contrasting with indicative *are*), but the *be* here is not inflectionally distinct from that of [*It is important*] *to be careful* or that of [*It is essential*] *that he be careful*: no verb in English has different forms in these three constructions, and hence there is no justification for saying that they differ with respect to verb inflection. Rather, there is a single inflectional form appearing in a range of syntactically distinguishable constructions. This form (here called the 'base form,' as it is identical with the lexical stem of the verb), is one of the markers of the imperative clause type in English, but there is no place in the grammar of English for an imperative verb category.

It is also common for imperatives to differ from declaratives with respect to the treatment of negation. In English the differences are fairly minor (the subject usually follows the *don't*, as in *Don't you touch it!*, and *do* is used more extensively, as noted above), but often they are significantly greater, with separate negative markers in the two types. The constructions associated with positive and negative directives may be so different (e.g., involving different verb-forms, as in Greenlandic or Latin) that they need to be assigned to distinct clause types, imperative for the positive, prohibitive for the negative.

Utterances with imperative form have directive force except where other factors override the clause type. Two such cases (besides the echo-inquiry mentioned above) involve wishes and coordination: (a) the imperative is conventionally used for a quite limited range of wishes, such as *Sleep well*; *Get well soon*; *Have a good weekend*, etc. (these involve events that are not normally conceived of as being within the control of the addressee(s), and hence a directive interpretation is blocked); and (b) when an imperative is coordinated with another clause it may be pragmatically equivalent to a conditional, e.g. *Do that again and you'll regret it* 'If you do that again, you'll regret it.' Although there is directive force here (I am likely to be threateningly telling you not to do *that* again), it is conveyed by the whole coordinative construction: there is no force of any kind attaching to the imperative clause itself. It should also be noted that imperatives are quite naturally used in making challenges (*Catch me if you can*), giving permission (*Help yourself if you need any more*), or merely indicating acceptance (*Go ahead if you insist* [*but I think you're making a mistake*]): it is questionable, at best, whether these can be properly subsumed under the concept of directive. (On this and other issues concerning the imperative construction, see the excellent study in Davies 1986.)

1.6 Interrogatives

English has two subtypes of interrogative, 'closed' and 'open' (14) and (15):

(a)	Are they dead?	Closed	(14)
(b)	Are they alive or dead?		
	Who are they?	Open	(15)

The name 'closed subtype' derives from the fact that such clauses are characteristically used to ask questions with a closed set of answers, either 'yes' and 'no,' as in (14a), or a set given in an *or*-coordination, e.g., 'alive' and 'dead' in (14b). Grammatically, they are marked (in main clauses) by verb–subject order. A special feature of English is that only a small number of verbs, mainly auxiliaries, can precede the subject: compare *Can she swim?* with **Swims she?* Where the corresponding declarative contains no such verb, *do* is added to satisfy this syntactic requirement: *Does she swim?* Since the unmarked order is subject–verb, many grammars describe the interrogative in terms of a syntactic process of subject–auxiliary inversion. (There are problems associated with this term since the main verb *be*, and also *have* under certain conditions, likewise undergo inversion; for this reason some grammars (e.g., Quirk, et al. 1985) use the English-specific term 'operator' rather than the general term 'auxiliary' for the class of verbs in question.)

Examples (14a) and (b) are commonly called respectively 'yes/no interrogative' and 'alternative interrogative' (or, more often, 'yes/no question' and 'alternative question'), with no broader term covering them both. The former is very much more frequent than the latter, and a common practice is therefore to present the major division within interrogatives as being between the yes/no subtype (14a) and the open subtype (15), with alternatives like (14b) introduced later (if at all) as a relatively minor third category. There can be no doubt, however, that from a grammatical point of view (14a) and (b) do belong together in a single class opposed to (15): thus a more general category of closed interrogative is required to cover them both. They both lack the interrogative phrase of the open type; as main clauses they both have inversion, and as subordinate clauses they are both introduced by *whether* or *if* ([*He doesn't know*] *whether they are dead/whether they are alive or dead*). It is arguable, moreover, that they should not even be regarded as distinct subtypes of closed interrogative, that the difference between them is not strictly a matter of clause type at all. For the *or* may coordinate not just elements within a clause, as in (14b), but complete clauses, as in *Are they alive or are they dead?* Like (5) above, this consists formally of two closed interrogative clauses, but expresses a single question; whereas (5) was a yes/no question, this is an alternative one, but this distinction clearly applies to the coordinative constructions as wholes, not to the separate clauses. The labels yes/no and alternative will accordingly be applied here just to kinds of question, not to subtypes of interrogative clause.

Now to the examination of open interrogatives. More commonly used terms are 'information question,' 'special question,' 'partial question,' 'question-word question,' '*wh*-interrogative/question.' The term 'open' reflects the fact that the interrogatives are characteristically used for questions where the set of answers is open-ended, as in (15). Other factors may close the set, as in *When are you going, today or tomorrow?*, where the addition of *today or tomorrow* in a loose appositional relation to *when* yields an alternative question. Given the distinction between general and language-particular definitions, however, this is no problem: the general term open interrogative reflects the fact that these clauses are characteristically used to express open questions, while the classification of individual examples is determined by reference to the language-particular grammatical criteria, and by these criteria the example clearly belongs with (15).

The grammatically distinctive property of open interrogatives is the presence of an interrogative word: *who, what, which, why*, etc. (The spelling of these words provides, of course, the basis for the *wh-* label, but this English bias makes it an unsatisfactory term for a general category.) The interrogative words occur as or within phrases filling a range of functions within the structure of the clause: subject (*Who/Which one* [*did it?*]), object (*What/Whose car* [*did you borrow?*]), predicative (*Who/How old* [*is she?*]), time adjunct (*When/What time* [*are you going?*]), and so on. They thus combine two roles: one as a marker of open interrogative clause type, one as a pronoun, determiner, temporal adverb, etc., with functions that can also be filled by noninterrogative words. A special case is where the two roles are associated with different clauses, as in *What do you think she said?* Here the *what* marks the main clause as interrogative but at the same time functions as object of *said* in the subordinate clause.

For some of the interrogative words there is a corresponding noninterrogative indefinite: *someone* corresponds to *who*, *something* to *what*, *somewhere* to *where*, and so on. If one substitutes the indefinite for the interrogative, the result is what is commonly called the presupposition of the question. For example, *Who has taken my umbrella?* presupposes *Someone has taken my umbrella*: if I ask that question I will normally be taking it for granted that someone has taken my umbrella, so that the information I am seeking is simply the identity of that person (this is the basis for the term 'partial question,' mentioned above as one of those sometimes used for the open interrogative category). *Which* differs from the other interrogative words in that it indicateas a selection from a definite set specified in an *of*-phrase, as in *Which of these approaches would you recommend?*, or merely implicit in the context, as in *Which approach would you recommend?*—compare *What approach would you recommend?*, where there need be no already defined set of approaches to choose from.

In all the examples so far the interrogative phrase has occupied initial position, but this is not quite an obligatory feature of the construction: particularly in a context of sustained inquiry, examples like *And so he must have left at approximately what time*, [*would you say?*] are perfectly possible. Normally, however, the interrogative phrase does come first, and this is commonly handled by postulating a transformation that moves it to initial position from an

underlying position determined by its noninterrogative role, e.g., from the unmarked position for an object (shown by '____') in *What did you say ____ to the inspector?* The movement of a nonsubject phrase to front position is accompanied by the subject–auxiliary inversion that is the sole marker of the closed interrogative type: compare *Have you seen something?* (closed) and *What have you seen?* (open).

All languages, it may be assumed, provide the means to ask both closed and open questions. They do not all, however, have both closed and open interrogatives. It has already been noted that intonation alone can be used to express a closed question, and languages (such as Modern Greek) where this is the sole device used for that purpose will not have a grammatical category of closed interrogative. Languages which do have this category usually mark it by one or more of three grammatical devices:

(a) an interrogative particle or clitic, usually appearing in a fixed position in the clause, typically first, second (for enclitics), or last (e.g., initial *est-ce que* in French, second position *li* in Serbo–Croat, initial *sé* or *ǹjé* or final *bí* in Yoruba);
(b) an interrogative verb-form (as in Greenlandic or Blackfoot);
(c) fronting of the verb (as in English).

Open interrogatives are marked by an interrogative word distinguishable from the particles or clitics just mentioned in that they have a dual role, as explained above; the construction may or may not also be marked by an interrogative particle/clitic, interrogative verb-form, or verb fronting. Again there are languages (such as Hopi) which lack these special dual-role interrogative words and hence have no open interrogative category: for open questions they simply use an indefinite in a declarative with rising intonation or in a closed interrogative. (Note that utterances of this kind in English, e.g., *You're going somewhere?* or *Are you going somewhere?*, will often be responded to as though they were open questions, i.e., with information about the destination; in this case the open question is conveyed indirectly, rather than directly by means of the open interrogative *Where are you going?*) Moreover, though it is semantically justifiable to regard closed and open questions as subclasses of question, it should not be assumed that in all languages which do have both closed and open interrogatives there will always be grammatical justification for regarding them as subclasses of a larger interrogative class. In English, justification for the larger class is found in the fact that subject-auxiliary inversion is a major marker of both subtypes (inversion is also found in declaratives, as in *Never before had she tried so hard*, but this case of inversion, unlike interrogative inversion, occurs also in subordinate clauses: *He remarked that never before had she tried so hard*). In French, both subtypes can be marked by the particle *est-ce que*. In Greenlandic, both have interrogative verb-forms. But there need be no such structural feature common to both—e.g., in languages (such as Yoruba) where the closed type is marked by a particle, the open type by a dual-role interrogative word.

There are, however, cases where the interrogative clause type is overridden in the determination of illocutionary force. A distinction has been made between the semantic category of question and the illocutionary category of inquiry; interrogatives almost always express questions, but questions are quite often expressed with other illocutionary intentions than inquiry—in various expository genres, for example, one might pose a question to direct the audience's attention to the issue that one proposes to discuss. The focus here will be on three special cases where an interrogative is typically used without inquiry force. In the first place, interrogatives are often used as directives: *Can/ Could/Will/Would you pass the salt?*; *Would you mind opening the door?*; *Would you be so good as to turn on the light?* Such clauses are typically used not to elicit answers but as requests—to pass the salt, open the door, turn on the light. A condition for complying with a request is an ability and willingness to do so, and a question concerning this ability or willingness can be used as an indirect way of making the request—politer, typically though not invariably, than the use of an imperative precisely because of its indirectness (cf. Davies 1986: ch. 2). The directive intention can be explicitly signaled by means of *please*: *Would you please hurry*. Some forms of expression are more idiomatically used in this way than others which are semantically equivalent—e.g., *can you . . .* rather than *are you able to . . . .* Most of them involve closed interrogatives, but examples are also found in the open type, notably *why* + negative, as in *Why don't you come with us next time?*

Second, interrogatives can be used to express rhetorical questions, questions whose answer is pragmatically so obvious that uttering the question indirectly conveys the answer, i.e., has the indirect force of a statement: *Who cares, anyway?* (answer: *no one*). Arguably a special, and very frequent, case of this is the exclamatory use of closed interrogatives: *Aren't they small!*; *Am I hungry!* Note that although the first of these is negative and the second positive, the implied statements are in both cases positive: *They are (remarkably) small*; *I am (remarkably) hungry*. The exclamatory component is commonly signaled prosodically, and the exclamatory-assertive force may be explicitly indicated by a special intensifying use of *ever*: *Am I ever hungry!*

Third, mention should be made of the special use of elliptical interrogatives as 'tags,' as in *She has agreed, hasn't she? They don't like it, do they?* The two clauses are in a close paratactic relation and the illocutionary force attaches to the construction as a whole rather than separately to the two component clauses. The force depends on the intonation: roughly, a rising tag asks whether the first proposition is in fact true, while a falling tag seeks agreement with the first proposition, about which the speaker is in little or no doubt. Where the tag has the same polarity as the first clause, as in *(So) you told her, did you?*, there is really no inquiry force at all: it is hardly asking for an answer. The speaker is not in doubt about the truth of the first proposition, and the tag has an emotive role, indicating (in combination with the prosody) the speaker's attitude, very often one of disapproval, sarcasm, or the like.

1.7 Exclamatives

Exclamatives in English are marked by a fronted exclamative phrase containing *how* or *what*: *How well she sings!*; *What a fantastic time we had!* How and what belong also to the class of interrogative words, and this close affinity between exclamatives and interrogatives is a widespread feature in the world's languages (cf. Elliott 1974). There are,

however, differences between interrogative and exclamative *how/what*. When modifying the verb, interrogative *how* is an adverb of manner (as in *How did he do it?*), whereas exclamative *how* is an adverb of degree (as in *How he hated them!*). Exclamative *what*, also concerned with degree, functions as determiner in NP structure and in count singular NPs precedes the indefinite article (*What a pathetic proposal they made!*); interrogative *what*, concerned with identity, can function as head in NP structure (*What would you propose?*) or as a determiner mutually exclusive with *a* (*What proposal would you make?*). A further difference is that exclamatives usually have the basic subject–verb order; inversion is not altogether excluded, and when it occurs there is potential ambiguity between the two constructions: *How often have I told you not to do that!/?*

Exclamatives have an exclamatory meaning, but 'exclamation' is not an illocutionary category, for any of the major illocutions can have an exclamatory component of meaning overlaid upon it. This is why exclamatory statement was given as the characteristic use of exclamatives. *What on earth is it?* would be an exclamatory inquiry, *Get the hell out of here!* an exclamatory directive, but in these cases the exclamatory component of meaning is not grammaticalized into a distinct clause type category, as it is in the *how/what* construction. With statements, moreover, there are many other ways of conveying exclamatory meaning than by the use of the exclamative clause type—e.g., by prosodic modulation or by means of intensifiers (*I was so hungry!*; *He made such a fuss!*; *It's absolutely delicious!*): exclamatives thus account for only quite a small proportion of exclamatory statements.

2. Clause Subordination
2.1 Desententialization

It was noted at the outset that when a clause is subordinated it generally loses the illocutionary force that it would normally have if uttered on its own as a sentence. If I utter *Kim is downstairs* on its own I normally make a statement, committing myself to the truth of the proposition that Kim is downstairs, but there is no such statement, no such commitment, when I utter it as a subordinate clause, i.e., as part of some larger clause: [*Max thinks*] *Kim is downstairs*; [*If*] *Kim is downstairs* [*we can ask her*]. This loss of illocutionary force is one aspect of the 'desententialization' that characteristically accompanies the subordination of a clause—i.e., the loss of features of interpretation and/or form that are associated with a clause standing alone as a sentence (see Lehmann 1988; also Palmer 1987).

As further illustration of the change in interpretation that may accompany subordination, consider (16)–(17):

Come in before it rains. (16)

If you told Max you were now better, he might not believe you. (17)

In (16) *it rains* is interpreted significantly differently than it would be as a main (i.e., nonsubordinate) clause, for in (16) one understands some potential future event of raining. With respect to the time of the event, it is closer in meaning to *It will rain* than to *It rains* as a main clause, but it differs in modality, as reflected in the absence of *will*. The main clause would (normally) be used as a statement: *will* is then pragmatically required to express the appropriate predictive modality, for in main clauses a nonmodal form is used for future events only when they are scheduled or determined in advance, as in *The sun sets at 4.55 tomorrow*; in subordinate (16), however, the modal is not needed because the 'rain' proposition is not being asserted. In (17) the meaning expressed by the past tense inflection in *told* is one of modality rather than time: the speaker presents your telling Max (a potential future event) as less likely than in the present tense construction *if you tell Max . . .* ; in main clauses, by contrast, *told* can only have a past time meaning. The other subordinate clause in (17), *you were now better*, is an example of what is traditionally called 'indirect reported speech' (though the term is too narrow: thoughts, feelings, etc. can be reported as well as speech). And here too a past tense may have a different interpretation than is normal for main clauses. In (17) the past tense in *were* does not indicate that the time of your being better is past: the time is present, but it is expressed as present relative not to the time of uttering (17) but to the time of the *told* clause. The tense is thus not a deictic past but an underlying present that has been 'backshifted,' changed from present to past, to agree with the past tense reporting verb *told* (for fuller discussion of tense in reported speech, see Comrie 1985).

In many languages the interpretive differences between the subordinate clauses in (16)–(17) and main clauses would be accompanied by formal differences (e.g., subjunctive as opposed to indicative verb forms), but the English examples illustrate the point that there can be desententialization without formal internal marking. Prototypically, however, subordination is marked in the internal structure of the clause. The major internal markers of subordination are of the same general kind as those mentioned in Sect. 1 as distinguishing clause types, but they differ of course in specifics. They include:

(a) verb-form—it is common for various verb inflections to be characteristic of subordinate clauses, notably nonfinite and subjunctive forms; contrast, for example, subordinate [*I remember*] *there being some debate on the issue* with main *There was some debate on the issue* (cf. Palmer 1986: 156–63, 172–74);

(b) special closed class words—most obviously subordinating conjunctions (e.g., *that/whether*, as in [*He wasn't sure*] *that/whether it was true*), and relative words (*who, which, where*, etc., as in [*The man*] *who broke it* [*was arrested*]);

(c) order—as in the contrast between main *What can we do about it?* and subordinate [*I wonder*] *what we can do about it* (a more striking example is provided by German, where the verb occurs in final position in subordinate clauses but in second position in declarative main clauses);

(d) omission of elements—subordinate clauses commonly lack structural elements that would appear in a corresponding main clause; contrast main *I met her* and subordinate [*It was nice*] *meeting her*, which has no subject.

2.2 Finite and Nonfinite Clauses

One important form of desententialization is nonfiniteness. Main clauses are characteristically finite, whereas subordinate clauses may be finite or nonfinite (18) and (19):

(a) [I'm glad] that she will be present.	Finite	(18)
(b) [I'm keen] for her to be present.	Nonfinite	

(a) [The guy] who was leading them [stumbled].	Finite	(19)
(b) [The guy] leading them [stumbled].	Nonfinite	

Nonfinite subordinate clauses thus differ more radically in structure from comparable main clauses than do finite ones. In (18), for example, the comparable main clause is *She will be present*; the finite subordinate (a) differs from this simply in the presence of the subordinating conjunction *that*, which is, moreover, omissible; the nonfinite subordinate (b), on the other hand, contains the conjunction *for*, the special infinitival marker *to*, and has its subject in the accusative case (*her*, not *she*). Furthermore, a number of verbal contrasts can be made in (a) but not (b): *will be* can be replaced by *may be, was, is*, etc., but equivalent replacements are not available in (b). And, in (18b) the subject is omissible when it is recoverable from the 'superordinate' clause (i.e., the one in which the subordinate clause is embedded): [*I'm keen*] *to be present*. The same points apply to (19), where the comparable main clause is *the guy was leading them*. Finite (a) differs simply in the substitution of the relative pronoun *who* for the subject. Nonfinite (b), however, lacks a subject altogether, and also the auxiliary verb—and hence it additionally lacks such verbal contrasts as those available in (a) between *was leading, led, leads, will lead, should lead*, etc. To a large extent, the differences are a matter of a nonfinite construction being reduced in various ways, with some elements omitted, some contrasts not available. There is a natural link between these features and subordination, for some of the information that in a main clause environment has to be explicitly expressed if it is to be conveyed can in a subordinate environment be left implicit, inferable from the superordinate context. It was noted in considering (18b) that the subject may be recoverable in this way, and the same applies (though much less frequently) to the object or complement of a preposition: e.g., in [*Bill found the instructions hard*] *to follow* the missing object is recovered from *the instructions*, as the subject is from *Bill*. Similarly with various features of meaning involving time and modality. Compare, for example, [*I regret*] *discussing it with him* (past time) with [*I propose*] *discussing it with him* (modalized future) or [*She was the first one*] *to do it* ('She did it') with [*She is the one*] *to do it* ('She should do it').

Traditionally, the general terms finite and nonfinite are applied initially to verb-forms, and then derivatively to clauses, so that a finite clause will be defined as one containing a finite verb. The grammatical sense of finite is related to its everyday sense of 'limited'; more specifically, as applied to Latin, finite verb-forms are limited with respect to (i.e., inflect for) the categories of person and number. For example, the present active indicative forms of the verb *laudo* 'praise' are *laudo* (1st sg), *laudas* (2nd sg), *laudat* (3rd sg), etc., hence finite, whereas the present active infinitive form is invariably *laudare*, hence nonfinite.

This is a very narrow definition, and there are languages where it does not yield satisfactory results. In Portuguese, for example, the infinitive inflects for person/number under certain conditions, yet the infinitive is normally the prototypical nonfinite form. Conversely, there are languages such as Japanese where there is no person/number inflection on the verb at all, but one would not want to say that all clauses in such languages were nonfinite. There are likewise problems in applying the definition as it stands to English because of the very small amount of person–number differentiation it displays: verbs other than *be* have just a two-way contrast between 3rd sg (e.g., *takes*) and not 3rd sg (*take*) in the present tense and no contrasts at all in the past tense or elsewhere. Traditional grammars of English avoid this problem by postulating a massive amount of syncretism (i.e., distinguishing forms when there is no overt difference). Thus the *be* of *He insists that I be told* is analyzed as a 1st sg form, that of *He insists that you be told* a 2nd sg or 2nd pl form, and so on, so that these verbs then qualify as finite. This, however, is to force English into an alien mold. There is no verb exhibiting any person/number contrasts in this construction, and hence no justification for saying that these categories apply: *be* is simply the invariable base form of the verb (cf. Sect. 1.5 above). It is arguable that in English the primary contrast in the system of verb inflection is between the tensed forms (*am, is, are, was, were*) and the nontensed forms (*be, being, been*) and that it is at the level of clause structure rather than that of verb inflection that the category of finiteness can be useful if its interpretation is broadened somewhat, especially if one allows for varying degrees of finiteness instead of insisting on an all-or-nothing contrast of finite vs. nonfinite.

Fully finite clauses are those displaying the full range of verbal contrasts characteristic of declarative main clauses; in English this comprises the set of tensed clauses, i.e., clauses containing a tensed verb-form. The nontensed base form is found in such constructions as (20)–(21):

(a) Be careful. (20)
(b) [It is essential] that they be told.
(c) Even if they be found guilty, [they will still deserve our sympathy].

(a) For them to be seen together [would be very dangerous]. (21)
(b) [I won't let] them be insulted.

Traditionally the clauses in (20) are finite, those in (21) nonfinite, and although they all contain the same verb-form, this analysis can be retained and justified on the grounds that the constructions in (20) are significantly closer to fully finite clauses than are those in (21). First, the imperative (20a) is like a tensed clause in taking auxiliary *do* in negatives and emphatic positives (cf. Sect. 1.5); it is the only nontensed construction with this property and thus may be regarded as coming second on the scale of finiteness. Imperatives, moreover, are virtually restricted to main clauses, whereas nonfinites are, as noted, normally subordinate. And second, (20b and c) are similar to tensed clauses in that they take nominative subjects (thus *they* in contrast to accusative *them* in (21)); the *be*, moreover, is here replaceable by tensed *is* or *should be* without any further change.

The four main kinds of nonfinite constructions traditionally distinguished are exemplified for English in (22)–(25):

[He enjoyed] writing the letter. (22)

[The guy] writing the letter [couldn't spell]. (23)

[She had lost the letter] written by her father. (24)

[It is essential] for her to write the letter. (25)

The verb-form *writing* is traditionally analyzed as a gerund in (22) and a present participle in (23). A gerund is a verb-form with some functional resemblance to a noun, while a participle is one with some functional resemblance to an adjective. Thus in (22) *writing the letter* is complement of the verb *enjoyed*, comparable therefore to a noun (phrase), whereas in (23) it modifies *guy*, the prototypical modifier of a noun being an adjective (phrase). In such languages as Latin the gerund and present participle are overtly distinct, but there is no such distinction in English and thus application of the traditional analysis to English again involves unjustifiable syncretism. Most modern grammars of English accordingly have a single inflectional category for the two instances of *writing*; it is usually called a participle, though it is arguable that a compound term 'participle-gerund' would better indicate its status, bringing out that it corresponds to both forms in languages where they are distinct. Modern grammars often use the derived term 'gerundive' for the clause level construction of (22), but in the absence of any clear difference in internal structure it is difficult and unnecessary to draw a systematic distinction between participial and gerundive clause constructions in English (cf. also Sect. 2.4 below). Turning now to (24), the form *written* is used in the passive construction (as here) and in the perfect ([*Her father has*] *written* [*the letter*]); the traditional term for it is 'past participle,' contrasting with the 'present participle' *writing*: they are both nontensed forms. Some grammars distinguish them as 'ing-participle' and 'en-participle' or simply 'ing-form' and 'en-form,' but these will obviously not serve as general terms, and the traditional terms continue to be widely used in spite of the problems they raise. Finally the *write* of (25) is traditionally analyzed as an infinitive form; it has been argued here that it is not a distinct verb-form in English and should be subsumed under the base form, but one can validly apply the term 'infinitival' to the clause-level nonfinite construction of (25) and (21) since there are structural features distinguishing it from finite (20). The infinitive is the unmarked nonfinite form, lacking the positive properties of participles or gerunds; often it is associated with a more hypothetical, modalized meaning than these latter—compare, for example, [*She is the one*] *to do it* vs. [*She is the one*] *doing it*.

2.3 Subordinate Clause as a Relational Category

The preceding sections looked at ways in which the subordinate status of a clause may be reflected in its internal structure, but it was noted that there is not always any internal difference between a subordinate clause and a main one. It follows that subordinate clause is essentially a relational category, defined primarily by reference to the larger construction in which it appears rather than in terms of its own structure. A subordinate clause is thus one contained within a larger, superordinate, clause. Nevertheless, it is because subordination is characteristically marked internally that subordinate clauses constitute a significant syntactic class. There is no comparable marking of superordinate clauses: the classes one needs to distinguish, therefore, are subordinate clauses and main clauses, with the latter defined negatively as not subordinate. Not all main clauses are superordinate (since they frequently do not contain any subordinate clause within them, as in (1)), and not all superordinate clauses are main (because subordination is 'recursive': in (17), for example, *if you told Max you were now better* is superordinate to *you were now better*, yet is itself subordinate to the main clause that forms the whole sentence).

Matters are complicated, however, by the fact that there is sometimes conflict between the external and internal aspects of subordination. This is illustrated in such samples as (26), in contrast to (27):

(a) [The issue is] what should we tell her? (26)
(b) To think that I was prepared to trust a guy like that!

(a) [The issue is] what we should tell her. (27)
(b) How amazing it is that I was prepared to trust a guy like that!

In (26a) *what should we tell her?* is externally subordinate by virtue of being complement to *is* (hence part of the clause with *is* as verb), but it has the inverted subject-auxiliary order that is characteristic of interrogative main clauses: subordinate interrogatives normally have the form shown in (27a). Conversely, (26b) is not externally subordinate but has an infinitival structure, which is characteristic of subordinate clauses: compare the finite main clause in (27b). There is no established terminology for handling these relatively exceptional constructions; as priority has been given to external features in the definitions, one might speak of *what should we tell her?* in (26a) as a 'structurally incongruous' subordinate clause in contrast to the 'structurally congruous' *what we should tell her* in (27a), and similarly for the main clauses (26b) and (27b) respectively. (Structurally incongruous indirect reported speech is not always clearly distinct from direct reported speech, at least in the spoken language: compare [*She asked*] *what he does*, indirect/congruous; [*She asked*] *what does he do* indirect/incongruous; [*She asked,*] '*what does he do?*,' direct.)

It has been said that a subordinate clause is one contained within a larger clause, but this definition is in need of some elaboration. One issue concerns the difference between such examples as (28) and (29):

Ed joined the club because he was bored. (28)

Ed joined the club although he had little spare time. (29)

The *because*-clause in (28) can be made focus of a cleft-construction (*It was because he was bored that Ed joined the club*) and it can figure as one of the alternatives in an alternative question (*Did Ed join the club because he was bored or because he wanted to get fit?*), but the *although*-clause in (29) cannot (**It was although he had little spare time that Ed joined the club*; **Did Ed go out although he had little spare time or although he was lazy?*). These facts suggest that the *because*-clause is more deeply embedded than the *although*-clause. It is arguable that the subordinate clause is functioning as modifier within the predicate in (28), but not in (29): in the latter it is an immediate constituent of the whole sentence. The status of the *because*-clause as an element within a larger clause will then be unproblematic, but for the *although*-clause in (29) to qualify one must allow that the whole sentence has the form of a clause even though its structure is head + modifier, not subject + predicate: it will be a clause because its head element, *Ed joined the club*, is a clause (of subject + predicate structure). But relatively fine details of constituent structure are involved here where the analysis will depend heavily on the theoretical model adopted: the proposal just made

is acknowledged to be problematic. (Some works, e.g, Halliday 1985; Matthiessen and Thompson 1988, distinguish two kinds of clause subordination, 'embedding' and 'hypotaxis': only the former satisfies the definition of subordination given here, with hypotaxis being a matter of combining one clause with another in a structure which is not itself a clause; for a critique, see Huddleston 1988: Sect. 2.2.)

A further issue concerns the distinction between subordination and coordination—e.g., between (29) and (30):

He joined the club but he had little spare time. (30)

In (29) *although he had little spare time* satisfies the definition of subordinate clause under the interpretation suggested above; in (30), by contrast, *but he had little spare time* does not satisfy the definition because the construction of which it is a part is not itself a clause, but a combination of two clauses of equal syntactic status. The question arises, however, as to how to justify assigning different structures to (29) and (30) in this way.

Notice that the concept of desententialization applies to coordination as well as to subordination: the *but*-clause no more forms a sentence on its own than does the *although*-clause. The degree to which a clause loses the properties of a sentence is typically greater when it is subordinated than when it is coordinated, but coordinative desententialization may nevertheless be clearly apparent in the interpretation or form of a clause. There has already been discussion (Sect. 1.5) of how coordination can lead to a loss of separate illocutionary force in examples like (5) or *Do that again and you'll regret it*. The chief effect on form is loss of elements through ellipsis, as in [*Tim needed three attempts*] *but his sister only two*; this kind of reduction excludes any possibility of defining main clauses in terms of an ability to stand alone as a sentence.

One clear difference between (29) and (30) is that the *although*-clause can be fronted, whereas the *but*-clause cannot: *Although he had little spare time he joined the club*; **But he had little spare time he joined the club*. It is common for dependent elements to be able to occur before or after their head, but comparable structural variation is not found in coordination. A second important difference emerges when one considers *although* and *but* in combination with the relative construction: [*Ed,*] *who joined the club although he had little spare time* vs. [*Ed,*] *who joined the club but who had little spare time*. In the *although*-construction relativization involves changing the first *he* to *who*, but not the second, whereas in the *but*-construction both are changed. This brings out the coordinative nature of *but*: the items it joins have to be of like syntactic status, either both main clauses, as in (30), or both relative clauses, as here. Because the *although*-clause is, by contrast, subordinate, it does not have to be of the same status as the one with which it is in construction, and hence relativization of the latter leaves it unaffected. (For a fuller discussion of the subordination-coordination distinction, see Quirk, et al. 1985: 918–28; Palmer 1986: 199–207.)

2.4 The Classification of Subordinate Clauses

Subordinate clauses are traditionally classified on the basis of functional similarities to three of the major parts of speech:

(a) [I remember] that she slapped him.   Nominal   (31)
(b) [They arrested the man] who attacked us.   Adjectival
(c) [She left] before it was over.   Adverbial

In (a) *that she slapped him* functions as object of *remember*, a function primarily associated with nouns (or NPs): compare [*I remember*] *her reaction*. In (b) *who attacked us* modifies *man*, and the prototypical modifier of a noun is an adjective: compare [*They arrested the*] *aggressive* [*man*]. In (c) *before it was over* modifies the verb, a function that figures in the traditional definition of the adverb: compare [*She left*] *early*.

This kind of analysis raises a number of problems, however. Note, first, that such a clause as *that she slapped him* can also be used 'adverbially,' as in [*He behaved so badly*] *that she slapped him*. It is necessary to describe the structure of the larger construction, saying here, for example, that the subordinate clause is dependent on *so* and that in (31a) it is object of *remember*, but once the function has been given nothing is added by saying that it is adverbial in one and nominal in the other. As noted above, subordinate clauses form a significant syntactic class because they prototypically differ in form from main clauses, but from the point of view of form there is no difference between the two occurrences of *that she slapped him* and hence we have no reason to assign them to different classes. What is important is the distinction between this kind of clause and that found in (31b), and so on. Second, and conversely, this type of classification will separate [*I have spent*] *what you gave me*, (31b) and [*He put it back*] *where he had found it* as respectively nominal, adjectival, and adverbial, but from the point of view of their structure they belong together, as relatives. (Traditional grammar does have a class of relative clauses, but it does not fit in well with the function-based classification, as these examples show; moreover, it remains unclear where in the latter scheme relative clauses with a clause as antecedent should be placed, as in [*I'll come at six tomorrow,*] *which will give us more time*, for there is no close analogy with any word class here.)

For these reasons, the classification given in (31) will be abandoned, and focus placed instead on classes based on structural likenesses, with attention limited to finite clauses. The major subclasses appropriate for English are illustrated in (32):

(a) [I couldn't obtain the book] which he   Relative   (32)
    recommended.
(b) [I'm not as fit as] I was then.   Comparative
(c) [He doesn't know] that he is dying.   Content

Relative clauses are distinguished by the fact that they contain a relative word or a gap ('zero' element) anaphorically related to an antecedent in the superordinate clause. Subordinate (32a), for example, differs from the main clause *he recommended the book* in that it has the relative pronoun *which* (in initial position) instead of the ordinary NP *the book* (in the basic, postverbal, object position), and the *which* receives its interpretation from the head of the NP in which the clause is embedded. The relative word may be a pronoun (*which, who, whom, whose*), an adverb (*when, where, why*, as in [*I remember the time*] *when I first met her*, etc.), or a determiner (*whose* or *which*, as in [*He may be here*], *in which case we can ask him*, where the anaphoric phrase *in which case* is interpreted as 'if he is here'). The gap construction is seen in [*I couldn't obtain the book*] *he*

recommended: this differs from (32a) in that the relative phrase is missing. Traditional grammar includes among the relative pronouns the *that* introducing relative clauses like [*I couldn't obtain the book*] *that he recommended*; modern grammars more often equate it with the subordinating conjunction introducing content clauses like (32c), and under this analysis *that*-relative clauses will belong with the gap construction, having no overt relative phrase.

Comparative clauses, which follow either *as* or *than*, differ internally from main clauses by virtue of their reduction by anaphoric ellipsis. Example (32b), for example, has ellipsis of the predicative complement: one understands, from the antecedent in the superordinate clause, 'I was fit then' (or rather something like 'I was x fit then,' where 'x' represents an unspecified degree modifier: the comparison is between the degree to which I am fit now and the degree to which I was fit then). There is no suggestion, of course, that anaphoric ellipsis is restricted to subordinate clauses. Subordination nevertheless creates a particularly favorable environment for ellipsis in that missing elements will be readily recoverable from the superordinate clause. The fine details of what can or must be left out in comparative clauses are, moreover, unique to that construction.

Content clauses form what can be regarded as the residual class of finite subordinate clauses: they lack the special structural features of the relative and comparative classes. Compare, for example (33):

(a) [He grumbled about the pies] I had   Relative   (33)
    eaten the day before.
(b) [He ate as many pies as] I had eaten   Comparative
    the day before.
(c) [He didn't tell her] I had eaten the   Content
    day before.

In (a) there is a gap created by the missing relativized object: the closest main clause equivalent is *I had eaten the pies the day before*. Example (b) exhibits again comparative ellipsis: the closest main clause this time is *I had eaten that many pies the day before* (substituting *that* for the unspecified degree modifier). Example (c) lacks these special features and in fact, being a very simple example, is not structurally distinct from a main clause (though *that* could be inserted as a marker of subordination, as in (32c)).

In the generative literature content clauses are normally called 'complement clauses.' Jespersen's (see *Jespersen, Otto*) term 'content clause' is preferred here, partly because 'complement' is a functional (relational) label, whereas the concern here is with a classification of clauses based on internal properties, partly because the clause class in question is not restricted to complement function. Content clauses commonly occur as subject, as in *That he was lying* [*was obvious*]. It is true that some scholars subsume subject under the concept of complement, but that is by no means a majority view. Moreover, there are other constructions where content clauses are clearly not complements: [*He had invited his mother,*] *that she might see the situation for herself*; [*I'm inviting her,*] *whether you approve or disapprove*.

One construction now widely analyzed as involving a content clause, but handled very differently in traditional grammar, is illustrated in (34):

He left before the meeting ended.   (34)

The traditional analysis (which was implicitly followed in

Sect. 2.3) takes the subordinate clause to be *before the meeting ended* (hence 'adverbial'), with *before* a subordinating conjunction, like the *that* of (32c). This, however, is to treat the *before* very differently from that of *He left before the end of the meeting*, where it is a preposition (and where, implicitly, *the end of the meeting*, unlike *the meeting ended* in (34), is a constituent). The criteria for distinguishing in practice between prepositions and subordinating conjunctions are extremely complex (note, for example, that the *while* of *while eating it* is said to be a conjunction whereas the *before* of *before eating it* is a preposition), and many grammarians now include most of the traditional subordinating conjunctions (though not *that*, *whether*, and one or two more) in the class of prepositions. In this analysis, *the meeting ended* in (34) will be a content clause functioning as complement to *before*. Prepositions—like verbs, nouns, and adjectives—will now be subclassified according to what kinds of complement they can have. Thus *underneath* takes NPs, *while* takes content clauses or nonfinites with a participle–gerund verb-form, *before* any of these three kinds, and so on.

2.5. Clause Type in Finite Subordinate Clauses

As remarked at the outset, clause type contrasts are found in subordinate clauses as well as in main clauses, as seen in example (35):

(a)	[No-one knew] that he'd chosen a young manager.	Declarative (35)
(b)	[No-one knew] if he'd chosen a young manager.	Closed interrogative
(c)	[No-one knew] which young manager he'd chosen.	Open interrogative
(d)	[No-one knew] what a young manager he'd chosen.	Exclamative

Again a distinction must be made between structurally congruous and structurally incongruous subordinate clauses. The latter include such constructions as [*I may be a little late,*] *in which case please do start without me* (imperative relative) or colloquial [*We must hurry*]—*because didn't you say it started at six?*; here there is syntactic subordination but from a communicative point of view the subordinate clauses have the same status as main clauses, being invested with their own illocutionary force. Such exceptional constructions will be set aside, and henceforth attention will be restricted to structurally congruous subordinate clauses. The only clauses of this kind where the type system applies are content clauses.

Although there are clear similarities between the type systems in main and subordinate clauses, there are also significant differences. These have to do with: (a) the set of terms in the system; (b) the structural features marking the various types; (c) the meaning. Points (a) and (c) merit brief comment.

Imperative clauses in English (and indeed in most languages) figure only in the main clause system. The utterance of imperative *go away* can be reported as *He told me to go away*, and for this reason this latter construction has sometimes been treated as containing a subordinate imperative. The subordinate clause, however, is simply the infinitival *to go away*, which also occurs in many environments that have no connection with the imperative (e.g., *I'm hoping to go away*). The directive meaning of the original is

captured in the reporting verb *told* in the superordinate clause, not in a special type of subordinate clause. Another construction that has been regarded as a subordinate imperative is illustrated in [*She demanded/It is important*] *that he go away* (also (20b) above). Like a main clause imperative this has a base-form verb, but the differences between the two constructions are nevertheless far too great for it to be validly classified as a subordinate imperative. Most notably, it allows the full range of subjects found in declaratives, whereas imperatives take only a subset, so that there are innumerable examples without main clause counterparts: [*it is essential*] *that there be a doctor present/that it not be raining*, and so on. Accordingly these subordinate clauses will be regarded as simply nontensed declaratives—the base-form verb does not constitute a distinct clause type marker as it is also found (though somewhat archaically) in interrogatives (*whether that be so*).

As for meaning, the subordinate types are of course less closely related to illocutionary force than the main clause types. Subordinate declaratives normally express propositions, as do main declaratives; but whereas the proposition expressed in a main declarative is normally taken as the content of the speaker's statement, the way the proposition expressed in a subordinate declarative is taken depends on properties of the superordinate clause. Thus *She knows he is ill* and *She is staying here because he is ill* both entail *he is ill*, whereas *She thinks he is ill* and *We're in trouble if he is ill* do not: this follows from the semantic properties of *know*, *think*, *because*, and *if*. The same applies, essentially, to exclamatives. Subordinate interrogatives can generally be paraphrased as *the answer to the question '. . .'*: e.g., *She asked/told me who he is = She asked/told me the answer to the question 'Who is he?'* Thus with a main interrogative the speaker characteristically expresses the question with the force of an inquiry, with the aim of eliciting an answer from the addressee, but with a subordinate interrogative the question is integrated into the semantic structure of the superordinate clause. (It must be remembered, however, that a single question may be expressed by a coordination of interrogatives, as [*He didn't know*] *whether it was genuine or whether it was a hoax*.)

The choice of clause type in subordinate clauses is generally constrained by the governing verb, adjective, noun, or preposition. Although *know* allows all three primary types, as illustrated in (35), *matter* takes (in subject function) only declaratives and interrogatives, *wonder* takes only interrogatives, *expect* only declaratives, and so on. The close semantic relation between exclamatives and declaratives is again reflected in the fact that all items taking exclamatives also take declaratives. But the two subtypes of interrogative do not have identical distributions: such items as *amazing*, for example, take the open but not the closed subtype (*It's amazing who they invited/*whether they invited him*). (For fuller discussion of type selection, see Grimshaw 1979.)

Bibliography

Comrie B 1985 *Tense*. Cambridge University Press, Cambridge
Comrie B (ed.) 1987 *The World's Major Languages*. Croom Helm, London
Davies E 1986 *The English Imperative*. Croom Helm, London
Elliott D E 1974 Toward a grammar of exclamations. *Foundations of Language* **11**: 231–46

Geluykens R 1988 On the myth of rising intonation in polar questions. *JPrag* **12**: 467–85

Grimshaw J 1979 Complement selection and the lexicon. *LIn* **10**: 279–326

Halliday M A K 1985 *Introduction to Functional Grammar.* Arnold, London

Huddleston R 1988 Constituency, multi-functionality and grammaticalization in Halliday's Functional Grammar. *JL* **24**: 137–74

Lehmann C 1988 Towards a typology of clause linkage. In: Haiman J, Thompson S A (eds.) *Clause Combining in Grammar and Discourse.* Benjamins, Amsterdam

Lyons J 1966 Towards a notional theory of the parts of speech. *JL* **2**: 209–36

Lyons J 1977 *Semantics.* Cambridge University Press, Cambridge

Lyons J 1981 *Language, Meaning and Context.* Fontana, London

Matthiessen C, Thompson S A 1988 The structure of discourse and 'subordination.' In: Haiman J, Thompsons A (eds.) *Clause Combining in Grammar and Discourse.* Benjamins, Amsterdam

Palmer F R 1986 *Mood and Modality.* Cambridge University Press, Cambridge

Palmer F R 1987 The typology of subordination: Results, actual and potential. *TPhS*: 90–109

Quirk R, Greenbaum S, Leech G, Svartvik J 1985 *A Comprehensive Grammar of the English Language.* Longman, London

Sadock J M, Zwicky A M 1985 Speech act distinctions in syntax. In: Shopen T (ed.) *Language Typology and Syntactic Description*, vol. I. Cambridge University Press, Cambridge

Schneider R, Tuite K, Chametzky R 1982 *Papers from the Parasession on Nondeclaratives.* Chicago Linguistics Society, Chicago, IL

Ultan R 1978 Some general characteristics of interrogative systems. In: Greenberg, J H (ed.) *Universals of Human Language*, vol. 4. Stanford University Press, Stanford, CA

R. D. Huddleston

Serbia: Language Situation

At the time of writing there is some uncertainty about the political future of all of the six republics that comprised the former Yugoslavia, and this applies to Serbia which, before the disintegration of Yugoslavia, had within it two autonomous provinces—Kosovo and Vojvodina. Within the boundaries of Serbia as they stood at the beginning of the period of unrest, the majority of the population (1991: 9,791,745) speak Serbo–Croat, for which in this case a more acceptable label may be assumed to be Serbian. The most widely spoken minority languages are Hungarian (in the northern province of Vojvodina; 430,946 out of a population of 2,012,517 in 1991) and Albanian (in the southern province of Kosovo; 1,607,690 out of a population of 1,954,747 in 1991). There are smaller numbers of Romanian and Bulgarian speakers.

See also: Serbo-Croat; Yugoslavia.

Serbo–Croat

Serbo–Croat is spoken by four groups of peoples within the former Yugoslav federation: Serbs, Croats, Montenegrins, and Muslims (the official 'nationality' of Muslim Serbo-Croat speakers in the republic of Bosnia–Hercegovina). It is also spoken by the 20 percent of the population who declared themselves 'Yugoslavs' in the 1981 census. There are some 17 million speakers in all. 'Serbo–Croat' (or Serbo–Croatian) is the name by which the language is known abroad. More locally it may also be referred to as Croato–Serbian, Serbian or Croatian, Croatian or Serbian, Serbian and Croatian, Croatian and Serbian, reflecting the equal status in law of the two components, individually termed the 'western' and the 'eastern variant.' This situation is changing, however, and with the break-up of the federation and independence of Croatia, 'Croatian' and 'Serbian' may well become established as official terms. But, while it is politically expedient to emphasize the differences between the two variants, the suggestion that they amount to two distinct languages remains linguistically untenable.

Serbo–Croat belongs, with Bulgarian, Slovene, and Macedonian, to the South Slav branch of the Slavonic language family. The first written records are eleventh-century inscriptions in stone in both the Glagolitic and related Cyrillic scripts. The cultural division between the two variants reflects their history: the western Latin-script culture of Croatia, in the orbit of the Catholic church and later the Habsburg Monarchy; and the eastern, Cyrillic, Byzantine, Orthodox culture of Serbia, more or less stagnant during the centuries of Ottoman occupation.

Dia-system: Serbo–Croat is the most heterogeneous Slavonic dia-system, with an exceptionally large variety of dialects, some with 6–7 cases, some with 4, and a great variety of verbal tense. At the same time, these dialects have a striking degree of connectedness, containing characteristic features which distinguish Serbo–Croat from all other Slavic languages. One of these is its complex, archaic, prosodic system, in which stress position, vocalic quantity (length/shortness) and tone (rising/falling) are marked. The traditional accents are—long falling: *nôć*; short falling: *kȕća*; long rising: *réka*; short rising: *òstati*.

There are not many minimal pairs. Examples would be 'grȃd' (hail) and 'grâd' (town); '*päs*' (dog) and '*pâs*' (belt, waist; pass); the sentence '*Sâm sȁm.*' (I am alone).

Morphology. The structure has remained complex, although one feature of Old Slavonic—the dual—has disappeared from the declensions and conjugations of all Serbo–Croat dialects. Case and verbal endings and accent shifts are the main morphological categories.

Word order is free, with the exception of strict rules governing the position of enclitics. These are verbal and pronominal short forms and the interrogative and reflexive particles.

Orthography. The systematization of the Serbo–Croat vernacular was carried out in the mid-nineteenth century on phonetic principles, with one letter corresponding to one sound, making its orthography one of the most consistent in Europe. There is exact correspondence between the two scripts so that transliteration from one to the other is straightforward.

There are three symbols unique to Serbo–Croat: **ć, ħ; dj, ђ; dž, ņ.**

Western variant. Od dviju sjevernih skupina, tj. istočne i zapadne, južna se razlikuje nizom osobina. (1)

Eastern variant.
(*This may equally well be written in the Latin script*)

Од двеју северних скупина, тј. источне и западне, јужна се
разликује низом особина.   (2)

Literal translation. The Southern Slavonic group is
distinguished from the two Northern groups, i.e., the Eastern
and Western, by a series of features.

C. Hawkesworth

Serial Verbs

The term 'serial verbs' has been used for a number of superficially similar constructions in various languages, including
West African languages of the Kwa group, Atlantic Creole
languages (which derive some of their lexicon and, arguably, some of their syntax from Kwa), Tok Pisin (Melanesian Pidgin English), and Chinese. There is no agreed
definition of serial verb, but generally constructions which
are so labeled are those which allow two or more verbs
(other than auxiliaries) within a single noncomplex sentence
or clause, with no overt signs of coordination.

1. Descriptive Problems

If self-embedding of sentences and coordination of sentences are universal properties of language, then all languages have the possibility of two or more—in theory,
infinitely many—verbs within one sentence. However, there
are usually morphological or syntactic markers of coordination or subordination, for example, the conjunction *and* or
a dependent verb form (in English, the infinitive form
marked by *to*) which distinguishes the embedded from the
matrix sentence. 'Serial verb constructions' do not show
morphological signs of coordination or subordination
within the sentence. This is true both of sentence (1) from
Mandarin Chinese, a language with little inflectional morphology, and sentence (2) from Akan (a Kwa language of
Ghana), which has person, number, and tense marking:

Tā   tiāntiān hùi-kè   xiě   xìn   (1)
s/he daily   receive-guest write letter
'Every day she receives visitors and writes letters.'

ɔde   pono   no   baae   (2)
3PERS-take-PAST table the come-PAST
'S/he brought the table.'

While sentence (1) could be regarded simply as involving
an unmarked coordination of verb phrases, in (2), the sense
of the sentence requires the translation 'S/he brought the
table'; the two verbs, *de* and *baae* are interpreted as parts
of the same action, which involves 'taking' and 'coming.'
Both verbs have past tense marking.

An even clearer indication that the verbs in a construction like (2) have a joint interpretation is found in (3), also
from Akan:

migyee   no   midii   (3)
I-accept him I-eat
'I believe him.'

In (3), the interpretation 'believe' is an idiomatic one
derived from the combination of the verbs meaning 'accept'
and 'eat.'

This suggests that at least some 'serial' combinations,

e.g., (3), have their own, unitary lexical entry, while others,
perhaps, like (2), are produced by a lexical redundancy rule
which permits verbs of a certain class (e.g., verbs of motion)
to be followed by certain other verbs (in this case, the verbs
meaning 'come' and 'go,' which provide an indication of
direction). This is reminiscent of the verbal affixes of languages like German which are attached by a productive
lexical rule to verbs of an appropriate meaning class (e.g.,
hin 'away from' to motion verbs).

In the case of sentence (1), the interpretation is clearly
that of two separate but contemporaneous actions, and
there are no restrictions on the classes of verbs which may
appear in either the first or second verb position. There
seem to be no grounds for postulating any lexical rules
relating the two verbs; in fact, this may be a case of coordination without morphological marking. It may be a completely distinct phenomenon from the Akan examples (2)
and (3). However, Akan also permits coordination-like
serial constructions, as in (4):

Yɛsɔrɛɛ   ntɛm kɔɔ   ofie   (4)
we-arise-PAST quick go-PAST home
'We arose quickly and went home.'

Meanwhile, constructions exist in Mandarin which
(though not traditionally called serial) involve the use of a
second verb as a direction marker:

Tā   ná   zhūozi   dào   wūzi-li   qù   (5)
s/he carry table   'to'   room-in go
'She carried the table into the room.'

In Akan, there are some constructions which are ambiguous
between 'unitary action' and 'two action' readings:

Amma   frɛɛ   Kofi   baae   (6)
(name) call-PAST (name) come-PAST
(a) 'Amma called Kofi towards her.'
(b) 'Amma called Kofi and came.'

In 6(a), *Kofi* (the second noun phrase, NP2) is interpreted
as the subject of *baae* (second verb, V2). In 6(b), NP1 is
interpreted as subject of V2. Sentences like (6) thus seem
to display ambiguity between an interpretation like that of
(2) and an interpretation like that of (4). This suggests that
at least two different structures may be involved; coordination of verb phrases in (1), (4), and (6) with interpretation
(b), and some kind of subordination or embedding in (2),
(3), (5), and 6(a).

Different constructions display different behavior
depending on whether the verbs involved are transitive or
intransitive. For example, in Sranan, a Creole of Surinam,
the verb *puru* 'remove' often follows a 'handling' verb, as
in (7):

A   hari a   ston   puru   na   ini a   olo   (7)
s/he pull the stone remove LOC   in   the hole
'He pulled the stone out of the hole.'

Puru on its own is always transitive; however, when used
as V2 in a series, it may not have a following object, but
must 'share' its object with V1. The verb *trowe* 'eject' in (8)
behaves like *puru*; however *naki* 'hit,' which is also transitive, is allowed to have its own object, and takes the object
of *fringi* and *trowe* as its subject.

A   fringi a   ston trowe naki a   bon   (8)
s/he throw the stone eject hit   the tree
'She threw the stone at the tree (and hit it).'

Ston in (8) thus plays the double role of object of *fringi* and *trowe*, and subject of *naki*. In this respect, a transitive verb + object like *naki a bon* behaves like an intransitive, taking the object of an earlier verb as its subject, cf. (9):

A   fringi a   ston fadon   (9)
s/he throw the stone fall
'She threw the stone down.'

What examples like (7), (8), and (9) have in common is that there is a strong lexical connection between the two or three verbs involved. In effect, each verb provides a complement to the preceding one, and there are restrictions on which may occur with which: *fringi fadon* is acceptable and normal, but **hari fadon* is not. This suggests that the syntactic structure of sentences of this type must: (a) allow for two or more verbs within the simple sentence; (b) permit lexical relations of subcategorization to hold between them; (c) allow the relation 'subject-of' to hold between, in principle, any NP in the sentence and a verb to its right; which NP is subject of which verb will depend on the transitivity of the verbs in the series.

Condition (b) requires that serial structures should be constrained in such a way as to allow verbs to select the class of other verbs in the series. In terms of most currently accepted theories of phrase structure, this would mean that they cannot occur on different branches of a coordinate structure.

One phrase structure schema which has been proposed for serial verbs by several authors is a right-branching one involving a phrase structure produced by a rule like (10):

VP → V XP VP where X is N or P.   (10)

The category here shown as VP cannot be what is traditionally meant by VP (i.e., the constituent containing the verb and all the phrases which it subcategorizes), since in a serial sequence like this each verb may have at most one object or prepositional phrase associated with it. Most serializing languages, however, seem to have verbs similar to English *put* and *give* which subcategorize a following NP and PP or two NPs. But in a series, these verbs may have only one NP or PP complement, as in the Akan example (11):

Ogyaw   ne   sika mãã   me   (11)
he-leave-PAST his money give-PAST me
'He left me his money.'

In (11), *mãã* 'gave' may have only one object NP, the 'indirect' object *me*, although *mãã* when not in a series may have both a direct and an indirect object: *ɔmãã me sika* 'he gave me money.'

A schema like (10) has the advantage that, within various widely accepted syntactic theories, it permits lexical relations and relations like 'subject-of' and 'object-of' to hold between verbs in the series. It also captures the intuition that verbs (or verb phrases) function as complements to verbs earlier in the sequence. However, there is no general agreement that (10) is a correct representation for any or all serial constructions. Other linguists have suggested structures involving multiple embedded sentences or verb phrases with relations of subject and object control holding

between NPs and verbs embedded below them, in a manner similar to the English *promise* and *persuade*. Yet other solutions have been proposed within the framework of government and binding (see, for example, Byrne 1987; see also *Government*; *Binding*). Which structure is seen as 'correct' must be held, at this stage, to be largely a consequence of the proponent's theoretical orientation. There is also no general agreement on whether serial constructions are a unitary phenomenon across languages, or whether there are several different kinds of structure involved. In the latter case different languages would be expected to display different ranges of construction types.

For some linguists working within the framework of generalized phrase structure grammar (see *Generalized Phrase Structure Grammar*), the schema (10) occurs even in nonserializing languages like English. On this view, auxiliaries are just a special subclass of verbs which subcategorize for a following verb; the schema (10) thus permits the production of a series of auxiliaries and main verbs like *must begin talking*, etc. If this is the correct analysis of auxiliaries, it must apply to serializing languages (which also have auxiliaries) as well. However, the type of serial verb structures just discussed do not seem in general to have anything in common with 'auxiliary–main verb' constructions. As will be clear from the discussion below, there is usually a lexical relationship between the verbs in a true series, with the choice of later verbs being restricted by the semantic properties of the earlier verbs. Auxiliaries, however, do not seem to be interdependent in this way with their main verbs: any main verb may follow any auxiliary verb. It seems necessary to make a clear distinction between 'auxiliary verbs' and 'serial verbs.'

2. Typology of Serial Constructions

Serial constructions can be classified into different types on the basis of the functions of the verbs in the series relative to one another. For example, in (2), (4), (5), and (6) above, V2 is 'come' or 'go' and serves as a directional complement to V1. What is remarkable is that these construction types occur with such regularity in languages which otherwise have little in common, cutting across language families, regional boundaries, and syntactic and morphological typologies. In this section some common serial construction types will be listed, with examples of each.

2.1 'Go' or 'Come' as a Directional Complement

This is so common that it seems to appear in every serializing language. Sentences (2), (4), (5), and (6) above are examples.

2.2 Other Complements to Motion Verbs

These vary from language to language; for example, Sranan has /puru/ 'remove,' usually translatable by 'out of,' and *naki* 'hit' for the goal of a verb denoting propulsion (examples (7) and (8)). Akan has *bɔ* 'strike' and *wɔ* 'pierce,' the choice of these being determined by the nature of the action (12–13):

Kofi tow   bo   no bɔɔ   Amma   (12)
      throw-PAST stone the hit-PAST
'Kofi threw the stone at Amma (and hit her).'

Kofi tow   agyan no wɔɔ   Amma   (13)
      throw-PAST arrow the pierce-PAST
'Kofi shot Amma with an arrow.'

2.3 Instrumental Constructions using 'Take'

How these should be analyzed is not clear, but similar constructions occur in many languages. 'Take' as V1 marks the instrument of the action denoted by V2. This Yoruba example is typical (14):

Mo fi   ada   ge   igi   (14)
I   take machete cut tree
'I cut the tree with a machete.'

2.4 Object Marking with 'Take'

This has the form 'take' NP V2 e ... where NP is the semantic object of V, and e is the empty 'object slot' of V2. 'Take' acts as a dummy verb to front the object of V2. Where V2 is ditransitive, its second object may appear after it in the normal position. The example is from Akan:

Wɔ de   no   too   Adow   (15)
they-take-PAST him name-PAST Adow
'They named him Adow.'

2.5 'Give' as a Dative and Benefactive Marker

The Akan sentence (11) above illustrates the verb 'give' used as a dative marker with a V1 denoting a transfer. Note that the transfer does not involve a literal 'giving.' Perhaps by extension of this use, 'give' may be used as a benefactive marker in some languages; cf. the Akan example (16):

ɔyɛɛ   adwuma mã   ne   nua   (16)
he-do work   give his brother
'He works for his brother.'

2.6 Comparative Constructions

A verb meaning 'pass' or 'surpass' may be used to form comparatives, for example, in Yoruba:

omo   náà gbon   jù   asarun   (17)
child the clever surpass tsetse-fly
'The child is cleverer than the tsetse fly.'

2.7 Lexical Idioms

These include a diverse collection of expressions, usually involving two verbs. Sentence (3) shows how the verbs function in series. Table 1 gives examples of lexical idioms from two West African languages and an Atlantic Creole.

Table 1.

Language	V1		V2		Combined meaning
Anyi-Baule	*kã*	'touch'	*klè*	'show'	'say, tell'
	bɔ	'hit'	*nĩã*	'look'	'taste' (liquid)
Yoruba	*là*	'cut open'	*yé*	'understand'	'explain'
	rí	'see'	*gbà*	'take'	'receive'
Sranan	*bro*	'breathe, blow'	*kiri*	'kill'	'blow out'
	anga	'hang'	*kiri*	'kill'	'crucify, hang'

3. Historical Perspective

There is good evidence to suggest that in some cases, particular verbs which participate in serial constructions have been 'reanalyzed' as members of another category, i.e., have changed their syntactic role into another one consistent with the sequences in which they typically occur. Instances of change from verb to preposition, verb to complementizer, verb to conjunction, and verb to tense marker appear to have taken place.

3.1. Reanalysis as a Gradual Process

In Sranan, it appears that while *gi* 'give' is a verb for all speakers, for some speakers it is a preposition as well. This is illustrated by (18), which is acceptable to all Sranan speakers, and (19), which shows clefting (a diagnostic for prepositional phrases) which is acceptable to some:

A   ben   tyari nyan gi   en   (18)
s/he PAST carry food give him/her
'S/he brought him/her food.'

Na gi   en   a   ben   tyari nyan   (19)
BE give him/her s/he PAST carry food
'It was to him/her that s/he brought food.'

(See Muysken 1978, and Sebba 1987 for discussion.)

In (18), the role of *gi* is ambiguous between that of (serial) verb and preposition, but in (19) it can only be a preposition. Thus there is a situation typical of cases where 'reanalysis' is claimed for serial verbs. The serial use of the verb is not lost, but it is reanalyzed *in some contexts* and may belong to more than one category in the grammars of some speakers.

Where verbs carry obligatory marking of tense, person, etc., a serial verb in the course of reanalysis will lose these, possibly by stages; and further loss of phonetic material may follow as well. Several such cases of reanalysis of verbs as prepositions, comitative markers, and (in one case) a subordinating conjunction are described by Lord (1973) as having occurred in the Kwa languages Yoruba, Gã, Ewe, and Fon. By a similar process the verb 'say' appears to have become a complementizer in many Kwa languages, and is also used as such in some Atlantic Creoles, although evidence for historical development is lacking in the latter. The situation is complicated by the existence of complementizers homophonous with 'to say' in many Bantu languages, which (though distantly related to Kwa) do not have serial verbs.

There are reports from a number of languages of past tense or perfective markers homophonous with a verb meaning 'finish.' This phenomenon does not appear to be confined to languages otherwise regarded as verb serializing, but where the language has serial constructions the position of the 'finish' tense marker is usually consistent with it having once been a verb in series.

3.2 Chinese 'coverbs'

Chinese has a large class of preposition-like words which are homophonous with verbs with related meanings—for example, *yòng* 'use' (verb), 'with' (preposition); *dào* 'arrive, to'; *zài* 'be-at, at.' These verbs are traditionally termed 'coverbs' because, while functioning as prepositions in one context, they are clearly verbs in another. Chinese grammar provides few criteria for distinguishing between verbs and other categories, particularly if one allows for the possibility of verb serialization. One possibility is that a general reanalysis has taken place at an earlier stage of Chinese, whereby certain [V NP] sequences were reinterpreted as [P NP] sequences, with a corresponding reinterpretation of VP to PP.

In what may be a similar type of reanalysis, the word *bǎ*, originally a verb meaning 'take, hold, use' has become an untranslatable 'object marker,' as in (20)—compare the object-marking 'take' of sentence (15):

Tā   bǎ   chìchē   màile
s/he BA   car   sell-PAST
'S/he sold the car.'

4. Serial Verbs: Function and Purpose

In languages where they do occur, serial constructions may carry a heavy functional load, doing, for example, the work of prepositions and syntactic markers, as well as participating in productive lexical processes and allowing for the expansion of the lexicon through idiomatic collocations. While historically, reanalysis of individual verbs which participate in serial constructions seems to be common, the loss of serial structures altogether is so far undocumented. Rather, certain verbs undergo reanalysis and may have multiple category membership, while the serializing capacity of the language remains otherwise unchanged.

One aspect of serial constructions which has attracted attention recently is their prevalence in creole languages (both of the Atlantic zone and the Pacific, although these are historically unlikely to be connected). Bickerton 1981 regards serial verbs as a *necessary* component of creole grammars, since 'verb serialization is the only solution to the problem of marking cases in languages which have only N and V as major categories.' In other words, serial verbs are a consequence of a language lacking, inter alia, the category 'preposition,' this lack being characteristic, in Bickerton's hypothesis, of the earliest stage of creoles (see *Prepositions and Prepositional Phrases*).

While there are no clear cases of existing languages which use serial constructions but lack prepositions, there is at least one clear case of a verb-serializing language where the number of arguments per verb is strictly limited to two (the subject and one other). In this language, Ijọ (of Nigeria), verbs may not subcategorize both a direct and an indirect object. Instead, two verbs are required in series, each with its own object. Here serialization may be seen as compensating for a restriction on phrase structure which would otherwise prevent the expression of certain actions requiring three or more participants.

Thus it seems that some languages, such as English, permit just one main (i.e., nonauxiliary) verb per simple sentence, but allow verbs to have several arguments. Other languages permit more than one main verb per simple sentence, but have tighter restrictions on the number of arguments per verb. Thus different languages map meanings on to syntactic structure in different ways. Serial verbs are one aspect of this.

See also: Pidgins and Creoles; Pidgins, Creoles and Change.

Bibliography

Bickerton D 1981 *Roots of Language*. Karoma Press, Ann Arbor, MI
Byrne F 1987 *Grammatical Relations in a Radical Creole: Verb Complementation in Saramaccan*. Benjamins, Amsterdam
Lefebvre C (ed.) 1991 *Serial Verbs: Grammatical, Comparative and Cognitive Approaches*. Benjamins, Amsterdam
Lord C 1973 Serial verbs in transition. *Studies in African Linguistics* **4**(3): 269–96
Muysken P 1978 *Serial Verbs in the Creole Languages*. University of Amsterdam, Amsterdam
Sebba M 1987 *The Syntax of Serial Verbs*. Benjamins, Amsterdam

M. Sebba

Set Theory

A set is an abstract object formed entirely and exclusively from other objects. These other objects are called its members or elements, and may themselves be sets. When an object *d* is an element of a set *s*, this is written as: $d \in s$. Normally it is assumed that there are no infinite chains of members of sets. The process of going from a set to one of its elements can only be repeated a finite number of times, after which one is left with the set that has no members, the empty set, or with an object which is not itself a set. Although sets have finite depth, they may be infinitely wide; they may contain infinitely many members.

Set theory was invented by the German mathematician Georg Cantor (1845–1918) in order to get a firmer grasp on the concept of infinity. By use of sets and their sizes, Cantor transcended the realm of finite mathematical objects to discern an endless array of infinities with quite peculiar properties. For example, adding two sets *A* and *B* of the same infinite size, a set *C* is obtained that contains precisely the members of *A* and *B* and which is still of the same size. At the time Cantor first published his ideas they were not uncontroversial, but nowadays one often quotes Hilbert: 'Nobody can expel us from the paradise created by Cantor.'

1. Comprehension and Separation

The reason why sets are of interest to linguists is that they provide formal structures which can be used, for example, in the formal study of grammars, or to model the meanings of expressions. To do so, one has to have the means to specify which set is intended. In the case of finite sets this can be done by enumeration of their elements, for example:

$$A = \{3, 8, 11\}$$

Infinite sets can only be determined by enumeration if dots are used as shorthand:

$$B = \{2, 3, 5, 7, 11, \ldots\}$$

This notation is rather informal, in that it suggests rather than specifies the property an object has to have in order to be counted as an element of the set. In defining sets by abstraction, which works both for finite and infinite sets, explicit use is made of this property:

$$B = \{x \mid x \text{ is a prime number}\}$$

The intimate connection between properties and sets can be stated in the form of an axiom:

Axiom 1.1 (comprehension) *For each property $\mathcal{P}$, the collection of objects that have $\mathcal{P}$ is a set; notation: $\{x \mid \mathcal{P}(x)\}$.*

For example, the property *to be different from itself* does not hold of any object and gives the empty set $\emptyset$.

In 1901 Russell noted that the axiom of comprehension is too strong; it yields set theory inconsistent. The reasoning that shows this, uses the property *not to be a member of itself*. On the basis of the axiom of comprehension $R =$

$\{x \mid x \notin x\}$ would be a set. There are two possibilities: R is or is not a member of itself. In case it is, R has the property that delineates R, so that R is not a member of itself. But no object can both have and lack a property. The other possibility has to obtain: R is not a member of itself. This, however, makes R satisfy its defining property, so that it is a member of itself after all. Since both possibilities lead to contradiction, R cannot exist.

There are several ways to bypass this dilemma, but most often Zermelo's solution is opted for. He suggests the axiom of comprehension be replaced by the axiom of separation:

Axiom 1.2 (separation) *For each property $\mathscr{P}$ and set S, the elements of S that have $\mathscr{P}$ form a set; notation: $\{x \in S \mid \mathscr{P}(x)\}$.*

The important difference between the axiom of comprehension and of separation is of course that the latter is restricted to another set. It can only be used to form sets if a set is already given. For example, from the set of natural numbers—the set $\{0, 1, 2, 3, \ldots\}$, commonly denoted by $\mathscr{N}$—one may separate the set of odd numbers: $\{x \in \mathscr{N} \mid x$ is odd$\}$. The properties mentioned in the axiom of separation are normally restricted to those specifiable by means of a first-order formula $\phi(x)$ (see *First Order Logic*). In this manner an axiom-scheme results, which gives an axiom for each such formula. But realists concerning mathematical objects would in principle allow properties which do not correspond to linguistic items (see *Realism*).

2. Extensionality

A familiar philosophical dictum runs: no entity without identity. In particular, when do two properties specify the same set? The answer is given as the axiom of extensionality, which states that a set is fully determined by its elements:

Axiom 2.1 (extensionality) *For each set A and B, A is identical to B if A and B have the same members.*

Since identical objects share all their properties, the converse holds as well: A and B have the same members if they are identical. Due to the axiom of extensionality, it does not make a difference in what order the elements are specified, or if elements are named more than once: $\{1, 2, 3\} = \{3, 1, 2\}$ and $\{1, 2\} = \{1, 2, 1\}$. Indeed, the manner in which the elements of a set are determined is immaterial to the set itself: sets are extensional objects (see *Intension; Intensionality*).

3. Power Sets and Boolean Operations

A more formal way to state that A is identical to B is: if for each element x, $x \in A$ if and only if $x \in B$, then $A = B$. This points to another important relation that may obtain between two sets, namely *to be a subset of*. The set A is a subset of B—notation: $A \subseteq B$—if and only if all members of A are also members of B. The set of all subsets of a set A is the power set $\wp(A)$:

$$\wp(A) = \{B \mid B \subseteq A\}$$

In case $A \subseteq B$ while there is an element of B not in A, A is called a proper subset of B; notation: $A \subset B$.

Separation and forming power sets are means to obtain new sets from given ones. Such means are also provided by the Boolean operations: difference, intersection, and union:

Difference	$A \setminus B = \{x \mid x \in A \text{ and } x \notin B\}$
Intersection	$A \cap B = \{x \mid x \in A \text{ and } x \in B\}$
Union	$A \cup B = \{x \mid x \in A \text{ or } x \in B\}$

Sometimes these operations are defined relative to a set E. In that case the difference $A \setminus E$ is also written as $\bar{A}$, A^c, or as A', and is called the complement of A (relative to E).

Intersection, union, and complementation have some noteworthy properties and interactions, which are intimately connected to the logic of the constants *and*, *or*, and *not* (see *Propositional Calculus*):

Idempotentcy	$A \cap A = A$
	$A \cup A = A$
Commutativity	$A \cap B = B \cap A$
	$A \cup B = B \cup A$
Associativity	$(A \cap B) \cap C = A \cap (B \cap C)$
	$(A \cup B) \cup C = A \cup (B \cup C)$
Distributivity	$A \cap (B \cup C) = (A \cap B) \cup (A \cap C)$
	$A \cup (B \cap C) = (A \cup B) \cap (A \cup C)$
Absorption	$A \cap (A \cup B) = A$
	$A \cup (A \cap B) = A$
De Morgan laws	$\overline{A \cap B} = \bar{A} \cup \bar{B}$
	$\overline{A \cup B} = \bar{A} \cap \bar{B}$
Law of double negation	$\bar{\bar{A}} = A$
Laws of $\varnothing$	$A \cup \varnothing = A$
	$A \cap \varnothing = \varnothing$
	$A \cap \bar{A} = \varnothing$

Where the sets A, B, and C are taken from the power set $\wp(E)$, the set E functions as a so-called 'unit element' which satisfies the additional three laws:

$$A \cup E = E; A \cap E = A; A \cup \bar{A} = E$$

When taken together, these laws are the axioms of Boolean Algebra. In particular, $\langle \wp(E), \cup, \cap, {}^-, \varnothing, E \rangle$ is a Boolean Algebra for each set E.

The above notions of intersection and union are finitary; they enable one to compute the intersection or union of, at most, finitely many sets. The intersection $A_1 \cap \ldots \cap A_n$, for instance, can be determined by handling two sets at a time (due to associativity and commutativity, the order in which this is done does not matter, it need not be indicated by parenthesis). However, there are also infinitary versions of these operations:

Definition 3.1 (infinitary intersection and union) *Let A_i be a set, where $i \in I$ and I is a nonempty indexset. The intersection of the A_i—notation: $\bigcap \{A_i \mid i \in I\}$ or $\bigcap_{i \in I} A_i$—contains all elements which the A_i have in common, and is defined by:*

$$\bigcap_{i \in I} A_i = \{x \mid \text{For all } i \in I: x \in A_i\}$$

The union of the A_i—notation: $\bigcup \{A_i \mid i \in I\}$ or $\bigcup_{i \in I} A_i$—contains all elements which occur in at least one A_i, and is defined by:

$$\bigcup_{i \in I} A_i = \{x \mid \text{There is an } i \in I: x \in A_i\}$$

The infinitary Boolean operations satisfy laws analogous to the ones already given (see Suppes 1972). Note that the indexset I is required to be nonempty. The reason is that the property 'For all $i \in I: x \in A_i$' could otherwise be vacuously true (see *First Order Logic*) and hence $\bigcap_{i \in I} A_i$ would be the universal class:

$$\{x \mid x \text{ is an object}\}$$

However, the universal class cannot be a set, for the axiom of separation relativized to this set would be equivalent to the axiom of comprehension and give rise to the Russell paradox as before.

4. Relations

One of the reasons why set theory received much attention at the turn of the century is that it seemed possible to reduce all mathematical concepts and reasoning to it. Mathematicians such as Dedekind, Frege, and Peano showed that this is indeed true for so-called classical mathematics. This logicist program—where principles were called logical which later were called set theoretical, the border is indeed a bit vague—was carried out in detail in Russell and Whitehead's monumental *Principia Mathematica* (1913), except for one step. The reduction was to the theory of sets and of relations, but it took an ingenious 'trick' of Wiener, devised in 1914, to show that relations can be seen as a special kind of sets.

A relation is a set of ordered 'tuples,' where an ordered tuple is a sequence of objects $\langle a_1, \ldots, a_n \rangle$ so that:

$$\langle a_1, \ldots, a_n \rangle = \langle b_1, \ldots, b_n \rangle \text{ if and only if } a_1 = b_1 \text{ and } a_n = b_n$$

In contrast with sets, the repetition and order of objects in a tuple do matter. In particular, $\langle a, a \rangle \neq \langle a \rangle$ and $\langle a, b \rangle \neq \langle b, a \rangle$. In the case of ordered pairs, where $n = 2$ in the above scheme, it can be shown that the next set has the property required of such pairs:

$$\langle a, b \rangle = \{\{a\}, \{a, b\}\}$$

(The definition comes from Kuratowski, not from Wiener.) By use of this definition, n-tuples can be obtained in a systematic way as follows:

$$\langle a_1, \ldots, a_n \rangle = \langle a_1, \langle \ldots, \langle a_{n-1}, a_n \rangle \rangle \rangle$$

If $n = 0$, this is the empty sequence $\langle \rangle$, which is identified with the empty set. Also, $\langle a \rangle$ is identified with a. One-membered tuples are thus different from one-membered sets, the so-called 'singletons,' for $\{a\}$ is different from a.

Now that ordered tuples are available, the notion of a Cartesian product can be defined:

Definition 4.1 (Cartesian products) *The Cartesian product of the sets A_1 and . . . and A_n is the set:*

$$A_1 \times \cdots \times A_n = \{\langle a_1, \ldots, a_n \rangle \mid a_1 \in A_1 \text{ and} \ldots \text{ and } a_n \in A_n\}$$

For every set A and every $n \in \mathcal{N}$, A^n is the set of all n-tuples over A:

$$\underbrace{A \times \cdots \times A}_{n \text{ times}}$$

Relations are subsets of such sets:

Definitions 4.2 (relations) *R is an n-place relation on A if and only if $R \subseteq A^n$. R is said to have arity n.*

In case of a two-place relation R, one often writes aRb for $\langle a, b \rangle \in R$. A two-place relation R can have several properties, e.g.:

Reflexive	For all x: xRx
Irreflexive	For all x: not xRx
Transitive	For all x, y, z: if xRy and yRz, then xRz
Antisymmetric	For all x, y: if xRy and yRx, then $x = y$
Symmetric	For all x, y: if xRy, then yRx

A relation which is reflexive, transitive, and antisymmetric is called a partial order. The relation $\subseteq$ on the set $\wp(E)$ is an instance of a partial order, and so is the relation *to be smaller than or equal to* on the set of natural numbers. A strict partial order is a relation which is irreflexive and transitive. An example is $\subset$ on $\wp(E)$, or *to be smarter than*

on the set of human beings. An equivalence relation is reflexive, transitive, and symmetric. *To be as intelligent as* is an equivalence relation on the set of postdocs. If R is an equivalence relation on a set A and $a \in A$, then $[a]_R = \{b \in A \mid aRb\}$ is called the equivalence class of a. The set $[a]_R$ contains the elements which are the same as far as R is concerned, and A is said to be partitioned by R:

Definition 4.3 (partitions) *A set $\mathcal{P} \subseteq \wp(E)$ is a partition of A if and only if:*

- $\varnothing \notin E$;
- $\bigcup \mathcal{P} = E$;
- *For all x, $y \in \mathcal{P}$: $x \cap y = \varnothing$*

To continue the example, postdocs can be divided in non-overlapping groups according to their IQ. More formally, the partition induced by an equivalence relation R on A is: $\{[a]_R \mid a \in A\}$. Conversely, each partition $\mathcal{P}$ of A induces the equivalence relation $R_{\mathcal{P}}$ defined by:

$$xR_{\mathcal{P}}y \text{ if and only if } \textit{there is an } A \in \mathcal{P} \text{ such that } x \in A \text{ and } y \in A$$

5. Functions

As it turns out, a function can be seen as a special kind of relation:

Definition 5.1 (functions) *f is a function from A to B if and only if:*
- *$f \subseteq A \times B$;*
- *for every $a \in A$ there is exactly one $b \in B$ with $\langle a, b \rangle \in f$.*

The relation 'tail of' between dogs and tails is a function, for every dog has exactly one tail (possibly the empty one), but the relation 'ears of' between dogs and ears is no function.

The notation for 'f is a function from A to B' is $f: A \to B$. The set A is the domain of f, dom(f), and B its codomain, codom(f). The domain of a function f may be a Cartesian product. If so, one usually writes $f(x_1, \ldots, x_n)$ instead of $f(\langle x_1, \ldots, x_n \rangle)$. Addition, for example, is a function from ordered pairs of natural numbers to natural numbers.

For each $a \in A$, $f(a)$ is the unique b in B such that $\langle a, b \rangle \in f$. The function f is said to map the argument a onto the value b. The range of f is the subset of its codomain B defined by:

$$\mathrm{ran}(f) = \{b \in B \mid \text{There is an } a \in A \text{ with } f(a) = b\}$$

In case $f: A \to B$ and $g: B \to C$, one defines the composition $f \circ g: A \to C$ of f and g by: $f \circ g(a) = g(f(a))$. Note that composing functions is associative. On the set of human beings, the function 'maternal grandfather of' is the composition of the function 'father of' and 'mother of,' since 'maternal grandfather' means 'the father of the mother of.'

The set $\{f \mid f: A \to B\}$ of all functions from A to B is denoted by B^A. Characteristic functions are functions which have the set $\{0, 1\}$ as their codomain; they are used often in logical semantics (see *Formal Semantics*; *Characteristic Function*). The set $\{0, 1\}$ is sometimes written as 2. Thus, $f: A \to 2$ is a characteristic function, and 2^A denotes the set:

$$\{f \mid f: A \to \{0, 1\}\}$$

of all characteristic functions with domain A. Each $f \in 2^A$ characterizes the set $B_f = \{a \in A \mid f(a) = 1\}$. Conversely, each set $B \subseteq A$ determines the characteristic function $\chi_B: A \to 2$ with for all $d \in A$:

$$\chi_B(d) = \begin{cases} 1 & \text{if } d \in B \\ 0 & \text{if } d \notin B \end{cases}$$

The next definition isolates some important kinds of function:

Definition 5.2 (surjections, injections, bijections) *A function* $f: A \to B$ *such that* $\text{rng}(f) = B$ *is called a surjection of A onto B. In other words,* $f: A \to B$ *is a surjection if for every* $b \in B$ *there is an* $a \in A$ *with* $f(a) = b$.

A function $f: A \to B$ *such that for every* $a, b \in A$, *if* $f(a) = f(b)$ *then* $a = b$, *is called an injection or a one-one mapping of A into B. So,* $f: A \to B$ *is an injection if for every* $b \in \text{rng}(f)$ *there is exactly one* $a \in A$ *with* $f(a) = b$.

A function $f: A \to B$ *which is both an injection and a surjection, is called a bijection. That is,* $f: A \to B$ *is a bijection if for every* $b \in B$ *there is exactly one* $a \in A$ *such that* $f(a) = b$ *(see Bijection).*

For instance, the relation *to begin with* between British words and letters is a surjection; the relation *to be the negation of* on the set of predicate logical formulas is an injection; and the relation *to be identical to* on the human beings is a bijection.

6. The Size of Sets

Cantor used bijections to give formal content to saying that two sets have the same size: a set A is equinumerous with B if and only if there is a bijection $f: A \to B$. For example, $\{1, 2, 3\}$ is as large as $\{a, b, c\}$, since $f(1) = c, f(2) = a, f(3) = b$ defines a bijection.

A set A is finite if there is an $n \in \mathcal{N}$ so that A is equinumerous with $\{m \in \mathcal{N} \mid m < n\}$; otherwise A is infinite. The alphabet is finite but the set of all possible words, i.e., all finite strings of letters, is not. The set $\mathcal{N}$ of natural numbers is of course also infinite. The size of $\mathcal{N}$ is in fact the smallest form of infinity, and the sets that are equinumerous with $\mathcal{N}$ are called countably infinite. The sets O and E of the odd and the even numbers are countably infinite; via $f(n) = 2n + 1$ and $g(n) = 2n$, respectively. Note that O and E can be used to show the peculiarities of infinities named in the introduction of this article. For 'adding' these sets, that is: taking $O \cup E$, gives $\mathcal{N}$ which is as large as either O or E.

The size of a set A is also called its 'cardinality,' denoted by $|A|$. Cantor's theorem implies that there are other cardinalities than the finite and the countably finite. In fact, the sizes of sets are unlimited. The proof of this theorem is as important as the theorem itself, since it makes use of a so-called diagonalization argument:

Theorem 6.1 (Cantor) *For each set A, there is no bijection from A to* $\wp(A): |\wp(A)|$ *is always larger than* $|A|$.

PROOF. The theorem holds in case $A = \varnothing$, for then $\wp(A) = \{\varnothing\}$. In case $A \neq \varnothing$, $q: A \to \wp(A)$ defined by $q(a) = \{a\}$ is an injection, which shows that $|\wp(A)|$ is at least as large as $|A|$. However, these cardinalities cannot be equal, for the assumption that there is a bijection $f: A \to \wp(A)$ leads to a contradiction. In terms of such an f one defines:

$$C = \{b \in A \mid b \notin f(b)\}$$

(Note that C is similar to Russell's class R, which is obtained by taking A to be the universal class and f the identity function: $f(d) = d$.) For all elements a in A, one has:

$$a \in C \text{ if and only if } a \notin f(a)$$

Since f is a bijection, it is also a surjection; hence, there should be a member a of A such that $f(a) = C$. Is $a \in C$? If

so, $a \notin f(a)$. But $f(a) = C$, which contradicts $a \in C$. So $a \notin C$ has to be the case. But from this and $C = f(a)$, it follows that $a \in C$, which is impossible. Both options lead to contradiction, and therefore no such bijection can exist. QED

A consequence of this theorem is that there are uncountable infinite sets; $\wp(\mathcal{N})$ is an example, and $\wp(\wp(\mathcal{N}))$, and so forth. For those who accept its proof, the theorem discloses Cantor's paradise with its endless array of ever larger kinds of infinity (see *Intuitionism*; *Deviant Logics*).

Bibliography

Potter M D 1991 *Sets: An Introduction.* Clarendon, Oxford
Shoenfield J R 1977 Axioms of set theory. In: Barwise J (ed.) *Handbook of Mathematical Logic.* North-Holland, Amsterdam
Suppes P 1972 *Axiomatic Set Theory.* Dover, New York

J. van der Does

Sex Differences

In practically every society, women and men tend to use language in slightly different ways, and some societies have been reported to have distinct women's and men's speech. However, the two sexes can communicate freely with each other in all societies, and both the magnitude and significance of sex differences in language have been debated by scholars.

1. Evidence of Sex Differences in Language

Ann Bodine (Thorne and Henley 1975) distinguishes two kinds of sex differences in language: sex-exclusive and sex-preferential. 'Sex-exclusivity' means that certain linguistic forms are reserved for the use of one sex or the other, while 'sex-preferential' means that one sex tends to use them more often than the other. Sex-exclusivity is rarely found in European languages, but anthropological research early in the twentieth century seemed to indicate that several non-European languages exhibited it to a marked degree. However, classic anthropology assumed that cultures were highly regular and could be studied through limited observation and a few key native informants. Thus, many features of non-European cultures may have been reported as more absolute than they really were, sex differences in language among them. Modern anthropologists employ more systematic methods for examining cultural patterns, including techniques comparable to random survey sampling, and they find sex-preferential differences far more commonly than sex-exclusive.

1.1 Non-European Languages

Cameron has reviewed the well-known example of the Caribs, after whom the Caribbean Sea was named. In 1665, women and men of this society were said to use different phonologies and lexicons, and the missionaries who noticed this believed it was explained by historical events. Supposedly, men from the Arawak tribe had invaded, exterminating the male Caribs and seizing the women. Each sex kept its own language. Mothers taught Carib to their daughters, and fathers taught Arawak to their sons. Subsequently, scholars proposed the alternative theory that distinctly different gender roles had produced different lexicons: because men and women did very different things, they used different words. In the 1920s, Otto Jespersen (see *Jespersen, Otto*) suggested that because women stayed at home while the men went hunting, women indulged in idle chatter and men learned to communicate efficiently to coordinate their actions. Cameron finds the specifics of this theory sexist, but praises the emphasis upon social role rather than historical accident as the source of sex differences in language.

It is difficult to evaluate linguistic data collected so long ago, but Mary R. Haas has studied similar phenomena in several living languages, including Koasati, a Muskogean language that persists in southwestern Lousiana. The most obvious sex difference is the fact that men often add or substitute *s* at the ends of words, under certain rule-guided situations. For example, 'If the women's form has the falling pitch-stress on its final syllable and ends in a short vowel followed by *l*, the men's form substitutes the high pitch-stress for the falling pitch-stress and an *s* for the *l*.' That is, the women say *lakawwil* 'I am lifting it,' while the men say *lakawwis*. One of Haas's male informants even commented that he did not like men's speech, because it 'has too much *sss*.' Interestingly, these differences were most noticeable among older informants, and younger women spoke almost identically with the men, suggesting that the marked sex differences were in the process of disappearing.

Among major modern languages said to have sex-exclusive as well as sex-preferential norms is Japanese. Although Japanese prefer to avoid direct pronomial reference, many pronomial forms are available to them. Both sexes may use the first-person pronoun *watakushi*. But *atashi* is a first-person pronoun primarily used by females, except sometimes employed by males such as traditional merchants and entertainers, while *boku* and *ore* are used exclusively by males. Second person pronouns are seldom used except when it is necessary to indicate a particular individual or in formal or honorific speech (see *Honorifics*). But at those times, *anata* can be used by a speaker of either sex. When speaking to social equals or inferiors of either sex, however, a man can employ *kimi* as the second person pronoun. For example, a husband may call his wife *kimi*, while she calls him *anata*.

Many Japanese nouns are rendered more polite by prefixing *o*, and women apparently do this more frequently: *kashi* versus *okashi* 'sweets.' In colloquial settings, men often end sentences with *da*, a contraction of *desu*, while women seldom do this. Women more often end sentences with the particles *ne* and *nano*. But these often-cited differences are sex-preferential rather than sex-exclusive. Indeed, the closer one looks at non-Western languages, the less one is convinced that they possess significant sex-exclusivity.

In studying speech in Western Samoa, Ochs found it difficult to disentangle sex differences from differences of social context and rank. This highly stratified society distinguishes *matai* 'titled persons' from those of lower rank, and the overwhelming majority of *matai* are men. In one analysis of 135 clauses of speech of listeners to personal narratives, 63 percent of male listeners expressed sympathy, compared with 83 percent of female listeners. But the men could be divided into titled and untitled groups, while the women research subjects were all wives of matai, and these titled men expressed sympathy with the narrator only 42 percent of the time. Samoan is an ergative language, treating subjects of intransitive sentences differently from subjects of transitive sentences and often placing them in the same category as direct objects. In family interactions, men use ergative case marking about as often as do women, but in nonfamily settings the men are far more likely to do this. Word order also differed, the men being more likely to employ Verb–Subject–Object than women, and less likely to employ Subject–Verb–Object, but sex differences are confounded by the fact that more of the men's speech was made in formal settings. Ochs concludes that Samoan men and women may indeed have been socialized to speak differently, but that other social parameters, including some like situational role that interact in complex ways with sex, are also important determinants of language.

1.2 European Languages

It is widely believed that European languages lack sex differences, at least in comparison to the languages of exotic cultures. However, variations in female/male speech found in European languages involve sex-preferential differences, arguably of substantial magnitude. There are no forms associated exclusively with one sex or the other, but there are tendencies for women or men to prefer certain forms. Following are examples of sex-preferential differences in English language that have been cited by various authors.

Several studies indicate that women in the USA use more hyperbolical expressions than do men, while men swear and curse more often. Women are more likely to adhere to standard speech, both in vocabulary and pronunciation, while men more often employ slang words and variant pronunciations. For example, women are more likely to pronounce the *g* in the present participle ending-*ing*. Thus, the speech of women is more correct in being traditionally associated with grammar books and middle-class upward mobility. A parallel can be drawn to the fact that men are more likely to violate criminal laws of the society, just as they are more apt to violate language customs.

The fact that a difference is sex-preferential rather than sex-exclusive does not render it trivial. Robin Lakoff is among the authors who argued most strenuously that sex-preferential differences are important in English, rendering the female register less assertive and direct than the male register. Women, she believes, frequently use empty words or imprecise intensifiers like 'adorable,' 'lovely,' and 'divine.' Women more commonly employ tag-questions, sentences half way between statements and questions, formed either by speaking a statement with the rising inflection typical of a question at the end, or by tagging a short question such as 'isn't it?' on the end of a statement. In many ways, Lakoff said, women hedge their statements.

Sally McConnell-Ginet (Thorne, et al. 1983) argues that much of the sex difference would not be revealed in ordinary written transcripts of speech, because it is intonational. She notes that women tend to use more changes of pitch and loudness; compared to men they employ more and different 'tunes' or 'speech melodies.' Perhaps falsely, the male monotone is perceived to be evidence of self control, while the female volatility in intonation is perceived as emotionality.

Authors who have attempted to summarize research on these points often comment that the research to date has been insufficient for definite conclusions on sex differences in the English language. Some of the most influential publications have been based on little more than the author's personal impressions; Lakoff says that her primary research method is introspection. A number of studies have failed to sustain her claim that women more frequently use tag-questions, for example, some finding the exact opposite. When systematic methods of research are used, substantial sex differences are often not found (Brouwer, et al. 1979).

One difficulty with much of the research is that scholars trained in one kind of methodology, for example, literary criticism or traditional linguistics, may fail to realize that their research topic requires other methods, such as random sampling of the population. Often the research fails to control for other factors that produce speech differences, such as social context (formal, conversational, or slang), characteristics of the speaker other than sex (age, occupation, social class), or the sex of the person spoken to. Even when proper precautions are taken, research studies done with different subjects under different conditions may disagree, suggesting that the phenomena are rather more complicated than some authors believed. Popular stereotypes have also been put into question by the body of research, such as the notion that women are more talkative than men. Summarizing a great quantity of literature, Thorne, et al. (1983) note that few expected sex differences have been firmly established by empirical studies of isolated variables.

2. Explanations of Sex Differences

Many theories have been proposed to explain why women and men may differ in the language they use. Barbara and Gene Eakins (1978) have categorized the causes of sex differences postulated by these theories into six overlapping groups: innate differences, personality, cultural elaboration, division of labor by sex, male dominance, and differing value systems.

Innate differences are biological in nature, represented by different reproductive systems, physiques, hormonal balances, and possibly different structures in the brain. While some minor differences in communicative style might be influenced by such factors, social scientists examining sex differences in language have largely discounted biological causes of vocabulary and other significant verbal phenomena.

Many different theories of personality have been proposed, but Eakins and Eakins focus on biologically based perspectives that view an adult's habitual patterns of thought and behavior as rooted in but not identical to his or her genetic inheritance. They note that it is very difficult to distinguish innate from learned patterns, and they argue that cultural stereotypes and social pressures have the power to override genetic differences.

Ray Birdwhistell (1970) suggests that kinesic sex variations are cultural elaborations of biological differences, displays that announce a person's gender to his or her audience. Humans, Birdwhistell notes, are only moderate in sexual dimorphism, males and females having very much the same physical form. Lacking gaudy plumage to distinguish females from males, humans are forced to employ body position, movement, and expression for gender display. Similarly, differences in voice tone or any other verbal characteristics could serve as distinct markers of the speaker's sex. Even the subtle variations called 'personality,'

shaped by female and male socialization to alternate stereotypes, can serve this function. The fact that cultures may vary with respect to which linguistic features distinguish the sexes does not invalidate this theory, because a variety of differences in language may be functionally equivalent, achieving the same goal of sex display.

All societies practice division of labor by sex and age (van den Berghe 1973), assigning very different social roles to persons in different age and sex categories. Since the second half of the nineteenth century, sociologists have argued that the growth of populations, trade routes, and technical capabilities have greatly expanded other divisions of labor. From this they have deduced that the sex-based division of labor should be much less pronounced in modern than in preindustrial societies. However, the sexes remain unequally represented in most occupations, and significant division of labor within the household persists. This means that, on average, women and men continue to play significantly different roles in society. Each role will be associated with topics of discussion, a style of speech, a distinctive vocabulary, and even a different repertoire of nonverbal communication.

Feminist writers have indicted male dominance as the chief cause of language differences between the sexes. To the extent that language reflects the structure of society, an unequal society will have an unequal language. Thorne and Henley (1975: 15) argue that male dominance has powerfully shaped the meaning of words referring to both sexes:

> Words associated with males more often have positive connotations: they convey notions of power, prestige, and leadership. In contrast, female words are more often negative, conveying weakness, inferiority, immaturity, a sense of the trivial.

On the basis of research that documented substantial linguistic sex differences in Norwich, UK, Peter Trudgill (1972) argued that women find it necessary to secure their social status through language, because their subordinate position in society closes off other options. Therefore, women use forms associated with the prestige standard more frequently than do men.

If the style and form of language are greatly determined by the values of the speaker, then different value systems possessed by the two sexes will produce linguistic differences (see *Values*). Florence Kluckhohn (1953) has argued that a culture may possess two quite different value systems, a dominant orientation and a variant orientation. The former is reserved for people of higher rank, primarily males, while the latter is assigned to people of lower rank, including most females. The dominant value orientation stresses individual achievement and emphasizes the future, while the latter stresses group identity and the present. In effect, a person following the dominant value orientation says 'I will,' while a person following the variant value orientation says 'we are.' The dominant value orientation is active and assertive, while the variant value orientation is subservient and responsive.

A seventh theory, not mentioned by Eakins and Eakins, holds that sex differences in language are caused by more rapid change in the language of one sex than another. Haas (1964), for example, argues that women speakers of Koasati use forms that are more archaic than those employed by men, or, conversely, that the speech of men changed more rapidly than that of women. Among speakers of Yana (a

California language), she reports, the situation appears to be reversed, with men speaking in more archaic forms and women leading the pace of linguistic change.

An eighth theory notes that people will come to be more different in speech the greater the social distance between them (see *Sociometry*). If women primarily speak with other women, and men with other men, then the social gap between the two sexes may become linguistic as well. Changes in vocabulary or any other aspect of language that start among members of one sex will have difficulty jumping over to the other sex, especially if they arise from random linguistic drift and have no functional significance for communication. This theory can usefully be combined with several of the others, providing a mechanism unrelated to social role or power that can magnify differences between the sexes that might originate in their roles or power positions.

Finally, social groups may use distinctive language to assert their solidarity, and either sex may thus develop unique ways of communicating among itself (Cameron and Coates 1989). Centuries ago, Japanese court ladies developed a special vocabulary that was imitated by other classes of women for whom the elite ladies were a reference group (Shibamoto 1985). By using this elegant, refined vocabulary, women could assert solidarity both with other women and with the elite.

3. Language Competence

One of the most heavily researched yet undecided questions is whether the sexes differ in their linguistic competence. Educators commonly believe that girls develop verbal skills more rapidly than boys, with the latter catching up partly or completely some time in adolescence. Girls are said to learn to talk at an earlier age, to produce longer utterances, and to be more proficient in language skills throughout childhood. If true, this could explain why the speech of adult women is closer to the official standard; they learned it better and earlier because they were more adept at verbal learning.

However, many critics have found fault with the research studies on which these impressions were based. Ronald Macaulay (1977) complained that reported differences often failed to meet elementary tests of statistical significance and that different tests of language ability give different results. Furthermore, one does not know whether to remove from the comparisons the somewhat greater percentage of boys who display definite speech disorders or behavior problems; perhaps 'normal' girls should be compared with 'normal' boys, and the apparent fact that a greater percentage of males are identifiably 'abnormal' should not be allowed to make it seem that the sexes in general differ in linguistic ability. In their influential survey of psychological differences between the sexes, Eleanor Maccoby and Carol Jacklin (1974) concluded that properly conducted studies revealed very little differences in verbal skills from about age 3–11, but they felt that girls surpassed boys in early adolescence.

While many writers want to see physiological causes behind the alleged sex differences in language, such as different degrees of lateralization in the brains of females and males, one could just as easily point to childhood socialization. Thus, other writers suggest that mothers talk more to their daughters than to their sons, or that sons will not as readily imitate their mothers' speech because they identify with their fathers, and the fathers are not home as much of the time to teach them. The response of the serious student of language must be to remain quite skeptical of claimed sex differences in linguistic ability, to encourage the development of more reliable tests of linguistic proficiency, and to avoid attributing sex differences in adult language to differences in verbal competence during childhood.

Bibliography

Berghe P van den 1973 *Age and Sex in Human Societies*. Wadsworth, Belmont, CA

Birdwhistell R 1970 *Kinesics and Context*. University of Pennsylvania Press, Philadelphia, PA

Brouwer D, Gerritsen M, De Haan D 1979 Speech differences between women and men: On the wrong track? *LiS* 8: 33–50

Cameron D 1985 *Feminism and Linguistic Theory*. Macmillan, London

Cameron D, Coates J 1989 Some problems in the sociolinguistic explanation of sex differences. In: Coates J, Cameron D (eds.) *Women in Their Speech Communities*. Longman, London

Coates J 1986 *Women, Men, and Language: A Sociolinguistic Account of Sex Differences in Language*. Longman, London

Eakins B W, Eakins R G 1978 *Sex Differences in Human Communication*. Houghton Mifflin, Boston, MA

Haas A 1979 Male and female spoken language differences: Stereotypes and evidence. *Psychological Bulletin* **86**: 616–26

Haas M R 1964 Men's and women's speech in Koasati. In: Hymes D (ed.) *Language in Culture and Society*. Harper and Row, New York

Ide S, Hori M, Kawasaki A, Ikuta S, Haga H 1986 Sex difference and politeness in Japanese. *International Journal of the Sociology of Language* **58**: 25–36

Kluckhohn F R 1953 Dominant and variant value orientations. In: Kluckhohn C, Murray H A (eds.) *Personality in Nature, Society, and Culture*. Knopf, New York

Kramarae C 1981 *Women and Men Speaking*. Newbury House, Rowley, MA

Kramarae C 1982 Gender: How she speaks. In: Ryan E B, Giles H (eds.) *Attitudes Towards Language Variation*. Edward Arnold, London

Lakoff R 1975 *Language and Women's Place*. Harper and Row, New York

Macaulay R K S 1977 The myth of female superiority in language. *Journal of Child Language* 5: 353–63

Maccoby E E, Jacklin C N 1974 *The Psychology of Sex Differences*. Stanford University Press, Stanford, CA

Ochs E 1987 The impact of stratification and socialization on men's and women's speech in Western Samoa. In: Philips S U, Steele S, Tanz C (eds.) *Language, Gender, and Sex in Comparative Perspective*. Cambridge University Press, Cambridge

Scherer K R, Giles H (eds.) 1980 *Social Markers in Speech*. Cambridge University Press, Cambridge

Shibamoto J S 1985 *Japanese Women's Language*. Academic Press, New York

Smith P M 1979 Sex markers in speech. In: Scherer K R, Giles H (eds.) *Social Markers in Speech*. Cambridge University Press, Cambridge

Smith P M 1985 *Language, the Sexes and Society*. Basil Blackwell, Oxford

Spender D 1985 *Man Made Language*. Routledge and Kegan Paul, London

Thorne B, Henley N (eds.) 1975 *Language and Sex: Difference and Dominance*. Newbury House, Rowley, MA

Thorne B, Kramarae C, Henley N (eds.) 1983 *Language, Gender, and Society*. Newbury House, Rowley, MA

Trudgill P 1972 Sex, covert prestige, and linguistic change in the urban British English of Norwich. *LiS* 1: 179–95

E. O. Bainbridge

Sex and Language

Interest in the sex and language issue has been prominent in linguistic research since the 1960s, no doubt as a result of the revival of the feminist movement in the same period. Language structure and language use were felt to support and reinforce age-old attitudes towards sex identity and sex roles which, in the case of women, were considered unfair and discriminatory. The new word 'sexism' (on the model of 'racism') was coined to convey the notion that there is widely spread antiwomen bias, particularly in texts influencing public opinion such as children's books, textbooks, and advertisements. The amount of published work in this field is vast and covers a variety of topics.

1. The Manifestation of Sex in Language: Gender

Gender (see *Gender and Language*) a secondary grammatical category whether as congruence of word endings or as a matter of selection, appears in a variety of languages. The first case is typically exemplified by the Romance languages, while the second corresponds to English, where gender is shown, mostly, if not exclusively, as pronoun selection.

The particular morphemes signaling gender belong to the set of classifiers (see *Classifier Languages*) which, in a variety of languages, categorize entities according to some physical criteria, functional criteria (e.g., tools, means of transport), or social relevance (e.g., animacy, status). Classifiers are commonly interpreted as mirroring the cultural ecology of given societies, and that is why, presumably at a very early stage of development, some societies found a hierarchical classification desirable along the scale of animacy whose main components from highest to lowest degree are: human, animate, inanimate. However, apart from these clear-cut categories, finer distinctions can also be found. An example could be the sexual differences that underlie gender systems (Comrie 1981).

The key concept, as far as the sex and language issue is concerned, is the hierarchical display of the system which embodies, at a very deep semantic level, the symbolization of sexual distinctions, a process with several linguistic consequences. To begin with, words with potential male or female referents—as indicated by their gender endings— may take over the connotations associated with men and women respectively and, once these connotations have been acquired, they can in turn be projected to nonhuman beings. This can be clearly seen in prosopopoeia or personification of inanimate beings, whereby the personified entities are attributed to the physical or psychical qualities stereotypically associated with males or females. This phenomenon poses translation problems whenever two languages diverge in word gender. A characteristic example is *sin* which is feminine in German (*die Sünde*) but masculine in Russian (*grex*). French audiences of Ingmar Bergman's film *The Seventh Seal* sharply felt the incoherence between the character of Death, performed by a man under the influence of the Swedish masculine name, and the subtitles referring to it as feminine (Yaguello 1987). The same sort of incongruence was experienced by Spanish audiences.

Sex-related associations have been observed and explained by language experts and native language users alike. It is precisely in languages lacking obligatory gender morphemes that speakers have a real choice. In English, assigned gender has been used to achieve stylistic effects in poetry, and to convey psychological attitudes in ordinary language. Thus present-day American speakers attach the masculine qualities of strength and mobility to the horse, whereas a motorcycle may be attributed feminine sleekness. Explanations or rather rationalizations for the various choices reveal stereotypical perception of sex-related qualities. In English, the ocean, in spite of the permanent association of water with feminity, is assigned the masculine gender on account of its power; the feminine moon is presented as passive and unstable whereas the masculine sun is seen as an active fecundating force. Experimental work (Ervin 1962) shows that speakers even assign sexual connotations to meaningless made-up words, on account of their endings only, thus confirming the intuitive perception of a polar opposition between the sexes in terms of features such as tallness, strength, boldness on the one hand and beauty, weakness, gentleness on the other.

Gender distribution implies, almost without exception, that the masculine form acts as the unmarked member of the polarity, that is, it stands for the whole set. This has caused extensive debate and controversy, since in generic reference (see *Reference, Philosophical Issues concerning*) the seeming neutrality actually disguises reference only to males, a phenomenon known as pseudo-genericity, the effect of which is to efface or obscure the presence of women in society. Of course, this is a matter of degree and depends on several pragmatic factors not well understood yet. For instance German *der Ehepartner* 'the spouse,' may be interpreted relationally and therefore more abstractly and neutrally than *der Boxer* 'the boxer' in which case a clear and concrete male image is evoked even if both expressions were meant as generic terms. This alleged invisibility of women has attracted a great deal of attention on the part of feminist linguists, and has become a favorite target for reform projects.

2. Linguistic Variation According to Sex

Long before reliable evidence was available from linguistic research, people held and still hold intuitive opinions and assumptions with respect to the linguistic behavior of either sex. Prescientific views such as this one are dealt with in folklinguistics, and irrespective of their objectivity they have proved to be extremely persistent. In experimental research conducted to compare stereotypes of male and female speech (Kramer 1974), men were described as using simpler, more direct and assertive language whereas women tended to adorn their speech and use soft, evaluative adjectives such as 'nice' or 'pretty.' The experiment indeed supported long-rooted beliefs in 'harsh versus polished' speech as the dominant masculine and feminine features.

Such views link up with a long chain of descriptions and opinions, a number of which lack adequate statistical evidence, even though they represent widespread notions.

Until recently, a large number of linguistic surveys reflected the assumption that men's speech was the norm and, consequently, women's speech was studied in terms of deviation (see *Norm*) or altogether ignored. However, in the early 1990s, studies, heavily influenced by the feminist movement reflect, in turn, the dominant interpretations of women's status. The first or 'difference' approach emphasizes the idea that men and women belong to separate subcultures and their respective differences in speech mirror specific membership features. The second or 'dominance' approach interprets linguistic differences in terms of men's dominance and women's subordination.

It seems that the conclusions of sound linguistic research have failed to prove any clear-cut and sharp differences in the speech of men and women. Comprehensive surveys, however, point to some sex-related characteristics. Specific features in pronunciation seem to be scarce, although in a few languages, mostly Native American, they occur often enough to serve as constant markers of sex (see *Sex Differences*). Specificities mentioned in various sources are the omission of a given sound by one sex and variation in the position or manner of sound articulation. Formal differences are also limited to the omission of some suffixes by one sex or the use of a few sexexclusive words, such as several dozen Carib terms. No significant contrasts have been found in syntactic patterning although lexical variation is quite common in interjections, particles, personal pronouns, and kinship terminology. For example, Thai and Japanese exhibit sexexclusive particles and personal pronouns. As for the majority of full content words, variation is rather sexpreferential than sexexclusive, e.g., Japanese verbs, adjectives, and adverbs show different suffixes for men and women; nouns are marked by women's honorific prefixes. In a large number of widely separated languages, men and women use different kinship terms. To put it in Western terms, brother and sister would use different words for what in the English system would be considered the same family relationship. In some of the so-called primitive societies, traces of linguistic segregation are found, with taboo restrictions applying mostly to women. On the other hand, the males are the ones who keep ceremonial and magico–religious languages to themselves.

Almost no study on language and sex fails to mention Jespersen's pioneer treatment of women's language (Jespersen 1922; see *Jespersen, Otto*). He finds the most significant differences between the speech of either sex precisely in the fields of vocabulary and style. Women use more innocent and euphemistic words than men and also shrink from coarse and gross expressions. In general, women use fewer lexical items, are less prone to lexical innovation, and their speech is punctuated by numerous evaluative adverbials ('vastly,' 'to a large degree'). As far as syntax is concerned, more intricate and involute structures are found in men, who are also the best punsters. Whatever their statistical accuracy, Jespersen's opinions have had a long life in linguistic literature.

A present-day author who has dealt with linguistic variation very influentially is Robin Lakoff (1975). Her overall claim is that women's language as a whole reveals women's social powerlessness and is thus dominated by stylistic features signaling insecurity and lack of assertiveness. Female language is consequently heavily influenced by the pragmatic principle of politeness (see *Politeness*; *Relevance*), which basically rules adaptative social behavior.

Some prominent features are: the use of hedges, e.g., 'sort of,' 'kind of,' hypercorrect grammar, polite formulae, empty evaluative adjectives of the type 'charming,' 'sweet,' etc. In sum, structural, lexical, or intonational signals of tentativeness and hesitancy. However, these features are not characteristic of the speech of all women nor are they restricted to female speakers.

Among the features mentioned above, there is one that has received a great deal of critical attention on account of its social implications. This feature is 'hypercorrection'—both in grammar and pronunciation—which has been described as compliance with standard, socially prestigious norms. Several surveys conducted in the UK show that whenever different variants are found and one of them can be labeled as prestigious, it is typical that it should be female speakers who use it. Nonstandard, nonprestige forms seem to be associated not only with working-class speakers but also with male speakers. Interesting explanations have been advanced for this seemingly odd behavior. Whereas standard forms carry overt prestige, nonstandard, specifically working-class forms, carry covert prestige. Accordingly, a large number of male speakers are more concerned with the acquisition of covert prestige as a signal of group solidarity than with attaining social status, as it is usually defined. This suggests an interesting intersection of sex and class membership, since working-class features appear to symbolize masculinity of a highly stereotyped form, associated with roughness, toughness, and physical strength.

However, the linguistic behavior of either sex cannot be fully accounted for in terms of each group trying deliberately to adopt given social norms of whichever origin. Rather, men's loyalty to the speech of their peers may be the result of the close-knit social network to which men have traditionally belonged and helping to maintain vernacular speech norms. In so far as women themselves leave their home isolation and integrate in more articulate social networks, the situation shows hints of fast change. Apart from group membership, the conditions of data collecting might also affect the alleged results. It might happen that women are just as nonstandard as men in casual, relaxed speech, only they are less likely to exhibit their spontaneous speech style when interviewed by a linguistic researcher, especially a male investigator.

With respect to topics of conversation, it appears that the speech of women shows a preference for family and interpersonal relations, while men seem more concerned with more general aspects of community life such as local politics and sports. Again, the influence of sex roles is keenly felt.

The biological foundations of sexually differentiated behavior have been and probably will remain an open question. Investigations of boys' and girls' utterances in the preverbal phase of language development show that already during the first months of their life female and male babies seem to behave differently.

It was observed that boys scream more than girls; girls vocalize more often than boys. Nevertheless, other studies, opposed to these repeatedly made observations, do not record any differences in the vocalization frequency of boys and girls (Klann-Delius 1981) and it remains controversial whether these vocalizations serve communicative functions. Investigations of sex differences in the phase of language development in late childhood generally maintain a more rapid acquisition process and higher verbal productivity in girls than in boys. Both sexes are said to differ in their intellectual characteristics, with mature males being relatively more able spatially and mature females more able verbally. This generalization may be supported by the fact that male children are stricken by language disabilities at least twice as often as female children. Thus, although the importance of socialization processes cannot be denied, biological factors are no doubt also involved.

3. The Image of the Sexes in Language

To the extent that language acts as a filter in our perception of reality, it can be said to convey predetermined and rather stable attitudes towards either sex which can be described as asymmetry, manifested by the respective symbolic value associated with the masculine and feminine worlds, as stated in Sect. 1. Moreover, asymmetry is also shown in the process of pejoration or derogation of feminine words with no parallel in their masculine counterparts.

This overall asymmetry has been explained (Giraud 1972) as a result of the influence of the body, its parts, and functions in the shaping of myths and archetypal models, which in turn pervade literary canons and religious scriptures. In otherwise largely divergent social systems, language has reflected notions of male supremacy based upon the characteristics of male sexuality, as experienced by males themselves, and upon the unique generative power attributed to the male, albeit unsupported by scientific research. In fact, the feminine role in reproduction was virtually ignored until relatively recent times, to such an extent that the prevalent analogy for human reproduction was that of vegetal growth, dominated by forceful images of the seed and the soil and other related physical phenomena. These notions supported the creation of a symbolic network in which men are enshrined as powerful, creative elements whereas women are conceptualized as passive, pliable receptacles.

However, the relevance of political explanations of women subordination cannot be denied. Engel's linking of the role of women to that of the proletariat has been an attractive model, which a large number of feminist linguists and critics have found extremely congenial, since from the very beginning, the feminist movement has been prone to stress its own nexus with the rest of human situations marked by inequality, in particular, social and racial discrimination. Moreover, a large number of feminists have also been militants in the various leftist parties.

The explanatory force of political interpretations notwithstanding, anthropological data seem to offer a better account of such worldwide, cross-cultural facts in terms of the symbolic projection of biological phenomena, as experienced by males and, more important, as interpreted by males. Sexual intercourse between man and woman has acted as a symbol of the agent and patient relationship. Languages have thus developed a constellation of binomial oppositions, modeled on this contrast, with a clear bias for the masculine sexual (and by extension social) role. Within the constellation of oppositions there are pairs of words of the type: 'subject–object,' 'knowledge–ignorance,' 'order–chaos,' 'energy–matter,' 'spirit–flesh,' 'day–night.' The so-called feminine member of the pair (the second)

invariably denotes a concept evaluated as negative or inferior.

This powerful symbolic dichotomy, which permeates anthropological literary and religious worldviews, was endorsed by psychoanalysis. Freud's description of woman as the deprived member of the human couple confirms the asymmetrical notions inherited from the past. Psychoanalysis has thus reinforced age-old views of masculine identity as a symbolic shaping force, the female difference being defined in terms of 'lack' rather than 'otherness.' Aspects of this school appeal to some writers, particularly French feminist writers who think it illumines the identity of women's literary voice.

The encapsulation by language of ancestral views on sexual prominence determines consistent lexical asymmetries. It is a widespread cross-cultural phenomenon that words related to men, men's occupations and the like remain relatively stable in their meanings for centuries whereas those denoting women and their world have undergone degeneration. Typical deterioration processes (MacDougald 1961) exemplify the fate of a large number of words. For example, 'tart' referring to a small pie or pastry was first applied to a young woman as a term of endearment, next to young women who were sexually desirable, then to women who were careless in their morals, and finally to women of the street.

Other terms, originally denoting either men or women, became pejorative when they narrowed their scope to refer only to women. Such is the case in the notorious examples of 'witch' or 'spinster.' In addition, there are asymmetric pairs of masculine/feminine words in which the feminine member invariably denotes lower status or conveys unfavorable associations, e.g., 'governor/governess,' 'king/queen,' 'master/mistress,' etc.

Not surprisingly, in the very large number of words that languages develop to designate sexual organs, the difference in assigned value is sharply shown. Men's genitals are associated with positively evaluated entities or situations whereas female organs convey negative perspectives.

Synchronically, however, it is uncertain whether language users are aware of the strong prejudice underlying a large number of lexical choices. Prejudice, in spite of its dark blinding force, is not fixed for ever in the history of humankind.

4. In Search of Balance

The pervasive cross–cultural discriminatory attitudes described above could not fail to bring about, in militant feminist groups, a reaction in favor of some sort of reform which would, on the one hand, remove sexism from language and, on the other, free women from the constraints of a medium ill-suited to express their own separate but equal identity. The theory underlying this view is that readjustments in language will eventually bring about isomorphic changes in the perception and conceptualization of the world itself. This assumption, to be sure, has never been accepted without challenge.

One general target for reform has been the so-called invisibility of women. This phenomenon is related to the topic of pseudo–genericity, stated in Sect. 1. The best-known and so far most successful reform attempts have taken place in English-speaking countries, which can be explained not only on account of the vitality of their feminist movements, but also in terms of the structure of English, a language not encumbered with morphological gender. The other main target has been the pejorative associations constantly attached to words related to women and women's world. In nonsexist guidelines several proposals have been put forward, in the hope that the misleading effects of pseudo-genericity and negative bias would be eventually redressed (Miller and Swift 1989).

Strategies can be illustrated by the proposals directed towards replacement of pseudo–generic '-man' (both as a bound and as a free morpheme). These proposals are representative of the main trends found in reform movements. One trend is towards divergence and consequently a tendency towards the use of words unambiguously marked for gender is recommended. Along these lines, words such as 'spokeswoman' and 'saleswomen' could be used besides the traditional 'spokesman' and 'salesman,' even though this usage may induce employers to adopt two separate pay scales, as feminist researchers duly noticed. The other trend is towards convergence, that is: the selecting of true generic, sex-inclusive words such as 'member of Congress,' 'representative' or 'congressional,' instead of 'congressman.'

Similar solutions are advanced for pronominal generic reference. Either 'he/she' or 's/he' are made available or else sex identification is obliterated by the use of generic 'they,' a respectable usage endorsed by some traditional grammars.

Reform is more troublesome in languages with morphological gender (e.g., German, Italian, Spanish) since they possess few common or sexinclusive words and their only way out for comprehensive generic reference is to keep one gender form (usually the masculine one) which falls back into pseudo-genericity. Another alternative is to specify both the masculine and the feminine words (or at least both masculine and feminine endings). This type of rather cumbersome solution is adopted in restricted contexts when the speaker deliberately wants to sound nondiscriminatory. For instance, the Spanish Minister for Education when speaking on TV about educational reform was heard to say: '*las niñas y los niños españoles necesitan una nueva ley*' (Spanish girls and boys need a new law). This is a particularly enlightening example because in addition to the specification of both genders he also reversed the traditionally established order of the pair by using the feminine term first, in a clear attempt towards open-mindedness and progressiveness.

A set of words which has proved hard to deal with is the group of terms for jobs and occupations. The use of feminine endings, allowed by the morphological structure of the language and even encouraged by sanctioning institutions such as academies, is not however as straightforward as it may seem. The feminine counterpart of a masculine term may be used to designate the wife of the man practicing the occupation or else the form potentially fit to appear as the feminine of a given job title has often been preempted by the corresponding name of an instrument, container, or product. Quite often the feminine forms have taken on derogatory or facetious connotations, sharing the common fate of so many feminine terms.

In English speaking countries the direction is rather towards sexneutral language for jobs, e.g., 'flight attendant,' 'salesperson,' 'fisher.' In other countries such as Israel and the former Soviet Union feminizers seem to enjoy great productivity and the same trend can be detected in Western European countries with gendered languages, albeit cases of divided usage still persist.

Whether masculine endings per se are responsible for pseudo-genericity remains a debatable issue. One may wonder if, for instance (Cameron 1985), the word 'astronaut' despite not having overt markers of masculinity is used by most people as if it were masculine only. There is some evidence that this is indeed the case with a number of words that are not linguistically gender-marked. The explanation for this fact seems to lie on the role of prototypes (see *Prototype Semantics*) in concept formation, according to which paradigmatic instances (see *Paradigms*) of some category are the central and most representative members of that category.

While men remain specially prominent, due to circumstances of whatever kind, they will stand out as prototypes. This very fact suggests that changes in behavior which would make women more conspicuous in all sorts of jobs may eventually bring about the correlative changes in conceptualization, thus bypassing the need for linguistic reform.

With respect to the removal of negative connotations, the prospects are promising. Changes in usage as distinct from morphosyntactic changes are easy and spread quickly through the mass media. One outstanding example is that of 'reclamation' or reinvesting a given derogatory word with a more positive meaning. The proud use of 'black' by militants in Negro civil rights' movements in the 1960s has become a classic example. Nonsexist vocabulary is increasingly being used in major channels of communication and nondiscriminatory forms of address make their way into official documents (notably the EC) which in turn influences ordinary usage.

A much thornier issue is that of women's alienation from language, that is the alleged difficulty in expressing female identity by means of a man-shaped medium. Feminist criticism, however, asserts that the real obstacle in expressing women's consciousness is not language inefficiency as such, but rather that women have been denied the full resources of language and forced into silence, euphemism, and circumlocution. The recent movement for revisionist mythmaking, that is re-examining the foundations of traditional myths, may no doubt mold cultural values truer to the real two-sexed human species.

Bibliography

Cameron D 1985 *Feminist Linguistic Theory*. MacMillan, London
Comrie B 1981 *Language Universals and Linguistic Typology*. Basil Blackwell, Oxford
Ervin S M 1962 The connotations of gender. *Word* **18**: 249–61
Giraud P 1972 *Semiologie de la Sexualité*. Payot, Paris
Jespersen O 1922 *Language, Its Nature, Development and Origin*. Allen and Unwin, London
Klann-Delius G 1981 Sex and language acquisition—is there any influence? *JPrag* **5**: 1–27
Kramer C 1974 Folklinguistics. *Psychology Today* **8**: 82–85
Lakoff R T 1975 *Language and Woman's Place*. Harper and Row, New York
MacDougald D 1961 Language and sex. In: Ellis A, Abarbanel A (eds.) *The Encyclopedia of Sexual Behavior*, vol. 2. Hawthorne Books, New York

Miller C, Swift K 1989 *The Handbook of Non sexist Writing*. The Women's Press, London
Yaguello M 1987 *Les Mots et les Femmes*. Payot, Paris

C. Olivares

Seychelles: Language Situation

At least 95 percent of the 67,000 inhabitants (1990) of the Republic of the Seychelles, which is made up of more than 100 islands scattered over the western Indian Ocean, speak Seychelles Creole French, said to be closely related to Chagos Creole, the main language of the five islands in the Chagos group, which are administered by Seychelles. In 1981, five years after Independence, Creole was made the official language of Seychelles, replacing English and French. All three languages can be used in the National Assembly. English is the main language of instruction in the schools, but Creole has been progressively introduced for this purpose during the 1980s. It has also been increasingly used by the Catholic Church, tending to replace French. Newspapers are mainly trilingual. Radio and television programs are broadcast in Creole, French, and English.

Bibliography

Franda M 1982 *The Seychelles: Unquiet Islands*. Westview Press, Boulder, CO

Shared Knowledge

'Shared knowledge' is one of a number of different terms (such as presupposition (see *Presupposition*), given information, background information, common ground) which have been used to refer to the knowledge, beliefs, and/or discourse entities common to both speaker and addressee. Shared knowledge may be based on general cultural knowledge shared by all members of the same speech community or on more specific experiences shared by speech participants, including information derived from the immediate physical environment and preceding utterances in the discourse (see *Discourse*). While there is some question as to whether 'shared knowledge' is the most appropriate term for describing the phenomenon at issue here, or indeed whether there is a unitary phenomenon involved here at all, it is clear that assumptions about what is shared by the speaker and addressee in a discourse are involved in both the production and interpretation of natural language utterances. Shared knowledge plays a crucial role in resolving ambiguity, in the appropriate use of specific linguistic constructions, and in defining general conditions for successful communication (e.g., knowledge of the language itself and of appropriateness conditions for the performance of various illocutionary acts such as requesting or promising).

1. What is Shared—Knowledge or Beliefs, Propositions or Entities?

The term 'knowledge' implies knowledge of some fact. As a condition for successful communication, however, what is crucial is not whether a particular proposition actually is true, but whether it is believed to be true by the participants in a discourse. This suggests that shared knowledge is a pragmatic relation holding between language users and their beliefs about the world. Sperber and Wilson (1986) define an even weaker notion of 'mutual manifestness' which includes not only what speech participants believe, but what they are capable of believing. Others have argued that truth is not a factor here at all, since what is shared is not a proposition, but rather familiarity with some entity (cf. Prince 1981). A number of problems associated with the notion of shared knowledge disappear on this latter view. These include the fact that something can be assumed for the purpose of conversation even though none of the speech participants believes it to be true, as well as the fact that shared knowledge is not necessarily associated with certain constructions in all contexts (see Gundel 1985).

2. How is Knowledge Shared? The Problem of Infinite Regress

It has been suggested that in order for speaker and hearer to know which assumptions they share, they must make higher order assumptions about these assumptions. Thus, in order for successful communication to take place, it is not only necessary that both speaker and hearer know some proposition (p), but that each knows that the other knows that p and that each knows that the other knows that he/she knows that p, and so on ad infinitum. Shared knowledge of this infinitely regressive sort was termed 'mutual knowledge' by Schiffer (1972). Since the mutual knowledge requirement is unrealistic from a processing point of view, Clark and Marshall (1981) propose that such knowledge is not a reality but 'an ideal people strive for because they will want to avoid misunderstanding whenever possible' (p. 27). Speech participants will thus behave as if they have mutual knowledge, even though they cannot conclusively establish its existence. Sperber and Wilson (1986) argue, on the other hand, that 'there is no indication that any particular striving after mutual knowledge goes on' (p. 19) and that 'mutual knowledge is a philosopher's construct with no close counterpart in reality' (p. 38). They propose that their own concept of 'mutual manifestness' is not open to the same psychological objections as mutual knowledge, since a claim that an assumption is mutually manifest is not a claim about actual mental states or processes.

3. Degrees of Shared Knowledge: One Phenomenon or Many?

The concept of shared knowledge is crucial in describing appropriateness conditions for a number of constructions across languages. These include definite reference, focus and topic constructions, cleft sentences, contrastive stress, and pronominal forms (see *Topic, Focus, and Word Order*). The type or degree of shared knowledge which is required, however, may differ from one construction to another. For example, the demonstrative determiner *that* in *That cake we had was good* is appropriate only if the referent of the noun phrase which contains it is familiar to both speaker and addressee (see *Determiners*; *Nouns and Noun Phrases*). On the other hand, appropriate use of a demonstrative pronoun like *that* in *That was good* requires not only that the referent be known or familiar, but that it be present in the immediate linguistic or extralinguistic context (see *Context*). And the referent of an unstressed personal pronoun like *it* in *It was good* requires that the speaker's attention actually be focused on the referent at the current point in the discourse. In order to account for such facts, it is necessary to distinguish different ways in which knowledge can be shared. Much of the current research on shared knowledge is devoted to the question of how many different degrees of knowledge need to be distinguished and what particular constructions are correlated with these different degrees across languages (see Gundel, et al. 1990).

See also: Pragmatics; Reference Group; Text Pragmatics; Context; Discourse; Conversation Analysis; Communication; Stress: Functions.

Bibliography

Clark H H, Marshall C R 1981 Definite reference and mutual knowledge. In: Joshi A K, Webber B L, Sag I A (eds.) *Elements of Discourse Understanding.* Cambridge University Press, Cambridge
Gundel J K 1985 'Shared knowledge' and topicality. *JPrag* **9**: 83–107 (issue devoted to Shared Knowledge)
Gundel J K, Hedberg N, Zacharski R 1990 Givenness, implicature and the form of referring expressions in discourse. In: Hall K, et al. (eds.) *Proceedings of the 16th Annual Meeting of the Berkeley Linguistics Society.* Berkeley, CA
Kreckel M 1981 *Communicative Acts and Shared Knowledge in Natural Discourse.* Academic Press, London
Prince E 1981 Towards a taxonomy of given-new information. In: Cole P (ed.) *Radical Pragmatics.* Academic Press, New York
Schiffer S R 1972 *Meaning.* Clarendon Press, Oxford
Smith N (ed.) 1982 *Mutual Knowledge.* Academic Press, London
Sperber D, Wilson D 1986 *Relevance: Communication and Cognition.* Harvard University Press, Cambridge, MA

J. K. Gundel

Shaw, George Bernard (1856–1950)

World-famous as a playwright and sage, and a key figure in the history of Fabian socialism, George Bernard Shaw earns his place in this Encyclopedia as author of *Pygmalion*, which provides a classic, entertaining introduction to sociolinguistics, through his will which made provision for a new, phonemically based English alphabet, and through his lifelong habit of making challenging public pronouncements about language use.

He was born in Dublin on July 26, 1856 and settled in London in 1876. His interest in phonetics and elocution had been aroused during a brief spasm of formal education (1867–68) by a nephew of Alexander Melville Bell (see *Bell, Alexander Melville*), inventor of 'visible speech.' Early years of poverty in London were employed in novel-writing, devilling at music criticism, and frequenting meetings of various societies, some at University College London. Thus he got to know F. J. Furnivall of the New Shakespeare and Philological Societies, who gave him uncongenial work making a glossary and index to the Hunterian Club edition of Thomas Lodge. He met Henry Sweet (see *Sweet, Henry*) in 1879, corresponded with him later, and wanted to set up a Chair for him at the London School of Economics—into which Sweet would not be persuaded. Meanwhile Shaw

made his first reputation through the regular reviewing of music and drama which came his way with the help of William Archer, respected critic and translator of Ibsen who happened also to be Secretary to a Society for Simplified Spelling. Contrarily, Shaw decided that simplified spelling was not radical enough as an answer to the problems of English orthography.

His first play (*Widowers' Houses*) was performed quietly in 1892. In 1898 he started a lifelong habit of publishing his dramatic texts with accompanying prefaces. His remarks on Cockney dialect in *Three Plays for Puritans* (1901) set off a newspaper correspondence, during which Shaw turned his ripostes into a campaign for a more rational orthography. (His letters, with other pieces on related topics, have been conveniently collected by Tauber in *Bernard Shaw on Language*.) In Act II of *Major Barbara* (1905, when he had made his triumphant breakthrough on the stage), set in a poor quarter of London, he introduces a passage of dialect in the international phonetic alphabet, translates it for the uninitiated, then resumes his earlier practice of using the symbols of the conventional alphabet to give a phonic approximation. This respelling proved baffling to some actors and has frightened off readers ever since, though the difficulty vanishes with perseverance.

Pygmalion, which Shaw disingenuously described as a play about phonetics, was first published in German in 1913, the year after Henry Sweet's death. In the same year it brought him his greatest success yet on the English stage, later becoming much more widely known as a film and, after his death, in the musical version *My Fair Lady*. Shaw acknowledged that Henry Higgins was based to a considerable extent on Sweet. (It has been argued more recently that Daniel Jones (see *Jones, Daniel*) was a living model he could not name without causing misunderstanding.) For all its ironic similarity to the Cinderella plot, the play opens up questions of the interrelation of language with social structures and cultural values, moving from the observation of regional dialects to explore questions of language and social class, language and gender, linguistic fashions, demotic speech as a force for change, etc.

Shaw's most frequently quoted dictum on speech occurs in an addition he made to his preface to *Pygmalion* in 1942: 'it is impossible for an Englishman to open his mouth without making some other Englishman despise him.' This reflects years of experience on an Advisory Committee on Spoken English to the British Broadcasting Company, as Chairman from 1930 to 1937. Although its declared purpose was simply to advise announcers on pronunciation, the Committee's authority, within the ethos of liberal consensus prevailing at the BBC under Lord Reith, did much to establish a standard of 'BBC English' (received pronunciation) which widely influenced speech habits across the population, gradually giving way with the spread of television.

Shaw's public stature was confirmed by the award of the Nobel Prize for Literature in 1926. He advertised that he was setting up a Trust in his will whereby the bulk of his fortune, accumulating from royalties, should be used for the introduction of a completely new English alphabet. The weaknesses of the campaign which occupied his mind greatly in his last years were: insufficient attention to the different problems of writers and readers and to the psychology of reading; an objection to any association of the proposed alphabet with children learning to read; and opposition to the specific schemes of the Simplified Spelling Society which had the expertise to make his intentions effective. After his death in 1950, two of the institutions which would be residuary legatees if the Trust failed (the British Museum and Royal Academy of Dramatic Art) contested the will and succeeded in leaving the alphabet project with a budget inadequate for anything like the full program of research and promotion Shaw had wanted. The visible result was an edition of *Androcles and the Lion* printed in a modification of Kingsley Read's system of 48 graphemes. This has become just such a curiosity as Shaw feared (see *Spelling Reform Proposals: English*).

Bibliography

Ducat V 1989 Bernard Shaw and the King's English. In: Crawford F D (ed.) *Shaw Offstage*. Pennsylvania State University Press, University Park, PA

Holroyd M 1988–92 *Bernard Shaw: A Biography*, 4 vols. Chatto and Windus, London

Laurence D H 1983 *Bernard Shaw: A Bibliography*, 2 vols. Clarendon Press, Oxford

Samson G 1985 *Writing Systems*. Hutchinson, London

Saxe J 1936 *Bernard Shaw's Phonetics: A Comparative Study of Cockney Sound Changes*. Allen and Unwin, London

Shaw G B 1962 *Androcles and the Lion*, with parallel text in Shaw's Alphabet and reading key. Penguin Books, Harmondsworth

Shaw G B 1965–88 *Collected Letters*, 4 vols. Max Reinhardt, London/Viking, New York

Shaw G B 1970–74 *Collected Plays and Their Prefaces*, 7 vols. Max Reinhardt/The Bodley Head, London, Sydney, Toronto

Tauber A (ed.) 1965 *George Bernard Shaw on Language*. Philosophical Library, New York/Peter Owen, London

Wearing J P, Haberman D C, Adams E B 1985–87 *Shaw: An Annotated Bibliography of Writings About Him*, 3 vols. Northern Illinois University Press, Dekalb, IL

M. Morgan

Sheridan, Thomas (1719–88)

Thomas Sheridan, actor, elocutionist, and orthoepist, was born in Dublin in 1719. He was the son of Thomas Sheridan (1637–1738), an eminent schoolmaster, and the father of Richard Brinsley Sheridan, dramatist. At the age of 13 he was sent to Westminster School, but remained there only two years as a result of his father's financial difficulties. He afterwards returned to Dublin, where he was on the foundation of Trinity College, taking his BA in 1739. His early career was upon the stage, and he traveled to England again in 1744, performing at Covent Garden and Drury Lane. He later became manager of the Theatre Royal in Dublin for eight years. His longstanding interest in oratory and elocution led him, however, to give up the stage and embark upon a (highly successful) career as a teacher and lecturer on elocution. He lectured to popular acclaim in Bath, Edinburgh, London, Oxford, and Cambridge, the universities of the latter two cities conferring honorary degrees upon him in recognition of his merits in this sphere,

and George III likewise choosing to bestow a pension upon him. Boswell, among many others, took elocution lessons from Sheridan.

Sheridan's interest in the spoken language led him to publish a number of works on this subject; his *Course of Lectures on Elocution* was published in 1762, and eight subsequent editions followed before the turn of the century. His main work on pronunciation is the *General Dictionary of the English Language* of 1780, which makes explicit his standardizing ideals in terms of accent; as he states on the title page 'one main object . . . is, to establish a plain and permanent standard of pronunciation.' Sheridan thus aimed to improve the language by fostering nonlocalized norms of accent, seeking to codify, and disseminate, patterns of phonemic propriety. He developed a detailed system of transcription to this end, employing numerical diacritics by which he indicated the pronunciation of individual words; the use of this throughout his extensive dictionary stands as an important development within lexicographical history. His dictionary provides a wealth of information on the spoken language of the late eighteenth century, as well as upon attitudes to language, and especially accent, at this time. Prescriptive ideals ensure a strong normative bias, though the way in which socially normative pressures are likewise exploited renders his work of particular interest. He also wrote a number of works on education in which he presented the teaching of the spoken language as an essential part of knowledge for the student.

Sheridan's works include the *Dissertation on the Causes of the Difficulties, which occur, in learning the English Tongue*, of 1761, which sets out the need to redeem the contemporary neglect of pronunciation, and stands in the same relationship to his later dictionary of 1780 as does Johnson's own *Plan* of 1747 to his *Dictionary* of 1755 (see also *Johnson, Samuel*); his *Lectures on the Art of Reading* of 1775, as well, of course, as the various editions of his *Lectures on Elocution* and the *General Dictionary of the English Language*. His popularity and reputation are clear in the late eighteenth and nineteenth centuries, and, as Boswell records in his *Life of Johnson*, he was recognized as 'a man of literature . . . [who] had considerably improved the arts of reading and speaking with distinctness and propriety.'

Bibliography

Benzie W 1972 *The Dublin Orator: Thomas Sheridan's Influence on Eighteenth-century Rhetoric and Belles Lettres*. University of Leeds School of English, Leeds

Chalmers A 1812–17 *The General Biographical Dictionary*. Nichols, London

Rose H J 1853 *A New General Biographical Dictionary*. Fellowes, London

Sheridan T 1762 *A Course of Lectures on Elocution*. Dodsley, London

Sheridan T 1780 *A General Dictionary of the English Language*. Dodsley, London

L. C. Mugglestone

Shilha

SEE Berber

Shinmura, Izuru (1876–1967)

Izuru Shinmura was a Japanese linguist and author of *Kōjien* (*Dictionary of the Japanese Language*). Born in Yamaguchi, Japan on October 4, 1876, he studied linguistics with Kazutoshi Ueda (see *Ueda, Kazutoshi*) and graduated from the Department of Hakugengaku (*Sprachenkunde*, in the sense of linguistics), Imperial University of Tokyo, in 1899. After teaching at the same university as assistant professor (among his pupils was K. Kindaichi (see *Kindaichi, Kyosuke*)), he was sent abroad as a Japanese government grantee and studied from 1907–09 in the UK, France, and Germany, notably with Hermann Paul (see *Paul, Hermann*) in Leipzig. He was Professor of Linguistics at the Imperial University of Kyoto from 1909–36 and Professor Emeritus there after being succeeded by Hisanosuke Izui. He was awarded the degree of DLitt in 1910 and the Cultural Medal in 1956, and elected a member of the Imperial Academy in 1928. He became president of the Linguistic Society of Japan at its foundation in 1938 (it began with 30 members and by 1992 had 1,300), and remained so until his death on August 17, 1967.

His principal work, *Kōjien* (literally 'a wide garden of words') is a one-volume encyclopedic dictionary of the Japanese language, which sold nine million copies between 1955–91. It contains 220,000 lemmata, including proper names; second and later editions were revised by his second son, the Romanist Takeshi Shinmura.

Other principal works (all in Japanese) include *Tōhō gengoshi sōkō* (*Papers in the History of Asian Languages*) 1927, a collection of 34 articles (including a comparison of Japanese and Korean numerals, Manchurian philology, genealogy of Japanese, contacts with the Ainu language); *Tōa gogenshi* (*Essays in the Etymology of East Asian Languages*) 1930; *Nanban sarasa* ('nanban' is etymologically 'southern barbaroi,' 'sarasa' is a silk cloth) the book is an introduction to things European, especially Portuguese, Spanish, and Christian, 1924; *Nippon Kirishitan Bunkashi* (*History of Christian Culture in Japan*), 1941. All these works, articles, and essays are collected in the *Complete Works of Izuru Shinmura* (1971–73).

Bibliography

Kindaichi K, et al. 1969 Obituaries of I. Shinmura. *Gengo Kenkyu* **54**: 1–38

Shinmura I 1971–73 *Complete Works*, 15 vols. Chikuma Shobo, Tokyo

Shinmura I 1991 *Kōjien*, 4th edn. Iwanami Shoten, Tokyo

T. Shimomiya

Shintō

Shintō, the indigenous religion of Japan centered on the relationship between the Japanese people and the native deities, *kami*, is closely associated, both at national and local community levels, with issues of Japanese identity and with social and cultural belonging. With no fixed doctrines, its focus is primarily expressed in ritual actions that are concerned with the celebration and promulgation of life, and with issues of spiritual purity and ritual performances that uphold and maintain the relationship between the human world and the world of the *kami*. Although its influence on the Japanese language has never been as pronounced as that of the imported religion Buddhism (see *Buddhism, Japanese*), it has nonetheless played a role in the development of philological studies in Japan as well as producing important texts and specialist vocabulary.

1. Shintō: Meaning and Derivation

The word 'Shintō' itself comes from two Sino–Japanese ideograms in their *on* (Japanese approximations of the original Chinese) readings. The first, *shin* (Chinese *shen*), also has the Japanese reading *kami*, the word used to refer to Shintō deities or powers, and the second *tō* (Chinese *tao* or *dao*), whose *kun* or Japanese reading is *michi*, means 'way' or 'path.' Together they signify the *kami no michi*, or *Shintō*, the 'way of the *kami*,' a word developed to identify the rather amorphous and undifferentiated native Japanese religious tradition centered on its native *kami* from the new religious entities and traditions, notably Buddhism, that were introduced to Japan from the Asian mainland from the sixth century AD onwards. Shintō as a named and identifiable entity thus evolved as a result of this cultural interaction with the outside. Although thereby identified as separate from the continental traditions and as specific to the Japanese experience, Shintō has generally existed in tandem with Buddhism in a mutually interpenetrating process. This interpenetration has not, however, prevented each from retaining its separate identity and form, including specialized linguistic forms.

2. Textual Traditions, Forms of Prayer and Linguistic Specialities

The introduction of Buddhism and the Chinese writing system provided the means by which a Shintō textual tradition and prayer forms specific to Shintō could be established and recorded. Because the myths and legends associated with Shintō were written at the instigation of the Imperial Court, they tended to legitimate the rule of the Imperial household as well as posit a special relationship of descent between the Japanese and their *kami*. The major text, the *Kojiki* or 'Record of Ancient Affairs,' and the *Nihon Shoki* or *Nihongi* ('Chronicles of Japan'), were written in the early eighth century in a Classical Japanese style strongly influenced by Chinese (indeed the *Nihongi* also contains sections from Chinese and Korean classical works) and describe the creation of Japan by the *kami*, the prominence of Amamterasu the Sun Goddess, and the descent of the Imperial lineage from her.

The adopted writing system provided the vehicle through which to record the *norito*, the sacred incantations and prayers used in Shintō rituals. According to the *Kojiki*, the first *norito* date from the mythical period of Japanese history described in the *Kojiki*, although in reality the earliest recorded extant examples only date to the early tenth century. *Norito* developed their own specialized style and linguistic structure, making use of the textual form of ideograms but adopting it into a style specific to Shintō ritual and terminology. In particular they used Chinese ideograms not simply in terms of meaning but also as phonetic devices: various grammatical nuances, such as verb endings and particles were denoted by ideograms inserted in the text in reduced size, to indicate that they were to be read for their sound rather than meaning. While the use of ideograms indicates the extent to which the indigenous religion was dependent on the linguistic forms provided by the adopted writing system to express itself, the specialized structure of *norito* equally reflects a dynamic within Shintō to create its own linguistic forms that could continue to differentiate it from Buddhism.

Shintō has also developed its own ritual vocabulary that serves to distinguish it both from Buddhism and from everyday affairs. Much of this revolves around taboos, either of words associated with death (a taboo subject in Shintō) or of words associated with Buddhism. In ritual terms, also, specialized Shintō terms are used for everyday words so as to differentiate them from ordinary life and transpose them to the purified realms of the *kami*. Many foodstuffs, for example, which are important offerings in Shintō rites, have Shintō as well as ordinary names: rice wine, for example, is normally known as *sake* but in Shintō contexts is called *miki*.

3. Linguistic Studies and the Purity of Language

Its close associations with Japanese identity have often placed Shintō in the forefront of moves to assert the indigenous culture over and against any external influences. Shintō itself was largely an amorphous tradition until attempts were made by various scholars and nationalists from the eighteenth century onwards to codify it as part of a wider design to distinguish Japanese from Chinese and continental influences in Japanese culture, and to attempt to assert the superiority of the former over the latter. Prominent in this was Motoori Norinaga (1730–1801) whose studies of early Japanese texts and pre-Buddhist Japanese as part of his endeavors to assert the culturally unique content of Shintō were—despite their chauvinistic themes—a major starting point for modern philological understandings of the Japanese language.

In the following centuries until 1945, Shintō was a focal rallying point for successive governments in their attempts to assert the purity of Japanese cultural identity over and against the outside world, and this led to further codifications of Shintō and the formation of state Shintō (*kokka Shintō*). While the attempts made by the government, especially in the 1930s and 1940s, to 'purify' Japanese by excising foreign loanwords have no direct and overt connection to Shintō in religious terms, the close association between the Shintō of that period and the state, and Shintō's association with and legitimation of concepts of Japanese national identity, did mean that Shintō had some influence in this issue.

Since 1945 and the legal separation of religion and state, Shintō has reverted more clearly to its basic connections with local communities and with rites, festivals, and celebrations. Nonetheless, its continuing and underlying associations with issues of purity and identity mean that its potential as a rallying point and medium for the expression of nationalistic reactions to the increasing numbers of loanwords in Japanese, and hence its subliminal influence and image as a defender of the purity of the Japanese language, cannot entirely be dismissed. This is perhaps somewhat ironic considering that its linguistic influences were never as far-reaching as those of Buddhism and that its very emergence as a named entity was very much dependent on the tools provided by Japan's cultural borrowings from Chinese culture.

Bibliography

Herbert J 1967 *Shinto*. Stein and Day, New York
Miller R A 1967 *The Japanese Language*. University of Chicago Press, Chicago, IL
Ono S 1962 *Shinto: The Kami Way*. C. E. Tuttle, Rutland, VT
Sonoda M (ed.) 1988 *Shintō: Nihon no minzoku shūkyō*. Kōbundō, Toyko

I. Reader

Shklovsky, Viktor Borisovich (1893–1984)

Viktor Shklovsky, one of the pioneers of the so-called 'formal method' of literary study, was also one of the first Russian literary theorists to become known to Western European readers, mainly through two seminal essays, 'Art as Technique' (1917) and 'Sterne's *Tristram Shandy* and the Theory of the Novel' (1921), both reprinted in Lee Lemon and Marion Reis's pioneering volume (1965). The former examines not so much 'technique' as 'the device' (a better translation of the Russian *priyom*). This, together with its 'motivations,' are taken to be the determining factors of the literary text. The latter piece takes Sterne's novel as 'typical' of prose narrative because it negotiates multiple narrative positions in relation to a series of digressions and indirections that plot event time against narrative time, playing off voice against text with a minimal regard for 'verisimilitude.'

Already controversial, and allied to the literary avant-garde (especially futurism), Shklovsky left Russia for Berlin in the early 1920s, publishing there in 1923 a remarkable succession of volumes (*The Knight's Gambit*; *A Sentimental Journey: Memoires*; *Zoo, or Letters Not About Love*; *Literature and Cinema*). These books were partly made up of pieces already written, and in some cases published, in the Soviet Union. Returning home, he followed up with *Theory of Prose* (1925), and *The Third Factory* (1926). He wrote at all times with great fluency, and the idea of the 'sentimental journey' shaped many of his books; like Nabokov, with whom he had much in common, he saw his life and works as complementary facets of a continuing narrative. His earliest volumes are a major modernist achievement; but even while writing them he was already struggling, under increasing political pressure, to subject his 'intrinsic' aesthetics to the constraints of literary history and biography and to push the formalist link with futurism further toward the kind of synthesis aimed at by his friend Mayakovsky, about whom he wrote at length (*Mayakovsky and His Circle* 1940). (Mayakovsky's theoretical *How are Verses Made?* is strongly influenced by Formalism.) In his *Left Front* period, Shklovsky developed his 'subversive' theory of parody as the manifestation of a renewal of the 'higher' genres by the infiltration of 'popular' forms and modes. From the outset, his unsystematic contributions to theory were dominated by his (much-abused) idea of the centrality to literary language of what he calls 'defamiliarization,' a concept based on the textual 'shifts' and plays of difference which subsequently attracted the attention of poststructuralism. 'Intertextuality,' the 'dialogic principle' (which Bakhtin developed from formalist analyses of the relation of plot to story), and the 'voicing' (*skaz*) which preoccupied Boris Eikhenbaum, are all foreshadowed by Shklovsky. Such homespun Shklovskyan terms as 'staircase construction,' 'retardation,' and 'making complicated' (*On the connection between devices of Sjuzhet construction and general stylistic devices* 1919) paved the way for a more broadly based theory of 'differences' in, for example, his work on Eisenstein in *The Hamburg Reckoning* (1928), and his books on classic Russian prose, which culminated in a study of Pushkin (1937), of Pushkin, Gogol, Lermontov, Turgenev, Tolstoy, and Chekhov (1953), and of Tolstoy (1963). At the same time, especially during the 1930s and in response to crude Marxist denunciations of 'formalism,' Shklovsky spent more and more of his time on reviewing, and on writing film scenarios which met with a mixed reception. One of the most engaging writers of literary theory of the twentieth century, and abused by the Marxists, he (ironically) never quite lived down the accusation of having capitulated to Stalinist pressure.

Bibliography

Bann S, Bowlt J E (eds.) 1973 *Russian Formalism*. Scottish Academic Press, Edinburgh

Lemon L T, Reis M J (eds.) 1965 *Russian Formalist Criticism: Four Essays*. University of Nebraska Press, Lincoln, NB

Mayakovsky V 1990 (trans. Hyde G M) *How are Verses Made?* The Bristol Press, Bristol

Sheldon R (ed.) 1977 *Viktor Shklovsky*. Ardis, Ann Arbor, MI

Shklovsky V B 1974 (trans. Feiler L) *Mayakovsky and his Circle*. Pluto Press, London

G. M. Hyde

Shorthand

1. Definitions

Shorthand is a style of writing in which briefer movements of the pen are used than for longhand; it also usually involves notating the phonemic elements of a language rather than the orthography. The term has also come to be applied to the mechanical production of text, without the use of a pen or other writing implement, in which a coded phonemic representation of the language is prepared (see Sect. 9). Synonyms for 'shorthand' are 'stenography' (but see also Sect. 9) and, in earlier times, 'tachygraphy' and 'brachygraphy.' This article will consider three types of shorthand: shorthand in its traditional sense; shortened longhand; and machine shorthand.

2. Uses and Users

Shorthand is used mainly in courts of law, parliaments, and newspaper and office contexts to record speech verbatim; a decline in its use in favor of other methods of reducing speech to writing is, however, noticeable. With the increasing use of dictation machines, word-processors, and laptop computers—especially by nonsecretarial staff in offices—the need for shorthand appears to be diminishing, particularly in the USA. For senior secretarial posts in the UK (at least), it does, however, remain an absolutely essential skill.

The type of system used varies from country to country (even from district to district), and depends on local traditions and facilities, particularly the availability of teachers, manuals, etc. A survey carried out in 1990 with the assistance of the European Association of Professional Secretaries and Professional Secretaries International revealed that, of the English systems, *Gregg* is dominant in North America, and *Pitman* and *Teeline* in Britain. Other languages use either an adaptation of *Pitman* or a native system (e.g., *Melin* in Sweden, *Deutsche Einheitskurzschrift* in the German-speaking countries, *Fællessystemet* in Denmark, *Duployé* in France).

Occasionally, specialist shorthands have been devised for purposes other than the representation of speech: for example, for transcribing musical sounds or the choreograph positions and movements of ballet.

3. Characteristics

Hundreds of different shorthand systems have been devised over more than two millennia (see Sect. 4). Nevertheless, the range of possible abbreviated pen-strokes that can be employed to transcribe speech is relatively small. Some, indeed, can be found in other systems of writing: for example, the use of contractions in classical and medieval manuscripts, and in modern English (e.g., NB, PS, &, and @; see also *Palaeography*). The possibility of omitting certain vowel diacritics in the writing of some Semitic languages has a parallel in all shorthands.

The direction of writing of almost all shorthands is from left to right, but the method of joining symbols together (e.g., a vowel to a consonant) can often lead to the writing direction having to diverge 45° or more from the horizontal: in Gregg Shorthand, JUXTAPOSITION is ; in Pitman

2000 Shorthand, PERSEVERINGLY is ; and in Teeline

Shorthand, ENTHUSIASTICALLY is .

The choice of pen-strokes has generally been based on those employed for either the normal longhand writing style of languages like English and Russian (a tilted ellipse), or the radii and arcs of a circle. The Gregg Shorthand system uses the former (sometimes called a 'cursive' shorthand); the Pitman Shorthand system uses the latter (a 'geometric' shorthand). (Both are, in fact, varieties of geometric forms, but the established terminology of 'cursive' and 'geometric' will be retained here.) Informally, one can say that one *writes* Gregg, but *draws* Pitman (see further Sects. 5 and 6).

The position of the beginning of a stroke in relation to the baseline ('x-line') can be significantly varied—this is a notable feature of Pitman Shorthand. Strokes may be made lightly or more firmly, giving the possibility of two visually distinct forms—'shading' is a feature of Pitman Shorthand. The size of symbols may be expanded or contracted to indicate particular phonemic sequences. Symbols (especially of vowels) may be joined to or disjoined from an adjacent consonant.

4. History

The earliest attested use of a shorthand is for Greek of the fourth century BC. By the second century AD, Greek shorthand was in daily use throughout the Greek-speaking world. It was based not on a segmental, but a syllabic, analysis of the language. The most widely known shorthand system of the Classical world was, however, a Latin one, the 'Notæ Tironianæ' or 'Tironian Notes,' attributed to Marcus Tullius Tiro (63 BC). Tiro taught the system to others, and transcriptions of parts of the speeches made by various Roman politicians and statesmen have survived. Roman shorthand-writers were known as '*exceptores*' or '*notarii.*' Tiro's system was used in many parts of the Roman Empire, and survived, with modifications, into the Middle Ages, when it was used for the verbatim transcription not only of political speeches, but also of clerical sermons (for example, of certain Protestant Reformers).

The second half of the sixteenth century saw the development of new shorthand systems as well as, concurrently, of various cipher systems (used, for example, in diplomatic work). For a time, the two types of writing were considered equatable: compare the situation in the late twentieth century, where text written in shorthand is meaningless to all but a small minority of the population. In 1588, the first modern shorthand, by the English doctor and cleric Timothy Bright (ca. 1551–1615), was published under the name of *Characterie*. Compared with all later systems, its notable feature was the assigning of a shorthand outline to a word according to its semantic content. For example, the words for 'winter,' 'spring,' 'summer,' and 'fall' differ only slightly from one another. Bright's system was geometric, whereas an almost contemporary cypher system of 1590 by Peter Bales, by contrast, was cursive.

During the two centuries following Bright's *Characterie*, shorthand systems were devised primarily for English. Between 1602 and 1837 (the date of publication of Isaac Pitman's *Stenographic Sound-Hand*), nearly 200 systems were published, some of them passing through numerous editions and reprints. Several of the most important in terms of influencing the design of later systems and of the public's acceptance of shorthand-writing as a professional activity were those by John Willis (1602), Thomas Shelton (1641), William Mason (1682), John Byrom (1767), and Samuel Taylor (1786). For details, see Butler (1951) and Johnen (1940).

Adaptations of English shorthands 'o other languages were published from the seventeenth century onwards. For example, Samuel Taylor's *Essay* of 1786 was adapted to French, German, Italian, Latin, Portuguese, Spanish, and Swedish. Several of the major nineteenth-century European shorthands had their roots, directly or indirectly, in various English systems. The cursive *Deutsche Redezeichenkunst* was devised by Franz Xaver Gabelsberger (1789–1849) and first published in 1834; it was later adapted for languages as diverse as Norwegian, Greek, and Finnish. For the Hispanic languages of Europe and South America, the geometric *Taquigrafía castellana*, published in 1803 by Francisco de Paula Martí (1761–1827), was preeminent. In French-speaking countries, the favored system was *Sténographie*

Duployé (1867), by Emile Duployé (1833–1912) and his three brothers (see further Navarre 1909).

Although shorthands have been devised for languages outside the Indo–European group (e.g., Arabic, Finnish, and Turkish), the concept of shorthand as a rapid writing system has been actualized almost entirely within the Indo–European group: not specifically because of the linguistic structure of the languages, but rather because of the commercial and political importance associated with many of them, especially English.

5. Gregg Shorthand

Gregg Shorthand was the invention of the Irishman and shorthand-writer, John Robert Gregg (1867–1948), who emigrated to the USA in the late nineteenth century; it was originally entitled *Light-Line Phonography* (1888). A measure of its quality is the fact that few changes have needed to be made to it in the light of extensive practical experience over the past century and more. Its latest version at the time of writing was *Series 90*, first published in 1978.

The natural movements of the pen when writing longhand provide the shapes for almost all of its symbols: from the very first edition of the work, Gregg used the slogan 'One slope, one position, one thickness' to emphasize how different his shorthand was from Pitman and many of the other 'geometric' systems. Users find that they can generally retain most of the pen-movements used in their personal versions of orthographic longhand.

It is based on a deliberately incomplete phonemic analysis of English—more especially, that of a rhotic accent, very probably Gregg's own Irish variety. Certain distinctions, which would have to be included in a complete phonemic analysis, are, simply, missing. Thus, no distinction is drawn between the /θ/ of THINK and the /ð/ of THEN, on the grounds that the distinction is not of major importance in the functioning of any accent of English; a single symbol (or rather two positional allographs) does duty for both phonemes. Similarly, there is no need to distinguish between /s/ and /z/: contextual information will disambiguate a form when the text is being read back. And yet, no single symbols exist to represent /w/ and /j/: depending on the following vowel sound, different symbols have to be used.

The desire to achieve economy in the range of symbols is most marked with the vowels. Only nine vowels require to be written: four 'monophthongs' (/eɪ/ and /oʊ/ are counted as such) and four diphthongs. A small circle ○ stands for /ɪ/, /ɛ/, /iː/, /ɜː/, and /j/ (followed by one of these four vowels). A larger circle ○ stands for /æ/, /ɑː/, /eɪ/, and /j/ (followed by one of these three vowels). A small, deep hook ∪ is used for /ɒ/, /ɔː/, and /oʊ/. The same symbol, but upside down, ∩ stands for /ʊ/, /uː/, and /ʌ/. Unstressed /ə/ is a dot ·, while /aɪ/, /aʊ/, /ɔɪ/, and /juː/ use an abbreviated combination of the 'monophthong' symbols. Behind this classification of vowel sounds lies an older and simpler analysis: 'labial' vowels are represented by hooks and 'lingual' vowels by circles.

The distinction within the consonant system between pairs of phonemically 'voiced' and 'voiceless' sounds is handled by length: most of the voiced sounds are written

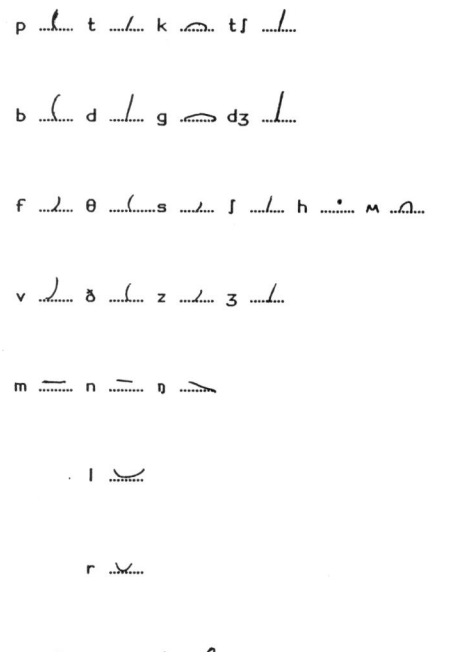

Figure 1. The consonant phonemes of Gregg Shorthand.

longer than their voiceless equivalents (see Fig. 1). Altogether, three degrees of length can be employed: compare, for instance, ⟩ for /s/ and /z/, ⟩ for /f/, and ⟩ for /v/ (SIGN 𝒶 FINE 𝒶 VINE 𝒶).

Like all other shorthands, Gregg's employs deliberate shortening of the phonemic structure of words to allow faster speeds to be achieved. Single symbols can represent entire morphemes: for example, the small circle ∘ (/i:/ etc.) for the {ly} in FAIRLY ⟋, and /b/ for {ible} in SENSIBLE . An /s, z/ symbol, deliberately disjoined from the previous symbol, stands for the two morphemes {ings}: for example, DEALINGS is written as . Lengthened symbols are allocated special values: for example, the /ŋ/ symbol ⌣ of SING is lengthened to give the sequence /ŋk/ in a word like SINK. A series of contractions of this sort, together with single symbols for frequently occurring entire words, means that the shorthand can be written at speed. Speeds in excess of 250 words per minute have been reported.

6. Pitman Shorthand

Pitman Shorthand was devised by the Englishman Isaac (later Sir Isaac) Pitman (1813–97); it will be discussed in terms of its latest version as at the time of writing, known as *Pitman 2000* and first published in 1975. (The differences between it and its immediate predecessor, *Pitman New Era* (1923–75), are, generally, fairly slight.) The importance of 'shading' as a feature of the system (see below) demands that Pitman be written very lightly with either a pencil or a fine ballpoint.

Pitman 2000, like all versions of Pitman Shorthand since 1837, is based on a phonemic analysis of English. The accent is similar to that of certain North American accents of English—not by design, but by the need to retain the rhotic distribution of /r/ in line with the orthography. (Nonrhotic learners, for example, in Australia, England, and Wales, usually have no difficulty in accepting the nominal existence of a postvocalic /r/ in the shorthand outline of a word like WORK, where none is pronounced in their speech. The same applies to nonrhotic learners of *Gregg*.)

Consonant symbols are straight strokes, curved strokes, or hooks attached to strokes. In phonetic terms, these correspond to the categories of (a) plosives and affricates (straight downstrokes), (b) fricatives (except for /h/, but including one form of /r/) (curved downstrokes), (c) nasals (curved horizontal strokes), (d) approximants (excepting one form of /r/) (hook + upstrokes), (e) lateral (curved upstroke), and (f) other forms of /r/ (straight upstroke). The difference between each type of curved downstroke depends on its position in relation to the circumference of a circle (see Fig. 2). In order to facilitate the writing of the phoneme in particular contexts, some consonants have more than one symbol, for example, /s/, /n/, and /r/.

The distinction between phonemically voiced and voiceless sounds is indicated by the use of 'thick' strokes for the former and 'thin' for the latter (= 'shading'): see Fig. 2. This applies only to those pairs of phonemes where the distinction is operative; the lack of a distinction in English between voiced and voiceless nasals, for example, allows shading to be used to distinguish between alveolar and velar nasals: see /n/ and /ŋ/ in Fig. 2.

Some consonant sequences require special symbols to be written. For the /w/ in QUESTION or LINGUISTIC, a hooked allograph of /w/ is used. (In *Gregg*, equally, a different allograph of /w/ is used.) The sequencing of /v/ and /r/ in a word like UNIVERSITY is written as a /vr/ cluster, with the stressed vowel omitted and with a special positional allograph of /r/ attached to the *beginning* of the /v/.

In words like DIRECTOR and AGRICULTURE , the final syllables ⟨-tor⟩ and ⟨-ture⟩ are represented by lengthening the final consonant of the preceding syllable. Conversely, shortening ('halving') of a symbol will indicate the presence of a following /t/, or /d/: for example, WAIT, MAD, END. Where an /n/ co-occurs closely with an /s/ followed by other consonants (e.g., in AGAINST, SPINSTER, EXPENSES), special allographs are used.

The symbols for /t/ and /d/ are also used to mark past tenses of weak verbs: FACED , NAMED , DATED . A shortened /mn/ indicates the morpheme {ment} as in SHIPMENT; /l/ stands for {ly} as in SOFTLY , and for {ally} as in STATISTICALLY .

Many frequently used words in English have special 'short forms,' some of which bear a resemblance to an aspect of their pronunciation: a short /t/ stands for BUT, (/θ/) for THINK. Others, such as for AND and for OF, are arbitrary. In predictable collocations, an entire

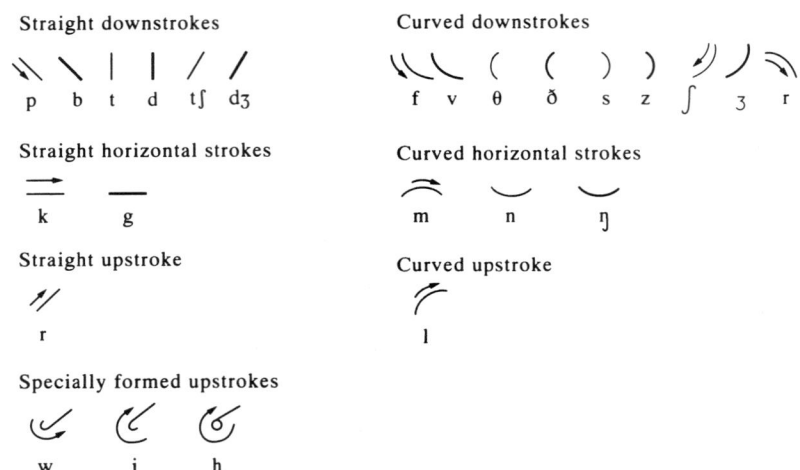

Figure 2. The consonant phonemes of Pitman Shorthand. The arrow beside certain symbols indicates the direction of the pen-stroke.

word may be omitted (e.g., 'the' in 'for the first time'). Sounds may be omitted—and, indeed, should be—if this will allow a faster but still interpretable outline to be written.

Special punctuation and capitalization marks are used, of which the most important are × for a period and a subscript sloping equals ...to indicate a capital. Where it may be necessary to mark the juxtaposition of vowel sounds at a syllable boundary (e.g., in CREATE /kri:eɪt/...), a special disjunction marker v is used.

The symbols for vowels (monophthongs and diphthongs) follow a logical schema. A light dot or dash indicates a relatively short or checked vowel (ɪ, ɛ, æ, ɒ, ʌ, ʊ), a heavy dot or dash a relatively long or free vowel (i: eɪ, ɑ:, ɔ:, oʊ, u:). With the exception of the heavy dot for /ɑ:/, all dots indicate front vowels, all dashes back vowels. The other diphthongs, /aɪ/, /ɔɪ/, and /aʊ/, are written with a small v in different positions; similarly the [ɪu:] sequence (corresponding to /ju:/) in a word like REFUSE. (The centering diphthongs of nonrhotic accents, for example RP /ɪə/, are treated as sequences of vowel + /r/.)

'Positioning' is another key feature of Pitman's system. The position of the dot or dash next to a consonant symbol indicates the tongue-height of the adjacent vowel. If, however, the vowel symbol is omitted, then the positioning of the consonant symbol relative to the writing line still allows the vowel to be interpreted within a narrow range of possibilities. Tongue-height does not, however, equate with tongue-height in articulatory terms, but, acoustically, with the first formant of the vowel: compare SIT ..., SET ..., SAT ... (In the first edition of the shorthand, in 1837, vowel positioning did correspond to tongue-height; in later editions, the positions were reversed.)

Accents of English may differ from one another in vowel system and distribution: for the Pitman shorthand-writer, such differences can be overlooked. Thus, for example, the lack of a contrast between NOT and NAUGHT in Scottish English, although noticeable to a Scot learning Pitman, is ultimately of negligible importance, since both outlines would be written in first position.

7. Teeline Shorthand

Teeline shorthand, devised by James Hill (1908–71), an English shorthand-teacher, and first made public in 1966 (although its origins go back more than 25 years earlier), takes its name from the letter ⟨t⟩, the cross-stroke of which is used to represent a ⟨t⟩ in the shorthand (see Hill and Bowers 1983). In some respects, the shorthand should be considered a faster written version of orthographic longhand rather than a phonetic shorthand proper (see Sect. 8). Some longhand forms are retained, with their orthographic values, for example, c, x; others are cut-down letters, for example, e.g. < from ⟨k⟩ and / from the first stroke of a copperplate longhand ⟨r⟩. The symbol s is retained but its value is that of ⟨sh⟩ (or, when part of a contraction, /ʃ l/). Alphabetic s is, however, written as a small circle ∘ (a reduced-sized ⟨o⟩). As in all shorthands, some single symbols can stand for whole words: < (⟨k⟩) for KIND, × for ACCIDENT. Some characters are formed by superimposing a symbol: the word OR is written with these two letters, but in the form ...⌀...

Since Teeline is predominantly based on the orthographic, not phonemic, forms of words, a good knowledge of traditional orthography is needed in order to write it fluently and at speed. For example, the words UNCLE and CHEQUE, although both containing a /k/, are written with a symbol identifiable as a ⟨c⟩ (in UNCLE) and a quite different one approximating to the shape of ⟨qu⟩ (in CHEQUE): ⟨symbol⟩, UNCLE; ⟨symbol⟩ CHEQUE. (The final ⟨e⟩ of CHEQUE is disregarded.)

As in all shorthands, vowels are omitted wherever possible, thus allowing most words to be written relatively quickly. NAME, for example, is reduced to the letters NM, which in turn are written as ⟨n⟩ and ⟨m⟩ (versions of ⟨n⟩ and ⟨m⟩); when joined together, they give ⟨symbol⟩.

Shortening and lengthening of symbols allows a variety of letter-sequences to be written. A lengthened ⟨m⟩, that is, ⟨symbol⟩, stands for ⟨m⟩ + ⟨r⟩ (as in Mr), but it also serves, without the capitalization marker, as the contracted form of the word METER. Conversely, a shortened ⟨m⟩, written in superscript position, gives the {ment} morpheme of words like SHIPMENT and PARLIAMENT.

Enlargement and stretching of a ⟨c⟩ to gives the sequence ⟨cm⟩ (as in COME). An extended ⟨l⟩ symbol, standing for ⟨l...r⟩, can be used in words such as CLEAR and TAILOR.

Some symbols, rather than being written in joined-up form, are deliberately disjoined from the preceding symbol (cf. both Gregg and Pitman). For example, the word TABLE consists of ⟨t⟩ followed by a disjoined ⟨a⟩ (standing for ⟨able⟩).

The popularity of Teeline, especially in Britain, can be judged by the number of secretaries who use it. Learning-time is generally considered to be less than that required for Gregg or Pitman. On the other hand, the fastest speed attainable (200 words per minute) cannot match the 250 wpm possible with Gregg or the 350 wpm with Pitman New Era. (In practice, however, even in verbatim court-reporting situations, speeds of over 200 wpm are rarely needed.)

8. Shortened Longhand

Many systems of shortened longhand have appeared in print, all having the aim of providing a rapid method of writing which can be learned more quickly than a short-hand. The most famous is perhaps *Speedwriting*, devised by Emma Belle Dearborn and first published in 1924. As many as possible of the genuinely unnecessary pen-strokes of longhand are removed; a phonemic base is also notice-able. Thus, the letter ⟨i⟩ is undotted, ⟨t⟩ uncrossed, the word LEVEL contains only ⟨lvl⟩, and WRITTEN ⟨rtn⟩. A later work, *Agiliwriting* (Gresham 1990), is designed to be used in conjunction with a computer program. The writer can produce a handwritten text or, better still, type the text straight into a word-processor, but in a reduced longhand form. A sentence such as 'We are pleased to inform you that we can immediately supply the computer you require' would be entered at the keyboard as 'Wrpltnfmu thtwcn imdytly sply th cmpwtr u rqr': the program then converts the reduced forms into their normal forms before printing out the sentence (see also Sect. 9).

9. Machine Shorthand

Since the nineteenth century, various devices have been manufactured to replace the pencil or other writing imple-ment for taking shorthand. The Stenograph, first patented in the USA by Miles Marshall Bartholomew (1844–?) in 1879, has undergone many developments, latterly and most significantly in an easily portable and computer-assisted form (see Glassbrenner and Sonntag 1992). The Palantype, first introduced into Britain in 1946 and the result of modi-fying the Grandjean machine used in France, is a second such device (Arnott 1987). Both provide highly efficient methods of taking shorthand; 'stenotypists' and 'palantyp-ists' routinely achieve speeds of over 200 wpm. Both mach-ines are used extensively in courts of law and parliaments in various countries, as well as in some business contexts.

The stenograph has 23 keys, the Palantype 29; the layout in both cases, however, is quite unlike that of a standard typewriter keyboard (see Arnott 1987). Speech is 'entered' in quasi-phonemic form as syllables or larger units; where necessary, combinations of letters stand for single phonemes. Any combination of keys can be depressed simultaneously—the analogy of playing a chord in music is relevant. The syllable /faɪnd/, for example, is keyboarded on the Stenograph as FAEUND, on the Palantype as FAINT+ (the + indicates 'voiced'). Prevocalic consonants in a syll-able are entered with the fingers of the left hand; postvocalic consonants with those of the right; vowels with the two thumbs. Various shortforms and abbreviations are used with both systems.

Basically, two forms of output are available: either a transcript of the 'coded' words on a piece of paper tape (which must then be interpreted and typed into a traditional orthographic form), or a computer file, subsequently con-verted into traditional orthography by the dictionary com-ponent of the program before being displayed on a computer screen for editing and thereafter printing.

Bibliography

Arnott J L 1987 A comparison of Palantype and Stenograph keyboards in high-speed speech output systems. In: Steele R D, Gerrey W (eds) *Proceedings of the 10th Annual Conference on Rehabilitation Technology (RESNA '87)*, vol. 7. Washington DC

Bright T 1558 *Characterie, an Arte of Shorte, Swifte, and Secrete Writing by Character.* Windet, London

Butler E H 1951 *The Story of British Shorthand.* Pitman, London

Byrom J 1767 *The Universal English Short-hand.* Harrop, Manchester

Glassbrenner M S, Sonntag G A 1992 *Computer-compatible Steno-graph Theory*, 2nd edn. Stenograph Corporation, Mount Prospect

Gregg J R 1888 *Light-Line Phonography: The Phonetic Handwrit-ing.* Light-Line Phonography Institute, Liverpool

Gregg J R, Leslie L A, Zoubek C E 1978 *Gregg Shorthand.* McGraw-Hill, New York

Gresham A 1990 *Agiliwriting. The Readable Shorthand of the English Language.* Agilityping Ltd, London

Hill I C, Bowers M 1983 *Teeline.* rev. edn. Heinemann Educa-tional, London

Johnen C 1940 *Allgemeine Geschichte der Kurzschrift*, 4th edn. Apitz, Berlin

Mason W 1682 *Arts Advancement; Or, The Most Exact, Lineal, Swift, Short, and Easy Method of Short-Hand-Writing Hitherto Extent.* Mason, London

Melin O W 1927 *Stenografiens Historia.* Nordiska Bokhandeln, Stockholm

Navarre A 1909 *Histoire générale de la sténographie et de l'écriture à travers les âges.* Institut sténographique de France, Paris

Pitman I 1837 *Stenographic Sound-Hand.* Bagster, London

Pitman Publishing Ltd 1982 *PITMAN 2000 Shorthand. First Course,* 2nd edn. Pitman, London

Shelton T 1641 *Tachygraphy, The Most Exact and Compendious Methode of Short and Swift Writing that Hath Ever Yet Beene Published.* Cartwright, London

Speedwriting Division of The Bobbs-Merrill Company Inc. 1977 *Principles of Speedwriting, college edn.* Bobbs-Merrill Com-pany, Indianapolis, IN

Taylor S 1786 *An Essay Intended to Establish a Standard for an Universal System of Stenography.* Bell, London

Willis J 1602 *The Art of Stenographie, Teaching by Plaine and Certaine Rules . . . the Way of Compendious Writing. Whereunto is Annexed a Very Easie Direction for Stenographie, or, Secret Writing.* Willis, London

M. K. C. MacMahon

Sibata, Takesi (1918–)

Takesi Sibata was born in Nagoya, Japan, on July 14, 1918. He is one of the leading linguists in Japan, and has been a pioneering figure in many fields of linguistics. He graduated from the University of Tokyo with a BA in linguistics in 1942, and in 1969 received his LittD from the same university. His major fields cover Turkish, linguistic geography, sociolinguistics, onomastics, and Japanese lexicology. Sibata worked for the National Institute for Japanese Language Research from 1949–64. His main work there was the preparation of the massive *Nihon Gengochizu* (*Japanese Linguistic Atlas*) which was published in six volumes from 1966–75. Parallel with this work, he carried out other intensive fieldwork on linguistic geography in Itoigawa area, Niigata Prefecture, with several collaborators. The unique feature of the survey was a microscopic survey of every inhabitant in the area. Through the analysis of the survey he has developed an original method of linguistic geography, the outline of which can be seen in Sibata (1969). The publication of the whole work is now in progress in the form of Sibata (1988–).

Sibata was professor at Tokyo University of Foreign Languages from 1964–68. He then became Professor of Linguistics at the University of Tokyo, 1968–79, and he was chairman of the Department of Linguistics from 1969–78. In the field of sociolinguistics, he put forward a new point of view from which to survey people's verbal behavior in every aspect of everyday life: when and how people speak, listen, write, read, and keep silence. This whole complex of activities is called in Japanese '*gengo seikatsu*' which literally means 'verbal life.'

Sibata has also contributed greatly to the development of Japanese lexicology and lexicography. He is a co-editor for several Japanese dictionaries, and was especially responsible for the description of word accents and the meanings of loanwords. As a perceptive analyst of Japanese word meanings, he has produced three volumes on word meanings with the collaboration of other analysts. He has been instrumental in the development of semantic analysis of both Common Japanese and some regional dialects. His work in this area is collected in Sibata (1988).

Since 1966 he has been a member of the Committee for Japanese for Broadcasting at Nihon Hōsō Kyōkai (Japanese Broadcasting Corporation), and a member of the government committee for Japanese language policy.

Bibliography

Sibata T 1969 *Gengochirigaku no Hōhō*. Chikuma Shobo, Tokyo
Sibata T 1978 *Shakaigengogaku no Kadai*. Sanseido, Tokyo
Sibata T 1988 *Goiron no Hōhō*. Sanseido, Tokyo
Sibata T 1988– *Itoigawa Gengochizu*, 3 vols. Akiyama Shoten, Tokyo

T. Kunihiro

Sībawayhi (eighth century AD)

Though not an Arab himself—his mother tongue was Persian—Abū Bishr 'Amr ibn 'Uthmān ibn Qanbar Sībawayhi was the first to compile an exhaustive description of Arabic based on a coherent theory of language. Born in the second half of the eighth century AD, he came to Basra to study religion and law, but is said to have turned to grammar after committing a solecism himself. He died in about 793 AD, just after his great master al-Khalīl ibn Ahmad (see *Al-Khalil*), aged forty or so.

He left only one work, so singular that it never had a title but came to be known as *Kitāb Sībawayhi* 'Sībawayhi's Book' or simply *al-Kitāb* 'The Book.' Although Sībawayhi reveals a considerable debt to his predecessors, most clearly to al-Khalīl, his originality cannot be doubted: he goes far beyond the speculations even of such a genius as al-Khalīl and his innovative achievement is virtually unchallenged in the Arab tradition, where the *Kitāb* has been called the 'Qur'ān of grammar.'

Drawing on an established technical vocabulary and a somewhat primitive grammatical legacy, as well as al-Khalīl's teachings on phonology (some of which he evidently discarded) and substitutability, Sībawayhi applied the fruits of his own study of the law to produce a descriptive grammar of Arabic which has not yet been superseded. Its underlying assumption is that *kalām* 'speech' is a form of behavior which can be regulated in the same way as the legal system regulates all social behavior. Linguistic acts are thus categorized by the following ethico-legal criteria: *hasan/qabīh* 'good/bad' for the structurally correct/incorrect, *mustaqīm* 'straight, right' for the semantically successful, and *muhāl* 'wrong, absurd' for the incomprehensible utterance. Speech need not be 'good' to be 'right': ill-formed utterances can convey meaning and well-formed ones can fail to do so. Every speech element has a 'status' *manzila* which determines its 'place' *mawdi*, that is its function in the utterance, exactly as lawyers determine the status and function of legal acts, with analogy *qiyās* as the organizing methodology in both domains. The most impressive development of these principles is unquestionably the theory of '*amal* 'operation,' the idea that each element of an utterance acts upon its neighbor, from which it follows that on the level of surface structure speech falls naturally into binary units, one active 'operator' *āmil*, the other passive, 'operated on' *ma'mūl f īhi*. This purely horizontal metaphor has no connection at all, scientifically or etymologically, with the Latin *regere* 'to govern,' a misperception which has long obscured the nature of Arabic grammatical theory in the West.

By the same token it is futile to look for Greek or other outside influences in the earliest Arabic grammar: Sībawayhi establishes on the first page of the *Kitāb* that there are only three parts of speech, *ism* 'noun,' *fi'l* 'verb' and the semantically and morphologically indeterminate *harf* 'particle.' He has no tripartite tense system, no verbal moods, no passive voice in the modern sense, no adverbs, no prepositions, in short there is hardly a trace of foreign influence on Sībawayhi. For him language was simply one 'way' of behaving (compare with *Sunna*, the 'Way' of the orthodox 'Sunni' Muslim), and his word for 'way,' *nahw*, in the end became the name for 'grammar' per se. However, the *Kitāb* was too descriptive for the normative demands of Islamic civilization and prescriptive grammar subsequently triumphed: in the eventual displacement of Sībawayhi's key behavioral term *kalām* 'speech' by the logically inspired concept of *jumla* 'sentence,' a completely different approach to language can be perceived.

Bibliography

Carter M G 1973 An Arab grammarian of the eighth century AD *JAOS* **93**: 146–57
Diem W 1983 Bibliographie/Bibliography: Sekundärliteratur zur einheimischen arabischen Grammatikschreibung. In: Versteegh C H M, Koerner K, Niederehe H-J (eds.) *The History of Linguistics in the Near East.* John Benjamins, Amsterdam
Jahn G 1895–1900 *Sībawaihi's Buch über die Grammatik, übersetzt und erklärt.* Reuther and Reichard, Berlin
Troupeau G 1976 *Lexique-index du Kitāb de Sībawayhi.* Klincksieck, Paris

M. G. Carter

Sierra Leone: Language Situation

Sierra Leone has a population of some four million people over a land area of 71,740 square kilometers, giving a density of some 55 persons per square kilometer on the average. There are 18 languages, distributed as shown in Table 1. (The percentages in Table 1 are derived from the 1963 census figures. It is unlikely the picture has changed significantly.)

Eight of the languages: Susu, Yalunka, Mandingo, Kono, Vai, Loko, Mende, and Kuranko, belong to the Mande language group which stretches from Senegal to Sudan. Seven others are Niger–Congo languages within the African fragmentation belt, namely: Temne, Kisi, Krim, and Gola belonging to the Mel group, as well as Fula (Pulaar), Kru, and Limba. Sherbro and Galinas also may belong here but their affinities are unknown. Krio is an English-related creole language which has strong affinities with Aku, Fernandino, and Weskos in the Gambia, Equatorial Guinea, and Cameroon respectively.

Krio is the lingua franca of Sierra Leone but this language has only recently received recognition as a language in its own right. Two other nonindigenous languages exist. Arabic is a language of religion but also of some business at grassroots level (see *Arabic*). English is the official and international language of government, business and administration, broadcasting and journalism, and education.

The population density figure, as well as a century-old tradition of social mobility, indicate that there is a fair amount of language contact, resulting in widespread bilingualism/multilingualism. The order is that of English (for the educated), Krio, Mende or Temne (the largest languages), then the mother tongue if different. Incidentally, this pattern also represents the hierarchy of language status.

Even so, and perhaps because of a much older tradition of group consciousness, dialectal differences tend to be marked especially for the larger languages. Thus Mende has at least six distinct dialects (Ko, Sewama, Komboya, Kpa, Sherbro, and Wanjama Mende), Temne has three (Konkay, Yoni, and Gbembeli Temne), and Limba has four (Safroko, Wara-wara, Tonko, and Biriwa Limba). The comparatively large number of the languages themselves, as well as the tendency towards dialectal preservation, have been factors in hindering language development in Sierra Leone. Another factor has been the status of English as an elitist language.

Linguistic studies began early in the twentieth century with Koelle's *Polyglotta Africana* (see *Koelle, Sigismund Wilhelm*) but slowed drastically, so that over the years language development work has depended upon the isolated and unsystematic efforts of only some foreign scholars— the small linguistics department of the University is of very recent creation. Consequently most of the languages have not been properly described. Thus, for example, attempts since the mid to late 1970s to use Mende, Temne, Krio, and Limba as instructional media in primary education, through the government's Sierra Leone Indigenous Languages Project, have so far not succeeded, very largely because of a lack of the necessary linguistic backup materials—for example, a dictionary and a grammar of Limba are not even available. However, recommended orthographies are available for nine of the languages, and these are used in literacy materials production and programs.

Illiteracy remains widespread, despite efforts since the early 1960s to eradicate it. The rates are 69.3 percent men, 88.7 percent women, and overall 79.3 percent. Little printed literature is available in the languages; and the Bunumbu Press, the sole rural press which used to publish literacy and postliteracy materials as well as a rural newspaper in eight languages, has been dormant though there are plans for its revival during the 1990s. The government is beginning to place much emphasis on universal literacy and the use of national languages in education.

The teaching of French (and French only), as a second language in addition to English, continues to be encouraged at the national university and in all secondary schools.

See also: Niger–Congo Languages.

Bibliography

Dalby D 1977 *Language Map of Africa and Adjacent Islands.* International African Institute, London
Fyle C The use of the mother tongue in education in Sierra Leone. In: Bamgbose (ed.) 1976 *Mother Tongue Education, The West African Experience.* Hodder and Stoughton, London/ UNESCO Press, Paris
UNESCO 1985 *African Community Languages and Their Use in Literacy and Education.* UNESCO Regional Office, Dakar
UNESCO 1991 *World Education Report.* UNESCO, Paris

C. N. Fyle

Table 1.

Language	% of population using language	Language	% of population using language
Mende	29.9	Mandingo	2.3
Temne	24.4	Kisi	2.2
Limba	8.1	Krio	1.9
Kono	4.6	Yalunka	0.7
Kuranko	3.6	Krim	0.4
Sherbro	3.3	Vai	0.2
Susu	3.0	Gola	0.2
Fula	3.0	Kru	0.2
Loko	2.9	Galinas	0.1

Sievers, Eduard (1850–1932)

Sievers, Germanic philologist and phonetician, was born on November 25, 1850 in Lippoldsberg near Hofgeismar/Kassel. He received private tuition at first, and then, in 1866, finished his secondary education at the Lyceum Fridericianum in Kassel. He studied classical, Germanic, and Semitic philology at Leipzig under the patronage of F. K. T. Zarncke (1825–91), with whom he graduated in 1870, and G. K. W. A. Ebert (1820–90). In 1870 he went to Berlin to study Anglo–Saxon with K. V. Müllenhoff (1818–84). He traveled to England for several months in 1871, staying in Oxford and London, where he became acquainted with Henry Sweet (see *Sweet, Henry*) and F. J. Furnivall (1825–1910). In the same year he was appointed associate professor of German philology at the University of Jena. In 1874 he received calls to Freiburg and Greifswald, which he declined. He was appointed full professor in 1876. In 1881 he was offered a professorship and the post of head of the Department of German at Harvard University, but he refused (he also refused the renewed offer in 1886). In 1882 he was appointed full professor of Germanic Philology at the University of Tübingen, in 1887 at the University of Halle, and in 1892 at the University of Leipzig. He retired in 1922 and died on March 30, 1932 in Leipzig.

Sievers's scientific career falls into two clearly distinct periods: one that is characterized by the neogrammarian approach to language study while the other—after the beginning of the twentieth century—is almost completely devoted to the so-called 'Schallanalyse.'

His first scientific occupations involved the study of the earliest Germanic texts together with authoritative editions of Tatian and Heliand (cf. for example, Sievers (ed.) 1878), publications on accent and phonology of the Germanic languages and on German grammar, and participation in the edition of Old High German glosses (cf. Steinmeyer and Sievers (eds.) 1879–1922). His important and strictly neogrammarian grammar of Anglo–Saxon (Old English) (Sievers 1882) was to a certain degree inspired by H. Sweet's editions of early Old English texts. On the basis of materials from Old English, Old High German, and the Nordic languages Sievers propounded in his Old Germanic metrics (Sievers 1893) a 5-type classification of alliterating verse, grounded on a typology of sentence accentuation and linked to features of Old Indic metrics. While the first edition of his main contribution to linguistics—the *Grundzüge* (Sievers 1876)—followed to a certain extent the work done by E. W. Brücke (see *Brücke, Ernst*) and K. L. Merkel (1812–76) and still depended upon the IE vowel system established by the previous generation of linguists, the second edition is amply revised by utilizing the research results of H. Sweet and A. M. Bell (see *Bell, Alexander Melville*), especially the articulatory classification of sounds. In his approach to phonetics Sievers treats every individual sound as fully determined by its respective sound system, but as disclosing its ultimate peculiarities to the trained ear of the phonetician only. In the succeeding editions of his *Grundzüge* he concentrated more and more on suprasegmental features, and finally on the role of the *Sprachmelodie* (speech modulation) as the main factor in the phonetic structuring of speech. This line of research dominated the second period of his scientific life and resulted in a preoccupation with rhythmic and melodic studies. He completely changed his scientific orientation and refused to revise works he had written prior to 1901. He turned to conceive of speech as a psychophysiological unity of (audible) sound and (visible) muscular tension of the whole body (gesture), and tried to systematize the individual and typical forms of speech production combined with the underlying so-called 'personal curves': i.e., recurrent movements which might be used even in textual criticism as proof of authenticity (cf. Sievers 1924).

Bibliography

Frings T 1934 Eduard Sievers, geboren zu Lippoldsberg a.d. Weser am 25 November 1850, gestorben zu Leipzig am 30 März 1932. In: *Berichte über die Verhandlungen der sächsischen Akademie der Wissenschaften zu Leipzig. Philologisch-historische Klasse (BVSAW)* **85(1)**: 1–56

Karg-Gasterstädt E 1834 Schriften (E Sievers'). In: *BVSAW. Phil.-hist. Kl.* **85(1)**: 57–92

Sievers E 1876 *Grundzüge der Lautphysiologie zur Einführung in das Studium der Lautlehre der indogermanischen Sprachen.* Breitkopf and Härtel, Leipzig

Sievers E (ed.) 1878 *Heliand.* Buchhandlung des Waisenhauses, Halle

Sievers E 1882 *Angelsächsische Grammatik.* Max Niemeyer, Halle

Sievers E (ed.) 1892 *Tatian. Lateinisch und altdeutsch mit ausführlichem Glossar*, 2nd edn. Schöningh, Paderborn

Sievers E 1893 *Altgermanische Metrik.* Max Niemeyer, Halle

Sievers E 1924 Ziele und Wege der Schallanalyse. Zwei Vorträge. In: *Stand und Aufgaben der Sprachwissenschaft. Festschrift für Wilhelm Streitberg.* Carl Winter's Universitätsbuchhandlung, Heidelberg

Steinmeyer E von, Sievers E (eds.) 1879–1922 *Die althochdeutschen Glossen gesammelt und bearbeitet*, vols. 1–5. Weidmann, Berlin

K. Grotsch

Siger de Courtrai (d. 1341)

Siger de Courtrai studied in Paris around 1300. He is known to have returned to Paris in 1315. From 1305 to ca. 1330 he was Dean of Chapter of the Church of Our Lady at Courtrai (Flanders). During the provisorate of Radulphus Brito, Siger was procurator of the college of the Sorbonne. His *Sophismata* were written before his *Summa Modorum Significandi*, but were not dated. He was influenced by Albertus Magnus and Thomas Aquinas, and was more conservative than Brito. He also wrote commentaries on the logical works of Aristotle. He belongs to the 'middle' group of Modistae (see *Linguistic Theory in the Later Middle Ages*).

Bibliography

Bursill-Hall G L 1971 *Speculative Grammars of the Middle Ages.* Mouton, The Hague

Grabmann M 1922 *Die Entwicklung der mittelalterlichen Sprachlogik.* Druck und Kommissionsverlag der Fuldaer Actiendruckerei, Fulda

Pinborg J 1967 *Die Entwicklung der Sprachtheorie im Mittelalter.* Aschendorff, Münster
Siger de Courtrai 1913 *Summa modorum significandi. Sophismata.* Institut supérieur de philosophie de l'université, Leuven
Siger de Courtrai 1977 *Summa modorum significandi. Sophismata.* Benjamins, Amsterdam
Trentman J 1976 Speculative grammar and transformational grammar: A comparison of philosophical presuppositions. In: Parret H (ed.) *History of Linguistic Thought and Contemporary Linguistics.* De Gruyter, Berlin

Sign

Although there is a general if only implicit agreement in modern linguistics that natural languages are a specific kind of sign system, there is hardly any mention of the notion of 'sign' in contemporary theoretical and philosophical linguistic literature. It is absent from modern grammatical and phonological theory, even from semantics. Saussure (see *Saussure, Ferdinand(-Mongin) de*) represented an old tradition in saying that 'Language is a system of signs expressing ideas' (1922: 33). He even invisaged a universal theory of the use of signs in societies, a 'semiology,' of which linguistics would be a part. But linguistics, as it subsequently developed, did not become a branch of such a semiology. On the contrary, the sign was quietly dropped from linguistic theory. Only in the collection of approaches falling under the name of semiotics was Saussure's suggestion of a universal semiology followed up. But semiotics, it is fair to say, falls outside linguistics proper, having a literary rather than a linguistic orientation (see *Semiotics*). Given the central importance of the notion of sign in earlier linguistic theorizing, its eclipse in twentieth-century linguistics calls for an explanation. A closer look at the history of the philosophy of signs and the definitional and notional problems involved will reveal why modern linguistics, in particular formal semantics, feels ill at ease with this notion. It will also show that there is a price to pay for its neglect.

From classical antiquity till quite recently, the notion of sign played an important role in both religious and philosophical thinking. In philosophy, two main traditions can be distinguished in the way this notion has been approached through the centuries. The first, which here is termed the 'associative tradition,' goes back to Aristotle (see *Aristotle*) and takes the defining characteristic of a sign to be its property of 'standing' for something else. The second has its origins in ancient Stoic thinking and sees a sign primarily as a perceptible object or event from which something else can be 'inferred' in virtue of the perceiver's inductive, empirical world knowledge. This is termed the 'inferential tradition.' These two traditions were, though clearly distinct, not totally separated: they kept influencing each other through the ages.

The former, associative, tradition led to a concept of sign that was so general as to lose relevance, while the latter, though relevant and specific, involved notions and perspectives that found no place in the intellectual climate of either behaviorist linguistics or model-theoretic semantics. One would expect the cognitive turn taken in psychology after 1960 to have made at least the inferential tradition respectable again, but, in spite of the psychologists' beckoning, theoretical linguistics became increasingly formalistic and inward-looking, while formal semantics simply remained uninterested in the cognitive dimension of language.

1. The Associative Tradition

The associative tradition originates with Aristotle, who says:

> Sounds are tokens ('sýmbola') of the experiences of the soul, and so are letters of sounds. And just as not everybody uses the same letters, sounds are also used differently. However, what those are primarily signs ('sēmeîa') of are the same experiences of the soul for everybody, and the things ('prágmata') of which these are likenesses ('homoiṓmata') are likewise the same for all.
>
> (*De Interpretatione*: 1, 16a4)

Thus, sounds 'symbolize' thoughts and graphemes 'symbolize' sounds; both 'signify' thoughts and concepts, which in turn 'represent' the objectual world; sounds and graphemes vary cross-linguistically, but thoughts and objects do not.

It is important to realize that Aristotle had to improvise terminologically. The terms *sýmbolon*, *sēmeîon*, and *homóiōma* still lacked any standardized philosophical meanings. Accordingly, it was necessary to improvise likewise in the English translation, choosing the approximate equivalents 'token,' 'sign,' and 'likeness,' respectively. In any case, Aristotle's followers and interpreters have tended to take these terms as largely synonymous, the common denominator being the relation of *standing for*. Ockham, commenting on this Aristotelian passage, uses one pair of terms only, 'signum' and 'signify,' and, no doubt correctly, extends Aristotle's analysis with an element of 'subordination':

> I shall not speak of the sign in such a general way. We say that sounds are signs that are subordinated to intentional concepts, not because the sounds primarily signify, in the proper sense of the word 'signum', the concepts, but because sounds are used to signify precisely those things which are signified by the mental concepts.
>
> (*Summa Totius Logicae*: I, 1 ,4)

Locke in his *Essay Concerning Human Understanding* elaborates Ockham's idea further:

> The use, then, of words, is to be sensible marks of ideas; and the ideas they stand for are their proper and immediate signification.... Words, in their primary or immediate signification, stand for nothing but *the ideas in the mind of him that uses them*, how imperfectly soever or carelessly those ideas are collected from the things which they are supposed to represent.... But though words, as they are used by men, can properly and immediately signify nothing but the ideas that are in the mind of the speaker; yet they in their thoughts give them a secret reference to two other things. First, *They suppose their words to be marks of the ideas in the minds also of other men, with whom they communicate*: for else they should talk in vain, and could not be understood.... Secondly, Because men would not be thought to talk barely of their own imagination, but of things as really they are; therefore they often suppose the *words to stand also for the reality of things*. (italics original)
>
> (Locke, Book III: ch. 2)

Locke's terminology is clear and virtually modern. Words are perceptible forms that 'stand for' or are 'marks of' ideas and nothing but ideas, i.e., concepts and propositions, which are nonperceptible. These in turn may stand for whatever is in the real world, and the latter property is often functionally primary. What the relation of standing for amounts to is largely left open.

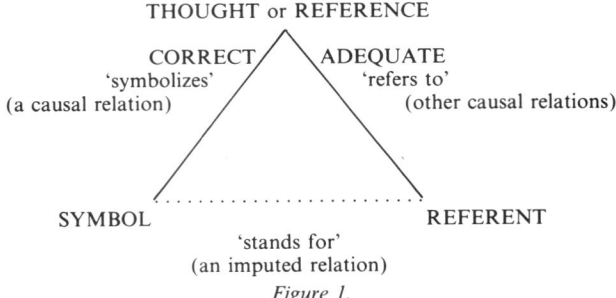

THOUGHT or REFERENCE

CORRECT / \ ADEQUATE
'symbolizes' / \ 'refers to'
(a causal relation) / \ (other causal relations)

SYMBOL .... REFERENT
'stands for'
(an imputed relation)

Figure 1.

C. S. Peirce carries this through to its logical conclusion. Taking over Locke's lack of specificity regarding the relation of standing for, Peirce presents the following definition, or description, of what constitutes a sign:

A sign, or *representamen*, is something which stands to somebody for something in some respect or capacity. It addresses somebody, that is, creates in the mind of that person an equivalent sign, or perhaps a more developed sign. That sign which it creates I call the *interpretant* of the first sign. The sign stands for something, its *object*. It stands for that object not in all respects, but in reference to a sort of idea, which I have sometimes called the *ground* of the representamen. 'Idea' is here to be understood in a sort of Platonic sense, very familiar in everyday talk. (italics original)

(Hartshorne and Weiss 1931, vol. II: 135)

In his article 'Sign' in *The Encyclopedia of Philosophy* (1967), Alston comments (p. 438) that Peirce's definition can be summarized as '*x* stands for *y* (for a person *P*).' This, he says, can be taken in an 'ideational sense': 'When *P* becomes aware of *x*, it calls *y* to mind,' or in a 'behavioral sense': 'When *P* perceives *x*, he is led to make some behavioral response appropriate to *y*.' Both interpretations are associative: no notion of rule-governed inference is involved. The latter interpretation is obviously behaviorist, well-known, for example, from chapter 2 in Bloomfield's *Language* (1933). The former interpretation, in terms of associative psychology, is found in the famous triangle (Fig. 1) presented by Ogden and Richards (1923: 11), which is, in principle, a summing up of Locke's analysis.

On both interpretations, however, Alston observes (p. 438), 'there are grave difficulties.' The ideational account is so general that it risks being weakened 'to the point that anything becomes a sign of anything.' The behavioral account is, says Alston, even less adequate. For example, 'It would be very odd for one to respond to a diagram of a high compression engine in anything like the way he responds to the engine itself,' though, clearly, the diagram *stands for* the engine. One is thus led 'to ask whether there is any interesting single sense in which one thing stands for another,' which makes it doubtful whether any useful notion of sign will come about when this associative line of analysis is pursued. Alston, who rests heavily on Peirce's approach, thus appears to admit to some skepticism about the usefulness of a notion of sign thus explicated.

2. The Inferential Tradition

Perhaps surprisingly, however, Alston fails to mention the inferential tradition in the philosophy of signs, which started with the Stoics (see *Aristotle and the Stoics on Language*). The crucial difference with the associative tradition is that the relation of standing for is replaced, and thereby

specified, by the relation of 'providing knowledge of the reality of.' On this account, a sign is a perceptible form or event *S* whose perception enables the perceiver *P* to make a reliable inference about some nonperceptible state of affairs or event *N* in the actual world beyond the immediate inference of the reality of *S*. *N* here is perceived as the 'significate' of *S* (more or less the '*signifié*' in Saussure's definition of the linguistic sign). The 'meaning' of S is its property of allowing for the reliable inference of the reality of the significate.

P's inference is justified by his inductively acquired knowledge of systematic co-occurrences, in particular causes and effects, in the world. The theory of signs is thus part of epistemology. When the inference to *N* is certain, there is then a sign in the full sense. When the inference is merely probabilistic and needs further confirmation (for example when S is part of a syndrome), there is a 'symptom.'

As Kneale and Kneale report (1962: 140–41), the Stoics developed their notion of sign in connection with their investigations into the nature of the logical form of the conditional: 'if A then B.' In normal usage, conditionals involve an element of epistemic necessity in that the consequent is taken to be somehow necessitated by, or follow from, its antecedent. Suppose there is a sound conditional, i.e., a conditional grounded in sound induction. Let the antecedent A describe a perceptible and the consequent B a nonperceptible state of affairs or event. Then, if A is true, B follows, and one can say that A describes a sign *S* and B its significate *N*. Clearly, the inference is made, i.e., the sign is interpreted, only if *P* recognizes the conditional as sound. If *P* lacks the knowledge required for the inference from *S* to its significate, he will fail to understand *S*. The logical form of the epistemically grounded conditional thus describes the nature and the functioning of the sign.

A conditional like 'If it is day it is light' therefore cannot describe the working of a sign since the consequent clause describes a state of affairs which is necessarily perceptible whenever the state of affairs described by the antecedent clause is (Kneale and Kneale 1962). But a conditional like 'If he shouts he is angry' will, if sound, describe a sign whenever the antecedent is perceptibly true, since though the consequent will also be true it will not be true in virtue of direct perception.

The significate, moreover, must be part of present reality. That is, it must be a fact of the present or past. Whenever the significate's description refers to a future fact, the significate must be taken to be a present state of affairs that will inevitably lead to the effect described. For example, when a cloud is correctly interpreted as a sign of impending rain, the significate must be taken to be the present state of the atmosphere, which is such that rain will inevitably follow, even though the conditional is of the form 'If there is a cloud it will rain.'

The main propagator of the Stoic analysis of the sign has been St Augustine, in whose theology signs were a central element. The definition and analysis of this notion is a recurrent theme in his numerous writings, for example, 'A sign is something which shows itself to the senses and beyond itself something else to the knowing mind' (*Dialectica*: ch. 5).

It may be observed, at this point, that Augustine's analysis of the sign, like that developed in the Stoa (in so far as it can be reconstructed from the mainly secondary sources), does not distinguish between cases where the non-perceptible fact, the 'something else,' causes (or motivates) the perceptible fact and those where the perceptible fact causes the nonperceptible 'something else.' When the former relation holds it is perfectly natural to speak of the perceptible element as a sign. But when the perceptible fact is itself the cause of the something else, so that perception of the cause induces certain knowledge (prediction) of the effect to come, it seems less natural to speak of a sign, even though the Stoic-Augustinian analysis allows for it. For example, on seeing a man jump from the roof of a tall building, one knows that he will die. Yet, it seems inappropriate, or anyway less appropriate, to say that the man's jump is a sign of his imminent death. It is, therefore, perhaps useful to add the following criterion to the analysis of the sign: if a causal relation is involved between a perceptible and a nonperceptible fact, then, for the perceptible fact to function as a sign it must be caused by the imperceptible fact, and not vice versa. Mere systematic co-occurrence seems insufficient as a criterion.

3. Signs: Natural and Conventional

Augustine amply discusses the Stoic distinction between *natural* and *conventional signs* (e.g., in *De Doctrina Christiana*, Book II: chs. 1–4). It is mainly through the enormous influence of his writings that this distinction became commonplace through the ages. It amounts to the following. Natural signs result from world knowledge. They need not be learned separately, as signs: factual knowledge suffices. For anyone who knows that smoke cannot come about unless as a result of combustion, smoke is a sign of (signifies) fire. Analogously, footprints signify the past passing of an animal or person, and the distant hum of aircraft may, in certain contexts, be a sign of a state of affairs that will soon lead to bombing. Or the presence of a limousine adorned with white flowers signifies, in certain cultures, that a wedding is being celebrated.

A conventional sign, on the other hand, results from a convention to produce a given form with the intention of making it known to an informed perceiver that the producer takes a particular stance with regard to a particular thought. Thus, the producer of a conventional sign can make it known that he commits himself to the truth of the thought expressed, or wishes it to be made true, or wants to be informed about its truth-value, etc. (see *Speech Act Theory—An Overview*; *Speech Acts and Grammar*). Emotions usually find a natural, nonconventional expression, but articulated, i.e., propositional, thoughts cannot, on the whole, be read off the body of the person thinking. Since it is often important that others know of a person that he entertains a particular thought in a particular mode (as an assertion, a wish, an order, a question, etc.), communities select certain forms that cannot easily occur unless as a result of a conscious decision to produce them. These forms are then assigned to certain thoughts, including their mode of entertainment, so that the members of the community in question know with reasonable certainty that when someone produces a form S, he entertains the thought T conventionally associated with S. The inference is certain to the extent that it is certain that S cannot have been produced other than by conscious decision, barring possible errors or random processes.

4. A Language as a Conventional Sign System

Comprehension of a conventional sign S consists in the reconstruction of S's significate, the underlying thought, by the perceiver. A system of forms allowing for structural articulations that map onto articulated, propositional thoughts in regular ways is a (natural or artificial) language. For a language to bring about a regular correspondence between forms and thoughts it must have well-defined 'building blocks' (lexical words, that is), which can be combined into full signs (sentences) and correspond regularly with structural parts of thoughts, in particular 'predicates' (in the sense of bundles of satisfaction conditions). It is customary to speak of conventional signs not only when referring to full sentences but also in the case of lexical words.

To be able to interpret a conventional sign one must know the convention according to which its mental significate, whether full thought or predicate, has been fixed. In the case of a language, this 'convention' consists of a rule system or 'grammar' mapping sentences and thought schemata onto each other, in combination with a 'lexicon,' which lists the words to be used in the sentences of the language. Although it is widely accepted nowadays that world knowledge is a necessary prerequisite for the adequate comprehension of sentences, there still is a fundamental difference between world knowledge and linguistic knowledge. The former is about facts irrespective of conventional sign systems. The latter is specifically about conventional linguistic sign systems.

5. The Referential Aspect

Thoughts are by their very nature intentional, i.e., about something. This may be termed their 'referential aspect.' It follows that the reconstruction of a given thought by a perceiving subject necessarily involves a copying of its referential aspect. In fact, in most speech situations the perceiver will not be primarily interested in the speaker's thought but rather in what the thought is about, i.e., its referential aspect. The transfer of thought is often only a means towards the end of organizing the actual world. This is what made Ockham introduce his notion of subordination, the fact that, as Locke said, men 'often suppose the words to stand also for the reality of things,' as seen above. The referential aspect, though primarily a property of thoughts (and their predicates), thus automatically carries over to sentences and words. But it must be remembered, as Locke keeps stressing, that linguistic forms possess their referential aspect only as a derived property, mediated by the thoughts and their predicates (ideas), which carry the referential aspect as their primary property.

An adequate analysis of the notion of sign helps to see language and language use in their proper ecological setting. When language is used the listener (reader) makes a mental reconstruction of the thought process expressed by the speaker (writer), including the latter's commitment or stance ('mode of entertainment') with regard to what is referred to. In principle, the certainty systematically induced by the occurrence of a linguistic sign in virtue of the conventional sign system at hand extends primarily only to the presence of the thought process concerned. Any relation to the real world is mediated by the thought processes, and any certainty about real world conditions induced by a linguistic message depends on external factors such as the speaker's reliability, not on the linguistic system in terms of which the message is presented.

6. The Price for Neglecting the Notion of Sign

This obvious and important fact has, however, not always been recognized. There is a tradition, which originated with Descartes (see *Descartes, René*) and has had something of a career in the philosophy of perception, where conventional linguistic signs are taken as prototypical of, or at least parallel to, the physical sense data impinging on the senses. At the beginning of his essay 'The world, or essay on light,' Descartes argues, in the wider context of his rationalist theory of innate ideas, that physical sense data have nothing in common with the mental sensations or ideas evoked by them. Hence, he concludes, the mental sensations must have an independent source, besides the physical stimuli, which determines their qualities. This independent source is a set of innate principles and ideas. In setting up his argument he draws a parallel with words:

> You know well that words, which bear no resemblance to the things they signify, nevertheless succeed in making us aware of them, often even without our paying attention to the sounds or syllables. Whence it may happen that having heard a stretch of speech whose meaning we understood full well, we cannot say in what language it was pronounced. Now, if words, which signify nothing except by human convention, suffice to make us aware of things to which they bear no resemblance, why could not Nature also have established a certain sign that makes us have the sensation of light even though this sign has nothing in itself resembling this sensation? Is this not also how she has established laughs and tears, to let us read joy and sadness on the faces of men? (author's translation)
>
> (Adam and Tannery, vol. xi: 4)

This parallel between linguistic signs on the one hand and sense data on the other is, of course, entirely spurious and confused. Descartes himself seems somewhat unconvinced by it as well. He continues to say that some might object that in the case of speech sounds the parallel is not the awareness of things but rather the 'acoustic image' that corresponds to the sound. Even so, he says, it all happens in the mind, and he cuts the argument short not wishing 'to lose time over this point.'

Nevertheless, 'this analogy will make quite a career in seventeenth and eighteenth century theories of perception (e.g., those of Berkeley and Reid) and, with new theoretical implications, it will also figure prominently in Helmholtz's cognitive theory of perception' (Meijering 1981: 113). Quite recently it was seen cropping up again in Fodor's book *The Modularity of Mind*:

> Now about language: Just as patterns of visual energy arriving at the retina are correlated, in a complicated but regular way, with certain properties of distal layouts, so too are the patterns of auditory energy that excite the tympanic membrane in speech exchanges. With, of course, this vital difference: What underwrites the correlation between visual stimulations and distal layouts are (roughly) the laws of light reflectance. Whereas, what underwrites the correlation between token utterances and distal layouts is (roughly) a convention of truth-telling.

> . . . Because that convention holds, it is possible to infer from what one hears said to the way the world is.
>
> (1983: 45)

This analogy is clearly misguided. It rests on the false parallel between 'distal layouts' in the case of visual perception and the things, states of affairs, or events talked about in the use of language. What underwrites the correlation between token utterances and distal layouts is the laws of propagation and impingement of sound. In the auditory case the 'distal layouts' are nothing but the organisms or mechanisms through or with which the sounds in question are produced, not the reference objects, states of affairs, or events referred to (cp. Seuren 1985: 53–54). While Descartes confused world facts with mental representations, Fodor confuses them, more in the behaviorist vein, with the physical source of sense data. Closer reflection on the nature of the sign would have kept these authors from such aberrations.

It would also have had a beneficial effect on formal semantics (see *Formal Semantics*) and philosophy of language (see *Philosophy of Language*) as these disciplines have been practiced over the past decades. There, full attention is paid to the referential aspect of linguistic forms, at the expense of their status as signs. The vast bulk of all efforts at formalization has concentrated on model theory, the formal, and definitely not causal, relation between linguistic structures and their possible denotations in some real or hypothetical world. All of formal semantics consists of a calculus of 'extensions' in possible worlds (see *Extensionality*). Very little effort has gone into the formalization of the sign process, the way uttered sentences are reconstructed by hearers, to be integrated into any available long-term fund or store of 'encyclopedic' world knowledge on the one hand, and short-term knowledge of what has been built up in preceding discourse on the other. It is only in recent developments of discourse semantics (see *Discourse Semantics*) that attempts are being made at developing formal theories of these cognitive interpretative processes.

Bibliography

Adam C, Tannery P (eds.) 1909 *Œuvres de Descartes*, vol. xi. Léopold Cerf, Paris
Alston W P 1967 Sign and symbol. In: Edwards P (ed.) *The Encyclopedia of Philosophy*, vol. vii, pp. 437–41. Macmillan, New York, and London
Bloomfield L 1933 *Language*. Holt, New York
Fodor J A 1983 *The Modularity of Mind: An essay on faculty psychology*. MIT Press, Cambridge, MA
Hartshorne C, Weiss P 1931 *Collected Papers of Charles Sanders Peirce*, 2 vols. Harvard University Press, Cambridge, MA
Kneale W, Kneale M 1962 *The Development of Logic*. Clarendon Press, Oxford
Meijering T C 1981 Naturalistic epistemology: Helmholtz and the rise of a cognitive theory of perception (Doctoral dissertation, University of California)
Ogden C K, Richards I A 1923 *The Meaning of Meaning: A Study of the Influence of Language upon Thought and of the Science of Symbolism*. Kegan Paul, London
Saussure F de 1922 *Cours de linguistique générale*, 2nd edn. Payot, Paris
Seuren P A M 1985 *Discourse Semantics*. Blackwell, Oxford

P. A. M. Seuren

Sign Bilingualism: Issues

Sign language bilingualism remains a poorly understood topic despite the fact that the great majority of signers, be they deaf, hearing-impaired, or hearing, are indeed bilingual. Their bilingualism is a form of minority language bilingualism in which the members of the linguistic minority, and more rarely, members of the majority, acquire and use in their everyday life both the minority language (sign language) and the majority language (in a signed, spoken, or written form). Sign language bilingualism can also involve the knowledge and use of two or more different sign languages, British and French Sign Languages, for example, but this is a less common type of bilingualism.

1. Sign Bilingualism as a Form of General Bilingualism

On the societal level, the similarities between sign language bilingualism and spoken language bilingualism have been studied in some depth (see *Deaf Community: Structures and Interaction*; *Deaf Community and Culture: USA*). On the individual level, it is clear that like spoken language bilinguals (see *Individual Bilingualism*), sign language bilinguals have a unique and specific linguistic configuration. The competencies they have developed in their languages, in all of their various modalities, are in large part due to the access they have had to the two languages, their need for them and their capability of acquiring them. It is now evident that the early acquisition of a minority language (sign language in case of deafness) prepares the child linguistically and cognitively to learn the majority language (at least in its written and signed variety). As adults, sign language bilinguals interact both with monolinguals and other bilinguals. When they are communicating with the former they restrict themselves to one language (for example, a written form of the majority language) and deactivate the other language. As with other types of bilinguals, however, deactivation is never total as can be seen in static and dynamic interferences. At other times, sign language bilinguals find themselves in a bilingual mode, that is, with other bilinguals who share their two languages—sign language and the majority language—and with whom they can mix their languages. Here, depending on such factors as the person(s) being addressed, the situation, the topic, the function of the interaction, etc., they choose a base language which is usually in a manual modality (the natural sign language of the community, or a signed version of the spoken language). Then, according to various momentary needs, and by means of signing, fingerspelling, mouthing, etc., they bring in the other language in the form of code-switches or borrowings. The result has been called contact signing.

2. The Uniqueness of Sign Language Bilingualism

Although the bilingualism of a sign language minority shares many characteristics with the bilingualism of a spoken language minority, there are a number of aspects that are unique to the sign language minority. Among these are: a wider diversity of language skills and language behavior within the group of sign language bilinguals given that they have acquired their languages at various ages and in different fashions (see *Sign Language Acquisition*; *Sign Language Acquisition: Development of Attention*); a failure

by some of these bilinguals, due to their hearing impairment, to attain a high level of fluency in their majority language, especially in its spoken modality; a maintenance of bilingualism within the sign language minority (other bilingual minorities often shift to a form of monolingualism over time, either in the majority language, in the minority language, or in some other form of language); finally, a failure so far to obtain the right to become bilingual. Unlike members of spoken language minorities who have the right, in fact the duty, to become bilingual, members of the sign language minority do not have this right—many are still brought up as monolinguals in the majority language.

The linguistic patterns of language knowledge and use also appear to be somewhat different, and probably more complex, than in spoken language bilingualism. When a sign language bilingual is observed using sign language with one interlocutor, a form of signed spoken language with another interlocutor, a mixture of the two with a third, and a form of simultaneous communication (sign and speech) with a fourth, the patterns of interaction cannot be explained easily with what has been learned about spoken language bilingualism. It would appear that a number of underlying factors are at work here. First, there is the bilingual's actual knowledge of the two languages—sign language and the majority language. This competence, in terms of rules and lexical knowledge, needs to be isolated and characterized in linguistic terms, independently of language use. Second, there are the modalities or channels of production: manual (body, face), oral (speech, mouthing with or without voice), written, etc. Some of these modalities are more appropriate for one language, but others, such as the manual modality, can be used by one or the other language. How these modalities are combined during an interaction, as they often are by sign language bilinguals, is of particular interest. Third, there is the actual presence of the other language as when, in a bilingual communication mode, one language has been chosen as the base language and the other language is brought in at different moments. This can take place sequentially (as in code-switching from signing to fingerspelling) or simultaneously (signing and mouthing with or without voice, for example). It is as yet unclear how the two languages are interacting during this type of simultaneous bimodal communication.

3. Future Research

Many issues relating to sign language bilingualism need further study. Among these are: the bilingual's linguistic knowledge independent of language use; the various types of language and modality interactions that take place during production in a monolingual and a bilingual mode; the perception and production of simultaneous bimodal utterances; the characterization and process of interference in the production of the minority and majority language; the sign–speech bilingualism of hearing people (children of deaf parents, interpreters, educators, parents of deaf children) and finally, the interplay between bilingualism and biculturalism.

Bibliography

Grosjean F 1987 Bilingualism. In: *Gallaudet Encyclopedia of Deaf People and Deafness*, vol 3. McGraw-Hill, New York

Grosjean F 1992 The bilingual and the bicultural person in the hearing and in the deaf world. In: *Sign Language Studies*

Lucas C (ed.) 1989 *The Sociolinguistics of the Deaf Community.* Academic Press, New York

Volterra V, Erting C (eds.) 1990 *From Gesture to Language in Hearing and Deaf Children.* Springer, Berlin

F. Grosjean

Sign Language

The term 'sign language' is used with a variety of meanings: to the layman it often means the kind of gestures people use when they travel abroad and have to communicate with people who do not share a common spoken language; it is also used to refer to the gesture systems used by specific groups (e.g., saw mill sign language). However, the term as used here will be restricted to a class of languages found amongst deaf communities throughout the world: languages which parallel spoken languages in complexity and structural features. Sign language is learned as a first language by deaf children in deaf families and it occurs in communities with their own recognizable culture. Although existing within the larger speaking community, sign languages are not derived from, and are unrelated to, the spoken languages in their countries.

1. History and Development

Despite the lack of appropriate technology in the past for recording sign language data the use of sign can be traced to the earliest civilizations. Knowledge of sign language use dates back at least 2,000 years in the Western world, and probably even earlier in Chinese writings. The Mishnah of the late second century (a complilation of Jewish oral law) makes reference to the valid use of signing by deaf people for legal purposes:

> A deaf-mute may communicate by signs and be communicated with by signs.
>
> (*Gitt* 5: 7; Danby 1933: 312)

> If a man that was a deaf-mute married a woman that was of sound senses, or if a man that was of sound senses married a woman that was a deaf-mute, if he will he may put her away, and if he will he may continue the marriage. Like as he married her by signs so he may put her away by signs.
>
> (*Yeb.* 14: 1; Danby 1933: 240)

Plato, in the *Cratylus*, refers to significant movements of head, hand, and body made by the dumb, and St Augustine describes a deaf person who could understand others and express himself by means of gestures. However, rarely did these authors give any information on the nature of the signing or give any description of the signs themselves. Without a written form, there has been no means of capturing these early perceptions.

A major difficulty in understanding the way in which sign might have been used is the habitual confusion between signs and gestures. Signs are, of course, a subset of human gestures, just as phonemes are a subset of human sounds. Signs are distinguished from gestures by having an internal structure composed of elements which form a system of contrasts, and whose usage is rule-governed.

Only in the late twentieth century has it been recognized that gestures are not universal. In the same way, signs have often been assumed to be part of a universal communication system. Throughout history, philosophers and linguists have considered the possibilities of creating a universal system for communication. While in recent centuries artificial spoken languages have been created with the aim of enabling international communication, sign language has often been seen as an already-existing universal language. Sir Richard Paget (who later collaborated with a deaf man, Pierre Gorman, in creating an artificial sign system to represent English visually; see *Paget, Sir Richard Arthur Surtees (Bart.)*) follows a very old tradition in proposing that a sign language 'might be taught . . . to all children . . . . If this were done in all countries . . . there would be a very simple international language by which the different races of mankind, including the deaf, might understand one another' (Paget 1953: xvi, cited in Knowlson 1965).

While universality has been one major concern (see *Universal Language Schemes in Seventeenth-century Britain*), there has also been a great deal of interest in the question of how languages arose initially (see *Origins of Language; Origin of Language Debate*). The supposed primitiveness and universality of sign language was a source for the belief that the earliest human language was sign.

1.1 Origins of Sign Language

It is likely that gestures were a major part of the communication of early primitive nonspeaking man, just as they are among modern primates (Hewes 1976). Some modern hunter–gatherer groups (such as Australian Aborigines) use supplemental communication systems which are sign-like (see *Alternate Sign Languages*) and there are also records of American Indian signs (see Fig. 1).

The origins of human language are unlikely to be fully resolved by examination of existing sign languages. In contrast, however, with the abandonment of interest in theories of language origin in the early nineteenth century, the grammars and lexical formation principles of sign languages do illuminate how languages can come into being.

In theories about the gestural origin of language, physical actions (of a gestural form) were claimed to predate verbal communication (as they appear to do in ontogenetic development). The competing view was that speech developed directly from nonverbal cries; gesture was an independent meaning system. The fact that most people gesture and that children naturally develop gesture alongside speech acquisition supported this notion of the subsidiary nature of communication which was not speech.

Probably the best-known philosopher concerning himself with issues of whether speech or gesture was primary was Condillac (1746; see *Condillac, Etienne Bonnot de*). He believed that images (the basis of thought) could not always be represented in speech and might be more related to gestures. The predominance of serial speech communication had created the impression that alternatives such as sign, which might be more image-related and were non-serial in construction, could not be considered language.

Diderot (1751; see *Diderot, Denis*) considered that the sign language of deaf people might prove to be a source of learning about the natural order of thought in language.

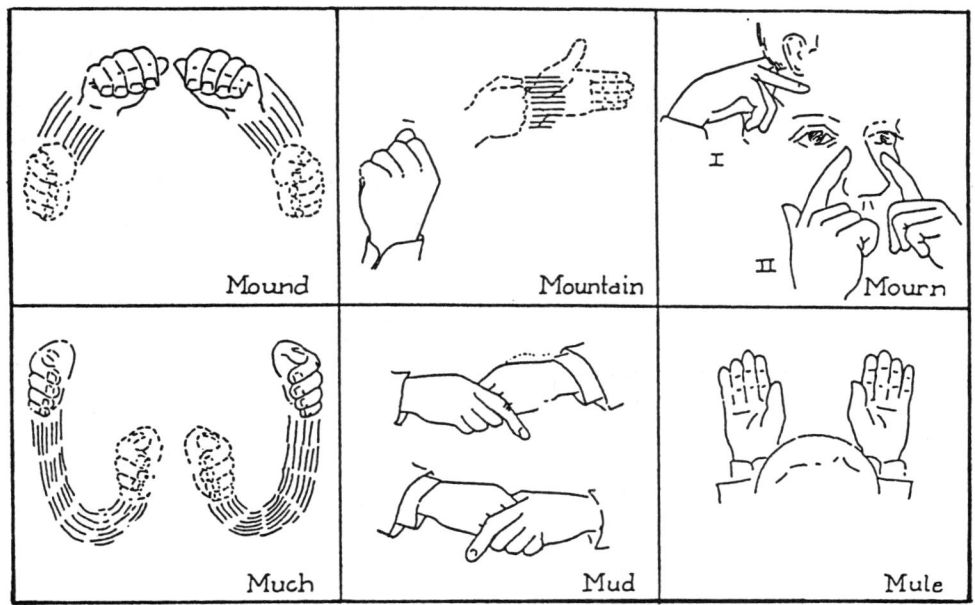

Figure 1. American Indian signs (from Tomkins 1927).

Others followed this line of reasoning. Tylor, a British anthropologist (1874), using notes he had made on a trip to Germany and in subsequent contact with deaf children in the UK, presented an examination of the structure of sign language and its role in deaf education. While recognized as complex, sign was still seen only as gesture and as a lower level form of communication when compared with speech. Stout (1899) described his theory that signs develop from iconic representations to cognitive symbols which gradually form a language. His perceptions were based on observations from a deaf man.

From the late nineteenth century until the second half of the twentieth century these arguments were lost. Saussurean linguistics (see *Saussurean Tradition in Twentieth-century Linguistics*), with its emphasis on the arbitrariness of the symbol–referent relationship, and the preoccupation of modern linguistics with speech as the primary form of language, led to a suppression of interest in research in sign languages; deaf people were regarded as living in a world with no thought or language.

Leonard Bloomfield's statement is a good example of the view of linguistics in the first part of the twentieth century:

Some communities have a gesture language which upon occasion they use instead of speech; such gesture languages have been observed among the lower-class Neapolitans, among Trappist monks (who have made a vow of silence), among the Indians of our western plains ... and among groups of deaf mutes.

It seems certain that these gesture languages are merely developments of ordinary gestures and that any and all complicated or not immediately intelligible gestures are based on the conventions of ordinary speech. Even such an obvious transference as pointing backward to indicate past time, is probably due to a linguistic habit of using the same word for 'in the rear' and 'in the past.' Whatever may be the origins of the two, gesture has so long played a secondary role under the dominance of language that it has lost all traces of independent character.

(Bloomfield 1933: 39)

As Hewes points out:

Impressed by the apparent arbitrariness of most spoken languages, it has been argued that such arbitrariness is an essential criterion for language or that a high degree of iconicity would interfere with understanding. The sign languages of the deaf are dismissed as crude, rudimentary, and if their users are unable to communicate except in such languages they display various serious cognitive handicaps.

(Hewes 1976: 409)

Sign language has endured a period 'underground' as educators and through them, parents, adopted this linguistic view. Sign had no linguistic status and maintained only a curiosity value as a remnant of some primitive communication system. Only in the past thirty years have attitudes changed and research been possible (see *Sign Language Research: Issues and Priorities*). However, research on sign languages as a way of exploring universals of language has not regained the interest it held between the seventeenth and nineteenth centuries.

1.2 Universals and Early Sign Descriptions

The belief in gesture and sign language as being a single universal language first appeared in post-Renaissance texts on rhetoric. The earliest English source (1644) is John Bulwer's *Chirologia: or the Natural language of the Hands. Composed of the Speaking Motions, and Discoursing Gestures thereof. Whereunto is added Chironomia: or the Art of Manuall Rhetoricke etc.* Bulwer (1644: 5) describes hundreds of gestures of the hands and fingers as proof of the existence of this universal language: 'A notable argument we have of this discoursing facilities of hand is ... the wonder of necessity which nature worketh in men that are borne deafe and dumbe; who can argue and dispute rhetorically by signs.'

His second book, *Philocophus, or the Deafe and Dumbe Man's Friend by J.B., surnamed the Chirosopher (1648)* is the first book specifically mentioning deaf persons, being dedicated to two deaf brothers. In the dedication, Bulwer states:

What though you cannot express your minds in those verbal contrivances of man's invention, yet you want not speeche, who have your whole body for a tongue, having a language more naturall and significant, which is common to you with us, to wit, gesture, the generall and universal language of human nature.

You already can express yourselves so truly by signes, from a habit you have gotten by using always signes, as we do speeche: nature also recompensing your want of speeche, in the invention of signes to express your conceptions.

This language you speak so purely that I who was the first that made it my Darling Study to interpret the naturall richnesse of our discoursing gestures . . . am fully satisfied that you want nothing to be perfectly understood, your mother tongue administering sufficient utterance upon all occasions.

He was not the first to make observations similar to this—25 years earlier, in Spain, Juan Pablo Bonet (1620) had drawn attention to the status of gesture as a natural language. He developed a manual alphabet which was 'so well adapted to nature that it would seem as if this artificial language had been derived from the language of nature, or that from this, since visible actions are nature's language.'

Dalgarno (1661; see *Dalgarno, George*), a Scottish educator, developed another manual alphabet (see *Fingerspelling, two-handed*) and observed the lack of connection between sign language and spoken language: 'The deaf man has no teacher at all, and though necessity may put him upon contriving and using a few signs, yet those have no affinity to the language by which they that are about him do converse amongst themselves' (p. 3). In the eighteenth century there were important developments in France, where the Abbé de L'Epée had founded a school for the deaf in Paris. He also described sign as universal language:

On a souvent désiré une langage universelle, avec le secours de laquelle les hommes de toutes les nations pourraient s'entendre les uns les autres. Il me semble qu'il y a longtemps qu'elle existe, et qu'elle est entendue partout. Cela n'est pas étonnant: c'est une langue naturelle. Je parle de la langue des signes.

[A universal language has often been wished for, with the help of which men of all nations could understand each other. It seems to me that for a long time such a language has existed, which is understood everywhere. That is not surprising: it is a natural language. I am speaking of sign language.]

With the abandonment of linguistic interest in sign language, from the late eighteenth century onwards, interest in sign language was only found within deaf education.

2. The Community of Signers

Sign-language-using populations are found throughout the world. Although there have been some hearing populations using sign languages for social or cultural reasons—such as the Martha's Vineyard signers of the last century (Groce 1986) and certain aboriginal groups in Australia (see *Alternate Sign Languages*), sign languages are almost exclusively the domain of Deaf people. Fluency in a sign language is one of the main identifiers of Deaf community membership. The signs meaning 'Deaf' (member of the Deaf community), as opposed to deaf (having a hearing impairment)—'STRONG-SIGN' in British Sign Language and 'PRODUCE-SIGN'—in American Sign Language indicate this (see Fig. 2).

Sign language use alone does not determine membership of the Deaf community; there are also the criteria of hearing loss and perhaps most important, social identification. Because of the history of oppression of Deaf people, members of the community may be defined by their distance from 'hearingness' (see *Deaf Community and Culture: USA; Deaf Community: Structures and Interaction*).

3. Sign Structure: Phonetics and Phonology in Sign Language

Sometimes termed 'chirology' (from the Greek *cheir* 'hand'), the study of the constituents of signs has been one of the major concerns of linguistic research since the 1960s (see *Sign Language Research: Issues and Priorities; Sign Language: Developments in Sublexical Analysis of Signs*). The term 'phonology' is used in the context of sign language research to emphasize the parallels in structure between spoken and sign languages at this level. Before Stokoe (1960), signs had been regarded as unanalyzable, unitary gestures, and therefore as containing no level analogous to the phonological. Stokoe's contribution was to recognize that American Sign Language (ASL) signs could be viewed as compositional, with subelements contrasting with each other, and thus unlike gestures. More recent research has sought to apply approaches to phonological theory in spoken languages, such as autosegmental phonology, to sign structure.

3.1 Arbitrariness in Phonology

A major issue for sign language phonologists is whether there is meaning at the sublexical level. Signs with shared sublexical features (e.g., handshape or location) often share some feature of meaning. Many signs located at the forehead relate to cognitive activity (THINK, REMEMBER, LEARN, STUPID, CLEVER, IMAGINE, DREAM, WORRY, etc.). In British Sign Language (BSL) the handshape of little finger extended from the fist is found in such signs as BAD, POISON, ILL, WRONG, END, ARGUE, CURSE, SOUR, EVIL, etc., while signs made with the handshape of thumb extended from the fist include GOOD, HEALTH, RIGHT, AGREE, KNOW, and so on (see Fig. 3).

3.2 Iconicity

Research on sign language in the 1960s and 1970s often made what appears to be an overly strong case for arbitrariness and absence of iconicity as an organizing principle. Because of the need to argue the case for the acceptance of sign languages as real languages, those features of sign language which differed from spoken language were minimized. With the subsequent recognition and acceptance of sign languages there has been a willingness to explore the modality-specific features of languages and this has led to renewed interest in iconicity and visual imagery as an organizing principle in sign language. The Saussurean emphasis on the arbitrariness of the link between the form of the linguistic symbol and its referent has had a number of effects on linguists' views. Those nonarbitrary relationships found in spoken languages, such as sound symbolism and

(a) BSL THROW–SIGN

(b) ASL STRONG–SIGN

Figure 2. Signs for 'Deaf' in British and American sign language.

onomatopoeia, tend to be regarded as odd exceptions (certainly not counterexamples) and as somewhat marginal. It is perhaps not surprising that visual languages exhibit more iconicity than auditory languages—objects in the external world tend to have more visual than auditory associations. However, because of the importance attached to the concept of arbitrariness in spoken language, the presence of iconicity in sign languages has been considered as making sign languages uniquely different from spoken languages.

The very frequent occurrence of nonarbitrary symbol–referent relationships in sign languages were seen as proof of the marginal nature of sign languages as human languages. About 50 percent of basic sign vocabulary appears to be iconic, at least in the sense that naive nonsigners will agree on the nature of the imagery when told the meaning of a sign (Klima and Bellugi 1979). The presence of iconicity in signs does not appear, however, to affect the learnability of signs or their subjection to regular processes of historical change.

It is important to emphasize that while sign languages may not show an arbitrary link between symbol and referent or form and meaning, this link is as conventionalized as in spoken languages. It is also important to note that just as speakers of English may not be aware of the sound symbolism in such words as 'wring,' 'writhe,' 'wrist,' etc., so too signers may not be aware of the iconic origins of signs. There remains a great deal of research to be done on the role and status of iconicity in sign language.

3.3 Constraints on Sign Form

Constraints on sign forms arise from two sources: physical limitations and language-specific restrictions. In the first group are those constraints relating to sign production and reception. It has been noted that all locations on the body are not equally available for signs; unlike gesture and mime, signs are limited to an area bounded by the top of the head, the hips, and the width of extended elbows. Within this space, the greatest number of contrasting locations are found on the face.

Other issues of interest in relation to sign production have only just begun to be investigated. One interesting question arises from the relationship between mouth and hand movements. Many signs are accompanied by obligatory mouth patterns (not derived from spoken languages). These mouth movements appear to match certain features of hand movements, such as 'opening,' 'continuous,' and 'punctual' (see Fig. 4).

Battison (1978) proposes two constraints on sign form in ASL which also appear to hold for other sign languages. The 'symmetry condition' states that if both hands move in a two-handed sign, they must both have the same handshape and the same movement. The 'dominance condition' states that when the location of a sign is a passive hand, the handshape of the passive hand must either be identical to that of the active hand, or be one of a set of unmarked handshapes. Later research has shown that while this constraint seems to operate in all sign languages, the inventory

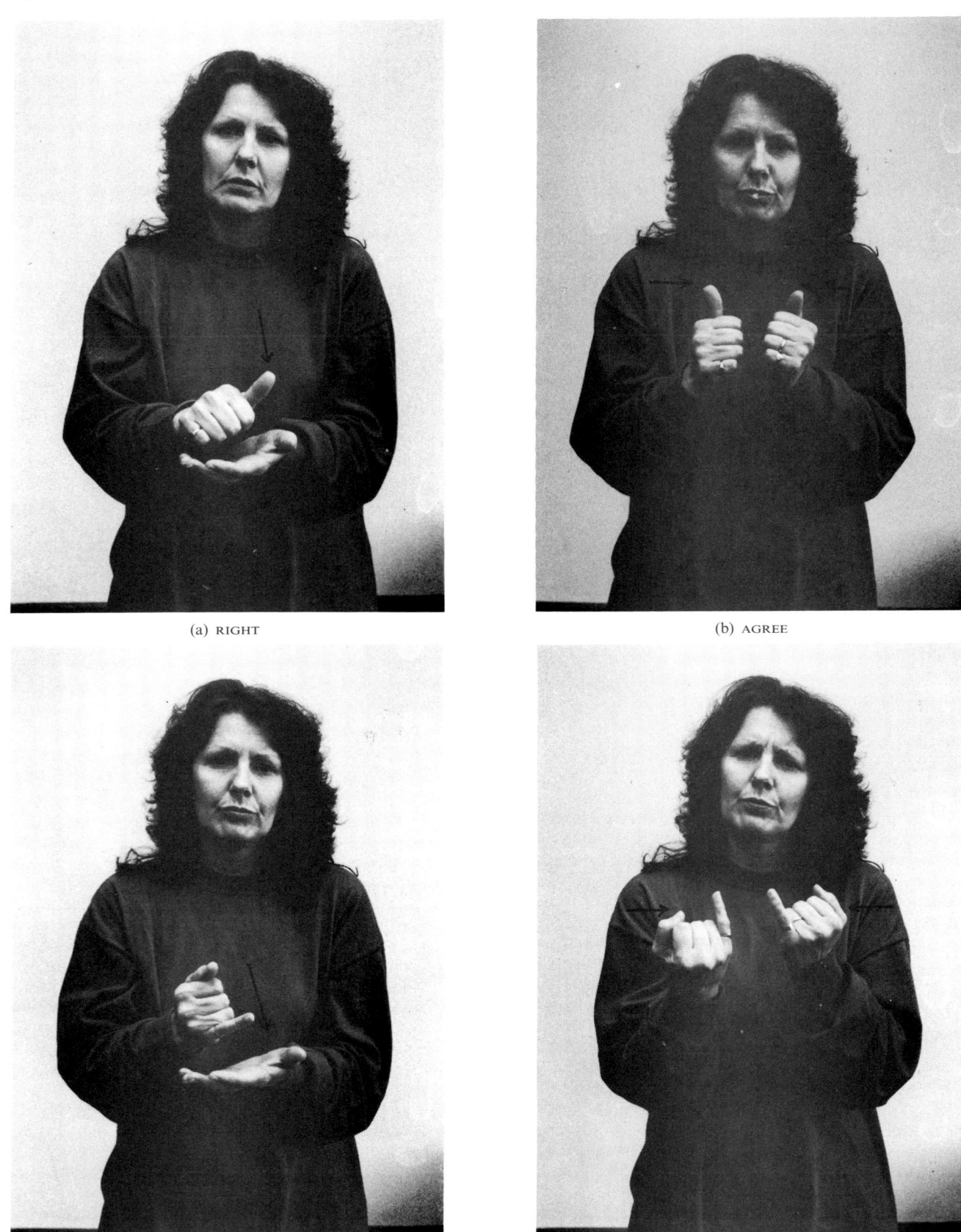

(a) RIGHT

(b) AGREE

(c) WRONG

(d) ARGUE

Figure 3. Signs with 'good' and 'bad' handshapes.

(a) THERE–IS and SHHH

(b) SUCCESS and PAH

Figure 4. Mouth and hand patterns linked (from Schermer 1990).

of unmarked handshapes differs from language to language. It is of interest to note that while it is common to see two hands with different handshapes, in different locations, and with different movements, such structures always reflect some syntactic, rather than lexical form.

Phonological processes operate on the citation forms of signs; amongst those studied are change of location and deletion of hand. Signs tend to move towards the center of signing space and for contact with a location to be lost. It is also common for one hand to be deleted in two-handed signs. Liddell and Johnson (1985) discuss at length a whole series of phonological processes in ASL, including movement epenthesis, metathesis, gemination, perseveration, and anticipation.

3.4 Historical Change in Sign Form

Frishberg (1975) decribes the changes ASL has undergone and Woll (1985) describes changes in BSL over the past 150 years. New signs are often created using iconic imagery, but these new signs soon begin to alter to assimilate to constraints in the language. For example, the BSL sign MOTORCYCLE has its origin in the representation of holding the handlebars of a motorcycle and turning the accelerator. This violates the symmetry condition mentioned earlier, in that only the right hand moves. The sign has therefore changed, so that both hands move. The effects of these

changes has been to reduce the link with the original mime of operating a motorcycle.

Another common change is the movement of signs from the periphery to the center of signing space. This change can be seen taking place in informal conversation: the sign KING, located in citation form on the top of the head is often signed at the side of the head above the ear. This shift can ultimately result in changes in citation forms. Signs (in BSL) which were formerly located at the top of the head are now signed in the space in front of the body (PERHAPS); signs located on the upper arm have moved to the forearm; signs located at the forearm have moved to the wrist (TROUBLE, POLICE, BLUE).

A third change in signs is deletion of the nondominant hand, changing two-handed signs to one-handed signs. Sometimes this has taken place in signs where both hands are active (SCHOOL, FISH, LIVE); it can be seen taking place where one hand serves as a passive base for the active hand (TRUE, WRONG). This reduction does not occur in signs with alternating movements (see Fig. 5).

Assimilation to constraints on sign form can be seen most clearly in compound signs. These are composed of two free morphemes occurring in combination. Research on STS (Swedish Sign Language; Wallin 1983) has distinguished between compounds borrowed from Swedish such as SJUK/HUS from Swedish *sjukhus* 'hospital' and 'genuine' STS compounds. He lists such compounds (translated into

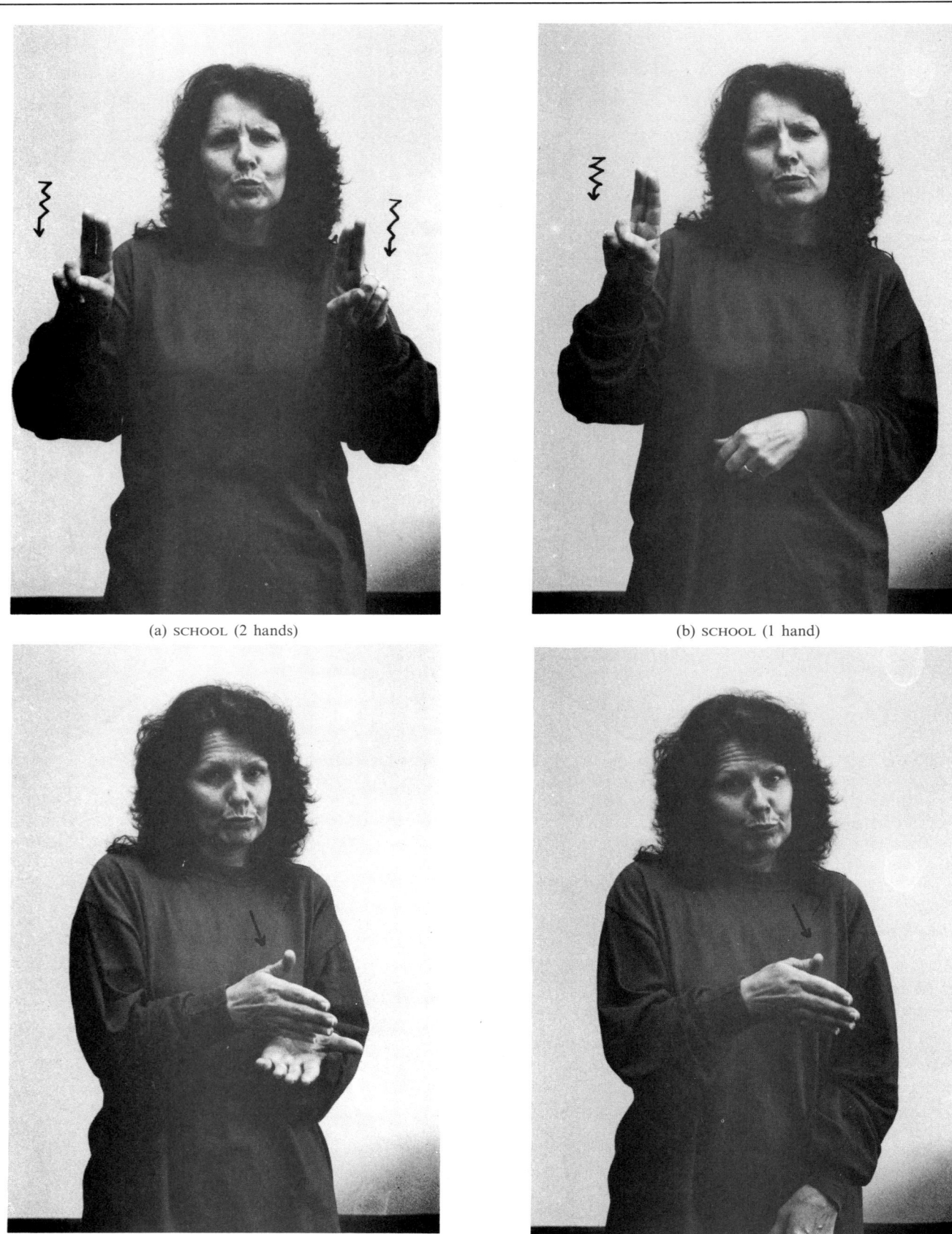

(a) SCHOOL (2 hands)

(b) SCHOOL (1 hand)

(c) TRUE (2 hands)

(b) TRUE (1 hand)

Figure 5. Deletion of nondominant hand.

English glosses) as COFFEE/SIGN (cafe), EAT/PECK (hen), SEE/BORROW (imitate), THINK/EMPTY (forget) and THINK/TIRED (absent-minded). The order of elements in compounds (see Fig. 6) is determined by their height in signing space, with the higher sign preceding the lower. Compounds in BSL most often serve one of two functions: as category terms composed of two exemplars of members of the category (MOTHER/FATHER (parents), TABLE/CHAIR (furniture), MAN/WOMAN (people)), or for certain abstract concepts (THINK/TRUE (believe), SAY/KEEP (promise)). In contrast to the appearance of the two signs when they appear independently, in the compound there are a number of changes reflecting assimilation of movement, handshape, and location. Most prominently, the length of time taken for the articulation of the first sign in a compound is greatly reduced compared to the articulation time of the sign occurring alone.

3.5 Borrowing from Spoken Languages

All signers live among hearing populations using spoken languages, and have some degree of access to the language of the hearing population. This contact is manifested in a number of areas, of which two will be discussed here: fingerspelling and loan-translations.

3.5.1 Fingerspelling

Most deaf populations in Western countries make use of fingerspelling (often confused by the public with sign language) which represents the standard written language through a series of hand configurations and movement. There are many different manual alphabets (and some syllabaries) in use through the world. These can serve as a source for loan signs. Factors affecting the creation of loan signs from fingerspelling (see *Fingerspelling: One-handed*) relate both to features of sign language and to features of fingerspelling form. It appears, for example, that neither ASL nor BSL creates verbs from fingerspelled forms. When fingerspelled words are borrowed into a sign language they begin to change form to accommodate to sign constraints and may ultimately become unrecognizable by users of the language as having originated in fingerspelling.

Battison (1978) defined loan signs in ASL as those in which the letter or letters from a fingerspelled word have become modified to be part of the sign language itself, and as not containing more than two letters. Within Battison's definition, movement or changed place of articulation must be added to the basic letter handshape. For a language such as BSL, making use of a two-handed alphabet, many of the loan examples would not meet Battison's criteria. Many loan signs in languages using two-handed alphabets, such as Norwegian and British Sign Languages, consist of the initial letter of the word together with a modified movement. In other cases historical records demonstrate that through folk etymology a fingerspelling handshape is imposed on an already existing sign . Thus, the bilingualism of the majority of signers means that fingerspelling serves as a continual source for new signs as well as for code-switching.

3.5.2 Loan Signs

Apart from fingerspelled loan signs derived from written words, a few signs are borrowed by translation from spoken words. These are found most frequently in place names and proper names, and are often treated as humorous. Examples include 'Manchester,' signed as MAN CHEST or 'Newcastle' as NEW CASTLE. A variant of this process can be seen in the use of the sign PISTOL for 'Bristol.' Here the mouth pattern in articulating the word 'Bristol' is similar to that in 'pistol.'

4. Sign Language Grammar

The function of grammar in a spoken language may be regarded as organizing nonlinear meanings into a linear order, and the function of a grammar in a sign language as organising nonlinear meanings into both spatial and linear order. Those features common to both signed and spoken languages reflect, in this view, nonmodality-specific universals of language.

The presentation of grammatical data from sign language is thus hampered by the difficulty of presenting transcriptions so that they represent both linear and simultaneous data. Examples below make use of both illustrations and glosses, in which English words will be used to represent signs, with inflections in which the form of a sign is altered, and nonmanual elements of sign strings, marked as super- or subscripts.

4.1 Bound Forms

The description of signs so far has mainly involved signs which occur as free forms. Bilingual signers can produce citation forms of these signs in response to the question 'What is the sign for *x*?' Other signs occur only in bound forms, and a number of these will be discussed briefly. The first example below, in Sect. 4.1.1, adds a movement morpheme to a verb stem consisting of a handshape and location; the second example, in Sect. 4.1.2, adds a handshape morpheme to a noun stem consisting of a location and movement; the third example, *wh*-conversion, may more properly be described as derivational, rather than inflectional, but operates in the same way, adding a handshape and movement to a location.

4.1.1 Negative Incorporation

Research on ASL, BSL, and LSF (French Sign Language) has revealed a process in these three languages by which certain verbs are converted to negatives through the addition of a bound form (Deuchar 1987). In ASL and LSF this is an 'outward twisting movement of the moving hand(s) from the place where the sign is made' (Woodward and de Santis 1977); in BSL negative incorporation 'involves the modification of the affirmative of a sign including a movement of upwards rotation of the hand, and change of handshape, if applicable, from a closed to an open handshape' (Deuchar 1987).

Negative incorporation can be applied only to a small class of verbs, which can generally be described as 'experiential' (in BSL, such verbs as KNOW, WANT, LIKE, POSSIBLE, AGREE, GOOD; see Fig. 7).

4.1.2 Numerical Incorporation

Certain signs in BSL such as YEARS-OLD, POUNDS (£), O'CLOCK, YEARS-AHEAD, YEARS-PAST, DAYS-AHEAD,

(a) THINK

(b) TRUE (2 hands)

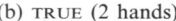

(c) BELIEVE

Figure 6. Compound signs.

(a) LIKE

(b) NOT LIKE

Figure 7. Negative incorporation.

DAYS–PAST, WEEKS–AHEAD, WEEKS–PAST and WEEKS–DURATION obligatorily incorporate a numeral affix into the sign root. Strings such as *FIVE WEEKS–AHEAD or *THREE YEARS–OLD (with the sign for, e.g., FIVE followed by the uninflected signs WEEKS–AHEAD) are ungrammatical, in contrast to FIVE–WEEKS–AHEAD (see Fig. 8).

4.1.3 Wh-questions

Wh-questions in BSL are formed with signs which can be glossed as HOW–OLD, WHO, HOW–MANY, WHEN, WHERE and HOW–MUCH. The majority of these have spread fingers and wiggling movement. This handshape and movement are the same as in the sign MANY. The sign WHEN, for example, has the same location as DAYS–PAST and DAYS–AHEAD; the sign HOW–OLD the same location as YEARS–OLD, and HOW–MANY the same location as the cardinal numbers. These forms may therefore be analyzed as similar to those which accept numeral incorporation, but with MANY rather than a numeral incorporated (see Fig. 9).

4.2 Plurals

Those sign languages studied so far exhibit three mechanisms for the formation of plural forms of nouns: reduplication of movement, reduplication of handshape, and addition of a quantity marker. With a few exceptions, most signs can pluralise in only one of these ways.

4.2.1 Reduplication of Movement

In pluralization by reduplication of movement, speed of movement is nonsignificant (in contrast to inflection of verbs) and the movement is repeated with a slight shift of location for each repetition (in BSL, for example, BOOK, CHILD, HOUSE, IDEA; see Fig. 10).

4.2.2 Reduplication of Handshape

In pluralization by reduplication of handshape, a one-handed sign is pluralized by articulating the sign with both hands and alternating movement (AEROPLANE, CUP). Like reduplication of movement, there is often some distributional meaning attached to this form of reduplication (CUPS–ALL–OVER–THE–PLACE).

4.2.3 Addition of Quantifier

Some signs cannot reduplicate either handshape or movement. Plurality in these nouns (MAN, CAR, SHIRT) is expressed by the addition of a quantifier such as MANY or a numeral.

The assignment of signs to one of these three classes is not related to a sign's meaning, but is linked to its derivational origin and to its formational properties. Signs with a repeated movement in citation form tend not to inflect by reduplication: signs with continuous contact between the hand and a body part are less likely to inflect by redupli-

(a) FIVE

(b) WEEKS–AHEAD

(c) FIVE WEEKS–AHEAD

Figure 8. Numeral incorporation.

(a) YESTERDAY

(b) WHEN

Figure 9. Wh-questions.

cation than those in neutral space (as signs in BSL have moved towards neutral space since the eighteenth century, some now reduplicate for plurals which did not do so formerly). Nouns formed by a derivational process from verbs do not take reduplication of movement, even where they are located in neutral space (CAR derived from DRIVE, BROOM derived from SWEEP).

4.3 Verbs and Space

It has been claimed that there are two distinct uses of space in sign languages. The first is a type of mapping of inherent spatial relationships among objects in the real world (topographical space), and the second is an internal representation for syntax based on abstract linguistic syntactic properties (syntactic space). In this second use of space, locations are assigned to grammatical subjects and objects, and verbs move towards, from, and between these locations. One simple way to distinguish the two is that in the first, the referent is *at* a location, while in the second, the referent *is* the location. Some features of verb classes relating to these different uses of space will be discussed here; see Padden (1990) and Liddell (1990) for detailed discussion of these issues).

Sign languages exhibit three verb classes: plain or invariant verbs, agreement verbs, and spatial verbs. Plain verbs exhibit no inflection for person or number and do not accept any locative affixes (BSL signs LIKE, TASTE,

DREAM). Agreement verbs inflect for person, number, or aspect, but do not accept locative affixes (BSL signs GIVE, TELEPHONE, SHOW). The third group, spatial verbs, do not inflect for person, number, or aspect, but do accept locative affixes (BSL signs MOVE, CARRY, HIT).

This third group has also been analyzed as forming a predicate classifier system (McDonald 1983; Supalla 1986). Verb stems for movement and location, based on the shape of the involved object, combine with affixes which signal adverbial, pronominal, and aspectual information. Five subsets of spatial verbs have been suggested:

(a) predicates with locative affixes, MOVE, PUT;

(b) predicates with locative, instrument-classifier, and manner affixes, CARRY BY HAND;

(c) predicates with locative, manner, and noun-classifier affixes, VEHICLE–MOVE, PERSON–MOVE;

(d) predicates with locative classifiers on the body, HIT–IN–THE–EYE, POINT–A–GUN–AT–SOMEONE'S–HEAD;

(e) predicates with locative affixes and body-part noun classifiers, CLENCH–FIST.

The contrast between the agreement and spatial verbs can be seen in Fig. 11 in the examples of the signs GIVE (agreement) and CARRY-BY-HAND (spatial). In 'He gives her [something]' the starting point of the movement identifies the subject and the final point of the movement identifies the indirect object. The first and last positions of the verb

(a) IDEA   (b) IDEAS

Figure 10. Plurals with movement reduplication.

are therefore person-agreement morphemes. In 'He carries [it] by hand from A to B,' the starting point of the movement identifies the starting location of the object and the final point of the movement identifies the final location of the object. The first and last positions of the verb are therefore locative morphemes.

This view of handshape as representing a member of a class of nouns in polymorphemic verbs has also been extended to a more general view of handshapes as proforms. Engberg–Pedersen (1987) has proposed a three-way classification of handshapes in Danish Sign Language. Some handshapes which occur in nouns cannot occur with the same meaning in predicates. The example in Fig. 12, *DENMARK SEA-SURROUND ('Denmark is surrounded by the sea'), is ungrammatical. Other handshapes occur both in nouns and in predicates. For example, the handshape found in TREE can occur both in the noun TREE and in predicates such as TREE-FALL ('the tree fell'). A third group of handshapes occur in predicates but not in the associated nouns: CAR TURN-LEFT ('the car turned left').

Forms can be described in terms of shape (see Fig. 13): 'two-dimensional' (flat hand representing WALL, TABLE, POSTCARD, BICYCLE) and 'three-dimensional' (clawed hand representing CAKE, BALL). There is a second group which relates to the handling properties of objects. These give us such forms as 'handle a compact or small cylindrical object' (DAGGER, LAWNMOWER (= handle), 'handle a thin, flattish object' (PAPER, CLOTH), 'handle a round

object' (KNOW, BALL, LID), 'handle a small object' (COIN, FLOWER), 'handle a small narrow object' (PLUG, SWITCH).

The development of frozen forms (see Fig. 14) can produce abstract verbs, nouns, or prepositions (ON = flat, wide object). In ASL, the form labeled as 'handle a compact or small cylindrical object' is used in such signs as PRACTICE, MAKE, and WORK. It appears impossible to predict which forms will 'freeze' in which way: the BSL sign WITH derives from the form 'handle a thin, flattish object'; the ASL sign WITH derives from the form 'handle a compact or small cylindrical object.' The ASL sign FALL has the properties *individual, flat, narrow*, but is used with nouns which do not have those properties, such as APPLE (see Fig. 14). The BSL sign CHOOSE, which has the properties *whole, circular, two-dimensional*, can be used with nouns as diverse as DRESS, FRUIT, BOX, etc.

4.4 Aspectual Inflection

The incorporation of aspect affixes into verb stem markers has been mentioned briefly in the section above. In this section, aspect and manner marking will be discussed more fully. Those sign languages studied so far all show complex marking of aspect on the verb, incorporating information regarding manner, frequency, and duration of an activity. This is normally accomplished by altering the movement of the verb itself. An exception is perfective aspect, which

<table>
<tr><td>(a) 'He gives it to her'</td><td>(b) 'He carries it from here to there'</td></tr>
</table>

Figure 11. Agreement versus spatial verbs.

in BSL is largely lexicalized, marked by the addition of the verb FINISH as an auxiliary to the main verb of the sentence. (FINISH can also occur on its own as a main verb.) Deuchar's (1984) data includes such sentences as I KILL ALL FINISH ('I've killed all [the weeds]'), SUGAR PUT–IN FINISH ('I've put in the sugar') and 3-PERSON SAY YOU ALL READ FINISH ('He says, "Have you finished reading all [of the newspaper"]?'). While her data do not include any examples of FINISH co-occurring with present or future time reference (thus suggesting that FINISH might be a tense marker) other researchers have found examples without past time reference such as BUTTONS PUT–IN–A–ROW FIN-ISH, DRAW–SMILE FINISH ('he puts the buttons in a row,' 'then draws a smile') or MUST EGG BEAT FINISH ('you must beat the eggs [first]') which confirm her interpretation of FINISH as a perfective aspect marker (see Fig. 15).

Intensity is marked by changes in speed, size, and force with which the verb is articulated. This gives such contrasts as STUDY/CRAM, JOG/RUN/SPRINT. Duration and frequency are marked by reduplication or elongation of the verb movement. Of the three major categories of morphological process two, reduplication and modification, are used far more frequently than the other, affixation. Bergman (1983) has focused on five morphological markers for aspect in STS: fast reduplication, slow reduplication, initial stop, doubling, and initial hold.

In Fig. 16, the verb LOOK–AT is shown in its uninflected form, together with the forms showing fast reduplication (='look at again and again') and slow reduplication (='look at for a long time'). These terms were first used for ASL by Fischer (1973), and Bergman (1983) has used the same terms for Swedish Sign Language. However, in BSL the two patterns do not differ so much in speed, but in their differing cyclic structures. In slow reduplication, there are pauses between each repetition of the verb; in fast reduplication, there is even movement, with less sense of cycles having intervening pauses.

An important observation first made by Supalla and Newport (1978), in describing aspect in ASL verbs, is that reduplication does not apply to the citation form of the sign, but to its underlying form. For example, in BSL the citation form of the sign WALK contains a repeated movement. If this were simply reduplicated we would have four movements. Instead, movement occurs only three times in the reduplicated form. This suggests that reduplication is added to a single underlying movement rather than the repeated movement of the citation form.

The meanings associated with slow and fast reduplication vary according to the semantics of the verb. Punctual verbs in BSL, such as JUMP, normally undergo only fast reduplication with the meanings of regularity, repetition of the action, or frequency; durational verbs, such as WAIT, undergo both fast and slow reduplication. Fast reduplication suggests habitual action; slow reduplication of durational verbs conveys continuous action. Stative verbs like ANGRY or INTERESTED can undergo slow reduplication

(a) DENMARK

(b) *DENMARK SURROUNDED BY SEA

(c) TREE

(d) TREE FALL

Figure 12. **Handshape** classes.

(a) FLOWER

(b) WRITE A POSTCARD

Figure 13. Proform handshapes.

only; this is understood as intensifying the verb (VERY–ANGRY, REALLY–INTERESTED).

The combination of inflection for role and aspect can result in visually complex configurations where the use of two hands and their orientations indicates reciprocity of action, and the movement pattern indicates inflection for durative aspect.

4.5 Pronominalization

There is a debate as to whether sign languages distinguish only between first person and all other persons, or whether there is a basically three-way contrast between first, second, and others. For the purposes of this discussion, a three-way distinction will be adopted.

First and second person pronouns always have a deictic function; third, fourth, and additional person pronouns can be either deictic or anaphoric. Anaphoric pronouns can only occur following the localization of the referent noun in the location assigned to the pronoun. Nouns articulated in the space in front of the body are, for example, moved to third person space; nouns located on a body part would be followed by an indexing of third person space. This assignment of location to a referent (see Sect. 4.3 above) then continues through the discourse until it is changed. To indicate anaphoric reference, the signer indexes the location previously assigned to that referent. In an example from Deuchar (1984: 97): TWO THREE FOUR HELP HE MARSHAL KNOW IT USED TO IT ('He helps to marshal numbers two,

three, and four. He knows it, he's used to it'), the anaphoric pronoun HE refers to someone named earlier in the discourse. The same person is the subject of the verbs KNOW and USED–TO, so the pronoun can be deleted as the referent of HE has remained unchanged. The pronouns IT in KNOW IT, etc. are not deleted since they are not part of the same topic.

The operation of anaphora, participant role marking, classifiers, inflection for aspect, and the availability of two articulators can all be seen in the following BSL example 'The woman keeps hitting the man.' In this, the sign MAN is articulated with the left hand, followed by the 'person' classifier, located to fourth person space. The left hand remains in the 'person' classifier handshape and fourth person location, while the remainder of the sentence is signed. The sign WOMAN is articulated with the right hand, followed by the 'person' classifier, located to third person space. The verb HIT, an agreement verb, is then articulated, moving on a track from the subject (third person) to object (fourth person). This movement is reduplicated (see Fig. 17).

lh: MAN CL-person INDEX$_4$

rh: WOMAN CL-personINDEX$_{33}$HIT$_{4f.redup}$

4.6 Sign Order

In an early study of ASL, it was suggested that 'the basic word-order in ASL is Subject–Verb–Object' (Fischer 1975).

3905

(a) APPLE

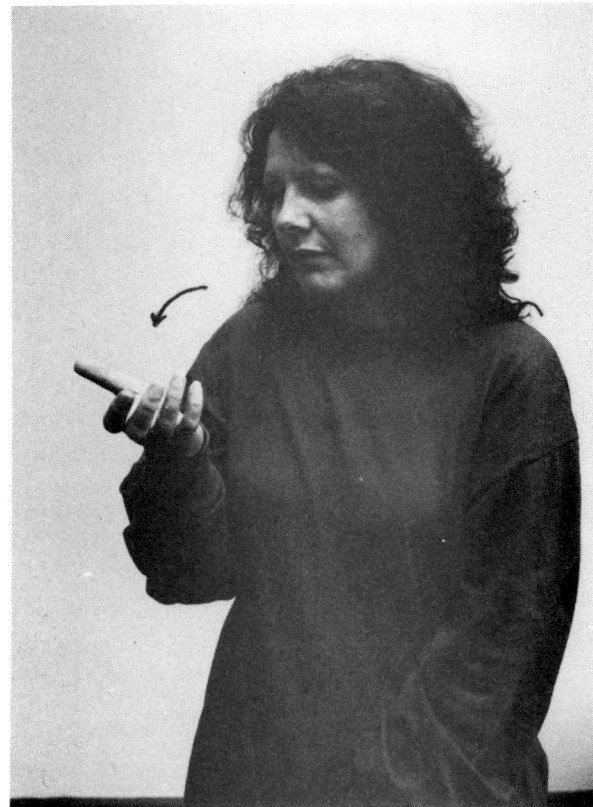

(b) APPLE FALL

Figure 14. Frozen forms.

Work has been undertaken on sign order in other languages and there is now evidence that different sign languages may differ in preferred order. In BSL, Deuchar (1983) has suggested that sign order is best described in terms of topic–comment structure, using Li and Thompson's (1976) criteria for identifying a topic-prominent language, such as the absence of passive constructions, the absence of dummy subjects such as 'there' and 'there is,' and the existence of 'double subject' constructions, with the topic followed by the subject. 'The woman hits the man,' shows typical order in BSL. Deuchar has related this topic–comment preference to the status of BSL as a language used mostly for informal conversation. In contrast, experimental studies of Italian Sign Language and Swiss–German Sign Language by Boyes-Braem (1987) have indicated that Italian signers show a preference for Subject-Verb-Object ordering, while the Swiss subjects show a topic-comment preference.

4.7 Simultaneity

The discussion on sign order obscures the important observation that linear order is not the only available dimension in which syntax can occur. In sign languages, the availability of two articulators moving in visible space offers opportunities for constructions which cannot occur in spoken languages, such as the simultaneous articulation of a noun with one hand and its modifier with the other, as in:

lh: BOY ⎫
          ⎬ 'small boy'
rh: SMALL ⎭

or

lh: BORN ⎫
          ⎬ 'born deaf'
rh: DEAF ⎭

While opportunities for simultaneous modification are limited, because of the necessity of having two one-handed signs, there is a substantial role for nonmanual behaviors occurring simultaneously with manual signs in such processes as the marking of questions, negation, size, and intensity. These can be seen to parallel prosodic aspects of spoken language such as stress, intonation, and tone.

4.8 Nonmanual Question Marking

Yes/no questions in BSL are most frequently formed without the use of manual question markers, but with a specific marking of facial expression which occurs simultaneously with the manual part of the sentence. In complex sentences with 'embedding, the nonmanual question markers occur only over the duration of the clause being questioned:

```
                   q.....................................
lh: WITH PAT GO/PAT STAY THERE

rh:                              YOU RETURN
```

When you go with Pat, will she stay while you come back?

FINISH

Figure 15. BSL sign FINISH.

This facial expression has as its most prominent feature raised eyebrows. *Wh*-questions are also accompanied by specific facial activity; this normally consists of furrowed eyebrows. This division is not absolute, however, and appears to be related to the information load of the question. Where *wh*-questions have the function of checking information already received, for example, raised brows would normally be present. This finding has led to the suggestion that rather than describing these brow patterns as nonmanual grammar, they should be regarded as some marker of pragmatic function, independent of grammatical structure.

4.9 Nonmanual Negation

There are a number of signs expressing negation: for example, in BSL, NEVER, NOTHING, NOT and NOT–YET (NOT–YET is mainly used as a marker of imperfective aspect), but negation is also frequently accomplished by the use of nonmanual activity (headshaking) superimposed on the manual component of the signing:

neg...................

SIGN TEACH VOICE
SOUND

I teach signing with no voice and no sound.

As with question marking, the nonmanual feature extends over the portion of the utterance being negated.

4.10 Other Nonmanual Activity

Investigations on other roles of nonmanual activity have been undertaken. Liddell (1980) and Deuchar (1984) suggest that head nods may function as assertion markers in ASL and BSL respectively. Liddell's claim that nonmanual marking of restrictive relative clauses takes place in ASL is disputed by Deuchar (1984) and Thompson (1977) who argue that this marking is at discourse level, and identifies material mentioned earlier in the discourse or present in the context, which the signer desires to make prominent. In other work on nonmanual activities, Baker and Padden (1978) have studied those features which occur at the juncture of 'if' and 'then' clauses and at the relinquishing of a turn by a signer.

5. Neurolinguistic Features

When first rediscovered in the 1970s, sign language posed interesting questions not only for linguists but for psychologists and neurological scientists. At first glance, sign language appears to have a fundamental difference in neurological terms: all spoken languages have a left hemisphere localization and damage to areas of this side of the brain create major difficulties in language use; sign language, on the other hand, appeared to have all the hallmarks of right hemisphere functioning—it was visual, spatial, and appeared to require the manipulation of hands and body in space. Are sign languages a class of languages with a localization in the right hemisphere?

Early research on the presentation of visual sign stimuli to right and left visual hemifields seemed to confirm this divergence of function and localization. However, these experiments were based on static sign pictures and the effects which were found tended to be weak, as did the deaf people's effects in written language localization. When moving stimuli were used, the effects began to reverse. Deaf people functioned rather better in identifying signs presented to the left side of the brain, just as they did with words.

Work by Ursula Bellugi and colleagues at the Salk Institute in the USA has taken this investigation further. By examining patients with various forms of brain damage they were able to make deductions on the functioning of sign language (Bellugi and Klima, 1990). They were able to separate patients with a right-hemisphere lesion and those with a left-hemisphere lesion. The latter showed sign language aphasia with a varying effect on sign production, sign syntax, length of utterance and parameters of sign formation. The former showed little effect on these factors of sign use and it was concluded that they were not sign aphasic. However, they did show clear deficits in spatial processing.

From these results Bellugi and Klima were able to describe the differences between spatial syntax and spatial mapping. The former is a major feature of *signed language* where the use of space has a grammatical function; the latter concerns the description of objects and events in space (see Sect. 4.3 on syntactic space). While left-hemisphere damaged patients had problems in using space in a syntactic way to create scenes, it was the right-hemisphere damaged patients who had the major difficulties in describing, for example, the layout of their rooms. Where space is a matter of imaging and then representing physical layout, right

(a) LOOK–AT

(b) LOOK–AT (fast reduplication)—again and again

(c) LOOK–AT (slow reduplication)—for a long time

Figure 16. The verb LOOK–AT.

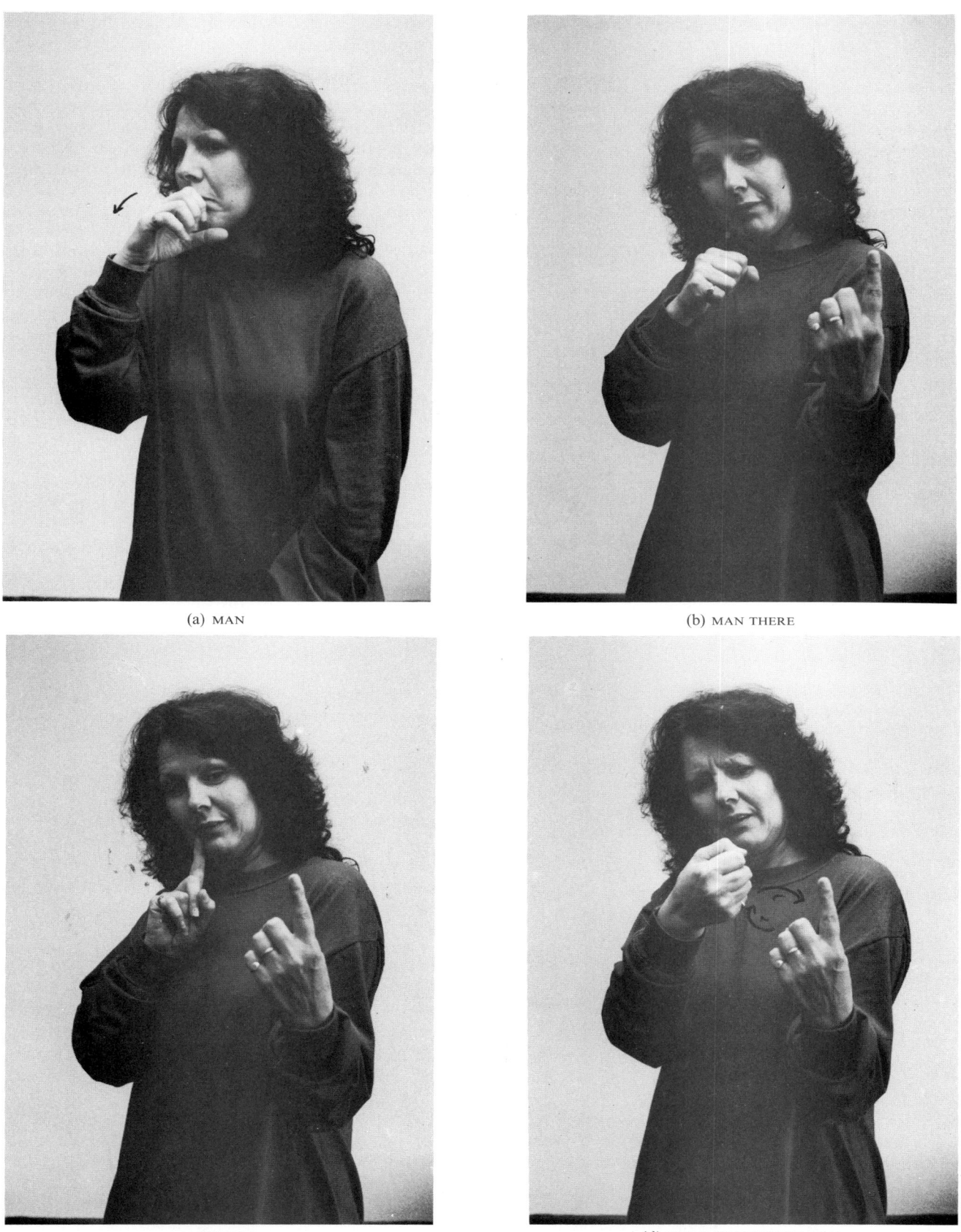

(a) MAN

(b) MAN THERE

(c) WOMAN

(d) KEEPS HITTING THE MAN

Figure 17. Sign sequence 'the woman keeps hitting the man.'

hemisphere processes are implicated; where syntactic functions of space are involved, it is the left hemisphere which is called into play.

Linked to these findings has been the contrasting use of facial expression for affect and for linguistic functions. Deaf people are sensitive to facial affect just as hearing people are and deaf children seem to develop a sensitivity to this in their early years (see *Language Acquisition in the Child*). Bellugi and others have been able to show how these uses of facial expression seem to interact with hemispheric lesions. Again they confirm the notion that linguistic functions of visual stimulation are localized in the left hemisphere and affect perception is localized in the right.

The evidence seems very clear: speech processing is not necessary for the development of hemisphere specialization and sign language follows a similar pattern to that of spoken language.

6. Sign Learning

Deaf people learn to sign in a natural way through interaction with other members of the community. However, for hearing people (who are learning sign), the length of residence in the Deaf community is usually very short. Teachers or parents frequently study sign language at lunchtimes or at evening sessions of short duration. There is no *Deafland* (although this has been proposed by some writers) and as a result culture and community life are rarely sampled whilst learning sign. The vast resource of people, customs, culture, and literature which is available for the learners of say, French, is simply not there for those who wish to learn a sign language.

Hearing people usually have poor skills in sign language and this has a major impact on the lives of Deaf people. In power relations, hearing people usually dominate. When they sign badly to a Deaf person the latter is rarely in a position to correct and so errors which would otherwise be corrected in peer interaction are left untouched and are often consolidated in the hearing person because 'the Deaf person has seemed to understand' (see *Sociolinguistics of Sign*).

Teaching method has been poorly developed, often consisting of no more than vocabulary learning. As linguistic knowledge develops, grammar is taught within an immersion environment. Many countries do not yet have a tradition of Deaf people teaching sign language but programes such as that described by Denmark (1990) have become more common in Western countries and are leading to a major shift in the perception of sign language both by hearing and by Deaf people.

7. Sign in Education

The educational arena has long been the battleground of Deaf people's hopes and fears. While linguists have studied and learned from the language, educators have been constrained by a special education model of deviance and remediation. They work in a context where 90 percent of deaf children are born in hearing families where there is no history of deafness. A deaf baby is seen as an abnormality. Education has embraced this view and has worked to eradicate the abnormality. Since the beginning of education for

the deaf in the mid-eighteenth century, the key focus has been on the learning of the spoken and written language of the majority. This has become the focus of much ill-informed debate and the cycles of educational belief which have gone from sign methodology to speech-only have done great damage to the development of Deaf people. de l'Epée was a key figure in the development of deaf people in the eighteenth century and of signing in education throughout Europe. His late vocation to deaf children led him to develop a signed method to teach literacy to the deaf child (see *Sign Languages in Europe: History and Research*). The ideas of de l'Epée spread throughout Europe but were contested by the German approach, led by Heinecke, which held that only an oral approach which suppressed signing would be in the long-term interest of deaf children. The 'combined method' was developed in the UK as something of a balance against these overwhelming polarized views. For most of the nineteenth century, sign approaches held sway in the UK, in the USA, and in other parts of Europe. Yet there was also a tendency to revert to a speech-only approach. This began to occur en masse towards the end of the century and the congress in Milan in 1880 is considered something of a turning point when the Italian-dominated Congress resolved to banish sign language altogether. Coupled with the growing linguistic pressure to recognise only spoken language, attitudes to sign in education and then in society have been passionately negative for most of this century.

A significant factor in this has been the advance of technology and latterly, and perversely, the advance of the civil rights movement. Schools in the nineteenth century attracted students on the basis of their performance with their current pupils. Often there were open days where the successes were paraded. Since the audience were likely to be hearing speakers, the emphasis was on showing how well the pupils had learned to speak and to write (the former being more significant). What became apparent was that late deafened or partially hearing pupils were more impressive than those with severe and profound losses. Oralism grew on the strength of the performance of these pupils. By the end of the nineteenth century, it was becoming possible to diagnose children more effectively and to discover the hearing loss earlier; between the World Wars, hearing aids came to be developed and were in circulation in Western countries after World War II. These factors led to a refining and strengthening of the oral position as more appropriate targeting of speech training could be done. Because of the nature of the distribution of extent of hearing loss there were more children who had partial losses than those with profound losses and gradually the 'oral successes' could be transferred to the mainstream setting as a vindication of the policies of denial of sign. Unfortunately, those Deaf children with a profound loss suffered extensively from this speech orientated curriculum.

The Civil Rights Movement in the late 1960s, while opening up the possibilities of recognition as a minority group, also posed a major problem. Civil Rights, when applied by the parents, were seen as a right to 'normal education.' While the study of sign gathered strength in the mid-1970s the movement toward normalized education in mainstream schools gathered pace. Parents were offered education in ordinary schools as a way of demonstrating the normality of their child. Rarely in these circumstances, did the child have access to sign and was increasingly unlikely to meet other deaf children. For many deaf people, this was a return to the situation before deaf schools had been founded where deaf people had little interaction with others and had no opportunity to develop sign—the same situation as in the eighteenth century. Ladd (1991) describes his experience in mainstream education and the socialization and language problems which it caused.

In the mid-1980s, a movement towards bilingualism was proposed which has begun to find models in schools for the deaf and in mainstream schools, where Deaf adults are given a role as teachers and assistants. Coupled with the problems of hearing people's attempts at mastery of sign, the meaningful access to language for Deaf children remains somewhat patchy.

It is the aim of most education systems to ensure competence in speech-related activities; curriculum access and learning itself tend to be secondary goals. To maintain this position in the face of growing advocacy of sign, educators developed various forms of systematic sign–speech mixes, whereby the teacher is able to speak and to sign at the same time. However, it is the underlying structure of the spoken form which dominates; the sign component is bolted on as and when it fits. Even in highly systematic systems where markers are invented to deal with divergence between sign and speech, the pressures of the teaching situation lead to the selective omission of the sign component. Not suprisingly, although this 'total communication' has an effect on behavior and personal development, it has not yet been able to demonstrate significant progress in language areas. New approaches to bilingualism in Scandinavia and in the USA have made sign language a central feature and have begun to see learning as the priority. It is these models which now dominate the debate on sign methods in education.

Interest in sign language has been relatively recent but considerable progress has been made. Sign language work challenges many of the assumptions about the dominance of speech and allows beliefs about how spoken language determines cognition to be examined. In addition, it provides a fascinating study of a unique class of languages used by a similarly defined minority group in each country of the world.

Bibliography

Baker C, Padden C 1978 Focusing on the nonmanual components of American Sign Language. In: Siple P (ed.) *Understanding Language through Sign Language Research.* Academic Press, New York

Battison R 1978 *Lexical Borrowing in American Sign Language.* Linstok Press, Silver Spring, MD

Bellugi U, Klima E 1990 Properties of visual spatial languages. In: Prillwitz S, Vollhaber T (eds.) *Sign Language Research and Application.* Signum, Hamburg

Bergman B 1983 Verbs and adjectives: Morphological processes in Swedish Sign Language. In: Kyle J G, Woll B (eds.) *Language in Sign.* Croom Helm, London

Bloomfield L 1933 *Language.* Holt, Rinehart and Winston, New York

Bonet J P 1620 *Reduccion de las Letras y Arte para Enseñar a ablar los mudos.* Francisco Abaraca de Angulo, Madrid

Boyes-Braem P 1987 Semantic roles in Italian Sign Language and in German Swiss Sign Language. (Unpublished paper presented at the 1987 International Pragmatics Conference, Antwerp)

Bulwer J B 1644 *Chirologia: Or the Natural Language of the Hands.* Whitaker, London

Bulwer J B 1648 *Philocophus: Or the Deafe and Dumbe Man's Friend.* Humphrey Moseley, London

Condillac J 1746 *An Essay on the Origin of Human Knowledge.* Scholars' Facsimiles and Reprints, Gainsville, FL

Conrad R 1979 *The Deaf School Child.* Harper and Row, London

Dalgarno G 1661 *Ars Signorum, Vulgo Character Universalis et Lingua Philosophica.* Hayes, London

Danby H 1933 *The Mishnah.* Oxford University Press, Oxford

Denmark A C 1990 British Sign Language tutor training course. In: Prillwitz S, Vollhaber T (eds.) *Sign Language Research and Application.* Signum, Hamburg

Deuchar M 1983 Is BSL an SVO language? In: Kyle J G, Woll B (eds.) *Language in Sign.* Croom Helm, London

Deuchar M 1984 *British Sign Language.* Routledge and Kegan Paul, London

Deuchar M 1987 Negative incorporation in three sign languages. In: Kyle J G (ed.) *Sign and School.* Multilingual Matters, Clevedon

Diderot J 1751 Letter on the deaf and dumb. In: Caldwell R L 1971 Structure de la lettre sur les sourds et muets. *Studies on Voltaire and the 18th Century* 84: 109–22

Engberg-Pedersen E 1987 Proforms in morphology, syntax and discourse (Unpublished paper)

l'Epée Abbé de 1776 *Instruction of the Deaf and Dumb by Means of Methodical Signs: The True Manner of Instructing the Deaf and Dumb Confirmed by Long Experience.* Le Crozet, Paris

Fischer S D 1973 Two processes of reduplication in American Sign Language. *Foundations of Language* 9: 469–80

Fischer S D 1975 Influences on word order change in American Sign Language. In: Li C (ed.) *Word Order and Word Order Change.* University of Texas Press, Austin, TX

Frishberg N 1975 Arbitrariness and iconicity in ASL. *Language* 51: 696–719

Groce N 1986 *Everyone Here Spoke Sign Language.* Harvard University Press, Cambridge, MA

Hewes 1976 The current status of the gestural theory of language origin. In: Harnad S R, Steklis H D, Lancaster J (eds.) *Origins and Evaluation of Language and Speech.* New York Academy of Sciences, New York

Klima E, Bellugi U 1979 *The Signs of Language.* Harvard University Press, Cambridge, MA

Knowlson J R 1965 The idea of gesture as a universal language in the XVIIth & XVIIIth Centuries. *Journal of the History of Ideas* 4: 420–508

Kyle J G 1989 Sign Language as cognition for deaf people. *Applied Cognitive Psychology* 3: 109–25

Kyle J G, Woll B (eds.) *Language in Sign.* Croom Helm, London

Ladd P 1991 In: Gregory S, Taylor J (eds.) *Being Deaf.* Pinter, London

Li C N, Thompson S A 1976 Subject and topic: A new typology of language. In: Li C N (ed.) *Subject and Topic.* Academic Press, New York

Liddell S K 1980 *American Sign Language Syntax.* Mouton, The Hague

Liddell S K 1990 Four functions of a locus: Re-examining the structure of space in ASL. In: Lucas C (ed.) *Sign Language Research: Theoretical Issues.* Gallaudet University Press, Washington, DC

Liddell S K, Johnson R E 1985 American Sign Language: The phonological base (Unpublished paper, Gallaudet University)

McDonald B 1983 Levels of analysis in sign language research. In: Kyle J G, Woll B (eds.) *Language in Sign*. Croom Helm, London

Padden C 1990 The relation between space and grammar in ASL verb morphology. In: Lucas C (ed.) *Sign Language Research: Theoretical Issues*. Gallaudet University Press, Washington, DC

Schermer G 1990 *In Search of a Language: Influences from Spoken Dutch on Sign Language of the Netherlands*. Elswoon, Delft

Stokoe W C 1960 Sign Language Structure: An Outline of the Visual Communication System of the American Deaf. Studies in Linguistics, Occasional Paper 8, University of Buffalo, New York

Stout G F 1899 *A Manual of Psychology*. University Correspondence College Press, London

Supalla E, Newport E L 1978 How many seats in a chair? The derivation of nouns and verbs in American Sign Language. In: Siple P (ed.) *Understanding Language through Sign Language Research*. Academic Press, New York

Supalla T 1986 The classifier system in ASL. In: Craig T C (ed.) *Noun Classes and Categorization: Typological Studies in Language*. John Benjamin, Philadelphia, PA

Thompson J 1977 The lack of subordination in American Sign Language. In: Friedman L A (ed.) *On the Other Hand: New Perspectives on American Sign Language*. Academic Press, New York

Tomkins W 1927 *Universal Indian Sign Language of the Plains Indians of North America*. Tomkins, San Diego, CA

Tylor E B 1874 *Researches into the Early History of Mankind*. Murray, London

Wallin L 1983 Compounds in Swedish Sign Language in historical perspective. In: Kyle J G, Woll B (eds.) *Language in Sign*. Croom Helm, London

Woll B 1985 Change in British Sign Language. *Final Report to the Leverhulme Trust*

Woodward J and de Santis S 1977 Negative incorporation in French and American Sign Languages. *Language in Society* 6: 379–88

B. Woll
J. G. Kyle

Sign Language Acquisition

Despite the expectation that proficiency in all languages is achieved in a rather similar way, there are certain features which make sign languages different from spoken languages. First, they are realized in a different medium—that is, visual–spatial, rather than auditory–oral; and second, sign languages develop in children whose parents are initially unable to use the language with them—90 percent of deaf children are born to hearing parents.

The characteristics of sign language itself are adequately described in other contributions (see *Sign Language, Sign Language Research: Issues and Priorities*) and it can be seen that the grammar of sign language is very different. Just as it has taken linguists rather longer to focus on spoken language acquisition after they have examined the structures and functioning of languages, so it is that there has been relatively little study of sign language acquisition. One of the reasons has been the lack of situations where the recording can take place. Deaf children who will develop sign language occur in only one in 2,000 births, and those born into deaf families (deaf children with deaf parents—*dcdp*) occur perhaps once in 40,000 births. The natural language situation of parent passing on the language to the child is rare. Studies of individual children are still the norm and continuous studies of 5 children from an early age (e.g., Ackerman, et al. 1991) are large.

Where it has been possible to record deaf children from an early age a number of striking findings can be reported.

1. Joint Reference

The ability of a hearing parent to discuss an object or event while a child is observing, is an important feature of interaction in infancy and early childhood; if a deaf child engages with an object, however, the communication channel (visual) is cut off. Research by Kyle, et al. (1988) suggests that deaf mothers overcome this problem by signing rather less than hearing mothers speak, but also by referring to objects prior to engaging with them. So in a task, which involves directing the child's gaze, deaf mothers characteristically refer to the object when they have eye contact with the child and then point to it. While the child is looking, the mother does not communicate and only as the child's eye contact is returned, is any further information provided by the mother. The purpose of this sort of interaction, which appears very limiting by hearing-speaking standards, is to establish attention routines such that much more extended interaction and turn-taking can occur in the second year as language develops. It is noticeable that hearing mothers of deaf children do not naturally develop this skill (see *Sign Language Acquisition*).

2. Motherese

Just as one can detect baby talk in hearing interaction, similar characteristics are found in the interaction with dcdp. Signs are lengthened in duration, extended in space, and manipulated in space (perhaps to increase attention); signs are displaced from their normal location to locations appropriate to the child's attention, for example, the mother will sign key concepts on top of a picture book. Signs can also be made 'on the child' and manipulated as in a game, for example, the sign DUCK (made by opening and closing the hand in the manner of a duck's beak) can be used as if the imaginary duck was pecking at the child. One further significant feature is that not only does the mother model signs for the child, she can model the signs *on* the child—she takes the child's hands and moves them in an appropriate way for that sign.

3. Emerging Signs

Just as with hearing children, signs begin to emerge reliably around one year. There is considerable variation in this in even the few studies which have been reported (Bonvillian, et al. 1983, Harris, et al. 1987; Kyle, et al. 1988). Some deaf children are reported as signing prior to one year and others do not produce the first sign until 17 months. Because of the relatively few home situations which have been studied, it is not obvious whether this variation is random within a norm or whether there are specific interaction factors in the home.

First signs tend to be object signs (seen around 11 months of age, Ackerman, et al. 1991) although in the earliest stage these are difficult to distinguish from gestures (hearing children also gesture and these can be detected from 15 months—Acredolo and Goodwyn 1988).

These early signs are poorly articulated in terms of handshape, location, and movement. Parents interpret the sign from the context and frequently provide a correction. It appears that signs are prelexical (as with words; see also Nelson and Lucariello 1985) until around 16 months of age when they begin to be generalized and where overextension can be noted.

4. Sign Combinations

As with words in hearing children signs come to be combined, but appear to pass through an intermediate stage prior to emerging as two-sign combinations. This intermediate stage is one of bracketing. In this, dcdp combine single signs with points, that is, a gesture signifying a location, usually made with the index finger as:

POINT *SIGN* POINT or *SIGN* POINT *SIGN*

before they move to sign$_1$ sign$_2$.

At this time the signs begin to develop into two- and three-sign utterances. However, it would also seem that sign utterances tend to be shorter than corresponding length of utterance in words. This may be partly due to the fact that the signs are more densely packed as units, but it is also likely to be a function of the relatively shorter conversation length possible for a young child when he/she has to engage in eye contact throughout the exchange.

5. Question Development

An interesting feature of sign competence is the use of question forms. Sign languages generally have *wh*-forms, but are most likely to indicate questions by the use of nonmanual markers (notably use of eyebrows). Initial work on the acquisition of question forms suggests that deaf children and their caregivers tend to avoid such question marking and the only distinguishing feature of a question appears to be the 'terminal hold'—the holding of the last sign for an extended period while maintaining eye contact. One possible explanation is that deaf children tend to learn the emotive connotations of the face before they learn its use for nonmanual grammar. Early sign questions if marked by knit brows would be interpreted emotionally by the young child. As a result question marking in the early stages has to adopt a different framework.

6. Gesture to Sign

Notable in the research is an examination of the continuity–discontinuity debate, whereby gestures can be considered to lead naturally into signs (speech) or are seen to diverge from the beginning. Petitto (1986) has reported the development of the gesture for self, prior to the development of the signs for I and YOU. The gestural stage of indicating self is generally a period of correct use, but the child then passes through a period of misattributing the sign I to others, and YOU to self. Only gradually does the child emerge from this 'confusion' to produce the correct signs for I and YOU.

From the findings of Volterra (1983) which indicate that hearing children, while able to use gesture, do not progress to the stage of combining referential gestures (which deaf children do), we can see how sign language acquisition work casts some light on the roots of language development.

7. Sign in School

Beyond this period there has been more concern with the applied field of education as the deaf child will be admitted into educational programs from as early as two years of age. Although one can see the sophisticated use of sign by dcdp (deaf children from deaf families), there can be significant problems for deaf children in hearing families. Here it is often the case that 'sign supported speech' forms are used by the hearing adults around the child.

Hoiting and Loncke (1990) have analyzed the typically atypical language learning situation of the deaf child. Characteristically it incorporates language input from both sign and speech and also may be presented in forms which mix both. Nevertheless, they conclude that the cognitive–linguistic system of deaf children is more linked to sign language than to spoken language. Deaf children do separate spoken forms from sign forms from an early age and peer interaction is most often sign dominated.

In an examination of sign competence in deaf children in school programs where sign was used, Kyle (1990) reports a pattern which indicates learning over time in the program, but disappointing levels of mastery of sign grammar. Features such as the use of spatial grammar (location of actions, objects, and people in space) and movement parameters (where movement and direction indicate aspect and person of the verb) are incompletely understood by deaf children up to the age of 10 years (although this does not apply to dcdp who are more advanced). Since a great deal of early interaction will deal with objects and story sequences this could prove to be a significant obstacle to learning. In effect, in the programs studied, the sign acquisition of the children was not adequate as a result of the nature of the input by adults—a fact also reflected in Johnson, et al. (1989). Loncke, et al. (1990) also investigated the acquisition of grammar in dchp (deaf children with hearing parents) in contrast to dcdp. They found problems in the former's use of morphosyntactic operations, while the latter seem to incorporate them in their signing from the age of 6 years onwards.

Sign development can be seen to reach levels comparable to spoken language but the process whereby this point is reached differs between deaf and hearing children. In most education systems at present, only those from deaf families are likely to achieve natural sign competence at a rate comparable to hearing children. It can be expected that components of sign morphology and syntax will be acquired rather late (at school rather than at home) by the majority of deaf children.

Bibliography

Ackerman J, Kyle J G, Woll B, Ezra M 1991 Lexical acquisition in sign and speech. In: Lucas C (ed.) *Sign Language Research: Theoretical Issues*. Gallaudet University Press, Washington, DC

Acredolo L, Goodwyn S 1988 Symbolic gesturing in normal infants. *Child Development* **59**: 450–66

Bonvillian J D, Orlansky M D, Novak L L 1983 Early sign language acquisition and its relation to cognitive and motor development. In: Kyle J G, Woll B (eds.) *Language in Sign.* Croom Helm, London

Harris M, Clibbens J, Tibbits R, Chasin J 1987 Communication between deaf mothers and their deaf infants. In: Griffiths P, Local J, Mills A (eds.) *Proceedings of the Child Language Seminar.* University of York, York

Hoiting N, Loncke F 1990 Models of acquisition and processing of multilingual and multimodal information. In: Prillwitz S, Vollhaber T (eds.) *Current Trends in European Sign Language Research.* Signum, Hamburg

Johnson R, Liddell S, Erting C 1989 *Unlocking the Curriculum.* Gallaudet Research Institute, Washington, DC

Kyle J G 1990 *BSL Development, Final Report.* Centre for Deaf Studies, Bristol

Kyle J G, Woll B, Ackerman J 1988 *Gesture to Sign and Speech, Final Report to ESRC.* Centre for Deaf Studies, Bristol

Loncke F, Quertinmont S, Ferreyra P 1990 Deaf children in schools: More or less native signers. In: Prillwitz S, Vollhaber T (eds.) *Current Trends in European Sign Language Research.* Signum, Hamburg

Nelson K, Lucariello J 1985 The development of meaning in first words. In: Barrett M D (ed.) *Children's Single Word Speech.* Wiley, New York

Petitto L 1986 Knowledge of language in signed and spoken language acquisition. In: Woll B (ed.) *Language Development and Sign Language,* ISLA Monograph. Centre for Deaf Studies, Bristol

Volterra V 1983 Gestures, signs and words at two years. In: Kyle J G, Woll B (eds.) *Language in Sign.* Croom Helm, London

J. G. Kyle

Sign Language Acquisition: Development of Attention

The interactive patterns established between mothers and infants, long before the infant begins to use language, have been thought to provide an environment conducive to language acquisition. Without conscious effort, mothers appear to adjust their communicative style to maximize the chances of their infants decoding the language input. One of the most important ways in which they accomplish this is by making their language input relevant to the child's activities. This is achieved by mothers talking to their infants about objects or activities to which they are both paying attention, thus providing optimum conditions for the child to grasp the connection between language and experience. When mother and infant are hearing, these situations are easily created. Attention is focused visually on an object or activity and the mother provides the verbal message at the same time, without disrupting the child's activities. The relationship between maternal speech and familiar objects and events is therefore readily established.

Deaf mothers also use language to talk about objects and actions which currently interest the child. However, when the language used is signed rather than spoken, the attentional demands are very different. Interactions in sign language require visual attention to the 'speaker.' The child must therefore divide attention between that which is being communicated about and the communication itself. Consequently, language input and attention to the referent occur sequentially rather than simultaneously, making the task of grasping the connection between language and experience much more complex. In this situation the child must shift attention (hence disrupting activities), retain information in memory, and integrate information from activities and language input. Despite these extra cognitive demands, children of deaf parents appear to acquire sign language as quickly and effortlessly as children of hearing parents acquire spoken language. The need for divided attention does not therefore appear to be an impediment to language development.

1. Management of Interactions during Periods of Joint Attention

The difficulties associated with divided attention are, in fact, largely resolved for the child by the mother using strategies which bring her signs into the nonverbal context. The cognitive demands on the child are therefore reduced by minimizing the need to switch attention and making the relationship between the signs and the object of communication more apparent. The methods used by the mothers to achieve these ends can be divided roughly into two groups; those which depend upon displacing the location in which signs are made, and those which require manipulation of the child's attention.

In conversations between adults, signs are usually made in the space in front of the signer's chest. The formation of some signs also requires contact with specific areas on the signer's body. When deaf mothers talk to their infants they frequently shift the location of the signs so that they are made within the child's signing space rather than the mother's. This is frequently observed when the child is sitting on the mother's knee and the mother reaches round in front of the child to sign. The mother may also make contact with the child's body rather than her own in producing a sign, or may make the sign for an object on the object itself. She may even use the object in the production of the sign, for example, making the sign for NOISY while holding a rattle in her signing hand.

Other ways of bringing signs into the child's visual field do not require distortion of the sign but entail manipulation of the child's attention. The mother may, for example, move her hands or body to ensure that her signed communication is within the child's visual field. Alternatively she may move objects so that they are within her signing space or move the child so that he/she can attend to both the object and the sign. The child's attention may also be obtained by waving a hand in front of the child, tapping the child, or banging on the floor.

All of these strategies enable the child to see both the sign and what it refers to, thus increasing the probability of a connection being made between the two and establishing the basis for language development.

The approaches outlined above are used most effectively when the child is young and relatively immobile. As the child becomes active and no longer remains close to the mother such methods become less practical, hence the child must increasingly take responsibility for dividing attention if language development is to continue. At this stage mothers shift their signing from the displaced locations back to the conventional signing space. However, they also incorporate into their communicative style a number of mechanisms which help the child to regulate divided attention. One of the most important of these is the use of a language structure called 'bracketing.' This involves signing the name of an object, followed by pointing to the object then naming it again or, conversely, pointing to an object, which is already occupying the child's attention, signing the name or a comment, and again pointing to the object. The mother's hand movements therefore orchestrate the child's attentional shifts and also provide repeated information to reduce the burden on memory and emphasize the link between the referent and the sign. Deaf mothers typically monitor the child's activity but wait for him or her to look at them before providing any information. In general they communicate with their children less frequently than hearing mothers, although their communication is usually both relevant and salient and as a result it is likely to hold the child's attention.

In summary, for the child who is acquiring sign language the problem of dividing visual attention between the context of communication and the communication itself is initially largely resolved by the mother, who takes responsibility for producing signs close to the referent and within the child's visual field. The mother also uses strategies which actively teach the child a system for dividing attention. Much of the cognitive burden involved in using divided attention is therefore removed from the child, leaving him/her free to decode the relationship between language and experience.

Bibliography

Harris M, Clibbins J, Chasin J, Tibbitts R 1989 The social context of early sign language development. *First Language* **9**: 81–97

Woll B, Kyle J 1989 Communication and language development in children of deaf parents. In: Tetzchner S von, Siegel L, Smith L S (eds.) *The Social and Cognitive Aspects of Normal and Atypical Language Development*. Springer-Verlag, New York

Wood D, Wood H, Griffiths A, Howarth I 1986 *Teaching and Talking with Deaf Children*. John Wiley and Sons, Chichester

H. Mohay

Sign Language: Developments in Sublexical Analysis of Signs

All human languages are structured by grammars which include rules that govern the organization of meaningless phonological elements into morphemes and words, the organization of individual meaningful elements to form complex words, and the organization of words into still larger units such as phrases and sentences. Although the world's spoken languages vary in a multitude of ways, current linguistic theory holds that behind the variation lies a set of universals which result from the human brain's biological predisposition to structure language in specific ways. The recent recognition that sign languages are fully legitimate human languages opened a door to a previously unanalyzed set of languages which also vary widely from one to another, but which are produced in another modality. Sign languages are produced by movements of the hands, arms, body, and face, and perceived by the eyes. There is essentially no overlap between the physiological means used to produce and perceive spoken languages and the physiological means used to produce and perceive sign languages. This difference in production and perception could have major consequences in terms of the way that sign languages are structured. Thus the analysis of the sublexical structure of sign languages has the potential to add a new dimension to our understanding of the cognitive mechanisms which underlie language.

1. First Evidence of Sublexical Structure

Prior to the work of William C. Stokoe Jr there was no evidence that signs were any different from other types of gestures. The individual gestures of a policeman directing traffic or an umpire at a football game have never been considered language-like in their structure, but Stokoe (1960) and Stokoe, et al. (1965) argued that the signs of a sign language are different from other types of gestures and should be regarded as having an abstract sublexical structure parallel to that which underlies words in spoken languages (see *Sign Language Research: Issues and Priorities*). Stokoe analyzed signs as decomposable into a limited number of abstract parts which he called 'cheremes.' The first syllable of the term 'chereme' was taken from the first syllable of a Homeric Greek word meaning 'handy' and the suffix -eme was used to show that the abstract units which underlie signs are meant to be parallel to phonemes in spoken languages. Stokoe's work on the structure of American Sign Language (ASL) made it clear that sign languages were real human languages rather than coded representations of the spoken language or simply a nonlinguistic gesture system.

In Stokoe's analysis ASL signs are decomposable into three types of cheremes. He identified 12 location cheremes, 19 handshape cheremes, and 24 movement cheremes. The cheremes in these limited sets are meant to combine with one another to form all the lexical signs in ASL. This theoretical model of sign structure gained worldwide acceptance and has been used to describe signs from a multitude of sign languages. In spite of its widespread acceptance, however, its usage has tended to be restricted to the description of citation form signs. The sign language literature reveals scant application of this model in the description or analysis of phonological or morphological problems. This is surprising since, for spoken languages, the use of phonological representations in the description and solution of phonological and morphological problems is the norm.

2. Comparing Phonemes and Cheremes

One aspect of Stokoe's analysis of cheremes demonstrated a clear parallel with phonemes in spoken languages. In both cases a limited number of abstract parts in different combinations produces the entire vocabularies of the languages involved. The parallel breaks down, however, when one looks at the distribution of phonemes and cheremes. Phonemes combine with one another in sequence. The English phonemes /k/, /æ/, and /t/, for example, combine in sequence to produce the phonemic representation of the English word 'cat.' Cheremes, however, combine without sequence into a simultaneous bundle of features. The logic which justified this view can be seen in the description of the ASL sign BLACK, produced by brushing the index finger extended from a closed fist from left to right against the forehead. In Stokoe's theory, the cheremes ' ∩ ' (forehead),

'G $_<$' (fist with extended index finger [G] pointing left [$_<$]), '>' (rightward movement), and 'x' (contact), combine as an unordered bundle of cheremes to produce the sign BLACK. It is evident that the handshape does not precede the movement and neither does the movement precede the handshape. In fact, the handshape is present through the movement. Similarly, the location does not precede the movement, but rather, is the site at which the movement takes place. The two movement cheremes in the sign BLACK are also not sequential. The hand moves to the right while it makes a brushing contact with the forehead.

The preceding description of the sign BLACK illustrates a fundamental difference between the proposed sublexical organization of cheremes in a sign language and phonemes in a spoken language. Words of a spoken language show sequential contrast provided by sequentially organized segments (consonants and vowels). Cheremes are not organized sequentially, and therefore, in this analysis, signs are incapable of showing this type of contrast.

3. Segmenting Signs according the Movements and Holds

Although the theoretical basis for Stokoe's model required that all the cheremes be organized simultaneously rather than sequentially, this principle was not always followed in practice. The sign CHICAGO, for example, is produced with a rightward movement followed by a downward movement, WHEN is produced with a circular movement followed by a contacting movement, and ALSO is produced with a contacting movement followed by a rightward movement, followed by yet another contacting movement. The importance of sequence for these signs stood in direct conflict with the theoretical assumptions of the cheremic model, yet there was no obvious alternative to that model.

Liddell (1984) introduced a theoretical model of sign structure which segments signs based on sequences of movement. The model divides segment types into two broad categories: M (movement), where the hands move along a path, and H (hold), where the hand remains stationary. Just as phonemes in spoken languages are composed of features which specify the state of the vocal tract during that segment (i.e., degree of closure of the vocal tract, lip rounding, position of the tongue, state of the glottis, etc.), each M or H segment consists of features which specify the state of the ASL articulatory system during that segment (movement type, handshape, orientation of the hands, etc.). Many of the units identified by Stokoe are still important in this model but they have a different status. Under this proposal handshape features, for example, do not constitute units parallel to phonemes, but rather constitute a set of features which specifies only a subset of the information required for a complete segment.

Under the new segmental theory, the sign BLACK consists of two segments, M and H. During the initial M an '1' handshape makes a brushing contact with the forehead and during the H the '1' handshape remains stationary near the forehead. The sign DROP is an HMH sign. During the initial H an 'S' handshape is held ahead of the torso. During the M the hand moves downward and the handshape changes to a '5.' During the final H the hand remains in its new position with a '5' handshape. WHEN is an MMH sign, produced with a circular movement of a '1' handshape followed by a straight movement of that hand toward the

fingertip of the stationary '1' handshape of the base hand, followed by a hold with the two fingertips in contact. A typical sign consists of two or more segments in sequence. Single segment signs are comparatively rare in sign languages, as they are in spoken languages.

This segmental theory of sign structure allows one to see signs, like spoken words, as organized sequences of segments. The proposal that there are two main segment types in sign language suggests another interesting parallel with spoken languages, where vowels and consonants constitute the two main segment types. ASL movements and holds, like vowels and consonants in spoken languages, are also subject to restrictions on their sequencing. Although MH and HM seem equally simple to produce, overwhelmingly two-segment signs are ordered MH rather than HM. For three-segment signs again a single order predominates: HMH. For four-segment signs the order MHMH predominates. This makes it appear that ASL has fairly strict morpheme structure constraints.

This theory had immediate application to a variety of structural problems which were not readily addressable under the 'simultaneous cheremes' theory. First, it legitimized signs like WHEN and ALSO, which are clearly produced with sequences of movement. It also legitimized signs like THREE, produced with no hand movement at all. In the 'simultaneous chereme' theory, a sign like THREE was not considered to be a well-formed sign since there was no chereme which caused the hand to remain stationary. Such a sign is a simple hold in the MH theory of sign structure.

4. Alternate Theories of Segmentation

The idea that signs could be segmented has sparked considerable research into theories on how best to accomplish the segmentation. The MH theory of segmentation has been developed into a multitiered autosegmental representation (Liddell and Johnson 1989). In this model movement features reside on a segmental tier while handshape, placement, location, orientation, and nonmanual features reside on separate tiers, independent of the number of segments. Several alternative theories, also using autosegmental representations, have also been developed. Two alternative theories maintain that 'holds' are not segment types. One theory lets movement and location determine the number of segments, while handshape features reside on tiers which are independent of the number of segments (Sandler 1986). The other segments sign according to movement and position and include tiers which determine a moraic syllable structure (Perlmutter 1992). While these two theories maintain that 'holds' are not segment types, another theory maintains that 'hold' is the only segment type and that 'movement' is not a segment type (Stack 1988; Hayes 1992). Still another theory holds that sequential patterning within the sign can be handled through nonsegmental syllabic representations (Wilbur 1992).

5. A Structural Difference between Signs and Words

There remains a very interesting difference between the abstract sublexical structure proposed for signs and those proposed for spoken languages based on the different potential of signed and spoken languages to show contrast. In a sign language the hand acts as a mobile articulator which can been viewed as parallel in a sense to the tongue as a moving articulator in the vocal tract. In ASL the hand can contact more than 50 distinct locations on the body and still more in the space ahead of the body. In contrast to this the tongue makes contact at a relatively small number of distinctive locations within the vocal tract for any given spoken language. Further, while the shape of the tongue is not generally distinctive in spoken languages, sign languages use a very large number of distinctive handshapes. In addition, sign languages can use two hands, often with different handshapes. Keeping in mind these differences, it is interesting to compare the number of distinctive segments used in the two modalities. The total number of distinctive consonants and vowels used by any given spoken language is typically under 50. Although there are not yet accurate counts, the number of distinctive segments used in any given sign language appears to be many times this number.

6. The Future

Research is still in the very early stages of development of theories of sign language phonology but it appears that the 'phonological' structures of sign languages are remarkably like those seen in spoken languages. Given the total lack of overlap in production and perception between signed and spoken languages one might have expected enormous differences. Continued research in this area can be expected to lead to a clearer picture not only of the ways in which signed phonologies are like spoken language phonologies but also of the ways that the two differ. This will lead us closer to understanding the truly universal aspects of grammars as well as those aspects of grammar which are dependent on the modality of transmission and perception.

Bibliography

Coulter G R (ed.) 1992 *ASL Phonology*. Academic Press, New York
Hayes B 1992 Against movement. In: Coulter G R (ed.) 1992
Liddell S K 1984 THINK and BELIEVE: Sequentiality in American Sign Language signs. *Language* **60(2)**: 372–99
Liddell S K, Johnson R E 1989 American Sign Language: The phonological base. *Sign Language Studies* **64**: 195–278
Perlmutter D 1992 Nucleus vs. satellite in ASL syllable structure. In: Coulter G R (ed.) 1992
Sandler W 1986 The spreading hand autosegment of American Sign Language. *Sign Language Studies* **50**: 1–28
Stack K 1988 Tiers and syllable structure in American Sign Language: evidence from phonotactics. (Master's thesis, University of California)
Stokoe W C Jr 1960 *Sign Language Structure: An Outline of the Visual Communication Systems of the American Deaf*, Studies in Linguistics: Occasional Papers **8**. University of Buffalo, Buffalo, NY
Stokoe W C Jr, Casterline D, Croneberg C 1965 *A Dictionary of American Sign Language on Linguistic Principles*. Gallaudet College Press, Washington, DC
Wilbur R B 1992 Move the holds & hold the movements—syllables & segments in ASL. In: Coulter G R (ed.) 1992

S. Liddell

Sign Language Morphology

A study of the many signed languages created by deaf people has shown that the structure, content, and processes of language in a modality where the articulators are the hands, arms, face, and body, and where perception is accomplished through vision, are highly similar to those in the spoken modality. In addition, sign language research has helped to differentiate linguistic universals which are modality-specific, occurring only in spoken language, and those which are present as true universals, occurring in both the spoken and signed language modality. Such information demonstrates the validity of an innate, partially predetermined biological program for language creation and acquisition, independent of the modality or channel used to communicate.

The study of regular meaning-bearing aspects of a single sign in signed languages affords the opportunity to investigate the validity of language universals at this level of analysis. In pursuit of this goal, linguists studying signed languages have been investigating the range of meanings within the complex signs of signed languages, the mechanisms for sign formation, and the grammatical processes which operate upon single roots in these languages. In addition, the comparative study of different signed languages contributes information on the validity of typological categorizations of languages at the morphological level, and, especially with signed languages, information about the underlying physiological motivations for differing types of languages at the morphological level.

Early research into the sign language used in the USA (American Sign Language, ASL) focused upon providing evidence within a structuralist framework that a signed language exhibited language-like characteristics and organized itself into structures and levels which were similar to those of spoken languages (see *Sign Language Research: Issues and Priorities*).

The data and level of analysis described led to a characterization of the ASL sign as the smallest unit of meaning with variations in form signaling unrelated lexical items. Subsequent research into the single sign across a wider range of ASL data and data from other signed languages established the fact that signs are composed of an internal composition of morphemes and that internal variations in the form of a single sign stem accomplished a variety of grammatical functions analogous to those found in the grammars of morphologically complex spoken languages (see *Sign Language*; *Sign Language: Developments in Sublexical Analysis of Signs*).

Research into the various signed languages of the world seems to indicate a similar state of affairs at the morphological level across signed languages. It has been shown that the larger musculature of the hand and arms requires comparatively more time for each muscular gesture than the smaller musculature within the vocal tract (Bellugi and Fischer 1972). It has been suggested that the concomitant need for an optimal proposition length for cognitive processing mandates a high degree of simultaneity of expression and hence a complex morphology within the single sign.

As research proceeded, careful analysis of signs with similar handshapes, locations or movements, and repetition patterns revealed regular patterns of composition, inflection, and derivation within the predicate and nominal systems of the languages. Examples henceforth will be drawn from a number of different signed languages.

Research has shown the predicate systems of many signed languages to exhibit complex inflections for person and number agreement. These inflections take the form of particular configurations of location on the signer's body and in the space around it and movement patterns through the space around a signer's body. In terms of agreement for person, it is well established that the system of reference rests on a 'structured use of space' (Loew 1984), wherein abstract loci in the space around a signer's body are established through various indexing devices and then incorporated into the predicate via direction or location of eye-gaze while signing the predicate, direction of movement of the predicate sign, or location of predicate sign production. As an example, the ASL sign usually translated as 'ask' or 'ask a question' is depicted in Klima and Bellugi (1979: 278) as having a differing direction of motion and initial and final location of the moving hand to signal the meanings of 'I asked you,' 'I asked him,' and 'You asked me' (see *Sign Language*).

Many signed languages have also been shown to mark distributional and temporal aspect as inflections which alter the predicate sign. This is accomplished through cyclic patterns of repeated motions in signing. Klima and Bellugi (1979: 293) depict various forms of the ASL sign translated as 'look at' inflected for a variety of temporal aspects, such as protractive, durational, incessant, continuative, etc. In each case, a distinct physiological path and manner of repeated movement, or lack of movement, which differs from the punctual form, consistently signals a particular meaning related to temporal aspect. In the case of durational aspect, for example, the movement is made in a small, smooth, oval path which is repeated.

In addition to these sorts of inflections, the predicate systems of some signed languages have been shown to include predicates which are complex compositions, including a wealth of information concerning arguments of the predicate such as size and shape, handling, path of motion, and position in space. Example languages are ASL, Thai Sign Language, Swedish Sign Language, British Sign Language (BSL), Italian Sign Language, and Danish Sign Language (e.g., McDonald 1982; Engberg-Pedersen and Pedersen 1985). One example of such a predicate sign, literally rendered as 'a two-dimensional object be located,' comes from Swedish Sign Language and is depicted in Wallin (1990: 136). In this polymorphemic sign, a flat hand, oriented palm downward, with the fingertips facing away from the signer's body, undergoes a 'placing' motion with a definite, abrupt endpoint in the space in front of the signer's body. Without analyzing the movement aspect of the sign, the handshape itself is shown to be polymorphemic in Wallin's research. The flat hand indicates a saliently two-dimensional object, the palm-down orientation signals an object not easily movable, and the fingertips oriented away from the signer signal that the largest dimension of the object is perpendicular to the signer's body. With reference to such systems, several researchers have made an analogy with the predicate classifier systems of the languages in the Athabaskan family, in which the predicates are composed of morphemes signaling the shape, consistency, animacy, and handling of objects, as well as morphemes indicating their location, manner of movement, extension, direction of movement, and spatial arrangement (Supalla 1986; McDonald 1982; Schick 1990).

Research has also revealed synchronic and diachronic processes active in the expansion of the lexicons of many signed languages. Two such processes are the derivation of new sign forms from an existing sign and the restructuring of two existing signs to form compound signs. In the first process, research from ASL, BSL, and New Zealand Sign Language (NZSL) indicates that a pattern of repeated motion which is different in quality derives nouns in these signed languages (Supalla and Newport 1978; Collins-Ahlgren 1990; Kyle and Woll 1985). Supalla and Newport depict and describe related noun–verb pairs in ASL (1978: 108). In one example, they depict the verb translated as 'fly' or 'go by plane,' a sign produced with a fluid continuous manner and a single movement. The related noun, translated as 'airplane,' exhibits a tense, restrained manner and a repeated movement with the handshape and general location remaining constant. As with other natural languages, adequate explanation of the variety of related inflected nouns and verbs in signed languages requires the postulation of abstract underlying forms and ordered derivational rules which apply cyclically. For ASL, an underlying form which specifies place of articulation, handshape, orientation, shape of movement, directionality, and a single movement is postulated. An ordered derivational process first adds a specification for a restrained manner for nouns or a continuous manner for verbs. The resulting form is termed a sign unit, which then is subject to rules deriving basic surface signs or a variety of inflected forms for nouns and verbs.

Many signed languages show evidence of a compounding process. This process has been shown to be similar to that which occurs in spoken languages. Two- and three-sign phrases or lists undergo restructuring through assimilation and deletion, and are often reanalyzed as single, monomorphemic lexical items. In NZSL, Collins-Ahlgren (1990: 298) illustrates that the sign meaning 'parents' is a compound sign derived from the signs meaning 'mother' and 'father' via a deletion rule for repeated movement-hold sequences in either part of a compound sign, and a deletion rule for noncontacting hold segments of a sign (see *Sign Language: Developments in Sublexical Analysis of Signs*). Essentially, the two-sign sequence is restructured to conform to what might be termed the morpheme structure constraints of the signed language.

Research into the morphology of signed languages includes both descriptive and theoretical aspects. Research into the linguistic systems of many signed languages endeavors to understand and describe the precise form–meaning correspondences of the complex inflections for predicate–argument agreement or case-marking, and the composition of classifier predicates. At a higher level of description, work proceeds on the classification and categorization of predicates in signed languages. As accurate, precise data accumulate in signed language research, they add to the specificity of characterization of the innate bioprogram for language in two ways. First, the further specification of substantive linguistic universals through study of signed language data adds to knowledge of the salient aspects of human language. An example of this sort of research is Supalla (1990), which describes possibly universal restrictions on the representation of simultaneous referent properties in language. Second, research which attempts to capture language structures and processes within the framework of existing formal models examines the adequacy of such models for a natural signed language and adds to knowledge of the possible structures and processes which constitute human language.

Bibliography

Bellugi U, Fischer S D 1972 A comparison of sign language and spoken language: Rate and grammatical mechanisms. *Cognition* **1**: 173–200

Collins-Ahlgren M 1990 Word formation processes in New Zealand sign languages. In: Fischer S D, Siple P (eds.) 1990

Engberg-Pedersen E, Pedersen A 1985 Proforms in Danish Sign Language. In: Volterra V, Stokoe W (eds.) 1983 SLR *Sign Language Research*. Linstok Press, Silver Spring, MD

Fischer S D, Siple P (eds.) 1990 *Theoretical Issues in Sign Language Research vol. 1: Linguistics*. University of Chicago Press, Chicago, IL

Klima E, Bellugi U 1979 *The Signs of Language*. Harvard University Press, Cambridge, MA

Kyle J G, Woll B 1985 *The Study of Deaf People and Their Language*. Cambridge University Press, Cambridge

Loew R 1984 Roles and reference in American Sign Language: A developmental perspective (Doctoral dissertation, University of Minnesota)

McDonald B H 1982 Aspects of the ASL predicate system (Doctoral dissertation, State University of New York)

Schick B 1990 Classifier predicates in American Sign Language. *IJAL* **1(1)**: 15–40

Supalla T 1986 The classifier system in American Sign Language. In: Craig C (ed.) *Noun Classes and Categorization*. John Benjamins, Philadelphia, PA

Supalla T 1990 Serial verbs of motion in ASL. In: Fischer S D, Siple P (eds.) 1990

Supalla T, Newport E 1978 How many seats in a chair? The derivation of nouns and verbs in ASL. In: Siple P (ed.) *Understanding Language through Sign Language Research*. Academic Press, New York

Wallin L 1990 Polymorphemic predicates in Swedish Sign Language. In: Lucas C (ed.) *Sign Language Research: Theoretical Issues*. Gallaudet University Press, Washington, DC

B. H. McDonald

Sign Language Research: Issues and Priorities

Sign language research only began in the 1960s, but sign languages from virtually every part of the world are now under study or have been studied. Some of this research is purely scientific, intended to gain knowledge about language or cognition or social interaction; some of it is applied, intended to improve educational, interpreting, counseling, or other services for deaf people. The research is also varied in its focus, which may be on: (a) the structure of gesturally expressed languages; (b) the normal communication or the special needs of persons who cannot hear; (c) a particular culture (e.g., that of Australian Aborigines) in which sign language is used despite easy access to a spoken language; or (d) hope that discoveries about sign language will support a language theory. Anthropological, linguistic,

psychological, sociological, and other methods have been used in sign language research (see *Sign Language*).

Much of the literature of sign language research appears in the issues of *Sign Language Studies* (1972–). Begun as a semiannual international journal under the auspices of the Indiana University Research Center for Language Sciences, *SLS* was published by Mouton for 3 years. In 1975 Linstok Press began, and continues, to publish the journal as a quarterly. In 1987, *Das Zeichen*, a quarterly devoted to sign language and deaf communication, began publication in Hamburg. The International Sign Linguistics Association began publishing a quarterly newsletter, *Sign Post*, in 1990; a journal is to follow.

1. Issues

Sign language research almost began in 1880, with the first report to the Smithsonian Institution from the Bureau of Ethnology (Mallery 1881); but in that year, educators of the deaf in a world congress at Milan, declared that 'sign language has no legitimate place in the education or the lives of deaf people' (Elliott 1882). The central issue, whether sign language should be studied, or have any notice taken of it at all, was thus effectively closed in 1880.

Eighty years later, however, a related issue was directly addressed: whether a sign language might be a language as structural linguists then defined language (Trager and Smith 1951). Trager had defined language as 'an arbitrary system of vocal symbols by means of which members of a culture carry on all the activities of that culture.' It was proposed to falsify that hypothesis by proof that the arbitrary symbols need not be vocal. When examined the language of American deaf people proved to have a structure like that of other languages, at the word level (Stokoe 1960), and at the level of phrases and sentences (Stokoe 1972). Since then research has convinced anthropologists, linguists, and psychologists—with very few exceptions—that sign languages are indeed languages.

An important distinction affecting all sign language research was made by Kendon (1988): sign languages are either 'primary' (used by persons as their first or only language), or 'alternate' (used by persons who also have a spoken language they could use). A research issue now being addressed is how a sign language relates, if it does, to a spoken language—either the one spoken by hearing people in the vicinity of primary (deaf) signers or the one spoken alternatively by the signers themselves.

There are also bogus issues to be dealt with, widely held notions that: (a) sign language users from anywhere can understand sign language users from anywhere else; and (b) the signs of a sign language simply and directly look exactly like what they mean. Research is continually correcting these misconceptions. Sign languages differ just as do vocally expressed languages. When deaf users of different sign languages congregate, they do seem to establish comfortable communication more readily than do speakers in similar situations (Jordan and Battison 1976). This may be because they are accustomed to gaining linguistic information by sight not sound and because as part of a (possibly oppressed) minority they share a bond lacked by hearing people without a common spoken language. Communication depends more on willingness to communicate than on having a language in common.

Signs of a sign language, like signs generally, may signify as icons, indices, or symbols (Peirce 1935–66); for example, in sign language, a sign meaning 'ball' may enclose (iconically) a spherical space with the hands, or a sign meaning 'see' may bring one or more fingers (as index) close to the eye; but the majority of signs are simply symbols and relate to what they signify arbitrarily, by convention only. Because they are part of a language, however, the actual signs meaning 'ball' or 'see' in different primary sign languages may be differently formed; they thus retain some iconic or indexic force but have become symbolic. Vocabularies of sign languages, because they are directed to the sense of vision instead of hearing, naturally have more iconic and indexic (or 'transparent') signs than spoken languages are likely to have onomatopoeic words. But just how languages, signed or spoken, mean is still a basic issue for research.

2. Priorities

In the first phase of sign language research, it was thought necessary to show how the structure of a particular sign language resembled the structure of spoken languages. This first phase also coincided with the appearance and rise of a new linguistic theory: that the abstract rules of language generally are in the human brain from birth and that social interaction has only the slightest interest for the study of language so conceived. Consequently, much research has been devoted to finding exact parallels in sign language with every feature and relationship posited in each most recent addition to the theory. Now that sign languages are widely recognized as languages, however, the effort to show similarity risks being overemphasized. When languages use different senses for reception and different mechanisms for expression, information about these differences may be more important than similarity.

From the beginning it was necessary to have some kind of notation for discussing signs and the way they are formed and combined. Also at the outset, those who supported research on the sign language of US deaf people were desirous of having 'a standard.' This was some years before new ways of studying variation within languages became a focus of linguistic research. A dictionary, it was thought, could help to reduce the troublesome variation characteristic of signing. The colloquial signing (learned from their older schoolmates) by students in schools for the deaf around the country varied widely from the formal signing of their deaf teachers, some of whom had learned signs in a tradition going back through Hotchkiss to Gallaudet to Clerc to Sicard (see Lane 1984).

The notation system developed for the 1960 monograph had given graphic symbols to the hand configurations, the actions, and the locations of manual signs. It was put to use in compiling the desired dictionary (Stokoe, et al. 1965). Since this first dictionary to list the signs (and not to treat them as glosses for words listed) appeared, a number of dictionaries of national sign languages have been published. Such recording of sign lexicons is admirable, but in some quarters, dictionary preparation has focused a great deal of attention on sign notation, and considerable effort has been spent on devising a definitive notation (or even a cursive writing) for sign language. This may be a mistake in priority, however, as the differences between noting on

paper in two dimensions changes in sound and changes in a signer's appearance may be too great for any such attempt to succeed. However, the very rapid development of electronic means for recording, playing back, analyzing, and altering visual information may well prove more useful to sign language research than an adaptation of the methods that led to the International Phonetic Alphabet for speech sounds. At a number of research centers attention is being given to the use of this new technology.

It is very likely that use of the new technology will add to knowledge of the natural history of sign languages in ways that earlier research could not, for the reason that a notation system inevitably reflects whatever analysis has been made. The essential and distinctive elements of signs were first called 'aspects' and put at three: configuration, location, and action, called *dez*, *tab*, and *sig* in the first monograph and dictionary. The elements have also been called 'major and minor parameters' and put at four or more ('hand configuration, orientation, place of articulation, and movement' and possibly region contacted and contacting element; Klima and Bellugi 1979). But all these, of course, apply to manual signs only. Because there is a large and important nonmanual component, in primary sign languages certainly (Baker and Cokely 1980), Stokoe has come to favor only a binary analysis, into 'what acts' and 'its action.' The immediate advantage of this reduction is that it applies equally well to nonmanual and manual signs; meanwhile, it leaves digital analysis of videotaped live signing to supply, as it uniquely can, instantly reproducible evidence of what actually happens.

A major priority for sign language research is what new information about language it can disclose. Already it has made clear that hearing and speech are separate systems, neither essential to language itself. It has thus disclosed that language is a deeper, more cerebral system than hearing and speech. To a limited degree, this information has been applied to show educators of deaf children that intensive training in audiology and speech therapy may be less useful for the children's teachers than knowledge about language and communication and cognition. There is need for still more application of this nature, and for sign language research directed at the individual, at the acquisition of a primary sign language, at the learning of a second language through literacy, at the processing of information received by sight and transmitted by gestures. A promising new approach considers language as gestures, whether made to be seen or made where they cannot be seen—in the vocal tract. Sign language research may also find evidence in gestural action and social interaction that languages have evolved from human communication without need for having the human brain prenatally supplied with the universal rules of language.

A promising area for future research will join sign language research with research in cognitive psychology, especially that focused on the perception of gestures, whether of vocal or other systems, memory, cognitive maps, and the interaction of information. To this end, researchers have begun comparing myographic recordings made of speakers' and signers' relevant musculature (Wilcox 1992).

Bibliography

Baker C, Cokely D 1980 *American Sign Language: A Teacher's Resource Text on Grammar and Culture*. T. J. Publishers, Silver Spring, MD

Das Zeichen 1987 Zentrum für Deutsche Gebärdensprache, Hamburg

Elliott R 1882 The Milan congress and the future of the education of the deaf and dumb. *American Annals of the Deaf* **27**: 146–58

Jordan I K, Battison R M 1976 A referential communication experiment with foreign sign languages. *Sign Language Studies* **10**: 69–80

Kendon A 1988 *Sign Languages of Aboriginal Australia.* Cambridge University Press, Cambridge

Klima E S, Bellugi U 1979 *The Signs of Language.* Harvard University Press, Cambridge, MA

Lane H L 1984 *When the Mind Hears: A History of the Deaf.* Random House, New York

Mallery G 1881 *Sign Language among North American Indians.* US Bureau of American Ethnology, Washington, DC

Peirce C S 1935–66 *Collected Papers of Charles Sanders Peirce,* 8 vols. Harvard University Press, Cambridge, MA

Sign Language Studies 1972 Linstok Press, Burtonsville, MD

Sign Post 1990– Deaf Studies Research Unit, Durham

Stokoe W 1960 *Sign Language Structure,* Studies in Linguistics: Occasional Papers 8. University of Buffalo, Buffalo, NY

Stokoe W 1972 *Semiotics and Human Sign Languages.* Mouton, The Hague

Stokoe W, Casterline D, Croneberg C 1965 *A Dictionary of American Sign Language on Linguistic Principles.* Gallaudet University Press, Washington, DC

Trager G L, Smith H L 1951 *An Outline of English Structure,* Studies in Linguistics: Occasional Papers 3. Battenburg Press, Norman, OK

Wilcox S 1992 *The Phonetics of Fingerspelling.* Benjamins, Amsterdam

W. C. Stokoe

Sign Languages in Asia

At least half of the world's deaf population lives in Asia (with 30,000 deaf babies born every year in China alone), and yet knowledge of their sign languages (henceforth SL) is very limited. Apart from some preliminary studies on the SL of China, Taiwan, Hong Kong, India, Japan, and Thailand, SL in Asia remain largely unexplored. Surprisingly, not only are the SL of small countries like Nepal ignored, but even Vietnamese and Indonesian SL are not mentioned in the *Gallaudet Encyclopedia of Deaf People and Deafness* (1987).

Although gestures can be an individual's inventions, the formation of a SL requires at least a small community as its cradle, and this is often provided by schools for the deaf. However, in Asia these schools came to existence only towards the end of the nineteenth century, immediately after the Milan Congress which adopted the oralist approach. This oralism was then propagated in Asia through Western educators. Consequently, the use of SL in schools for the deaf in China, Vietnam, India, and later Sri Lanka, Indonesia, and elsewhere in the region was discouraged or even prohibited until recently. Though Japan's deaf education was initiated in 1875 by Taishiro Jurukawa, a primary school teacher in Kyoto, its initial manual method gave way to oralism around the 1920s.

Despite this straitjacket of oralism, SL continue to develop within the deaf community, particularly in specialized schools where deaf children learn signs from their peers. Sadly, enrollment covered only 5.1 percent of the deaf children in India and 6 percent in China in the 1980s (though 15 percent were expected in China in 1990). Repeated failures and frustrations experienced by both teachers and deaf pupils and the lack of hearing aids have forced most of the education authorities to accept SL as the main teaching medium.

Teaching staff members are dominated by hearing people who tend to communicate with their deaf pupils by signing their vernacular. Thus in schools, a natural SL and a signed vernacular are always in juxtaposition. Their difference is less glaring in lexicon than in syntax. Preliminary analyses of SL in Vietnam, China, Taiwan, Japan, Hong Kong (Yau 1982), and India (Vasishta, et al. 1982) have shown that 'locative—subject—object—verb' and 'modified—modifier or quantifier' are the basic temporal sign orders in these SL. This is particularly true when the verb is intrinsically directional, such as *bite, hit, catch, sit,* etc. The same orders were found in the historical syntax of American SL (Fischer 1975) and French SL (Valade 1854). These orders also constitute the major features of the spontaneous syntax in SL created by illiterate Chinese and Amerindian adults who are deaf from birth, and live isolatedly within a hearing community (Yau 1992). Thus, only a few more SL remain to be verified before these sign orders are confirmed as the general syntactic pattern in Asian SL.

Indian, Pakistani, Bangladeshi, Sri Lankan, and Nepalese SL belong to the same family. This is also the case with SL used in Hong Kong, Singapore, and China. The history of SL in Asia is closely related with Western missionary activities. The first school for the deaf in Vietnam was set up by Father Azéma of the French Foreign Missions in 1886. In China the first school was established by two American Presbyterian missionaries, Annetta Thompson Mills and her husband C. R. Mills. Colonialism also affected the development of Asian SL. Thus Taiwanese SL is more related to Japanese SL than to Chinese SL. Due to the Japanese occupation, about 50 percent of the lexicon of Korean and Taiwanese SL is of Japanese origin (compared with less than 10 percent of signs borrowed from the French in Vietnamese SL according to a preliminary survey). Moreover, since the late 1960s, American economic supremacy has enabled American SL to exercise strong influence in Malaysia, the Philippines, Indonesia, and part of India (Bombay). Future typological studies on SL in the area have to take this new factor into account.

'Fingerspelling' is another consequence of European influence, next to oralism. British, Dutch, and French manual alphabets were introduced respectively to India, Indonesia, and Vietnam. In countries within the sphere of Chinese ideographs, fingerspelling encounters strong resistance. In China, Taiwan, and Japan signers prefer to imitate characters or write them in the air or on the palm. In the *Chinese Sign Language* (1990) there are 59 such imitations, compared with 26 in Japanese and 24 in Taiwanese SL (Smith, et al. 1979). Nevertheless, the manual alphabet is exploited as a sign-creating device in China, and 458 initialized signs (14.8 percent), have been newly introduced, mainly in the domain of politico–philosophical terminology, kinship terms, names of provinces, metals, etc. Excessive use of initialized signs is observed in Malaysian (Kuala Lumpur) SL. The worst case is the Philippine SL lexicon compiled by US Peace Corps Volunteers (Macfadden, et al. 1977) where about half of the 1,164 entries carry the initials of the corresponding English words, and almost as many are American loan-signs!

As early as 1961, China published her first SL lexicon, containing some 2,000 items. In its latest version (1990), the content is expanded to 3,095 illustrated signs, with the focus placed on word–sign correspondences. The signs are arranged according to semantic categories. Other dictionaries or lexicons for SL in Japan (1970), Taiwan (Smith, et al. 1979), Hong Kong (Goodstadt 1970), Thailand (Suwanarat, et al. 1986) and Pakistan (Hussain and Aziz 1989) are also available. The Indonesian and Vietnamese SL lexicons are now in preparation. But for countries like Bangladesh with 95 percent of her deaf population living in ignorance, and a total of only 941 books published in 1988, such a project would be unaffordable.

Only a few in-depth sociolinguistic studies on SL, e.g., Peng (1974), Yau and He (1989) have so far been published outside Asia. Observations on syntax usually creep into introductions in SL dictionaries. Most educators, language planners and SL researchers concentrate their efforts on compiling dictionaries so that hearing parents and teachers can learn to understand their deaf youngsters, since special courses on SL are generally lacking in Asia, as reported recently by the World Federation for the Deaf. These dictionaries also provide a lexicon to meet the demand for court and TV news interpretation. In the case of China, the aim of publishing such a dictionary is also to impose a standard SL. Important dialectal differences persist nevertheless, as revealed in Yau and He 1987 (cf. also Vasishta, et al. 1985 for Indian varieties). Research should be done promptly before sign dialects melt into the language planning pot.

Bibliography

Chinese Sign Language 1990 Association of the Deaf in China
Cleve J V Van (ed.) 1987 *Gallaudet Encyclopedia of Deaf People and Deafness.* McGraw-Hill, New York
Fischer S 1975 Influences of word order change in American Sign Language. In: Li C N (ed.) *Word Order and Word Order Change.* University of Texas Press, Austin, TX
Goodstadt R Y C 1970 *Speaking with Signs: A Sign Language Manual for Hong Kong's Deaf.* Government Printer, Hong Kong
Hussain M T, Aziz D 1989 *Relationships in Sign Language.* ABSA Research Group, Karachi
Macfadden J, et al. 1977 *Sign as You Speak.* Southeast Asian Institute for the Deaf, Philippines
Our Sign Language: Illustration of the Word for the Deaf in Japan 1970 Alliance of the Deaf, Tokyo
Peng F C C 1974 Kinship signs in Japanese Sign Language. *Sign Language Studies* 5: 31–47
Smith W H, et al. 1979 *Shou neng sheng chyau.* Deaf Sign Language Research Association, Taipei
Suwanarat M, et al. 1986 *The Thai Sign Language Dictionary,* Book 1. National Association of the Deaf in Thailand and International Human Assistance Programs, Thailand
Valade Y L R 1854 *Etudes sur la lexicologie et la grammaire du langage naturel des signes.* Librairie philosophique de Ladrange, Paris
Vasishta M, et al. 1982 *An Introduction to Indian Sign Language.* Sign Language Research, College Park, MD
Vasishta M, et al. 1985 *An Introduction to the Bangalore Variety of Indian Sign Language,* Monograph no. 4. Gallaudet Research Institute, Washington, DC
Yau S-C 1982 Constraints on basic sign order and word order universals. In: M R (ed.) *Nonverbal Communication Today: Current Research.* Mouton, The Hague
Yau S-C, He J X 1987 Chinese place names in CSL. In: *Shou yu long.* Kexue puji chubanshe, Guangzhou
Yau S-C, He J X 1989 How deaf children in a Chinese school get their name signs. *Sign Language Studies* 65: 305–22
Yau S-C 1992 *Création gestuelle et débuts du langage.* Ecole des Hautes Etudes en Sciences Sociales, Paris

Yau Shun-chiu

Sign Languages in Australasia

Australia has two signing traditions: the alternate sign languages of Aboriginal Australians which are gestural codes used to represent spoken languages, and the primary sign language of deaf Australians which is an autonomous language in its own right.

Alternate sign languages are still found in the North Central Desert area of Australia but knowledge and use of them is waning (see *Alternate Sign Languages*). They are used by people who are perfectly able to hear and speak but who sign in observation of speech taboos. Recent extensive documentation and analysis reveal alternate sign languages to be formationally constrained in the same kinds of ways as primary sign languages (e.g., in terms of handshapes, significant locations, and movement types). These alternate sign languages follow closely the word-order and morphology of the various spoken languages they are used to represent. Surprisingly, virtually no use of facial expression is made in the Aboriginal sign languages in sign formation or in signed discourse. In contrast, facial expression is vitally important as a grammatical device in the primary sign languages of the deaf.

The Australian sign language of the deaf (called 'Auslan') has evolved from the sign languages brought to Australia during the nineteenth century from Britain and Ireland. The first two Australian schools for the deaf were established by deaf people, themselves British immigrants, very early in the history of the community (1860). In addition, Irish Catholics introduced Irish signs and the one-handed alphabet which they had in turn borrowed from French sign language. The two-handed alphabet (see *Fingerspelling: Two-handed*) and the BSL-based signs have nonetheless always formed the basis of the sign language of the Australian deaf community despite some borrowing of Irish signs.

Since the schools for the deaf played a seminal role in forging and sustaining the deaf community and standardizing sign usage, the subsequent rise of oralist philosophies from the late nineteenth century until the 1970s placed great stress on the signing community. Indeed, vigorous oralism in the Catholic school system has meant that the Irish strand of Australian signing has all but died out. Other traumas to the sign language of the deaf community emerged in the 1960s and 1970s as moves were made to close residential schools for the deaf and introduce 'signed English.' Though signed English legitimated the role of manual communication in education, its introduction was traumatic in that it introduced new signs and undermined the existing sign language of the community. Despite these stresses Auslan has managed to survive in the deaf community itself, being handed down in deaf families and taught to deaf children in school playgrounds.

An Auslan dictionary was the first product of recent linguistic research into the language. Together with other preliminary research into grammatical organization in Auslan a picture of the language is beginning to emerge. Not surprisingly, Auslan appears to be very much like other sign languages such as ASL and BSL. It is, of course, clearly related to the latter.

Auslan has developed a number of complex grammatical processes and markings that are not found in the spoken language of the surrounding community. Some of these linguistic mechanisms seem to have been developed in exploitation of the visual gestural modality in which the language is articulated. In particular and among others, they include the possible articulation of signs with reference to various loci in the signing space for pronominal reference and verb agreement, and the articulation of verb signs with various spatial and movement contours to convey aspectual information. Other linguistic mechanisms exploited in Auslan are also found in spoken languages. For example, the linear order of constituents is significant (though in Auslan this appears to be primarily a function of information structure in the clause rather than grammatical relations), and the manipulation of intonation contours (i.e., facial expression) is similarly used for the grouping and hierarchical ordering of clauses (e.g., subordination), the marking of clause type (e.g., interrogative), and the encoding of interpersonal meanings (e.g., assessment of probability). However, while these linguistic functions are also regularly encoded in the constituent structure of spoken languages, it is not yet clear whether or not some of the lexis and morphosyntax also used to realize these linguistic functions in Auslan represent a borrowing from English.

Auslan is perfectly adequate for everyday conversation, abstract talk, linguistic art, and humor. It has a large and productive vocabulary in areas in which it is used. Until recently, however, Auslan has not been regularly used as the linguistic vehicle in a number of domains and therefore often relies on lexical borrowing from English, usually by fingerspelling but also by mouthing, to augment its vocabulary. Auslan itself does not have a written form nor does it have some of the functional varieties of language often associated with literacy. English itself (both written English and signed English) is the language of literacy for Auslan signers. Importantly, the face-to-face nature of all signed exchanges may impact structurally on the language as there is no imperative to lexicalize and/or grammaticalize in the morphosyntax that which context and intonation might otherwise adequately convey.

Close historical and cultural ties between Australia and New Zealand mean that there are strong similarities between sign language in both countries. However, a powerful oralist tradition in New Zealand, coupled with a small population base, adversely affected the signing community. The introduction of signed English in Australia in the 1970s was cosponsored by New Zealand interests. In recent years both countries have experienced the impact of signed English and the cultural and linguistic influence of ASL.

Bibliography

Johnston T A 1989 *Auslan Dictionary: A Dictionary of the Sign Language of the Australian Deaf Community*. Deafness Resources Australia, Sydney

Johnston T A 1989 Auslan: The sign language of the Australian Deaf community (Doctoral dissertation, University of Sydney)

Kendon A 1988 *Sign Languages of Aboriginal Australia: Cultural, Semiotic and Communicative Perspectives*. Cambridge University Press, Cambridge

T. A. Johnston

Sign Languages in Europe: History and Research

In a strict sense there is no history of sign language in Europe. The information lies embedded in the history of the schools for the deaf in the different countries. Two names and one major event can serve to mark this shortest of overviews, namely Charles Michel de l'Epée of Paris, France, versus Samuel Heinicke of Leipzig, Germany, with their opposite educational philosophies on the one hand, and the convention of Milan, Italy, with its famous—or infamous—resolution on the other.

De l'Epée (1712–89) taught the deaf to read and write French, forgoing speech and using their signs as an obvious natural education tool. Heinicke (1723–90) was not the first but certainly the best known educator to take speech and speech reading as the prime educational goal. Whereas de l'Epée departed from what agreed naturally with the deaf, Heinicke's first concern was their better integration in hearing society. These two philosophies have marked the fundamental controversy on the education of the deaf over the nineteenth and twentieth centuries. They spread, from Paris over France and into parts of Spain, Portugal, Italy, French Switzerland, and, moreover, to the USA; and from Leipzig over the German-speaking countries like the German federal States and Austria, and also into the Low Countries, Scandinavia, and the UK. At the Milan convention (1880), a majority of strongly speech-biased participants voted their preference for speech over sign, in a resolution which has deeply influenced the European education of the deaf and created the negative image of signing for nearly a century thereafter. The teaching of language through speech became the educators' prime objective; the use of sign, as primitive and sublinguistic, had to be avoided, or—at the most and as a last resort—to be restricted to mentally impaired pupils.

In opposition to the USA, where at least most state schools favored a combined, simultaneous use of speech and signs, accepting signing as a natural means of communication outside the classroom, the great majority of their European counterparts tended to adhere to strict oralism, discouraging and even suppressing all use of sign. This did not prevent deaf children everywhere, in Europe as much as in the USA, from following their nature. But it stands to reason that without any feedback and support from adults, the signing of the former remained primitive and underrated, as something to be ashamed of, even by the deaf themselves. Consequently, the higher social status of signing deaf adults and their organizations in the USA has been one of several reasons for the emergence of sign language research (SLR) in that continent in the 1960s and 1970s, prior to similar research in Europe. So, the history of sign in Europe is, paradoxically, a history of early educational acceptance in some countries in the nineteenth century, followed by overall suppression for almost a century thereafter of signing as an acceptable means of deaf communication and as a helpful educational tool. The view was that signing was not worth any serious attention, far less any scientific research. Because it was primitive and sublinguistic, the existence of a sign language as a complete natural language was a priori impossible.

A dramatic turnabout occurred in the 1970s and 1980s, however. Following American initiatives at first, SLR has emerged in some European countries and, little by little, made progress. Its first results, everywhere without exception, have been the discovery of the existence of true sign languages, warranting the proposition that all countries do have them, even if they are not yet aware of them. This is grosso modo the case in the countries east of the former iron curtain, where no SLR has been reported to date. Since SLR in Europe is still in its formative stage, one can hardly speak of its recent history in a strict sense; at the most, one can point to some trends, giving the European endeavors some characteristics of their own.

European SLR centers now in existence are usually small, sometimes restricted to one or two researchers. In such cases the distinction between a center and an individual is hard to make. A center can be firmly and permanently based, e.g., in a university context, or organized on a private, sometimes insecure base; in some cases it is related to a school for the deaf or to a social center for deaf adults, with educational or social applications in its research.

Rather than just enumerating lists of European SLR locations, preference is given here to elaborating upon some specific characteristics of European SLR. This does not imply that European SLR does not cover common, well-defined subject matter. Nowadays it is carried out in all the main research fields of sign linguistics (morphophonology, syntax—including nonmanual features—and semantics), sign psycholinguistics (acquisition, perception and production, iconicity, laterality), sociolinguistics (variation, dialects, bilingualism, interference, discourse) and lexicology (dictionary, notation, computer storage).

Compared to American SLR, it can be seen that the following areas of research receive more specific attention in European SLR: (a) lexicography, (b) acquisition in relation to the education of the deaf child, (c) nonmanual features.

1. Lexicography

It stands to reason that beginning SLR starts with an inventory of the lexicon—as did Stokoe for ASL in the early 1960s. His dictionary was innovative and linguistically well received; however, it distanced itself from numerous practical sign dictionaries already in existence which were all English based—not to say biased—and in frequent use. In most European countries no such popular dictionaries—giving a first, basic inventory of signs—were readily available, or were suppressed if they had been available in

the past. An additional problem was the fact that Europe had not one but many spoken languages, and that, consequently, historical sign inventories were based on different languages. So the first task several European SL researchers set themselves was to take stock of the signs, both practically and scientifically, which meant making a first inventory that was usable in educational and social settings. Late twentieth-century lexicology and its efficient means of notation and computerized storage, had to be combined with convenience in different contexts (the use of sign in schools, home training programs, interpreters' schooling and performance in various situations). This has been a focus of attention in the Hamburg University Center for German Sign Language and Communication of the Deaf (with over 40 collaborators) and the Dutch Foundation for the Deaf and Hard of Hearing Child in collaboration with the General Linguistics Institute of the University of Amsterdam, Holland. A lone researcher (who unfortunately died in 1991) was Paul Jouison, of the Bordeaux School for the Deaf (France), who by himself developed a meticulous and intricate notation system that accounted for all aspects of deaf-to-deaf communication.

2. Sign Language Acquisition in Relation to the Education of Young Deaf Children

As has been stated in the foregoing, sign communication among deaf adults was looked down upon for over half a century in European countries, as an unwanted result of weakhearted, unsuccessful oral education, as an indication of lower intellectual competence or as evidence of an additional handicap. This was even the case among most of the deaf themselves. They believed that good oral skills were the indispensable first conditions for success and true happiness, and, consequently, for complete integration into hearing society. Signing became a form of unacceptable behavior, to be avoided at all costs. Deaf clubs, where signing remained the acceptable but hidden means of communication, were often avoided by upper- and middle-class deaf. In that way the low social and intellectual status of signing became a self-fulfilling prophesy.

The result was that for decades no sociologist, psychologist, linguist, or any otherwise engaged scientist would even think of investigating this primitive, sublinguistic substitute for normal human communication.

However, the only group of professionals engaged with the deaf to be confronted regularly with signing were the educators. In every school for the deaf (especially in the residential schools—the majority) the struggle between natural tendencies and educational demands was a daily issue. The adage was: signs are like weeds, they threaten to suffocate the harvest and should be destroyed. It took an unbiased field linguist more or less by accident to notice the gap between the primitive and awkard oral language production of deaf pupils and their fluent communication among themselves, leading to the hypothesis that possibly two languages might be involved. Three years of research led to the conclusion that at least some features of a visual linguistic system were involved (Tervoort 1953). Stokoe and Tervoort met first in 1957, at Gallaudet. They acknowledged the different attitudes towards sign research in the two continents. In the USA, SLR was beginning to come of age and was developing fast, concentrating on adult use in its pure, unadulterated form, and removed from educational implications. Whereas in Europe, educationally oriented research into signing among deaf children was acceptable as long as it served the final goal of oral education in a better way. The results of Tervoort's second study, based on a comparison of the developmental features of the linguistic competence of some 50 American and Dutch school age (7 to 17 years) deaf students, showed the value of sign but remained an isolated case (Tervoort 1975).

Around that time, in the middle 1970s, however, the poor results of oral teaching had become so evident that many European schools for the deaf began to have second thoughts about the supposedly negative influence of signing. The philosophy of Total Communication (TC), originating from American schools, seemed a more promising alternative. Obviously, educationally oriented research was needed to support that claim. Whereas American SLR kept its distance from educational issues, and some European research centers began to follow suit, a considerable issue for sign research was speech-only versus the new TC-approach. It took some time for the two research concerns to meet and merge, i.e., applied educational research involving the use of sign, and theoretically oriented SLR. Many European centers remain interested in both, e.g., the Linguistic Institutes of the Universities of Stockholm, Helsinki, Trondheim, Amsterdam, Brussels, the Centre for Deaf Studies of the University of Bristol, the Institute of Psychology CRN of the University of Rome, the German Center for SLR of the University of Hamburg. Some centers are involved in socially oriented research, e.g., the Center of TC for the Deaf in Copenhagen, the Deaf Studies Research Unit of the Department of Sociology of the University of Durham.

Most recently, a synthesis is in view between theoretical and applied SLR. As far as sign language acquisition in relation to the education of young deaf children is concerned, TC (in terms of its application—Signed English, Signed German, Signed Dutch) is seen as a transitory compromise, unsatisfactory as a permanent answer, and to be replaced by the use of sign language—BSL, GSL, SLN, and so on. The major educationally oriented SLR issue has become the theme of bilingualism. The ultimate educational consequence of the social reality of the two worlds deaf people live in, has to be their bilingual education.

3. Nonmanual Features

From the beginning of SLR in the 1960s, it has been acknowledged that not only the hands and fingers but also the whole body, especially the head and the face, have their indispensable functions in conveying the complete message. The hands, as the main articulators, initially had most of the linguists' attention. It took researchers some time to realize that in communication between deaf people body language, specifically eye gaze, mime and facial expressions, not only exert the usual psychological functions—seeking or avoiding contact, questioning, doubting or negating what is being communicated, as well as expressing joy, fear, sadness, anger—but can also be part of the language in a conventionalized, arbitrarily rule-governed way. Initial American research into this matter dissociated itself explicitly from including any remnants of speech. Movements of the mouth and lips were accepted as part of the language only insofar as they did not originate from (the teaching of) the spoken language. Speech which never could become part of a sign language as such, was an axiomatic point of departure. If it appeared to be part of the exchange between deaf people anyhow, it had to be considered a foreign element, a case of language borrowing, or rather of language interference, where a spoken element prevented the mouth from executing the required mimics. This standpoint was characteristic for the first period of theoretically oriented search for the abstract, pure ASL. At present it seems removed from the reality of what actually happens, even in ASL.

In more orally oriented Europe, speech elements far more often do find their way into the authentic communication of the deaf among themselves, to the extent that they are fully incorporated in the language and sometimes assume new functions they do not have in the spoken language. The moment field linguists succeeded in obtaining videotapes of true, unbiased sign language communication between deaf persons (e.g., by letting deaf technicians do the recording), oral features comparable to the typical ASL characteristics, American researchers had found, had to be distinguished from features originating from speech teaching, the most important conclusion being that both types are authentic elements of the sign language as such. New approaches in the fields of bilingualism, interlanguage, pidgins, and creoles facilitated the search for the linguistic account of these phenomena. Vogt-Svendsen (1984) of the Linguistics Department of the University of Trondheim, as well as Schermer (1990) and Coerts (1992) of the Institute of General Linguistics of the University of Amsterdam have carried out extensive research into these typically European aspects of SLR.

4. Conclusion

This overview unfortunately stands out by its incompleteness. It is impossible to give, in a few pages, a reasonably full account of SLR in Europe, its historical background, its coming of age in the 1980s, and its present state, as it is carried out in many places by a growing number of dedicated scholars. The emphasis has been placed on a few research issues which seem to be more typically European than others. This by no means implies that research into other aspects is less important: they might even be more so, but less characteristic of what happens in Europe.

Bibliography

Ahlgren I, Bergman B (eds.) 1980 *Papers from the First International Symposium on Sign Language Research*. Swedish National Association of the Deaf, Leksand

Coerts J 1992 Nonmanual grammatical markers: An analysis of interrogatives, negations and topicalisations in sign language of the Netherlands. (Doctoral dissertation, University of Amsterdam)

Edmondson W H, Karlsson F (eds.) 1990 *SLR'87: Papers from the Fourth International Symposium on Sign Language Research, Lappeenranta, Finland July 15–19, 1987*. Signum Press, Hamburg

Kyle J, Woll B (eds.) 1983 *Language in Sign: Papers from the Second International Symposium on Sign Language Research*. Croom Helm, London

Loncke F, Boyes Braem P, Lebrun Y (eds.) 1984 *Recent Research on European Sign Languages*. Swetz & Zeitlinger, Lisse

Prillwitz S, Vollhaber T (eds.) 1990 *Current Trends in European Sign Language Research: Proceedings of the Third European Congress on Sign Language Research, Hamburg July 26–29, 1989.* Signum Verlag, Hamburg

Schermer T M 1990 In search of a language: Influences from spoken Dutch on sign language of the Netherlands. (Doctoral dissertation, University of Amsterdam)

Stokoe W, Volterra V. (eds.) 1985 *SLR '83: Proceedings of the* III *International Symposium on Sign Language Research.* Linstok Press, Silver Spring, MO

Tervoort B T (ed.) 1986 *Signs of Life: Proceedings of the Second European Congress on Sign Language Research.* The Dutch Foundation for the Deaf and Hearing Impaired Child, The Institute for General Linguistics of the University of Amsterdam, The Dutch Council of the Deaf, Amsterdam

Tervoort B T 1953 *Structurele Analyse van Visueel Taalgebruik binnen een Groep Dove Kinderen,* vols. I and II. North-Holland, Amsterdam

Tervoort B T 1975 *Developmental Features of Visual Communication: A Psycholinguistic Analysis of Deaf Children's Growth in Communicative Competence.* North-Holland, Amsterdam

Vogt-Svendsen M Word-pictures in Norwegian Sign Language (NSL): A preliminary analysis. In: *Working Papers in Linguistics* 2. University of Trondheim, Trondheim

B. T. Tervoort

Sign Languages in South America

Sign language research in South America is incipient. Findings to date indicate that the continent's sign languages are autonomous systems: that is, they appear to be distinct languages rather than dialects of one source language (see *Sign Language*; *Sign Language Acquisition*). Nevertheless, due to language contact, some linguistic interference may be observed near international boundaries. For instance, the Brazilian sign language (LSCB) used in southern Brazil has imported some lexical items from Uruguay and Argentina. By the same token, linguistic interference from Brazil and Argentina can be noted in Uruguay. These influences are, however, basically restricted to the level of borrowed lexical items. Sign language work has begun in most countries—published data is available from Argentina, Uruguay, Chile, Puerto Rico, and Venezuela, as well as Brazil.

Since no grammars or dictionaries have yet been completed for these languages, one source of comparison has been fingerspelling. The fingerspelling alphabet employed in each country may indicate the source of a modern sign language, as fingerspelling is the result of language contact as well as of past contact between educators and the deaf (see *Fingerspelling: One-handed*).

Fingerspelling forms in Venezuela, Chile, and Brazil, plus one of the two forms used in Uruguay, are very similar and all one-handed; they would appear to have originated from French, Spanish, and/or USA alphabets. However, in Argentina and in Salto, Uruguay, fingerspelling is bimanual and relies on head-touching as well. This may reflect the influence of the ancient Italian manual alphabet.

Although Brazil's first Deaf Club was founded with the help of deaf people from Argentina, this appears to have had no influence on fingerspelling, since the alphabets used

in these two nations are distinctly different. Italian educators traveled to Argentina at the time that schools for the deaf were founded there, introducing their kind of fingerspelling. Through language contact, this variety spread into the Salto region, in neighboring Uruguay. The same may have occurred with French educators in Brazil, and Spanish educators in Venezuela and Montevideo.

The Brazilian Kaapor Sign Language (LSKB) does not use fingerspelling. This indigenous people has never had any schools, nor has it had contact with educators who could have introduced the system. Research on Brazilian Sign Language is perhaps the furthest developed.

Researchers of LSCB and LSKB have discovered certain features unique to one or the other of these two Brazilian sign languages:

(a) *Time*: Like most other known sign languages, LSCB uses a horizontal time line, with past located in the back, future in the front, and present in the same plane as the signer's body. In LSKB, however, the time line is vertical, with future at the top, present at the center of the signer's trunk, and past evidently unmarked, as in the oral Kaapor language.

(b) *Negation*: LSCB uses five negative forms, 'negative' defined here as a form that contradicts or is the opposite of a 'positive' term: (i) the lexical sign NOT, which may follow or precede a verb or adjective; (ii) a kind of suprasegmental marker that occurs simultaneous with the sign (shaking the head from side to side); (iii) a negative marker that incorporates the NOT sign movement with lexical items like HAVE; (iv) a negative movement marker, away from the body, which affects signs whose movement occurs at or towards the body, such as with WANT, KNOW, and LIKE; and (v) an inversion of movement in any direction, which occurs with the negative poles of such signs as POSSIBLE, ALREADY, and SUCCEED— that is, IMPOSSIBLE, NOT-YET, and NOT-SUCCEED. The negative markers (iii)–(v)—called 'negative incorporation'—also occur in American Sign Language (ASL).

(c) *Classifiers*: All but two LSCB classifiers are quite similar to ASL classifiers. ASL presents a 3-Cl (classifier with hand configuration 3)[1] for vehicles, while LSCB uses the B-Cl. But LSCB also has a classifier not found in the literature on ASL or European sign languages: the Y-Cl, which is used for fat people; for fine clothes, food, and objects; and for objects of irregular shape such as high-heeled shoes, submarines, and aircraft (see Fig. 1).

(d) *Pronominal system*: The LSCB pronominal system is very rich. There are two forms for the first person singular: a G_1-hand pointing toward the signer and a B-hand touching the signer's chest, the latter being the emphatic form. The third person present can be expressed using two signs: one is a polite form in which a G_1-hand is pointed at the third person, but touching the palm of the left B-hand, which 'shields' the action; the other consists of a G_1-hand pointed directly at the third person present. The other pronominal signs present a peculiar form but are similar to those of other sign languages.

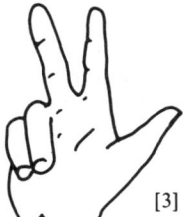 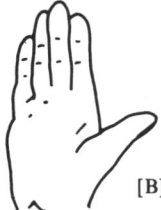  

[3] [B] [Y] [G₁]

Figure 1.

(e) *Modals*: LSCB modals are abstract despite their iconicity (see also *Iconicity*). Although iconicity was long believed to be the opposite of abstractness, LSCB data shows that iconicity can serve semantic purposes—that is, it can serve to build basic meanings in semantic domains. Lakoff and Johnson (1980) point out that several semantic fields are based on orientational metaphors, for example, 'up' and 'down.' In LSCB, the majority of the root or deontic modal signs use either neutral space or the left (nondominant) hand as point of articulation. Hands and energetic movements seem to play a relatively important role in signing these modals. In the epistemic system, most signs consist of nonenergetic movements using the head as point of articulation. This can be characterized as iconicity, and can be associated with two metaphors: 'the head' and 'hands in action.' The first constitutes the basis of epistemic modals (certainty, probability, or possibility in reasoning processes); the second is the orientational metaphor of deontic modals (obligation, permission, and ability in the real world). Deontic modals correspond to a concrete level of actions close to sociophysical forces or causality of events and action, while epistemic modals correspond to an intellectual level related to the causality of reasoning processes.

The study of LSCB modals uncovers evidence which reinforces Lyons's (1977) idea that there are only two systems of modality in natural languages: epistemic and deontic. An orientational metaphor for alethic concepts has not been found in LSCB.

(f) *Politeness*: A comparison of gestural-visual and oral-auditive languages reveals that language modality constrains the structure and rules of linguistic interaction. For example, unlike oral languages, LSCB uses no vocatives (proper names and other expressions with a politeness function) in referring to an addressee in a request. In LSCB, deixis and pointing are not considered impolite in situations where it would be inappropriate to use pure pronouns in Portuguese, or even ruder actually to point. The only case in which pointing is interpreted as impolite in LSCB is when there is no intimacy, or at least a certain level of familiarity, between the signer and the person pointed at; in this case, the polite form mentioned above would be employed, with the left B-hand hiding the pointing act.

Portuguese and LSCB politeness strategies show some similarities—that is, formal polite expressions meaning 'please' or 'excuse me,' requests for permission, hints, modals, etc. In the same way that intonation has a major politeness function in Portuguese requests, LSCB signers use facial expressions that become more accentuated as the request becomes 'more difficult' (i.e., when social distance and the power relationship between the sender and the addressee are greater and when what is requested has a higher cost). In these cases, the movement of the sign is also altered, becoming shorter and softer.

These strategies may be common to several sign languages; if that is true, they may be the result of constraints imposed by the gestural-visual modality of language. But the strategies may also be cultural, and if so, one would expect to see parallels between them and Portuguese intonation.

Bibliography

Lakoff G, Johnson M 1980 *Metaphors We Live By*. University of Chicago Press, Chicago, IL

Lyons J 1977 *Semantics*, 2 vols. Cambridge University Press, Cambridge

L. Ferreira Brito

Signal Processing for Speech

To understand much about the generation and recognition of speech sounds, both by humans and machines, one first needs an intuitive feeling for a range of more general signal processing concepts. These in turn rest on a set of mathematical ideas; and this may present a problem for those who find mathematics unattractive. The first few sections of this article therefore try to provide a nonrigorous intuitive introduction to the mathematical ideas that will be needed in the rest of the article. Readers who feel comfortable with the topics covered are invited to skip these sections.

The rest of the article offers an introduction to signal processing techniques relevant to speech. There are no detailed recipes for implementing these techniques, and there is no attempt to give a comprehensive account of all the methods commonly used, nor to provide rigorous proofs of the results quoted. However, if the aim of providing an intuitive understanding of the basic ideas of the field is successful, readers should have the background required for the other articles on speech technology, and those who need more detailed information on signal processing techniques should have the framework necessary to acquire it (see *Speech Coding and Compression, Stochastic Techniques for Automatic Speech Recognition, Speech Recognition, Automatic: Rule Based Methods, Neural Net and Connectionist Methods in Speech Recognition and Synthesis*.)

1. Differentiation and Integration

Imagine a car gaining speed on a straight road, causing the occupants to be pulled back into the seat. By reading the speedometer once and then again ten seconds later, one can make an estimate, $\hat{a}$, of the acceleration in mph/hr as the difference in the speedometer readings, δV, say 5 mph, divided by the time difference, δt, in this case $\frac{1}{360}$ of an hour. That is:

$$\hat{a} = \frac{\delta v}{\delta t} = 5 \times 360 = 1{,}800 \text{ mph/hr}$$

But, particularly if there are gear changes, the acceleration will not be constant over the ten seconds, so $\hat{a}$ represents its average value. Yet it is its *instantaneous* value that is felt as a force. Notionally, this value can be approached by taking measurements over progressively shorter intervals. Of course, this quickly becomes impracticable as the diminishing speed differences are swamped by the inaccuracies in speedometer readings. An expression can be written down, however, for the instantaneous acceleration, $\hat{a}$, namely:

$$a = \lim_{\delta t \to 0} \frac{\delta v}{\delta t} = \frac{dv}{dt}$$

Acceleration is said to be the *differential* of the speed with respect to time. Differentiation represents the rate of change of one variable with respect to another variable on which it depends.

Although a here is the result of a limiting process that cannot be fully replicated in practice, it does have a clear physical meaning, and it can be measured in other ways. For example, by measuring the force due to acceleration with a spring gauge a good estimate can be obtained of this instantaneous acceleration without reference to the speedometer or to a watch.

Now suppose that we also want to know how far the car has traveled over the ten-second period. If the speed were constant, we could simply multiply that speed by the time, that is, by 1/360. However, since it is varying, we have to take shorter intervals of time, δt, over which the speed, which we can write as $v(t)$, will have varied less. We can then get an approximation to the distance traveled by adding up the distances traveled in each δt in the ten seconds. Our approximation of treating v as constant over the time δt clearly gets better as δt gets shorter, and gets perfect as δt tends to zero, though the number of terms we would then have to add tends to infinity. We can write this as:

$$s = \lim_{\delta t \to 0} \sum_{t=0}^{t=10} v(t)\delta t = \int_{t=0}^{t=10} v(t)\, dt$$

The distance traveled is said to be the 'integral' of the speed with respect to time. Integration represents the accumulated effect of one variable with respect to another on which it depends.

In the same way, we could get a rough estimate of the speed change over the ten seconds by sampling the acceleration measured by the spring gauge at a series of instants separated by short time intervals, δt, multiplying these values by δt and summing them. Again, the result becomes exact as δt tends to zero; and we can say that the speed change is the integral of the acceleration over time. (If the acceleration had been tracked from when the car was stationary, we could say that the speed itself was the integral of the acceleration with respect to time; but in our case to get the final speed we have to add a constant to our integral, namely the speed at the start of the ten seconds.)

We have just seen that, within a constant, the speed is the integral with respect to time of the acceleration; and previously that acceleration is the differential with respect to time of speed. This inverse relationship between the integral and the differential is quite general: apart from the loss of information about the constant (the initial speed in the car example) the processes of integration and differentiation cancel each other out exactly.

If distance traveled is the integral of the speed with respect to time, speed must, by the inverse relationship, be the differential of distance with respect to time, i.e., $v = ds/dt$. But acceleration is the differential of speed with respect to time, so it must be the *double* differential of distance with respect to time, which we write as $a = d^2s/dt^2$. Distance, speed and acceleration form a series of parameters related to each other in one direction by progressive differentiation with respect to time, and therefore in the other direction by progressive integration with respect to time.

2. Means, Variances, Correlations, and Covariances

To characterize the values of a particular quantity, say the market value of houses in a neighborhood, we would probably want to start by describing the typical value. By far the commonest way of doing this is to compute the average of mean—simply the sum of all the values divided by the number of such values. We can write this as:

$$\bar{x} = \frac{1}{N} \sum_{i=1}^{i=N} x_i$$

where N is the number of houses and x_i is the value of the ith house.

Occasionally, alternative measures of the typical value are used. Suppose, for example, the houses in a neighborhood were mostly inexpensive, but a single mansion affected the mean enough to distort the impression of the typical house value. In this case, the 'median' value would be more informative. The median is the point below which half the values occur, and, of course, above which half the values occur. Its great merit is that it is unaffected by atypical extreme values. Its weaknesses are that it makes less efficient use of all the information available than does the mean, and it is less easy to manipulate mathematically.

The next most basic descriptor of the distribution of values would measure how closely the values cluster about their typical value. An obvious choice for this descriptor might seem to be the average difference of the individual values from the mean without regard to the sign of the difference. This 'mean deviation,' however, turns out to be less useful than the average squared difference from the mean, called the 'variance' and frequently represented by the symbol σ^2. The square root of the variance, σ, is called the 'standard deviation.' Such a measure of spread about the mean is not too useful if instead of clustering about their mean the individual values cluster into two or more separate groups (in the house example, for instance, there might be just two basic designs) but when the distribution of values has just one clear peak, and when the values are arranged roughly symmetrically about this peak, the variance is a good measure of spread. In particular, values are often found to follow a symmetrical bell-shaped distribution, known as a 'normal' or 'Gaussian' distribution. For such a distribution, the probability of obtaining any specific value can be calculated if the mean and variance are both known.

If we are interested in two variables—perhaps the floor area of a house and its market value—we might ask whether knowing one allows us to make a better guess of the value of the other. The relationship between the two variables may be complex, but most often we look for a simple, 'linear,' relationship between them of the form $y = ax + c$. We can take the variables x and y and subtract their means from them. This process does not affect the properties we are interested in here, but it makes the behavior easier to picture, and it makes the mathematical expressions simpler. The constant, c, for instance, in the expression linking x and y becomes zero and disappears.

In general, knowing x will not allow us to predict y perfectly. Rather, we can write for the ith values of x and y, that $y_i = ax_i + e_i$, where e_i is the error in this particular prediction. The amount of error depends on how closely related x and y are and on the value we choose for a. Usually, a is chosen to minimize the average squared error, which we can write as $\langle e_i^2 \rangle$, where the averaging implied by the pointed brackets is over i, that is, over all pairs of values. This 'least squared error' criterion is common in statistics and in signal processing. In signal processing, the 'power' in a signal depends on the average squared value of the signal, so we can describe the least squared error criterion as a minimum error power criterion. The process of deriving a in this way is known as 'linear regression,' and a is a regression coefficient. The expression for a turns out to be:

$$a = \frac{\sum xy}{\sum x^2} \text{ or in simpler notation } \frac{\langle xy \rangle}{\sigma_x^2}$$

By analogy with the variance, which in the new notation we could write as $\langle x^2 \rangle$, $\langle xy \rangle$ is called the 'covariance' of the variables x and y.

The linear predictability of one variable from another is measured by the 'correlation coefficient.' When the value of this statistic is at one of the extreme ends of its range, namely ± 1, one variable can be perfectly predicted from the other using a linear relationship; and when it has a value of 0, knowing the value of the first variable is of no help in predicting the value of the second by means of a linear relationship. The sign of the correlation coefficient is negative when an increase in one of the variables is linked to a decrease in the other, and positive when they increase together, as house prices and floor areas would. The expression for the correlation coefficient, ρ, is $\rho = \langle xy \rangle / \sigma_x \sigma_y$. We can see the validity of this expression for the maximum case, since if y is perfectly predictable from x then $y = ax$ exactly. Then $\langle xy \rangle = a \langle x^2 \rangle = a\sigma_x^2$ and $\sigma_y = a\sigma_x$, so $\sigma_x \sigma_y = a\sigma_x^2$, and $\rho = 1$. When the values of the variables are symmetrically distributed about their means, we can also see the validity of the expression for the minimum case, since for any value of x the corresponding value of y is equally likely to be negative or positive, so the average value of xy is zero, making $\langle xy \rangle$, and hence ρ, zero. Although the proof is different, the result remains true when there is no symmetry about the means.

If x and y are represented as coordinates on a pair of rectangular axes, we can construct other pairs of rectangular axes that are rotated with respect to x and y. The information originally contained in the variables x and y would then be contained in a new pair of variables, x' and y', that are a linear combination of x and y; that is, $x' = ax + by$. As the axes are rotated, the variances of the corresponding variables will change, but the sum of the two variances remains the same; i.e., $\sigma_x'^2 + \sigma_y'^2 = \sigma_x^2 + \sigma_y^2$. It turns out that with the pair of rotated axes for which the difference between $\sigma_x'^2$ and $\sigma_y'^2$ is a maximum, $\langle x'y' \rangle = 0$, i.e., the variables are uncorrelated.

Everything discussed so far about single variables and pairs of variables extends to arbitrary numbers of variables. The mean, a single number for a single variable, becomes for n variables, a vector defining a point in n-dimensional space. The variance and covariance properties can be represented by a table symmetrical about the diagonal from the upper-left to the lower-right corner called a 'covariance matrix.' Its diagonal elements are the variances of the individual variables, and its ijth element is the covariance $\langle x_i x_j \rangle$ between the ith and jth variables x_i and x_j. For the generalization of the Gaussian distribution, the 'multivariate Gaussian,' the distribution is completely defined by its mean vector and its covariance matrix.

Just as a pair of variables can be converted by rotation to a new pair where correlation is absent, so any set of variables can be converted by rotations to a new set where there is no correlation between any pair. The only nonzero terms in the covariance matrix then lie along the diagonal. The new variables are called 'principal components.' As with the two-variable case, the total variance, i.e., the sum of the diagonal terms of the covariance matrix, is unchanged, and the separation between the largest and smallest variance is maximized. In fact, the first i principal components out of n contain the largest possible proportion of the total variance in the n variables that can be obtained using linear combinations. Principal components are an efficient way of representing information: first, because it is more efficient to represent information with uncorrelated variables; and second, because the lower principal components often have very low variance and can be replaced by their means without much loss of information. Indeed, judged by the least squares criterion, and allowing only linear combinations of the original variables, the first i principal components constitute the best way of representing the information contained in n variables with just i variables, the remaining $n - i$ being replaced by their means. Since the process of transforming to principal components is reversible, we can encode data efficiently in terms of principal components and later transform back to the original set of variables.

3. Autocorrelation, Crosscorrelation, and Convolution

Given an ordered sequence of values we might look for correlations between pairs of values with a particular separation. Daily maximum temperatures, for example, might be expected to show a correlation with the same measurements a year later. We have seen how the correlation between pairs of variables can be measured by multiplying together corresponding values and summing the result. The same approach can be taken with sequences, so we can compute:

$$r(i) = \frac{1}{N} \sum_{j=1}^{j=N} x(j)x(j+i)$$

where $r(i)$, the ith autocorrelation coefficient, measures the correlation between pairs of ordered samples of the variable x that are i samples apart. This definition differs slightly from that for the ordinary correlation coefficient where we scale by the range of the variables by dividing by $\sigma_x \sigma_y$. We could choose to do the same thing here. Assuming, apart from its periodic properties, that the sequence is not changing over time, the variance in the sequence will not be affected by delays, so the scale factor is just σ_x^2, or $r(0)$—the power in the sequence.

The zeroth autocorrelation coefficient, $r(0)$, effectively measures the correlation of a variable with itself; and since it cannot be more correlated with any time-displaced version, $r(0)$ represents the largest possible value of the autocorrelation coefficients of a sequence of values. If the values in the sequence are changing only slowly, $r(1)$ and other low-delay coefficients will be positive and have values close to $r(0)$.

An ordered set of values that exactly repeat themselves after a delay of say M samples is said to be a periodic sequence with period M. For such a sequence, $r(M) = r(0)$. Indeed, if the sequence repeats after M samples, it must also repeat after $2M$ samples, $3M$ samples, etc.; so $r(nM) = r(0)$ for any integer n, provided the sequence continues for long enough. (For simplicity, all the discussion so far has assumed that the sequences are long enough that complications from end effects can be ignored.)

The concept of autocorrelation can be extended from sequences of discrete samples to continuous waveforms. The separations we can investigate are then no longer limited to integer values, and the autocorrelation properties of a waveform are represented by a continuous-valued function $r(\tau)$, where τ is the separation in time over which the correlation is being measured. Equally, the summation used in the discrete-sample case becomes an integral, so $r(\tau) = \int x(t)x(t+\tau)\,dt$.

In voiced speech, the vocal tract is excited by the quasi-periodic closure of the vocal cords. Unless the vocal tract is changing its shape very quickly, the resulting speech waveform approximately repeats itself following each closure. The repetition rate is called the 'fundamental frequency,' and many applications of speech signal processing involve its determination. The autocorrelation function of the speech waveform is one way of doing so, since the repetition of the waveform will result in a peak at a time delay corresponding to successive vocal cord closures and at integer multiples of this delay.

When periodicity is sought using autocorrelation, the waveform is multiplied with a delayed version of itself. One might ask why we do not seek periodicity by subtracting the waveform from a delayed version of itself and finding the delay values at which the waveform cancels itself out: subtraction is a simpler computation than multiplication. Such an approach, followed by the computation of the average absolute magnitude of the difference function (and therefore called AMDF) works well with perfectly periodic waveforms; but in speech the shape of the waveform is often repeated periodically but its scale varies over time,

and subtraction then fails to produce cancellation. AMDF is therefore generally used only in combination with other processing.

Just as a waveform can be correlated with itself, it can also be correlated with another waveform as a function of relative delay. We can write this as $c(\tau) = \int x(t)y(t+\tau)\,dt$ where the two waveforms being crosscorrelated are $x(t)$ and $y(t)$. Crosscorrelation is rarely used in speech signal processing except in multisensor methods for noise reduction and beam forming.

A closely related process to crosscorrelation, namely 'convolution,' is, however, central to much speech processing. Formally, the convolution, $y(t)$, of a waveform $x(t)$ with a second waveform $h(\tau)$ is $y(t) = \int x(t-\tau)h(\tau)\,d\tau$. This definition is suitable for one-dimensional signals such as a speech waveform; but one of the clearest examples of convolution occurs in two dimensions. Imagine a camera whose lens is slightly out of focus for the scene being photographed. A point of light arriving from the scene will appear on the film spread into a small round blur. The whole image on the film can be interpreted as being composed of a set of such points of light varying in color and intensity and with each point spread by the blurring pattern. The set of points corresponds to the image that would be obtained if the camera were in focus, and the actual image is the sum of the overlapping blurred points; that is, the convolution of the focused image and the blurring pattern.

4. Sine Waves and Fourier Analysis

If we take a point on the circumference of a rotating circle lying in a vertical plane and plot its height as a function of time, the periodic curve traced out is a sine wave (see Fig. 1). The maximum vertical excursion, i.e., the radius of the circle, is the 'amplitude' of the sine wave; the repetition rate of the waveform, i.e., the number of rotations of the circle in unit time, is the 'frequency'; and the angle at a given instant between the point on the circle and the horizontal diameter is the 'phase' of the waveform. When the phase angle is zero, the vertical height of the point on the circle is zero; it then moves to the maximum positive vertical height when the phase equals 90°, and so on round the circle. A 'cosine' wave is a sine wave with its phase advanced by 90°: it therefore has its maximum positive value when the phase is zero, and moves down through zero to its

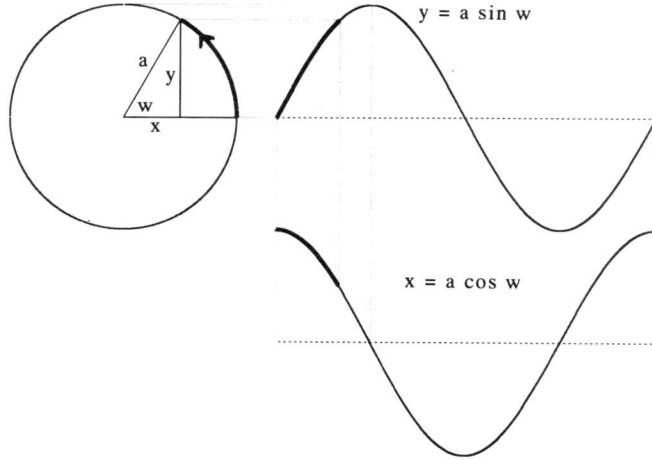

Figure 1. Sine and cosine waves traced out by motion around a circle.

maximum negative value, and so on. If the sine wave is the vertical projection of the location of the point, the cosine wave is its horizontal projection. The sine and cosine functions are written: $a\sin(2\pi ft + \phi)$ and $a\cos(2\pi ft + \phi)$ respectively, where a is the amplitude, f the frequency, and ϕ the phase at time $t = 0$. Frequencies are measured in cycles per second, or *Hertz*, abbreviated as *Hz*.

Why should sine waves (and 'spectra,' which are a description of a signal in terms of sine waves) play a central role in signal processing? The answer lies in three linked properties. The first of these is that differentiating a sine wave results in another sine wave of the same frequency. The amplitude is changed to $2\pi fa$, and the phase is advanced by 90°. The phase shift occurs because the fastest rate of change is when the value of the sine wave is zero, i.e., when the phase is 0° or 180°, and it is zero when the sine wave has its peak value, i.e., 90° later. The multiplication of the amplitude by f is intuitively obvious, since if the frequency of a sine wave is increased by a factor n, n times as many cycles fit into a given time period and the rate of change of the waveform with time must have increased by the same factor. Integration, as the inverse of differentiation, results in the amplitude being divided by $2\pi f$ and in a phase delay of 90°.

The sine wave is the only periodic waveform to preserve its form under differentiation. But there is a nonperiodic waveform with the same property, namely the 'exponential' function, a^x, for which differentiation results in the same function multiplied by a constant. When $a = e$, an irrational number approximately equal to 2.72, the multiplicative constant is 1. The rate of increase of the exponential e^x at any point is therefore equal to its value at that point. By setting $x = ct$, we can generalize the exponential to e^{ct} (Fig. 2a). The rate of growth is then still proportional to the current value, but it is scaled by the constant c. That is, the differential with respect to t is ce^{ct}.

Sine waves and exponentials frequently appear multiplied together in signal processing. The waveform produced by a simple resonator ringing freely (e.g., the sound wave produced by a tuning fork after being struck), has the form $e^{ct}\sin(2\pi ft)$ (Fig. 2b). Since such a freely ringing resonance must be losing energy and be therefore decaying (it is said to be 'damped,' from the image of damping a fire), the constant c in the expression must have a negative value. Indeed, this is the usual case, for if c is positive the waveform grows unbounded, and the process generating it is said to be 'unstable.' The product of a decaying exponential

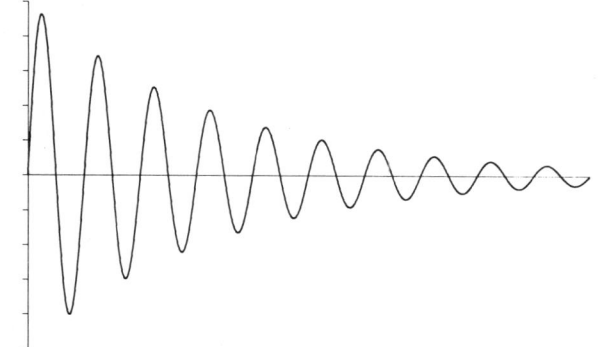

Figure 2b. Exponentially decaying sine wave (damped sinusoid) $e^{ct}\sin(2\pi ft)$.

and a sine wave is called a 'damped sinusoid.' The expression for the exponential is often written $e^{-2\pi bt}$, where b is now a positive constant for a stable process, and the 2π multiplier puts b into the same units as the frequency, f.

A large proportion of the processes applied to signals share the properties of being 'linear' and 'time invariant.' A process is time-invariant if the result of subjecting a signal to it is the same whenever the signal is presented. Some important processes in speech signal processing, e.g., the acoustic effect of the vocal tract and its synthetic analogues, are not strictly time invariant. However, for the purposes of the discussion here 'time invariant' means that the parameters of the process do not change appreciably over the timescale defined by the frequencies and rates of exponential decay needed to describe the signal. In these terms, most, though not all, processes in speech signal processing are time invariant.

Linearity means that if a waveform $x(t)$ is produced when a waveform $u(t)$ is presented to a process, and $y(t)$ when $v(t)$ is presented, then the result of presenting $u(t) + v(t)$ will be to produce the waveform $x(t) + y(t)$. It is as though the two waveforms pass through the process without noticing the presence of the other. A subsidiary property is that changing the size of the input by a constant scaling factor will have exactly the same scaling effect on the output from the process. Amplifiers and graphic equalizers in consumer audio systems are linear systems—unless the volume is turned up so loud that they overload. They are also time invariant—until the settings of the controls are changed. On the other hand, a half-wave rectifier (a process that lets through only positive signals) is not linear, since the polarity of the sum of two signals, and hence the response of the process, depends on the relationship between them.

The second major property of a sine wave is that when it is presented to any linear time-invariant process the output is always a sine wave of possibly different amplitude and phase but of the same frequency. This property, which follows from the differentiation property, is shared by no other periodic waveform, and otherwise only by exponentials and by the product of an exponential and a sine wave: a sine wave passed through a graphic equalizer will preserve its appearance, but a square wave will not in general come out looking square.

The third property, which again follows from the first, is 'orthogonality.' A pair of functions $\phi(x)$ and $\psi(x)$ are said to be orthogonal over the interval from a to b if:

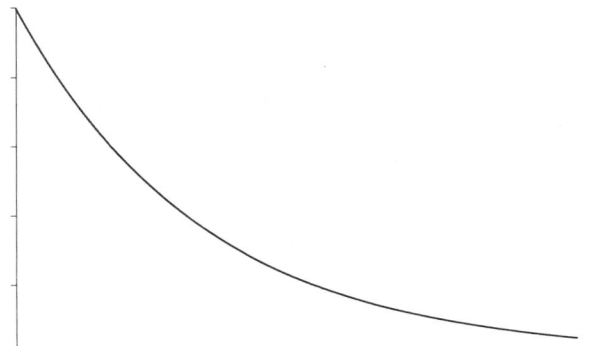

Figure 2a. Decaying exponential, e^{ct}, with a negative value for c.

$$\int_{x=a}^{x=b} \phi(x)\psi(x)\,dx = 0 \quad \text{while} \quad \int_{x=a}^{x=b} \phi(x)^2\,dx = p \quad \text{and}$$

$$\int_{x=a}^{x=b} \psi(x)^2\,dx = q$$

where p and q are both nonzero. It is always possible to scale the functions to make p and q equal to one. This process is called normalization, and the resulting functions are said to be 'orthonormal.'

Two sine waves of different frequency are orthogonal to each other over an interval that exactly spans a whole number of periods of both waveforms. For example, if this interval is one second, a sine wave of frequency 1 cycle per second, i.e., 1 Hz, is orthogonal to a sine wave of 2, 3, 4, and indeed any whole number of cycles per second. This property holds equally for pairs of cosine waves and for a sine wave and a cosine wave; and in this last case it remains true even when the two frequencies are the same.

In the example just given, the 1 Hz wave, the lowest possible frequency of a waveform that is periodic over a one-second interval, is known as the 'fundamental,' and the waves at exact multiples of this frequency are said to be 'harmonics' of this fundamental. In the vocabulary of music they are called 'overtones.'

Sine waves are not the only family of periodic waveforms to be orthogonal to each other, though most such families are not. For example, symmetrical square waves, with equal positive and negative portions, do not form an orthogonal set.

With one minor qualification, the set of sine and cosine waves that have a whole number of periods in a particular interval form a complete orthogonal (or when suitably scaled, orthonormal) basis set over that interval. This means that any waveform that is periodic over the interval can be produced by adding together proportions of the sine and cosine waves.

Moreover, the proportion of any given component can always be uniquely determined by what amounts to correlating the composite waveform with the particular component, which, if normalized, has effectively had its variance set to one. We can see how this works by writing the composite waveform in terms of its components. That is, $f(x) = \sum a_n \phi_n(x)$, where $\phi_n(x)$ is the nth orthonormal (scaled sine or cosine) waveform. Then:

$$\int \phi_n(x)f(x)dx = \int \phi_n(x)\sum_k a_k \phi_k(x)dx = \sum_k a_k \int \phi_n(x)\phi_k(x)dx$$

$$= a_n \int \phi_n(x)^2 dx = a_n$$

This way of determining the proportions of the various components in a composite waveform works for any set of orthonormal functions, but when the set consists of sines and cosines the process is known as 'Fourier analysis' and the resulting a_n are said to be the coefficients of a 'Fourier series.'

The qualification on completeness mentioned above is that to construct waveforms with a nonzero mean we have to include in the basis set an additional waveform which is simply a constant. Such a waveform can be viewed as a cosine waveform of frequency zero, and it is orthogonal to the other sine and cosine waveforms in the set. The

corresponding zero-frequency component in the composite waveform is often loosely called the 'DC component.'

The separation in frequency between sine or cosine waves that form an orthogonal set depends on the range over which all the members of the set are periodic. As we saw earlier, if this range is 1 second, the frequencies are separated by 1 Hz. If the range is 10 seconds, the lowest frequency that is periodic over the range is 0.1 Hz, the next 0.2 Hz, then 0.3 Hz, and so on. The separation is therefore 0.1 Hz. In general, the separation between adjacent frequencies is inversely proportional to the range, i.e., to the repeat period of the composite periodic waveform that we need to represent. As this period tends to infinity, the frequency separation tends to zero. Thus, to represent a waveform whose repeat period is infinite (i.e., an 'aperiodic' waveform) we need a continuous spectrum of sine and cosine waves instead of the discrete series needed for periodic waveforms.

Where in the discrete case we might express the proportion of the nth sine wave as s_n, the equivalent information in the continuous case is expressed by the density of the sine waves, $s(f)$, at the frequency f. Otherwise, the technique for determining the presence in the composite waveform of a particular frequency is much the same as for the discrete case except that the integration is over an infinite range. The reconstruction of the composite waveform, which consists of a summation in the discrete case, becomes an integration in the continuous case. Any waveform, which is a function of time, can thus be represented as a pair of sine and cosine densities, which are themselves functions of frequency; and from any pair of functions of frequency can be generated a function of time, namely a waveform. This reversible transformation between the time and frequency domains is called a 'Fourier transform.'

Reversing a Fourier transform to obtain a time waveform from a continuous spectrum involves multiplying the sine and cosine densities, $s(f)$ and $c(f)$, by the corresponding sine and cosine functions, $\sin(2\pi ft)$ and $\cos(2\pi ft)$, and integrating over frequency. The transformation from the frequency domain to the time domain is thus much the same as that from the time to the frequency domain with the roles of time and frequency exchanged.

5. Properties of Fourier Transforms

It was shown in the previous section that any periodic waveform can be expressed in terms of a discrete series of sine and cosine waves, and that any aperiodic waveform can be expressed in terms of a continuous distribution of sine and cosine waves. The properties discussed in this section apply to both.

The first of these properties is 'linearity.' Since we can express any waveform as a sum or integral of sine and cosine waves, the sum of two waveforms can be expressed as the sum of the corresponding sine and cosine components. The Fourier transform of the sum of two waveforms is therefore the sum of the two individual Fourier transforms, and if a waveform is scaled by a particular factor, its Fourier transform is scaled by the same factor.

The previous section discussed several properties of sine waves. Yet another property of sine waves offers an alternative means of representing the Fourier transform: if two sine waves of possibly different amplitude and phase but of the same frequency are added together, the result is another sine wave of the same frequency. Since a cosine wave is simply a sine wave with a 90° phase shift, adding a cosine and sine wave of the same frequency results in a phase-shifted sine wave. If the amplitude of the original sine wave is s and that of the cosine wave, c, the amplitude of the resulting wave is $\sqrt{s^2 + c^2}$. The proof of this result is a little complicated, but roughly, sine and cosine waves, being projections onto the vertical and horizontal axis of a point on a circle, can be seen as two sides of length s and c of a right-angled triangle. The amplitude of the combined waveform is then the length of the hypotenuse, given by the Pythagorean theorem. The phase of the combined waveform is the angle between this hypotenuse and the side of length c, which can be written $\tan^{-1} s/c$.

The combining properties of sine and cosine waves of the same frequency lead to an alternative way of describing the spectrum corresponding to any waveform. Instead of representing the sine and cosine spectra separately, they can be combined and represented by the resulting phase and amplitude at each frequency, that is, by the 'phase spectrum' and its 'amplitude spectrum'—or, by squaring the amplitude, its 'power spectrum.' The description of a waveform in these terms is often more useful than the original separate sine and cosine description. For example, since, our ears are insensitive to the relative phases of components at well-separated frequencies, sounds including speech are often represented in terms of their power spectrum, ignoring the phase spectrum. Indeed, in speech processing the word 'spectrum' without qualification is synonymous with the amplitude or power spectrum.

The linearity property discussed above does not apply to the phase and power spectrum representation: if two waveforms are added, the resulting phase spectrum is not the sum of the two individual phase spectra. The resulting power spectrum is also not strictly the sum of the individual power spectra, though it is often taken to be, since if there are no long-term phase relationships between corresponding components in two waveforms, the power spectra (though not the amplitude spectra) can be added.

The total power in a waveform, computed by squaring and integrating the waveform over time, is equal to the total power in the spectrum, computed by integrating the power spectrum over frequency. This fairly unsurprising result goes under the name of 'Parseval's theorem.'

This article attempts to avoid the complication of so-called imaginary and complex numbers, which are extensively used in Fourier analysis and in signal processing in general; but it is as well to know that the description of the spectrum in terms of sine and cosine amplitudes rather than power and phase is called the 'complex spectrum.' Complex analysis leads to the concept of negative as well as positive frequencies, with the power spectrum being symmetrical about frequency zero.

Since $\cos(x) = \cos(-x)$, cosines are said to be 'symmetrical' functions, while $\sin(x) = -\sin(-x)$, and sines are said to be 'antisymmetrical.' These properties have implications for Fourier transforms. If we multiply a symmetrical function by a sine wave and integrate from $-\infty$ to $+\infty$, the part from $-\infty$ to 0 will exactly cancel the part from 0 to $+\infty$, so the only nonzero terms in the Fourier transform of a symmetrical function are cosine terms, and can be called a 'cosine transform.' It need be evaluated only over the positive half of the range of the function using cosine waves that span multiples of half a period rather than a full period. Similarly, the Fourier transform of an antisymmetrical function contains only sine terms and also need only be evaluated over half the usual range. In the power/phase representation of the spectrum, the phase spectrum of a symmetrical function is entirely zero. As has been shown, the power spectrum itself is a symmetrical function, so the Fourier transform of the power spectrum contains only cosine terms.

If we displace a waveform in time, the power spectrum, which is concerned only with relationships within the waveform, will be unchanged. The phase spectrum, however, will be changed. Since the rate of change of phase with respect to time is proportional to the frequency, a time shift results in phase shift that is proportional to the frequency; except, of course, that when the phase reaches 360° it returns to zero.

It turns out that the Fourier transform of the power spectrum is the autocorrelation function, and vice versa. This result is intuitively reasonable, because the autocorrelation function is concerned only with the correlation between events separated by a particular delay and not with their absolute location in time, and the power spectrum is equally independent of the absolute timing of events.

It was shown in the previous section that differentiating a sine wave produces the corresponding cosine wave multiplied by $2\pi f$. Since sines and cosines differ only in phase, if a waveform is differentiated the effect on its amplitude spectrum is to scale each component by a factor proportional to the frequency of the component. For example, if a component is a factor of two (i.e., one 'octave') higher than another its relative amplitude will be increased by a factor of two (and the relative power by a factor of four) when the waveform is differentiated. Over a broad range of frequencies the long-term average amplitude spectrum of speech is approximately inversely proportional to the frequency. Differentiating the speech waveform therefore provides a roughly flat average spectrum. This useful and common procedure is called 'preemphasis.' Integration of the waveform has, of course, the opposite scaling effect on the amplitude spectrum.

If we know the effects that a particular linear time-invariant system imposes on a sine and cosine wave at any frequency, the so-called 'transfer function' of the system, we can determine exactly what it will do to any waveform that is presented to it. This is done by first analyzing the waveform into its spectrum, effecting the changes, and then reconstructing the modified waveform. With the complex spectrum, the process amounts simply to a scaling of each component. It is more usual, however, to think of the transfer function in terms of the amplitude and phase spectrum, where the effect of the system appears as a scaling of the amplitude and a shift added to the phase at each frequency. The transfer function provides a powerful technique for characterizing linear time-invariant signal processing elements. It is the primary reason why sine waves play such a central role in signal processing.

The final property of Fourier transforms to be discussed in this section, the 'convolution theorem,' is probably the most important for speech processing. If a waveform consists of the product of two other waveforms, say $f(t)$ and $\phi(t)$, then its Fourier transform is the convolution of the individual Fourier transforms of $f(t)$ and $\phi(t)$. The converse is also true; that is, if a waveform consists of the convolution of two waveforms, say $f(t)$ and $\phi(\tau)$ (note that we need the separate time variable τ because convolution deals with relative times), the Fourier transform of the composite waveform consists of the product of the Fourier transforms of $f(t)$ and $\phi(\tau)$. The importance of the first of these properties will appear in the section on windowing below, and the second when impulse responses are discussed.

6. Windowing

Of course, the idea of integrating from minus infinity to plus infinity is not a practically realizable operation. Furthermore, we have been assuming in our discussion both of Fourier transforms and of autocorrelation that the properties of waveforms do not change over time. But any signal that is transmitting information must be continually changing, and the speech waveform is no exception. Speech sounds cannot be assumed to stay constant for more than a few hundred milliseconds at most. If we are to apply Fourier techniques to speech, some method is therefore needed of carrying out a Fourier analysis of a nonperiodic waveform over a finite time interval.

One way of carrying out the analysis over a finite interval is simply to restrict the integrals to this interval. From the discussion above of the Fourier properties of periodic waveforms, this action is equivalent to asserting that the waveform repeats itself with a period equal to the interval; and this may not be a good model of how the waveform behaves outside the interval. Moreover, to retain the orthogonality of the sine and cosine waves, only frequencies that correspond to a whole number of periods within the interval can be used. This means that the spectrum is sampled at a set of discrete frequencies whose regular spacing is inversely proportional to the length of the interval.

Apart from this restriction on the frequencies available, other effects of restricting the integrals to a finite interval can be determined by noting that at the allowed frequencies it would be equivalent to integrating over the infinite range if the waveform were zero outside the finite interval, since regions where the waveform is zero will contribute nothing to the integral. The waveform could be given this property by multiplying it by another waveform whose value is one inside the interval and zero outside it. Such a waveform applied to another signal is called a 'rectangular window.' From the convolution theorem, the Fourier transform of the windowed waveform is the convolution of the Fourier transform of the unwindowed waveform and that of the window itself.

The Fourier transform of a rectangular window is shown in Fig. 3a. Remembering the effect of convolution in the optical case, we can see that the broad central peak in the transform of the window will blur or smooth the spectrum of the waveform. The surrounding, subsidiary peaks, called 'sidelobes,' present more of a problem because they cause particular parts of the unwindowed spectrum to be folded back on itself, creating spurious spectral structure.

We might imagine that rather than making a waveform go abruptly and discontinuously to zero it would be better

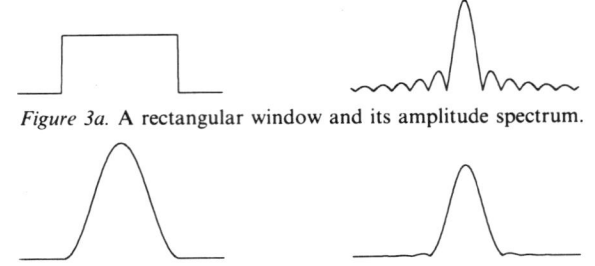

Figure 3a. A rectangular window and its amplitude spectrum.

Figure 3b. A raised-cosine (von Hann) window and its amplitude spectrum.

to apply the transition to zero smoothly with a window tapered at both ends. It turns out indeed that tapered windows have smaller sidelobes. The best tapered window shape to use depends on the criterion adopted: minimization of the largest sidelobe, of the sum of all sidelobes, of the width of the central peak, etc. However, by far the commonest windows used in speech processing are, 'raised cosine' windows, which consist of a single cycle of a cosine wave symmetrical about its highest value and raised so that it is positive over the whole period. In the von Hann window (often called the 'Hanning' window) the raised cosine goes exactly to zero at the ends of the window, while in the Hamming window it has a small positive value at its ends. Raised-cosine windows have a broader central peak but much smaller sidelobes than a rectangular window (see Fig. 3b).

Whatever shape of window is used, it is the length of the analysis interval that controls the degree of detail that can be seen in the spectrum, since a long interval will result in the spectrum being sampled at closely spaced intervals, and in the Fourier transform of the window being correspondingly narrow, limiting its blurring effect on the spectrum. On the other hand, any changes in the characteristics of the waveform over time will be smoothed away over a long analysis interval. There is therefore a tradeoff between the fine spectral resolution of long windows, and the fine temporal resolution of short windows. A plosive burst, for example, which is sudden and brief with little spectral detail to be discerned, is best analyzed with a short window; while an analysis of a long steady vowel might require the spectral detail provided by a long window.

7. Some Particular Fourier Transforms

7.1 Sine Wave

From the orthogonality property, the power spectrum of a pure sine or cosine wave is clearly a spike, or 'impulse,' at the frequency of the wave. Because the power spectrum is symmetrical about frequency zero, there is a second spike at the corresponding negative frequency. The spectrum of a damped sinusoid will be discussed when resonances are studied more closely.

7.2 Impulse

An impulse at $t = 0$ is symmetrical in time, and its complex spectrum can consequently have only cosine terms. The phase spectrum is therefore zero for all frequencies, and since $\cos(0) = 1$ independently of frequency, the power spectrum is a constant whose value depends on the size of the impulse. From the effects of time displacement on Fourier

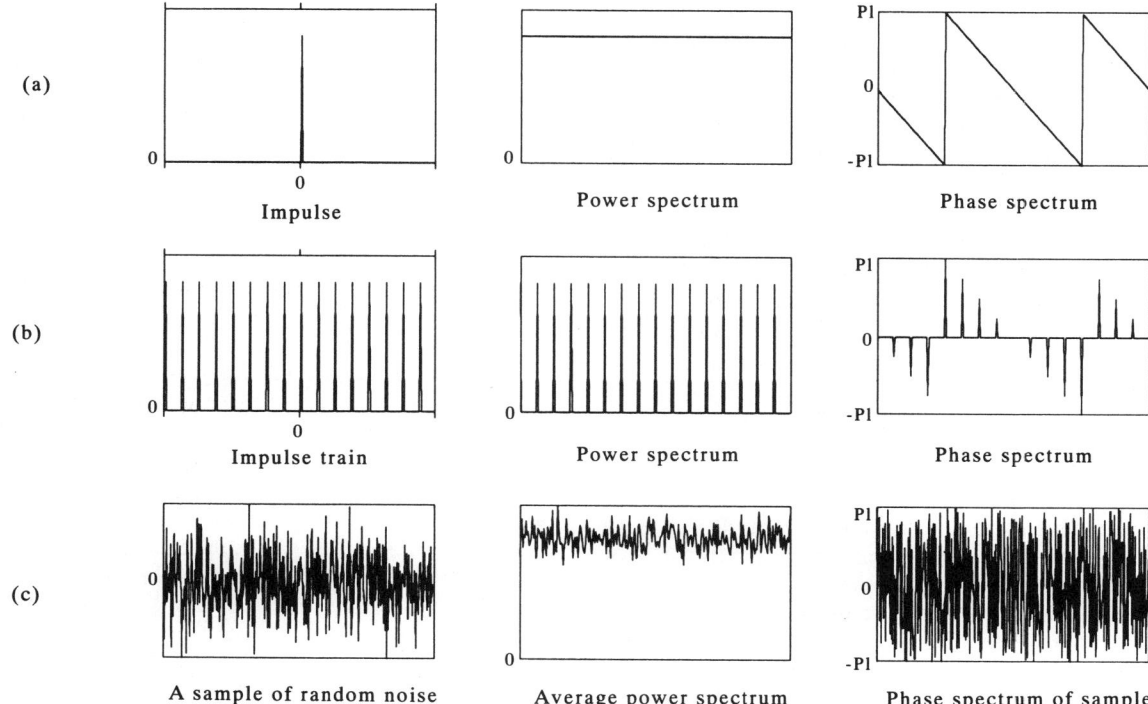

Figure 4. Power and phase spectra for some basic waveforms: (a) an impulse delayed from $t = 0$; (b) a sequence of regularly spaced impulses delayed from $t = 0$ (note that the phase is defined only when the power is nonzero); (c) a portion of white noise (the power spectrum was averaged over several such portions).

transforms discussed earlier, an impulse at some other time has the same power spectrum, and its phase spectrum is a linear ramp falling to $-180°$ $(-\pi)$, jumping instantaneously to $+180°(\pi)$, and falling to 360° again (Fig. 4a).

A series of equally spaced impulses, being periodic, has nonzero components only at a discrete set of frequencies (see Fig. 4b). As with all periodic waveforms, the separation in frequency between the nonzero components is inversely proportional to the repeat interval; that is, to the separation in time between the impulses. Otherwise, the power and phase spectrum share the properties of the single impulse, with, for example, all nonzero components of the power spectrum having equal values.

7.3 White Noise

A waveform corresponds to white noise if its value at any instant is of no help in predicting its value at any other instant. The autocorrelation function of white noise is therefore zero except at $\tau = 0$. This is identical to the auto-correlation function of a single impulse, so the power spectrum of white noise must be identical to that of the impulse, i.e., uniform across all frequencies. Indeed, white noise takes its name by analogy with white light, notionally equally intense at all frequencies.

White noise is distinguished from an impulse by its phase spectrum, which is random. Also, noise being by definition noisy, any finite windowed portion of white noise will not have a perfectly uniform power spectrum, but the fluctuations from uniformity will be random (Fig. 4c).

It is possible to take white noise and change the relative intensities of various frequency components, e.g., by integrating or differentiating the waveform. In the resulting

'colored noise' there is a degree of predictability between samples, but the phase of the components drifts randomly over time.

8. The Impulse Response

It has been shown that the effect of a linear time invariant system on any waveform can be computed by transforming the waveform into its amplitude and phase spectrum, applying the effect of the transfer function of the system to the spectrum, and reconstructing the waveform corresponding to the modified spectrum. Since an impulse at $t = 0$ has a phase spectrum of zero and a uniform amplitude spectrum at all frequencies, which can be scaled to unity, the spectrum of an impulse that has passed through a particular system *is* the transfer function of that system. The impulse response of a system, the waveform resulting when an impulse is presented to the system, is therefore a time-domain representation of the transfer function.

The process of applying the effect of the transfer function to a complex spectrum consists of multiplying the sine and cosine spectra by a pair of scaling functions. From the convolution theorem, such multiplication in the frequency domain is equivalent to convolving the waveform with the Fourier transform of the transfer function, namely the impulse response.

This convolution of the input waveform with the impulse response has an intuitive interpretation, which can be reached by imagining a waveform being composed of a series of impulses of varying height (this is easier to picture with the discretely sampled waveforms discussed later). Each impulse passing through the linear time-invariant system is transformed into a scaled, time-delayed version of the impulse response, and these overlapping waveforms add up to give the result of passing the whole original waveform through the system. This process is a one-dimensional analogue of the convolution of a blurring pattern with a sharp image by imagining the image being composed of a sum of blurred points of varying intensity.

We therefore have the option of applying the effect of a linear time-invariant system of known transfer function without needing to transform the input waveform into the frequency domain. We can design the characteristics of a system in terms of the effect on the amplitude and phase spectrum yet realize the effect by convolution in the time domain.

9. Resonances

As has been shown, a stable resonance has an impulse response of the form $e^{-2\pi ct}\sin(2\pi ft)$. The Fourier transform of this product of a sine wave and an exponential is the convolution of the two individual transforms. It has been shown that the power spectrum of a sine wave consists of an impulse at $\pm f$. That of an exponential is a symmetrical bell-shaped curve with a peak of height inversely proportional to c^2 located at frequency zero and falling to half its peak value at frequency $\pm c$. The convolution of the two transforms results in two bell-shaped curves centered on $\pm f$. (This is strictly true only for $f \gg c$; otherwise, the two bell-shaped curves interact with each other, causing the two peaks in the power spectrum to be shifted toward zero frequency.)

Depending, then, on the value of c, a resonance may have a transfer function that responds strongly over a narrow range of frequencies, or more weakly over a broader range. The parameter c is consequently called the 'bandwidth' of the resonance.

An intuitive picture of the dependence on c comes from considering a resonance in an acoustic tube of uniform cross-sectional area with partial reflections at both ends—rather like the vocal tract making a schwa vowel sound [ə]. If a sine wave is applied to this tube at a frequency matching a resonance, the incident wave will have added to it delayed versions that have traveled up and down the tube one or more times. When the frequency of the sine wave exactly matches a resonance of the tube, the delayed versions of the sine wave will be exactly in phase with the incident wave. They will add together and enhance the amplitude of the sine wave. The amplitude of the delayed versions decreases with the delay at a rate that depends on c, so a small value of c causes the sine wave at a resonant frequency to be strongly enhanced.

If, however, the frequency of the sine wave does not correspond to a resonance, the delayed versions will not be in phase with the incident wave. Writing the phase mismatch of a wave traveling up and down the tube once as θ, which is proportional to the frequency mismatch with the resonance, the wave delayed twice as long by traveling up and down the tube twice will have a phase mismatch of 2θ, that delayed three times as long 3θ, and so on. Eventually the phase mismatch will be so great that the delayed versions will be in antiphase with the incident waveform and will act to reduce its amplitude. If the frequency difference from the resonance is small, it will take long delays to reach these destructive phase shifts, and unless c is very

small the delayed waveform will have decayed to insignificance before it happens.

In summary, for small c there is strong amplification at the resonant frequency, but even at small differences from this frequency the effect of the constructive delayed versions will be largely canceled by the destructive delayed versions, leaving little net amplification. On the other hand, for large values of c the amplification at resonance will be small, but even at large frequency differences from resonance the effect will remain constructive because only delayed versions corresponding to few reflections and therefore small phase shifts will be retained.

In addition to resonances there are 'antiresonances.' If an impulse passes through a resonance and the resulting decaying sinusoid then passes through the antiresonance with the same frequency and bandwidth, the impulse is restored to its original values. When two linear time-invariant systems follow each other in this manner, they are said to be 'in series' or 'in cascade,' and their transfer functions can be combined: their effects on the power spectrum of the signal passing through them are multiplied together, and their effects on the phase spectrum are added together. The transfer function of an antiresonance must therefore have a multiplicative effect on the power spectrum that is the reciprocal of that of the corresponding resonance, and the phase shifts it imposes must be equal and opposite to that of the resonance. An antiresonance therefore imposes a bell-shaped dip on the power spectrum. Naturally, the null effect of such a resonance–antiresonance combination holds for all waveforms presented to it, and it holds whether the resonance is encountered first or second.

For reasons related to the complex number theory mentioned earlier, resonances and antiresonances are often called 'poles' and 'zeroes' respectively; or more strictly, pole and zero pairs, since every pole or zero at a positive frequency must have a partner at the corresponding negative frequency. The only exception to this rule occurs at zero frequency: a single pole of zero bandwidth at zero frequency corresponds to integration, and single zero to differentiation, and there are finite-bandwidth generalizations of these processes.

Multiple resonances can be combined by placing them in series, and they can also be combined 'in parallel': that is, the input waveform is split and presented to all the resonances simultaneously with the outputs from the resonances then being summed. The series arrangement appears as multiple convolutions of impulse responses in the time domain and as multiplications of transfer functions in the frequency domain. On the other hand, the effect of the parallel arrangement is to sum the impulse responses and therefore to sum the transfer functions in the complex spectrum representation.

In the series formulation the effect on the power spectrum of the composite system is determined completely by the frequencies and bandwidths of the resonances. In the parallel formulation, on the other hand, the relative contribution of the individual resonances can be controlled by scaling their outputs prior to summing.

An all-series arrangement can be found that is exactly equivalent in its effect to any parallel arrangement of resonances, but the series version will in general contain antiresonances as well as resonances. This point is important in the analysis of nasalized speech sounds.

10. Filters

A filter is in general a device that allows some objects to pass through it while preventing others. In signal processing a filter originally signified a system that passed certain frequencies and blocked others. Thus there are 'low-pass filters,' which block components above a given frequency, 'high-pass filters,' which block components below a given frequency, 'band-pass filters,' which block components outside a given band of frequencies, and 'band-stop filters,' which pass components outside a given band. The term has, however, been generalized to include such apparent absurdities as 'all-pass filters,' whose effect is purely on the phase spectrum of the signal presented to them. The term 'filter' encompasses any linear time-invariant signal processing system that alters the power or phase spectrum in any way except the trivial ones corresponding to a simple scaling or delay applied to the waveform. A single resonance or antiresonance would thus be regarded as a filter, as would a differentiating device applying pre-emphasis to a speech signal.

Filters in the classic sense, especially low-pass filters, remain, however, an important class within the wider sense of the term. The ideal low-pass filter would pass all components up to the cutoff frequency without imposing any change in amplitude or any delay differences between these components, and all components above the cutoff frequency would be blocked completely. One can compute the impulse response of such a filter and show that it would impose an infinite delay on the signal passing through it. Real low-pass filters do not have absolutely sharp boundaries between the region where components are passed (the pass band) and the one where they are blocked (the stop band). Their design is a compromise between various factors: the sharpness of the cutoff, amplitude variation in the pass band (pass-band ripple), delay variation in the pass band (phase distortion), leakage of components in the stop band, complexity of the filter, and the overall delay that it imposes. Similar remarks apply to high-pass and the other types of filters designed to pass components in particular bands.

It was seen in the previous section that an impulse passing through a resonance will be restored to its original state by passing through the corresponding antiresonance. A resonance by the wider definition is a filter, and the corresponding antiresonance, capable of canceling the effect of the resonance and restoring any waveform to its original state is its 'inverse filter.' In general, the inverse of any filter made up of resonances and antiresonances in series can be constructed by replacing every resonance and antiresonance by its corresponding antiresonance and resonance respectively. There are, however, two qualifications to this statement. First, the resonance corresponding to a particular antiresonance may be unstable, i.e., its exponential term may be rising instead of falling. The inverse filter then risks being unstable. Second, if a filter reduces the amplitude of a component so much that it is lost in the inevitable noise present in any signal processing system, the component cannot be restored by an inverse filter.

So far, this section has dealt only with linear filters, which are by far the most common type. However, one kind of nonlinear filter is sufficiently widely used in speech processing to merit description here. It is used with certain parameters, such as the fundamental frequency and the frequencies of vocal tract resonances, that vary smoothly most of the time but occasionally make an abrupt jump to another smooth sequence at, for example, a stop release, or the onset of voicing, or of nasality. Errors made by processors trying to track such parameters often consist of one or two values that depart wildly from an otherwise smooth sequence that is then resumed. What is needed is a filter that accepts the real, step-like changes in the parameter values but rejects the spurious, impulse-like events. The 'median smoother' does this. It takes a window of, say, five consecutive parameter values and replaces the sample at the middle of the window by the median of the five values. The window then advances one sample and the process is repeated. Such a filter leaves unchanged a uniformly rising or falling sequence, including any step jump in the sequence. However, one or two isolated wild values would be replaced by the median over the window, i.e., by values within the smooth sequence. By contrast, a linear smoothing filter would blur both the step and the isolated wild excursion.

11. Logarithmic Scales

The power in waveforms and in power spectra is normally measured in 'decibels' (dB), which are based on a logarithmic (or log) scale. To see the reasons, some properties of logarithms need to be reviewed.

If $x = 10^u$, then, $u = \log_{10} x$ (or in words, u is said to be 'log to the base 10 of x'). The variable u is defined only for $x > 0$, but within this region the pairs of numbers x and u have a one-to-one relationship, and an increase in x implies an increase in u. This means that no information is lost by transforming x to its logarithmic equivalent, u. The motivation for doing this is that multiplying a pair of numbers in the original ('linear') representation corresponds to adding them in the logarithmic representation. To see this, consider a second variable y, for which $y = 10^v$, then $xy = 10^u 10^v = 10^{u+v}$, so $\log xy = u + v = \log x + \log y$.

An amplifier will scale up a waveform, and hence the power in the waveform, by a fixed amount. On a log scale, the amplifier adds a constant to the power. Similarly, the effect of a filter of multiplying each frequency component by a particular amount appears in the log spectrum as the addition of a particular amount. When filters are cascaded, their combined effect on the log power spectrum is found by summing the individual effects, which is generally easier to imagine than the compound multiplication of individual effects on the linear spectrum. A simple scaling of a waveform will change the shape of a linear power spectrum, but will simply shift a log power spectrum up or down leaving its shape otherwise unchanged.

For these reasons, power relationships are generally measured in logarithmic, decibel units. Two linear powers x and y differ by n dB if $10\log_{10} x/y = n$. Consequently, if x is 10 times greater than y, the difference is 10 dB. A power ratio of 2 corresponds to 3 dB, 4 to 6 dB, and 100 to 20 dB. Similarly, a power ratio of 0.5 corresponds to -3 dB, 0.1 to -10 dB, etc. It is worth emphasizing that the decibel is a unit of *relative* not absolute power, and that it is a unit of relative *power* not amplitude, so 6 dB corresponds to an amplitude ratio of 2 not 4.

If a series of numbers has a constant ratio between consecutive pairs (e.g., 1, 10, 100, 1,000, 10,000, . . .) then their logarithms will have constant differences between them (e.g., 0, 1, 2, 3, 4 . . .). Thus an exponential growth or decay appears as a linear increase or decrease on a log scale; and the effect of differentiating a waveform, described earlier as causing the relative power in its spectrum to be increased by a factor of four per octave, can be restated as adding 6 dB per octave.

A second set of motivations for using log scales comes from the properties of human hearing. Perceptual loudness corresponds more closely to log power than to linear power (though it is closer still to the cube root of the power). In measuring the loudness of sound an absolute dB scale is used, which relates the power in a sound to the power of a sound considered to be close to the threshold of human hearing.

Similarly, human perception of frequencies corresponds more closely to a logarithmic than to a linear scale. The octaves used in musical scales, for example, represent, as has already been shown, equal frequency ratios, and are therefore equally spaced on a log frequency scale. Various methods of measuring human frequency resolution arrive at scales that are not perfectly logarithmic. A frequency scale widely used in speech recognition, the 'technical mel' scale, corresponds to linear frequency up to 800 or 1,000 Hz, and to log frequency above this value.

A log scale effectively compresses the differences between large numbers and expands the differences between small ones. One consequence of this property is that averaging in the linear and log domains gives different results. Averaging a set of n logged numbers, i.e., computing their *arithmetic mean* is equivalent to multiplying the numbers together in the linear domain and taking the nth root of the product, i.e., taking their *geometric mean* and then taking the log of the result. The geometric mean can never be greater than the arithmetic mean, and is particularly sensitive to small numbers (consider what happens when one of the numbers is zero). An average log spectrum is therefore much more sensitive to the weak parts of the spectrum than an average linear spectrum.

In particular, as $x \to 0$, $\log x \to -\infty$. Since practical signal processing systems cannot deal with infinite quantities, data to be transformed to a log domain must first be given a lower bound, either by setting a threshold below which the data cannot fall, or by adding a small constant to all its values.

If we take the log of the sum of two numbers, one of which is much larger than the other, the compression effect means that the influence of the smaller number is negligible. That is, $\log (x + y)$ approximates $\log x$ if $x \gg y$. This has implications for the log power spectra of speech plus broadband noise. In regions where the noise energy predominates, the speech energy cannot be detected, and in regions where the speech energy is markedly greater than the noise, the noise can be neglected. Consequently, to limit irrelevant fluctuations in regions where the speech level lies below the noise level, the linear power spectrum is often stabilized by adding a constant offset or by applying a threshold at a level related to the expected noise level.

12. Digital Signal Processing

So far, this article has dealt mainly with continuous variables: with 'analogue' signal processing. This does not seem unreasonable, since speech production is an analogue process. However, most modern speech signal processing is carried out digitally; i.e., with quantities being given discrete, numerical values.

A waveform, for example, is represented digitally by discrete values in two senses. First, instead of being a continuous function of time, the waveform is sampled at discrete, usually regularly spaced, instants. Second, the instantaneous amplitude of the waveform at each such instant is represented by the closest of a set of numerical values. If a waveform is digitized simply for storage or transmission, it may be more efficient to arrange the numerical values on a nonuniform scale (so-called A-law or μ-law coding) closer to a log scale; but if significant processing is involved, equally spaced values are normally used. The values are typically all the integers in the range -128 to $+127$ (8-bit coding), -2048 to $+2047$ (12-bit coding), or -32768 to $+32767$ (16-bit coding). The effect of approximating the continuously valued amplitude by the nearest discrete value resembles adding white noise, called 'quantization noise,' to the waveform, except that the noise appears only when the waveform is changing its value. Clearly, provided the waveform has been appropriately scaled to fill the numerical range available, the more levels there are, the closer is the approximation, and the greater is the ratio of true signal power to noise power (called the signal-to-noise ratio or SNR).

The effects of discrete sampling in time are more profound. Imagine, for example, a sine wave whose frequency is equal to the sampling frequency. Because of its periodicity, every time it is sampled the value will be the same. Clearly, such a sampled waveform cannot be distinguished from a constant, i.e., from a sine wave at zero frequency. It turns out that if a waveform has no components above half the frequency at which it is sampled, it can in principle be perfectly reconstructed after digitization. If, however, the waveform contains frequencies spanning a wider frequency range than this, the reconstructed waveform will be distorted by a process known as 'aliasing.' If the sampling frequency is f_s, a component originally at frequency $f_s + \varepsilon$ will reappear after digitization and reconstruction as an analogue waveform as a component at frequency $f_s - \varepsilon$. It is as though frequencies are reflected in a mirror at f_s. Aliasing adds a characteristic distortion to digitized speech: a high-frequency ringing a little like the sound of a finger being dragged over the teeth of a metal comb.

To ensure that aliasing is avoided, the analogue signal to be digitized has first to be low-pass filtered. Since low-pass filters can never be perfectly sharp, the cutoff frequency of the filter must be set at a value somewhat below f_s. The reconstruction process will also generate spurious components, though this time they lie above f_s. They must similarly be removed by analogue low-pass filtering. In some extremely low-cost speech output devices the additional expense of analogue low-pass filtering may be prohibitive, and spurious high-frequency components cause distortion.

Provided that the frequencies being considered are small in relation to f_s, digital filters behave much like analogue filters, but differences occur when one observes the spectrum at frequencies comparable to half the sampling frequency or when there are resonances or antiresonances in this region. For example, just as differentiation imposes a 6 dB/octave rising slope on the spectrum, so its digital equivalent (namely subtraction of consecutive samples) imposes the same slope at low frequencies, but the slope gradually decreases over the spectrum, falling to zero at f_s.

It has been shown that in the analogue world single poles and zeros can occur only at zero frequency. In the digital world they can also occur at f_s: a zero-bandwidth zero at f_s, for example, is realized by *adding* rather than subtracting consecutive samples.

Since they form a model for other digital filters, a closer look is needed at how the digital equivalents of differentiation and integration are realized. If the nth input sample to a digital filter is written as x_n and the nth output sample as y_n, then the digital equivalent of differentiation is: $y_n = x_n - x_{n-1}$ and the digital equivalent of integration is: $y_n = x_n + y_{n-1}$. In the differentiation-like process corresponding to a single zero, the output thus depends only on the current input sample and on the previous input sample. By contrast, the integration-like process corresponding to a single pole depends on the current input and on the previous *output* sample. In the latter case the output of the process is thus fed back to contribute to the input for the next sample.

In a digital realization of a resonance, corresponding to a pair of poles instead of the single pole of an integrator, the feedback is from the previous output sample and the one before that. For example, an undamped resonance at one-sixth the sampling frequency can be represented as:

$$y_n = x_n + y_{n-1} - y_{n-2} \tag{1}$$

while the corresponding antiresonance can be represented by the equation:

$$y_n = x_n - x_{n-1} + x_{n-2} \tag{2}$$

The reader might like to check that equation 1 turns an impulse sequence $\{\ldots 0\,1\,0\,0\,0\,0\,0\,0\,0\ldots\}$ into the sequence $\{\ldots 0\,1\,1\,0\,-1\,-1\,0\,1\,1\ldots\}$, which fits a sine wave of the required frequency; and that presenting this latter sequence to equation 2 restores the impulse.

The sequence will also return to its original form, of course, if it passes through the resonance and antiresonance in the opposite order. In this case, the intermediate sequence at the output of the antiresonance is $\{\ldots 0\,1\,-1\,1\,0\,0\,0\,0\,0\ldots\}$, i.e., the response of the antiresonance to the unit impulse has just three nonzero samples and their values are just the multipliers applied to the samples, the 'coefficients' appearing in equation 2.

This is a general result, valid for any resonance and antiresonance. Different frequencies and different bandwidths result in different coefficients appearing on the right-hand side of equations 1 and 2, corresponding to the different impulse responses.

Furthermore, a series of p antiresonances has an impulse response $2p + 1$ samples long, corresponding to the composite convolution of the p individual impulse responses. Such a $2p$th-order 'finite-impulse-response' (or FIR) filter can be represented by a process of the form of equation 2 but with $2p + 1$ terms with coefficients equal to its impulse response. This generalization is written as:

$$y_n = a_0 x_n + \sum_{i=1}^{i=p} a_i x_{n-i} \tag{3}$$

where a_i is the ith value of the sampled impulse response.

Such filters are attractive partly because they can be designed simply by specifying the required impulse response, or even by specifying the transfer function and converting it to an impulse response, which may then need to be truncated.

Similarly, a series of p resonances can be represented by a process that is a generalization of equation 1, namely:

$$y_n = a_0 x_n - \sum_{i=1}^{i=p} a_i y_{n-i} \tag{4}$$

with coefficients that are the result of convolving the coefficients in the equations for the individual resonances. However, these coefficients do not correspond directly to the impulse response of the filter but rather to that of its inverse filter. The impulse response of the all-pole filter, like those of the individual resonances, is in principle 'infinite'; and the filter is therefore said to be a $2p$th-order 'infinite-impulse-response' (IIR) filter. It will be seen later that the coefficients can, nevertheless, be derived from its impulse response. Because in such filters previous outputs contribute to the computation of the current output sample, they are also known as 'recursive filters.'

The most general form of a digital filter contains both resonances and antiresonances and can be written as:

$$y_n = a_0 x_n + \sum_{i=1}^{i=p} a_i x_{n-i} - \sum_{i=1}^{i=p} b_i y_{n-i} \tag{5}$$

Because the process defined by equation 3 can be viewed as the computation of a moving average, and that defined by equation 4 as linear regression applied across delayed values of the same variable—autoregression—the process defined by equation 5 can be described as an 'autoregressive moving average' or ARMA. With filters of the form of equations 3 or 4, there are straightforward techniques for deducing the coefficients a_i from the effects of the filters on waveforms; but with ARMA processes there are no such techniques.

Fourier analysis can be carried out in the digital domain. The integration over time needed to determine the spectral components in the analogue case is replaced by a summation over the discrete samples in the digital case. The result of such a 'discrete Fourier transform' or DFT is a spectrum defined only up to half the sampling frequency.

When the number of samples in the analysis interval is a power of two, a particularly efficient method of computing the DFT known as the 'fast Fourier transform' or FFT can be used. If there are n samples in the analysis interval, the computational cost of computing an ordinary DFT is proportional to n^2 while that of an FFT is roughly proportional to $n\log n$. Since, as seen above, the log function flattens out for large numbers, the advantage of the FFT increases with larger analysis intervals.

13. The Source-filter Model of Speech Production

The source of acoustic energy in voiced speech sounds is the larynx, where the vocal cords open and close on average 100 times a second in the speech of a man and on average twice as frequently in that of a woman. Although this 'fundamental frequency' is continually varying, it generally varies smoothly; so, as seen in the discussion of autocorrelation, over short periods the source of energy in voiced sounds can be treated as periodic.

In voiceless sounds, on the other hand, the source of acoustic energy is typically a constriction in the vocal tract resulting in turbulence as air is forced through it, and hence in an aperiodic, noise-like acoustic excitation.

In both cases, the acoustic energy passes into an acoustic tube consisting of the vocal tract downstream of the source and acting as a filter. A crucial property in the study of acoustic speech production is that to a good approximation the source and the filter behave independently of each other. This is not the case for all acoustic systems consisting of a source and a filter. For example, in brass and woodwind instruments the rate of vibration of the source, the lips and the reed respectively, is controlled by the resonances of the tube which follows it.

An acoustic wave travels in space, and the 'wavelength' of such a wave, the length of one cycle of the wave, is given by the speed of sound in the medium divided by the frequency of the wave. When the velum (the soft palate) is raised, the vocal tract forms an unbranched tube; and the acoustic properties of such a tube are simple provided that its lateral dimensions are small compared with the wavelengths being considered. Since the frequencies of major phonetic significance in voiced speech are concentrated below 3 kHz, corresponding to a wavelength of about 10 cm, this condition is largely satisfied. The acoustic properties are then characterized completely by the cross-sectional area of the tube as a function of distance along it, and its exact shape can be ignored.

Within an appropriately restricted frequency range, such a narrow unbranched tube is equivalent to a set of resonances in series, to an all-pole filter. It is also equivalent to a tube consisting of a series of cylinders of different diameters joined together, the number of such sections being equal to the order of the filter. In such a tube it is the reflections occurring in the acoustic wave at the abrupt boundaries between the cylinders that give rise to the resonances. Consequently, instead of defining the properties of the filter in terms of the frequencies and bandwidths of the resonances, they can be equivalently defined by the ratios of the cross-sectional areas of the cylinders or, more commonly, by the 'log area ratios,' or by the degree of reflection at each boundary, the 'reflection coefficients,' which are derived directly from the area ratios.

When the velum is lowered, air can flow through the nasal cavity and out through the nostrils. The vocal tract then becomes a branched tube, having resonances in parallel and consequently having zeros in the transfer function.

The transfer function of the vocal tract gives rise to peaks in the power spectrum of speech sounds known as formants. In nonnasalized sounds, where the all-pole model applies, formants correspond closely to the resonances of the vocal tract. Indeed, the term 'formant' is often used as a synonym for vocal tract resonance. The phonetic identity of voiced speech sounds has been found to be tightly linked to the frequencies of the first three formants and to their changes over time. On the other hand, the bandwidths of vocal tract resonances, which generally increase with frequency, have little phonetic influence.

In the central, schwa vowel [ə], the cross-sectional area of the vocal tract is uniform. Such a uniform tube closed at one end (the larynx) and open at the other (the mouth) has a set of resonances, equally spaced in frequency. For a typical man's vocal tract length of 17.5 cm, the lowest resonance (corresponding to the first formant) is located at 500 Hz, with the succeeding resonances being at 1.5 kHz, 2.5 kHz, etc. Since these frequencies are inversely proportional to the length of the tube, they are typically 10 to 15 percent higher in women, whose vocal tracts tend to be shorter by these proportions.

In voiced sounds, the power spectrum of the excitation signal resulting from the interrupted airflow through the vocal cords decreases at around 12 dB per octave. However, since the lips form a small opening compared with the important wavelengths in speech, the mouth behaves like an earphone heard from a distance and radiates high frequencies more efficiently than low frequencies, causing a 6 dB per octave rise in the power spectrum. Consequently, the excitation viewed from outside the mouth appears to have a power spectrum that decreases at roughly 6 dB per octave.

In principle, an inverse filter can be applied to the speech waveform to undo the effect of the vocal tract and recover the excitation signal. To see the airflow through the vocal cords as a function of time, this inverse filter must include an integrator to counter the lip radiation effect. However, it is sometimes useful to view the waveform in a form in which its power spectrum is flat; and this is achieved by replacing the integrator by a differentiator.

In normal phonation (so-called 'modal' voice) most of the acoustic activity in the spectrally flattened version of the voiced excitation signal occurs at the instants when the vocal cords close and suddenly shut off the airflow. The signal can therefore be approximately represented as a series of impulses located at these instants, though less intense activity is present throughout the cycle of opening and closure (the so-called 'glottal' cycle). Moreover, this representation is quite invalid for other modes of phonation including falsetto, breathy, and creaky voice.

14. Spectral Analysis of Speech

Analyses of the short-term power spectrum of the speech signal are used in speech coding for efficient transmission, in speech recognition, and in providing representations, known as 'spectrograms,' for visual inspection. Spectrograms conventionally represent time on the horizontal axis and frequency on the vertical axis. The power at any instant and frequency is then commonly represented on a gray scale, with white corresponding to least power and black to most power. Increasingly, color scales are being used in place of gray scales, and three-dimensional representations have also been used.

An obvious and direct method of analysis is to derive log power spectra from Fourier transforms of sequences of overlapping, windowed sections of waveform. The resulting pattern for steady-voiced speech depends critically on the length of the window. If it spans two or more glottal cycles, the speech signal appears to repeat itself. The power spectrum then appears as a set of impulses broadened by the effect of the window and appearing at all integer multiples of the fundamental frequency. In spectrograms, these harmonics of the fundamental frequency appear as roughly horizontal stripes. The intensity of each harmonic then depends on the power spectrum of an excitation cycle multiplied by the transfer function of the vocal tract at the frequency of the harmonic.

If, on the other hand, the window length for the Fourier transform is shorter than a glottal cycle, no harmonic structure will appear at the fundamental frequency. However, as such a short window advances, the power in the portion of waveform that it spans will vary at the fundamental frequency. In this case, the power spectrum, instead of being modulated in frequency, is now modulated in time and vertical stripes appear in spectrograms. Formant structure is easier to read in these low resolution spectrograms, and their better time resolution shows sudden events such as plosive releases more clearly.

A second, closely related analysis technique uses sets of overlapping band-pass filters arranged in parallel (a so-called 'filter bank'). The waveform output of each filter is converted to a measure of short-term power or amplitude by first squaring or rectifying it and then smoothing the result by low-pass filtering.

If the filters have narrow bandwidths, their impulse response will not decay to a negligible value from one closure of the vocal cords to the next. Consequently, the effects of sequential glottal cycles add together, and the result depends on their relative phase. The output will be strongest when the phases are equal, i.e., when the filter center frequency is an integer multiple of the excitation frequency, a harmonic of the fundamental frequency. Broad filters, on the other hand, have rapidly decaying impulse responses that do not give rise to harmonic structure but cause the excitations to appear as energy pulses. In this respect, filter banks parallel the behavior of high and low resolution Fourier analyses.

To reflect a property of the ear, the bands of filter banks often get wider and more widely spaced at high frequencies. Fourier analysis cannot incorporate this property directly; but the result may be achieved indirectly in a simulated filter bank, constructed from a weighted sum of groups of components of the power spectrum. Strictly, simulated filter banks differ from real ones in that they ignore the phase relationships between the components grouped together in each band; but this difference seems to have little practical importance.

15. Linear Prediction

Equation 4 says that the value of a sample at the output of an all-pole filter could be predicted from a linear combination of the current input sample and a set of previous output samples given the appropriate set of coefficients, a_i. Since the vocal tract can be regarded as an all-pole filter for unnasalized vowels, its output should be predictable in this way. However, even for this restricted range of speech sounds, the prediction cannot be exact. First, the characteristics of the vocal tract vary over time; second, the values of the input samples are unknown, i.e., the excitation due to the vocal cords; and third, however carefully they are recorded, the output samples are inevitably corrupted by noise, if only quantization noise.

Linear predictive coding (LPC; see also *Speech Coding and Compression*) assumes that the excitation contains no short-term correlations and is therefore spectrally flat. Effectively, this means that the excitation is assumed to be a single impulse on each closure of the vocal cords in voiced speech and white noise in voiceless speech. Then for a portion of speech waveform typically 25 ms long and preemphasized so as to make the excitation appear spectrally flat,

LPC finds the values of the coefficients that give the best prediction according to the least-squared-error criterion, as seen in the discussion on linear regression above. Indeed, finding the best values for the coefficients is a linear regression problem.

The solution to this problem depends on the autocorrelation properties of the portion of waveform; and the two main LPC methods differ in the way that they estimate these autocorrelation properties, in particular how they deal with the ends of the portion of waveform being analyzed, and whether they are sensitive to an evolution in the autocorrelation statistics over the portion of waveform being analyzed. The 'covariance' method, which is sensitive to changes over time, gives an exactly accurate analysis of an ideal waveform provided that the order of the analysis fits the number of resonances that generated the waveform; but with real speech waveforms it may occasionally specify an unstable filter, requiring stability checks and corrections to be included if a speech waveform is to be resynthesized from such an analysis. On the other hand, the analyses provided by the computationally simpler and more widely used 'autocorrelation' method, which takes as input an ordinary windowed autocorrelation function, are always only approximate, but the resulting filters are guaranteed to be stable.

The order of the LP analysis needed to give a good analysis depends on the number of resonances in the frequency range represented in the digitized waveform, and hence on the sampling rate. With extremely carefully recorded preemphasized speech, using short analysis windows covering not more than one glottal cycle, good results are obtained when the analysis order is equal to the sampling rate expressed in kHz, i.e., when the number of resonances in the LPC analysis equals the expected number of vocal tract resonances. However, to give a more robust analysis, the order is usually increased by 2, i.e., 10th order at 8 kHz sampling and 12th order at 10 kHz sampling.

As well as fitting a particular model to the waveform, LPC can also be interpreted as a method of fitting an all-pole model of predetermined order to the power spectrum of the waveform being analyzed. However, since it is the intense parts of the spectrum that have most influence on the waveform, the least-squares fit to the waveform does not correspond to a least-squares fit to the spectrum, but rather to fitting the intense parts, in the neighborhood of formant center, frequencies, as accurately as possible at the expense of the fit to the less intense parts lying between the formants. This is useful from a perceptual viewpoint, since our auditory system behaves similarly. As a result, LPC can be reasonably effective even with sounds such as nasal consonants for which the all-pole assumption is quite invalid.

The coefficients, a_i, produced by a linear prediction analysis can be used to derive the frequencies and bandwidths of the resonances in the filter that they define, and they can be converted to reflection coefficients or to log area ratios.

The predictor coefficients can also be used to construct the power spectrum. When such a spectrum is compared with a corresponding spectrum derived from a Fourier transform, an apparent paradox arises. The spectral resolution of a Fourier transform is proportional to the length of waveform analyzed: a 256-sample window, for example, will produce just 128 equally spaced spectral components.

The frequency resolution of a Fourier analysis of a speech waveform with a long analysis window is further limited by the harmonic structure imposed by the periodic excitation. Yet a linear prediction analysis carried out on, say, 40 samples produces a smooth power spectrum defined at any frequency required, including those at which the harmonic structure would permit no energy. The source of this paradox is that while the Fourier analysis imposes no assumptions on the waveform, the linear prediction assumes an all-pole filter and attempts to compute its transfer function. The transfer function of this filter is defined at all frequencies, and is free of the harmonic structure, which is due to the periodicity of the excitation.

In a process of the form of equation 4, the predictor coefficients operate as an all-zero inverse filter applied to samples of the preemphasized speech waveform, x_n, x_{n-1}, etc., to produce an estimate of the excitation waveform, y_n, called the linear prediction 'residual.' This signal can also be seen as the difference between the current speech sample, x_n, and the value predicted from the earlier samples, and would be zero if the prediction were perfect. The residual is therefore also called the 'error signal.'

If the residual is used as the input, x_n, to the all-pole filtering process described by equation 3, the original speech waveform will be recovered. As a method of encoding the speech waveform, however, this is not attractive, because it takes as much information to store or transmit the residual as it does for the waveform, and the predictor coefficients are needed in addition. Most often, the residual for voiced speech is stylized as a single impulse repeated at the fundamental frequency and for voiceless speech as white noise. These forms are consistent with the assumptions made in the derivation of the predictor coefficients.

At some cost in the amount of information needed, the quality of the reconstructed speech waveform can be improved by supplying a somewhat more complex excitation signal using, for instance, several impulses in each glottal cycle ('multipulse' LPC), or selecting portions of the excitation signal from a library of possible forms ('codebook-excited' LPC or CELP). Such methods, which are growing in popularity as increasingly powerful digital signal processing hardware makes them practicable, are able to cope with the inevitable deviations from the all-pole assumption made by LPC by effectively supplying an FIR filter through the excitation signal.

In analyzing a power spectrum, a filter bank can confine its analysis to selected portions of the spectrum and use different spectral resolution at different frequencies. Standard LPC, on the other hand, must analyze the whole spectrum up to half the sampling frequency and must give equal weight to all frequencies in its all-pole spectral fit. However, a technique called 'selective LPC' is free of these limitations. Recalling that the autocorrelation function is the Fourier transform of the power spectrum, and that autocorrelation-method LPC takes the autocorrelation function as input, an LPC analysis of a modified spectrum can be performed by taking its Fourier transform and using this quasi-autocorrelation function as the input to the LPC. Of course, one of the theoretical justifications for LPC, namely that it matches the waveform generated by an all-pole vocal tract filter, applies only to unmodified spectra but, if LPC is viewed simply as a technique for fitting a smooth, simple

shape to a power spectrum, selective LPC is a perfectly valid technique. In a method called 'perceptual linear prediction' (PLP) selective LPC is applied to the output of a filter bank with perceptually spaced and shaped channels.

16. The Cepstrum

The excitation in a steady voiced sound is periodic, and its power spectrum can be written as the product of a set of impulses at the harmonics of the fundamental, $p(f)$, and a function, $q(f)$, changing slowly with frequency that describes the intensity of the harmonics. Since the speech spectrum, $s(f)$, is the product of this excitation spectrum and the shaping effect of the vocal tract, $v(f)$, we can write $s(f) = v(f)q(f)p(f)$. If we take the cosine transform of $s(f)$, we get the autocorrelation function. If we take the log of $s(f)$ before the cosine transform, we also get a function of time delay, τ, but the product of the terms composing $s(f)$ now becomes a sum, and from the linearity properties of Fourier transforms, we can write $S(\tau) = V(\tau) + Q(\tau) + P(\tau)$, where $S(\tau)$ is the cosine transform of $\log s(f)$, etc.

It is easier to imagine the properties of $S(\tau)$ if we think of the log spectrum as though it were a waveform and $S(\tau)$ its 'spectrum.' $S(\tau)$ is called the 'cepstrum,' i.e., 'spectrum' with the first syllable reversed; and by extension, (τ), corresponding to frequency in the spectrum, is called the 'quefrency,' while the equivalent of filtering for the spectrum is called 'liftering.'

The effect of the harmonic structure, $P(\tau)$, appears as a set of impulses at integer multiples of the glottal period, i.e., at quefrencies above 8 to 10 ms for a man. On the other hand, $V(\tau)$ and $Q(\tau)$ correspond to the smooth modulation of the log power spectrum (sometimes called the spectral envelope) and have only low-quefrency terms. At least for the lower fundamental frequencies typical of a man, the contributions to the cepstrum of P and of Q and V together do not overlap in quefrency.

The cepstrum therefore offers a means of separating the harmonic fine structure of the spectrum from the spectral envelope. The cepstral peaks corresponding to the fundamental frequency are much sharper than those occurring in the autocorrelation function, which are blurred by the effects of the envelope. Equally, reconstruction of the spectrum by inverse transformation from the low-quefrency terms offers a theoretically ideal means of removing the harmonic fine structure without (in contrast to LPC) having to impose assumptions about the form of the spectrum apart from that of smoothness.

In practice the situation is not so perfect. As has been shown, logarithms of small numbers have to be limited. Apart from numerical limitations, noise in the weak parts of the spectrum between harmonics makes it necessary to threshold the log spectrum. The separation between the envelope and the harmonic structure is then no longer exact, though it remains substantial.

There is a second, quite separate motivation for the cepstrum. While the variations in adjacent components in the power spectrum of a portion of speech waveform, or in the outputs of adjacent channels of a filter bank are highly correlated, it turns out that the low-quefrency terms of the cepstrum are uncorrelated with each other. This means that the low-quefrency cepstrum components form an approximation to a principal components representation of the speech spectral envelope; that is, something close to a maximally compact description.

When using the cepstrum to track fundamental frequency, it is convenient to think of it in terms of a quasi-continuous time-delay variable, τ. The cepstrum, being the result of an analysis of a finite frequency range, is, however, necessarily discrete, and the low-quefrency components are usually identified by their component number as C_0, C_1, C_2, etc.

The zeroth cepstrum coefficient, C_0, represents the average log spectrum. C_1 is the result of correlating the positive-frequency half of the log spectrum with a half-cosine wave running from +1 at zero frequency to +1 at half the sampling frequency. It therefore provides a measure of the balance between high and low-frequency energy in the log spectrum. Similarly, C_2 measures the balance between the energy in the center of the log spectrum and that at the two ends. Generally, C_n represents the effect of cross-correlation with a cosine wave that crosses the zero axis n times.

The uncorrelated property of cepstrum coefficients extends to cepstra derived by taking the cosine transform of the log-energy outputs of a filter-bank, even when the filter bank uses a nonuniform, perceptual scale (giving so-called 'mel-frequency cepstrum coefficients' or MFCC's), and it extends to cepstra derived from a linear prediction or PLP analysis.

Low-quefrency cepstrum coefficients are widely used in speech recognition partly because they form a compact representation and partly because their uncorrelated nature makes it possible by scaling to give them desirable statistical properties that are denied to direct representations of the log power spectrum. Discussion of these properties is outside the scope of this article.

17. Auditory Models

Auditory modeling is a point of view, not a specific technique like LPC. Its proponents can argue that modeling human hearing, particularly for automatic speech recognition, is likely to be fruitful because humans do far better than current machines at recognizing even nonsense words, where higher-order linguistic processes have no part to play.

This argument is persuasive because speech certainly evolved after hearing, which is similar in other animals who do not of course speak. Speech must therefore have adapted to the properties of human hearing; and it would be surprising to find reliable cues to phonetic identity in the speech signal that human ears cannot detect. Note that there is no parallel with flying: air did not adapt to suit the properties of birds' wings; rather, birds evolved a solution to a predefined problem, namely locomotion through air, and humans invented others, none of which involve 747s flapping their wings.

The problems start when trying to decide which properties to model, and whether to model physiological mechanisms or psychoacoustic results. Moreover, many properties are disputed; and including one property while omitting another, or while passing the result of the analysis to a recognition process quite different from that in the brain may be harmful.

Sometimes, physiology and psychoacoustics lead to similar conclusions, as they have for physiologically and psychoacoustically derived frequency scales. When a sine-wave stimulus is presented to the ear, the basilar membrane in the cochlea (the inner ear) moves in response to it. The location of peak motion along the membrane depends on the frequency of the stimulus, and the distance between peak locations corresponding to equal steps in frequency becomes more compressed at higher frequencies. The relationship between distance and frequency is close to that predicted from psychoacoustic properties such as the ability of listeners to detect small frequency differences in sine waves. It has been generally found that in speech recognition and speech coding the use of a frequency scale that compresses higher frequencies is helpful, and this might be seen as a victory for the proponents of the incorporation of auditory properties. However, it is conceivable that the advantage of frequency scales that compress higher frequencies stems not from properties of speech perception but from speech production, since, for example, formant bandwidths increase with frequency. Support for this contention comes from a finding that the best frequency scale for recognizing female speech is different from that for male speech, and that it differs in a way predictable from the differences in formant frequencies.

Certainly, the incorporation features that have only a physiological manifestation seems less strongly motivated. A particular physiological mechanism may result from peculiarly biological constraints on signal processing, much as wheels are ruled out for mechanical processing in living things. What is a good solution for highly miniaturized, massively parallel but slow and possibly noisy physiological processing system might be a very bad solution for quiet, fast but relatively bulky and simple hardware.

One such a feature may be the half-wave rectification observed in the cells along the basilar membrane (so-called inner hair cells) which convert vibrations into electrical signals. How these signals are subsequently processed is not yet clear. Some processes (such as the determination of the frequency of a sine by measuring the time difference between successive peaks) are simpler and more accurate with half-wave rectification than with full-wave rectification, where the negative parts of a signal are inverted in sign rather than being set to zero; while others (such as estimating the amplitude of the sine wave) would work better with full-wave rectification. Yet half-wave rectification is used both in auditory models where the subsequent processing benefits from it and in models where it would be expected to be less effective than full-wave rectification—and indeed where experimental results have shown this to be so. Retention of half-wave rectification in these circumstances seems to stem from a mystical belief in physiological modeling. Copying another superficial physiological property by painting the microphone flesh-colored would be less damaging to the final performance!

Several auditory properties have already been widely incorporated into speech recognition systems, sometimes for explicit auditory modeling reasons and sometimes for purely pragmatic reasons. The acoustic analyses used in virtually all systems respond to the power spectrum and not to the phase spectrum of speech sounds, and to the log power spectrum rather than the linear power spectrum. As seen above, many use a perceptual frequency scale, and most of the more effective systems reflect the ear's sensitivity to spectral change as well as to the properties of static spectra. These properties are taken for granted and are not regarded in themselves as constituting auditory modeling, which, like the epithet 'advanced technology' is a moving target.

The basilar membrane appears to behave like a filter bank with many heavily overlapping channels, each of which has an asymmetrical response shape, with a sharp cutoff on the high frequency side and a relatively slow rolloff on the other side of the peak response frequency. However, incorporation of such response shapes into speech recognizers has had little effect. The same is true of careful modeling of perceptual loudness as a function both of the intensity and the frequency of the input stimulus. Such properties surely need to be combined with other auditory properties before there is hope of seeing any benefit from them.

Over the critical frequency range for voiced speech sounds, inner hair cells tend to fire in synchrony with the motion of the basilar membrane at the point where they are attached to it. It is therefore possible that subsequent processing in the auditory system could recover the dominant frequency at each point along the membrane from the intervals between successive nerve impulses. Some models have attempted to carry out a similar synchrony or dominant frequency analysis. While there are some encouraging signs that this may be helpful, the results in general are mixed.

Piecemeal introduction of imperfectly understood auditory properties is by no means guaranteed to be helpful. However, there seems little doubt that a more complete understanding of human speech signal processing will ultimately help automatic speech recognition. In the meantime, even imperfect auditory models may themselves shed light on the system they seek to reproduce.

Acknowledgements

The author is grateful to Paul van Mulbregt and John Bridle for helpful suggestions on the text, and to John Bridle for help in producing the figures.

See also: Speech Coding and Compression; Speech Synthesis; Speech Recognition: Stochastic Techniques; Neural Net and Connectionist Methods in Speech Recognition and Synthesis; Speaker-adaptation Techniques in Speech Recognition; Speaker Normalization Techniques in Speech Recognition; Speech Recognition, Automatic: Knowledge-based Methods.

M. J. Hunt

Sikhism

Sikhism has always had a close territorial connection with the Panjab, still the homeland of the great majority of Sikhs. The historic link between Sikhism and Panjabi, while undeniably close, is however more complex than their close modern identification might suggest.

1. The Scriptural Language of the Sikhs

One of the most vital religious currents in medieval North India was the reformist monotheism of the lower caste Sants, whose hymns were composed in the dialectically mixed idiom loosely termed 'Santbhāṣā.' Very much in general line with those of the Sants, though distinguished by their exceptionally coherent articulation, the teachings of Gurū Nānak (1469–1539), the founder of the Sikh faith who was born in Shekhupura district west of Lahore, were similarly couched in a mixed poetic language well suited to extend their geographical appeal. Since Gurū Nānak's magnificent hymns formed the model for his immediate successors whose compositions are collected in the *Ādi Granth*, the Sikh scripture assembled by Gurū Arjan (1563–1606), their language may properly be termed the sacred language of the Sikhs (SLS) (Shackle 1983), a distinctive variety of Santbhāṣā.

Drawing freely for its technical lexicon upon assimilated Perso–Arabic loans besides the usual Sanskritic *tatsama* vocabulary (Shackle 1981), the core dialectal elements of SLS are Nānak's own speech and the Kharī bolī lingua franca, in roughly equal measure. The parallel use of such 'Old Panjabi' and 'Old Hindi' elements is exemplified by many common alternations, e.g., PRES 1SG *karāṃ/karaüṃ*, 3PL *karanhi/karaṃhi*. The location of Nānak's own dialect in the borderland between central Panjabi and the western 'Lahndā' dialects with their typical sigmatic future is reflected in further alternations, e.g., FUT 3SG *karegā/karasī*. More peripheral dialectal components are drawn from the Siraiki of Multan to the west, and Braj bhāṣā to the east.

Apart from this dialectal mixture, the most striking feature of SLS from a modern perspective is its marked archaism (Shapiro 1987), notable in its retention of the morphologically important final short vowels since lost in modern Panjabi, e.g., SG DIR *guru*, SG OBL/Pl DIR *gura*, SG LOC/INSTR *guri*, versus modern *gur[ū]*. By making recourse to modern patterns of postpositional extension redundant, this permits a conciseness of expression more typical of older Apabhraṃśa norms than of later Indo–Aryan, where such characteristic constructions as the loc abs (e.g., *satiguri miliai* 'through the True Guru's meeting') have long been unfamiliar.

2. The Gurmukhi Script and Postscriptural Literature

The *Ādi Granth* is written in the Gurmukhi script, whose standardization is attributed to the second Gurū, Angad (1504–52). This is superficially similar to Nagari, albeit with the confusing assignation of different values to identical graphs (e.g., Gurmukhi [s p m] = Nagari [m dh bh]) and the addition of a separate sign for [ṛ]. In such characteristics as the general avoidance of consonant clusters, Gurmukhi is however closer to original Brahmi norms than to learned South Asian scripts of the Nagari type. Gurmukhi may rather be regarded as occupying an intermediate position between the latter and the commercial shorthands known in the Panjab as *laṇḍe*, which it resembles in the alphabetic order of its 35 letters and their distinctive names. These features, plus the reduction of vowel-bearers to three and of the sibilants to a single graph, are seen in the first five letters of the alphabet: *ūrā* [u], *airā* [a], *īṛī* [i], *sassā* [s], *hāhā* [h].

Religions tend to be linked more closely to scripts than to languages (see *Alphabet: Religious Beliefs*), and postscriptural Sikh literature is recorded in the same sacred

Gurmukhi ('from the mouth of the Gurū'), irrespective of its language. The seventeenth-century prose hagiographies (called *janamsākhī*, already show many more modern features, with increasing confusion in the notation of final short vowels indicating their gradual disappearance in contemporary speech.

Though not included in the *Ādi Granth*, particular liturgical importance attaches to the compositions of the tenth and last Gurū, Gobind Singh (1666–1708). Born in Patna and throughout his life involved in the militant struggle against the Muslim imperial power which was to dominate Sikh affairs throughout the eighteenth century, Gobind Singh wrote not in SLS but in Braj bhāṣā, then the premier non-Muslim literary language of North India. Much of the later Sikh literature down to the time of the kingdom of Maharājā Ranjīt Singh (1799–1839) was similarly composed in Braj bhāṣā, though recorded in Gurmukhi.

3. Reformist Sikhism and the Rise of Modern Standard Panjabi

The British conquest of the Panjab in 1849 reduced the Sikhs to the unprivileged status of a minority to both Muslims and Hindus. From the 1870s the assimilationist claims of revivalist Hinduism were vigorously combated by the Sikh reformers of the Singh Sabhā movement. This religious controversy quickly assumed a linguistic dimension, as Panjabi Hindus identified with Hindi while the Sikhs identified with Panjabi (Brass 1974).

Owing much to the conscious efforts of such reformist writers as Vīr Singh (1872–1957), a modern standard Panjabi based on the central Mājhī dialect was evolved, drawing increasingly on Sanskrit rather than Perso–Arabic for its learned vocabulary (Shackle 1988). Although very different in character from SLS, the continued use of the Gurmukhi script (with the addition of appropriately standardized diacritics) has aided this modern Panjabi in becoming the unquestioned language of contemporary Sikhism.

Campaigns to secure its official recognition continued after Indian independence, until the demand for a Sikh-majority state, made politically acceptable by being defined as one with Panjabi as its official language, was eventually achieved in 1966. In the Sikh diaspora in Britain and North America, too, claims for its recognition overseas are frequently raised, in spite of the growing importance of English even within nonliturgical parts of the temple services themselves.

See also: Panjabi; India.

Bibliography

Brass P R 1974 *Language, Religion and Politics in North India.* Cambridge University Press, Cambridge

Shackle C 1981 *A Gurū Nānak Glossary.* School of Oriental and African Studies, London

Shackle C 1983 *An Introduction to the Sacred Language of the Sikhs.* School of Oriental and African Studies, London

Shackle C 1988 Some observations on the Evolution of Modern Standard Punjabi. In: O'Connell J T (ed.) *Sikh History and Religion in the Twentieth Century.* University of Toronto, Toronto

Shapiro M C 1987 Observations on the core language of the *Ādigranth Berliner. Indologische Studien* 3: 181–93

C. Shackle

Silence

Silence, perhaps because it seems the antithesis of linguistic form, has long been neglected in the study of language. Nevertheless, it forms an essential part of communication, and speech communities differ as much in the uses and interpretations they give to silence as they do in regard to the linguistic forms that they use. Silence is thus better seen as the complement to sound; an awareness of its potential functions, structures, and meaning therefore necessarily becomes as relevant to the study of linguistic communication as the recognition of clauses, lexical networks, and intonation is now.

1. Societal Patterning of Silence

At a societal level, patterning in the use of silence generally relates to dimensions of social organization, to community attitudes, and to such macrofunctions as social control, ritual interaction with the supernatural, and establishment or reinforcement of group identity. In part this patterning is determined by the institutions of a specific society, and the functional meaning of silence can only be understood in relation to particular institutional contexts. These contexts may be as various as physical locations, ritual performances, or the enactment of social roles/relationships. Communication may be proscribed, for example, between a commoner and a chief, or a man and his mother-in-law, while membership in certain religious groups may require a vow of silence.

Where institutionally determined power is accorded voice, silence is often indicative of passivity and powerlessness. Thus women may keep silent in the presence of men, or children in the presence of adults. The opposite is the case in settings where self-exposure is required, however, and where the listener sits in silent judgment: e.g., religious confession, psychotherapy, bureaucratic interviews, and jury trials (Gal 1989).

In some cases, the interpretation of silence may be institutionally defined by a society's covenants and laws. In the USA, for instance, suspected legal offenders must be explicitly informed that they have the 'right to remain silent' to avoid self-incrimination, while instances of implicit silence (i.e., nondisclosure) in business transactions have been ruled to constitute active concealment and fraud. In some societies, silence in interpersonal interaction may be invoked as a powerful instrument of social control (e.g., 'shunning' among the Inuit, the Igbo, or the Amish).

Many societal patterns of silence are also determined by members of a group in relation to dynamics of social organization. Patterns may be situational, as when access to speaking privilege in public forums is allocated by group decision and others must remain silent, or normative, as when differential speaking privileges are allocated to individuals or classes of individuals.

The amount of talk versus silence that is prescribed is closely tied to social values and norms. The relative value of talk or silence in a society may be partly inferred from whether one or the other is ascribed to its rulers, priests, and sages. The value of silence may also be found in proverbs: e.g., 'Silence is golden' (English); 'Because of the mouth the fish dies' (Spanish); 'The way your eyes look can say more than your mouth' (Japanese); and 'Man becomes wise through the ear' (Persian).

Additionally, cultural understandings regarding the contextual or interactional interpretation of silence may be made explicit in the choice of adjectives coupled with the term 'silence' itself (e.g., 'ominous silence,' 'worshipful silence,' 'eerie silence,' 'smug silence,' 'thoughtful silence,' 'pregnant silence') or may be implied by terms used to describe people who exhibit relatively silent behavior (e.g., 'taciturn,' 'reserved,' 'secretive,' 'circumspect'). Differing group norms of appropriateness for speaking versus maintaining silence can give rise to cross-cultural misunderstanding, as when 'friendliness' is equated differently with one or the other in a conversation, or 'sincerity' and 'politeness' in a business or political encounter.

Societal norms for the use and interpretation of silence inevitably influence artistic expression, with painters, poets, authors, composers, and playwrights using pauses and silences, or their visual and orthographic counterparts, for aesthetic effect. Silence, like other components of communication, may also serve amusement functions, often as a key element of joke and story telling. One of the most successful jokes performed on radio by Jack Benny (a USA comedian who cultivated the image of being miserly) was his long silence in response to a robber's directive, 'Your money or your life!'

2. Individual and Small Group Patterning of Silence

At the level of individuals and small interacting groups within a society, patterning of silence occurs in relation to expression and interpretation of personality, and to microfunctions related to participants' purposes and needs. Bruneau (1973) terms these 'psycholinguistic' and 'interactive' silences, which include an array of functions ranging from defining the role of auditor in a communicative exchange, to providing social control, to demonstrating deference, to indicating emotional closeness, to managing personal interaction. Jensen (1973) presents a similar array, categorizing functions as 'linkage,' 'affecting,' 'revelational,' 'judgmental,' and 'activating.'

Some interactional functions of silence may be viewed as primarily sociocontextual in nature: defining (e.g., status and role), structuring (e.g., situations), tactical (e.g., nonparticipation, avoidance, disapproval, mitigation, image manipulation), and phatic (emotional sharing); some as primarily linguistic: discursive (e.g., prayer, fantasizing, rehearsing) or propositional (e.g., negation, affirmation, refusal, acknowledgment); and some as primarily psychological (e.g., expression of anger, sorrow, embarrassment, joy, or fear). Some noninteractional functions of silence involve contemplative/meditative states, while others are inactive in nature.

While none of these listings is entirely comprehensive, such taxonomies provide a basis for recognizing and contrasting many potential functions of silence in relation to situational contexts of use.

3. Structures of Silence

A basic distinction should be made between silences which carry meaning, but not propositional content, and silent communicative acts which carry their own illocutionary force. The former include the pauses and hesitations that occur within and between turns of talking—the prosodic dimension of silence. Such nonpropositional silences may

be volitional or nonvolitional, and may convey a wide variety of meanings. The meanings carried by pauses and hesitations are generally affective in nature, and connotative rather than denotative. Their meanings are nonetheless symbolic and conventional, as is seen in the various patterns of use and norms of interpretation in different speech communities (see examples in Tannen and Saville-Troike 1985).

Silent communicative acts conveying either emotional or propositional content may be accompanied by meaningful facial expressions or gestures, but they may consist of silence unaccompanied by any visual cues. Even in a telephone conversation where no visual signals are possible, silence in response to a greeting, query, or request which anticipates verbal response is fraught with propositional meaning in its own right. Silence as part of communicative interaction can be one of the forms a 'speech' act may take—filling many of the same functions and discourse slots—and should be considered along with the production of sentence tokens as a basic formational unit of linguistic communication. Thus, silence on the part of an Arabic or Japanese woman in response to a proposal of marriage implies consent, while in many speech communities a silent response to a request to borrow money or for a favor would be interpreted as a refusal.

Silence may even carry grammatical and lexical meaning within the sentence. One form of the *wh-* question in English, for instance, is a fill-in-the-blank structure, e.g., 'And your name is . . . ?' (said with nonterminal intonation), meaning 'What is your name?' Utterances may be completed in silence when the topic is a particularly delicate one or the word which would be used is taboo, or when the situation is emotionally loaded and the speaker is 'at a loss' for words. The Japanese term *haragei* 'wordless communication' captures the essence of this latter type of silence.

Silence over longer segments of communication may convey a more generalized meaning, as in 'sulking' to express disapproval of others' behavior, or silent attentiveness during relatively long stretches of speaking to convey listener interest and respect. (The same absence of conversational backchannel noise in some speech communities (e.g., African–American) would convey disinterest or hostility.)

Entire communicative events without sound are also common. Especially in ritual contexts, silence may be conventionally mandated as the only form which could achieve the event's communicative goals. Thus we find the invocation in Judeo–Christian ritual: 'The Lord is in His holy temple; let all the earth keep silence before Him.'

4. Interpretation and Production of Silence in Communicative Events

Appropriate participation in communicative events requires recognition of the components which are likely to be salient to members of the speech community within which the event occurs (Saville-Troike 1989). Each component that can call for a different form of speech can also permit or prescribe silence. These include the extrapersonal context, as well as the status and role-relationships of the participants: the genre, topic, or setting (time and place) may be designated as inappropriate for vocal interaction. The sequence of communicative acts in an event includes turn-taking and overlap phenomena, which include silence on the prosodic dimension. Maintaining silence between turns may be an indication of politeness (e.g., among the Navajo), or a violation of norms of interaction. Rules for appropriate interpretation and production of speech include knowing the properties relating to silence which should be observed in different types of speech situations, as well as the potential significance of silence in negotiating meaning within any specific interaction. Finally, as an overarching consideration, successful communication requires shared knowledge and cultural presuppositions which allow inferences to be drawn about the unsaid as well as the said.

Almost all research on child-language development has focused on how children learn to speak. But an essential part of children's acquisition of communicative competence is learning when not to talk, and what silence means in their speech community. Because cultural beliefs, values, and practices are integrally involved in the process, socializing young children to the use of silence may be considered part of the transmission of world view. This question remains largely unexplored in the early 1990s, but constitutes a promising direction for future cross-cultural studies of silence.

Bibliography

Bruneau T J 1973 Communicative silences: Forms and functions. *Journal of Communication* **23**: 17–46

Dauenhauer B P 1980 *Silence: The Phenomenon and Its Ontological Significance*. Indiana University Press, Bloomington, IN

Gal S 1989 Between speech and silence: The problematics of research on language and gender. *Papers in Pragmatics* **3**(1): 1–38

Jensen J V 1973 Communicative functions of silence. *ETC: A Review of General Semantics* **30**: 249–57

Saville-Troike M 1989 *The Ethnography of Communication*, 2nd edn. Basil Blackwell, Oxford

Tannen D, Saville-Troike M (eds.) 1985 *Perspectives on Silence*. Ablex, Norwood, NJ

Traber M (ed.) 1982 *Media Development* **29**(4) [Issue devoted to Silence in Communication.]

M. Saville-Troike

Silvestre de Sacy, Baron Antoine-Isaac (1758–1838)

The French Orientalist, Silvestre de Sacy was born on April 21, 1758, the second son of a Paris notary. His father died when de Sacy was 7 and, because of his delicate health, he was educated at home, acquiring a deep knowledge of Greek and Latin, which latter he wrote fluently in his scholarly works. At the age of 12 he met the Benedictine Dom Berthereau, then engaged on a study of Arab historians of the Crusades, who fired his first enthusiasm for Eastern languages.

De Sacy studied in succession Hebrew, Syriac, Chaldean, Samaritan, Arabic, and Ethiopic, and at the same time learned Italian, Spanish, English, and German. His first scholarly work was done on a Syriac MS, while his first published work was a Latin translation of two Samaritan letters originally written to J. J. Scaliger (1793; see *Scaliger, Joseph Justus*). He was then studying Persian and Turkish. In 1785 he was admitted to the Académie des Inscriptions,

where he began work on two major studies on the breaking of the dam of Ma'rib and the earliest Arabic literature, only published much later. He was also given the task of preparing a descriptive catalogue of Arabic and Persian MSS in French libraries. While continuing to work in Samaritan studies, de Sacy was now led to an interest in pre-Islamic Persian antiquities, working on the inscriptions of Naqsh-i Rustam and Bīsutūn (the latter without success) and Pahlavi coinage. Next, he was drawn to what became a lifelong interest, the history and doctrines of the Druze. These years were spent in seclusion in the countryside, his scholarly work alternating with the cultivation of his garden.

In 1795, the Terror was over and de Sacy was appointed Professor of Arabic at the new Ecole des Langues Orientales Vivantes. One of the conditions of the appointment was that he should write an Arabic grammar but the preparatory work led him first to study what was then known as 'universal grammar,' and in 1799 he published his *Principes de Grammaire Générale*, which drew upon the ideas of the Port-Royal grammar (see *Port-Royal Tradition of Grammar*) and others. In 1806 he was made Professor of Persian at the Collège de France, but despite his new duties he continued with his work on Arabic. The first edition of his three-volume *Chrestomathie arabe* appeared in 1806, followed in 1810 by his *Grammaire arabe*. In the same year he published a translation of 'Abd al-Latīf al-Baghdādī's *K. al-Ifāda wa-al-I 'tibār* (*Relation d'Egypte*) and began work on a major series of studies on the law of property in Egypt from the Arab conquest.

De Sacy had never hidden his royalist principles, and soon after the Restoration he was made Prefect of the University of Paris, and a series of academic honours followed, culminating in his ennoblement in 1832. Major publications of this period were his editions of *Kalīla wa-Dimna* (1816), 'Afttār's *Pand-Nama* (1819), and Harīrī's *Maqāmāt* (1822), a revised and expanded edition of his *Anthologie* (1829) and *Grammaire* (1831), an edition of the *Alfiyya* (1833), and his last work, the two-volume *Exposé de la religion des Druzes* (1838). A projected third volume was cut short by his death on February 21, 1838.

De Sacy's learned output was vast and varied, and in his youth especially his restless temperament took him from one field to another; his best work was done in later life. More even than this, however, de Sacy's main services to Middle Eastern studies probably lay in his textbooks and the outstanding scholars whom he taught. Among many others, these included Flügel, Kosegarten, Quatremère, de Slane, and Fleischer. The enormous expansion of Arabic studies in the nineteenth century owed almost everything to the groundwork laid by Silvestre de Sacy.

Bibliography

Centenaire de Silvestre de Sacy 1938 *Comptes rendus des séances de l'Académie des Inscriptions et Belles-lettres*

Reinaud J T 1838 Notice historique et littéraire sur le Baron Silvestre de Sacy, lue à la séance générale de la Societé Asiatique, le 25 juin 1838. *Journal Asiatique* **3**(6): 113–95. (English transl. *Asiatic Journal* **27**: 115–29; 182–97)

M. V. McDonald

Sindhi

Sindhi belongs to a family of the Indo–Aryan languages. According to Grierson (1919), it is 'a member of the north-western, outer-circle of the Indo–Aryan vernaculars spoken in British India.'

One comes across diverse writing systems used for Sindhi until the time of the British conquest of Sind. In addition to various forms of Devanagari and Launda scripts such as Khudawadi, Shikarpuri, Sakhru, Thattai, Larai, Sewhani, and Memaniko, Perso–Arabic and Gurumukhi characters also are used for Sindhi religious and literary writings. It was in 1851 that the British government decided to adopt Arabic script for the purposes of their administration. But the use of Devanagari and Gurumukhi continued for religious purposes, and Launda for commercial purposes.

According to the census report of India (1991), there are about 2.6 million people who speak Sindhi in India. It may be regarded as the mother tongue of another 15 million people who live in Sind province in Pakistan.

The difference between the Indian Sindhi and that of Pakistan has been fast increasing on the subcontinent since the advent of Independence in 1947. During the first half of the twentieth century, the language of literature and formal discourse was pre-eminently dominated by Perso–Arabic influences. Even in the 1990s, the Sindhi language in Pakistan continues to lean heavily toward Perso–Arabic and Urdu styles to identify itself with Islamic culture; whereas the Sindhi language in India does not show much resistance to borrowings from Sanskrit and Hindi. Obviously, the use of Perso–Arabic elements in the colloquial as well as written Indian Sindhi language has been very much on the decline. This change is well reflected, for example, in the phonological patterns of Indian Sindhi as shown below:

(a) The Perso–Arabic borrowed sounds [x] and [ɣ] are fast losing their distinctiveness in modern Indian Sindhi. These two sounds most often occur in free variation with [kʰ] and [g] respectively in the speech of bilingual immigrants. For all practical purposes, however, they have disappeared from the speech of the younger generation.

(b) The distribution pattern of Sindhi distinctive sounds is affected to a great extent.

According to the sound laws of Sindhi, every word must end in a vowel. All consonant sounds, therefore, occur only in the word-initial and word-medial position. There are, however, a large number of borrowed words from Persian (including Arabic) and English, used very frequently in modern Indian Sindhi wherein consonant sounds do occur in the word-final position; e.g., [xɔf] (fear), [ɣəlɘt] (wrong), [bəraɟ] (a dam over a river).

A young Sindhi speaker, generally, tends to add a short vowel, either [ə], [ɪ], or [ʊ] at the end of these loan words to fit these into the overall phonotactic patterns of Sindhi.

The process of development thus has resulted in a deepening of the influence of Sanskrit and Hindi on Sindhi in India, and that of Persian, Arabic and Urdu on Sindhi in Pakistan.

Bibliography

Grierson Sir G A 1919 *Linguistic Survey of India. Vol.8 (1): Indo-Aryan Family North Western Group: Sindhi and Lahanda*. Office of the Registrar General and Census Commissioner, Calcutta

P. Nihalani

Singapore: Language Situation

The language situation in Singapore (area 618 km^2; population in the early 1990s 3,000,000) is complex. Several unrelated languages, each with its own literary tradition, are spoken by three major ethnic groups: Chinese (77.7 percent), Malay (14.1 percent), and Indian (7.1 percent). Generally, the ethnic Chinese speak one or more Chinese dialects, for example, Hokkien, Teochew, Cantonese, Hainanese, Hakka, and Foochow; the ethnic Malay speak Austronesian languages, for example, Malay, Javanese, and Boyanese; and the ethnic Indians speak Dravidian and Indo–Aryan languages, for example, Tamil, Malayalam, Hindi, Panjabi, Bengali, Telugu, Gujarati, and Sindhi.

There are four official languages: Malay (the national language), Mandarin, Tamil, and English. The single most important language is English, which is used in the public domains of transactions, employment, education, media, government, law, and religion, and in the private domains of family and friendship.

Published data on the language situation in Singapore are limited to censuses and census reports, questionnaires and small-scale interviews, and observations by scholars. They are further restricted to the study of official languages. The lingua francas are English and Mandarin for the better-educated, and Malay and Hokkien for the less well-educated.

The choice of language spoken at home depends on six factors: the person spoken to, the person speaking, type of family nucleus, household income, ethnicity, and the educational attainment of the head of the household (Tay 1983: 91–92). The principal languages most commonly reported to be spoken at home are: a Chinese dialect, Mandarin, English, Malay, and Tamil. Since the early 1980s, the use of Mandarin and English as home languages has increased while the use of Chinese dialects at home has dropped. Malay is the predominant language of the Malay households.

The incidence of multilingualism is 24 percent by households and 27 percent by individuals. The major types of multilingualism are: Mandarin and Chinese dialects, English and Chinese dialects, Mandarin and English, two or more Chinese dialects, English and Malay, English and Tamil.

The medium of instruction in all schools is English; a second official language is used to teach several subjects. The bilingual policy in education requires proficiency in English and one other official language up to secondary-school level. University education is entirely in English. A third language, usually Japanese, French, or German, is taught in selected schools.

The general literacy rate is high (90.1 percent). The rank order of official languages in which people are literate is: Chinese, English, Malay, Tamil. Literacy in English (65 percent) has increased for Chinese, Malays, and Indians. Multiliteracy is also on the increase, especially among the younger age group. The Chinese are predominantly literate in Chinese only or in both Chinese and English, and the Malays in Malay only or in both Malay and English, while the Indians are more literate in English than Tamil.

Bibliography

Afendras E A, Kuo E C Y 1980 *Language and Society in Singapore*. Singapore University Press, Singapore
Tay M W J 1983 *Trends in Language, Literacy and Education in Singapore*. Department of Statistics, Singapore

M. W. J. Tay

Singular/General Proposition

Many propositions depend for their truth values on facts about particular individuals, but only singular propositions are directly *about* individuals. The proposition that the President of the USA is not tall, depends for its truth value on the height of a particular person, e.g., George Bush, but it is not directly about him (though it is directly about the USA). If Bush were never to have existed, the proposition that the President of the USA is not tall would still exist and could be stated in the same way; it is not *internally* related to Bush; it is not identified by reference to Bush, but only to the property of being the President of the USA; it might have been true even if Bush were tall (so long as the President of the USA was not). The proposition that George Bush is not tall, on the other hand, is internally related to Bush. It is directly *about him*; it could not be stated (in the same way) if he never had existed; it is identified by reference to him; it could not be true unless Bush himself was not tall. Singular propositions are those of this latter kind, which are directly about particular individuals. General propositions are about no particular individuals, but only about properties. Some paradigm general propositions are that all snow is white, and that the shortest spy is human. Paradigm singular propositions include that the earth is round, and that Nixon was President of the USA. In theories of structured propositions, singular propositions are held to contain the individuals they are about as constituents, whereas general propositions contain only properties.

See also: Proposition; Properties and Predication: Formal Theories; Reference, Philosophical Issues concerning.

Bibliography

Evans G, McDowell J (eds.) 1982 *The Varieties of Reference*. Clarendon Press, Oxford

M. Crimmins

Sinhala

Sinhala (Sinhalese), one of the two official national languages of Sri Lanka (Ceylon), is spoken by 11,000,000 Sinhalese, who constitute 74 percent of the island's population (1981). While Sinhala is spoken only in Sri Lanka, Tamil, the other official language, is also the state language of Tamil Nadu in India. The rise of Sinhala nationalism has led, on the one hand, to the resurgence of Sinhala as a medium of communication, education, and administration, and, on the other, to political and ethnic conflicts with the Tamils.

Sinhala has given rise to a new language Divehi, the language of the Maldives; a new brand of English, Sri Lankan English; and the creole of the Vaedda tribe, the island's vanishing aboriginals (see de Silva 1972). The variety of Sinhala which Sri Lankan bilinguals use, Singlish, accommodates with ease English words within Sinhala grammar.

1. Genetic Affinities

Sinhala is an Indo–European language belonging to the Indo–Aryan subfamily. Genetically, its closest relatives are Bengali in eastern India, and Gujarati in western India. The origin of the name 'Sinhala' is traced back to Vijaya, the legendary founder of the Sinhala race. The arrival of Vijaya and his 700 followers from northern India in the sixth century BC marks the first wave of Aryan migrations to the island. Their descendants were called Sinhala perhaps in recognition of the ancestral myth that Vijaya was the grandson of a lion, *sinha*, who roamed the jungles of Bengal. The language that these Aryan settlers developed, under the impact of subsequent waves of migration and the influence of languages of pre-Vijayan inhabitants such as the Nagas, Yakshas, and Rakshashas, came to be known as Sinhala.

2. History

Geiger divides the history of Sinhala into four periods:
  (a) Sinhalese Prakrit (200 BC to fourth or fifth century AD);
  (b) Proto–Sinhalese (fourth or fifth to eighth century AD);
  (c) Medieval Sinhalese (eighth to thirteenth century);
  (d) Modern Sinhalese (thirteenth century onward).

3. Sinhala Writing

The earliest extant Sinhala writings are found in inscriptions engraved below the dripline in caves donated to Buddhist monks as dwelling places. The credit of introducing this system of writing goes to Sage Mahinda, the head of the first Indian Buddhist mission responsible for the establishment of Buddhism on the island in the third century BC. The script used was that known as Brahmi, which was also used by the Indian emperor Asoka in his edicts. However, in view of certain differences that exist between the Asokan and Sri Lankan Brahmi scripts, epigraphists believe that the art of writing had been practiced in Sri Lanka even before the advent of Buddhism. This script, influenced later by other Indian scripts such as the Pallava Granta, gave rise to the modern system of writing. Sinhala has an extant written literature dating from about the ninth century AD.

3.1 Alphabet

Sinhala writers use an alphabet of 58 letters: 16 vowels and 42 consonants (Fig. 1). Vowels use two kinds of symbols: one when they occur initially in words, and the other, resembling diacritical marks, when they occur after consonants. Sinhala typewriters and word-processors have successfully accommodated these conventions of writing.

Figure 1. Sinhala alphabet.

ශ්‍රී ලංකාව   සිංහල

Sri Lanka   Sinhala

Figure 2. A sample of Sinhala writing.

4. Structure

Sinhala is structurally an Indo–Aryan language, with a phonological system evolved from Sanskrit through gradual changes following regular sound laws, and a grammatical system exhibiting categories such as number, gender, and case similar to other Indo–Aryan languages. Its vocabulary is full of derivatives and loans from Sanskrit and Pali. Owing to its close contact with Tamil, Sinhala shares some linguistic features of Dravidian, thus providing an excellent example of linguistic convergence.

4.1 Phonology

Spoken Sinhala contains 40 segmental phonemes: 14 vowels and 26 consonants, including a set of 4 'prenasalized' plosives or 'prenasals' peculiar to Sinhala. The vowels are either short or long:

short	a	ae	i	u	e	o	ə		(1)
long	aː	aeː	iː	uː	eː	oː	əː		

The consonants are given in Fig. 3.

4.2 Morphology and Syntax

Sinhala morphology is basically inflectional. Nominal inflection involves categories such as gender, number, and case. 'Gender' is twofold: 'animate' or 'inanimate':

Animate	put-aː	(the son)	put-ek	(a son)	(2)
Inanimate	pot-ə	(the book)	pot-ak	(a book)	

Animate nouns are either 'masculine' or 'feminine':

Masculine	koll-a	(the lad)	koll-ek	(a lad)	(3)
Feminine	kell-ə	(the lass)	kell-ak	(a lass)	

'Number' is threefold: 'singular definite,' 'singular indefinite,' or 'plural':

Sg def	put-aː	pot-ə	(4)
Sg indef	put-ek	pot-ak	
Plural	put-t-u	pot	

Case also shows an 'animate/inanimate' distinction. Animate nouns have five cases, and inanimate nouns have four cases:

Nominative	putaː	(the son)	potə	(the book)	(5)
Dative	putaː -tə		potə-tə		
Genitive	putaː -ge		pot-eː		
Ablative	putaː -gen		pot-en		
Vocative	put-eː				

The Sinhala verbal system is more complex and intricate.

One of the more interesting subsystems is that which involves the terms 'transitive' and 'intransitive' on the one hand, and 'volitive' and 'involitive' on the other. These morphological categories also have bearings on syntactic structures, as exemplified by the following sentences, which use the pair of verbs aha-nava (transitive–volitive) and aehe-nava (intransitive–involitive).

(a) Transitive–volitive sentence:

> miniha sinduva **ahanava**   (6)
> man-the song-the listen
> 'The man listens to the song (and he does so voluntarily).'

(b) Intransitive sentence:

> sinduva **aehenava**   (7)
> song-the hear
> 'The song is heard.'

(c) Involitive sentence:

> minihatə   sinduva **aehenava**   (8)
> man-the-DAT song-the hear
> 'The man hears the song (involuntarily).'

An interesting syntactic feature of the involitive sentence is that its 'subject' is a 'dative noun.' Sinhala has many types of sentences in which dative nouns function as subjects, a feature which Sinhala (9) shares with Tamil (10):

> Sinhala: **matə** putek innava   (9)
> I-DAT son-a exists
> 'I have a son.'

> Tamil: **enakku** oru-mahan irukku   (10)
> I-DAT a-son   exists
> 'I have a son.'

4.3 Vocabulary

The vocabulary of Sinhala is an index to the cultural history of its speakers. While the largest core of words are of Sanskritic origin, the others trace their origins to Pali, Tamil, Portuguese, Dutch, and English.

5. Diglossia

Sinhala diglossia exhibits two main varieties: spoken Sinhala and literary Sinhala. They differ not only in their form and structure but also in their typical uses and functions. Literary Sinhala is generally considered the 'higher' variety in that its structure is closer to the classical literary idiom. It is used in all forms of nonfictional writing, including news bulletins, and in electronic media. News is read rather than spoken. Different genres of fiction use a mixture of both: literary Sinhala for narration and spoken Sinhala for dialog. Spoken Sinhala is used in all face-to-face communication.

	bilabial	labiodental	dental	cerebral	palatal	velar
plosive						
voiceless	p		t	ṭ	c	k
voiced	b		d	ḍ	j	g
prenasalized	ṁb		ṅd	ṅḍ		ṅg
nasal	m		n		ɲ	ŋ
fricative		f	s		ś	h
lateral			l			
trill				r		
semivowel		v				y

Figure 3. Sinhala consonants.

6. Grammatical Studies

The earliest extant Sinhala grammar is *Sidat Sangaraṭva*, written in the thirteenth century. Although some scholars maintain that the original aim of this work was to serve as a guide for versification, rather than as a manual of grammar, it is still considered the most important traditional grammar of the language. In the twentieth century, Munidasa Kumaratunga and W.F. Gunawardhana made valuable contributions to Sinhala grammatical studies. With the establishment of linguistics as an autonomous subject in the universities, spoken Sinhala has become the focus of serious academic analysis. A comprehensive Sinhala dictionary is nearing completion at the time of writing (the early 1990s). Among the issues in Sinhala linguistics are alphabetic reform, Romanization, use of spoken grammar in preference to the literary idiom, and standardization of grammar.

Bibliography

Disanayaka J B 1991 *The Structure of Spoken Sinhala*, vol. 1. National Institute of Education, Sri Lanka

Gair J W 1970 *Colloquial Sinhalese Clause Structures*. Mouton, The Hague

Geiger W 1938 *A Grammar of the Sinhalese Language*. Colombo

Reynolds C H B 1980 *Sinhalese: An Introductory Course*. School of Oriental and African Studies, University of London, London

Silva M W S de 1972 *Vedda Language of Ceylon* (*Texts and Lexicon*). Kitzinger, Munich

J. B. Disanayaka

Sino–Tibetan Languages

Sino–Tibetan is a family of languages spoken in much of eastern Asia and southeast Asia. It ranks second only to Indo–European in terms of number of speakers, mainly due to Chinese, which has well over a billion speakers. This family was formerly also called Indo–Chinese, but the term 'Sino–Tibetan' has come to be universally used.

Various attempts have been made to link Sino–Tibetan genetically to other languages. In 1920, the American linguist Sapir (see *Sapir, Edward*) suggested that these languages were related to the Na–Dene languages of North America. He was especially impressed by some lexical and morphological similarities between Tibetan and Tlingit. The Russian linguist Starostin (1984) discusses the possible relationship between Sino–Tibetan and Yeniseian and North Caucasus languages. Chang (1988) examines the link between Chinese and Indo-European. The French linguist Sagart (1993) offers additional evidence connecting Chinese and Austronesian, a link suggested by Conrady in 1916. It is difficult to assess these hypotheses with confidence, as Sino–Tibetan studies are at an early stage in the 1990s. Stronger grounds may eventually emerge for separating similarities which are due to diffusion from those which are due to common inheritance.

The internal composition of Sino–Tibetan is clearer, though there is by no means any general consensus. An early proposal is due to Li, who in 1937 divided the family into four branches: Sinitic, Tibeto–Burman, Kam–Tai, and Miao–Yao. This proposal still serves as the major working hypothesis for linguists in China at the time of writing (Ma 1991). Western scholarship, on the other hand, has been much influenced by the views of Benedict, who excludes the Kam–Tai and Miao–Yao languages, attributing their similarities to diffusion. Instead, he proposes the inclusion of a group of Karen languages, which are mostly spoken in northern Burma. This latter framework is accepted, for instance, in Ruhlen (1991).

Within this framework, Ruhlen lists some 300 languages for Sino–Tibetan. This is a vast linguistic area which goes southward along the Irrawady River and the Salween River (called the Nu Jiang in China) to the Bay of Bengal, westward along the Himalayas, and eastward to the northeast corner of China, stretching across some 3,500 miles. In addition, Tibetan was carried deeper into India by the fourteenth Dalai Lama in 1959, transplanting some 100,000 speakers. On a yet grander scale, Chinese has been carried by several tens of millions of people who have emigrated to all the continents of the world since the mid-nineteenth century.

The great majority of Sino–Tibetan languages are tribal languages, with speakers numbering in the thousands or tens of thousands. They include goat-herders in the mountains of Nepal and former head-hunters in the jungles of

Assam. There are a few languages, however, which number over 1,000,000 speakers. These include Burmese, with some 30,000,000 speakers, as well as Tibetan, Yi (previously called Lolo), Tujia, Bai, Hani, etc.

The Sinitic languages have by far the largest numbers of speakers. For historical reasons, these languages are generally known as Chinese dialects, even though their diversification began well before 1000 AD and their mutual intelligibility is low. The dominant dialect group is Mandarin, with over 700,000,000 native speakers. In China, Modern Standard Chinese, which is the variety of Mandarin largely based on Beijing speech, is called Putonghua, or 'Common Language.' In addition, the traditional division is into these six dialect groups: Wu, Gan, Xiang, Min, Yue, and Kejia, each with tens of millions of speakers.

Although most of the Sino–Tibetan languages have acquired writing systems only in the late twentieth century, an exceptional case is Naxi, a Burman language of southwest China, which independently invented its own pictographic orthography some centuries back. Another independently invented orthography, based on a Chinese model, was that of the Xixia (Tangut) kingdom in 1036. The kingdom was founded by a Tibetan people in northwestern China. After its conquest by the Mongols in 1227, the orthography fell into disuse.

The three major literary traditions which continue in the 1990s are Tibetan, Burmese, and Chinese. For Tibetan, the earliest reference to writing is in the ancient historical annals, reporting that in the year 655 the prime minister wrote down some royal commands. The earliest extant Tibetan writing is an inscription on a pillar, dated to 767. For Burmese, the earliest extant inscription dates to around 1112. Modern Burmese writing, like the Tibetan orthography, is based on an Indic prototype. However, they make very distinct visual impressions: Tibetan writing is angular and square, while Burmese writing is circular and flowing.

Of all the writing systems in use in the world, the Chinese system reaches furthest back in time. The name 'China' and the stem 'Sino-' probably derive from the name of the Qin dynasty (221–207 BC). In China, the writing system as well as the dialects are associated with the succeeding Han dynasty, whence the names *hanzi* and *hanyu* for the written and spoken forms respectively. However, Chinese writing dates back considerably before that. An extensive set of inscriptions made on bronze, stone, and animal bones dates back well over 3,000 years. A small set of modern Chinese characters traces back to pictograms, such as those for natural objects, for example, sun, moon, mountain, rain, water; or for body parts or for animals, for example, eye, hand, heart, horse, sheep. The great majority of Chinese characters, however, are morphosyllabic compounds formed from two parts, each part typically a character in its own right: a radical and a phonetic.

The radicals all have semantic content; for instance, all 10 of the examples given above serve as radicals. Since 1615, a set of 214 radicals (also called significs) has been in common use. The characters in a Chinese dictionary are grouped according to these radicals. The phonetic is a character used in the compound for its syllabic value only. An example of such a morphosyllabic compound is the character for 'ocean,' which has the 'water' radical on the left and the character for 'sheep' on the right serving as the phonetic. Since the character for 'sheep' is pronounced /iaŋ/, the reader can infer that the character for 'ocean' is also pronounced like /iaŋ/.

Since the early twentieth century, scholars have searched for cognates to verify the Sino–Tibetan hypothesis. This typically involves comparing reconstructed Chinese forms with written Tibetan, which fortunately is very conservative phonetically. Some of the first successes were basic words such as these:

English	Chinese	Tibetan	(1)
I	*ngag*	*nga*	
two	*ni*	*gnyis*	
three	*sam*	*gsum*	
five	*ngag*	*lnga*	
eye	*myak*	*mig*	
fish	*ngyag*	*nya*	
kill	*srat*	*bsad*	

Since then, due to contributions from many scholars, the list has grown significantly, with many items buttressed with words from other languages. Coblin's handlist of 1986, for instance, contains some 500 cognate sets.

In addition to lexical evidence from the basic vocabulary, there are several structural features which characterize most Sino–Tibetan languages. For instance, Gong has compared the vowel systems of the three major languages in the family. The structural features are largely areal as well, and some can also be found in the neighboring Altaic and Austric languages. One structural feature is the extensive use of tone on single syllables, which is implemented primarily by variations in the pitch of the voice. However, a few languages in the Karen and Tibeto–Burman groups do not have tones, for example, the Purik and Ambo varieties of Tibetan. For the majority of Sino–Tibetan languages that do have tones, the number of distinct tones may vary from 2 to over 10.

In Putonghua, for example, there are four distinct tones. The words for 'mother, hemp, horse, scold' are all pronounced with the sequence /ma/, and are minimally distinguished by tone. These are illustrated in Fig. 1, where the curves represent the pitch values extracted by computer from the voice of the author of this article. Words in tone languages, therefore, are built from tones as well as from consonants and vowels.

In some cases, tones perform grammatical functions alongside the lexical ones. In Putonghua, for example, a noun can be derived from the corresponding verb by changing to the falling tone: *shu* ('number'), *shan* ('fan'), *lian* ('chain'), *mo* ('grindstone'). As another example, consider Yi, a Burman language in southwest China. It is reported that in the Liangshan variety of this language, the first person pronoun is /nga/. With a mid-level tone it means 'I,' with a high level tone it means 'my,' and with a low falling tone it means 'me.' However, inflectional morphology of this sort is relatively uncommon in Sino–Tibetan, whether the alternation is by tone or by consonant and vowel.

Another structural feature found in many Sino–Tibetan languages is the use of noun classifiers (also called measure words). Classifiers are found in English only for mass nouns, as in 'a grain of sand,' 'a sheet of paper,' etc. Though this use is a relatively late development in some Sino–

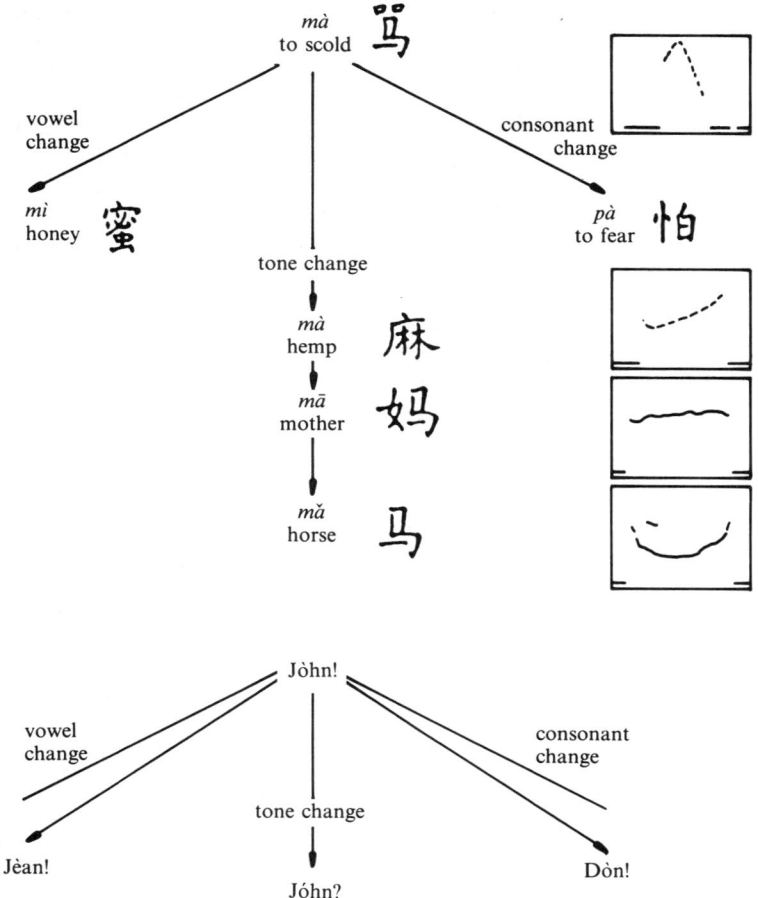

Figure 1. Illustration of the four tones of Putonghua. The curves in the four boxes are based on the fundamental frequency of the voice as extracted by computer. Taken from Wang (1991: 57).

Tibetan languages, it has spread to many neighboring languages, such as Japanese and Vietnamese. In these languages, virtually all nouns require such classifiers when they are preceded by certain modifiers, such as demonstratives or numbers. A language typically has several dozens of classifiers to go with various classes of nouns. For example, in the grammar by Chao (1968), which is a classic work in the field, one finds 72 such classifiers for Chinese nouns.

Sino–Tibetan is one of the most important language families in the world, for its large number of speakers and for its diverse civilizations and cultures. Considering the fact that the field is quite young, most proposals for external affiliations and internal subgroupings must be considered working hypotheses rather than solid conclusions. Deeper studies, in collaboration with the allied fields of anthropology and population genetics, will permit verification of these hypotheses, and will reveal much about the development of the human species in Asia.

Bibliography

Benedict P 1972 *Sino–Tibetan: A Conspectus*. Cambridge University Press, Cambridge

Chang T T 1988 *Indo-European Vocabulary in Old Chinese*, Sino-Platonic Papers 7. University of Pennsylvania Press, Philadelphia, PA

Chao Y R 1968 *A Grammar of Spoken Chinese*. University of California Press, Berkeley, CA

Coblin S 1986 A sinologist's handlist of Sino–Tibetan lexical comparisons. Monumenta Serica Monograph **18**

Gong H-C 1980 A comparative study of the Chinese, Tibetan and Burmese vowel systems. *Bulletin of the (Taiwan) Institute of History and Philology* **51**: 455–90

Li F-K 1973 Languages and dialects of China. *Journal of Chinese Linguistics* **1**: 1–13

Ma Xueliang 1991 *A General Introduction to Sino–Tibetan Languages*. Peking University Press, Beijing

Ruhlen M 1991 *A Guide to the World's Languages*, vol. 1. Stanford University Press, Stanford, CA

Sagart L 1993 Chinese and Austronesian: Evidence for a genetic relationship. *Journal of Chinese Linguistics* **21**: 1–65

Sapir E 1984 The Sapir–Kroeber correspondence. In: Golla V (ed.) *Survey of California and Other Indian Languages*, Report 6. University of California Press, Berkeley, CA

Starostin S A 1984 On the hypothesis of a genetic connection between the Sino–Tibetan languages and the Yeniseian and North Caucasian languages. In: *Lingvisticheskaja rekonstrukcija i drevnejshaja istorija vostoka*, Moscow.

Sun H 1989 Language planning in China. *Journal of Chinese Linguistics* **17**: 1–49

Wang W S-Y 1991 *Explorations in Language*. Pyramid Press, Taipei

W. S.-Y. Wang

Siouan Languages

At the time of earliest contact with Europeans (mostly seventeenth century) the Siouan-speaking peoples were found in an arc extending from the northern high plains of North America east and southward along the prairie–plains border to the mouth of the Arkansas River, with enclaves in the southeast. These languages generally bear the names of the Native American tribes that speak them.

1. Subgroups, Locations, and Speaker Statistics

The languages fall into three major subgroups named after the river valleys in which they are projected to have been spoken in prehistoric times.

Missouri River Siouan includes Crow, still spoken in southeastern Montana by perhaps 4,000 persons of all ages, and Hidatsa in North Dakota with approximately 125 speakers, all adults.

Mississippi Valley Siouan is itself split into three major groups, Dakotan, Chiwere–Winnebago, and Dhegiha. Dakotan is spoken by over 9,000 persons of all ages in several dialects including Dakota, Lakota, and Nakoda scattered across northern Nebraska, Minnesota, the Dakotas, Montana, Manitoba, Saskatchewan, and Alberta. The Chiwere dialects are Ioway, Otoe, and Missouria, spoken originally in Iowa and northern Missouri. The Missourias joined the Otoes and all three tribes were moved to Oklahoma where there are still a very few elderly speakers. Winnebago, originally spoken in Wisconsin, is still spoken by adults both there and in Nebraska. The Dhegiha dialects are Omaha–Ponca, Kansa, Osage, and Quapaw. Omaha–Ponca is still spoken by perhaps 150 adults of both tribes in their ancestral home, Nebraska, and near Ponca City, Oklahoma. Kansa, originally of northeast Kansas, no longer has fluent speakers, while Osage, originally of southwest Missouri, has a handful of elderly speakers in northeast Oklahoma. Quapaw, originally found in eastern Arkansas, now in northeast Oklahoma, lacks fluent speakers.

Ohio Valley Siouan, often called southeastern Siouan, is extinct but once comprised three languages, Biloxi in southwest Alabama, Ofo in Mississippi, and Tutelo–Saponi, in Virginia. There were a few Tutelo speakers living with the Cayuga in Ontario as recently as the early 1980s. Some linguists consider Tutelo a separate subgroup of Siouan.

The Mandan language, with only a handful of speakers in North Dakota, is considered a separate subgroup by some and a close relation of Mississippi Valley Siouan by others.

The Dakotan, Chiwere, and Dhegiha dialects or languages share a certain amount of mutual intelligibility, but there is little or no intelligibility between these subgroups or between other Siouan languages.

2. External Relationships

The Siouan family is related to the extinct Catawban languages of the Carolina Piedmont. These included Catawba and Woccon and a number of unattested languages said by explorers to have been similar. Sapir (1929; see *Sapir, Edward*) proposed more distant links to Yuchi, and to the Iroquoian and Caddoan language families, but there is no real agreement among specialists on any of these.

3. Grammatical and Phonological Features

Grammatically, the Siouan languages are of the active-stative or split intransitive type in which, roughly speaking, the subjects of stative verbs and objects of active transitive verbs are marked alike, while the subjects of active verbs (both transitive and intransitive) are marked differently. All have the basic word order subject–object–verb (SOV) along with many of the other syntactic orderings that verb-final languages tend to have, postpositions, main verb-auxiliary verb, possessor-noun (inalienable), subordinate clause-main clause. All are mildly agglutinating in their morphological structures, mark person, number, aspect, mode, and pronominal case in their verb morphologies, and permit compounding as a form of noun incorporation. Many of the languages have fairly complex phonological inventories including aspiration, glottalization, and nasalization contrasts for three or four places of articulation among consonants and length contrasts for five oral and three nasal vowels.

4. Future Scholarship

Siouan scholarship is presently flourishing. New dictionaries are being or have recently been elaborated for Crow, Hidatsa, Mandan, Dakota, Chiwere, Winnebago, Kansa, and Quapaw, along with grammars of Crow, Hidatsa, Chiwere, Omaha, and Biloxi. A comparative Siouan dictionary is nearing completion. The Dakota grammar of Boas and Deloria (1941) is, however, still arguably the best grammar of any Native American language and can be recommended to the educated layman as well as to professional linguists.

Bibliography

Boas F, Deloria E 1941 *Dakota Grammar*, vol. XXIII, Second Memoir. Memoirs of the National Academy of Sciences, Washington, DC
Chafe W L 1976 *The Caddoan, Iroquoian and Siouan Languages*, State of the Art Reports 3. Mouton, The Hague
Sapir E 1929 Central and North American Indian languages. *Encyclopædia Britannica*, 14th edn., vol. 5, pp. 128–41

R. L. Rankin

Situation Semantics

The term 'situation semantics' covers a variety of theories and conceptions of meaning and the logic of information, and, particularly, the development of a partial semantics for natural language. Within this context, situations are the basic building blocks of reality. They constitute the cornerstones of a theoretic framework that allows for an integrated classification of the world, of meaning, and of the mental states that cognitive beings can be in.

At the heart of the enterprise lies the work of the founding fathers of situation semantics: Jon Barwise and John Perry. In the early 1980s they launched a campaign for a more 'realistic,' situation-based semantics, and against traditional formal semantic theories which were rejected as too coarse-grained. A series of publications culminated in the still canonical book on the subject: *Situations and Attitudes* (Barwise and Perry 1983; *S&A* henceforth). The book introduced the basic themes which, even 10 years after, continued to engage the situation semantic entrepreneurs.

In this article some of those themes are addressed. In the first section, the key notions 'meaning,' 'realism,' 'partiality,' and 'relativity' are explained. The second section is a short introduction to situation theory, a theory of the classification of reality and meaning. Then there is a sketch of how a situation theoretic semantics of natural language can be built up, including a treatment of the notoriously problematic 'propositional' attitude reports. The last section surveys a number of extensions and developments.

1. Key Notions

1.1 Meaning and Information

Traditionally, formal semantics has focused on developing a theory of truth and truth-preserving inference. The descriptive content of an indicative sentence is explained in terms of its truth conditions, and an inference is called 'valid' if the truth conditions of the premises are at least as strong as the truth conditions of the conclusion.

Situation semantics is more ambitious. Following Dretske (1981), who takes information as the basic notion of the domain of knowledge and communication, it considers a semantics based on truth conditions much too abstract for the analysis of everyday reasoning and the exchange of information in natural language. Instead, it tries to supply a general theory of information extraction and processing which applies to linguistic information exchange as a special case. Within such a theory, truth and validity will only be derivative.

The guiding idea is that meaning is not some idealized or idealizable relation between language and the world, but a very real thing in the world itself. The world is full of information: events happening in one part of the world carry information about events in other parts of the world, and living organisms are able to pick up such information and react accordingly. For instance, the presence of smoke may carry the information that there is fire, and, likewise, the exclamation 'Fire!' may inform us about the same thing: that there is a fire. Individuals seeing the smoke, or hearing somebody shout 'Fire!' may well be disposed to run away. In both cases, the informational link can be expressed by the word 'means': smoke means fire and 'Fire!' means fire. Of course, smoke's (naturally) meaning fire and Fire!'s (conventionally) meaning fire are not the same thing, but they are 'very much the same' from the perspective of an information-processing agent. Situation theory classes the different species of informational links under a common genus. These links may be natural laws, but they are also linguistic conventions.

1.2 Realism and Attunement

Mere regularities do not give rise to meaning. One can speak of meaning when organisms become 'attuned' to the regularities in their environment, and start to anticipate events on the basis of obtaining events.

Basically then, meaning is taken to be a discriminated relation between real events or situations. However, the perceptual and cognitive capacities of living organisms

enable a more fine-grained classification of their environment. Organisms may individuate objects, relations, and locations, and classify situations according to whether they support the state of affairs that certain objects stand in certain relations at certain locations. Yet, these objects and relations are considered 'real,' since they are 'uniformities' across situations. Hence, meanings can be derivatively, but realistically, seen as relations between compounds of aspects of real events, between situations of certain types.

1.3 Partiality and Situations

The most important feature of situation semantics is its partiality. In general, information is a partial description of situations, which are themselves parts of the world. This is consistent with the general idea that meaning is situated in reality. First, information for living organisms concerns their environment, the part of reality in which an organism finds itself. Second, the regularities that enable organisms to extract information obtain between (types of) situations, not between complete worlds. Besides, these regularities usually hold only in parts of the world, for instance in the natural environment of the individual. As was pointed out, the relevant regularities for organisms are generally not full-blown natural laws; they include conventional regularities connecting utterances with the things they mean.

1.4 Relativity and Efficiency

The notion of meaning as a relation between situations is another hallmark of the theory. In the situation semantic perspective it is not sentences that convey information or entail one another, but statements, i.e., sentences uttered on a specific occasion. Linguistic meaning is a relation between utterance situations and interpretations, and the meaning of an assertively used indicative sentence ϕ is a relation between situations in which ϕ is uttered on the one hand, and the collection of described situations that constitute ϕ's interpretation on the other. This relational account of meaning sheds new light on the so-called 'efficiency of language.' This phenomenon, more familiarly known as 'context dependence,' is the connection between described situations and the (partial) contexts in which language is used. For example, it is (part of) the meaning of the personal pronoun 'I' that it refers to the speaker—not some unique speaker in the whole wide world, but the unique speaker in an utterance situation. More generally, the notion of meaning as a relation between (types of) situations can exploit all kinds of facts in the utterance situation which are relevant for establishing the interpretation of that utterance.

2. Situation Theory

The major tenet of situation theory is that reality consists of situations. Situations can be perceived and stand in causal relations to one another. They exhibit uniformities to living organisms. The basic uniformities that human beings recognize are individuals ($a, b, \ldots$), n-ary relations ($r^n, \ldots$, where $n \geq 0$), and locations ($l, l', \ldots$). These uniformities we find reflected in human languages. Individuals are thought of as the real things known to us, which figure in different situations. Relations (including properties) are also seen as invariants across real situations. Locations are taken to be regions of space–time. They may temporally precede, and spatially or temporally overlap or include one another.

From these 'primitives' and $\{0, 1\}$, an additional set of 'polarity markers' ($\{$no, yes$\}$ in *S&A*), other situation theoretic objects can be built up. First, sequences of basic information units, 'infons,' are constructed: $\langle\!\langle R^n, l, a_1, \ldots, a_n; i\rangle\!\rangle$ consisting of an n-ary relation R^n, a location l, a sequence of n individuals $a_1, \ldots, a_n$, and a polarity marker i. Such sequences reflect the fact that the individuals $a_1, \ldots, a_n$, do (in case $i = 1$) or do not (in case $i = 0$) stand in relation R^n at location l in some situation. (In *S&A* the location argument of an infon is fronted: $\langle l, \langle R^n, a_1, \ldots, a_n; i\rangle\rangle$. In more recent work, it has become optional.) For instance, the infon $\langle\!\langle LOVES, here\&now, Jon, John; 1\rangle\!\rangle$ reflects the fact Jon loves John here and now, and $\langle\!\langle LOVES, here\&now, Jon, John; 0\rangle\!\rangle$ reflects the fact that Jon does not love John here and now. Notice that facts are talked about here without making reference to situations. The connection between facts and the reality of situations comes about by what is called the 'supports'-relation. If an infon i is a fact in a real situation s, then s is said to support i, which is written as: $s \models i$. So if $s \models \langle\!\langle LOVES, here\&now, Jon, John; 0\rangle\!\rangle$, then in s Jon does not love John at the location here and now. Furthermore, $s \models \langle\!\langle LOVES, here\&now, Jon, John; 0\rangle\!\rangle$ itself is called a proposition which is either true or false.

Infons are the basic information units of situation theory. More complex information is gathered in sets of infons, called 'abstract situations.' So real situations, parts of the world which are recognized as such by agentive organisms, are distinguished from abstract situations (or just 'situations'), mathematical compounds of primitives abstracted from real situations. Notice that real situations are even more primitive than the theoretical primitives from which abstract situations are built up. (In *S&A*, abstract situations are called 'courses of events.' Certain courses of events are called 'states of affairs,' situations whose infons all have the same location argument.) Abstract situations s may also be said to support an infon i, where, of course, $s \models i$ if and only if $i \in s$. Furthermore, real and abstract situations can be related in the following way. An abstract situation s corresponds to a real situation $\boldsymbol{s}$ iff for all infons $i: i \in s \Leftrightarrow \boldsymbol{s} \models i$. If an abstract situation corresponds to some real situation then it is said to be 'actual.' A weaker notion is in use as well. An abstract situation s classifies a real situation $\boldsymbol{s}$ iff for all infons i: if $i \in s$ then $\boldsymbol{s} \models i$. In case an abstract situation classifies some real situation, then it is called 'factual.' In a sense, then, an actual situation is some kind of complete factual situation: if some situation s is factual, then there is some actual situation s' such that $s \subseteq s'$.

A situation can leave the issue whether certain individuals stand in a particular relation undecided. Neither $\langle\!\langle WALK, here\&now, Jon; 1\rangle\!\rangle$ nor $\langle\!\langle WALK, here\&now, Jon; 0\rangle\!\rangle$ needs to be a member of s, and this possibility captures the credited partiality of real situations. But it is also possible that both an infon and its negation are an element of a situation. This possibility does not seem to be grounded in reality. (However, in the context of attitude reports (cf. below) this possibility might be useful again.) An important notion, therefore, is that of a coherent situation: a situation s is coherent if, for no $R^n, l, a_1, \ldots, a_n$, both

$\langle\!\langle R^n, l, a_1, \ldots, a_n; 1\rangle\!\rangle$ and $\langle\!\langle R^n, l, a_1, \ldots, a_n; 0\rangle\!\rangle$ are in s. It will be assumed that all actual situations are coherent.

It was said above that meaning in situation semantics is, basically, a relation between situations, a relation which itself is considered 'real.' However, in order to account for this relation, more complex uniformities need to be introduced—so-called 'situation types.' For that purpose 'basic indeterminates' (also called 'parameters') are introduced. These are abstract stand-ins for real primitives: $\boldsymbol{a}, \boldsymbol{b}, \ldots$ for individuals; $\boldsymbol{r}, \boldsymbol{r}', \ldots$ for relations; and $\boldsymbol{l}, \boldsymbol{l}', \ldots$ for locations. An indeterminate (or 'parametrized') infon is a sequence $\langle\!\langle R^n, l, a_1, \ldots, a_n; i\rangle\!\rangle$ where $R^n, l, a_1, \ldots, a_n$ are indeterminates or real primitives, and i is a polarity marker. A 'situation-type' (or 'parametrized situation') is a set of indeterminate infons, i.e., an abstract situation in which zero or more indeterminates are substituted for real primitives. An example: situation-type $S = \{\langle\!\langle LOVES, \boldsymbol{l}, \boldsymbol{a}, \boldsymbol{b}; 1\rangle\!\rangle\}$ contains one indeterminate infon $\langle\!\langle LOVES, \boldsymbol{l}, \boldsymbol{a}, \boldsymbol{b}; 1\rangle\!\rangle$, with three indeterminates: $\boldsymbol{l}, \boldsymbol{a}$, and $\boldsymbol{b}$. Note that, since every infon is also an indeterminate infon (one with zero indeterminates), every situation is a situation type.

Situation types are conceived of as uniformities in their own right. They may be used to classify situations and can be linked up with situations using anchors. 'Anchors' are partial functions from individual, relation, and location indeterminates to individuals, relations, and locations, respectively. An anchor f is a total anchor for situation-type S if f is defined on all indeterminates in S. Write $S[f]$ for the situation-type S' which results from simultaneously substituting $f(x)$ for x in S for all indeterminates x in the domain of f. Then can be defined: s is of type S (also written as $s: S$) if there is a total anchor f for S such that $S[f] \subseteq s$. For instance, $f = \{\langle \boldsymbol{l}, here\&now\rangle, \langle \boldsymbol{a}, Jon\rangle, \langle \boldsymbol{b}, John\rangle\}$ is a total anchor for situation-type $S = \{\langle\!\langle LOVES, \boldsymbol{l}, \boldsymbol{a}, \boldsymbol{b}; 1\rangle\!\rangle\}$, and $S[f] = \{\langle\!\langle LOVES, here\&now, Jon, John; 1\rangle\!\rangle\} = s$. Since $S[f] = s$, s is of type S. However, observe that also $s' = \{\langle\!\langle LOVES, here\&now, Jon, John; 1\rangle\!\rangle, \langle\!\langle SMOKE, there\&then; 0\rangle\!\rangle\}$ is of type S.

The notion 'constraint' models the idea that meanings reside in the world, as regularities which allow attuned agents to derive information about situations from situations. It is a fact that situations of a certain kind entail the presence of situations of another kind. In situation theory this fact is captured by infons of the form $\langle\!\langle INVOLVES, S, S'; 1\rangle\!\rangle$. S and S' are situation-types and *INVOLVES* is a primitive binary relation between situation-types. Infons of this form are called (unconditional) constraints. However, constraints by themselves do not constrain reality. The factuality of an infon $\langle\!\langle INVOLVES, S, S'; 1\rangle\!\rangle$ as such is no guarantee that situations of type S' always come along with situations of type S. It is only in structures of situations that constraints correspond to regularities between situations. Structures of situations are models of reality. In keeping with the slogan 'Reality consists of situations—individuals having properties and standing in relations at various spatiotemporal locations' (*S&A*: 7), a 'structure of situations' $\boldsymbol{M}$ is a collection of abstract situations, i.e., a collection of sets of infons. $\boldsymbol{M}$ consists of a collection, M, of factual situations, with a nonempty subcollection, M_0, of actual situations. It observes four conditions:

(a) every s in M is coherent;

(b) if $s \in M_0$ and $s' \subseteq s$, then $s' \in M$;

(c) if X is a sub*set* (with stress on *set*) of M, then there is an $s \in M_0$ such that $\bigcup X \subseteq s$ ($\bigcup X$ is the set of infons i for which there is an $s \in X$ such that $i \in s$);

(d) if C is a constraint in M, then M respects C.

Condition (a) states that reality is consistent. Condition (b) models the fact that parts of real (actual) situations are also (factual) situations. Condition (b) requires that the infons involved in a 'set' of factual situations be also members of an actual situation. Recall that M_0 was defined as a 'collection' of abstract situations, so it need not be a set—it could be a proper class: too large to be countenanced as a set. But if M_0 actually were a set, then (c) would entail the existence of a situation $s \in M_0$ such that $\bigcup M_0 \subseteq s$, so $\forall s' \in M_0: s' \subseteq s$. Such a situation, if present, might be called a world in M.

Condition (d) relates constraints to the regularities in reality that underlie the possibility of extracting information about situations from other situations. Intuitively, if constraints are conceived of as laws, what this clause says is that reality behaves in conformity with the laws it contains. The relevant notion of a structure of situations M respecting such a constraint is therefore defined as follows: M respects $\langle\!\langle INVOLVES, S, S'; 1 \rangle\!\rangle$ iff $\forall s \in M_0; \exists s' \in M: \forall f:$ if f is an anchor for exactly the indeterminates of S, and $S[f] \subseteq s$, then $\exists g: (S'[f])[g] \subseteq s'$. This says that for every situation of type S there is a situation s' of type S' such that all ways of anchoring S in s are ways of (partially) anchoring S' in s'.

Notice that S and S' are arbitrary situation-types, so S' can contain indeterminates absent from S. In Barwise and Perry (1983: 146), this is considered 'a mistake.' Accordingly, Barwise (1989: 114) simply stipulates that every parameter in S' will also be a parameter in S. This enables us to simplify the definition considerably: M respects $\langle\!\langle INVOLVES, S, S'; 1 \rangle\!\rangle$ iff $\forall s \in M_0: \exists s' \in M: \forall f:$ if $S[f] \subseteq s$, then $S'[f] \subseteq s'$. For example, the constraint $\langle\!\langle INVOLVES, \{\langle\!\langle SMOKE, l, 1 \rangle\!\rangle\}, \{\langle\!\langle FIRE, l, 1 \rangle\!\rangle\}; 1 \rangle\!\rangle$ is respected by M iff $\forall s \in M_0: \exists s' \in M: \forall f:$ if $\{\langle\!\langle SMOKE, l, 1 \rangle\!\rangle\}[f] \subseteq s$, then $\{\langle\!\langle FIRE, l, 1 \rangle\!\rangle\}[f] \subseteq s'$. This amounts to $\forall s \in M_0: \exists s' \in M: \forall l:$ if $\{\langle\!\langle SMOKE, l; 1 \rangle\!\rangle\} \subseteq s$, then $\{\langle\!\langle FIRE, l; 1 \rangle\!\rangle\} \subseteq s'$. So, for every situation s in M_0 with smoke at a number of locations, there is a situation s' in M with fire at those locations.

Having defined the notion 'M respects C,' what the interpretation of situations is given a certain constraint can be defined. The 'interpretation' of a situation s of type S with respect to a constraint C, $[s]_C$, where $C = \langle\!\langle INVOLVES, S, S'; 1 \rangle\!\rangle$, is the collection of situations s' such that $\forall f:$ if f anchors exactly the indeterminates of S and $S[f] \subseteq s$, then s' is of type $S'[f]$.

So, for $C = \{\langle\!\langle INVOLVES, \{\langle\!\langle SMOKE, l, 1 \rangle\!\rangle\}, \{\langle\!\langle FIRE, l, 1 \rangle\!\rangle\}; 1 \rangle\!\rangle$, and $s = \{\langle\!\langle SMOKE, here\&now; 1 \rangle\!\rangle\}$, $[s]_C$ is the collection of all situations s' such that $\{\langle\!\langle FIRE, here\&now; 1 \rangle\!\rangle\} \in s'$. In other words, the interpretation with respect to C of a situation with smoke here and now consists of involved situations with fire here and now.

3. Situation Semantics

Assuming that linguistic meanings of expressions are conventional constraints on utterances and that the primary function of language is to convey information, situation semantics describes the meaning of an assertively used indicative sentence ϕ as a relation $u[\phi]s$ between situations u in which ϕ is uttered and situations s described by such utterances. This is called 'the relational theory of meaning.' In other semantic approaches, the constraints ϕ puts on u have been put away in so-called 'context sequences.' Within situation semantics, the context of a sentence is the same type of thing as the thing the sentence is about, which allows an account of the 'efficiency of language' alluded to above.

An utterance situation u comprises the utterance of an expression ϕ (an aspect of u which is made explicit in the notation '$u[\phi]s$' we use) by one speaker to one addressee at one location. Moreover, u determines a number of 'speaker connections,' which specify the referents the speaker intends to denote by uttering certain subexpressions of ϕ. For instance, they specify the intended referents of proper names and the (temporal) locations that serve as intended referents of tenses of verbs.

The 'meanings' of lexical and compound expressions exploit these features of u. For example, a sentence like 'I am stroking Jackie' is assigned the meaning $u[I$ *am stroking Jackie*$]s$ iff $\langle\!\langle STROKE, l, a, b; 1 \rangle\!\rangle \in s$, where $l = u(am)$, l temporally overlaps with the location of u, a is the speaker in u, and $b = u(Jackie)$. The interpretation of coordinated sentences is straightforward: $u[\phi$ *and* $\psi]s$ iff $u[\phi]s$ and $u[\psi]s$; $u[\phi$ *or* $\psi]s$ iff $u[\phi]s$ or $u[\psi]s$.

A 'statement' consists of the utterance of an indicative sentence ϕ in an utterance situation: $u: \phi$. Whereas sentences have meanings, a statement $u: \phi$ is assigned an 'interpretation' $[u: \phi] = \{s \mid u[\phi]s\}$. The interpretation of the statement $u:$ *I am stroking Jackie* is the collection of situations s such that $\langle\!\langle STROKE, l, a, b; 1 \rangle\!\rangle \in s$, where l, a, b are as above. This collection contains possible situations, but also impossible (incoherent) ones. Notice that for simple positive sentences ϕ like 'I am stroking Jackie,' $[u: \phi]$ is 'persistent': if $s \in [u: \phi]$ and $s \subseteq s'$, then $s' \in [u: \phi]$. Truth is a property of statements, not of sentences. A statement $u: \phi$ is 'true' in M iff there is an s such that $s \in M_0$ and $s \in [u: \phi]$.

In keeping with the underlying philosophy, there are two notions of logical consequence for statements. If Φ and Ψ are statements, then Ψ is a 'strong consequence' of Φ iff $[\Phi]$ is a subcollection of $[\Psi]$, and Ψ is a 'weak consequence' of Φ iff Ψ is true in every M where Φ is true. The notion of strong consequence is relevant for the logic of information containment: if someone knows that Φ, and Ψ is a strong consequence of Φ, then (s)he knows that Ψ. The notion of weak consequence is more traditional. If Φ is true, and Ψ is a weak consequence of Φ, then Ψ must be true as well. Note, however, that the weak consequences of a statement do not completely coincide with the consequences in classical logics.

The relational theory of meaning, in which u and s are the same type of thing, easily explains the phenomenon of 'inverse information.' An utterance can convey information about a described situation, but also about the utterance situation. Suppose someone next door says 'I am Jon.' This utterance describes situations in which the speaker of the utterance is called Jon. However, for someone who knows Jon, the utterance may convey information about the utterance situation: he is speaking there! Note that this information is not part of the linguistic interpretation of the utterance.

From the outset, situation semantics has been concerned with attitude reports, utterances of sentences containing verbs like 'see (that),' 'know that,' 'believe that,' which are used to report perception and cognition. The seminal paper 'Scenes and Other Situations' (1981, reprinted in Barwise 1989) studies the semantics of sentences reporting visual perceptions. Syntactically, one can distinguish at least two kinds of those reports. In (1), the verb 'see' has an untensed sentence (or 'naked infinitive') as its complement; in (2), it selects a *that*-complementizer followed by a tensed sentence:

> John saw Jackie bite Molly   (1)

> John saw that Jackie bit Molly   (2)

Semantically, 'epistemically neutral' 'see' can be contrasted with 'epistemically positive' 'see that': 'To prove the first (and weaker) claim, one has to show that [John] had his eyes open and functioning, and that an event of a certain sort was taking place before him. To prove the stronger claim, one needs to prove something about what he recognized and what thoughts were going through his mind' (S&A: 179). *See-* reports like (1) are considered paradigmatic for a semantics of the attitudes. One reason for this is that they report, in a sense, the most realistic attitude; what is seen is real. Another reason is that they have the least controversial semantic properties, like:

(a) *Veridicality*: if a sees ϕ, then ϕ^*, where ϕ^* is the tensed version of ϕ. *Jackie sees Molly scratch. So, Molly scratches.* (ϕ must be a sentence giving rise to a persistent interpretation. It does not follow that if Alice is seeing no one walk on the road, then no one is walking on the road.);

(b) *Conjunction Distribution*: if a sees ϕ and ψ, then a sees ϕ and a sees ψ;

(c) *Disjunction Distribution*: if a sees ϕ or ψ, then a sees ϕ or a sees ψ.

Properties like these should shed light on the proper treatment of *see*-reports. Standard possible world semantics assumes that the semantic value of embedded clauses is the set of possible worlds in which they are true. This leads to the problem that if a sees ϕ and ϕ is logically equivalent to ψ, then a sees ψ. Hence, *John saw Jackie bite Molly* entails *John saw Jackie bite Molly and Tully scratch or not scratch*, since *Jackie bite Molly* and *Jackie bite Molly and Tully scratch or not scratch* denote the same set of possible worlds.

In the special case of verbs like 'see,' this assumption has even worse implications. Using veridicality, conjunction distribution, and disjunction distribution, one can derive 'omnipercipience' ('you've seen one, you've seen them all'): if for some ϕ, a sees ϕ, then for all true ψ, it must hold that a sees ψ.

Situation semantics solves those problems by assigning clauses a more fine-grained semantic value: situations. *See* denotes a primitive relation, SEE, between a location, an individual (the agent), and a situation. The infon $\langle\!\langle SEE, l, a, e; 1\rangle\!\rangle$ corresponds to the fact that a sees e at l, and *see*-reports are interpreted in the following way: $u[$*John is seeing Jackie bite Molly*$]s$ iff $\langle\!\langle SEE, l, a, s'; 1\rangle\!\rangle \in s$ and $\langle\!\langle BITE, l, b, c; 1\rangle\!\rangle \in s'$, where $l=u(is)$, l temporally overlaps with the location of u, $a=u(John)$, $b=u(Jackie)$, and $c=u(Molly)$.

It is easy to see that this analysis validates conjunction and disjunction distribution. However, veridicality is not yet guaranteed. If $\langle\!\langle SEE, l, a, s'; 1\rangle\!\rangle \in s$, and s is actual, nothing follows about s' being actual or factual; s' is just a possible (or even impossible) situation doing duty as a constituent of a fact. To get veridicality, a constraint is needed: $\langle\!\langle INVOLVES, S, S'; 1\rangle\!\rangle$, with $S=\{\langle\!\langle SEE, \boldsymbol{l}, \boldsymbol{a}, \boldsymbol{s}; 1\rangle\!\rangle\}$ and $S'=\boldsymbol{s}$ (where $\boldsymbol{s}$ is a situation indeterminate).

The effect of this constraint is that for every actual s', there is a factual s'' such that for all locations l, individuals a, and situations s such that $\{\langle\!\langle SEE, l, a, s; 1\rangle\!\rangle\} \subseteq s'$, it holds that $s \subseteq s''$. Every factual situation is a subset of an actual situation. So, if the interpretation of the embedded sentence is persistent, then the fact that it contains a factual situation entails that it also contains an actual situation. Hence, the sentence must be true.

'Less realistic' attitude reports like 'Jon believes that Jackie bites Molly' obey different semantic principles. Veridicality does not apply to *believe that*-reports, since one can believe things that are not true. Neither does disjunction distribution: it is possible that 'Jon believes that Jackie or Molly has fleas' is true, whereas both 'Jon believes that Jackie has fleas' and 'John believes that Molly has fleas' are false. On the other hand, conjunction distribution is valid for *believe that*.

Situation semantics not only wants to account for these logical facts, but also for the way in which attitude reports are used in explanations of what people think and do. There is, for example, a big difference between John believing that Jon is ill and Jon believing that Jon (i.e., he himself) is ill. Yet on an account which construes believing as a relation between individuals and situations, John and Jon stand in exactly the same relation to the same situations if they both believe that Jon is ill, though Jon is the one to get up and go see the doctor. There is some intuitive sense in which John and Jon have different beliefs (i.e., are in different mental states) if they both believe that Jon is ill. Accordingly, situation semantics analyses *believe that*-reports in terms of represented belief.

The basic idea is to use situation-types to classify both what is believed and how it is believed. This does justice to the commonsense intuition that there are different ways of believing the same thing. Individuals a at locations l are in 'cognitive states': frames of mind which are related to the world by a setting. A frame of mind is given by a situation-type S, and a setting consists of an anchor f (assume that f is a total anchor for S). A belief, therefore, is a pair $\langle S, f\rangle$, written as $\langle\!\langle BR, l, a, S, f; 1\rangle\!\rangle$ (BR abbreviates 'represented belief').

Now, John's believing at l in s that Jon is ill at l' can be rendered as: $\langle\!\langle BR, l, John, S, f; 1\rangle\!\rangle \in s$, where $S=\{\langle\!\langle ILL, \boldsymbol{l}, \boldsymbol{a}; 1\rangle\!\rangle\}$, $f(\boldsymbol{l})=l'$, and $f(\boldsymbol{l})=Jon$. The fact that Jon is in a different mental state from John when he believes that Jon is ill is expressed by using the *role i* in his frame of mind, an indeterminate associated with the agent of a situation. (Roles will be discussed below.)

The semantics of *believe that*-reports is phrased in terms of situation-types and anchors. It is simply required that the agent has some belief $\langle S, f\rangle$ such that the anchoring of S by f classifies the interpretation of the embedded sentence. On this analysis, if a believes that ϕ, and the statement that ψ is a strong consequence of the statement that ϕ, then a

believes that ψ. So, conjunction distribution is valid (whereas disjunction distribution and veridicality fail).

4. Extensions and Developments

Barwise and Etchemendy's *The Liar* (1987) is a thorough study of the liar paradox and related cases of circularity or self-reference. Assertions like 'I am now lying, 'What I am now saying is false,' This proposition is not true' are paradoxical, since if they were true, then what they claim would have to be the case, and so they would be not true. Conversely, if they are not true, then what they claim to be the case is in fact the case, so they must be true. Whereas the liar paradox has been known since antiquity, no satisfactory analysis of it has yet been given. In formal semantic practice, one usually follows Tarski's (1956) approach of avoiding the paradox by denying languages their own truth predicate. Saul Kripke, however, has shown that circular reference of the sort involved in the liar is not only a much more common phenomenon than had been supposed, but also that whether a given utterance is paradoxical may well depend on nonlinguistic, empirical facts. Ergo: 'there can be no syntactic or semantic "sieve" that will winnow out the "bad" cases while preserving the "good" ones' (Kripke 1975). Barwise and Etchemendy's analysis of languages that admit circular reference and contain their own truth predicate supplements situation theory with the theory of non-wellfounded sets developed by Peter Aczel.

Aczel (1988: ii) introduces nonwell-founded ('extraordinary') sets with a quotation from Mirimanoff (1917): 'Let E be a set, E' one of its elements, E'' any element of E', and so on. Call a *descent* the sequence of steps from E to E', E' to E'', etc. . . . I say that a set is *ordinary* when it only gives rise to finite descents; I say that it is *extraordinary* when among its descents there are some which are infinite.' The standard system of axiomatic set theory, ZFC, includes the foundation axiom FA. This axiom expresses that all sets are ordinary (i.e., wellfounded), thus giving rise to the familiar 'cumulative hierarchy of sets.' Instead, Aczel proposes an antifoundation axiom (AFA) which entails the existence of non-wellfounded sets such as Ω: the unique set such that $\Omega = \{\Omega\}$. Using a version of Aczel's set theory with atoms, Barwise and Etchemendy arrive at a notion of circular situations and circular propositions. On their view, truth is not a property of sentences, but of statements or propositions. Sentences may well fail to express a proposition, and so fail to have a truth value. This does not hold for propositions, the kind of thing asserted by a successful statement: if a proposition is not true, then it is false. *The Liar* discusses two accounts of the relation between sentences and the propositions they express, the Russellian and the Austinian view.

According to the Russellian view, sentences are used to express propositions, claims about the world, and these claims are true just in case the world is as it is claimed to be. Relevant is that the truth of the proposition is arbitrated by the world as a whole. On the Russellian analysis, the liar sentence 'This proposition is not true' expresses the unique (non-wellfounded) proposition f satisfying $f = [FALSE\ f]$.

According to the truth scheme introduced by Austin (1961), an assertively used declarative sentence S contributes two things: the descriptive conventions of language yield a certain type of situation S that is expressed by ϕ, whereas the demonstrative conventions refer to an actual, 'historic' situation s. So, an Austinian proposition can be written as a claim $s:S$ (cf. Sect. 2 above). The rule of truth is simply that $s:S$ is true if s is of type S. This holds in general, independently of the presence of indexical expressions in ϕ. On the Austinian analysis, there are many different propositions that can be expressed using the liar sentence.

Comparing the two accounts, Barwise and Etchemendy show that while the Russellian view is crucially flawed in limiting cases, the Austinian view can be seen as a refinement which avoids the paradox while providing a straightforward understanding of the semantic intuitions that give rise to it.

On the basis of various examples involving inherently circular situations (aspects of perceptual knowledge, self-awareness, Gricean intentions of speakers and hearers, shared information), Barwise (1989: ch. 8) argues that reality, unlike the cumulative hierarchy of sets, is not wellfounded. Consistent with the assumption that situations are parts of reality (families of facts) that can be comprehended as completed totalities, i.e., as sets, this article has been modeling situations as sets of infons, and infons as sequences $\langle\!\langle R^n, l, a_1, \ldots, a_n; i \rangle\!\rangle$ consisting of an n-ary relation R^n, a location l, a sequence of n arguments $a_1, \ldots, a_n$ (the constituents of the infon, which can be primitives, situations, or situation-types), and a polarity marker i. Now, if this sort of set theoretical model is to be used, then non-wellfounded sets are essential when circular situations are to be represented. Thus it should be possible that a situation s contains infon $\langle\!\langle R^n, a_1, \ldots, a_n; i \rangle\!\rangle$ as a member, while s itself also is (a constituent of a member of . . .) a member of a_1 or . . . or a_n.

In an interesting case study of non-wellfoundedness, Barwise (1989: ch. 9) addresses the phenomenon of common knowledge, which is crucial for an understanding of communication. Common knowledge arises for instance when a card player (Jon, say), receives a card (e.g., the queen of clubs) that everyone (viz., Jon and John) can see. The orthodox 'iterate' account analyzes this in terms of an infinite hierarchy of iterated attitudes: (0) Jon has the queen of clubs; (1) Jo(h)n knows Jon has the queen of clubs: (2) Jo(h)n knows that Jo(h)n knows that Jon has the queen of clubs; and so on. Barwise contrasts this account with non-wellfounded approaches, and shows that it is inadequate. Moreover, it turns out that common knowledge is better analyzed in terms of shared information.

In spite of its pervasively indexical, 'efficient,' character (witness the speaker connections), the situation semantics outlined in Sect. 3 is essentially Russellian. More recent contributions, however, have incorporated the inherently indexical Austinian approach sketched in the present section. Gawron and Peters (1990), a book on quantification and anaphora, is a case in point.

Situation semantic accounts of anaphora and quantification make frequent use of so-called 'restricted parameters' or 'roles' (see *S&A*: 80–90; Gawron and Peters 1990; Devlin, et al. and Westerståhl in Cooper, et al. 1990). A restricted parameter is an indeterminate subscripted by a situation-type that contains the indeterminate. The idea is that the situation-type restricts the domain of things onto which the indeterminate can be anchored. If r is a restricted indeterminate x_S, then an anchor f for r in situation s must be such that f anchors all parameters in S (among which may be restricted ones), $S[f] \subseteq s$, and $f(r) = f(x)$. Suppose $S = \langle\!\langle MAN, x, 1 \rangle\!\rangle$; then x_S can only be anchored to individuals a in s if a is a man in s. It is clear that restricted parameters introduce a form of restricted existential quantification. For instance, the proposition $s \vDash \{\langle\!\langle WALKS, x_S; 1 \rangle\!\rangle\}$, where S is as above, expresses that in s an individual a walks who is a man. Notice that s itself is not required to contain the information that a is a man, provided that some other situation s' does (Devlin, in Cooper, et al. 1990: 84). Instead of situation-types it is also possible to have propositions as restrictions on parameters (Gawron and Peters 1990). Such a proposition explicitly addresses a resource situation where the restriction is required to be satisfied. For example, if r is the parameter $x_{s \vDash S}$, where S is as above, then $s \vDash \langle\!\langle WALKS, r, 1 \rangle\!\rangle$ expresses that someone who is a man in s walks in s. (Resource situations were already introduced in *S&A*. These situations are exploited by speakers and they figure as a kind of domains for reference and quantification.)

Gawron and Peters (1990; and in Cooper, et al. 1990) give a more or less uniform treatment of natural language noun phrases using restricted parameters. Proper names, pronouns, definite, and indefinite descriptions contribute restricted parameters to the interpretations of sentences. A use of the proper name 'John' introduces a parameter $x_{(r \vDash \langle\!\langle NAMED, x, 'John' \rangle\!\rangle)}$ that restricts x to be anchored to an individual named 'John' in the resource situation. Definite descriptions like 'the dog' introduce a parameter that is restricted to be anchored to the unique dog in a resource situation, if there is one. The content of the pronoun 'she' is captured with a parameter that is restricted to be anchored to females in a resource situation. Here the utterance situation (Gawron and Peters use the term 'circumstances') contains the information whether the pronoun is used deictically or anaphorically, and what the resource situation is. The first person pronoun I yields a parameter restricted to be anchored to its utterer. Anaphoric pronouns are simply reused parameters, with additional restrictions due to their gender.

An interesting possibility is that an anaphoric pronoun may pick up a parameter associated with either the argument slot of a verb or the noun phrase that fills the argument slot. This enables Gawron and Peters to treat so-called 'sloppy' readings of sentences like 'Only John expected that he would lose.' On the sloppy reading John is the only one that expected 'himself' to lose. Here the pronoun is linked up with the subject–argument–role of the *EXPECT*-relation. On the strict reading, where the pronoun is coparametric with the subject 'John' itself, nobody expected that John would lose, except John.

Gawron and Peters (1990) also treat quantified noun phrases. A quantified phrase like 'Every N' is analyzed in terms of a determiner relation with a domain-type constructed from the common noun N. A determiner is a relation between properties and this relation is said to hold of the domain-type and the property expressed by the surrounding utterance. Circumstances determine which part of the utterance is in the scope of the quantifier, and hence

resolve possible scope ambiguities. Essential in this treatment is the restriction that a determiner like *EVERY* holds of two properties P_1 and P_2 if all objects that have property P_1 also have property P_2. Again, the first property (the domain-type) is constructed relative to a resource situation for the utterance.

In their contribution to Cooper, et al. (1990), Gawron and Peters treat quantified noun phrases more on a par with nonquantified noun phrases. Quantified noun phrases initially contribute a parameter r to the interpretation of an utterance, with a restriction imposed by their common noun. The determiner is interpreted as a property of properties P which relates the appropriate anchors of r (the anchors that satisfy the restriction on x) to the objects having P. A generalization of this mechanism allows a treatment of the so-called 'donkey-anaphor' *it* in a sentence like 'Every farmer who owns a donkey beats it.' (For alternative treatments of quantification within situation semantics see Barwise and Perry in Cooper 1985: 144–47; Cooper 1987; Devlin in Cooper, et al. 1990. Fenstad, et al. (1987) treat donkey-anaphora as well; see also *Quantifiers*.)

Bibliography

Aczel P 1988 *Non-Well-Founded Sets*. CSLI Publications, Stanford, CA

Austin J L 1961 Truth. In: Urmson J O, Warnock G J (eds.) *Philosophical Papers*. Oxford University Press, Oxford

Barwise J 1989 *The Situation in Logic*. CSLI Publications, Stanford, CA

Barwise J, Etchemendy J 1987 *The Liar: An Essay on Truth and Circularity*. Oxford University Press, New York

Barwise J, Perry J 1983 *Situations and Attitudes*. Bradford Books, MIT Press, Cambridge, MA

Cooper R (ed.) 1985 Situations and attitudes. aPh 8: 1

Cooper R 1987 Preliminaries to the treatment of generalized quantifiers in situation semantics. In: Gärdenfors P (ed.) *Generalized Quantifiers: Linguistic and Logical Approaches*. Reidel, Dordrecht

Cooper R, Mukai K, Perry J (eds.) 1990 *Situation Theory and its Applications*, vol. 1. CSLI Publications, Stanford, CA

Dretske F I 1981 *Knowledge and the Flow of Information*. Basil Blackwell, Oxford

Fenstad J E, Halvorsen P K, Langholm T, Van Benthem J (eds.) 1987 *Situations, Language and Logic*. Reidel, Dordrecht

Gawron J M Types, contents and semantic objects. *LaPh* 9: 427–76

Gawron J M, Peters S 1990 *Anaphora and Quantification in Situation Semantics*. CSLI Publications, Stanford, CA

Kripke S 1975 Outline of a theory of truth. *The Journal of Philosophy* 72: 690–716

Langholm T 1988 *Partiality, Truth and Persistence*. CSLI Publications, Stanford, CA

Pratt I 1987 Constraints, meaning and information. *LaPh* 10: 299–324

Stalnaker R C 1986 Possible worlds and situations. *Journal of Philosophical Logic* 15: 109–23

Tarski A 1956 The concept of truth in formalized languages. In: *Logic, Semantics, Metamathematics*. Clarendon Press, Oxford.

P. J. E. Dekker
H. L. W. Hendriks

Slang: Sociology

Slang is more a sociological than a purely linguistic idea and is best understood in the theory of modern society and culture. Dictionaries usually define slang with at least two senses. First, slang is the special, restricted speech of subgroups or subcultures in society and, second, it is a highly informal, unconventional vocabulary of more general use. This article is concerned with both senses, but especially with why and how restricted subgroup speech becomes general slang. Slang in use is a marker of social differences and, as such, is a vocabulary that has become used and understood with social purpose beyond the boundaries of the subgroup that originated the lexical items or their special meanings.

1. Origins

Slang first emerged in abundance where diverse peoples met at the cultural crossroads of the ancient market city; it flourished in the more diverse and occupationally interdependent medieval city. For the same but more complex reasons in the nineteenth century, slang became part of the life of modern cities, or more validly today, of modern society in general. By its very nature slang emerges from the organization of diverse society and in small ways serves both to maintain and to change social structures, or the power relationships among social groups. Slang is a necessary and inevitable cultural product of a plural, complex, dynamic, and highly interdependent modern society.

The word 'slang,' of uncertain origin, has been dated to about 1750 and was soon thereafter defined at least once as 'street language.' Slang originally denoted cant, or the restricted speech of the low, often criminal classes of society. However, the idea of slang gradually evolved to denote other subcultural speech, both high and low, as well as more general but unconventional vocabulary. By 1890 slang had taken on its present sense of a level of language below standard and of a body of lexemes derived from yet lower and more restricted levels of speech. The more general idea of popular speech, which includes slang, is today coming into a newer and wider use by language scholars. Popular speech encompasses older forms of folk speech, which are associated with rural society and with the oral tradition, and newer forms of folk speech, often slang, which are associated with cities and modern society and with the mass media. Popular speech includes both spontaneous folk expressions and popular locutions prompted by the mass media. Sociologically speaking, slang is the urban part of popular speech and has historically found many of its incentives and referents in the socially diverse urban setting.

2. The Late Twentieth-century Idea of Slang

Slang is not a class of lexemes that can be described and then circumscribed and does not differ from standard or other levels of speech in any purely linguistic characteristic. Every effort to define slang as a kind of vocabulary has failed to cast a net wide and fine enough to catch all that looks, feels, sounds, and works like slang. The indefinite class of words labeled slang in general dictionaries or included in any dictionary of slang will testify to this problem. Nonetheless, dictionaries usually characterize slang by describing its informality, unconventionality, ephemerality, ellipsis, bizarre metaphors, playfulness, and the like. People of a Whitmanesque bent have said that slang is the poetry of everyday life and the free and natural speech of the common people. While slang expression is acute, the metaphors occasionally brilliant, and it sometimes alliterates and rhymes, slang is more a level or register of speech than a poetic form of the folk.

For practical lexicographers, slang is a 'place,' a way station and a proving ground for cheeky new words and phrases. The label of 'slang' is a necessary one for lexicographers who are obliged to indicate levels of usage to guide dictionary users. The most neutral and unassailable definition of slang is simply that of a level of usage (Flexner 1974). Slang is 'below' standard and 'correct' informal usages and socially is less acceptable in formal discourse. On the other hand, slang is more widely used or at least more widely understood than restricted subgroup speech, such as regional and social dialects, argot, cant, or jargon. In this sense, slang is 'above' subcultural speech, where so much slang began its upward and outward-bound career into general usage.

Viewed as a level of usage, slang is vocabulary in limbo. Slang is, so to speak, applicant language that is awaiting acceptance or rejection by standard usage, or endlessly awaiting neither—and perhaps quiet withdrawal. Slang has at least four resolutions (Maurer and High 1980). If an item of slang proves durable and virtuous in the usage of the general public and, to a lesser extent, in the eyes of arbiters of elite usage, it may enter standard usage, as much slang has and does all the time (e.g., *movies*). Or it may remain slang for years, decades (e.g., *cool* 'very good'), or even centuries (e.g., *to snitch* 'to inform'). Or it may be tried out, found wanting, redundant, or boring, and returned to the worldly regions of its subcultural origins, or perhaps just assigned the stigma of datedness (e.g., *to dig* 'to understand'). Much slang just disappears, not to be heard from again (*wizard* or *some pumpkins!* 'superb!'), unless resuscitated in later years (*pig*, 'a policeman' in the 1840s, was revived over a century later in the 1960s). All this is only the beginning of the story. Slang is too vital an idea to rest easily under the umbrella of popular speech or upon a rung on the social ladder of usage.

3. The Interactional Uses of Slang

The view of slang as a level of usage, or as a marker of social position in systems of difference, often of vertical stratification, however, opens the way to see the distinctive uses of slang in social interaction and foreshadows its larger sociology. The difference between standard, proper, or elite speech, on the one hand, and low, unconventional slang, on the other, provides the tension that enables slang to serve as a language of social opposition. The role of slang in subcultural confrontation has long been known but perhaps not generally appreciated. Slang is a class of language used, among other social and psychological uses, to deny allegiance to genteel, elite, and proper society and to its standard linguistic forms. Slang is thus used to assert social opposition, ranging from the most vicious and hostile verbal aggression to the gentlest, teasing contrariness and playful disruptiveness. The utterance of subcultural words and phrases is also a way to seek bonds with sympathetic others and, as a new group, to oppose or just to break with the dominant tone of discourse. Slang in any case is used earnestly or playfully in order to lower, or to shift laterally, the register of discourse.

Dumas and Lighter have articulated this view and call for the retention of the concept of slang in linguistics to denote a functional category of lexemes that 'are identifiable primarily by the intent (or perceived intent) of the speaker or writer to break with established linguistic convention.' They also note another basic distinction of most slang: 'Slang characterizes a referent; jargon and standard English only indicate it' (Dumas and Lighter 1978: 13). The social utility of slang, then, lies in the disruptive rhetoric it produces and using the speech of stigmatized subcultures is one way to lower the register of discourse.

Slang also facilitates a variety of distinctive interactions in modern society, insofar as it retains widely recognizable subgroup origins and meanings. Slang is used to manage the multiple, overlapping, and shifting identities of modern life—a world of 'masks and mirrors.' A skill of city living, for those who adventure into its diversity, is knowing the sucultural talk of other groups. This knowledge is a way to attribute meaning to the seeming jumble and noise of modern life. The anonymity and public life of the large city, especially, offer many opportunities for interactional games, deceptions, identity switches, and opportunities for impression management for either fun or profit, and slang with subcultural associations facilitates these manipulations. Slang, for example, may be used to signal that the speaker is conversant with, or maybe even belongs to, a subculture of titillating or prestigeful reputation. The use of subcultural speech becoming slang, then, is often a tame adventure in verbal slumming, or in social climbing.

4. The Essential Urbanness of Slang

Modern slang is a distinct level or register of language that arose during the Great Transformation from homogeneous rural to heterogeneous urban society. While in principle, general slang can arise in any situation of social difference, the modern industrial city in the nineteenth century intensified every material condition that creates slang: the aggregation of large and variegated social groupings, their proximity and high visibility to one another, the complexity of their economic interdependencies, and the necessity and desirability of contact and exchanges of every sort. Heavy migration and settlement in ethnic enclaves of the great cities influenced slang throughout the nineteenth century and are influencing it again in the 1990s. To this potent mix was added the intensifying ingredient of common knowledge of the city through the mass media, especially the newspapers and the comics and, in another medium, the popular cultures of minstrelsy and vaudeville.

The lexicographer Stuart Berg Flexner developed the idea of slang in diverse society (Flexner 1974). General slang and other nonstandard varieties of language can arise only in the presence of third parties or subgroups in society—the primitive urban situation. Flexner suggested a simple sociology of number, in both the grammatical and numerical senses, that is reminiscent of the triadic theory of the German sociologist Georg Simmel (Wolff 1950: 135–36). Slang develops when the conversation between the first and second persons, who have agreed upon a common language, begins to include the speech of third parties or subgroups and thus to allude to other, external meanings and realities. General slang is, thus, an epiphenomenon of diverse urban society and, by sociological definition, can exist only in plural societies of multiple, interacting social worlds.

Historically, cities have been generators of cultural and technological innovation, new forms of social organization, new social varieties, new forms of inequality and, thus, of lexical innovation to express these new thoughts and new social objects. American slang, however, is often traced to the period after the War of 1812 when the old frontier set the emerging tone of American speech with, in H. L. Mencken's words, 'its disdain of all scholastic rules and precedents, its tendency toward bold and often bizarre tropes, its rough humors, its not infrequent flights of what might be called poetic fancy, its love of neologisms for their own sake.' Yet 'to the immigrants who poured in after 1850, even the slums of the great Eastern cities presented essentially frontier conditions' (Mencken 1963: 148).

Language scholars of a social bent have long associated slang with cities and urban society. John Camden Hotten, the London publisher and lexicographer of slang, in 1859 wrote in the preface to his early compilation that the most favorable conditions for the appearance of slang are those of 'crowding and excitement, and artificial life' (Hotten 1859: 35). Or, to elaborate this observation for the end of the twentieth century, slang grows from the density, intensifications, and social releases of urban life, in contrast to life in traditional, homogeneous, or rural communities. The philologist George Philip Krapp wrote that, in general, slang 'is found in the speech of persons whose social relations are extensive, varied, and animated. It is the product of the city rather than the country, of sophisticated rather than naive society' (Krapp 1925: 317). Eric Partridge, noting the presence of slang in Ancient Greek and Latin, wrote that 'knowing the characteristics of urban life, we may assume that slang dates from the massing of populations in cities' (Partridge 1963: 37).

Yet general slang can arise in markedly nonurban places, as Partridge and others so abundantly found in the military where slang served as a freemasonry of speech among persons of diverse backgrounds. Slang can arise in any place that simulates the social diversity of the cities and where diverse peoples meet, even at rural crossroads, or in any situation where people of different social ranks meet and, at least initially, culturally oppose one another. In principle, general slang can arise from the most rudimentary differences of social role, in any situation where third-group locutions can be introduced.

Large metropolitan centers have been the most fertile producers of slang about all things. Anglo–American commentators on slang throughout the nineteenth century regularly associated slang with big cities, especially New York and London. Early lexicographers collected the distinctive vocabularies of various urban groups; they noted the role of the printed mass media in the diffusion of slang; they contrasted stable rural dialect with the bizarre fleeting talk of the big cities; they noted the origins and use of slang in high society as well as in low; they understood its uses in social opposition; and they glimpsed the principles of diffusion. Population density and crowd psychology in the streets did the job of circulating slang that mass communication does in the late twentieth century. In 1852 Charles Mackay, in his essay 'The popular follies of great cities,' marveled at how the catch phrases, such as *quoz, Oh, what a shocking bad hat!*, and *flare up*, seized the lower orders of London. 'London is particularly fertile in this sort of phrase,' Mackay wrote, 'which springs up suddenly, no one knows in exactly what spot, and pervades the whole population in a few hours, no one knows how' (Mackay 980: 620).

Throughout the modern period down to, say, 1950 one may well be struck by the number of words and phrases in slang that denote the essences of city life. Segmental, impersonal, and often exploitative social relations were expressed in the idea of the city as a *jungle*, an employment agency as a *slave market*, or in the irony of *my uncle* 'a pawnbroker.' An awareness of class and ethnic differences were expressed in hundreds of well-known ethnic slurs and similar class derogations. Personal appearances and styles of dress as seen in city streets are recorded in terms such as *plug ugly, jelly bean, dude*, and *gussied up*. A variety of urban social locations and roles were expressed in *lounge lizard, ritzy, rubbernecker, skid row, coontown, black-and-tan dive, the 'burbs*, and in other slang denotations of urban class and status. Unconventional styles of life and bizarre occupational specializations were denoted in *panhandler, mushroom faker, taxi dancer*, and *sandwich man*. The importance of money is apparent in the many slang synonyms for money, often ill-gotten, and the lavish spending of it (*big spender* and *butter-and-egg man*). Sexual and other social relations that are casual, segmental, impersonal, commercial, and exploitative are implicit in *sugar daddy, gold digger, hooker, pimp, bouncer, puller-in*, or *steerer*. New experiences of every kind in the industrial city, including its machines, were amply denoted in slang: *bus, taxi, el, rattler* 'a streetcar,' *skyscraper*, or *an Ameche* (passingly, 'a telephone' about 1940 and an allusion to the actor Don Ameche who played the inventor Alexander Graham Bell in a popular movie).

Moreover, the semantics of slang, especially its names for kinds of people (ethnic, class, and other social types), display a pervasive structure of vertical stratification and binary opposition, frequently expressed in invidious distinctions between 'Us' and 'Them.' Slang is greatly about the new and different and, in the social realm, often expresses stressful social relations and a dislike for the unlike.

5. The Urban Sociology of Slang

Slang derives from the multiple subcultures of urban, that is to say modern, society. For the most part it denotes vocabulary that has diffused through and perked up into wider use from myriad intersecting social circles. The neoclassical or subcultural theory of urbanism explains how cities create a variety of subgroups and subcultures that vary in number directly with population size (Fischer 1975). Large cities attract as migrants large numbers of different kinds of people, who then join and enlarge the diversity of groups already in the city. The greater numbers of people with specialized interests in cities provide the sufficient numbers or 'critical masses' that enable subcultures to sustain and intensify. Eventually, nascent subgroups within larger subcultures reach the numbers necessary and sufficient for even more specialized interest groups to break away and form yet other subcultures.

The many direct and indirect contacts and communications among most subgroups in the dense, compact, intensely interactive market city, as people learn more and more about one another, cause some subcultures to become more alike, in some cases even to assimilate or merge into one. Other groups recoil from the culture clash they experience and, as a result, entrench, reaffirm their original identities, and become even more different than before. The city, precisely because of its large size, density, and social variety, creates a continual process of sustaining, reinforcing, and creating ethnic groups, social classes, styles of life, and every imaginable kind of subculture, including many so-called deviant ones. As a necessary part of this process, many meanings are exchanged, which results in the learning and diffusion of borrowed subcultural words and phrases. The creation of subcultural speech, intergroup contact, and the diffusion of these words through intersecting social networks into wider usage, or into general slang, recapitulate and illustrate Fischer's modified theory of urbanism and may be taken as a special application of it.

Most general slang comes from the restricted, special vocabularies of these many subgroups in modern society and becomes slang as it diffuses through the word-of-mouth networks and between the intersecting social circles that lace together much of the whole society. The diffusion of lexical innovation follows the same principles that govern the diffusion of any cultural innovation: it spreads in direct proportion to population density, intensity of communication and—above all—perceived usefulness in social interaction. In this way, restricted subcultural usages pass into general or at least into wider usage, often with the augmentation and amplification of the mass media.

In the process of diffusion, the subcultural expression becoming general slang often changes meaning to some degree, usually widening in denotation and connotation, and so becoming useful in more social situations. If the word or phrase proves useful or amusing in its new social setting, it may pass further into more and more circles until it reaches a wide enough audience, who at least understand its meaning, to say that it is in general slang and part of the general culture. If such slang stays in wide use for decades, it may lose its subcultural associations and seem just to be there in the language, its subgroup origins remote or forgotten.

More than half of historical American slang, it has been estimated, came from the chiefly male subcultural speech of lumberjacks, railroaders, musicians, hoboes, sportsmen, show business, teenagers, college students, ethnic minorities, the military, and various deviant subcultures, such as criminals and drug users (Flexner 1960). Subcultures, as the prefix of the term implies, were once thought of as little social worlds that were 'below' the general culture or ones that were marginal to society or isolated within it. The idea of subcultures more validly embraces all subgroups of society, including social classes, genders, variant sexual interests, all majority and minority ethnic groups, regional groups, age groups, and a host of occupational, life-style, and consumer cultures, as well as all the groups more traditionally described as subcultures. A subgroup is any set of people generally linked in communication and bound by a common interest. These groups vary greatly in their level of organization and degree of self-consciousness. Ultimately, almost any distinguishing set of common experience and meaning can be described as a subculture of a subgroup.

Everyone, it follows, belongs to multiple, overlapping subgroups and subcultures, the number depending on the variety and breadth of their interests and social engagements. The general culture of a society is the meanings and values that most of its subcultures have in common, and this includes its language and general slang.

Many subcultures, some of which may be called speech communities, have their own dialects or varieties of English in degrees of distinction from standard speech. Each variety, and most are merely nascent, may include distinctive pronunciations, special words or special meanings of ordinary words, or even grammatical differences. These special words, or as often ordinary words with special meanings, sometimes escape their little social circles or leak into one or more intersecting or tangential circles, where they are provisionally adopted. The subcultures of male homosexuals, drug users, and lower-class blacks are examples of leaky subcultures whose special words and phrases diffused into the general culture and its slang in the 1960s and 1970s (Maurer and High 1980). Previously, these subcultures were structurally tighter, or more isolated, and their words leaked out slowly and were transmitted largely by word-of-mouth. The diffusion, or at least knowledge, of their norms was accompanied by the diffusion of their language, especially through the mass media. In the early 1990s such stigmatized subcultures are much less isolated and more subgroups of all kinds are leaking lexical expressions of their cultures—and leaking them faster—especially through television and the movies. Adopting slang, heard either in interpersonal or in mass communications, is a traditional way young people flirt with forbidden and other attractive subcultures.

The mass media can bring almost instant lexical diffusion. Mass-communicated slang and neologisms initially leapfrog communities and are introduced at once into many thousands of local social circles. If they catch on in many of these circles, they have a big headstart in the diffusion process and spread even further by word-of-mouth, now able to go like multiple brushfires through the verbal culture of a society. Slang-like advertising slogans, for example, are repeatedly reimplanted in local networks, from which they are sometimes spread from person to person. In modern societies laced together by the mass media, folk lexical culture (categories invented by people) blends with mass lexical culture (categories invented by media writers for people). This is how almost all new words now spread, slang or not.

6. Slang in the Late Twentieth Century

In the past slang has been used more by men than by women and more by younger than by older people. In this sense, general slang itself was a semirestricted vocabulary of youthful male subculture and reflected its distinctive social construction of reality. But this is changing as gender and age subcultures merge a little in their social experiences. Much historical slang came from stressful male social worlds of the barroom and brothel, the life of tramps and hoboes, rough occupations, the military, sports, and deviant subcultures. Sociolinguists report that, until the 1970s at least, women used less slang than men and, even if they knew its meaning, used it in fewer social situations. Proper English signaled proper behavior, and the avoidance of slang reflected the greater pressures on women toward conventional behavior, at least in mixed company.

These subcultural walls are breaking down as women move into male preserves and so into situations of greater cultural variety and clash, which prompted male slang in the first place. Even low-register sexual and scatological expressions used as slang hardly raise an eyebrow in gatherings of sophisticated young men and women. Such vulgar and taboo expressions were formerly the restricted speech of male subculture, which is today losing its exclusiveness and isolation. Yet slang remains to some extent the province of the young—of socially engaged young men and women. The cultural boundaries of yet other social categories—ethnic, class, style of life—are weakening as well.

In the more self-conscious atmosphere of cultural and linguistic relativism, slang is more acceptable in many situations, is no longer so shocking, and in a functional sense is ceasing to be slang—in a kind of postmodernist collapse of old social categories. At one time all slang, echoing rebellion and disrespect, might have raised eyebrows in the most formal contexts. But in the 1990s some of the norms and useful parts of the language of deviant subgroups have been absorbed by straight society. The former, critical distinction of these different registers is diminishing. Slang depends on social differences, often tense hierarchies. If the norms and language of low-status outgroups were ever totally absorbed by elite ingroups, 'slang and gentility would die together' (Sledd 1965: 699). But new social differences and hierarchies are continually arising. Slang will certainly retain a role in the inevitable cultural conflict among them.

See also: Sex Differences; Sociology in Language; Subcultures and Countercultures.

Bibliography

Dumas B K, Lighter J 1978 Is *slang* a word for linguists? *AS* **53**: 5–17
Fischer C S 1975 Toward a subcultural theory of urbanism. *American Journal of Sociology* **80**: 1319–41
Flexner S B 1960 Preface. In: Wentworth H, Flexner S B (eds.) *Dictionary of American Slang*. Crowell, New York
Flexner S B 1974 Slang. *Encyclopaedia Brittanica*, vol. 16
Hotten J C 1859 *The Slang Dictionary*. Chatto and Windus, London
Krapp G P 1925 *The English Language in America*, vol. 1. Century, New York
Mackay C 1980 *Memoirs of Extraordinary Popular Delusions and The Madness of Crowds*. Bonanza, New York
Maurer D W, High E C 1980 New words—Where do they come from and where do they go? *AS* **55**: 184–94
Mencken H L 1963 *The American Language*, 4th ed. Knopf, New York
Partridge E 1963 *Slang To-Day and Yesterday*, 3rd edn. Bonanza, New York
Sledd J 1965 On not teaching English usage. *English Jo* **54**: 698–703
Wolff K H (ed.) 1950 *The Sociology of Georg Simmel*. Free Press, New York

I. L. Allen

Slavic Languages

The Slavic languages are traditionally divided into three major groups on linguistic, geographical, and cultural grounds. These three groups are: the East Slavic languages, consisting of Russian (more precisely Great Russian, but this term is now rare), Belorussian (or Byelorussian, formerly also called White Ruthenian), and Ukrainian (formerly also called Ruthenian); the South Slavic languages, consisting of Bulgarian (with Macedonian), Serbo–Croat (sometimes also called Serbocroatian and realized in its Serbian and Croatian variants), and Slovene (sometimes called Slovenian); and the West Slavic languages, consisting of Czech, Slovak, Polish, Lusatian (sometimes called Sorbian or Wendish) with its now distinct variants of Lower Lusatian and Upper Lusatian, Polabian (died out toward the middle of the eighteenth century), and Cassubian (whose status as an individual Slavonic language is controversial). The term 'Slavonic' in relation to language is the British English term for 'Slavic' which is used elsewhere in the English-speaking world.

The Slavic languages are a branch of the Indo–European language family, and thus they share a remote common origin with English. Within this superordinate grouping they share a particular affiliation with the Baltic languages.

The Slavic languages are in official use in Russia, Bulgaria, former Yugoslavia, the Czech Republic, Slovakia, and Poland. Russian is the main and official language of the CIS stretching from European Russia through Siberia to the Pacific Ocean (more than 130 million native speakers). Belorussian is, alongside Russian, the official language of the Belorussian Republic (about 9 million native speakers). Ukrainian is, alongside Russian, the official language of the Ukrainian Republic (about 40 million native speakers). Bulgarian is the official language of the Republic of Bulgaria (about 8.5 million native speakers). Macedonian is the official language of the Republic of Macedonia (about 1.5 million speakers). Serbo–Croat, as a blanket language of the largest and central parts of former Yugoslavia, is the official language of the republics of Serbia, Croatia, Bosnia–Herzegovina and Montenegro (above 15 million native speakers). Slovene is the official language of the republic of Slovenia (about 1.5 million native speakers). In the Czech Republic Czech is the official language (about 9.5 million native speakers) and Slovak is the official language of Slovakia (above 4.5 million native speakers). Polish is the official language of the Polish Republic (about 35 million native speakers). Upper and Lower Lusatian are regional and also literary languages in the southeast of the former GDR (about 100,000 native speakers). Polabian used to be a regional language, although not in official or literary use, in north Germany but has been totally superseded by German. Cassubian is a regional language spoken in north Poland, also without the status of an official or literary language (about 150,000 speakers).

The Slavic languages are rather homogeneous in their grammatical structure with the striking exception of Bulgarian (with Macedonian). They are synthetic languages (Bulgarian has become an analytic one) with a high degree of inflection in all the relevant word classes, which make them comparable to Latin in their complexity.

The common origin of all the Slavic languages is the hypothetical language called Proto-Slavic or Common Slavic. This language is presumed to have been spoken in the original territories of the Slavs, i.e., between twentieth century Warsaw and Kiev, north of the Carpathians and south of the Baltic Sea. Common Slavic is not attested by written documents because it antedates any Slavic alphabet, but it can be convincingly reconstructed on the basis of a comparative study of the Slavic languages and their documented history. Mention of the ancient Slavs has been made from as early as the fifth century BC by Greek and subsequently Roman writers and historians. The first known contacts of the Slavs and their language was with the Baltic peoples and languages. Further ancient linguistic contacts with consequential borrowings took place with the Iranian languages to the north of the Black Sea and Dacian in the south. A certain number of borrowings from the Germanic languages are dated from the second to the fourth centuries AD: first from Gothic as spoken in eastern Europe and later from Old Saxon, Frankish, and the Bavarian dialects of Old High German.

The location of the ancient Slavs is reconstructed on the basis of two main hypotheses which situate them: (a) as a compact ethnic group between the rivers Vistula and Oder with further expansions at the beginning of the first millennium AD toward the Danube and the Balkans in the south, the valley of the river Dnieper and beyond it in the east, and in the west beyond the river Oder; (b) on the territories between the Western Bug and the Middle Dnieper, with the river Pripet in the north and the forest and steppe regions on the right-hand side of the river Dniester in the south; this latter hypothesis is corroborated by geographical terms used in Proto-Slavic, mainly those designating swamps and forests, and the absence of words designating mountain chains.

After the disintegration of Indo–European, Proto-Slavic and Proto-Baltic developed certain common features which support the hypothesis of a common Proto-Slavic–Baltic language. These features include stress shifts occurring in both groups, the development of compound adjective forms with the help of the anaphoric pronoun, the use of the genitive after negation, and many common items in the lexicon. However, later investigations tend to explain these common features by mutual interpenetration after the disintegration of Indo–European.

For the reconstruction of Proto-Slavic the earliest written Slavic language going back to the second half of the ninth century, Old Church Slavonic (sometimes also called Old Slavonic or Old Bulgarian), is of the utmost interest, as well as certain archaic Slavic dialects and the oldest written documents of the individual Slavic languages. Slavic toponyms and borrowings in surrounding languages provide evidence on the chronology of certain phonetic developments in Slavic itself.

In discussing initial dialectal differentiations within Proto-Slavic the term 'macrodialect,' which denotes a large linguistic territory with common features with an internal division into smaller areas, seems appropriate. The comparative study of the Slavic languages and their dialects reveals that by the fifth century Proto-Slavic was divided into an eastern and a western macrodialect on the one hand and into a northern and southern one on the other. At the end of the Proto-Slavic era, i.e., between the sixth and ninth centuries, three new macrodialects took shape which were the final forerunners of the twentieth century East, South, and West Slavic languages.

See also: Balto–Slavonic Languages; Belorussian; Bulgarian and Macedonian; Czech; Polish; Russian; Serbo-Croat; Slovak; Slovene.

Bibliography

Bray R G A De 1969 *Guide to the Slavonic Languages*, 2nd rev. edn. London
Dvornik F 1962 *The Slavs in European History and Civilization*. New Brunswick
Entwistle W J, Morison W A 1964 *Russian and the Slavonic Languages*, 2nd rev. edn. London
Stone G, Worth D (eds.) 1985 *The Formation of the Slavonic Literary Languages*. Columbus

T. Henninger

Slips of the Tongue

Certain errors in speech, like *You have hissed all my mystery lectures* for *You have missed all my history lectures*, are sometimes called slips of the tongue (or spoonerisms, after the Reverend William Spooner of Oxford University, whose speech is reputed to have been riddled with them). But the term 'slip of the tongue' is somewhat misleading. Analysis of large numbers of errors shows that, far from involving just the placement of the tongue in the articulatory tract, these mistakes in speaking can also take place during the cognitive process of planning an utterance for production. As a result, they provide evidence about what the planning process involves: what kinds of elements are represented, how they are represented, what planning steps must be carried out, what information is available to support computation at each step, and what particular aspects of utterances cause trouble for the planning mechanism. In addition, error patterns have been used to make inferences about the brain mechanisms involved in the control of speaking, about the mental lexicon, and about the articulatory process itself.

1. Sublexical Errors

Of particular interest from the point of view of models of production planning are errors that break a word up into smaller elements by moving or changing some of its sounds, as in the spoonerism cited above. Errors of this kind are sometimes called sublexical errors or phonological errors, and it is somewhat surprising that they occur at all. It would be easy to imagine that once a speaker knows which words will appear in an utterance and where they will appear, no further processing is required to ensure that the individual subparts of words appear in the right order. After all, the order of the component sounds of a word is part of its definition: *apt* is a different word from *pat*, and both differ from *tap*, partly because of the order of their sounds. This shows that the order of a word's subparts must be an aspect of its stored mental representation. Despite this fact, however, errors that break up target words show that individual phonemes (and other subparts of words) undergo considerable processing of their own. Errors like:

shu flots (for *flu shots*)
feed Handrew _ot dogs (for *feed Andrew hot dogs*) and
spack rices (for *spice racks*)

(Crompton 1982)

show that there is an extensive amount of processing to be done at the phonological level even after the words that are to be used in an utterance have been identified by the speaker.

Research in linguistic theories of phonology, in psychological theories of cognitive processing, and in acoustic phonetics since the 1960s has shown that the retrieval of word forms from the mental lexicon and their integration into sentential contexts involves a number of tasks, including the serial ordering of segmental information, the interaction of segmental information with adjacent segmental context, and the integration of segmental and prosodic information. These and other aspects of phonological processing are sometimes referred to as 'phonological encoding.' The study of sublexical speech errors has provided evidence for models of these phonological aspects of the production planning process, because errors exhibit highly systematic behavior that can be most easily explained if one adopts certain views about the planning process for normal, fluent, error-free speech. In this way, the study of speech errors resembles the study of related areas of speech pathology, aphasia, typing errors, errors in American Sign Language, and action planning errors (like putting the cat in the refrigerator and the milk bottle outside before going to bed). Researchers use the regularities in error patterns to infer what the normal processing mechanisms are like, on the assumption that an error usually results from a small perturbation in a mechanism which has otherwise functioned in the normal way. Thus, an error not only reveals the disturbed aspect of the process; it also reflects the constraints imposed by the remaining intact, nonperturbed aspects of the planning process.

2. Representation of Linguistic Elements in Phonological Encoding

One of the most striking aspects of sublexical speech errors is the evidence which they provide for the claim that the discrete units proposed by linguists for the formal statement of grammars play a role in the cognitive process of speech production planning. In fact, one of the works that introduced linguists and psycholinguists to the wealth of error data is Fromkin (1973). This observation is particularly important because the ongoing speech signal, like the movements of the articulatory tract, is relatively continuous. Even the discontinuities that the signal does display do not reflect in any straightforward way the discrete distinctive features, phonemic segments, syllable onsets and rhymes, morphemes, and words that make up the vocabulary of linguistic descriptions. Sublexical errors provide compelling evidence that many of these elements play a role in the psycholinguistic process of sentence planning, even if they are not apparent in the observable wave forms and muscle movements of speech.

Error evidence also suggests that different units can play different roles in production planning. That is, linguistic elements can show themselves in error patterns in several different ways: as the elements that move or change in errors; as the representational dimensions of those elements; or as the larger structures that constrain the error interactions among smaller elements. In addition, as will be seen, not every element suggested by error patterns corresponds to a linguistically motivated unit.

3. Methods

3.1 Collection

Sublexical errors come in many different varieties; so, in order to see their patterns and regularities clearly, it is necessary to analyze a large number of them. The first substantial corpus on record was collected in German by Meringer and published in 1896. Inspired by his example, researchers have collected corpora of errors of all types from the speech that they hear around them, including several in American English and British English, others in Dutch, Spanish, and German, and smaller collections for a few other languages, including Japanese and Portuguese. Some collections contain 10,000 or more errors. The most extensive analyses have been done for corpora in American English, in which sublexical errors have been found to make up more than 40 percent of errors.

Collection by simple listening yields a large number of errors, because it allows collectors to harvest the data from the sea of conversational and presentational speech that surrounds them every day. But this method has some problems as well as advantages. To be entered into a collection, an error must be noticed by the observer and correctly remembered, and both of these processes may be subject to bias. For example, it may be easier to remember an error that forms a real word, like *some lumber scattered across the lamp* (*ramp*), and harder to recall one that forms a nonsense word like *traditional fatterns as a function of* . . . (*patterns*). Or, it may be more difficult to notice an error that occurs late in a word, as in *You wouldn't laft* (*last*), but easier if the error occurs at the beginning, as in *tweezers or needle-nosed twiers* (*pliers*). As a result, error collections may not always reflect the actual distribution of error varieties in language use.

For these reasons, many investigators view collections of errors from running speech as the source of hypotheses to be tested in the laboratory, with experiments that elicit speech under controlled conditions. Elicitation experiments often involve either tongue-twisters (i.e., particularly difficult patterns of sound alternation) or priming certain sound sequences, to increase the rate at which sublexical errors occur. This method has difficulties of a different kind: it is not altogether clear that speech produced from controlled scripts in front of a laboratory tape recorder invokes the same processing mechanisms that normal spontaneous speech employs. For example, presenting the speaker with the written form of the word may change some aspects of the planning process (although other aspects are presumably identical for reading aloud and speaking from intention). The ideal collection method would involve a task or topic that imposes some control on the words, sounds, and structures that the speaker uses, allowing the experimenter to collect specific kinds of error data, yet requires production of fully spontaneous speech in conditions that absorb attention and prevent selfconsciousness. Such methods have not yet come into widespread use by the time of writing, so most error studies rely on corpora collected by ear (or in a few cases by tape recorder, which permits acoustic analysis) or on errors elicited by reading aloud under challenging conditions.

3.2 Classification

Whether gathered from spontaneous speech or elicited in experiments, errors must be categorized so that similar types can be grouped together for analysis. Traditionally, categorization involves the dimensions of error type, error unit, error context, error result, and the target/source relationship. The nature of the change from the intended utterance to the error must first be identified as an exchange (like the spoonerisms cited above), a substitution (e.g., *the yongest* for *longest*), an addition (e.g., *a capracity crowd* for *capacity*; see Stemberger and Treiman (1986) for discussion), an omission (e.g., *the conf_icting claims* for *conflicting*), or a shift (e.g., *I figured hout _ow to* for *figured out how to*). This is the error type, and provides information on the kinds of processes that manipulate individual elements during the planning process. An additional type of error, the word blend, merges the first part of one word with the second part of another, as in *the two tyles of speech* (*types + styles*). Second, one must identify the size of the element that is moved, substituted, added, or deleted: whether a single distinctive feature (e.g., *leezer shoots* for *leisure suits*), a single phonemic segment (e.g., *Get your tar cowed away* for *car towed*), a syllable or syllabic subunit (e.g., an onset, as in *Claude and Moey* for *Maud and Chloë*), or a morpheme (e.g., *Chew out what you are spitting* for *Spit out what you are chewing*). Or, the error may affect some other fragment of a word that does not correspond to a linguistically defined element (e.g., *cassy put* for *pussy cat*, or *Groyota Tappone* for *Grappone Toyota*). This is the error unit, and provides insights into the representational elements that play an active role in production planning. Third, the context in which the error occurs includes facts like the form class and prosodic character of the words involved, the position of the error element in the phrase, word, or syllable, the grammatical role of the words in their phrases, etc. These facts suggest the kinds of information that are available to the processor when the errors occur. Fourth, the result of the error needs to be identified: whether it is a phonotactically permissible word shape in English; whether it can be characterized as a real word of English; if so, whether it is of the same form class as the target word; whether it is complete, or interrupted; and, if interrupted, where in the structure it is interrupted. Such observations are relevant to the monitoring mechanisms involved in the production process. The final dimension of categorization, the error–source relationship, applies only to errors which reflect an interaction between two elements or locations in an utterance, like an exchange, shift, anticipation, or perseveration. It involves questions such as the distance between an error and its presumed source element (both in absolute terms and in terms of the types of boundaries between them), the similarity of the error and source contexts, and whether the source precedes or follows the error in the utterance. This dimension provides information about a number of aspects of production planning, including the size of the planning span, the factors that cause difficulty for the planning mechanism, and the distinctness or modularity of different components of the model.

Like the collection methods, the classification methods for sublexical errors confront difficulties. Many, if not most, sublexical errors are ambiguous, some in several ways at once. For example, the error *most highly-played payer* for *highly paid player* is ambiguous as to type and unit: it may be viewed as an exchange of the two syllable onsets /p/ and /pl/, a shift of the single segment /l/ to a later location, an exchange of the two root morphemes *play* and *pay*, or even a substitution of the two intrusion words *played* and *payer* for the two target words *paid* and *player*. Another common form of ambiguity is found in incomplete errors like *tup of—cup of tea*. Here, the speaker noticed and interrupted either the exchange *tup of kea* or the anticipatory substitution *tup of tea*, so it is difficult to know whether this error should be grouped with other exchanges or with other substitutions. Yet another kind of ambiguity involves multiple possible sources, as in *that kind of thing keems to be coming out* for *seems to be coming*: this error could be either an anticipatory substitution from *coming* or a perseveratory substitution for *kind*. These examples illustrate only some of the ambiguities that are commonly observed.

The careful categorizer has two possible solutions to the problems raised by classification ambiguity. The first is to restrict analyses to a small set of errors that is as free as possible from ambiguity, and the second is to classify ambiguous errors separately, and carry out critical analyses both with and without the ambiguous sets. Fortunately, many errors provide useful information despite their ambiguities; for example, the error *a tup of—cup of tea* may be ambiguous with respect to type, but it nevertheless illustrates the fact that single phonemic segments can interact, because the nature of the error unit is relatively clear.

4. Errors as Evidence for Models of the Phonological Encoding Process

Despite the difficulties, analysis of errors collected and categorized in these ways has made it possible to construct and evaluate models of the phonological aspect of the production planning process, and to answer a number of specific questions about the mechanisms and representations involved. Levelt's (1989) summary makes it clear just how complex and multifaceted this phonological planning must be. He describes three major tasks that must be accomplished during the phonological planning of individual words, each with several subparts: (a) morphological and metrical spellout, which integrates the addressing information for the forms of successive lexical categories in the surface structure of an utterance into the appropriate slots in that structure, providing the information necessary for looking up and spelling out the stored metrical and morphological composition of each word; (b) segmental spellout, which integrates the morphemes (stems, prefixes, and suffixes) into their appropriate slots in the developing representation, providing the information necessary for looking up and spelling out the segmental composition of each word; and (c) phonetic spellout, which integrates the syllabic constituents of onset, nucleus, and rhyme into the syllable slots provided by the metrical spellout, and provides the information necessary for looking up the phonetic programs for those elements. To this, Levelt adds an extra step for spelling out complex syllabic constituents like onset consonant clusters. In addition, there is another layer of processing to generate phonetic plans for connected speech over an entire phrase or larger constituent. Connected speech processing includes segmental and morphological accommodations (such as cliticization and adjustments of adjacent segments at word boundaries) which integrate a word into its surrounding segmental context, and prosodic planning which integrates the metrical structure of individual words into the prosodic structure of the utterance as a whole. Confronted by this array of complex requirements, it is no wonder that the processing mechanism occasionally misfires and produces an error. Perhaps the surprising fact is that this does not happen more often.

Many of these steps are suggested by detailed acoustic phonetic analysis, which has revealed just how different the phonetics of words can be when produced in sentential context, as compared to citation forms. Other aspects of the model are suggested by constraints and regularities that have been observed in collections of sublexical errors. These insights facilitate ruling out some models of phonological planning, and suggest possible components for others.

One of the first insights gained from error analysis was described by Lashley (1951), who noted that errors often involve the anticipation of a target element, that is, the production of the element at a point earlier than its expected location in the utterance, as in exchanges (e.g., *They don't have any wails to tag* for *tails to wag*), anticipatory substitutions (e.g., *yast year* for *last year*), and anticipatory shifts (e.g., *twenty-wunch in__* for *twenty-one inch*). Lashley pointed out that anticipatory errors demonstrate that at the time a speaker is producing an earlier word in an utterance, a representation has already been formed of later words in the utterance, sometimes quite a few words later, as shown by errors like *large purz with lots of fur* (*paws*). This observation rules out models in which each word is retrieved just as the preceding word is produced; at least some aspects of the later word must be available well before its target moment.

Anticipatory errors also show that selecting and ordering the elements of an utterance is not equivalent to producing them. Instead, it must be the case that speakers construct a plan, and the execution of that plan lags behind its construction in time. This claim is supported by complete exchange errors (spoonerisms) like *Beel fetter?* (*feel better*) and other examples given at the beginning of this article. These two-part errors show that the planning framework being developed by the speaker is represented separately from the planning elements that participate in errors. If the plan consisted simply of a string of elements to be executed, with no further structure, then the early execution of /b/ in place of the target /f/ would remove /f/ from the plan, leaving no empty 'slot' behind at its later target location. As a result, the displaced segment /f/ would have no particular home; it might appear in some random location, or it might fail to appear at all, so that the later string -*etter* could be produced without any initial element. But this does not occur in sublexical errors. Instead, one sees exchanges like *beel fetter* (in which the displaced earlier target /f/ fills the later slot) or anticipatory substitutions like *beel better* (in which the intruding segment /b/ appears again in its own later slot), but not like *beel _etter* (where the displaced target element fails to appear or appears at some random location). In other words, the slot is represented separately from its content element, and demands to be filled one way or another.

These arguments suggest two conclusions about the speech planning process: planning involves construction of a representation that precedes the actual articulation of speech; and this representation includes a structural framework that is separate from the phonological entities that will fill it. In addition, error observations suggest that there is a serial ordering process that associates the phonological entities with their appropriate locations or order in the framework. One is then led to hypothesize about the nature of this phonological frame, of the phonological units that will fill it, and of the serial ordering process that integrates them. As the summary from Levelt suggests, one attractive hypothesis for the serial ordering process of already-ordered elements of words is that production planning requires the meshing of two separate representations: the syntactic–morphological information in the surface structure of the utterance, and the prosodic information in the intonational and rhythmic structure of the utterance.

The nature of the elements that undergo this ordering process, however, are a matter of dispute, as is the nature of the planning frame. Dell (1986; 1988) has argued for syllabic subunits of onset, nucleus, and rhyme, and proposed a syllabic template frame to receive them, while Shattuck-Hufnagel (1979) suggests a word-based set of target phonemes to be integrated into a metrically and intonationally structured prosodic frame. A second sharp distinction between models is their degree of modularity. Like Stemberger (1985), Dell works in the theoretical domain of spreading activation models, in which information flows freely between levels of representation. He proposes a serial ordering mechanism which transfers information from the individual, segment-specific nodes that represent the long-term stored knowledge of the speaker about the words of the language, in a network of interconnected nodes. On this view, activated word nodes, segment nodes, and feature nodes spread their activation freely through the network, so that activity at the word-selection level influences activity in related phonemic segments nodes, and vice versa. Shattuck-Hufnagel, in the spirit of Garrett's (1975) modular approach to production planning, suggests a serial ordering process that transfers information from target word representations that have been developed specifically for the utterance that is being planned; in this approach, the transfer mechanism is not influenced by information available to other levels of processing. This model primarily describes error interactions among the set of sublexical elements that form the targets for a particular utterance, rather than interactions among stored representations of the language as a whole. Both models, however, hypothesize that information about sublexical elements is transferred into a planning framework made up of larger constituents.

The nature of the representations involved in this process is revealed in part by the way in which different linguistic elements behave in sublexical errors. For example, the elements that are most commonly moved, added, deleted, and substituted are individual phonemic segments, and combinations of segments that correspond to syllabic subunits like onsets. On the other hand, a whole syllable like *-raffe* in *giraffe* is very seldom moved in an error. When a syllable does move in an error, it usually corresponds to an entire word or morpheme; its status as a syllable is most likely accidental. Unambiguous errors that move just one distinctive feature are also rare, although they are attested, as in *ponato* for *tomato* (where the place features for /t/ and

/m/ appear to have exchanged). On the other hand, the similarity between two phonemic segments that interact in an error can often be expressed by just a single feature, suggesting that features do play some kind of a role in the processing representation. This combination of facts is compatible with a model of serial ordering in which features, segments, and syllables play quite different roles: segments provide the information which is actually transferred from one representation to another, features serve as the identifying dimensions that specify and differentiate the segment representations, and syllables (or perhaps hierarchical structures of syllables like metrical feet) define the organizing framework which guides the serial ordering process. Shattuck-Hufnagel (1992) has shown experimentally that word structure also plays a role in constraining sublexical error interactions, suggesting a complex interaction between word structure and metrical structure in sublexical serial ordering.

A pervasive characteristic of sublexical errors is that they are governed by powerful regularities which can only have arisen from the influence of the representations and mechanisms involved. For example, it was seen above that two interacting segments often share most of their distinctive feature values. In addition, interacting segments very often share identical contexts. That is, when two consonants exchange, they are often followed by the same vowel, as in *for the focal volds* (*vocal folds*). (It is unlikely that this is an exchange of the two sequences /vo/ and /fo/, since sequences that have different vowel nuclei so rarely exchange.) Similarly, two interacting elements usually come from the same position, whether initial, for example, *the Sicks and the Kneltics* (*Knicks and the Celtics*), or final, for example, *I have a stick neff* (*stiff neck*). These similarity constraints on the interacting target segments themselves and on their contexts reveal that the representational facts like intrinsic segmental similarity, surrounding phonemic context, and position in the larger word or syllable all influence the operation of the serial ordering mechanism.

The position in which an element occurs also affects error frequency. For example, word-initial consonants are more likely to interact in errors than are medial or final consonants; up to 80 percent of consonant exchange errors occur between pairs of initial consonants, although they make up a far smaller proportion of the consonants in running speech. This disproportionate representation suggests that initial segments are especially confusable with each other, perhaps because the serial ordering mechanism selects among these elements as a set.

So, intrinsic similarity constraints between an error element and the intrusion element that displaces it provide information about the representation of those elements, and context similarity constraints between the error and the source reveal something about the planning frames. Other aspects of error patterns help to illuminate distinctions among the mechanisms that integrate planning elements into planning frames, and suggest the order in which these different mechanisms operate. For example, crosscategorizing errors by element and type highlights the contrast between word exchange errors (which often cross clause boundaries and respect grammatical category) and segment exchanges (which usually occur within a phrase between two words not of the same grammatical category). Garrett

(1980) suggests that this contrast reflects a distinction in the processing level at which these two classes of errors occur. Segmental exchanges, like *a gudget bap* (*budget gap*), are more likely to involve initial consonants, while segmental substitutions which anticipate or perseverate a target segment, like *consumer attormey* (*consumer attorney*), are more evenly distributed across word positions. Shattuck-Hufnagel (1992) suggests that this difference may arise because there is a separate processing mechanism for integrating word-onset consonants with the frame, and this mechanism is particularly susceptible to exchange errors.

Observations of phonetic accommodation in errors also argue for an ordering of processing steps. In errors like *Even the best team losts* (*teams lost*), the /z/ that would have been appropriate for the target *-ms* context is replaced by the /s/ appropriate to the new *-sts* context. Such accommodations show that the morphemes for verb tense and number, for the plural forms of nouns, and for the indefinite article fit the form of the error rather than the original target. This means that the phonetic forms of these morphemes are determined at a later processing stage, after the error occurs. Garrett (1980) argues that such accommodation occurs after segmental serial ordering not only in errors, but also during the normal production planning process. Finally, Meyer (1991) has shown in priming experiments involving naming that the subportions of a word are not encoded all at once or in random order, but sequentially.

Two more aspects of error patterns that provide evidence for processing mechanisms are observations on monitoring, and determinations of what makes errors more likely. Monitoring for errors clearly occurs, since speakers regularly detect and correct many of the errors they make, and Laver (1980) has proposed a neurolinguistic model of both pre- and postarticulatory monitoring. The phenomenon of reblending leftover segments (as in *a back—patch of cigarettes*, for *batch* and *pack*) also suggests that the serial ordering mechanism keeps track of segments as they are used. Levelt (1983) and Nooteboom (1973) also discuss monitoring mechanisms. Unanswered questions include what factors influence the likelihood that the speaker will detect and correct an error, and what determines how far back in the utterance the correction will begin.

Claims about what makes it more or less likely that an error will occur have been made from several points of view, reflecting different models of the processing mechanisms involved. They range from general psychological factors like unconscious Freudian influences (*I'll leave the key under the mattress* for *doormat*) or distracted attention, to specifically structural claims that difficulty will arise with alternating patterns of alternation (*she sells sea shells*) or when two competing plans are similar enough to provoke partial selection of each one (*symbol* and *emblem* share number of syllables, stress pattern, and the segments *-mb-*, possibly provoking the word blend *symblem*). A critical question that bears on the dispute between modular and spreading activation models of production planning is whether similarities at several different levels can influence an error that occurs at one level, for example, whether sound similarity, meaning similarity, and pragmatic context can all influence the misselection of a word.

5. Relation to Long-term Stored Knowledge: The Mental Lexicon

The phonological planning process draws on many aspects of the speaker's stored knowledge of the language, and the lexicon is one for which errors have provided a considerable amount of information. For example, Cutler and Isard (1980) have shown that when lexical stress errors occur (e.g., *photo*GRAPHY for *pho*Tography), it is almost always the case that another form of the root exists with its lexical stress on the wrongly stressed syllable, in this case *photo*GRAPHic. They argue that this error pattern supports the claim that information about lexical stress is stored in the lexicon, rather than being computed after lexical retrieval. Levelt (1992) suggests that the metrical structure of a word, for example, the number of syllables it contains, and its lexical stress pattern, is stored in the lexical entry separately from the segmental contents. In his model, the metrical frame is retrieved and processed separately from its phonological contents as part of the prosodic planning frame of the utterance. Fay and Cutler (1977) observe that when a substituted word is similar in form to the target word, the similarity involves initial segments, syllable structure and stress, and grammatical category. They argue that these similarity constraints on errors show that the lexicon is organized for retrieval according to these parameters.

6. Relation to Other Aspects of Language Processing

Spoken errors provide not only a useful window into the operation of spoken language production mechanisms, but also an interesting comparison with other aspects of language production. For example, MacNeilage (1964) has shown that typing errors often show a strong influence of the finger motor control systems quite different from the position similarity constraints on spoken sublexical errors. Newkirk, et al. (1982) analysed errors in American Sign Language, and found evidence that the gestures used in that system, like the phonemic segments of spoken language, have internal structure. The ASL elements appear to be characterized in terms of the three parameters of hand configuration, place of articulation, and movement.

Comparisons between errors in aphasic and normal speech have shown both differences (e.g., more errors in selecting elements from long-term storage and fewer interaction errors among target elements in the utterance, for some aphasic speakers; see Talo 1982) and striking similarities (e.g., in the details of lemma selection errors; see Garrett 1992). Saffran, et al. argue that, if care is taken to select patients with relevant deficits, evidence from agrammatic speakers supports many of the claims made for processing components and their order of application in models of normal production processing, for example, that syntactic allomorphs receive their phonological specification after lexical insertion.

A final source of data for comparison with slips of the tongue in normal speakers is found in studies of speakers' abilities to take words apart into smaller fragments and manipulate them systematically. Observational studies of language games, like Pig Latin, supplemented with experimental studies of sublexical manipulation (as in Treiman 1984), support the claim that speakers represent the structure of both words and syllables in the process of production planning.

7. Summary

Sublexical production errors in spoken language are not cases of random disorganization; instead, they are governed by stringent constraints, which provide information about the representations and mechanisms involved in the phonological aspects of normal, error-free planning for production. Analysis of large numbers of sublexical errors has shown that, between the speakers' identification of word candidates for the utterance and activation of the appropriate articulatory muscles, a complex planning process unfolds. Error patterns provide evidence for an active role in this process for many linguistic constructs. Error data also suggests a separate representation of planning frames and their contents, and a number of distinct and ordered steps in the phonological planning process.

However, interpretation of this data by different researchers has resulted in a variety of planning models. A deeper understanding of this evidence will require analysis of a larger number of errors, in a variety of languages, supplemented by experiments using both improved methods of error elicitation and precise methods for determining the time course of production planning events. The task is to develop a model of the normal, error-free production planning process for which the error patterns observed are natural consequences; analysis of the sublexical errors known as slips of the tongue can provide both the initial building blocks and some of the refining tools for this challenging enterprise.

Bibliography

Butterworth B (ed.) 1980 *Language Production, vol. I: Speech and Talk.* Academic Press, New York
Cutler A (ed.) 1982 *Slips of the Tongue, and Language Production.* Mouton, The Hague
Cutler A, Isard S D 1980 The production of prosody. In: Butterworth B (ed.) 1980
Dell G 1986 A spreading activation theory of retrieval in sentence production. *Psychological Review* 93: 283–321
Dell G 1988 The retrieval of phonological forms in production: Tests of predictions from a connectionist model. *Journal of Memory and Language* 27: 124–42
Fay D A, Cutler A 1977 Malapropisms and the structure of the mental lexicon. *LIn* 8: 505–20
Fromkin V A 1971 The non-anomalous nature of anomalous utterances. *Lg* 47: 27–52
Fromkin V A (ed.) 1973 *Speech Errors as Linguistic Evidence.* Mouton, The Hague
Fromkin V A (ed.) 1980 *Slips of the Tongue, Eye, Ear, and Hand.* Academic Press, New York
Garrett M F 1975 The analysis of sentence production. In: Bower G H (ed.) *The Psychology of Learning and Motivation.* Academic Press, New York
Garrett M F 1980 Levels of processing in sentence production. In: Butterworth B (ed.) 1980
Garrett M F 1992 Disorders of lexical selection. *Cognition* 42: 143–80
Lashley K 1951 The problem of serial order of behavior. In: Jeffress L (ed.) *Cerebral Mechanisms in Behavior.* Wiley, New York
Laver J 1980 Monitoring systems in the neurolinguistic control of speech production. In: Fromkin V A (ed.). 1980
Levelt W J C 1983 Monitoring and self-repair in speech. *Cognition* 14: 41–104
Levelt W J C 1989 *Speaking: From Intention to Articulation.* MIT Press, Cambridge, MA
Levelt W J C 1992 Accessing words in speech production. *Cognition* 42: 1–22
MacNeilage P 1964 Typing errors as clues to serial ordering mechanims in language behavior. *L & S* 7: 144–59
Meringer R, Mayer K 1896 *Versprechen und Verlesen.* Goschensche Verlag, Stuttgart
Meyer A 1991 The time course of phonological encoding in language production: Phonological encoding inside the syllable. *Journal of Memory and Language* 30: 69–89
Nooteboom S 1973 The tongue slips into patterns. In: Fromkin V A (ed.) 1973
Shattuck-Hufnagel S 1979 Speech errors as evidence for a serial order mechanism in sentence production. In: Cooper W E, Walker E C T (eds.) *Sentence Processing: Psycholinguistic Studies Presented to Merrill Garrett.* Erlbaum, Hillsdale, NJ
Shattuck-Hufnagel S 1992 The role of word structure in segmental serial ordering. *Cognition* 42: 213–59
Stemberger J 1985 An interactive activation model of language production. In: Ellis A (ed.) *Progress in the Psychology of Language,* vol. 1. Erlbaum, London
Stemberger J, Treiman R 1986 The internal structure of word-initial consonant clusters. *Journal of Memory and Language* 25: 163–80
Treiman R 1984 On the status of final consonant clusters in English syllables. *Journal of Verbal Learning and Verbal Behavior* 23: 343–56

S. Shattuck-Hufnagel

Slovak

Slovak is a Slavic language, spoken by five million people in Slovakia. About a million Slovaks live outside Slovakia, mainly in USA, Canada, and Hungary, and many continue to use their native language.

1. History

The first attestations of Slovak are place names and personal names in local Latin documents dating from the eleventh century. In the fourteenth century, Czech started to be used as the literary language in Slovakia, but its adaptation to the Slovak environment led to the appearance of discernible Slovak morphological and phonological features. The first attempt at introducing Slovak as a written language by the Catholics in western Slovakia in the seventeenth and eighteenth centuries was unsuccessful. A uniform Standard Slovak was established in the middle of the nineteenth century. In 1918, after the formation of Czechoslovakia, it became the official language of Slovakia; until then, Hungarian had been the only official language.

2. Writing

Slovak is written with the Latin alphabet. There are three digraphs ch [x], dz [dz], dž [dʒ]. Palatal consonants are written with diacritic marks (č, dž, š, ž, t', d', n', l'). However, when *t, d, n, l* are followed by *i, í* and *e,* they are pronounced as palatal, without indication in spelling: [ɟeci] 'children,' spelled *deti.* The acute accents represent length.

3. The Place of Slovak within the Slavic Language Group

Slovak belongs to the western Slavic language group, together with Czech, Polish, Kashubian, Lower and Upper

Sorbian, and extinct Polabian. Czech and Slovak are more similar and closer to each other than any other pair of Slavic languages. They are mutually intelligible and share about 90 percent of their vocabulary. The phonological and morphological system of Standard Slovak, based on the central Slovak dialect, differs from the western and eastern Slovak dialects and from Czech by the presence of certain features which unite it with the southern Slavonic languages: e.g., (a) reflexes *raT-*, *laT-* of Common Slavonic **orT-*, **olT-*, cf. Slovak *rastiem* 'I grow,' Serbo–Croat *rastem*, but Czech *rostu*; (b) result of the so-called Second Palatalization: /x/ > /s/, instead of /š/, NOM SG *mucha*, DAT LOC SG *muse*, but Czech *mouše*; (c) simplification of clusters *-tl-*, *-dl-*, cf. Slovak *salo* 'fat,' but Czech *sádlo*. The origin of these 'yugoslavisms' is still a matter of dispute.

4. Phonology

The consonantal system is characterized by the voice/voiceless opposition, the palatal/nonpalatal opposition is limited to four pairs only. Standard Slovak has six short vowels /i/, /e/, /æ/ (spelled *ä*), /a/, /o/, /u/, five long vowels /iː/, /eː/, /aː/, /oː/ (only in loanwords), /uː/, and four diphthongs /ia/, /ie/, /iu/, /uo/ (represented as *ô*). There is also a syllabic /r̩/ and /l̩/ short and long, e.g., *zrno* 'grain,' GEN PL *zŕn*.

A peculiar feature of the central Slovak dialect is so-called 'rhythmic law,' a rule according to which, within the boundaries of a word, two historically long syllables cannot follow one another, therefore the vowel in the second syllable (often a suffix) is shortened, e.g., *dáva* 'he gives' but in the western Slovak dialect and Czech *dává*. The diphthongs function as long vowels. The stress is relatively weak and fixed on the first syllable. Monosyllabic prepositions form a single unit with the following word and carry the stress, e.g., *pod stôl* ['potstṷol] 'under the table.' Monosyllabic personal pronouns and some forms of the verb *byt'* 'to be' are enclitics.

5. Morphology and Syntax

Slovak morphology is similar to Czech; however, it is less archaic, more modified by paradigmatic leveling and the generalization of endings. There are six cases: nominative, accusative, genitive, dative, locative, and instrumental (the vocative survives in few masculine nouns only); singular and plural numbers, and three genders with the subcategory of animacy in the masculine nouns. The adjectival declensions differ from the nominal declensions. The occurrence of long vowels, characteristic of the adjectival declension, is constrained by the rhythmic rule.

The verbal system of Slovak is very similar to the verbal system of Czech. The main difference is the generalization of the 1 SG PRES IND ending *-m* in all verbal classes, e.g., *píšem* 'I write,' but Czech *píši* or *píšu*. The basic pattern is SVO. However, as in all Slavic languages, the word order is flexible.

Bibliography

Bray R G A de 1980 *Guide to the West Slavonic Languages*. Slavica Publishers, Columbus, OH

Krajčovič R 1975 *A Historical Phonology of the Slovak Language*. Carl Winter Universitätsverlag, Heidelberg

Mistrík J 1988 *A Grammar of Contemporary Slovak*. Slovenské pedagogické nakladateľstvo, Bratislava

Mistrík J 1989 *Basic Slovak*. Slovenské pedagogické nakladateľstvo, Bratislava

Short D 1990 Czech and Slovak. In: Comrie B (ed.) *The World's Major Languages of Eastern Europe*. Routledge, London

V. Čapková

Slovak Republic

SEE Czech Republic and Slovak Republic: Language Situation

Slovene

The official language of Slovenia, Slovene (or Slovenian, as it is also known) is spoken by about 2,000,000 people in Slovenia and adjacent regions of Italy, Austria, and Hungary, and by another 400,000 emigrés, especially in the USA, Canada, Australia, and Argentina. It is a South Slavic language (see *Slavic Languages*), most closely related to Serbo–Croatian Kajkavic dialects (see *Serbo-Croat*); northern Slovene dialects show transitional features to West Slavic. The earliest Slovene settlements were in the sixth century AD. Since the early Middle Ages these lands have been controlled by speakers of German, Italian, and Hungarian; a control which restricted the use of Slovene to localized varieties, which were often isolated and developed idiosyncratically. There are few extant Slovene texts from before the Reformation; the earliest is the *Freising Fragments* (ca. 1000 AD). In the sixteenth century a written form of Slovene was developed by Protestant writers and some 50 books were printed in that language. The Counter-Reformation decelerated the expansion and codification of the standard language, but this was developed and finally adopted by the Slovene intelligentsia in the nineteenth century.

The writing system is Latin-based, with diacritics for showing consonantal and (to avoid ambiguity only) vocalic distinctions. Slovene is the only Standard Slavic language with eight distinct stressed vowels, /i e ɛ a ə ɔ o u/, and with neither palatalized nor (other than /j/) palatal consonants. Two prosodic systems are sanctioned, one with distinctive pitch, the other without. Morphologically, all the Common Slavic categories are well represented: unusually for Slavic, the dual number is maintained (in both nominal and verbal systems); there is little case syncretism; and the vocative is lost. Verbally, both supine and infinitive are still used. Unusual syntactic features include a highly constrained system of clitics and the so-called 'orphan accusative': masculine/neuter adjectives, when used pronominally as direct objects, occur with what is historically the genitive ending. Sample (here, in the prosodic system without distinctive pitch): *V mesto greva kupovat božična darila. Kateri avto bova vzela?—Zelenega, če ga želita.* /'wmestɔ 'greva kupɔ'vat bɔ'ʒitʃna da'rila ka'teri 'awtɔ 'bova 'wzela zɛ'lɛnɛga tʃɛ ga ʒɛ'lita/

V	mesto	greva	kupovat	božična	darila.
Into	town	we-2-go	to-buy	Christmas	presents.

Kateri	avto	bova	vzela?
Which	car	we-2-shall	take?

Zelenega, če ga želita.
Green,   if it you-2-want.

'We (two) are going to town to buy Christmas presents. Which car shall we take?'—'The green one, if you (two) want it.' Here, *greva, bova vzela* are 1st dual and *želita* is 2nd dual: precisely two persons are implied. *Kupovat* is the supine (cf. infinitive *kupovati*); pronominal *zelenega* has the originally genitive ending (cf. accusative *zeleni* in the attributive adjectival form); and *ga* is the unstressed proclitic for 'it.'

The relatively small area of the Slovene lands and small number of Slovene speakers are characterized by a heterogeneity of dialects that is unique in Slavic; there is some lack of mutual comprehension. Slovene-speakers in adjoining areas of Italy, Austria, and Hungary have faced considerable assimilatory pressure from the respective majorities in these areas, especially during the 1920–45 period; in some jurisdictions, this pressure still obtains in the 1990s. Within Slovenia, 70 years' political coexistence with speakers of Serbo–Croatian effected some (but limited) linguistic influence.

Bibliography

Comrie B, Corbett G 1993 *The Slavonic Languages*. Routledge, London

T. Priestly

Slovenia: Language Situation

Following the breakup of Yugoslavia in 1992, Slovenia became a separate independent republic. At the time of writing there is some confusion about future political boundaries in the region formerly covered by Yugoslavia, and movements of refugees make precise statements about languages spoken in a given area difficult. Within the boundaries of Slovenia as they stood at the beginning of the period of unrest, 90 percent of the population speak the South Slavonic language Slovene.

See also: Slovene; Yugoslavia.

Small Group Research

At the dawn of human history, before agriculture had made large societies possible, every human being lived within a small group of people that hunted and gathered together, sharing all aspects of their lives. Citizens of modern societies tend to belong to several small groups simultaneously, of different kinds and with different memberships, most making only slight demands upon the individuals who comprise them. The characteristic of small groups most important for the study of language is 'solidarity,' the extent to which the individuals who belong are bound tightly together into a social unit, and modern groups tend to be much lower in solidarity than the prehistoric hunting band. Stephen Wilson identified six dimensions of solidarity that together provide a useful rubric for considering linguistic aspects of small groups: interaction, norms, status structure, goals, cohesiveness, and awareness of membership.

1. Interaction

'Interaction' is defined as the process of mutual communication between individuals, often leading to interdependence between them. Among sociologists, there is some disagreement about the way that interaction creates a social bond. Members of the school of thought called 'symbolic interactionism' (see *Symbolic Interactionism*) believe that humans have a natural hunger for language-encoded meaning, and that this alone is sufficient to explain why individuals who have communicated extensively with each other will tend to orient themselves toward each other's perceptions and desires. Scholars in the 'exchange theory' (see *Exchange Theory*) tradition consider the words exchanged between people less important than the rewards, and they hold that a person becomes bonded to another as a result of the valuable things (including verbally communicated information as well as material goods) that have been received. Certainly, individuals who do not interact cannot be said to be members of the same small group.

'Interaction process analysis' (see *Interaction Process Analysis*), devised by Robert F. Bales in the late 1940s, is one of a number of techniques for studying interaction rates and patterns in small groups, employing highly trained observers who identify the smallest atoms of communication, 'unit acts,' and assign them to one of a set of 12 categories (Hare 1976). The simplest of the many other such techniques is that developed by Eliot D. Chapple around 1940, who divided all interaction into just two categories, action and silence. Using a device called the 'interaction chronograph' to help with the timing and data recording, Chapple would observe two-person interactions, focusing on when each person spoke.

Bales's system of categories inspired other researchers to invent their own schemes for identifying types of communication, based either on theories or on statistical analysis of data. Timothy Leary proposed a set of 16 psychological mechanisms that could be seen in interaction, including narcissistic reflexes (boast, act proud, narcissistically exhibitionistic) and docile reflexes (act in an over-respecting manner, docilely conform). Richard D. Mann's system of 16 categories was designed to analyze 'communicative acts,' defined as single speeches or bursts of sentences within which the expressed feelings are uniform, directed by a member of the group to its leader. Three of these are in the area of authority relations: showing dependency, showing independence, and showing counterdependency.

A vast body of research has been done with these social–psychological schemes for categorizing communicative acts, much employing Bales's system or adaptations of it. One can focus either on the kinds of unit acts the group primarily produces, for example, expressing solidarity versus hostility, or on the distribution of unit acts across the individual members. Then one can study such things as the way in which a group accomplishes a set task, the balance between task accomplishment and emotional gratification, the emergence of leadership, and the processes that establish norms.

2. Norms

'Norms' are authoritative standards of behavior, principles of right action binding upon the members of a group, including rules governing proper speech. As defined by

George Homans (1950: 123), a norm 'is an idea in the minds of the members of a group, an idea that can be put in the form of a statement specifying what the members or other men should do, ought to do, are expected to do, under given circumstances.' The fact that a norm can be expressed as a statement does not mean that norms are learned primarily as statements communicated verbally, nor that they are encoded in memory as strings of words. In exchange theory, norms are learned through experiencing contingencies of reward and punishment, a process that can take place without use of language, as it does among pigeons and mice in psychological experiments. The extent to which all human norms are linguistic phenomena, not those concerning speech alone, remains an open question deserving scientific attention.

Some norms are very general, established by the society as a whole to cover a wide range of circumstances. An example is the biblical commandment, 'Thou shalt not take the name of the Lord thy God in vain.' Others are very specific, belonging to only a small group of people and concerning a limited range of circumstances. As reported by Homans, a particular group of nine factory workers attaching wires to telephone switching equipment had established a norm to call a man who made more than 825 connections an hour a 'rate-buster,' and someone who made less than 825, a 'chiseler.'

2.1 Norm Standardization

Among the most enduring themes of small group research is the way an individual's behavior changes as the result of belonging to a group, which can be conceptualized as the emergence and acceptance of norms. In the 1920s, Floyd Allport did many experiments on how people performed language-related tasks, to study 'social facilitation,' an increase in performance caused by the mere presence of other people. For example, research subjects were given a piece of paper with a single word written at the top and were asked to write as many disconnected words below it as they could in the time allotted. Most of them wrote more words while working in the presence of others, but they were judged to write words of a more personal nature while alone.

In another of Allport's experiments, subjects were given either mechanical tasks (such as crossing out vowels in newspaper stories), problem-solving tasks (writing statements disproving didactic passages from ancient philosophers), and judgment tasks (such as judging the relative pleasantness of a series of odors). For part of the time they did these jobs alone, and the rest of the time they were working in the presence of other research subjects. Interestingly, results depended upon the nature of the task. Subjects crossed out vowels more rapidly when working with others than when alone, and they wrote longer arguments in the group situation. However, arguments written while alone were deemed to be of higher quality. Judgments of the pleasantness of odors were less extreme when made in a group than when alone.

The most famous experiment in this tradition was done in the 1950s by Solomon Asch. Each research subject was placed in a group of six people, unaware that the other five were confederates of the experimenter. They were shown a series of cards, each with lines drawn on it, and asked to say which of three lines was the same length as a fourth. As the session progressed the confederates began unanimously giving the wrong answer, and the real research subjects, whose turn came last, were left in the quandary whether to accede to the judgment of the majority or to disagree. Much of the time, they expressed agreement with the confederates, but interviews with the subjects revealed that they often harbored private disagreements but conformed in what they said because they wanted to avoid appearing different from the rest of the group.

When participation in a group tends to reduce the extremes of individual speech or action, processes of standardization are at work. Homans noted that individuals who interact frequently tend to become similar to each other in their behavior and attitudes. Among the examples he offered, linking speech and action, was research done in a special test room at the Western Electric Company, where women were rapidly assembling electrical relays. The work required such concentration that the women could converse with only their nearest neighbors. Analysis of output rates showed that women working next to each other had unconsciously learned to work at almost identical rates. In this case, conversation had unintentionally standardized work patterns, but frequent interaction also has the power to standardize speech itself.

In the early 1960s, social psychology experimenters reported a phenomenon they called the 'risky shift,' in which research subjects accepted greater risks when they were making decisions in groups than when they were deciding alone. Later research found that some decisions were made more cautiously by groups than by individuals. This led to the realization that a group's norms are not simply the average or sum of the wishes of the individuals who constitute the group. Under a variety of circumstances, extreme norms of one kind or another may emerge from the complex web of social interaction in groups of high solidarity.

When a group of people who work closely together is under great stress, extreme pressures toward uniformity of opinion may arise. Irving Janis has called this 'groupthink' and argued that it often leads to very bad decisions. Members limit their discussion to but a few of the many alternatives open to them, fail to admit disadvantages of the course they have chosen or advantages of courses they have not initially considered, and avoid obtaining information that might provide a more realistic basis for evaluation. They show great interest in facts and opinions that appear to support their plans, and they ignore contrary data. They fail to deliberate possible barriers to success and are unprepared to deal with them when they arise. Individuals within the group who disagree are either excluded from the discussion or voluntarily suppress their own reservations. Among the examples of groupthink analyzed by Janis are the discussions in the advisory cabinets of American presidents Kennedy and Johnson that led to an abortive invasion of Cuba and to costly prolongation of the Vietnam War.

2.2 Communication Norms

Susan Shimanoff has suggested that there are seven types of communication rules established by small groups, each specifying desired behavior for one part of the following: (a) who says, (b) what, (c) to whom, (d) when, (e) with what duration and frequency, (f) through what medium, (g) by what decision-procedure. Formally constituted committees often have elaborate rules concerning who is 'speaker' or who 'has the floor,' but almost all groups possess habits and expectations about who will speak under a specified set of circumstances. Other norms define the limits of what shall be spoken about, for example, whether obscenities are prohibited or encouraged. In a weight-control group, Overeaters Anonymous, members may talk about food in generic terms ('refined carbohydrates,' 'junk food') but are enjoined from naming particular foods ('pizza,' 'twinkies'). The person to whom an utterance is usually addressed may be the designated leader, someone who has been temporarily recognized as having the floor, an individual member with a personal interest in the topic, or the membership as a whole. Groups differ in their preferences for each of these alternatives.

Some group norms concern who speaks when and what is said when. Groups may even differ in how they talk about these timing norms. Legend has it that a joint British–American committee of the military high command in World War II fell into deadlock because their dialects of English had opposite meanings for the term to *table* a topic. For the British, *table* meant to place a topic on the agenda, while for the Americans it meant to remove it from consideration indefinitely. Groups vary in the standards they set for duration and frequency of speech. Many legislatures follow elaborate procedures for allocating debating time, and even highly informal groups discourage individuals from 'hogging the floor' or 'talking out of turn.'

Although talking is the typical medium of communication in small groups, many in business and government also employ memos or even lengthy documents, perhaps to lay the basis for oral discussion or to provide a record of positions taken and decisions made. Norms concerning the proper medium may punish persons who write their messages in an oral group, or persons who fail to write when they are expected to. Norms concerning decision-procedures are the political culture of the group, specifying whether a vote should be taken and how, informally conferring decision power on a few individuals, or requiring consensus of the entire group. Decision-procedure rules may exist to modify the six other types of communication rules, for example, requiring a two-thirds vote to end a filibuster. While it is easiest to illustrate communication norms with examples from deliberative bodies that possess written rules, presumably every small group with some measure of solidarity possesses all seven kinds.

3. Status Structure

The word 'status' is often used to refer to a rank in a hierarchy, but in sociology it has a more general meaning, referring to any position in a social structure which defines a set of expectations for a person occupying it. In the USA the status of Supreme Court Judge is different from that of Senator, because they play very different roles in writing and interpreting legislation and they gain their positions through very different social processes, but the two may be of equal rank. Each status has certain rights and obligations, and satisfying the obligations attendant on a particular status is equivalent to playing the social role associated with it (see *Role Theory*). Informal small groups often lack

explicit statuses, but as a group grows, a set of statuses tends to crystalize out while power differentials and division of labor become institutionalized. In modern bureaucracies, a formal structure of statuses is often outlined in an organizational chart and spelled out in detailed documents. But even in casual groups lacking any written records, members can usually say who occupies the leadership positions.

Among the most active fields for research on leadership in small groups is 'administrative science,' the study of effective and efficient management of businesses and other formal organizations. Like many other applied fields which lack clear criteria for evaluating the truth of ideas, administrative science is highly susceptible to fads, and many of its most popular notions about language and communication are based on rather shaky scientific foundations. One of the hottest continuing debates is the degree to which managers should share information and decision-making responsibilities with subordinates.

In 1960, Douglas McGregor distinguished two management philosophies he called 'theory X' and 'theory Y.' Theory X managers believe people are not to be trusted, so they keep close watch on their subordinates, avoid sharing responsibility and information with them, and are traditional authoritarian bosses. This means they tend to give detailed and complete instructions to their subordinates, setting explicit standards for performance in achieving the management-defined goals which they monitor with formal statistics. Theory Y managers, in contrast, believe their underlings can generally be trusted with responsibility, so they share more information and create a work environment in which people can best meet their own personal goals by working hard for the goals of the organization. Thus they give only general instructions, depending upon the subordinates to work out details, employing group discussion and informal verbal feedback to maintain work momentum.

Clearly, these are two competing quasipolitical ideologies—authoritarianism versus egalitarianism—and McGregor was probably asserting his own values rather than reporting scientific findings when he claimed that theory Y was more effective. In recent years, this belief has resurfaced many times with many labels (Tubbs 1988). David Bradford and Allan R. Cohen urge managers to be 'developers,' that is, to assist their subordinates in growing as human beings and to give them considerable freedom to solve problems in their own way. Among the paradoxes of the developer approach is the belief that managers increase their own power by giving subordinates greater powers.

Theory X is comparable to Machiavellianism, the philosophy of Niccolò Machiavelli, and some researchers have used a Machiavellianism scale developed by Richard Christie to measure this untrusting style of management. Among the scale's items are several maxims concerning speech: 'Never tell anyone the real reason you did something unless it is useful to do so.' 'It is wise to flatter important people.' Machiavellians are expected to agree with these two statements, and to disagree with the proposition, 'There is no excuse for lying to someone else.' The theory X manager may not be a liar, but he does not expect other people to do what they say, and he monitors their actual behavior closely rather than trusting their words.

In contrast to these one-sided analyses, 'contingency

theories' note that different styles of leadership are effective under different conditions. Paul Hersey and Kenneth Blanchard stress the importance of the degree of maturity of the followers in determining which of four kinds of management is appropriate: telling, selling, participating, and delegating. People who are both unable and unwilling to take responsibility must simply be *told* what to do. Subordinates of slightly greater maturity must be *sold*; they still need directive management but will be more fully committed to the task if they can be convinced to 'buy into' desired behaviors by the explanations of their boss. A nondirective 'participating' style will help motivate persons of moderate to high maturity, through effective two-way communication with the leader. Finally, tasks can simply be 'delegated' to fully mature subordinates who can be trusted to accomplish them without much direction, explanation, or two-way communication with the manager. This analytic scheme expands the two categories of McGregor's analysis into four, and avoids the unwarranted assumption that one is best under all conditions.

John Kotter, Leonard Schlesinger, and Vijay Sathe note that management occasionally need to change the organization they direct in a significant way, and that several tactics may be used to overcome employees' resistance, depending upon a variety of factors. When speed is essential and the managers possess considerable power, the right tactic may be coercion, but this can leave a residue of anger. Education/communication may be the right approach when resistance to change is based on lack of correct information, and once persuaded, people may actively help implementation of the change; however, this tactic is typically quite slow. Negotiation is best in situations where one group is bound to lose as a result of the change, and where they have power to resist. Tactical schemes like this are Machiavellianism of a higher order, because communication rules are treated as contingent upon the manager's analysis of the most effective way to control subordinates, not determined by invariant norms. Honesty is treated as only one of a number of good policies, the best only under certain circumstances.

4. Goals

In many cases, a group is a set of people with a common goal, but other groups may never have defined a goal, and the members of many groups may have personal goals that conflict with those of other members. Goals vary from the most specific, to the most general, what are often called values (see *Values*). High-solidarity groups tend to have many defined goals rather than just a few, a consensus on what the goals are rather than a disagreement, cooperative rather than competitive goals, and motives oriented toward their group rather than each member being concerned only with himself or herself. Many groups define their goals at the moment they come into being, for example, business and special interest clubs, but others experience a sometimes lengthy process of searching for goals.

Albert K. Cohen has analyzed the way 'mutual conversion' can create a group and give it distinctive goals, if a number of individuals with similar problems of social adjustment come into communication with one another. This takes place in tiny, even imperceptible steps, as one individual expresses a hope or plan and receives positive feedback in the form of similar hopes and plans from the others. Cohen believed that all human action is an ongoing series of efforts to solve problems, but he focused on the specific frustrations of lower-class adolescent boys who experienced repeated failures to meet the standards of middle-class culture, especially in school where particular kinds of verbal facility are demanded. Unable initially to express their frustrations to each other, these boys will congregate in groups and begin to share various escapades in which they explore alternative, even deviant patterns of behavior. Together, they gradually redefine conventional standards as bad and erect a new set of standards which they can successfully meet. The result is a delinquent gang (see *Subcultures and Countercultures*). Mutual conversion can occur with many other kinds of group, and Cohen's analysis sensitively describes how tentatively the parties may grope their way to a consensus.

Similarly, Richard Cloward and Lloyd Ohlin argued that youth whose attempts to achieve the goals valued by society have been thwarted may collect into delinquent gangs that seek these or other goals by deviant means. If theft or vice can provide the money and status desired by these adolescents, they will create a 'criminal' gang. But for many of them, success will be as hard to attain through crime as it was through attending school, and they will be forced to set new goals, such as violent defense of their city block against other gangs, and they will become a 'conflict' gang. If beaten in this attempt, or if the members of the adolescent group lack the strength and skill for fighting, they will become a 'retreatist' gang, descending into drug addiction or losing a sense of personal and collective goals altogether.

George Homans explained that groups exist as a means by which members can cooperatively extract resources from the environment and defend against threats. In meeting these goals, the members develop what Homans called the 'external system,' a set of social relations that allows the group to survive in its environment. As members interact, however, they come to value each other not merely as means for coping with the environment, but for their own sakes and for the social and emotional rewards they can provide each other. Thus arises the 'internal system' of the group, social relations not primarily conditioned by the external environment, often purely verbal in nature, such as pleasant conversation and joking. While the internal system can take on a life of its own, it will eventually die if the external system fails to achieve its goals.

Parallel to the different goals that groups may have are the various goals researchers pursue in studying them. Sociologists by the score have examined delinquent gangs, both because deviant behavior provides a certain journalistic excitement and because the conventional society feels gangs are a serious problem. Those who have studied psychotherapy groups typically had the goal of evaluating or promoting the particular brand of therapy, and research in business and industry sought information about how to increase profitability. The artificial groups created in social psychology laboratories contributed to the development and testing of often rather narrow theories about group dynamics.

5. Cohesiveness

'Cohesiveness' is sometimes defined as the degree to which members are attracted to their group, but a definition that has been especially productive for research is the degree to which members are tied to each other by social bonds. Sociometry (see *Sociometry*) is a set of methods for measuring the social bonds within a group, whether by simply asking each individual which others he or she especially likes or by observing which persons tend to interact most with each other. If a group is high in solidarity, its members will be connected by strong social bonds, and many researchers have used cohesiveness as a synonym for solidarity.

One language-related field of research that has made especially good use of analysis in terms of social bonds is the sociology of religion (Stark and Bainbridge 1985). A popular slogan holds that 'the family that prays together stays together,' and many studies have shown that religious belief and practice are powerfully connected to the strength and structure of social relationships. Kevin Welch assessed the role of interpersonal bonds in sustaining commitment to orthodox beliefs among members of mainline denominations in the United States, finding strong positive correlations between various measures of orthodoxy and the proportion of one's best friends who are members of one's own religious congregation. Also, the greater the number of nonchurch organizations and clubs the person belonged to, the lower his or her orthodoxy.

Members of highly cohesive religious groups are more likely than others to proselytize, to pray, and to profess their faith with confidence. Rodney Stark examined the effects social context had on religious experiences, moments when the individual believed he or she had a personal encounter with the supernatural, finding that people who had such experiences were highly concentrated among those whose closest friends were members of the same religious group. Thus, conversations with God are facilitated by communication with fellow believers; or, unusual psychological states are more likely to be defined as religious in nature if the person belongs to a cohesive group that wants to interpret them that way. But it is also true that religious groups that provide many shared spiritual experiences, whether formal rituals or informal gatherings, tend thereby to create a sense of communion and thus cohesiveness between members.

Among the best explanations of conversion to small, radical religious groups—'sects' and 'cults'—is the process of recruitment through social bonds. The model that has received the most attention was proposed by John Lofland and Rodney Stark, and it has guided many subsequent research studies. Combining social bond analysis with other factors, it has seven steps:

(a) The person must suffer enduring, acutely-felt tensions which derive from a discrepancy between the person's current life conditions and those he deeply desires.

(b) The person possesses a religious problem-solving perspective, a way of understanding life events that defines their causes in supernatural terms.

(c) Dissatisfied with the help received from a current religious group, the person defines himself as a religious seeker on a quest for a new religious group.

(d) The person encounters the sect or cult at a turning point, which may combine a period of weak social attachments with the termination of old lines of action, as may come with divorce, school graduation, or a new job.

(e) A strong emotional social bond develops with members of the radical religious group.

(f) Emotional social bonds with nonmembers are lost, weakened, or neutralized by being defined as irrelevant to the person's needs at the moment.

(g) Intensive interaction with members of the group inculcates its beliefs and turns the person into a committed member ready to recruit others to the new faith.

This analysis places great emphasis on social interaction with members of the group. An alternative theory, which has been used to explain conversion to various political creeds as well as religious faiths, postulates that converts are emotionally vulnerable to ideological appeals, because they suffer intense personal deprivations, causing unendurable frustration. The person will then encounter an ideology that explains this suffering in ways flattering to the sufferer and offers an apparent solution to the person's problems. The Lofland–Stark theory incorporates these ideas, but argues that they are not enough, and subsequent research has supported this assertion. Apparently it is not sufficient to hear 'the word.' Rather, one must develop social bonds with current believers who draw one into a small, like-minded group, and only then does one listen receptively to the word and eventually accept it. In general, membership in a group precedes acceptance of its beliefs and practices.

6. Awareness of Membership

Charles Horton Cooley wrote on *primary groups*, those characterized by intimate face-to-face association, and said membership in one 'involves the sort of sympathy and mutual identification for which *we* is the natural expression.' The 'sense of we-ness' or 'we-feeling,' as it has been called by sociologists, is a variable that is strong in some small groups but weak in others, measurable in part by members' use of the first person plural in talking about it. Another marker of significant we-feeling is the possession of a name for the group.

Names, of course, tell us much about the image members have of their own group and how they want outsiders to regard them. 'Hell's Angels' must be both terrifying and important. Members of the 'Cornbelt Lapidary and Geological Society' profess a rather specialized set of harmless interests and live in an informally defined region notable for growing corn. Churches that call themselves 'Christian Science,' 'Divine Science,' or 'Religious Science' are apparently modern creations that seek some of the prestige that science has had in recent years.

Rodney Stark studied the names adopted by novel American religious cults in different periods, finding that the proportion with innocuous, Christian-sounding names was nearly twice as high early in the century as it was after 1950. Among some of the older names that apparently provided camouflage to protect the cults from public outrage were Universal Christ Church, Liberal Catholic Church, and Congregational Church of Practical Theology, actually deviant cults in the spiritualist, theosophical, and psychic traditions, respectively. More recently, cults have been happy to be known publicly by names such as

Enchanted Moon Coven or Church of Satanic Brotherhood, a sign that society is far more tolerant of religious deviance than formerly.

As Stephen Wilson explains, many social psychologists have equated awareness of membership in a group with morale, but morale has proven very difficult to measure. If one simply asks people whether they belong to a highly prestigious group, many will profess membership who do not seem really to belong. A group toward which people orient their action and which sets standards for their behavior, even if they are not in all the senses discussed here members of the group, is a 'reference group.' Actual membership in a small group involves all six of the dimensions of solidarity, not awareness alone. Calling oneself a member is not enough.

The research on small groups is vast; A. Paul Hare's 1976 bibliography lists fully 6,037 publications, but he ignores most of those done by sociologists and others on natural groups in the field, concentrating instead on laboratory experimental studies. A considerable fraction of this scholarship concerns language, but few of the authors have an awareness of membership in the profession of linguistics. Nonetheless, students of language would have much to learn from examination of small group research; many of these studies should be renamed linguistic, and small group researchers would benefit from realization of the contributions that linguistics could make to their work.

See also: Social Psychology; Sociology in Language.

Bibliography

Blumberg H H, Hare A P, Kent V, Davies M F (eds.) 1983 *Small Groups and Social Interaction*. Wiley, New York
Cartwright D, Zander A (eds.) 1968 *Group Dynamics: Research and Theory*. Harper and Row, New York
Christie R, Geis F L 1970 *Studies in Machiavellianism*. Academic Press, New York
Cloward R A, Ohlin L E 1960 *Delinquency and Opportunity*. Free Press, New York
Cohen A K 1955 *Delinquent Boys*. Free Press, New York
Hare A P 1976 *Handbook of Small Group Research*. Free Press, New York
Homans G C 1950 *The Human Group*. Harcourt Brace, New York
McGregor D 1960 *The Human Side of Enterprise*. McGraw-Hill, New York
Shaw M E 1981 *Group Dynamics: The Psychology of Small Group Behavior*. McGraw-Hill, New York
Shimanoff S B 1984 Coordinating group interaction via communication rules. In: Cathcart R S, Samovar L A (eds) *Small Group Communication: A reader*. William C. Brown, Dubuque, IA
Stark R, Bainbridge W S 1985 *The Future of Religion*. University of California Press, Berkeley, CA
Tubbs S L 1988 *A Systems Approach to Small Group Interaction*. Random House, New York
Wilson S 1978 *Informal Groups: An Introduction*. Prentice-Hall, Englewood Cliffs, NJ

W. S. Bainbridge

Smith, Adam (1723–90)

Adam Smith, best known as a political economist, wrote an important essay on the formation of languages. He speculated upon different principles of linguistic structures and suggested an order of genetic priority among them.

Smith was born at Kirkcaldy, Scotland, in 1723. He studied at Glasgow and then (1740–47) at Oxford. He became (1751) professor, first of logic and later of moral philosophy, at Glasgow. His *Theory of Moral Sentiments* (1759), based upon the concept of sympathy, established his reputation. He subsequently resigned his professorship and spent some years (up to 1766) as tutor to the Duke of Buccleuch. He then returned to Kirkcaldy and passed ten years writing his *Inquiry into the Nature and Causes of the Wealth of Nations* (1776). For this pioneering study he soon became famous. He spent some time in London, where he was elected to both Samuel Johnson's club and the Royal Society. He was appointed (1778) a commissioner of customs for Scotland and returned to Edinburgh, where he died in 1790.

Smith's interest in language probably began while he was at Oxford. Student notes on his lectures from 1762–63 show that he was then addressing the question of the origin of language. His published work in the field of linguistics is largely confined to one relatively short essay, the *Considerations concerning the First Formation of Languages*. This appeared first in the *Philological Miscellany* (1761) and again as an appendix to the third (1767) edition of the *Theory of Moral Sentiments*.

Smith's concern is with the evolution of linguistic types once the process of language development had begun. He therefore makes a number of assumptions about our perception of reality and initial linguistic operations. Man, Smith assumes, originally perceives reality as made up of objects and events, and has the ability to bestow names upon what he perceives. Upon this basis Smith offers an evolutionary account of how, within a framework of developing mental powers, increasingly complex linguistic structures might have been achieved. In so doing he remains very much within the terminological boundaries of traditional grammar, in effect producing an outline of the evolution of the various parts of speech from the primal name.

The first words, he says, would have been 'denotations' of particulars (i.e., proper names). By subsequent operations of 'generalization' and 'comparison,' mental classification of particulars would be achieved and common nouns introduced as names for classes of objects. The classification of objects entails perception of differences of quality and relation among them, and inflection of nominal roots might be used to reflect some of these differences. At a later stage, as man developed increasing powers of 'abstraction,' adjectives and prepositions would be invented for this purpose. In a very similar way Smith then explains how verbs and verb phrases might have evolved from names originally bestowed upon events. The earliest verbs would have been 'impersonal,' but gradually verb stems conjugated to express differences of agent, number, tense, and mood would have evolved. More 'abstract' forms, using pronouns and auxiliaries, would have developed, Smith suggests, with tribal movements as nonnative speakers took over and simplified the original complex structures.

Smith's essay distinguishes between two linguistic types, that which relies upon inflection of stems, and that which employs instead a wide range of adjectives, prepositions, adverbs, pronouns, and auxiliaries. Smith distinguishes between these types, which later writers labeled 'synthetic' and 'analytic' respectively, in terms of the degree of mental 'abstraction' required for their employment. The synthetic type, he thinks, must have been the earlier. He offers a 'maxim' that 'the more simple any language is in its composition [i.e., its use of diverse parts of speech], the more complex it must be in its declensions and conjugations,' and vice versa. He concludes with an aesthetic evaluation of the two types, preferring the synthetic on stylistic grounds.

Smith was one of a number of writers thinking along these lines in the mid-eighteenth century. He cites Rousseau and almost certainly owes something to Condillac. By the 1790s the ideas he discusses had become commonplace, and although few writers refer explicitly to his essay it was widely known.

See also: Condillac, Etienne Bonnot de; Rousseau, Jean-Jacques; Origin of Language Debate.

Bibliography

Berry C J 1974 Adam Smith's *Considerations* on language. *Journal of the History of Ideas* 35: 130–38

Coseriu E 1968 Adam Smith und die Anfänge der Sprachtypologie. In: *Wortbildung, Syntax und Morphologie: Festschrift zum 60. Geburtstag von Hans Marchand*. Mouton, The Hague

Land S K 1986 *The Philosophy of Language in Britain*. AMS Press, New York

Lightwood M B 1984 *A Selected Bibliography of Significant Works about Adam Smith*. University of Pennsylvania Press, Philadelphia, PA

Smith A 1980 *The Glasgow Edition of the Works and Correspondence of Adam Smith*. Clarendon Press, Oxford

S. K. Land

Smith, Henry Lee (1913–72)

Henry Lee Smith, Jr ('Haxie' to his colleagues, friends, and family), linguist, educator, and US State Department Foreign Service officer, was born on July 11, 1913, in Morristown, NJ, son of Henry Lee Smith and Elise Garr Henry. He was educated at Gilman Country School, Baltimore, MD, then at Princeton University, from where he graduated BA *summa cum laude* Phi Beta Kappa in 1935, MA in 1937, and PhD in Oriental languages and literature in 1938. He was a Charlotte Elizabeth Procter fellow in 1937–38. He was awarded an honorary LittD degree from Wagner College (Staten Island, New York) in 1961 and a postdoctoral fellowship in linguistics by the University of Edinburgh, UK, during his last sabbatical leave in 1970.

Smith was a major in the US Army from 1942–46, and was the officer in charge of the language section of the Information and Education Division, Army Service Forces. Cofounder of the Foreign Service Institute School of Language and Linguistics (1946–56) and of the FSI School of Languages, he was the first director (1946–56) and dean (1955–56) of the School. Previously, he had been a lecturer in English at Barnard College, Columbia University (1938–40) and an instructor of English at Brown University (1940–42). He was the chairman and cofounder (in 1956, with George L. Trager; see *Trager, George L.*) of the Department of Anthropology and Linguistics at the University of Buffalo (later State University of New York at Buffalo), chairman of the Department of Anthropology

(1964–65), and director of the Program in Linguistics (1967–68), but resigned that post to resume his research and teaching as Professor of Linguistics and English, an appointment which he had held since coming to the university in 1956. He died very suddenly on December 13, 1972, survived by his wife, Virginia von Wodtke Smith (deceased October 26, 1987) and four children: Heather Smith Kleiner, Marshall, Randolph, and Letitia.

His contributions to the discipline of linguistics left an indelible mark on the field. The development of the Army Language Program, also known as the 'Intensive Language Program,' which he directed, accelerated the course of language acquisition at a time when language learning and crosscultural understanding were becoming imperative for survival in a smaller world. The tools and techniques produced under his direction, using native speakers as informants for 22 different languages, are still available and in use in the early 1990s. An outgrowth of this project was the development of a system of linguistic analysis that he called 'aspectualism,' in which he demonstrated a tripartite, 27-level framework that achieved a more finely focused view into the structure of language than had previously been defined.

Introduced in the analysis was the concept of the 'morphophone,' which demonstrated, for instance, how two different phonemes in the same environment in a certain lexical item could be understood as expressions of the same morphophone unit, thereby making two different dialects mutually intelligible. A series of publications, beginning in 1951 with *An Outline of English Structure* (with George L. Trager), and including 'The concept of the morphophone' (1967) and 'The morphophone and English dialects' (1972), traces the development of this idea. *Linguistic Science and the Teaching of English* (1956) and *The Linguistic Readers* (1963–67), a beginning reader series co-written by Smith, further explore the theory of the morphophone and its usefulness in enhancing the understanding of language structure. 'Dialects of English' (1969) explains and discusses the theory of the morphophone and its application to dialectology.

In his memorable and highly effective speaking style, Henry Lee Smith told the world about linguistics, when it was still a relatively unknown and poorly understood discipline, through literally hundreds of lectures, workshops, and conferences. A guest much in demand on educational television and radio, he prepared and presented *Language and Linguistics*, a 13-part series on Educational Television that was also widely used in classrooms over a period of years. Among the many special lectures he gave were those at Harvard University, Princeton University, and Gallaudet College, a school for the hearing-impaired in Washington, DC. He conducted a well-known radio program, 'Where Are You From?' from 1939–41 on WOR, New York City. He was listed in *Marquis Who's Who*, *Who's Who in the East*, and *American Men of Science*, and was a member of the American Association for the Advancement of Science, the Linguistic Society of America, the American Anthropological Association, the Cosmos Club in Washington, DC, and many other civic and professional societies.

Henry Lee Smith was a vivid and distinguished figure in the various worlds of which he was a part. Interrupted in mid-career and somewhat surprised by death, he was still deeply involved in his teaching and research. He had often expressed the hope that his students would continue on the path he had laid out.

Bibliography

Farley-Winer C A 1992 Henry Lee Smith Jr (1913–72). A *Nachruf* twenty years after. *HL* **19**(1): 187–98 (includes a bibliography)

Smith H L 1956 *Linguistic Science and the Teaching of English.* Harvard University Press, Cambridge, MA

Smith H L 1967 The concept of the morphophone. *Lg* 43(1): 306–41

Smith H L 1969 Dialects of English. In: Morris W (ed.) *American Heritage Dictionary.* American Heritage/Houghton Mifflin, Boston, MA

Smith H L 1972 The morphophone and English dialects. In: Davis L M (ed.) *Studies in Linguistics in Honor of Raven I. McDavid Jr.* University of Alabama Press, Tuscaloosa, AL

Smith H L, Trager G L 1951 *An Outline of English Structure.* Battenberg Press, Norman, OK

C. A. Farley-Winer

Social Class

Although social class is one of the key sociological concepts in language studies, there is little agreement or clarity about the meaning of the term. Linguists frequently research class differences in speech, syntax, and grammar without their criteria for classification, leaving unspecified the underlying social causes of the variations they report. For Marxists, class refers to ownership or control of the means of production (factories, land, tools, etc.), with the fundamental cleavage dividing the owners and managers of large corporations from the class of proletarian wage earners. Other theorists use class to refer to unequal bargaining positions in markets for labor and capital, with the population stratified along multiple and cross-cutting dimensions of inequality rather than sharply divided into polarized groups. The causal order is also generally unclear; do distinct class voices reflect material divisions that correspond to class inequalities, or do material circumstances reflect differences in the possession of language skills and styles required for upward mobility? Finally, is the distinctive language of the lower classes indicative of cultural deficit and deprivation, or do such claims reflect the class bias of the scholars who advance them? These controversies have been particularly sharp surrounding the eminent work of Basil Bernstein, perhaps the foremost theorist of the language of class.

1. From Static Taxonomy to Historical Change

References can be found in both the scholarly and popular literatures not only to blue-collar workers but also students, the aged, the handicapped, ethnic groups, women, welfare recipients, and renters as subordinate classes. At a minimum, the term class implies only that certain people share a distinctive attribute of interest to the observer, hence the diverse assortment of people who find themselves 'classified.' While Marxists emphasize property relations as the defining attribute, others include knowledge and skill, authority, and more recently, power and cultural capital.

Some see class inequality as evidence of injustice, the monopolization of valued resources by a privileged minority. Others see class differentiation as a natural and highly functional expression of individual differences in taste and talent.

These diverse usages should not tempt us to search for an inflexible formula or authoritative definition that might give the term greater coherence. Models of the class structure are not descriptive typologies or taxonomic schemas but rather theories of social and political contestation and historical change. A social class is more than a category; each grouping implies a corresponding theory about the importance and unequal distribution of the defining attribute. Hence, there is a need to examine the origins of fundamental inequalities in the social division of labor and the processes that perpetuate them. The reader can then use and interpret the term more effectively, particularly in sociolinguistic applications. Special emphasis will thus be placed on the role played by language—how these inequalities are manifested in distinctive voices and how these in turn promote, attenuate, or alter the reproduction of class inequalities over time.

2. Class According to Marx and Weber

Marx devoted a lifetime of intellectual labor to unraveling what he saw as the central paradox of human history: humans must work in order to live, yet the more they labor, the stronger become the forces that compel them to work. The problem centers on the alienation of propertyless producers from the means of production they create and on which they depend for survival. The products of their labor belong not to them but to those who own the land, factories, equipment, tools, and materials, all of which are themselves products of labor but now confront their makers as something hostile and alien. In Marx's Hegelian language, the creative process is turned upside down in an inversion of subject and predicate such that 'man's own deed becomes an alien power opposed to him which enslaves him instead of being controlled by him' (1978: 160). In capitalist production, the dependence of the propertyless proletarian on the means of production owned by capital also leaves the worker unable to command remuneration for a day's labor commensurate with what the capitalist could obtain in selling what the worker produced in a day. Reduced to homogeneous raw material, the producers are themselves consumed by the very productive forces they have created. In brief, the workers forge their own chains.

Indeed, the producers are dominated not only by the means of production but by all that they have produced, including politics and religion. The creators of God are thus banished from the real world to the garden of Eden: the more of himself man attributes to God, Marx writes, 'the less he retains in himself. The worker puts his life into the object, but now his life no longer belongs to him but to the object' (1978: 72). Similarly, the dependence of the producers on the propertied class for survival causes the economic interests of that class to take on the appearance of the universal interests of society, the interests that are in turn sanctioned by the state, even when it is democratically controlled. As the embodiment of this universal interest, 'the executive of the modern State is but a committee for managing the common affairs of the whole bourgeoisie' (1978:

475). Contrary to what is often crudely portrayed by his critics, no conspiracy by a prescient ruling class is implied by Marx's famous dictum. Nor are the masses brainwashed by the bourgeoisie. While 'the ideas of the ruling class are in every epoch the ruling ideas,' their dominion is always subject to contestation. The antagonism of interest between the propertied class and the producers creates the material basis for often bloody class struggle, with the potential to transform the property relations that are the root of the conflict.

Marxists in the late twentieth century, faced with the embarrassment of classifying salaried managers and professionals as wage-earning proletarians, have broadened the meaning of relationship to the means of production to include both ownership and control (Wright 1979). This elaboration of the classical doctrine resonates with Marx's early emphasis on the domination of the producers by the products of their own labor and also has important ramifications for the socialist agenda; it is not enough for the workers to own collectively the means of production, they must also control it, which implies not only a democratic state but also a democratic enterprise. The failure of that vision to survive the test of practical politics in the twentieth century, in both East and West, has motivated continuing efforts to rethink Marxist class theory. Nevertheless, the political systems of most of the industrial democracies are closely tied to class-specific constituencies, and Marx's seminal contribution remains the single most important intellectual influence on contemporary applications.

The neo-Marxist distinction between ownership and control owes extensively to a prominent non-Marxist, Ralf Dahrendorf, who argued that property is merely a special case of a more fundamental class relation based on authority. Dahrendorf's command class may be found not only in the process of production but in all 'imperatively coordinated associations,' including schools and churches. While this seems to imply an even broader and more radical agenda for the class struggle, Dahrendorf draws the opposite conclusion. The ubiquity of the command class means that opportunities exist for subordinates in one sphere of social life to serve as bosses in another. These cross-cutting cleavages suggest not class polarization but rather a pluralist model of highly stable industrial democracies.

The German sociologist Max Weber (see *Weber, Max*), whose stature in class theory rivals that of Marx, also challenged the assumption that class societies tend towards polarization and irreconcilable conflict. Weber countered that property relations need not correspond to other dimensions of social stratification, namely political power and social prestige; that is, the correspondence between class, status, and power is empirically and historically variable.

Marxists from the second half of the twentieth century generally agree, but insist that there are structural, economic limits on the political power of the working class, even where labor parties have enjoyed decades of uninterrupted political rule, as in social democratic Sweden. Efforts to redistribute profit and protect workers from the threat of the sack ultimately confront the inexorable logic of the competitive market, a conclusion that conservative economists readily affirm.

Weber also broadened the Marxist notion of property. Like Marx, Weber believed that '"Property" and "lack of property" are ... the basic categories of all class situations' (1978: 927). By this Weber means specifically a market situation, that is, a bargaining position in markets for labor, capital, or credit. Like Marx, Weber saw the propertyless as powerless in the bargaining encounter, but he differs in that his notion of property is more nuanced. For Weber, Marx's proletariat is not one but two classes, those who possess a marketable skill and those with only their raw labor power to sell. The bargaining power of the unskilled laborer is vastly inferior to that of the expert machinist. Weber thus introduces the idea that knowledge, educational credentials, and skill can be marketable assets comparable to physical means of production and therefore relevant to the differentiation of classes. This has become one of the primary interests of contemporary class theorists, with important implications for the role of language, to be addressed momentarily.

As Weber seems to have recognized, his theory of market situation suggests gradational stratification rather than classification. The market capacities associated with the level of skill or the value of accumulated assets form a continuum with no intrinsically meaningful categories. In what sense then can Weberian classes be understood as qualitatively distinct? The solution proposed by Weber is the concept of *social* class based on the probability of movement from one position to another. Social classes can then be differentiated within a continuum of market capacities by mobility patterns: 'the totality of those class situations within which individual and generational mobility is easy and typical' (1978: 302). Social classes are thus characterized by common socioeconomic backgrounds as these open/restrict access to a given set of market positions. While inherited wealth may be the most obviously important, what has fascinated class theorists of the late 1980s and early 1990s is the inheritance and accumulation of cultural capital: educational credentials, knowledge and skill in the symbolic manipulation of language and figures, verbal style and proficiency, cultural taste, and knowledge of how to play the educational game.

3. Classes of Persons and Classes of Positions

Weber's distinction between economic classes defined by market situation and social classes bounded by mobility barriers introduces a dimension of class analysis that is largely missing from Marxist accounts: the social and cultural backgrounds of the incumbents of class positions. For Marxists, it is the inequality of positions within the social division of labor, and not the inequality of persons in access to those positions, that motors history. Hence 'individuals are dealt with only in so far as they are the personifications of economic categories, embodiments of particular class-relations and class-interests' (Marx 1978: 297).

This approach has informed numerous empirical studies that demonstrate pronounced differences in political and ideological alignment that reflect the interests inscribed in what structuralists call the empty places of the division of labor, empty in that it matters not who fills them. Simply put, the job makes the man, independently of the social and cultural orientations that incumbents may bring with them to their positions. Put the children of workers in executive positions and they will think and act not like their parents but like their golf partners. Hence, social closure and class inheritance are not necessary to reproduce the class structure.

Writers working in the Weberian tradition, on the other hand, are more likely to think in terms of classes of persons defined by their access to valued resources, not classes of positions defined by locations in the social division of labor. Persons, as the units of class analysis, provide the nodal points at which the vocational dimensions of class intersect with inequalities outside the workplace, like differential access to marriage partners, private clubs, residential neighborhoods, and social networks. From Hollingshead's Elmtown to Warner and Lunt's Yankee City, these classic studies aggregate classes from the similarities of personal attributes affecting individual life-chances and social standing, in which family and education, as well as wealth and occupation, are what usually matter.

In broad strokes, this theoretical perspective places the social and cultural composition of classes at the center of class analysis and draws particular attention to problems of social mobility and status attainment. Incumbents do more than vivify their parts in a structural *deus ex machina*. Classes differ in their ideology, life-style, and voice because they systematically recruit incumbents with distinctive social and cultural backgrounds. Social closure is therefore essential to the reproduction of class. While acknowledging the Marxist canon that classes 'share a common function in the broad social division of labor,' the Ehrenreichs reject what they see as a 'vocational approach to class,' because it 'leaves out everything else which shapes a person's political consciousness and loyalties—their . . . social and cultural existence' (Ehrenreich and Ehrenreich 1979). Social closure based on exclusionary practices also entails intentional collective action, such that consciousness is a constitutive element of social class and not an epiphenomenon as assumed by structural Marxism, an approach that the eminent British sociologists Anthony Giddens and Frank Parkin claim vitiates class as a tool of empirical analysis. It is not incumbency of position in a formally defined structure but rather the organized effort to monopolize and usurp access that usually corresponds to political alignment and behavior.

Personal attributes that typify locations may also produce an association between persons and positions such that members acquire the class outlook of the positions typified by their background—the positions where they 'belong' as signified by their cultural marker. Members of an ethnic or other cultural collectivity historically associated with particular places in the division of labor may identify with the position signified not by where they are but by who they are, that is to say, not by their own class-structural location but by the location of those persons with whom they associate and typically interact. For example, one widely cited study suggests that middle-class blacks are more likely than whites in comparable class locations to identify with the working or lower class. Studies of over-education have also found that college-educated respondents are more likely to identify as middle or upper class than others in similar blue-collar occupations, suggesting that membership in the middle class is based on the possession of credentials and not actual location in the social division of labor.

4. Knowledge Workers on the Road to Class Power

The rise of the new middle class is clearly one of the most important changes in the class structure of the advanced industrial societies, both East and West. The class is new in that its members derive their power, prestige, and overall life chances not from the sale of material commodities, as did the old petty bourgeoisie of family owned and operated businesses, but as salaried knowledge workers.

The term 'new class' was first proposed by Djilas in his pioneering work on the former state elites in Eastern Europe. The term was imported to the West by theorists of postindustrialism who broadened the concept to refer to structural changes in the social division of labor in both the public and private sectors: the separation of ownership and control, the growth of the public and nonprofit sectors, and the increasing centrality of highly specialized knowledge. The rapid ascension of these new administrative and professional positions has aroused the hopes and fears of left and right as they hazard the prospects of a robust and liberal counterweight to the political influence of business. Prominent neoconservatives like Peter Berger and Irving Kristol predict a political inversion in which these purveyors of symbolic knowledge supplant the proletariat as the major antagonists of capitalism. Others, including some neo-Marxists, claim only that large sections may be a potentially vital (if unstable) ally of the working class in countering the power of propertied interests (Wright 1979).

New-class opposition to corporate prerogatives, market logic, and entrepreneurial values has been attributed to the material interests of credentialed knowledge workers who find their road to power and privilege blocked by the propertied class, much as the bourgeoisie once confronted an older aristocracy. Those 'with an interest in having privilege based on educational credentials,' Berger hypothesizes, tend toward 'a general antagonism . . . against the capitalist market system that, in principle, is open to anyone regardless of education' (1986: 69–70). Moreover, 'like all rising classes, the knowledge class rhetorically identifies its own class interests . . . with the downtrodden (just as the early bourgeoisie did in its conflict with the *ancien régime*).' This opposition is reflected in and reinforced by what Alvin Gouldner (1979) has called a 'culture of critical discourse' that questions tradition, deference to authority, inherited privilege, and the voice of money rather than reason.

Neoconservative writers have also emphasized the role of the state as the Trojan horse of the intellectuals on the road to class power. As Berger argues, the growth of the state and nonprofit sectors provides the structural basis for the emergence of a counterelite that opposes propertied interests and supports state intervention on behalf of those perceived as victims of market inequity. Those whose work and advancement is not governed by the logic of commodity production may be less likely to accept the necessity or desirability of profit-centered activity and more disposed toward criticism of entrepreneurial values. However, critics such as Daniel Bell and C. Wright Mills have sharply questioned the independence of managers and highly paid professionals from the propertied interests that support them and with whom they socialize and marry.

These controversies have animated a plethora of empirical studies by leading researchers, including Samuel Stouffer and Seymour Martin Lipset. Evidence abounds of widespread support among college-graduate professionals for left-of-center positions on social issues: personal freedom, racial and cultural tolerance, rights of women and minorities, environmental and consumer protection, and antimilitarism. However, there is little evidence to suggest that either higher education or professional position promote antipathy toward business or free enterprise or support for greater economic equality.

Framed by Gouldner's theory of a culture of critical discourse, consistent cross-national evidence of the subjective salience of occupational self-direction suggests a plausible interpretation of new-class dissent on social issues. Melvin Kohn, who pioneered these studies, has accumulated, over three decades and in a variety of countries in the East and West, a vast archive of evidence pointing to the psychological impact of the experience of self-directed work (Kohn 1977). His extensive research reveals striking class differences in the exercise of critical discourse: tolerance, intellectual skepticism, moral flexibility, openness to social change, and a critical orientation towards tradition and authority. Classes differ ideologically not only because incumbents have different material interests, but also because they experience systematically different social relationships, from which they draw different generalizations about the world and their relationship to it, minimizing the dissonance between the values inscribed in their occupational roles and those in the world outside. Hence those required to submit in the workplace are uncomfortable with self-directed inquiry, situationist ethics, and scientific uncertainty, while those in jobs that entail the exercise of discretionary responsibility find moral majorities equally bothersome.

Although Kohn and his associates do not test the implications of their model for class differences on social issues, other studies find strong support for the effects of occupational self-direction in promoting greater openness to social change. However, there is no evidence that this extends to an antibusiness animus. The weight of the evidence so far leans heavily to the conclusion that the rising middle class provides a powerful constituency for social reform but is unlikely to challenge the power and privilege of the propertied class.

Others have suggested reversing the causal order in Kohn's model. The personality traits associated with occupational self-direction may instead be acquired long before entering the workplace, through processes of socialization in the home and school. In their influential critique of the educational system, Bowles and Gintis contend that middle-class families tend to have children in student-centered, inquiry-oriented classrooms that model the employee-centered social relations of the office. In contrast, working-class children are more likely to find themselves in teacher-centered schools oriented toward discipline and compliance, corresponding to the more authoritarian social relations of the shop floor. As a result, despite class similarities in native intelligence, schools reinforce psychic and cultural differences that limit both the aspirations and opportunities of the less privileged. This view of the educational system, not as the great equalizer but as the axial mechanism for class inheritance, has provided the point of departure for important sociolinguistic studies of class attainment.

5. The Theory of Discursive Capital

The rise of a new middle class, endowed with cultural rather than material assets, has altered the process by which class inequalities are reproduced over time. Although cultural stocks like educational credentials, knowledge, and manners are highly marketable, they differ from material assets in that they cannot be readily probated. As a result, family socialization and education have attracted considerable scholarly attention as vehicles of class inheritance. It is in this context that theories of linguistic class differences assume special prominence. Basil Bernstein's work on the accumulation of what he calls 'discursive resources' represents one of the leading contributions, as well as one of the most controversial.

Following Emile Durkheim, the influential French sociologist of the late nineteenth century, Bernstein argues that a more complex and fully differentiated division of labor entails changes in family interactions and corresponding linguistic codes. The simpler the social division of labor, Bernstein writes, the more restricted the coding orientation. The more complex the social division of labor, the more elaborated the coding orientation. These distinct semiotic grammars in turn facilitate or restrict access to locations in the division of labor, thereby reproducing and legitimating class inequalities across the generations (1981: 327–32).

The theory begins with a Weberian concept of a positively privileged class whose position is based on the possession of marketable knowledge, skills, and credentials, with access largely controlled by the educational system. Bernstein argues that the family relationships in this class differ fundamentally from the interpersonal relationships in working-class families. The latter are characterized by closed, position-oriented family relations in which interactions are determined by ascribed status as parent–child and male–female. The closed, position-oriented working-class relationships foster communalized roles outside the family that require consensus among the interactants, shared cultural history, similarity of experiences, and common assumptions that family members do not need or want to articulate, a pattern Durkheim called 'mechanical solidarity.'

According to Durkheim, mechanical solidarity derives from similarities in roles and functions, in which common experiences and shared identities bind members to the collectivity, as exemplified by tribal systems. This contrasts with what he called 'organic solidarity,' which derives from highly differentiated, interdependent roles, with bonds based on mutual need rather than identity of position. Mechanical solidarity is centered on the group, within which members are interchangeable parts. Organic solidarity is centered instead on the indispensability of specialized roles, leading to what Durkheim called the cult of the individual.

This cult of the individual, Bernstein argues, is more likely to typify middle-class families. They tend to exhibit open, person-oriented interactions, in which decisions are open to discussion and criticism, with less deference to the position of the speaker. Roles are more flexible and status within the family is negotiated rather than ascribed. Hence children can shape their role in the family so as to reflect their individual social and cognitive attributes and unique experiences. The open, person-oriented middle-class relationships carry over into what Bernstein characterizes as individualized roles outside the family that permit and encourage differences among interactants in backgrounds, cultural assumptions, and points of view.

Bernstein also follows Durkheim in the emphasis he places on the social structuring of meanings and on their diverse but related contextual linguistic realizations. Bernstein's approach is thus diametrically opposed to the Whorfian school which sees language as primary to the structuring of social relationships, determining the conceptualization and ordering of experience. Here it is the other way around. Distinctive patterns of interpersonal relationships provide different opportunities for the use of language. The interpersonal relationships in which working-class children communicate involve 'restricted codes' in which the speakers rely on shared understandings, with implicit meanings that speakers find difficult to articulate directly. 'The most general condition for the emergence of this code is a social relationship based upon a common, extensive set of closely shared identifications, and expectations self-consciously held by the members . . . . The meanings are likely to be concrete, descriptive, or narrative rather than analytical or abstract . . . there will be a low level of vocabulary and syntactic selection; and *the unique meaning of the individual is likely to be verbally implicit*' (Bernstein 1966: 256–57).

Conversely, the individualized roles of the middle-class family, where the intent of the other person cannot be taken for granted, are conducive to *elaborated codes*, with a more complex grammatical sentence structure and more subordinate clauses, adverbs, and adjectives. Communication among highly differentiated roles requires speakers to be more explicit about meanings, with fewer assumptions about the common base of knowledge and experience on which speakers might rely.

These elaborated codes in turn reinforce a self-directed relationship with others. 'The user of an elaborated code comes to perceive language as a set of theoretical possibilities available for the transmission of unique experience,' Bernstein continues. 'The concept of self, unlike the self-concept of a speaker limited to a restricted code, will be verbally differentiated, so that it becomes, in itself, the object of specialized perceptual activity.'

The argument has striking implications for theories of the new middle class. Gouldner, for example, cites Bernstein's concept of elaborated codes as key to the critical discourse of the intellectuals. The model also addresses Kohn's research on occupational self-direction, suggesting that linguistic elaboration may account for the widely observed correspondence between self-directed work and ideational flexibility, openness to change, tolerance of diversity, and intellectual skepticism. What appear to be the psychological consequences of occupation may turn out to be latent cultural attributes, embedded in speech patterns, that incumbents bring with them to the job.

However, the major application of the model has been as an explanation for class differences in educational success. Elaborated codes facilitate expression of complex and abstract ideas valued by the school, while the grammatical structure of the restricted code inhibits logical reasoning, promotes inconsistency, and limits interest in generalization, thereby precluding discursive inquiry and compromising the probability of academic achievement. 'If a child is to succeed as he progresses through school,' Bernstein concludes, 'it becomes critical for him to possess, or at least to be oriented towards, an elaborated code' (1966: 259).

Bernstein's novel and provocative explanation for the meritocratic reproduction of class inequality has motivated a new cottage industry of empirical studies. Bernstein's own investigations report that British upper-class children are significantly more likely to use elaborated codes, passive voice, and first-person pronouns, even when nonverbal IQ is controlled. Another 5-year British study found that compared to working-class mothers, middle-class mothers favor abstract and implicit definitions over explicit and concrete definitions, and favor open-ended, heuristic answers to children's questions. An Australian study of 96 high-schoolers showed distinct social class differences in verbal linguistic coding.

Nevertheless, many others have found that Bernstein's model fits the data rather poorly and have had difficulty replicating his results, especially outside the UK. One study of the speech of 39 British 11-year-olds found no rigidity in the lower working-class children's speech, nor persistence of any restricted and elaborated codes. Similar findings have been reported from Australia. An American study of written language usage of 100 high school freshmen found no relationship between parental socioeconomic status and word usage or sentence structure. Several other US studies have also failed to show any direct relationship between social class and children's verbal communicative styles. Neither social control strategies nor school achievement scores were differently related to elaborated and restricted variants. An Israeli study of formal and informal speech situations for 72 male 12-year olds found no support for the claim that lower class children have less access to an elaborated code.

Thorlindsson's (1987) study of 338 Icelandic 15-year olds represents one of the most thorough and exhaustive attempts to fully test Bernstein's model. Thorlindsson found that linguistic elaboration does not play its predicted role, with no significant association with either social class, family interaction patterns, or scholastic achievement.

These inconsistent results may indicate substantial measurement error in key variables like linguistic elaboration and child-centered family interactions. Investigators disagree over the need to test spoken versus written language, the use of formal and informal contexts, and whether young children or parents should provide data on parental roles in the family. Thorlindsson also suspects that Bernstein's findings among British children reflect peculiarities of British upper-class values as these are reflected in the schools.

6. The Deficit Controversy

The empirical problems have been overshadowed by the other major criticism of Bernstein's work. His theory has invited interpretation and sharp controversy as a deficit theory of academic failure among working-class youth. Deficit theories, critics charge, blame the victims for conditions that are imposed on them and over which they exercise no real control. Class inequalities may then be rationalized as natural expressions of innate differences rather than outcomes of a competitive struggle.

Critics such as Gecas complain that restricted codes imply that the user could be expected to have lower cognitive abilities of abstract reasoning and analytic thinking. Bernstein is thus regarded as lending support to controversial theories of cultural inferiority such as those of Bereiter and Engelmann who hold that the dialect of blacks in the USA is not merely an underdeveloped version of standard English, but basically a nonlogical mode of expressive behavior.

Although Bernstein has been roundly criticized for advocating a deficit interpretation, it is clear even in his early writings that this is a serious distortion of his intent. Bernstein never contends that working-class children are cognitively deficient but only that they lack the opportunities for language use that middle-class children experience. To begin with, restricted codes are used at some time by all members of society, Bernstein emphasizes, including the middle class. 'Children socialized within middle class and associated strata can be expected to possess both an elaborated and a restricted code; while children socialized within some sections of the working class strata, particularly the lower working class, can be expected to be limited to a restricted code' (1966: 259).

This limitation is not a matter of ability. Working-class children are fully capable of using elaborated codes but lack opportunities to do so. Those thrust into highly differentiated roles have no choice but to respond to the needs for specialized communication inscribed therein. 'The orientation towards these codes, both elaborated and restricted, may be independent of the psychology of the child, independent of his native ability,' Bernstein continues, 'governed entirely by the form of the social relation, or more generally by the quality of the social structure.' The problem is not innate ability but rather unequal access to different speech systems based on status position in a given social structure, such that children may adopt quite different social and intellectual procedures, despite a common potential. Thus Bernstein concludes that:

> the relative backwardness of lower working class and rural children may well be a form of culturally induced backwardness which is transmitted to the child through the linguistic process. The code the child brings to the school symbolizes his social identity. It relates him to his kin and to his local social relations. The code progressively orients the child towards a pattern of relationships which constitute for him his psychological reality, and this reality is reinforced every time he speaks.

In his later work, Bernstein underscores the point that the differences are based on power, not cognitive function. Using less neutral terminology, Bernstein argues that class relations 'generate, distribute, reproduce, and legitimate distinctive forms of communication, which transmit dominating and dominated codes . . . [that function as] culturally determined positioning devices' (Bernstein 1981: 327).

For example, Labov's (1972) study of language use among black gang members suggests that the experimental setting can generate the linguistic deficit that the investigator is seeking to measure. Labov found that when an inner-city black child is interviewed by an educated white person using elaborated codes, the child defends himself against what is perceived as an unsympathetic and probably hostile person by resorting to monosyllabic expression and minimal response. Labov then replaced the interviewer with an unthreatening black person who allows the child's best friend to come along and who sits on the floor with the children and shares a snack. The child then becomes verbally enterprising and shows no cognitive deficiency. Labov concludes that the social situation is the principal determinant of verbal behavior. Once this is taken into account,

street dialect appears to be structurally equivalent to standard English, the speech patterns merely alternative expressions of the same latent linguistic construction.

Other studies also call into question the assumption that working-class children are victims of class-based socialization patterns. In his compelling ethnography of a white working-class gang in a British factory town, Willis (1977) shows how the gang members construct what he calls a counterschool culture in active defiance of dominant patterns that threaten their gendered self-esteem. The boys do not passively adopt coding orientations that handicap them in the schools; they not only know how to use elaborated codes, they delight in exaggerated mimicry of the ineffectual ambience projected by 'proper' expression. From this perspective, the concreteness of their discourse expresses their potency, while the official language of the school provides an endless source of ridicule that delights the boys and ritually affirms their masculine prowess. The paradox is that the boys are condemned to follow their parents into stultifying and low-paying jobs not because the school fails to appreciate their obvious ability and creativity, but because they reject the school as a scam designed for fools and a threat to their authenticity as concrete actors. To return to Marx, it would seem that the inversion of subject and predicate in the world of work leaves the boys with no choice but to speak in their own voice, a voice that mocks the ineffectual white-collar world and celebrates the robust efficacy of manual labor, echoing the sturdy proletarians depicted in the murals of socialist realism. But the celebration is cut short when the boys soon discover that life does not imitate art.

See also: Weber, Max.

Bibliography

Berger P 1986 *The Capitalist Revolution*. Basic Books, New York

Bernstein B 1966 Elaborated and restricted codes: An outline. *Social Inquiry* **36**(2): 126–33

Bernstein B 1981 Codes, modalities, and the process of cultural reproduction: A model. *Language in Society* **10**(3): 327–63

Dahrendorf R 1959 *Class and Class Conflict in Industrial Society*. Stanford University Press, Stanford

Ehrenreich B, Ehrenreich J 1979. In: Walker P (ed.) *Between Labor and Capital*. South End Press, Boston, MA

Gouldner A 1979 *The Future of Intellectuals and the Rise of the New Class*. Seabury Press, New York

Kohn M L 1977 *Class and Conformity: A Study in Values, with a Reassessment*, 2nd edn. University of Chicago Press, Chicago, IL

Labov W 1972 The logic of nonstandard English. In: Giglioli P P (ed.) *Language and Social Context*. Penguin Books, Harmondsworth

Marx K 1978 Manifesto of the Communist Party. In: Tucker R C (ed.) *The Marx–Engels Reader*, 2nd edn. Norton, New York

Thorlindsson T 1987 Bernstein's sociolinguistics: An empirical test in Iceland. *Social Forces* **65**(3): 695–718

Weber M 1978 (transl. Fischoff E, et al.) *Economy and Society: An Outline of Interpretative Sociology*. University of California Press, Berkeley, CA

Willis P E 1977 *Learning to Labor*. Columbia University Press, New York

Wright E O 1979 *Class Structure and Income Determination*. Academic Press, New York

M. W. Macy

Social Networks

Dialectological and historical linguistic research has consistently revealed the persistence, often over centuries, of low status and nonlegitimized dialects and languages in rural and urban communities, despite pressure from powerful standard languages like English and French. In contemporary western society where nonstandard dialects are publicly and generally stigmatized, such pressure is exerted in many ways—for example, through the educational system, through social and economic penalties springing from public use of nonstandard dialects, and through the language used and attitudes expressed in the broadcast and printed media. An individual's social network is quite simply the sum of relationships which he or she has contracted with others, and social network analysis examines the differing structure and properties of social networks. Such analysis has been applied in dialectology to explicate the day by day social mechanisms which allow speakers to maintain their nonstandard dialects, despite pressure from national standard languages. Conversely, change in the operation of these social mechanisms has been used to elucidate the phenomenon of linguistic change.

1. The Concept of Social Network

Social network analysis of the kind which is particularly relevant to dialectology originates in anthropological research, mainly during the 1960s and 1970s. Procedures for analyzing the social networks of individuals were developed as a result of dissatisfaction with what some anthropologists saw as an overreliance on highly abstract social concepts (such as that of social class) in accounting for differences in everyday social behavior. Personal networks were generally seen as contextualized within this broader social framework, which constantly constrained behavior. However, it was 'bracketed off' to allow attention to be concentrated on developing less abstract modes of analysis which could account more immediately for the variable behavior of individuals. A fundamental postulate of network analysis is that individuals create personal communities which provide them with a meaningful framework for solving the problems of their day to day existence (Mitchell 1986: 74), and this kind of focus makes it very suitable for studying small and relatively well-defined urban and rural communities.

A social network may be seen as a boundless web of ties which reaches out through a whole society, linking people to one another, however remotely. But for practical reasons social networks are generally 'anchored' to individuals, and interest focuses on relatively 'strong' first-order network ties—i.e., those persons with whom an individual directly interacts. Second-order ties are those to whom the link is indirect (see Fig. 1). This principle of 'anchorage' effectively limits the field of network studies, generally to something between 20 and 50 individuals. Thus, for example, if the objective was to look comparatively at the network structures of 40 speakers of a nonstandard urban dialect, one way to proceed would be to discover the 20 individuals whom each saw as his or her most significant daily contacts. Then the contrasts between these various 'networks' of 20 could be examined with respect to linguistically relevant characteristics such as whether they were dialect speakers

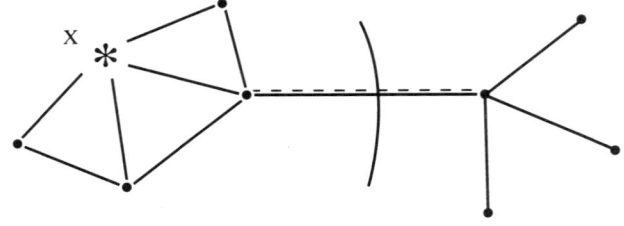

Figure 1. High-density personal network structure, showing first and second order zones. X is the focal point of the network.

or not, kin or not, had contacts with each other or not, and so on. In fact this is parallel to the procedure adopted by the social anthropologist Clyde Mitchell in a 1980s study of homeless women in Manchester, UK. His interest is in the effects of their personal network structures upon the length of time they are homeless. A different way of examining network structure is described in Sect. 2.

1.1 Multiplexity and Density as Properties of Networks

The two concepts of 'multiplexity' and 'density' are of critical importance in a comparative analysis of social networks. In a maximally dense and multiplex network, everyone would know everyone else (density), and the actors would know one another in a range of capacities (multiplexity). Social anthropologists now generally agree that a social network of a dense, multiplex type, which in effect constitutes a bounded group, has the capacity to impose general normative consensus upon its members. The idealized maximally dense and multiplex network is shown in Fig. 2.1 in contrast with a loose-knit, uniplex type of network (Fig. 2.2). Close-knit networks, which will of course vary in the extent to which they approximate to such a representation, have the capacity to maintain and even enforce local conventions and norms—of dress, religion, and general behavior, for example—and linguistic norms are no exception to this generalization. Close-knit networks are very common worldwide in low-status communities, both rural and urban, and they flourish in the absence of social and geographical mobility. It has been argued that close-knit networks with their characteristic reciprocity and solidarity

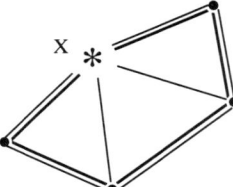

Figure 2.1 High-density, high-multiplexity personal network structure: X is the focal point of the network.

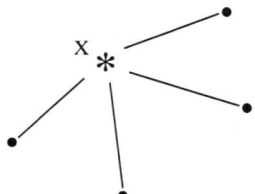

Figure 2.2 Low-density, uniplex personal network structure: X is the focal point of the network.

ethic constitute a basic survival and support mechanism in poor communities in the absence of material resources. It will be shown in Sect. 2 how the characteristics of such networks are important in encouraging the long-term survival of socially disfavored dialects.

2. Social Networks and Language Variation

In this section some applications of the network concept in dialectology will be described, with particular reference to small-scale close-knit communities. Particular attention will be given to a study carried out in the mid-1970s of the urban dialect of Belfast, Northern Ireland (see Milroy and Milroy 1978; Milroy 1987). This research is in the quantitative tradition developed by William Labov (see *Labov, William*). Using the concept of the sociolinguistic variable, the language patterns of 46 speakers from three inner-city communities were examined. Eight phonological variables (seven vowel variables and one consonant variable) were selected for analysis in relation to the network structure of individual speakers; all were quite characteristic of the dialect. Speakers varied, however, in the extent to which they used the vernacular realization of these variables; they were not isolated individuals, but had contracted long-standing social ties with each other within their neighborhoods. All three communities, Ballymacarrett, Clonard, and Hammer, were poor working-class communities where the informal social structure corresponded to the dense, multiplex, often kin-based patterns, described by many investigators as characteristic of long-established working-class communities (see, for example, Young and Wilmott 1962). The communicative pattern which recurs in these accounts is one of persons interacting mostly within a clearly-defined territory, tending to know each others' social contacts (i.e., having relatively dense social networks) and tending to be linked to each other by multiplex ties.

Although this dense, multiplex network structure was evident in all three communities (in very sharp contrast to middle-class neighborhoods) the extent to which individuals were linked to local networks varied considerably. Some people, for example, worked outside the area and had no local kin and no local ties of friendship, while others were linked to local networks in all these capacities. These differences in personal network structure, which appeared to spring from many complex social and psychological factors, were related to a number of other variables, such as the age and sex of the speaker and the type of locality. For example, young men seemed on the whole to contract denser and more multiplex network ties than young women, and urban redevelopment programs which relocated communities in outer urban areas seemed to have the effect of disrupting long-term network ties. Social network structure is also class-related in that middle-class networks are more frequently loose-knit. This point is returned to below.

2.1 Measuring Social Network Structure

Although when considered in terms of their social class they formed a very homogeneous group, the Belfast working-class speakers varied in their use of the linguistic variables, some sounding very much more vernacular than others. The device used to examine the relationship between this linguistic variation and variation in network structure was a six-point network strength scale which measured speakers'

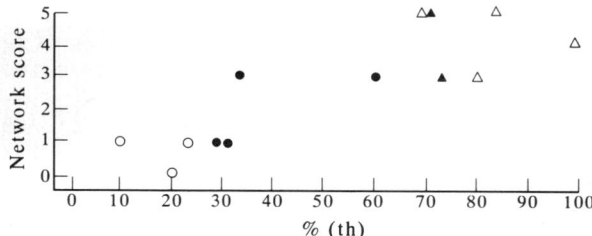

Figure 3. Ballymacarrett—individual scores on network strength scale.

network characteristics on various indicators of multiplexity and density. Two examples of these indicators are kin orientation and territorially based friendship ties (see Milroy 1987: 141 for full details). Since this network strength scale quantified the extent to which speakers interacted with others in the community and the strength of the ties contracted there, it could be interpreted as a measure of the pressure exerted by the close-knit network upon its members. A series of statistical tests revealed a strong correlation between personal network structure and patterns of language use, even allowing for the interaction of other social variables such as the age and the sex of the speaker; the strongest dialect speakers were those whose informal social ties were the strongest. Fig. 3 illustrates this relationship in Ballymacarrett, in showing a tendency for speakers who are plotted high on the vertical axis also to be plotted towards the right of the graph. The linguistic behavior at issue is the presence versus absence of the consonant [ð] intervocalically in such words as *mother, brother.* Deletion scores for each speaker, whose age group and sex are also specified, are plotted as percentages against his or her network strength score. It is on the basis of such language/network relationships that the close-knit network may be viewed as an important social mechanism of dialect maintenance, encouraging the long-term survival of nonstandard and socially disfavored language varieties.

2.2 Applications of the Network Concept in Small-scale Communities

Apart from its potential for explaining why nonstandard dialects persist, a network approach has been found methodologically useful for investigations of subgroups in the population in situations where a social class model such as that provided by William Labov (1972) in his study of the urban dialect of New York City is less practical. This happens when the class distribution of the speakers to be studied is uneven, as is the case with most nonstandard dialect speakers. A network analysis has several rather obvious methodological advantages in such situations, which can be stated quite briefly. First, it provides a useful means of studying relatively small, self-contained groups in more detail than is possible within a large-scale survey framework such as Labov's. Second, it provides a means of approaching an analysis where the concept of social class is difficult to apply; this is a problem commonly encountered by researchers studying minority ethnic groups, migrants, rural populations, or populations in nonindustrialized societies (see, for example, Horvath 1985). Finally, network analysis offers a procedure for dealing with variation between speakers at the level of the individual rather than the group. These points are all relevant to the studies by Edwards

(1986) of the language of British black adolescents and by Bortoni-Ricardo (1985) of changes in the language of rural migrants to a Brazilian city. A brief review of these studies follows.

One of the limitations on choice of method encountered by Edwards was that since there is no enumerated list of British black persons (even assuming that this is a well-defined category), a sample frame could not be constructed to allow speakers from the British black community to be systematically sampled from a range of social classes. Even if the use of social class as a speaker variable were feasible in this rather fundamental practical sense, it would in any case be unlikely to yield much insight into the interplay between social and linguistic differentiation. This is for the rather obvious reason that a social class index cannot distinguish in an illuminating way between members of a group who are mostly unemployed or concentrated in low-status occupations. But since it seems to be possible to analyze the black community as a whole as consisting of overlapping sets of relatively close-knit groups, the network variable is, as Edwards found, rather more helpful in describing the relationship between linguistic variability and the social characteristics of speakers.

The crucial variable from a dialectologist's point of view underlying any measure of personal network structure is degree of integration into a close-knit group. However, the same indicators (see the description in Sect. 2.1 of two of those used in Belfast) are not necessarily relevant to different groups. Even if attention is confined to the UK, membership of groups associated with religious institutions might well be irrelevant in a contemporary northern English coal-mining community, but highly relevant in a Midlands' black community such as the one Edwards studied. In fact the indicators used by Edwards were chosen for their capacity to distinguish between individuals who associated themselves to varying degrees with the norms and values of the black community; of particular importance is the distinction between black and nonblack ethnicity. For this reason, Edwards's indicators were designed to measure in various ways the extent to which speakers had contact with black friends and neighbors and participated in black social activities. Whether or not the speakers were employed at all was also taken into account, since employment will almost always involve fairly extended interaction with nonblack individuals. In fact, the index of integration into the black community which was constructed using these indicators correlated well with the extent to which the individual speakers used the 'patois' characteristic of that community.

Bortoni-Ricardo's account of the sociolinguistic adjustment of rural migrants to Brazlandia, a satellite city of Brasilia, is a particularly interesting and innovative application of the network concept. A survey based on a social class analysis is not appropriate or feasible for a sociolinguistic study carried out in Brazil; the chief objections are that the notion of a continuum is neither congruent with the sharp distinction between rich and poor, nor does it adequately discriminate between the individuals studied, all of whom were relatively poor. Bortoni-Ricardo did not posit a linguistic movement by the migrants in the direction of an urban standardized norm (of Portuguese) of the kind familiar in studies using the social class variable; taking the group's own linguistic norms as a starting point, she

examined the extent to which speakers had moved away from their stigmatized Caipira dialect.

Bortoni-Ricardo's main hypothesis about change in social structure associated with the change from rural to urban life is that it involves a move from an 'insulated' network consisting largely of kinsfolk and neighbors to an 'integrated' urban network where the links will be less multiplex and associated with a wider range of social contexts. The linguistic counterpart of this process is analyzed as one of dialect diffuseness—a movement away from the norms of the Caipira dialect. Two separate network indices are used to measure the changing patterns of the migrants' social relationships; the first is the integration index and the second the urbanization index. The integration index expresses numerically certain relevant characteristics of the three persons with whom each migrant most frequently interacts—for example, whether or not they are kinsfolk, or whether the ties have been contracted in the premigration period. The score assigned to each migrant is intended to characterize progress in the transition from an insulated to an integrated type of network, and as such is a tool capable of investigating loose-knit types of personal network structure (see further below). As Bortoni-Ricardo shows, integration scores correlate with a linguistic movement away from the norms of the Caipira dialect.

The urbanization index is designed to supplement this structural measure, representing the extent to which the members of each migrant's personal network are integrated into urban life. A number of indicators are used to compute this index, two of which are educational level and occupational mobility; the indicators are selected for their capacity to measure the extent to which the persons with whom a migrant customarily interacts is integrated into (i.e., participates in) urban life.

From both a methodological and a theoretical point of view, Bortoni-Ricardo's work is particularly interesting. In developing two types of index it extends the application of the network variable beyond an analysis of small, close-knit groups of the kind described so far to consider the extent to which individuals have detached themselves from such groups. The theoretical significance of this advance is explored below. Section 3 will concentrate on the theoretical implications of the link between a close-knit network structure and language maintenance and its obvious corollary; that a loosening of close-knit ties is likely to be associated with linguistic change.

3. Strong and Weak Network Ties: Theories of Language Maintenance and Language Change

A general methodological problem associated with the use of the network variable is that although it can be readily operationalized as described above to study speakers whose networks are of a relatively close-knit type, it cannot easily handle socially and geographically mobile speakers whose personal network ties are not predominantly dense or multiplex. However, such persons make up a substantial proportion of the population in a postindustrial society, particularly in cities. Loose-knit networks are hard to deal with chiefly because social network analysis involves comparing speakers who differ from each other in certain respects—for example, in respect of the multiplexity of the ties which they have contracted at the workplace—but are still similar enough in other related ways to make such a comparison meaningful. For example, it is evident that relative to someone who has changed employment and place of residence several times, the networks of the Belfast inner-city speakers described in Sect. 2.1 are all close-knit. While one might make this general point and follow through its implications in a comparison of, for example, these speakers with residents of lower middle-class areas of the city, it is much less easy to see how the relatively loose-knit network structures of individual lower middle-class speakers might meaningfully be compared with each other. This problem was encountered in an attempt to apply social network analysis in the prosperous Berlin suburb of Zehlendorf (Dittmar and Schlobinski 1988).

In Belfast, language variation in two lower middle-class areas, Braniel and Andersonstown, was analyzed to supplement the inner-city studies described Sect. 2.1. Many of the Braniel and Andersonstown speakers owned cars and telephones, which they used as a means of maintaining important personal ties over long distances, but the capacity of these 'distance' ties to influence their behavior (linguistic or otherwise) is not clear. Some speakers seemed to be relatively exposed to standardizing mainstream influences, in that they had contracted few personal ties which were likely to exert normative pressure on their behavior; but in any case the geographical spread of the ties contracted by most Braniel and Andersonstown speakers made them difficult to investigate. In general, however, these individuals seemed less likely than the inner-city speakers to be subject to the pressures of their personal networks and more likely to be subject to a less localized outside influence, which in turn exposes them to external pressure from a linguistic standard.

3.1 The Importance of Weak Ties in Elucidating Linguistic Change

Loose-knit networks are likely to play an important part in the construction of a theory of linguistic diffusion and change, at the level of theory, although they are difficult to analyze empirically (but see the discussion above of Bortoni-Ricardo's study of rural immigrants to a Brazilian city). Following Granovetter's work (1973) Milroy and Milroy (1985) have argued that 'weak' and apparently insignificant interpersonal ties (of 'acquaintance' as opposed to 'friend,' for example) are important channels through which innovation and influence flow from one close-knit group to another, linking such groups to the wider society. To support this argument, a detailed quantitative analysis of the history and present-day distribution of three Belfast phonological variables is presented. The spread of one of them apparently across sectarian lines of demarcation to penetrate the dialect of young speakers is difficult to explain except in such terms. The change involved is a realization of a limited set of lexical items such as *pull*, *put*, *foot* with an unrounded rather than a rounded vowel. This weak-tie model of change and diffusion is also applied to account for the tendency of some languages to be more resistant to change than others (Icelandic versus English, for example), the general argument being that a type of social organization which is based on overlapping close-knit networks will inhibit change, while one based on

mobility (for whatever reason), with a concomitant weakening of network ties, will facilitate it. Weak intergroup ties are argued to be critical in transmitting innovations from one group to another, despite the rather general common-sense assumption in sociolinguistic and dialectological work that strong ties fulfil this role. For example, in suggesting that the network concept is important for a theory of linguistic diffusion, Downes (1984: 155) assumes that it is strong ties which will be relevant, and Labov (1980: 261) presents a model of diffusion and change where the innovator is seen as an individual with strong ties both inside and outside a local group.

Although the idea that innovations are transmitted through weak network links may at first sight seem counterintuitive, a little thought suggests that it is plausible. First of all, it is likely (in the networks of mobile individuals at least) that weak ties are more numerous than strong ties. Second, many more individuals can be reached through weak ties than through strong ties; consider, for example, the links set up by participants at academic or business conferences, which link cohesive groups associated with each institution and through which new ideas and information pass. Conversely, information relayed through strong ties tends not to be innovatory, since those linked by strong ties tend to share contacts (that is to belong to overlapping networks). Thus, mobile individuals who have contracted many weak ties, but as a consequence of their mobility occupy a position marginal to any given cohesive group, are in a favorable position to diffuse innovation. Interestingly, this conclusion is in line with the traditional assumption of historians of language that the emergent, mobile merchant class were largely responsible for the appearance of Northern (and other) dialectal innovations in Early Modern (Standard) English (see, for example, Baugh and Cable 1978: 194).

The norm-enforcing capacities of groups built up mainly of strong ties partly explains why innovators are likely to be persons weakly linked to the group; indeed, using a measure of network strength, the Belfast community studies described in Sect. 2.1 showed that susceptibility to outside influence increased in inverse proportion to strength of tie with the group. Where groups are loose-knit—that is linked internally mainly by weak ties—they are therefore likely to be generally more susceptible to innovation. This conclusion is consistent with Labov's principle that innovating groups are located centrally in the social hierarchy, in his terms upper-working or lower-middle class (Labov 1980: 254). For it is likely that in British (and probably also North American) society close-knit networks are located primarily at the highest and lowest strata, with a majority of socially and geographically mobile speakers falling between these two points.

3.2 An Apparent Problem: The Weak Tie Model of Diffusion and Change

One apparent difficulty with a theory which argues that innovators are only marginally linked to the group is in explaining how they can successfully diffuse innovations to more central members; two related points are relevant here. First, since resistance to innovation is likely to be strong in a norm-conforming group, a large number of persons will have to be exposed to it and adopt it in the early stages for it to spread successfully. Now in a mobile postindustrial society, weak ties are likely to be very much more numerous than strong ties. Thus, an innovation like the Cockney merger between /v/:/ð/ and /f/:/θ/ reported in Norwich teenage speech (Trudgill 1986: 54ff.) which appears to 'jump' over a considerable distance is likely to be transmitted through a great many weak links between Londoners and Norwich speakers. Trudgill's suggestion of tourists and football supporters as individuals who might contract such links and transmit the change is quite consistent with the model outlined in this section. Second, persons central to a close-knit, norm-enforcing group are likely to find innovation a risky business; but adopting an innovation which is already widespread on the fringes of the group is very much less risky. Thus, instead of asking how central members of a group are induced to accept an innovation from marginal members, this can be viewed as a prudent strategy on their part. For it is likely that a necessary (but not sufficient) condition for the ultimate adoption of a candidate innovation is that it is positively evaluated, either overtly or covertly. Thus, Norwich speakers, whether they are central or marginal to their local groups, in some sense view vernacular London speech as desirable—more desirable than the speech of other cities. Central members of a group diminish the risk of potentially deviant activity by adopting an innovation from persons who are already linked to the group, rather than by direct importation.

This weak tie model of linguistic change remains to be developed further. However, it seems to be capable of illuminating some puzzling patterns of variation and change which are difficult to explain in terms of the usual unqualified assumption that linguistic change is encouraged by frequency of contact and relatively open channels of communication, and discouraged by boundaries of one sort or another, or weaknesses in lines of communication.

4. Social Network, Social Class, and the 'Quantitative Paradigm'

An extension of network analysis which focuses on the properties of weak ties provides a crucial link with the variable of social class, which is used extensively in social dialectology to account for variation in urban dialects. Social anthropologists have linked the variables of class and network by arguing that class differences in small communities begin to emerge over time as the proportion of multiplex relationships declines. Such observations suggest a route for constructing a two-level sociolinguistic theory, linking small-scale structures such as networks in which individuals are embedded and act purposively in their daily lives with larger scale social structures (classes) which determine relationships of power at the institutional level. Such a dual level of analysis is needed in order to understand the frequently reported tendency of speakers of urban vernaculars to downgrade their dialects (describing them as 'sloppy,' 'vulgar,' and the like) while nevertheless continuing to speak them in the face of intense standardizing pressure. Recall that while strong ties give rise to a local cohesion of the kind described in inner-city Belfast, they lead paradoxically to overall fragmentation. It is this potential for explaining both patterns—local stability and cohesion versus overall fragmentation and conflict—which allows

network analysis to be related to macro-level social structure.

Some comments made about network models assume that they cannot easily be linked with class-based analyses of language variation because they are concerned only with strong ties in close-knit communities. Network is frequently seen as a microsociological concept, while class is macrosociological. While this is a reasonable point if network analysis is applied only to close-knit communities, an analysis of loose ties provides a link between the two levels. Furthermore, an initial concentration on network, which emphasizes the extent of local fragmentation in socially stratified societies, suggests that a social class model based on conflict is more appropriate for urban dialectological work than one based on consensus. A number of researchers have been critical of the currently widely accepted consensus model which underlies the work of Labov.

It was pointed out in Sect. 3 that an analysis which makes use of the weak-tie concept agrees with a Labovian class-based analysis in locating linguistic innovators centrally in the class structure. For in British and North American society at least close-knit networks are located primarily in the highest (most powerful) and lowest (least powerful) classes; with regard to the former, consider Mills's (1956) description of the USA power elite. The majority of socially and geographically mobile speakers falls between these two points. Thus, if a network analysis is extended to include an examination of loose-knit network types, which are susceptible to outside (frequently standardizing) influences, it is plain that network-based and class-based analyses are not contradictory as is sometimes suggested; rather they complement each other. This suggests the possibility of an integrated analysis of the relationship between language variation and social structure, combining the variables of social class and social network. Such an analysis would present particular social groups as both internally structured and connected to each other with varying proportions of strong and weak ties.

4.1 Class-related Types of Social Network

The characteristic network structure of distinguishable social groups is certainly related to social class variation (and indeed to other intersecting social variables such as gender and ethnicity) and is likely to have a powerful effect on the kind of dialect spoken both by individuals and by the group as a whole. For example, ethnic subgroups in Britain such as the black speakers studied by Edwards have a predominantly strong-tie internal structure, but seem to be linked with relatively few weak ties to white working-class groups. These white groups in turn might have a similar internal network structure but have more weak-tie links with other white working-class groups. Vertical links to middle-class groups are likely to be fewer (this seemed to be the case in Belfast) and moreover to be frequently institutional in content (to such persons as doctors, lawyers, teachers, welfare personnel, and the like). Middle-class groups for their part—professional, neighborhood, and friendship groups—are characterized by a higher proportion of weak ties internally than working-class groups; hence the problems of studying them systematically in network terms in Zehlendorf, Berlin, and in outer-city Belfast.

However the controversial concept of social class is interpreted and however close-knit networks are investigated and described, Granovetter's concept of the weak tie can be used to link close-knit community level groupings to more abstract institutional structures. A network perspective on social dialects attributes the behavior of speakers to the constraining effects of the network, or the diminution of those effects which enables standardizing linguistic influences to permeate communities. This avoids a direct appeal to the notion of prestige as defined by the perceived attributes of speakers who are seen to *belong* to different status groups. Social class is viewed as a structural concept rather than a set of labels which might be attached to particular individuals. Thus, local and individual social and linguistic behavior is not seen as directly related to class but as mediated through smaller scale network structures.

See also: Semiotic Anthropology; Sociology in Language; Phonology; Historical Linguistics: History; Comparative Linguistics: History.

Bibliography

Baugh A C, Cable T 1978 *History of the English Language*, 3rd edn. Routledge and Kegan Paul, London

Bortoni-Ricardo S M 1985 *The Urbanisation of Rural Dialect Speakers: A Sociolinguistic Study in Brazil*. Cambridge University Press, Cambridge

Ditmarr N, Schlobinski P 1988 *The Sociolinguistics of Urban Vernaculars*. de Gruyter, Berlin

Downes W 1984 *Language and Society*. Fontana, London

Edwards V 1986 *Language in a Black Community*. Multilingual Matters, Clevedon, Avon

Granovetter M 1973 The strength of weak ties. *American Journal of Sociology* **78**: 1360–80

Horvath B 1985 *Variation in Australian English*. Cambridge University Press, Cambridge

Labov W 1972 *Sociolinguistic Patterns*. Pennsylvania University Press, Philadelphia, PA

Labov W (ed.) 1980 *Locating Language in Time and Space*. Academic Press, New York

Milroy J, Milroy L 1978 Belfast: Change and variation in an urban vernacular. In: Trudgill P (ed.) *Sociolinguistic Patterns in British English*. Arnold, London

Milroy J, Milroy L 1985 Linguistic change, social network and speaker innovation. *JL* **21**: 339–84

Milroy L 1987 *Language and Social Networks*, 2nd edn. Blackwell, Oxford

Mills C W 1956 *The Power Elite*. Oxford University Press, Oxford

Mitchell J C 1986 Network procedures. In: *The Quality of Urban Life*. de Gruyter, Berlin

Rickford J 1986 The need for new approaches to social class analysis in linguistics. *Language and Communication* **6(3)**: 215–21

Trudgill P 1986 *Dialects in Contact*. Blackwell, Oxford

Young M, Wilmott P 1962 *Family and Kinship in East London*. Penguin, Harmondsworth

A. L. Milroy

Social Problems

Scholarship on social problems have undergone a transformation that has led to a fresh emphasis on the importance of language in defining problems and in shaping social responses to them. Formerly, social problems were defined as undesirable social conditions, but questions were raised about the logic of this conception. In particular, critics argued that problems and the responses to them were socially constructed—that problems were literally problematic. For students of language, the aspects of this process of construction that are of greatest interest include the rhetorical idioms of problems discourse, counter-rhetorical strategies that may be employed to refute these idioms, the recurrent motifs that efficiently express aspects of a social problem, and the claims-making styles in which the rhetoric may be expressed.

1. The Sociological Background

The constructionist approach to the study of social problems emerged out of a recognition that the field was constituted in atheoretical fashion, being typically consigned to the indifferent care of authors of textbooks for use in lower division social science service courses. A prominent exception was the influential theoretical statement offered by Merton and Nisbet, especially in the 1971 edition of their text, *Contemporary Social Problems*. Their formulation, however, suffered from a fundamental ambiguity with respect to the definition of social problems that they proposed. The logic of the distinction they proposed, between what they term 'manifest' and 'latent' social problems, led them to the view that in some instances the members' definitions are acceptable as the bases for identifying social problems, but in other instances they are not. It is not clear, however, on what bases the sociologist's definitions (i.e., latent social problems) are privileged over those of ordinary members of society (i.e., manifest).

Building on the work of Waller (1936), Fuller and Myers (1941), Blumer (1971), and others, Spector and Kitsuse (1977) critically examined this ambiguity and proposed a reformulation that stressed the importance of distinguishing between 'social conditions' and 'social problems.' They argued that the social conditions that ordinary members of society invoke as occasions for their collective activities should be considered, for purposes of analysis, 'putative' social conditions. Spector and Kitsuse reasoned that social problems, like categories of deviance, are characteristically imbedded in moral, political, and social controversies in which assumptions and methodologies, constitutive of 'the facts' and what they mean, are central to their status as problems. That is, these assumptions and methodologies *constituted* social problems and were thus the proper focus for constructionist analysis.

In addressing this field, however, too frequently the research stance of the sociological analyst, no less than the discursive practices of the nonsociologist, implicitly if not explicitly reflect definitional commitments. It is because of this practical orientation that the conception of social conditions as putative has been interpreted by some constructionists as questioning the corresponding reality of such imputations. Thus, Spector and Kitsuse's recommendation to focus on the interactional processes through which definitions and claims are constructed by members (and sociologist-as-participants) shifted to questions concerning the empirical bases of the putative social conditions—that is, what are the grounds for the members' claims that social problems exist as described? Lacking 'good enough' grounds for being taken at face value, members are 'set up,' their claims 'ironicized,' or 'explained away' (Pollner 1978). As a consequence, the social constructionist project's more radical, language-based concerns remain underdeveloped, displaced by research and analysis reflective of the very definitional ambiguity in Merton and Nisbet that *Constructing Social Problems* rejected and proposed to move beyond.

It is in this context that the methodology and explanatory format of 'case studies' (e.g., Conrad 1975; McCrea 1983; Pfohl 1977) concerned with the sociohistorical contexts of social problems definitions have been criticized as inconsistent with the epistemological bases of constructionism (Woolgar and Pawluch 1985a, b; see also Hazelrigg 1986; Pfohl 1985; Schneider 1985b). The logic of this criticism argues the fundamental importance of sustaining the analytic distinction between the moral conceptions and interpretive practices of everyday member/participants in their social problems activities and the sociologists' descriptions of members' constructions. Inasmuch as the research phenomenon consists of members' claims-making activities, understood as a specific variety of communication, then the theoretical task of reconstructing members' interpretive and rhetorical resources is displaced when sociologists—by endorsing some while discrediting other claims—engage in the very practices that they should be describing (see Schneider 1985a for a survey of the constructionist literature on social problems).

The formulation that follows suggests a line of research that conceives of claims-making as a process of rhetorical construction in which members invoke, appropriate, and inflect vernacular expressions and understanding to assert and confirm the legitimacy of their social concerns and moral sensibilities. The inventory of specific idioms, styles, and so forth offered is composed of ideal types and thus stands to be refined, reconceived, and/or elaborated upon through empirical research and further theoretical reflection.

2. Rhetorical Idioms

Members' claims-making activities are directed at expressing their concerns about states of affairs—'condition-categories'—that they conceive to be undesirable. Claims-making activities problematize such condition-categories by making use of a corpus of mundane discursive strategies that render the conditions describable and remediable 'moral objects.' Thus, social constructionists study social problems as they are brought into being through participants' distinctive ways of speaking and reasoning about, and acting upon, symbolically demarcated social realities.

Rhetorical idioms function as moral vocabularies, providing participants with sets or clusters of themes or sacred symbols capable of endowing claims with wide-ranging significance. They are also commonsense constructions of moral competence in the sense that their idiomatic usage carries the implication that auditors are obliged to honor the value expressed in the claim, and hence the claim itself. The idioms are mainly concerned with establishing, not the magnitude of social problems, but rather their normative tenor. That is, the rhetorical idioms are useful in clarifying and evoking the ethos implicit in the claim. This is especially facilitated by each idiom's characteristic set of positive and negative terms, that is, the idiom's preferred objects of veneration and scorn.

2.1 Loss

The rhetoric of loss is not employed to express mourning over the extinction of something but rather to inveigh against its devaluation. One of its central images is that of humans as custodians or guardians of some unique and sacred thing or quality. It is by virtue of the loss of prestige or value accorded to the sacred object that its existence is threatened, with the concomitant implication that such negligence is deeply revealing of our character in the eyes of some future judge. This rhetoric works most idiomatically with moral objects (condition-categories) that can be interpreted to qualify as forms of perfection in some sense or other. The positive terms composing the idiom's moral vocabulary include 'innocence,' 'beauty,' 'nature,' and 'civilization.' Negative terms consequently cite types of contamination or imperilment culminating in devaluation: 'sin,' 'pollution,' 'decadence,' 'desecration,' and 'commercialization.'

Symbols expressive of protection constitute key elements in this rhetorical idiom's narrative kit, enabling the evocation of the heroism of the rescuer. Indeed, although 'Operation Rescue' is the name chosen by the now well-publicized antiabortion organization, it is a name that is paradigmatic of the idiom's characteristic rhetoric and could probably be applied or adjusted to fit other condition-categories by claimants who use the rhetoric of loss, for example, the 'Save the Planet' slogan of the environmentalists and the 'Save the Schools' cry of antibusing parents. When articulated idiomatically, the rhetoric of loss suggests a posture of vigilance that is heroic rather than merely reactionary. Such an impression is assisted by the premise that the sacred objects (e.g., 'great books') or beings (e.g., 'spotted owls') cannot save or help themselves and so must have the claimants acting on their behalf to protect their elevated symbolic positions and interests.

2.2 Entitlement

Whereas the rhetoric of loss is rooted in a language of altruism and social responsibility to something other than the claimant's own interests, the rhetoric of entitlement emphasizes the virtue of securing for all persons, including the claimants (and in some instances including other forms of life, as in the rights of animals and trees), equal institutional access as well as the unhampered freedom to exercise choice of self-expression, whatever form that may take. The sensibility expressed by this idiom is egalitarian and relativistic. It is egalitarian in its aversion to forms of discrimination against categories of people. Thus, its negative terms are emblematic of forms of discrimination: 'intolerance,' 'oppression,' 'sexism,' 'racism,' 'ageism,' and even 'speciesism.' The idiom's positive terms stem from its relativist philosophy: 'lifestyle,' 'diversity,' 'choice,' 'tolerance,' 'empowerment.' Characteristic here are symbols of liberation that can evoke the value in recognizing others' dignity or rights to personal freedom. Thus, reference to figures like President Lincoln or Dr Martin Luther King calls forth the nobility and personal cost in struggling to expand such rights as well as the historic mission of which the current claims-making activities are a part. This long progressive march of history furnishes narrative frameworks that enable the emergence of the idiom's preferred pejorative: 'reactionary,' an epithet used against counterclaimants (or abstract figures of infamy) who would like to 'turn back the clock' on the democratization of society.

2.3 Endangerment

Whereas the rhetoric of entitlement is applied most idiomatically when the condition-category is elaborated upon as an instance of injustice or inhibition of expressive freedom, the rhetoric of endangerment is suited to being applied to condition-categories so as to articulate threats to the health and safety of the human body. This rhetorical idiom is a relative of entitlement discourse inasmuch as the presumption is that individuals have the right to be safe from harm, to have good health, and to be shielded from preventable or reducible types of bodily risk. However, the rhetoric of endangerment is composed of a cluster of themes and symbols distinct from those associated with the rhetoric of entitlement. Because the urgency of its moral discourse is due less to issues regarding obstacles to freedom and equality than to optimal bodily function and health care, the rhetoric of endangerment can elaborate claims that are in extreme tension with the rights to privacy and expression that are advanced by entitlement discourse.

The idiom's positive terms characteristically combine hope with the prestige of medical reason: 'hygiene,' 'prevention,' 'fitness,' 'nutritiousness.' Its negative terms pinpoint the processes that medically warrant fear: 'disease,' 'pathology,' 'epidemic,' 'malignancy.' Yet while claims employing the rhetoric of endangerment are most idiomatic when delivered in scientific style, language, and reasoning, or when endorsed by medical authorities, they are not immune to being answered. The counter-rhetoric of the telling anecdote described below is a characteristically vernacular way of responding to endangerment claims. In addition, this idiom's applications are often limited to conditioncategories that can be shown to impinge on secondary parties (e.g., 'bystanders,' 'the general population,' 'innocent victims'), precisely because of its bodily centered individualism. In the absence of an analysis linking a private act to a public consequence, the person who insists that the pleasures derived from engaging in the problematic practice (e.g., smoking) outweigh the extended lifespan promoted by the cessation of the practice, is understood to be making a personal decision that must finally be respected, though not necessarily admired.

2.4 Unreason

Of course, 'self-destructive' or 'reckless behavior' may in and of itself become the problematic category, a sign of a less than total mastery of one's powers of intellect. This type of claim utilizes the rhetoric of unreason, which draws upon a hermeneutics of paranoia, interpreting conditioncategories in terms that highlight concerns about being taken advantage of, of being manipulated, 'brainwashed,' or transformed into a 'dupe' or 'fool.' The rhetoric of unreason is premised upon an idealized relationship between the self and the state of knowing; instances where that proper relationship is being undermined or destroyed are

elaborated with reference to such spectres as subliminal messages, conspiracies, mind-altering drugs, hidden forces, and the mesmerizing powers of advertising.

Certain categories of persons are understood to require greater vigilance in regard to the issues encapsulated by this kind of discourse. Those who can be said to be 'trusting,' 'naive,' 'innocent,' 'uneducated,' 'uninformed,' 'desperate,' and so forth can be 'taken advantage of' as 'easy prey,' 'vulnerable' to being manipulated by persons or institutions of greater power or authority. 'Children' provides a paradigmatic vernacular resource for articulating this rhetorical idiom. Playing off the understanding that children are as yet 'unformed,' and interjecting into social problems discourse the suggestive question, 'What about the children?,' directs auditors to extrapolate the worst case scenario: what a child would end up like were he to mature under the tutelage or influence of the pernicious experience.

2.5 Calamity

Unlike the four rhetorical idioms so far discussed, the rhetoric of calamity is distinguished by being composed of metaphors and reasoning practices that evoke the unimaginability of utter disaster. This kind of articulation may be of greatest utility when the social problems language game is especially crowded with a panoply of claims-making movements vying for attention, when claimants are 'coming out all over,' so to speak. Claimants using this idiom will recognize the existence of other claims-making activities directed at nominally unrelated condition-categories, yet cast them into perspective by demonstrating how those other moral objects are contingent upon the existence of their condition-category. The one is either symptom, effect, or logically subordinate to the other. Thus, it is poverty that generates urban crime, drug abuse, poor schools, and teenage pregnancies; it is the problem of the greenhouse effect that stands to create disasters of every imaginable kind; it is AIDS that threatens to create disease on an epidemic scale, an overburdened medical system, explosive insurance premiums, and gay-bashing.

The rhetoric of calamity does not elevate a specific kind of moral system, as do the other idioms. It recognizes that moral reasoning may differ between allies, but the implication of the rhetoric of calamity is that now is not the time for sorting out ethical grounds: there will be time enough later for mere talk; now is the time for action. Thus, the idiomatic expression 'the crisis of X' will be understood to mean that inattention to the condition will only result in creating other social problems at an exponential rate, or exacerbate existing ones to the point of intractability.

2.6 Linguistic Functions of Idioms

The thematic complexes termed 'rhetorical idioms' are vernacular resources, each serving as a kind of narrative kit through which is articulated a condition-category's socially problematic and justifiably treatable status. Analytically, they locate one area in which the central insight of social constructionism—that claims-making activities constitute social problems—can be investigated. When social constructionism investigates members' usage of these rhetorical sets, the questions raised concern not specific conditions but the varieties of claims that the idioms can usefully express. For example, what makes a claim idiomatic in the first place would appear to involve a certain kind of readability, a usage of the language that is both symbolically coherent and morally competent. Given that premise, one can inquire as to what it is that members know when they hear a claim as especially edifying, moving, or insightful, on the one hand, or 'far out,' incomprehensible, or mistaken, on the other. The utility of the rhetorical idioms derives from the discursive materials they provide to claimants to structure and lend urgency to their claims, but presumably those materials cannot be applied in random fashion. The conventions underlying the idiomatic elaboration of condition-categories constitute one aspect of the subject matter. Artfulness consists of stretching and moving the boundaries of what can be construed as idiomatic.

What kinds of semiotic operations does a condition-category undergo as it is moved from one rhetorical idiom to another? Are some kinds of condition-categories more versatile or adaptable in this regard than are others? What are the distinctive kinds of vulnerabilities that each idiom poses for claimants and claims? What are the various ways in which idioms may be combined? What kinds of atrocity tales (Best 1987) do the various idioms accommodate? Does sponsorship (or disallowance) of a given claim under one of the rhetorical idioms entail sponsoring (or disallowing) other claims directed at other condition-categories that are drawing upon the same rhetorical idiom? What are the ways in which this is managed? To what extent is intractability in social problems discourse contingent on participants' usage of different rhetorical idioms? What vernacular resources do members have access to for countering a claim while retaining moral standing? It is to the latter question that we turn in our discussion of counter-rhetorical strategies.

3. Counter-rhetorical Strategies

If rhetorical idioms can render claims both symbolically coherent and morally competent, then auditors are obliged, as members of the same cultural community the claimant has invoked, either to convey sympathy or else to have good reasons for refraining from doing so. Rhetorical idioms usually posit hierarchies of value (e.g., 'freedom' over 'oppression') with which it is difficult to disagree without discrediting oneself; to invert the hierarchy is to marginalize oneself as a postscript in the causes of social problems. Countering claims thus entails an artfulness that comes with being versed in the uses of certain vernacular resources, especially since counterclaimants can, under certain circumstances, be told that 'if you're not part of the solution, then you're part of the problem.'

To be sure, alternative rhetorical idioms can be used to counter claims. Idioms other than the one implicit in a claim are useful in shifting the focus of discourse from the condition-category the claimant has singled out to the meaning of the claimant's claims-making itself. An example: the 'War on Drugs,' initiated under the Reagan and Bush administrations in the USA in the 1980s, was itself rendered problematic when civil libertarians cited the intrusiveness of such measures as drug-testing in the workplace (Staudenmeier 1989). In this case the rhetoric of entitlement (viz., the right to privacy) was evoked to counter a claim arguably rooted in a rhetoric of endangerment.

A similar discursive move was made by critics of anti-abortion claimants, the charge being that one kind of moral belief (itself not disputed) was taking precedence over another to the point of usurpation (e.g., the blocking of entrances to abortion facilities by protestors).

Whereas the rhetorical idioms are drawn upon in efforts to amplify and justify one's claims while seeking to sway others to sympathetic stances, counter-rhetorics block either the attempted characterization of the condition-category, or the call to action, or both. These rhetorical strategies are generalized ways of speaking as morally competent counterclaimants, and thus can be articulated with regard to a variety of provisionally problematized condition-categories. The strategies fall into two classes: (a) sympathetic counter-rhetorics that accept, in part or whole, the problematic status of the condition-category, but which in effect block the request for remedial activities; and (b) unsympathetic counter-rhetorics, which countenance neither the proposed characterization and evaluation nor the suggested remedies.

3.1 Naturalizing

First, there is the sympathetic counter-rhetorical move. Naturalizing is a move that accepts the assessment proposed while rejecting the call for action by normalizing the very condition-category that claimants seek to render problematic and/or undesirable. If the condition-category (e.g., 'sexism') is an instance of how the world 'naturally' is, then calls for remedies are hopelessly naive. Yet the user of this gambit runs the risk of being labeled a 'cynic' or 'pessimist,' labels that acquire negative connotations when directed at certain categories of persons in certain settings, such as politicians during re-election campaign debates.

3.2 Costs

Second, one might use the counter-rhetoric of 'the costs involved.' The upshot of this technique is to assert that the problematic condition-category must be lived with rather than remedied through the claimant's specific measures, either because 'two wrongs don't make a right,' or because the claimed benefits would not outweigh their costs. Saving the spotted owl might result in 'costing' 30,000 logging jobs; implementing civil rights legislation to eradicate racism in the workplace might involve 'reverse discrimination'; pornography is the 'price' of free speech. While the counter-rhetoric of naturalizing is fairly unequivocal about the inevitability of our suffering the condition-category, there is some imprecision in the 'costs involved' gambit. Adapting to the pre-existing is implied in the first, contemplating a 'trade-off' is encouraged in the second; meaning that one might well find the costs involved are not so costly after all.

3.3 Impotence

A third way to accept the claimants' complaint or dissatisfaction with a condition-category while withholding support for remedial action lies in declaring impotence. This entails registering one's moral sympathy while pointing to an impoverishment of resources at hand for adequately addressing the problem. Those who declare impotence, in either personal or institutional capacities, may be subject to charges of merely giving 'lip service' to the problem and become objects of distrust. Indeed, officials may in turn become the object of claims-making activities for their very declared impotence. This occurred when missing children advocates turned their attention to the government itself for its inept, confusing, or unresponsive styles of bureaucratic record-keeping: thus the FBI became part of the problem of missing children (Best 1987).

3.4 Perspectivizing

The fourth sympathetic counter-rhetorical strategy is perspectivizing. This form of talk is possible because the social problems process is premised on the object–subject distinction (Pollner 1978). That is, it consists of observing that the claimant's account is a characterization of a state of affairs which is distinct from that state of affairs itself. The claim is characterized as an opinion. In the locution 'You're entitled to your opinion,' the counterclaimant avers the right of the claimant to participate in the social problems process while simultaneously placing a check on that participation by implying the counterclaimant need not, as a matter of opinion, subscribe to either the same view or the call for remedies. Perspectivizing is in effect a mundane form of relativism. And claimants who proceed to insist that such a relativizing characterization reflects a lack of moral competence may open themselves up to being considered intolerant of differing opinions. In this way, this strategy has an affinity with the rhetorical idiom of entitlement noted above. Thus, this rhetoric is being employed whenever counterclaimants make reference to lifestyle as a legitimation of a series of activities: that the condition in question is a lifestyle is supposed to guarantee its propriety.

3.5 Tactical Criticism

A fifth counter-rhetorical style in this category is tactical criticism. Tactical critics accept the characterization of the condition-category being proffered, but demur in the means claimants employ. 'Yes, gays and lesbians are oppressed, but do those activists have to be so militant and strident about publicizing the fact?' is an example here. Tactical critics can either imply their status as a potentially supportive group of fellow travelers, or suggest that the means claimants are employing might themselves be viewed and treated as a social problem (as when AIDS activists who disrupt religious services or block traffic are characterized by fellow travelers as a 'fringe element' that is potentially dangerous, both to society and to the cause). Of all sympathetic counter-rhetorical moves, this one carries the possibility of being seen as the least hostile by claimants, for the 'counterclaimant' is both sympathetic with the effort to problematize and indicates a willingness to discuss tactics.

3.6 Antipatterning

Then there are the unsympathetic counter-rhetorical strategies. These oppose the condition-category's candidacy as a social problem and therefore also reject the call for remedial activities. First, antipatterning holds that the claim has not in fact characterized a full-scale social problem at all, but rather is focused on something akin to 'isolated incidents.' This was a characteristic response to charges of racial harassment on US college campuses heard during the 1980s. Or, it might be held that victims of magnetic radiation were merely 'unlucky' in developing cancer (Brodeur 1990). Claimants may interpret the gist of the counterclaim as suggesting that the incidence of the phenomenon has been exaggerated, or its nature misunderstood. In this usage, antipatterning serves in effect as a challenge for the claimant to verify the magnitude of the condition-category, or specify the meaning of the terms being used to link instances of the condition-category into a social pattern worthy of attention. This can thus engender 'hairsplitting' debates over the meaning of a key term employed by claimants ('What counts as sexual harassment?' or 'How should one define racism?') or a kind of numbers game ('Are there 300,000 or 3 million homeless persons?').

3.7 Telling Anecdote

The telling anecdote presumes to invalidate a claim by recounting an instance, for example, a personal experience or something that the media has treated as a novel case, which questions the generality of the claimant's analysis. To a charge that the business world practices sex discrimination, the anecdotal response can be, 'But what about all of those women executives they show on TV?' To the charge that smoking is a problem since it causes cancer can come the response, 'My grandfather smoked two packs a day and lived a good 80 years and then some.' The telling anecdote thus holds the claims-maker's characterization accountable to invariability instead of likelihood. Therefore claims couched in the language of scientific generalization are particularly susceptible to the usage of this strategy.

3.8 Insincerity

In using the counter-rhetoric of insincerity the counterclaimant either intimates or declares that the claimant's characterization is suspect because of a 'hidden agenda' on his part: namely that his social problems activity is really a way of advancing or guaranteeing his career, power, or wealth. The logic of this device presumes that self-interest and moral standing are incompatible: claims forwarded by the self-interested are more indicative of private ambitions than the public good. Thus, prolife men are involved in the movement to reassert masculine privilege; social workers trumpet poverty programs because it further solidifies their source of income; civil rights leaders aren't really interested in ending racism because, should they realize that goal, their political power and leadership positions would be undermined (Steele 1988). This form of talk can have an accusatory, *ad hominem* tone, often delivered in the shape of sincerity tests: 'If prolifers really cared about children, then why don't they do something about malnutrition or children in poverty?' 'If antivivisectionists really cared about animal rights, then why don't they wear synthetic fibers on an exclusive basis?' Tone is important: a mild tone suggests inconsistency on the claimant's part, while caustic modulation leaves the impression that he is a hypocrite.

3.9 Hysteria

The counter-rhetoric of hysteria is unsympathetic inasmuch as its usage implies the moral judgment of the claimants is not based in a sound assessment of the condition but is under the influence of nonrational, even irrational factors. Thus, the economy of the USA may not really be in a recession, though ironically the nervous perceptions of panicky stockholders might induce one; the involvement of 'Hollywood liberals' in efforts to save the Amazon rainforest is yet another demonstration of their susceptibility to 'faddish causes'; Evangelical Fundamentalists are on a 'crusade' against pornography because of a 'suspicious' obsession with sexuality nurtured by their leaders. The counter-rhetoric of hysteria characterizes the claimants as members of a social category, and then dismisses their claims as 'typical' expressions of 'bleeding heart liberals,' 'narrow-minded religious fundamentalists,' or 'crazy environmentalists.' In these cases, auditors are instructed to note that the claims display features of the claimants' subcultures, rather than matters of concern to the 'mainstream' of society.

Whether the counter-rhetorics be sympathetic or not, they are all ways of phrasing responses to claims, and the format that they have in common is, 'yes, but. . . .' That is, the value is honored but the claim is not. Each counter-rhetoric carries its own shadings of meaning, and therefore conceivably preferable and less preferable uses. Theoretical reconstruction of social problems discourse can proceed by investigating the kinds of uses the strategies are good for, and the kind for which they fall flat. How are they adapted to different condition-categories, rhetorical idioms, settings, and claims-making stylistics? What do participants know when they read a counterclaim as an indication of the speaker's moral incompetence? The matter of marginality in social problems discourse is a subject of great interest; here it is enough to note that counterclaimants always skirt having their moral standing questioned, and thus their capacity for being participants in social problems discourse in the first place. To study counter-rhetorics is to study how credibility is sustained by virtue of being well versed in the vernacular.

4. Motifs

Motifs are recurrent thematic elements and figures of speech that encapsulate or foreground some aspect of a social problem. They are not complexes of moral discourse in the same sense as rhetorical idioms; rather, they are a kind of generic vocabulary that is of service in claims-making, each term or phrase being inflected because situated in one kind of idiom instead of another. The study of social problems motifs directs attention to the application of morally imbued metaphors and phrases in claims-making.

Examples of motifs include: 'epidemic,' 'menace,' 'scourge,' 'casualties,' 'tip of the iceberg,' 'the war on (drugs, poverty, crime, gangs),' 'abuse,' 'hidden costs.' Some of these terms refer to kinds of moral agents, others to practices, and still others to magnitudes. What is entailed in using these terms in one's moral discourse? How do descriptive requirements shift when something is proposed to constitute a 'scandal,' for example, then a 'crisis'? One set of issues raised concerns the versatility of members' vocabularies within the constraints imposed by their vernacular origins and idiomatic logic. As an example, consider the metaphor of the 'ticking timebomb,' a phrase commonly employed in a variety of claims-making contexts, with respect to diverse condition-categories, and under the auspices of different rhetorical idioms. Urban

poverty, depletion of the ozone layer, and AIDS are often spoken of as ticking timebombs, but why would it be unusual to find abortion associated with that metaphor, even though the politics of abortion might well be? What do condition-categories have to be conceived to share such that they can be said to involve a common motif? What features are shared by those to which no such motif can be applied? What would be an innovative usage of a motif? What do such innovative applications and adaptations involve as symbolic operations? How important is freshness in the use of motifs, as opposed to clichéd applications?

Motifs also raise questions regarding their symbolic currency, or why some are prized while others are considered best avoided. Indeed, the identical motif may undergo such a transformation of value. Thus, Holstein and Miller (1990) provide a reconstruction of members' various usages of the motif 'victim,' describing how it is that victim identity is sometimes considered helpful or enlightening, and other times pointedly not, because the connotations of the victim motif vary when positioned amid diverse kinds of claims. In this sense, then, motifs direct us to observe how the terms of social problems discourse are fine-tuned and symbolic implications are contained. Whether studied for their grammar or utility, motifs afford an avenue for appreciating what claimants do when they make claims.

5. Claims-making Styles

The concept of claims-making styles also suggests an appreciative research agenda, for it makes problematic the tendency for constructionists to focus on state-centered discourse, or favor legal-rational claims and criteria over claims-making embodying alternative forms of knowing and representation.

In connection with claims-making activities, the noun *styles* raises issues regarding how various groupings of the claimant's bearing, tone, sensibility, and membership category can inform both a claim's general appearance and specific content as well as instruct auditors on how the claim should be interpreted. As a transitive verb, 'style' refers to the act of fashioning a claim that is consistent with the conventions of claims-making styles, as when one styles, say, a scientific claim. The task is to specify, first of all, the kinds of styles that are evident across the range of social problems discourses; second, to discern the practices constitutive of the various styles; and third, to comprehend the range and shadings of meaning that these genres of moral representation are capable of conveying. In other words, how is style useful?

5.1 The Scientific Style

For example, what is going on when a claimant is described or recognized as speaking in a 'scientific style?' The frame of reference being invoked probably includes certain typification: a bearing that is disinterested; a tone that is sober; and a vocabulary that is technical and precise. Presumably, anecdotes should serve prefatory or illustrative purposes only, thus humanizing or making accessible the presentation, but such anecdotes should be incidental to the substance of the claims produced. Similarly, to be too rhetorical, political, or poetic, can be taken to be a liability, a departure from the hallmark of the style. The point of the style is not to fashion emotive imagery or reveal the personal stamp of its authors, but rather be anonymous, even styleless, while diminishing uncertainty about the properties of condition-categories. It is quite evident that many practitioners of claims-making recognize the importance of scientific style for lending 'objectivity' to their claims. Thus, examining how members communicate 'scientifically' is relevant for the realization of an interactionist formulation of the social problems process.

The scientific method is, analytically, subsumed under the concept scientific style, and it is not given any greater theoretical significance than any other body of practices associated with a particular kind of style. Given this comparative level of analysis, the point is not that some styles seem to be more often effective in weighty settings, but that research must recognize the importance of studying alternative or oppositional styles as well as less weighty settings.

In addition to the scientific style of claims-making, it is appropriate to point to what might count as specific kinds of styles in claims-making. Such a listing is undertaken for illustrative purposes only, to suggest the range of interactional practices that we can concern ourselves with describing.

5.2 The Comic Style

Under the term 'comic style' are included those practices by which members foreground absurdities in certain positions, highlight the hypocrisies of claimants or counterclaimants, or draw upon some measure of irony or sarcasm to point up a particular moral. Comic styles represent interesting problems of claim-readability inasmuch as the aesthetic imperative of making a good joke can come into conflict with the practical goal of building a constituency. Requirements that humor not be 'off-color,' a 'cheap shot,' or a 'low blow' are apparently conventionally present, even though what counts as being in poor taste is itself variable. Another issue is whether there are circumstances under which the comic style seems most pointed or strategic. That is, with respect to what kinds of categories does it make the most difference? Is it a style better suited to claiming or counterclaiming?

Consider how the comic style of caricature might be used to fashion a counterclaim by an *ad absurdum* extension of claims couched in the entitlement idiom. Thus, efforts by gay educators in California to include recognition of the contribution of gays in high-school history textbooks (as a way of empowering gay teenagers) were countered by such rhetorical questions as 'Should we mention the contributions of pedophiles and prostitutes as well?' Implied in this rhetorical gambit are two subtexts: first, a moral equivalence between gays and pedophiles that would presumably embarrass proponents of the project; second, that history textbooks would by the logic of entitlement soon take on the character of a perverts' gallery, and thus could not be placed in the hands of the impressionable young. This counterclaim charges those who press such entitlement claims with creating a 'slippery slope' from which there would be no return—evoking the spectre of nihilism. Thus, the central concept of the entitlement idiom's remedial vocabulary—the expansion of rights—is countered in this instance by exposing the absurd, the unidiomatic lengths to which the rhetoric of entitlement can be taken.

5.3 The Theatrical Style

The 'theatrical style' encompasses those instances of claims-making that make a point of illustrating the group's moral posture in the very way in which the claim is represented. The AIDS organization Act-up's various 'actions,' such as 'die-ins,' are dramatizations of the condition being contested. 'Guerrilla theater' activists also seek to become living illustrations of their claim's substance, such as when an anti-Miss California Pageant demonstrator in Santa Cruz, California, dressed up in a bathing suit consisting of pieces of meat. Theatrical styles seem to have gained wider usage, so that what might once have been, and probably still is, the preferred style of artists and other cultural workers, has filtered out to other segments of society. Thus, 'Operation Rescue' demonstrations against legalized abortion have featured such actions as symbolic mass funerals. The danger in this style is inscrutability, especially when the symbolic stagings carry the burden of being presented before a broader public. In that event, literary critics or social scientists may be brought in to translate for the public the allegorical or symbolic meaning embedded in the representation, or the integrity of the speech style itself, as when Henry Louis Gates, Jr testified on behalf of rap musicians '2 Live Crew' in a 1990 obscenity trial. ('Rapping' is best considered a 'subcultural style' in our scheme, however.)

5.4 The Civic Style

The 'civic style' of claims-making entails making claims that have what we call 'the look of being unpolished.' That is, the civic style lends to claims the tenor of being 'honest,' 'sincere,' 'upright,' 'unstylized.' Where extensive preparation is clearly the rule in the theatrical style, claimants using the civic style should aim to be interpreted as participating in social problems discourse out of spontaneous moral indignation or outrage. To appear too well organized or 'too slick' is to be part of an 'interest group.' The civic style involves trading off an ideal of the 'common,' 'decent folk,' and its character is often used as the face of commonsense morality, especially in such popular culture icons as the film *Mr Smith Goes to Washington*.

5.5 The Legalistic Style

The 'legalistic style' is premised on the notion that the claimant is in fact speaking on behalf of another party, a defendant or plaintiff, and that the merits of that party's case are consistent with rights and protections embodied in the law. The reason that the legalistic style is not subsumed under the theatrical style, in spite of the courtroom theatrics of attorneys, is because a legalistic-styled claim is presumably neither allegorical nor symbolic, but rather particular, specific, and analogic with the full weight and prestige of institutional justice supporting it.

5.6 The Subcultural Style

Finally, a possible category that might provide a linkage between social constructionism and cultural studies: 'subcultural style.' It is possible that various segments of society—whether self-defined by class, race, ethnicity, gender, sexual orientation, or geographical location—tend to evolve unique or local (Geertz 1983) ways of commenting on the larger social world. Possible connections that might be considered: the relationship between 'camp' and moral positioning; the styles of moral discourse evolved in such dialogical situations as 'self-help groups,' or consciousness-raising sessions; and the claims-making formats nurtured by bilingualism or the use of nonstandard English. The value of including the category of subcultural style is that it reminds us of something easily overlooked: social problems discourse occurs in all manner of forums and among a wide range of persons. The concerns that these diverse people may have in commenting on, and their characteristic ways of describing, the symbolic order in which they are involved are not necessarily apparent if one takes state-sponsored or, for that matter, media-sponsored discourse as offering a point of entry into the sociology of contemporary moralities. Thus, in her study of news organizations, Tuchman (1978: 139) found that the women's movement's consciousness-raising sessions were not amenable to the conventional formats of news reporting. As she puts it, 'The reporter could not draw on narrative forms embedded in the web of facticity to frame seemingly "formless kind of talk" as a topic—a news story she could tell.'

6. Conclusion

By investigating vernacular resources as they are adapted to the social problems process, social constructionists stand to develop what might be called an 'ethnography of moral discourse.' In particular, the discursive practices through which claims are constituted reveal the language and reasoning which members are capable of appropriating, developing, and inflecting in a variety of subtle and distinctive ways. The task of theory and research is to note the differences in the meaning and consequences that members' uses of vernacular forms can have for the character of society's social problems. The study of the vernacular constituents of social problems provides new ways of conceiving the subject matter, as well as indicating the necessity for rethinking or refining the theoretical language employed to reconstruct those social interactions that can be called claims-making activities.

See also: Medicalization; Social Psychology; Sociology in Language; Symbolic Crusades; Symbolic Interactionism.

Bibliography

Best J 1987 Rhetoric in claims-making: Constructing the missing children problem. *Social Problems* **34**: 101–21
Blumer H 1971 Social problems as collective behavior. *Social Problems* **18**: 298–306
Brodeur P 1990 Annals of radiation: Calamity on Meadows Street. *The New Yorker*
Conrad P 1975 The discovery of hyperkinesis: Notes on the medicalization of deviant behavior. *Social Problems* **23**: 12–21
Fuller R C, Myers R R 1941 The natural history of a social problem. *American Sociological Review* **6**: 320–28
Geertz C 1983 *Local Knowledge: Further Essays in Interpretive Anthropology*. Basic Books, New York
Hazelrigg L 1986 Is there a choice between 'constructionism' and 'objectivism'? *Social Problems* **33**: 1–13
Holstein J, Miller G 1990 Rethinking victimization: An interactional approach to victimology. *Symbolic Interaction* **13**: 103–22
McCrea F B 1983 The politics of menopause. *Social Problems* **31**: 111–23
Merton R K 1971 Introduction: The sociology of social problems. In: *Contemporary Social Problems*, 3rd edn. Harcourt, Brace and World, New York
Pfohl S J 1977 The 'discovery' of child abuse. *Social Problems* **24**: 310–23
Pfohl S J 1985 Toward a sociological deconstruction of social problems. *Social Problems* **32**: 228–32
Pollner M 1978 Constitutive and mundane versions of labeling theory. *Human Studies* **I**: 269–88
Schneider J W 1985a Social problems theory: The constructionist view. *Annual Review of Sociology* **1**: 209–27a
Schneider J W 1985b Defining the definitional perspective of social problems. *Social Problems* **32**: 232–37
Spector M, Kitsuse J I 1977 *Constructing Social Problems*. Cummings, Menlo Park, CA
Staudenmeier W J 1989 Urine testing: The battle for privatized social control during the 1986 war on drugs. In: Best J (ed.) *Images of Issues: Typifying Contemporary Social Problems*. Aldine de Gruyter, New York
Steele S 1988 I'm black, you're white, who's innocent? *Harper's Magazine* **June**: 45–53
Tuchman G 1978 *Making News: A Study in the Construction of Reality*. Free Press, New York
Waller W 1936 Social problems and the mores. *American Sociological Review* **1**: 922–34
Woolgar S, Pawluch D 1985a Ontological gerrymandering: The anatomy of social problems explanations. *Social Problems* **32**: 214–27
Woolgar S, Pawluch D 1985b How shall we move beyond constructionism? *Social Problems* **33**: 159–62

P. R. Ibarra
J. I. Kitsuse

Social Psychology

Social psychology is an interdisciplinary academic field, lying between psychology and sociology, with less substantial connections to economics and to literature. At many universities, competing social psychology courses are taught in both the psychology and sociology departments, and on rare occasions joint departments in social relations have been founded. The division between psychology and sociology is so extreme that it has become fashionable to speak of 'two social psychologies' rather than one. Despite its fragmentation, social psychology speaks with a strong voice on the importance of language in human relations, and many of its theories and research findings should be of direct concern to linguistics. Several essays in this *Encyclopedia* examine in detail aspects of the social psychology of language, and this essay provides an overview. After sketching the structure of the field, a sampling of major language-related topics will be considered: the social psychology of speech, attitudes, symbolic interactionism, meaning, and microsociology.

1. The Structure of Social Psychology

Stephan and Stephan say that sociological social psychology concerns social experience stemming from individuals' participation in groups, social interaction, the effects on both of these of the cultural environment, and the emergence of social structure from interaction. In contrast, psychological social psychology focuses on the thoughts, feelings, and behaviors of individuals as influenced by others. In sociology, Stephan and Stephan contend, two distinct schools of thought exist: symbolic interactionism, which holds that reality is socially constructed through the meanings people communicate, and the personality and society perspective, which emphasizes the attitudes and values that individuals derive from their cultures. Psychological social psychology seems even more diverse, including social learning theory, exchange theory, role theory, and attribution theory.

While such a typology can have heuristic functions, no single conceptual division of the field has achieved wide consensus. Not only is it difficult to map social psychology at a given point in time, but as Sahakian's review of the history of the field proves, its contours and divisions have changed over the decades. A. M. McMahon and a number of other authors have argued that social psychology of all varieties experienced a crisis in the late 1970s, when many critics charged that the field had lost sight of fundamental questions, and the knowledge gained by each successive research project seemed to illustrate the law of diminishing returns.

George Homans (see *Homans, George C.*) frequently remarked that human beings must have always known the chief truths concerning social behavior, or else they would not have been able to sustain successful relations with each other. If true, this observation sets sharp limits to the achievements possible for academic social science. Prior to the late 1970s, however, social psychologists had made striking claims for a number of rather counterintuitive theories, and part of the crisis that followed may merely have been their empirical disproof.

McMahon says that psychological social psychology was dominated by two classes of theorizing: trait theories of individual behavior and field theory. Trait theories assert that social conditions shape individuals, giving them distinct personalities or attitudes that become fixed and thus render behavior consistent across many very different situations. When human behavior was found to be significantly inconsistent, and attitudes refused to stabilize in study after study, trait theories lost ground. Field theory asserts that the proper unit of analysis is the social system, but beyond this its advice has not been clear and its influence has faded as its terminology has been replaced by fresher metaphors.

Sociological social psychology, for McMahon, either borrowed its perspectives from psychology, in which case it suffered the same crisis, or drew upon the often compatible sociological schools of thought known as 'symbolic interactionism' and 'structural functionalism.' In textbooks of a generation ago, symbolic interactionism was used to explain individual-level phenomena, while structural functionalism explained phenomena on the societal level. Supposedly, society was a structure of institutions, organized around a coherent set of values and beliefs, that served vital functions for the entire system. Individuals were socialized, greatly through symbols exchanged during social interaction, to play their necessary roles in the institutions. However, in the 1960s structural functionalism crashed, its theories seeming either factually wrong or vacuous, and its relative political conservatism was no longer attractive to the increasingly radical sociologists. Symbolic interactionism has retreated from its partnership with the now bankrupt structural functionalism, and it continues to be a vital school of thought recruiting new scholars and publishing at a great rate. Yet its theories have never been particularly adapted to unambiguous empirical testing, and the increasing quantification and empiricism of the main journals shunted symbolic interactionism over to the sidelines.

2. The Social Psychology of Speech

A few older textbooks on social psychology contain distinct sections on language, notably the excellent texts by Roger Brown and by Krech, et al., but most textbooks of the late 1980s and early 1990s disperse their material on language across several chapters ostensibly devoted to other topics. For example, studies on interpersonal influence are found throughout these texts, offering many insights that might be applied to linguistic analysis of accommodation (see *Accommodation in Communication*), the adjustment of speech to match that of persons with whom one is speaking.

The study of psychopathology has particularly generated theory and research concerning language. Psychotherapy (see *Psychotherapy*), the talking cure, assumes that emotional problems are sufficiently language-rooted that the insight or catharsis that can come from talking about them is curative. The theory of the double bind (see *Double Bind*), to mention a specific example, asserts that mental problems can arise from contradictory messages imposed on a powerless person by a powerful one. One form of therapy, albeit a deviant one, was explicitly linguistic in nature, the general semantics (see *General Semantics*) movement that asserted that all human social and emotional pathologies resulted from misuse of language. Research has also been conducted on deception, the conscious use of language to misinform the listener, including a large body of studies on the so-called Machiavellian personality who habitually lies (Christie and Geis 1970; Hyman 1989).

Social psychologists have learned about language not only by studying it, but also by perfecting research methods that rely heavily upon it. For example, interviewers have been forced to learn how to maximize rapport with their research subjects, thus gaining general insights into how successful communication can be achieved. Richard A. Berk and Joseph M. Adams have suggested four principles of establishing rapport with respondents who are apt to be suspicious of the researcher: always be honest, be prepared to inconvenience oneself as a sign of commitment, always keep one's word, and speak in as flattering terms as possible, consistent with plausibility.

Berk and Adams have also listed techniques for establishing respect and acceptance. While it is important for an interviewer dealing with subjects who speak a different language to communicate in their terms, the interviewer should not adopt the slang style of the subjects unless it is very natural for the interviewer. The subjects may appreciate the special effort the interviewer makes to learn their language, but they know the interviewer is not a member of their group and may be offended by a pretense of membership. Other language-related techniques include remaining unshaken even when one hears things that are very shocking to the researcher's personal standards, and occasionally revealing some intimate facts about oneself in recognition that really successful communication requires a reciprocal relationship between the speakers.

Raymond L. Gordon has identified eight factors that inhibit communication in interviews: competing demands for time made by activities outside the interview, threats to the person's ego that various topics may constitute, etiquette rules that prohibit saying certain kinds of things in public or to certain kinds of people, the pain of recounting past traumatic experiences, simple forgetting, confusion about the chronological order of events, inferential confusion about the meaning of events, and unconscious behavior patterns that set hidden agendas for the conversation. The best antidotes to these inhibitors are eight facilitators: the respondent's desire to fulfill expectations, the recognition he or she seeks from the interviewer, altruistic appeals that stress the ultimate values served by the interview, sympathetic understanding of what the person expresses, the new experience that an interview affords, emotional catharsis, the opportunity to place memories and feelings in a meaningful context with an intelligent listener who asks guiding questions, and extrinsic rewards such as money paid for talk.

3. Attitudes

Perhaps the most widely used concept in psychological social psychology is *attitude*, often defined as the positive or negative evaluation of an object, with anything, tangible or intangible, capable of being the object of an attitude. As the term is generally used, each person is presumed to possess a large number of attitudes that can be expressed almost instantly in words and that are the key determinants of behavior with regard to the object. People who say they favor political party X can be expected to vote for it; people who express positive atitudes toward particular foods are likely to eat them. The standard way of measuring attitudes is through self-report questionnaires or interviews, and the underlying assumption of this research is that attidues are coded verbally in the brain, thus making them linguistic phenomena.

Linguists have begun systematic research on attitudes towards speech styles (see *Speech Styles: Attitudes and Inferences*), in light of the fact that speakers and dialects are often evaluated harshly if they do not meet some set of standards applied by listeners. Standard psychological experimental methodology has been applied to this topic, through the matched guise technique (MGT), described by Peter Ball and Howard Giles. Respondents are played a set of recordings of voices and asked to judge the speakers' capabilities, personalities, emotional states, and various other social and linguistic characteristics. The challenge in such a method is to control for differences in the speakers' voices that are unrelated to the independent variable in question. In MGT, speakers are chosen to make the recordings who are capable of speaking in two distinctly different ways, for example equally fluently in French or English, thus matching all voice characteristics other than the one under examination.

Perhaps the classic example of social psychological research on attitudes is the work on attitude change that was performed at Yale University around 1950, still relevant and constantly being extended in the 1990s. Two of the experiments done at Yale by Carl I. Hovland and his associates will demonstrate the wide range of language-related phenomena that were studied, one concerning the credibility of communicators, and the other exploring the role of public proclamations in stabilizing attitudes. In an experiment reported by Hovland, et al., a recorded lecture about juvenile delinquency was played to high school students who were asked to judge how fair it was. The first of three experimental groups was told that the speaker was a judge in a juvenile court, someone who was a real expert on the topic, and highly respectable as well. A second group thought the speaker was an ordinary member of a radio program's studio audience, and a third group was told that the speaker was a former juvenile delinquent currently awaiting trial on a charge of drug peddling. The judge was considered fair by 73 percent of the subjects, and 63 thought the ordinary person was fair, but only 29 percent gave a favorable rating to the accused drug pedlar. The vast literature of similar studies that have followed on from the Yale research support and give scientific specificity to the commonsense notion that speech has a variable impact on listeners, depending upon who speaks it.

The second attitude change experiment divided student respondents into two groups who were given a pair of lectures on the issue of the voting age, which was 21 years old at the time of the study. In the first phase of the experiment, the subjects heard a speech giving one side of a debate on voting age. Then the students were asked whether they agreed or disagreed with the following statement: 'The voting age should be reduced from 21 years to the draft age of 18 years.' After that, they all wrote an essay, giving their views on the voting age debate. The second phase consisted of another speech, giving the other side of the voting age debate. Finally, the students were asked again to state their view on whether the voting age should be reduced from 21 to 18.

The experimental manipulation concerned the essay the student wrote at the end of the first phase. Half of the students were told to sign their essays and were informed that they would appear in the next issue of the school newspaper, while the other half of the respondents were left to believe that their essays and opinions were private. The researchers hypothesized that making a public commitment to an opinion reduced the chances that a person would change his or her views subsequently. Indeed, among the group that signed their essays and believed they would be published, only 14 percent changed their opinion to agree with the second speaker, while in the control group, 41 percent did so. Thus, expressing an attitude in public strengthens the individual's commitment to it.

Research on attitudes is conducted at such a high rate in the late twentieth century, that the *Annual Review of Psychology* summarizes it regularly (Cooper and Croyle 1984; Chaiken and Stangor 1987; Tesser and Shaffer 1990). Yet serious questions remain about the efficacy of the concept. In particular, questions continue to be raised about the connection between attitudes and behavior (see *Attitudes and Behavior*), and many studies indicate that what people say and what they do are quite different things. Certainly the concept of attitude asserts a theory about the power of language, and much research on the topic will be of interest to linguists.

4. Symbolic Interactionism

Symbolic interactionism (see *Symbolic Interactionism*) is a distinct school of thought, acknowledging a unified heritage that many say began with George Herbert Mead (see *Mead, George Herbert*). Although some symbolic interactionists have accepted the canons of positivist science, others, notably Herbert Blumer (see *Blumer, Herbert*), believe that social reality is too multifaceted and fluid to be captured in a few rigid hypotheses. Some of the most influential members of this school, Erving Goffman (see *Goffman, Erving*), for example, offer suggestive interpretations of the meaning of human behavior and symbolic expression, but refuse to subject them to any process of unequivocal evaluation. To that extent, symbolic interactionism is more like poetry or music than it is like the natural sciences.

Some writers distinguish two brands of symbolic interactionism, the Chicago School, which stresses interpretation of humanly constructed meanings to the exclusion of hypothesis testing, and the Iowa School, which allows the possibility of logically framing and empirically testing somewhat general statements about human behavior. But in all its manifestations, symbolic interactionism offers a sharp critique of the currently dominant approach in the central sociology journals, which stresses the computerized analysis of frequently superficial numbers far removed from the richness of human meanings.

Among the early concepts that continue to have great influence is definition of the situation (see *Definition of the Situation*), proposed by Thomas and Znaniecki in 1918. The meaning of something does not immediately announce itself to us, but must be read into every situation, typically on the basis of the culture shared by participants and prior experiences of the individuals. To some extent, such definitions are arbitrary, and there are always alternative definitions that fit a situation equally well. But once a definition has been adopted, it conditions people's actions, feelings, and further perceptions.

Among the most important entities that requires definition is the self (see *Self: Definition of*). A glance at an English dictionary reveals that *self* appears in literally hundreds of compounds, from *self-abandoned* to *self-worship*, and it primarily serves to indicate reflexivity. As George Herbert Mead analyzed it, this reflexivity is both subject and object, the first person in both nominative and objective cases, the *I* contemplating the *me*. Clearly, there are several ways one might analyze *self* linguistically, and in various usages it is frequently listed as pronoun, adjective, noun, and even verb. As a noun, it is an abstraction referring to the entire person of an individual. Symbolic interactionists have both examined the concept closely and employed it to great effect in their analyses of individual behavior and of society. As Hazel Marcus and Elissa Wurf (1987) noted, social psychologists of several varieties have come to see self-concepts as dynamic, multifaceted, and implicated in social phenomena of all kinds.

Among the ways a self can manifest itself is through the playing of roles, and role theory (see *Role Theory*) has been developed and applied by literally hundreds of symbolic interactionists. Language enshrines many roles, such as 'father,' 'mother,' 'priest,' 'judge,' and 'teacher.' The complete set of roles in a society provides a kind of social grammar, defining how persons (rather than words) are supposed to interact, and they are among the most thoroughly linguistic of social phenomena. Many sociologists argue that social roles are scripted by society and define *role* as 'a set of expectations governing the behavior of persons holding particular positions in society; a set of norms that defines how persons in a particular position should behave' (Stark 1989: 686). Symbolic interactionists have given rather more stress to the capacity of individuals to script their own roles, for example, through constant *impression management* intended to give the most favorable impression of oneself to others, and to the way that the roles in a particular social group are constantly undergoing change. In the extreme, it can be argued that the self is nothing more than the set of roles played by a given person.

The self comes into existence through interaction with others, and the other, as an alternate self, comes into existence reciprocally through the same process. Important in symbolic interactionism is the concept of the *generalized other*, a kind of indefinite second person that represents the shared perspective of all the particular others who interact with the self. By taking that perspective, in the imagination, a person can view himself from outside as it were, thus attaining a clear concept of self. At one level, the generalized other can represent all of humanity minus one, but there also can exist several more limited generalized others, including groups that serve as reference points for the definition of the self.

A reference group (see *Reference Group*) is a category of persons, real or imaginary, toward whom the individual orients his behavior and which he uses to define himself. Often, the individual desires the approval of the reference group and tries to become a worthy member of it. A negative reference group, however, is a category of people one wishes to disassociate from, and one method to achieve this is to broadcast the twin message that the traits of the group are abhorrent and that one possesses very different traits. For years, reference group theory has been influential in business marketing research, and advertising is often designed to communicate messages associating a product with groups that are positive reference groups for many consumers.

Early in the twentieth century, symbolic interactionism greatly influenced educational theory in the United States, and in diluted and often unrecognized forms, it continues in the 1990s to shape discourse about the means by which good citizens and responsible adults are created. Many community leaders, social workers, and journalists talk the language of symbolic interaction without necessarily understanding its technical meaning or the relatively distinct philosophy of life embodied in it. In sociology, symbolic interactionism has been important in shaping conceptions of values (see *Values*), and it has contributed to our understanding of the role of symbols in social conflict through labeling theory (see *Schütz, Alfred*) of deviant behavior and the analysis of social movements as symbolic crusades (see *Symbolic Crusades*).

5. Meaning

Not surprisingly, *meaning* is one of the most difficult words to define, especially as it is used in social psychology to refer to humanly constructed frameworks for perception, emotion, and action. A dictionary may say that meaning is what is conveyed by language, but how this 'what' exists apart from the language that conveys it is not clear, and the meaning of *meaning* has been the special focus of ethnomethodology, attribution theory, and branches of semantics that spread into social psychology.

Ethnomethodology (see *Ethnomethodology*) is a school of sociology concerned with how human beings make sense of their everyday lives, and like symbolic interactionism, it stresses the processes by which people achieve definitions of objects, roles, and even the internal states of their own minds. Of particular interest to linguists, ethnomethodology was in great measure the source of the movement known as 'conversation analysis' (see *Conversation Analysis*). Ethnomethodology is distinct from symbolic interactionism both in arising from German philosophical roots rather than American ones, and for giving rather greater emphasis to the internal subjectivity of the individual, and less to the role of the other. Indeed, while symbolic interactionist George Herbert Mead was concerned with how other people participate in the building of an individual's self, ethnomethodological precursor Alfred Schütz (see *Schütz, Alfred*) wrote about how a person gains insight into other's subjectivity through consideration of his or her own.

Richard Hilbert has argued that ethnomethodology (including conversation analysis) should not be considered a part of social psychology because it transcends the distinction between microsociology and macrosociology, and yet with its emphasis on the contents of the human mind and its empirical emphasis on the details of interactions between individuals, it seems appropriate to consider it here.

A classic empirical study in the ethnomethodological tradition was Peter McHugh's experiment that ostensibly studied a new method of counseling. Each research subject sat alone in a room, speaking into a microphone about his personal problems and asking questions answerable by 'yes' or 'no.' After the counselor in another room responded, the research subject was supposed to say aloud what the answer meant to him, then proceed to present more of his problems and ask further yes–no questions. In fact, the yes–no answers were given according to a prearranged pattern, and had nothing to do with the questions asked. The fact that the subjects typically found the answers meaningful was interesting, but the study also allowed close examination of the frameworks people used to construct the meaning they believed they had found.

Many ethnomethodological studies have concerned direction-giving of one kind or another. In one design, the researcher telephones various businesses, asking directions for how to come over but continually failing to understand them; this forces the unwitting research subjects on the other end of the phone to struggle to orient the caller in terms of landmarks or abstract principles like compass directions. A less intrusive method is to listen in on the radio messages used to dispatch taxicabs. One researcher merely observed what medical personnel said to patients who were awakening from general anaesthesia, words apparently chosen to reorient the person and prevent them from panicking and thrashing around.

Ethnomethodology is in great measure based on phenomenology (see *Phenomenology*), a philosophical tradition associated with Edmund Husserl. For example, a technique of philosophical analysis called 'reduction' can be adapted to the study of the meaning of concepts. In reduction, one contemplates a particular concept, noting all the characteristics that seem associated with it. Then one mentally examines each characteristic in the list, determining whether the concept in question could exist without it, and crossing the characteristic off the list if it could. Eventually, one arrives at an irreducible list of attributes of the concept in question, a pristine definition of it shorn of all nonessentials.

What is a telephone call? The phone rings, someone picks it up, and a person says 'Hello.' That's a phone call. But is the ring essential? No; there could be a flashing light, or other signal. Is some kind of signal necessary? Perhaps; that question needs further study. Is it essential for there to be something to pick up? No. Must there be someone on the other end of the line? Yes. Must that person be aware that there is somebody on this end of the line? Yes. Is the exchange of words necessary? Eventually, after close thought to resolve any ambiguities, reduction would produce the essential definition of *telephone call*. In their empirical research, ethnomethodologists force ordinary people to act out this procedure, or they watch them employing their *ethnomethods* to make sense out of natural problems of definition that present themselves in the world of everyday life.

In psychological social psychology, the 1970s and 1980s saw the emergence of a major approach to meaning called attribution theory (see *Attribution Theory*). When it first emerged in the 1960s, attribution theory had some similarities to ethnomethodology; both stressed the ways people make sense of their surroundings and both made radical claims about the novelty of their findings. For example, attribution theorists frequently asserted that people do not know their own minds but infer their attitudes on the basis of observing their own behavior or being told by others how they felt.

A host of experimental studies seemed to confirm this diagnosis of human self-ignorance. Subjects given injections of epinephrine felt and behaved quite differently, depending on what they had been told the effects would be or on how the experimenter's confederate behaved. Subjects who had received a series of painful electric shocks could endure more or less further pain depending on whether they were told they had been assisted in tolerating the earlier shocks by a drug. Despite initial appearances, attribution theory turned out not to be one of the faddish excesses of the 1960s, but a solid contribution, and in the 1990s it can now be seen that much work before the 1960s actually laid the basis for the recent developments. Attribution theory focuses most closely on the social and psychological processes by which people define the causes of events, but its ideas are remarkably similar to those of contemporary symbolic interactionism, except supported by a far stronger empirical research program.

Another development in psychological social psychology that focuses on meaning is the research technique known as the 'semantic differential' (see *Semantic Differential*). It consists of a set of paired opposites, such as good–bad and happy–sad, presented as questionnaire scales. The respondent is required to rate a concept on each of these scales, and statistical analysis then maps the concept along three dimensions: evaluation, potency, and activity. Widely used in a variety of studies conducted in many languages, the semantic differential is believed to measure the connotative meaning of terms. Very recently, as John Digman reports, the three semantic dimensions have been related to a system of five dimensions of personality that has achieved much consensus among psychologists: extraversion/introversion, friendliness/hostility, conscientiousness, neuroticism, and intellect. Digman further notes that the personality typologies employed both by psychologists and by ordinary people are rooted in language and may be little more than the system human language possesses for classifying human behavior.

6. Small Groups and Other Microstructures

At present, judging from course enrolments and book sales, the psychological brand of social psychology is more popular than the sociological brand, and thus perhaps it is more influential. However, much of the work done in sociology that could be called social psychology is given other names. Rodney Stark (1989: 682–83), among others, calls it 'microsociology,' which he defines as 'the study of small groups and of face-to-face interaction among humans,' to be contrasted with macrosociology, 'the study of large groups and even of whole societies.' Much microsociological research is performed in the field, for example, observational studies of families, religious groups, or deviant subcultures, while psychological social psychology is more wedded to the laboratory and to the experimental method. Some varieties of microsociology eschew psychology altogether, if by 'psychology' is meant the study of the individual psyche, and focus instead on the structure of social relations in small groups and networks.

In both sociology and psychology, small group research (see *Small Group Research*) has been carried out vigorously for many decades. Groups establish norms concerning proper language; the status structure of groups often demands deferential or commanding language, and groups shape the language of members through cohesive social relations and the socialization of values. Among the research techniques developed to study communication patterns in small groups, interaction process analysis (see *Interaction Process Analysis*) is notable not only for its great influence but also for providing a novel theory of the categories of speech.

Microsociologists have become increasingly dissatisfied with the concept of group, however, noting that many of the stable social relationships that affect the individual occur in open structures that might better be called 'networks.' Sociometry (see *Sociometry*) is the technique for studying social networks, and the measurement of linguistic influence across complex social structures has progressed considerably in recent years.

Some scholars, in both psychology and sociology, prefer to begin their analysis with the exchanges that take place between individuals, and exchange theory (see *Exchange Theory*) has become a prime rallying point for social psychologists who emphasize the economic nature of human behavior. Like symbolic interactionism, exchange theory focuses on the give and take that transpires between individuals, but it ignores symbols in favor of rewards, whether tangible or intangible. Thus, exchange theory appears to give a lesser role to language than do the other perspectives described above. In the extreme, as practiced by George Caspar Homans, exchange theory is thoroughly behavioristic, denying the importance of the subtle contents of the human mind, words included.

7. Conclusion

The diversity of social psychology is at once a blessing and a curse. Few practitioners are aware of the potentially great value of uniting social psychology with linguistics, and those few can at best create narrow bridges between their own particular subfields or schools of thought and scholarly linguistics. Thus, a convergence of social psychology and linguistics will be difficult to achieve. However, language plays such a tremendous role in so many branches of social psychology, and a variety of its theories and research traditions have so much insight and information to offer linguists, that a marriage of the disciplines is worth promoting.

See also: Sociology in Language.

Bibliography

Ball P, Giles H 1988 Speech style and employment selection: The Matched Guise Technique. In: Breakwell G M, Foot H, Gilmour R (eds.) *Doing Social Psychology: Laboratory and Field Exercises.* Cambridge University Press, Cambridge

Berk R A, Adams J M 1970 Establishing rapport with deviant groups. *Social Problems* **18**: 102–17

Brown R 1965 *Social Psychology.* Free Press, New York

Chaiken S, Stangor C 1987 Attitudes and attitude change. *Annual Review of Psychology* **38**: 575–630

Christie R, Geis F L 1970 *Studies in Machiavellianism.* Academic Press, New York

Cooper J, Croyle R T 1984 Attitudes and attitude change. *Annual Review of Psychology* **35**: 395–426

Digman J M 1990 Personality structure: Emergence of the five-actor model. *Annual Review of Psychology* **41**: 417–40

Engel J F, Blackwell R D, Kollat D T 1978 *Consumer Behavior.* Dryden Press, Hinsdale, IL

Gordon R L 1969 *Interviewing: Strategy, Techniques, and Tactics.* Dorsey, Homewood, IL

Hilbert R A 1990 Ethnomethodology and the micro–macro order. *American Sociological Review* **55**: 794–808

Hovland C I (ed.) 1957 *The Order of Presentation in Persuasion.* Yale University Press, New Haven, CT

Hovland C I, Janis I L, Kelley H H 1953 *Communication and Persuasion.* Yale University Press, New Haven, CT

Hyman R 1989 The psychology of deception. *Annual Review of Psychology* **40**: 133–54

Krech D, Crutchfield R S, Ballachey E L 1962 *Individual in Society.* McGraw-Hill, New York

Marcus H, Wurf E 1987 The dynamic self-concept: A social psychological perspective. *Annual Review of Psychology* **38**: 299–337

McHugh P 1968 *Defining the Situation: The Organization of Meaning in Social Interaction.* Bobbs-Merrill, Indianapolis, IN

McMahon A M 1984 The two social psychologies: Postcrisis directions. *Annual Review of Sociology* **10**: 121–40

Mead G H 1934 *Mind, Self, and Society.* University of Chicago Press, Chicago, IL

Ryan E B, Giles H 1982 *Attitudes Toward Language Variation.* Edward Arnold, London

Sahakian W S 1982 *History and Systems of Social Psychology.* Hemisphere, Washington, DC

Schütz A 1967 *The Phenomenology of the Social World.* Northwestern University Press, Evanston, IL

Snyder M 1977 Impression management. In: Wrightsman L S (ed.) *Social Psychology.* Brooks/Cole, Monterey, CA

Stark R 1989 *Sociology.* Wadsworth, Belmont, CA

Stephan C W, Stephan W G 1985 *Two Social Psychologies.* Dorsey, Homewood, IL

Tesser A, Shaffer D R 1990 Attitudes and attitude change. *Annual Review of Psychology* **41**: 479–523

W. S. Bainbridge

Socialization

Socialization is the process of internalization through which human beings become members of particular cultures, learning how to speak as well as how to act and think and feel. The term 'language socialization' is used more often for the primary socialization that takes place during childhood within the family (for which Schieffelin and Ochs 1986, is the best short review); but it should also refer to secondary socializations throughout life to specialized forms and uses of language in school, community, and work settings.

Language socialization is a more inclusive term than language acquisition, emphasizing pragmatic as well as syntactic and semantic competence; it is the preferred term in linguistic anthropology, sociolinguistics (see *Sociolinguistics*), and culturally oriented psychology.

1. Relationships between Language and Socialization

Language relates to socialization in three ways. First, language is the primary medium for socialization into culture; that is, there is socialization by or through language, where language is the means. Second, there is socialization for language, where situation-specific and culture-specific language use is the outcome. Third, there is socialization about language in the form of knowledge about, and attitudes toward, language forms and functions. While these three aspects of socialization occur together in real life, they are often studied separately, and by different research techniques.

2. Socialization through Language

Language plays an especially important role in socialization because it is such a pervasive and orderly feature of everyday life in every culture (Sapir 1962). Three characteristics of language contribute to this role: its propositional nature makes possible explicit cultural instruction; its reference to the non-here-and-now permits the sharing of memories and knowledge of the past, plans for the future, and imagined worlds; its indexicality (see *Deixis*) means that units of language, such as terms of address or speaking one dialect rather than another, point to culturally interpreted aspects of the nonverbal world. (Ochs 1990 discusses this last, and more subtle, relationship.)

3. Socialization for Language

Learning to speak is never simply a matter of learning a particular language or dialect—i.e., the words, syntactic patterns, and accent spoken in a particular community; it also involves learning multiple registers, i.e., particular ways of using language in particular settings within that community.

When one shifts registers, one also often shifts what one is talking about, and the values and beliefs implicit in those words. For this reason, Gee uses the term 'discourses' for 'forms of life which integrate words, acts, values, beliefs, attitudes, and social identities' (1989: 6–7; see *Discourse*). He then distinguishes primary and secondary discourses (including literacy in the latter), and also dominant and nondominant discourses according to their social prestige and power (see *Literacy*; *Power and Language*).

Even young children exhibit some register variation—for example, by speaking differently to adults or their peers (reviewed in Andersen 1990). For most people, secondary socialization in additional registers continues into adulthood, as they acquire new ways of speaking in new roles. Examples include the nearly universal, but culturally expressed, roles of student (Cazden 1988) or parent (Snow and Ferguson 1977); professions such as doctor or lawyer (Philips 1982); age-specific rhetorical styles such as 'the talk of the elders of bygone days' in Mexicano communities in the southwestern USA (Briggs 1986); and occasional oral tasks like chairing meetings, or conducting sociolinguistically appropriate interviews in a particular speech community (Briggs 1986).

Most research on language socialization is ethnographic. But experimental situations such as role playing can reveal register knowledge for roles never enacted in reality. Andersen (1990) provides both a research review of such knowledge in children, and a report of experimental research in which 4- to 7-year-old children gave a doctor puppet lower pitch and more imperatives and questions when talking to a nurse, and gave the nurse more polite requests to the doctor.

4. Socialization about Language

Socialization about language includes both knowledge and attitudes. One kind of metapragmatic knowledge is evidenced in the way speech is reported in narrative (see *Metapragmatics*). Whereas 7- and 10-year-old children frame direct speech, usually with 'said,' 4-year-olds often provide no verbal framing but sometimes differentiate voices by pitch (Hickman 1985).

Other kinds of knowledge become important when children enter school and confront the task of learning to read (see *Pedagogy*; *Children's Early Reading Development*). Where alphabetic orthographies are used, learners must become aware of the sounds in oral language and their relationship to letters; and even teachers, whose mental representation of language has been influenced by experience with written texts, may have to learn to distinguish the number of phonemes in a word from the number of letters (see *Text*; *Phoneme*; *Written and Spoken Language: Relationship*).

As with oral language, 'literacy socialization' is a more inclusive term than 'literacy acquisition': while the latter may refer only to learning to encode, decode, and comprehend print; the former points also to uses of reading and writing for different purposes in different settings.

Attitudes toward language can often be inferred from observations of which forms available in an environment are in fact learned, and from spontaneous comments about other people's oral or written language use. More systematic study of language attitudes requires more experimental techniques, often by social psychologists. One widely used technique is the matched guise in which subjects evaluate messages spoken in different languages or dialects but, unknown to the subjects, by a single speaker.

5. Environmental Influences on Language Socialization

There is general agreement that primary socialization occurs through participation, and through interaction between children and more mature speakers, both adults and peers. In fact, family and community settings for the virtually universally successful process of language socialization are often cited as the prototype of effective learning environments. While implicit immersion in language-related activities is certainly crucial, there is also evidence that more explicit tuition also occurs, e.g., in elicited imitation routines found in many cultures in which an adult will direct a child to say a word or phrase (Ochs 1990).

How secondary socializations can be aided in school is less clear, and educational controversies continue over the most effective combination of implicit immersion and explicit instruction. Heath (1983) gives a vivid picture of primary socialization in three communities that differ in race and social class, and an optimistic report of how teachers adapted their teaching for more effective secondary language socialization in school—including getting learners to 'become ethnographers' and study language use themselves.

In the study of language socialization, gender differences in ways of speaking—sometimes referred to as gender-lects—are especially interesting because most children are exposed to both men's and women's speech during their primary socialization (see *Sex Differences*). Differential socialization cannot, therefore, be explained by differential exposure (Warren-Leubecker and Bohannon 1989).

6. Socialization and Resistance

Many writers on language socialization imply that language socialization is always successful as long as the learning environment is at least minimally adequate. But resistance does occur. Familiar examples are immigrant children resisting speaking the language of their primary socialization at home, if the language of the school is also the language of the wider society, or nondominant dialect speakers resisting speaking a standard dialect despite its availability at school and on television.

Writing about the more general field of the socialization of cognition Goodnow (1990: 280) states: 'I seek an account of socialization that goes beyond saying that the individual must be regarded as agent or actor, or that influences are bidirectional... [E]ven if much of one's life is spent in puppet fashion, there remain at least the occasional times when one notices the strings and decides to cut them.'

Of all forms of learning, language is closest to one's social and individual identity; and that identity helps to account for both resistance and learning, and is also their result. In Sapir's words, 'In spite of the fact that language acts as a socializing and uniformizing force, it is at the same time the most potent single known factor for the growth of individuality' (1962: 19).

Bibliography

Andersen E S 1990 *Speaking with Style: The Sociolinguistic Skills of Children*. Routledge, London
Briggs C L 1986 *Learning to Ask: A Sociolinguistic Appraisal of the Role of the Interview in Social Science Research*. Cambridge University Press, Cambridge
Cazden C B 1988 *Classroom Discourse*. Heinemann, Portsmouth, NH
Gee J P 1989 Literacy, discourse, and linguistics: An introduction. *Journal of Education* 171: 5–17
Goodnow J L 1990 The socialization of cognition. In: Stigler J W, Shweder R A, Herdt G (eds.) *Cultural Psychology: Essays In Comparative Human Development*. Cambridge University Press, Cambridge
Heath S B 1983 *Ways with Words: Language, Life, and Work in Communities and Classrooms*. Cambridge University Press, Cambridge
Hickmann M 1985 Metapragmatics in child language. In: Mertz E, Parmenter (eds.) *Semiotic Mediation: Sociocultural and Psychological Perspectives*. Academic Press, Orlando, FL
Ochs E 1990 Indexicality and socialization. In: Stigler J W, Shweder R A, Herdt G (eds.) *Cultural Psychology: Essays on Comparative Human Development*. Cambridge University Press, Cambridge
Philips S U 1982 The language socialization of lawyers: Acquiring the cant. In: Spindler G (ed.) *Doing the Ethnography of Schooling*. Holt, Rinehart and Winston, New York
Sapir E 1962 In: Mandelbaum D G (ed.) *Culture, Language, and Personality: Selected Essays*. University of California Press, Berkeley, CA
Schieffelin B, Ochs E 1986 Language socialization. *Annual Review of Anthropology* 15: 163–91
Snow C E, Ferguson C A (eds.) 1977 *Talking to Children: Language Input and Acquisition*. Cambridge University Press, Cambridge
Warren-Leubecker A, Bohannon J N 1989 Pragmatics: Language in social contexts. In: Gleason J B (ed.) *The Development of Language*, 2nd edn. Merrill, Columbus, OH

C. B. Cazden

Sociolinguistics

Sociolinguistics is the subdiscipline of linguistics which deals with the relationships between language and society. It has close connections with the social sciences, in particular, sociology, anthropology, social psychology, and education and encompasses the study of multilingualism, social dialects, conversational interaction, attitudes to language, language change, and much more. Sometimes the field is subdivided into macro- and microsociolinguistics (as reflected, for example, in Fasold 1984, 1990), with the macro-domain sometimes also referred to as the sociology of language. Macrosociolinguistics takes society as its starting point and deals with language as a pivotal factor in the organization of communities. Microsociolinguistics begins with language and treats social forces as essential factors influencing the structure of languages. Some also distinguish between theoretical and applied sociolinguistics (Trudgill 1984). The former is concerned with formal models and methods for analyzing the structure of speech communities and speech varieties, and providing a general account of communicative competence. Applied sociolinguistics deals with the social and political implications of fundamental inequalities in language use in various areas of public life, for example, school, courts, etc.

1. Macrosociolinguistics, Speech Communities, and Communicative Competence

The notions of 'speech community' and 'communicative competence' are fundamental to macrosociolinguistics, which is concerned with the way in which social groups organize their linguistic repertoires. A speech community is not necessarily coextensive with a language community. A speech community is a group of people who do not necessarily share the same language, but share a set of norms and rules for the use of language. The boundaries between speech communities are essentially social rather than linguistic. The term 'language' is, from a linguistic point of view, a nontechnical notion since there is no objective way to determine when two varieties are sufficiently similar to warrant calling them the 'same' language.

The very concept of discrete languages is probably a European cultural artefact fostered by processes such as literacy and standardization (see *Standardization*). Any attempt to count distinct languages will be an artefact of classificatory procedures rather than a reflection of communicative practices. In many parts of the Pacific there are extensive chains of interrelated varieties with no clear internal boundaries. In Papua New Guinea people pay very great attention to small linguistic differences in differentiating themselves from their neighbors. People insist they speak a different language from the next village, although there is often a high degree of mutual intelligibility. Degree of mutual intelligibility is greatly affected by the extent of social and other contact between the groups concerned and does not necessarily have much to do with objective linguistic differences' (see *Mutual Intelligibility*).

Prague School linguists introduced the notions of *Sprechbund* and *Sprachbund* (with a *Sprechbund* involving shared ways of speaking which go beyond language boundaries, and *Sprachbund*, relatedness at the level of linguistic form). A *Sprachbund* and a *Sprechbund* may not necessarily coincide. Dorian (1981) has discussed a case where membership in a community is established and maintained primarily in terms of interactional rather than language norms. In some bilingual Gaelic/English communities along the east coast of Sutherland she found that speakers who had only a receptive competence in Gaelic nevertheless shared in conversations and interactions with more fluent speakers. Even though they did not control the language well enough to use it, they understood what went on and what was appropriate. They had communicative competence even though their grammatical competence was weak.

The term 'communicative competence' is used by sociolinguists such as Hymes (1972) to refer to a speaker's underlying knowledge of the rules of grammar (understood in the widest sense to include phonology, grammar, lexicon, and semantics) and rules for their use in socially appropriate circumstances. The notion is intended to replace Chomsky's dichotomy between competence and performance. The knowledge of rules of grammar is what Chomsky calls competence (as distinct from performance, which refers to how the rules of grammar are used). Speakers draw on their competence in putting together grammatical sentences, i.e., those which can be derived by the rules of grammar. Not all grammatical sentences can be used in the same circumstances. Thus, '*Close the window*' and '*Would you mind closing the window please?*' are both grammatical sentences of English, but they differ in terms of their appropriateness for use in particular situations. Speakers rely on their communicative competence in choosing what to say, as well as how and when to say it.

2. Multilingualism and Diglossia

Not all speech communities are organized in the same way. Widespread bilingualism and multilingualism are actually more common than monolingualism. It has been estimated that there are some four to five thousand languages in the world but only about 140 nation-states. About half the world's population is bilingual and bilingualism is present in practically every country in the world. With the formation of new nation-states, the question of which language (or which version of which one) will become the official national language arises and has often led to bitter controversy. Even countries with more than one official language, such as Canada, have not escaped attempts by various factions to gain political advantage by exploiting issues of language loyalty.

A distinction can be drawn between individual and societal multilingualism. Some countries such as Canada are officially bilingual in English and French, although not all Canadians are bilingual. There are many more French Canadians who learn English as a second language than English Canadians who learn French. In other countries such as India there is a high degree of individual bilingualism with the average person knowing at least two languages.

In many multilingual communities speakers switch among languages or varieties as monolinguals switch among styles. Often each language or variety serves a specialized function and is used for particular purposes. This situation is known as 'diglossia.' An example can be taken from Arabic-speaking countries in which the language used at home may be a local version of Arabic. The language that is recognized publicly, however, is Modern Standard Arabic, which takes many of its normative rules from the Classical Arabic of the Qur'ān. The standard language is used for 'high' functions such as giving a lecture, reading, writing, or broadcasting, while the home variety is reserved for 'low' functions such as interacting with friends at home.

The high (H) and low (L) varieties differ not only in grammar, phonology, and vocabulary, but also with respect to a number of social characteristics, namely, function, prestige, literary heritage, acquisition, standardization, and stability. L is typically acquired at home as a mother tongue and continues to be used throughout life. Its main uses are in familial and familiar interactions. H, on the other hand, is learned later through schooling and never at home. H is related to and supported by institutions outside the home. The separate domains in which H and L are acquired immediately provide them with separate institutional support systems. Diglossic societies are marked not only by this compartmentalization of varieties, but also by restriction of access. Entry to formal institutions such as school and government requires knowledge of H.

The extent to which these functions are compartmentalized can be illustrated in the importance attached by community members to using the right variety in the appropriate context. An outsider who learns to speak L and then uses it in a formal speech will be ridiculed. Speakers regard H as superior to L in a number of respects. In some cases H is regarded as the only 'real' version of a particular language to the extent that speakers claim they do not speak L. Sometimes the alleged superiority is avowed for religious and/or literary reasons. For example, the fact that Classical

Arabic is the language of the Qu'rān endows it with special significance. In other cases a long literary tradition backs the H variety, e.g., Tamil. There is also a strong tradition of formal grammatical study and standardization associated with H (see *Diglossia*).

The analogy has been extended to other communities in which the varieties in diglossic distribution have the status of separate languages, such as Spanish and Guaraní (an Indian language totally unrelated to Spanish) in Paraguay. Spanish serves here as the high variety and is used for high functions. The notion is also sometimes extended to include more than two varieties or languages which participate in such a functional relationship; for example, in Tunisia, French, Classical, and Tunisian Arabic are in 'triglossic' distribution, with French and Classical Arabic sharing H functions. The term 'polyglossia' ('many tongues') has also been used to refer to cases such as Singapore where many varieties coexist in a functional relationship.

3. Language Shift and Death

Macrosociolinguistics also studies the factors which promote the maintenance and shift or death of languages. Language shift generally involves bilingualism (often with diglossia) as a stage on the way to eventual monolingualism in a new language. Typically a community which was once monolingual becomes bilingual as a result of contact with another (usually socially more powerful) group and becomes transitionally bilingual in the new language until their own language is given up altogether. In some cases shift occurs as a result of forced or voluntary immigration to a place where it is not possible to maintain one's native language, e.g., Italians in the United States, or as a result of conquest, e.g., the Gaels in Scotland and Ireland. The loss of a language in this way is termed language death. Many factors are responsible for language shift, for example, religious and educational background, settlement patterns, ties with the homeland (in the case of immigrant bilingualism), extent of exogamous marriage, attitudes of majority and minority language groups, government policies concerning language, and education, etc.

Where large groups of immigrants concentrate in particular geographical areas, they are often better able to preserve their languages, e.g., third generation Chinese Americans who reside in Chinatowns have shifted less toward English than their age-mates outside Chinatowns. Often a shift from rural to urban areas triggers a language shift, e.g., in Papua New Guinea, where Tok Pisin (an English-based pidgin used as a lingua franca) is the language most used in the towns, many children grow up not speaking their parents' vernacular languages. When a language serves important religious functions, as German does among the Pennsylvania Dutch, it may stand a better chance of survival.

The inability of minorities to maintain the home as an intact domain for the use of their language has often been decisive for language shift. There is a high rate of loss in mixed marriages, e.g., in Wales, where if Welsh is not the language of the home, the onus for transmission is shifted to the school. Identification with a language and positive attitudes toward it cannot guarantee its maintenance. In Ireland the necessity of using English has overpowered antipathy toward English and English speakers. In some cases speakers may be forbidden to use their language altogether,

for example, the Kurds in Turkey at one time. In a community whose language is under threat, it is difficult for children to acquire the language fully.

Languages undergoing shift often display characteristic types of changes such as simplification of complex grammatical structures. These changes are often the result of decreased use of the language in certain contexts which may lead to a loss of stylistic options. In some Native American Indian languages of the southwestern United States complex syntactic structures have become less frequent because the formal and poetic styles of language are no longer used.

The degree of linguistic assimilation may serve as an index of social assimilation of a group. It depends on many factors such as receptiveness of the group to the other culture and language, possibility of acceptance by the dominant group, degree of similarity between the two groups, etc. Albanian speakers who emigrated to Greece have more readily given up their language and assimilated than have Albanian speakers in Italy, where attitudes toward diversity are more favorable (see *Language Maintenance, Shift and Death*).

4. Lingua Francas, Pidgins, and Creoles

In some multilingual communities speakers who do not share a native language use a 'lingua franca' to communicate in certain contexts, such as in commercial transactions. The chosen lingua franca can be indigenous to an area, as Swahili is to Africa, or nonindigenous, as English is to India. It may be but does not have to be the native language of any of the speakers (see *Lingua Franca*).

In some cases a new language called a 'pidgin' may arise. A pidgin is a contact language drawing on elements from at least two, but usually more languages, which is normally not the native language of any of its speakers. It exists as a marginal language to fulfill certain restrictive communicative functions among people who have no common language. Often, though not always, where pidgins develop, one group is socially superior, and their language is sufficiently inaccessible to the other group(s) that there is little motivation or opportunity to improve performance. Where communication needs are minimal and confined to a few basic domains such as work and trade, a defective version of language can be functionally adequate. Many pidgin languages arose in the context of contact between European colonizers who enslaved or employed the colonized population on plantations (see *Pidgins and Creoles*).

The languages from which the pidgin is derived are simplified, and vocabulary and grammatical complexities have been reduced. A pidgin is characterized by a small vocabulary of between a few hundred and a thousand or so words drawn largely from the superstrate language (the language of the socially dominant group), and a reduction of many grammatical features such as inflectional morphology. The grammar typically comes largely from the substratum language(s) of the socially subordinate group. In addition to retaining some features found in the input varieties, speakers must bring some general and possibly innate principles to bear on the task of learning to communicate under such circumstances. Often vocabulary and pronunciation conventions from other languages (other than the one on which the pidgin is based) are introduced into the pidgin by those who use it.

As with other lingua francas, the uses and occasions for using a pidgin will partly depend on how widely it is known. This will determine the degree of expansion of the language. Pidgins can be classified into different types according to their phase of development: jargon, stable pidgin, extended pidgin, and creole. Each stage is characterized by a gradual increase in overall complexity.

When a pidgin is nativized and becomes the primary language of a speech community, it is termed a 'creole.' Creolization may occur at any stage in the development of a pidgin from jargon to expanded pidgin. It involves both linguistic expansion and extension of functions for which a language is used. Depending on the stage at which creolization occurs, different types of structural expansion are necessary before the language can become an adequate primary language for a speech community. In the case of Jamaican Creole it is believed that a rudimentary pidgin creolized within a generation and then began to decreolize. Tok Pisin, however, first stabilized and expanded before becoming creolized (see *Tok Pisin*). In such cases there are very few linguistic differences between the pidgin and creole and the transition between these two stages is gradual rather than abrupt.

The term 'creolization' is also more generally applied to cases where borrowing disrupts the continuity of historical transmission of a language and the result is a creole-like language variety, but one which does not have a prior pidgin history. Some have argued that Middle English is a creole due to contact with Norse during the Viking period and French after the Norman Conquest. In addition to massive lexical borrowing, many of the changes which took place led to the simplification of English grammar, for example, loss of inflectional endings. It is not clear that these changes were due solely to language contact since other languages have undergone similar restructurings in the absence of contact.

The names given to pidgin and creole languages by linguists refer to their location and their principal lexifier language (i.e., the language from which they draw most of their vocabulary). Thus, Jamaican Creole English refers to the creole spoken in Jamaica, which is English-based or draws most of its vocabulary from English. Haitian Creole French is the name given to the creole language spoken in Haiti, which draws most of its vocabulary from French and is French-based. Papuan Pidgin English refers to the pidgin spoken in what was formerly the Territory of Papua, draws most of its vocabulary from English, and is therefore termed an English-based pidgin. English-based creoles are used in West Africa, Cameroon and Sierra Leone, and throughout the Caribbean and Pacific. Spanish- and Portuguese-based creoles are widely used in Asia. Three Portuguese creoles are in use in islands off the West African coast, i.e., Cape Verde, Annobon, and São Tomé. Papiamentu is the only such creole in the Caribbean spoken by the inhabitants of the Southern Caribbean Dutch-owned islands of Aruba, Bonaire, and Curaçao. A Dutch-based creole called Negerhollands ('Black Dutch') is spoken by a small number of speakers in the Virgin Islands. Non-European language-based creoles can be found in Africa and the South Pacific, e.g., Swahili in parts of Africa where it is used as a trade vernacular, and Hiri Motu in Papua New Guinea (see *Hiri Motu*).

Following the creolization of a pidgin, a postcreole continuum may develop when, after a period of relatively independent linguistic development, a postpidgin or postcreole variety comes under a period of renewed influence from the lexifier language. The postcreole continuum is a chain of language varieties which links a creole (also known as the 'basilect') to its superstrate language (also known as the 'acrolect') via intermediate varieties called 'mesolects,' e.g., the Jamaican postcreole continuum. Compare these Guyanese English Creole forms for standard English 'I gave him': basilect, *mi gii am*; mesolect, *a giv im*; and acrolect, *a geev him*. The differences between coexistent varieties in a creole continuum are generally greater than might be expected in an ordinary community fragmented by normal processes of dialect formation, particularly in terms of the amount and degree of syntactic and semantic variation. Decreolization may obscure the creole origins of a variety, as in the case of Black English in the United States.

The field of pidgin and creole studies has been rapidly expanding as linguists interested in language acquisition, language change, and universal grammar have taken more notice of these languages, which were neglected until the twentieth century because they were not regarded as full-fledged languages. Because these pidgins and creoles arise and then often expand rapidly, they provide excellent testing ground for theories of historical change. These languages have also attracted the attention of sociolinguists due to the amount of variation found in them (Romaine 1988; Holm 1989).

5. Microsociolinguistics and the Study of Social Dialects

Linguistic diversity occurs in monolingual speech communities too. The most substantial body of work which is unequivocally thought of as sociolinguistic is the research on urban social dialects, particularly in the English-speaking world.

It has been known for some time that differences in language are tied to social class. Ross (1956) suggested that certain lexical and phonological differences in English could be classified as U (upper class) or non-U (lower class), e.g., *serviette* versus *table-napkin*, which he described as perhaps the best known of all linguistic class indicators of England. Previously most studies were concerned with regional variation (see *Dialect and Dialectology*). Labov's work in New York City was the first to introduce a systematic methodology for investigating social dialects (see *Labov, William*). His book, *The Social Stratification of English in New York City* (1966), was the first large scale sociolinguistic survey of an urban community. Unlike dialectologists, who generally chose one person as representative of a particular area, Labov carried out tape-recorded interviews with 103 informants who had been chosen by random sample as being representative of the various social classes, ages, ethnic groups, etc to be found in New York City.

Previous investigations had concluded that the speech of New Yorkers appeared to vary in a random and unpredictable manner. Sometimes they pronounced the names *Ian* and *Ann* alike and sometimes they pronounced postvocalic /r/ in words such as *car*, while at other times they did not. This fluctuation was termed 'free variation' because there did not seem to be any explanation for it. Labov, however, showed that when such free variation in the speech of and between individuals was viewed against the background of the community as a whole, it was not free, but rather conditioned by social factors such as social class, age, sex, and style in predictable ways. Thus, while idiolects considered in isolation might seem random, the speech community as a whole behaved regularly. Using Labov's methods, one could predict that a person of a particular social class, age, sex, etc would not pronounce postvocalic /r/ a certain percent of the time in certain situations. Through Labov's introduction of methods for investigating social dialects by correlating sociolinguistic variables with social factors, sociolinguists have been able to build up a comprehensive picture of social dialect differentiation in the United States and Britain in particular, and other places, where his studies have been replicated.

In order to demonstrate a regular relationship between social and linguistic factors, one has to be able to measure them in a reliable way. The principal social dimensions sociolinguists have been concerned with are social class, age, sex, and style. Of these, social class has been the most researched. Many sociolinguistic studies have started by grouping individuals into social classes on the basis of factors such as education, occupation, income, etc, and then looked to see how certain linguistic features were used by each group. The method used by Labov to study the linguistic features was to select items which could be easily quantified, in particular, phonological variables such as postvocalic /r/, which was either present or absent. This was one of the first features to be studied in detail by Labov and other sociolinguists.

Varieties of English can be divided into two groups with respect to their treatment of this variable: those that are r-pronouncing (rhotic) and those that are not r-pronouncing (nonrhotic). In the late twentieth century in Britain accents that have lost postvocalic /r/ as a result of linguistic change generally have more prestige than those, like Scottish English, that preserve it. In many parts of the United States the reverse is true, although this has not always been the

Table 1. Percent of postvocalic /r/s pronounced.

New York City	Reading	Social class
32	0	upper-middle class
20	28	lower-middle class
12	44	upper-working class
0	49	lower-working class

case (see *Dialect and Dialectology*). Table 1 compares the pronunciation of postvocalic /r/ in New York City with that of Reading (based on research by Trudgill 1974). The results show that in New York City the lower one's social status, as measured in terms of factors such as occupation, education, and income, the fewer postvocalic /r/s one uses, while in Reading the reverse is true.

Like many features investigated by sociolinguists, the pronunciation of postvocalic /r/ shows a geographically as well as socially significant distribution. This difference among dialects of English is the result of a linguistic change involving the loss of /r/ following a consonant, but not a vowel, which began centuries ago in southeast England and spread north and west. The distribution of postvocalic /r/ in the United States reflects the history of settlement patterns of colonists from different parts of Britain and Ireland. Because the relevant linguistic factor for this

change was the presence or absence of a consonant in the immediately following word (cf., for example, *car engine* versus *car key*), a so-called 'linking /r/' appears in nonrhotic accents before words beginning with a vowel. Subsequently, this pattern seems to have been restructured and generalized so that /r/ is inserted in many contexts before a vowel where historically it was never present, e.g., *the idea of it* becomes *the idear of it* and *Shah of Iran* becomes *Shar of Iran*. This phenomenon is known as 'intrusive r.'

Just as the diffusion of linguistic features may be halted by natural geographical barriers, it may also be impeded by social class stratification. Similarly the boundaries between social dialects tend for the most part not to be absolute. The pattern of variation for postvocalic /r/ shows fine stratification or continuous variation along a linguistic dimension (in this case a phonetic one) as well as an extralinguistic one (in this case social class). The indices go up or down in relation to social class, and there are no sharp breaks between groups. A major finding of urban sociolinguistic work is that differences among social dialects are quantitative and not qualitative.

There are many other variables in English which show similar sociolinguistically significant distributions, such as those studied by Trudgill (1974) in Norwich in an urban dialect study modeled after Labov's. Trudgill examined three consonantal variables which varied with social class.

Table 2. Percent of non-RP forms in Norwich.

Social class	(ing)	(t)	(h)
upper-middle class	31	41	6
lower-middle class	42	62	14
upper-working class	87	89	40
middle-working class	95	92	59
lower-working class	100	94	61

Table 2 shows the results for (ing), (t), and (h). The numbers show the percentage of non-RP (received pronunciation) forms used by different class groups. RP is the speech variety used by those educated at public schools and is not tied to any particular locality. The variable (ing) refers to alternation between alveolar /n/ and a velar nasal /ŋ/ in words with -*ing* endings such as *reading, singing*, etc. Table 2 shows that the lower a person's social status, the more likely he/she is to use a higher percentage of alveolar rather than velar nasal endings. This is often referred to popularly as 'dropping one's g's.' It is a well known marker of social status over most of the English-speaking world. The variable (h) refers to alternation between /h/ and lack of /h/ in words beginning with /h/ such as *heart, hand*, etc. Unlike RP, most urban accents in England do not have initial /h/ or are variable in their usage of it. For these speakers who 'drop their h's,' *art* and *heart* are pronounced the same. Again, the lower a person's social status, the more likely he/she is to drop h's. Speakers in the north of England, Scotland, and Ireland retain /h/, as do speakers of American English. The variable (t) refers to the use of glottal stops instead of /t/. Most speakers of English glottalize final /t/ in words such as *pat*. In many urban dialects of British English, however, glottal stops are more widely used, particularly by younger working class speakers in London, Glasgow, etc. Trudgill and others have found that working class speakers are fairly consistent users of glottal stops as allophones for (t).

By comparing the results Trudgill obtained for the use of glottal stops in Norwich with those for (ing) and (h), some interesting conclusions can be drawn about the way language and social class are related in Norwich. Looking first at frequency, even the middle class in Norwich uses glottal stops very frequently, i.e., almost 50 percent of the time, but this is not true of (h). There is no reason to assume that every instance of variation in language will correlate with social structure in the same way or to the same extent. Most sociolinguistic variables have a complicated history. Some variables will serve to stratify the population more finely than others; and some cases of variation do not seem to correlate with any external variables, e.g., the variation between /i/ and /ɛ/ in the first vowel of *economic*. Phonological variables tend to show fine stratification and there is more socially significant variation in the pronunciation of English vowels than in consonants. In the case of glottal stop usage, what is socially significant is how frequently a person uses glottal stops in particular linguistic and social contexts. The use of glottal stops is particularly socially stigmatized in medial position, e.g., *bottle, butter*. A hierarchy of linguistic environments can be set up which seems to apply to all speakers. Glottal stops are more likely to occur in the following environments:

most frequent	word final + consonant	e.g., *that cat*
	before syllabic nasal	e.g., *button*
	word final + vowel	e.g., *that apple*
	before syllabic /l/	e.g., *bottle*
least frequent	word medially	e.g., *butter*

Although all speakers are affected by the same internal constraints in the same way, they apply at different frequency levels, depending on social class membership and

Table 3. Incidence of glottal stops in all environments compared to medial position.

Class	I	IIa	IIb	III	Total
all environments	48.4	72.9	84.3	91.7	74.3
medial position	0	7.2	42.5	68.8	29.6

other external factors. Table 3 shows the incidence of glottal stops in relation to social class in Glasgow for all environments compared with that occurring only in medial position (based on Macaulay 1977). Class I is the highest and contains professional people, while Class III is the lowest and contains unskilled workers. The results show that glottal stops are the norm for this community (74.3 percent), if all the environments are considered. Even the highest social class uses glottal stops nearly half the time and the lowest class, almost all the time. However, if medial position is considered, the highest social class uses no glottal stops in this environment, while the lowest class uses 68.8 percent.

The view of language which emerges from the sociolinguistic study of urban dialects is that of a structured but variable system, whose use is conditioned by both internal and external factors. The use of other variables can be more sharply socially stratifying. That is, a large social barrier between the middle class and the working class may be reflected in the usage of some linguistic feature. In English such features are more likely to be grammatical or syntactic, such as the use of multiple negation (e.g., *I don't want no trouble*), than pronunciation variables. Table 4 shows the

Table 4. Verbs without *-s*.

Class	Detroit	Norwich
upper-middle class	1	0
lower-middle class	10	2
upper-working class	57	70
middle-working class		87
lower-working class	71	97

results of a study of a grammatical variable in Detroit and Norwich (based on the Detroit dialect survey, Wolfram 1974; Trudgill 1974). The variable concerns the use of nonstandard third person singular present tense verb forms without *-s*, e.g., *he go*. Only working-class speakers use these forms with any great frequency and this is more so in Norwich than in Detroit. The gap between the middle and working class norms is also greater in Norwich than in Detroit reflecting the greater social mobility of the American social system. There are also other varieties of British English, e.g., in parts of the north, southwest, and south Wales, where the present tense paradigm is regularized in the opposite direction and all persons of the verb take *-s*, i.e., *I goes, you goes, he goes*, etc.

Not only do some of the same linguistic features figure in patterns of both regional and social dialect differentiation, but they also display correlations with other social factors. The intersection of social and stylistic continua is one of the most important findings of quantitative sociolinguistics: namely, if a feature occurs more frequently in working-class speech, then it will occur more frequently in the informal speech of all speakers. Table 5 shows this for the variable (ing). The behavior of each social class group varies according to whether its style is casual or formal. Style can range from formal to informal depending on social context, relationship of the participants, social class, sex, age, physical environment, and topic. Although each class had different average scores in each style, all groups style shift in the same direction in their more formal speech style, i.e., in the direction of the standard language. This similar behavior is an indication of membership in a speech community. All groups recognize the overt greater prestige of standard speech and shift toward it in more formal styles.

Some deviations in this pattern have been observed, as in Fig. 1 (from Labov 1972: 125), which shows the stylistic distribution of postvocalic /r/ in New York City. The highest and lowest groups have the shallowest slopes, but the second highest group in the social hierarchy, the lower-middle class, shows the most radical style shifting, exceeding even the highest status group in their use of postvocalic /r/ in the most formal style. Labov calls this the 'crossover pattern' and takes it to be a manifestation of 'hypercorrection.' The behavior of the lower-middle class is governed by their recognition of an exterior standard of correctness and their insecurity about their own speech. The use of postvocalic /r/ is seen by them as a prestige marker

Table 5. Percent of forms without final *g* (results from Trudgill 1974).

	Style	
Social class	casual	formal
middle-middle class	28	3
lower-middle class	42	15
upper-working class	87	74
middle-working class	95	88
lower-working class	100	98

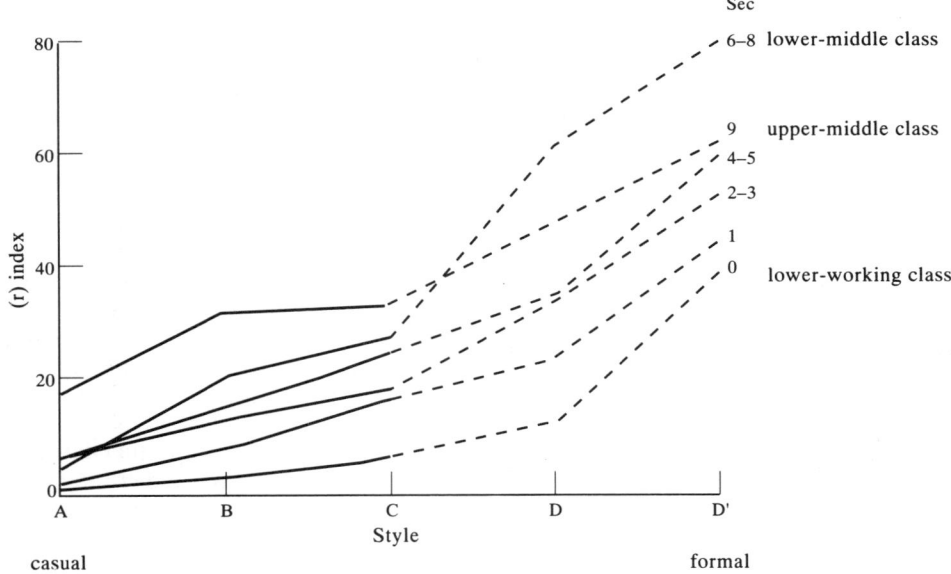

Figure 1.

of the highest social group. In their attempt to adopt the norm of this group, they manifest their aspirations of upward social mobility, but they overshoot the mark. The clearest cases of hypercorrection occur when a feature is undergoing change in response to social pressure from above, i.e., a prestige norm used by the upper class. In New York City the new /r/ pronouncing norm is being imported into previously nonrhotic areas of the eastern United States.

Hypercorrection by the lower-middle class accelerates the introduction of this new norm. By contrast, (ing) shows no such hypercorrection and is not undergoing any linguistic change. It is a stable social and stylistic marker and has been for centuries as far as can be told. Another type of hypercorrection actually results in the production of forms which are incorrect. In New York City highly stigmatized pronunciations such as *toity toid street* (for *33rd Street*) are popularly associated with the so-called Brooklyn accent (although in fact are more widespread throughout working-class speech of the city). Speakers who wish to dissociate themselves from this way of speaking often 'correct' forms which contain the sound ⟨oi⟩, so that *toilet* becomes *terlet* and *boil* becomes *berl*. Speakers alter these sounds because they are aware of the 'toity toid' stereotype, which to them suggests that ⟨oi⟩ is an incorrect pronunciation of ⟨er⟩, so they correct all cases where ⟨oi⟩ occurs to ⟨er⟩. In cases like *terlet*, this produces a form which is not only hypercorrect, but also nonexistent in the more prestigious form of speech which these speakers are trying to emulate. These hypercorrections often become so common that they too have now become stereotypes.

There is also a connection between patterns of social stratification and gender. A number of sociolinguistic studies have found that women tend to use higher status variants more frequently than men. This pattern was found, for example, with both postvocalic /r/ and (ing). An example can be seen in Table 6, which shows the results for multiple negation for male and female speakers in Detroit. Women of each social class group use the more standard

Table 6. Multiple negation in Detroit.

Class	Men	Women
upper-middle class	6.3	0
lower-middle class	32.4	1.4
upper-working class	40.0	35.6
lower-working class	90.1	58.9

variants more often than men of equal status. The variable is more sharply stratifying for women than for men, and the biggest gaps occur in the lower-middle class and lower-working class. Labov also found that women tended to hypercorrect more than men. Similar results have been found in other places, such as Sweden. Some researchers have argued that, in the case of spoken English at least, men's and women's speech are two distinct varieties of language. Studies have shown differences in phonological features, intonation patterns, choice of vocabulary (certain adjectives and intensifiers appear more frequently in women's speech), use of tag questions (addition of a question—such as *isn't it?*—to a statement in order to get agreement of affirmation, something women seem to do more than men), and other features. Many studies arose out of the women's liberation movement and were concerned to show the sexist bias in language, e.g., the use of *he* as a generic pronoun as in *Will everyone take his seat?* (see Spender 1980).

Research on urban dialects has now established a number of sociolinguistic patterns, i.e., regular, recurrent correlations between language and external factors such as social class, style, age, sex, etc. (see Labov 1972). Labov has identified a number of types of variables, e.g., indicators, which show regular distribution over socioeconomic, ethnic, or age groups, but are used by each individual more or less in the same way in any context; stereotypes, socially marked forms stereotyped by society such as Brooklyn *toity toid* and *terlet*, which may or not conform to any objective reality; and markers, such as (ing), which are stable reflectors of social class and style. Sociolinguistic patterns are acquired quite early in some communities. Romaine (1984: ch. 4) found gender, style, and social class differentiation in evidence in Scottish schoolchildren as young as six years old. Many of these children also were aware of the social significance of variants. In other communities such awareness may develop later. The age distribution of a variable may be an important clue to ongoing change in a community. While some patterns of age grading (i.e., variation in relation to age) may reflect a passing fad or simply be repeated anew in each generation, other cases may represent change in progress. This can only be determined by comparing the usage of speech communities at two points in time. Only then can it be established if contemporary variation is a stage in longterm change. One of the first demonstrations of age grading in the transmission of change is found in a study done in the Swiss village of Charmey in 1905 by Gauchat. Gauchat found fluctuation among the middle generation of speakers with respect to the use of both old and new norms as exemplified in the speech of the older and younger generations respectively. Another investigation some 25 years later demonstrated that the variant used by the younger generation had established itself as the new norm. Both studies showed the importance of variation and age grading as a mechanism of change.

The social dimensions of linguistic change were explored in more detail by Labov on Martha's Vineyard, a small island community off the coast of Massachusetts, where a group of fishermen were introducing increasingly centralized vowels in words such as *night* and *house* (see Labov 1972: ch. 1). Such variants had not been recorded by earlier dialect geographers and were new to the community. Labov found a strong correlation between the degree of centralization and the extent to which speakers identified with life on the island and wanted to remain.

Quantitative sociolinguistic work has led to considerable understanding of how linguistic change might proceed in a functional system by means of internal and external structuring of inherent variability which shows directional gradience though social groups, geographical space, and time (see Weinreich, et al. 1968). Research indicates that formal styles and high registers are more conservative, while informal speech draws on the latest innovations. Sometimes items lag behind in certain changes and remain in the speech of older people as stylistic variants. New variants often appear first in casual speech, while older ones remain in more emphatic formal styles. Formal styles may provide a locus for the introduction of prestige changes. It was well known to dialectologists studying regional dialects that older male informants from rural areas were often the best sources of conservative speech. Women, on the other hand, have been often observed to introduce new prestige variants. Change may come from both above and below in the social hierarchy. At the time when postvocalic /r/ was lost in many varieties of English, discrimination by accent became an important issue. Some associated the loss of /r/ with the working class Cockney speech of London. Henry Alford wrote in 1864 (*A Plea for the Queen's English*) that the loss of /r/ is a worse fault than the misuse of the aspirate /h/. He quotes extensively from a letter professedly from a correspondent in the House of Commons to the effect that: 'Woe betide any unfortunate member if he strews the floor with his "aitches": the laughter is open and merciless: but the honourable members may talk of "lawrr" of the land, scawn the "idear" with perfect impunity.' Although Alford denounces this as 'enough to make the hair of anyone but a well seasoned Cockney stand on end,' it is evident from this and other examples that the vocalization of /r/, /h/ dropping, and the phenomenon of intrusive /r/ were widespread in the best society in nineteenth-century England. These features may originally have made their way into the language via the lower classes and would be examples of change from below. At the moment sociolinguistic patterns are rough guidelines based on generalizations from the studies available. Part of the problem in making extrapolations from these patterns to build a theory is that the relationship between language and social structure may vary considerably, both synchronically and diachronically.

Contact between groups in urban society may also accelerate the use of nonstandard features and in some cases inhibit change toward the standard. In Wolfram's (1974) study of Puerto Rican speakers in New York City, it emerged that Puerto Ricans who were in contact with black speakers deleted final *t/d* more often (e.g., fas' train, gol' watch) than blacks or whites or Puerto Ricans who did not socialize with blacks. The people with whom one interacts are a powerful source of influence on speech. The concept of social network, adopted from anthropology into sociolinguistics, takes into account different socializing habits of individuals and their degree of involvement in local community. The use of network as an analytical construct does not require grouping individuals into social classes. Networks may cut across social class boundaries and they may also reveal differences within social classes. Milroy (1980), who used network analysis in Belfast, found that two women who lived in the same type of housing in the same area and had similar employment, nevertheless, behaved quite differently linguistically. One was much more standard in her speech than the other. Their socialization patterns were, however, clearly very different. The woman whose speech was more nonstandard was a member of a local bingo-playing group and had extensive kin ties in the area. The more standard speaker had no kin in the area and did not associate with local people. Milroy found that those with high network scores indicating the strength of association with the local community used more local, nonstandard forms of speech. Those whose networks were more open and less locally constrained used more standard speech. Networks in which individuals interact locally within a well-defined territory and whose members are linked to each other in several capacities, e.g., as kin, neighbor, workmate, etc, act as a powerful influence on the maintenance of local norms. If these networks are disrupted, then people will be more open to the influence of standard speech. Speakers use their local accents as a means of affirming identity and loyalty to local groups. There is a broad link between network and social class to the extent that middle-class speakers tend to have looser networks than the working class. However, dense networks may also be found at the upper levels of society, as in Britain, where the so-called 'old boy network,' whose members have usually been educated at English public schools and at Oxbridge, gives rise to an equally distinctive speech variety, RP. Milroy also found that more men than women had dense networks, which suggests an explanation for some of the patterns of sex differentiation found by other sociolinguists.

Since the study of language varieties has taken a central place in sociolinguistics, sociolinguists have produced formal models of variation which try to incorporate information about the social and linguistic constraints on variables. Labov proposed that variable rules are a fundamental part of both grammar and competence. The formula for a variable rule is:

$$A \rightarrow \langle B \rangle / \underline{\quad} \begin{Bmatrix} \text{linguistic constraints} \\ \text{social constraints} \end{Bmatrix}$$

This states that feature A variably becomes B in a particular context in accordance with social and linguistic constraints which are ranked hierarchically. The social constraints may be social class membership, age, sex, etc, while the linguistic constraints are system-internal and are the environments in which the variable occurs, e.g. before/after a vowel, etc. Various mathematical procedures are used to compute the values and weightings attached to the different constraints. This is generally known as 'variable rule analysis' (sometimes also VARBRUL) and is especially popular in North American quantitative sociolinguistics. Variable rule analysis incorporates multivariate statistics and assigns probabilities to constraints. Variable rules, however, pose substantial philosophical, psychological, and linguistic questions about the forms of grammars, nature of rules and representations, and the role they play in characterizing human competence. Some have objected to them because autonomous models of grammar rule out the possibility that probabilities of rule application have any place in formal grammars which aim to model competence, which is seen as invariant. It is not clear what a sociolinguistic grammar as opposed to a traditional grammar would look like (Romaine 1985). Others object more specifically to the idea that explanations for variability can be found in social rather than purely linguistic factors (see *Dialect and Dialectology*). Such disputes are indicative of the fact that not all scholars are agreed on the boundaries and relationship between linguistics and sociolinguistics. Downes (1984: 15), for instance, argues that sociolinguistics is that branch of linguistics which studies 'just those properties of language and languages which require reference to social, including contextual factors, in their explanation.' Others such as Hymes (1974) would be unhappy with the characterization of sociolinguistics as a subdiscipline of linguistics and have proposed instead a 'socially constituted' theory of language. Hymes rejects the notion that language has an existence apart from the social reality of its users. Similarly, Labov (1972) professes that he has resisted the term 'sociolinguistics' because it 'implies that there can be a successful linguistic theory of practice that is not social.'

6. Practical Applications

Sociolinguistic research, in particular on social dialects, has had many practical implications since it is concerned with fundamental inequalities in language use. Language has often been cited as the main cause for the greater rate of school failure among minority and working-class children. Because schools measure success in terms of mastery of standard English (or whatever the accepted language of the society is), nonstandard speech is seen as illogical. There is similar prejudice and intolerance of minority languages such as Panjabi in Britain and Spanish in the United States. Sociolinguists such as Labov have, however, argued that nonstandard speech forms are just as structurally complex, rule-governed, and capable of expressing logical arguments as standard English (Labov 1969). Moreover, because such varieties play an important role in speaker identity, change toward standard English may be resisted. Labov found that in inner city areas black youths who socialized in street gangs were those who used the most nonstandard forms of speech and were most opposed to the value system of the school. Not only did they have the highest rate of failure, but they were also regarded as those most likely to fail by their teachers. Labov concluded that negative attitudes toward nonstandard speech were more decisive in determining school outcomes than the actual linguistic differences between standard and nonstandard speech. Political mobilization of linguistic minorities and legislation prompted by equality of opportunity has led in some places to the development and funding of programs aimed at rectifying linguistic inequalities. In some cases, however, the courts have become battlegrounds for issues, which, although not primarily linguistic, have had fundamental linguistic implications. The Ann Arbor decision on Black English in the United States is an example of litigation brought under Equality of Opportunity legislation, which makes no mention of language. It guarantees simply that no one shall be denied equal educational opportunity on account of race, color, sex, or national origin. Black parents filed a suit against the school board for failure to take into account the linguistic background of their children. The issue of language, in particular, the autonomy of Black English, became salient in this case because it was argued that a language group, i.e., speakers of Black English, coincided with a racial group. The Ann Arbor case probably could not have occurred or been won without the research done on social dialects in the 1960s and 1970s, which supported the argument that Black English was not a deficient, but only different, linguistic system. The judge, who ruled in favor of the black parents and their children, was clearly influenced by the expert testimony of sociolinguists.

Bibliography

Dorian N C 1981 Language death. In: *The Life Cycle of a Scottish Gaelic Dialect.* University of Pennsylvania Press, Philadelphia, PA

Downes W 1984 *Language and Society.* Fontana, London

Fasold R 1984 *The Sociolinguistics of Society.* Blackwell, Oxford

Fasold R 1990 *The Sociolinguistics of Language.* Blackwell, Oxford

Holm J 1989 *Pidgins and Creoles*, 2 vols. Cambridge University Press, Cambridge

Hudson R A 1990 *Sociolinguistics.* Cambridge University Press, Cambridge

Hymes D 1972 On communicative competence. In: Pride J B, Holmes J (eds.) *Sociolinguistics.* Penguin, Harmondsworth.

Hymes D 1974 *Foundations in Sociolinguistics.* University of Pennsylvania Press, Philadelphia, PA

Labov W 1966 *The Social Stratification of English in New York City.* Center for Applied Linguistics, Washington, DC

Labov W 1969 On the logic of non-standard English. In: *Georgetown Monographs on Language and Linguistics, 22.* Georgetown University Press, Washington, DC

Labov W 1972 *Sociolinguistic Patterns.* University of Pennsylvania Press, Philadelphia, PA

Macaulay R K S 1977 *Language, Social Class, and Education: A Glasgow Study.* University of Edinburgh Press, Edinburgh

Milroy L 1980 *Language and Social Networks.* Blackwell, Oxford

Romaine S 1982 *Sociolinguistic Variation in Speech Communities.* Edward Arnold, London

Romaine S 1984 *The Language of Children and Adolescents.* Blackwell, Oxford

Romaine S 1985. Variable rules, O.K.? Or Can there be sociolinguistic grammars? *Language and Communication* 5: 53–67

Romaine S 1988 *Pidgin and Creole Languages.* Longman, London

Romaine S 1989 *Bilingualism.* Blackwell, Oxford

Ross A S C 1956 U and non-U. In: Mitford N *Noblesse Oblige.* Hamish Hamilton

Spender D 1980 *Man Made Language.* Routledge, London

Trudgill P 1974 *The Social Differentiation of English in Norwich.* Cambridge University Press, Cambridge

Trudgill P 1983 *Sociolinguistics.* Penguin, Harmondsworth

Trudgill P 1984 *Applied Sociolinguistics.* Academic Press, New York

Weinreich U, Labov W, Herzog M 1968. Empirical foundations for a theory of language change. In: Lehmann W P, Malkiel Y (eds.) *Directions for Historical Linguistics.* University of Texas Press, Austin, TX

Wolfram W 1974 *A Sociolinguistic Description of Detroit Negro Speech.* Center for Applied Linguistics, Washington DC

S. Romaine

Sociolinguistics and Language Change

It may seem surprising to the lay person that orthodox historical linguistics has not taken very much account of social factors in attempting to explain linguistic change. Some experts insist that social factors are of little relevance, and that the causes of change are to be found in phenomena that are more central to language structure, for example, 'natural' phonetic processes. However, there is one important difficulty, which applies especially to the explanation of *sound* change. This is that if one does not take social factors into account, there appears to be little reason why sound change (and some other kinds of change) should take place at all. If, at some place and time, the sound [a] should change to [o] in all relevant words, the language has not gained anything by the change, as one tiny segment of sound cannot be 'better' or more efficient than another. Indeed, it can be argued that change is dysfunctional, since, when a change is introduced by some section of a speech community, it is in principle possible that the new form will not be immediately understood. However, change is continuously in progress, and its operation has greatly altered the sound systems and structural characteristics of languages in the course of history: Old and Middle English, for example, were clearly very different in pronunciation and grammar from twentieth-century English, and language change can be very rapid.

It seems that the causes of change are not to be found in the structure of languages as such, but in the behavior of speakers. As speakers in social groups manifestly attach great social importance to quite small differences in pronunciation, which are arbitrary in linguistic terms (i.e., one sound is just as good as another), sociolinguists argue that

collecting and analyzing the language of live speakers in social groupings can be used to advance the understanding of the causes of linguistic change. The basic problem to be solved is known as the 'actuation problem,' and it can be stated thus:

> Why do changes in a structural feature take place in a particular language at a given time, but not in other languages with the same feature, or in the same language at other times?

Thus, one might ask why the French language has lost many final consonants in the course of history, while Spanish and Italian have preserved them, and (at the dialectal level) why some dialects of English have lost final and preconsonantal [r] in words such as *car, card*, while others (for example, Scottish and North American English) have retained it. Although the actuation problem cannot be completely solved, sociolinguists attempt to come closer to understanding it.

Most changes in language, as far as is known, take place without self-conscious attempts being made by speakers to implement them; yet, paradoxically, they must in some way be implemented through speaker activity, as the new forms are accepted and used by new generations of speakers. Self-conscious institutional intervention in language is generally known as 'language planning.' Another phenomenon that may be brought about by institutional intervention is language standardization (see *Standardization*); from a sociolinguistic point of view, standardization can be seen as an attempt to impose uniformity on a phenomenon which is by nature variable (language), and part of its purpose is to prevent linguistic change. Sociolinguists have up until the time of writing been mainly interested in change that comes about 'naturally,' without conscious intervention.

Three main approaches can be distinguished. The first is associated with the work of anthropological linguists, and focuses on 'language shift'—the replacement of one language by another, perhaps with discernible effects on one or both languages. Work in this tradition traces the replacement patterns as they progress through bilingual populations. It is typically found that some social groups (e.g., females as against males, or a particular social class) lead in the shift, and that the recessive language is replaced by the incoming language in different social situations at different rates: for example, the recessive language normally persists in domestic environments after it has been replaced in most other functions. The study of recessive languages in these situations is referred to as the study of 'language death' (see *Language Death*). Typically, these languages undergo a great deal of internal change during the process.

The second approach to language change focuses on monolingual situations in much greater linguistic detail, and is associated with the name of William Labov. It can be called quantitative social dialectology (see *Urban Dialectology*), as it makes use of quantification to reveal patterns of variation in terms of the social characteristics of the speakers studied—age, sex, and social class, for example. By this means, linguistic changes in progress can be detected and traced in fine detail as they diffuse in an orderly way through populations of speakers (see *Lexical Diffusion*). These studies usually focus on quite small communities of speakers, and they have shown that, in order to understand linguistic changes, one must first think of changes as coming about in the speech community rather than in the national language as a whole. That is, changes originate not in 'English,' but in some localized variety of English. From localized situations, they may diffuse much more widely, and these wider patterns of diffusion are also studied.

The third relevant approach concerns Pidgin and Creole languages (see *Pidgins, Creoles, and Change*). Like the first approach, this involves contact between languages, except that the replacement of one language (an established native language) is abrupt—it is brought about by upheaval of populations who are then thrown together with strangers in situations where there is no common language. Creoles are normally based on colonial languages such as English or Portuguese, with much reduced syntax. Pidgin and Creole studies have greatly advanced the understanding of universals of language change, particularly syntactic universals.

So far, theoretical advances in traditional historical linguistic concerns have come mainly from work in the second approach above. They have been chiefly concerned with sound change and have borne in mind the traditional neo-grammarian axioms, which propose that sound change is phonetically gradual and lexically abrupt. In this view, change is believed to proceed by imperceptible degrees affecting all members of a word-class at the same time (e.g., all words with the vowel [a], as in *bat, bad, hand*, etc.). Many sociolinguistic patterns, however, have proved to be different from this: they are lexically gradual and phonetically abrupt, and sound change is often observed to spread gradually through the relevant lexicon, affecting some words before others. Similarly, phonetic differences are not necessarily imperceptible, but may be quite marked. The relevance of these traditional concerns is a matter of debate; what is certainly clear is that sound change is *socially* gradual. It spreads gradually through populations of speakers.

Influenced by Labov, many attempted accounts of language change have used social class as a background to their arguments. Change has been seen as spreading upward and downward from some central point in the social-class hierarchy, and social-class differentiation seems to have been thought of as a cause of change. Sex differentiation in language has also been cited as an equally important variable in linguistic change, as males and females are always found to differ in speech, usually with females using more 'careful' or less 'vernacular' speech than males.

Argumentation based on the idea of varying solidarity within and between communities and operationalized in terms of social network (see *Social Networks*) has been used to propose a theory that can account for different language situations—encompassing those studied by the three approaches enumerated above. This suggests that, as close and solidary personal ties in communities result in dialect maintenance and resistance to change, linguistic change is facilitated by the development of large numbers of weak ties. If this model is used in interpretation, it appears to account in a coherent way for situations of different orders of magnitude. It is proposed that:

> Linguistic change is slow to the extent that the relevant populations are well established and bound by strong ties, whereas it is rapid to the extent that weak ties exist in populations.

Although traditional historical linguistics neglected speakers (partly because it did not have access to tape recorders), languages that have no speakers do not change. A theory of change must therefore have a place for speakers, and it has been proposed that a distinction should be drawn between innovations and changes in language. An innovation is an act of the speaker, which may or may not lead to a *change*, which is something that is embedded in the language system. In order to make progress here, one must attempt to understand the way in which some innovations in some circumstances can become changes, whereas others fall away without trace. Although the actuation problem is still a very long way from being solved, it is to be hoped that the typical sociolinguistic focus on speaker behavior will make further contributions to linguists' understanding of the nature of linguistic change.

See also: Sociolinguistics; Sociolinguistics and Language Change.

Bibliography

Aitchison J 1991 *Language Change: Progress or Decay?*, 2nd edn. Cambridge University Press, Cambridge
Labov W 1972 *Sociolinguistic Patterns*. University of Pennsylvania Press, Philadelphia, PA
Milroy J 1992 *Linguistic Variation and Change*. Basil Blackwell, Oxford
Trudgill P 1986 *Dialects in Contact*. Basil Blackwell, Oxford

J. Milroy

Sociolinguistics of Sign

Natural sign languages are autonomous linguistic systems, independent of the spoken languages with which they may coexist in a given community. As sign languages are full-fledged autonomous linguistic systems shared by communities of users, the sociolinguistics of sign languages can be described in ways which parallel the description of the sociolinguistics of spoken languages. That is, the sociolinguistics of sign languages concerns the interrelationship of sign language and social structure. As with spoken languages, sign languages are at once used to communicate information and to define the social situation, i.e., to make statements about individual identity, group loyalties, and one's relation to one's interlocutors. The sociolinguistics of sign languages includes the study of regional and social variation, bilingualism and language contact phenomena, language maintenance and choice, language attitudes, language policy and planning, and discourse analysis. However, it is very important to understand that while each of these areas has relevance for deaf communities, the sociolinguistics of sign is a relatively young discipline and there exist few if any empirical studies in some of these areas.

1. Regional and Social Variation

Regional and social variation in sign languages has been described mainly at the phonological and lexical levels, and to a lesser extent at the morphological and syntactic levels (see *Dialect and Dialectology*). Variation at the phonological level involves variation in the production of the component parts of signs such as handshape, location, palm orientation, nonmanual signals, and segmental structure. For example, the American Sign Language (ASL) signs

FUNNY, BLACK, and CUTE might be produced with the thumb extended or with the thumb closed; the ASL signs BORED and DEAF might be produced with the little finger extended or with the little finger closed; the ASL sign WEEK might be produced with the palm of the dominant hand facing upward or the palm facing downward; the ASL sign KNOW might be produced on the forehead or on the cheek. Lexical variation concerns different signs for the same concept. Regional differences have been described in British Sign Language (BSL), for example, between Reading and York for the signs LEARN, SUNDAY, and WHO (Deuchar 1984: 131). Lexical variation in BSL has also been described by Kyle and Woll (1985). Lexical variation has also been looked at in New Zealand Sign Language, Italian Sign Language, Dutch Sign Language, Swiss German Sign Language and Swiss French Sign Language, Brazilian Sign Language, and ASL. Variation in terms of ethnicity has been looked at by Woodward (1976) and Aramburo (1989), i.e., differences between black and white signers in the USA. Gender variation has been looked at in ASL, in Chinese Sign Language, and in Irish Sign Language. However, social variation in terms of socioeconomic status (i.e., the classic Labovian type of sociolinguistic analysis; see *Labov, William*) or in terms of social networks such as have been described for spoken languages has yet to be described systematically for sign languages.

2. Bilingualism and Language Contact Phenomena

There exist different kinds of bilingualism in deaf communities. For one, most deaf individuals have at least some exposure to the spoken language of the majority community in which they live. This exposure may be primarily exposure to the written form of the majority language, although in many countries a signed code to manually represent the spoken majority language has been devised, with signs invented to represent the bound morphemes of the spoken language. A discussion of bilingualism in deaf communities necessarily requires a re-examination of the term 'bilingual' as it has been used to describe spoken language communities. This is because many deaf people with a firm command of the written version of the majority spoken language choose not to use their voices because they are not able to hear themselves and hence monitor the volume or pitch of their speech. Bilingualism in deaf communities does not necessarily include *speaking* the languages in question, at least not in the way that the term *speaking* is generally understood by linguists.

There are many occasions for language contact in deaf communities. Fig. 1 presents a model of the linguistic outcomes of language contact. A fundamental distinction is made between a situation involving contact between two sign languages and a situation involving contact between a sign language and a spoken language, a distinction necessary because of the difference in modality between sign and spoken languages. Naturally, the situation is not entirely straightforward, as two sign languages may be in contact, both of which may incorporate outcomes of contact with their respective spoken languages, outcomes which may then play a role in the contact between the two sign languages.

As can be seen from Fig. 1, the outcomes of contact between two sign languages parallel the outcomes that have been described for contact between spoken languages, namely lexical borrowing of various kinds, code-switching and code-mixing, foreigner talk, interference, pidgins and creoles, and mixed systems. Again, it should be remembered that while there is much anecdotal evidence for many of these outcomes, there are not many empirical studies of the outcomes of contact between two sign languages. Signers borrow the signs from one language into their own; bilinguals may code-switch and code-mix elements from two sign languages; a signer may alter his signing and simplify it when signing to a nonnative, and signers may show interference from one sign language when using another. Signers have been observed to have 'accents.' As concerns contact between a sign language and a spoken language, a distinction is made between outcomes which reflect literal adherence to the spoken language criteria defined for those outcomes. For example, code-switching would mean ceasing signing and beginning to talk. This is distinct from unique phenomena that occur, such as contact signing, as observed in the American deaf community: the simultaneous production of ASL lexical forms in English word order with mouthing of English words, with the possible inclusion of inflected ASL verbs and ASL nonmanual signals. Some analyses have characterized this as a pidgin but more recent analyses find the features of this kind of signing to be inconsistent with the features of pidgins (Lucas and Valli 1992). Fingerspelling is also a unique phenomenon, because although the forms are part of the natural sign language—i.e., the handshape, the location, orientation, and the segmental structure—it is a representation of the writing system of the majority spoken language (see *Fingerspelling: One-handed*). Signers in contact with languages which use the Roman alphabet fingerspell, but signers in contact with Arabic, Russian, Japanese, and Chinese also represent the writing systems of their respective spoken languages (see *Sign Languages in Asia*). Other unique phenomena include the English sometimes produced by the children of deaf adults (CODA-speak, Jacobs 1992), and the English of typed telephone conversations that often incorporates features of ASL (Mather 1991).

3. Language Maintenance and Choice

Typically, the use of natural sign languages has been restricted to a very limited set of functions and has been totally excluded from the educational process. Such a sociolinguistic situation has led to the characterization of language use in the deaf community as diglossic, the majority spoken language being the H variety and the natural sign language being the L variety (Stokoe 1969; see also *Sociolinguistics*). There is a lot of evidence that some signers clearly see their natural sign language as appropriate only for intimate, informal situations, and the signed version of the majority spoken language as appropriate for public, formal situations, be the interlocutors hearing or deaf. However, as many countries around the world begin to use natural sign languages in deaf education, these sign languages are acquiring functions that they have not had before, and the spoken or signed version of the majority spoken languages may lose functions they once had or be restricted to the functions of reading and writing. Because of the clear need in deaf communities for both a natural sign language and for some form of the majority spoken

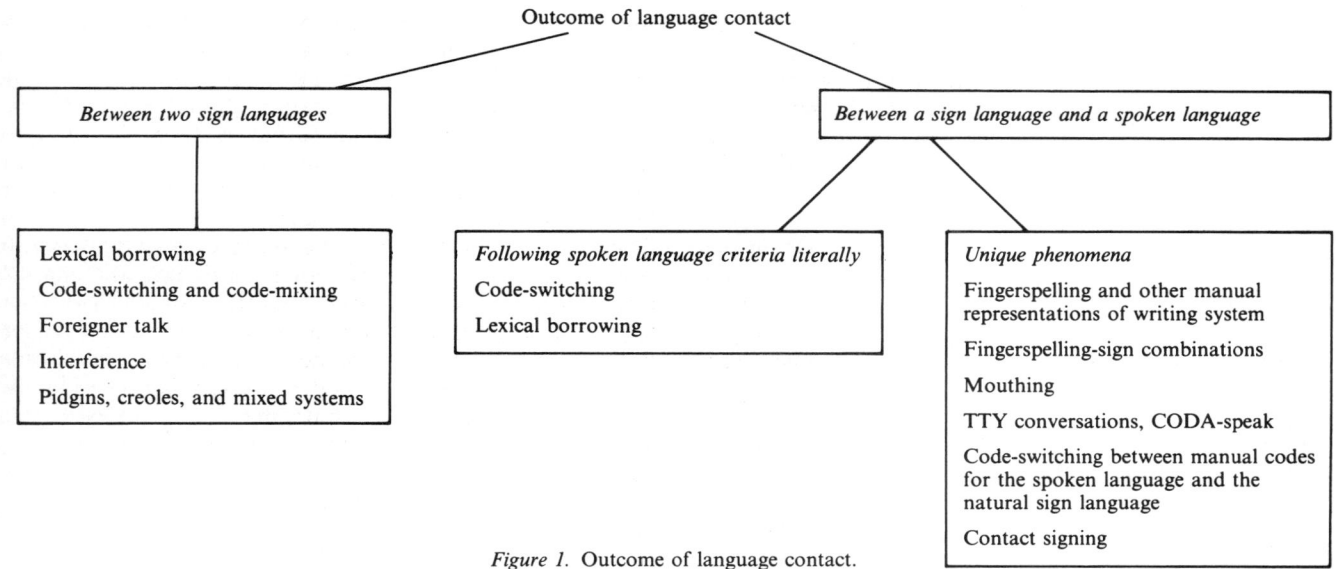

Figure 1. Outcome of language contact.

language, the situation in most deaf communities can be characterized as one of maintained bilingualism. Unlike many minority languages in a majority language situation, it would not appear that natural sign languages are in any danger of disappearing.

4. Language Attitudes

Language attitude studies in deaf communities concern signers' attitudes toward their natural sign language and toward the majority spoken language, attitudes toward users of the sign and spoken language, attitudes of teachers of the deaf and professionals toward natural sign languages, attitudes toward the invention and introduction of new signs, and attitudes toward the outcomes of language contact (Kannapell 1989). Language attitude studies often reveal conflicting attitudes toward the natural sign language and the majority spoken language in a given community, as a result of lack of recognition of the status of the sign language as a viable and autonomous linguistic system. That is, pride with respect to the sign language may co-occur with an attitude that its use reveals a lower educational level or even lower intelligence in the user, while use of a signed version of the majority spoken language may be viewed as evidence of good education and superior intelligence. Pride with respect to the natural sign language may coexist with the misconception that it is not a real language or is a deficient form of the spoken majority language.

5. Language Policy and Planning

Language planning has been defined as deliberate decision making in response to language problems. Deaf communities have very often been perceived as the sites of language *problems*, particularly as concerns the education of deaf children, for the obvious reason that deaf children do not have easy access to the spoken majority language as a medium of instruction. Approaches since the 1970s have involved the invention of manual codes to represent the majority spoken language and may involve the simultaneous production of the spoken language and the sign language, referred to as sign-supported speech (Johnson, et al. 1989). However, many deaf communities around the world are beginning to use the natural sign language of the community as the medium of instruction. All of these approaches have implications for language planning, either in the invention of manual codes for educational use, or in the use of the natural sign language for functions it has not previously had. This may entail expanding the lexicon of the natural sign language, an expansion which leads to other language planning issues, such as whether signs should be invented for new concepts or whether new concepts should be represented with fingerspelling. Issues of access and hence of language policy and planning are not limited to deaf education. For example, providing deaf adults with full access to the business of the majority language community—i.e., media, government, the law, medical care—entails decisions as to how linguistic access will be provided: whether closed-captioning is preferable for television news to a sign language interpreter; whether a sign language interpreter, if provided, should use the natural sign language or a signed version of the spoken majority language; what the interpreting policy should be in an international gathering of deaf people—the natural sign language of the location of the gathering or an international variety or both. These are all issues that are the subject of debate in many deaf communities around the world.

6. Discourse Analysis

As with spoken languages, the discourse of natural sign languages is structured and subject to sociolinguistic description (see *Pragmatics*). Signers use natural sign languages and choices between natural sign languages and other kinds of signing to make statements about who they are, what their group loyalties are, how they perceive their relationship to their interlocutors, and what kind of speech event they consider themselves to be involved in. Sign languages are used to establish or reinforce social relations and to control the behavior of others. Sign language discourse has internal structure and is governed by norms such as how many people sign at once, how much one person should sign, what can be signed about in public, how a conversation should be entered or left, how turns should be allocated, how repairs should be undertaken, and so forth. Topic and the world knowledge that individuals bring to the discourse may also structure it (Roy 1989), and sign language discourse can be described in terms of register variation (Lawson 1981; Deuchar 1984; Zimmer 1989). The concept of 'language as skilled work' is applicable to sign languages, as skill is demonstrated both in everyday use of language and in special forms such as storytelling and poetry.

Bibliography

Aramburo A J 1989 Sociolinguistic aspects of the black deaf community. In: Lucas C (ed.) *The Sociolinguistics of the Deaf Community*. Academic Press, San Diego, CA

Battison R 1978 *Lexical Borrowing in American Sign Language*. Linstock Press, Silver Spring, MD

Battison R, Markowicz H, Woodward J 1975 A good rule of thumb: Variable phonology in American Sign Language. In: Shuy R W, Fasold R W (eds.) *New Ways of Analyzing Variation in English*. Georgetown University Press, Washington, DC

Davis J 1989 Distinguishing language contact phenomena in ASL interpretation. In: Lucas C (ed.) 1989

Deuchar M 1984 *British Sign Language*. Routledge and Kegan Paul, London

Hansen B 1980 Research on Danish sign language and its impact on the deaf community. In: Baker C, Battison R (eds.) *Sign Language and the Deaf Community*. NAD, Silver Spring, MD

Jacobs S 1992 Coda talk column. *Coda Connection* 9(1)

Johnson R, Liddell S, Erting C 1989 *Unlocking the Curriculum*. Gallaudet University Press, Washington, DC

Kannapell B 1989 An examination of deaf college students' attitudes toward ASL and English. In: Lucas C (ed.) 1989

Kyle J G, Woll B (eds.) 1983 *Language in Sign: An International Perspective on Sign Language*. Croom Helm, London

Kyle J G, Woll B (eds.) 1985 *Sign Language: The Study of Deaf People and Their Language*. Cambridge University Press, Cambridge

Lawson L 1981 The role of sign in the structure of the deaf community. In: Woll B, Kyle J, Deuchar M (eds.) 1981

Llewellyn-Jones P, Kyle J, Woll B 1979 Sign language communication (Unpublished paper presented at the International Conference on Social Psychology and Language, Bristol)

Lucas C (ed.) 1989 *The Sociolinguistics of the Deaf Community*. Academic Press, San Diego, CA

Lucas C, Valli C 1992 *Language Contact in the American Deaf Community*. Academic Press, San Diego, CA

Mather S 1991 The discourse marker OH in typed telephone conversations among deaf typists (Doctoral dissertation, Georgetown University)

Nowell E 1989 Conversational features and gender in ASL. In: Lucas C (ed.) 1989

Ramsey C 1989 Language planning in deaf education. In: Lucas C (ed.) 1989

Roy C 1989 Features of discourse in an American Sign Language lecture. In: Lucas C (ed.) 1989

Schermer T 1990 *In Search of a Language: Influences from Spoken Dutch on Sign Language of the Netherlands*. Eburon, Delft

Stokoe W C 1969–70 Sign language diglossia. *Studies in Linguistics* **21**: 27–41

Stokoe W C (ed.) 1980 *Sign and Culture: A Reader for Students of American Sign Language*. Linstok Press, Silver Spring, MD

Sutton-Spence R, Woll B, Allsop L 1990 Variation and recent change in fingerspelling in British Sign Language. *Language Variation and Change* **2**: 313–30

Woll B, Kyle J, Deuchar M (eds.) 1981 *Perspectives on British Sign Language and Deafness*. Croom Helm, London

Woodward J C 1976 Black southern signing. *LiS* **5**: 211–18

Zimmer J 1989 Toward a description of register variation in American Sign Language. In: Lucas C (ed.) 1989

C. Lucas

Sociology of Knowledge

The sociology of knowledge is concerned with investigating the extent of the presumed influence of people's concrete social existence on their knowledge, thought, consciousness, beliefs, and culture in general. Traditionally, this quest has been variably seen as a charge for the analysis and elucidation of the 'social frameworks' or 'social contexts' of knowledge, the 'social determination' of thought and consciousness, or the 'social origins' of ideas. However, these expressions demarcate theoretical programs that are different in the intended scope and intensity of their applications.

1. Historical Background

The term 'sociology of knowledge' was first introduced in the 1920s by Max Scheler and Karl Mannheim, as if to mark explicitly the sociological turn within a larger enterprise that was directed towards the analysis of knowledge and culture (a) in philosophico–anthropological terms (i.e., the then prevailing expressions of *Lebensphilosophie* and of social phenomenology, as in the work of Eduard Spranger) or (b) on the basis of the principles of *historicism* (exemplified at that time in the work of Ernst Troeltsch and Georg Lukàcs). Considered then somewhat strictly, the 'sociology of knowledge' addresses primarily—and in a more robust sense—the issue of the specific sociostructural frameworks and determinations of ideas; the historicist approach purports to capture the spirit of a given epoch (*Zeitgeist*) as a unity of meaning and as a culmination of concrete historico–cultural development; while the philosophico–anthropological approach is oriented toward the phenomenological discovery of the constitutive grounds of the social life-world, the recovery of its humanizing, moral meaning and, thus, also the rehabilitation of knowledge in virtue of the proper human interests it ought to serve. Notwithstanding, this analytical demarcation of the official originators of the sociology of knowledge, Scheler opted for the marriage of the sociological and phenomenological approaches, Mannheim of the sociological and historicist ones. As a result, their methods and conceptual systems differ considerably. Sociologists of knowledge seem to use concurrently a variety of images and arguments derived from the above three perspectives, so that, quite often, there is only a loose family resemblance between their respective views.

The sociology of knowledge has a long history. Several pre-Socratic philosophers, for example, held that gods were made in the image of humans and given names by them, not the other way around. In the *Republic*, Plato expresses the opinion that the material interests and artifactual practices of the working classes affect not only their bodies but their souls as well, rendering them unfit to pursue and gain any higher form of knowledge. In *Theaetetus*, too, the sophist Protagoras holds the view that 'man is the measure of all things' and that things appear to be different to various individuals seen from their diverging points of view. Moreover, the sophists have been hailed as the true precursors of modern rhetoricians and social epistemologists and Protagorean relativism is once more made respectable in the current postpositivist milieu.

Starting with the early Italian Renaissance, political realists and humanists were quick to point out the inevitable diversity of opinion prevailing on the basis of national culture, station in life, or the follies of man. One recalls Erasmus' brilliant praise of the latter, or Boccaccio's or Chaucer's vivid descriptions of the opinions and life-styles of different classes of people in their times. In his *Discourses* as well as in *The Prince*, the sharp and observant Machiavelli made clear the difference between the way rulers in the palace thought about public affairs as opposed to the way the people in the marketplace thought. Political leaders needed *virtù* ('vitality, forcefulness'), not virtues; they had to be virtuosi, possessing and using power/knowledge and looking after the interests of their regime of force. Bacon, though a scientific rationalist, still lamented the fact that the growth of knowledge was inhibited by certain general inclinations of the human mind, which he called 'Idols'; the source of these was the human constitution itself, especially the distorting faculty of perception (the Idols of the Tribe); each person's idiosyncracy (the Idols of the Den); human interactions, exchanges, and influences (the Idols of the Market Place); and the preexisting, false and dogmatic, and in any case conventional, systems of philosophy (the Idols of the Theater). Bacon, however, still thought that these sources of error could be corrected and true scientific knowledge achieved as a result of consistent pursuit of the methodological canons of modern science, the *novum organum*.

With Vico and Hegel the modern historicist program has been put in place. Vico's attack on the Cartesian program rested on his principle of *verum factum*: the true (*verum*) and the made (*factum*) were for him interchangeable. Facts as well as mathematical systems were human historical constructions and as such conventional forms of knowledge and, quite often, fallible or limited. Truth was historically bounded and reflected both the particular system of meaning of an epoch as well as the location of that epoch within cyclical time, the *corsi e recorsi* of history. In the former sense, all aspects of a society's life in a given epoch are intrinsically connected and correspond to each other, so that knowledge itself always relates and corresponds to the particular type of religion or law, economic or political organization, general manners or styles of thought and action, and so forth. With Hegel, this historicist program is pushed in a more dialectical, quasilinear direction. The 'ruse of Reason' operating behind people's back brings about not only the particular 'Zeitgeists' but also the fallibly and as yet incompletely unfolding meaning of History. Philosophy is the reconstruction of the History of Philosophy. Knowledge is the reconstruction of the History of Knowledge, still limited and bound to the concerns and experiences of the present.

With the left-Hegelians, with Feuerbach, and especially with Marx, the emphasis shifted for the first time from the historical and cultural to the political and economic. This was the beginning of the materialist conception of history, of politics, and of culture. In the *German Ideology*, Marx describes this shift as follows: 'Men are the producers of their conceptions, ideas, etc.—real, active men, as they are conditioned by a definite development of their productive forces and of the intercourse corresponding to these, up to its furthest forms.' 'Life is not determined by consciousness, but consciousness by life.' And in the preface to *A Critique of Political Economy*, he says: 'The mode of production of material life conditions the social, political, and intellectual life process in general. It is not the consciousness of men that determines their being, but, on the contrary, their social being that determines their consciousness.' These Marxist theses have been canonized as the 'hard core' of the contemporary, narrower and notably strong program in the sociology of knowledge.

Unquestionably, the first persistent efforts to produce a systematic theoretical and methodological framework for the sociology of knowledge were those of Karl Mannheim. His important work on ideology and utopia is still highly regarded, notwithstanding a number of inherent difficulties and ambiguities. Mannheim, presumably apprehensive of the implications of extreme relativism derived from the historicist program, shifted the focus of analysis from the *particular* conception of ideology (interest-based, conscious beliefs; deception) to that of *total* ideology (the total structure of the mind of an age or a group; *Weltanschauungen*). He also proposed the development of an *evaluative* total conception: the recovery of historical and cultural truth by the 'unattached intelligentsia' ('free-floating intellectuals') resulting from the critical comprehension and application of his 'relationism'—admittedly, a thorny, undeveloped project. By late twentieth-century standards, Mannheim's position is quite tame for another reason as well; namely, because he thought that, in contrast to the historical–cultural sciences, the natural and formal sciences are not 'existentially determined.' This position has been rejected by many contemporary sociologists of knowledge.

2. General Conceptions of Human Knowledge

For the purpose at hand, it can be simply argued that, in the course of intellectual history, both asocial and social conceptions of the grounds of knowledge have been elaborated. The former, of course, are quite hostile to the spirit and practices of the sociology of knowledge, the latter its offshoots.

Asocial conceptions of knowledge have privileged either (a) the 'sentient' constitutional characteristics of humans as natural beings, (b) their 'prudential' dispositions in the life-world, or, finally, (c) their special 'rational' qualities. In all these cases, reference is made to the species-specific characteristics, dispositions, and qualia of humans, to 'abstract man' fully or largely devoid of concrete historico–social existence. Thus were created the empiricist, the pragmatist–instrumentalist, and the rationalist epistemologies of the modern world and their more complex mixtures, the Kantian, the logical positivist, and the Popperian epistemologies. In all these cases, knowledge is conceived as objective, true or tending asymptotically towards truth, cumulative, produced on the basis of rational methodological canons, justifiably held. Sometimes a distinction is made between the 'context of discovery' of truth, which is somewhat tinted by 'external' psychological or sociological processes, and the 'context of justification,' which obeys the 'internal' logic and canons of proper philosophical or scientific thinking. The latter is treated as totally asocial, unassailable as the citadel of Reason, a Third World in itself.

Against this prevailing orthodoxy of philosophers and scientists, this excessive prejudice of moderns in favor of the ideals of Reason and Progress, social scientists of different persuasions counterposed theories of knowledge of an explicitly social character. These differ, to begin with, in the *scale* of their reference, on the basis of which can be distinguished five primary orientations.

First, there are those social views of knowledge that have a *quasitranscendental* grounding. Emile Durkheim's posit, in his *Elementary Forms of the Religious Life*, that all categories of thought originate in social, collective experience *illo tempore* is an exemplary case in point. The work of Claude Lévi-Strauss affords another example of a transcendentalist view, located ambivalently between the respective conceptions of Kant and Durkheim. German cultural philosophical anthropology, for example, the work of A. Gehlen and E. Rothacker, provides another case. The movement of J. Habermas towards 'Universal Pragmatics' has been also thought of as exhibiting transcendental commitments. Even the work of H. G. Gadamer and C. Taylor on recovering through history the meaning of humanity has been construed by critics as quasitranscendental in inspiration. In all these cases objectivity is presumably recovered/reconstructed by a thorough analysis of the primordial social and/or the transhistorical experience of the human race.

Second, there are those social views of knowledge that can be thought of as *global* forms of *historicism*, the historicism of Hegel, Comte, Croce, and perhaps Marx, forms that have been attacked by F. A. Hayek and Karl Popper. These forms of global historicism are characterized (a) by their favoring of some sort or another of 'methodological holism' over 'methodological individualism,' and (b) by their positing of special 'laws of development' of social entities, laws that are not reducible to any laws of individual behavior and which can offer grounds for predicting the next developmental stage of these entities. All the same, theories of knowledge inscribed in these forms of global or developmental historicism are still fallibilist, involving the social conditioning of ideas, and offering only a limited kind of historically reconstructed objectivity. Consider here Marx's qualified thoughts on this issue. In a 'Letter to Annenkov' (McLellan 1977: 192–94), while criticizing Proudhon's views, Marx asserts that the categories of thought 'are no more eternal than the relations they express. They are historical and transitory products.' Also, in the 1872 Preface to *Capital*, Marx cites approvingly the review of his book, published in a St Petersburg newspaper, which correctly attributes to Marx the view that abstract laws (of economic or any other aspect of life) do not exist: 'On the contrary,' says the reviewer, 'in his [Marx's] opinion every historical period has laws of its own . . . As soon as society has outlived a given period of development, and is passing over from one given stage to another, it begins to be subject also to other laws.' 'The scientific value of such inquiry,' further states the reviewer, 'lies in the disclosing of the special laws that regulate the origin, existence, development, death of a given social organism and its replacement

by another and higher one.' To this Marx only adds that that is exactly his dialectic method (McLellan 1977: 419).

Third, there are those social conceptions of knowledge that emphasize the embeddedness of knowing within a given *Lebenswelt*, in a spatiotemporally concrete society. Here must be cited once more the Durkheimian legacy according to which a society is defined by its ways of acting, thinking, and feeling, all three intricately connected. The late Wittgensteinian philosophy—and its Winchian extension—with its emphasis on 'forms of life' and 'language games,' also addresses knowledge as a life-form, as a shared way of doing and knowing-in-doing, as opposed to the philosophers' constructed abstractions (Bloor 1983). Schutzian phenomenology, ethnomethodology, and affine orientations in cultural anthropology, have all contributed to the conceptualization of knowledge as correlative to language, social practice, and culture. From this vantage point, the alleged distinctions between everyday general practices and specialized practices such as, for example, those of scientists, mathematicians, and philosophers have been minimized, if not totally eliminated. It will be seen shortly how the so-called 'strong program' of the sociology of knowledge informing the specialized field of the 'sociology of scientific knowledge' (SSK) rests on the above working presumption.

Fourth, there are those social conceptions of knowledge that can be thought of as *local* forms of *historicism*. Radical notions of historicism, such as Dilthey's, are *contextual* in method and emphasize the 'uniqueness' of specific sociocultural configurations in every particular epoch. A concrete society in a concrete space–time has unique properties, cultural meanings, *Zeitgeist*. Particular conceptual structures and modes of knowing, and therefore also objectified forms of knowledge, are associated with every such social context. Objectivity is internal to it. From the outside there is no objective knowledge, except perhaps the limited knowledge afforded by hermeneutical methods and the merging of horizons of our time with those of the other epoch. Even the sciences of nature exhibit a great degree of incommensurability across epochs. From the point of view of this contextual historicism, transitions from one epoch to another do not follow developmental laws—as in the case of global, developmental historicism—but are rather idiosyncratic; at the very best, they may exhibit 'transvaluations' (Nietzsche) or 'elective affinities' (Weber). This conception, therefore, is the prototype of sociocultural relativism.

Fifth, and finally, there are those social conceptions of knowledge that can be called *social structural*. Very central here, of course, is the Marxist theory that class fashions ideology and that class interests inform particular ideas and modes of thought—the basic core of the sociology of knowledge in the strict sense of this term. Marx's own and a plethora of other Marxist analyses have not only stressed the class production of ideological beliefs but also of the metaphysical foundations of philosophies, literary and artistic modes of expression, and scientific orientations (for example, of individualism, atomism, aggregative rather than structural social sciences, reductionism as the general model of science, and so on). Besides class, ethnoracial structural distinctions have been proposed as explaining different modes of acting, thinking, and feeling. Increasingly too, many arguments and descriptive studies by feminist writers (for example, A. Jaggar, J. Sayers, S. Harding, among others) have raised the specter of a gender determination of knowledge, though, admittedly, this research program is, in the early 1990s, still in its incipient phase.

3. The Social Context of Ideas: The General Model

Conceived broadly, as R. K. Merton recognized, the sociology of knowledge posits a special, determinative 'relation' between 'social context' and 'knowledge.' It therefore structures itself on a three-dimensional space, the axes of which measure: (a) the *scale* of the 'social context,' (b) the *scope* (*breadth*) of the latter's influence over the various forms of ideas and knowledge, and (c) the *intensity* (*depth*) of that influence. Above were presented five distinct social conceptions of knowledge, each one of which focuses on a unique, scaleable social-conceptual domain. Attention will now be turned to the general consideration of the 'relation' obtaining between 'social context' and 'knowledge.'

In the asocial conceptions of knowledge the demarcation between, on the one hand, logic, method, and/or valid perception and, on the other, subjective or social experience and associated interests is said to be absolute. Thus, philosophers of science have defended until recently the rigid distinction between internalist ('context of justification') and externalist ('context of discovery') discourses, exorcizing the latter out of the domain of science. In contrast, a variety of sociologies of knowledge, some softer, others more predatory, aided nowadays by many postpositivist philosophical views, have attacked this internal–external demarcation and insisted on the social character of all ideas and modes of thought. Four positions can be distinguished regarding the extent and nature of influence of the social context on ideas, along a continuum of decreasing intensity.

The strongest claims maintain that every aspect of knowledge, including its *cognitive content*, are affected by the general human condition and the given historical context, social practices, and structural locations of knowledge producers and users. The so-called 'strong program' of the sociology of knowledge, especially as it has been applied to scientific knowledge (D. Bloor, B. Barnes, H. Collins, B. Latour, among others) and the more traditional Marxist sociology of knowledge are exemplary instances of this position.

The second, somewhat less radical position maintains that the effects of the historico–social context are to a certain extent indirect: they condition the *informal modes of reasoning*, *feeling*, *and acting* of concrete groups and individuals, though the latter's self-conceptions and active interventions may mediate that influence to a larger or lesser degree. Neo-Marxist versions of the sociology of knowledge (such as, for example, that of Lucien Goldmann), even when extending in the Gramscian direction of positing hegemonic struggles of class-based knowledge/powers (as in the work of Stuart Hall), have disavowed any direct, mechanistic as it were, class determination of ideas. Nonetheless, even though structural determination per se may be said to be mediated, the strong social character of the process of knowledge production is still never in doubt. This is true in the case of both Marxist and non-Marxist viewpoints. In the latter instance, the influence—among others—of M. Polanyi's notion of 'tacit knowledge' and of the Kuhnian framework regarding the composition and change of scientific 'paradigms' is considerably evident. Q.

Skinner's so-called 'contextualist' proposal to investigate the tradition-reflecting 'habits of thought and behavior' of social actors in their particular historical context is a case in point; Latour and Woolgar's (1979) view of the scientific laboratory as a collection of informal procedural rules of method as well as a collection of 'inscription devices' is another. Also, the more recent works of H. Garfinkel and his students M. Lynch and E. Livingston bring quite forcefully to focus the procedural skills used by knowledge producers in the particular local phenomenologies of science.

The third and more moderate position in the sociology of knowledge investigates the many ways in which the 'social context' affects 'knowledge' by *determining the possibility space itself*, though perhaps not the content of ideas developed within that possibility space. This determination may be the function of various organizational factors, of the sociocultural and material interests of producers, supporters, and users of knowledge and culture, of their conjunctural-strategic system of relations and actions, and other such relevant social factors. The social space is seen as defining the possible questions that can be raised in principle (G. Bachelard's 'problematique'); the topics, canonized methods, and theoretical discourses that may be realistically included in the agendas of knowledge producers as a result of considerable politico-symbolic power struggles (from M. Foucault's Nietzschean power/knowledge 'projects' to the more traditional notions of topic-selection and the hierarchization of research priorities); and the critical dimensions of problem-weighting and theory-choice implicated in the search for knowledge and in the acceptance and justification of knowledge beliefs, especially given the thorny notions of the 'underdetermination of theory by facts' and the, at least relative, 'determination of facts by theory' (the Duhem–Quine Thesis and its extensions by M. Hesse and other philosophers). Studies in this more modest tradition usually stress the 'elective affinity' between social interests and the orientations of knowledge production (studies linking the seventeenth-century commercial-shipping interests in navigation, cargo stability, and protection to the development of Newtonian science), or that between some given knowledge beliefs and later cognitive orientations and social practices (Weber's linkage of the protestant ethic with the emergence of the capitalist spirit). Sometimes, the argument gets even stronger, as when certain organizational aspects of cultural production are said to affect the forms and content of knowledge or of various other cultural products; M. Useem's work on the state production of social knowledge and M. Baxandall and L. Greenfeld's explanations of the accelerated development of artistic styles in the cases of the limewood sculptors of Renaissance Germany and of the French Impressionist painters (all cited in Kuklick 1983) respectively are good examples of this tendency. However, this territorially important claim of the sociology of knowledge will not be broadly accepted until it can be shown persuasively that the content of knowledge in the physical sciences is also affected by this or that aspect of social life, that is, that—as the constructionists maintain—there is no internal rational process in scientific development immune from such influences.

The final position, somewhat in the margins of the sociology of knowledge, argues the vanguard thesis that even historical reconstructions of 'rationality' principles and ensuing historical reconstructions of relevant criteria of cultural meaning (in hermeneutics) and of scientific appraisals (in the philosophy of science) are fallible, socially bound in, at least, a global historicist sense, and open to contestation and differential valuation. This point has been brought home by I. Lakatos and has been supported and pushed further by R. Rorty and other pragmatist philosophers. J. Margolis, for example, has correctly argued that all second-order inquiries, reconstructions, and the like, are always dependent on previous first-order inquiries, and therefore they cannot be said to be fully autonomous in respect to the latter; on this argument, then, the formal always trades on the informal, the reconstruction on the primary practice. This form of *social pragmatism* guarantees the ineliminative nature of the sociology of knowledge.

4. The Objects of Social Determination

The sociology of knowledge has been concerned, not so much with the subjective and embodied forms of culture (for example, P. Bourdieu's notion of 'habitus') or the experiences of everyday life, as with what Mannheim has called 'objective culture,' i.e., political ideologies, religion, art, and science, to name the more distinct cases. Obviously, the intensity of determination of these objective cultural products varies, perhaps along a continuum. Thus, political ideologies are taken by sociologists of knowledge to be fully determined by the social context in which they emerge, even in the strictest sense of direct class determination. Religion has also been thought by many as more or less fully determined by for example primordial social experience (Durkheim), the general human condition (Feuerbach, Freud), historico-political forces (the young Hegel), structurally imposed 'false consciousness' (Marx). The same holds for broad historical ideologies of a philosophico–anthropological nature, such as conservativism (Mannheim), humanism (Nietzsche, Althusser), or general self-conceptions of particular epochs (Scheler). Already there is here a perception that the influence of the social context on the content of these cultural products is somewhat mediated by the limited historical self-reflection of humans. This holds even more true in the case of the arts and of literature, where ideological and other axiological elements are intertwined with internalist processes (textual and intertextual linkages, personal and interpersonal elements of expressive styles). The crux of the matter, however, remains the status of the natural sciences; here, the strong program of the sociology of scientific knowledge presses the challenge against the established view, advocating that these too are socially determined to the utmost. The question, nonetheless, is still open and the debate between rationalists (for example Martin Gardner, Larry Laudan) and social constructionists (David Bloor, Harry Collins) rages on. On the other hand, many postpositivist philosophers have already reached a more compromising position within the framework of what has been variably described as 'internal realism' (H. Putnam), 'social pragmatism' (R. Rorty, A. MacIntyre, R. Bernstein), or 'robust relativism' (J. Margolis); these positions are in principle hospitable to a temperate version of the sociology of knowledge. It could be argued, therefore, that the grounds of the latter are quite secure and the enterprise seems more promising now than ever before.

See also: Ethnomethodology; Scientific Nomenclature; Sociology in Language; Conceptual Systems; Weber, Max.

Bibliography

Barnes B, Bloor D 1982 Relativism, rationalism, and the sociology of knowledge. In: Hollis M, Lukes S (eds.) *Rationality and Relativism.* Blackwell, Oxford

Barth H 1977 *Truth and Ideology.* University of California Press, Berkeley, CA

Bloor D 1976 *Knowledge and Social Imagery.* Routledge and Kegan Paul, London

Bloor D 1983 *Wittgenstein: A Social Theory of Knowledge.* Columbia University Press, New York

Collins H, Pinch T J 1982 *Frames of Meaning: The Social Construction of Extraordinary Science.* Routledge and Kegan Paul, London

Couzens Hoy D (ed.) 1986 *Foucault: A Critical Reader.* Blackwell, Oxford

D'Amico R 1989 *Historicism and Knowledge.* Routledge, London

Hekman S J 1986 *Hermeneutics and the Sociology of Knowledge.* Polity Press, Cambridge

Garfinkel H, Lynch M, Livingston E 1981 The work of a discovering science construed with materials from the optically discovered pulsar. *Philosophy of the Social Sciences* 11: 131–58

Goldmann L 1964 *The Hidden God: A Study of Tragic Vision in the Pensées of Pascal and the Tragedies of Racine.* Routledge and Kegan Paul, London

Hall S 1980 Recent developments in theories of language and ideology: A critical note. In: *Culture, Media, Language.* Hutchinson, London

Hall S 1984 The Problem of Ideology. In: Mathews B (ed.) *Marx 100 years on.* Lawrence and Wishart, London

Kuklick H 1983 The sociology of knowledge: Retrospect and prospect. *Annual Review of Sociology* 9: 287–310

Kuhn T S 1962 *The Structure of Scientific Revolutions.* University of Chicago Press, Chicago, IL

Latour B, Woolgar S 1979 *Laboratory Life: The Social Construction of Scientific Facts.* Sage, Beverly Hills, CA

Laudan L 1977 *Progress and Its Problems.* University of California Press, Berkeley, CA

Lynch M 1985 *Art and Artifact in Laboratory Science.* Routledge and Kegan Paul, London

Mannheim K 1952 *Essays on the Sociology of Knowledge.* Routledge and Kegan Paul, London

Mannheim K 1972 *Ideology and Utopia: An Introduction to the Sociology of Knowledge.* Routledge and Kegan Paul, London

Mannheim K 1982 *Structures of Thinking.* Routledge and Kegan Paul, London

Margolis J 1986 *Pragmatism Without Foundations.* Blackwell, Oxford

McLellan D 1977 *Karl Marx: Selected Writings.* Oxford University Press, Oxford

Merton R K 1968 The sociology of knowledge. In: *Social Theory and Social Structure.* Free Press, New York

Rouse J 1987 *Knowledge and Power.* Cornell University Press, Ithaca, NY

Scheler M 1980 *Problems of a Sociology of Knowledge.* Routledge and Kegan Paul, London

Simonds A P 1978 *Karl Mannheim's Sociology of Knowledge.* Clarendon Press, Oxford

Stehr N, Meja V 1984 *Society and Knowledge.* Transaction, New Brunswick, NJ

Wolff K H 1971 *From Karl Mannheim.* Oxford University Press, New York

K. M. Kontopoulos